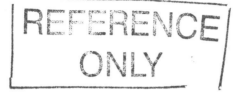

# HALSBURY'S
# Laws of England

## FIFTH EDITION
## 2019

## Volume 76

This is volume 76 of the Fifth Edition of Halsbury's Laws of England containing the titles MINES, MINERALS AND QUARRIES and MISREPRESENTATION .

This volume replaces the titles of the same names contained in volume 76 (2013). Upon receipt of volume 76 (2019), the old volume 76 (2013) may be archived.

For a full list of volumes comprised in a current set of Halsbury's Laws of England please see overleaf.

Fifth Edition volumes:

1 (2017), 1A (2017), 2 (2017), 3 (2011), 4 (2011), 5 (2013), 6 (2018), 7 (2015), 8 (2015), 9 (2017), 10 (2017), 11 (2015), 12 (2015), 12A (2015), 13 (2017), 14 (2016), 15 (2016), 15A (2016), 16 (2017), 17 (2017), 18 (2009), 19 (2011), 20 (2014), 21 (2016), 22 (2012), 23 (2016), 24 (2010), 25 (2016), 26 (2016), 27 (2015), 28 (2015), 29 (2019), 30 (2012), 31 (2012), 32 (2019), 33 (2017), 34 (2011), 35 (2015), 36 (2015), 37 (2013), 38 (2013), 38A (2013), 39 (2014), 40 (2014), 41 (2014), 41A (2014), 42 (2018), 43 (2018), 44 (2018), 45 (2019), 46 (2019), 47 (2014), 47A (2014), 48 (2015), 49 (2015), 50 (2016), 50A (2016), 51 (2013), 52 (2014), 53 (2014), 54 (2017), 54A (2017), 55 (2012), 56 (2017), 57 (2018), 60 (2018), 61 (2010), 61 (2018), 61A (2018), 62 (2016), 63 (2016), 64 (2016), 65 (2015), 66 (2015), 67 (2016), 68 (2016), 69 (2018), 70 (2018), 71 (2013), 72 (2015), 73 (2015), 74 (2011), 75 (2013), 76 (2019), 77 (2016), 78 (2018), 79 (2014), 80 (2013), 81 (2018), 82 (2018), 83 (2018), 84 (2013), 84A (2013), 85 (2012), 86 (2017), 87 (2017), 88 (2012), 88A (2018), 89 (2018), 90 (2018), 91 (2012), 92 (2015), 93 (2017), 94 (2017), 95 (2017), 96 (2018), 97 (2015), 97A (2014), 98 (2019), 99 (2018), 99A (2018), 100 (2018), 101 (2018), 102 (2016), 103 (2016), 104 (2014)

Consolidated Index and Tables:

2018 Consolidated Index (A–E), 2018 Consolidated Index (F–O), 2018 Consolidated Index (P–Z), 2019 Consolidated Table of Statutes, 2019 Consolidated Table of Statutory Instruments, 2019 Consolidated Table of Cases (A–G), 2019 Consolidated Table of Cases (H–Q), 2019 Consolidated Table of Cases (R–Z, ECJ Cases)

Updating and ancillary materials:

2019 annual Cumulative Supplement; monthly Noter-up; annual Abridgments 1974–2018

May 2019

# HALSBURY'S
# Laws of England

## Volume 76

2019

Members of the LexisNexis Group worldwide

| | |
|---|---|
| United Kingdom | RELX (UK) Ltd, trading as LexisNexis, 1–3 Strand, London WC2N 5JR and 9–10 St Andrew Square, Edinburgh EH2 2AF |
| Australia | Reed International Books Australia Pty Ltd trading as LexisNexis, Chatswood, New South Wales |
| Austria | LexisNexis Verlag ARD Orac GmbH & Co KG, Vienna |
| Benelux | LexisNexis Benelux, Amsterdam |
| Canada | LexisNexis Canada, Markham, Ontario |
| China | LexisNexis China, Beijing and Shanghai |
| France | LexisNexis SA, Paris |
| Germany | LexisNexis GmbH, Dusseldorf |
| Hong Kong | LexisNexis Hong Kong, Hong Kong |
| India | LexisNexis India, New Delhi |
| Italy | Giuffrè Editore, Milan |
| Japan | LexisNexis Japan, Tokyo |
| Malaysia | Malayan Law Journal Sdn Bhd, Kuala Lumpur |
| New Zealand | LexisNexis New Zealand Ltd, Wellington |
| Singapore | LexisNexis Singapore, Singapore |
| South Africa | LexisNexis, Durban |
| USA | LexisNexis, Dayton, Ohio |

| | |
|---|---|
| FIRST EDITION | *Published in 31 volumes between 1907 and 1917* |
| SECOND EDITION | *Published in 37 volumes between 1931 and 1942* |
| THIRD EDITION | *Published in 43 volumes between 1952 and 1964* |
| FOURTH EDITION | *Published in 56 volumes between 1973 and 1987, with reissues between 1988 and 2008* |
| FIFTH EDITION | *Published between 2008 and 2014, with reissues from 2014* |

© 2019 RELX (UK) Ltd

A CIP Catalogue record for this book is available from the British Library.

ISBN 978-1-4743-1260-8

ISBN for the set: 9781405734394
ISBN for this volume: 9781474312608
Typeset by LexisNexis
Printed and bound by CPI Group (UK) Ltd, Croydon, CR0 4YY

Visit LexisNexis at www.lexisnexis.co.uk

# HALSBURY ADVISORY BOARD

# MINES, MINERALS AND QUARRIES

**Consultant Editor**

ANDREW FRASER-URQUHART, QC, MA,
of the Middle Temple, Barrister

# MISREPRESENTATION

**Consultant Editor**

JOHN CARTWRIGHT, BCL, MA,
Emeritus Professor of the Law of Contract, University of Oxford;
a Solicitor of the Senior Courts of England and Wales

The law stated in this volume is in general that in force on 1 April 2019, although subsequent changes have been included wherever possible.

Any future updating material will be found in the Noter-up and annual Cumulative Supplement to Halsbury's Laws of England

# TABLE OF CONTENTS

# HOW TO USE HALSBURY'S LAWS OF ENGLAND

## Volumes

Each text volume of Halsbury's Laws of England contains the law on the titles contained in it as at a date stated at the front of the volume (the operative date).

Information contained in Halsbury's Laws of England may be accessed in several ways.

*First, by using the tables of contents.*

Each volume contains both a general Table of Contents, and a specific Table of Contents for each title contained in it. From these tables you will be directed to the relevant part of the work.

**Readers should note that the current arrangement of titles can be found in the Noter-up.**

*Secondly, by using tables of statutes, statutory instruments, cases or other materials.*

If you know the name of the Act, statutory instrument or case with which your research is concerned, you should consult the Consolidated Tables of statutes, cases and so on (published as separate volumes) which will direct you to the relevant volume and paragraph.

(Each individual text volume also includes tables of those materials used as authority in that volume.)

*Thirdly, by using the indexes.*

If you are uncertain of the general subject area of your research, you should go to the Consolidated Index (published as separate volumes) for reference to the relevant volume(s) and paragraph(s).

(Each individual text volume also includes an index to the material contained therein.)

## Updating publications

The text volumes of Halsbury's Laws should be used in conjunction with the annual Cumulative Supplement and the monthly Noter-up.

*The annual Cumulative Supplement*

The Supplement gives details of all changes between the operative date of the text volume and the operative date of the Supplement. It is arranged in the same volume, title and paragraph order as the text volumes. Developments affecting particular points of law are noted to the relevant paragraph(s) of the text volumes.

*For narrative treatment of material noted in the Cumulative Supplement, go to the annual Abridgment volume for the relevant year.*

*Destination Tables*

In certain titles in the annual *Cumulative Supplement,* reference is made to Destination Tables showing the destination of consolidated legislation. Those Destination Tables are to be found either at the end of the titles within the annual *Cumulative Supplement,* or in a separate *Destination Tables* booklet provided from time to time with the *Cumulative Supplement.*

*The Noter-up*

The Noter-up is issued monthly and notes changes since the publication of the annual Cumulative Supplement. Also arranged in the same volume, title and paragraph order as the text volumes, the Noter-up follows the style of the Cumulative Supplement.

*For narrative treatment of material noted in the Noter-up, go to the annual Abridgment volume for the relevant year.*

# REFERENCES AND ABBREVIATIONS

ACT ........................... Australian Capital Territory
A-G ........................... Attorney General
Admin ........................ Administrative Court
Admlty ....................... Admiralty Court
Adv-Gen ..................... Advocate General
affd ........................... affirmed
affg ........................... affirming
Alta .......................... Alberta
App ........................... Appendix
art ............................ article
Aust .......................... Australia
B  ............................. Baron
BC ........................... British Columbia
C .............................. Command Paper (of a series published before 1900)
c .............................. chapter number of an Act
CA ............................ Court of Appeal
CAC .......................... Central Arbitration Committee
CA in Ch ..................... Court of Appeal in Chancery
CB ........................... Chief Baron
CCA .......................... Court of Criminal Appeal
CCR .......................... County Court Rules 1981 (as subsequently amended)
CCR .......................... Court for Crown Cases Reserved
CJEU ......................... Court of Justice of the European Union
C-MAC ....................... Courts-Martial Appeal Court
CO ............................ Crown Office
COD .......................... Crown Office Digest
CPR ........................... Civil Procedure Rules
Can ........................... Canada
Cd ............................ Command Paper (of the series published 1900–18)
Cf ............................. compare
Ch ............................ Chancery Division
ch ............................ chapter
cl ............................. clause
Cm ........................... Command Paper (of the series published 1986 to date)
Cmd .......................... Command Paper (of the series published 1919–56)
Cmnd ......................... Command Paper (of the series published 1956–86)
Comm ........................ Commercial Court

| | |
|---|---|
| Comr | Commissioner |
| Court Forms (2nd Edn) | Atkin's Encyclopaedia of Court Forms in Civil Proceedings, 2nd Edn. See note 2 post. |
| CrimPR | Criminal Procedure Rules |
| DC | Divisional Court |
| DPP | Director of Public Prosecutions |
| EAT | Employment Appeal Tribunal |
| EC | European Community |
| ECJ | Court of Justice of the European Community (before the Treaty of Lisbon (OJ C306, 17.12.2007, p 1) came into force on 1 December 2009); European Court of Justice (after the Treaty of Lisbon (OJ C306, 17.12.2007, p 1) came into force on 1 December 2009) |
| EComHR | European Commission of Human Rights |
| ECSC | European Coal and Steel Community |
| ECtHR Rules of Court | Rules of Court of the European Court of Human Rights |
| EEC | European Economic Community |
| EFTA | European Free Trade Association |
| EGC | European General Court |
| EWCA Civ | Official neutral citation for judgments of the Court of Appeal (Civil Division) |
| EWCA Crim | Official neutral citation for judgments of the Court of Appeal (Criminal Division) |
| EWHC | Official neutral citation for judgments of the High Court |
| Edn | Edition |
| Euratom | European Atomic Energy Community |
| EU | European Union |
| Ex Ch | Court of Exchequer Chamber |
| ex p | ex parte |
| Fam | Family Division |
| Fed | Federal |
| Forms & Precedents (5th Edn) | Encyclopaedia of Forms and Precedents other than Court Forms, 5th Edn. See note 2 post |
| GLC | Greater London Council |
| HC | High Court |
| HC | House of Commons |
| HK | Hong Kong |
| HL | House of Lords |
| HMRC | Her Majesty's Revenue and Customs |
| IAT | Immigration Appeal Tribunal |
| ILM | International Legal Materials |

INLR .......................... Immigration and Nationality Law Reports
IRC .......................... Inland Revenue Commissioners
Ind ........................... India
Int Rels...................... International Relations
Ir ............................ Ireland
J ............................. Justice
JA ........................... Judge of Appeal
Kan .......................... Kansas
LA ........................... Lord Advocate
LC ........................... Lord Chancellor
LCC .......................... London County Council
LCJ .......................... Lord Chief Justice
LJ ........................... Lord Justice of Appeal
MR .......................... Master of the Rolls
Man .......................... Manitoba
n.............................. note
NB .......................... New Brunswick
NI............................ Northern Ireland
NS............................ Nova Scotia
NSW.......................... New South Wales
NY........................... New York
NZ........................... New Zealand
OHIM........................ Office for Harmonisation in the Internal Market
OJ............................ The Official Journal of the European Union
                            published by the Publications Office of the
                            European Union
Ont .......................... Ontario
P............................. President
PC............................ Judicial Committee of the Privy Council
PEI........................... Prince Edward Island
Pat .......................... Patents Court
q............................. question
QB ........................... Queen's Bench Division
QBD.......................... Queen's Bench Division of the High Court
Qld .......................... Queensland
Que .......................... Quebec
r............................. rule
RDC.......................... Rural District Council
RPC.......................... Restrictive Practices Court
RSC.......................... Rules of the Supreme Court 1965 (as subsequently
                            amended)
reg .......................... regulation
Res........................... Resolution
revsd......................... reversed

| | |
|---|---|
| Rly | Railway |
| s | section |
| SA | South Africa |
| S Aust | South Australia |
| SC | Supreme Court |
| SI | Statutory Instruments published by authority |
| SR & O | Statutory Rules and Orders published by authority |
| SR & O Rev 1904 | Revised Edition comprising all Public and General Statutory Rules and Orders in force on 31 December 1903 |
| SR & O Rev 1948 | Revised Edition comprising all Public and General Statutory Rules and Orders and Statutory Instruments in force on 31 December 1948 |
| STI | Simon's Tax Intelligence (1973–1995); Simon's Weekly Tax Intelligence (1996-current) |
| Sask | Saskatchewan |
| Sch | Schedule |
| Sess | Session |
| Sing | Singapore |
| TCC | Technology and Construction Court |
| TS | Treaty Series |
| Tanz | Tanzania |
| Tas | Tasmania |
| UDC | Urban District Council |
| UKHL | Official neutral citation for judgments of the House of Lords |
| UKPC | Official neutral citation for judgments of the Privy Council |
| UN | United Nations |
| V-C | Vice-Chancellor |
| Vict | Victoria |
| W Aust | Western Australia |
| Zimb | Zimbabwe |

NOTE 1. A general list of the abbreviations of law reports and other sources used in this work can be found at the beginning of the Consolidated Table of Cases.

NOTE 2. Where references are made to other publications, the volume number precedes and the page number follows the name of the publication; eg the reference '12 Forms & Precedents (5th Edn) 44' refers to volume 12 of the Encyclopaedia of Forms and Precedents, page 44.

NOTE 3. An English statute is cited by short title or, where there is no short title, by regnal year and chapter number together with the name by which it is commonly known or a description of its subject matter and date. In the case of a foreign statute, the mode of citation generally follows the style of citation in use in the country concerned with the addition, where necessary, of the name of the country in parentheses.

NOTE 4. A statutory instrument is cited by short title, if any, followed by the year and number, or, if unnumbered, the date.

# TABLE OF STATUTES

# TABLE OF STATUTORY INSTRUMENTS

# TABLE OF PROCEDURE

## Civil Procedure

## Practice Directions relating to Civil Procedure Rules 1998, SI 1998/3132 (CPR)

# TABLE OF CASES

PARA

## D

PARA

## G

## H

PARA

## O

## S

PARA

# MINES, MINERALS AND QUARRIES

# 1. SCOPE OF THE TITLE, ADMINISTRATION AND TERMINOLOGY

## (1) Scope of the title and administration

### 1. Scope of title.

This title covers mining and quarrying generally but also includes the significant changes that have occurred over the years to the coal-mining industry[1]. It also covers ownership[2], rights affecting mines in general[3], disposition of land and mines[4], the right to work minerals[5], opencast working of coal[6], the regulation of mines and quarries[7], ironstone district restoration[8], the treatment of former mining land[9] and local rights and customs in relation to mines, minerals and quarries[10].

1 See PARAS 48–51 et seq.
2 See PARA 3 et seq.
3 See PARA 114 et seq.
4 See PARA 282 et seq.
5 See PARA 352 et seq.
6 See PARA 413 et seq.
7 See PARA 517 et seq.
8 See PARA 580 et seq.
9 See PARA 582 et seq.
10 See PARA 585 et seq.

### 2. The Secretary of State and the Welsh Ministers.

The administration of the coal-mining industry was initially the responsibility of the Mines Department of the Board of Trade, and over the years ministerial functions have been transferred[1] to the Minister of Fuel and Power[2] (who became the Minister of Power[3]), the Minister of Technology[4], the Secretary of State for Trade and Industry[5], the Secretary of State for Energy[6], then once again the Secretary of State for Trade and Industry[7] who was redesignated the Secretary of State for Business, Enterprise and Regulatory Reform. then the Secretary of State for Energy and Climate Change; they are now predominantly vested in the Secretary of State for Business, Energy and Industrial Strategy[8].

Functions in relation to mining which were initially the responsibility of the Minister of Town and Country Planning[9] were transferred to the Minister of Local Government and Planning[10] (later the Minister of Housing and Local Government[11]), then to the Secretary of State for the Environment[12], and subsequently this became the responsibility of the Secretary of State for the Environment, Transport and the Regions[13]. Functions of the Secretary of State for the Environment, Transport and the Regions have been divided between the Secretary of State for Transport, Secretary of State for Housing, Communities and Local Government and the Secretary of State for Environment, Food and Rural Affairs[14]. Health and safety functions are now mainly carried out by the Health and Safety Executive, which is the responsibility of the Department for Work and Pensions[15].

Older statutes refer to specific ministers or government departments[16], but many modern statutes refer simply to 'the Secretary of State' without reference to a particular department or ministry. 'Secretary of State' means one of Her Majesty's principal Secretaries of State[17]; the office of Secretary of State is a unified office, and in law each Secretary of State is capable of performing the functions of all or any of them[18].

Many statutory functions vested in Ministers of the Crown are now exercisable in relation to Wales by the Welsh Ministers[19]. Functions transferred include specified functions under the Inclosure Act 1845[20]; the Inclosure Act 1859[21]; the Opencast Coal Act 1958[22]; the Mines (Working Facilities and Support) Act 1966[23]; the Mines and Quarries (Tips) Act 1969[24]; the Local Government Act 1972[25]; the Acquisition of Land Act 1981[26]; the Town and Country Planning Act 1990[27]; the Water Industry Act 1991[28]; the Water Resources Act 1991[29]; the Clean Air Act 1993[30], the Coal Industry Act 1994[31]; and the Environment Act 1995[32]. Legislation enacted following the establishment of the Welsh Assembly Government which confers functions on the Secretary of State and the Welsh Ministers often refers to those bodies collectively as 'the appropriate national authority', and that expression is used throughout this title to cover any situation where the function in question is exercised in relation to England by the Secretary of State and in relation to Wales by the Welsh Ministers, and also where the functions may be carried out jointly[33].

1   As to the transfer of functions generally see CONSTITUTIONAL AND ADMINISTRATIVE LAW vol 20 (2014) PARA 380 et seq.
2   See the Ministry of Fuel and Power Act 1945 s 1, Sch 1 (repealed); and the Ministers of the Crown (Minister of Fuel and Power) Order 1942, SR & O 1942/1132 (lapsed).
3   See the Minister of Fuel and Power (Change of Style and Title) Order 1957, SI 1957/48 (lapsed).
4   See the Minister of Technology Order 1969, SI 1969/1498 (superseded in part and remainder lapsed).
5   See the Secretary of State for Trade and Industry Order 1970, SI 1970/1537 (lapsed).
6   See the Secretary of State (New Departments) Order 1974, SI 1974/692 (superseded in part and remainder lapsed).
7   See the Transfer of Functions (Energy) Order 1992, SI 1992/1314. As to the Secretary of State for Trade and Industry see COMPETITION vol 18 (2009) PARA 5.
8   The Department for Business, Energy and Industrial Strategy is responsible for policy issues in relation to the continuing UK coal industry and also the delivery and policy of matters arising from the restructuring of the coal industry under the Coal Industry Act 1994.
9   See the Minister of Town and Country Planning Act 1943 s 1 (repealed).
10  See the Transfer of Functions (Minister of Health and Minister of Local Government and Planning) (No 1) Order 1951, SI 1951/142 (lapsed).
11  See the Minister of Local Government and Planning (Change of Style and Title) Order 1951, SI 1951/1900 (lapsed).
12  See the Secretary of State for the Environment Order 1970, SI 1970/1681 (amended by amended SI 1999/1820, SI 2001/1149 and superseded in part).
13  See the Secretary of State for the Environment, Transport and the Regions Order 1997, SI 1997/2971.
14  See the Secretaries of State for Transport, Local Government and the Regions and for Environment, Food and Rural Affairs Order 2001, SI 2001/2568 (amended by SI 2002/2626). On the dissolution of the Ministry of Agriculture, Fisheries and Food, the functions of the Minister of Agriculture, Fisheries and Food were transferred to the Secretary of State for Environment, Food and Rural Affairs: see the Ministry of Agriculture, Fisheries and Food (Dissolution) Order 2002, SI 2002/794 (amended by SI 2009/463; and SI 2015/191).
15  See the Legislative Reform (Health and Safety Executive) Order 2008, SI 2008/960; and HEALTH AND SAFETY AT WORK vol 52 (2014) PARA 326 et seq. The Department for Work and Pensions is the successor to the Department for Education and Employment. It was created in 2001 when that department and the former Department of Social Security were restructured.
16  The Mining Industry Act 1920 and the Coal Act 1938 (now repealed) referred to the Board of Trade. The Coal Industry Nationalisation Act 1946, the Miners' Welfare Act 1952 and the Mines and Quarries Act 1954 referred to the Minister of Fuel and Power. The Opencast Coal Act 1958, the Mines (Working Facilities and Support) Act 1966, the National Coal Board (Additional Powers) Act 1966 and the Coal Industry Act 1967 referred to the Minister of Power. The Mineral Workings Act 1951 referred to the Minister of Local Government and Planning. The Mines and Quarries (Tips) Act 1969 referred to the Minister of Housing and Local Government.

17 See the Interpretation Act 1978 s 5, Sch 1.
18 See CONSTITUTIONAL AND ADMINISTRATIVE LAW vol 20 (2014) PARA 153.
19 Such statutory functions, so far as exercisable in relation to Wales, were transferred to the National Assembly for Wales by the National Assembly for Wales (Transfer of Functions) Order 1999, SI 1999/672, art 2, Sch 1; and the National Assembly for Wales (Transfer of Functions) Order 2000, SI 2000/253, art 2, Sch 1. Pursuant to the establishment of the Welsh Assembly Government under the Government of Wales Act 2006 Pt 2 (ss 45–92) (see CONSTITUTIONAL AND ADMINISTRATIVE LAW vol 20 (2014) PARA 373 et seq), such functions, including functions under subordinate legislation, so far as exercisable in relation to Wales, are now almost exclusively the responsibility of Welsh Ministers (ie the First Minister and the Welsh Ministers established under ss 46, 48: see s 45(2); and CONSTITUTIONAL AND ADMINISTRATIVE LAW vol 20 (2014) PARAS 375). Further transfers of ministerial functions to the Welsh Ministers may be effected by Order in Council pursuant to s 58, Sch 3 paras 1–8. As to provisions as to the exercise of the transferred functions see Sch 11 paras 33–35 (in the case of functions originally transferred to the Assembly by Order in Council under the Government of Wales Act 1998 s 22) or the Government of Wales Act 2006 Sch 3 para 9 (in the case of functions subsequently transferred to the Welsh Ministers by Order in Council under Sch 3 paras 1–8).
  Any enactment which charges the payment of any sum on the Consolidated Fund or requires or authorises the payment of any sum from that Fund, or requires or authorises the payment of any sum out of money provided by Parliament, ceases to have effect in so far as that sum is payable by the Assembly: s 89. As to the Consolidated Fund see CONSTITUTIONAL AND ADMINISTRATIVE LAW vol 20 (2014) PARA 480; PARLIAMENT vol 78 (2018) PARA 847 et seq.
20 As to the Inclosure Act 1845 see PARAS 313–315; and COMMONS vol 13 (2017) PARA 319 et seq.
21 As to the Inclosure Act 1859 see PARA 313; and COMMONS vol 13 (2017) PARA 319 et seq.
22 As to the Opencast Coal Act 1958 see PARA 413 et seq.
23 As to the Mines (Working Facilities and Support) Act 1966 see PARA 380 et seq.
24 Ie except the Mines and Quarries (Tips) Act 1969 Pt I (ss 1–10) (see PARAS 520–558). As to the Mines and Quarries (Tips) Act 1969 generally see PARA 520 et seq.
25 As to the Local Government Act 1972 see PARAS 558, 574; and LOCAL GOVERNMENT vol 69 (2018) PARA 38 et seq.
26 As to the Acquisition of Land Act 1981 see PARAS 430, 442; and COMPULSORY ACQUISITION OF LAND.
27 As to the Town and Country Planning Act 1990 see PARA 352 et seq; and PLANNING.
28 As to the Water Industry Act 1991 see eg PARAS 135, 438; and WATER AND WATERWAYS vol 100 (2018) PARAS 476 et seq, 137 et seq, 318 et seq; WATER AND WATERWAYS vol 101 (2018) PARA 719 et seq.
29 As to the Water Resources Act 1991 see eg PARA 533; and WATER AND WATERWAYS vol 100 (2018) PARA 342 et seq; WATER AND WATERWAYS vol 101 (2018) PARA 719 et seq.
30 Ie except the Clean Air Act 1993 ss 30–32, 36(6) and 48. See PARA 277.
31 Ie the Coal Industry Act 1994 ss 53, 54 (see PARAS 354, 355). As to the Coal Industry Act 1994 generally see PARA 52 et seq.
32 As to the Environment Act 1995 see eg PARA 352; and ENVIRONMENTAL QUALITY AND PUBLIC HEALTH vol 45 (2010) PARA 68 et seq; PLANNING; WATER AND WATERWAYS.
33 National Assembly for Wales (Transfer of Functions) Order 1999, SI 1999/672, art 4.

## (2) Terminology

### (i) Mines and Quarries

**3. Meaning of 'mine'.**
In a document or statute 'mine' takes its meaning from the other words used in the document or statute, and from its factual context[1]. The word 'mine' is not a definite term, but is susceptible of limitation or expansion according to the intention with which it is used[2]. 'Mine' originally meant an underground excavation made for the purpose of getting minerals[3], but in particular contexts

the word has been given differing meanings. Thus it has been interpreted so as to include a place where minerals commonly worked underground are in the particular case being worked on the surface, as in opencast coal workings and in certain ironstone mines[4].

It may also denote a stratum, vein or seam of mineral, as in the phrase 'all that mine, vein, or seam of coal'[5]. If, in such a case, the mine is unopened[6], it is clear that the word is used in the sense of a stratum of mineral[7]. Where so used, the primary meaning of 'mine' is that of a vein or seam, but it may be used in a wider sense to denote a number of veins or seams[8], or in a narrower sense to denote only that part of a vein or seam which is within a particular tenement[9].

A further meaning of 'mine' includes not only the mineral deposits but also so much of the adjoining strata, whether above or below, as it may be necessary to remove for the purpose of working the mineral in a proper manner[10]. The word has also been given, in some cases, a meaning which includes, in addition to the mineral itself, the space created as the mineral is being worked, and the space left when the mineral has been worked out[11].

Where the word 'mine' occurs in legislation it may be used in a special sense and it is sometimes expressly defined. Examples[12] of such legislation are the Mines and Quarries Act 1954[13], the Coal Industry Act 1994[14] and the Town and Country Planning (General Permitted Development) Order 1995[15]. 'Mine' is often defined by reference to the minerals extracted[16].

1   See, on the construction of documents generally, *Investors Compensation Scheme Ltd v West Bromwich Building Society* [1998] 1 All ER 114–115, [1998] 1 WLR 896 at 912–913, HL, per Lord Hoffmann.

2   *Glasgow Corpn v Farie* (1888) 13 App Cas 657 at 675, HL, per Lord Watson; *Midland Rly Co v Haunchwood Brick and Tile Co* (1882) 20 ChD 552 at 555 per Kay J; *South Staffordshire Mines Drainage Comrs v Grosvenor Colliery Co Ltd* (1961) 125 JP 484 at 485, CA, per Sellers LJ.

3   *Glasgow Corpn v Farie* (1888) 13 App Cas 657 at 670, HL, per Lord Halsbury LC, and at 676 per Lord Watson; *Bell v Wilson* (1866) 1 Ch App 303 at 308 per Turner LJ. Some authorities indicate that this original meaning of 'mine' is to be regarded as the primary or ordinary meaning: *Midland Rly Co v Haunchwood Brick and Tile Co* (1882) 20 ChD 552 at 555 per Kay J; *Glasgow Corpn v Farie* at 683 per Lord Herschell (dissenting), and at 687 per Lord Macnaghten; *Midland Rly Co and Kettering, Thrapston and Huntingdon Rly Co v Robinson* (1889) 15 App Cas 19 at 34, HL, per Lord Macnaghten (dissenting); but these last two authorities have been said not to be of general effect: see *South Staffordshire Mines Drainage Comrs v Grosvenor Colliery Co Ltd* (1961) 125 JP 484 at 485, CA, per Sellers LJ. See also *South Staffordshire Mines Drainage Comrs v Elwell & Sons* (1927) 97 LJKB 13 at 15, CA, per Bankes LJ; and cf *NSW Associated Blue-Metal Quarries Ltd v Federal Comr of Taxation* (1956) 94 CLR 509, [1956] ALR 286, Aust HC. As to the meaning of 'minerals' see PARA 10.

4   *South Staffordshire Mines Drainage Comrs v Grosvenor Colliery Co Ltd* (1961) 125 JP 484, CA; *Glasgow Corpn v Farie* (1888) 13 App Cas 657 at 678, HL, per Lord Watson, and at 684 per Lord Herschell (dissenting); and see *Sim v Evans* (1875) 23 WR 730; and *Rogers (Inspector of Taxes) v Longsdon* [1967] Ch 93 at 110, [1966] 2 All ER 49 at 57 per Stamp J. See also the cases cited in PARA 4. As to the opencast working of coal see PARA 413 et seq.

5   *Lord Abinger v Ashton* (1873) LR 17 Eq 358 at 369 per Jessel MR; *Ramsay v Blair* (1876) 1 App Cas 701 at 705, HL, per Lord Selborne; *Midland Rly Co v Haunchwood Brick and Tile Co* (1882) 20 ChD 552 at 555 per Kay J; *Glasgow Corpn v Farie* (1888) 13 App Cas 657 at 677, HL, per Lord Watson, and at 687 per Lord Macnaghten; *Batten Pool v Kennedy* [1907] 1 Ch 256 at 266 per Warrington J.

6   As to open and unopened mines see PARA 5 et seq.

7   *Ramsay v Blair* (1876) 1 App Cas 701 at 705, HL, per Lord Selborne; *Midland Rly Co v Haunchwood Brick and Tile Co* (1882) 20 ChD 552; *Glasgow Corpn v Farie* (1888) 13 App Cas 657 at 687, HL, per Lord Macnaghten. A grant of 'lands and mines', where some of the mines are open, includes, however, only the open mines: *Astry v Ballard* (1677) 2 Mod Rep 193; and see *Newton, Chambers & Co Ltd v Hall* [1907] 2 KB 446 at 458, 459 per Bray J. Where 'mine' is used

to express the substance as distinct from the working, it may be confined to substances to be got by mining in the ordinary sense of that term, and not by open working on the surface: see *Tucker v Linger* (1882) 21 ChD 18 at 36, CA, per Sir George Jessel MR; affd (1883) 8 App Cas 508, HL.

8    *Spencer v Scurr* (1862) 31 Beav 334.

9    *Ivimey v Stocker* (1865) 1 Ch App 396 at 407 per Lord Cranworth LC; *Van Mining Co v Llanidloes Overseers* (1876) 1 Ex D 310 at 319 per Mellor J. See also *R v Foleshill Inhabitants* (1835) 2 Ad & El 593.

10   *Batten Pooll v Kennedy* [1907] 1 Ch 256; following *Proud v Bates* (1865) 34 LJ Ch 406; *Duke of Hamilton v Graham* (1871) LR 2 Sc & Div 166; *Eardley v Granville* (1876) 3 ChD 826; and distinguishing *Ramsay v Blair* (1876) 1 App Cas 701, HL. As to the construction of roads by a person having a right of property in a mine see PARA 255.

11   *Bowser v Maclean* (1860) 2 De GF & J 415 at 420; *Proud v Bates* (1865) 34 LJ Ch 406 at 411; *Duke of Hamilton v Graham* (1871) LR 2 Sc & Div 166; *Ramsay v Blair* (1876) 1 App Cas 701 at 705, HL, per Lord Selborne; *Glasgow Corpn v Farie* (1888) 13 App Cas 657 at 687, HL, per Lord Macnaghten; *Batten Pooll v Kennedy* [1907] 1 Ch 256 at 267 per Warrington J.

12   See also the statutory definitions of 'mines and minerals' in PARA 10.

13   'Mine' means an excavation or system of excavations (including all excavations to which a common system of ventilation is provided) made for the purpose of, or in connection with, the extraction, wholly or substantially by means involving persons working below ground, of minerals (in their natural state or in solution or suspension) or mineral products: Mines and Quarries Act 1954 s 180(1) (substituted by SI 2014/3248). In the Management and Administration of Safety and Health at Mines Regulations 1993, SI 1993/1897, 'mine' means a mine within the meaning of the Mines and Quarries Act 1954: Management and Administration of Health and Safety at Mines Regulations 1993, SI 1993/1897, reg 2(1) (substituted by SI 1995/2005). In some instances, health and safety regulations use the word 'mine' in special senses: see the Management and Administration of Safety and Health at Mines Regulations 1993, SI 1993/1897; and HEALTH AND SAFETY AT WORK vol 52 (2014) PARA 313; HEALTH AND SAFETY AT WORK vol 53 (2014) PARA 702.

     For the purposes of the Mines and Quarries Act 1954, so much of the surface (including buildings, structures and works on it) surrounding or adjacent to the shafts or outlets of the mine as is occupied together with the mine for the purpose of, or in connection with, the working of the mine, the treatment, preparation for sale, consumption or use, storage or removal from the mine of the minerals or products thereof gotten from the mine or the removal from the mine of the refuse thereof, is deemed to form part of a mine (s 180(3)(a); and see HEALTH AND SAFETY AT WORK vol 52 (2014) PARA 313); provided that premises in which a manufacturing process is carried on otherwise than for the purpose of the working of the mine or the preparation for sale of minerals gotten from it are not, for these purposes, deemed to form part of the mine (see s 180(3) proviso (amended by SI 1999/2024); and HEALTH AND SAFETY AT WORK vol 52 (2014) PARA 313). 'Shaft' means a shaft the top of which is, or is intended to be, at the surface: s 182(1). A conveyor or aerial ropeway provided for the removal from the mine of minerals or refuse from it is deemed to form part of the mine: see s 180(6) (amended by SI 1999/2024).

     Premises exclusively occupied by the owner of the mine for the time being used for depositing refuse from it are also deemed to be part of the mine, and premises for the time being used for depositing refuse from two or more mines, being premises occupied by the owner of one of those mines (either exclusively or jointly with the owner of the other or any of the others) are deemed to form part of such one of those mines as the Health and Safety Executive may direct: see the Mines and Quarries Act 1954 s 180(4) (s 180(4), (5) amended by virtue of SI 1974/2013; and SI 1999/2024); and HEALTH AND SAFETY AT WORK vol 52 (2014) PARA 313.

     A railway line serving a single mine (not being a railway line falling under the Mines and Quarries Act 1954 s 180(3) or a railway line belonging to a railway company) is deemed to form part of the mine, and such a railway line jointly serving two or more mines is deemed to form part of such one of them as the Health and Safety Executive may direct: s 180(5) (amended by SI 1999/2024); and see HEALTH AND SAFETY AT WORK vol 52 (2014) PARA 313. 'Railway company' means any persons authorised by an enactment to construct, work or carry on a railway; and 'enactment' includes a provision of an order or scheme made under or confirmed by an Act: Mines and Quarries Act 1954 s 182(1) (definition amended by the Transport Act 1962 s 95(2), Sch 12 Pt II).

     As to the Health and Safety Executive see HEALTH AND SAFETY AT WORK vol 52 (2014) PARA 326 et seq.

14 'Coal mine' includes: (1) any space excavated underground for the purposes of coal-mining operations and any shaft or adit made for those purposes; (2) any space occupied by unworked coal; and (3) a coal quarry and opencast workings of coal: Coal Industry Act 1994 s 65(1). As to the meaning of 'coal-mining operations' see PARA 51.

15 'Mine' means any site on which mining operations are carried out: see the Town and Country Planning (General Permitted Development) Order 1995, SI 1995/418, art 1(2); *English Clays Lovering Pochin & Co Ltd v Plymouth Corpn* [1974] 2 All ER 239 at 242, [1974] 1 WLR 742 at 745, CA; definition of 'mine' not confined to surface manifestation at a site (see *Harworth Estates Ltd v Secretary of State for Housing, Communities and Local Government* (unreported, refusal of permission, CA, 18 September 2018) and PLANNING.

16 As to the meaning of 'minerals' see PARA 10. 'Mines' means mines of coal, ironstone, slate and other minerals: see the Acquisition of Land Act 1981 s 3, Sch 2 para 1(2); the Water Industry Act 1991 s 188, Sch 14 para 7(1); the Water Resources Act 1991 s 182, Sch 23 para 7(1) (amended by the Environment Act 1995 s 120(1), Sch 22 para 128). See also the High Peak Mining Customs and Mineral Courts Act 1851 and the Derbyshire Mining Customs and Mineral Courts Act 1852 which define 'mine' or 'mines', and 'vein' or 'veins' as a mine or mines, vein or veins of lead ore, and include parts of or shares in any mine or vein as well as entire mines and veins, and all minerals containing lead ore: High Peak Mining Customs and Mineral Courts Act 1851 s 2; Derbyshire Mining Customs and Mineral Courts Act 1852 s 2. As to lead mining in Derbyshire see PARA 592 et seq.

## 4. Meaning of 'quarry'.

'Quarry' usually implies surface workings of minerals, leaving no roof overhead[1]. The manner in which the minerals are extracted is not, however, a conclusive test in distinguishing a quarry from a mine[2]. Thus in some circumstances surface workings are regarded as mines[3], while 'quarry' may be used to denote workings for slate even where they are carried on almost exclusively underground[4], although it has been held that a slate quarry worked by means of underground levels is a mine[5]. A sand or gravel pit may be a quarry, but workings in a heap of furnace slag are not[6].

For the purposes of the Quarries Regulations 1999[7], 'quarry' means:

(1)    an excavation[8] or system of excavations made for the purpose of, or in connection with, the extraction of minerals[9] or products of minerals, being neither a mine nor merely a well or borehole or a well and borehole combined[10];

(2)    any reclamation site[11] from which minerals are being extracted for sale or further use[12]; or

(3)    any disused tip[13] which is not at a mine being worked[14] from which minerals are being extracted for sale or further use[15].

Notwithstanding head (1) above[16], 'quarry' does not include:

(a)    an excavation or system of excavations made for the purpose of or in connection with the extraction of such minerals or products of minerals where the exclusive purpose of that extraction is to enable the minerals or products of minerals so extracted to be used for the purpose of carrying out any building, civil engineering or engineering construction work on the site at which the extraction has taken place[17];

(b)    a public road[18]; or

(c)    a railway line which is exclusively under the control of a railway company[19], or a person who carries on an undertaking which consists of, or the main activity or one of the main activities of which consists of, the management of a network[20].

For these purposes, the following are deemed to form part of a quarry:

(i)    so much of the surface (including buildings, structures and works thereon) surrounding or adjacent to the quarry as is occupied for the purpose of, or in connection with: (A) the working of the quarry[21]; (B) the consumption, use, storage or preparation for sale of the minerals or products thereof extracted from the quarry[22]; or (C) the removal from the quarry of any substance extracted from the quarry[23]; and

(ii)    any tip (A) for the time being used in conjunction or connection with the operation of the quarry; or (B) whether or not it is for the time being in use, situated on premises occupied by the operator of the quarry[24].

1    *Darvill v Roper* (1855) 3 Drew 294; *Bell v Wilson* (1866) 1 Ch App 303 at 309, CA, per Turner LJ; *Glasgow Corpn v Farie* (1888) 13 App Cas 657 at 677, HL, per Lord Watson, and at 684 per Lord Herschell (dissenting). See also *Jones v Cwmorthen Slate Co Ltd* (1879) 5 Ex D 93, CA; *Earl of Jersey v Neath Poor Law Union Guardians* (1889) 22 QBD 555, CA; *Rogers (Inspector of Taxes) v Longsdon* [1967] Ch 93, [1966] 2 All ER 49.

2    *Glasgow Corpn v Farie* (1888) 13 App Cas 657 at 678, HL, per Lord Watson, and at 684 per Lord Herschell (dissenting); *Sim v Evans* (1875) 23 WR 730; *Jones v Cwmorthen Slate Co Ltd* (1879) 5 Ex D 93, CA; *Midland Rly Co and Kettering, Thrapston and Huntingdon Rly Co v Robinson* (1889) 15 App Cas 19 at 26, HL, per Lord Herschell, and at 33 per Lord Watson; *South Staffordshire Mines Drainage Comrs v Elwell & Sons* (1927) 97 LJKB 13 at 15, CA, per Bankes LJ; *South Staffordshire Mines Drainage Comrs v Grosvenor Colliery Co Ltd* (1961) 125 JP 484 at 485, CA, per Sellers LJ; *Rogers (Inspector of Taxes) v Longsdon* [1967] Ch 93 at 113, [1966] 2 All ER 49 at 59 per Stamp J; *NSW Associated Blue-Metal Quarries Ltd v Federal Comr of Taxation* (1956) 94 CLR 509, [1956] ALR 286, Aust HC. As to the meaning of 'mine' see PARA 3; and as to the meaning of 'minerals' see PARA 10.

3    See PARA 3.

4    *Glasgow Corpn v Farie* (1888) 13 App Cas 657 at 684, HL, per Lord Herschell (dissenting).

5    *Sim v Evans* (1875) 23 WR 730 (a decision under the Metalliferous Mines Regulation Act 1872 (repealed)).

6    *Scott v Midland Rly Co* [1901] 1 KB 317, DC (gravel or sand pit); *Scott v Midland Rly Co* (1897) 61 JP 358, DC (furnace slag), both decisions under the Quarries Act 1894 (repealed); and see *Airdrie, Coatbridge and District Water Trustees v Lanarkshire Assessor* 1908 SC 596, a decision under the Lands Valuation (Scotland) Act 1854 (repealed).

7    Ie the Quarries Regulations 1999, SI 1999/2024. As to the scope and application of the Quarries Regulations 1999, SI 1999/2024, see PARA 520.

8    'Excavation' means any place at the quarry where minerals are or have been extracted and includes the ground, faces or sides of the quarry and any other incline; and 'minerals' includes stone, slate, clay, gravel, sand and other natural deposits except peat: Quarries Regulations 1999, SI 1999/2024, reg 2(1).

9    Ie whether in their natural state or in solution or suspension: see the Quarries Regulations 1999, SI 1999/2024, reg 3(1)(a).

10    Quarries Regulations 1999, SI 1999/2024, reg 3(1)(a).

11    For this purpose, 'reclamation site' means a site where the extraction of minerals forms part of the process whereby that site is restored for agricultural, industrial or domestic use: see the Quarries Regulations 1999, SI 1999/2024, reg 3(1)(b).

12    Quarries Regulations 1999, SI 1999/2024, reg 3(1)(b).

13    'Tip' means an accumulation or deposit of any substance at a quarry (whether in a solid or liquid state or in solution or suspension) and includes, but is not limited to, over-burden dumps, backfill, spoil heaps, stock piles and lagoons, and where any wall or other structure retains or confines a tip then it must be deemed to form part of the tip: Quarries Regulations 1999, SI 1999/2024, reg 2(1). As to disused tips see PARA 558 et seq.

14    Ie within the meaning of the Mines Regulations 2014, SI 2014/3248, reg 2(2) (see HEALTH AND SAFETY AT WORK vol 53 (2014) PARA 702): see the Quarries Regulations 1999, SI 1999/2024, reg 3(1)(c) (amended by SI 2014/3248).

15    Quarries Regulations 1999, SI 1999/2024, reg 3(1)(c) (amended by SI 2014/3248).

16    Ie the Quarries Regulations 1999, SI 1999/2024, reg 3(1)(a).

17    Quarries Regulations 1999, SI 1999/2024, reg 3(2)(a).

18    Quarries Regulations 1999, SI 1999/2024, reg 3(2)(b). 'Public road' means a highway maintainable at public expense within the meaning of the Highways Act 1980 s 329 (see HIGHWAYS, STREETS AND BRIDGES vol 55 (2012) PARA 251): Quarries Regulations 1999, SI 1999/2024, reg 2(1).

19 'Railway company' means any person authorised by an enactment to construct, work or carry on a railway and for the purposes of this definition the expression 'enactment' includes a provision of an order or scheme made under or confirmed by an Act: Quarries Regulations 1999, SI 1999/2024, reg 2(1).

20 Quarries Regulations 1999, SI 1999/2024, reg 3(2)(c). 'Network' means a network within the meaning of the Railways Act 1993 s 83(1) (see RAILWAYS AND TRAMWAYS vol 86 (2017) PARA 81): Quarries Regulations 1999, SI 1999/2024, reg 3(2)(c).

21 Quarries Regulations 1999, SI 1999/2024, reg 3(3)(a)(i).

22 Quarries Regulations 1999, SI 1999/2024, reg 3(3)(a)(ii).

23 Quarries Regulations 1999, SI 1999/2024, reg 3(3)(a)(iii).

24 Quarries Regulations 1999, SI 1999/2024, reg 3(3)(b)(i), (ii). For the purposes of the Quarries Regulations 1999, SI 1999/2024:

    (1) where a tip is for the time being used in conjunction or connection with the operation of two or more quarries and is situated on premises occupied exclusively by the operator of one of those quarries, it must be treated as forming part of that quarry unless:

        (a) the operator of one of the other quarries in conjunction or connection with which the tip is for the time being used has agreed that the tip should be treated as forming part of the quarry of which he is the operator (reg 3(4)(a)(i)); and

        (b) notice to that effect has been given to the Health and Safety Executive by that operator (reg 3(4)(a)(ii));

    (2) where a tip is for the time being used in conjunction or connection with the operation of two or more quarries and is situated on premises occupied jointly by the operators of two or more of those quarries, the last-named operators must, for the purposes of the Quarries Regulations 1999, SI 1999/2024, be treated as being in joint and several control of that tip and as being jointly and severally responsible for it unless:

        (a) the said operators have agreed that one of their number should be treated as being in control of that tip and responsible for it (reg 3(4)(b)(i)); and

        (b) notice to that effect has been given to the Health and Safety Executive by the operator who is to be so treated (reg 3(4)(b)(ii)).

Upon receipt of a notice given in accordance with head (1)(b) or head (2)(b), the tip named in that notice is to be treated as forming part of the quarry specified in the notice: reg 3(5). As to the Health and Safety Executive see HEALTH AND SAFETY AT WORK vol 52 (2014) PARA 326 et seq.

## 5. Open and new mines, quarries and active and dormant mineral sites.

A mine[1] is said to be open when it has been devoted by a person lawfully entitled to do so to the purpose of making a profit by the working and sale of the minerals in it[2]. The question what is an open mine derives such importance as it has from its bearing upon the rights of limited owners[3]. The mine, if open at the time of the creation of limited estates, remains an open mine[4]. Under the old law[5] a mine might be opened, during the subsistence of the limitations under which such estates arose, either by a person having an estate enabling him to do so, as a tenant in tail in possession[6], or a person specially empowered, as a trustee having power to work[7] or lease mines[8].

The rules which apply to mines have been held to apply similarly to quarries[9] and other open workings, such as brickfields[10] or gravel pits[11].

For the purposes of provisions relating to the review of old mineral planning permissions and the periodic review of mineral planning permissions ('ROMP applications')[12], distinction is made between active and dormant mineral sites[13]. A dormant site is a site[14] in, on or under which no mineral development had been carried out to any substantial extent at any time beginning on 22 February 1982 and ending with 6 June 1995 otherwise than by virtue of a planning permission[15] which is not a relevant planning permission[16] relating to the site[17].

1 As to the meaning of 'mine' see PARA 3.

2 *Elias v Griffith* (1878) 8 ChD 521 at 532, CA; affd on another point sub nom *Elias v Snowdon Slate Quarries Co* (1879) 4 App Cas 454, HL. As to the meaning of 'minerals' see PARA 10.

3 See PARAS 289–290, 368 et seq. As to the rights of limited owners generally see SETTLEMENTS.

4   *Greville-Nugent v Mackenzie* [1900] AC 83, HL. Mines the working of which has been for a time suspended because of a diminished price to be got for the mineral or some other temporary cause are to be regarded as opened mines: *Greville-Nugent v Mackenzie* at 90. See also PARA 8. As to the statutory power to grant mining leases see PARA 289; and SETTLEMENTS.
5   As to the present law see PARA 282; and SETTLEMENTS.
6   *Clavering v Clavering* (1726) 2 P Wms 388.
7   *Chaytor v Trotter* (1902) 87 LT 33, CA.
8   *Daly v Beckett* (1857) 24 Beav 114; *Earl Cowley v Wellesley* (1866) LR 1 Eq 656; *Campbell v Wardlaw* (1883) 8 App Cas 641, HL.
9   *Elias v Griffith* (1878) 8 ChD 521 at 532, CA; affd on another point sub nom *Elias v Snowdon Slate Quarries Co* (1879) 4 App Cas 454, HL. See also now the Quarries Regulations 1999, SI 1999/2024; and PARA 520.
10   *Earl Cowley v Wellesley* (1866) LR 1 Eq 656; *Miller v Miller* (1872) LR 13 Eq 263.
11   *Huntley v Russell* (1849) 13 QB 572. As to peat see *Coppinger v Gubbins* (1846) 3 Jo & Lat 397.
12   Ie for the purposes of the Environment Act 1995 Sch 13, Sch 14: see PLANNING vol 82 (2018) PARAS 665 et seq, 933 et seq. As to ROMP applications see PARA 353; and PLANNING vol 82 (2018) PARA 99 et seq.
13   As to the meaning of 'mineral site' see PLANNING vol 82 (2018) PARA 665.
14   Ie a 'Phase I' or 'Phase II' site: see PLANNING vol 82 (2018) PARA 666.
15   As to the meaning of 'planning permission' see PLANNING vol 81 (2018) PARA 160.
16   As to the meaning of 'relevant planning permission' see PLANNING vol 82 (2018) PARA 665.
17   Environment Act 1995 Sch 13 para 1(1), Sch 14 para 3; and PLANNING vol 82 (2018) PARA 666.

## 6.   What is an open mine.

Whether a mine is open or not is a question of intention[1], which may be evidenced in various ways. If the mine has been worked with a view to profit it is open, even if no profit has in fact been made[2]. Sale of the products is not a necessary criterion of profit: use of the products (otherwise than for some restricted purpose) is sufficient[3]. It is open if it is included in a lease, reserving a share of profits, under which the lessee has worked[4], or in an agreement for a lease where a dead rent has become payable and workings are approaching by instroke[5], or if a proper working shaft has been sunk to the seam[6], even if no coal is in fact hewn[7].

1   *Chaytor v Trotter* (1902) 87 LT 33, CA. As to the meaning of 'mine' see PARA 3.
2   *Elias v Griffith* (1878) 8 ChD 521, CA; affd on appeal sub nom *Elias v Snowdon Slate Quarries Co* (1879) 4 App Cas 454, HL.
3   *Elias v Snowdon Slate Quarries Co* (1879) 4 App Cas 454 at 465, HL, per Lord Selborne. As to examples of workings for a restricted purpose see PARA 7.
4   *Elias v Snowdon Slate Quarries Co* (1879) 4 App Cas 454, HL; *Dashwood v Magniac* [1891] 3 Ch 306 at 327–328, CA, per Chitty J, and at 360–361 per Bowen LJ.
5   *Re Kemeys-Tynte, Kemeys-Tynte v Kemeys-Tynte* [1892] 2 Ch 211; and see *Stoughton v Leigh* (1808) 1 Taunt 402. As to the meaning of 'instroke' see PARA 327.
6   *Chaytor v Trotter* (1902) 87 LT 33, CA.
7   *Re Morgan, Vachell v Morgan* [1914] 1 Ch 910, CA.

## 7.   Workings which do not render a mine open.

It is not every working that will render a mine open[1]. Thus the mine is not open if the working is wrongful[2], or purely experimental[3], or for a restricted purpose, as for fuel or to repair a particular tenement[4]. The grant of a limited right, such as a grant to tenants of the right to scrape or scour for coal on the outcrop, is also insufficient[5], and so are workings by a person having a statutory right independently of the owner[6]. As a rule, the existence of an open mine on one part of an estate does not make the other mines open mines[7], especially where the estate is severed by land in different ownership[8].

1   As to the meaning of 'mine' see PARA 3.
2   *Bartlett v Phillips* (1859) 4 De G & J 414; *Ecclesiastical Comrs v Wodehouse* [1895] 1 Ch 552.

3  *Chaytor v Trotter* (1902) 87 LT 33, CA.
4  *Elias v Snowdon Slate Quarries Co* (1879) 4 App Cas 454, HL; and see *Campbell v Wardlaw* (1883) 8 App Cas 641 at 645, HL, per Lord Blackburn.
5  *Stepney v Chambers* [1866] WN 401.
6  *Huntley v Russell* (1849) 13 QB 572 (highway surveyors taking gravel for public purposes); and cf *Ross v Adcock* (1868) LR 3 CP 655 at 669, 670.
7  *Campbell v Wardlaw* (1883) 8 App Cas 641, HL.
8  *Re Maynard's Settled Estate* [1899] 2 Ch 347; and see *Lloyd-Jones v Clark-Lloyd* [1919] 1 Ch 424, CA.

## 8. When a mine ceases to be open.

It is a question of degree whether a mine which has once been opened but which has not been worked for a time ceases to be an open mine[1]. Interruption of working for a moderate period will not necessarily be treated as evidence of abandonment so as to prevent the mine remaining open[2]. Nor will the cessation of working for a longer period where the cessation is due to an unremunerative market for the produce[3]. But if a mine has not been worked for a very long period, for example a century, or has been abandoned for the benefit of the inheritance, it ceases to be an open mine[4].

1  *Bagot v Bagot, Legge v Legge* (1863) 32 Beav 509; *Greville-Nugent v Mackenzie* [1900] AC 83, HL; and see *Viner v Vaughan* (1840) 2 Beav 466. As to the meaning of 'mine' see PARA 3.
2  *Re Chaytor* [1900] 2 Ch 804, where a mine was still held to be open after workings had been interrupted for 17 years.
3  *Bagot v Bagot, Legge v Legge* (1863) 32 Beav 509.
4  *Bagot v Bagot, Legge v Legge* (1863) 32 Beav 509.

## 9. Opening of new mines.

When a mine is open, the sinking of a new pit in the same vein or seam, or breaking ground in a new place in the same rock, is not necessarily opening a new mine[1]. However, the sinking of a shaft for the purpose of working a mineral not worked in an existing open mine is an opening of a new mine[2].

1  *Clavering v Clavering* (1726) 2 P Wms 388; *Spencer v Scurr* (1862) 31 Beav 334; *Bagot v Bagot, Legge v Legge* (1863) 32 Beav 509; *Earl Cowley v Wellesley* (1866) LR 1 Eq 656 at 659; *Elias v Snowdon Slate Quarries Co* (1879) 4 App Cas 454, HL. As to the meaning of 'mine' see PARA 3.
2  *Spencer v Scurr* (1862) 31 Beav 334. As to the meaning of 'minerals' see PARA 10.

### (ii)  Minerals

## 10. Meaning of 'minerals'.

'Minerals' admits of a variety of meanings, and has no general definition[1]. Whether in a particular case a substance is a mineral or not is primarily a question of fact[2]. The test is what 'minerals' meant at the date of the instrument concerned[3] in the vernacular of the mining world, the commercial world and among landowners[4], and in case of conflict this meaning must prevail over the purely scientific meaning[5]. Nevertheless, 'minerals' is capable of limitation or expansion according to the intention with which it is used[6], and this intention may be inferred from the document itself or from consideration of the circumstances in which it was made[7]. In the case of the document itself, the inference may be drawn from a comparison with other parts of the document[8] or from the immediate context[9]. In a reservation of minerals out of a grant of land, the rules of construction describing the substances reserved are the same whether the grant is made by instrument between the parties or by statute[10]. In looking at the circumstances in which the document was made, regard must be had to the relative position of the parties interested, and to the substance of the transaction or arrangement which the instrument or statute embodies[11]. The fact that the owner of minerals is not entitled to get them by surface workings is not sufficient to restrict the meaning of 'minerals'[12]; but the meaning may be restricted by proof of a custom the existence of which is incompatible with the prima facie meaning[13], or by particular circumstances showing that not all the minerals were intended to be referred to[14].

In considering liquid and fugacious substances, such as oil or natural gas, cases which dealt with solid substances should be approached with some caution because different considerations may apply[15].

'Mines' is frequently found in collocation with 'minerals', as in the term 'mines and minerals' or its equivalents[16]. As so used 'mines' does not narrow the meaning of 'minerals', and the term is wide enough prima facie to include even those minerals which can only be got by surface workings[17]. 'Minerals' does not comprise the space occupied or formerly occupied by mineral substances, even though 'mines' may do so[18].

'Minerals' has been expressly defined for the purposes of certain statutes, for example the Mining Industry Act 1926[19], the Atomic Energy Act 1946[20], the Mines and Quarries Act 1954[21], the Opencast Coal Act 1958[22], the Mines (Working Facilities and Support) Act 1966[23], and the Town and Country Planning Act 1990[24]. 'Mines and minerals' has been defined for the purposes of the property legislation of 1925[25]. 'Hard mineral resources' has been defined for the purposes of the Deep Sea Mining (Temporary Provisions) Act 1981[26].

1    *North British Rly Co v Budhill Coal and Sandstone Co* [1910] AC 116 at 130, HL, per Lord Gorell; *Caledonian Rly Co v Glenboig Union Fireclay Co* [1911] AC 290 at 299, HL, per Lord Loreburn LC; *Earl of Lonsdale v A-G* [1982] 3 All ER 579 at 609, [1982] 1 WLR 887 at 924 per Slade J.

2    *Great Western Rly Co v Carpalla United China Clay Co Ltd* [1910] AC 83, HL; *Staples v Young* [1908] 1 IR 135, Ir CA; *George Skey & Co Ltd v Parsons* (1909) 101 LT 103; *Symington v Caledonian Rly Co* [1912] AC 87, HL (and see also *Caledonian Rly Co v Symington* (1913) 2 SLT 294 (further hearing)); *Waring v Foden* [1932] 1 Ch 276, CA; *A-G for Isle of Man v Moore* [1938] 3 All ER 263 at 267, PC. Expert evidence is therefore admissible on the issue: *Waring v Foden* at 302 per Romer LJ; *A-G for Isle of Man v Moore* at 267, 268; and see CUSTOM AND USAGE.

3    Evidence of the vernacular meaning at the date of trial may justify the assumption that there was a similar vernacular usage at the date of the grant: *Caledonian Rly Co v Glenboig Union Fireclay Co* [1911] AC 290 at 299, HL, per Lord Loreburn LC; *Earl of Lonsdale v A-G* [1982] 3 All ER 579 at 609, [1982] 1 WLR 887 at 924 per Slade J. As to the construction of instruments according to contemporary usage see DEEDS AND OTHER INSTRUMENTS vol 32 (2012) PARAS 404, 407.

4    This criterion was first suggested by James LJ in *Hext v Gill* (1872) 7 Ch App 699 at 719, but at 712 Mellish LJ formulated the test of whether the substance could be worked for the purpose of profit (cf PARA 6). The test of Mellish LJ as reported in 7 Ch App at 712 omits, perhaps because of a transcription error, a material passage which appears in other reports of *Hext v Gill* in 41 LJ Ch 761 at 762, 27 LT 291 at 295 and 20 WR 957 at 960; but there seems no indication that the omission has been noticed in any subsequent case. In any event there is a substantial weight of authority to show that the criterion suggested by James LJ is to be preferred: see *Glasgow Corpn v Farie* (1888) 13 App Cas 657, HL; *Re Todd, Birleston & Co v North Eastern Rly Co* [1903] 1 KB 603, 606, 607, CA, per the Earl of Halsbury LC; *North British Rly Co v Budhill Coal and Sandstone Co* [1910] AC 116, HL; *Caledonian Rly Co v Glenboig Union Fireclay Co* [1911] AC 290, HL; *Waring v Foden* [1932] 1 Ch 276, CA; *A-G for Isle of Man v Moore* [1938] 3 All ER 263 at 267, PC; *Borys v Canadian Pacific Rly Co* [1953] AC 217 at 223, [1953] 1 All ER 451 at 455, PC; *Earl of Lonsdale v A-G* [1982] 3 All ER 579 at 609, [1982] 1 WLR 887 at 925 per Slade J. Nevertheless, the purpose of profit may still have some bearing: see *North British Rly Co v Budhill Coal and Sandstone Co* at 132 per Lord Gorell; *O'Callaghan v Elliott* [1966] 1 QB 601 at 608, [1965] 3 All ER 111 at 113, CA, per Lord Denning MR; *Earl of Lonsdale v A-G* at 609 and 925 per Slade J. Similarly, the question whether the substance concerned has any rare or exceptional quality or value, as distinct from being part of the ordinary soil, may also be relevant: see *North British Rly Co v Budhill Coal and Sandstone Co*; *Great Western Rly Co v Carpalla United China Clay Co Ltd* [1910] AC 83, HL; *Caledonian Rly Co v Glenboig Union Fireclay Co*;

*Symington v Caledonian Rly Co* [1912] AC 87, HL; *Borthwick-Norton v Gavin Paul & Sons* 1947 SC 659, Ct of Sess; *O'Callaghan v Elliott*; and *Earl of Lonsdale v A-G*.

5  *Borys v Canadian Pacific Rly Co* [1953] AC 217 at 223, [1953] 1 All ER 451 at 455, PC.

6  *Glasgow Corpn v Farie* (1888) 13 App Cas 657 at 675, HL, per Lord Watson. The test of intention is objective: *Earl of Lonsdale v A-G* [1982] 3 All ER 579 at 610, [1982] 1 WLR 887 at 925 per Slade J.

7  See *Commonwealth of Australia v Hazeldell Ltd* [1921] 2 AC 373, PC; *Earl of Lonsdale v A-G* [1982] 3 All ER 579 at 609, [1982] 1 WLR 887 at 925 per Slade J.

8  *Wainman v Earl of Rosse* (1848) 2 Exch 800.

9  *A-G for Isle of Man v Mylchreest* (1879) 4 App Cas 294, PC; *Barnard-Argue-Roth-Stearns Oil and Gas Co Ltd v Farquharson* [1912] AC 864, PC.

10  *North British Rly Co v Budhill Coal and Sandstone Co* [1910] AC 116 at 127, HL, per Lord Loreburn LC, and at 138 per Lord Shaw of Dunfermline; *Great Western Rly Co v Carpalla United China Clay Co Ltd* [1910] AC 83, HL; *Glasgow Corpn v Farie* (1888) 13 App Cas 657 at 672, HL, per Lord Halsbury LC; *Waring v Foden* [1932] 1 Ch 276. It is submitted that the dicta to the contrary of Lord Herschell in *Midland Rly Co and Kettering, Thrapston and Huntingdon Rly Co v Robinson* (1889) 15 App Cas 19 at 27, HL, and of Buckley J in *Great Western Rly Co v Blades* [1901] 2 Ch 624 at 632 do not represent the law: see *Waring v Foden* at 288 per Lord Hanworth MR.

11  *Glasgow Corpn v Farie* (1888) 13 App Cas 657 at 675, HL, per Lord Watson; *Waring v Foden* [1932] 1 Ch 276, CA. As to the meaning of 'minerals' in building contracts see BUILDING CONTRACTS vol 6 (2018) PARA 234.

12  *Bell v Wilson* (1866) 1 Ch App 303; *Hext v Gill* (1872) 7 Ch App 699; cf *Earl of Lonsdale v A-G* [1982] 3 All ER 579 at 609, [1982] 1 WLR 887 at 924.

13  *A-G for Isle of Man v Mylchreest* (1879) 4 App Cas 294, PC; *Tucker v Linger* (1882) 21 ChD 18, CA (on appeal (1883) 8 App Cas 508, HL).

14  *Darvill v Roper* (1855) 3 Drew 294.

15  *Earl of Lonsdale v A-G* [1982] 3 All ER 579 at 610, [1982] 1 WLR 887 at 925 per Slade J.

16  Eg the term 'mines of coal, ironstone, slate or other minerals': see the Railways Clauses Consolidation Act 1845 s 77; the Acquisition of Land Act 1981 s 3, Sch 2 para 1(2); the Water Industry Act 1991 s 188, Sch 14 para 7(1); the Water Resources Act 1991 s 182, Sch 23 para 7(1) (substituted by the Environment Act 1995 s 120(1), Sch 22 para 128). As to the meaning of 'mine' see PARA 3.

17  *Hext v Gill* (1872) 7 Ch App 699; *Midland Rly Co v Haunchwood Brick and Tile Co* (1882) 20 ChD 552; *Glasgow Corpn v Farie* (1888) 13 App Cas 657 at 690, HL, per Lord Macnaghten; *Midland Rly Co and Kettering, Thrapston and Huntingdon Rly Co v Robinson* (1889) 15 App Cas 19, HL; *Great Western Rly Co v Carpalla United China Clay Co Ltd* [1910] AC 83, HL; cf *Earl of Lonsdale v A-G* [1982] 3 All ER 579 at 609, [1982] 1 WLR 887 at 924.

18  *Ramsay v Blair* (1876) 1 App Cas 701, HL; *Ballacorkish Silver, Lead and Copper Mining Co v Harrison* (1873) LR 5 PC 49; and see *Batten Pooll v Kennedy* [1907] 1 Ch 256. See also PARA 5.

19  For the purposes of the Mining Industry Act 1926 s 23(1) 'minerals' includes petroleum within the meaning of the Petroleum Act 1998 Pt I (ss 1–9) (see ENERGY AND CLIMATE CHANGE vol 44 (2011) PARA 1030): Mining Industry Act 1926 s 23(6) (added by the Petroleum Act 1998 s 50, Sch 4 para 1). The Mining Industry Act 1926 s 23(1) imposes on persons sinking bore holes for the purpose of searching for or getting minerals obligations to give certain facilities to the Natural Environment Research Council: see PARA 356.

20  'Minerals' includes all substances obtained or obtainable from the soil by underground or surface working: Atomic Energy Act 1946 s 18(1); and see ENERGY AND CLIMATE CHANGE vol 44 (2011) PARA 790.

21  'Minerals' includes stone, slate, clay, gravel, sand and other natural deposits except peat: Mines and Quarries Act 1954 s 182(1); and see HEALTH AND SAFETY AT WORK vol 52 (2014) PARA 313.

22  'Minerals' includes stone, slate, clay, gravel, sand and similar deposits: Opencast Coal Act 1958 s 51(1); and see PARA 434.

23  'Minerals' includes all minerals and substances in or under land obtainable by underground or by surface working: see the Mines (Working Facilities and Support) Act 1966 s 14(1).

24  'Minerals' includes all substances of a kind ordinarily worked for removal by underground or surface working, except it does not include peat cut for purposes other than sale: Town and Country Planning Act 1990 s 336(1) (amended by the Planning and Compensation Act 1991 s 21, Sch 1 para 12(c)); and see PARA 352; and PLANNING vol 81 (2018) PARA 8.

25 'Mines and minerals' includes any strata or seam of minerals or substances in or under any land and powers of working and getting the same: see the Law of Property Act 1925 s 205(1)(ix); the Trustee Act 1925 s 68(6) (both amended by the Trusts of Land and Appointment of Trustees Act 1996 s 25(2), Sch 4); and the Land Registration Act 2002 s 132(1). 'Mines and minerals' means mines and minerals whether already opened or in work or not, and includes all minerals and substances in, on, or under the land obtainable by underground or by surface working: see the Settled Land Act 1925 s 117(1)(xv); and the Universities and College Estates Act 1925 s 43(vii) (amended by the University and College Estates Act 1964 s 4(1)).

26 'Hard mineral resources' means deposits of nodules containing (in quantities greater than trace) at least one of the following elements: manganese, nickel, cobalt, copper, phosphorus and molybdenum: Deep Sea Mining (Temporary Provisions) Act 1981 s 1(6); and see INTERNATIONAL RELATIONS LAW vol 61 (2010) PARA 175.

## 11. Particular minerals.

The numerous cases in which specific substances have been decided or assumed to be or not to be minerals must be considered[1] as decisions on the particular facts[2]. Thus in particular circumstances the following substances have been held or assumed to be minerals: asphalt[3]; basalt[4]; bog-earth[5]; brick-clay[6]; brine[7]; calc spar and calk (barytes)[8]; clay, whether common[9], china[10], London[11] or terra cotta[12]; copper[13]; felsite[14]; fireclay[15]; freestone[16]; gravel[17]; granite[18]; gypsum[19]; ironstone[20]; kieselguhr (diatomite)[21]; lead[22]; limestone[23]; loam[24]; marble[25]; marl[26]; peat-earth[27]; petroleum and natural gas[28]; pitch[29]; salt[30]; sand[31]; sandstone[32]; shale[33]; stone[34]; tin[35]; and whinstone[36].

On the other hand, the following substances, which include some of those already listed above, have been held or assumed in particular circumstances not to be minerals: brick-earth (although described as valuable)[37]; clay in the popular sense[38]; clay of great thickness[39]; freestone[40]; furnace slag[41]; gravel[42]; limestone[43]; natural gas[44]; oil[45]; oil shale[46]; salt (obtained from lime)[47]; sand[48]; sandstone[49]; stone[50]; and tap-cinder (obtained in the manufacture of pig-iron)[51].

1 Ie for the reasons stated in PARA 10.
2 In some cases the courts, in formulating the issues of fact, have adopted the test of profit arrived at by Mellish LJ in *Hext v Gill* (1872) 7 Ch App 699 at 712. It is submitted that in view of the weight of authority against this test (see PARA 10) such cases must be treated with caution, even on their facts. Substances which, on the test of profit, have been held or stated to be minerals include brick-clay (*Earl of Jersey v Neath Poor Law Union Guardians* (1889) 22 QBD 555, CA; *Shaftesbury v Wallace* [1897] 1 IR 381); brick-earth (*Tucker v Linger* (1882) 21 ChD 18 at 36, CA, per Jessel MR (on appeal (1883) 8 App Cas 508, HL); *Robinson v Milne* (1884) 53 LJ Ch 1070); clay (*Loosemore v Tiverton and North Devon Rly Co* (1882) 22 ChD 25 at 42, 43 per Fry J); china clay (*Hext v Gill* at 712 per Mellish LJ); coal (*Johnstone v Crompton & Co* [1899] 2 Ch 190); coprolites (*A-G v Tomline* (1877) 5 ChD 750 at 762 per Fry J; cf *Dant v Moore* (1863) 9 LT 381); flints under the surface (*Tucker v Linger* (1882) 21 ChD 18, CA; on appeal (1883) 8 App Cas 508 at 512, HL, per Lord Blackburn); limestone (*Fishbourne v Hamilton* (1890) 25 LR Ir 483); red rock (*Johnstone v Crompton & Co* [1899] 2 Ch 190); and sand (*Tucker v Linger* (1882) 21 ChD 18 at 36, CA, per Jessel MR; on appeal (1883) 8 App Cas 508, HL). Substances which, on that test, have been held or assumed not to be minerals include blue brick clay (*Great Western Rly Co v Blades* [1901] 2 Ch 624); clay and sandstone (*George Skey & Co Ltd v Parsons* (1909) 101 LT 103); flints, dug up in the ordinary course of ploughing (*Tucker v Linger* (1882) 21 ChD 18 at 36, CA, per Jessel MR (but see on appeal (1883) 8 App Cas 508, HL)); and sand (*Staples v Young* [1908] 1 IR 135, Ir CA).
3 *Trinidad Asphalt Co v Ambard* [1899] AC 594 at 602, PC.
4 *Re Woodside's Estate* [1929] NI 75, NI CA.
5 *Earl Cowley v Wellesley* (1866) as reported in 35 Beav 635.
6 *Marquis of Salisbury v Gladstone* (1860) 6 H & N 123 at 127, Ex Ch, per Wightman J (on appeal (1861) 9 HL Cas 692); *Midland Rly Co v Miles* (1886) 33 ChD 632 at 642 per Stirling J.
7 *A-G v Salt Union Ltd* [1917] 2 KB 488.
8 *Stokes v Arkwright* (1897) 66 LJQB 845, DC.
9 *Midland Rly Co v Haunchwood Brick and Tile Co* (1882) 20 ChD 552.
10 *Great Western Rly Co v Carpalla United China Clay Co Ltd* [1910] AC 83, HL.

11 *Errington v Metropolitan District Rly Co* (1882) 19 ChD 559 at 571, CA, per Jessel MR.
12 *Ruabon Brick and Terra Cotta Co v Great Western Rly Co* [1893] 1 Ch 427 at 463, CA, per A
    L Smith LJ.
13 *North British Rly Co v Budhill Coal and Sandstone Co* [1910] AC 116 at 133, HL, per Lord
    Gorell; *Bishop of Winchester v Knight* (1717) 1 P Wms 406.
14 *Anstruther's Trustees v IRC* 1912 SC 1165, Ct of Sess.
15 *Caledonian Rly Co v Glenboig Union Fireclay Co* [1911] AC 290, HL; *Midland Rly Co v Checkley*
    (1867) LR 4 Eq 19.
16 *Bell v Wilson* (1866) 1 Ch App 303; *Mawson v Fletcher* (1870) 6 Ch App 91 at 95 per Mellish LJ;
    *Glasgow and South Western Rly Co v Bain* (1893) 21 R 134, Ct of Sess; *Symington v Caledonian
    Rly Co* [1912] AC 87, HL (and see *Caledonian Rly Co v Symington* (1913) 2 SLT 294 (further
    hearing)).
17 *Earl Cowley v Wellesley* (1866) LR 1 Eq 656 at 659 per Lord Romilly MR; *Midland Rly Co v
    Checkley* (1867) LR 4 Eq 19; *Errington v Metropolitan District Rly Co* (1882) 19 ChD 559 at 571,
    CA, per Jessel MR; *Scott v Midland Rly Co* [1901] 1 KB 317, DC.
18 *A-G v Welsh Granite Co* (1887) 35 WR 617, CA; *Anstruther's Trustees v IRC* 1912 SC 1165, Ct
    of Sess.
19 *General Accident Fire and Life Assurance Corpn Ltd v British Gypsum Ltd* [1967] 3 All ER 40,
    [1967] 1 WLR 1215.
20 *Midland Rly Co and Kettering, Thrapston and Huntingdon Rly Co v Robinson* (1889) 15 App Cas
    19, HL; *Midland Rly Co v Checkley* (1867) LR 4 Eq 19.
21 *Re Chichester-Clark's Estate* [1937] NI 98.
22 *North British Rly Co v Budhill Coal and Sandstone Co* [1910] AC 116 at 133, HL, per Lord
    Gorell.
23 *Midland Rly Co v Checkley* (1867) LR 4 Eq 19; *Mawson v Fletcher* (1870) 6 Ch App 91 at 95 per
    Mellish LJ; *Dixon v Caledonian and Glasgow and South Western Railway Companies* (1880) 5
    App Cas 820, HL (cf *North British Rly Co v Budhill Coal and Sandstone Co* [1910] AC 116 at
    124, HL); *Midland Rly Co and Kettering, Thrapston and Huntingdon Rly Co v Robinson* (1889)
    15 App Cas 19, HL; *Edinburgh and District Water Trustees v Clippens Oil Co* (1898) 25 R 504,
    Ct of Sess; and see *Commonwealth of Australia v Hazeldell Ltd* [1921] 2 AC 373, PC.
24 *Earl Cowley v Wellesley* (1866) as reported in 35 Beav 635.
25 *Midland Rly Co v Checkley* (1867) LR 4 Eq 19 at 25 per Lord Romilly MR.
26 *Midland Rly Co v Checkley* (1867) as reported in 36 LJCh 380 at 382 per Lord Romilly MR.
27 *Earl Cowley v Wellesley* (1866) as reported in 35 Beav 635.
28 *Knight Sugar Co Ltd v Alberta Rly and Irrigation Co* [1938] 1 All ER 266, PC; and see *Borys v
    Canadian Pacific Rly Co* [1953] AC 217, [1953] 1 All ER 451, PC; *Ontario Natural Gas Co v
    Smart* (1890) 19 OR 591.
29 *Trinidad Asphalt Co v Ambard* [1899] AC 594, PC.
30 *North British Rly Co v Budhill Coal and Sandstone Co* [1910] AC 116 at 133, HL, per Lord
    Gorell.
31 *Hanmer v Chance* (1864) 11 LT 667 at 669, 670 (on appeal (1865) 4 De G J & Sm 626); *Earl
    Cowley v Wellesley* (1866) as reported in 35 Beav 635; *Nisbet Hamilton v North British Rly Co*
    (1886) 13 R 454, Ct of Sess; *Scott v Midland Rly Co* [1901] 1 KB 317, DC.
32 *Greville v Hemingway* (1902) 87 LT 443.
33 *Earl of Hopetoun v North British Rly Co* (1893) 20 R 704 at 711, Ct of Sess; *Edinburgh and
    District Water Trustees v Clippens Oil Co* (1898) 25 R 504, Ct of Sess.
34 *Earl of Rosse v Wainman* (1845) 14 M & W 859 (on appeal sub nom *Wainman v Earl of Rosse*
    (1848) 2 Exch 800); *Micklethwait v Winter* (1851) 6 Exch 644; *Nisbet Hamilton v North British
    Rly Co* (1886) 13 R 454, Ct of Sess.
35 *North British Rly Co v Budhill Coal and Sandstone Co* [1910] AC 116 at 133, HL, per Lord
    Gorell.
36 *Forth Bridge Rly Co v Dunfermline Guildry* 1909 SC 493 (cf *North British Rly Co v Budhill Coal
    and Sandstone Co* [1910] AC 116 at 124, HL, per Lord Loreburn LC); *Anstruther's Trustees v
    IRC* 1912 SC 1165, Ct of Sess; and see *Caledonian Rly Co v Symington* (1913) 2 SLT 294 at 305
    per Lord Cullen.
37 *Church v Inclosure Comrs* (1862) 11 CBNS 664; *Re Todd, Birleston & Co and North Eastern Rly
    Co* [1903] 1 KB 603, CA.
38 *A-G for Isle of Man v Mylchreest* (1879) 4 App Cas 294, PC; *Glasgow Corpn v Farie* (1888) 13
    App Cas 657, HL.
39 *Re Todd, Birleston & Co and North Eastern Rly Co* [1903] 1 KB 603, CA.
40 *Menzies v Earl of Breadalbane and Holland* (1822) 1 Sh Sc App 225; *Hamilton v Bentley* (1841)
    3 Dunl 1121, Ct of Sess.
41 *Scott v Midland Rly Co* (1897) 13 TLR 398.

42   *Waring v Foden* [1932] 1 Ch 276, CA.
43   *Darvill v Roper* (1855) 3 Drew 294; *Brown v Chadwick* (1857) 7 ICLR 101; *Countess of Listowel v Gibbings* (1858) 9 ICLR 223.
44   *Barnard-Argue-Roth-Stearns Oil and Gas Co Ltd v Farquharson* [1912] AC 864, PC; *Earl of Lonsdale v A-G* [1982] 3 All ER 579, [1982] 1 WLR 887.
45   *Earl of Lonsdale v A-G* [1982] 3 All ER 579, [1982] 1 WLR 887.
46   *Marquis of Linlithgow v North British Rly Co* 1912 SC 1327; affd on other grounds [1914] AC 820, HL.
47   *Re Dudley's Settled Estates* (1882) 26 Sol Jo 359.
48   *A-G for Isle of Man v Mylchreest* (1879) 4 App Cas 294 at 305, PC; *Waring v Foden* [1932] 1 Ch 276, CA; *Borthwick-Norton v Gavin Paul & Sons* 1947 SC 659; *MacDonald v Inverness-shire Assessor* 1954 SC 89.
49   *North British Rly Co v Budhill Coal and Sandstone Co* [1910] AC 116, HL.
50   *Nisbet Hamilton v North British Rly Co* (1886) 13 R 454, Ct of Sess.
51   *Boileau v Heath* [1898] 2 Ch 301; cf *Elwes v Brigg Gas Co* (1886) 33 ChD 562 at 566–567 per Chitty J.

## 12. Onus of proof.

The onus of proof that a particular substance was, at the date of the document to be construed, or is, at the present day, regarded as a mineral is upon those raising the contention[1], and the court may be justified in assuming that the meaning of 'minerals' at the date of the document in question was the same as it is at the present day unless there is evidence to the contrary[2]. Where, however, there is a contract for sale, the meaning to be applied will be the meaning at the date of the contract, even though a considerable period elapses before the formal conveyance is executed[3].

1   *North British Rly Co v Budhill Coal and Sandstone Co* [1910] AC 116 at 134, HL, per Lord Gorell. As to the meaning of 'minerals' see PARA 10.
2   *Caledonian Rly Co v Glenboig Union Fireclay Co* [1911] AC 290 at 299, HL, per Lord Loreburn LC; *Earl of Lonsdale v A-G* [1982] 3 All ER 579 at 609, [1982] 1 WLR 887 at 924 per Slade J.
3   *Marquis of Linlithgow v North British Rly Co* 1912 SC 1327; on appeal [1914] AC 820, HL.

## 13. Meaning of 'mineral substances'.

For all practical purposes 'minerals' and 'mineral substances' are synonymous terms, and the meaning of 'mineral substances' depends on the expressed or implied intention with which the words are used, as much as 'minerals', and accordingly what is said in the authorities as to the meaning of 'minerals'[1] applies with equal force to 'mineral substances'[2].

1   See PARAS 10–11.
2   *Waring v Foden* [1932] 1 Ch 276, CA.

### (iii) Other Terms

## 14. Meanings of 'bed', 'seam' and 'vein'.

In a legal document, the context may show that the word 'bed' or 'seam', instead of bearing its normal meaning of a layer or member of a series of stratified rocks, is used to designate a deposit consisting of two or more strata of mineral separated by thin layers of other rock, for example shale, as distinguished from any one layer of mineral. In such a case 'vein' is sometimes applied to each of the layers of minerals comprised in the seam[1].

1   See *Brewer v Rhymney Iron Co* [1910] 1 Ch 766 at 775. See also PARAS 3, 149. As to the meaning of 'minerals' see PARA 10.

## 15. Meanings of 'colliery' and 'coal measures'.

'Colliery' includes or may include all contiguous and connected veins[1] and seams of coal which are worked as one concern, together with the workings and machinery necessary for working the minerals[2] and the business of selling the coal worked[3]. 'Coal measures' has been held to include those identifiable seams of coal which are or might be worth mining[4].

1 See PARA 3.
2 *Hodgson v Field* (1806) 7 East 613 at 620; *Chaytor v Trotter* (1901) 87 LT 33 at 35. As to the meaning of 'minerals' see PARA 10.
3 *Gloucester County Bank v Rudry Merthyr Steam and House Coal Colliery Co* [1895] 1 Ch 629, CA.
4 *Earl of Lonsdale v A-G* [1982] 3 All ER 579 at 617, [1982] 1 WLR 887 at 935 per Slade J.

## 16. Meaning of 'pit'.

'Pit' has no precise meaning. In reference to underground workings it can denote not only the shafts but also the underground workings to which they give access[1]. It can also describe workings on the surface, whether the mineral is taken from the bottom or the sides of the workings[2].

1 See *Lofthouse Colliery Ltd v Ogden* [1913] 3 KB 120 at 123, a case decided under the Coal Mines (Minimum Wage) Act 1912 (repealed).
2 *Ellis v Bromley Local Board* (1876) 45 LJ Ch 763 at 764, CA, per Mellish LJ. As to the meaning of 'minerals' see PARA 10.

## 17. Meaning of 'land' and cognate terms.

Prima facie 'land' or 'lands' includes everything on or under the surface[1], although this meaning has in some cases been held to have been restricted by the context[2]. 'Soil' is apt to denote the surface and everything above and below it[3], but similarly its meaning may be restricted by the context so as to exclude the mines[4]. 'Subsoil' includes everything from the surface to the centre of the earth[5]; and 'surface' may include, in addition to the actual plane surface, all the land except the mines[6], or the soil overlying the minerals[7]. The word 'stratum' may be used in legislation in a special sense[8]. 'Close'[9], 'tenement'[10] and 'hereditament'[11] are sufficiently wide to include the mines.

1 *Newcomen v Coulson* (1877) 5 ChD 133 at 142, CA; Shep Touch (7th Edn) 90; *Campbell v Leach* (1775) Amb 740 at 748; *Railways Comr v Valuer-General* [1974] AC 328 at 351–354, PC. 'Lands' as used in the Railways Clauses Consolidation Act 1845 s 6 includes mines: see *Smith v Great Western Rly Co* (1877) 3 App Cas 165, HL. As to the meaning of 'land' see further eg LANDLORD AND TENANT vol 62 (2016) PARAS 1, 17. See also REAL PROPERTY AND REGISTRATION vol 87 (2017) PARAS 6–7.
2 *Thursby v Churchwardens of Briercliffe-with-Extwistle* [1895] AC 32, HL; and see *R v West Ardsley Inhabitants* (1863) 4 B & S 95; *Railways Comr v Valuer-General* [1974] AC 328, PC. 'Land' has been statutorily defined: see eg the Law of Property Act 1925 s 205(1)(ix) (see REAL PROPERTY AND REGISTRATION vol 87 (2017) PARA 7); the Opencast Coal Act 1958 s 51(1) (see PARA 414); and the Town and Country Planning Act 1990 s 336(1) (see PLANNING vol 81 (2018) PARA 3) (this definition is applied by the Mineral Workings Act 1951 s 41: see PARA 581).
3 *Thomson v St Catharine's College, Cambridge* [1919] AC 468 at 480, HL, per Lord Finlay; and see *Townley v Gibson* (1788) 2 Term Rep 701 at 706; *Pretty v Solly* (1859) 26 Beav 606; *Wakefield v Duke of Buccleuch* (1867) LR 4 Eq 613 (affd sub nom *Duke of Buccleuch v Wakefield* (1870) LR 4 HL 377).
4 *Pretty v Solly* (1859) 26 Beav 606; *Wakefield v Duke of Buccleuch* (1867) LR 4 Eq 613 (affd sub nom *Duke of Buccleuch v Wakefield* (1870) LR 4 HL 377). As to the meaning of 'mine' see PARA 3.
5 *Cox v Glue* (1848) 5 CB 533.
6 *Pountney v Clayton* (1883) 11 QBD 820 at 839, 840, CA.
7 *Humphries v Brogden* (1850) 12 QB 739. As to the meaning of 'minerals' see PARA 10.

8  *Railways Comr v Valuer-General* [1974] AC 328 at 353–354, PC (a case on the Valuation of Land Act 1916 (New South Wales)).
9  *Cox v Glue* (1848) 5 CB 533; and see LANDLORD AND TENANT vol 62 (2016) PARA 154.
10 *Loosemore v Tiverton and North Devon Rly Co* (1882) 22 ChD 25 at 43; on appeal sub nom *Tiverton and North Devon Rly Co v Loosemore* (1884) 9 App Cas 480, HL.
11 *Dunn v Birmingham Canal Co* (1872) LR 8 QB 42 at 48, Ex Ch.

# 2. OWNERSHIP

## (1) Property in Mines; Presumption of Ownership

### 18. Presumption arising from surface ownership.

Mines, quarries and minerals in their original position are part and parcel of the land[1]. Consequently the owner of surface land is entitled prima facie to everything beneath or within it, down to the centre of the earth[2]. This principle applies even where title to the surface has been acquired by prescription[3], but it is subject to exceptions. Thus, at common law, mines of gold and silver belong to the Crown[4], and by statute unworked coal which was, at the restructuring date, vested in the British Coal Corporation is vested in the Coal Authority[5]. Any minerals removed from land under a compulsory rights order for opencast working of coal become the property of the person entitled to the rights conferred by the order[6]. The property in petroleum existing in its natural condition in strata is vested by statute in the Crown[7].

If an estate in fee simple in land is acquired by enlargement of a long term, the estate thus acquired includes the mines and minerals which at the time of enlargement had not been severed in right or in fact, or had not been severed or reserved by an Inclosure Act or award[8].

1   See *Wilkinson v Proud* (1843) 11 M & W 33; *Williamson v Wootton* (1855) 3 Drew 210 at 213; *Kerr v Pawson* (1858) 25 Beav 394 at 406. As to the meaning of 'mine' see PARA 3; and as to the meaning of 'quarry' see PARA 4. As to the meaning of 'minerals' see PARA 10.
2   *Rowbotham v Wilson* (1860) 8 HL Cas 348 at 360 per Lord Wensleydale; *Mines Case* (1567) 1 Plowd 310, Ex Ch; *Lewis v Branthwaite* (1831) 2 B & Ad 437 at 443; *Keyse v Powell* (1853) 2 E & B 132; *Pountney v Clayton* (1883) 11 QBD 820 at 839, CA, per Bowen LJ; and see *Curtis v Daniel* (1808) 10 East 273; *Rowe v Grenfel* (1824) Ry & M 396; *Egremont Burial Board v Egremont Iron Ore Co* (1880) 14 ChD 158.
3   *Seddon v Smith* (1877) 36 LT 168, CA; cf *Walker v Jeffreys* (1842) 1 Hare 341 at 349.
4   *Mines Case* (1567) 1 Plowd 310 at 336. As to the law relating to royal mines and prerogative rights of mining see CROWN AND CROWN PROCEEDINGS vol 29 (2014) PARA 132 et seq.
5   The ownership of unworked coal which had been alienated by the Coal Commission under the Coal Act 1938 s 17(3) (repealed) did not vest in the National Coal Board (later renamed the British Coal Corporation: see PARA 49) under the Coal Industry Nationalisation Act 1946 s 5, Sch 1 (repealed) and so did not pass to the Coal Authority under the Coal Industry Act 1994 s 7(3) (see PARA 66). Accordingly, such coal remains in private hands.
     As to the restructuring date (ie 31 October 1994) see PARA 50. As to the Coal Commission and the British Coal Corporation see PARAS 49–50; and as to the Coal Authority see PARA 52 et seq. As to coal in the continental shelf see PARA 24.
6   See the Opencast Coal Act 1958 s 10(1); and PARA 434.
7   See ENERGY AND CLIMATE CHANGE vol 44 (2011) PARA 1039.
8   See the Law of Property Act 1925 s 153(10); and REAL PROPERTY AND REGISTRATION vol 87 (2017) PARA 84.

### 19. Rebuttal of presumption of ownership.

The ownership in mines[1] under land may be severed from the ownership of the surface[2], and the mines so severed are a separate tenement, capable of being held for the same estates as other hereditaments[3], and with similar incidental rights of ownership[4]. It follows that the presumption arising from surface ownership[5] may be rebutted by evidence showing that the ownership of the surface has been severed from that of the underlying mines, as by a conveyance or demise of land excepting the mines, or of the mines excepting the surface[6], or by Act of Parliament[7]. The presumption may also be rebutted by evidence of a long and continuous enjoyment of the mines by persons other than the owners of the surface[8]. The different strata of a parcel of land may likewise be shown to be in different ownership[9]; and proof of ownership of a mine under any parcel of land does not raise any presumption or afford any evidence regarding ownership of the surface[10], or of ownership of the other mines under the same parcel of land[11].

1  As to the meaning of 'mine' see PARA 3.
2  *Barnes v Mawson* (1813) 1 M & S 77; *Rowe v Grenfel* (1824) Ry & M 396; *Harris v Ryding* (1839) 5 M & W 60; *Cox v Glue* (1848) 5 CB 533; *Humphries v Brogden* (1850) 12 QB 739; *Keyse v Powell* (1853) 2 E & B 132. See further PARA 306.
3  *Port v Turton* (1763) 2 Wils 169; *Stoughton v Leigh* (1808) 1 Taunt 402.
4  *Duke of Hamilton v Graham* (1871) LR 2 Sc & Div 166; *Seaman v Vawdrey* (1810) 16 Ves 390 at 392; *Rowbotham v Wilson* (1857) 8 E & B 123, Ex Ch (affd (1860) 8 HL Cas 348). See also PARA 114.
5  See PARA 18.
6  *Harris v Ryding* (1839) 5 M & W 60; *Cox v Glue* (1848) 5 CB 533.
7  Eg severance of mines has been effected by numerous Inclosure Acts: see COMMONS vol 13 (2017) PARA 397. See also PARA 310 et seq.
8  *Rowe v Grenfel* (1824) Ry & M 396; *Cox v Glue* (1848) 5 CB 533; and see CIVIL PROCEDURE vol 12 (2015) PARA 730.
9  *Cox v Glue* (1848) 5 CB 533.
10 *Tyrwhitt v Wynne* (1819) 2 B & Ald 554.
11 *London and North Western Rly Co v Howley Park Coal and Cannel Co* [1911] 2 Ch 97 at 111, CA, per Cozens-Hardy MR, and at 131 per Buckley LJ; on appeal sub nom *Howley Park Coal and Cannel Co v London and North Western Rly Co* [1913] AC 11, HL.

## 20.  Ownership of coal.

By statute, the fee simple in all coal[1] and mines of coal[2], with the exception of certain retained interests[3] and statutory rights but including certain other property and rights, vested in the Coal Commission on 1 July 1942 and compensation was paid for the interests so acquired[4]. When the coal industry was nationalised[5] the proprietary rights of the Coal Commission and colliery concerns[6] (including retained interests) in unworked coal[7], mines of coal[8] and in certain associated minerals were transferred to the National Coal Board[9], which was later renamed the British Coal Corporation[10]. On the subsequent restructuring of the coal industry[11] the interests of the British Coal Corporation in unworked coal and coal mines were transferred to the Coal Authority[12].

1  As to the meaning of 'coal' for these purposes see PARA 48.
2  As to the meaning of 'mine of coal' for these purposes see PARA 48.
3  As to retained interests see PARA 48.
4  See the Coal Act 1938 s 3(1) (repealed); and PARA 48.
5  Ie by the Coal Industry Nationalisation Act 1946: see PARA 49.
6  As to the meaning of 'colliery concern' see PARA 49.
7  As to the meaning of 'coal' for these purposes see PARA 49.
8  As to the meaning of 'mine of coal' for these purposes see PARA 49.
9  See the Coal Industry Nationalisation Act 1946 s 5(1), Sch 1 (repealed); and PARA 49.
10 See the Coal Industry Act 1987 s 1 (repealed); and PARA 49.
11 Ie under the Coal Industry Act 1994: see PARAS 50, 51 et seq.
12 See the Coal Industry Act 1994 s 7(3); and PARA 66. As to the Coal Authority see PARA 52 et seq.

## 21.  Profits à prendre affecting minerals.

The right to enter upon another person's land and extract minerals[1], as distinguished from the ownership of a stratum of minerals in another person's land[2], is a profit à prendre[3] and may be created by grant, statute or prescription[4].

A common case of a profit à prendre in respect of minerals is a right for freehold tenants of a manor to cut turf[5] and dig loam, sand and gravel out of the waste[6].

1  As to the meaning of 'minerals' see PARA 10.
2  *Wilkinson v Proud* (1843) 12 LJ Ex 227; *Duke of Sutherland v Heathcote* [1892] 1 Ch 475 at 483, CA.
3  As to profits à prendre generally see REAL PROPERTY AND REGISTRATION vol 87 (2017) PARA 974.
4  A profit à prendre cannot be claimed by custom, except in certain mining localities and in the case of copyholders claiming the right to a profit à prendre in the waste of the manor which they hold: *Goodman v Saltash Corpn* (1882) 7 App Cas 633 at 648, HL; *Gateward's Case* (1607) 6 Co Rep 59b; *A-G v Mathias* (1858) 4 K & J 579; *Alfred F Beckett Ltd v Lyons* [1967] Ch 449 at 474, [1967] 1 All ER 833 at 846, CA, per Harman LJ, and at 482 and 851 per Winn LJ; and see CUSTOM AND USAGE; REAL PROPERTY AND REGISTRATION vol 87 (2017) PARA 976. As to acts of ownership supporting the existence of a custom see PARAS 27–28. As to customs in particular localities see PARA 585 et seq.
5  See COMMONS vol 13 (2017) PARA 356 et seq.
6  *Warrick v Queen's College, Oxford* (1871) 6 Ch App 716; *Betts v Thompson* (1871) 6 Ch App 732 at 739; *Heath v Deane* [1905] 2 Ch 86. As to rights of common in the soil see COMMONS vol 13 (2017) PARA 364 et seq.

## 22.  Mines under highways.

Prima facie, mines[1] situate beneath a highway are owned by the owners of the land adjoining the highway on either side, the point of division being the centre of the road[2]. The presumption is a deduction from the doctrine that a conveyance of land bounded by a highway passes the soil of a moiety of the highway[3]. The presumption does not apply in the case of a railway[4] or canal[5]. Nor does it apply to a road set out under an Inclosure Act; in this case the property in the mines prima facie remains in the lord of the manor[6].

Statutory protection is accorded to the rights of the owners of mines and minerals under certain highways vested in a highway authority[7].

1  As to the meaning of 'mine' see PARA 3.
2  *Goodtitle d Chester v Alker* (1757) 1 Burr 133; *Baird v Tunbridge Wells Corpn* [1894] 2 QB 867 at 883, CA, per A L Smith LJ (on appeal sub nom *Tunbridge Wells Corpn v Baird* [1896] AC 434, HL); and see HIGHWAYS, STREETS AND BRIDGES.
3  *Chamber Colliery Co Ltd v Rochdale Canal Co* [1895] AC 564 at 584, HL, per Lord Macnaghten. See HIGHWAYS, STREETS AND BRIDGES.
4  *Thompson v Hickman* [1907] 1 Ch 550.
5  *Chamber Colliery Co Ltd v Rochdale Canal Co* [1895] AC 564, HL.
6  *Seddon v Smith* (1877) 36 LT 168, CA. The ownership of the mines is often a question of the construction of the particular Act: see *Poole v Huskinson* (1843) 11 M & W 827; *Haigh v West* [1893] 2 QB 19 at 29, CA; and COMMONS vol 13 (2017) PARA 320.
7  See the Highways Act 1980 s 335, referring to highways vested in a highway authority by virtue of any provision of Pt XII (ss 238–271); and HIGHWAYS, STREETS AND BRIDGES. The minerals must be got so as not to damage the road: see *A-G v Conduit Colliery Co* [1895] 1 QB 301, DC. If the road is damaged the measure of damages is the cost of making an equally commodious road: *Lodge Holes Colliery Co Ltd v Wednesbury Corpn* [1908] AC 323, HL. As to the meaning of 'minerals' see PARA 10.

## 23.  Mines beneath rivers and seashore.

The mines[1] beneath the bed of a non-navigable river belong prima facie to the owners of the adjoining land as owners of the bed of the river[2]. Mines under navigable rivers[3], under the shore between low water mark and ordinary high water mark (known as the foreshore)[4], and under the bed of the sea adjoining the shore[5] belong, prima facie, to the Crown as the owner of the beds of navigable rivers, of the foreshore and of the sea bed[6]. Mines under the foreshore may, however, be shown to belong to the adjoining owner[7].

1   As to the meaning of 'mine' see PARA 3.
2   *Chamber Colliery Co Ltd v Rochdale Canal Co* [1895] AC 564, HL; and see WATER AND WATERWAYS vol 100 (2018) PARA 265 et seq. As to mineral rights under the Water Industry Act 1991 and the Water Resources Act 1991 see WATER AND WATERWAYS vol 101 (2009) PARA 492 et seq.
3   *Lyon v Fishmongers' Co* (1876) 1 App Cas 662, HL.
4   *Lopez v Andrew* (1826) 3 Man & Ry KB 329n; *A-G v Chambers* (1854) 4 De GM & G 206; *A-G v Emerson* [1891] AC 649 at 654, HL.
5   *A-G v Chambers* (1854) 4 De GM & G 206.
6   See CROWN AND CROWN PROCEEDINGS vol 29 (2014) PARA 156 et seq. The prima facie title of the Crown no longer holds good, however, in the case of foreshores on the coast of Cornwall: see CROWN AND CROWN PROCEEDINGS vol 29 (2014) PARA 161.
7   *A-G v Hanmer* (1858) 27 LJ Ch 837 (on appeal (1859) 4 De G & J 205); and see *Calmady v Rowe* (1844–48) 6 CB 861; *Lord Advocate v Lord Blantyre* (1879) 4 App Cas 770, HL; *Lord Advocate v Young, North British Rly Co v Young* (1887) 12 App Cas 544, HL; *Lord Advocate v Wemyss* [1900] AC 48, HL; *Constable v Nicholson* (1863) 14 CBNS 230. As to the rights of user of the foreshore granted to persons entitled, in right of or under the Crown, to or to the management of minerals in or under the foreshore or adjacent land managed by the Crown Estate Commissioners see CROWN AND CROWN PROCEEDINGS vol 29 (2014) PARA 156 et seq.

## 24.   The continental shelf and territorial waters.

Any rights exercisable by the United Kingdom[1] outside territorial waters[2] with respect to the sea bed and subsoil and their natural resources, other than coal, are vested by statute in the Crown[3]. For the purposes of exploiting certain coal under the territorial sea and coal in designated areas[4] of the continental shelf, various interests and rights are vested by statute in the Coal Authority[5].

1   As to the meaning of 'United Kingdom' see PARA 48.
2   As to territorial waters see INTERNATIONAL RELATIONS LAW vol 61 (2010) PARA 121 et seq.
3   Continental Shelf Act 1964 s 1(1). See also CROWN AND CROWN PROCEEDINGS vol 29 (2014) PARA 156 et seq; INTERNATIONAL RELATIONS LAW vol 61 (2010) PARAS 163, 172. As to the registration of offshore installations and safety measures see ENERGY AND CLIMATE CHANGE vol 44 (2011) PARA 1081 et seq.
4   As to certain areas, known as 'designated areas', within which these rights are exercisable see ENERGY AND CLIMATE CHANGE vol 44 (2011) PARA 1040. See also PARA 66.
5   See the Coal Industry Act 1994 s 8; and PARAS 66–68. As to the Coal Authority see PARA 52 et seq.

## 25.   Land held by limited owners.

Where mines[1], whether as part of the land or as a separate tenement, are held for an estate for years or from year to year, the right of possession in the mines, and in the space formerly occupied by minerals[2] which have been worked, is vested in the termor or tenant from year to year, as the case may be[3].

1   As to the meaning of 'mine' see PARA 3.
2   As to the meaning of 'minerals' see PARA 10.
3   *Attersoll v Stevens* (1808) 1 Taunt 183; *Lewis v Branthwaite* (1831) 2 B & Ad 437; *Keyse v Powell* (1853) 2 E & B 132; *Raine v Alderson* (1838) 6 Scott 691; *Milne v Taylor* (1850) 16 LTOS 172; and see PARA 368; and REAL PROPERTY AND REGISTRATION; SETTLEMENTS.

## 26.   Mines under enfranchised land.

The law on mines and minerals in or under land of former copyhold and customary freehold tenure, and the effect of enfranchisement, are dealt with elsewhere in this title[1].

1   See PARA 309. As to the rights conferred by statute to work coal in former copyhold land see the

Coal Industry Act 1994 ss 49, 50, Sch 7; and PARA 397 et seq. As to copyhold generally see CUSTOM AND USAGE; REAL PROPERTY AND REGISTRATION vol 87 (2017) PARA 36 et seq.

## 27. Title presumed from acts of ownership.

Acts of ownership exercised over mines[1] or quarries[2] may, apart from statute, in the absence or inadequacy of rebutting evidence, give rise to a presumption of ownership[3], even in favour of a mere wrongdoer or trespasser[4], or an adverse title may be acquired[5]. There may also be evidence of a custom regarding the working of minerals[6] in a manor[7] or some other area[8] in which customary rights prevail.

1  As to the meaning of 'mine' see PARA 3.
2  As to the meaning of 'quarry' see PARA 4.
3  *Hanmer v Chance* (1865) 4 De GJ & Sm 626.
4  *Ashton v Stock* (1877) 6 ChD 719 at 726, obiter, per Hall V-C.
5  *Thew v Wingate* (1862) 10 B & S 714; *Smith v Stocks* (1869) 10 B & S 701 (highway authority by ceasing to use such allotments and obtaining its materials elsewhere, lost its right to extract such materials and an adverse title was acquired against it); and see LIMITATION PERIODS vol 68 (2016) PARA 1082.
6  As to the meaning of 'minerals' see PARA 10.
7  *Warrick v Queen's College, Oxford* (1871) 6 Ch App 716; *Heath v Deane* [1905] 2 Ch 86 at 93. As to proof see COMMONS vol 13 (2017) PARA 366 et seq.
8  *A-G v Mathias* (1858) 4 K & J 579. As to customary rights generally see CUSTOM AND USAGE.

## 28. Extent of area affected by presumption from acts of ownership.

As the act of working minerals[1] constitutes a removal, pro tanto, of that which gives a particular place its value, the question arises how far constructive possession of a wider area can be inferred from actual possession of a limited area. Thus acts of taking or dealing with minerals under certain land are evidence of the ownership of the minerals under other land within the same boundaries[2], and if possession is taken under a document constructive possession will be inferred of so many seams[3] or such areas[4] as are intended to be comprised in the document, but mere trespass on a neighbouring mine for longer than the prescription period gives no title to that mine[5]. Generally, where title is established or evidenced by lapse of time, constructive possession of an area wider than that actually worked will only be inferred in cases where such an inference is necessary to give effect to contractual obligations or to preserve the good faith and honesty of a bargain[6].

1  As to the meaning of 'minerals' see PARA 10.
2  *Barnes v Mawson* (1813) 1 M & S 77; *Tyrwhitt v Wynne* (1819) 2 B & Ald 554 (waste of manor); *Doe d Earl of Falmouth v Alderson* (1836) 1 M & W 210 (tin bounds); *Wild v Holt* (1842) 11 LJ Ex 285; *Taylor v Parry* (1840) 9 LJCP 298. See, however, PARA 21.
3  *Low Moor Co v Stanley Coal Co Ltd* (1876) 34 LT 186, CA.
4  *Davis v Shepherd* (1866) 1 Ch App 410.
5  *Earl of Dartmouth v Spittle* (1871) 19 WR 444; *Ashton v Stock* (1877) 6 ChD 719; *Thompson v Hickman* [1907] 1 Ch 550. As to the meaning of 'mine' see PARA 3.
6  *Glyn v Howell* [1909] 1 Ch 666 at 678 per Eve J; and see *M'Donnell v M'Kinty* (1847) 10 ILR 514. As to the presumption of ownership of undersea mines in Scotland see *Lord Advocate v Wemyss* [1900] AC 48, HL.

## (2) Rights Incidental to Ownership

### (i) Possession

### 29. Recovery of possession.

Proceedings may be instituted by the owner for recovery of possession if a trespasser is in possession of a mine[1]. The claim may relate to the surface and the mines beneath[2], or to the mines alone, whether open[3] or unopened[4]. Thus a coal mine or a salt pit[5], a mine under a tin bound, though not the tin bound[6], a stratum of coal[7], and mining liberties appurtenant to land may be the subject of such proceedings[8]; but a claim to possession may not be brought in respect of a liberty to get minerals alone, for this is an incorporeal hereditament[9]. If a tenant works a quarry[10] when the right to the stone is reserved by the lease, the landlord may maintain an action for conversion[11].

1 As to the meaning of 'mine' see PARA 3.
2 *Crocker v Fothergill* (1819) 2 B & Ald 652; *Harebottle v Placock* (1604) Cro Jac 21; *Goodtitle d Chester v Alker* (1757) 1 Burr 133. As to trespass see TORT vol 97 (2015) PARA 525 et seq.
3 *Sayer v Pierce* (1749) 1 Ves Sen 232; *Wilkinson v Proud* (1843) 11 M & W 33 at 38. As to open and unopened mines see PARAS 5–9.
4 See *Doe d Lord v Kingsbury* (1848) 10 LTOS 442; *Low Moor Co v Stanley Coal Co Ltd* (1875) 33 LT 436 (affd (1876) 34 LT 186, CA).
5 *Comyn v Kyneto* (1607) Cro Jac 150; *Andrews v Whittingham* (1692) Carth 277.
6 *Doe d Earl of Falmouth v Alderson* (1836) 1 M & W 210. As to tin bounds see PARAS 588–591.
7 *Earl of Dartmouth v Spittle* (1871) 19 WR 444 at 445 per Kelly CB.
8 *Crocker v Fothergill* (1819) 2 B & Ald 652 at 661 per Holroyd J.
9 *Crocker v Fothergill* (1819) 2 B & Ald 652; *Doe d Hanley v Wood* (1819) 2 B & Ald 724; *Low Moor Co v Stanley Coal Co Ltd* (1876) 34 LT 186 at 189, CA. The right to get coal in another's land may be acquired by prescription: *Wilkinson v Proud* (1843) 11 M & W 33. As to incorporeal hereditaments see REAL PROPERTY AND REGISTRATION vol 87 (2017) PARA 12; and as to the acquisition of a profit à prendre by prescription see REAL PROPERTY AND REGISTRATION vol 87 (2017) PARA 803.
10 As to the meaning of 'quarry' see PARA 4.
11 *Brown v Chadwick* (1857) 7 ICLR 101 at 108; and see PARA 31. As to the action of conversion see TORT vol 97 (2015) PARA 604 et seq.

### 30. Effect of non-user of right to get minerals.

The title of the owner of mines[1] and minerals[2] having the right to enter and get the minerals is not barred by the simple omission to exercise his right[3]. Similarly, the right to work a mine is not lost by simply ceasing to work it[4]. Moreover, if a trespasser to a mine abandons possession before he has acquired a title, time does not continue to run in his favour even if there is no new act of ownership by the rightful owner[5].

1 As to the meaning of 'mine' see PARA 3.
2 As to the meaning of 'minerals' see PARA 10.
3 *M'Donnell v M'Kinty* (1847) 10 ILR 514; *Smith v Lloyd* (1854) 9 Exch 562; *Trustees, Executors and Agency Co Ltd v Short* (1888) 13 App Cas 793 at 799, PC; *Seaman v Vawdrey* (1810) 16 Ves 390 at 392; *Jamieson v Harvey* [1876] WN 277, HL; *Adair v Shaftoe* (circa 1790), cited in *Norway v Rowe* (1812) 19 Ves 144 at 156 per Lord Eldon LC. See further LIMITATION PERIODS vol 68 (2016) PARA 1082.
4 *Low Moor Co v Stanley Coal Co Ltd* (1876) 34 LT 186, CA; and see *Heath v Deane* [1905] 2 Ch 86. As to rights to work minerals see PARA 352 et seq.

5   *Trustees, Executors and Agency Co Ltd v Short* (1888) 13 App Cas 793, PC. It has been stated that
    when a lease of mines has been granted and there is no entry by the grantee within the time of
    limitation, the grantee's rights against the lessor are barred at the expiration of the statutory
    period: *Keyse v Powell* (1853) 2 E & B 132 at 147. This seems not to be the case, however, when
    the lessor is not in actual possession: see LIMITATION PERIODS vol 68 (2016) PARA 1082.

## 31.   Abandonment of right to get minerals.

If the right to work minerals[1] is granted for a term of years, the right is not
waived or abandoned during the term, even where the grantee has ceased working
for many years[2]. A presumption of right arises from possession[3] apart from the
Limitation Act 1980[4], but the title to minerals will be extinguished if possession
is abandoned by the owner and another has actual possession for the statutory
period[5].

1   As to the meaning of 'minerals' see PARA 10.
2   *Crang v Adams* (1776) 5 Bro Parl Cas 588.
3   *Hodgkinson v Fletcher* (1781) 3 Doug KB 31 at 33.
4   See LIMITATION PERIODS vol 68 (2016) PARA 1018 et seq.
5   See LIMITATION PERIODS vol 68 (2016) PARA 1077; and *Smith v Stocks* (1869) 10 B & S 701
    (actual possession by stranger of gravel pit and road to it).

### (ii)   Rights against Persons Wrongfully Taking Minerals

## 32.   Property in abstracted minerals.

At common law, when part of the realty is severed and converted into a chattel,
it becomes immediately the property of the person who was the owner of the land
whilst it remained a portion of the land[1]. However, the damages to which the
owner is entitled against a person wrongfully taking minerals[2] are based (in the
absence of fraud or negligence) on what the owner has lost, which is the value of
the mineral as it existed unworked in the pit[3].

1   *Livingstone v Rawyards Coal Co* (1880) 5 App Cas 25 at 39, HL, per Lord Blackburn. As to
    property in mining refuse see *Boileau v Heath* [1898] 2 Ch 301.
2   As to the meaning of 'minerals' see PARA 10.
3   See *Jegon v Vivian* (1871) 6 Ch App 742 at 760 per Lord Hatherley LC; *Livingstone v Rawyards
    Coal Co* (1880) 5 App Cas 25 at 40, HL, per Lord Blackburn; *Peruvian Guano Co Ltd v Dreyfus
    Bros & Co* [1892] AC 170n at 175n, HL, per Lord Macnaghten. As to the rules governing the
    measure of damages generally see PARA 40 et seq. See also PARA 374.

## 33.   Claim for an account.

A claim may be maintained for an account of minerals wrongfully abstracted[1].
In such a claim the defendant is required to account for the value of the mineral
raised, that is to say the market price or value after making just allowances[2].
When a mine[3] is held in trust for co-owners, one of the equitable co-owners who
has not consented to the grant by the others of a licence to work may have an
account against the licensee[4].

Such a claim for an account is available not only against the wrongdoer but
also, after his death, against his personal representatives[5].

1   *Phillips v Homfray* [1892] 1 Ch 465 at 470, CA, per Lindley LJ; *Dean v Thwaite* (1855) 21 Beav
    621; *Llynvi Co v Brogden* (1870) LR 11 Eq 188; *Jegon v Vivian* (1871) 6 Ch App 742 at 762; *Job
    v Potton* (1875) LR 20 Eq 84 at 99; *Ecclesiastical Comrs for England v North Eastern Rly Co*
    (1877) 4 ChD 845 at 868; *Ashton v Stock* (1877) 6 ChD 719 at 727; *Joicey v Dickinson* (1881)
    45 LT 643, CA. See also PARA 374. As to the meaning of 'minerals' see PARA 10.
        The circumstances of the case may sometimes, however, be so complex that the owner of the
    minerals may be without a remedy. If a person sinks a shaft on his own land and pumps brine from
    it, both of which acts are prima facie lawful, the acts do not of necessity become unlawful merely

because it turns out that the brine obtained may be the result of dissolution of rock in another person's property. It may be impossible to ascertain the source of the brine, although it may be possible, by tracing subsequent subsidences of the surface, to form some judgment as to the area from which salt rock has been dissolved. To such an abnormal case it is practically impossible to apply the ordinary principles of law relating to underground property: see *Salt Union Ltd v Brunner, Mond & Co* [1906] 2 KB 822. In this respect there is no difference in principle between mineral more or less in suspension, as running silt, and mineral in solution, as brine. If, however, the silt is only wet sand, a claim for wrongful removal will lie: see *Salt Union Ltd v Brunner, Mond & Co; Jordeson v Sutton, Southcoates and Drypool Gas Co* [1898] 2 Ch 614 (affd [1899] 2 Ch 217, CA); *Trinidad Asphalt Co v Ambard* [1899] AC 594, PC; cf *Lotus Ltd v British Soda Co Ltd* [1972] Ch 123, [1971] 1 All ER 265; *Fletcher v Birkenhead Corpn* [1906] 1 KB 605 (affd [1907] 1 KB 205, CA); *English v Metropolitan Water Board* [1907] 1 KB 588. As to the action of account generally see EQUITABLE JURISDICTION vol 47 (2014) PARA 49 et seq.

2　See *Phillips v Homfray* [1892] 1 Ch 465 at 470, CA, per Lindley LJ; and PARA 40.

3　As to the meaning of 'mine' see PARA 3.

4　*Job v Potton* (1875) LR 20 Eq 84 at 96, considered in *Glyn v Howell* [1909] 1 Ch 666 at 677; see also *Denys v Shuckburgh* (1840) 4 Y & C Ex 42. The result of the 1925 property legislation is that beneficial joint tenants and tenants in common are beneficiaries under a trust. This does not affect their right to an account inter se, and may in certain circumstances afford an added right to an account as against the trustee: see TRUSTS AND POWERS vol 98 (2013) PARA 1 et seq. As to the rights of co-owners see further PARA 363 et seq; and as to licences see PARA 346 et seq.

5　*Bishop of Winchester v Knight* (1717) 1 P Wms 406; *Phillips v Homfray* [1892] 1 Ch 465 at 470, CA, per Lindley LJ. See also the Law Reform (Miscellaneous Provisions) Act 1934 s 1(1) (amended by the Law Reform (Miscellaneous Provisions) Act 1970 s 7(2), Schedule; and the Administration of Justice Act 1982 s 75(1), Sch 9 Pt I); and WILLS AND INTESTACY vol 103 (2016) PARA 1277 et seq.

## 34. Injunctions.

An injunction may be obtained to restrain future working[1]. This jurisdiction was first exercised on account of the irreparable injury to the property, as a mine[2]; and on the principle that a mine is regarded as a species of trade[3]. Where the application is to stay waste it must be made promptly[4].

1　See the Senior Courts Act 1981 s 37; and CIVIL PROCEDURE vol 12 (2015) PARA 1084. See also *Trinidad Asphalt Co v Ambard* [1899] AC 594, PC; *Ashton v Stock* (1877) 6 ChD 719 at 725 per Hall V-C; *Phillips v Homfray, Fothergill v Phillips* (1871) 6 Ch App 770; *Wright v Pitt* (1870) LR 12 Eq 408; *Hilton v Woods* (1867) LR 4 Eq 432 at 440 per Malins V-C; *Wilson v Grey* (1866) LR 3 Eq 117 at 121 per Stuart V-C; *Ackroyd v Briggs* (1865) 13 LT 521; *Hunt v Peake* (1860) John 705 at 713. In a proper case the court will make an order for an early trial: *Grey v Duke of Northumberland* (1809) 17 Ves 281. See also PARA 374; and CIVIL PROCEDURE vol 12 (2015) PARA 1155 et seq.

2　As to the meaning of 'mine' see PARA 3.

3　*Flamang's Case* (circa 1783) cited in 7 Ves 308. As to the extension of the remedy by injunction so as to apply in case of trespass as well as waste see *Mitchell v Dors* (1801) 6 Ves 147; *Crockford v Alexander* (1808) 15 Ves 138; *Earl of Cowper v Baker* (1810) 17 Ves 128; *Thomas v Oakley* (1811) 18 Ves 184. As to the circumstances in which a receiver may be appointed see RECEIVERS.

4　*Hilton v Earl Granville* (1841) Cr & Ph 283; and see CIVIL PROCEDURE vol 12 (2015) PARA 1159.

## 35. Claims for conversion and for money had and received.

The owner of minerals[1] which have been wrongfully abstracted may also bring a claim of conversion against the wrongdoer[2] or, if the wrongdoer has sold the minerals, a claim for money had and received[3], but not for use and occupation[4]. The claim for money had and received will also lie against the personal representatives of the wrongdoer in respect of the proceeds of minerals raised before his death[5]. No direct evidence of the actual sum received is necessary[6].

1　As to the meaning of 'minerals' see PARA 10.

2　*Martin v Porter* (1839) 5 M & W 351; and see TORT vol 97 (2015) PARA 604 et seq.

3   See *Powell v Rees* (1837) 7 Ad & El 426 at 428 per Lord Denman CJ; and CONTRACT.
4   *Phillips v Homfray* [1892] 1 Ch 465 at 472, CA, per Lopes LJ.
5   *Powell v Rees* (1837) 7 Ad & El 426 at 428 per Lord Denman CJ.
6   *Powell v Rees* (1837) 7 Ad & El 426.

## 36.  Damages for trespass.

The owner of minerals[1] which have been wrongfully abstracted may bring a claim for damages for trespass[2], but actual possession is necessary to maintain this form of claim[3]. If a tenant is in possession the landlord may sue for injury to the reversion[4], but not for a trespass which is not shown to injure the reversion[5]. A person in possession with an exclusive right to take minerals[6], and a person entitled under the Limitation Act 1980, may maintain a claim of trespass[7]. A claim for damages for trespass, or for damage to the land by working the minerals, or for compensation for the use of roads and passages[8], is maintainable after the death of the wrongdoer[9].

1   As to the meaning of 'minerals' see PARA 10.
2   See *Martin v Porter* (1839) 5 M & W 351; *Morgan v Powell* (1842) 3 QB 278; *Clegg v Dearden* (1848) 12 QB 576; *Brain v Harris* (1855) 10 Exch 908; *Hunter v Gibbons* (1856) 1 H & N 459; *Earl of Dartmouth v Spittle* (1871) 19 WR 444; *Eardley v Granville* (1876) 3 ChD 826.
3   *Cox v Glue* (1848) 5 CB 533 at 549, 550 per Wilde CJ; and see *Wallis v Hands* [1893] 2 Ch 75 at 85, 86; *Ocean Accident and Guarantee Corpn v Ilford Gas Co* [1905] 2 KB 493 at 497, 498, CA, per Collins MR.
4   *Raine v Alderson* (1838) 6 Scott 691; *Harker v Birkbeck* (1764) 3 Burr 1556 at 1563 per Lord Mansfield CJ, where it was held that an action on the case was maintainable. See also *Wood v Morewood* (1841) 3 QB 440n.
5   *Cooper v Crabtree* (1882) 20 ChD 589, CA.
6   *Low Moor Co v Stanley Coal Co Ltd* (1875) 33 LT 436 (affd (1876) 34 LT 186, CA); and see *Eardley v Granville* (1876) 3 ChD 826 at 833 per Jessel MR.
7   *Low Moor Co v Stanley Coal Co Ltd* (1875) 33 LT 436; affd (1876) 34 LT 186, CA.
8   Formerly an action was not maintainable after the death of the wrongdoer for damage to the land by working the minerals, or for compensation for the use of roads and passages: see *Phillips v Homfray* (1883) 24 ChD 439, CA (affd (1886) 11 App Cas 466, HL); *Phillips v Homfray* (1890) 44 ChD 694 (affd [1892] 1 Ch 465, CA).
9   See the Law Reform (Miscellaneous Provisions) Act 1934 s 1(1) (amended by the Law Reform (Miscellaneous Provisions) Act 1970 s 7(2), Schedule; and the Administration of Justice Act 1982 s 75(1), Sch 9 Pt I); WILLS AND INTESTACY vol 103 (2016) PARA 1277 et seq. As to the limitation period applicable where proceedings are brought after the death of the wrongdoer see LIMITATION PERIODS vol 68 (2016) PARA 916.

## 37.  Liability of mortgagee.

A mortgagee[1] of leaseholds in possession may be accountable for the wrongful working of a mine[2] by a sub-lessee[3], and a mortgagee, although not in possession, who authorises the working, is accountable in a redemption claim[4]. If the mortgagor is in possession, however, the mortgagee is not liable for wrongful working by the mortgagor, even where he receives the proceeds, unless he knows that the working is wrongful[5].

1   As to mortgagees generally see MORTGAGE vol 77 (2016) PARA 101 et seq.
2   As to the meaning of 'mine' see PARA 3.
3   *Taylor v Mostyn* (1886) 33 ChD 226, CA.
4   *Hood v Easton* (1856) 2 Giff 692 at 701.
5   *Powell v Aiken* (1858) 4 K & J 343; *Elias v Griffith* (1878) 8 ChD 521 at 528, CA.

## 38.  Access to and inspection of mine.

Where workings have taken place wrongfully, the owner of the mines[1] and minerals[2] may obtain liberty of access for the purpose of stopping up passages into his mine[3]. In a proper case, an order for inspection of the defendant's mine through his pits may be obtained on interim application[4]. Such an order is granted with all necessary incidental powers, so that all obstructions will be directed to be removed except where such removal will occasion danger to life or destruction of the mine[5]. The order has usually been granted subject to conditions; for example, the applicant must give reasonable notice in writing of the time at which it is proposed to inspect[6], and of the names and descriptions of the persons who are to make the inspection, subject to objection by the respondents[7]; the inspection may be limited to a certain part of the mine only; no unnecessary damage to the respondent's property or interference with his proper mining operations may be allowed[8]; security may be required against damage caused by the inspection[9]; and the costs of the inspection may have to be provided for in any event[10]. Inspection has usually been authorised only for the purpose of ascertaining the boundary of the applicant's mine[11], and the extent of the trespass[12].

1   As to the meaning of 'mine' see PARA 3.
2   As to the meaning of 'mineral' see PARA 10.
3   *Phillips v Homfray, Fothergill v Phillips* (1871) 6 Ch App 770 at 776; see also *Plant v Stott* (1869) 21 LT 106 at 107.
4   CPR 25.1; CPR 25.5; and see CIVIL PROCEDURE vol 12 (2015) PARAS 566, 573. See also *Earl of Lonsdale v Curwen* (1799) 3 Bligh 168n; *Cooper v Ince Hall Co* [1876] WN 24; *Whaley v Brancker* (1864) 10 Jur NS 535; *Bennitt v Whitehouse* (1860) 28 Beav 119 at 122; and see *Bradford Corpn v Ferrand and Shipley UDC* (1902) 86 LT 497; *Lumb v Beaumont* (1884) 27 ChD 356 at 358. The court also has powers to order an inspection of property before proceedings are started: see the Senior Courts Act 1981 s 33 (amended by SI 1998/2940); CPR 25.1 (1)(i), (j), 25.4 (1)(b), (2), 25.5. As to orders for inspection of property generally see CIVIL PROCEDURE vol 12 (2015) PARA 572.
5   *Walker v Fletcher* (1804) 3 Bligh 172n; *Ennor v Barwell* (1860) 1 De GF & J 529; *Bennett v Griffiths* (1861) 3 E & E 467; *Lumb v Beaumont* (1884) 27 ChD 356; *Earl of Lonsdale v Curwen* (1799) 3 Bligh 168n.
6   *Bennitt v Whitehouse* (1860) 28 Beav 119.
7   *Walker v Fletcher* (1804) 3 Bligh 172n; *Lewis v Marsh* (1849) 8 Hare 97; *Ennor v Barwell* (1860) 1 De GF & J 529.
8   *Cooper v Ince Hall Co* [1876] WN 24.
9   *Bennett v Griffiths* (1861) 3 E & E 467.
10   *Mitchell v Darley Main Colliery Co* (1883) 10 QBD 457, DC; *Cooper v Ince Hall Co* [1876] WN 24.
11   *Lewis v Marsh* (1849) 8 Hare 97 at 100; *Cooper v Ince Hall Co* [1876] WN 24.
12   *Bennitt v Whitehouse* (1860) 28 Beav 119 at 123; *Cooper v Ince Hall Co* [1876] WN 24.

### 39. Disclosure of documents.

Production and inspection of the defendant's title deeds for the purpose of ascertaining boundaries may be obtained, liberty being given to seal up all but the parcels and plans[1]. In a claim for an account of minerals[2] in which the defendant denies the claimant's title without pleading his own, a request for information as to the defendant's title may be allowed[3].

1   *Wayne's Merthyr Co v Powell's Dyffryn Steam Coal Co* [1880] WN 141 (affd [1880] WN 159, CA); *Ponsonby v Hartley* [1883] WN 13 (affd [1883] WN 44, CA); *Jenkins v Bushby* (1866) 35 LJ Ch 400. As to disclosure and requests for information generally see CIVIL PROCEDURE vol 12 (2015) PARAS 621 et seq, 1020.
2   As to the meaning of 'minerals' see PARA 10.
3   *Cayley v Sandycroft Brick, Tile and Colliery Co* (1885) 33 WR 577; and see CIVIL PROCEDURE.

### 40. Measure of damages.

By the rules of equity in claims of account, which are applicable in all courts[1], the claimant is entitled to the market value of the minerals at the pit's mouth subject to certain allowances. The defendant may be allowed the cost of hewing and bringing to bank if he has acted inadvertently[2], or under a belief of title in good faith[3], or fairly and honestly[4], or in cases of mere mistake in circumstances where there is no suggestion of fraud[5], or where the mineral was worked under an expectation in good faith of a contract which the mineral owner knew would be acted on at once[6]. This rule is applicable to cases when the mineral owner stands by and sees the mineral worked without interfering[7]. However, the cost of hewing is not allowed to the defendant when he has acted fraudulently[8], negligently[9] or wilfully[10], or in a manner wholly unauthorised and unlawful[11]; but even then the defendant is not deprived of the cost of bringing the mineral to bank[12]. This measure of damages has been applied where the defendants had, with the landowner's permission, driven headings into an adjoining mine during negotiations for a lease and continued the working without the landowner's knowledge after they had declined to accept the lease[13]; where, after preliminary workings in expectation of a lease, the intending lessee continued the workings after it was found that the intending lessor had no power to grant a lease[14]; where the defendant worked a neighbouring mine knowing the boundaries of his own[15]; and even in a case of inadvertent working[16]. These principles apply to claims in the winding up of a company[17]. The measure of damages is not affected by a covenant which binds the claimant to use any mineral got upon the premises[18]. Where the mineral could have been worked only by the trespasser, damages have been assessed in accordance with the value of the royalty paid for the surrounding field of minerals[19], but a trespasser who is allowed disbursements for hewing and bringing to bank is not entitled to any profit or trade allowance[20].

1   *Peruvian Guano Co Ltd v Dreyfus Bros & Co* [1892] AC 166 at 175, HL, per Lord Macnaghten. Before 1875 the damages recoverable for wrongfully working minerals depended upon the form of claim adopted: see *Peruvian Guano Co Ltd v Dreyfus Bros & Co* at 175; *Martin v Porter* (1839) 5 M & W 351; *Wild v Holt* (1842) 9 M & W 672; *Morgan v Powell* (1842) 3 QB 278 (but cf *Wood v Morewood* (1841) 3 QB 440n (trespass)); *Jegon v Vivian* (1871) 6 Ch App 742 at 761, 762; *Livingstone v Rawyards Coal Co* (1880) 5 App Cas 25 at 40, HL, per Lord Blackburn. As to the meaning of 'minerals' see PARA 10.
2   *Hilton v Woods* (1867) LR 4 Eq 432.
3   *Hilton v Woods* (1867) LR 4 Eq 432; *Jegon v Vivian* (1871) 6 Ch App 742 at 761; *Elias v Griffith* (1878) 8 ChD 521 at 529, CA; *Ashton v Stock* (1877) 6 ChD 719.
4   *Wood v Morewood* (1841) 3 QB 440n.
5   *Re United Merthyr Collieries Co* (1872) LR 15 Eq 46. See also *Bulli Coal Mining Co v Osborne* [1899] AC 351 at 362, PC.
6   *Trotter v Maclean* (1879) 13 ChD 574 at 587; *Townend v Askern Coal and Iron Co* [1934] Ch 463.
7   *Jegon v Vivian* (1871) 6 Ch App 742 at 762; *Trotter v Maclean* (1879) 13 ChD 574 at 587. The principle thus adopted is that if the wrongful act is shown to have been committed inadvertently, and there are no circumstances which a court of equity would consider to affect the case, just allowance is to be made for outlay on the wrongdoer's part, and as far as possible there is to be returned to the rightful owner the full value of that which cannot be restored to him in specie: see *Livingstone v Rawyards Coal Co* (1880) 5 App Cas 25, HL; *Dreyfus Bros & Co v Peruvian Guano Co Ltd* (1889) 42 ChD 66 at 76; *Peruvian Guano Co Ltd v Dreyfus Bros & Co* [1892] AC 166, HL; *Eden v North Eastern Rly Co* [1907] AC 400, HL. The owner has no right to follow the severed minerals into whatever place they may be carried, or in whatever circumstances they may come to be disposed of, and to fasten upon any increment of value which from exceptional circumstances may be found to attach to those minerals. The test is what may fairly be said to have been the value of the mineral to the person from whose property it was taken at the time it was taken: *Livingstone v Rawyards Coal Co* at 32 per Earl Cairns LC. In such cases the value is estimated on the basis that no impediment exists which would prevent the owner from himself working the minerals. Where such an impediment exists, account may be taken of it.
8   *Ecclesiastical Comrs for England v North Eastern Rly Co* (1877) 4 ChD 845; *Joicey v Dickinson* (1881) 45 LT 643, CA; *Bulli Coal Mining Co v Osborne* [1899] AC 351 at 362, PC; and see *Cassell & Co Ltd v Broome* [1972] AC 1027 at 1129, [1972] 1 All ER 801 at 873, HL, per Lord Diplock.

9   *Wood v Morewood* (1841) 3 QB 440n.

10  *Martin v Porter* (1839) 5 M & W 351; *Trotter v Maclean* (1879) 13 ChD 574 at 588; *Phillips v Homfray* (1890) 44 ChD 694 at 701 (affd [1892] 1 Ch 465, CA).

11  *Llynvi Co v Brogden* (1870) LR 11 Eq 188.

12  *Trotter v Maclean* (1879) 13 ChD 574 at 586; *Joicey v Dickinson* (1881) 45 LT 643 at 644, CA; but see *Livingstone v Rawyards Coal Co* (1880) 5 App Cas 25 at 34, HL, per Lord Hatherley, and at 39 per Lord Blackburn; *Job v Potton* (1875) LR 20 Eq 84 at 91, 97; *Plant v Stott* (1869) 21 LT 106.

13  *Phillips v Homfray, Fothergill v Phillips* (1871) 6 Ch App 770 at 771; subsequent proceedings *Phillips v Homfray* (1890) 44 ChD 694.

14  *Trotter v Maclean* (1879) 13 ChD 574 at 588.

15  *Joicey v Dickinson* (1881) 45 LT 643, CA.

16  *Ecclesiastical Comrs for England v North Eastern Rly Co* (1877) 4 ChD 845. This decision was disapproved in *Bulli Coal Mining Co v Osborne* [1899] AC 351, PC. See also LIMITATION PERIODS vol 68 (2016) PARAS 993, 1225.

17  *Re United Merthyr Collieries Co* (1872) LR 15 Eq 46; *Bulli Coal Mining Co v Osborne* [1899] AC 351, PC.

18  *Ashton v Stock* (1877) 6 ChD 719 at 726.

19  *Livingstone v Rawyards Coal Co* (1880) 5 App Cas 25, HL; see also *Townend v Askern Coal and Iron Co* [1934] Ch 463.

20  *Re United Merthyr Collieries Co* (1872) LR 15 Eq 46.

## 41. Interest.

The circumstances in which the court may grant interest on damages awarded are dealt with elsewhere in this work[1]. It seems that interest may be allowed also in a claim for an account arising out of a trespass[2].

1  See DAMAGES vol 29 (2014) PARA 635; FINANCIAL INSTRUMENTS AND TRANSACTIONS vol 49 (2015) PARA 90 et seq. Where an inquiry as to damages is directed and the order does not contain a direction for payment, the order is not one within the Judgments Act 1838 s 18, so as to render interest on the damages payable from the date of the order: *Ashover Fluor Spar Mines Ltd v Jackson* [1911] 2 Ch 355; and see CIVIL PROCEDURE vol 12A (2015) PARA 1235.

2  *Phillips v Homfray* [1892] 1 Ch 465, CA.

## 42. Abstraction by railway authority.

If a railway authority, after giving notice to treat, removes minerals[1] not included in the notice, and the removal is not necessary for making the railway, damages can be recovered, and the landowner is not obliged[2] to take compensation[3].

1  As to the meaning of 'minerals' see PARA 10.

2  Ie under the Railways Clauses Consolidation Act 1845 s 6: see RAILWAYS AND TRAMWAYS vol 86 (2017) PARAS 299, 432.

3  *Tiverton and North Devon Rly Co v Loosemore* (1884) 9 App Cas 480, HL.

## 43. Consequential damage.

Damages are recoverable for consequential injury resulting from the wrongful working of minerals[1], for example for injury caused to houses on the surface[2], for subsidence of the surface caused by the removal of support[3], for minerals rendered unworkable[4], and for letting in water[5]. If damages are recovered for letting in water, there is no further liability for continuing damage from flooding through the same aperture[6]. Damages are recoverable for the loss of pitch which the defendant, by removing lateral support, has caused to flow upon his land and appropriated[7]. This principle does not apply when the defendant has pumped brine upon his own land which in part results from dissolution of the claimant's rock[8]. An inquiry has been directed as to damages beyond the removal of the minerals occasioned by working the mines[9], as to damage by reason of the manner in which the wrongdoers worked the minerals[10], and as to damage by reason of the wrongdoers having broken through the boundary[11]; and compensation may be obtained as for a wayleave when the trespasser has wrongfully carried minerals through the mine[12].

1   As to the meaning of 'minerals' see PARA 10.
2   *Livingstone v Rawyards Coal Co* (1880) 5 App Cas 25 at 33, HL; *Hunt v Peake* (1860) John 705. See PARAS 184–186.
3   *Trinidad Asphalt Co v Ambard* [1899] AC 594, PC; *Lodge Holes Colliery Co Ltd v Wednesbury Corpn* [1908] AC 323, HL (measure of damages where highway is let down is the cost of making an equally commodious road). As to subsidence damage see PARA 182 et seq.
4   *Plant v Stott* (1869) 21 LT 106; *Williams v Raggett* (1877) 25 WR 874.
5   *Phillips v Homfray, Fothergill v Phillips* (1871) 6 Ch App 770 at 776; *Taylor v Mostyn* (1886) 33 ChD 226, CA; *Plant v Stott* (1869) 21 LT 106. See PARA 267.
6   *Clegg v Dearden* (1848) 12 QB 576. See PARA 269.
7   *Trinidad Asphalt Co v Ambard* [1899] AC 594, PC.
8   *Salt Union Ltd v Brunner, Mond & Co* [1906] 2 KB 822 at 831; and see *Lotus Ltd v British Soda Co Ltd* [1972] Ch 123, [1971] 1 All ER 265. See also PARA 33.
9   *Jegon v Vivian* (1871) 6 Ch App 742. As to the meaning of 'mine' see PARA 3.
10  *Phillips v Homfray, Fothergill v Phillips* (1871) 6 Ch App 770.
11  *Llynvi Co v Brogden* (1870) LR 11 Eq 188 at 192.
12  *Martin v Porter* (1839) 5 M & W 351; *Jegon v Vivian* (1871) 6 Ch App 742 at 762; *Phillips v Homfray, Fothergill v Phillips* (1871) 6 Ch App 770 at 776. See PARAS 261–262.

## 44.   Entitlement to damages recovered as between limited owners.

If a lease with liberty to dig for minerals amounts to an absolute sale of all the minerals[1], the lessee is entitled as between himself and the lessor to retain the whole damages recovered by him from a trespasser who has worked the minerals[2].

If a tenant for life is not impeachable for waste he is entitled to compensation recovered from a trespasser in respect of minerals worked during the life tenancy[3]. If, on the other hand, the tenant for life is impeachable for waste, damages recovered are capital money[4].

1   As to the nature of a mining lease see PARA 318. As to the meaning of 'minerals' see PARA 10.
2   *Attersoll v Stevens* (1808) 1 Taunt 183. As to the respective rights of lessor and lessee see PARA 36.
3   *Re Barrington, Gamlen v Lyon* (1886) 33 ChD 523. As to the powers of a tenant for life see PARA 368 et seq; and SETTLEMENTS. As to the phasing out of strict settlements and trusts for sale see the Trusts of Land and Appointment of Trustees Act 1996 s 2, Sch 1; and REAL PROPERTY AND REGISTRATION vol 87 (2017) PARA 102 et seq; SETTLEMENTS; TRUSTS AND POWERS vol 98 (2013) PARAS 1, 151.
4   *Re Barrington, Gamlen v Lyon* (1886) 33 ChD 523 at 527; and see *Bewick v Whitfield* (1734) 3 P Wms 267 at 268.

## 45.   Loss of remedies by lapse of time.

By statute a claim of tort may not normally be brought more than six years after the cause of action accrued[1], and a claim for an account may not be brought after the expiration of any statutory time limit applicable to the claim which is the basis of the duty to account[2]. In a claim of tort in respect of the wrongful working of minerals, time normally runs from the date of the working[3]. The onus is on the defendant to show what portion of minerals found to have been abstracted was taken before the commencement of the six-year period[4]. Where, however, the claimant's right of action has been concealed by the defendant's fraud, time does not begin to run until the claimant has discovered the fraud or could with reasonable diligence have discovered it[5]. Moreover, if the person to whom a cause of action accrues is under a disability, the claim may normally be brought at any time before the expiration of six years from the date when the person ceased to be under a disability or died[6].

In the case of a subsidence of the surface caused by the lawful working of minerals, time normally runs from the date of the subsidence[7], but when subsidence results from the act of a trespasser, the cause of action is the trespass and time runs from that[8].

The Limitation Act 1980 does not affect the prerogative right of the Crown or of the Duke of Cornwall to any gold or silver mine[9].

1   See the Limitation Act 1980 s 2; and LIMITATION PERIODS vol 68 (2016) PARA 979.
2   See the Limitation Act 1980 s 23; and LIMITATION PERIODS vol 68 (2016) PARA 1008. See also *Denys v Shuckburgh* (1840) 4 Y & C Ex 42; *Dean v Thwaite* (1855) 21 Beav 621; *Dawes v Bagnall* (1875) 23 WR 690; *Ashton v Stock* (1877) 6 ChD 719; *Glyn v Howell* [1909] 1 Ch 666. As to the principle that a mortgagee in possession is bound to account for all rents and profits received during his possession see LIMITATION PERIODS vol 68 (2016) PARA 1116.
3   See LIMITATION PERIODS vol 68 (2016) PARA 993. As to the meaning of 'minerals' see PARA 10.
4   *Dean v Thwaite* (1855) 21 Beav 621; *Trotter v Maclean* (1879) 13 ChD 574 at 585 per Fry J.
5   See the Limitation Act 1980 s 32; and LIMITATION PERIODS vol 68 (2016) PARA 1220 et seq. As to the conflict which formerly existed between the courts of law and equity as to the effect of fraudulent concealment see LIMITATION PERIODS vol 68 (2016) PARA 1220.
6   See the Limitation Act 1980 s 28; and LIMITATION PERIODS vol 68 (2016) PARAS 1168, 1175.
7   *Darley Main Colliery Co v Mitchell* (1886) 11 App Cas 127, HL; *West Leigh Colliery Co Ltd v Tunnicliffe and Hampson Ltd* [1908] AC 27, HL; and see LIMITATION PERIODS vol 68 (2016) PARA 921. As to the position where there is a continuance of damage see DAMAGES vol 29 (2014) PARA 338; LIMITATION PERIODS vol 68 (2016) PARA 921. As to subsidence damage see PARA 182 et seq.
8   See LIMITATION PERIODS vol 68 (2016) PARA 993.
9   See the Limitation Act 1980 s 37(6). As to the application of the Act to the Crown see LIMITATION PERIODS vol 68 (2016) PARA 903. As to the prerogative right to mines of gold or silver see CROWN AND CROWN PROCEEDINGS vol 29 (2014) PARA 132.

## 46.   Effect of release.

A release from liability for wrongful acts does not extend to wrongful abstraction carried on during negotiations for the release and after the boundaries have been settled[1].

1   *Ecclesiastical Comrs for England v North Eastern Rly Co* (1877) 4 ChD 845.

## 47.   Criminal proceedings.

In certain circumstances criminal proceedings for theft may be instituted against a person who appropriates anything forming part of land by severing it or causing it to be severed, or after it has been severed[1]. Such proceedings may be instituted also for destruction of or damage to property in defined circumstances[2].

1   See the Theft Act 1968 s 4(2)(b); and CRIMINAL LAW vol 25 (2016) PARA 319.
2   See the Criminal Damage Act 1971 s 1; and CRIMINAL LAW vol 25 (2016) PARA 391 et seq.

# 3. COAL MINING INDUSTRY

## (1) Historical Development

**48. Transfer of interests to the Coal Commission.**

There was no central administration of the coal-mining industry until 1920, when the Mining Industry Act 1920 established the Mines Department of the Board of Trade in order to secure the most effective development and utilisation of the mineral resources of the United Kingdom and the safety and welfare of those engaged in the mining industry[1]. The Mining Industry Act 1926 and the Coal Mines Act 1930 (both now repealed) provided machinery for reorganisation of the coal-mining industry, and in 1937 a coal holdings register was established so that persons having a proprietary interest in coal and mines of coal in Great Britain[2] and in certain associated minerals could apply for registration of their interests[3]. The following year, the Coal Act 1938 (now repealed) made provision for the public ownership of unworked coal[4] (but not of the industry itself) and established the Coal Commission as a body corporate[5]. On 1 July 1942[6], there vested in the Coal Commission the fee simple in all coal[7] and mines of coal[8] as existing at that date together with all other interests except retained interests[9] then subsisting in any such coal or mine[10]. The Coal Commission also acquired certain annexed property and rights, and certain rights to withdraw support[11]. Compensation was payable for the interests[12] so acquired[13]. The Board of Trade's functions in relation to the provision of the coal holdings register were also transferred to the Coal Commission at that time[14].

1   See the Mining Industry Act 1920 s 1 (repealed). 'United Kingdom' means Great Britain and Northern Ireland: Interpretation Act 1978 s 5, Sch 1. 'Great Britain' means England, Scotland and Wales: Union with Scotland Act 1706, preamble art I; Interpretation Act 1978 s 22(1), Sch 2 para 5(a). Neither the Channel Islands nor the Isle of Man are within the United Kingdom. See further CONSTITUTIONAL AND ADMINISTRATIVE LAW vol 20 (2014) PARA 3.

2   Ie England, Scotland and Wales.

3   See the Coal (Registration of Ownership) Act 1937 (repealed).

4   The provisions relating to the unification of coal-mining royalties in the Coal Act 1938 extended also to land belonging to the Crown or the Duchy of Cornwall (see s 42 (repealed)) and, subject to certain exceptions, to land in the Forest of Dean or any other part of the Hundred of St Briavels (see s 43 (repealed); and PARA 609). The Coal Industry Act 1994 makes transitional provisions and savings in relation to the repeal of the Coal Act 1938: see the Coal Industry Act 1994 s 67(7), Sch 10 paras 1–5.

5   See the Coal Act 1938 s 1, Sch 1 (both repealed).

6   Ie the vesting date under the Coal Act 1938 s 3(2) (repealed).

7   For the purposes of the Coal Act 1938, 'coal' (1) meant bituminous coal, cannel coal and anthracite; but (2) where minerals or substances other than those were comprised in a lease subsisting at the valuation date (ie 1 January 1939: see s 3(2) (repealed)) which conferred a right to work and carry away both that coal, or anthracite and those other minerals or substances, also included those other minerals or substances unless they were excluded by a direction given by the Coal Commission, and included any of those other minerals or substances which would normally be worked by surface workings not in association with that coal or anthracite unless they were excluded by direction given by the Coal Commission on application of a person interested; and (3) except in the case of references to the making merchantable or disposing of coal, meant unworked coal, ie not so severed as to have become a chattel: see ss 3(4)(a), (b), (c), 44(1) (repealed). The inclusion of 'minerals or other substances' in the definition of 'coal' did not apply to gold, gold ore, silver or silver ore: s 42(1) proviso (repealed).

8   For the purposes of the Coal Act 1938, 'mine of coal' meant a space which was occupied by coal or which had been excavated underground for a coal-mining purpose, and included a shaft and an adit made for a coal-mining purpose; and 'coal-mining purpose' meant searching and boring for, winning, working, getting, carrying away, making merchantable or disposing of coal: see s 44(1) (repealed).

9　The following were retained interests which did not vest in the Coal Commission:
　　(1)　interests arising under a coal-mining lease (subject to certain exceptions) (see Coal Act 1938 s 5(1), (2), (3), (5) (repealed));
　　(2)　a right to work granted by a working facilities order in so far as it created an interest in any coal or mine of coal (see s 5(4) (repealed));
　　(3)　retained copyhold interests, ie interests in coal or a mine of coal in or under land formerly copyhold which were preserved to the tenant on enfranchisement, except where the tenant had by custom or otherwise (except by virtue of a coal-mining lease) the right to work coal in or under the land without the lord's licence (see s 5(6) (repealed));
　　(4)　an interest in coal or a mine of coal arising under a coal-mining lease the lessee under which was a committee appointed for the purposes of a drainage scheme under the Mining Industry Act 1920 s 18 ((repealed) (see the Coal Act 1938 s 34(2) (repealed)).
　　It was within the competence of the Coal Commission to acquire: (a) a retained copyhold interest in coal or a mine of coal; (b) certain interests in any minerals or substances other than coal that were capable of being economically gotten in association with the coal being worked; and (c) the benefit of any right to be exercised in respect of any land for a coal-mining purpose: see s 32(1) (repealed). The only retained interest which remains extant is a retained copyhold interest: see PARA 397 et seq. The Coal Industry Act 1994 ss 49, 50, Sch 7 make provision in regard to the working of coal in former copyhold land: see PARA 397 et seq. As to copyhold land generally see CUSTOM AND USAGE; REAL PROPERTY AND REGISTRATION vol 87 (2017) PARA 36 et seq.
10　See the Coal Act 1938 s 3(3) (repealed).
11　See the Coal Act 1938 ss 3(1), 4, Sch 2 (all repealed). As to the statutory right to withdraw support from land in relation to coal mining see PARA 176 et seq.
12　All such rights and liabilities conferred on the Coal Commission were registrable as overriding interests: see the Coal Act 1938 s 41 (repealed). As to overriding interests see now the Land Registration Act 2002 ss 11, 12, 29, 30, Sch 1, Sch 3; and REAL PROPERTY AND REGISTRATION vol 87 (2017) PARAS 351 et seq, 451, 453.
13　See the Coal Act 1938 s 6 (repealed).
14　See the Coal Act 1938 s 35(1) (repealed).

## 49.　The National Coal Board (later renamed the British Coal Corporation).

The Coal Industry Nationalisation Act 1946[1] effected the nationalisation of the coal-mining industry as from 1 January 1947[2], and established the National Coal Board[3] as a body corporate[4]. On that date there vested in the National Coal Board all the interests in unworked coal[5] and in mines of coal[6], of colliery concerns[7] and of the Coal Commission[8] and, subject to certain provisions[9], certain interests which under the Coal Act 1938 were retained interests[10]. Compensation was payable[11] for the wide range of assets[12] so transferred.

The National Coal Board was charged with the duties of: (1) working and getting the coal in Great Britain[13] to the exclusion[14] of any other person[15]; (2) securing the efficient development of the coal-mining industry[16]; and (3) making supplies of coal available in such quantities and at such prices as seemed to it best calculated to further the public interest, including the avoidance of any undue or unreasonable preference or advantage[17]. It was also given ancillary functions including the carrying on of such activities as appeared to it to be requisite, advantageous or convenient for it to carry on for or in connection with those duties[18].

Having been thus divested of its interests, the Coal Commission was dissolved on 1 April 1947[19]. The National Coal Board was later given additional powers with respect to petroleum[20], and also with respect to other minerals discovered in the course of searching or boring for, or working and getting coal[21]. In 1987 the National Coal Board was renamed the British Coal Corporation[22] and continued to exercise its existing functions[23] and powers[24] under that name until privatisation[25].

1 The Coal Industry Nationalisation Act 1946; the Coal Industry Act 1949 Pt I (ss 1–8); the Coal Industry (No 2) Act 1949; the Coal Industry Acts 1951, 1956, 1960, 1961; the Coal Consumers' Councils (Northern Irish Interests) Act 1962; the Coal Industry Acts 1962, 1965, 1967, 1971, 1973, 1975; the National Coal Board (Additional Powers) Act 1966; the National Coal Board (Finance) Act 1976; and the Coal Industry Acts 1977, 1980, 1982, 1983, 1985, 1987, 1990 and 1992 were cited together as the Coal Industry Acts 1946 to 1992: see the Coal Industry Act 1992 s 3(2) (repealed). The Acts listed are all repealed from different dates and not all the repeals were effective at the date at which this volume states the law.

2 Ie the primary vesting date: see the Coal Industry Nationalisation Act 1946 s 5(1) (repealed); s 63(1) (repealed by the Coal Industry Act 1994 Sch 11 Pt III as from a day to be appointed under s 68); and the Coal Industry Nationalisation (Primary Vesting Date) Order 1946, SR & O 1946/1986 (spent).

3 See the Coal Industry Nationalisation Act 1946 s 1(1) (repealed). The National Coal Board was renamed the British Coal Corporation in 1987.

4 See the Coal Industry Nationalisation Act 1946 s 2(1) (repealed). As to the constitution of the National Coal Board and the salaries paid to its members see the Coal Industry Nationalisation Act 1946 s 2 (repealed); and the Coal Industry Act 1949 s 1 (repealed). As to administration matters including the appointment and tenure of members, disclosure of information and procedural requirements for meetings see the Coal Industry Nationalisation (National Coal Board) Regulations 1946, SR & O 1946/1094 (lapsed) (made under the Coal Industry Nationalisation Act 1946 s 2(7) (repealed)). Significant changes have now been made to its membership by the Coal Industry Act 1994: see s 23; and PARA 88.

5 For the purposes of the Coal Industry Nationalisation Act 1946, 'coal' meant bituminous coal, cannel coal and anthracite: s 63(1) (repealed by the Coal Industry Act 1994 Sch 11 Pt III as from a day to be appointed under s 68).

6 For the purposes of the Coal Industry Nationalisation Act 1946, 'mine of coal' meant a space occupied by unworked coal or excavated underground for the purposes of colliery activities, and included a shaft or adit made for those purposes, a coal quarry and opencast workings of coal: s 63(1). 'Colliery activities' meant searching or boring for, winning, working or getting coal, bringing it to the surface, treating it and rendering it saleable, and included depositing spoil arising from working coal or from any other of these activities: s 63(1).

7 Certain liabilities for subsidence were transferred from colliery concerns to the National Coal Board at this time: see the Coal Industry Nationalisation Act 1946 s 48 (repealed). For the purposes of the Coal Industry Nationalisation Act 1946, 'colliery concern' meant a company whose business included the working of coal (excluding working undertaken to dig or carry away coal in the course of activities other than colliery activities, and working undertaken only as ancillary to the working of minerals other than coal), and any other person whose business included such working of coal: s 63(1).

8 As to the Coal Commission see PARA 48. All interests of the Coal Commission not otherwise vested in the National Coal Board (ie by the Coal Industry Nationalisation Act 1946 s 5 (repealed) in land or other fixed property and in moveable property; and the property in, and the right to possession of, records and other documents which were vested in the Coal Commission were also vested in the National Coal Board (see the Coal Act 1938 s 14 (repealed); and the Coal Industry Nationalisation Act 1946 s 38(1) (repealed)), as were contracts to which the Coal Commission had been a party (see s 38(2) (repealed)), and the Commission's compensation functions under the Coal Act 1938 (see the Coal Industry Nationalisation Act 1946 s 38(3) (repealed)). The rights and powers of the Coal Commission in relation to the use of underground land were similarly transferred in accordance with s 8 (repealed).

9 Ie the provisions of the Coal Industry Nationalisation Act 1946 s 36 (repealed).

10 Coal Act 1938 s 5(1), Sch 1 para 1(1) (both repealed). On 1 January 1947 all retained interests, with the exception of retained copyhold interests, vested in the National Coal Board. As to retained interests under the Coal Act 1938 see PARA 48. The statutory vesting of coal in the National Coal Board did not extend to the interests of persons other than the Coal Commission in any coal or mine of coal used immediately before 1 January 1947 exclusively or mainly in the course of activities other than colliery activities: see the Coal Industry Nationalisation Act 1946 s 36(1) (repealed).

11 See the Coal Industry Nationalisation Act 1946 ss 10–25 (repealed).

12 Certain assets were transferred subject to an option (see the Coal Industry Nationalisation Act 1946 s 5(2), (3), Sch 1 Pts II, III, IV (all repealed)) and certain others were transferred without option (see s 5(1), Sch 1 Pt I (both repealed)). In addition to the assets described in s 5, Sch 1 (both repealed), interests of colliery concerns in patents for inventions and copyrights for designs intended for use or application or capable of being used or applied in connection with colliery production activities vested in the National Coal Board at the option of the Board or of the owners, subject to arbitration in the case of objection: see s 6 (repealed). Rights and liabilities under certain contracts mentioned in Sch 2 (repealed) were transferred to the extent mentioned in that Schedule subject to the right of the National Coal Board to disclaim certain contracts: see s 7 (repealed). All the assets, property, rights and liabilities other than those of the Coal Commission were referred to as 'transferred interests': see s 9(2) (repealed). Regulations (all now spent) were made to ascertain particulars of the transferred assets: see s 9(1), (4) (repealed).

13 The National Coal Board was later given power to do anything outside Great Britain whether or not related to working and getting coal in Great Britain, which appeared to it requisite, advantageous or convenient and which it was required or authorised to do in Great Britain, provided it had the consent of the Secretary of State and, if capital expenditure was involved, also the approval of the Treasury: see the Coal Industry Act 1977 s 11 (as originally enacted). Section 11 is already partly repealed and the remainder is repealed by the Coal Industry Act 1994 Sch 11 Pt III as from days to be appointed. As to the Secretary of State see PARA 2. As to the Treasury see CONSTITUTIONAL AND ADMINISTRATIVE LAW vol 20 (2014) PARAS 262–265. As to the meaning of 'Great Britain' see PARA 48.

14 This provision was subject to certain exceptions. In particular, it did not make it unlawful to dig or carry away coal that was necessary to be dug or carried away in the course of activities other than colliery activities; and interests of persons other than the Coal Commission in any such coal or in a mine of coal used immediately before 1 January 1947 exclusively or mainly in the course of such other activities were excepted from vesting in the National Coal Board under the Coal Industry Nationalisation Act 1946 s 5 (repealed): see s 36(1) (repealed). It was also within the power of the National Coal Board to grant licences to others for the working and getting of coal: see s 36(2), (2A), (3) (repealed). Licences under these provisions were granted in respect of the Forest of Dean: see PARA 607 et seq. As to the continuation of licences granted under these provisions as authorisations under the Coal Industry Act 1994 Pt II (ss 25–36) see s 25(3), (4); and PARA 89.

15 Coal Industry Nationalisation Act 1946 s 1(1)(a) (repealed).

16 Coal Industry Nationalisation Act 1946 s 1(1)(b) (repealed).

17 Coal Industry Nationalisation Act 1946 s 1(1)(c) (repealed).

18 See the Coal Industry Nationalisation Act 1946 s 1(2)–(4) (as originally enacted) (now repealed).

19 See the Coal Industry Nationalisation Act 1946 s 38(5) (repealed); and the Coal Commission (Dissolution) Order 1947, SR & O 1947/396 (spent). The Coal Commission's reserve fund had been wound up and transferred to the National Coal Board on 30 March 1947 by Treasury direction under the Coal Industry Nationalisation Act 1946 s 38(4) (repealed).

20 See the National Coal Board (Additional Powers) Act 1966 ss 1, 2 (both repealed); and the Coal Industry Act 1977 s 9(1)–(4) (repealed). As to petroleum production generally see ENERGY AND CLIMATE CHANGE vol 44 (2011) PARA 1029 et seq.

21 See the Coal Industry Act 1977 s 10 (as originally enacted) (now repealed).

22 See the Coal Industry Act 1987 s 1 (partly repealed and the remainder is repealed by the Coal Industry Act 1994 Sch 11 Pt III as from a day to be appointed). The change of name took effect on 5 March 1987 (the day on which the Coal Industry Act 1987 came into force), although the name 'British Coal' had been used for trading purposes since June 1986. The records of the British Coal Corporation are public records for the purposes of the Public Records Act 1958: see s 10, Sch 1 para 3 Table Pt II; and CONSTITUTIONAL AND ADMINISTRATIVE LAW vol 20 (2014) PARA 343. As to the dissolution of the British Coal Corporation see PARA 88.

23 These functions included: (1) searching and boring for coal in Great Britain (originally this was to the exclusion of any other person but that restriction was removed with effect from 31 October 1994 (see PARA 50) by the Coal Industry Act 1994 s 7(2), Sch 11 Pt II); (2) treating, rendering saleable, supplying and selling coal; (3) producing, manufacturing, treating, rendering saleable, supplying and selling products of coal; (4) producing or manufacturing any goods or utilities of a kind required by the British Coal Corporation for or in connection with the working or getting of coal or any other of its activities, or which could advantageously be produced or manufactured by the Corporation by reason of its having materials or facilities for their production or manufacture in connection with the working or getting of coal or any other of its activities, and supplying and selling goods or utilities so produced or manufactured; (5) activities which could advantageously be carried on by the British Coal Corporation with a view to making the best use of its assets; and

(6) activities conducive to advancing the skill of persons employed for the purposes of any of those activities, or the efficiency of equipment and methods to be used for them, including the provision by the British Coal Corporation itself, and its assisting the provision by others, of facilities for training, education and research: see the Coal Industry Nationalisation Act 1946 s 1(2) (repealed).

24 The British Coal Corporation had power to do anything and to enter into any transaction (whether or not involving the expenditure, borrowing or lending of money, the acquisition of any property or rights, or the disposal of any property or rights not in its opinion required for the proper discharge of its duties) which in its opinion was calculated to facilitate the proper discharge of its duties or the carrying on of its ancillary activities or was incidental or conducive to that purpose: see the Coal Industry Nationalisation Act 1946 s 1(3) (repealed).

The stated policy of the British Coal Corporation was to secure, consistently with the proper discharge of its duties: (1) the safety, health and welfare of persons in its employment; (2) the benefit of the practical knowledge and experience of such persons in the organisation and conduct of the operations in which they were employed; and (3) that the revenues of the Corporation were not less than sufficient to meet all its outgoings properly chargeable to revenue account (including provisions in respect of its obligations under the Coal Industry Nationalisation Act 1946 ss 28, 29 (repealed)) on an average of good and bad years: see s 1(4) (repealed).

25 As to the restructuring of the coal industry under privatisation see PARAS 50, 51 et seq. As to the restructuring of the British Coal Corporation's functions under the Coal Industry Act 1994 see PARA 71.

## 50. Privatisation of the coal industry.

The privatisation of the coal industry was introduced in two stages. The first stage occurred in 1990 with the raising of the limits on the number of men who could be employed underground or, as appropriate, the tonnage of coal to be got from an opencast operation[1] worked in accordance with a licence granted by the British Coal Corporation[2]. This made it possible for reasonably substantial mines to be worked otherwise than by the British Coal Corporation. The British Coal Corporation therefore granted licences to independent operators enabling the continued working of a number of underground mines which had previously been worked by the British Coal Corporation but which it would otherwise have closed permanently. In those cases, it leased the surface land at mines concerned to the relevant operator. In 1993 the restrictions on the permitted hours of work below ground in coal mines[3] were removed[4].

The second stage of privatisation was the passing of the Coal Industry Act 1994[5] which provided for the coal industry to return to the private sector, operating under a licensing system[6]. The way had been paved the previous year by the British Coal and British Rail (Transfer Proposals) Act 1993 which enabled the British Coal Corporation to act in relation to government proposals for the transfer of its functions, property, rights and liabilities to another body or person[7]. The Coal Industry Act 1994 established the Coal Authority[8], which on 31 October 1994[9] succeeded to the interests of the British Coal Corporation in unworked coal and coal mines[10]. The Coal Industry Act 1994 introduced a prohibition from that date on the carrying on of coal-mining operations[11] otherwise than under a licence granted under the Act, or, subject to certain qualifications, under a licence granted under the Coal Industry Nationalisation Act 1946[12]. At that time the British Coal Corporation remained the largest operator of coal mines, and the Secretary of State[13] granted licences[14] to the British Coal Corporation in respect of its mines (both underground and opencast). Contemporaneously with the grant of those licences, the Coal Authority granted leases of the relevant coal and coal mines to the British Coal Corporation[15]. The Secretary of State also granted a number of conditional licences[16] to the British Coal Corporation; and the Coal Authority granted to the British Coal Corporation options for leases of the coal relevant to those conditional licences. Subsequently, the coal-mining undertaking of the British Coal Corporation with the assets attributable to it (including the licences, conditional licences, leases and options for leases) was vested, by restructuring schemes made by the Secretary of State[17], in separate companies wholly owned by the Crown, known as 'successor companies'[18]. The Coal Authority assumed powers and duties relating to licensing these successor companies before they were then sold[19]. The Coal Authority also took on the responsibility for certain subsidence damage claims[20] and the provision of information[21].

The European Commission approved the plan to modernise, rationalise and restructure the coal industry as complying with the objectives of making the United Kingdom coal industry fully competitive with coal prices on international markets and privatising the British Coal Corporation[22], and it therefore authorised the grant by the United Kingdom government of financial aid to the coal industry in relation to the associated costs and liabilities[23].

The vast majority of the British Coal Corporation's interests were transferred by a series of restructuring schemes and what remained were only very limited residual functions and powers[24]. The British Coal Corporation was eventually dissolved on 27 March 2004[25].

1  See the amendments which were made by the Coal Industry Act 1990 s 4(1) (now repealed) to the Coal Industry Nationalisation Act 1946 s 36(2) (now repealed).
2  Ie a licence granted under the Coal Industry Nationalisation Act 1946 s 36 (repealed). As to the British Coal Corporation see PARA 49. As to such licences see PARA 49.
3  Ie the restrictions contained in the Coal Mines Regulation Act 1908 (repealed).
4  See the Coal Industry Act 1992 s 2 (repealed).
5  The Coal Industry Act 1994 received Royal Assent on 5 July 1994. As to the restructuring of the coal industry under privatisation see PARA 51 et seq.
6  See PARA 89 et seq.
7  See the British Coal and British Rail (Transfer Proposals) Act 1993 (repealed).
8  As to the Coal Authority see PARA 52 et seq.
9  Ie the date appointed as the 'restructuring date' under the Coal Industry Act 1994 s 7(1): see s 65(1); and the Coal Industry (Restructuring Date) Order 1994, SI 1994/2553.
10 See the Coal Industry Act 1994 s 7(3). The retained copyhold interests which had not vested in the National Coal Board were unaffected by the transfer of the British Coal Corporation's interests to the Coal Authority: see PARA 397 et seq. As to retained interests see PARA 48.
11 As to the meaning of 'coal-mining operations' see PARA 51.
12 See the Coal Industry Act 1994 s 25(1), (3), (4); and PARA 89 et seq. The licensing provisions referred to are those of Pt II (ss 25–36). Note that the limits on the number of men who could be employed underground or, as appropriate, the tonnage of coal to be got from an opencast operation under the Coal Industry Nationalisation Act 1946 s 36 (repealed) which had hitherto applied to the licensing powers of the British Coal Corporation had been removed since 5 July 1994: see the Coal Industry Act 1994 s 7(1).
13 As to the Secretary of State see PARA 2.
14 The relevant licences were granted to the British Coal Corporation by the Secretary of State in exercise of his powers under the Coal Industry Act 1994 s 26(6) (see PARA 90). As to the licensing of coal-mining operations see PARA 89 et seq.
15 Ie by direction of the Secretary of State under the Coal Industry Act 1994 s 6(1): see PARA 65.
16 Ie licences which contained conditions under which the authorisation was postponed until the fulfilment of specified requirements. As to the conditions which may be included in licences see PARAS 95–96.
17 Ie under the Coal Industry Act 1994 s 12 (see PARA 72). As to restructuring schemes see PARA 72.
18 As to successor companies see PARA 74.
19 See PARA 74.
20 These were broadly those not in areas of then current mining. As to subsidence damage by coal mining see PARAS 62, 200 et seq.
21 As to the Coal Authority's duties regarding the provision of information see PARAS 107–108.
22 See EC Commission Decision 94/574/ECSC (OJ L220, 25.8.94, p 12).
23 Financial aid was authorised in relation to: (1) contributions to pension schemes for former

workers of the British Coal Corporation and their dependants (see PARA 80 et seq); (2) exceptional social welfare benefits for workers who lost their jobs as a result of the restructuring, rationalisation and modernisation of the United Kingdom coal industry (see PARA 86 et seq); (3) concessionary fuel entitlement for former British Coal Corporation workers and their dependants (see PARA 78); (4) compensation for industrial injury and damage to health for former workers of the British Coal Corporation and their dependants (see PARA 75); (5) the costs from the residual activities of the British Coal Corporation (see PARA 76 et seq); and (6) environmental damage caused by mining activities before privatisation: see EC Commission Decision 97/577/ECSC (OJ L237, 28.8.97, p 13).

24 As to the restructuring of the British Coal Corporation's functions see PARA 71. The remaining empowering statutory provisions, although still extant, are now prospectively repealed by the Coal Industry Act 1994 Sch 11 Pt III from a day to be appointed (see PARA 49). See eg the Coal Industry Nationalisation Act 1946 s 37, Sch 2A (superannuation); s 41 (variation of trusts); s 56 (restrictions on disclosure of information); s 59 (prosecutions and offences); s 60 (service of notices etc); s 61 (arbitration); s 62 (regulations); the Coal Industry Act 1949 s 4 (superannuation); the Coal Industry Act 1962 s 2 (financial year); the Coal Industry Act 1971 s 7 (directions by the Secretary of State); s 8 (annual accounts); s 9 (issues out of Consolidated Fund); the Coal Industry Act 1973 s 1 (capital reconstruction); s 2 (borrowing powers of the British Coal Corporation and its subsidiaries); s 10 (membership limits); s 11 (administrative expenses); the Coal Industry Act 1977 s 7 (payments to redundant workers); s 13 (Secretary of State's administrative expenses); the Coal Industry Act 1985 s 3 (payments to redundant workers); the Coal Industry Act 1987 s 3 (grants for workforce redeployment and reduction); s 4 (pit closures); ss 5, 8 (see PARA 87) (participation by representative organisations in the management of trusts and bodies connected with the coal industry).

25 Ie the date appointed as the 'dissolution date' under the Coal Industry Act 1994 s 23 for the dissolution of the British Coal Corporation: see s 23(2); and the Coal Industry Act 1994 (Commencement No 7) and Dissolution of the British Coal Corporation Order 2004, SI 2004/144, art 3. As to the British Coal Corporation see PARAS 49–50. As to the dissolution of the British Coal Corporation see PARA 88.

# (2) Reorganisation of the Coal-mining Industry

## (i) Introduction

### 51. The Coal Industry Act 1994.

The main purposes of the Coal Industry Act 1994[1] are to provide for the establishment of the Coal Authority[2] and for the restructuring of the coal industry[3]. To achieve this the Coal Industry Act 1994 provides for the transfer of property, rights and liabilities[4] of the British Coal Corporation[5] and its wholly-owned subsidiaries to other persons[6], and for the British Coal Corporation to lose its exclusive powers and duties of searching for, boring for, working and getting the coal in Great Britain[7]. The Coal Industry Act 1994 also provides for the dissolution of the British Coal Corporation[8], and makes provision for the licensing of coal-mining operations[9] as well as making various other consequential changes to the law[10].

1 Coal Industry Act 1994 s 68(1). The provisions of the Coal Industry Act 1994 are brought into force on a number of different dates. The following provisions of the Coal Industry Act 1994 came into force on the passing of the Act (ie 5 July 1994): ss 7–9, 12–14, 17, 54, 62–66, 67(2)–(6), (8), Sch 2, Sch 11 Pt I: s 68(6). The following provisions of the Act came into force on the restructuring date (ie 31 October 1994: see PARA 50): ss 10, 11, 18, 23, 31–34, 36, 38–44, 48–53, 55, 67(1), (8) (for certain purposes only), Schs 6, 7, 8, 9 (for certain purposes only), Sch 11 Pt II: s 68(2) (amended by the Gambling Act 2005, s 356(4), Sch 17; and the Planning (Consequential Provisions) (Scotland) Act 1997, s 3, Sch 1, Pt 1). The following provisions of the Coal Industry Act 1994 came into force on the dissolution date ie 27 March 2004: s 67(1), (8) (for certain purposes only), Sch 9 (for certain purposes only), Sch 11 Pt IV: s 68(3).

Apart from the above provisions, the Coal Industry Act 1994 comes into force on such days as the Secretary of State may by order made by statutory instrument appoint: see s 68(4), (5). As to the Secretary of State see PARA 2. The following commencement orders have been made under the Coal Industry Act 1994: the Coal Industry Act 1994 (Commencement No 1) Order 1994, SI 1994/2189; the Coal Industry Act 1994 (Commencement No 2 and Transitional Provisions) Order 1994, SI 1994/2552; the Coal Industry Act 1994 (Commencement No 3) Order 1994, SI 1994/3063; the Coal Industry Act 1994 (Commencement No 4) Order 1995, SI 1995/159; the Coal Industry Act 1994 (Commencement No 5) Order 1995, SI 1995/273; the Coal Industry Act 1994 (Commencement No 6) and Membership of the British Coal Corporation (Appointed Day) Order 1995, SI 1995/1507; and the Coal Industry Act 1994 (Commencement No 7) and Dissolution of the British Coal Corporation Order 2004, SI 2004/144.

As to the provisions which do not apply to Scotland see the Coal Industry Act 1994 s 68(7), (7A) (s 68(7) amended by the Water Act 2003 s 85(3); the Coal Industry Act 1994 s 68(7A) added by the Water Services etc (Scotland) Act 2005 s 30(3)). The Coal Industry Act 1994 does not apply to Northern Ireland, with the exception of the following provisions: (1) ss 7–9, 12, 13, Sch 2; (2) ss 20, 21, Sch 4; (3) certain provisions of Sch 1; (4) certain provisions of Sch 9; (5) the repeal of certain enactments; (6) so much of Pt IV (ss 57–68) as is required for the purpose of giving effect to the extension to Northern Ireland of the provisions mentioned in the preceding paragraphs: s 68(8). The Coal Industry Act 1994 extends to the Isle of Man for the purpose of giving effect there to the repeal of the Territorial Sea Act 1987 s 2(3), to the Coal Industry Act 1994 s 67(7), Sch 10 para 10 and to so much of any restructuring scheme or any agreement under s 13 (see PARA 72) as relates to rights mentioned in Sch 10 para 10; and, subject to Sch 10 para 10, that repeal accordingly includes the repeal of the Territorial Sea Act 1987 s 2(3) as it extends to the Isle of Man by virtue of the Territorial Sea Act 1987 (Isle of Man) Order 1991, SI 1991/1722.

As to the Secretary of State's power to make orders under the Coal Industry Act 1994 see s 67.

2   As to the Coal Authority see PARA 52 et seq.

3   Coal Industry Act 1994, long title.

4   'Liability', in relation to the transfer of liabilities from one person to another or to the modification of any liability, does not include any criminal liability: Coal Industry Act 1994 s 65(1). 'Modifications' includes additions, alterations and omissions: s 65(1).

5   As to the British Coal Corporation see PARAS 49–50.

6   Coal Industry Act 1994, long title. 'Subsidiary' and 'wholly-owned subsidiary' have the same meanings given by the Companies Act 2006 s 1159 (see COMPANIES vol 14 (2016) PARA 22): Coal Industry Act 1994 s 65(1) (definition amended by SI 2009/1941).

7   Those powers and duties were imposed by the Coal Industry Nationalisation Act 1946 s 1(1)(a) (repealed), and ceased as from the restructuring date (ie 31 October 1994: see PARA 50): Coal Industry Act 1994 s 7(2). As to the meaning of 'Great Britain' see PARA 48.

8   Coal Industry Act 1994, long title. As to the dissolution of the British Coal Corporation see PARA 88.

9   See the Coal Industry Act 1994 Pt II (ss 25–36); and PARA 89 et seq. 'Coal-mining operations' includes: (1) searching for coal and boring for it; (2) winning, working and getting it (whether underground or in the course of opencast operations); (3) bringing underground coal to the surface, treating coal and rendering it saleable; (4) treating coal in the strata for the purpose of winning any product of coal and winning, working or getting any product of coal resulting from such treatment; and (5) depositing spoil from any activities carried on in the course of any coal-mining operations and draining coal mines, and an operation carried on in relation to minerals other than coal is a coal-mining operation in so far as it is carried on in relation to those minerals as part of, or is ancillary to, operations carried on in relation to coal: s 65(1). 'Coal' means bituminous coal, cannel coal and anthracite: s 65(1). References to the treatment of coal in the strata are to be taken not to include references to any operations which (a) are carried on in relation to coal in or to which any oil or gas that exists in its natural condition in the strata is absorbed or adsorbed; and (b) are so carried on wholly for the purpose of winning or getting that oil or gas: s 65(2). 'Oil or gas' means (i) any mineral oil or any relative hydrocarbon which, in its natural state, is not a solid; or (ii) methane or any other natural gas: ss 9(6), 65(2). In the context of an Act dealing with mining operations and mineral extraction, the word 'spoil' meant a substance produced as a result of mining or mineral extraction that was not the primary target of the operations: see *MMC Midlands Ltd v Revenue and Customs Comrs* [2009] EWHC 683 (Ch), [2009] STC 1969.

10  Coal Industry Act 1994, long title. As to the consequential changes to the law see s 52(2), Sch 8 (amendments to the Opencast Coal Act 1958: see PARA 413 et seq); Coal Industry Act 1994 s 67(1), Sch 9 (minor and consequential amendments); s 67(7), Sch 10 (transitional provisions and savings); s 67(8), Sch 11 (repeals).

## (ii) The Coal Authority

### A.    ESTABLISHMENT AND CONSTITUTION

## 52. Establishment and purposes of the Coal Authority.

The Coal Industry Act 1994 established the Coal Authority[1] as a body corporate for the purpose of:

(1)    holding, managing and disposing of interests[2] and rights in or in relation to the unworked coal[3] and other property which is transferred to or otherwise acquired by it by or under the Coal Industry Act 1994[4];

(2)    carrying out functions with respect to the licensing of coal-mining operations[5];

(3)    carrying out functions with respect to coal-mining subsidence and in connection with other matters incidental to the carrying on of any opencast or other coal-mining operations[6];

(4)    facilitating the establishment and maintenance of arrangements for the information to which persons are to be entitled under the Coal Industry Act 1994 to be made available to them[7]; and

(5)    carrying out the other functions conferred on it by virtue of the Coal Industry Act 1994[8].

1   In the Coal Industry Act 1994, the Coal Authority is referred to as 'the Authority': see s 65(1). At the date at which this volume states the law, the principal office of the Coal Authority is 200 Lichfield Lane, Mansfield, Nottinghamshire NG18 4RG.
2   'Interest' in relation to land includes estate: Coal Industry Act 1994 s 65(1). References to the creation, in favour of any person, of an interest in property include references to the vesting in that person of a freehold or leasehold interest in property: s 65(3).
3   As to the meaning of 'coal' see PARA 51.
4   Coal Industry Act 1994 s 1(1)(a). As to the membership of the Coal Authority see s 1(2)-(4), Sch 1 paras 1, 2. As to officers and employees of the Coal Authority see Sch 1 para 3.
5   Coal Industry Act 1994 s 1(1)(b). As to the meaning of 'coal-mining operations' see PARA 51.
6   Coal Industry Act 1994 s 1(1)(c). As to subsidence by coal mining see PARA 200 et seq.
7   Coal Industry Act 1994 s 1(1)(d).
8   Coal Industry Act 1994 s 1(1)(e).

## 53. Relationship with the Crown.

The Coal Authority is not to be regarded as the servant or agent of the Crown, or as enjoying any status, immunity or privilege of the Crown; or by virtue of any connection with the Crown, as exempt from any tax, duty, rate, levy or other charge whatsoever, whether general or local; and nor is the Authority's property to be regarded as property of, or property held on behalf of, the Crown[1].

1   Coal Industry Act 1994 s 1(5).

## 54. Proceedings.

Subject to certain provisions[1], the Coal Authority regulates its own procedure (including quorum)[2]. Anything authorised or required by or under any enactment to be done by the Authority may be done by any of its members, officers or employees who has been authorised for the purpose, whether generally or specially, by the Authority[3].

A member of the Authority who is in any way directly or indirectly interested in any matter that is brought up for consideration at a meeting must disclose the nature of his interest to the meeting[4]. Where such a disclosure is made, it must be recorded in the minutes of the meeting and the member in question must not take part in any deliberation or decision of the Authority with respect to that matter if either (1) it relates to any application made to the Authority or to any licence or contract which the Authority has granted or entered into or is considering granting or entering into[5]; or (2) the Authority determines that the nature of the matter, the extent of the member's interest and any prejudicial effect of his joining in the consideration of that matter are such that the member should not take part[6].

The validity of any of the Authority's proceedings is not affected by a vacancy amongst its members, by any defect in the appointment of a member or by any contravention of the requirement[7] relating to giving notice of interest[8].

Minutes must be kept of its proceedings[9], and are evidence of those proceedings if they are signed by a person purporting to have acted as chairman of the proceedings to which the minutes relate or of any subsequent proceedings in the course of which the minutes were approved as a correct record[10].

The application of the Authority's seal must be authenticated by the signature[11] of any member, officer or employee of the Authority who has been authorised for the purpose, whether generally or specially, by the Authority[12]. Every document purporting to be an instrument made or issued by or on behalf of the Authority and to be duly executed under its seal, or to be signed or executed by a person authorised by the Authority for the purpose, must be received in evidence and treated, without further proof, as being so made or issued unless the contrary is shown[13].

1   Ie subject to the Coal Industry Act 1994 s 1(6), Sch 1 paras 5–12: see Sch 1 para 4.
2   Coal Industry Act 1994 Sch 1 para 4.
3   Coal Industry Act 1994 Sch 1 para 5.
4   Coal Industry Act 1994 Sch 1 para 6(1). For these purposes, a general notification given at a meeting of the Authority by any of its members to the effect that (1) he is a member of a specified body corporate or firm; and (2) he is to be regarded as interested in any matter involving that body or firm which falls to be considered after the giving of the notification, is to be regarded as a sufficient disclosure of his interest in relation to any such matter: Sch 1 para 6(3). A member who is required to make a disclosure at any meeting need not attend in person in order to make the disclosure if he takes reasonable steps to secure that the disclosure is made by a notice which is taken into consideration and read at the meeting: Sch 1 para 6(4).
5   Coal Industry Act 1994 Sch 1 para 6(2)(a).
6   Coal Industry Act 1994 Sch 1 para 6(2)(b).
7   Ie the Coal Industry Act 1994 Sch 1 para 6. 'Contravention' includes a failure to comply: s 65(1). The Coal Authority has adopted a Code of Practice in line with guidance set out in Annex C to the White Paper 'The Governance of Public Bodies: A Progress Report' (Cm 3557) (1997).
8   Coal Industry Act 1994 Sch 1 para 7.
9   Coal Industry Act 1994 Sch 1 para 8(1).
10  Coal Industry Act 1994 Sch 1 para 8(2). Where minutes of any such proceedings have been so signed, those proceedings are, unless the contrary is shown, deemed to have been regularly convened and constituted: Sch 1 para 8(3).
11  For these purposes the reference to the signature of a person includes a reference to a facsimile of a signature by whatever process reproduced; and 'signed' is to be construed accordingly: Coal Industry Act 1994 Sch 1 para 9(3).
12  Coal Industry Act 1994 Sch 1 para 9(1).
13  Coal Industry Act 1994 Sch 1 para 9(2).

## 55.   Finances and accounts.

The Secretary of State[1] may, after consultation with the Coal Authority, determine[2] the financial duties of the Authority, and different determinations may be made for different functions and activities of the Authority[3]. Such a determination may (1) relate to a period beginning before the date on which it is made[4]; (2) contain supplemental provisions[5]; and (3) be varied by a subsequent determination[6]. The Secretary of State must give the Authority written notice of every such determination and the Authority must conduct its finances in accordance with the determinations of which it has been given notice[7].

The Secretary of State must, in respect of each accounting year[8], pay to the Authority such amount as he may determine[9] to be the amount required by the Authority for the carrying out during that year of its functions under the Coal Industry Act 1994[10]. Except so far as the Secretary of State may otherwise direct, sums received by the Authority in the course of carrying out its functions are to be paid by the Authority to the Secretary of State[11].

The Authority must keep proper accounts and records in relation to its accounts[12], and in respect of each accounting year, must prepare a statement of accounts in such form, and within such period after the end of that year, as the Secretary of State may, with the approval of the Treasury, direct[13]. On or before 31 August following the end of every accounting year, the Secretary of State must send a copy of that year's statement of accounts to the Comptroller and Auditor General[14], who must examine, certify and report on the statement and lay copies of it and of his report before each House of Parliament[15].

1   As to the Secretary of State see PARA 2.
2   The approval of the Treasury is required for the making of a determination under the Coal Industry Act 1994 s 1(6), Sch 1 para 13: Sch 1 para 13(4).
3   Coal Industry Act 1994 Sch 1 para 13(1).
4   Coal Industry Act 1994 Sch 1 para 13(2)(a).
5   Coal Industry Act 1994 Sch 1 para 13(2)(b).
6   Coal Industry Act 1994 Sch 1 para 13(2)(c).
7   Coal Industry Act 1994 Sch 1 para 13(3).
8   For these purposes, 'accounting year' means the period beginning with the day on which the Authority is established (see PARA 52) and ending with the financial year current on that date, and each successive financial year: Sch 1 para 14(5). 'Financial year' means the 12 months ending with 31 March: s 65(1).
9   The approval of the Treasury is required for the making of a determination, or the giving of any direction, under the Coal Industry Act 1994 Sch 1 para 14: Sch 1 para 14(4). The Authority is required to set out in its annual report all determinations that are made under Sch 1 Pt II: see s 60(2)(a); and PARA 56.
10  Coal Industry Act 1994 Sch 1 para 14(1). Any sums required by the Secretary of State for making such a payment is to be paid out of money provided by Parliament: Sch 1 para 14(3).
11  Coal Industry Act 1994 Sch 1 para 14(2). Any sums so received by the Secretary of State are to be paid into the Consolidated Fund: Sch 1 para 14(3). As to the Consolidated Fund see CONSTITUTIONAL AND ADMINISTRATIVE LAW vol 20 (2014) PARA 480; PARLIAMENT vol 78 (2018) PARA 847 et seq.
12  Coal Industry Act 1994 Sch 1 para 15(1)(a).
13  Coal Industry Act 1994 Sch 1 para 15(1)(b). Before such date after the end of every accounting year as the Secretary of State may direct, the Authority must send to the Secretary of State a copy of the statement of accounts prepared in respect of that accounting year: Sch 1 para 15(2). As to the Treasury see CONSTITUTIONAL AND ADMINISTRATIVE LAW vol 20 (2014) PARAS 262–265.
14  Coal Industry Act 1994 Sch 1 para 15(3). As to the Comptroller and Auditor General see CONSTITUTIONAL AND ADMINISTRATIVE LAW vol 20 (2014) PARAS 494–496.
15  Coal Industry Act 1994 Sch 1 para 15(4). The Authority's annual report must incorporate the statement of accounts prepared by it in respect of the accounting year ending with the financial year in question, together with a copy of the report on those accounts which is required to be laid before Parliament under Sch 1 para 15(4): see s 60(2)(b); and PARA 56.

## 56.   Annual report on the activities of the Coal Authority.

As soon as reasonably practicable after the end of each financial year[1] the Coal Authority must prepare a report[2] on its activities during that year and send a copy to the Secretary of State[3], who must, as soon as reasonably practicable after he has received it, lay a copy of it before each House of Parliament[4]. The Authority must arrange for copies of every annual report to be published in such manner as it considers appropriate for securing that the information contained in it is available to the persons likely to be interested in it[5], and must also send the Secretary of State as many copies of the published report as he requires[6].

1 As to the meaning of 'financial year' see PARA 55.
2 The Authority's annual report must set out (1) all directions under the Coal Industry Act 1994 ss 1(6), 6, 60, Sch 1 Pt II paras 13–15 (see PARA 55); and (2) all such determinations under Sch 1 Pt II (see PARA 55), as have been given to it or made during the financial year to which the report relates: s 60(2)(a). It must incorporate the statement of accounts prepared by the Authority in respect of the accounting year ending with the financial year in question, together with a copy of the report on those accounts which is required to be laid before Parliament under Sch 1 para 15(4) (see PARA 55): s 60(2)(b). The report must otherwise be in such form, and contain such information, as may be specified in a direction given to it by the Secretary of State: s 60(2)(c). As to the Secretary of State see PARA 2. The information contained in the Authority's annual report must not include any information excluded by virtue of s 57(3) or s 57(4) from the information which is to be made available in pursuance of arrangements under s 57 (see PARA 107): s 60(3). However, this does not prevent the inclusion in the Authority's annual report of any information which has already been made public by virtue of any statutory provision: s 60(4). In consequence of the Coal Mining Subsidence Act 1991 s 49 (see PARA 253), it is not necessary for the Authority's annual report to include any report on the operation of that Act: Coal Industry Act 1994 s 60(5).
3 Coal Industry Act 1994 s 60(1).
4 Coal Industry Act 1994 s 60(6).
5 Coal Industry Act 1994 s 60(7)(a).
6 Coal Industry Act 1994 s 60(7)(b).

## 57. Coal-mining museum report.

The Secretary of State[1] must, in addition to laying the annual report on the activities of the Coal Authority[2] before Parliament, prepare and lay a report relating to coal-mining museums. He is required, as soon as reasonably practicable after the end of the period of three years beginning with the restructuring date[3], to prepare and lay before Parliament a report setting out particulars of:

(1) the financial assistance provided during that period to coal-mining museums, so far as it has involved the making of payments for that purpose to any person by the Secretary of State[4];

(2) the manner in which the provision of that financial assistance has been administered[5]; and

(3) the use to which that financial assistance has been put by the coal-mining museums which have received it[6].

1 As to the Secretary of State see PARA 2.
2 See PARA 56.
3 Ie 31 October 1994: see PARA 50.
4 Coal Industry Act 1994 s 61(a).
5 Coal Industry Act 1994 s 61(b).
6 Coal Industry Act 1994 s 61(c).

B. DUTIES AND POWERS

## 58. Duties with respect to licensing.

The Coal Authority has two classes of duty which affect the manner in which it carries out its functions in relation to licensing coal-mining operations[1].

The first class comprises the duty of the Authority to carry out its licensing functions[2] in the manner that it considers is best calculated to secure, so far as practicable:

(1) that an economically viable[3] coal-mining industry[4] in Great Britain[5] is maintained and developed by the persons authorised[6] to carry on coal-mining operations[7];

(2)     that such persons are able to finance both the proper carrying on of the coal-mining operations that they are authorised to carry on and the discharge of liabilities arising from the carrying on of those operations[8]; and

(3)     that persons to whom obligations are owed[9] in respect of subsidence damage[10] caused at any time[11] do not sustain loss in consequence of any failure by a person who is or has been a licensed operator[12] to make such financial provision for meeting present and future liabilities as might reasonably have been required of that person[13].

The second class comprises the duty, subject to certain provisions[14], of the Authority, in carrying out its licensing functions, to have regard to the desirability of securing:

(a)     that persons authorised[15] to carry on coal-mining operations are persons who have at their disposal such experience and expertise in the carrying on of such operations as are appropriate for ensuring that any authorised operations are properly carried on[16]; and

(b)     that competition is promoted between the different persons carrying on, or seeking to carry on, coal-mining operations[17].

Similarly, it is also the duty of the Authority, in carrying out its licensing functions in cases where it appears that subsidence damage may be caused to any land or other property that does not consist in unworked coal[18] or in a coal mine[19], to have regard to the extent of the damage which is likely to be caused, and to the character of the land or other property in question and to the uses to which it is or is likely to be put[20].

1   The first class of duty is a positive duty to carry out various functions in the manner the Coal Authority considers best calculated to secure certain precise objectives (see the Coal Industry Act 1994 s 2(1)). The second class is a less positive duty for the Authority merely to have regard to the desirability of securing certain less precise objectives (see s 2(2), (3)). As to the meaning of 'coal-mining operations' see PARA 51.

2   Ie under the Coal Industry Act 1994 Pt II (ss 25–36) (see PARA 89 et seq): s 2(1).

3   It is submitted that the words 'economically viable' given their ordinary meaning and applied to the industry as a whole, are not inconsistent with the failure of individual operators; cf Coal Industry Act 1994 s 3(5); PARA 59. See also *Nocton Ltd v Water Hall Group plc* [1997] EGCS 97.

4   'Coal-mining industry' is not defined in the Coal Industry Act 1994.

5   As to the meaning of 'Great Britain' see PARA 48.

6   Ie authorised under the Coal Industry Act 1994 Pt II: see s 2(1)(a).

7   Coal Industry Act 1994 s 2(1)(a).

8   Coal Industry Act 1994 s 2(1)(b).

9   An obligation may be owed by virtue of the Coal Industry Act 1994 s 43 (see PARA 204) or contractually.

10  As to the meaning of 'subsidence damage' see PARA 203. As to subsidence damage by coal mining see PARA 200 et seq.

11  Ie whether before or after the passing of the Coal Industry Act 1994 (ie 5 July 1994): see s 2(1)(c).

12  'Licensed operator' means any person who is for the time being either (1) authorised by a licence under the Coal Industry Act 1994 Pt II to carry on coal-mining operations to which s 25 applies (see PARA 89); or (2) authorised by virtue of s 25(3) to carry on any such operations: s 65(1).

13  Coal Industry Act 1994 s 2(1)(c). As to subsidence provisions see ss 42–48; and PARA 203 et seq.

14  Ie the Coal Industry Act 1994 s 4 (see PARA 60): see s 2(2).

15  Ie by virtue of the Coal Industry Act 1994 Pt II: see s 2(2)(a).

16  Coal Industry Act 1994 s 2(2)(a).

17  Coal Industry Act 1994 s 2(2)(b).

18  As to the meaning of 'coal' see PARA 51.

19  As to the meaning of 'coal mine' see PARA 3.

20  Coal Industry Act 1994 s 2(3).

## 59. Duties with respect to property.

It is the duty of the Coal Authority, in carrying out its functions[1] of holding, managing and disposing of interests and rights in or in relation to the unworked coal[2] and other property which is transferred[3] to or otherwise acquired[4] by it, to have regard to: (1) the need to co-ordinate its practice in relation to relevant property dealings[5] with the carrying out of its licensing functions[6]; and (2) the need to secure the safety of members of the public[7].

Subject to certain provisions[8], it is the duty of the Authority, so far as practicable, to make available for acquisition by others such of its land and other property as (a) does not consist in an interest in any unworked coal or coal mine[9]; (b) is not being put to a use which justifies its retention by the Authority[10]; and (c) in the opinion of the Authority, is unlikely to be required for any such use[11].

Where the Authority disposes of any interests or rights in or in relation to any land or other property, it must secure the best terms reasonably available for the disposal[12], and, in the exercise and performance of its powers and duties with respect to its land and other property, it must have regard to the desirability of the exploitation, so far as that is economically viable[13], of coal-bed methane in Great Britain[14].

It is the duty of the Authority, in formulating any proposals for works on or in relation to any of its land or other property which has been (but is no longer) used for the carrying on of any coal-mining operations to (i) have regard to the desirability of preserving natural beauty, of conserving flora and fauna and geological or physiographical features of special interest and of protecting sites, buildings, structures and objects of architectural, historic or archaeological interest[15]; and (ii) take into account the effect of the proposals on the natural beauty of any area or on any such flora, fauna, features, sites, buildings, structures or objects[16].

1  Ie the functions mentioned in the Coal Industry Act 1994 s 1(1)(a) (see PARA 52): see s 3(1).
2  As to the meaning of 'coal' see PARA 51.
3  See the Coal Industry Act 1994 s 7(3); and PARA 66.
4  See the Coal Industry Act 1994 s 5(2) (see PARA 63); s 12 (see PARA 72).
5  For these purposes, 'relevant property dealings', in relation to the Coal Authority, means the grant of such interests and rights in or in relation to its land or other property as appear to it to be appropriate for the purpose of enabling or facilitating its use for, or in connection with, the carrying on of any coal-mining operations: Coal Industry Act 1994 s 3(8). As to the meaning of 'interest' see PARA 52; and as to the meaning of 'coal-mining operations' see PARA 51.
6  Coal Industry Act 1994 s 3(1)(a). The licensing functions referred to are those under Pt II (ss 25–36) (see PARA 89 et seq): see s 3(1)(a).
7  Coal Industry Act 1994 s 3(1)(b).
8  Ie the Coal Industry Act 1994 s 3(4): see s 3(3).
9  Coal Industry Act 1994 s 3(2)(a). As to the meaning of 'coal mine' see PARA 3.
10  Coal Industry Act 1994 s 3(2)(b). For the purposes of s 3(2) the only uses for land and other property which justify its retention by the Authority are: (1) use by any person for or in connection with the carrying on of any coal-mining operations; and (2) use by the Authority in connection with the administration of its own activities or with the management of the land and other property which it is entitled to retain or is unable to dispose of: s 3(3). For this purpose the management of land and other property includes the performance of every obligation to which the Authority is subject in relation to any of that land or other property: s 3(3).
11  Coal Industry Act 1994 s 3(2)(c).
12  Coal Industry Act 1994 s 3(4).
13  As to the meaning of 'economically viable' see PARA 58.
14  Coal Industry Act 1994 s 3(5). As to the meaning of 'Great Britain' see PARA 48. Section 3(4), (5) is subject to s 3(6), which provides that it is the duty of the Authority, in determining the terms on which it may dispose of any interest or right in or in relation to any unworked coal or coal mine to a person who requires the interest or right for purposes connected with activities to be carried

on under the authority of a licence under the Petroleum Act 1998 s 3 (see ENERGY AND CLIMATE CHANGE vol 44 (2011) PARA 1046), to act in accordance with such arrangements and principles as it may, with the approval of the Secretary of State, have determined for the purposes of the Coal Industry Act 1994 s 3(5): s 3(6) (amended by the Petroleum Act 1998 s 50, Sch 4 para 38(2)). As to the Secretary of State see PARA 2.

15  Coal Industry Act 1994 s 3(7)(a). As to areas of outstanding beauty see OPEN SPACES AND COUNTRYSIDE vol 78 (2018) PARA 443 et seq; as to nature conservation see OPEN SPACES AND COUNTRYSIDE vol 78 (2018) PARA 422 et seq; and as to ancient monuments and archaeological areas see NATIONAL CULTURAL HERITAGE vol 77 (2016) PARA 1006 et seq. See also PLANNING.
16  Coal Industry Act 1994 s 3(7)(b).

## 60.  Duty with respect to safety.

It is the Coal Authority's duty in conjunction with the Health and Safety Executive[1], to prepare and from time to time revise a document setting out such means as may, be agreed between the Authority and the Executive for securing co-operation and the exchange of information between them[2]; and without prejudice to the effect or operation of any relevant statutory provisions[3] to conduct itself in the carrying out of its functions in accordance with any agreement contained in that document[4].

As soon as practicable after agreement is reached for the purposes of the preparation or revision of such a document, the Authority must send a copy of the document or, as the case may be, of the revised version of it to the Secretary of State[5], who must lay the copy before each House of Parliament[6].

1  As to the Health and Safety Executive see HEALTH AND SAFETY AT WORK vol 52 (2014) PARA 326 et seq.
2  Coal Industry Act 1994 s 4(1)(a) (amended by SI 2008/960).
3  Ie within the meaning of the Health and Safety at Work etc Act 1974 Pt I (ss 1–54) (see HEALTH AND SAFETY AT WORK vol 52 (2014) PARA 302 et seq): see the Coal Industry Act 1994 s 4(1)(b).
4  Coal Industry Act 1994 s 4(1)(b). The document contains undertakings:
   (1)  by the Coal Authority and the Health and Safety Executive to co-operate with each other on the exchange of information necessary to enable both organisations to carry out their functions efficiently and effectively, and to appoint liaison officers to be responsible for doing so;
   (2)  for the Coal Authority to provide the Health and Safety Executive with information relating to details of any licence application, licence granted, change of licensee and any other significant change to a licence; any permission to drill; details of any freehold sale of unworked coal and, at the request of the Health and Safety Executive, any other information in its possession which is of particular relevance to the health and safety of persons engaged in, or who may be affected by, coal-mining operations;
   (3)  for the Coal Authority to notify the Health and Safety Executive promptly of any information which comes to its attention which may be relevant to the health and safety of persons engaged in, or who may be affected by, coal-mining operations, and to notify any licensee of the name and address of the local Health and Safety Executive inspector;
   (4)  for the Health and Safety Executive to provide the Coal Authority with any information or technical advice reasonably requested by it in connection with its licensing functions (see PARA 58) and property functions (see PARA 59), including any action the Health and Safety Executive takes or proposes to take which may materially affect coal-mining operations, and any information on abandoned mines or other workings provided to the Health and Safety Executive; to draw the attention of the Coal Authority to any other information which it believes is relevant to the licensing and property functions of the Coal Authority, including details of any information received by the Health and Safety Executive of the start or cessation of coal-mining operations, or the abandonment of a mine or coal quarry.
   The provision of information in head (2) is subject to the provisions of the Coal Industry Act 1994 s 57 (see PARA 107), s 58 (see PARA 97), and s 59 (see PARA 108).
   The Agreement is to be reviewed annually, and may be amended or reviewed at any time by agreement of the Coal Authority and the Health and Safety Executive.

5	As to the Secretary of State see PARA 2.
6	Coal Industry Act 1994 s 4(2).

## 61. Power with respect to coal mine water discharge.

The Coal Authority may take such action as it considers appropriate, if any, for the purpose of preventing, or mitigating the effect of, the discharge of water from a coal mine[1] into or on to any land or into any controlled waters[2].

If the Authority is of the opinion that a discharge of water from a coal mine into or on to any land or into any controlled waters has caused, is causing or is likely to cause (1) serious pollution of the environment; or (2) danger to life or health, the Authority may, for any specified purpose[3], in writing authorise a person to exercise, in accordance with the terms of the authorisation, any of the following powers[4]:

(a)	to enter at any reasonable time (or, in an emergency, at any time and, if need be, using reasonable force) any premises[5] which the authorised person has reason to believe it is necessary for him to enter[6];

(b)	to use a vehicle or a boat to do so[7];

(c)	on entering any premises by virtue of head (a) above, to take with him any other person authorised by the Authority and, if the authorised person reasonably believes he is likely to be obstructed, a constable and any equipment or materials needed for any purpose for which the power of entry is being exercised[8];

(d)	to make such examination and investigation as may in any circumstances be necessary[9];

(e)	to take such measurements and photographs and make such recordings as he considers necessary for the purpose of any examination or investigation under head (d) above[10];

(f)	to take samples, or cause samples to be taken, of any articles or substances found in or on any premises which he has power to enter, and of the air or water or land in, on, or in the vicinity of, the premises[11];

(g)	to require any person to give him such facilities and assistance with respect to any matters or things within that person's control or in relation to which that person has responsibilities as are necessary to enable the authorised person to exercise any of the powers so conferred on him[12].

The Authority may be authorised by the Secretary of State[13] to purchase compulsorily any land anywhere in England and Wales where he is of the opinion that the purchase is required by the Authority for the purpose of preventing, or mitigating the effect of, a discharge of water from a coal mine; and the discharge has caused, is causing or is likely to cause significant pollution of controlled waters or serious harm to human health[14]. Such a power[15] includes the power to authorise the acquisition of interests in, and rights over, land by the creation of new interests and rights; and by authorising the acquisition by the Authority of any rights over land which is to be or has been acquired by the Authority, to provide for the extinguishment of those rights[16].

1	References to coal mines are to coal mines vested in the Coal Authority: Coal Industry Act 1994 s 4A(2)(b) (s 4A–4C added by the Water Act 2003 s 85(1); Coal Industry Act 1994 s 4A(2) amended by the Energy Act 2011 s 115(2)). As to the meaning of 'controlled waters' see the Water Resources Act 1991 s 104; and ENVIRONMENTAL QUALITY AND PUBLIC HEALTH vol 45 (2010) PARA 289 (definition applied by the Coal Industry Act 1994 s 4A(2)(a)).

2	Coal Industry Act 1994 s 4A(1). As to power with respect to coal mine water discharge similar power in relation to Scotland see ss 4D–4G (ss 4D–4F added by the Water Services etc (Scotland) Act 2005 s 30(1); Coal Industry Act 1994 s 4G added by the Energy Act 2011 s 116(1)).

3   The purposes are (1) to determine the extent of the pollution or of the danger, or the likelihood of serious pollution or such danger; (2) to determine whether, and, if so, how, the Authority should exercise its power under the Coal Industry Act 1994 s 4A; (3) to take action under s 4A: s 4B(2).

4   Coal Industry Act 1994 s 4B(1). The powers which are conferred in relation to any land by s 4B include power, for the purposes mentioned in s 4B(2) (1) to carry out experimental borings or other works on those premises; and (2) to install, keep or maintain monitoring and other apparatus there: s 4B(4).

5   'Premises' includes any land, vehicle or vessel, and any plant which is designed to move or be moved (whether or not on roads): Coal Industry Act 1994 s 4B(9). In relation to any premises belonging to or used for the purposes of the United Kingdom Atomic Energy Authority, s 4B(1)–(3) has effect subject to the Atomic Energy Authority Act 1954 s 6(3) (which restricts entry to such premises where they have been declared to be prohibited places for the purposes of the Official Secrets Act 1911): Coal Industry Act 1994 s 4B(7).

6   Coal Industry Act 1994 s 4B(3)(a). Except in an emergency, in any case where it is proposed to enter any premises used for residential purposes, or to take heavy equipment on to any premises which are to be entered, any entry by virtue of s 4B is only effected (1) after the expiration of at least seven days' notice of the proposed entry given to a person who appears to the authorised person in question to be in occupation of the premises in question; and (2) either with the consent of a person who is in occupation of those premises or under the authority of a warrant by virtue of Sch 1A: s 4B(5). Except in an emergency, where an authorised person proposes to enter any premises and (a) entry has been refused and he reasonably believes that the use of force may be necessary to effect entry; or (b) he reasonably believes that entry is likely to be refused and that the use of force may be necessary to effect entry, any entry on to those premises by virtue of s 4B must be effected only under the authority of a warrant by virtue of Sch 1A: s 4B(6). As to further provision with respect to powers of entry see s 4B(8), Sch 1A (Sch 1A added by the Water Act 2003, s 85(2), Sch 5).

7   Coal Industry Act 1994 s 4B(3)(b).

8   Coal Industry Act 1994 s 4B(3)(c).

9   Coal Industry Act 1994 s 4B(3)(d).

10  Coal Industry Act 1994 s 4B(3)(e).

11  Coal Industry Act 1994 s 4B(3)(f).

12  Coal Industry Act 1994 s 4B(3)(g).

13  As to the Secretary of State see PARA 2.

14  Coal Industry Act 1994 s 4C(1). Without prejudice to the generality of s 4C(1), the land which the Authority may be authorised under s 4C(1) to purchase compulsorily includes land which is or will be required for the purpose of being given in exchange for, or for any right over, any other land which for the purposes of the Acquisition of Land Act 1981 is or forms part of a common, open space or a fuel or field garden allotment: Coal Industry Act 1994 s 4C(3). The Acquisition of Land Act 1981 applies to any compulsory purchase under the Coal Industry Act 1994 s 4C(1) of any land by the Authority; and the Acquisition of Land Act 1981 Sch 3 applies to the compulsory acquisition under the Coal Industry Act 1994 s 4C(1) of rights by the creation of new rights: s 4C(4). As to modifying enactments relating to compensation and the provisions of the Compulsory Purchase Act 1965 in their application in relation to the compulsory acquisition under the Coal Industry Act 1994 s 4C(1) of a right over land by the creation of a new right see s 4C(5), Sch 1B (Sch 1B added by the Water Act 2003, s 85(2), Sch 6).

15  Ie the power under the Coal Industry Act 1994 s 4C(1).

16  Coal Industry Act 1994 s 4C(2).

## 62.   Duties in relation to subsidence damage.

The Coal Authority has a number of duties in relation to subsidence damage imposed upon it by the Coal Mining Subsidence Act 1991 and the Coal Industry Act 1994, including the duty to take appropriate action to remedy such damage and to provide such additional remedies as may be required from time to time[1]; the duty to comply with the statutory requirements in relation to providing information relating to subsidence[2] and the forwarding of damage notices[3]; the duty of furnishing the subsidence adviser with information and assistance[4] and complying with the statutory requirements relating to the subsidence adviser and the Arbitration Body[5]; making such reports as the Secretary of State[6] may direct[7]; and maintaining drainage works in accordance with the Doncaster Area Drainage Act 1929[8].

The Authority may take such action as it considers appropriate, if any (1) with respect to subsidence arising otherwise than in connection with coal-mining; (2) for the purpose of preventing, or mitigating the effect of, the discharge of water other than from a coal mine into or on to any land or into any controlled waters[9].

1 See PARA 203 et seq. As to subsidence damage by coal mining see PARA 200 et seq.
2 See PARA 207. As to the Coal Authority's duties in relation to making such information publicly available see PARA 107.
3 See PARA 210.
4 See PARA 208.
5 See PARAS 208, 250. As to the Arbitration Body see PARA 250.
6 As to the Secretary of State see PARA 2.
7 See PARA 253.
8 See PARA 244.
9 Coal Industry Act 1994 s 4CA(1) (added by the Energy Act 2011 s 115(1)). The powers conferred on the Authority by the Coal Industry Act 1994 s 4CA(1) do not affect any other function of the Authority: s 4CA(2).

### 63. General powers.

Subject to certain restrictions[1], the Coal Authority has power to do anything which, in its opinion, is calculated to facilitate, or is conducive or incidental to, the carrying out of its functions[2]. In addition to this general power, the Authority has certain express powers which may be exercised subject to restrictions[3].

The Authority's powers include power, for the purposes of or in connection with the carrying out of its functions (1) to acquire land by agreement and to hold and dispose of land; and (2) in exercise of rights attached to its interests[4] in land, or of any such rights in relation to other land as are granted to it by the owner or occupier, to carry out any works on or with respect to land[5].

Where the Authority has land which it is required under the Coal Industry Act 1994 to make available for acquisition by others, its powers include: (a) power, in exercise of any rights attached to its interest in the land, to develop or improve the land, or to join with others in developing or improving the land, with a view to its disposal for use or enjoyment by another; and (b) power by agreement to acquire other land with a view (with or without developing or improving it) to disposing of the other land together with the land in question[6].

The powers of the Authority include power to enter into arrangements with a person who is or has been a licensed operator[7] to act on that person's behalf in relation to certain matters[8], and also include power, where it provides a service to anyone in the course of the exercise or performance of its powers or duties, or receives any application for the grant of, or any offer for, any such interest or right in or in relation to any of its land or other property[9] as may be required by any person for the purpose of exploring for coal[10] or of carrying on coal-mining operations, to make a charge for the provision of that service or, as the case may be, for considering that application or offer[11].

1 Ie the Coal Industry Act 1994 s 5(6), (7) (see PARA 64): see s 5(1).
2 Coal Industry Act 1994 s 5(1). The Secretary of State has power to give the Coal Authority directions of a general character as to the carrying out of its functions: see s 6(1); and PARA 65. As to the Secretary of State see PARA 2. As to the functions of the Coal Authority see PARA 52.
3 For the Authority's express powers see Coal Industry Act 1994 s 5(2)–(5). Section 5(2)–(5) is without prejudice to the generality of s 5(1): s 5(9). The powers contained in s 5(2) are subject to the restrictions of s 5(6), (7) (see PARA 64) and the powers contained in s 5(3) are subject to the restrictions of s 5(7) (see PARA 64).
4 As to the meaning of 'interest' see PARA 52.
5 Coal Industry Act 1994 s 5(2).

6   Coal Industry Act 1994 s 5(3).
7   As to the meaning of 'licensed operator' see PARA 58. As to the licensing of coal-mining operations see PARA 89 et seq. As to the meaning of 'coal-mining operations' see PARA 51.
8   See the Coal Industry Act 1994 s 5(4). The matters referred to in the text are: (1) the giving and publication of notices under or for the purposes of s 38 (rights to withdraw support) (see PARA 176 et seq) or s 49 (rights to work coal in former copyhold land) (see PARA 397 et seq) or any provisions of the Coal Mining Subsidence Act 1991 (see PARA 201 et seq); or (2) the handling of any matter arising under the Coal Mining Subsidence Act 1991 and the performance of that person's obligations in relation to any subsidence damage: Coal Industry Act 1994 s 5(4).
9   As to the vesting of assets in the Coal Authority see PARA 66.
10   As to the meaning of 'coal' see PARA 51.
11   Coal Industry Act 1994 s 5(5).

## 64. Restrictions affecting the Coal Authority's general powers.

The Coal Authority does not have power[1]:

(1)      for commercial purposes or with a view to itself using any coal[2] or product of coal, to carry on any coal-mining operations[3] consisting in:

     (a)      the winning, working or getting (with or without other minerals[4]) of any coal[5];

     (b)      the treatment of coal in the strata[6] for the purpose of winning any product of coal[7]; or

     (c)      the winning, working or getting of any product of coal resulting from such treatment[8]; or

(2)      with a view to any such operations being so carried on by the Authority or any other person, to explore for coal or[9] to take any steps for the benefit of another for obtaining planning permission or any other authorisation required for carrying on coal-mining operations[10].

The Authority must not, except with the agreement of the Secretary of State[11], acquire any land or acquire or hold shares in or other securities of any body corporate or otherwise become a member of a body corporate, or lend money to any person or guarantee or otherwise provide security for a loan made to any person[12].

1   As to the general powers of the Coal Authority see PARA 63.
2   As to the meaning of 'coal' see PARA 51.
3   As to the meaning of 'coal-mining operations' see PARA 51.
4   As to the meaning of 'minerals' see PARA 10.
5   Coal Industry Act 1994 s 5(6)(a)(i).
6   As to references to 'treatment of coal in the strata' see PARA 51.
7   Coal Industry Act 1994 s 5(6)(a)(ii).
8   Coal Industry Act 1994 s 5(6)(a)(iii).
9   This is subject to the Coal Industry Act 1994 s 5(4) (see PARA 63): see s 5(6)(b).
10   Coal Industry Act 1994 s 5(6)(b).
11   As to the Secretary of State see PARA 2.
12   Coal Industry Act 1994 s 5(7). The consent of the Treasury is required for the giving of the Secretary of State's agreement under this provision: s 5(8). As to the Treasury see CONSTITUTIONAL AND ADMINISTRATIVE LAW vol 20 (2014) PARAS 262–265.

## 65. Directions given to the Coal Authority by the Secretary of State.

The Coal Authority must comply with such directions of a general character as may be given to it by the Secretary of State[1] with respect to the carrying out of any of its functions, or to its activities generally[2]. The Authority must also comply with such specific directions as may be given to it by the Secretary of State with respect to:

(1)      whether or not it exercises any of its powers and the manner in which any of its powers is to be exercised[3];

(2)     the manner in which any of its duties is to be performed[4]; or

(3)     any other conduct by the Authority in connection with the carrying out of any of its functions or with its activities generally[5].

Directions by the Secretary of State[6] may be given, in relation to any information which is in the possession of or available to the Authority, requiring it to publish the information in such manner as may be described in the direction[7]. The Authority may also be required to furnish such information, together with such explanations as he may reasonably require, to the Secretary of State[8]. However, a direction may not authorise the publication of any information if, apart from the direction, the publication of that information would be in contravention[9] of arrangements for keeping certain information confidential[10].

Except in an emergency, the power to give a direction is exercisable only after consultation with the Authority[11].

1   As to the Secretary of State see PARA 2.
2   Coal Industry Act 1994 s 6(1). As to the functions of the Coal Authority see PARA 52.
3   Coal Industry Act 1994 s 6(2)(a).
4   Coal Industry Act 1994 s 6(2)(b).
5   Coal Industry Act 1994 s 6(2)(c).
6   Ie under the Coal Industry Act 1994 s 6: see s 6(3).
7   Coal Industry Act 1994 s 6(3)(a).
8   Coal Industry Act 1994 s 6(3)(b).
9   As to the meaning of 'contravention' see PARA 54.
10  Coal Industry Act 1994 s 6(4). As to the duty to keep certain information confidential see s 59; and PARA 108.
11  Coal Industry Act 1994 s 6(5).

C.     VESTING OF ASSETS IN THE COAL AUTHORITY

## 66. Vesting of assets in the Coal Authority.

On the restructuring date[1] the British Coal Corporation's[2] interests in unworked coal[3] and coal mines[4], including its interests in any coal that (notwithstanding having been worked at some time) was so attached to or incorporated in any coal mine or other land as to be, in law, a part of it, vested without further assurance in the Coal Authority[5].

Subject to certain provisions[6], the interests in unworked coal and coal mines which vested in the Corporation immediately before the restructuring date were deemed to include: (1) the interests and rights of a freehold owner[7] in and in relation to any such coal under the territorial sea adjacent to the United Kingdom[8] as well as coal with respect to which the Corporation had rights[9] immediately before that date[10]; and (2) the exclusive right, for the purposes of the rights of the United Kingdom[11] and without the consent of the Secretary of State, of authorising the carrying on, in relation to the coal in any designated area[12], of any of the coal-mining operations[13] or of any operation carried on for the purpose of searching or boring for coal[14].

1   Ie 31 October 1994: see PARA 50. In appointing a date as the restructuring date, the Secretary of State had to be satisfied that such schemes were or were to be made under the Coal Industry Act 1994 s 12 (see PARA 72) as would ensure that the Coal Authority would be entitled or subject, from that date, to all such property, rights and liabilities as it would require for carrying out the functions which were to become its functions on that date: see s 7(5). As to the Secretary of State see PARA 2.
2   In the Coal Industry Act 1994, the British Coal Corporation is referred to as 'the Corporation': see s 65(1). As to the British Coal Corporation see PARAS 49–50.
3   As to the meaning of 'coal' see PARA 51.
4   As to the meaning of 'coal mine' see PARA 3.

5 Coal Industry Act 1994 s 7(3). This provision has effect subject to ss 8, 9 (see PARAS 67–69) and to the powers conferred by virtue of s 12(1) (see PARA 72): s 7(4). The ownership of unworked coal which had been alienated by the Coal Commission under the Coal Act 1938 s 17(3) (repealed) did not vest in the National Coal Board (later renamed the British Coal Corporation: see PARA 49) under the Coal Industry Nationalisation Act 1946 s 5, Sch 1 (repealed) and so did not pass to the Coal Authority under the Coal Industry Act 1994 s 7(3). Accordingly, such coal remains in private hands.

6 Ie the Coal Industry Act 1994 s 9 (see PARAS 68–69): see s 8(1).

7 References in the Coal Industry Act 1994 s 8 to the interests and rights of a freehold owner are to be construed, in relation to any coal the interests or rights in or in relation to which fall to be determined according to the law of Scotland, as references to the interests and rights of an owner: s 8(6) (amended by the Abolition of Feudal Tenure etc (Scotland) Act 2000 s 76(1), Sch 12 para 56(1), (2)).

8 As to the meaning of 'United Kingdom' see PARA 48.

9 Ie by virtue of the Continental Shelf Act 1964 s 1 (see PARA 24) as read with the Territorial Sea Act 1987 s 2(3) (repealed: see PARA 51): see the Coal Industry Act 1994 s 8(1)(a).

10 Coal Industry Act 1994 s 8(1)(a).

11 Ie mentioned in the Continental Shelf Act 1964 s 1(1) (see PARA 24): see the Coal Industry Act 1994 s 8(1)(b).

12 For these purposes, 'designated area' means any area which is for the time being both outside the territorial sea adjacent to the United Kingdom and comprised in an area designated (whether before or after the beginning of the restructuring date) under the Continental Shelf Act 1964 s 1(7) (see ENERGY AND CLIMATE CHANGE vol 44 (2011) PARA 1040): Coal Industry Act 1994 s 8(5).

13 Ie coal-mining operations to which the Coal Industry Act 1994 s 25 (see PARA 89) applies: see s 8(1)(b). As to the meaning of 'coal-mining operations' see PARA 51.

14 Coal Industry Act 1994 s 8(1)(b). Section 7(3) does not vest in the Authority any interest or rights in or in relation to any coal or coal mines outside Great Britain and the territorial sea adjacent to Great Britain except those mentioned in s 8(1)(b): see s 8(2); and PARA 68. As to the future vesting of coal beneath extensions to the territorial sea see PARA 67.

## 67. Future vesting of coal beneath extensions to territorial sea.

Where, on the coming into force on or after the restructuring date[1] of any relevant Order in Council[2], any area outside the United Kingdom[3] and the territorial sea adjacent to the United Kingdom is brought within that territorial sea, that Order in Council has the effect of vesting the interests and rights of a freehold owner[4] in and in relation to coal[5] under the seabed in that area in such person as may be specified in the Order in Council or, if no person is so specified, in the Coal Authority[6]. However, nothing is to be vested in any person[7] which would have been excluded[8], had the Order in Council come into force before the restructuring date, from the interests and rights which were deemed to be vested in the British Coal Corporation immediately before that date[9].

1 Ie 31 October 1994: see PARA 50.

2 Ie under the Territorial Sea Act 1987 s 1 (see WATER AND WATERWAYS vol 100 (2018) PARA 38): see the Coal Industry Act 1994 s 8(3).

3 As to the meaning of 'United Kingdom' see PARA 48.

4 As to the interests and rights of a freehold owner see PARA 66.

5 As to the meaning of 'coal' see PARA 51.

6 Coal Industry Act 1994 s 8(3).

7 Ie by virtue of the Coal Industry Act 1994 s 8(3): see s 8(4).

8 Ie by virtue of the Coal Industry Act 1994 s 9 (see PARAS 68–69): see s 8(4).

9 Coal Industry Act 1994 s 8(4). As to the British Coal Corporation see PARAS 49–50.

## 68. Exclusions from vesting of coal.

Interests[1] or rights in or in relation to any coal[2] or coal mines[3] outside Great Britain[4] and the territorial sea adjacent to Great Britain, with the exception of the exclusive right[5] without the consent of the Secretary of State[6] of authorising the carrying on, in relation to the coal in any designated area[7], of any of the coal-mining operations[8] or of any operation carried on for the purpose of searching or boring for coal[9], are excluded from vesting[10] in the Coal Authority[11].

The interests and rights which are vested or deemed to be vested in the British Coal Corporation[12] immediately before the restructuring date[13] are declared not to have included: (1) any interest in, or any entitlement to an interest in, any oil or gas[14] which, in its natural condition in strata, is or becomes absorbed in or adsorbed to any coal[15]; or (2) any right, without a licence[16], to search for, bore for or get any oil or gas which is or becomes so absorbed or adsorbed[17]. Accordingly, nothing in any enactment or subordinate legislation relating to interests in or in relation to any coal, or in or in relation to any oil or gas is to be taken to have prevented any such interest as is mentioned in head (1) above from having become or from continuing to be an interest or entitlement of the Crown[18]. Those exclusions[19] do not give rise to any liability in respect of the winning, working, treatment, getting or disposal of (a) any of that coal having oil or gas occluded in it at the time of its being brought from the strata to the surface or, as the case may be, of its treatment in the strata[20]; or (b) any product of that coal resulting from any such treatment, where the coal in question was won, worked, treated or got in pursuance of any interests or rights which were vested or deemed to be vested in the British Coal Corporation immediately before the restructuring date[21].

1   As to the meaning of 'interest' see PARA 52.
2   As to the meaning of 'coal' see PARA 51.
3   As to the meaning of 'coal mine' see PARA 3.
4   As to the meaning of 'Great Britain' see PARA 48.
5   Ie for the purposes of the rights of the United Kingdom mentioned in the Continental Shelf Act 1964 s 1(1) (see PARA 24): see the Coal Industry Act 1994 s 8(1)(b). As to the meaning of 'United Kingdom' see PARA 48.
6   As to the Secretary of State see PARA 2.
7   As to the meaning of 'designated area' see PARA 66.
8   As to the meaning of 'coal-mining operations' see PARA 51.
9   See the Coal Industry Act 1994 s 8(1)(b).
10  Ie under the Coal Industry Act 1994 s 7(3) (see PARA 66): see s 8(2).
11  Coal Industry Act 1994 s 8(2).
12  As to the British Coal Corporation see PARAS 49–50.
13  Ie 31 October 1994: see PARA 50.
14  As to the meaning of 'oil or gas' see PARA 51.
15  Coal Industry Act 1994 s 9(1)(a).
16  Ie under the Petroleum Act 1998 s 3: see the Coal Industry Act 1994 s 9(1)(b). As to the grant of such licences see ENERGY AND CLIMATE CHANGE vol 44 (2011) PARA 1046 et seq.
17  Coal Industry Act 1994 s 9(1)(b) (amended by the Petroleum Act 1998 s 50, Sch 4 para 38(3)(b)). This provision is expressed to be without prejudice to the Petroleum Act 1998 s 9(1) which provides that nothing in the Petroleum Act 1998 is to be construed as imposing any liability on any person where petroleum is set free in the course of mining and other lawful operations (see ENERGY AND CLIMATE CHANGE vol 44 (2011) PARA 1043): see the Coal Industry Act 1994 s 9(1) (amended by the Petroleum Act 1998 s 50, Sch 4 para 38(3)(a)).
18  Coal Industry Act 1994 s 9(2).
19  Ie the exclusions confirmed by virtue of the Coal Industry Act 1994 s 9(1), (2).
20  As to the meaning of 'treatment of coal in the strata' see PARA 51.
21  Coal Industry Act 1994 s 9(3).

### 69. Exploitation of oil and gas in coal mines.

So long as the Coal Authority retains the interest[1] of a freehold owner in any coal[2] or coal mine[3] vested in it[4], it is entitled by virtue of such ownership to grant such rights in relation to that coal or coal mine as are required by any person for the purpose, under the authority of any licence[5], of searching for, boring for or getting any oil or gas[6] in that coal or coal mine[7]. Such a grant is, in favour of that person, binding on any other person who has or acquires an interest or right in or in relation to the coal or coal mine in question; but is without prejudice, in a case where there is a person other than the Authority with an interest or right in that coal or coal mine at the time of the grant, to any such person's rights as against the Authority in respect of: (1) any interference by virtue of the grant with the enjoyment of his interest or right; or (2) any contravention of an undertaking given in relation to that interest or right[8].

1   As to the meaning of 'interest' see PARA 52.
2   As to the meaning of 'coal' see PARA 51.
3   As to the meaning of 'coal mine' see PARA 3.
4   Ie by virtue of the Coal Industry Act 1994 s 7(3) (see PARA 66).
5   Ie a licence which has been or may be granted to that person under the Petroleum Act 1998 s 3: see the Coal Industry Act 1994 s 9(4). As to the grant of such licences see ENERGY AND CLIMATE CHANGE vol 44 (2011) PARA 1046 et seq.
6   As to the meaning of 'oil or gas' see PARA 51.
7   Coal Industry Act 1994 s 9(4) (amended by the Petroleum Act 1998 s 50, Sch 4 para 38(3)(b)).
8   Coal Industry Act 1994 s 9(5). As to the meaning of 'contravention' see PARA 54.

**70.  Protection for certain interests in coal and coal mines.**
Where the ownership[1] of any coal or coal mine was vested in the British Coal Corporation[2] immediately before the restructuring date[3], and has not, at any time on or since that date, become vested in a person other than the Corporation or the Coal Authority by virtue of being conveyed or transferred to that person either by the Authority or the Corporation, or in accordance with a restructuring scheme[4], there are certain protections against acquisition[5].

First, no interest or right adverse to the title of the Authority or the Corporation in any such coal or coal mine[6] is capable of being acquired under the provisions concerning time limits on actions to recover land and extinction of titles[7]. Secondly, subject to an exception relating to compulsory purchase for purposes of underground gas storage[8], where any power to acquire land compulsorily is conferred by or under any enactment[9], that power is not exercisable on or after the restructuring date in respect of any such coal or coal mine except in so far as (1) the coal is coal that it is necessary to dig or carry away in the course of operations for the purposes of which the power is conferred; or (2) the coal mine is one that it is necessary to use in the course of any such operations[10].

These protections[11], in their application to England and Wales, do not restrict the acquisition of any such liberty, privilege, easement, advantage or other right[12] as adversely affects any such coal or coal mine and is either annexed to any land or, without being so annexed, is acquired under any enactment[13].

1   This reference to the ownership of any coal or coal mine is a reference, in relation to England and Wales, to the interest of the freehold owner of that coal or coal mine: Coal Industry Act 1994 s 10(7)(a). As to the meaning of 'coal' see PARA 51; as to the meaning of 'coal mine' see PARA 3; and as to the meaning of 'interest' see PARA 52.
2   As to the British Coal Corporation see PARAS 49–50.
3   Ie 31 October 1994: see PARA 50.
4   Ie under the Coal Industry Act 1994 s 12. As to restructuring schemes see PARA 72.
5   See the Coal Industry Act 1994 s 10(1).
6   Ie any coal or coal mine to which the Coal Industry Act 1994 s 10 applies: see s 10(2).
7   Coal Industry Act 1994 s 10(2)(a). The provisions referred to are the Limitation Act 1980 s 15 or s 17 (see LIMITATION PERIODS vol 68 (2016) PARAS 1018, 1093): see the Coal Industry Act 1994 s 10(2)(a).
8   The exception mentioned in the text is in relation to the power under the Gas Act 1965 s 13(8) (see

ENERGY AND CLIMATE CHANGE vol 43 (2011) PARA 462) which may be conferred on a public gas supplier to acquire compulsorily for purposes connected with underground gas storage land which is the site of a well, borehole or shaft: see the Coal Industry Act 1994 s 10(3).

9   This includes, unless it otherwise provides, an enactment passed after 5 July 1994 (ie the date of the passing of the Coal Industry Act 1994): see s 10(3).

10  Coal Industry Act 1994 s 10(3).

11  Ie the Coal Industry Act 1994 s 10(2), (3): see s 10(4).

12  For these purposes the reference to a liberty, privilege, easement, advantage or other right being annexed to any land is a reference to its appertaining to that land or any part of it, to its being demised, occupied or enjoyed with that land or any part of it or to its being reputed or known as part or parcel of the land or as appurtenant to the land or to any part of it: Coal Industry Act 1994 s 10(6).

13  Coal Industry Act 1994 s 10(4).

### (iii) Restructuring of the British Coal Corporation's Undertaking

#### A. IN GENERAL

## 71. Restructuring of the functions of the British Coal Corporation.

Since the restructuring date[1] the British Coal Corporation[2] continued to exist[3] but with its functions confined to: (1) carrying on its undertaking[4] for the time being; and (2) managing and otherwise dealing with the interests and rights in or in relation to property which were for the time being vested in it, in such manner as, having regard to what was economically viable, it considered best calculated for securing the following purposes[5]:

(a)   that all of the Corporation's undertaking and property is in due course transferred out of the ownership and control of the Corporation[6];

(b)   that any transfers for the removal of any of that undertaking or property from the ownership or control of the public sector are on the best available terms[7]; and

(c)   that the Corporation's undertaking and property are put to the best available use for so long as they remain in its ownership or under its control[8].

Where the Secretary of State[9] notified his opinion to the Corporation as to (i) what is economically viable in any case; (ii) the activities most likely to secure that any transfer for the removal of any of the Corporation's undertaking, or any property, from the ownership or control of the public sector are to be on the best available terms; or (iii) the best available use to which any of the Corporation's undertaking or property may be put while owned by or under the control of the Corporation, the Corporation was required to accept that opinion[10].

It was the duty of the Corporation to comply with such general or specific directions with respect to the exercise of any of its powers, or otherwise with respect to the carrying on of any of its activities, which may be given to it at any time by the Secretary of State[11].

Since the restructuring date, certain of the Corporation's powers continued to be exercisable by it for the purposes of carrying out its reduced functions[12]. Various restructuring schemes[13] transferred its property, rights and liabilities to other parties[14] and the Corporation was reduced to a mere formal existence as a shell. Until its eventual dissolution[15], its only real function was to hold and deal with any residual liabilities which it may be found to have retained notwithstanding the restructuring schemes[16].

1   Ie 31 October 1994: see PARA 50.

2   As to the British Coal Corporation see PARAS 49–50.

3   Ie until its eventual dissolution on the dissolution date: see PARA 50. As to the dissolution of the British Coal Corporation see PARA 88.

4   'Undertaking', in relation to the British Coal Corporation, includes the undertakings of its wholly-owned subsidiaries: Coal Industry Act 1994 s 65(1). As to the meanings of 'subsidiary' and 'wholly-owned subsidiary' see PARA 51.

5   Coal Industry Act 1994 s 11(1). This provision is without prejudice to any powers conferred on the Corporation by the British Coal and British Rail (Transfer Proposals) Act 1993 (now repealed): Coal Industry Act 1994 s 11(9).

    The requirement for the matters secured under the Coal Industry Nationalisation Act 1946 s 1(4) (now repealed) which specifies policy objectives for the Corporation, to be secured consistently with the proper discharge of the Corporation's duties under s 1(1) (repealed) has effect since the restructuring date as a requirement for those matters to be secured consistently with the carrying out of the Corporation's functions under the Coal Industry Act 1994 s 11(1): s 11(5).

6   Coal Industry Act 1994 s 11(2)(a).

7   Coal Industry Act 1994 s 11(2)(b).

8   Coal Industry Act 1994 s 11(2)(c).

9   As to the Secretary of State see PARA 2.

10   Coal Industry Act 1994 s 11(3). The consent of the Treasury is required for the giving of any such notification; and the power of the Secretary of State to give such a notification is exercisable, except in an emergency, only after consultation with the Corporation: see s 11(8). As to the Treasury see CONSTITUTIONAL AND ADMINISTRATIVE LAW vol 20 (2014) PARAS 262–265.

11   Coal Industry Act 1994 s 11(7). The Secretary of State's power to give such directions is exercisable, except in an emergency, only after consultation with the Corporation: see s 11(8). As to agreements binding the manner and circumstances in which the Secretary of State exercised his power to give such directions see s 13; and PARA 72.

12   See the Coal Industry Act 1994 s 11(4). The powers referred to are as follows: (1) the powers conferred on the Corporation by the Coal Industry Nationalisation Act 1946 s 1(2) (repealed) (see PARA 49) (incidental activities) and described there as functions; (2) those conferred on the Corporation by s 1(3) (repealed) (power to enter into certain transactions); and (3) a power, so far as not comprised in the powers mentioned in heads (1) and (2), to carry on any activities consisting in or connected with the working or getting of coal: Coal Industry Act 1994 s 11(4). However, since the restructuring date the Corporation (a) has not been entitled to carry on any coal-mining operations in respect of which a licence under the Coal Industry Act 1994 Pt II (ss 25–36) is required except under and in accordance with such a licence; (b) no longer has the powers with respect to petroleum conferred on it by the National Coal Board (Additional Powers) Act 1966 (repealed) and the Coal Industry Act 1977 s 9 (repealed) (see PARA 49); and (c) has no power, by virtue of the Coal Industry Act 1994 s 11(1)–(5) to carry on any business which it would not have had power to carry on apart from that Act: s 11(6). 'Business' includes any trade or profession: s 65(1).

13   As to restructuring schemes see PARA 72.

14   Eg to the successor companies (see PARAS 50, 74), the Coal Authority (see PARA 52 et seq) and the Secretary of State (see PARA 2).

15   The British Coal Corporation was eventually dissolved on 27 March 2004 ie the date appointed as the 'dissolution date' under the Coal Industry Act 1994 s 23 for the dissolution of the British Coal Corporation: see s 23(2); and the Coal Industry Act 1994 (Commencement No 7) and Dissolution of the British Coal Corporation Order 2004, SI 2004/144, art 3. As to the dissolution of the British Coal Corporation see PARA 88.

16   See further PARA 72.

## 72. Restructuring schemes.

The Secretary of State[1] had power, at any time before the restructuring date[2], to make a restructuring scheme[3] providing for the creation[4], in favour of (1) the British Coal Corporation[5]; or (2) any person to whom any part of the Corporation's undertaking[6] was to be transferred on that date in accordance with such a scheme, of such interests[7] and rights in or in relation to any of the property transferred[8] to the Coal Authority as he thought appropriate for the purposes of the Corporation's functions on and after that date or for the purposes of the carrying on by that person of the part of the Corporation's undertaking which was to be transferred to him[9].

In addition, the Secretary of State may from time to time make a scheme for the transfer of property, rights and liabilities[10] from the Corporation or any of its wholly-owned subsidiaries[11] to the Authority or to any one or more other persons who have entered into an agreement[12] to accept the transfers; or who otherwise appear to him to be persons in whom it is appropriate to vest the property, rights and liabilities in question[13]. However, a restructuring scheme must not[14] contain any provision in accordance with which any person other than the Secretary of State, the Coal Authority, the British Coal Corporation or any of its wholly-owned subsidiaries, or a company wholly owned by the Crown[15], becomes entitled or subject to any property, rights or liabilities unless it appears to the Secretary of State that that person consented to the provisions of the scheme so far as they relate to him[16]. However, the consent of any person is not required to so much of any restructuring scheme as relates to property, rights or liabilities to which that person is already entitled or subject; and appears to the Secretary of State to be made for purposes that are no more than supplemental or incidental to the other provisions of the scheme[17].

The Secretary of State, in exercising his powers to make a restructuring scheme in accordance with which any person other than (a) the Secretary of State, the Coal Authority, the British Coal Corporation or any of its wholly-owned subsidiaries, or a company wholly owned by the Crown; or (b) a body of whom all the members are appointed by a Minister of the Crown, becomes subject to any liabilities, must have regard to the fact that it would not be appropriate for the scheme to provide for the transfer of any of those liabilities to any person except where it is reasonable to believe that that person is a person able to finance their discharge[18].

The Secretary of State must retain and preserve a copy of every restructuring scheme[19] and, at the request of any person who, in accordance with such a scheme, has become entitled to any interest or right in or in relation to any property, must furnish that person with a list of the names and addresses of the other persons who have become entitled to interests or rights in or in relation to property in accordance with that or with any other such scheme[20].

Specific provision is made in the Coal Industry Act 1994 for the organisation of restructuring schemes[21]. In particular, provision is made for: regulating their contents and effect[22]; the division of property by such schemes[23]; the property to which a scheme may relate[24]; supplemental provisions of schemes[25]; duties in relation to foreign property[26]; the modification of the effect of a scheme by agreement[27]; the application of transfer of undertakings provisions[28]; compensation[29]; and the notice to be given to persons affected by a scheme[30]. Provision is also made in the Coal Industry Act 1994 for the treatment for taxation purposes of property transferred by a restructuring scheme to a public-sector body[31].

The Secretary of State may enter into any such agreement with another person as he thinks fit for the purpose of accepting or imposing contractual obligations with respect to anything connected with: (i) the manner and circumstances in which his powers relating to restructuring schemes[32] are to be exercised; and (ii) the property, rights or liabilities to which any proposed restructuring scheme relates[33].

The Corporation and the Authority must furnish the Secretary of State with all the information and other assistance he requires to make a restructuring scheme or agreement[34], or to exercise any of his powers in relation to any such scheme[35].

The property, rights and liabilities of the British Coal Corporation were transferred by a succession of such restructuring schemes and the residuary body that remained was eventually dissolved[36].

1 As to the Secretary of State see PARA 2.
2 Ie 31 October 1994: see PARA 50.
3 'Restructuring scheme' means a scheme under the Coal Industry Act 1994 s 12: s 65(1). The consent of the Treasury was required for the making of any such scheme: Coal Industry Act 1994 s 12(3). As to the Treasury see CONSTITUTIONAL AND ADMINISTRATIVE LAW vol 20 (2014) PARAS 262–265.
4 Ie as from the restructuring date.
5 As to the British Coal Corporation see PARAS 49–50.
6 As to the meaning of 'undertaking' see PARA 71.
7 As to the creation of an interest in property see the Coal Industry Act 1994 s 65(3); and PARA 52. As to the meaning of 'interest' see PARA 52.
8 Ie under the Coal Industry Act 1994 s 7(3) (see PARA 66): see s 12(1).
9 Coal Industry Act 1994 s 12(1). The restructuring schemes dealt with the transfer of the British Coal Corporation's unsold property interests including operational land associated with working collieries or opencast sites, liability sites and land which British Coal could not itself sell prior to 20 December 1997, disused colliery sites, recreational land and rescue stations. As to further information regarding restructuring schemes see the Department of Energy and Climate Change's website.
10 As to the meaning of 'liability' see PARA 51.
11 As to the meanings of 'subsidiary' and 'wholly-owned subsidiary' see PARA 51.
12 Ie under the Coal Industry Act 1994 s 13: see s 12(2).
13 Coal Industry Act 1994 s 12(2). The persons to whom a transfer may be made by virtue of head (1) in the text include the Secretary of State himself: s 12(2).
14 Ie by virtue of the Coal Industry Act 1994 s 12(2): see s 12(4).
15 A company is to be regarded as wholly owned by the Crown at any time if it is: (1) a company limited by shares in which there are at that time no issued shares held otherwise than by, or by a nominee of, the Treasury, the Secretary of State or any other company wholly owned by the Crown; or (2) a company limited by guarantee of which no person other than the Treasury or the Secretary of State, or a nominee of the Treasury or the Secretary of State, is a member: Coal Industry Act 1994 s 65(4). 'Company' has the same meaning as in the Companies Act 2006 s 1(1) (see generally COMPANIES vol 14 (2016) PARA 21): Coal Industry Act 1994 s 65(1) (definition amended by SI 2009/1941). The Companies Acts (as defined by the Companies Act 2006 s 2) (see COMPANIES vol 14 (2016) PARA 13) have effect in relation to a company that (a) is wholly owned by the Crown; and (b) has been notified by the Secretary of State that it is a company to which it is proposed to transfer any part of the Corporation's undertaking, as if references to a shadow director did not include the Treasury or any Minister of the Crown: Coal Industry Act 1994 s 65A (added by SI 2007/2194).
16 Coal Industry Act 1994 s 12(4).
17 Coal Industry Act 1994 s 12(5).
18 Coal Industry Act 1994 s 12(6).
19 Coal Industry Act 1994 s 12(7)(a).
20 Coal Industry Act 1994 s 12(7)(b).
21 See the Coal Industry Act 1994 s 12(8), Sch 2.
22 See the Coal Industry Act 1994 Sch 2 para 1.
23 See the Coal Industry Act 1994 Sch 2 para 2.
24 See the Coal Industry Act 1994 Sch 2 para 3.
25 See the Coal Industry Act 1994 Sch 2 para 4.
26 See the Coal Industry Act 1994 Sch 2 para 5.
27 See the Coal Industry Act 1994 Sch 2 para 6. As to the meaning of 'modifications' see PARA 51.
28 See the Coal Industry Act 1994 Sch 2 para 7. The transfer of undertakings provisions referred to in Sch 2 para 7 is the Transfer of Undertakings (Protection of Employment) Regulations 1981, SI 1981/1794, which has now been replaced by the Transfer of Undertakings (Protection of Employment) Regulations 2006, SI 2006/246. As to transfers of undertakings generally see EMPLOYMENT vol 39 (2014) PARA 136 et seq.
29 Coal Industry Act 1994 Sch 2 para 8.
30 Coal Industry Act 1994 Sch 2 para 9.

31 See the Coal Industry Act 1994 s 21, Sch 4. 'Public-sector body' means the Treasury or any
   Minister of the Crown, the Coal Authority, a local authority, any company which is wholly owned
   by the Crown or any body which is not a company but is established by or under any enactment
   for the purpose of carrying out functions conferred on it by any enactment or subordinate
   legislation: Sch 4 para 1(2).
       In particular, provision is made in relation to corporation tax (including provisions relating to
   chargeable gains (see Sch 4 paras 2–10 (Sch 2 para 2 amended by the Finance Act 2008 Sch 2 para
   70(c))); transfers of trading stock (see Sch 4 para 11); transfer of rights to receipts (see Sch 4 para
   12); transfer of liabilities (see Sch 4 para 13); losses to be retained by the predecessor (see Sch 4
   para 14); charges on leases granted at an undervalue (see Sch 4 para 15); group relief (see Sch 4
   para 16); special provision for successor companies (see Sch 4 para 17 (amended by the Income
   Tax (Trading and Other Income) Act 2005 Sch 1 Pt 2 para 474)); leased assets (see Sch 4 para 18);
   capital allowances (see Sch 4 paras 19–22 (amended by the Capital Allowances Act 2001 s 578,
   Sch 2 para 93(2)–(14))); exchange gains and losses (see the Coal Industry Act 1994 Sch 4 para 23);
   transfers of property in coal and lease back (see Sch 4 para 24); modifications of restructuring
   schemes (see Sch 4 para 25)); and stamp duty and stamp duty reserve tax (see Sch 4 paras 26–28).
32 Ie by virtue of the Coal Industry Act 1994 s 12: see s 13(1).
33 Coal Industry Act 1994 s 13(1). Such an agreement may provide for the making of payments to
   the Corporation or the Secretary of State (by way of consideration or otherwise) in respect of
   anything created or transferred in accordance with a restructuring scheme (s 13(2)) and may also
   contain provision in pursuance of which the Secretary of State binds himself as to the manner and
   circumstances in which he exercises his power to give directions under s 11(7) (see PARA 71) (s
   13(3)). The consent of the Treasury was required for the making of such an agreement: s 13(4).
   Any sums received by the Secretary of State in pursuance of such an agreement are to be paid into
   the Consolidated Fund: s 13(5). As to the Consolidated Fund see CONSTITUTIONAL AND
   ADMINISTRATIVE LAW vol 20 (2014) PARA 480; PARLIAMENT vol 78 (2018) PARA 847 et seq.
34 Ie under the Coal Industry Act 1994 s 13: see s 14(1).
35 Coal Industry Act 1994 s 14(1). Such assistance includes: (1) assistance required by the Secretary
   of State in connection with the exercise of any power conferred on him by s 26(6) (see PARA 90);
   and (2) the taking of any step which the Corporation has power to take for the purpose of
   facilitating the implementation of any proposals of the Secretary of State which involve the
   inclusion of anything in the scheme or agreement or otherwise relate, in connection with the
   making of the scheme or agreement, to the Corporation's undertaking: s 14(2). The obligations of
   the Corporation under s 14 include a duty to secure, so far as practicable, that its subsidiaries
   furnish all such information and assistance as the Secretary of State requires to make any such
   scheme or agreement, or to exercise any such power: s 14(3). A duty to furnish information or
   assistance, or to secure that it is furnished, must be performed within such period after the
   requirement giving rise to the duty as the Secretary of State may allow: s 14(4).
36 The British Coal Corporation was eventually dissolved on 27 March 2004 ie the date appointed
   as the 'dissolution date' under the Coal Industry Act 1994 s 23 for the dissolution of the British
   Coal Corporation: see s 23(2); and the Coal Industry Act 1994 (Commencement No 7) and
   Dissolution of the British Coal Corporation Order 2004, SI 2004/144, art 3. As to the dissolution
   of the British Coal Corporation see PARA 88.

## 73. Contracts transferred to the Coal Authority under a restructuring scheme.

As a matter of practice, where real or personal property which was transferred
to the Coal Authority[1] by a restructuring scheme[2] was affected by any contract to
which the British Coal Corporation[3] was a party, the rights and obligations of the
corporation under such contracts were transferred to the Authority[4].

1  As to the Coal Authority see PARA 52 et seq.
2  As to restructuring schemes see PARA 72.
3  As to the British Coal Corporation see PARAS 49–50.
4  The Corporation's rights and obligations under contracts for the repair of subsidence-damaged
   properties were also transferred to the Coal Authority. As to subsidence damage by coal mining see
   PARA 200 et seq.

## 74. Successor companies.

The companies[1] which, when they were wholly owned by the Crown[2], became
entitled or subject in accordance with any restructuring scheme[3] to any property,

rights or liabilities are known as 'successor companies'[4]. Provision was made in the Coal Industry Act 1994 for the financial structure of these companies and related matters[5], and the Secretary of State[6] was required, with the consent of the Treasury, to set target investment limits for government holding in successor companies limited by shares[7]. The target investment limit in relation to the government shareholding in each successor company was set at one-half of 1 per cent of the voting rights exercisable in all circumstances at general meetings of the company in question[8].

The Coal Authority[9] assumed powers and duties relating to licensing[10] the successor companies before they were then sold[11].

1 As to the meaning of 'company' see PARA 72.
2 As to the meaning of 'company wholly owned by the Crown' see PARA 72.
3 As to restructuring schemes see PARA 72.
4 Coal Industry Act 1994 s 65(1). The following successor companies took over those mines that were, on the restructuring date, in the ownership of the British Coal Corporation: Annesley Bentinck Colliery Ltd; Central and Northern Mining Ltd (renamed RJB Mining (UK) Ltd on 30 December 1994); the South Wales Regional Coal Company Ltd (renamed Celtic Energy Ltd on 3 January 1995); the Scottish Coal Company Ltd; and Tower Colliery Ltd. As to the British Coal Corporation see PARAS 49–50. As to the restructuring date (ie 31 October 1994) see PARA 50.
5 See the Coal Industry Act 1994 s 15, Sch 3 para 2 (Sch 3 para 2 amended by SI 2009/1941), (initial government holding in successor companies); Coal Industry Act 1994 Sch 3 para 3 (government investment in successor companies); Sch 3 para 4 (exercise of functions through nominees); Sch 3 para 5 (payment of dividends into Consolidated Fund); Sch 3 para 6 (amended by SI 2008/948) (distributable reserves of successor companies); Coal Industry Act 1994 Sch 3 para 7 (amended by SI 2008/948) (temporary restrictions on borrowing of successor companies); Coal Industry Act 1994 Sch 3 para 8 (government lending to successor companies); Sch 3 para 9 (Treasury guarantees for loans made to successor companies); Sch 3 para 10 (limit on government financial assistance for successor companies). As to the Consolidated Fund see CONSTITUTIONAL AND ADMINISTRATIVE LAW vol 20 (2014) PARA 480; PARLIAMENT vol 78 (2018) PARA 847 et seq. As to the Treasury see CONSTITUTIONAL AND ADMINISTRATIVE LAW vol 20 (2014) PARAS 262–265.
6 As to the Secretary of State see PARA 2.
7 See the Coal Industry Act 1994 s 16. As to the meaning of 'the government shareholding' see s 16(2).
8 See the Coal Industry (Coal Mining Successor Companies Target Investment Limit) Order 1995, SI 1995/1477, art 2, Schedule. The order came into force on 23 June 1995: art 1.
9 As to the Coal Authority see PARA 52 et seq.
10 Ie by granting licences under the Coal Industry Act 1994 Pt II (ss 25–36): see PARA 89 et seq.
11 The sales took effect and the companies ceased to be wholly owned by the Crown on the following dates: Tower Colliery Ltd on 23 December 1994; RJB Mining (UK) Ltd and The Scottish Coal Company Ltd on 30 December 1994; South Wales Regional Coal Company Ltd on 31 December 1994; and Annesley Bentinck Colliery Ltd on 25 April 1995: see the Coal Industry (Coal Mining Successor Companies Target Investment Limit) Order 1995, SI 1995/1477, Schedule.

## 75. Compensation claims.

On 1 January 1998, the health compensation liabilities of the British Coal Corporation[1] were transferred to the Secretary of State[2] by a restructuring scheme[3]. Industrial injury actions have been brought regarding various work-related conditions, such as lung diseases[4] and vibratory white finger[5].

The Coal Liabilities Unit[6] deals with potential new liabilities arising from injuries or illness following employment by British Coal and its predecessors. It oversaw the administration of the two compensation schemes, one for chronic obstructive pulmonary disease and one for vibration white finger. Claims handling agreements were negotiated for the two schemes which included information on how claims would be dealt with, the medical assessment process and how much compensation a claimant would have expected if a claim through the courts was pursued[7]. Both schemes have now concluded[8] and claims have to be made through the courts.

1 As to the British Coal Corporation see PARAS 49–50.
2 As to the Secretary of State see PARA 2.
3 As to restructuring schemes see PARA 72.
4 See eg *Re British Coal Respiratory Disease Litigation* (23 January 1998, unreported), QBD; *Griffiths v British Coal Corpn* [2001] EWCA Civ 336, [2001] 1 WLR 1493, 60 BMLR 188).
5 See eg *Armstrong v British Coal Corpn* [1997] 8 Med LR 259, (1996) Times, 6 December, CA.
6 Ie on behalf of the Department of Energy and Climate Change. See PARA 2.
7 The chronic obstructive pulmonary disease agreement was signed in September 1999 and the vibration white finger agreement was signed in January 1999. As to the interpretation of the claims handling agreement which governs the compensation of miners and their families see *AB v British Coal Corpn* [2007] EWHC 1407 (QB), [2007] All ER (D) 366 (Jun).
8 The chronic obstructive pulmonary disease scheme ended on 31 March 2004 and the vibration white finger scheme ended on 1 May 2009.

### B. FINANCIAL ARRANGEMENTS IN CONNECTION WITH RESTRUCTURING

## 76. Grant-making powers.

The Secretary of State[1] is prohibited from including provision in any restructuring scheme[2] for the transfer to any person of a right to certain grants or other payments[3], and from making any such grant or payment at any time after the appointed date[4].

The grants and payments referred to above are:

(1) payments under the provisions relating to payments providing reimbursement of contributions to early retirement benefits[5];

(2) payments under the provisions relating to payments towards mineworkers' pension scheme deficiency[6];

(3) grants under (a) the provisions relating to pit closure grants for certain financial years[7]; or (b) the provisions relating to grants in respect of expenditure referable to costs incurred in those financial years or in respect of other approved expenditure[8];

(4) such payments under a scheme made in pursuance of the provisions relating to payments to redundant workers or in respect of arrangements relating to concessionary coal[9];

(5) grants under the provisions relating to grants for workforce redeployment and reduction etc[10];

(6) grants under the provisions relating to deficiency grants to the British Coal Corporation[11].

1 As to the Secretary of State see PARA 2.
2 As to restructuring schemes see PARA 72.
3 Coal Industry Act 1994 s 17(1)(a). As to the European Commission's authorisation of grants to the coal industry by the United Kingdom government see PARA 50.
4 Coal Industry Act 1994 s 17(1)(b). The appointed date referred to in the text is such date as the Secretary of State may by order made by statutory instrument appoint for the purposes of s 17(1)(b); but different dates might be appointed for these purposes in relation to different grants and payments: s 17(1). At the date at which this volume states the law no such order had been made.
    As to the power of the Secretary of State to make payments by way of grant with a view of reducing or eliminating deficit on cash flow for any accounting period see PARA 77.
5 Coal Industry Act 1994 s 17(2)(a). The provisions referred to in head (1) in the text are the Coal Industry Act 1967 s 4 (repealed) or the Coal Industry Act 1982 s 3 (repealed).
6 Coal Industry Act 1994 s 17(2)(b). The provisions referred to in head (2) in the text are the National Coal Board (Finance) Act 1976 s 2 (repealed).

7   Ie the Coal Industry Act 1977 s 6 (repealed).
8   Coal Industry Act 1994 s 17(2)(c). The provisions referred to in head (b) in the text are the Coal
    Industry Act 1987 s 4 (repealed).
9   Coal Industry Act 1994 s 17(2)(d). The provisions referred to in head (4) are the Coal Industry Act
    1977 s 7 (repealed) (as may be made otherwise than to persons to whom the scheme applies in
    accordance with s 7(1) (repealed)).
10  Coal Industry Act 1994 s 17(2)(e). The provisions referred to in head (5) are the Coal Industry Act
    1987 s 3 (repealed).
11  Coal Industry Act 1994 s 17(2)(f). The provisions referred to in head (6) are the Coal Industry Act
    1990 s 1 (repealed).

## 77. Residual payments grant.

The Secretary of State[1] has power, with the approval of the Treasury, to make
payments by way of grant (known as 'residual payments grant')[2] to the British
Coal Corporation[3], or to any successor company[4] which is for the time being
wholly owned by the Crown[5], with a view to reducing or eliminating any amount
falling to be shown in any accounts of the Corporation or that company as a
deficit on its cash flow for any accounting period[6]. Payment of residual payments
grant is made by advancing sums during any accounting period in anticipation of
what appears will be the deficit on cash flow for that period[7].

Where payments by way of residual payments grant have been made to the
Corporation or any successor company and it appears to the Secretary of State
that, after those payments have been taken into account in relation to the relevant
accounting period[8], there is a surplus on its cash flow for that accounting period
or for any subsequent accounting period, an amount equal to whichever is the
smaller of:

(1)     so much of the aggregate amount of payments made by way of grant to
        the Corporation or, as the case may be, that company as has not already
        been repaid; and

(2)     the amount of the surplus,

must be paid by the Corporation or, as the case may be, that company to the
Secretary of State[9].

No amount is payable to the Secretary of State in respect of any surplus on the
cash flow of any successor company for any accounting period ending after the
company has ceased to be wholly owned by the Crown, but a successor company
which has ceased to be so owned is required to produce accounts for the period
between the end of its previous accounting period and the time when it ceased to
be wholly owned by the Crown[10].

1   As to the Secretary of State see PARA 2.
2   Any sums required by the Secretary of State for making any such grant are to be paid out of money
    provided by Parliament: Coal Industry Act 1994 s 18(7). As to the European Commission's
    authorisation of grants to the coal industry by the United Kingdom government see PARA 50.
3   As to the British Coal Corporation see PARAS 49–50.
4   As to the meaning of 'successor company' see PARA 74.
5   As to the meaning of 'company wholly owned by the Crown' see PARA 72.
6   Coal Industry Act 1994 s 18(1). For these purposes, 'accounting period', in relation to the
    Corporation or any successor company, means any period for which the Corporation or that
    company is required by or under any enactment to produce accounts: s 18(8).
        Residual payments grant is not payable to any person in respect of any deficit which appears
    to the Secretary of State to be attributable to any failure of the Corporation to be paid, or to apply
    for, any amount which could have been paid, or would have been payable, to the Corporation by
    way of any payment or grant mentioned in s 17(2) (see PARA 76): s 18(3).
7   Coal Industry Act 1994 s 18(2).
8   Ie the accounting period in respect of which the payments were made: see the Coal Industry Act
    1994 s 18(4).

9   Coal Industry Act 1994 s 18(4). Such sums bear interest at such rate as the Secretary of State, with
    the consent of the Treasury, determines: s 18(5). Any sums received by the Secretary of State by
    virtue of s 18(4), (5) are to be paid into the Consolidated Fund: s 18(7). As to the Consolidated
    Fund see CONSTITUTIONAL AND ADMINISTRATIVE LAW vol 20 (2014) PARA 480;
    PARLIAMENT vol 78 (2018) PARA 847 et seq. As to the Treasury see CONSTITUTIONAL AND
    ADMINISTRATIVE LAW vol 20 (2014) PARAS 262–265.
10  Coal Industry Act 1994 s 18(6). As to the dates on which the successor companies ceased to be
    wholly owned by the Crown see PARA 74.

## 78.   Concessionary coal.

Under arrangements with the British Coal Corporation[1] certain persons
received either concessionary coal[2] or payments in lieu of it. Following the
restructure of the coal industry, the Secretary of State[3] may, out of money provided
by Parliament, make such payments[4] to such persons as he may think fit for the
purpose of securing:

(1)     that supplies of concessionary coal are made on and after the
        restructuring date[5] to persons who would have received such supplies
        from the Corporation under relevant arrangements[6] if those
        arrangements had not been affected by steps taken in connection with
        the restructuring of the coal industry[7];

(2)     that provision is made for sums to be paid in lieu of concessionary coal
        to such persons[8]; and

(3)     that provision is made for sums to be so paid to persons who (but for
        any steps so taken) would, under relevant arrangements, have received
        payments in lieu of concessionary coal[9].

In relation to an entitlement to concessionary coal[10] or payments in lieu of
concessionary coal:

(a)     arising in connection with employment by a company which on 1
        January 2014 was carrying on the business of deep coal-mining in the
        United Kingdom; and

(b)     which is not being met otherwise than by virtue of this provision,

the Secretary of State may, out of money provided by Parliament, make such
payments as the Secretary of State considers appropriate for the purpose of
securing that such an entitlement is met[11].

1   As to the British Coal Corporation see PARAS 49–50.
2   'Concessionary coal' means coal or other solid fuel supplied free of charge or at reduced prices:
    Coal Industry Act 1994 s 19(3).
3   As to the Secretary of State see PARA 2.
4   The consent of the Treasury is required for the making of payments under the Coal Industry Act
    1994 s 19: s 19(2). As to the European Commission's authorisation of grants to the coal industry
    by the United Kingdom government see PARA 50.
5   Ie 31 October 1994: see PARA 50.
6   'Relevant arrangements' means any arrangements which: (1) whether or not they are legally
    enforceable, are in operation immediately before the restructuring date; and (2) provide for the
    supply of concessionary coal or for the making of payments in lieu of concessionary coal: Coal
    Industry Act 1994 s 19(3).
7   Coal Industry Act 1994 s 19(1)(a).
8   Coal Industry Act 1994 s 19(1)(b).
9   Coal Industry Act 1994 s 19(1)(c).
10  Concessionary coal' means coal or other solid fuel supplied free of charge or at reduced prices:
    Small Business, Enterprise and Employment Act 2015 s 158(4).
11  Small Business, Enterprise and Employment Act 2015 s 158(1), (2). Payments under s 158 may be
    made only with the consent of the Treasury: s 158(3)

## 79. Extinguishment of loans to the British Coal Corporation.

Where any sum has been lent, whether before or after 5 July 1994[1], to the British Coal Corporation[2] out of money provided by Parliament, or any sum is for the time being to be taken as having been so lent, the Secretary of State[3] may by order[4] extinguish any present or contingent liabilities of the Corporation to make repayments of capital or payments of interest in respect of that sum[5].

1  Ie the date of the passing of the Coal Industry Act 1994.
2  As to the British Coal Corporation see PARAS 49–50.
3  As to the Secretary of State see PARA 2.
4  The consent of the Treasury is required for the making of such an order: Coal Industry Act 1994 s 20(4). The power to make an order is exercisable by statutory instrument subject to annulment in pursuance of a resolution of either House of Parliament: s 20(5). As to the Treasury see CONSTITUTIONAL AND ADMINISTRATIVE LAW vol 20 (2014) PARAS 262–265.
5  Coal Industry Act 1994 s 20(1). The liabilities of the British Coal Corporation to make repayments of capital of £1,598,400,000 and payments of interest of £34,466,803 in respect of sums lent to it out of money provided by Parliament pursuant to the Coal Industry Act 1980 s 2 (repealed) (loans to the British Coal Corporation out of votes) were extinguished by order: see the Coal Industry Act 1994 (British Coal Corporation) Extinguishment of Loans Order 1995, SI 1995/509.
     The Income and Corporation Taxes Act 1988 s 400(1) (restriction of tax losses in case of any write-off of government investment) has no effect in relation to any extinguishment of liabilities by an order under the Coal Industry Act 1994 s 20(1), and the Income and Corporation Taxes Act 1988 s 400(6) applies in relation to any such extinguishment as if the reference to the body in question were a reference to the Corporation: see the Coal Industry Act 1994 s 20(2), (3). The Income and Corporation Taxes Act 1988 s 400(1) has been repealed by the Corporation Tax Act 2010 Sch 1 Pt 1 para 38, Sch 3, Pt 1 and the relevant provision for these purposes is s 92 (loss relief to be reduced if government investment is written off). The Income and Corporation Taxes Act 1988 s 400(6) has also been repealed by the Corporation Tax Act 2010 Sch 1 Pt 1 para 38, Sch 3, Pt 1 and the relevant provision for these purposes is s 96 (interaction with other tax provisions). As to the write-off of government investment see the Corporation Tax Act 2010 Pt 4 Ch 7 (ss 92–96); and INCOME TAXATION vol 58A (2014) PARAS 1093, 1200.

### C.   SUPERANNUATION AND PENSIONS

## 80. Provision of benefits.

The Secretary of State[1] was empowered by the Coal Industry Nationalisation Act 1946 to make regulations for the purpose of providing pensions, gratuities and other like benefits for certain persons employed in or about the coal industry[2]. The British Coal Superannuation Scheme[3] and the Mineworkers' Pension Scheme[4] were approved under such regulations. In connection with the restructuring of the British Coal Corporation's undertaking[5], the Coal Industry Act 1994 makes provision in relation to the pensions paid to or in respect of its present and former employees and other persons[6]. In particular, notwithstanding the prospective repeal of their original empowering provision, the existing schemes[7] continue to have effect with certain modifications[8]. New trustees have been appointed for the scheme funds[9].

The Secretary of State has also made regulations[10] which secure the establishment of new pension schemes for employees transferred[11] to the private sector[12], and has also made regulations which impose restrictions and obligations for the purpose of protecting the rights in such pension schemes of persons so transferred[13].

1  As to the Secretary of State see PARA 2.
2  See the Coal Industry Nationalisation Act 1946 s 37 (amended by the Coal Industry Act 1949, s 4(3); the Coal Industry Act 1987 Sch 1 para 1(3), (4); and the Coal Industry Act 1987 s 1(2), Sch 1 para 1(3)). See also the Coal Industry Act 1949 s 4(4) (substituted by virtue of SI 1992/1314); and the Coal Industry Act 1965 s 4(1) (now repealed) which modified the scope of the regulations for certain purposes. As to the eligibility for superannuation rights see the Coal Industry

Nationalisation Act 1946 s 37(1A), Sch 2A (s 37(1A) added by Coal Industry Act 1977 s 12(1); Coal Industry Nationalisation Act 1946 Sch 2A added by Coal Industry Act 1977 s 12(1); amended by the Coal Industry Act 1987 s 1(2), Sch 1 para 1(3) and the Companies Act 1989, s 144(4), Sch 18, para 1). As to the Secretary of State's power to amend a scheme made under the Coal Industry Nationalisation Act 1946 s 37 so as to secure participation in any function conferred under it by any organisation which appears to him to represent a substantial proportion of its members see the Coal Industry Act 1987 ss 7, 8. These provisions (except for the Coal Industry Act 1965 s 4(1) which is now repealed) are all repealed by the Coal Industry Act 1994 s 67(8), Sch 11 Pt III as from a day to be appointed under s 68. At the date at which this volume states the law no such day had been appointed.

3    The British Coal Staff Superannuation Scheme was established on 1 January 1947 under the Coal Industry Nationalisation (Superannuation) Regulations 1946, SR & O 1946/2198.

4    The Mineworkers' Pension Scheme was established on 1 January 1952 under the Coal Industry Nationalisation (Superannuation) Regulations 1950, SI 1950/376.

5    As to the reorganisation of the coal industry under privatisation see PARAS 50, 51 et seq. The British Coal Corporation was dissolved on 27 March 2004 ie the date appointed as the 'dissolution date' under the Coal Industry Act 1994 s 23 for the dissolution of the British Coal Corporation: see s 23(2); and the Coal Industry Act 1994 (Commencement No 7) and Dissolution of the British Coal Corporation Order 2004, SI 2004/144, art 3. As to the British Coal Corporation see PARAS 49–50. As to the dissolution of the British Coal Corporation see PARA 88.

6    See the Coal Industry Act 1994 s 22(1), Sch 5 (Sch 5 amended by the Employment Rights Act 1996, s 240, Sch 1, para 64; and SI 2006/745). For the purposes of Sch 5, 'pension', in relation to any person, means a pension of any kind payable to or in respect of that person, including: (1) a lump sum, allowance or gratuity so payable; and (2) a return of contributions, with or without interest or any other addition: Sch 5 para 1(1).

7    'Existing scheme' means any scheme having effect by virtue of regulations made under the Coal Industry Nationalisation Act 1946 s 37 for purposes relating to pensions, gratuities or other like benefits (ie the British Coal Superannuation Scheme and the Mineworkers' Pension Scheme): Coal Industry Act 1994 Sch 5 para 1(1).

8    See the Coal Industry Act 1994 Sch 5 para 2(1), (2); the British Coal Staff Superannuation Scheme (Modification) Regulations 1994, SI 1994/2576, regs 1, 3, 4; and the Mineworkers' Pension Scheme (Modification) Regulations 1994, SI 1994/2577, regs 1, 3, 4. As to the modification of existing schemes see PARA 82.

9    The British Coal Staff Superannuation Scheme Trustees Limited was appointed by the Secretary of State to be sole trustee of the British Coal Staff Superannuation Scheme: see the British Coal Staff Superannuation Scheme (Modification) Regulations 1994, SI 1994/2576, reg 4, Schedule para 1A. The Mineworkers' Pension Scheme Trustees Limited was appointed by the Secretary of State to be sole trustee of the Mineworkers' Pension Scheme: see the Mineworkers' Pension Scheme (Modification) Regulations 1994, SI 1994/2577, reg 4, Schedule para 5A.

10    As to the power to make regulations under the Coal Industry Act 1994 Sch 5 see PARA 81.

11    Ie by virtue of the coming into force of any provisions of a restructuring scheme in accordance with which a person other than the Coal Authority becomes the employer in place of the British Coal Corporation or one of its wholly-owned subsidiaries; or by a company's having ceased at any time on or after the restructuring date (ie 31 October 1994: see PARA 50) to be a subsidiary of the British Coal Corporation: Coal Industry Act 1994 Sch 5 para 3(2). As to restructuring schemes see PARA 72. As to the Coal Authority see PARA 52 et seq. As to the meanings of 'subsidiary' and 'wholly-owned subsidiary' see PARA 51.

12    See the Coal Industry Act 1994 Sch 5 paras 3, 5; the Industry-Wide Coal Staff Superannuation Scheme Regulations 1994, SI 1994/2973 (amended by SI 2001/3649); the Industry-Wide Mineworkers' Pension Scheme Regulations 1994, SI 1994/2974 (amended by SI 2001/3649; and SI 2004/3379); and PARA 83. These regulations respectively establish new schemes in which the participants in the British Coal Staff Superannuation Scheme and the Mineworkers' Pension Scheme are able to participate. Both sets of regulations came into force on 15 December 1994: Industry-Wide Coal Staff Superannuation Scheme Regulations 1994, SI 1994/2973, reg 1; Industry-Wide Mineworkers' Pension Scheme Regulations 1994, SI 1994/2974, reg 1.

13    See the Coal Industry Act 1994 Sch 5 paras 4, 5 (Sch 5 para 4 amended by the Employment Rights Act 1996, s 240, Sch 1, para 64; and SI 2006/745); the Coal Industry (Protected Persons) Pensions Regulations 1994, SI 1994/3070; and PARA 84. The regulations came into force on 24 December 1994: reg 1.

## 81. Secretary of State's power to make regulations.

The powers of the Secretary of State[1] to make regulations under the provisions of the Coal Industry Act 1994 relating to the pension provisions in connection with the restructuring of the coal industry[2] are exercisable by statutory instrument subject to annulment in pursuance of a resolution of either House of Parliament[3]. Any such power includes power to make different provision for different cases or different purposes, and to make such supplemental, incidental, consequential and transitional provision as the Secretary of State considers appropriate in relation to the provision contained in any such regulations[4]. These powers include power, for the purpose of giving effect to any option[5], to provide for the modification[6] of the contracts of employment of persons who become participants in a scheme established in pursuance of any such regulations[7]; and power to require any dispute arising under or in relation to any such regulations to be referred to arbitration[8].

Regulations may have effect from a date prior to their making, but they must not place any person other than (1) the Secretary of State; (2) the Coal Authority[9]; (3) the British Coal Corporation[10] or any of its wholly-owned subsidiaries[11]; or (4) a company wholly owned by the Crown[12], in a worse position than he or it would have been in if the regulations had been made so as to have effect only from the date they were made[13].

Where any modification of any existing scheme[14] confers any powers on the Secretary of State, those powers are to be treated as conferred for purposes that include securing that the trustees and other persons concerned in the administration of the scheme exercise and perform their powers and duties in such manner as appears to the Secretary of State to take account of the desirability (a) of preventing the Secretary of State from incurring any liability under certain arrangements[15]; (b) of keeping to a minimum the amount of any liability incurred under such arrangements[16]; and (c) of managing the scheme so as to produce the largest practicable surpluses at the times as at which determinations of any relevant surpluses[17] fall to be made[18].

Nothing in any enactment or rule of law prevents the Corporation, the trustees of any existing scheme, or any other person concerned in the administration of any such scheme, from giving the Secretary of State or other prescribed person the advice or assistance he reasonably requires to make any determination, apportionment, allocation or transfer, or give or issue any direction or certificate[19].

1  As to the Secretary of State see PARA 2.
2  Ie under the Coal Industry Act 1994 s 22(1), Sch 5: see Sch 5 para 5(1).
3  Coal Industry Act 1994 Sch 5 para 5(1).
4  Coal Industry Act 1994 Sch 5 para 5(2).
5  Ie an option afforded by virtue of the Coal Industry Act 1994 Sch 5: see Sch 5 para 5(3)(a).
6  As to the meaning of 'modifications' see PARA 51.
7  Coal Industry Act 1994 Sch 5 para 5(3)(a).
8  Coal Industry Act 1994 Sch 5 para 5(3)(b).
9  As to the Coal Authority see PARA 52 et seq.
10 The British Coal Corporation was dissolved on 27 March 2004 ie the date appointed as the 'dissolution date' under the Coal Industry Act 1994 s 23 for the dissolution of the British Coal Corporation: see s 23(2); and the Coal Industry Act 1994 (Commencement No 7) and Dissolution of the British Coal Corporation Order 2004, SI 2004/144, art 3. As to the British Coal Corporation see PARAS 49–50. As to the dissolution of the British Coal Corporation see PARA 88.
11 As to the meanings of 'subsidiary' and 'wholly-owned subsidiary' see PARA 51.
12 As to 'company wholly owned by the Crown' see PARA 72.
13 Coal Industry Act 1994 Sch 5 para 5(4).

14 As to the meaning of 'existing scheme' see PARA 80.

15 Coal Industry Act 1994 Sch 5 para 5(5)(a). The arrangements referred to in the text are those entered into as mentioned in Sch 5 para 2(9) (see PARA 82): see Sch 5 para 5(5).

16 Coal Industry Act 1994 Sch 5 para 5(5)(b).

17 As to the meaning of 'relevant surplus' see PARA 82.

18 Coal Industry Act 1994 Sch 5 para 5(5)(c).

19 Coal Industry Act 1994 Sch 5 para 5(6). The determinations etc which are referred to in the text are those for which provision is made under Sch 5: see Sch 5 para 5(6).

## 82. Modification of existing schemes.

The power to modify an existing scheme[1] by regulations[2] has not been exercisable since the end of the period of two years beginning with the restructuring date[3]. Before making any regulations in relation to an existing scheme the Secretary of State[4] had to consult with the British Coal Corporation[5] and the trustees for the time being of that scheme[6]. The power did not authorise the making of any modification[7] which, in relation to the person entitled to it, adversely affected so much of any pension right[8] as gave rise to any of the principal pension obligations[9] under that scheme[10].

The modifications of an existing scheme that could be made by regulations included modifications for any of the following purposes:

(1)　　for conferring power on the Secretary of State or any other prescribed[11] person to appoint trustees of the existing scheme or for requiring trustees to be appointed only in a prescribed manner and in prescribed circumstances, or with the approval of the Secretary of State or other prescribed person[12];

(2)　　for enabling a person who was entitled to appoint trustees of the existing scheme to remove trustees of the scheme from office[13];

(3)　　for requiring or enabling powers or duties of any person under the existing scheme to be exercisable or performed by or in accordance with the directions of prescribed persons or in prescribed circumstances, or to be exercisable or performed only in a prescribed manner or with the consent of prescribed persons[14];

(4)　　for providing that persons who became entitled in respect of any period of employment to be participants in another prescribed scheme were not, as from a determined time, entitled in respect of that period of employment to be participants in the existing scheme[15];

(5)　　for facilitating the transfer in prescribed circumstances to another scheme of (a) rights and liabilities under the existing scheme of any participant in the existing scheme who became a participant in the other scheme[16]; or (b) the benefit of any arrangements under which participants in the existing scheme were relieved from any obligation to make contributions[17];

(6)　　for the apportionment and allocation to particular rights and liabilities of assets[18] of the existing scheme and for the transfer of assets to other schemes[19];

(7)　　for restricting the persons who were to be able on and after the restructuring date to become participants in the existing scheme[20];

(8)　　for enabling management and administration expenses of the existing scheme to be met out of the assets of the scheme[21];

(9)　　for securing that the existing scheme continued to be approved for the purposes of the relevant enactments[22];

(10)　　for enabling the existing scheme to be wound up (in whole or in part) in prescribed circumstances[23].

The modifications of an existing scheme that could be made by regulations included modifications making such provision as the Secretary of State considered appropriate for cases where either (i) there were assets of the scheme representing a relevant surplus; or (ii) the assets of the scheme were insufficient for meeting pension obligations under the scheme[24].

Regulations made under these provisions could provide for any relevant apportionments, allocations[25] or determinations[26] to be made at prescribed times and by reference to the opinion of prescribed persons[27].

The Secretary of State may still, with the consent of the Treasury, enter into such arrangements as he may consider appropriate for guaranteeing or otherwise securing, in relation to any existing scheme, that the assets of the scheme are always sufficient for meeting the principal pension obligations and such other pension obligations under the scheme to which he considers such arrangements should apply[28].

1   As to the meaning of 'existing scheme' see PARA 80.
2   Ie under the Coal Industry Act 1994 s 22(1), Sch 5 para 2. The modified British Coal Superannuation Scheme (see PARA 80) is contained in the British Coal Staff Superannuation Scheme (Modification) Regulations 1994, SI 1994/2576, reg 4, Schedule (amended by SI 2001/3649). The modified Mineworkers' Pension Scheme (see PARA 80) is contained in the Mineworkers' Pension Scheme (Modification) Regulations 1994, SI 1994/2577, reg 4, Schedule (amended by SI 2001/3649; and SI 2004/3379). Both sets of regulations came into force on 31 October 1994: British Coal Staff Superannuation Scheme (Modification) Regulations 1994, SI 1994/2576, reg 1; Mineworkers' Pension Scheme (Modification) Regulations 1994, SI 1994/2577, reg 1.
3   Coal Industry Act 1994 Sch 5 para 2(14). However, this is without prejudice to any regulations made before the end of that period or to anything done (whether before or after the end of that period) under any regulations so made: Sch 5 para 2(14). As to the restructuring date (ie 31 October 1994) see PARA 50.
4   As to the Secretary of State see PARA 2.
5   The British Coal Corporation was dissolved on 27 March 2004 ie the date appointed as the 'dissolution date' under the Coal Industry Act 1994 s 23 for the dissolution of the British Coal Corporation: see s 23(2); and the Coal Industry Act 1994 (Commencement No 7) and Dissolution of the British Coal Corporation Order 2004, SI 2004/144, art 3. As to the British Coal Corporation see PARAS 49–50. As to the dissolution of the British Coal Corporation see PARA 88.
6   Coal Industry Act 1994 Sch 5 para 2(13).
7   As to the meaning of 'modifications' see PARA 51.
8   'Pension rights', in relation to any person, includes all forms of right to or eligibility for the present or future payment of a pension to or in respect of that person and any right of allocation in respect of the present or future payment of a pension: Coal Industry Act 1994 Sch 5 para 1(1).
9   'Pension obligation' means any present, future or contingent obligation to make a payment which is an obligation to which pension rights of the person to whom it is owed give rise: Coal Industry Act 1994 Sch 5 para 1(1). In Sch 5 para 2, references to the principal pension obligations under an existing scheme are references to the following:
    (1)   so much of any pension obligation arising under the scheme as derives neither from modifications of the scheme made on or after the restructuring date nor from any relevant surplus (Sch 5 para 2(16)(a));
    (2)   so much of any pension obligation arising under the scheme as represents the effect on any pension right giving rise to a pension obligation falling within head (1) of any decision before 1 September 1994 to appropriate any of a relevant surplus determined as at a time before 31 March 1994 to the payment of increases in any pensions payable in pursuance of that right (Sch 5 para 2(16)(b)); and
    (3)   so much of any pension obligation arising under the scheme as represents the effect on any pension right giving rise to a pension obligation falling within head (1) or head (2) of any provisions of the scheme, as modified on or after the restructuring date, which require that right to be varied from time to time by reference to fluctuations in any level of prices in Great Britain (Sch 5 para 2(16)(c)).

'Relevant surplus', in relation to an existing scheme, means any surplus determined as at any time on or after 31 March 1992 of the assets of the scheme over the amounts required, as at that time, for meeting the obligations which (apart from the surplus) either have arisen or may arise as pension obligations under the scheme: Sch 5 para 2(15). As to the meaning of 'Great Britain' see PARA 48. The British Coal Corporation was not entitled to apply any part of the British Coal Staff Superannuation Scheme's actuarial surplus in discharge or reduction of outstanding instalments of additional contributions required to meet the costs of providing enhanced benefits for members who were granted them on accepting voluntary redundancy before 5 April 1992: see *British Coal Corpn v British Coal Staff Superannuation Scheme Trustees Ltd* [1995] 1 All ER 912.

10 Coal Industry Act 1994 Sch 5 para 2(12).

11 'Prescribed' means prescribed by regulations made by the Secretary of State: Coal Industry Act 1994 Sch 5 para 1(1).

12 Coal Industry Act 1994 Sch 5 para 2(3)(a). As to the new trustees appointed see PARA 80.

13 Coal Industry Act 1994 Sch 5 para 2(3)(b).

14 Coal Industry Act 1994 Sch 5 para 2(3)(c).

15 Coal Industry Act 1994 Sch 5 para 2(3)(d).

16 Coal Industry Act 1994 Sch 5 para 2(3)(e)(i).

17 Coal Industry Act 1994 Sch 5 para 2(3)(e)(ii).

18 'Assets', in relation to any existing scheme, means all the assets for the time being held for the purposes of the scheme by the trustees of the scheme, including every interest in property and right to which the trustees of the scheme are for the time being entitled, together with any liabilities, not being liabilities in respect of pension obligations, to which any entitlement of the trustees to any of the scheme's assets is subject: Coal Industry Act 1994 Sch 5 para 1(1).

19 Coal Industry Act 1994 Sch 5 para 2(3)(f). The provisions referred to are those of Sch 5: see Sch 5 para 2(3)(f).

20 Coal Industry Act 1994 Sch 5 para 2(3)(g).

21 Coal Industry Act 1994 Sch 5 para 2(3)(h).

22 Coal Industry Act 1994 Sch 5 para 2(3)(i). 'The relevant enactments' means the Finance Act 2004 Pt 4 (ss 149–284) (pension schemes etc) and the Pension Schemes Act 1993 Pt III (ss 7–68) (so far as relating to occupational pension schemes within the meaning of that Act): Coal Industry Act 1994 Sch 5 para 1(1) (amended by SI 2006/745). Note that references in the Coal Industry Act 1994 Sch 5 to a scheme being approved for the purposes of the Pension Schemes Act 1993 Pt III are references to its being included in a contracting-out certificate having effect for the purposes of that Part: Coal Industry Act 1994 Sch 5 para 1(2). As to retirement benefit schemes and occupational pension schemes see WELFARE BENEFITS AND STATE PENSIONS vol 104 (2014) PARA 236 et seq.

23 Coal Industry Act 1994 Sch 5 para 2(3)(j).

24 Coal Industry Act 1994 Sch 5 para 2(4). These modifications might contain:

(1)    provision for a relevant surplus, and the assets representing it, to be apportioned between (a) the part (if any) of the surplus which was to be retained in a reserve ('an investment reserve') as an asset of the scheme, and (b) the remainder ('the distributable part') of the surplus (Sch 5 para 2(5)(a));

(2)    provision for the management of assets representing an investment reserve and for the manner in which any such assets were to be applied (Sch 5 para 2(5)(b));

(3)    provision for income accruing in respect of assets representing an investment reserve to be added to the reserve (Sch 5 para 2(5)(c));

(4)    provision for the manner in which assets representing the distributable part of a relevant surplus were to be applied (Sch 5 para 2(5)(d)); and

(5)    provision, for the purposes of any provision under heads (1)–(4), for modifying any decisions as to the way in which relevant surpluses determined as at times before the restructuring date, and the assets representing any such surpluses, were to be treated (Sch 5 para 2(5)(e)).

The provision as to the apportionment of any surplus or assets to an investment reserve that might be contained in such modifications was not to include any provision authorising the allocation to such a reserve of any part of a surplus determined as at a time after 31 March 1994, or of any assets representing any part of such a surplus, except where the allocation was made for making good amounts which (apart from any entitlement for which provision is made by virtue of Sch 5 para 2(7)) would have been comprised in the value of the reserve if assets representing any part of it had not been applied from the reserve in meeting a deficiency that arose as at any time by reason of the other assets of the scheme having been insufficient as at that time for meeting pension obligations under the scheme: Sch 5 para 2(6). The provision as to the application of assets representing an investment reserve that might be contained in such modifications included provision for the Secretary of State to become entitled where (i) any such arrangements as are mentioned in Sch 5 para 2(9) were entered into in relation to pension obligations under the scheme in question; and (ii) the value of the assets representing the reserve exceeded the aggregate amount required for the purposes for which the reserve had been retained, to assets of the scheme representing the amount of the excess or, where those purposes ceased, the value of the reserve: Sch 5 para 2(7). The provision as to the application of assets representing the distributable part of a relevant surplus that might be contained in such modifications included provision for the Secretary of State to become entitled where (A) the surplus was one determined as at a time on or after 31 March 1994; and (B) any such arrangements as are mentioned in Sch 5 para 2(9) were entered into in relation to pension obligations under the scheme in question, to assets of the scheme representing no more than one-half of the distributable part of that surplus: Sch 5 para 2(8).

25 Ie as mentioned in the Coal Industry Act 1994 Sch 5 para 2(1)–(10): see Sch 5 para 2(11).

26 Ie any determination for the purposes of any existing scheme of the amount of, or of any part of, any surplus or excess or of the assets for the time being to be treated as representing the whole or any part of any such surplus or excess; and the determination of any other matter falling to be determined for the purposes of any provision relating, in the case of any such scheme, to the management or application of the assets representing any reserve or surplus: see the Coal Industry Act 1994 Sch 5 para 2(11).

27 Coal Industry Act 1994 Sch 5 para 2(11).

28 Coal Industry Act 1994 Sch 5 para 2(9). Sums required by the Secretary of State for making any payment in pursuance of any such arrangements are to be paid out of money provided by Parliament; and any sums received by him by virtue of Sch 5 para 2(7) or Sch 5 para 2(8) are to be paid into the Consolidated Fund: Sch 5 para 2(10). As to the Consolidated Fund see CONSTITUTIONAL AND ADMINISTRATIVE LAW vol 20 (2014) PARA 480; PARLIAMENT vol 78 (2018) PARA 847 et seq.

## 83. Replacement schemes for employees transferred to the private sector.

The Secretary of State[1] may by regulations[2] make such provision as he thinks fit for securing that arrangements are made and implemented in relation to any existing scheme[3] for enabling participants in it to become participants in another pension scheme ('a new scheme') which is established, under and in accordance with the regulations, by the British Coal Corporation[4] or such other person as may be prescribed; and satisfies the statutory requirements by reference to that existing scheme[5]. This paragraph sets out the provisions that may be made in such regulations.

Where the employment of any participant in any existing scheme in relation to which a new scheme has been established[6] is affected (1) by the coming into force of any provisions of a restructuring scheme[7] in accordance with which a person other than the Coal Authority[8] becomes his employer in place of the Corporation or one of its wholly-owned subsidiaries[9]; or (2) by a company's[10] having ceased at any time on or after the restructuring date[11] to be a subsidiary of the Corporation[12], a duty arises to secure that the person to whom the duty is owed is afforded, and is entitled to exercise, an option of becoming a participant in the new scheme in respect of the employment to which he is transferred or, as the case may be, in respect of his continuation, after the time when the duty arises, in the employment in respect of which he is at that time participating in the existing scheme[13]. This duty is owed to the participant and to every person who at that time is a participant in that existing scheme in respect of his continuing employment with a person other than the Corporation or a subsidiary of the Corporation[14]. In a case where it is owed to a person who is transferred in accordance with a restructuring scheme from the employment of one person to the employment of another, the duty is owed by the person to whose employment he is transferred[15]. In any other case, it is owed by the person who, in relation to the employment to which the duty relates, is the employer of the person to whom the duty is owed[16].

A new scheme satisfies the statutory requirements by reference to an existing scheme ('the previous scheme') if it contains such provision[17] as may be prescribed for the following purposes[18]:

(a) that no person is able to participate in the new scheme as an employee unless he is a person falling within a certain provision[19];

(b) that the new scheme is and continues to be approved for the purposes of the relevant enactments[20];

(c) that the new scheme provides benefits to and in respect of participants in the new scheme which are no less advantageous than the benefits falling to be provided under the previous scheme as at the time immediately before the restructuring date[21]; and

(d) that the pension rights under the previous scheme of any person who becomes a participant in the new scheme in respect of any employment are capable, at that person's option, of being transferred so as to become rights under the new scheme[22].

1 As to the Secretary of State see PARA 2.
2 See the Industry-Wide Coal Staff Superannuation Scheme Regulations 1994, SI 1994/2973 (amended by SI 2001/3649) (which establish new schemes in which the participants in the British Coal Staff Superannuation Scheme are able to participate); and the Industry-Wide Mineworkers' Pension Scheme Regulations 1994, SI 1994/2974 (amended by SI 2001/3649; and SI 2004/3379) (which establish new schemes in which the participants in the Mineworkers' Pension Scheme are able to participate). Both sets of regulations came into force on 15 December 1994: Industry-Wide Coal Staff Superannuation Scheme Regulations 1994, SI 1994/2973, reg 1; Industry-Wide Mineworkers' Pension Scheme Regulations 1994, SI 1994/2974, reg 1. As to the British Coal Staff Superannuation Scheme and the Mineworkers' Pension Scheme see PARA 80.
3 As to the meaning of 'existing scheme' see PARA 80.
4 The British Coal Corporation was dissolved on 27 March 2004 ie the date appointed as the 'dissolution date' under the Coal Industry Act 1994 s 23 for the dissolution of the British Coal Corporation: see s 23(2); and the Coal Industry Act 1994 (Commencement No 7) and Dissolution of the British Coal Corporation Order 2004, SI 2004/144, art 3. As to the British Coal Corporation see PARAS 49–50. As to the dissolution of the British Coal Corporation see PARA 88.
5 Coal Industry Act 1994 s 22(1), Sch 5 para 3(1).
6 Ie in pursuance of regulations under the Coal Industry Act 1994 Sch 5: Sch 5 para 3(2).
7 As to restructuring schemes see PARA 72.
8 As to the Coal Authority see PARA 52 et seq.
9 As to the meanings of 'subsidiary' and 'wholly-owned subsidiary' see PARA 51.
10 As to the meaning of 'company' see PARA 72.
11 Ie 31 October 1994: see PARA 50.
12 For these purposes, where a company has ceased to be a subsidiary of the Corporation, the persons whose employment is to be treated as affected by the company's having ceased to be such a subsidiary are only the persons employed by that company at whichever is the later of the following times: (1) the time when the company ceased to be a subsidiary of the Corporation; and (2) the time when the company would so cease if any shares in the company which have at any time been transferred (whether in accordance with a restructuring scheme or otherwise) to any of the following persons: (a) the Treasury; (b) the Secretary of State; (c) a company wholly owned by the Crown; or (d) any nominee of the Treasury, the Secretary of State or a company wholly owned by the Crown, remained vested in the Corporation for so long after their transfer as they remain vested in any of the persons mentioned in heads (a)–(d): Coal Industry Act 1994 Sch 5 para 3(5). A person whose employment is affected by a company's having ceased to be a subsidiary of the Corporation is to be treated for these purposes as so affected only at whichever of the times mentioned in heads (1) and (2) is applicable in his case: Sch 5 para 3(5). As to the meaning of 'company wholly-owned by the Crown' see PARA 72. As to the Treasury see CONSTITUTIONAL AND ADMINISTRATIVE LAW vol 20 (2014) PARAS 262–265.
13 See the Coal Industry Act 1994 Sch 5 para 3(2), (3).
14 Coal Industry Act 1994 Sch 5 para 3(2).
15 Coal Industry Act 1994 Sch 5 para 3(4)(a).
16 Coal Industry Act 1994 Sch 5 para 3(4)(b).

17 Regulations prescribing the provision that must be contained in a scheme for it to satisfy the statutory requirements may provide for that provision to be determined by reference to such directions and certificates of the Secretary of State as may be given or issued to such persons, in such cases and in such manner as may be prescribed: Coal Industry Act 1994 Sch 5 para 3(9).

18 Coal Industry Act 1994 Sch 5 para 3(6).

19 Coal Industry Act 1994 Sch 5 para 3(7)(a). The provision referred to in the text is Sch 5 para 3(8), and a person falls within that provision if he is:
   (1)    one of the persons who, by virtue of Sch 5 para 3(2), is to be afforded the option of becoming a participant in the new scheme (Sch 5 para 3(8)(a));
   (2)    a person the duties of whose employment with the same employer have changed so that he has ceased to be eligible to participate in a scheme in relation to which he has been entitled to protection under Sch 5 para 4 (see PARA 84) but has become a person who satisfies, by reference to his new duties, a condition of eligibility for participation in the new scheme (Sch 5 para 3(8)(b)); or
   (3)    a person with pension rights as a result of having been a participant in an existing scheme who, at any time on or after the restructuring date, enters the employment of a person any of whose employees are already, in respect of their employment with that person, participants in the new scheme (Sch 5 para 3(8)(c)).
   As to the meaning of 'pension rights' see PARA 82.

20 Coal Industry Act 1994 Sch 5 para 3(7)(b). As to the meaning of 'relevant enactments' see PARA 82.

21 Coal Industry Act 1994 Sch 5 para 3(7)(c).

22 Coal Industry Act 1994 Sch 5 para 3(7)(d).

## 84.   Protection for rights under private sector schemes.

The Secretary of State[1] may, in relation to any replacement pension scheme for employees transferred to the private sector[2], and any prescribed scheme the establishment of which appears to the Secretary of State to be, or to have been required, for the purposes of any protection to which any person is entitled[3], impose by regulations[4] such restrictions and obligations as appear to him to be appropriate for the purpose of securing:

   (1)    that no person entitled to protection in relation to such a scheme is placed in any worse position[5] by reason of (a) any such amendment of the scheme as is made otherwise than in prescribed[6] circumstances and results in benefits under the scheme being reduced, or contributions by employees being increased; or (b) any winding-up, in whole or in part, of the scheme[7];

   (2)    that no person entitled to protection in relation to such a scheme is prevented from continuing to participate in or acquire pension rights under the scheme by reason of any change of employer which does not affect his continuity of employment[8]; and

   (3)    that no person entitled to protection in relation to such a scheme is prevented[9] from continuing to participate in or acquire pension rights under the scheme by reason of his having entered the employment of an employer who (a) opts to allow that person to continue, in respect of his employment with that employer, as a participant in that scheme; and (b) is able to exercise that option without the scheme ceasing to be registered or approved for the purposes of the relevant enactments[10].

Such regulations may make provision for securing that a person entitled to protection in relation to such a scheme who ceases, by reason of any change in the duties of his employment with the same employer, to be eligible to participate in that scheme, but who, by reason of the change, becomes a person who satisfies, by reference to his new duties, a condition of eligibility for participation in another such scheme, is afforded the equivalent protection with respect to his participation in the other scheme as was previously secured[11] with respect to his continuing participation in the scheme for which he has ceased to be eligible[12]. Regulations may also make provision for securing that individuals with pension rights under such a scheme are allowed to become participants in another such scheme or to renew their participation in the same scheme where, in prescribed cases, they enter the employment of a person any of whose employees are already, in respect of their employment with that person, participants in the other scheme or, as the case may be, in the scheme under which those rights subsist[13].

Regulations may impose duties[14] on (i) any person who has been or is for the time being the employer of a person entitled to protection in relation to any such scheme; and (ii) any persons by whom such an employer is or has been wholly owned[15]. They may also provide for the duties imposed by the regulations on any person to be owed to prescribed persons, including persons other than those who are or have been employed by that person or, as the case may be, by a company wholly owned by him[16].

Certain persons are entitled to protection in relation to any such scheme, except in so far as they cease to be so entitled[17]. A person entitled to such protection may elect, in the prescribed manner, that he is to cease to be entitled to that protection[18]. If any person who is entitled to protection by virtue of having exercised an option to become a participant in the scheme in respect of his employment, or having been a participant in the scheme in pursuance of regulations for the purpose of preserving the entitlement of that person to protection in relation to any other such scheme[19], ceases to be in continuous employment or voluntarily withdraws from that scheme, and the circumstances of that cesser or withdrawal are not such as may be prescribed, that person ceases to be entitled to that protection except as respects pension rights which have accrued to him before the time when he so ceases or withdraws[20]. Regulations may provide that no account is to be taken of any person's ceasing to be in continuous employment for such periods and in such circumstances as may be prescribed[21].

1   As to the Secretary of State see PARA 2.
2   Ie a scheme established in pursuance of regulations under the Coal Industry Act 1994 s 22(1), Sch 5 para 3(1) (see PARA 83): see Sch 5 para 4(1)(a).
3   Coal Industry Act 1994 Sch 5 para 4(1)(b).
4   See the Coal Industry (Protected Persons) Pensions Regulations 1994, SI 1994/3070, which are concerned with the industry-wide pension scheme established in accordance with the Industry-Wide Coal Staff Superannuation Scheme Regulations 1994, SI 1994/2973; and the industry-wide pension scheme established in accordance with the Industry-Wide Mineworkers' Pension Scheme Regulations 1994, SI 1994/2974.
5   The reference to being placed in any worse position is to be construed, in relation to a person entitled to protection by virtue of the Coal Industry Act 1994 Sch 5 para 4(6)(a) who ceases, after the exercise of the option made available to him in pursuance of Sch 5 para 3(2) to participate in or acquire pension rights under any scheme, as a reference to being placed in a position which is worse than his position immediately before he so ceases: Sch 5 para 4(10). As to the meaning of 'pension rights' see PARA 82.
6   As to the meaning of 'prescribed' see PARA 82.
7   Coal Industry Act 1994 Sch 5 para 4(2)(a).
8   Coal Industry Act 1994 Sch 5 para 4(2)(b).
9   Ie in a case not falling within head (2) in the text: see the Coal Industry Act 1994 Sch 5 para 4(2)(c).
10  Coal Industry Act 1994 Sch 5 para 4(2)(c) (amended by SI 2006/745). As to the meaning of 'relevant enactments' see PARA 82.
11  Ie by virtue of the Coal Industry Act 1994 Sch 5 para 4: see Sch 5 para 4(3).
12  Coal Industry Act 1994 Sch 5 para 4(3).
13  Coal Industry Act 1994 Sch 5 para 4(4).
14  These duties may be either as to the provision or amendment of any such scheme, the purchase of annuities, the making of payments or otherwise: see Coal Industry Act 1994 Sch 5 para 4(5)(a).

15 Coal Industry Act 1994 Sch 5 para 4(5)(a). For these purposes a company is wholly owned by any person if its members do not include any person other than (1) that person himself; (2) companies wholly owned by that person; and (3) persons acting on behalf of that person or a company wholly owned by that person: Sch 5 para 4(13).

16 Coal Industry Act 1994 Sch 5 para 4(5)(b).

17 See the Coal Industry Act 1994 Sch 5 para 4(6). The persons entitled to protection are: (1) every person who (a) has exercised an option conferred by virtue of Sch 5 para 3(2) (see PARA 83) to become a participant in the scheme in respect of his employment; or (b) is or has been a participant in the scheme in pursuance of any regulations made under Sch 5 para 4 for the purpose of preserving the entitlement of that person to protection in relation to any other scheme to which Sch 5 para 4 applies (Sch 5 para 4(6)(a)); and (2) every person who has pension rights under the scheme in consequence of the death of a person falling within head (1) (Sch 5 para 4(6)(b)). However, a person is not entitled to protection by virtue of head (2) except as respects the pension rights in respect of which he falls within that head: Sch 5 para 4(6). As to how a person ceases to be entitled to protection see Sch 5 para 4(7)–(9).

18 Coal Industry Act 1994 Sch 5 para 4(7).

19 Ie under the Coal Industry Act 1994 Sch 5 para 4(6)(a).

20 Coal Industry Act 1994 Sch 5 para 4(8). However, if such a person continues to be a participant in that scheme after such a change of employment as brings the case within Sch 5 para 4(2)(c), that person ceases to be entitled to that protection except as respects pension rights which have accrued to him before that change: Sch 5 para 4(9).

21 Coal Industry Act 1994 Sch 5 para 4(12). The Employment Rights Act 1996 Pt XIV Ch I (ss 210–219), except s 218(6), applies for the purposes of the Coal Industry Act 1994 Sch 5 para 4 as if Sch 5 para 4 were contained in the Employment Rights Act 1996: Coal Industry Act 1994 Sch 5 para 4(11) (amended by the Employment Rights Act 1996 s 240, Sch 1 para 64).

## 85. Benefits for redundant coal industry employees.

For the purpose of providing assistance to persons made redundant[1] by the closure of coal mines[2] or coking plants, the reduction in the number of persons employed at them or the consequent reduction in ancillary services and facilities, the Secretary of State[3] may, by order[4] make a scheme providing for payments, out of money provided by Parliament[5], to or in respect of prescribed[6] classes of persons who at any time between 17 July 1967 and 29 March 1987 (1) were employed at a coal mine or at any place of a prescribed class used for providing services or facilities ancillary to the working of one or more coal mines or were employed by any person carrying on in Great Britain[7] a business consisting wholly or mainly of the production of coke and were so employed either at a coking plant or at any place of a prescribed class used for providing services or facilities ancillary to the operation of one or more coking plants; and in either case (2) became redundant in prescribed circumstances[8].

Payments under a scheme are either payments by the Secretary of State to persons to whom the scheme applies or payments by the Secretary of State to the British Coal Corporation[9] in respect of the carrying out by the Corporation of arrangements relating to concessionary coal[10]; and the aggregate amounts of such payments are subject to specified limits[11]. However, as part of the restructuring of the coal industry, these provisions are repealed by the Coal Industry Act 1994 as from a day to be appointed.

1 As to redundancy generally see EMPLOYMENT vol 41 (2014) PARA 835 et seq.

2 As to the meaning of 'mine' see PARA 3.

3 As to the Secretary of State see PARA 2.

4 The power to make a scheme is exercisable by order contained in a statutory instrument, which may be varied or revoked by a subsequent order: Coal Industry Act 1977 s 7(7). An order may not be made unless a draft of it has been laid before and approved by the House of Commons: s 7(7). Section 7 is repealed by the Coal Industry Act 1994 s 67(8), Sch 11 Pt III as from a day to be appointed under s 68. At the date at which this volume states the law no such day had been appointed.

5 Coal Industry Act 1977 s 7(9).

6   Ie prescribed by a scheme under the Coal Industry Act 1977 s 7: s 7(8).

7   As to the meaning of 'Great Britain' see PARA 48.

8   Coal Industry Act 1977 s 7(1) (amended by Coal Industry Act 1980 s 7(1); and the Coal Industry Act 1985 s 3(1); prospectively repealed).
    The Redundant Mineworkers (Payments Scheme) Order 1968, SI 1968/987 (amended by SI 1971/553, SI 1972/335, SI 1973/1268); the Redundant Mineworkers (Payments Scheme) Order 1972, SI 1972/335 (amended by SI 1973/1268, SI 1976/495); and the Redundant Mineworkers and Concessionary Coal (Payments Schemes) Order 1973, SI 1973/1268 (all made under the Coal Industry Act 1967 s 3) were all continued in force by the Coal Industry Act 1977 s 7(10) but will lapse on the repeal of that section. The following orders have been made under s 7: the Redundant Mineworkers and Concessionary Coal (Payments Schemes) Order 1978, SI 1978/415 (amended by SI 1979/385; SI 1980/434; SI 1980/835; SI 1980/1984; SI 1981/482; SI 1982/407; SI 1987/1258; SI 1988/1252; and SI 1989/1201); and the Redundant Mineworkers (Payments Schemes) (Amendment and Consolidation) Order 1996, SI 1996/1288, but will lapse on the repeal of that section. The Redundant Mineworkers (Payments Schemes) (Amendment and Consolidation) Order 1996, SI 1996/1288, establishes a scheme which revokes and supersedes earlier schemes made under the Redundant Mineworkers and Concessionary Coal (Payments Schemes) Order 1983, SI 1983/506 (revoked) (the '1983 Scheme' for employees made redundant between 6 April 1983 and 1 April 1984); the Redundant Mineworkers and Concessionary Coal (Payments Schemes) Order 1984, SI 1984/457 (revoked) (the '1984 Scheme' for employees made redundant between 1 April 1984 and 30 March 1986); and the Redundant Mineworkers and Concessionary Coal (Payments Schemes) Order 1986, SI 1986/625 (revoked) (the '1986 Scheme' for employees made redundant between 30 March 1986 and 29 March 1987): see the Redundant Mineworkers (Payments Schemes) (Amendment and Consolidation) Order 1996, SI 1996/1288, arts 1–4. The termination dates of the earlier schemes remain the same for those entitled under them and are as follows: (1) 3 April 1999 for the 1983 Scheme; (2) 31 March 2001 for the 1984 Scheme; and (3) 30 March 2002 for the 1986 Scheme, provided in each case that the employee does not first reach the age of 65 (if a man) or 60 (if a woman): see art 5, Schedule para 9.

9   The British Coal Corporation was dissolved on 27 March 2004 ie the date appointed as the 'dissolution date' under the Coal Industry Act 1994 s 23 for the dissolution of the British Coal Corporation: see s 23(2); and the Coal Industry Act 1994 (Commencement No 7) and Dissolution of the British Coal Corporation Order 2004, SI 2004/144, art 3. As to the British Coal Corporation see PARAS 49–50. As to the dissolution of the British Coal Corporation see PARA 88.

10  Coal Industry Act 1977 s 7(2) (s 7(2), (4) amended by the Coal Industry Act 1987 s 1(2), Sch 1 para 34(1); prospectively repealed). 'Concessionary coal' means coal or other solid fuel supplied free of charge or at reduced prices: Coal Industry Act 1977 s 7(8). As to concessionary coal see PARA 78.

11  See the Coal Industry Act 1977 s 7(4), (5) (s 7(5) substituted by the Coal Industry Act 1980 s 7(3); amended by the Coal Industry Act 1983 s 4(1), (3); Coal Industry Act 1985 s 3(2); Coal Industry Act 1987 s 1(2), Sch 1 para 34(1); and SI 1986/631).

### D.   SOCIAL WELFARE

## 86.   Transfer of functions of the Coal Industry Social Welfare Organisation.

The miners' welfare fund was set up in 1920 for the improvement of social conditions of colliery workers[1]. When it was wound up on 1 July 1952, its property, rights and liabilities were divided between the British Coal Corporation[2] and the Coal Industry Social Welfare Organisation[3] in accordance with a scheme agreed between them[4]. Similarly, the property, rights and liabilities of the Miners' Welfare Commission, which had been set up in 1939[5], were transferred to the British Coal Corporation and the Coal Industry Social Welfare Organisation on the dissolution of the Commission on 1 July 1952[6].

On 23 March 1995 the functions of the Coal Industry Social Welfare Organisation were transferred to the trustees of the trust known as 'The Coal Industry Social Welfare Organisation'[7]. The Secretary of State has power by order to vary certain trusts[8] if it appears to him expedient in the interest of social welfare activities[9].

1   Ie under the Mining Industry Act 1920 s 20 (repealed).

2   The British Coal Corporation was dissolved on 27 March 2004 ie the date appointed as the 'dissolution date' under the Coal Industry Act 1994 s 23 for the dissolution of the British Coal Corporation: see s 23(2); and the Coal Industry Act 1994 (Commencement No 7) and Dissolution of the British Coal Corporation Order 2004, SI 2004/144, art 3. As to the British Coal Corporation see PARAS 49–50. As to the dissolution of the British Coal Corporation see PARA 88.

3   The Coal Industry Social Welfare Organisation was incorporated in 1952 as a company limited by guarantee registered under the Companies Acts. Following restructuring, the company was wound up.

4   See the Miners' Welfare Act 1952 s 2. The transfer included colliery welfare property (see ss 3–6), vocational education trusts (see s 7) and certain documents (see s 9). 'Colliery welfare property' means property representing an application of moneys standing to the credit of the miners' welfare fund, being property used for purposes conducive to the welfare of persons employed in or about coal mines in matters affecting their employment, and in particular includes property used for the following purposes: (1) the maintenance and operation in or about coal mines of pithead baths, drying rooms or canteens or of ancillary services; (2) the maintenance and operation of cycle stores, bus shelters or other similar facilities; (3) the maintenance and operation of medical treatment centres or other facilities for medical or therapeutic treatment; (4) the advancement of vocational education or training for the coal-mining industry (ss 3(1), 16(1), Sch 1 paras 1–3); but does not include property for the following purposes: (a) the maintenance and operation of recreation grounds, institutes, clubs or camps, and the encouragement or organisation of sports, games, holidays or other social or cultural activities; (b) the maintenance and operation of convalescent homes or ambulances, or the assistance of the sick and disabled otherwise than by the provision of such facilities as are mentioned in head (3); (c) the advancement of education or training, other than vocational training or training for the coal-mining industry (ss 3(1), 16(1), Sch 1 paras 5–7). 'Social welfare activities' means activities concerned with the maintenance or improvement of the health, social well-being, recreation or conditions of living of (i) persons employed in or about coal mines or otherwise employed under the Corporation; (ii) persons who have ceased to be so employed by reason of age or disability or, having ceased to be so employed for any reason, have not subsequently changed their occupation; or (iii) dependants of such persons, and in particular includes activities carried on for the purposes mentioned in heads (a)–(c): Miners' Welfare Act 1952 16(1). Provision was also made regarding the payment of grants by the Corporation: see s 13 (amended by the Coal Industry Act 1987 s 1(1), (2), Sch 1 para 3(a)).
    As part of the restructuring of the coal industry, the Miners' Welfare Act 1952 is repealed by the Coal Industry Act 1994 ss 22(2), 67(8), Sch 11 Pt III as from a day to be appointed by s 68.

5   Ie under the Mining Industry (Welfare Fund) Act 1939 s 2 (repealed).

6   See the Miners' Welfare Act 1952 ss 1(2), 8, 10.

7   Miners' Welfare Act 1952 ss 12(3), 15; Miners' Welfare Act 1952 (Transfer of Functions of Coal Industry Social Welfare Organisation) Order 1995, SI 1995/855, arts 1, 2. The trust is registered with the Charity Commissioners under the Charities Act 1993 with the number 1015581: Miners' Welfare Act 1952 (Transfer of Functions of Coal Industry Social Welfare Organisation) Order 1995, SI 1995/855, art 2. As to the registration of charities see CHARITIES vol 8 (2015) PARA 307 et seq.
    Despite the prospective repeal of the Miners' Welfare Act 1952, s 12(3) has effect pending its repeal as if the functions so transferred are all the functions of the Coal Industry Social Welfare Organisation, whether or not they arose under the Miners' Welfare Act 1952: Coal Industry Act 1994 s 22(3). In particular the repeal of the Miners' Welfare Act 1952 does not affect the application in relation to any trusts of the Recreational Charities Act 1958 s 2 (certain trusts for the purposes of welfare activities within the meaning of the Miners' Welfare Act 1952 to be charitable: see CHARITIES vol 8 (2015) PARA 51): Coal Industry Act 1994 s 67(7), Sch 10 para 8.

8   Ie any trust that subsisted before 1 July 1952 and is in force in respect of property consisting (1) of property representing an application of moneys standing to the credit of the miners' welfare fund; or (2) of such property mentioned in head (1) and other property held with it where the value of the property mentioned in head (1) substantially exceeds the value of the other property: see the Coal Industry Nationalisation Act 1946 s 41(1) (substituted by the Miners' Welfare Act 1952 s 11(1)). The Coal Industry Nationalisation Act 1946 s 41 is repealed by the Coal Industry Act 1994 s 67(8), Sch 11 Pt III as from a day to be appointed under s 68. At the date at which this volume states the law no such day had been appointed. The repeal of the Coal Industry Nationalisation Act 1946 s 41 is without prejudice to the continuing effect of any order made before that repeal under that section: Coal Industry Act 1994 Sch 10 para 7.

9 See the Coal Industry Nationalisation Act 1946 s 41(1); and the Miners' Welfare Act 1952 s 11(2). Certain conditions must be met before such an order may be made: see the Coal Industry Nationalisation Act 1946 s 41(2). Trusts so varied may be varied by a subsequent order: s 41(3).

## 87. Participation of employee organisations in trusts and social welfare bodies.

Where it appears to the Charity Commission[1] on an application by an employee organisation[2] that the members of the employee organisation or the members and their dependants constitute a substantial proportion of those who may benefit under a trust[3], and that neither the organisation nor its members are entitled to appoint any of the trustees of the trust[4], the Charity Commission may by order make a scheme amending the trust for the purpose of securing fair representation amongst the trustees of those persons employed in the coal industry who may benefit under the trust[5]. Such an amendment scheme may (1) make such provision as to the manner in which the trustees are to be appointed as the Charity Commission considers appropriate[6]; (2) restrict or remove any person's right to appoint a trustee[7]; (3) remove any trustee[8]; and (4) make such further amendments of the provisions regulating the trust as the Charity Commission considers appropriate[9]. The Charity Commission must not exercise its powers under this provision in any case which it considers, by reason of any special question of law or of fact which it may involve, more fit to be adjudicated on by the court[10].

1 As to the Charity Commission see CHARITIES vol 8 (2015) PARA 543 et seq.
2 'Employee organisation' means any organisation appearing to the Charity Commission to represent in respect of its employment a substantial number of persons whose employers are licensed operators, or who are all employed by the same licensed operator: Coal Industry Act 1987 s 5(4) (substituted by the Coal Industry Act 1994 s 67(1), Sch 9 para 36(b); and amended by the Charities Act 2006 Sch 8 para 80). As to the meaning of 'licensed operator' see PARA 58.
3 Ie any trust for purposes which are exclusively charitable according to the law of England and Wales (1) which is a trust of property wholly or partly representing an application of money from the miners' welfare fund constituted under the Mining Industry Act 1920 s 20 (repealed) or the Coal Industry Social Welfare Organisation; (2) which is a trust expressed to be for the benefit of (a) persons currently or formerly employed in the coal industry or any class of such persons or their dependants; or (b) members of the mining community in general or of the mining community of a particular area, whether or not any other persons are also beneficiaries; or (3) under the terms of which all or a majority of the trustees are appointed by the body mentioned in head (1) or are appointed by the British Coal Corporation and an employee organisation: Coal Industry Act 1987 s 5(3). The British Coal Corporation was dissolved on 27 March 2004 ie the date appointed as the 'dissolution date' under the Coal Industry Act 1994 s 23 for the dissolution of the British Coal Corporation: see s 23(2); and the Coal Industry Act 1994 (Commencement No 7) and Dissolution of the British Coal Corporation Order 2004, SI 2004/144, art 3. As to the British Coal Corporation see PARAS 49–50. As to the dissolution of the British Coal Corporation see PARA 88. References to the Coal Industry Social Welfare Organisation include references to the trustees of the trust known as the Coal Industry Social Welfare Organisation: see the Coal Industry Act 1994 Sch 9 para 36(a). As to the transfer of the functions of the Coal Industry Social Welfare Organisation to that trust see PARA 86.
4 References to the trustees of a trust include references to the members of any body a function of which is to hold property subject to the trust or to perform any administrative functions in relation to the trust and, in relation to the members of such a body, references to the appointment of trustees are to be construed as references to any corresponding procedure under the provisions relating to the constitution of the body: Coal Industry Act 1987 s 5(5).
5 Coal Industry Act 1987 s 5(1). Where any functions relating to a trust are exercisable by more than one body of trustees, the Charity Commission may disregard or have regard only to the members of one of those bodies: s 5(6).
6 Coal Industry Act 1987 s 5(2)(a) (amended by the Charities Act 2006 Sch 8 para 80).
7 Coal Industry Act 1987 s 5(2)(b).
8 Coal Industry Act 1987 s 5(2)(c).
9 Coal Industry Act 1987 s 5(2)(d) (amended by the Charities Act 2006 Sch 8 para 80).

10   See the Coal Industry Act 1987 s 5(7) (amended by the Charities Act 2006 s 75(1), Sch 8, para 80; and the Charities Act 2011 s 354(1), Sch 7 Pt 2 para 47). As to the meaning of court see the Charities Act 2011 s 353(1); and CHARITIES vol 8 (2015) PARA 177. This does not affect any other powers exercisable by the Charity Commission or the High Court in relation to trusts to which this provision applies: Coal Industry Act 1987 s 5(9).

     The Charities Act 2011 ss 70(1), 71, 73(1)–(6), 74, 88 and 89 apply in relation to the powers of the Commission and the making of schemes under the Coal Industry Act 1987 s 5 as they apply in relation to its powers and the making of schemes under the Charities Act 2011; and ss 337, 339 apply to orders and decisions under this section as they apply to orders and decisions under the Coal Industry Act 1987 s 5: s 5(8) (s 5(8), (8A) substituted by the Charities Act 2011 Sch 7 Pt 2 para 47). The Commission must not proceed under the Charities Act 2011 s 73 (as applied by the Coal Industry Act 1987 s 5(8)) without the same application and notice to the trustees of the trust in question, as would be required if the Commission was proceeding under the Coal Industry Act 1987 s 5(1); but on any application made with a view to a scheme under 5(1) the Commission may proceed under s 5(1) or under the Charities Act 2011 s 73 (as so applied) as appears to it appropriate: Coal Industry Act 1987 s 5(8A) (as so substituted). The provisions of the Charities Act 2011 Pt 17 Ch 2, Sch 6 (appeals and applications to Tribunal) apply in relation to an order made under the Coal Industry Act 1987 s 5 as they apply in relation to an order made under Charities Act 2011 s 69(1): Coal Industry Act 1987 s 5(8B) (added by the Charities Act 2011 Sch 7 Pt 2 para 47). As to the settlement of schemes by the Charity Commission see CHARITIES vol 8 (2015) PARA 189 et seq.

E.    DISSOLUTION OF THE BRITISH COAL CORPORATION

## 88. Reduction in membership and dissolution of the British Coal Corporation.

As soon after the restructuring date[1] as it appeared to the Secretary of State[2] that it was no longer necessary for the British Coal Corporation[3] to continue to exist, he could by order dissolve it[4]. Such an order[5] dissolved the British Coal Corporation on 27 March 2004[6].

Before making such an order, the Secretary of State consulted the Corporation and the Coal Authority[7]. The following changes[8] were made to the membership of the Corporation:

(1)      the minimum number of members of the Corporation, in addition to the chairman, was reduced to one[9];

(2)      the statutory requirements[10] as to the persons from amongst whom the members were to be appointed ceased to have effect[11];

(3)      there was no requirement for a member of the Corporation to be appointed to act as its deputy chairman[12]; and

(4)      the Secretary of State could, if he considered it appropriate to do so in consequence of the coming into force of any provision of the Coal Industry Act 1994 or of any restructuring scheme[13], by notice in writing remove from office any member of the Corporation, including the chairman[14].

It is expressly provided that certain statutory provisions continue to have effect notwithstanding any repeal that came into force on 27 March 2004[15].

1   Ie 31 October 1994: see PARA 50.
2   As to the Secretary of State see PARA 2.
3   As to the British Coal Corporation see PARAS 49–50.
4   See the Coal Industry Act 1994 s 23(2).

     Any power to make an order under the Coal Industry Act 1994 s 23 was exercisable by statutory instrument; and an order dissolving the Corporation may not be amended or revoked by any order made on or after the dissolution date: s 23(7). As to the effect of the dissolution on the preparation of accounts and the final report relating to the carrying out of the Corporation's functions for the financial year see s 23(3).

5  Ie the Coal Industry Act 1994 (Commencement No 7) and Dissolution of the British Coal Corporation Order 2004, SI 2004/144.

6  Ie the date appointed as the 'dissolution date' under the Coal Industry Act 1994 s 23 for the dissolution of the British Coal Corporation: see s 23(2); and the Coal Industry Act 1994 (Commencement No 7) and Dissolution of the British Coal Corporation Order 2004, SI 2004/144, art 3. As to the British Coal Corporation see PARAS 49–50.

7  Coal Industry Act 1994 s 23(4). As to the Coal Authority see PARA 52 et seq.

8  The appointed day for this purpose was 30 June 1995: see the Coal Industry Act 1994 (Commencement No 6) and Membership of the British Coal Corporation (Appointed Day) Order 1995, SI 1995/1507, art 3.

9  Coal Industry Act 1994 s 23(1)(a).

10 Ie the Coal Industry Nationalisation Act 1946 s 2(3) (repealed); and the Coal Industry Act 1949 s 1(2) (repealed): see the Coal Industry Act 1994 s 23(1)(b).

11 Coal Industry Act 1994 s 23(1)(b).

12 Coal Industry Act 1994 s 23(1)(c).

13 As to restructuring schemes see PARA 72.

14 Coal Industry Act 1994 s 23(1)(d). Where any person ceases, by virtue of s 23, to be the chairman or a member of the Corporation before his term of office would otherwise have expired the Secretary of State must, with the consent of the Treasury, determine an amount to be paid to that person by way of compensation for loss of office; and any amount so determined must be paid to that person (1) in the case of loss of office by virtue of a notice under s 23(1)(d), by the Corporation; and (2) in the case of loss of office by virtue of the dissolution of the Corporation, by the Secretary of State out of money provided by Parliament: s 23(5). As to the Treasury see CONSTITUTIONAL AND ADMINISTRATIVE LAW vol 20 (2014) PARAS 262–265.

15 Without prejudice to the generality of the powers conferred by virtue of the Coal Industry Act 1994 s 12 (see PARA 72), where provision is made by any restructuring scheme for the transfer to any person of any liability of the Corporation under s 23(5) or under the Coal Industry Nationalisation Act 1946 s 2(6) (repealed) (salaries, pensions etc for members), the provision in question has effect subject to the transfer, and the transferred liability continues to have effect notwithstanding any repeal that comes into force on the dissolution date: Coal Industry Act 1994 s 23(6).

## (iv)  Licensing of Coal-mining Operations

### A.   IN GENERAL

## 89.   Coal-mining operations to be licensed.

Coal-mining operations[1] which (1) consist in the winning, working or getting (with or without other minerals[2]) of any coal[3], in the treatment of coal in the strata[4] for the purpose of winning any product of coal or in the winning, working or getting of any product of coal resulting from such treatment[5]; (2) are carried on in relation to coal in any part of Great Britain[6], in relation to coal under the territorial sea adjacent to Great Britain or in relation to coal in any designated area[7]; and (3) are neither carried on exclusively for the purpose of exploring for coal nor confined to the digging or carrying away of coal that it is necessary to dig or carry away[8] in the course of activities carried on for purposes which do not include the getting of coal or any product of coal[9], must not, at any time on or after the restructuring date[10], be carried on by any person except under and in accordance with a licence[11].

No such licence, however, is required for the carrying on of any coal-mining operations by or on behalf of the Crown[12].

1  As to the meaning of 'coal-mining operations' see PARA 51.

2  As to the meaning of 'minerals' see PARA 10.

3  As to the meaning of 'coal' see PARA 51.

4  As to the meaning of 'treatment of coal in the strata' see PARA 51.

5  Coal Industry Act 1994 s 25(2)(a).

6   As to the meaning of 'Great Britain' see PARA 48.

7   Coal Industry Act 1994 s 25(2)(b). As to the meaning of 'designated area' see PARA 66 (definition applied by s 25(5)).

8   The similar words 'necessary to be dug or carried away' appear in the Railways Clauses Consolidation Act 1845 s 77 and in an identical provision in the Railways Clauses Consolidation (Scotland) Act 1845 s 70 (the railway company is not entitled to any mines of coal, ironstone, slate or other minerals under any land purchased by it, except only such parts of them as are necessary to be dug or carried away or used in the construction of the works, unless they have been expressly purchased: see the Railways Clauses Consolidation Act 1845 s 77; and PARA 142) and have been judicially considered in that context: see *Nisbet Hamilton v North British Rly Co* (1886) 13 R 454, Ct of Sess (a railway company which had constructed a railway in a cutting was entitled not only to the stone down to the foundation level of the railway line but also, many years later when the stone sides of the cutting had become unsafe through weathering, to remove such stone as was from time to time necessary for the continued safety of the line). It appears that the company itself, acting bona fide, is the judge of what is 'necessary'; and that the only evidence required is the bona fide opinion of its surveyor, engineer or other officer: cf *Errington v Metropolitan District Rly Co* (1882) 19 ChD 559 at 571, CA, per Jessel MR. See also the Coal Act 1938 s 17(1), (3) (repealed); the Coal Industry Nationalisation Act 1946 s 36(1) (repealed); s 63(1) (definition of colliery concern) (prospectively repealed); and PARA 49. See also PARAS 142, 305.

9   Coal Industry Act 1994 s 25(2)(c).

10   Ie 31 October 1994: see PARA 50.

11   Coal Industry Act 1994 s 25(1). The licensing provisions are contained in Pt II (ss 25–36). Where a licence from the British Coal Corporation to work or get coal (ie under the Coal Industry Nationalisation Act 1946 s 36(2) (repealed); see PARA 49) was in force immediately before the restructuring date, and that licence authorised the carrying on of any coal-mining operations as mentioned in heads (1)–(3) in the text, the authorisation contained in that licence has effect on and after that date as an authorisation for the carrying on of those operations without a licence under the Coal Industry Act 1994 Pt II and, accordingly, so as to prevent the carrying on of any operations under and in accordance with that authorisation from constituting a contravention (as to the meaning of which see PARA 54) of s 25(1): s 25(3). Where any authorisation has effect in accordance with this provision, it has effect, except to the extent that a restructuring scheme otherwise provides, subject to the same conditions and to the same powers of revocation and other provisions for expiry and termination as, immediately before the restructuring date, applied to the licence under the Coal Industry Nationalisation Act 1946 s 36(2) (repealed); but as if the powers of the Corporation under that licence were powers of the Coal Authority: Coal Industry Act 1994 s 25(4). As to the Coal Authority see PARA 52 et seq. The repeal of the Coal Industry Nationalisation Act 1946 s 36 is without prejudice to so much of any licence under s 36 as has effect (with any modifications) as a contract between the person to whom it is granted and the British Coal Corporation or, as the case may be, any person to whom the Corporation's rights and liabilities under the licence are transferred in accordance with a restructuring scheme: Coal Industry Act 1994 s 67(7), Sch 10 para 6.

12   Coal Industry Act 1994 s 66(3). As to the application of the Coal Industry Act 1994 to the Crown see PARA 112.

## 90. Power to grant licences.

The Coal Authority[1] has the power to grant a licence[2]. However, where provision is made by any restructuring scheme[3] for any interest[4] or rights in or in relation to any coal[5] or coal mine[6] to be created in any person's favour or to be transferred to any person, and that person requires the interest or rights to enable him to continue, resume or begin the carrying on[7] of any coal-mining operations[8], the Coal Industry Act 1994 has effect as if the Secretary of State[9], as well as the Authority, was entitled, at any time before the coming into force of the scheme, to exercise the Authority's power to grant a licence to that person authorising the carrying on of those operations and, for that purpose, was entitled to act on the Authority's behalf in the exercise of any of its other powers[10].

Without prejudice to the Authority's power (subject to its statutory duties with respect to licensing[11], property[12] and safety[13]) to take into account all such factors as it thinks fit in determining whether, and subject to what conditions, to grant a licence, the factors that may be taken into account include, in particular, the terms on which the applicant, or any other applicant with respect to the same area, is offering to acquire from the Authority such an interest in land comprised in the area with respect to which the application is made, or such rights in relation to coal in that area, as, apart from the need for a licence would entitle him to carry on the coal-mining operations to which the application relates[14].

1  As to the Coal Authority see PARA 52 et seq.
2  Coal Industry Act 1994 s 26(1). As to the requirement for a licence see PARA 89. If or to the extent that a licence under the Coal Industry Act 1994 Pt II (ss 25–36) authorises coal-mining operations in relation to coal in Wales, it has effect only if the Welsh Ministers notify the Authority that they approve the authorisation: Coal Industry Act 1994 s 26A (added by the Wales Act 2017 s 67).
3  As to restructuring schemes see PARA 72.
4  As to the meaning of 'interest' see PARA 52.
5  As to the meaning of 'coal' see PARA 51.
6  As to the meaning of 'coal mine' see PARA 3.
7  Ie whether from the coming into force of the scheme or from some future time: see the Coal Industry Act 1994 s 26(6).
8  As to the meaning of 'coal-mining operations' see PARA 51.
9  As to the Secretary of State see PARA 2.
10 Coal Industry Act 1994 s 26(6). In practical terms, this power will come to be exercisable after the dissolution date: see PARA 88.
11 Ie under the Coal Industry Act 1994 s 2 (see PARA 58).
12 Ie under the Coal Industry Act 1994 s 3 (see PARA 59).
13 Ie under the Coal Industry Act 1994 s 4 (see PARA 60).
14 Coal Industry Act 1994 s 26(2), (5).

## 91. Publication of licensing arrangements.

The Coal Authority[1] is under a duty to publish, from time to time, such details as it thinks fit of the manner in which it proposes to exercise and perform its powers and duties in relation to the licensing of coal-mining operations[2], and the arrangements it has made for purposes connected with the exercise and performance of those powers and duties[3]. These arrangements[4] include any made with respect to the receipt and consideration, together with any application for a licence, of any application to the Authority for such interests[5] or rights in or in relation to land or other property as the applicant may wish to acquire from the Authority for purposes connected with the operations to which the application for the licence relates[6]. The Authority must also publish model provisions for inclusion in licences and have regard to the published provisions in determining what provision to incorporate in any such licence[7].

Anything so published must be published in such manner, and periodically given such further publicity, as appears to the Authority to be appropriate for securing that it is brought to the attention of persons who are likely from time to time to be interested[8].

1  As to the Coal Authority see PARA 52 et seq.
2  Coal Industry Act 1994 s 30(1)(a). The powers and duties referred to are those under ss 25–29: see s 30(1). As to the meaning of 'coal-mining operations' see PARA 51.
3  Coal Industry Act 1994 s 30(1)(b). As to the information published with respect to the fixing of fees for handling applications for licences see s 26(4); and PARA 92.
4  Ie the arrangements referred to in the Coal Industry Act 1994 s 30(1)(b): see s 30(2).
5  As to the meaning of 'interest' see PARA 52.
6  Coal Industry Act 1994 s 30(2).
7  Coal Industry Act 1994 s 30(3). This provision is without prejudice to the generality of s 30(1) or to the Authority's power to incorporate such provision as it may think fit in any licence (see s 28(1); and PARA 95): s 30(3). As to the conditions that may be contained in a licence see PARAS 95–96.
8  Coal Industry Act 1994 s 30(4).

## 92. Applications for a licence.

An application for a licence[1] may be made by any person who has acquired, or is proposing to acquire (whether from the Coal Authority[2] or some other person) (1) such an interest[3] in land comprised in the area with respect to which the application is made; or (2) such rights in relation to coal[4] in that area, as, apart from the need[5] for a licence, would entitle him to carry on the coal-mining operations[6] to which the application relates[7].

Where any area of Great Britain[8], the territorial sea adjacent to Great Britain or the continental shelf is one (a) interests or rights in which may be acquired (in addition to any such rights as may be contained in a licence) from the Authority; and (b) in relation to which the Authority considers that it is appropriate to do so, the Authority may issue specific or general invitations for applications or, as the case may be, further applications to be made in respect of that area for the grant of licences[9].

An applicant for a licence must pay to the Authority such fee (if any) in respect of its handling of that application as, having regard to the nature of the application and any information published under statutory requirement to do so[10] with respect to the fixing of the fees for handling applications, the Authority may reasonably require[11].

1  Ie a licence under the Coal Industry Act 1994 Pt II (ss 25–36): see s 26(2).
2  As to the Coal Authority see PARA 52 et seq.
3  As to the meaning of 'interest' see PARA 52.
4  As to the meaning of 'coal' see PARA 51.
5  See the Coal Industry Act 1994 s 25(1); and PARA 89.
6  As to the meaning of 'coal-mining operations' see PARA 51.
7  Coal Industry Act 1994 s 26(2).
8  As to the meaning of 'Great Britain' see PARA 48.
9  Coal Industry Act 1994 s 26(3).
10  Ie under the Coal Industry Act 1994 s 30 (see PARA 91): see s 26(4).
11  Coal Industry Act 1994 s 26(4). The Coal Authority publishes from time to time a scale of such fees, details of which are available from its principal office: see PARA 52.

## 93. Authorisation contained in a licence.

The provisions of a licence[1] must specify or describe the coal-mining operations[2] which, subject to its conditions, are authorised by the licence[3]. The provisions included must identify the area of Great Britain[4], the territorial sea adjacent to Great Britain or the continental shelf where the operations are to be carried on[5], and may restrict the authorisation contained in the licence to operations carried on within a specified period or a period determined in a specified manner[6].

A licence may provide for the coming into force of the authorisation contained in it, or of any conditions or other provisions of it, to be postponed until after the acquisition by the holder[7] of the licence of any interest[8] or right in or in relation to any land or other property or until after such other specified requirements have been satisfied[9]. It may also provide for the licence to lapse if the interest or right is not acquired, or the other requirements are not satisfied, within a specified period[10].

The persons who, so long as the authorisation remains in force, are authorised to carry on the operations to which a licence relates are the holder of the licence and such other persons as may be authorised by the licence or, without any contravention[11] of the conditions of the licence, by the holder of the licence to carry on those operations on his behalf[12]. A licence may contain provision which,

in such cases, in such manner and subject to such conditions or consents as may
be specified in the licence, authorises the transfer of any person's rights and
obligations as holder of the licence to another person[13]. Particulars of every such
transfer must be registered with the Coal Authority[14].

1  Ie a licence under the Coal Industry Act 1994 Pt II (ss 25–36): see s 27(1).
2  As to the meaning of 'coal-mining operations' see PARA 51.
3  Coal Industry Act 1994 s 27(1).
4  As to the meaning of 'Great Britain' see PARA 48.
5  This may include restrictions as to the depth at which any operations are to be carried on: see the
   Coal Industry Act 1994 s 27(2).
6  Coal Industry Act 1994 s 27(2).
7  'Holder', in relation to a licence under the Coal Industry Act 1994 Pt II, means (whether or not the
   authorisation contained in the licence remains in force): (1) in a case where there has been no such
   transfer in relation to that licence as is mentioned in s 27(5)), the person to whom the licence was
   granted; and (2) in any other case, the person to whom the rights and obligations of the holder of
   that licence were last transferred: s 65(1).
8  As to the meaning of 'interest' see PARA 52.
9  Coal Industry Act 1994 s 27(3)(a).
10  Coal Industry Act 1994 s 27(3)(b).
11  As to the meaning of 'contravention' see PARA 54.
12  Coal Industry Act 1994 s 27(4). In the case of any licensed operator who is entitled to withdraw
   support from any land, the rights comprised in his entitlement are also exercisable by any person
   authorised as mentioned in s 27(4) to act on his behalf in the carrying on of any of the operations
   which the operator is authorised to carry on: see s 38(4); and PARA 176. As to the meaning of
   'licensed operator' see PARA 58.
13  Coal Industry Act 1994 s 27(5).
14  See the Coal Industry Act 1994 s 35(1)(c); and PARA 105. As to the Coal Authority see PARA 52
   et seq.

## 94.  Modification of a licence.

Conditions included in a licence[1] may contain provision for the authorisation[2]
contained in it, and any of the licence conditions[3] to cease to have effect, or to be
revoked or otherwise modified, at such times, in such manner and in such
circumstances as may be specified in or determined under the conditions[4]. In
addition, without prejudice to any condition contained in a licence, the conditions
and other provisions may be modified by the Coal Authority[5] with the agreement
of the holder of the licence[6].

1  Ie a licence under the Coal Industry Act 1994 Pt II (ss 25–36): see s 28(7).
2  See PARA 93.
3  Ie apart from any conditions included by virtue of the Coal Industry Act 1994 s 28(7): see s 28(7).
4  Coal Industry Act 1994 s 28(7).
5  As to the Coal Authority see PARA 52 et seq.
6  Coal Industry Act 1994 s 27(6). As to the meaning of 'holder' see PARA 93.

## 95.  Conditions of a licence.

A licence[1] may include such conditions as the Coal Authority[2], subject to its
having regard to its statutory duties with respect to licensing[3], property[4] and
safety[5] and to certain statutory provisions[6], may think fit[7].

Conditions included in a licence may contain provision requiring its holder[8] to
render to the Authority (1) payments on the grant or coming into force of the
licence[9]; and (2) payments while the licence is in force[10]. Such conditions may
contain provision requiring the holder of the licence to secure that agreements for
such purposes as may be specified in the conditions are entered into between the
holder of the licence and any other specified persons[11], and that the terms of those
agreements satisfy any specified requirements[12]. Conditions included in a licence

may also contain provision requiring the holder of the licence to comply with any direction given by the Authority as to matters specified in the licence[13].

Conditions included in a licence may contain provision for disputes between the Authority and the holder of the licence as to any matter to which the licence relates to be referred to the determination of such persons as may be specified in, or appointed in accordance with, the conditions[14]. Any dispute to which any such provision applies is to be determined accordingly[15].

Conditions may provide for the authorisation contained in the licence or any of its conditions to cease to have effect, or to be revoked or otherwise modified[16]. They may also provide for obligations imposed on any person by the conditions of the licence, and liabilities arising in respect of contraventions[17] by any person of those conditions, to continue in accordance with the licence provisions, and to be capable of arising, after the authorisation contained in the licence has been revoked or is otherwise no longer in force or, where they have already arisen, to continue after the holder's rights and obligations have been transferred to another person[18].

The Coal Authority, as a matter of practice, requires licensed operators[19] to enter into an agreement, the purpose of which is to regulate relationships between licensed operators whose respective mines interact, or have the potential to interact, with one another.

1  Ie a licence under the Coal Industry Act 1994 Pt II (ss 25–36): see s 28(1).
2  As to the Coal Authority see PARA 52 et seq.
3  Ie under the Coal Industry Act 1994 s 2 (see PARA 58).
4  Ie under the Coal Industry Act 1994 s 3 (see PARA 59).
5  Ie under the Coal Industry Act 1994 s 4 (see PARA 60).
6  Ie the Coal Industry Act 1994 ss 29–68: see s 28(1).
7  Coal Industry Act 1994 s 28(1). Sections 28(2)–(8), 29 (see PARA 96) are without prejudice to the generality of s 28(1): s 28(9). The conditions that may be included in a licence with respect to the carrying on of the coal-mining operations authorised by the licence include conditions having effect in relation to the carrying on, in association with those operations, of:
    (1)    coal-mining operations for which no authorisation is required (s 28(2)(a));
    (2)    coal-mining operations the authorisation for which is contained in another licence or is conferred by virtue of s 25(3) (see PARA 89) (s 28(2)(b)); or
    (3)    any activities carried on for purposes connected with any coal-mining operations to which the conditions relate (s 28(2)(c)).
    As to the meaning of 'coal-mining operations' see PARA 51.
8  As to the meaning of 'holder' see PARA 93.
9  Coal Industry Act 1994 s 28(3)(a).
10  Coal Industry Act 1994 s 28(3)(b). The Coal Authority publishes scales of such payments which are revised from time to time.
11  Coal Industry Act 1994 s 28(4)(a).
12  Coal Industry Act 1994 s 28(4)(b).
13  Coal Industry Act 1994 s 28(5).
14  Coal Industry Act 1994 s 28(6).
15  Coal Industry Act 1994 s 28(6).
16  See the Coal Industry Act 1994 s 28(7); and PARA 94.
17  As to the meaning of 'contravention' see PARA 54.
18  Coal Industry Act 1994 s 28(8).
19  As to the meaning of 'licensed operator' see PARA 58.

## 96. Conditions for the provision of security.

A licence[1] may include conditions which require the holder[2] of it to provide such security as may be so determined for his performance of any of the obligations to which he is or may become subject, either in accordance with the licence itself or otherwise by virtue of being the holder of it at any time[3]. Such security may be required, on or before the coming into force of the authorisation contained in the licence and at such subsequent times as may be determined by or under the conditions[4]. The licence may also include conditions which require the licence holder, for the purposes of that security and in relation to any property or rights in which it consists, to take such steps for or in connection with the establishment and maintenance of any trust or other arrangements as may be so determined[5].

Where such security for the performance of any person's obligations has been so provided[6] and any trust or other arrangements which have been established and maintained for the purposes of that security have been registered[7], certain restrictions apply as to the manner in which, and the purposes for which, that security and any property or rights in which it consists are to be applied and enforceable[8].

1   Ie a licence under the Coal Industry Act 1994 Pt II (ss 25–36): see s 29(1).
2   As to the meaning of 'holder' see PARA 93.
3   Coal Industry Act 1994 s 29(1)(a).
4   See the Coal Industry Act 1994 s 29(1).
5   Coal Industry Act 1994 s 29(1)(b).
6   Ie in accordance with any condition included by virtue of the Coal Industry Act 1994 s 29(1) in the licence: see s 29(2).
7   Ie under the Coal Industry Act 1994 s 35(1)(f) (see PARA 105): see s 29(2).
8   See Coal Industry Act 1994 s 29(2). The manner in which, and the purposes for which, that security and any property or rights in which it consists are to be applied and enforceable (whether in the event of that person's insolvency or otherwise) are to be determined in accordance with the trust or other arrangements and without regard to so much of the Insolvency Act 1986 or any other enactment or rule of law as, in its operation in relation to that person or any conduct of his, would prevent or restrict their being applied in accordance with the trust or other arrangements or would prevent or restrict their enforcement for the purpose of being so applied: s 29(2). As to the insolvency of licensed operators see PARA 98. As to insolvency generally see BANKRUPTCY AND INDIVIDUAL INSOLVENCY; COMPANY AND PARTNERSHIP INSOLVENCY.

**97.   Liability for inaccurate information furnished to the Coal Authority.**
Where the conditions of a licence[1] contain provisions stating (1) that information of a specified description which is furnished to the Coal Authority[2] in pursuance of the conditions of the licence may be disclosed by the Authority for specified purposes in pursuance of arrangements[3] for making information available[4]; and (2) that any information of that description that is disclosed by the Authority for any of those purposes is to be treated as information whose accuracy the operator has undertaken to secure[5], the following provisions apply.

The licensed operator[6] owes a duty to the Authority and to every person likely to be affected by any inaccuracy in information disclosed by the Authority for any of the specified purposes to exercise all due diligence to secure: (a) that the Authority is furnished, in accordance with the conditions of the licence, with all the information of the specified descriptions which the operator is required by those conditions to furnish to the Authority[7]; and (b) that the information of those descriptions which is furnished by the operator to the Authority is accurate in every material particular[8]. Where such a duty is owed by any person to another person, any breach of that duty which causes that other person to sustain loss or damage is actionable against the person in breach at the suit or instance of the other person[9]. However, a person is not liable for any breach of such a duty except (i) in respect of a disclosure of information made by the Authority for a specified purpose[10]; and (ii) to the Authority or the person to whom the disclosure was made[11].

These provisions are without prejudice to the liability of any person for breach of the duty to comply with an enforcement order[12].

1   Ie a licence under the Coal Industry Act 1994 Pt II (ss 25–36): see s 58(1). As to the conditions that may be contained in a licence see PARAS 95–96.
2   As to the Coal Authority see PARA 52 et seq.
3   Ie under the Coal Industry Act 1994 s 57 (see PARA 107): see s 58(1)(a).
4   Coal Industry Act 1994 s 58(1)(a).
5   Coal Industry Act 1994 s 58(1)(b).
6   As to the meaning of 'licensed operator' see PARA 58.
7   Coal Industry Act 1994 s 58(2)(a).
8   Coal Industry Act 1994 s 58(2)(b).
9   Coal Industry Act 1994 s 58(3).
10  Coal Industry Act 1994 s 58(4)(a).
11  Coal Industry Act 1994 s 58(4)(b).
12  Coal Industry Act 1994 s 58(5). As to enforcement orders under Pt II see PARA 99 et seq.

## 98.  Insolvency of licensed operators.

In general, a licence[1] and the obligations arising out of or incidental to it are not to be treated as property for the purposes of the Insolvency Act 1986[2]. However, where a licence authorises[3] the official receiver[4] or any person who is for the time being acting as an insolvency practitioner[5] in relation to the holder[6] of the licence to carry on any of the coal-mining operations[7] to which the licence relates or to transfer the rights and obligations of the holder of the licence to another person, he may do so[8].

Where, in the case of the winding up of a company which is or has been a licensed operator[9], the liquidator or official receiver sends certain documents or notices[10] to the registrar of companies[11], he must also send a copy to the Coal Authority[12].

In the case of any company which is either the holder of a licence[13], or a licensed operator[14], the Authority is included in the persons who are entitled to make certain applications[15] to cancel or defer the dissolution of a company[16].

1   Ie a licence under the Coal Industry Act 1994 Pt II (ss 25–36): see s 36(1).
2   As to insolvency generally see BANKRUPTCY AND INDIVIDUAL INSOLVENCY; COMPANY AND PARTNERSHIP INSOLVENCY.
3   Ie by virtue of the Coal Industry Act 1994 s 27(4) or s 27(5) (see PARA 93): see s 36(1).
4   As to the official receiver see BANKRUPTCY AND INDIVIDUAL INSOLVENCY vol 5 (2013) PARA 35 et seq; COMPANY AND PARTNERSHIP INSOLVENCY vol 16 (2017) PARA 416 et seq.
5   This reference to a person's acting as an insolvency practitioner is to be construed in accordance with the Insolvency Act 1986 s 388 (see BANKRUPTCY AND INDIVIDUAL INSOLVENCY vol 5 (2013) PARA 314; COMPANY AND PARTNERSHIP INSOLVENCY vol 16 (2017) PARA 10): Coal Industry Act 1994 s 36(7).
6   As to the meaning of 'holder' see PARA 93.
7   As to the meaning of 'coal-mining operations' see PARA 51.
8   Coal Industry Act 1994 s 36(1).
9   As to the meaning of 'licensed operator' see PARA 58.
10  The documents or notices referred to are:
    (1)    any such account or return as is mentioned in the Insolvency Act 1986 s 94(3) or s 106(3) (account of the winding up and return of final meeting or meetings) (Coal Industry Act 1994 s 36(2)(a));
    (2)    any notice for the purposes of the Insolvency Act 1986 s 172(8) (notice of final meeting and of its decisions) (Coal Industry Act 1994 s 36(2)(b));
    (3)    an application under the Insolvency Act 1986 s 202(2) (applications for early dissolution) (Coal Industry Act 1994 s 36(2)(c));
    (4)    a copy of such an order for dissolution of the company as is mentioned in the Insolvency Act 1986 s 204(4) (order for early dissolution in Scotland) (Coal Industry Act 1994 s 36(2)(d)); or

(5)    such a notice as is mentioned in the Insolvency Act 1986 s 205(1)(b) (notice that winding up complete) (Coal Industry Act 1994 s 36(2)(e)).

11 'Registrar of companies' has the same meaning as in the Companies Acts (see the Companies Act 2006 s 1060; and COMPANIES vol 14 (2016) PARA 126): Coal Industry Act 1994 s 36(7) (amended by SI 2009/1941).

12 Coal Industry Act 1994 s 36(2). Where the administrator of a company who has been a licensed operator files a notice with the registrar under the Insolvency Act 1986 s 8, Sch B1 para 84(1) (Sch B1 added by the Enterprise Act 2002 s 8, Sch 16) (see COMPANY AND PARTNERSHIP INSOLVENCY vol 16 (2017) PARA 283) he must at the same time send a copy to the Authority: Coal Industry Act 1994 s 36(2A) (added by the Enterprise Act 2002 s 248(3), Sch 17 para 48(1), (2)). A liquidator or administrator who contravenes the Coal Industry Act 1994 s 36(2) or s 36(2A) is guilty of an offence and liable, on summary conviction, to a fine not exceeding level 3 on the standard scale: s 36(3) (amended by the Enterprise Act 2002 Sch 17 para 38(1), (3)(a), (b)). However, it is a defence for that person to show that at the time of the contravention he did not know and had no grounds for suspecting that the company in question had ever been a licensed operator: s 36(4). As to the meaning of 'contravention' see PARA 54. As to the standard scale see SENTENCING vol 92 (2015) PARA 176.

13 Ie under the Coal Industry Act 1994 Pt II: see s 36(5)(a).

14 Ie by virtue of the Coal Industry Act 1994 s 25(3) (see PARA 89): see s 36(5)(b).

15 Ie under the Companies Act 2006 s 1029 (application to court for restoration to the register) (see COMPANIES vol 15A (2016) PARA 1718) (application to cancel the dissolution of a company) or under the Insolvency Act 1986 ss 201(3), 202(5), 204(5) or s 205(3) or s 205(5) (applications in the case of a winding up for the deferment of a company's dissolution): Coal Industry Act 1994 s 36(5) (amended by SI 2009/1941).

16 Coal Industry Act 1994 s 36(5).

B.    ENFORCEMENT OF LICENCE CONDITIONS

## 99. Power of the Coal Authority to make enforcement orders.

An enforcement order may be either final or provisional[1]. An enforcement order requires the person to whom it relates (according to the circumstances of the case) to do, or not to do, such things as are specified in the order[2]. It takes effect at such time, being the earliest practicable time, as is determined by or under the order[3], and may be revoked at any time by the Coal Authority[4].

Where the Authority is satisfied (1) that any person is carrying on, or is likely to carry on, any coal-mining operations[5] in contravention[6] of the statutory requirement for such operations to be carried on under and in accordance with a licence[7]; or (2) that any person is contravening, or is likely to contravene, any of the conditions of a licence[8], the Authority may make a final enforcement order to secure that there is no such contravention of that statutory requirement or, as the case may be, that the condition is complied with[9].

Where (a) it appears to the Authority that any person is carrying on, or is likely to carry on, any coal-mining operations in contravention of the statutory requirement for such operations to be carried on under and in accordance with a licence, or that any person is contravening, or is likely to contravene, any of the conditions of a licence[10]; and (b) it appears to the Authority that it is appropriate that a provisional enforcement order be made, the Authority may, instead of taking steps towards the making of a final enforcement order, by a provisional enforcement order make such provision in relation to the person in question as appears to it requisite for the purpose of securing that there is no such contravention of the statutory requirement to carry out coal-mining operations in accordance with a licence or, as the case may be, that the condition is complied with[11]. In determining whether it is appropriate that a provisional enforcement order be made, the Authority must have regard, in particular, to the extent to which any person is likely to sustain loss or damage in consequence of anything which, in contravention of the statutory requirement for such operations to be carried on under and in accordance with a licence[12] or the condition in question, is likely to be done, or omitted to be done, before a final enforcement order may be made[13].

Where a provisional enforcement order has been made, the Authority must consider whether, for the purpose of giving it final effect, it should be confirmed[14]. The Authority is entitled to confirm it, with or without modifications[15], if: (i) it is satisfied that the person to whom the order relates is carrying on, or is likely to carry on, any coal-mining operations in contravention of the statutory requirement to carry out coal-mining operations in accordance with a licence, or is contravening, or is likely to contravene, any of the licence conditions[16]; and (ii) the provision made by the order (with any modifications) is requisite for the purpose of securing that there is no contravention of the statutory requirement to carry out coal-mining operations in accordance with a licence or, as the case may be, that that condition is complied with[17].

The Authority may not make a final enforcement order or make or confirm a provisional enforcement order in relation to any person if it is satisfied that that person has agreed to take, and is taking, all such steps as it appears to the Authority for the time being to be appropriate for him to take for the purpose of securing that there is no contravention of the statutory requirement to carry out coal-mining operations in accordance with a licence, or that the condition in question is complied with[18]. Nor may the Authority make a final enforcement order or make or confirm a provisional enforcement order if it is satisfied that the contravention of the statutory requirement to carry out coal-mining operations in accordance with a licence, or the contravention of that condition is of a trivial nature[19].

The power to make an enforcement order does not prejudice the right of the Authority, where any sum is due to it under any condition in a licence, to enforce that condition in proceedings to recover that sum as an amount due to the Authority by virtue of an enactment[20].

1   'Enforcement order' means a final enforcement order or a provisional enforcement order; 'final enforcement order' means an order under the Coal Industry Act 1994 s 31 other than a provisional enforcement order; and 'provisional enforcement order' means an order under s 31 which, if not previously confirmed for the purpose of giving it final effect (see s 31(4)), will cease to have effect at the end of such period (not exceeding three months) as is determined by or under the order: s 31(7).
    The main practical differences between a provisional order and a final order are that the procedural requirements of giving notice and of specifying the period for the consideration of representations and objections (see s 32; and PARA 101) which apply to a final order do not apply to a provisional order. Also, a provisional order has effect only for a limited period and ceases to have effect at the end of the period (not exceeding three months) specified in the order (see s 31(7)). The Coal Authority must, in considering whether to make a provisional or a final order, have regard in particular to the extent to which any person is likely to sustain loss or damage in consequence of the unlicensed mining or, as the case may be, the breach of a particular licence condition (see s 31(3)). It is therefore suggested that a provisional order will be appropriate where the Authority considers it necessary to act quickly, whether to avoid such loss or damage, or for some other reason. As to the Coal Authority see PARA 52 et seq.
2   Coal Industry Act 1994 s 31(6)(a).
3   Coal Industry Act 1994 s 31(6)(b).
4   Coal Industry Act 1994 s 31(6)(c). As to the procedural requirements for revoking enforcement orders see PARA 102.
5   As to the meaning of 'coal-mining operations' see PARA 51.
6   As to the meaning of 'contravention' see PARA 54.
7   See the Coal Industry Act 1994 s 25(1); and PARA 89.
8   Ie under the Coal Industry Act 1994 Pt II (ss 25–36): see s 31(1). As to the conditions that may be

contained in a licence see PARAS 95–96.

9   Coal Industry Act 1994 s 31(1). This provision is subject to ss 31(2), (5), 32: see s 31(1).
10  See the Coal Industry Act 1994 s 31(1).
11  Coal Industry Act 1994 s 31(2). This provision is subject to s 31(5): see s 31(2).
12  See the Coal Industry Act 1994 s 25(1); and PARA 89.
13  Coal Industry Act 1994 s 31(3).
14  Coal Industry Act 1994 s 31(4).
15  As to the meaning of 'modifications' see PARA 51.
16  Coal Industry Act 1994 s 31(4)(a).
17  Coal Industry Act 1994 s 31(4)(b).
18  Coal Industry Act 1994 s 31(5)(a).
19  Coal Industry Act 1994 s 31(5)(b).
20  Coal Industry Act 1994 s 31(8). Sections 32, 33 (see PARAS 101–104) are also without prejudice
    to this right: see s 31(8).

## 100. Coal Authority's power to require information for the purposes of enforcement.

Where it appears to the Coal Authority[1] that there is, or may have been, a contravention[2] of the statutory requirement to carry out coal-mining operations[3] in accordance with a licence[4], or that any person is contravening, or may have contravened, any condition of a licence, the Authority may, for any purpose connected with its relevant enforcement functions[5], serve a notice[6] on any person[7]. The notice either (1) requires the person on whom it is served[8] to produce, at a specified time and place, to the Authority or to any person appointed by the Authority, any documents which are specified in the notice and are in that person's possession or under his control[9]; or (2) requires that person, if he is carrying on a business[10], to furnish the Authority, at a specified time and place and in a specified form and manner, with such information as may be specified in the notice[11]. However, no person is required to produce any documents which he could not be compelled to produce in civil proceedings in the court or, in complying with any requirement for the furnishing of information, to disclose any information which he could not be compelled to give in evidence in any such proceedings[12].

A person who, without reasonable excuse[13], fails to do anything required of him by such a notice is guilty of an offence and liable, on summary conviction, to a fine not exceeding level 5 on the standard scale[14]. A person who intentionally alters, suppresses or destroys any document which he has been required by notice to produce is guilty of an offence and liable on summary conviction, to a fine not exceeding the statutory maximum[15]; and on conviction on indictment, to a fine[16]. Proceedings for such offences are to be instituted in England and Wales only by, or on behalf of, the Coal Authority or the Director of Public Prosecutions[17].

If a person defaults in complying with such a notice, the court[18] may, on the application of the Authority, make such order as it thinks fit for requiring the default to be made good; and any such order may provide that all the costs of the application are to be borne by the person in default or by any officers of a company[19] or other association who are responsible for its default[20].

1   As to the Coal Authority see PARA 52 et seq.
2   As to the meaning of 'contravention' see PARA 54.
3   As to the meaning of 'coal-mining operations' see PARA 51.
4   See the Coal Industry Act 1994 s 25(1); and PARA 89. The licence referred to is a licence under Pt
    II (ss 25–36): see s 34(1).
5   Ie under the Coal Industry Act 1994 s 31 (see PARA 99): see s 34(1).
6   Ie under the Coal Industry Act 1994 s 34(2): see s 34(1).
7   Coal Industry Act 1994 s 34(1).

8   As to the service of documents see PARA 110.
9   Coal Industry Act 1994 s 34(2)(a). As to the disclosure of documents in a party's possession see CIVIL PROCEDURE vol 12 (2015) PARAS 621–628.
10   As to the meaning of 'business' see PARA 49.
11   Coal Industry Act 1994 s 34(2)(b).
12   Coal Industry Act 1994 s 34(3).
13   What amounts to 'reasonable excuse' is largely a matter of fact: *Leck v Epsom RDC* [1922] 1 KB 383. However, ignorance of the statutory provisions provides no reasonable excuse (*Aldridge v Warwickshire Coal Co Ltd* (1925) 133 LT 439, CA), nor does a mistaken view of those provisions (*R v Philip Reid* [1973] 3 All ER 1020, [1973] 1 WLR 1283, CA). Quaere whether reliance on the advice of an expert can amount to reasonable excuse: see *Saddleworth UDC v Aggregate and Sand Ltd* (1970) 69 LGR 103.
14   Coal Industry Act 1994 s 34(4). As to the standard scale see SENTENCING vol 92 (2015) PARA 176.
15   Coal Industry Act 1994 s 34(5)(a). As to the statutory maximum see SENTENCING vol 92 (2015) PARA 176.
16   Coal Industry Act 1994 s 34(5)(b).
17   Coal Industry Act 1994 s 34(7).
18   As to the meaning of 'the court' see PARA 103.
19   As to the meaning of 'company' see PARA 72.
20   Coal Industry Act 1994 s 34(6).

## 101. Notice requirements for enforcement orders.

Before making a final enforcement order[1] or confirming a provisional enforcement order[2], the Coal Authority[3] must give notice[4] to the person to whom the order relates and must consider any representations or objections which are made and not withdrawn[5]. The notice must state that the Authority proposes to make or confirm the order and set out its effect[6]. It must also set out:

(1)     any condition of the licence[7] for the purpose of securing compliance with which the order is to be made or confirmed[8];

(2)     the acts or omissions which, in the Authority's opinion, constitute or would constitute contraventions of the statutory requirement to carry out coal-mining operations[9] in accordance with a licence[10] or, as the case may be, that condition[11]; and

(3)     any other matters which, in the Authority's opinion, justify the making or confirmation of the order[12].

The notice must specify the period (which must not be less than 28 days from the date of the service) within which representations or objections with respect to the proposed order or proposed confirmation may be made[13].

The Authority, having given notice, may not make a final enforcement order with modifications[14] that are not contained in the notice or confirm a provisional enforcement order with any such modifications, unless the person to whom the order relates has consented to the modifications, or the Authority has complied with certain requirements[15].

As soon as practicable after making a final enforcement order or making or confirming a provisional enforcement order, the Authority must serve a copy of the order or, as the case may be, of the order as confirmed, on the person to whom it relates[16], and take such steps (if any) for publishing notice of the order and, where the case so requires, of its confirmation and any modifications subject to which it is confirmed as the Authority considers appropriate to bring the matters in the notice to the attention of persons likely to be affected by them[17].

1   As to the meaning of 'final enforcement order' see PARA 99.
2   As to the meaning of 'provisional enforcement order' see PARA 99.
3   As to the Coal Authority see PARA 52 et seq.

4   The notice is given by serving it, together with a copy of the proposed order (or in the case of the confirmation of a provisional order, a copy of the order as proposed to be confirmed) on the person to whom the order relates (Coal Industry Act 1994 s 32(2)(a)), and by taking such steps (if any) for publishing a copy of the notice as the Authority considers appropriate for the purpose of bringing the matters to which the notice relates to the attention of persons likely to be affected by them and of enabling them to make representations and objections within the period specified in the notice (s 32(2)(b)). As to the service of documents see PARA 110.
5   See the Coal Industry Act 1994 s 32(1).
6   Coal Industry Act 1994 s 32(1)(a).
7   As to the conditions that may be contained in a licence see PARAS 95–96.
8   Coal Industry Act 1994 s 32(1)(b)(i).
9   As to the meaning of 'coal-mining operations' see PARA 51.
10  See the Coal Industry Act 1994 s 25(1); and PARA 89.
11  Coal Industry Act 1994 s 32(1)(b)(ii).
12  Coal Industry Act 1994 s 32(1)(b)(iii).
13  Coal Industry Act 1994 s 32(1)(c).
14  As to the meaning of 'modifications' see PARA 51.
15  See the Coal Industry Act 1994 s 32(3). The requirements referred to in the text are as follows. The Authority must:
    (1)   serve on the person to whom the order relates such notice as appears to it requisite of its proposal to make or confirm the order with modifications (s 32(4)(a));
    (2)   in that notice specify the period (not being less than 28 days from the date of its service on the person to whom the order relates) within which representations or objections with respect to the proposed modifications may be made (s 32(4)(b));
    (3)   take such steps (if any) for publishing a copy of the notice as it considers appropriate for the purpose of bringing the proposal to the attention of persons likely to be affected by it and of enabling them to make representations and objections within the period specified in the notice (s 32(4)(c)); and
    (4)   consider any representations or objections which are duly made and not withdrawn (s 32(4)(d)).
16  Coal Industry Act 1994 s 32(5)(a).
17  Coal Industry Act 1994 s 32(5)(b).

## 102.   Revocation of enforcement orders.

The Coal Authority[1] may revoke an enforcement order at any time[2]. Before revoking an enforcement order, other than an unconfirmed provisional enforcement order[3], the Authority must give notice[4] stating that it proposes to revoke the order and setting out the effect of the order; and specifying the period (not being less than 28 days from the date of the service) within which representations or objections with respect to the proposed revocation may be made[5]. Before revoking the order, the Authority must also consider any representations or objections which are duly made and not withdrawn[6]. If, after giving the notice, the Authority decides not to revoke the order, it must give notice of its decision[7].

1   As to the Coal Authority see PARA 52 et seq.
2   Coal Industry Act 1994 s 31(6)(c). As to the meaning of 'enforcement order' see PARA 99.
3   As to the meaning of 'provisional enforcement order' see PARA 99.
4   Notice is given (1) by serving it on the person to whom the order relates (Coal Industry Act 1994 s 32(8)(a)); and (2) by taking such steps (if any) for publishing a copy of the notice as the Authority considers appropriate for the purpose of bringing the matters contained in the notice to the attention of persons likely to be affected by them and, in the case of a notice under s 32(6), of enabling them to make representations and objections within the period specified in the notice (s 32(8)(b)). As to the service of documents see PARA 110.
5   Coal Industry Act 1994 s 32(6).
6   Coal Industry Act 1994 s 32(6).
7   Coal Industry Act 1994 s 32(7).

## 103. Validity of enforcement orders.

Any person to whom an enforcement order[1] relates who is aggrieved[2] by the order and desires to question its validity on the ground that its making or confirmation was not within the statutory powers of the Coal Authority[3], or that any of the procedural requirements were not complied with in relation to it[4], may make an application to the court[5] within the specified time limit[6]. On any such application the court may, if satisfied that the making or confirmation of the order was not within those powers or that the interests of the applicant were substantially[7] prejudiced by a failure to comply with those requirements, quash the order or any provision of the order[8].

1   As to the meaning of 'enforcement order' see PARA 99.
2   As to persons aggrieved see CONSTITUTIONAL AND ADMINISTRATIVE LAW vol 20 (2014) PARA 634.
3   Ie within the powers conferred by the Coal Industry Act 1994 s 31 (see PARA 99): see s 33(1). As to the Coal Authority see PARA 52 et seq.
4   Ie the requirements of the Coal Industry Act 1994 s 32 (see PARAS 101–102): see s 33(1).
5   For these purposes, 'the court' means the High Court in relation to England and Wales and the Court of Session in relation to Scotland: Coal Industry Act 1994 s 33(8).
6   Coal Industry Act 1994 s 33(1). The validity of an enforcement order may not be questioned by any legal proceedings whatever, except as provided by s 33: s 33(3). The specified time limit is 42 days from the date of service of a copy of the order or, as the case may be, of the order as confirmed: s 33(1). As to the time within which an act must be done see TIME vol 97 (2015) PARA 336 et seq. As to challenges to the validity of orders under the Town and Country Planning Act 1990 s 288 see PLANNING vol 82 (2018) PARAS 1011, 1012.
7   'Substantial' has been held to mean 'considerable': see *Palser v Grinling* [1948] AC 291 at 317, [1948] 1 All ER 1 at 11, HL, per Viscount Simon; applied in *Atkinson v Bettison* [1955] 3 All ER 340 [1955] 1 WLR 1127, CA. 'Substantial' is a question of degree and therefore one of fact (*King Features Syndicate Inc v O and M Kleeman Ltd* [1941] AC 417, [1941] 2 All ER 403, HL; *Atkinson v Bettison*) and may be used in contradistinction to 'trivial and not worth consideration' (*Langham v City of London Corpn* [1949] 1 KB 208 at 213, [1948] 2 All ER 1018 at 1020, CA, per Birkett J).
8   Coal Industry Act 1994 s 33(2).

## 104. Effect of enforcement orders.

The obligation to comply with an enforcement order[1] is a duty owed to any person who may be affected by a contravention[2] of the order[3]. Any breach of this duty which causes the person to whom it is owed to sustain loss or damage is actionable against the person in breach at the suit or instance of that other person[4]. In any such proceedings it is a defence for the person by whom the duty is owed to show that he took all reasonable steps and exercised all due diligence[5] to avoid the contravention of the order[6].

Compliance with any enforcement order is enforceable by civil proceedings by the Coal Authority for an injunction or for any other appropriate relief[7]. This does not affect any right which any person to whom the duty to comply with an enforcement order is owed may have to bring civil proceedings in respect of any contravention or apprehended contravention of the order[8].

1   As to the meaning of 'enforcement order' see PARA 99.
2   As to the meaning of 'contravention' see PARA 54.
3   Coal Industry Act 1994 s 33(4).
4   Coal Industry Act 1994 s 33(5). It is submitted that the person by whom the duty is owed (ie the person under the obligation to comply with the enforcement order) can only be the person to whom the order relates, and is therefore the person whom the Coal Authority is satisfied is carrying on, or is likely to carry on, coal-mining operations in contravention of the licensing requirements contained in s 25(1) (see PARA 89), or whom the Authority is satisfied is contravening, or is likely to contravene, any of the provisions of a licence under Pt II (ss 25–36) (see s 31(1); and PARA 99).

As to the Coal Authority see PARA 52 et seq.

5   Whether or not the accused has exercised all due diligence is a question of fact: see *R C Hammett Ltd v Crabb* (1931) 145 LT 638, HL. The failure of the directors of a limited company to exercise due diligence is the failure of the company (*Pearce v Cullen* (1952) 96 Sol Jo 132) but the failure of subordinate managers and similar employees of a large-scale business to exercise due diligence is not necessarily the failure of the company (*Tesco Supermarkets Ltd v Nattrass* [1972] AC 153, [1971] 2 All ER 127, HL).

6   Coal Industry Act 1994 s 33(6).

7   Coal Industry Act 1994 s 33(7). As to injunctions generally see CIVIL PROCEDURE vol 12 (2015) PARA 1098 et seq.

8   Coal Industry Act 1994 s 33(7).

## (v) Registration and Information

### 105. Register of licences and orders.

The Coal Authority[1] is required to establish and maintain a register in which it enters particulars of:

(1)      every licence granted under Part II of the Coal Industry Act 1994[2] and every pending application for such a licence[3];

(2)      every licence under the Coal Industry Nationalisation Act 1946 in force immediately before the restructuring date[4] in pursuance of which any person is or has been entitled[5] to carry on coal-mining operations[6];

(3)      every transfer, in accordance with the provisions of a licence, of the rights and obligations of any person as the holder[7] of that licence[8];

(4)      every revocation of, or of the authorisation contained in, a licence falling within head (1) or head (2) above[9];

(5)      every other such modification[10] of a licence falling within head (1) or head (2) above as relates to the particulars of that licence which are entered in the register[11];

(6)      such trusts and other arrangements as for the time being have effect for the purposes of any security provided under the conditions included in licences[12] in pursuance of the Coal Authority's duty[13] to carry out its functions in the manner best calculated to secure, so far as practicable, that persons to whom obligations are owed in respect of subsidence damage[14] do not sustain loss in consequence of any failure by a licensed operator[15] to make such financial provision for meeting liabilities as might reasonably have been required of that person[16]; and

(7)      every enforcement order[17], every confirmation of a provisional enforcement order[18], the terms on which every confirmed order is confirmed and every revocation of an enforcement order[19].

The particulars entered in the register in relation to any licence are confined to:

(a)      the date of the grant of the licence and the time of the coming into force of the authorisation contained in the licence[20];

(b)      the identity of the person to whom the licence is granted and a description of any other persons who are entitled, under the licence, to carry on the coal-mining operations to which it relates[21];

(c)      the area to which the authorisation contained in the licence relates[22];

(d)      any restrictions contained in the licence as to the depth at which the coal-mining operations authorised by the licence may be carried on[23];

(e)      any other provisions of the licence restricting the authorised coal-mining operations to specified descriptions of operations[24];

(f)      any area designated by the licence as the area of responsibility[25] of the holder of the licence[26];

(g)      any provision included in the licence for the purposes of the provisions relating to the disclosure of information[27] and any conditions requiring the disclosure of information which may be of the description specified for those purposes[28]; and

(h)      any provisions of the licence for the expiry of the authorisation contained in the licence or for determining when an area ceases to be the area of responsibility of the holder of the licence[29].

The particulars entered in the register in relation to any pending application for a licence are confined to so much of the application as contains proposals with respect to any of the matters mentioned in heads (a) to (h) above[30].

The information contained in the register is, subject to certain exceptions, available to the public[31].

1   As to the Coal Authority see PARA 52 et seq.
2   Ie a licence under the Coal Industry Act 1994 Pt II (ss 25–36): see s 35(1)(a).
3   Coal Industry Act 1994 s 35(1)(a).
4   Ie a licence under the Coal Industry Nationalisation Act 1946 s 36(2) (repealed). As to the restructuring date (ie 31 October 1994) see PARA 50.
5   Ie by virtue of the Coal Industry Act 1994 s 25(3) (see PARA 89): see s 35(1)(b).
6   Coal Industry Act 1994 s 35(1)(b). As to the meaning of 'coal-mining operations' see PARA 51.
7   As to the meaning of 'holder' see PARA 93.
8   Coal Industry Act 1994 s 35(1)(c); and see PARA 93.
9   Coal Industry Act 1994 s 35(1)(d); and see PARA 93.
10   As to the meaning of 'modifications' see PARA 51.
11   Coal Industry Act 1994 s 35(1)(e). As to the modification of licences see PARA 94.
12   As to the conditions that may be contained in a licence see PARAS 95–96.
13   Ie under the Coal Industry Act 1994 s 2(1)(c) (see PARA 58): see s 35(1)(f).
14   As to subsidence damage by coal mining see PARA 200 et seq.
15   As to the meaning of 'licensed operator' see PARA 58.
16   Coal Industry Act 1994 s 35(1)(f). The particulars entered in the register in relation to any trust or other arrangements falling within head (6) in the text are confined to particulars identifying the form (but not the value or amount) of the security in question, the person who provided the security and the trustees or other person responsible for administering the security or determining the use to which it is put: s 35(4).
17   As to the meaning of 'enforcement order' see PARA 99. As to enforcement orders see PARA 99 et seq.
18   As to the meaning of 'provisional enforcement order' see PARA 99.
19   Coal Industry Act 1994 s 35(1)(g).
20   Coal Industry Act 1994 s 35(2)(a). As to the power to grant licences see PARA 90; and as to the authorisations contained in licences see PARA 93.
21   Coal Industry Act 1994 s 35(2)(b). As to applications for licences see PARA 92.
22   Coal Industry Act 1994 s 35(2)(c).
23   Coal Industry Act 1994 s 35(2)(d).
24   Coal Industry Act 1994 s 35(2)(e).
25   Ie under the Coal Industry Act 1994 s 37 (see PARA 205): see s 35(2)(f).
26   Coal Industry Act 1994 s 35(2)(f).
27   See the Coal Industry Act 1994 s 58; and PARA 97.
28   Coal Industry Act 1994 s 35(2)(g).
29   Coal Industry Act 1994 s 35(2)(h).
30   Coal Industry Act 1994 s 35(3).
31   See the Coal Industry Act 1994 s 57; and PARA 107.

## 106. Registration of rights.

The Coal Authority[1] is required to establish and maintain a register in which it enters particulars of certain notices, orders, designations, confirmations of orders and agreements[2]. It must also preserve a copy of every document particulars of which are entered in that register[3].

If any person furnishes the Authority with any information for these purposes which he knows to be false in a material particular, or recklessly furnishes the Authority with any information which is false in a material particular, he is guilty of an offence and liable on summary conviction, to a fine not exceeding the statutory maximum[4], and on conviction on indictment, to a fine[5].

1  As to the Coal Authority see PARA 52 et seq.
2  Particulars of the following are required to be entered in the register:
   (1)    every notice under the Coal Industry Act 1994 s 38 (right to withdraw support) (see
          PARA 176) a copy of which is sent to the Coal Authority by the person giving it (s
          56(1)(a));
   (2)    every notice published under the Coal Industry Act 1975 s 2 (repealed) (notices
          conferring right for the British Coal Corporation to withdraw support) (see PARA 176)
          a copy of which has been supplied to the Authority by the Corporation (Coal Industry
          Act 1994 s 56(1)(b));
   (3)    every public notice under the Coal Act 1938 Sch 2 para 6(2) (repealed) (withdrawal of
          support) a copy of which has been supplied to the Authority by the Corporation (Coal
          Industry Act 1994 s 56(1)(c));
   (4)    every notice given by the Authority under s 41 (revocation of right to withdraw support)
          (see PARA 178) (s 56(1)(d));
   (5)    every notice given for the purposes of s 49 (rights to work coal in former copyhold land)
          (see PARA 397) a copy of which is sent to the Authority by the person giving it (s
          56(1)(e));
   (6)    every notice published under the Coal Industry Act 1975 s 3 (repealed) (notices
          conferring right for the Corporation to work coal in copyhold land) (see PARA 397), a
          copy of which has been supplied to the Authority by the Corporation (Coal Industry Act
          1994 s 56(1)(f));
   (7)    every notice sent to the Authority under s 49(7), Sch 7 para 9 (see PARA 399) and so
          much of any information known to the Authority as (a) relates to any compensation paid
          under the Coal Industry Act 1975 s 3(4) (repealed) or to any agreement for the purposes
          of s 3, Sch 2 para 8 (repealed); and (b) is information which, in the case of any
          compensation or agreement under or for the purposes of the Coal Industry Act 1994
          Sch 7 Pt I (see PARA 398 et seq), would fall to be included in such a notice (s 56(1)(g));
   (8)    the following: (a) every compulsory rights order under the Opencast Coal Act 1958 (see
          PARA 431 et seq); (b) every order under s 15 (see PARA 424 et seq) or s 16 (see PARA
          430) (rights of way, drainage and water supply); and (c) every designation under s 39
          (see PARAS 420–421), in so far as it is an order or designation made by the Authority
          or an order or designation of which a copy has been supplied to the Authority by the
          Corporation (Coal Industry Act 1994 s 56(1)(h));
   (9)    every confirmation of an order mentioned in head (8)(a) or (b) and every notice or other
          document for the purposes of the Opencast Coal Act 1958 which is, or a copy of which
          is, sent to the Authority under the Opencast Coal Act 1958 or a copy of which has been
          supplied to the Authority by the Corporation (Coal Industry Act 1994 s 56(1)(i)); and
   (10)   every agreement entered into with a local planning authority for the purposes of the
          Opencast Coal Act 1958 s 15(5) (see PARA 424 et seq) (agreements as to the restoration
          of a right of way) (Coal Industry Act 1994 s 56(1)(j)).
   References to the supply to the Coal Authority by the British Coal Corporation of a copy of
   any document include references to the transfer in accordance with a restructuring scheme of
   possession of the document itself or of any copy of that document: s 56(6). The British Coal
   Corporation was dissolved on 27 March 2004. As to the dissolution of the British Coal
   Corporation see PARA 88. As to the British Coal Corporation see PARAS 49–50. As to copyhold
   land see CUSTOM AND USAGE; REAL PROPERTY AND REGISTRATION vol 87 (2017) PARA 36
   et seq.
3  Coal Industry Act 1994 s 56(4).
4  Coal Industry Act 1994 s 56(5)(a). As to the statutory maximum see SENTENCING vol 92 (2015)
   PARA 176.
5  Coal Industry Act 1994 s 56(5)(b).

## 107. Public access to information held by the Coal Authority.

The Coal Authority[1] is required to establish and maintain arrangements under which every person is entitled, in such cases, on payment to the Authority of such fee[2] and subject to such other conditions as the Authority may consider appropriate (1) to be furnished with certain information[3]; (2) to have the contents of so much of the records[4] maintained by the Authority as contains any such information made available to him, at such office of the Authority as it may determine, for inspection at such times as may be reasonable[5]; and (3) to make or be supplied with copies of, or of extracts from, so much of the records maintained by the Authority as contains any such information[6].

The information which must be made available in this way is: (a) that contained in the register of licences and orders[7]; (b) that contained in the register of rights[8]; and (c) any of the following information which is for the time being in the possession of the Authority:

(i)　　information about the geological or physiographical features or characteristics of any land in which any unworked coal[9] or any coal mine[10] is situated or of any other land[11];

(ii)　　information about the identity of the persons in whom interests[12] and rights in any unworked coal or coal mine have been vested[13];

(iii)　　the contents of the plans of any coal mines or coal workings[14];

(iv)　　any other information about proposals for the carrying on by any person of any coal-mining operations[15];

(v)　　information about any subsidence or subsidence damage[16] or about claims made under the Coal Mining Subsidence Act 1991[17]; and

(vi)　　information about such other matters as the Secretary of State[18] may prescribe by regulations[19].

The Authority must maintain such records of any information which comes into its possession and which falls into heads (a) to (c) above as it considers appropriate[20].

Certain designated types of information are, however, excluded from the information which is to be made available to any person in pursuance of these arrangements. In particular, the Authority is not required or authorised to disclose any information which relates to the affairs of an individual or specifically to the affairs of any body of persons (whether corporate or unincorporate), including the Authority itself, and which is not contained in the register of licences and orders or the register of rights, if the disclosure of that information would or might, in the opinion of the Authority, seriously and prejudicially affect the interests of the individual or body concerned[21]. Similarly, the arrangements do not require or authorise the Authority to disclose, without the consent of the person to whom it owes the obligation of confidence, any information which has been furnished to it under certain provisions[22] or which, under the provisions of the licence[23], agreement or undertaking given by the Authority to the applicant for the purposes of that application, is to be treated as subject to an obligation of confidence owed by the Authority to any other person[24]. However, the information that is to be excluded from that which is to be made available to any person in pursuance of these arrangements does not include any information that appears to the Authority to relate to matters which are or may be relevant to the safety of members of the public or of any particular individual or individuals other than the person whose consent is required for its disclosure[25].

1　As to the Coal Authority see PARA 52 et seq.
2　As to the charging of fees by the Coal Authority see PARA 63.

3  Coal Industry Act 1994 s 57(2)(a).
4  For these purposes, 'records' includes registers, maps, plans and accounts, as well as computer records and other records kept otherwise than in documentary form: Coal Industry Act 1994 57(8). Records of the Coal Authority are public records for the purposes of the Public Records Act 1958: see s 10, Sch 1 para 3 Table Pt II; and CONSTITUTIONAL AND ADMINISTRATIVE LAW vol 20 (2014) PARA 343.
5  Coal Industry Act 1994 s 57(2)(b).
6  Coal Industry Act 1994 s 57(2)(c).
7  Ie under the Coal Industry Act 1994 s 35 (see PARA 105).
8  Ie under the Coal Industry Act 1994 s 56 (see PARA 106).
9  As to the meaning of 'coal' see PARA 51.
10 As to the meaning of 'coal mine' see PARA 3.
11 Coal Industry Act 1994 s 57(1)(a).
12 As to the meaning of 'interest' see PARA 52.
13 Coal Industry Act 1994 s 57(1)(b).
14 Coal Industry Act 1994 s 57(1)(c).
15 Coal Industry Act 1994 s 57(1)(d). As to the meaning of 'coal-mining operations' see PARA 51.
16 As to the meaning of 'subsidence damage' see PARA 203. As to subsidence damage by coal mining see PARA 200 et seq.
17 Coal Industry Act 1994 s 57(1)(e).
18 As to the Secretary of State see PARA 2.
19 Coal Industry Act 1994 s 57(1)(f). The power to make regulations for these purposes is exercisable by statutory instrument subject to annulment in pursuance of a resolution of either House of Parliament: s 57(7). At the date at which this volume states the law no such regulations had been made.
20 Coal Industry Act 1994 s 57(6).
21 Coal Industry Act 1994 s 57(3). This provision is subject to s 57(5): s 57(3).
22 Ie (1) in pursuance of the provisions of a licence under the Coal Industry Act 1994 Pt II (ss 25–36); (2) in pursuance of any provisions of an agreement entered into in connection with, or with any proposals for, the carrying on of any activities in the course of any exploration for coal or of any activities for which a licence under the Petroleum Act 1998 s 3 (see ENERGY AND CLIMATE CHANGE vol 44 (2011) PARA 1046) is required; or (3) for the purposes of any application to the Authority for the grant of a licence under the Coal Industry Act 1994 Pt II, for the making of such an agreement or for the transfer or creation of any interests or rights in or in relation to any land: s 57(4)(a) (amended by the Petroleum Act 1998 s 50, Sch 4 para 38(4)).
23 Ie under the Coal Industry Act 1994 Pt II: see s 57(4)(b).
24 Coal Industry Act 1994 s 57(4)(b). As to the information to be kept confidential by the Authority see PARA 108. As to obligations of confidence generally see CONFIDENCE AND INFORMATIONAL PRIVACY vol 19 (2011) PARA 14 et seq.
25 Coal Industry Act 1994 s 57(5).

## 108.  Information to be kept confidential by the Coal Authority.

It is the duty of the Coal Authority[1] to establish and maintain such arrangements as it considers best calculated to secure that information which (1) is in its possession in consequence of either the carrying out of any of its functions or the transfer to it, in accordance with a restructuring scheme[2], of any records[3]; and (2) relates to the affairs of any individual or to any particular business[4], is not, during the lifetime of that individual or so long as that business continues to be carried on, disclosed to any person without the consent of that individual or, as the case may be, of the person for the time being carrying on that business[5]. This does not, however, authorise or require the making of arrangements which prevent the disclosure of information:

(a)    for the purpose of facilitating the carrying out by the Secretary of State[6], the Treasury or the Coal Authority of any of their functions under the Coal Industry Act 1994[7];

(b)    in pursuance of public access arrangements[8];

(c)    for the purpose of facilitating the carrying out by any relevant authority[9] of any of the functions in relation to which it is such an authority[10];

(d)    in connection with the investigation of any criminal offence or for the purposes of criminal proceedings[11];

(e)    for the purposes of any civil proceedings brought under the Coal Industry Act 1994 or any relevant enactment[12], of any proceedings before the Upper Tribunal[13] under the Coal Mining Subsidence Act 1991 or of any arbitration for which provision is made by regulations[14] in relation to disputes as to subsidence matters[15]; or

(f)    in pursuance of any European Union obligation[16].

These provisions do not limit the matters which may be contained in the annual report of the Coal Authority[17] or in a report on the operation of the Coal Mining Subsidence Act 1991[18]. Nor do they restrict or prohibit the disclosure of any information which has already been made public (i) as part of such a report[19]; (ii) in pursuance of any public access arrangements[20]; (iii) under any of certain specified provisions[21] requiring the publication of any notice or other matter[22]; or (iv) in the exercise of any power or the performance of any duty which is conferred or imposed on any person apart from the Coal Industry Act 1994[23].

The Secretary of State may by order modify these provisions[24] so as to add to or restrict the descriptions of disclosures which are to be excluded from any prohibition contained in these arrangements[25].

Where any licence[26] or any undertaking given by the Authority to an applicant[27] contains provision for any information furnished to the Authority to be treated as subject to such an obligation of confidence as restricts the disclosure or use of that information without the consent of the person to whom that obligation is to be owed, special provision applies[28]. In such a case, the requirement to comply with that obligation is a duty owed by the Authority to that person[29], and any such disclosure or use, in contravention[30] of that provision, of any information as causes the person to whom it is owed to sustain loss or damage is actionable against the Authority at the suit or instance of that person[31].

1    As to the Coal Authority see PARA 52 et seq.
2    As to restructuring schemes see PARA 72.
3    As to the meaning of 'records' see PARA 107 (definition applied by the Coal Industry Act 1994 s 59(9)).
4    As to the meaning of 'business' see PARA 71.
5    Coal Industry Act 1994 s 59(1).
6    As to the Secretary of State see PARA 2.
7    Coal Industry Act 1994 s 59(2)(a). As the extension of disclosure powers see the Anti-terrorism, Crime and Security Act 2001 s 17, Sch 4 Pt 1 para 35; and CRIMINAL LAW vol 25 (2016) PARA 463.
8    Coal Industry Act 1994 s 59(2)(b). The public access arrangements referred to in the text are those made under s 57: see PARA 107.
9    For the purposes of the Coal Industry Act 1994 s 59, every Minister of the Crown and local weights and measures authority in Great Britain is a relevant authority in relation to his or, as the case may be, its functions under any relevant enactment: s 59(3)(a). As to the meaning of 'Great Britain' see PARA 48. As to weights and measures authorities see WEIGHTS AND MEASURES vol 101 (2018) PARA 1019. The the Secretary of State, the Treasury, the Financial Conduct Authority and the Prudential Regulation Authority are relevant authorities in relation to their functions under the Financial Services and Markets Act 2000, the Consumer Credit Act 1974 and the enactments relating to companies and insolvency: Coal Industry Act 1994 s 59(3)(b) (substituted by SI 2002/1555; amended by the Financial Services Act 2012 Sch 18 para 80; and SI 2013/1882)). An inspector appointed under the enactments relating to companies, an official receiver and any recognised professional body for the purposes of the Insolvency Act 1986 s 391 (see BANKRUPTCY AND INDIVIDUAL INSOLVENCY vol 5 (2013) PARA 40) are relevant authorities in relation to

their functions as such: Coal Industry Act 1994 s 59(3)(c). Every enforcing authority, within the meaning of the Health and Safety at Work etc Act 1974 Pt I (ss 1–54), is a relevant authority in relation to its functions under any relevant statutory provision, within the meaning of that Act: Coal Industry Act 1994 s 59(3)(d). The Civil Aviation Authority is a relevant authority in relation to its functions under the Transport Act 2000 Pt I (ss 1–107): Coal Industry Act 1994 s 59(3)(dd) (added by SI 2001/4050). The following are relevant authorities in relation to all of their functions: (1) the Comptroller and Auditor General (see CONSTITUTIONAL AND ADMINISTRATIVE LAW vol 20 (2014) PARAS 494–496; PARLIAMENT vol 78 (2010) PARA 945); (2) the Health and Safety Executive (see HEALTH AND SAFETY AT WORK vol 52 (2014) PARA 326 et seq); (3) the Environment Agency (see ENVIRONMENTAL QUALITY AND PUBLIC HEALTH vol 45 (2010) PARA 68 et seq); (4) the Competition and Markets Authority (see COMPETITION vol 18 (2009) PARA 6 et seq) and the Gas and Electricity Markets Authority (see ENERGY AND CLIMATE CHANGE vol 42 (2011) PARA 202 et seq); (5) the Scottish Environment Protection Agency (see ENVIRONMENTAL QUALITY AND PUBLIC HEALTH vol 45 (2010) PARA 68); (6) Office for Nuclear Regulation (see ENERGY AND CLIMATE CHANGE vol 44 (2011) PARA 815A): Coal Industry Act 1994 s 59(3)(e)(i)–(vi) (amended by the Utilities Act 2000 s 3(2); the Enterprise Act 2002 s 278(1), Sch 25, para 32(2); Energy Act 2013 Sch 12 para 70; SI 1996/593, SI 1996/973, SI 1999/506, SI 2001/4050, SI 2002/1555; and SI 2008/960). The Natural Resources Body for Wales is a relevant authority in relation to its relevant transferred functions (within the meaning of the Natural Resources Body for Wales (Establishment) Order 2012, SI 2012/1903, art 11): Coal Industry Act 1994 s 59(3)(f) (added by SI 2013/755).

10 Coal Industry Act 1994 s 59(2)(c).

11 Coal Industry Act 1994 s 59(2)(d).

12 'Relevant enactment' means any of the following: (1) the Trade Descriptions Act 1968; (2) the Fair Trading Act 1973; (3) the Consumer Credit Act 1974; (4) the Control of Pollution Act 1974 Pt II; (5) the Estate Agents Act 1979; (6) the Competition Act 1980; (7) the Consumer Protection Act 1987; (8) the Electricity Act 1989; (9) the Water Resources Act 1991; (10) the Land Drainage Act 1991; (11) the Competition Act 1998; (12) the Enterprise Act 2002; (13) the Water Act 2003; (14) any subordinate legislation made for the purpose of securing compliance with Council Directive (EC) 2005/29 (OJ L149, 11.6.2005, p 22) concerning unfair business-to-consumer commercial practices in the internal market; (15) any subordinate legislation made for the purpose of securing compliance with Council Directive (EC) 2006/114 (OJ L376, 27.12.2006, p 21) concerning misleading and comparative advertising; (16) the Enterprise and Regulatory Reform Act 2013 Pts 3, 4; (17) the Water Act 2014: Coal Industry Act 1994 s 59(4) (amended by the Competition Act 1998 s 74(1), (3), Sch 12 para 18, Sch 14 Pt I; the Enterprise Act 2002 s 278(1), Sch 25 para 32(1), (2)(b); the Water Act 2003, s 101(1), Sch 7, Pt 2, para 31; SI 2008/1277; SI 2014/892; and SI 2017/506).

13 As to the Upper Tribunal see COURTS AND TRIBUNALS vol 24 (2010) PARA 883.

14 See eg the Coal Mining Subsidence (Arbitration Schemes) Regulations 1994, SI 1994/2566, made under the Coal Industry Act 1994 s 47(2); and PARA 250.

15 Coal Industry Act 1994 s 59(2)(e) (amended by SI 2009/1307).

16 Coal Industry Act 1994 s 59(2)(f) (amended by SI 2011/1043). 'European Union obligation' means such an obligation within the meaning of the European Communities Act 1972: see the Interpretation Act 1978 s 5, Sch 1 (definition amended by the European Union (Amendment) Act 2008 Schedule Pt 2).

17 Ie under the Coal Industry Act 1994 s 60 (see PARA 56): see s 59(5)(a).

18 Coal Industry Act 1994 s 59(5)(a). The report on the operation of the Coal Mining Subsidence Act 1991 is made under s 49 (see PARA 253): see the Coal Industry Act 1994 s 59(5)(a).

19 Coal Industry Act 1994 s 59(5)(b)(i).

20 Coal Industry Act 1994 s 59(5)(b)(ii). The public access arrangements referred to in the text are those made under s 57: see PARA 107.

21 Ie any provision of the Coal Industry Act 1994 s 31 (see PARA 99) or s 32 (see PARAS 101–102) or Pt III (ss 37–56) (see PARA 105 et seq): see s 59(5)(b)(iii).

22 Coal Industry Act 1994 s 59(5)(b)(iii).

23 Coal Industry Act 1994 s 59(5)(b)(iv).

24 Ie the Coal Industry Act 1994 s 59(2)–(5): see s 59(6).

25 Coal Industry Act 1994 s 59(6). The power to make such an order is exercisable by statutory instrument subject to annulment in pursuance of a resolution of either House of Parliament: s 59(6).

26 Ie under the Coal Industry Act 1994 Pt II: see s 59(7).

27 Ie under the Coal Industry Act 1994 s 57(4)(b) (see PARA 107): see s 59(7).

28 See the Coal Industry Act 1994 s 59(7). Section 59(7) does not apply, except in so far as the provisions of the licence or undertaking contain express provision to the contrary, to any disclosure of information which is for the time being excluded by virtue of s 59(2)–(5) from the prohibition contained in arrangements under s 59(1): s 59(8).
29 Coal Industry Act 1994 s 59(7)(a).
30 As to the meaning of 'contravention' see PARA 54.
31 Coal Industry Act 1994 s 59(7)(b).

### (vi) Supplemental Provisions

**109. Financial provisions.**
The following sums are to be paid out of money provided by Parliament:
(1)      any administrative expenses incurred by the Secretary of State[1] or the Treasury in consequence of the provisions of the Coal Industry Act 1994[2];
(2)      any sums required by any Minister of the Crown or government department for meeting obligations arising in consequence of that Minister or department becoming entitled or subject, in accordance with any restructuring scheme[3], to any property, rights or liabilities[4]; and
(3)      any increase attributable to the Coal Industry Act 1994 in the sums payable out of money so provided under any other Act[5].

1 As to the Secretary of State see PARA 2.
2 Coal Industry Act 1994 s 62(a).
3 As to restructuring schemes see PARA 72.
4 Coal Industry Act 1994 s 62(b).
5 Coal Industry Act 1994 s 62(c).

**110. Service of documents.**
Any document (except a document in relation to the service of which provision is made by rules of court[1]) required or authorised by virtue of the Coal Industry Act 1994 to be served[2] on any person may be served (1) by delivering it to him or by leaving it at his proper address[3] or by sending it by post to him at that address; (2) if the person is a body corporate, by serving it in accordance with head (1) above on the secretary or clerk of that body; or (3) if the person is a partnership, by serving it in accordance with head (1) above on a partner or a person having the control or management of the partnership business; and any document required or authorised to be served on the Coal Authority[4] or the British Coal Corporation[5] may be served by leaving it at, or sending it by post to, any office of the Authority or, as the case may be, of the Corporation[6].

1 Coal Industry Act 1994 s 63(5).
2 References in the Coal Industry Act 1994 s 63 to the service of a document on any person include references to the giving, making or sending to that person of any notice, direction, claim or request which is in writing: s 63(4). As to the service of documents generally see CIVIL PROCEDURE vol 11 (2015) PARA 244 et seq. See also COMPANIES vol 15 (2016) PARA 743.
3 For the purposes of the Coal Industry Act 1994 s 63 and the Interpretation Act 1978 s 7 (which relates to the service of documents by post) in its application to the Coal Industry Act 1994 s 63, the proper address of any person on whom a document is to be served is his last known address, except that (1) in the case of service on a body corporate or its secretary or clerk, it is the address of the registered or principal office of the body; and (2) in the case of service on a partnership or a partner or a person having the control or management of a partnership business, it is the address of the principal office of the partnership; and for these purposes the principal office of a company registered outside the United Kingdom, or of a partnership carrying on business outside the United Kingdom, is its principal office within the United Kingdom: s 63(2). If a person to be served with any document by another has specified to that other an address within the United Kingdom, other

than his proper address, as one at which he or someone on his behalf will accept documents of the same description as that document, that address must also be treated as a proper address of that person for these purposes and for the purposes of the Interpretation Act 1978 s 7 in its application to the Coal Industry Act 1994 s 63: s 63(3). As to the meaning of 'United Kingdom' see PARA 48.

4　As to the Coal Authority see PARA 52 et seq. As to the principal office of the Coal Authority see PARA 52.

5　As to the British Coal Corporation see PARAS 49–50.

6　Coal Industry Act 1994 s 63(1).

## 111. Offences by bodies corporate.

Where a body corporate is guilty of an offence under the Coal Industry Act 1994 and that offence is proved to have been committed with the consent or connivance of, or to be attributable to any neglect on the part of, any director, manager, secretary or other similar officer of the body corporate or any person who was purporting to act in any such capacity, then he, as well as the body corporate, is guilty of that offence and is liable to be proceeded against and punished accordingly[1]. Where the affairs of a body corporate are managed by its members this provision applies in relation to the acts and defaults of a member in connection with his functions of management as if he were a director of the body corporate[2].

1　Coal Industry Act 1994 s 64(1). As to the liability of companies for crimes and offences see COMPANIES vol 14 (2016) PARAS 312–317.

2　Coal Industry Act 1994 s 64(2).

## 112. Crown application.

The Coal Industry Act 1994 has effect in relation to any land or other property in which there is a Crown or Duchy interest[1] as it has effect in relation to land or other property in which there is no such interest[2]. So much of Coal Industry Act 1994 as contains provision for the modification of the rights or liabilities to which any person is or may become entitled or subject also binds the Crown[3].

1　'Crown or Duchy interest' means any interest belonging to Her Majesty or to the Duchy of Cornwall or any interest belonging to a government department or held in trust for the purposes of a government department: Coal Industry Act 1994 s 66(5). As to the meaning of 'interest' see PARA 52. As to Crown lands generally see CROWN AND CROWN PROCEEDINGS vol 29 (2014) PARAS 114 et seq, 192 et seq.

2　Coal Industry Act 1994 s 66(1).

3　Coal Industry Act 1994 s 66(2). Where the Coal Industry Act 1994 modifies any enactment in relation to which provision is made for its application to the Crown that differs from s 66, that provision and not s 66, has effect in relation to the modification: s 66(4).

## 113. Procedures for awarding supply and works contracts.

Member states of the European Community are required to co-ordinate procedures for the award of supply and works contracts by certain entities operating in the water, energy, transport and telecommunications sectors[1]. In the United Kingdom[2] the Utilities Contracts Regulations 2016[3] utilities have obligations in relation to how they award contracts for the supply of products, provision of services or the execution of works which are not specifically excluded.[4]. For the purposes of those regulations, a licensed operator[5] within the meaning of the Coal Industry Act 1994[6] is a utility in relation to the exploitation of a geographical area for the purposes of exploring for or extracting coal or other solid fuel[7].

The Utilities Contracts Regulations 2016 make provision relating to the scope of the Regulations, general rules and principles that apply to a procurement within the scope of the Regulation[8], rules to be followed in relation to a procurement[9]; procurement regimes for the procurement of social and other specific services and the use of design contests which impose less detailed requirements[10]recording and reporting information[11] and remedies (and their facilitation) in relation to such procurements[12].

1  See European Parliament and Council Regulation (EU) 2014/25 (OJ L94, 28.3.2014, p 243) on procurement by entities operating in the water, energy, transport and postal services sectors; and ENERGY AND CLIMATE CHANGE vol 42 (2011) PARA 26 et seq. See also See European Parliament and Council Directive (EU) 2014/55 (OJ L133, 6.5.2014, p 1) on electronic invoicing in public procurement (member states must adopt, publish and apply the laws, regulations and administrative provisions necessary to comply with Directive 2014/55 by 27 November 2018: art 11(1)); Commission Implementing Regulation (EU) 2016/7 (OJ L3, 6.1.2016, p 16) establishing the standard form for the European Single Procurement Document.

2  As to the meaning of 'United Kingdom' see PARA 48.

3  Ie the Utilities Contracts Regulations 2016, SI 2016/274, which came into force on 18 April 2016: see Utilities Contracts Regulations 2016, SI 2016/274, reg 1. These regulations implement the European Parliament and Council Directive (EU) 2014/55.

4  As to excluded contracts see the Utilities Contracts Regulations 2016, SI 2016/274, regs 18–25.

5  As to the meaning of 'licensed operator' see PARA 58.

6  As to the meaning of 'licensed operator' see PARA 58.

7  See the Utilities Contracts Regulations 2016, SI 2016/274, regs 5, 15.

8  See the Utilities Contracts Regulations 2016, SI 2016/274, Pt 1 (regs 1–42 ).

9  See the Utilities Contracts Regulations 2016, SI 2016/274, Pt 2 (regs 43–89 ).

10 See the Utilities Contracts Regulations 2016, SI 2016/274, Pt 3 (regs 90–97).

11 See the Utilities Contracts Regulations 2016, SI 2016/274, Pt 4 (regs 98–99 ).

12 See the Utilities Contracts Regulations 2016, SI 2016/274, Pt 5 (regs 100–119 ).

# 4. RIGHTS AFFECTING MINES IN GENERAL

## (1) Right of Support

### (i) Natural Right of Support

**114. General principles.**

At common law, where there has been severance of title and the surface and minerals are in different hands[1], ownership of the surface land carries prima facie a natural right of support which is a right to have the surface kept in its natural position and condition[2]. The right is not an easement but a natural right incident to the ownership of the soil[3].

There is no natural right of support for anything artificially constructed on land; such a right cannot exist *ex jure naturae* because the thing itself did not do so[4]. Thus any right to the support of such an artificial burden must be acquired as an easement[5].

Rights and obligations in regard to support may be varied by the instrument of severance of the surface and minerals[6] or by a separate instrument[7]. They may also be modified by custom[8].

In many circumstances the application of the common law principles is subject to statutory provisions[9]. By the effect of such provisions, or of subordinate instruments[10], rights and obligations in regard to support may be created[11], overridden[12] or varied[13], or new remedies may be established where the withdrawal of support has caused subsidence damage[14].

1   See PARA 19. As to the meaning of 'minerals' see PARA 10.
2   *Humphries v Brogden* (1850) 12 QB 739; *Bonomi v Backhouse* (1859) EB & E 646, Ex Ch (affd sub nom *Backhouse v Bonomi* (1861) 9 HL Cas 503); *Butterknowle Colliery Co Ltd v Bishop Auckland Industrial Co-operative Co Ltd* [1906] AC 305, HL. At the time when the principle was laid down it appears to have been assumed that minerals could always be worked commercially, to some extent, without letting down the surface, so that it may have seemed reasonable to infer an intention at the time of severance that they could be worked to that extent but no further: see *Warwickshire Coal Co Ltd v Coventry Corpn* [1934] Ch 488 at 508, CA, per Romer LJ. More recently the assumption has not been accepted: see eg *Welldon v Butterley Co Ltd* [1920] 1 Ch 130 at 141 per Astbury J (overruled on another point by *Warwickshire Coal Co Ltd v Coventry Corpn*); and see *Butterley Co Ltd v New Hucknall Colliery Co Ltd* [1909] 1 Ch 37 at 46, 47, CA, per Cozens-Hardy MR (affd [1910] AC 381, HL). Nevertheless whatever the reason of the principle, there is no doubt that it continues to exist: *Warwickshire Coal Co Ltd v Coventry Corpn* at 508 per Romer LJ. See also *Thomson v St Catharine's College, Cambridge* [1919] AC 468, HL; and PARA 197.
3   As to easements of support see REAL PROPERTY AND REGISTRATION vol 87 (2017) PARA 568.
4   *Wilde v Minsterley* (1639) 2 Roll Abr 564, Trespass (I); *Partridge v Scott* (1838) 3 M & W 220; *Dalton v Angus & Co* (1881) 6 App Cas 740 at 792, HL, per Lord Selborne LC; and see REAL PROPERTY AND REGISTRATION vol 87 (2017) PARA 904.
5   *Dalton v Angus & Co* (1881) 6 App Cas 740 at 792, HL, per Lord Selborne LC. See also PARA 121 et seq and, as to easements of support generally, REAL PROPERTY AND REGISTRATION vol 87 (2017) PARA 906. As to subsidence damage see PARA 182 et seq.
6   See *Rowbotham v Wilson* (1860) 8 HL Cas 348 (overruling the dictum of Lord Denham CJ in *Hilton v Earl Granville* (1844) 5 QB 701 at 730); and see *Bell v Love* (1833) 10 QBD 547 at 561, CA, per Baggallay LJ (on appeal sub nom *Love v Bell* (1884) 9 App Cas 286 at 293, HL, per Lord Selborne LC); *Davies v Powell Duffryn Steam Coal Co Ltd (No 2)* (1921) 91 LJ Ch 40, CA; *Harris v Ryding* (1839) 5 M & W 60; *Humphries v Brogden* (1850) 12 QB 739 at 757. See also PARAS 116, 127.

7  *Rowbotham v Wilson* (1856) 6 E & B 593 at 604 (affd (1857) 8 E & B 123 Ex Ch, (1860) 8 HL
   Cas 348); *Murchie v Black* (1865) 19 CBNS 190 at 205 per Erle CJ; cf *Richards v Harper* (1866)
   LR 1 Exch 199 at 205 per Martin B; *Sitwell v Earl of Londesborough* [1905] 1 Ch 460. See also
   PARA 127.
8  See PARA 134.
9  Such provisions are found both in statutes of general application and in local statutes, eg the
   Inclosure Acts (see PARA 127).
10 Eg compulsory purchase orders providing for the incorporation of the mining code of the
   Acquisition of Land Act 1981: see PARA 135.
11 See eg the Coal Industry Act 1994 ss 38–41; and PARA 176 et seq.
12 See eg the Mines (Working Facilities and Support) Act 1966 s 2(1)(a); and PARA 384.
13 See eg the Mines (Working Facilities and Support) Act 1966 s 7; and PARA 387.
14 See the Coal Mining Subsidence Act 1991; and PARA 200 et seq. The form of the Interaction
   Framework Agreement between the Coal Authority and operators who acquire a right to enter,
   extract or otherwise affect coal contains requirements as to notifications to be given and consents
   to be obtained where an operator intends to carry on operations which cause or may cause
   subsidence damage affecting other parties to the Agreement. As to the Coal Authority see PARA 52
   et seq.

## 115.  Rights of support from subjacent mines.

The principles which apply in respect of support from subjacent mines[1] which
are severed in ownership from the surface[2] are similar[3] to those which regulate the
mutual rights and liabilities of the owners of adjacent closes[4] in respect of lateral
support[5]. They apply also to the support of an underground stratum by a deeper
stratum[6] and to the support of surface land from mines under adjacent land[7].

1  As to lateral support from mines see *Whitehouse v Bayley* (1875) 34 LT 93; and see also *New Moss
   Colliery Ltd v Manchester Corpn* [1908] AC 117 at 122, HL, per Lord Loreburn LC; *Thomson v
   St Catharine's College, Cambridge* [1919] AC 468 at 502, HL, per Lord Sumner. As to the
   meaning of 'mine' see PARA 3.
2  See PARA 114. As to the persons who must provide support see PARA 118.
3  *Humphries v Brogden* (1850) 12 QB 739 at 744; *Pountney v Clayton* (1883) 11 QBD 820 at 839,
   CA, per Bowen LJ. As to the statutory right of licensees of the Coal Authority to withdraw support
   to enable coal to be worked see the Coal Industry Act 1994 ss 38–41; and PARA 176 et seq. As to
   the Coal Authority see PARA 52 et seq.
4  As to the meaning of 'close' see PARA 17.
5  As to the rights of adjoining owners of land to support, and as to the right of support for buildings
   see REAL PROPERTY AND REGISTRATION vol 87 (2017) PARA 900. As to the right of support in
   the case of walls see BOUNDARIES vol 4 (2011) PARA 371 et seq. See also Roll Abr 564, Trespass
   (I); Com Dig, Action upon the Case for a Nuisance (A); *Hunt v Peake* (1860) John 705; *Humphries
   v Brogden* (1850) 12 QB 739; *Caledonian Rly Co v Sprot (of Garnkirk)* (1856) 2 Macq 449 at
   450, HL, per Lord Cranworth LC; *North Eastern Rly Co v Elliot* (1860) 1 John & H 145 at 153
   per Page Wood V-C (affd 2 De GF & J 423); *Backhouse v Bonomi* (1861) 9 HL Cas 503 at 512,
   513 per Lord Cranworth; *Dalton v Angus & Co* (1881) 6 App Cas 740, HL; *Manchester Corpn
   v New Moss Colliery Ltd* [1906] 1 Ch 278 at 295 per Farwell J (revsd on other points [1906] 2
   Ch 564, CA; and sub nom *New Moss Colliery Ltd v Manchester Corpn* [1908] AC 117, HL).
6  See *Dixon v White* (1883) 8 App Cas 833 at 842, HL, per Lord Blackburn; *Butterley Co Ltd v New
   Hucknall Colliery Co Ltd* [1909] 1 Ch 37 at 48, CA, per Cozens-Hardy MR (affd [1910] AC 381
   at 386, HL, per Lord Macnaghten); cf [1908] 2 Ch 475 at 483 per Neville J; *Mundy v Duke of
   Rutland* (1883) 23 ChD 81, CA; and see PARA 114; and REAL PROPERTY AND REGISTRATION.
7  *London and North Western Rly Co v Howley Park Coal and Cannel Co* [1911] 2 Ch 97, CA; affd
   sub nom *Howley Park Coal and Cannel Co v London and North Western Rly Co* [1913] AC 11,
   HL.

## 116.  Nature of the right of support.

The right of support arises on the severance[1] of the surface and the minerals[2].
Thus the landowner may, on severance, by apt words convey the minerals with the
right to let down the surface in working them, or he may by means of exceptions
and reservations of minerals and powers of working them grant the surface so that

the right of support does not arise at all. In the latter case, there is no necessity for a regrant by the grantee of the surface of the right to let down the surface[3].

The right of support is independent of the nature of the strata[4], or the difficulty of propping up the surface, or the comparative values of the surface and the minerals[5]. It is impossible to measure out degrees to which the right may extend. Accordingly, the surface owner's right is not modified by the fact that the obligation not to cause damage by subsidence renders the effectual working of the underlying minerals impossible, as where the extent of pillars necessary to maintain the surface undamaged is such as to make the remaining minerals unprofitable to work[6]. Similarly there is no modification of the surface owner's right where the supported tenement contains strata of an unstable nature which shift or escape and cause subsidence if the adjoining owner excavates on his land[7].

1  See PARA 19.
2  See *Pountney v Clayton* (1883) 11 QBD 820 at 838, CA, per Bowen LJ. As to the meaning of 'minerals' see PARA 10.
3  *Davies v Powell Duffryn Steam Coal Co Ltd (No 2)* (1921) 91 LJ Ch 40, CA. It follows that the owner of the soil and minerals may grant the minerals and retain the right of support, or grant the surface with an express or implied right of support: see PARAS 127–128.
4  *Humphries v Brogden* (1850) 12 QB 739; *Rowbotham v Wilson* (1856) 6 E & B 593 at 601; affd on appeal (1857) 8 E & B 123, Ex Ch; (1860) 8 HL Cas 348.
5  *Humphries v Brogden* (1850) 12 QB 739.
6  *Wakefield v Duke of Buccleuch* (1867) LR 4 Eq 613 at 628, 638 per Malins V-C (affd sub nom *Duke of Buccleuch v Wakefield* (1870) LR 4 HL 377); *New Sharlston Collieries Co Ltd v Earl of Westmorland* (1900) [1904] 2 Ch 443n, HL.
7  See *Trinidad Asphalt Co v Ambard* [1899] AC 594 at 602, PC (fluid pitch); *Jordeson v Sutton, Southcoates and Drypool Gas Co* [1899] 2 Ch 217, CA; *Fletcher v Birkenhead Corpn* [1906] 1 KB 605 (affd [1907] 1 KB 205, CA (running silt)); *Salt Union Ltd v Brunner, Mond & Co* [1906] 2 KB 822 (brine pumped to surface); cf *Langbrook Properties Ltd v Surrey County Council* [1969] 3 All ER 1424, [1970] 1 WLR 161 (water).

## 117.  Limits to the natural right of support.

The natural right of support is not an interest in the subjacent mines[1] sufficient to entitle the surface owner to insist upon the minerals remaining unworked[2]. The owner of the minerals is entitled as an incident to the enjoyment of his property to get his minerals in a usual and proper course of working consistent with leaving support[3]; the minerals may be worked out completely provided adequate artificial support is substituted[4].

1  As to the meaning of 'mine' see PARA 3.
2  See *Bonomi v Backhouse* (1859) EB & E 646 at 655, Ex Ch; affd (1861) 9 HL Cas 503; *Dalton v Angus & Co* (1881) 6 App Cas 740 at 808, HL, per Lord Blackburn. As to the right to work minerals under the uninclosed waste of a manor see COMMONS vol 13 (2017) PARA 462. As to the meaning of 'minerals' see PARA 10.
3  *Rowbotham v Wilson* (1860) 8 HL Cas 348 at 360 per Lord Wensleydale; *Butterknowle Colliery Co Ltd v Bishop Auckland Industrial Co-operative Co Ltd* [1906] AC 305, HL; but see PARA 114. As to liability in respect of subsidence caused by coal mining see PARA 200 et seq; and as to liability in respect of subsidence caused by other mining operations see PARA 182 et seq.
4  *Harris v Ryding* (1839) 5 M & W 60 at 74, 76; *Humphries v Brogden* (1850) 12 QB 739 at 744; *Rowbotham v Wilson* (1857) 8 E & B 123 at 157, Ex Ch (on appeal (1860) 8 HL Cas 348); *Backhouse v Bonomi* (1861) 9 HL Cas 503. See also PARA 114; and REAL PROPERTY AND REGISTRATION vol 87 (2017) PARA 900.

## 118.  Persons who must afford support.

The land which is affected by the obligation to afford support is not limited to the land of the immediately adjoining owner if that land in its natural condition is insufficient of itself to afford the proper support. Therefore, all persons whose land in its natural state affords support are, for the purposes of support, adjoining owners or neighbours of the person whose land enjoys the support[1]. But if an adjoining piece of land which affords support is excavated, no right of support is automatically acquired against a more distant piece of land which in fact affords support in the altered circumstances[2].

1  *Birmingham Corpn v Allen* (1877) 6 ChD 284, CA.
2  *Birmingham Corpn v Allen* (1877) 6 ChD 284, CA; *Darley Main Colliery Co v Mitchell* (1886) 11 App Cas 127, HL; and see *Williams v Bagnall* (1866) 15 WR 272 at 276 per Page Wood V-C.

## 119.  Manner of severance immaterial.

The presumption that the surface owner is entitled to support from underlying minerals in different ownership does not depend on the manner of severance[1]. It applies whether the surface and minerals have been severed by a grant of mines and minerals apart from the land[2], or by a grant of the land with an exception of the mines and minerals[3]. The form of the instrument of severance is also immaterial; it may be a grant in fee simple[4], or a lease for a term of years[5] or it may be an Inclosure Act or award[6].

1  See PARAS 114–116. As to the meaning of 'minerals' see PARA 10.
2  *Dugdale v Robertson* (1857) 3 K & J 695; *Davis v Treharne* (1881) 6 App Cas 460, HL; *Pountney v Clayton* (1883) 11 QBD 820 at 838, CA, per Bowen LJ. As to the meaning of 'mines and minerals' see PARA 10.
3  *Harris v Ryding* (1839) 5 M & W 60; *Smart v Morton* (1855) 5 E & B 30 at 46 per Lord Campbell CJ; *Roberts v Haines* (1856) 6 E & B 643 at 654 per Coleridge J, and at 655 per Erle J (affd sub nom *Haines v Roberts* (1857) 7 E & B 625, Ex Ch); *Caledonian Rly Co v Sprot (of Garnkirk)* (1856) 2 Macq 449 at 451, HL, per Lord Cranworth LC; *Westhoughton UDC v Wigan Coal and Iron Co Ltd* [1919] 1 Ch 159, CA; *Warwickshire Coal Co Ltd v Coventry Corpn* [1934] Ch 488, CA; *Wath-upon-Dearne UDC v John Brown & Co Ltd* [1936] Ch 172.
4  *Harris v Ryding* (1839) 5 M & W 60; *Dixon v White* (1883) 8 App Cas 833, HL.
5  *Dugdale v Robertson* (1857) 3 K & J 695; *Davis v Treharne* (1881) 6 App Cas 460, HL.
6  *Roberts v Haines* (1856) 6 E & B 643; affd sub nom *Haines v Roberts* (1857) 7 E & B 625, Ex Ch.

## 120.  Onus of proving a right of support.

It is not necessary in pleading to allege, or in evidence to prove, any special origin for the natural right of support; the onus both in pleading and in proof is on those who deny the existence of the right in the particular case[1]. In the case of an easement of support[2], on the other hand, the acquisition of the right must be proved; but it is sufficient in pleading for the party claiming the right to allege that he is entitled to it; it is not necessary to allege facts from which a title to such right can be inferred as a matter of law[3]. This rule applies as against a defendant entitled to work the minerals[4]; as against a wrongdoer no allegation of right is necessary: de facto enjoyment of support is sufficient to maintain an action[5].

1  *Humphries v Brogden* (1850) 12 QB 739 at 742; *Dalton v Angus & Co* (1881) 6 App Cas 740 at 809, HL, per Lord Blackburn.
2  As to easements of support see PARA 121 et seq; and REAL PROPERTY AND REGISTRATION vol 87 (2017) PARA 900.
3  *Rogers v Taylor* (1858) 2 H & N 828; distinguishing *Hilton v Whitehead* (1848) 12 QB 734.
4  As to the meaning of 'minerals' see PARA 10.
5  *Jeffries v Williams* (1850) 5 Exch 792.

## (ii) Easement of Support

### 121. Support for artificial structures.

An easement of support for an artificial structure[1] may be created by grant, express[2] deemed[3] or implied[4], by prescription[5] or by statute[6]. But, although the natural and acquired rights thus differ in their origin, the acquired right is inseparable from, and, as between the parties concerned, is a mere enlargement of, the natural right[7]. Where a right of support for an artificial structure has been acquired by way of easement, the right does not extend so as to entitle the owner to increase the burden[8].

1   See PARA 114.
2   As to the creation of easements by express grant see PARA 123; and REAL PROPERTY AND REGISTRATION vol 87 (2017) PARA 750.
3   As to the creation of easements by deemed express grant see PARA 124; and REAL PROPERTY AND REGISTRATION.
4   As to the creation of easements by implied grant see PARAS 124–125; and REAL PROPERTY AND REGISTRATION vol 87 (2017) PARA 792.
5   As to the creation of easements by prescription see PARA 126; and REAL PROPERTY AND REGISTRATION vol 87 (2017) PARA 803.
6   As to the creation of easements by statute see REAL PROPERTY AND REGISTRATION vol 87 (2017) PARA 776. As to the creation of easements of support under the statutory mining codes see PARA 135 et seq. As to restrictions on working minerals required for support see PARAS 387–389.
7   *Bonomi v Backhouse* (1859) EB & E 646 at 654, 655, Ex Ch; affd sub nom *Backhouse v Bonomi* (1861) 9 HL Cas 503; and see *Humphries v Brogden* (1850) 12 QB 739 at 742.
8   See *Murchie v Black* (1865) 19 CBNS 190; *Angus v Dalton & Co* (1878) 4 QBD 162, CA (affd sub nom *Dalton v Angus & Co* (1881) 6 App Cas 740, HL); cf *Great Western Rly Co v Cefn Cribbwr Brick Co* [1894] 2 Ch 157.

### 122. Statutory grant of support.

A right of support of artificial structures is frequently created by statute, as where statutory undertakers are empowered to construct and maintain works of public utility, such as railways and canals, on the lands of private owners. In such cases the grant of the right to the support of the works will be presumed unless the provisions of the statute negative the inference[1].

1   See *Caledonian Rly Co v Sprot (of Garnkirk)* (1856) 2 Macq 449, HL; *Re Dudley Corpn and Earl of Dudley's Trustees* (1881) 8 QBD 86 at 93, CA, per Brett LJ; *Clippens Oil Co Ltd v Edinburgh and District Water Trustees* [1904] AC 64, HL; and see PARA 141; and REAL PROPERTY AND REGISTRATION vol 87 (2017) PARA 907. As to restrictions on working minerals required for support see also PARAS 387–389. Examples of a statutory liability to provide support are afforded by the Underground Works (London) Act 1956 s 5; and the Post Office Works Act 1959 s 3 (amended by the Post Office Act 1969 s 22(1)).

### 123. Express grant of support.

An easement of support for artificial structures may be the subject of an express grant or reservation. In the case of registered land, an express grant or reservation of such an easement must itself be registered even if the disposition in which it is made does not itself require to be registered[1]. The same object is sometimes attained, in dispositions of minerals[2], by a covenant which binds the mineral owner or the lessee not to work a certain part or certain parts of a seam or vein, or by a covenant to leave specified pillars unworked for the support of buildings. Such a restriction differs from a right to support in that it prohibits the mineral owner or the lessee from working or getting the minerals within those areas or pillars, irrespective of whether those areas or pillars are more or less than adequate for the support of the buildings, and also irrespective of whether or not substituted support by shoring or propping or otherwise would suffice. Sometimes the requisite pillars are excepted from the disposition³.

A perpetual restriction upon the working of mines⁴ may be imposed by statute, as where the statute imposes the obligation upon a mine owner not to work or get certain mines or minerals, and confers upon the surface owner the correlative right to insist upon the observance of the obligation⁵.

1   In the case of dispositions made on or after 13 October 2003, the day appointed for the Land Registration Act 2003 to come into force: see the Land Registration Act 2002 (Commencement No 4) Order 2003, SI 2003/1725, art 2(1). Requirements for the compulsory registration of expressly granted easements are contained in the Land Registration Act 2002 ss 4, 27: see REAL PROPERTY AND REGISTRATION vol 87 (2017) PARAS 324, 425–428.
2   As to the meaning of 'minerals' see PARA 10.
3   See PARAS 325 et seq, 342.
4   As to the meaning of 'mine' see PARA 3.
5   Eg under the Railways Clauses Consolidation Act 1845 s 78; and the Acquisition of Land Act 1981 s 3, Sch 2 para 3(3): see PARA 154. It is not possible to create such a perpetual restriction by a common law grant; such a grant would not bind the land in the hands of successive owners. Apart from statute, such a restriction can only be created by a covenant not to work the mines, which may be enforced in equity against successive owners as a restrictive covenant: see *Great Northern Rly Co v IRC* [1901] 1 KB 416 at 428, CA, per Collins LJ, and at 428–429 per Stirling LJ; cf *Leech v Schweder* (1874) 9 Ch App 463 at 475 per Mellish LJ. Such a restrictive covenant will only be enforceable against subsequent owners if appropriately registered against the burdened land: see REAL PROPERTY AND REGISTRATION vol 87 (2017) PARA 846.

## 124.   Implied grant of support.

An easement of support for artificial structures may be the subject of an implied or deemed¹ grant if and to the extent that a contrary intention is not expressed in the relevant disposition. It differs from a restriction imposed on the working of mines² in that it does not prohibit working within any area; the mine owner, as in the case of a natural right, is free to work, provided he substitutes efficient artificial support³. If the common owner of the land and the subjacent mines transfers the land to another, but at the same time retains his ownership of the mines, and, if at the time of the transfer, there are buildings on the land transferred, there will be implied, and deemed to be, a grant of an easement of support for the buildings from the subjacent mines, in the absence of any contrary intention expressed in the transfer⁴. No such implied or deemed easement would arise, however, if the common owner transferred the mines to another, retaining his ownership of the land and buildings; in such a case the easement would have to be expressly reserved in favour of the land and buildings retained⁵. Moreover, if the surface of the land is transferred with a view to building on it, or for any other specified use, which may render increased support necessary, there is implied a grant of support from the grantor's subjacent mines and adjoining land to the extent reasonably necessary for the use of the land for the purposes within the parties' contemplation at the date of the transfer⁶. Thus where land is acquired for constructing and maintaining a railway there is implied, in the absence of any provision to the contrary, a grant of such support as may be proper and necessary for the railway, however, the railway may be used and whatever the purposes to which it may be applied⁷.

An implied easement of support may arise even if the purpose for which the land is transferred should be expressed in the instrument of severance⁸. To ascertain the parties' common intention, evidence is therefore admissible to show the use which, to the knowledge of both parties, the person acquiring the land intended to make of it, and of the impossibility of making that use of the land, without the right claimed as arising by implication[9]. If both parties to a transfer of land (where the transferor retains ownership of the subjacent mines) contemplated that the land would in the future be subjected to an artificial burden, it is a legitimate inference that support for such a burden was intended to be granted, as where the surface of land is sold for development and the purchaser enters into restrictive covenants with the vendor in relation to that future development. In such a case an easement of support for that development is likely to be implied, and the vendor will be liable for any damage caused by the working of the subjacent mines retained in his ownership[10].

1   Law of Property Act 1925 s 62(2).
2   As to the meaning of 'mine' see PARA 3.
3   *Dalton v Angus & Co* (1881) 6 App Cas 740 at 830, HL, per Lord Watson. See also PARA 117.
4   *Dalton v Angus & Co* (1881) 6 App Cas 740 at 792, HL, per Lord Selborne LC. See also *Richards v Jenkins* (1868) 17 WR 30.
5   *Union Lighterage Co v London Graving Dock Co* [1902] 2 Ch 557, CA; and see REAL PROPERTY AND REGISTRATION vol 87 (2017) PARA 792.
6   *Caledonian Rly Co v Sprot (of Garnkirk)* (1856) 2 Macq 449, HL; *Dalton v Angus & Co* (1881) 6 App Cas 740 at 792, HL, per Lord Selborne LC.
7   *Caledonian Rly Co v Sprot (of Garnkirk)* (1856) 2 Macq 449, HL; *Great Western Rly Co v Cefn Cribbwr Brick Co* [1894] 2 Ch 157. The implication of a right of support does not, however, arise where the mining code of the Railways Clauses Consolidation Act 1845 applies as substituted by the Mines (Working Facilities and Support) Act 1923 s 15, except as provided in the code or as specially agreed: Railways Clauses Consolidation Act 1845 s 85E; and see PARA 174.
8   See *Siddons v Short* (1877) 2 CPD 572.
9   See, however, *Butterley Co Ltd v New Hucknall Colliery Co Ltd* [1909] 1 Ch 37 at 52, CA, per Farwell LJ; affd [1910] AC 381, HL.
10   *Berkley v Shafto* (1863) 15 CBNS 79.

## 125. Validity and extent of implied grant.

The implied grant is valid only to the extent that the grantor is able to grant it, so that, in the case of subjacent support, the doctrine of implied grant is confined to the case of the person who is the owner of both surface and subjacent mines[1] at the time of the severance. If the surface owner has no right to support, or has it for the land in its natural state only, a purchaser of the surface does not by implication purchase also the right to support for any burden he may place on the surface[2]. If, however, the surface owner is entitled to support for all purposes, he may transfer his right to a person who purchases the surface[3]; indeed, it will pass automatically to such a purchaser, unless a contrary intention is expressed.

The extent of the right to support arising by an implied grant created by statute on the purchase of surface land by statutory undertakers may, however, be much wider, so that the undertakers may acquire a right of support not merely against the vendor of the surface, but against owners of adjacent or subjacent land[4].

1   As to the meaning of 'mine' see PARA 3.
2   *Pountney v Clayton* (1883) 11 QBD 820 at 840, 841, CA, per Bowen LJ.
3   *Pountney v Clayton* (1883) 11 QBD 820 at 840, CA, per Bowen LJ; *Consett Waterworks Co v Ritson* (1889) 22 QBD 318 at 326 per A L Smith J; on appeal 22 QBD 702, CA.
4   See PARA 137.

## 126. Prescription.

Support for buildings may be acquired by prescription, either at common law or under statute[1], but the existence of any contract between the parties or a grant inconsistent with the claim prevents its acquisition; thus no right can be acquired if the surface owner is, by some instrument, expressly excluded from the natural right of support[2]. Similar principles apply in the case of land weakened by excavation of the subjacent mines[3]; if the subjacent mines afford adequate support for buildings before excavation, no right is acquired by prescription against a lateral owner, if the prescription period[4] has not elapsed since the excavation of the subjacent mines[5]; nor if the lateral owner was ignorant of the workings[6]. However, where buildings have been erected over partially excavated mines, a right is acquired after the prescription period against persons interested in the mines if, but for the working of the mines, the buildings would not have subsided[7].

1 *Dalton v Angus & Co* (1881) 6 App Cas 740, HL; and see REAL PROPERTY AND REGISTRATION vol 87 (2017) PARA 810 et seq.
2 See *Rowbotham v Wilson* (1856) 6 E & B 593 (affd (1857) 8 E & B 123, Ex Ch; (1860) 8 HL Cas 348).
3 As to the meaning of 'mine' see PARA 3.
4 See REAL PROPERTY AND REGISTRATION vol 87 (2017) PARA 761.
5 *Partridge v Scott* (1838) 3 M & W 220.
6 *Woodall v Hingley* (1866) 14 LT 167.
7 *Richards v Jenkins* (1868) 17 WR 30. As to subsidence damage see PARA 182 et seq. As to subsidence damage by coal mining see PARA 200 et seq.

### (iii) Modification of Rights

### 127. Variation of right to support.

An instrument of severance[1] or other instrument[2] varying the prima facie rights and obligations of the surface owner and the mineral owner[3] may do so in either affirmative terms or negative terms[4], and by express words or by necessary implication[5], whether the mines are granted with an exception of the surface or the surface is granted excepting the mines[6], and whether the instrument is a voluntary contract between the parties concerned or an Inclosure Act[7] or other statute[8]. A statute which does not itself provide for severance may nevertheless affect rights and obligations as to support[9]. Such rights and obligations may also be varied by custom[10].

1 See PARA 114.
2 See PARA 114.
3 See PARA 114. As to the meaning of 'minerals' see PARA 10.
4 See *Smith v Darby* (1872) LR 7 QB 716 at 724 per Blackburn J.
5 See *Smith v Darby* (1872) LR 7 QB 716 at 725 per Mellor J; *Aspden v Seddon* (1875) 10 Ch App 394; *Davis v Treharne* (1881) 6 App Cas 460, HL; *Dixon v White* (1883) 8 App Cas 833, HL; *New Sharlston Collieries Co Ltd v Earl of Westmorland* (1900) [1904] 2 Ch 443n, HL; *Butterknowle Colliery Co Ltd v Bishop Auckland Industrial Co-operative Co Ltd* [1906] AC 305, HL; *Butterley Co Ltd v New Hucknall Colliery Co Ltd* [1910] AC 381, HL.
6 *Dixon v White* (1883) 8 App Cas 833, HL; *Williams v Bagnall* (1866) 15 WR 272 at 275 per Page Wood V-C. See also PARA 21. As to the meaning of 'mine' see PARA 3.
7 See *Duke of Buccleuch v Wakefield* (1870) LR 4 HL 377; *Bell v Love* (1883) 10 QBD 547 at 558, 560, CA, per Baggallay LJ (on appeal sub nom *Love v Bell* (1884) 9 App Cas 286 at 297, HL, per Lord Watson); *Consett Waterworks Co v Ritson* (1889) 22 QBD 702, CA; *Butterknowle Colliery Co Ltd v Bishop Auckland Industrial Co-operative Co Ltd* [1906] AC 305, HL.
8 Eg statutes incorporating the mining codes: see PARA 135 et seq.
9 See eg the Mines (Working Facilities and Support) Act 1966 ss 1, 2, 7 (see PARA 380 et seq); and the Coal Industry Act 1994 ss 38–41 (see PARA 176 et seq).
10 See PARA 134.

### 128. Implied right to withdraw support.

The right to withdraw support may be conferred upon the mine owner by express words[1], but very frequently it arises by implication. Thus where the surface is transferred excepting the mines underneath, or the mines are transferred excepting the surface, it is a question of construction of the instrument of severance in each case whether by the express language of the transfer or exception, or by the general effect and intent of the instrument, there is a power to interfere with the support of the surface. The intention is to be gathered from the language of the instrument as a whole in the first instance[2], but evidence is admissible as to the circumstances in which the instrument was executed, including the facts known to the parties as to the practice of mining at the date of the instrument, in order to ascertain the sense in which the parties used the words employed by them to define their respective rights[3]. The burden of proof in all cases is on the party who claims that the common law right of support has been varied[4].

1    See eg *Whitehouse v Bayley* (1875) 34 LT 93, where an express power to withdraw vertical support did not confer upon a mine owner, who also owned the lateral mines, a power to withdraw lateral support. As to the meaning of 'mine' see PARA 3.

2    As to the general principles applicable to the interpretation of instruments see DEEDS AND OTHER INSTRUMENTS vol 32 (2012) PARA 364 et seq.

3    See *Dixon v White* (1883) 8 App Cas 833, HL; *New Sharlston Collieries Co Ltd v Earl of Westmorland* (1900) [1904] 2 Ch 443n, HL; *Bishop Auckland Industrial Co-operative Society Ltd v Butterknowle Colliery Co Ltd* [1904] 2 Ch 419 at 435, CA, per Vaughan Williams LJ (affd sub nom *Butterknowle Colliery Co Ltd v Bishop Auckland Industrial Co-operative Co Ltd* [1906] AC 305, HL); *Butterley Co Ltd v New Hucknall Colliery Co Ltd* [1909] 1 Ch 37 at 46, CA, per Cozens-Hardy MR, at 49 per Fletcher Moulton LJ, and at 51, 52–55 per Farwell LJ (on appeal [1910] AC 381 at 386–388, HL, per Lord Macnaghten); *Jones v Consolidated Anthracite Collieries Ltd and Lord Dynevor* [1916] 1 KB 123. As to what evidence is admissible see further DEEDS AND OTHER INSTRUMENTS vol 32 (2012) PARA 398 et seq.

4    *Davis v Treharne* (1881) 6 App Cas 460 at 466–468, HL, per Lord Blackburn; *Love v Bell* (1884) 9 App Cas 286 at 289, HL, per Lord Selborne LC. Thus it has been said that if the introduction in the instrument of severance of a clause to the effect that the mines must not be worked so as to let down the surface would not create an inconsistency with the actual clauses of the instrument, then the surface cannot be let down: *Butterknowle Colliery Co Ltd v Bishop Auckland Industrial Co-operative Co Ltd* [1906] AC 305 at 309, HL, per Lord Loreburn LC; and see *Thomson v St Catharine's College, Cambridge* [1919] AC 468, HL.

## 129. Implication from reservation of working powers.

The inclusion in the instrument of severance of a clause in the widest terms conferring general powers of working is not sufficient to rebut the presumption in favour of the surface owner; such a clause confers prima facie only the powers of working incident at common law to the ownership of mines[1]. An implication of the right to withdraw support may, however, be made from the reservation of working powers which existed before the severance, as where mines are excepted from a transfer of the surface, with a reservation of powers of working and getting the excepted minerals[2] in as full and ample a way as if the transfer of the surface had not been made, coupled or not with a provision for payment by the grantor of compensation for damage or injury done in the exercise of the reserved powers. In these circumstances there may be a necessary implication from the language used that the grantor should be entitled to let down the surface, if he is to be able to work and carry away the minerals as fully as he could have done before the transfer[3].

1    See *Harris v Ryding* (1839) 5 M & W 60; *Smart v Morton* (1855) 5 E & B 30; *Roberts v Haines* (1856) 6 E & B 643 (affd sub nom *Haines v Roberts* (1857) 7 E & B 625, Ex Ch); *Caledonian Rly Co v Sprot (of Garnkirk)* (1856) 2 Macq 449, HL; *Proud v Bates* (1865) 34 LJ Ch 406; *Buchanan v Andrew* (1873) LR 2 Sc & Div 286 at 290, HL, per Lord Selborne LC; *Bell v Love* (1883) 10 QBD 547, CA (affd *Love v Bell* (1884) 9 App Cas 286, HL); *New Sharlston Collieries Co Ltd v Earl of Westmorland* (1900) [1904] 2 Ch 443n, HL; *Bishop Auckland Industrial Co-operative*

*Society Ltd v Butterknowle Colliery Co Ltd* [1904] 2 Ch 419 at 435, CA, per Vaughan Williams LJ (on appeal sub nom *Butterknowle Colliery Co Ltd v Bishop Auckland Industrial Co-operative Co Ltd* [1906] AC 305 at 309, HL, per Lord Loreburn LC); *Butterley Co Ltd v New Hucknall Colliery Co Ltd* [1910] AC 381, HL. As to the meaning of 'mine' see PARA 3.

2   As to the meaning of 'minerals' see PARA 10.

3   See *Beard v Moira Colliery Co Ltd* [1915] 1 Ch 257, CA. The conveyance in this case contained a provision for payment of compensation for damage to the surface, and it was held that the decisions in *Love v Bell* (1884) 9 App Cas 286, HL, and *Butterknowle Colliery Co Ltd v Bishop Auckland Industrial Co-operative Co Ltd* [1906] AC 305, HL, were not to be extended to the construction of deeds contrary to the long established rule that ordinary words ought to be given their plain and ordinary meaning. See also *Brewer v Rhymney Iron Co* [1910] 1 Ch 766; *Davies v Powell Duffryn Steam Coal Co Ltd* [1917] 1 Ch 488, CA; *Davies v Powell Duffryn Steam Coal Co Ltd (No 2)* (1921) 91 LJ Ch 40, CA, where there was no provision for compensation for surface damage. These Court of Appeal decisions appeared to set at rest a point which had been in doubt since *Chamber Colliery Co Ltd v Twyerould* (1893) [1915] 1 Ch 268n, HL, where Lord Watson treated it as a question of some nicety whether similar words were sufficient to oust the common law right to support. In *New Sharlston Collieries Co Ltd v Earl of Westmorland* (1900) [1904] 2 Ch 443n, HL, Lord Halsbury LC expressed the opinion that such words were in themselves sufficient 'to carry you the whole way'. See further, however, *Wath-upon-Dearne UDC v John Brown & Co Ltd* [1936] Ch 172, where Luxmoore J, construing an Inclosure Act which included such words, held that the common law right of support was not displaced.

## 130.   Implication from knowledge of parties and mining practice.

An implication of the right to withdraw support may also be made where it is admitted or proved[1] that the parties entered into the transaction with the knowledge that it was impossible to work the mines without causing subsidence[2]. Such knowledge may be a matter of inference from mining practice at the date of severance[3].

1   Ie by relevant admissible evidence: see PARA 128.

2   *Butterley Co Ltd v New Hucknall Colliery Co Ltd* [1910] AC 381, HL; *Locker-Lampson v Staveley Coal and Iron Co Ltd* (1908) 25 TLR 136. As to the meaning of 'mine' see PARA 3. As to subsidence damage see PARA 182 et seq.

3   *Butterley Co Ltd v New Hucknall Colliery Co Ltd* [1909] 1 Ch 37, CA; affd [1910] AC 381, HL, where the evidence showed that at the date of severance it was a matter of common knowledge that it was impossible to work the minerals commercially without causing subsidence. The court therefore gave effect to the presumption that the parties intended the minerals to be enjoyed. A suggestion made in that case that there is a difference in principle between the right to support of overlying seams and the right to support of the surface is, it is submitted, untenable: see *Butterley Co Ltd v New Hucknall Colliery Co Ltd* at 386 per Lord Macnaghten. As to the inference of knowledge from evidence of mining practice see also *Locker-Lampson v Staveley Iron and Coal Co Ltd* (1908) 25 TLR 136; *Jones v Consolidated Anthracite Collieries Ltd and Lord Dynevor* [1916] 1 KB 123; *Welldon v Butterley Co Ltd* [1920] 1 Ch 130 (overruled on another point by *Warwickshire Coal Co Ltd v Coventry Corpn* [1934] Ch 488, CA); and cf *Wath-upon-Dearne UDC v John Brown & Co Ltd* [1936] Ch 172 (knowledge acquired after transaction not enough). As to the meaning of 'minerals' see PARA 10

## 131.   Implication from express covenants.

A covenant by lessees to work mines[1] fairly and regularly according to the best and most improved method in use in the district indicates an intention to authorise, even if it does not enjoin, the lessees to work on the longwall system if that is the best and most improved system in use in the district[2]. Further, a mining lease may impose on the lessee an obligation to perform certain acts which are plainly inconsistent with the support of the surface[3], as where the lessee is under covenant to work so as to produce from the mine the greatest quantity of merchantable coals from each of the seams, and is by the same instrument prohibited from working under a certain area in order that such area may be absolutely protected. Where a substantial area is so protected, the inference may be drawn that the part not specifically protected may be let down[4].

The protection of a specific area by the absolute prohibition of the working of minerals under it is not, however, necessarily inconsistent with the continuance of the common law right of support from the minerals outside that area[5]; the question is whether upon the construction of the instrument as a whole the common law right is excluded[6].

1   As to the meaning of 'mine' see PARA 3.
2   See *Butterley Co Ltd v New Hucknall Colliery Co Ltd* [1910] AC 381 at 389, HL, per Lord Atkinson; cf *Shafto v Johnson* (1863) 8 B & S 252n at 256n per Page Wood V-C; *Buchanan v Andrew* (1873) LR 2 Sc & Div 286 at 292, HL, per Lord Selborne LC. In *Davis v Treharne* (1881) 6 App Cas 460 at 464, HL, Lord Selborne considered that a covenant to work in 'the most usual and approved way of working' in the county related to the manner of working the mine for mining purposes, and did not affect the collateral obligation to support the surface, that there could not possibly be any local custom in such a district to disregard the right of the surface owner who was not a lessor of the mines, and that the position was no different if the surface owner was also lessor of the mines.
3   See *Davis v Treharne* (1881) 6 App Cas 460 at 469, HL, per Lord Watson.
4   See *Shafto v Johnson* (1863) 8 B & S 252n at 255n per Page Wood V-C. The same lease was considered in *Taylor v Shafto* (1867) 8 B & S 228. The reasoning of Page Wood V-C in *Shafto v Johnson* may perhaps explain the dictum of Lord Macnaghten in *Butterknowle Colliery Co Ltd v Bishop Auckland Industrial Co-operative Co Ltd* [1906] AC 305 at 313, HL, to the effect that an obligation in a lease to work out the minerals or to work the minerals in a prescribed manner is not sufficient to exclude the presumption that the surface is to be supported. It was this decision which led Neville J, in *Butterley Co Ltd v New Hucknall Colliery Co Ltd* [1908] 2 Ch 475 (revsd [1909] 1 Ch 37, CA), against his own inclination to find that the right of support was not excluded. Lord Macnaghten himself did not consider that the decision in *Butterley Co Ltd v New Hucknall Colliery Co Ltd* [1910] AC 381, HL (affg [1909] 1 Ch 37, CA) was in any way inconsistent with what he had said in *Butterknowle Colliery Co Ltd v Bishop Auckland Industrial Co-operative Co Ltd*; and see [1910] AC at 385. In *Markham v Paget* [1908] 1 Ch 697 at 710, Swinfen Eady J, on the authority of the same dictum, refused to imply, in an agreement for a lease, leave to work on the longwall system, which would necessarily cause subsidence, although the agreement provided that the lease should contain clauses and conditions usual in similar leases in the counties of Derby and Nottingham, and it was proved that working by the longwall system was the usual system in the district. As to the meaning of 'minerals' see PARA 10.
5   See *Haines v Roberts* (1857) 7 E & B 625, Ex Ch; *Dugdale v Robertson* (1857) 3 K & J 695.
6   See *Shafto v Johnson* (1863) 8 B & S 252n; *Chamber Colliery Co Ltd v Twyerould* (1893) [1915] 1 Ch 268n, HL; *Brewer v Rhymney Iron Co* [1910] 1 Ch 766 at 770 per Parker J.

**132. Implication from compensation provisions.**

Where the power of getting the minerals[1] is made subject to the payment of compensation for surface damage, the scope of the compensation clause may, in the absence of evidence as to the inevitability of subsidence, be material in considering the extent of the working powers granted or reserved[2]. It is not the function of a compensation clause to define or extend working powers[3]. If the clause is capable of being satisfied by construing it as a provision for compensation in respect of surface injury, caused by the exercise of surface powers, it will be so limited, even where it is wide enough in terms to include surface injury caused by subsidence[4]; if the clause does, in fact, cover injury by subsidence, it only provides a cumulative remedy[5]. In such a case it may refer to injury caused by accident or negligence[6], and a provision for compensation for injury caused by subsidence is not inconsistent with an obligation not to let down[7].

The clause may, nevertheless, be so framed as to explain the character and extent of the working powers[8]; thus where no surface powers are granted, but the powers of working are subject to the condition that compensation must be made for injury to buildings on the surface, it is a reasonable, if not a necessary, inference that the kind of working contemplated and sanctioned is such as would cause subsidence and injury to buildings on the surface[9]. On similar principles, where no surface powers are granted and the mine[10] owner is expressly exempted from liability in respect of injury to the surface and the buildings on it, the clause cannot be satisfied by injury other than subsidence, and a power to let down will be inferred[11].

1   As to the meaning of 'minerals' see PARA 10.
2   See *Executors of John Hargreaves Ltd v Burnley Corpn* [1936] 3 All ER 959 at 968, CA, per Slesser LJ.
3   *Love v Bell* (1884) 9 App Cas 286 at 299, HL, per Lord Watson. As to compensation clauses see PARA 340.
4   *Butterknowle Colliery Co Ltd v Bishop Auckland Industrial Co-operative Co Ltd* [1906] AC 305 at 309, 310, HL, per Lord Loreburn LC; and see *Harris v Ryding* (1839) 5 M & W 60; *Smart v Morton* (1855) 5 E & B 30; *Allaway v Wagstaff* (1859) 4 H & N 681; *Davis v Treharne* (1881) 6 App Cas 460, HL; *Mundy v Duke of Rutland* (1883) 23 ChD 81, CA; *Dixon v White* (1883) 8 App Cas 833, HL; *Sitwell v Earl of Londesborough* [1905] 1 Ch 460. As to subsidence damage see PARA 182 et seq.
5   *Harris v Ryding* (1839) 5 M & W 60.
6   See *Dixon v White* (1883) 8 App Cas 833, HL.
7   *New Sharlston Collieries Co Ltd v Earl of Westmorland* (1900) [1904] 2 Ch 443n, HL; see at 447n per Lord Davey, who seems to refer to a general provision which may include injury by subsidence, and not necessarily an express provision for compensation for injury caused by subsidence; *Davis v Treharne* (1881) 6 App Cas 460 at 467, 468, HL, per Lord Blackburn; *Butterknowle Colliery Co Ltd v Bishop Auckland Industrial Co-operative Co Ltd* [1906] AC 305 at 315, 316, HL, per Lord Davey.
8   *Love v Bell* (1884) 9 App Cas 286 at 299, HL, per Lord Watson.
9   *Aspden v Seddon* (1875) 10 Ch App 394; and see *Love v Bell* (1884) 9 App Cas 286 at 299, HL, per Lord Watson. See also *Smith v Darby* (1872) LR 7 QB 716; *Twyerould v Chamber Colliery Co* [1892] WN 27, CA (on appeal (1893) sub nom *Chamber Colliery Co v Twyerould* [1915] 1 Ch 268n, HL), where there were surface powers, but the compensation clause extended to injury done to buildings, and a right to cause subsidence was inferred. In *Duke of Buccleuch v Wakefield* (1870) LR 4 HL 377 (a case on an Inclosure Act), a power to cause subsidence was inferred; there was a wide compensation provision. The latter case is discussed in *Hext v Gill* (1872) 7 Ch App 699 at 716–717 per Mellish LJ, and in *Love v Bell* at 295, 296, 298 per Lord Watson; it stands by itself. See also *Butterknowle Colliery Co Ltd v Bishop Auckland Industrial Co-operative Co Ltd* [1906] AC 305 at 314, HL, per Lord Macnaghten, and at 316 per Lord Davey.
10  As to the meaning of 'mine' see PARA 3.
11  *Williams v Bagnall* (1866) 15 WR 272; *Buchanan v Andrew* (1873) LR 2 Sc & Div 286, HL.

### 133. Effect of absence of compensation provisions.

The absence of a provision for compensation is almost conclusive that the common law obligation is to continue[1], and the inadequacy or inappropriateness of the compensation, if applied to damage by subsidence, is cogent evidence that subsidence was not contemplated[2]. Thus a provision for a yearly payment to the surface occupiers for damage and spoil of ground during the time of working cannot apply to subsidence damage, for such damage injures the owner, and may not occur until the workings have ceased[3]; and a provision that compensation for injury to an allotment in the exercise of reserved mining powers should be made by a rateable levy, enforceable by distress, on the occupiers of other allotments within the township, cannot refer to subsidence, for it would compel temporary occupiers to pay for permanent damage[4].

1   See *Butterknowle Colliery Co Ltd v Bishop Auckland Industrial Co-operative Co Ltd* [1906] AC 305 at 315, HL, per Lord Davey; *Bell v Earl of Dudley* [1895] 1 Ch 182.
2   See *Butterknowle Colliery Co Ltd v Bishop Auckland Industrial Co-operative Co Ltd* [1906] AC 305 at 314, HL, per Lord Macnaghten. As to subsidence see PARA 182 et seq.
3   *Love v Bell* (1884) 9 App Cas 286, HL.
4   *Butterknowle Colliery Co Ltd v Bishop Auckland Industrial Co-operative Co Ltd* [1906] AC 305, HL.

## 134. Custom and prescription.

An alleged custom to work under the tenements of a manor or under an allotment of the waste so as to cause subsidence, but without payment of compensation, is unreasonable and void[1]; although a claim to cause subsidence, based on prescription or custom, may be good, if the exercise of the right is subject to the payment of compensation[2]. The custom alleged must be shown to have existed at the time of severance[3].

1 *Wolstanton Ltd and A-G of Duchy of Lancaster v Newcastle-under-Lyme Corpn* [1940] AC 860, [1940] 3 All ER 101, HL, approving *Hilton v Earl Granville* (1844) 5 QB 701 (tenements). See also *Bell v Love* (1883) 10 QBD 547, CA (affd sub nom *Love v Bell* (1884) 9 App Cas 286, HL); *Marquis of Salisbury v Gladstone* (1861) 9 HL Cas 692; *Blackett v Bradley* (1862) 1 B & S 940 (allotments). In *Gill v Dickinson* (1880) 5 QBD 159, DC, a case on the same Inclosure Act as *Blackett v Bradley* the custom was admitted, but the decision has been overruled on this point by *Butterknowle Colliery Co Ltd v Bishop Auckland Industrial Co-operative Co Ltd* [1906] AC 305, HL, a case on the same Inclosure Act.

2 As to custom see *Wolstanton Ltd and A-G of Duchy of Lancaster v Newcastle-under-Lyme Corpn* [1940] AC 860, [1940] 3 All ER 101, HL; *Aspden v Seddon, Preston v Seddon* (1876) 1 Ex D 496 at 510, CA, per Mellish LJ. See also *Duke of Buccleuch v Wakefield* (1870) LR 4 HL 377 at 395, 396, 399, per Lord Hatherley LC; and CUSTOM AND USAGE. As to prescription see *Rowbotham v Wilson* (1860) 8 HL Cas 348 at 363 per Lord Wensleydale; and REAL PROPERTY AND REGISTRATION. There can be no custom of a county to work to the prejudice of third persons: see *Davis v Treharne* (1881) 6 App Cas 460 at 464, HL, per Lord Selborne.

3 *Smart v Morton* (1855) 5 E & B 30.

# (2) Support and Compulsory Acquisition

### (i) In General

## 135. General statutory codes.

In modern statutes conferring powers for the construction and maintenance of railways and powers for the compulsory purchase of land[1] there are incorporated provisions of the Railways Clauses Consolidation Act 1845 or the Acquisition of Land Act 1981. Each of these Acts contains a group of sections dealing with mines and minerals known as a 'mining code'[2]. The mining code of the Acquisition of Land Act 1981 is a re-enactment in modern form of the code in the Railways Clauses Consolidation Act 1845[3].

The mining code of the Railways Clauses Consolidation Act 1845 was substantially modified[4] by the Mines (Working Facilities and Support) Act 1923, and the mining code as so modified is substituted[5] for the original code in the Railways Clauses Consolidation Act 1845 as incorporated in any Act, order or other instrument relating to a railway company passed or made on or after 18 July 1923[6] except in so far as the Act, order or other instrument provides to the contrary[7]. The code as substituted by the Mines (Working Facilities and Support) Act 1923 is itself replaced in relation to railway property by the continuing effect of an agreement[8] which was made[9] between the British Railways Board and the National Coal Board (later renamed the British Coal Corporation[10]).

A compulsory purchase order[11] may, as respects all or any of the land to which it relates, provide for the incorporation with it of the mining code of the Acquisition of Land Act 1981[12]. A local Act may incorporate the code of the Railways Clauses Consolidation Act 1845[13]; and model clauses prescribed for inclusion in ministerial orders authorising railways and tramways[14] provide for the incorporation of the code as substituted[15].

The relations of water and sewerage undertakers[16] and of the Environment Agency[17] with owners, lessees and occupiers of minerals are governed by the mining code of the Water Industry Act 1991 and the Water Resources Act 1991[18]. The code, which is dealt with elsewhere in this work[19], has a broad similarity to the codes referred to above, but differs in some respects[20].

1   As to compulsory acquisition of land generally see COMPULSORY ACQUISITION OF LAND.

2   Ie the Railways Clauses Consolidation Act 1845 ss 77–85; and the Acquisition of Land Act 1981 s 3, Sch 2. As to the meaning of 'mine' see PARA 3. The principal mining codes restrict the meaning of 'mine', at least for some purposes: see the Railways Clauses Consolidation Act 1845 s 77; the Acquisition of Land Act 1981 s 3, Sch 2 para 1(2); and PARAS 3, 142. As to the meaning of 'minerals' see PARA 10. See also PARAS 11–13.

3   See the Acquisition of Land Act 1981 Sch 2 Pt I para 1(1). Schedule 2 has effect subject to the Coal Industry Act 1994 s 10(3) (restriction on the circumstances in which powers of compulsory purchase are exercisable in respect of coal or coal mines) (see PARA 70): Acquisition of Land Act 1981 Sch 2 para 1(5) (amended by the Coal Industry Act 1994 s 67(1), Sch 9 para 27(3)).

4   See PARA 143 et seq.

5   The substituted code for railways represents a statutory compromise between railway authorities and mine owners agreed in consequence of the decision in *Howley Park Coal and Cannel Co Ltd v London and North Western Rly Co* [1913] AC 11, HL: see *London and North Eastern Rly Co v BA Collieries Ltd* [1945] AC 143 at 176, 177, [1945] 1 All ER 51 at 61, HL, per Lord Macmillan, and at 188, 189 and 68 per Lord Simonds (dissenting); *Thomas McGhie & Sons Ltd v British Transport Commission* [1963] 1 QB 125 at 178, [1962] 2 All ER 646 at 649 per Phillimore J.

6   Ie the date of the passing of the Mines (Working Facilities and Support) Act 1923. For an example of the incorporation of the unamended provisions of the Railways Clauses Consolidation Act 1845 see the Requisitioned Land and War Works Act 1948 s 15(3); and ARMED CONFLICT AND EMERGENCY vol 3 (2011) PARA 139.

7   See the Mines (Working Facilities and Support) Act 1923 s 15 (amended by the Decimal Currency Act 1969 s 10(1)). Where (1) a special Act, order, scheme or certificate confirmed by or having the force of an Act of Parliament relating to a railway company, passed or confirmed before 1 January 1924 (the date of commencement of the Mines (Working Facilities and Support) Act 1923: see s 18(2) (repealed)), incorporates the original mining code of the Railways Clauses Consolidation Act 1845, and does not prescribe any distance in lieu of the distance of 40 yards mentioned in the original mining code (see PARA 149); or (2) a special Act relating to a railway company, passed before 1 January 1924, does not incorporate the original mining code, but contains similar provisions, including a provision prescribing a distance of 40 yards, then such Act, order, scheme or certificate takes effect as from that date as if the new mining code were substituted for the original code as incorporated in the Act, order, scheme or certificate, or for the similar provisions contained in the special Act, as the case may be, subject to the Mines (Working Facilities and Support) Act 1923 s 16(2)–(4): s 16(1). See in particular the saving for rights acquired before 1 January 1924 in s 16(4); and PARA 175.

8   The agreement was dated 26 January 1982 and superseded an agreement dated 30 November 1959. It was expressed to be made in exercise of powers conferred by the Coal-Mining (Subsidence) Act 1957 s 6(4) (repealed). Similar powers are contained now in the Coal Mining Subsidence Act 1991 s 37(4): see PARA 246.

9   The agreement continues in effect subject to the provisions of transfer schemes made under the Railways Act 1993 Pt II (ss 84–116) and of a restructuring scheme made under the Coal Industry Act 1994 s 7. As to restructuring schemes see PARA 72.

10 See PARA 49.

11 Ie an order authorising a compulsory purchase: see the Acquisition of Land Act 1981 s 2(1); and COMPULSORY ACQUISITION OF LAND vol 18 (2009) PARA 557.

12 See the Acquisition of Land Act 1981 Sch 2 para 1(1). The incorporation may extend to Sch 2 Pt II (which re-enacts the Railways Clauses Consolidation Act 1845 s 77 (see PARA 142)) or to the Acquisition of Land Act 1981 Sch 2 Pts II, III (which together re-enact the Railways Clauses Consolidation Act 1845 ss 77–85 (see PARA 143 et seq)): Acquisition of Land Act 1981 Sch 2 para 1(1)(a), (b).

The Acquisition of Land Act 1981 is a consolidating statute and replaces, inter alia, the Acquisition of Land (Authorisation Procedure) Act 1946 (repealed). Compulsory purchase orders made before 30 January 1982 (the date of commencement of the Acquisition of Land Act 1981: see s 35(2)) could incorporate the mining code of the Railways Clauses Consolidation Act 1845 as originally enacted (see PARA 143 et seq): Acquisition of Land (Authorisation Procedure) Act 1946 s 1(3), Sch 2 para 7(1) (repealed). See further COMPULSORY ACQUISITION OF LAND vol 18 (2009) PARAS 503, 556.

13 See COMPULSORY ACQUISITION OF LAND vol 18 (2009) PARA 515.

14 Ie under the Transport and Works Act 1992 s 8, which empowers the Secretary of State to prescribe model provisions for incorporation in draft orders concerning the construction and operation of railways and other transport systems. As to the Secretary of State see PARA 2.

15 See eg the model clauses set out in the Transport and Works (Model Clauses for Railways and Tramways) Order 2006, SI 2006/1954, art 3(a), Sch 1; and RAILWAYS AND TRAMWAYS vol 86 (2017) PARAS 313–314.

16 Ie 'relevant undertakers' within the meaning of the Water Industry Act 1991: see WATER AND WATERWAYS vol 100 (2018) PARA 505.

17 As to the Environment Agency see ENVIRONMENTAL QUALITY AND PUBLIC HEALTH vol 45 (2010) PARA 68 et seq; WATER AND WATERWAYS vol 100 (2018) PARA 23.

18 See the Water Industry Act 1991 s 188, Sch 14; and the Water Resources Act 1991 s 182, Sch 23 (amended by the Environment Act 1995 s 120(1), Sch 22 para 128; and SI 2009/1307). The code is the same in each of the Acts and is a re-enactment, in modern form, of the codes of the Waterworks Clauses Act 1847 ss 18–27 (repealed) and the Water Act 1945 s 32, Sch 3 Pt IV (repealed): see further WATER AND WATERWAYS vol 101 (2018) PARA 758.

19 See WATER AND WATERWAYS vol 101 (2018) PARA 758 et seq.

20 See *London and North Western Rly Co v Howley Park Coal and Cannel Co* [1911] 2 Ch 97 at 124–125, CA, per Fletcher Moulton LJ; affd sub nom *Howley Park Coal and Cannel Co v London and North Western Rly Co* [1913] AC 11, HL.

## 136.   Special statutes.

Before the passing of the mining codes[1], special provisions relating to mines[2] and minerals[3] were inserted in special Acts authorising the making and maintenance of railways, canals, waterworks, sanitary works, highways and similar works. These provisions were not uniform in character and involved different results as to the relative rights of the surface owner and the mine owner, and consequently regard must be had to the provisions of each particular Act to determine the obligation of the mine owner to support the statutory works and his right to compensation[4].

1   See PARA 135.

2   As to the meaning of 'mine' see PARA 3.

3   As to the meaning of 'minerals' see PARA 10.

4   See eg *Knowles & Sons v Lancashire and Yorkshire Rly Co* (1889) 14 App Cas 248, HL; *Wyrley Canal Co v Bradley* (1806) 7 East 368; *Dudley Canal Navigation Co v Grazebrook* (1830) 1 B & Ad 59; *Cromford Canal Co v Cutts* (1848) 5 Ry & Can Cas 442; *North Eastern Rly Co v Crosland* (1862) 32 LJ Ch 353; *Elliot v North Eastern Rly Co* (1863) 10 HL Cas 333; *Dunn v Birmingham Canal Co* (1872) LR 8 QB 42, Ex Ch; *London and North Western Rly Co v Evans* [1893] 1 Ch 16, CA; *Chamber Colliery Co Ltd v Rochdale Canal Co* [1895] AC 564, HL; *New Moss Colliery Co v Manchester, Sheffield and Lincolnshire Rly Co* [1897] 1 Ch 725; *Glamorganshire Canal Navigation Co v Nixon's Navigation Co Ltd* (1901) 85 LT 53, CA; *London and North Western Rly Co v Walker* [1903] AC 289, HL; *Ilkeston Collieries Ltd v Grand Union Canal Co* (1946) 175 LT 12. See further PARAS 137–141.

## 137.   Rights on acquisition by statutory powers.

The rights of a corporation which acquires land or erects works on land in pursuance of statutory powers are the same as would be those of an ordinary individual acquiring the land or erecting the works, except so far as those rights are expressly varied or excepted by the statute under which the land is acquired, or by contract between the parties. Save in so far as that statute or contract does vary or except those rights, the corporation, as against the vendor, is entitled prima facie to such a measure of support to the land purchased from the land (including the subjacent mines[1] and minerals[2]) retained as is necessary for the land purchased in its condition at the time of the purchase or when applied to the purpose for which the land was expressly acquired[3]; and the compensation payable includes the loss of value of the mines due to the liability to leave support[4]. However, this presumption may be displaced if there is no provision for giving the owner compensation for imposing this burden on his land[5]. The position may be different with regard to the adjacent mines and minerals of an owner between whom and the statutory undertakers there is no privity. If there is no provision for compensation to the adjacent owner, a right of support will not be presumed[6], but it may be otherwise when there are compensation provisions which can be applied[7].

1  As to the meaning of 'mine' see PARA 3.
2  As to the meaning of 'minerals' see PARA 10.
3  *Caledonian Rly Co v Sprot (of Garnkirk)* (1856) 2 Macq 449, HL; *Elliot v North Eastern Rly Co* (1863) 10 HL Cas 333 (railways under special Acts); *Re Dudley Corpn and Earl of Dudley's Trustees* (1881) 8 QBD 86, CA (sewer under the Public Health Act 1875; see also PARA 176); *Normanton Gas Co v Pope and Pearson Ltd* (1882) 48 LT 666 (affd (1883) 52 LJQB 629, CA) (gas mains under special Act); *London and North Western Rly Co v Evans* [1893] 1 Ch 16, CA (canal under special Act); *Clippens Oil Co v Edinburgh and District Water Trustees* [1904] AC 64, HL (water pipes under special Act); cf *Dixon v White* (1883) 8 App Cas 833, HL; *Bell v Earl of Dudley* [1895] 1 Ch 182. As to the ordinary presumption see PARA 114 et seq.
4  *London and North Western Rly Co v Evans* [1893] 1 Ch 16, CA; *Glamorganshire Canal Navigation Co v Nixon's Navigation Co Ltd* (1901) 85 LT 53, CA. Where compensation has been assessed on the basis that a right of support exists no further claim for compensation in respect of such a right may be made when it is desired to work the minerals: *Great Western Rly Co v Cefn Cribbwr Brick Co* [1894] 2 Ch 157.
5  *London and North Western Rly Co v Evans* [1893] 1 Ch 16 at 28, CA, per Bowen LJ (approved generally in *Clippens Oil Co v Edinburgh and District Water Trustees* [1904] AC 64, HL); *Re Dudley Corpn and Earl of Dudley's Trustees* (1881) 8 QBD 86 at 93, 95, CA, per Brett LJ; *Benfieldside Local Board v Consett Iron Co* (1877) 3 Ex D 54. See also PARA 133.
6  *Metropolitan Board of Works v Metropolitan Rly Co* (1869) LR 4 CP 192, Ex Ch. This was a case of a sewer constructed under a special Act; the sewer might have been constructed of sufficient strength not to require the lateral support of which it was deprived: see *Roderick v Aston Local Board* (1877) 5 ChD 328 at 332 per Jessel MR; affd (1877) 5 ChD 328 at 333, CA. As to the construction of compensation clauses see PARAS 132–133.
7  See *Re Dudley Corpn and Earl of Dudley's Trustees* (1881) 8 QBD 86, CA, in conjunction with *Roderick v Aston Local Board* (1877) 5 ChD 328, CA, explained in *Jary v Barnsley Corpn* [1907] 2 Ch 600.

## 138. Special provisions as to support.

Railway Acts passed before the enactment of the general statutory code[1], canal Acts and other similar Acts usually contain specific provisions with regard to mines[2] and minerals[3]. Whether the undertakers acquire a right of support is then a question of the construction of the special provisions of the Acts[4]. The Acts may be divided into three classes:

(1)     those in which there is an immediate expressed or implied grant of the right of support, with an inherent right to immediate compensation on the part of the mine owner[5];

(2)     those in which the mine owner can compel the purchase of support when he is proceeding to work his minerals[6]; and

(3)     those under which the undertakers have a right, but are under no obligation, to purchase support when the minerals are about to be worked[7].

1  See PARA 135.
2  As to the meaning of 'mine' see PARA 3.
3  As to the meaning of 'minerals' see PARA 10.
4  *Cromford Canal Co v Cutts* (1848) 5 Ry & Can Cas 442; *Knowles & Sons v Lancashire and Yorkshire Rly Co* (1889) 14 App Cas 248, HL; *London and North Western Rly Co v Walker* [1903] AC 289, HL.
5  See PARA 139.
6  See PARA 140.
7  See PARA 141.

### 139.   Inherent right to immediate compensation.

A grant of the right of support will be presumed unless there is some provision inconsistent with the ordinary presumption as between grantor and grantee[1]. In addition there may be an express statutory liability imposed on the owner of the mine[2] not to injure the undertakers' works[3]; or he may be prohibited from working without the undertakers' consent and without giving security for damage done to their works[4]. In these cases the mine owner has an inherent right to immediate compensation for his obligation to leave support[5], and this is an item which falls to be included in the compensation paid on the acquisition of the land[6]. After the lapse of time, it will be presumed to have been so included[7] or to have been waived[8], even if it appears that the matter was not in fact considered at the time of the acquisition[9].

1  See *Caledonian Rly Co v Sprot (of Garnkirk)* (1856) 2 Macq 449, HL; *Elliot v North Eastern Rly Co* (1863) 10 HL Cas 333; *North Eastern Rly Co v Crosland* (1862) 4 De GF & J 550; *Benfieldside Local Board v Consett Iron Co* (1877) 3 Ex D 54 (highway). As to the ordinary presumption see PARA 114 et seq.
2  As to the meaning of 'mine' see PARA 3.
3  *Elliot v North Eastern Rly Co* (1863) 10 HL Cas 333; *North Eastern Rly Co v Crosland* (1862) 4 De GF & J 550.
4  *Caledonian Rly Co v Sprot (of Garnkirk)* (1856) 2 Macq 449, HL.
5  See *North Eastern Rly Co v Elliot* (1860) 1 John & H 145 at 153–154 per Page Wood V-C; affd 2 De GF & J 423 at 432 per Lord Campbell LC.
6  *Re Dudley Corpn and Earl of Dudley's Trustees* (1881) 8 QBD 86, CA.
7  *London and North Western Rly Co v Evans* [1893] 1 Ch 16, CA; *Clippens Oil Co v Edinburgh and District Water Trustees* [1904] AC 64 at 69, 70, HL, per the Earl of Halsbury LC, and at 71 per Lord Robertson.
8  *London and North Western Rly Co v Evans* [1893] 1 Ch 16, CA; *Clippens Oil Co v Edinburgh and District Water Trustees* [1904] AC 64, HL; and see *Glamorganshire Canal Navigation Co v Nixon's Navigation Co Ltd* (1901) 85 LT 53, CA.
9  *Glamorganshire Canal Navigation Co v Nixon's Navigation Co Ltd* (1901) 85 LT 53, CA.

### 140.   Power to compel assessment of compensation.

In some canal Acts there is imposed upon the owner of excepted mines[1] and minerals[2] an obligation not to injure the canal as a result of working the mines and minerals. As a rule the obligation is subject to a right on the part of the mine owner, if the result of his working will be to injure the canal or to flood his mines, to initiate proceedings for the assessment of compensation in respect of his obligation to leave support and to compel payment[3]. In such a case, if, instead of compelling the assessment of compensation, the mine owner proceeds to work and injures the canal, he is liable in damages[4]. Where, however, there are provisions for payment of compensation which apply to mines 'near or under' the canal[5], and the canal undertaker lawfully refuses to pay compensation, the owner of adjacent mines is not liable in damages on working and injuring the canal[6], even if he is also the owner of the subjacent mines[7].

1  As to the meaning of 'mine' see PARA 3. As to the meaning of 'mines and minerals' see PARA 10.
2  As to the meaning of 'minerals' see PARA 10.
3  *Cromford Canal Co v Cutts* (1848) 5 Ry & Can Cas 442.
4  *Knowles & Sons v Lancashire and Yorkshire Rly Co* (1889) 14 App Cas 248, HL.
5  See, however, *Manchester, Sheffield and Lincolnshire Rly Co v Johnson* (1883) 36 ChD 629n; *Evans v Manchester, Sheffield and Lincolnshire Rly Co* (1887) 36 ChD 626.
6  *Chamber Colliery Co Ltd v Rochdale Canal Co* [1895] AC 564, HL.
7  *New Moss Colliery Co v Manchester, Sheffield and Lincolnshire Rly Co* [1897] 1 Ch 725.

## 141.  Option to acquire support.

Some special Acts contain provisions similar to the provisions of the mining code[1]. The common law right of support is displaced from the moment when the owner of the mine[2] in good faith desires to work such of his minerals[3] as lie within the limits prescribed by the Act[4]. The undertakers then have an option, but are under no obligation, to purchase the minerals or to pay compensation in respect of their being left unworked. In these circumstances there may be no remedy available to the mine owner if his mines are flooded[5].

1  Where these Acts relate to a railway company and prescribe a distance of 40 yards (see PARA 149), the provisions of the mining code for railways, as substituted by the Mines (Working Facilities and Support) Act 1923, apply: see s 16(1); and PARAS 135, 142, 145 et seq.
2  As to the meaning of 'mine' see PARA 3.
3  As to the meaning of 'minerals' see PARA 10.
4  See *Dunn v Birmingham Canal Co* (1872) LR 7 QB 244 at 256 per Cockburn CJ (affd LR 8 QB 42, Ex Ch); *Ilkeston Collieries Ltd v Grand Union Canal Co* (1946) 175 LT 12.
5  See *Dunn v Birmingham Canal Co* (1872) LR 7 QB 244 at 256 per Cockburn CJ (affd LR 8 QB 42, Ex Ch); and the Acts considered in *Dudley Canal Navigation Co v Grazebrook* (1830) 1 B & Ad 59; followed in *Stourbridge Navigation Co v Earl of Dudley* (1860) 3 E & E 409, Ex Ch. See also the provisions for support of masonry referred to in *North Eastern Rly Co v Elliot* (1860) 1 John & H 145; affd 2 De GF & J 423. See also *Birmingham Canal Navigation Co v Earl of Dudley* (1862) 7 H & N 969 Ex Ch; *Birmingham Canal Navigation Co v Swindell* (1856) 7 H & N 980n; *Midland Rly Co v Checkley* (1867) LR 4 Eq 19 (lateral support).

## (ii)  Railways, Land Acquired under Compulsory Powers and Sanitary Works

## 142.  Minerals do not impliedly pass with the surface.

Under the mining codes[1], railway and other authorities are not entitled to any mines[2] of coal, ironstone, slate or other minerals[3] under land[4] which they have purchased, except such parts of the mines as are necessary to be dug or carried away or used in the construction of the works[5], unless those mines are expressly purchased; and, with those exceptions, all those mines are deemed to be excepted out of the conveyance of the land unless they are expressly named in it and conveyed by it[6].

1  See PARA 135. The codes are self-contained and complete, save as expressly varied by any special Act or agreement: *London and North Eastern Rly Co v BA Collieries Ltd* [1945] AC 143 at 180, [1945] 1 All ER 51 at 63, HL, per Lord Wright.
2  As to the meaning of 'mine' see PARA 3. As to the meaning of 'mines and minerals' see PARA 10.
3  As to the meaning of 'minerals' see PARA 10.
4  As to or the meaning of 'land' see PARA 143.
5  See the Railways Clauses Consolidation Act 1845 s 77. The re-enactment in the Acquisition of Land Act 1981 s 3, Sch 2 para 2 (see PARA 135) refers to 'minerals necessarily extracted or used in the construction of the undertaking'. As to the construction of the words in the Railways Clauses Consolidation Act 1845 s 77 see *Great Western Rly Co v Bennett* (1867) LR 2 HL 27 at

38 per Lord Chelmsford LC; *Errington v Metropolitan District Rly Co* (1882) 19 ChD 559, CA; *Nisbet Hamilton v North British Rly Co* (1886) 13 R 454, Ct of Sess.

For the corresponding provisions in the codes relating to water and sewerage undertakers and the Environment Agency see WATER AND WATERWAYS vol 101 (2018) PARA 759.

6   Railways Clauses Consolidation Act 1845 s 77; Acquisition of Land Act 1981 Sch 2 para 2(1), (2). As to whether, under the Railways Clauses Consolidation Act 1845 (as originally enacted), authorities acquiring land from persons having the surface only, but with a right of support, obtain that right with the surface, see *Great Western Rly Co v Fletcher* (1860) 5 H & N 689, Ex Ch; *Pountney v Clayton* (1883) 11 QBD 820 at 843, CA, per Bowen LJ; *Consett Waterworks Co v Ritson* (1889) 22 QBD 318 at 328, 329 per A L Smith J (on appeal 22 QBD 702, CA); *London and North Western Rly Co v Howley Park Coal and Cannel Co* [1911] 2 Ch 97 at 116, 121, 122, 124, 125, CA, per Fletcher Moulton LJ (affd sub nom *Howley Park Coal and Cannel Co v London and North Western Rly Co* [1913] AC 11 HL); and cf, as to the position created by the corresponding provision in the Waterworks Clauses Act 1847 s 18 (repealed), *New Moss Colliery Ltd v Manchester Corpn* [1908] AC 117, HL; *London and North Western Rly Co v Howley Park Coal and Cannel Co* at 110 per Cozens-Hardy MR, at 124–126 per Fletcher Moulton LJ, and at 130–131 per Buckley LJ; *Wath-upon-Dearne UDC v John Brown & Co Ltd* [1936] Ch 172; *Executors of John Hargreaves Ltd v Burnley Corpn* [1936] 3 All ER 959, CA. See also PARAS WATER AND WATERWAYS vol 101 (2018) PARA 759. As to wrongful abstraction of minerals by a railway authority see PARA 42.

## 143.   General effect of mining codes in relation to railways and compulsory acquisition of land.

Where the mining code of the Railways Clauses Consolidation Act 1845[1] or the mining code of the Acquisition of Land Act 1981 applies[2], the railway or other authority purchasing land[3] is under no necessity to lay out funds at the outset on the purchase of support from minerals[4] within the area of protection[5]: it may postpone such outlay until the mine owner desires to work the minerals[6]. The railway or other authority has no rights of subjacent or adjacent support from the minerals within the area of protection until and unless such support is acquired either by the purchase of the minerals[7] or by the payment of compensation for leaving the minerals unworked[8]. If the minerals are not purchased and the mine owner wishes to work his mines[9], then the occasion when the railway or other authority may acquire support arises; and if the authority, upon notice, does not wish to purchase such support, the mine owner may then remove the adjacent and subjacent support from minerals within the area of protection provided he works in the manner authorised by the code[10].

1   Ie the code either as originally enacted or as substituted by the Mines (Working Facilities and Support) Act 1923 s 15: see PARA 135.
2   See PARA 135.
3   In the mining code of the Railways Clauses Consolidation Act 1845 (both as originally enacted and as substituted), 'lands' includes messuages, land, tenements and hereditaments of any tenure: s 3. In the mining code of the Acquisition of Land Act 1981, 'land' includes messuages, tenements and hereditaments and, in relation to compulsory purchase under any enactment, includes anything falling within the definition of the expression in that enactment: s 7(1).
4   As to the meaning of 'minerals' see PARA 10.
5   As to the area of protection see PARA 149.
6   *Glasgow Corpn v Farie* (1888) 13 App Cas 657 at 675–676, HL, per Lord Watson; *Great Western Rly Co v Bennett* (1867) LR 2 HL 27; *Fletcher v Great Western Rly Co* (1859) 4 H & N 242 at 252 per Martin B, and at 253 per Watson B (affd sub nom *Great Western Rly Co v Fletcher* (1860) 5 H & N 689 at 698–699, Ex Ch, per Cockburn CJ); *Dunn v Birmingham Canal Co* (1872) LR 7 QB 244 at 256 per Cockburn CJ (affd LR 8 QB 42, Ex Ch); *Smith v Great Western Rly Co* (1877) 3 App Cas 165 at 175, HL, per Lord Cairns LC; *Dixon v Caledonian and Glasgow and South Western Railway Companies* (1880) 5 App Cas 820 at 832, HL, per Lord Selborne LC; *Midland Rly Co v Miles* (1885) 30 ChD 634 at 638 per Pearson J; *Midland Rly Co v Miles* (1886) 33 ChD 632 at 646 per Stirling J; *Midland Rly Co v Robinson* (1887) 37 ChD 386 at 395, CA, per Cotton LJ (affd (1889) 15 App Cas 19 at 28, HL, per Lord Herschell); *Consett Waterworks Co v Ritson* (1889) 22 QBD 318 at 328 per A L Smith J (on appeal 22 QBD 702, CA); *Ruabon*

*Brick and Terra Cotta Co v Great Western Rly Co* [1893] 1 Ch 427 at 454, CA, per Lindley LJ; *Re Lord Gerard and London and North Western Rly Co* [1895] 1 QB 459 at 465, CA, per Lord Esher MR; *Eden v North Eastern Rly Co* [1907] AC 400 at 407, HL, per Lord Macnaghten; *Rugby Portland Cement Co v London and North Western Rly Co* [1908] 2 KB 606 at 618, CA, per Farwell LJ; *Great Western Rly Co v Carpalla United China Clay Co Ltd* [1909] 1 Ch 218 at 230, CA, per Fletcher Moulton LJ (affd [1910] AC 83, HL); *North British Rly Co v Budhill Coal and Sandstone Co* [1910] AC 116 at 126, HL, per Lord Loreburn LC; *London and North Western Rly Co v Howley Park Coal and Cannel Co* [1911] 2 Ch 97 at 114, CA, per Fletcher Moulton LJ (affd sub nom *Howley Park Coal and Cannel Co v London and North Western Rly Co* [1913] AC 11, HL). Waterworks authorities are in a similar position: see *Holliday v Wakefield Corpn* [1891] AC 81 at 90, HL, per Lord Halsbury LC. See also WATER AND WATERWAYS vol 101 (2018) PARA 760.

7   See PARAS 142, 145–148.
8   See PARAS 157–159.
9   As to the meaning of 'mine' see PARA 3.
10   See PARA 160.

## 144. Effect of mining code on common law right of support.

The rights given by the mining code to the railway or other authority are in substitution for the common law rights of support, whether vertical or lateral, from minerals[1] within the area of protection[2]. The general effect of the code is to establish on a statutory basis the reciprocal rights of the railway or other authority and the mineral owners, and these rights are different from and inconsistent with the common law right of vertical and lateral support. In return for the servitude imposed on them, the mine owners have certain rights and privileges granted to them. Those rights and privileges are defined by statute, and are unaffected by any transactions between the railway or other authority and third persons[3].

1   As to the meaning of 'minerals' see PARA 10.
2   As to the area of protection see PARA 149.
3   See *Great Western Rly Co v Bennett* (1867) LR 2 HL 27; *Ruabon Brick and Terra Cotta Co v Great Western Rly Co* [1893] 1 Ch 427, CA; *Re Lord Gerard and London and North Western Rly Co* [1895] 1 QB 459 at 464, CA, per Lord Esher MR; *London and North Western Rly Co v Howley Park Coal and Cannel Co* [1911] 2 Ch 97 at 114, CA, per Fletcher Moulton LJ (affd sub nom *Howley Park Coal and Cannel Co v London and North Western Rly Co* [1913] AC 11, HL); and see *London and North Eastern Rly Co v BA Collieries Ltd* [1945] AC 143, [1945] 1 All ER 51, HL; cf *Ilkeston Collieries Ltd v Grand Union Canal Co* (1946) 175 LT 12. As to specific provision in the case of railways to which the code (see PARA 135) substituted by the Mines (Working Facilities and Support) Act 1923 s 15 applies see PARA 174.

## 145. Powers of railway or other authority to purchase mines.

Railway and other authorities empowered under the Lands Clauses Consolidation Act 1845 to purchase land, have power to purchase mines and minerals[1]. Where the mines and minerals belong to the same vendor as does the surface[2], the purchase of the mines and minerals is merely part of the purchase of the whole of the land, but the power extends also to cases where the mines and minerals and the surface are severed in ownership[3]. In the exercise of the power the authorities are not affected by the fact that the provisions of the mining codes[4] are applicable[5]. In any such purchase of land, however, the mines and minerals will not be included unless they are expressly conveyed[6]. The normal procedure is the purchase of the land without the mines and minerals, leaving the mines and minerals to be dealt with when the necessity for them arises[7].

1   See the Lands Clauses Consolidation Act 1845 s 6; *Errington v Metropolitan District Rly Co* (1882) 19 ChD 559, CA; and COMPULSORY ACQUISITION OF LAND vol 18 (2009) PARAS 550–551. As to the meaning of 'mine' see PARA 3; and as to the meaning of 'minerals' see PARA 10. See in particular PARA 10.

2   As to the meaning of 'surface' see PARA 17.
3   This is because 'lands' in the Lands Clauses Consolidation Act 1845 s 6 includes minerals:
    *Errington v Metropolitan District Rly Co* (1882) 19 ChD 559, CA; and see *Smith v Great Western
    Rly Co* (1877) 3 App Cas 165 at 180, HL, per Lord Cairns LC.
4   Ie the mining codes of the Railways Clauses Consolidation Act 1845 or of the Acquisition of Land
    Act 1981: see PARA 135.
5   *London and North Western Rly Co v Howley Park Coal and Cannel Co* [1911] 2 Ch 97 at 113,
    CA, per Fletcher Moulton LJ (affd sub nom *Howley Park Coal and Cannel Co v London and
    North Western Rly Co* [1913] AC 11, HL); and see *Errington v Metropolitan District Rly Co*
    (1882) 19 ChD 559, CA; *Midland Rly Co v Haunchwood Brick and Tile Co* (1882) 20 ChD 552
    at 556 per Kay J; *Pountney v Clayton* (1883) 11 QBD 820 at 833, CA, per Brett MR; *Holliday v
    Wakefield Corpn* [1891] AC 81 at 86, HL, per Lord Bramwell.
6   See PARA 142.
7   See *London and North Western Rly Co v Howley Park Coal and Cannel Co* [1911] 2 Ch 97, CA;
    affd sub nom *Howley Park Coal and Cannel Co v London and North Western Rly Co* [1913] AC
    11, HL.

## 146.   Mode of purchase.

The purchase may be by agreement or under the compulsory powers of the
railway or other authority[1] and the provisions of the empowering statute apply to
minerals[2] worked by surface workings as well as to those worked by underground
workings[3]. The mines[4] and minerals may be purchased as a separate tenement[5].
The mere fact that the authority has already purchased the surface does not
exhaust the power; the mines and minerals may be purchased at any time
subsequently within the period limited for the exercise of the power, and it is
optional on the part of the authority whether the whole, or a part only, of the
mines and minerals are purchased at any time[6].

1   See *London and North Western Rly Co v Howley Park Coal and Cannel Co* [1911] 2 Ch 97 at
    112, 113, CA, per Fletcher Moulton LJ; affd sub nom *Howley Park Coal and Cannel Co v London
    and North Western Rly Co* [1913] AC 11, HL.
2   As to the meaning of 'minerals' see PARA 10.
3   *Glasgow Corpn v Farie* (1888) 13 App Cas 657 at 678, HL, per Lord Watson.
4   As to the meaning of 'mine' see PARA 3.
5   *Errington v Metropolitan District Rly Co* (1882) 19 ChD 559, CA; *London and North Western
    Rly Co v Howley Park Coal and Cannel Co* [1911] 2 Ch 97 at 113, CA, per Fletcher Moulton LJ
    (affd sub nom *Howley Park Coal and Cannel Co v London and North Western Rly Co* [1913] AC
    11, HL); see *Great Western Rly Co v Bennett* (1867) LR 2 HL 27 at 40 per Lord Cranworth; and
    *Great Western Rly Co v Smith* (1876) 2 ChD 235 at 244, CA, per James LJ (affd sub nom *Smith
    v Great Western Rly Co* (1877) 3 App Cas 165, HL).
6   *Errington v Metropolitan District Rly Co* (1882) 19 ChD 559, CA; *Re Lord Gerard and London
    and North Western Rly Co* [1895] 1 QB 459 at 464, CA, per Lord Esher MR.

## 147.   Limits on exercise of powers.

The power to purchase is only exercisable in respect of mines[1] and minerals[2]
lying under land within the limits prescribed in the special Act, and the
compulsory power is only exercisable within the time prescribed by that Act[3].
After the expiration of the compulsory power, however, the railway or other
authority may at any time purchase the mines and minerals within those
prescribed limits by agreement[4]. In any event, the authority is empowered to make
such purchases, whether compulsory or voluntary, only for the purposes of the
works authorised to be constructed by it[5].

1   As to the meaning of 'mine' see PARA 3.
2   As to the meaning of 'minerals' see PARA 10.
3   *Errington v Metropolitan District Rly Co* (1882) 19 ChD 559, CA; *London and North Western
    Rly Co v Howley Park Coal and Cannel Co* [1911] 2 Ch 97 at 113, CA, per Fletcher Moulton LJ
    (affd sub nom *Howley Park Coal and Cannel Co v London and North Western Rly Co* [1913] AC
    11, HL). The usual time is three years after the passing of the special Act: see the Lands Clauses

Consolidation Act 1845 s 123; and COMPULSORY ACQUISITION OF LAND vol 18 (2009) PARA 617. The special Act is the Act which incorporates the statutory code.

4   *Thompson v Hickman* [1907] 1 Ch 550; *London and North Western Rly Co v Howley Park Coal and Cannel Co* [1911] 2 Ch 97, CA; affd sub nom *Howley Park Coal and Cannel Co v London and North Western Rly Co* [1913] AC 11, HL.

5   *Thompson v Hickman* [1907] 1 Ch 550; *London and North Western Rly Co v Howley Park Coal and Cannel Co* [1911] 2 Ch 97 at 113, CA, per Fletcher Moulton LJ (affd sub nom *Howley Park Coal and Cannel Co v London and North Western Rly Co* [1913] AC 11, HL); *Pountney v Clayton* (1883) 11 QBD 820 at 830 per Manisty J (on appeal 11 QBD 820 at 832, CA); *Re Lord Gerard and London and North Western Rly Co* [1894] 2 QB 915 (on appeal [1895] 1 QB 459, CA).

## 148. Authority is sole judge of its requirements.

The railway or other authority is the sole judge of what it requires, whether it requires only the surface[1], or the surface with the mines[2] and minerals[3], or only the mines and minerals, or only part of the mines and minerals, provided the authority acts in good faith; and the only evidence required is the opinion of the surveyor, engineer or other officer of the authority, unless the surface and mineral owners can show that the authority is not acting in good faith[4]. Want of good faith may be shown in various ways, for example by proving that the authority's object in taking the land is to use it for some collateral purpose; or by proving that the alleged purpose is so absurd, in the circumstances, that it cannot be in good faith[5]. It is not sufficient to say that the authority cannot want the mines and minerals at the time of the purchase of the surface merely because the railway or other works are sufficiently protected by the provisions of the mining code[6].

1   As to the meaning of 'surface' see PARA 17.
2   As to the meaning of 'mine' see PARA 3.
3   As to the meaning of 'minerals' see PARA 10.
4   *Errington v Metropolitan District Rly Co* (1882) 19 ChD 559 at 571, CA, per Jessel MR.
5   *Errington v Metropolitan District Rly Co* (1882) 19 ChD 559 at 571, CA, per Jessel MR.
6   See *Stockton and Darlington Rly Co v Brown* (1860) 9 HL Cas 246 at 256 per Lord Cranworth.

## 149. The area of protection.

The mining code of the Railways Clauses Consolidation Act 1845 as originally enacted and the mining code of the Acquisition of Land Act 1981[1] extend to the railway[2] or other undertaking[3] and the area within the prescribed distance[4] or, where no distance is prescribed, 40 yards from it[5].

Under the substituted code[6], the area of protection in relation to any seam[7] of minerals is the area comprising any railway or works of the authority and such a lateral distance therefrom, on all or both sides, as is equal at each point along the railway to one-half of the depth of the seam[8] at that point or 40 yards, whichever is the greater; and when the lateral distance exceeds 40 yards, the area of protection is divided into two areas: (1) an inner area consisting of the area comprising the railway or works and a distance of 40 yards therefrom on all sides; and (2) an outer area consisting of so much of the area of protection as is not included in the inner area[9].

1   See PARA 135.
2   'Railway' means the railway and works by the special Act authorised to be constructed: Railways Clauses Consolidation Act 1845 s 3.
3   In the mining code of the Acquisition of Land Act 1981, 'the undertaking' means the undertaking which the acquiring authority is authorised to carry out by the enactment under which the purchase is authorised, but the compulsory purchase order may include such modifications as may be specified in the order: s 3, Sch 2 para 1(4). In the Railways Clauses Consolidation Act 1845, 'the undertaking' means the railway and works of whatever description, by the special Act authorised to be executed: s 2.

4   Ie the distance prescribed by the special Act or, as the case may be, the compulsory purchase order:
    see the Railways Clauses Consolidation Act 1845 s 2; and the Acquisition of Land Act 1981 Sch 2
    para 1(3). As to the corresponding provisions in the codes relating to water and sewerage
    undertakers and the Environment Agency see WATER AND WATERWAYS vol 101 (2018)
    PARA 760.
5   See the Railways Clauses Consolidation Act 1845 s 78 (as originally enacted); and the Acquisition
    of Land Act 1981 Sch 2 para 1(3). A tenant for life may contract that a transaction affected by this
    provision is to take effect as if some distance other than 40 yards or the prescribed distance had
    been mentioned: see the Settled Land Act 1925 s 58(3); and SETTLEMENTS vol 91 (2012)
    PARA 689. As to a similar power in relation to certain universities and colleges see the Universities
    and College Estates Act 1925 s 17(3); and EDUCATION vol 36 (2015) PARA 1329. As to the
    measurement of distances see the Interpretation Act 1978 ss 8, 22(1), (2), Sch 2 para 3; and
    STATUTES AND LEGISLATIVE PROCESS vol 96 (2012) PARA 1218.
6   See PARA 135.
7   'Seam' in relation to minerals includes bed, lode or vein: Railways Clauses Consolidation Act 1845
    s 85D(1) (s 85D(1), (2) added by the Mines (Working Facilities and Support) Act 1923 s 15)). See
    also PARA 14. As to the meaning of 'minerals' see PARA 10.
8   For this purpose, the depth of a seam at any point of the railway is the distance between the rail
    level and the point where a line drawn vertically through the centre of the railway would first cut
    the seam of minerals, but, for the purpose only of ascertaining the area of protection, the distance
    is to be measured, where the railway is carried through a tunnel, from the point where the line
    would cut the natural surface of the land instead of from the rail level: Railways Clauses
    Consolidation Act 1845 s 85D(2). 'Surface' in relation to land includes any buildings, works or
    other things erected, constructed or growing on it: s 85D(1).
9   Railways Clauses Consolidation Act 1845 s 78(5). See also PARA 135.

## 150.  Notice of intention to work.

When a mine owner[1] desires to work minerals lying under[2] the area of
protection[3], he must give notice of his intention to the railway or other authority
before he begins to work[4]. This obligation to give notice is not affected by any
rights or obligations with regard to support which may exist outside the mining
code. Thus it makes no difference that the mine owner may already have the right
to let down the surface, either unconditionally or subject to the payment of
compensation, or that the railway or other authority is already entitled to
support[5]. The mine owner is entitled to give the notice even where he intends to
lease the minerals to some other person rather than work them himself[6].

If the mine owner works part of the minerals under the area of protection
without giving notice, he commits an illegal act, but he is not thereby precluded
from subsequently giving notice as regards the remaining part[7].

Even though a notice has been given and compensation received in respect of
one kind of mineral, such as coal or one seam of coal, the owner who then or
subsequently has the right to work another kind of mineral, such as ironstone or
another seam of coal, may subsequently give a notice and receive compensation in
respect of the latter mineral[8].

1   In the mining code of the Railways Clauses Consolidation Act 1845, 'mine owner' means the
    owner, lessee or occupier of mines or minerals (s 78 (as originally enacted)) or, in the case of a
    railway to which the substituted mining code applies (see PARA 135), includes the owner, lessee or
    other person entitled to get minerals: s 85D(1) (added by the Mines (Working Facilities and
    Support) Act 1923 s 15 (see PARA 135)). In the mining code of the Acquisition of Land Act 1981,
    'owner', in relation to mines or minerals, includes a lessee or occupier: s 3, Sch 2 para 1(2). See also
    the cases cited in PARA 154. As to the meaning of 'mine' see PARA 3; and as to the meaning of
    'minerals' see PARA 10.
2   In the mining code of the Acquisition of Land Act 1981, the term 'underlying' is used, which, in
    relation to mines or minerals, means mines or minerals lying under, or within the prescribed
    distance from, the undertaking: Sch 2 para 1(3). As to the meaning of 'undertaking' see PARA 149;
    and as to the prescribed distance see PARA 149.

3   As to the area of protection see PARA 149.
4   See the Railways Clauses Consolidation Act 1845 s 78 (as originally enacted); s 78(1) (substituted
    by the Mines (Working Facilities and Support) Act 1923 s 15)); the Acquisition of Land Act 1981
    Sch 2 para 3(1); and PARA 135. See also *Dixon v Caledonian and Glasgow and South Western
    Railway Companies* (1880) 5 App Cas 820 at 839, HL, per Lord Watson; *London and North
    Western Rly Co v Howley Park Coal and Cannel Co* [1911] 2 Ch 97 at 109, CA, per
    Cozens-Hardy MR (affd [1913] AC 11, HL).
        As to corresponding provisions in the mining codes relating to water and sewerage undertakers
    and the Environment Agency see WATER AND WATERWAYS vol 101 (2018) PARA 760. As to the
    variation of rights by agreement in the case of railways see PARA 171.
5   *London and North Western Rly Co v Howley Park Coal and Cannel Co* [1911] 2 Ch 97 at 109,
    CA, per Cozens-Hardy MR (affd sub nom *Howley Park Coal and Cannel Co v London and North
    Western Rly Co* [1913] AC 11, HL); and see *New Moss Colliery Ltd v Manchester Corpn* [1908]
    AC 117 at 122, HL, per Lord Loreburn LC. As to statutory savings of certain common law rights
    see PARA 172.
6   *Midland Rly Co and Keltering, Thrapston and Huntingdon Rly Co v Robinson* (1887) 37 ChD
    386, CA (affd (1889) 15 App Cas 19, HL); and see *Bolsover UDC v Bolsover Colliery Co Ltd*
    [1947] 1 All ER 130. The owner must in good faith intend that the minerals are to be worked: see
    PARA 151.
7   *Edinburgh and District Water Trustees v Clippens Oil Co* (1898) 25 R 504, Ct of Sess.
8   *Smith v Great Western Rly Co* (1877) 3 App Cas 165, HL; and see *Bolsover UDC v Bolsover
    Colliery Co Ltd* [1947] 1 All ER 130.

## 151.   Validity of notice.

The notice of intention to work[1] must be given at least 30 days before the
commencement of working[2], and must in all cases be sufficient in point of form[3].
It is not necessary to specify in the notice the particular seams which it is intended
to work[4]. The notice is not invalid merely because it is not intended to act upon
it at once; it is not necessary that there should be an intention to work
immediately, or apparently within what may be deemed a reasonable time, if there
is in fact an intention to work[5]. The giving of notice some considerable time
beforehand entails no hardship on the railway or other authority, for it is not
bound to give a counter-notice within 30 days; it may give it at any time[6].
Nevertheless the notice must in all cases be given in good faith[7]. To justify a mine
owner in giving the notice, there must be not only an expression of desire, but an
honest actual existence of intention, to work either by himself or by his lessee[8].

1   As to the notice of intention to work see PARA 150.
2   See the Railways Clauses Consolidation Act 1845 s 78 (as originally enacted); s 78(1) (as
    substituted by the Mines (Working Facilities and Support) Act 1923 s 15) (see PARA 135); and the
    Acquisition of Land Act 1981 s 3, Sch 2 para 3(1). See also *Great Western Rly Co v Bennett* (1867)
    LR 2 HL 27 at 42 per Lord Westbury.
        As to the corresponding provisions in the mining codes relating to water and sewerage
    undertakers and the Environment Agency see WATER AND WATERWAYS vol 101 (2018)
    PARA 760. As to the variation of rights by agreement in the case of railways see PARA 171.
3   *Dixon v Caledonian and Glasgow and South Western Railway Companies* (1880) 5 App Cas 820
    at 834, HL, per Lord Selborne LC. Notices or counter-notices and copies of them required or
    authorised to be served or given under the provisions of the Railways Clauses Consolidation Act
    1845 (as substituted by the Mines (Working Facilities and Support) Act 1923 s 15) with respect to
    mines lying under or near the railway must be in writing and are otherwise subject to the
    provisions of the Law of Property Act 1925 s 196 (replacing the Conveyancing Act 1881 s 67
    (repealed): see LANDLORD AND TENANT vol 62 (2016) PARA 512): Railways Clauses
    Consolidation Act 1845 s 85C (added by the Mines (Working Facilities and Support) Act 1923 s
    15)).
4   *Bolsover UDC v Bolsover Colliery Co Ltd* [1947] 1 All ER 130.
5   *Midland Rly Co and Keltering, Thrapston and Huntingdon Rly Co v Robinson* (1887) 37 ChD
    386, CA; affd (1889) 15 App Cas 19, HL.

6 *Dixon v Caledonian and Glasgow and South Western Railway Companies* (1880) 5 App Cas 820, HL; *Smith v Great Western Rly Co* (1877) 3 App Cas 165, HL. See also *Midland Rly Co and Keltering, Thrapston and Huntingdon Rly Co v Robinson* (1887) 37 ChD 386, CA; affd (1889) 15 App Cas 19, HL.
7 *Midland Rly Co and Keltering, Thrapston and Huntingdon Rly Co v Robinson* (1887) 37 ChD 386, CA (affd (1889) 15 App Cas 19, HL, per Kay J); *Midland Rly Co v Haunchwood Brick and Tile Co* (1882) 20 ChD 552 at 558.
8 *Midland Rly Co v Robinson* (1887) 37 ChD 386, CA (affd (1889) 15 App Cas 19, HL); *Eden v North Eastern Rly Co* [1907] AC 400 at 408, HL, per Lord Macnaghten; *Bolsover UDC v Bolsover Colliery Co Ltd* [1947] 1 All ER 130.

## 152. Limits of obligation to give notice.

The obligation to give notice of intention to work[1] does not extend to substances which are not minerals within the meaning of the mining code[2], even though they may be minerals apart from the code: such substances pass to the railway or other authority without express mention on the purchase of the surface lands[3]. The obligation also does not extend to substances (whether minerals or not) which do not lie within the area of protection[4], and there is no such obligation in respect of minerals lying under or near land which formerly belonged to a railway or other authority but which has been sold as superfluous[5].

1 As to the notice of intention to work see PARA 150.
2 As to what substances are minerals within the meaning of the code see PARA 142. As to the meaning of 'minerals' see PARA 10.
3 See *North British Rly Co v Budhill Coal and Sandstone Co* [1910] AC 116, HL.
4 *London and North Western Rly Co v Howley Park Coal and Cannel Co* [1911] 2 Ch 97 at 109, CA, per Cozens-Hardy MR; affd sub nom *Howley Park Coal and Cannel Co v London and North Western Rly Co* [1913] AC 11, HL. As to the area of protection see PARA 149.
5 *Pountney v Clayton* (1883) 11 QBD 820, CA; *London and North Western Rly Co v Howley Park Coal and Cannel Co* [1911] 2 Ch 97, CA (affd sub nom *Howley Park Coal and Cannel Co v London and North Western Rly Co* [1913] AC 11, HL).

## 153. Inspection of mine.

On receipt of the notice of intention to work[1] the railway or other authority may cause the mines[2] to be inspected by any person appointed by it for the purpose[3].

1 As to the notice of intention to work see PARA 150.
2 As to the meaning of 'mine' see PARA 3.
3 See the Railways Clauses Consolidation Act 1845 s 78 (as originally enacted); s 78(1) (as substituted by the Mines (Working Facilities and Support) Act 1923 s 15) (see PARA 135); and the Acquisition of Land Act 1981 s 3, Sch 2 para 3(2). As to the corresponding provisions in the mining codes relating to water and sewerage undertakers and the Environment Agency see WATER AND WATERWAYS vol 101 (2018) PARA 760. As to general rights of inspection see PARA 169.

## 154. Counter-notice.

Where the mining code of the Railways Clauses Consolidation Act 1845 as originally enacted[1] or the mining code of the Acquisition of Land Act 1981[2] applies, if it appears to the railway or other authority that the working of mines[3] or minerals[4] to which the notice of intention to work[5] relates is likely to damage the railway or other works, and if the authority is willing to make compensation for such mines and minerals to the mine owner, then the mine owner must not work them[6]. For the purposes of service of a counter-notice, the mine owner is the person who has the present right to work the minerals[7], even though he intends to grant a lease of the mines and not to work them himself[8].

In the case of railways and works to which the substituted mining code applies[9], if it appears to the railway or other authority that the working of any of the minerals to which the notice relates will be likely to damage the railway or works or any part of it or them, the authority may, at any time after the receipt of the notice, give a counter-notice to the mine owner requiring him to leave unworked all or any part of those minerals[10]. The counter-notice must specify the minerals so required to be left unworked and the particular portion of the railway or works for the support of which the specified minerals are required to be left unworked[11].

There is nothing to prevent the railway or other authority from giving a counter-notice as to part of the minerals at one time, and as to another part at another time, so as to enable them to limit the compensation payable at any time to such part only of the minerals as may be likely to be worked at once[12]. Where the 30 days have elapsed and the mine owner has begun to work the minerals specified in his notice, without a counter-notice, then, the counter-notice is out of time as to such portions as have been worked[13]. It is for the authority to decide whether or not the working of the minerals within the area of protection will damage the railway or works connected with it, and if the counter-notice is given in good faith it will not be set aside[14].

1   See PARA 135.
2   See PARA 135.
3   As to the meaning of 'mine' see PARA 3.
4   As to the meaning of 'minerals' see PARA 10.
5   As to the notice of intention to work see PARA 150.
6   See the Railways Clauses Consolidation Act 1845 s 78 (as originally enacted); and the Acquisition of Land Act 1981 s 3, Sch 2 para 3(3). The willingness of the authority to make compensation is in practice intimated by counter-notice: see eg *Howley Park Coal and Cannel Co v London and North Western Rly Co* [1913] AC 11 at 21–22, HL, per Viscount Haldane LC. For the corresponding provisions in the mining codes relating to water and sewerage undertakers and the Environment Agency see WATER AND WATERWAYS vol 101 (2018) PARA 760.
7   *Smith v Great Western Rly Co* (1877) 3 App Cas 165 at 178–180, HL, per Lord Cairns LC, at 185, 188 per Lord Penzance, and at 191 per Lord O'Hagan; *Eden v North Eastern Rly Co* [1907] AC 400 at 408, HL, per Lord Macnaghten.
8   *Midland Rly Co v Robinson* (1887) 37 ChD 386, CA (affd (1889) 15 App Cas 19, HL); and see *London and North Eastern Rly Co v BA Collieries Ltd* [1945] AC 143, [1945] 1 All ER 51, HL; and PARA 150.
9   See PARA 135.
10 See the Railways Clauses Consolidation Act 1845 s 78(2) (s 78(2), (3) substituted by the Mines (Working Facilities and Support) Act 1923 s 15) (see PARA 135). As to the requirements as to form and service of the counter-notice see PARA 151. On receipt of a counter-notice where the substituted code applies, the mine owner must serve a copy of it on the royalty owner, if any: Railways Clauses Consolidation Act 1845 s 78(3) (as so substituted). 'Royalty owner' includes any person entitled to receive a royalty in respect of minerals; and 'royalty' includes rent and any other reservation in respect of minerals by the acre, ton or otherwise: s 85D(1) (added by the Mines (Working Facilities and Support) Act 1923 s 15). As to the corresponding provisions in the mining codes relating to water and sewerage undertakers and the Environment Agency see WATER AND WATERWAYS vol 101 (2018) PARA 760.
11 Railways Clauses Consolidation Act 1845 s 78(2).
12 *Midland Rly Co v Robinson* (1887) 37 ChD 386 at 396, CA, per Cotton LJ, at 402 per Lindley LJ, and at 405 per Lopes LJ; affd (1889) 15 App Cas 19, HL.
13 *Dixon v Caledonian and Glasgow and South Western Railway Companies* (1880) 5 App Cas 820 at 832, HL, per Lord Selborne LC, and at 835 per Lord Blackburn; *Howley Park Coal and Cannel Co v London and North Western Rly Co* [1913] AC 11 at 22, HL, per Viscount Haldane LC.
14 Cf *Errington v Metropolitan District Rly Co* (1882) 19 ChD 559, CA; and see PARA 148.

## 155. Effect of counter-notice.

The service of the counter-notice[1] does not constitute a contract for sale and purchase of the minerals[2]; nor is it a step towards such a contract or towards expropriation. The minerals remain the property of the mine owner[3], notwithstanding the payment of compensation, which may be, and often is, equal to what the minerals would be worth if sold; but the mine owner may not remove them, nor may the railway or other authority[4]. It is immaterial that the minerals specified in the counter-notice may be more or less than are in fact necessary for the support of the works, or that artificial support of some kind or other may be sufficient where supplied[5]. The right thus conferred upon the authority is different from a right of support in that the obligation upon the mine owner is a restriction which cannot be created by common law grant[6]. A restriction for the compensation paid is not, therefore, chargeable with ad valorem stamp duty as on a conveyance[7].

1  As to the counter-notice see PARA 154.
2  As to the meaning of 'minerals' see PARA 10.
3  As to the meaning of 'mine owner' see PARA 150. As to the meaning of 'mine' see PARA 3.
4  Cf *Errington v Metropolitan District Rly Co* (1882) 19 ChD 559 at 575, CA, per Brett LJ; *Great Northern Rly Co v IRC* [1899] 2 QB 652 at 657, DC, per Darling J, and at 662 per Phillimore J (on appeal [1901] 1 KB 416 at 427, CA, per Collins LJ, and at 428–429 per Stirling LJ); *Bwllfa and Merthyr Dare Steam Collieries (1891) Ltd v Pontypridd Waterworks Co* [1903] AC 426 at 428, HL, per the Earl of Halsbury LC, at 431 per Lord Macnaghten, and at 432–433 per Lord Robertson; *Re Richard and Great Western Rly Co* [1905] 1 KB 68 at 70, CA, per Collins MR, and at 73 per Stirling and Matthew LJJ; *Eden v North Eastern Rly Co* [1907] AC 400 at 408, HL, per Lord Macnaghten, and at 411 per Lord Atkinson. Such minerals are sometimes referred to as 'sterilised' minerals.
5  *Great Northern Rly Co v IRC* [1901] 1 KB 416 at 427, CA, per Collins LJ, and at 428 per Stirling LJ.
6  *Great Northern Rly Co v IRC* [1901] 1 KB 416 at 428–429, CA, per Stirling LJ. It is similar to a restrictive covenant.
7  *Great Northern Rly Co v IRC* [1901] 1 KB 416 at 428, CA. Quaere, however, whether the compensation is not chargeable to stamp duty land tax as paid in respect of a land transaction which, subject to certain exemptions, includes the acquisition of the benefit of a restriction over land: see the Finance Act 2003 Pt 4 (ss 42–124); and STAMP TAXES vol 96 (2012) PARA 426.

## 156.  Restrictions on counter-notice.

Once given, a counter-notice[1] may not be withdrawn[2]. Like the notice of intention to work[3], it must be confined to substances which are minerals within the mining code[4] and lying within the area of protection[5]; it may not apply to substances within the area of protection which are not minerals within the code, or to substances (whether minerals or not) lying outside the area of protection[6].

1  As to the counter-notice see PARA 154.
2  *Edinburgh and District Water Trustees v Clippens Oil Co* (1902) 87 LT 275, HL; affg (1900) 3 F 1113, Ct of Sess.
3  As to the notice of intention to work see PARA 150.
4  As to such minerals see PARA 142. As to the meaning of 'minerals' see PARA 10.
5  *London and North Western Rly Co v Howley Park Coal and Cannel Co* [1911] 2 Ch 97 at 120, CA, per Fletcher Moulton LJ; affd sub nom *Howley Park Coal and Cannel Co v London and North Western Rly Co* [1913] AC 11, HL. As to the area of protection see PARA 149.
6  *London and North Western Rly Co v Howley Park Coal and Cannel Co* [1911] 2 Ch 97 at 110, CA, per Cozens-Hardy MR, and at 126 per Buckley LJ; affd [1913] AC 11, HL.

## 157.  Compensation.

Where the mining code of the Railways Clauses Consolidation Act 1845 as originally enacted or the mining code of the Acquisition of Land Act 1981 applies[1], compensation[2] is payable for the mines within the area of protection[3] comprised in the notice of intention to work[4] and which the railway or other authority requires to be left unworked[5].

Where the substituted code applies[6] and the railway or other authority has served a counter-notice[7] on the mine owner[8], the minerals[9] specified in the counter-notice must not be worked or got, and the authority must pay compensation[10] to the mine owner and the royalty owner, if any, for the loss caused by the specified minerals being left unworked[11].

1  See PARA 135.
2  The amount of the compensation is to be determined, in default of agreement, by the Upper Tribunal: see the Railways Clauses Consolidation Act 1845 s 78 (amended by the Compulsory Purchase Act 1965 s 39(3), Sch 7; and SI 2009/1307); and the Acquisition of Land Act 1981 s 3, Sch 2 para 3(4) (amended by SI 2009/1307). As to the Upper Tribunal see COURTS AND TRIBUNALS vol 24 (2010) PARA 883 et seq.
3  As to the area of protection see PARA 149. As to the meaning of 'mine' see PARA 3.
4  As to the notice of intention to work see PARA 150.
5  See the Railways Clauses Consolidation Act 1845 s 78 (as originally enacted); and the Acquisition of Land Act 1981 Sch 2 para 3(3). As to the corresponding provisions in the mining codes relating to water and sewerage undertakers and the Environment Agency see WATER AND WATERWAYS vol 101 (2018) PARA 760.
6  See PARA 135.
7  As to the counter-notice see PARA 154.
8  As to the meaning of 'mine owner' see PARA 150.
9  As to the meaning of 'minerals' see PARA 10.
10 The Railways Clauses Consolidation Act 1845 s 78A(1) (see PARA 135) provides that the compensation payable to the mine owner and the royalty owner respectively is to be determined, in default of agreement, by arbitration; but ; and the Transport Act 1962 s 95(3), Sch 12 Pt I (repealed), which repeals provisions of the Railways Clauses Consolidation Act 1845 dealing with arbitration. As to the meaning of 'royalty owner' see PARA 154. The arbitrator must state in his decision the tonnage of the specified minerals on which his award is based: s 78A(1) proviso (iv). As to statutory references to arbitration generally see ARBITRATION vol 2 (2017) PARA 501 et seq.
11 See the Railways Clauses Consolidation Act 1845 s 78(4) (substituted by the Mines (Working Facilities and Support) Act 1923 s 15). The substitution does not change the basis upon which compensation must be made: *London and North Eastern Rly Co v BA Collieries Ltd* [1945] AC 143 at 172, [1945] 1 All ER 51 at 59, HL, per Lord Thankerton, and at 176 and 61 per Lord Macmillan, approving the test laid down in *Bwllfa and Merthyr Dare Steam Collieries* (1891) *Ltd v Pontypridd Waterworks Co* [1903] AC 426, HL; and see PARA 158. The decisions on the old mining code are therefore of assistance in construing the substituted code.

## 158. Measure of compensation.

The compensation payable is that part of the entire value of the minerals[1] which is proportionate to the interest of the mine owner[2], and the difficulty of assessment in such cases is immaterial[3]. The compensation payable is full compensation[4], namely what the minerals would have sold for, if worked, less the cost of working them[5], although interest is not payable between the date of the notice of intention to work[6] and the date of assessment of compensation[7].

1  As to the meaning of 'minerals' see PARA 10.
2  As to the meaning of 'mine owner' see PARA 150.
3  *Smith v Great Western Rly Co* (1877) 3 App Cas 165, HL; *London and North Eastern Rly Co v BA Collieries Ltd* [1945] AC 143, [1945] 1 All ER 51, HL; cf *Consett Waterworks Co v Ritson* (1889) 22 QBD 318 at 333–336 per Cave J (on appeal 22 QBD 702, CA); and see *Great Western Rly Co v Smith* (1876) 2 ChD 235 at 252, CA, per Mellish LJ (on appeal sub nom *Smith v Great Western Rly Co* (1877) 3 App Cas 165, HL). As to apportionment as between reversioners among themselves see *Re Barrington, Gamlen v Lyon* (1886) 33 ChD 523; *Re Robinson's Settlement Trusts* [1891] 3 Ch 129 at 132, 133 per Chitty J; *Cardigan v Curzon-Howe* (1898) 14 TLR 550; *Re Fullerton's Will* [1906] 2 Ch 138.
4  See *Bwllfa and Merthyr Dare Steam Collieries (1891) Ltd v Pontypridd Waterworks Co* [1903] AC 426 at 430, HL, per Lord Macnaghten.

5   *Bwllfa and Merthyr Dare Steam Collieries (1891) Ltd v Pontypridd Waterworks Co* [1903] AC
    426, HL; *Smith v Great Western Rly Co* (1877) 3 App Cas 165 at 185, HL, per Lord Penzance;
    *Eden v North Eastern Rly Co* [1907] AC 400, HL; *Rugby Portland Cement Co v London and
    North Western Rly Co* [1908] 2 KB 606, CA; *London and North Eastern Rly Co v BA Collieries
    Ltd* [1945] AC 143, [1945] 1 All ER 51, HL; *Thomas McGhie & Sons Ltd v British Transport
    Commission* [1963] 1 QB 125, [1962] 2 All ER 646. The fact that the mine owner could have
    worked other mines in the neighbourhood or that, being a lessee, he could not have exhausted the
    minerals within the term of his lease, is immaterial: *Eden v North Eastern Rly Co* at 404 per Lord
    Loreburn LC. The physical conditions of the mine, including in particular the difficulties of
    working it, and the time when the minerals would in the ordinary course be worked so as to arrive
    at the present value, are matters to be considered: *Edinburgh and District Water Trustees v
    Clippens Oil Co* (1902) 87 LT 275 at 279, HL, per Lord Robertson; *Eden v North Eastern Rly Co*
    at 412 per Lord Atkinson. If the minerals have no value, no compensation in this respect is
    payable, but this can seldom happen, notwithstanding that the minerals may be worked at a loss
    (see *Rugby Portland Cement Co v London and North Western Rly Co* at 615 per Gorell Barnes
    P); but it may happen where the minerals cannot be worked (*Edinburgh and District Water
    Trustees v Clippens Oil Co* at 279 per Lord Robertson). The incidence of taxation must be taken
    into account (*Thomas McGhie & Sons Ltd v British Transport Commission*), and in a case falling
    within the substituted code (see PARA 135) account must also be taken of the possible contribution
    (see PARA 162) for which the mine owner might in the future have become liable under the
    Railways Clauses Consolidation Act 1845 s 79A (added by the Mines (Working Facilities and
    Support) Act 1923 s 15), if the coal covered by the counter-notice had been actually worked and
    damage to the railway and works of the railway authority had been caused by that working:
    *London and North Eastern Rly Co v BA Collieries Ltd.*
        The measure of compensation appears to be the same for all of the mining codes, including eg
    those relating to water and sewerage undertakers and the Environment Agency: see eg *Bwllfa and
    Merthyr Dare Steam Collieries (1891) Ltd v Pontypridd Waterworks Co* [1903] AC 426, HL;
    *Edinburgh and District Water Trustees v Clippens Oil Co* (1902) 87 LT 275 at 278, 279, HL, per
    Lord Robertson; and WATER AND WATERWAYS vol 101 (2018) PARA 758 et seq.
6   As to the notice of intention to work see PARA 150.
7   *Re Richard and Great Western Rly Co* [1905] 1 KB 68, CA; cf *Fletcher v Lancashire and Yorkshire
    Rly Co* [1902] 1 Ch 901.

## 159. Separate assessment of compensation.

Where compensation is payable under the substituted mining code[1] for the loss
caused by the specified minerals being left unworked[2], the compensation payable
to the mine owner[3] and the royalty owner[4] must, so far as it is payable in respect
of the value of specified minerals, be separately assessed[5].

The compensation payable[6] to the mine owner is a sum for each ton of the
specified minerals, the rate per ton in the case of minerals lying under the outer
area of protection being one-third of the rate which is or would be awarded in the
case of minerals lying under the inner area of protection[7]. The mine owner is also
entitled to be paid the amount of any increase in the cost of working any part of
his minerals (other than the specified minerals) which may have been caused by
the failure of the railway or other authority to give the counter-notice[8] within such
a reasonable time as would have enabled the mine owner to avoid the increase in
cost[9].

The compensation payable[10] to the royalty owner is based on the amount
which would have been received from time to time by way of royalty in respect of
the specified minerals if they had been worked out in the ordinary course, and the
royalties payable had been (1) in the case of such of the specified minerals as lie
under the inner area of protection, the same as those reserved by and payable
under the lease comprising the minerals and subsisting at the date of the
counter-notice[11]; and (2) in the case of such of the specified minerals as lie under
the outer area of protection, one-third of the royalties so reserved and payable
with a specified addition[12] to such one-third[13].

1   See PARA 135.

2 See PARA 158. As to the meaning of 'minerals' see PARA 10.

3 As to the meaning of 'mine owner' see PARA 150.

4 As to the meaning of 'royalty owner' see PARA 154. As to the meaning of 'royalty' see PARA 154.

5 Railways Clauses Consolidation Act 1845 s 78A(1) proviso (i) (s 78A added by the Mines (Working Facilities and Support) Act 1923 s 15) (see PARA 135).

6 Ie where payable under the substituted code: see PARA 135.

7 Railways Clauses Consolidation Act 1845 s 78A(1) proviso (ii). As to the inner and outer areas of protection see PARA 149. In *London and North Eastern Rly Co v BA Collieries Ltd* [1945] AC 143 at 168, 181, 182, [1945] 1 All ER 51 at 58, 64, HL, the interpretation of this provision was discussed obiter by Lord Thankerton and Lord Wright respectively. Lord Thankerton considered that the arbitrator's duty was to ascertain the value of the whole of the specified minerals, and to reduce that value to a rate per ton over the whole tonnage and to apply 100% of the rate to the tonnage lying under the inner area, and one-third of that rate to the tonnage lying under the outer area. Lord Wright thought that each ton of the specified minerals should be valued, but that when the arbitrator came to value the mineral in the outer area he should find what he would award for each ton of coal if it had lain in the inner area and then divide it by three.

8 As to the counter-notice see PARA 154.

9 Railways Clauses Consolidation Act 1845 s 78A(2) which provides also that in default of agreement the amount payable is to be determined by arbitration. See, however, PARA 157.

10 Ie where payable under the substituted code: see PARA 135.

11 Railways Clauses Consolidation Act 1845 s 78A(1) proviso (iii)(a).

12 Ie the equivalent of one old penny per ton.

13 Railways Clauses Consolidation Act 1845 s 78A(1) proviso (iii)(b).

## 160. Working without counter-notice.

Where the mining code of the Railways Clauses Consolidation Act 1845[1] or the mining code of the Acquisition of Land Act 1981 applies[2] there is no obligation on railway or other authorities to give a counter-notice[3] and pay compensation; they may allow the mine owner[4] to work the minerals[5]; and if a counter-notice is given as to part only of the minerals within the area of protection[6], it is only in respect of that part that compensation must be paid[7].

In the absence of a counter-notice or so far as the counter-notice does not extend, the mine owner may work the minerals within the area of protection which are comprised in the notice of intention to work[8]; but such working must be done in the manner proper and necessary for the beneficial working of them and according to the usual manner of working such minerals in the district[9].

The mine owner may accordingly work the minerals even though the surface is thereby destroyed[10]. It is, however, for the mine owner to show that his workings are proper, necessary and usual[11]. If the railway or other work is destroyed by the mining operations, the railway or other authority cannot be compelled to reinstate it[12]. However, where the substituted code applies[13], the authority may, however, stop the working at any time by giving a counter-notice[14].

1 Ie the code either as originally enacted or as substituted by the Mines (Working Facilities and Support) Act 1923 s 15: see PARA 135.

2 See PARA 135.

3 As to the counter-notice see PARA 154.

4 As to the meaning of 'mine owner' see PARA 150.

5 *Midland Rly Co v Miles* (1886) 33 ChD 632 at 638–639 per Stirling J; *Holliday v Wakefield Corpn* [1891] AC 81 at 87–88, HL, per Lord Bramwell, and at 97 per Lord Watson; *Re Lord Gerard and London and North Western Rly Co* [1895] 1 QB 459 at 466, 467, CA, per Lord Esher MR; *Manchester Corpn v New Moss Colliery Ltd* [1906] 2 Ch 564, CA (affd sub nom *New Moss Colliery Ltd v Manchester Corpn* [1908] AC 117, HL). As to the meaning of 'minerals' see PARA 10.

6 As to the area of protection see PARA 149.

7 *Midland Rly Co v Miles* (1886) 33 ChD 632 at 649–651 per Stirling J.

8 As to the notice of intention to work see PARA 150.

9  See the Railways Clauses Consolidation Act 1845 s 79; s 79(1) (ss 78(2), 79(1) substituted by the Mines (Working Facilities and Support) Act 1923 s 15) (see PARA 135); and the Acquisition of Land Act 1981 s 3, Sch 2 para 4(1). As to the corresponding provisions in the codes relating to water and sewerage undertakers and the Environment Agency see WATER AND WATERWAYS vol 101 (2018) PARA 760.

10  See *Ruabon Brick and Terra Cotta Co v Great Western Rly Co* [1893] 1 Ch 427 at 453–454, CA, per Lindley LJ, at 457–463 per Bowen LJ, and at 464–465 per A L Smith LJ; *London and North Western Rly Co v Howley Park Coal and Cannel Co* [1911] 2 Ch 97 at 109, CA, per Cozens-Hardy MR (affd sub nom *Howley Park Coal and Cannel Co v London and North Western Rly Co* [1913] AC 11, HL). As to the common law right of support where the substituted code applies see PARA 174.

11  See *Edinburgh and District Water Trustees v Clippens Oil Co* (1898) 25 R 504 at 516, Ct of Sess, per Lord Robertson. The position is different under the mining codes relating to water and sewerage undertakers and the Environment Agency: see WATER AND WATERWAYS vol 101 (2018) PARA 760.

12  *R v Great Western Rly Co* (1893) 62 LJQB 572, CA, where the plaintiffs, who were applying for mandamus, were the mine owners by whose operations the railway in question was destroyed: see *Ruabon Brick and Terra Cotta Co v Great Western Rly Co* [1893] 1 Ch 427, CA.

13  See PARA 135.

14  Railways Clauses Consolidation Act 1845 ss 78(2), 79(1).

## 161. Improper working.

The mining codes of the Railways Clauses Consolidation Act 1845[1] and the mining code of the Acquisition of Land Act 1981[2] provide that if any damage or obstruction is caused to the railway or other works by any improper working of the minerals[3] within the area of protection[4] the damage or obstruction must forthwith be repaired or removed, as the case may require, and the damage made good by the mine owner[5] at his own expense; and if the repair or removal is not done forthwith, or if the railway or other authority thinks fit, without waiting for it to be done by the mine owner, it may execute it and recover from the mine owner by action the expense occasioned[6].

1  Ie the code either as originally enacted or as substituted by the Mines (Working Facilities and Support) Act 1923 s 15: see PARA 135.

2  See PARA 135.

3  As to the meaning of 'minerals' see PARA 10.

4  As to the area of protection see PARA 149.

5  As to the meaning of 'mine owner' see PARA 150.

6  See the Railways Clauses Consolidation Act 1845 s 79 (as originally enacted); s 79(2) (substituted by the Mines (Working Facilities and Support) Act 1923 s 15) (see PARA 135); and the Acquisition of Land Act 1981 s 3, Sch 2 para 4(2). See also *Great Western Rly Co v Bennett* (1867) LR 2 HL 27 at 39 per Lord Chelmsford LC; *Midland Rly Co and Kettering, Thrapston and Huntingdon Rly Co v Robinson* (1889) 15 App Cas 19 at 27, HL, per Lord Herschell; *Ruabon Brick and Terra Cotta Co v Great Western Rly Co* [1893] 1 Ch 427 at 436, 441 per Kekewich J (affd [1893] 1 Ch 427 at 441, CA).

    As to the corresponding provisions in the mining codes relating to water and sewerage undertakers and the Environment Agency see WATER AND WATERWAYS vol 101 (2018) PARA 760.

## 162. Contribution to railway or other authority in respect of authorised working.

In the case of railways and works to which the substituted mining code of the Railways Clauses Consolidation Act 1845 applies[1], if a mine owner[2] works any minerals[3] lying under any part of the area of protection[4] in the authorised manner, he nevertheless becomes liable on demand by the railway or other authority to contribute towards the expenses properly incurred, or to be incurred[5], by the authority from time to time thereafter in making good any damage caused by the working to the railway or works of the authority (not being protected works comprised in any counter-notice[6] relating to the area of protection) the appropriate percentage[7], if any, of those expenses[8].

The liability of any mine owner under this provision, in respect of any part of the railway or works on which such expenditure has been incurred, is not to exceed a specified aggregate sum[9] for each ton of the commercially workable[10] minerals, gotten or ungotten, in such part of any seams[11] as lies under the area ascertained as respects the several seams in accordance with statutory rules[12], being seams which have been or are being worked under that area[13]. In ascertaining the aggregate sum, however, minerals gotten more than six years before the date on which a contribution is demanded by the authority under this provision are not to be taken into account[14].

1   Ie the code as substituted by the Mines (Working Facilities and Support) Act 1923 s 15: see PARA 135.
2   As to the meaning of 'mine owner' see PARA 150.
3   As to the meaning of 'minerals' see PARA 10.
4   As to the area of protection see PARA 149.
5   Thus apprehended or potential expenses may be taken into account: *London and North Eastern Rly Co v BA Collieries Ltd* [1945] AC 143, [1945] 1 All ER 51, HL; *Thomas McGhie & Sons Ltd v British Transport Commission* [1963] 1 QB 125, [1962] 2 All ER 646. See further PARA 158.
6   As to the counter-notice see PARA 154.
7   The appropriate percentage is such as is specified in the Railways Clauses Consolidation Act 1845 s 79A(1) (s 79A(1), (2) added by the Mines (Working Facilities and Support) Act 1923 s 15); and the Railways Clauses Consolidation Act 1845 Sch 1 (added by the Mines (Working Facilities and Support) Act 1923 s 15, Sch 1) according to the depth of the minerals being so worked: Railways Clauses Consolidation Act 1845 s 79A(1). As to the ascertainment of depth see PARA 149.
8   Railways Clauses Consolidation Act 1845 s 79A(1).
9   Ie the equivalent of six old pence.
10  As to the meaning of 'commercially workable' see *Griffiths v Rigby* (1856) 1 H & N 237 at 241 per Pollock CB; *Carr v Benson* (1868) 3 Ch App 524, CA.
11  As to the meaning of 'seam' see PARA 149.
12  Ie the rules contained in the Railways Clauses Consolidation Act 1845 s 79A(2); Sch 2 (substituted by the Mines (Working Facilities and Support) Act 1923 s 15, Sch 2): Railways Clauses Consolidation Act 1845 s 79A(2).
13  Railways Clauses Consolidation Act 1845 s 79A(2).
14  Railways Clauses Consolidation Act 1845 s 79A(2) proviso. Any dispute arising as to the amount of the expenses towards which a mine owner is liable to contribute or the amount of his contribution, or the amount to be deducted by a mine owner from the royalties payable to the royalty owner is to be settled by arbitration: s 79A(6). As to this amount see PARA 163. As to the meanings of 'royalty' and 'royalty owner' see PARA 154. As to arbitration see PARA 157.

### 163.  Mine owner's right of deduction from royalties.

Where the substituted mining code of the Railways Clauses Consolidation Act 1845[1] applies, any mine owner[2] making a contribution[3] in respect of authorised workings, being a lessee[4], is entitled to deduct from any royalties then or thereafter becoming due from him to the royalty owner under the lease, one-third part of the amount which he has so contributed[5]. Where, however, the royalty payable under the lease is less than a specified amount[6] per ton, the amount so deducted must not exceed the amount produced by multiplying one-third of such rate per ton by the tonnage of the minerals with reference to the aggregate amount of which the maximum liability of the mine owner is to be calculated[7]; and where the mine owner is entitled to make such a deduction, the sum reserved by and payable under the lease is deemed to be the net amount arrived at after making the deduction[8]. No such deduction is, however, allowed when the liability of the mine owner to the railway or other authority is a liability arising out of an arrangement between them with respect to the working of minerals under or near the railway or works[9].

1  Ie the code as substituted by the Mines (Working Facilities and Support) Act 1923 s 15: see PARA 135.
2  As to the meaning of 'mine owner' see PARA 150.
3  As to such contributions see PARA 162.
4  'Lessee' includes an under-lessee and a licensee: Railways Clauses Consolidation Act 1845 s 85D(1) (ss 79A, 85D added by the Mines (Working Facilities and Support) Act 1923 s 15) (see PARA 135). Where a single mine (see PARA 164) is held under leases granted by more than one lessor, any deductions which the mine owner is authorised to make are to be made from the royalties payable to such one or more of such lessors and, if more than one, in such proportions as, in default of agreement, may be determined by arbitration on the application of the mine owner or any of the royalty owners: Railways Clauses Consolidation Act 1845 s 79A(5). As to arbitration see, however, PARA 157. 'Lease' includes an under-lease or other tenancy and a licence: s 85D(1). As to the meanings of 'royalty' and 'royalty owner' see PARA 154.
5  See the Railways Clauses Consolidation Act 1845 s 79A(3). As to the settlement of disputes see PARA 162.
6  Ie the equivalent of six old pence.
7  See PARA 162.
8  See the Railways Clauses Consolidation Act 1845 s 79A(3).
9  See the Railways Clauses Consolidation Act 1845 s 79A(3) proviso. As to the power to vary rights by agreement see PARA 171.

## 164. Limitation of contribution in respect of single mine.

Where the substituted mining code of the Railways Clauses Consolidation Act 1845[1] applies, the liability of the mine owner[2] to contribute[3] in respect of authorised workings is subject to the following further limitation as respects damage done by workings in any single mine[4]. When the aggregate of the sums paid by him in satisfaction of that liability amounts to a sum equivalent to a specified amount[5] for each ton of commercially workable[6] minerals, gotten or ungotten, in such part of any seams[7] as lies within the mine and under an area extending laterally on both sides of the railway or works to a distance ascertained in accordance with a statutory rule[8] and extending longitudinally to a distance co-extensive with the portion of the railway lying over or adjacent to the mine, being seams which have been or are being worked under that area, the mine owner is not liable to make any further contribution[9] towards the expenses of making good any damage caused to any part of the railway or works by the working of such seams in that mine[10].

Where the liability of a mine owner to contribute in respect of authorised workings is reduced by the operation of this limitation in respect of a single mine, his right to make deductions from royalties[11] is proportionately reduced[12].

1  Ie the code as substituted by the Mines (Working Facilities and Support) Act 1923 s 15: see PARA 135.
2  As to the meaning of 'mine owner' see PARA 150.
3  As to such contributions see PARA 162.
4  For these purposes, all the minerals which the mine owner is entitled to work and which would have been, or would in the ordinary course of events and in accordance with good mining practice be, worked from the same shafts or adits are deemed to be a single mine: Railways Clauses Consolidation Act 1845 s 79A(4) (added by the Mines (Working Facilities and Support) Act 1923 s 15 (see PARA 135)). As to the meaning of 'mine' see PARA 3; and as to the meaning of 'minerals' see PARA 10.
5  Ie the equivalent of six old pence.
6  See PARA 162.
7  As to the meaning of 'seam' see PARA 149.

8	Ie the Railways Clauses Consolidation Act 1845 Sch 2 r 1 (Sch 2 added by the Mines (Working Facilities and Support) Act 1923 s 15, Sch 2).
9	Ie any further contribution under the Railways Clauses Consolidation Act 1845 s 79A: see PARA 162.
10	Railways Clauses Consolidation Act 1845 s 79A(4).
11	As to the meaning of 'royalty' see PARA 154. As to these deductions see PARA 163.
12	Railways Clauses Consolidation Act 1845 s 79A(4).

## 165. Notices and accounts with respect to damage.

In the case of railways and other works to which the substituted mining code applies[1], the railway or other authority must, when and so far as reasonable and practicable, give notice to the mine owner[2] and royalty owner[3], if any, affected, specifying particulars of: (1) the railway or works to which damage has been caused or to which damage is apprehended from the working of any minerals[4] under the area of protection[5] sufficient to enable the same to be identified[6]; (2) the nature of the damage or apprehended damage[7]; and (3) the nature of the works intended to be carried out for the purpose of making good or preventing the damage[8].

The authority must keep separate accounts differentiating the cost of the ordinary maintenance of the railway or works from the cost of making good any damage caused to the railway or works by the working of any minerals under the area of protection, and these accounts must, at all reasonable times, be open for inspection by or on behalf of a mine owner working minerals under or near the railway or works and the royalty owner, if any, of the minerals[9].

1	Ie the code as substituted by the Mines (Working Facilities and Support) Act 1923 s 15: see PARA 135.
2	As to the meaning of 'mine owner' see PARA 150.
3	As to the meaning of 'royalty owner' see PARA 154.
4	As to the meaning of 'minerals' see PARA 10.
5	As to the area of protection see PARA 149.
6	See the Railways Clauses Consolidation Act 1845 s 79B(1)(i) (s 79B added by the Mines (Working Facilities and Support) Act 1923 s 15) (see PARA 135).
7	See the Railways Clauses Consolidation Act 1845 s 79B(1)(ii).
8	Railways Clauses Consolidation Act 1845 s 79B(1)(iii).
9	Railways Clauses Consolidation Act 1845 s 79B(2).

## 166. Rights of access through specified minerals.

Where the mining code of the Railways Clauses Consolidation Act 1845[1] or the mining code of the Acquisition of Land Act 1981 applies[2], and the working of any minerals[3] is prevented by reason of a counter-notice[4], the mine owner[5] whose minerals extend so as to lie on both sides of the specified minerals[6] may cut and make such communication works[7] through the specified minerals and the strata above or below them as may be requisite to enable him to ventilate, drain and work his remaining minerals; but no such ways may be cut or made upon or so as to injure any part of the protected works[8].

1	Ie the code either as originally enacted or as substituted by the Mines (Working Facilities and Support) Act 1923 s 15: see PARA 135.
2	See PARA 135.
3	As to the meaning of 'minerals' see PARA 10.
4	As to the counter-notice see PARA 154.
5	As to the meaning of 'mine owner' see PARA 150.
6	The mining code of the Acquisition of Land Act 1981 uses the term 'protected minerals' which is defined as mines, measures or strata the working of which is prevented under s 3, Sch 2 para 3(3) (see PARA 157): Sch 2 para 5(4)(a); and see PARA 154.

7   In the mining code of the Acquisition of Land Act 1981, 'communication works' means airways, headings, gateways or water levels: Sch 2 para 5(4)(b). The mining code of the Railways Clauses Consolidation Act 1845 both as originally enacted and as substituted uses the terms 'airways, headways, gateways or water levels': see the Railways Clauses Consolidation Act 1845 s 80 (as originally enacted); s 80 (substituted by the Mines (Working Facilities and Support) Act 1923 s 15) (see PARA 135).

8   See the Railways Clauses Consolidation Act 1845 s 80 (as originally enacted); s 80; and the Acquisition of Land Act 1981 Sch 2 para 5(1). No such communication works may be of greater dimensions than 8 feet wide and 8 feet high (see the Railways Clauses Consolidation Act 1845 s 80 (as originally enacted); s 80 (as so substituted); and the Acquisition of Land Act 1981 Sch 2 para 5(2)). In the case of railways and other works to which the substituted code applies, no such communication works may be within 40 yards of any other such way, and if the top of the same is more than 160 yards below the average rail level, the width of the way may be 13 feet: Railways Clauses Consolidation Act 1845 s 80 (as so substituted). Where the mining code of the Railways Clauses Consolidation Act 1845 as originally enacted or the mining code of the Acquisition of Land Act 1981 applies, the special Act or compulsory purchase order, as the case may be, may prescribe other dimensions (see the Railways Clauses Consolidation Act 1845 s 80 (as originally enacted); and the Acquisition of Land Act 1981 Sch 2 para 5(2)); and the communication works must not impede passage on the protected works (see the Railways Clauses Consolidation Act 1845 s 80 (as originally enacted); and the Acquisition of Land Act 1981 Sch 2 para 5(3)).

   The mine owner may not enter upon and go over a railway to reach and work his mines on the other side: *Midland Rly Co v Miles* (1885) 30 ChD 634 per Pearson J; *Midland Rly Co v Miles* (1886) 33 ChD 632 at 643–644, 648–649 per Stirling J; and see *Re Lord Gerard and London and North Western Rly Co* [1894] 2 QB 915 at 921 per Kennedy J (affd [1895] 1 QB 459, CA).

   As to the corresponding provisions in the mining codes relating to water and sewerage authorities and the Environment Agency see WATER AND WATERWAYS vol 101 (2018) PARA 761.

## 167. Compensation for additional expenses and for severance.

Where the mining code of the Railways Clauses Consolidation Act 1845[1] or the mining code of the Acquisition of Land Act 1981 applies[2] and a counter-notice[3] has been given, the authority must from time to time pay to the mine owner[4] compensation in respect of the additional expenses and losses incurred by him in consequence of the counter-notice by reason of the continuous working of the mines[5] or minerals[6] being interrupted, or by reason of the mines or minerals being worked in the manner authorised and under the restrictions imposed by the mining codes[7]. Where, in the case of railways to which the substituted code[8] applies, the minerals specified in a counter-notice lie in different seams[9], the amount payable is to be calculated separately for each seam[10], but where any additional expenditure is incurred on works which serve more than one seam, that expenditure may be apportioned for these purposes between the seams[11].

In the cases of railways and other works to which the mining code of the Railways Clauses Consolidation Act 1845 as originally enacted or the mining code of the Acquisition of Land Act 1981 applies, compensation must also be paid in respect of any loss and additional expense incurred by reason of the severance of the land over the mines by the protected works, and for such mines or minerals not purchased by the undertakers as cannot be worked by reason of the making and continuance of the authority's works[12]. It is necessary[13], in order to entitle a mine owner to compensation under these provisions, that his mines should extend so as to lie on both sides of the protected works[14]. Compensation for severance is in addition to and not in substitution for the compensation provided by the code for leaving minerals unworked[15]. There is provision for the amount of the compensation to be settled by arbitration in case of dispute[16], although it may be that such amount is now to be settled by the Upper Tribunal[17].

1   Ie the code either as originally enacted or as substituted by the Mines (Working Facilities and Support) Act 1923 s 15: see PARA 135.

2   See PARA 135.

3  As to the counter-notice see PARA 154.
4  As to the meaning of 'mine owner' see PARA 150.
5  As to the meaning of 'mine' see PARA 3.
6  As to the meaning of 'minerals' see PARA 10.
7  See the Railways Clauses Consolidation Act 1845 s 81 (as originally enacted); s 81(1) (s 81 substituted by the Mines (Working Facilities and Support) Act 1923 s 15) (see PARA 135); and the Acquisition of Land Act 1981 s 3, Sch 2 para 6(1)(b), (c). In the case of railways to which the substituted mining code applies, the compensation is limited to the appropriate percentage of the additional expenses determined in accordance with the rules contained in the Railways Clauses Consolidation Act 1845 s 81(2), Sch 3 (added by the Mines (Working Facilities and Support) Act 1923 s 15, Sch 3): Railways Clauses Consolidation Act 1845 s 81(1), (2) (as so substituted).
      As to the corresponding provisions in the mining codes relating to water and sewerage undertakers and the Environment Agency see WATER AND WATERWAYS vol 101 (2018) PARA 762.
8  See PARA 135.
9  As to the meaning of 'seam' see PARA 149.
10 See the Railways Clauses Consolidation Act 1845 s 81(4).
11 See the Railways Clauses Consolidation Act 1845 s 81(4) proviso.
12 See the Railways Clauses Consolidation Act 1845 s 81 (as originally enacted); and the Acquisition of Land Act 1981 Sch 2 para 6(1)(a). As to the corresponding provisions in the mining codes relating to water and sewerage undertakers and the Environment Agency see WATER AND WATERWAYS vol 101 (2018) PARA 762.
13 Ie under the Railways Clauses Consolidation Act 1845 s 81 (as originally enacted) or the Acquisition of Land Act 1981 Sch 2 para 6.
14 See generally *Holliday v Wakefield Corpn* [1891] AC 81 at 88, HL, per Lord Bramwell; *Whitehouse v Wolverhampton and Walsall Rly Co* (1869) LR 5 Exch 6.
15 As to the code provisions for such compensation see PARAS 157–159. See also *Eden v North Eastern Rly Co* [1907] AC 400 at 408, HL, per Lord Macnaghten; *Midland Rly Co v Miles* (1886) 33 ChD 632; *Re Huddersfield Corpn and Jacomb* (1874) 10 Ch App 92.
16 See the Railways Clauses Consolidation Act 1845 s 81 (as originally enacted); s 81(3); and the Acquisition of Land Act 1981 Sch 2 para 6(2). For the corresponding provisions in the mining codes relating to water and sewerage undertakers and the Environment Agency see WATER AND WATERWAYS vol 101 (2018) PARA 762.
17 See further PARA 157. As to the Upper Tribunal generally see COURTS AND TRIBUNALS vol 24 (2010) PARA 883 et seq.

## 168.  Compensation to surface owners.

Where the mining code of the Railways Clauses Consolidation Act 1845[1] or the mining code of the Acquisition of Land Act 1981 applies[2] and any loss or damage is sustained by the owner, lessee or occupier of the land over minerals[3] comprised in a counter-notice[4] (not being the owner or lessee of the minerals) by reason of the making of communication works[5] where those works would have been unnecessary but for the prevention of the working of the minerals, the railway or other authority must pay full compensation to the owner, lessee or occupier of the surface[6] for the loss or damage[7].

1  Ie the code either as originally enacted or as substituted by the Mines (Working Facilities and Support) Act 1923 s 15: see PARA 135.
2  See PARA 135.
3  As to the meaning of 'minerals' see PARA 10.
4  As to the counter-notice see PARA 154.
5  As to the meaning of 'communication works' see PARA 166.
6  As to the meaning of 'surface' see PARA 149.
7  See the Railways Clauses Consolidation Act 1845 s 82 (as originally enacted); s 82 (substituted by the Mines (Working Facilities and Support) Act 1923 s 15) (see PARA 135); and the Acquisition of Land Act 1981 s 3, Sch 2 para 7(1), (2). Where the substituted code applies, the compensation is to be determined, in default of agreement, by arbitration: Railways Clauses Consolidation Act 1845 s 82 (as so substituted). As to arbitration see, however, PARA 157. There is no corresponding provision for compensation in the case of waterworks.

## 169. Rights of inspection.

Where the mining code of the Railways Clauses Consolidation Act 1845[1] or the mining code of the Acquisition of Land Act 1981 applies[2] the railway or other authority may, after 24 hours' notice, and in order to ascertain whether or not any mines[3] or minerals[4] are being worked or are about to be or have been worked[5] so as to damage the railway or works, enter upon any land through or near which the railway or works passes or is or are situate, being land in which the mines or minerals are being worked or lie, or are supposed to be worked or to lie, and may enter into and return from any such mines or minerals or the works connected with them, and for that purpose may make use of any apparatus or machinery belonging to the mine owner[6], and use all necessary means for discovering the distance from the railway or works to the parts of the mines or minerals which are being or have been worked or are about to be worked[7].

In the case of railways and works to which the substituted code applies[8] a similar right of inspection of the railway or works is given to the mine owner who desires to work minerals under or near the railway or works, and also to the royalty owner[9], if any, or any person duly authorised by either of them[10].

In the case of railways, refusal to allow such inspection[11] makes the person offending liable for each refusal to a penalty not exceeding level 2 on the standard scale[12].

1   Ie the code either as originally enacted or as substituted by the Mines (Working Facilities and Support) Act 1923 s 15: see PARA 135.

2   See PARA 135.

3   As to the meaning of 'mine' see PARA 3.

4   As to the meaning of 'minerals' see PARA 10.

5   These words are taken from the mining code of the Railways Clauses Consolidation Act 1845 s 83. In the Railways Clauses Consolidation Act 1845 s 83 (as originally enacted) the words are 'are being worked or have been worked'; and in the Acquisition of Land Act 1981 s 3, Sch 2 para 8(1) they are 'have been worked'.

6   As to the meaning of 'mine owner' see PARA 150.

7   See the Railways Clauses Consolidation Act 1845 ss 78, 83 (both as originally enacted); ss 78(1), 83(1) (both substituted by the Mines (Working Facilities and Support) Act 1923 s 15 (see PARA 135); and the Acquisition of Land Act 1981 Sch 2 para 8(1), (2)). The words 'are being or have been worked or are about to be worked' are taken from the Railways Clauses Consolidation Act 1845 s 83 (as substituted). Section 83 (as originally enacted) and the Acquisition of Land Act 1981 Sch 2 para 8(2) do not contain any reference to minerals which 'have been worked'.

     The code (as substituted) in the Railways Clauses Consolidation Act 1845 empowers the railway authority to inspect and take copies of so much of the working plans and sections of the mine as relate to minerals the working of which affects, has affected or may affect the railway or works (s 83(1) (as so substituted)); but otherwise the codes confer no right to a general inspection of the working plans: see *Eden v North Eastern Rly Co* [1907] AC 400 at 409, 410, HL, per Lord Macnaghten. As to the corresponding provisions in the mining codes relating to water and sewerage undertakers and the Environment Agency see WATER AND WATERWAYS vol 101 (2018) PARA 763.

8   See PARA 135.

9   As to the meaning of 'royalty owner' see PARA 154.

10   See the Railways Clauses Consolidation Act 1845 s 83(2).

11   Ie where the mining code of the Railways Clauses Consolidation Act 1845 as originally enacted or the mining code of the Acquisition of Land Act 1981 applies, inspection by the railway authority and, where the substituted code applies (see PARA 135), inspection by the railway authority, mine owner or royalty owner.

12   See the Railways Clauses Consolidation Act 1845 s 84 (as originally enacted) (amended by the Justices of the Peace Act 1949 s 46, Sch 7 Pt III; and the Criminal Justice Act 1982 s 46); Railways Clauses Consolidation Act 1845 s 84; and the Acquisition of Land Act 1981 Sch 2 para 8(3) (amended by the Criminal Justice Act 1982 s 46). As to the standard scale see SENTENCING vol 92 (2015) PARA 176.

In the case of refusal by the authority where the substituted code applies, the penalty is payable to the mine owner or royalty owner: Railways Clauses Consolidation Act 1845 s 84 (as so substituted). In all cases the penalty is recoverable by summary proceedings: s 145 (amended by the Summary Jurisdiction Act 1884 s 4, Schedule; the Statute Law Revision Act 1892; and the Transport Act 1962 ss 93(1), 95(1), (2), Sch 12, Pt II). The procedure is criminal, not civil: see *R v Paget* (1881) 8 QBD 151, DC.

## 170. Protection against improper working.

Where the mining code of the Railways Clauses Consolidation Act 1845[1] or the mining code of the Acquisition of Land Act 1981 applies[2], if any minerals[3] have been worked or are being worked contrary to the mining code or the special Act of a railway authority, the railway or other authority may give notice to the mine owner[4] requiring him to construct such works and to adopt such means as may be necessary or proper for making safe the railway or works and for preventing injury to them; and if he does not forthwith proceed to construct the works, the authority may construct the works and recover the expense of it from him by action[5].

1  Ie the code either as originally enacted or as substituted by the Mines (Working Facilities and Support) Act 1923 s 15: see PARA 135.
2  See PARA 135.
3  As to the meaning of 'minerals' see PARA 10.
4  As to the meaning of 'mine owner' see PARA 150.
5  See the Railways Clauses Consolidation Act 1845 s 85 (as originally enacted); s 85 (substituted by the Mines (Working Facilities and Support) Act 1923 s 15) (see PARA 135); and the Acquisition of Land Act 1981 s 3, Sch 2 para 9(1), (2).

## 171. Variation of rights by agreement.

Where the substituted mining code of the Railways Clauses Consolidation Act 1845 applies[1], a mine owner[2], a royalty owner[3] and the railway authority, or any two of them, may by agreement alter, extend or otherwise vary their respective rights under the code with regard to any minerals to which the code applies[4], but not so as to prejudice the right of any mine owner, royalty owner or authority not a party to the agreement without his or its consent[5].

1  Ie the code as substituted by the Mines (Working Facilities and Support) Act 1923 s 15: see PARA 135.
2  As to the meaning of 'mine owner' see PARA 150.
3  As to the meaning of 'royalty owner' see PARA 154.
4  As to the minerals to which the code applies see PARA 142. As to the meaning of 'minerals' see PARA 10.
5  See the Railways Clauses Consolidation Act 1845 s 85A (added by the Mines (Working Facilities and Support) Act 1923 s 15) (see PARA 135). The power of variation applies notwithstanding anything contained in the Act: Railways Clauses Consolidation Act 1845 s 85A. See also the Coal Mining Subsidence Act 1991 s 37(4); and PARA 246.

## 172. Saving of common law rights.

Where the substituted mining code of the Railways Clauses Consolidation Act 1845 applies[1], the code does not alter, diminish or affect any right to let down the surface[2], either unconditionally or subject to payment of compensation, or to any other condition, which a mine owner[3] or royalty owner[4] may possess, whether by statute, grant, lease, agreement or otherwise, derived from a title antecedent[5] to the acquisition by the railway authority of its interest in the surface, or conferred on him by a reservation contained in the grant to the authority, and a mine owner having such a title and having served a notice in accordance with the code with respect to the working of any minerals[6] is free to work any such minerals as to which a counter-notice[7] has not been received, discharged from all the restrictions and provisions of the code[8] other than those[9] relating to improper working[10]. If a counter-notice is served, however, the minerals to which the counter-notice relates are, for the purposes of assessment of compensation payable to the mine owner or royalty owner for leaving them unworked, deemed to be minerals lying wholly within the inner area of protection[11], and the appropriate percentage for the purposes of computing compensation for the additional expenses and losses incurred by the mine owner by reason of the counter-notice[12] is 100[13]. In such a case, even if the railway authority is already entitled to support by express grant, or by the exercise of its powers under the Railways Clauses Consolidation Act 1845, the mine owner is not absolved from the obligation of giving notice of intention to work, for the obligation is absolute[14].

1 Ie the code as substituted by the Mines (Working Facilities and Support) Act 1923 s 15: see PARA 135.
2 As to the meaning of 'surface' see PARA 149.
3 As to the meaning of 'mine owner' see PARA 150.
4 As to the meaning of 'royalty owner' see PARA 154.
5 If a mine owner surrenders his lease (the date of which is antecedent to the acquisition by the railway authority of the surface) and takes a new lease after the acquisition of the surface by the railway authority, his title is not then antecedent to the acquisition of the surface by the railway authority: see *London and North Eastern Rly Co v Hardwick Colliery Co Ltd* [1935] Ch 203.
6 As to the notice of intention to work see PARA 150. As to the meaning of 'minerals' see PARA 10.
7 As to the counter-notice see PARA 154.
8 As to these restrictions see PARA 160 et seq.
9 See PARA 161.
10 Railways Clauses Consolidation Act 1845 s 85B(2) (added by the Mines (Working Facilities and Support) Act 1923 s 15) (see PARA 135).
11 As to the area of protection see PARA 149.
12 As to such compensation see PARA 167.
13 Railways Clauses Consolidation Act 1845 s 85B(2). In assessing compensation it seems that account must be taken of the possible contribution for which the mine owner might in the future have become liable under s 79A if the coal covered by the counter-notice had been actually worked and damage to the railway had been caused by that working: *London and North Eastern Rly Co v B A Collieries Ltd* [1945] AC 143 at 173, [1945] 1 All ER 51 at 59, HL, obiter per Lord Thankerton.
14 Railways Clauses Consolidation Act 1845 s 78(1) (substituted by the Mines (Working Facilities and Support) Act 1923 s 15); and see the Mines (Working Facilities and Support) Act 1923 s 16(4); and PARA 175.

**173. Adjustments between mine owner and royalty owner.**
Where the substituted mining code of the Railways Clauses Consolidation Act 1845 applies[1], the code does not affect any agreement between the mine owner[2] and the royalty owner[3] for the payment of any rent or royalty[4], but the payment of compensation by the railway or other authority to the royalty owner in respect of any minerals extinguishes any liability by the mine owner to pay any royalty in respect of the same minerals[5], and the mine owner is entitled to make the normal deductions from royalties[6] notwithstanding anything in any agreement entered into before 1 August 1923[7], unless the agreement was made after 1 November 1912[8] and expressly or by necessary implication provided for the payment of royalties in respect of the minerals supporting the railway or works in the event of the mine owner working them in virtue of a right acquired by agreement or statute or otherwise, or for the payment of royalties in respect of those minerals whether or not they are worked[9].

If the exercise by the railway or other authority of the powers conferred upon it by the code as to minerals within the area of protection[10] will prevent the mine owner from producing such a quantity of minerals as at the royalty rate will equal the fixed or minimum rent[11] reserved by his lease, or otherwise occasions serious hardship having regard to his obligation to pay such rent, or owing to any provision in the lease restricting the time within which a deficiency due to previous short working may be made good, such adjustment must be made between the royalty owner and the mine owner as, in default of agreement, may be determined by arbitration[12].

1  Ie the code as substituted by the Mines (Working Facilities and Support) Act 1923 s 15: see PARA 135.
2  As to the meaning of 'mine owner' see PARA 150.
3  As to the meaning of 'royalty owner' see PARA 154.
4  Railways Clauses Consolidation Act 1845 s 85B(1) (s 85B added by the Mines (Working Facilities and Support) Act 1923 s 15) (see PARA 135). As to the meaning of 'royalty' see PARA 154.
5  Railways Clauses Consolidation Act 1845 s 85B(1) proviso (i). As to the meaning of 'minerals' see PARA 10.
6  Ie the deductions authorised by the Railways Clauses Consolidation Act 1845 s 79A(3): see PARA 163.
7  The Mines (Working Facilities and Support) Act 1923 was passed on 18 July 1923 and came into operation on 1 January 1924: s 18(2) (repealed).
8  Ie the date of the decision in *Howley Park Coal and Cannel Co v London and North Western Rly Co* [1913] AC 11, HL: see PARA 135.
9  Railways Clauses Consolidation Act 1845 s 85B(1) proviso (ii).
10  As to the area of protection see PARA 149.
11  As to the meanings of 'fixed rent' and 'minimum rent' see PARA 330.
12  Railways Clauses Consolidation Act 1845 s 85B(1) proviso (iii). As to arbitration see, however, PARA 157.

## 174.  Support apart from the code.

Where the substituted mining code of the Railways Clauses Consolidation Act 1845 applies[1] and except as expressly provided in the code or under any agreement between the railway or other authority and the mine owner[2], the mine owner, as between himself and the authority: (1) is not under any liability to leave support either inside or outside the area of protection[3]; and (2) is entitled to remove such support without being liable for any damage thereby caused to the railway or works or any part of them, provided the removal is done in a manner proper and necessary for the beneficial working of the minerals and according to the usual manner of working minerals in the district[4].

1  Ie the code as substituted by the Mines (Working Facilities and Support) Act 1923 s 15: see PARA 135.
2  As to the meaning of 'mine owner' see PARA 150.
3  Railways Clauses Consolidation Act 1845 s 85E(a) (added by the Mines (Working Facilities and Support) Act 1923 s 15 (see PARA 135). As to the area of protection see PARA 149.
4  Railways Clauses Consolidation Act 1845 s 85E(b). As to the right of support at common law see PARA 114 et seq. As to the meaning of 'minerals' see PARA 10.

## 175.  Rights acquired before 1 January 1924.

The substituted mining code of the Railways Clauses Consolidation Act 1845[1] does not take away, diminish or prejudicially alter or affect any estate, right or interest in minerals[2] which may have been acquired by a railway or other authority before 1 January 1924[3] under or by virtue of any express provision in any deed or contract, or under or by virtue of the exercise of its powers under the code as originally enacted[4], or any right of support from minerals which any such authority may have so acquired, or any compensation paid or payable by any such company in consequence of the exercise before 1 January 1924 of any of its powers under the original code[5]. The substituted code does not affect any agreement subsisting between a railway or other authority and a mine owner[6] or a royalty owner[7] on 1 January 1924 with regard to the working, or the leaving unworked, of minerals lying under or near to any railway or works of the authority, so long as the agreement remains in force, and any such agreement continues in force until determined by effluxion of time, or by the exercise of any power of determination conferred by it; and a new agreement may be entered into[8].

1   Ie the code as substituted by the Mines (Working Facilities and Support) Act 1923 s 15: see PARA 135.
2   As to the meaning of 'minerals' see PARA 10.
3   Ie the date of coming into force of the Mines (Working Facilities and Support) Act 1923: see PARA 173.
4   Ie the Railways Clauses Consolidation Act 1845 ss 78–85 (as originally enacted).
5   Mines (Working Facilities and Support) Act 1923 s 16(4)(a).
6   As to the meaning of 'mine owner' see PARA 150.
7   As to the meaning of 'royalty owner' see PARA 154.
8   Mines (Working Facilities and Support) Act 1923 s 16(4)(b).

## (3) Statutory Right to Withdraw Support: Coal Mining

**176. Extent of the right to withdraw support from land in relation to coal-mining operations.**

On and after the restructuring date[1], any licensed operator[2] is entitled, so far as may be reasonably requisite for the carrying on of any coal-mining operations[3] to which the licensing requirements apply[4], to withdraw support from certain land[5]. This provision applies to any land, not being land comprised in an underground coal mine[6], if:

(1)     a notice relating to that land has been given[7] and has come into force[8];
(2)     immediately before the restructuring date the British Coal Corporation was entitled under and in accordance with the statutory provisions then in force[9] to withdraw support from that land; or
(3)     certain transitional conditions relating to notice given before the restructuring date are satisfied[10],

and a right under this provision has effect whether the coal[11] in relation to which the operations concerned are carried on lies under the land to which this provision applies or under adjacent land[12].

1   Ie 31 October 1994: see PARA 50.
2   As to the meaning of 'licensed operator' see PARA 58. In the case of any licensed operator who is entitled by virtue of these provisions to withdraw support from any land, the rights comprised in his entitlement are also exercisable by any person authorised (ie as mentioned in the Coal Industry Act 1994 s 27(4): see PARA 93) to act on his behalf in the carrying on of any of the operations which the operator is authorised to carry on: s 38(4).
3   As to the meaning of 'coal-mining operations' see PARA 51.
4   Ie the Coal Industry Act 1994 s 25: see PARA 89.
5   Coal Industry Act 1994 s 38(1). Previous statutory provision for the withdrawal of support from land was contained in the Coal Act 1938 s 4, Sch 2 (repealed); and later in the Coal Industry Act 1975 s 2 (repealed), which conferred on the British Coal Corporation a right to withdraw support to enable coal to be worked, subject to the publication of notice in the London Gazette and on two successive weeks in local newspapers. The relevant date of publication for these purposes is the date on which the notice is published in the London Gazette or, if it is later, is first published in

the local newspapers: see s 2 (repealed). As to the British Coal Corporation see PARAS 49–50. Subject to the provisions of the Coal Industry Act 1994 s 38, the rights conferred by the Coal Industry Act 1975 s 2 (repealed) are not exercisable on or after the restructuring date: Coal Industry Act 1994 s 38(7).

6   'Underground coal mine' means any coal mine which is a mine within the meaning of the Mines and Quarries Act 1954 (see PARA 3): Coal Industry Act 1994 s 38(6). As to the meaning of 'coal mine' see PARA 3.

7   Ie in accordance with the Coal Industry Act 1994 s 39: see PARA 177.

8   A notice comes into force with whichever is the later of the following: (1) the expiry of the period of three months beginning with the day after the relevant date of publication; and (2) the time when particulars of the notice are first registered by the Coal Authority (ie in accordance with Coal Industry Act 1994 s 56: see PARA 106): s 38(3). 'Relevant date of publication', in relation to a notice under the Coal Industry Act 1975 s 2 (repealed), has the same meaning as in that provision; and, in relation to a notice under the Coal Industry Act 1994 s 38, means whichever is the later of (a) the date of the publication of the notice in the London Gazette; and (b) the date of the first of the publications in a local newspaper (ie for the purposes of s 39(3)(b): see PARA 177 head (b)): s 38(5). As to the Coal Authority see PARA 52 et seq.

   Where a copy of any notice under s 38 is sent to the Authority more than 14 days before the end of the period of three months mentioned in head (1) the duty of the Authority to enter particulars of that notice in the register (ie the register maintained under s 56: see PARA 106) must be discharged before the end of that period of three months: s 56(2). The Authority must not enter any particulars of any notice under s 38 in the register unless it is satisfied that the notice has been properly given in accordance with the requirements of the Coal Industry Act 1994, and that the posting requirements of s 39(4) (see PARA 177) have been complied with in relation to that notice: see s 56(3).

9   Ie the Coal Industry Act 1975 s 2 (repealed).

10  The conditions are that: (1) the relevant date of publication of a notice under the Coal Industry Act 1975 s 2 (repealed) relating to that land is a date not more than three months before the restructuring date; (2) the Corporation would (apart from the Coal Industry Act 1994 s 38(7) have become entitled as mentioned in head (2) in the text at the end of the period of three months beginning on the relevant date of publication; and (3) that period has expired: see s 38(2).

11  As to the meaning of 'coal' see PARA 51.

12  Coal Industry Act 1994 s 38(2).

### 177. Notices in connection with the statutory right to withdraw support.

No notice in connection with the right to withdraw support from land[1] may be given except: (1) by a person who, on the relevant date of publication[2], is a licensed operator[3] and as the holder of a licence[4] has an area of responsibility[5] that consists of or includes all the land to which the notice relates; or (2) by a person who, on that date, is authorised by such a licence, or by virtue of a licence originally granted by the British Coal Corporation[6], to carry on coal-mining operations[7] and has the approval of the Coal Authority[8] for the giving of a notice relating to the land in question[9].

The notice, which must contain certain information[10], is to be given by being published (a) in the London Gazette[11]; and (b) at least once in each of two successive weeks, in newspapers circulating in the locality where that land is situated[12]. Not later than the relevant date of publication of a notice[13], the person giving that notice must serve a copy on every planning authority[14] within whose area or district any part of the land to which the notice relates is situated; and must also post a copy or copies of the notice in some conspicuous place or places on that land[15].

1   Ie under the Coal Industry Act 1994 s 38: see PARA 176.

2   As to the meaning of 'relevant date of publication' see PARA 176.

3   As to the meaning of 'licensed operator' see PARA 58.

4   Ie under the Coal Industry Act 1994 Pt II (ss 25–36): see PARA 89 et seq.

5   As to the areas of responsibility see PARA 205.

6   Ie a licence granted under the Coal Industry Nationalisation Act 1946 s 36(2) (repealed), which

continues to have effect by virtue of the Coal Industry Act 1994 s 25(3): see PARA 89. As to the British Coal Corporation see PARAS 49–50.

7   Ie coal-mining operations to which the Coal Industry Act 1994 s 25 applies: see PARA 89. As to the meaning of 'coal-mining operations' see PARA 51.

8   As to the Coal Authority see PARA 52 et seq.

9   Coal Industry Act 1994 s 39(1).

10  A notice must (1) indicate the land to which it relates either by reference to a map or in any other manner which, in the circumstances, is sufficient to identify it; (2) identify the person by whom the notice is given, and summarise the respects in which the requirements of the Coal Industry Act 1994 s 39(1) are satisfied in relation to that person; and (3) state that there are proposals to carry on coal-mining operations which may require the exercise in relation to that land of the right to withdraw support mentioned in s 38(1) (see PARA 176): s 39(2).

11  Coal Industry Act 1994 s 39(3)(a).

12  Coal Industry Act 1994 s 39(3)(b).

13  Ie under the Coal Industry Act 1994 s 38: see PARA 176.

14  For these purposes, 'planning authority' means any local planning authority within the meaning of the Town and Country Planning Act 1990 (see PLANNING vol 81 (2018) PARAS 3, 160 et seq): see the Coal Industry Act 1994 s 39(5).

15  Coal Industry Act 1994 s 39(4).

## 178. Revocation of the statutory right to withdraw support.

The right of a licensed operator[1] to withdraw support[2] may, in relation to any land to which it applies, be revoked by a notice given by the Coal Authority[3]. Where the Coal Authority gives a notice in relation to any land to which the provisions concerning the right to withdraw support apply[4], those provisions cease to apply to that land in relation to any coal-mining operations[5] carried on after the relevant date of publication[6]. The Authority must not give such a notice unless it appears to it that there is not for the time being any person who is authorised[7] to carry on coal-mining operations which might involve the withdrawal of support from the land in question[8].

A notice under these provisions must indicate the land to which it relates, either by reference to a map or in any other manner which, in the circumstances, is sufficient to identify it[9]; and must state that the provisions giving rights to withdraw support[10] are to cease to apply to the land[11]. The notice must be published (1) in the London Gazette; and (2) at least once in each of two successive weeks, in newspapers circulating in the locality where that land is situated[12]. Not later than the relevant date of publication of the notice, the Authority must serve a copy of the notice on every planning authority[13] within whose area or district any part of the land to which the notice relates is situated[14].

1   As to the meaning of 'licensed operator' see PARA 58.

2   As to the statutory right of a licensed operator to withdraw support from land in relation to coal mining see PARAS 176–177.

3   As to the Coal Authority see PARA 52 et seq.

4   Ie the Coal Industry Act 1994 s 38: see PARA 176.

5   As to the meaning of 'coal-mining operations' see PARA 51.

6   Coal Industry Act 1994 s 41(1). 'Relevant date of publication', in relation to a notice under s 41, means whichever is the later of: (1) the date of the publication in the London Gazette (see head (1) in the text); and (2) the date of the first of the publications of that notice in local newspapers (see head (2) in the text): s 41(6).

      A revocation under s 41(1) is subject to the effect of any notice under s 38 (see PARA 176) which is given at any time after the relevant date of publication of the notice under s 41: see s 41(5).

7   Ie authorised by a licence under the Coal Industry Act 1994 Pt II (ss 25–36) or by virtue of s 25(3): see PARA 89 et seq.

8   Coal Industry Act 1994 s 41(2).

9   Coal Industry Act 1994 s 41(3)(a).

10  Ie the Coal Industry Act 1994 s 38: see PARA 176.

11 Coal Industry Act 1994 s 41(3)(b).
12 Coal Industry Act 1994 s 41(3)(c).
13 For these purposes, 'planning authority' means any local planning authority within the meaning of the Town and Country Planning Act 1990 (see PLANNING vol 81 (2018) PARAS 3, 160 et seq): Coal Industry Act 1994 s 41(6).
14 Coal Industry Act 1994 s 41(4). As to registration of the notice see s 56; and PARA 106.

**179. Savings for special cases.**
There are four special cases in which the right to withdraw support[1] is subject to specific restrictions or modifications.

First, where the British Coal Corporation[2] was bound, immediately before the restructuring date[3], by (1) the provisions of an agreement made between the Corporation (or any of its predecessors[4]) and a person who was interested in any land[5], which has effect so as to require the Corporation to comply with an undertaking (contained in the agreement) not to work any coal, not to work minerals or not to withdraw support from any land; or (2) any provisions containing any restriction, terms or conditions applicable to the working of coal by virtue of an agreement entered into after 1 July 1942 and before the restructuring date; or (3) the provisions of any coal-mining lease[6] prohibiting the withdrawal of support from any land specified in the lease, the right to withdraw support has effect subject to those provisions, but only so far as they have effect in relation to the Corporation or any other person who is for the time being bound by them[7].

Second, the provisions relating to the withdrawal of support from land do not affect any restrictions, terms or conditions applicable to the working of coal by virtue of a working facilities order[8], or by virtue of the restrictions on the working of coal which was vested in statutory undertakers[9]; and the right to withdraw support is without prejudice to the effect of any restructuring scheme[10] on any of those restrictions, terms or conditions[11].

Third, the provisions relating to the withdrawal of support from land have effect subject to any right[12] to which the activities of the Corporation were subject immediately before the restructuring date[13].

Fourth, nothing in the provisions relating to the withdrawal of support from land confers any entitlement to withdraw support in connection with the working of any coal or coal mines[14] comprised in land in the Forest of Dean or any other part of the area of what was the Hundred of St Briavels[15] in the county of Gloucester, being land in respect of which the privileges of free miners[16] are exercisable[17].

Nothing in the Coal Industry Act 1994 or in any other enactment may be taken as preventing any person from entering, at any time on or after the restructuring date, into an agreement by virtue of which he accepts a prohibition or restriction on the exercise of his rights[18] to withdraw support from land[19].

1  Ie the right granted under the Coal Industry Act 1994 s 38: see PARA 176.
2  As to the British Coal Corporation see PARAS 49–50.
3  Ie 31 October 1994: see PARA 50.
4  References in the Coal Industry Act 1994 s 40, in relation to an agreement which has effect with respect to the working of coal, to a predecessor of the Corporation are references to the Coal Commission or the person in whom the fee simple of the coal was vested when the agreement was entered into: s 40(5). As to the Coal Commission see PARA 48. As to the meaning of 'coal' see PARA 51.
5  'Interested' must be construed, in relation to a person referred to as interested in any coal or mine of coal, or in any other land, as referring to any person entitled to, or to exercise, or interested in, or in the exercise of, any estate, interest, charge or power (including an option or right of pre-emption, and including a contingent executory or future interest or a possibility coupled with

an interest whether or not the object of the gift or limitation of such interest or possibility be ascertained) in, on or over that coal or mine or that other land, as the case may be, or in, on or over the rents and profits thereof, otherwise than in respect only of the benefit of a servitude or restrictive covenant adversely affecting that coal or mine or that other land, as the case may be: Coal Act 1938 s 44 (repealed with savings) (definition applied by the Coal Industry Act 1994 s 40(1)). As to the meaning of 'coal' see PARA 48; and as to the meaning of 'mine of coal' see PARA 48.

6    'Coal-mining lease' means in relation to any coal a lease that confers a right to work and carry away that coal, and means in relation to any mine of coal a lease that confers a right to use it for a coal-mining purpose: Coal Act 1938 s 44 (repealed with savings) (definition applied by the Coal Industry Act 1994 s 40(1)).

7    Coal Industry Act 1994 s 40(1).

8    Ie an order made, whether before or after the restructuring date, under the Mines (Working Facilities and Support) Act 1966 s 1 or s 7: see PARA 380 et seq.

9    Ie the Coal Act 1938 s 33 (repealed) or any consent required by virtue of that provision: see further PARA 180.

10   As to restructuring schemes see PARA 72.

11   See the Coal Industry Act 1994 s 40(2).

12   Ie any such right as was referred to in the Coal Act 1938 s 34(1) (repealed) (rights of the Crown, local authorities, highway authorities or statutory undertakers). As to the saving of such rights see the Coal Industry Act 1994 s 67, Sch 10 para 4.

13   See the Coal Industry Act 1994 s 40(3).

14   As to the meaning of 'coal mine' see PARA 3.

15   As to the areas included in the Forest of Dean and the Hundred of St Briavels see PARA 607.

16   As to the meaning of 'free miner' see PARA 607.

17   Coal Industry Act 1994 s 40(4). As to mining in Gloucestershire generally see PARA 607 et seq.

18   Ie under the Coal Industry Act 1994 s 38: see PARA 176.

19   Coal Industry Act 1994 s 40(7).

## 180. Consent required for the working of coal previously vested in statutory undertakers.

Where any coal[1] which was vested in the British Coal Corporation[2] immediately before the restructuring date[3] is coal which cannot be worked without the consent of the person in whom any statutory undertaking is vested[4], the consent of the person in whom that undertaking is for the time being vested[5] continues to be required on and after that date for the working of that coal[6]. A consent so required must not be unreasonably withheld[7], but this does not preclude the right of any person whose consent is sought for these purposes (1) to give consent subject, so far as may be reasonably requisite (a) to a condition that the working of the coal must not be such as to let down any land in which that person is interested in respect of the undertaking in question or must be limited to working in particular places or in a particular manner; or (b) to other conditions or limitations as regards the working consented to or the payment of proper compensation for, or the making good of, damage arising from it; or (2) to require, as a condition of consent, payment of a reasonable sum in respect of any legal or other expenses incurred in connection with the consent[8]. These requirements are enforceable by the persons in whom the undertaking in question is for the time being vested; and are so enforceable in the same manner and (subject to any transfer of liabilities in accordance with a restructuring scheme[9]) against the same persons as it would have been enforceable[10] immediately before the restructuring date by the persons in whom that undertaking was vested at that time[11].

1    As to the meaning of 'coal' see PARA 51.

2    As to the British Coal Corporation see PARAS 49–50.

3    Ie 31 October 1994: see PARA 50.

4　Ie by virtue of the Coal Act 1938 s 33 (repealed). Under this provision, coal which was previously vested in statutory undertakers was subject to the restriction that the coal was not to be worked without the consent of the persons in whom the undertaking was for the time being vested: see s 33 (repealed). Such a restriction was enforceable by the persons in whom the undertaking was for the time being vested in the like manner and against the like persons as if it had been imposed by a covenant entered into by the Coal Commission on 1 July 1942: see s 33(6) (repealed). As to the Coal Commission see PARA 48. 'Statutory undertakers' meant a local authority, company or other body or person authorised by or under an Act of Parliament, or an order having the force of an Act of Parliament, to construct, work, or carry on a railway, canal, inland navigation, dock, harbour, tramway, gas, electricity, water, sewage disposal, or other public undertaking: see s 33(1) (repealed).

5　If at any time the undertaking in question is vested in a person having no interest in land supported by that coal, consent for the working of the coal ceases from that time to be required: Coal Industry Act 1994 s 67, Sch 10 para 3(2).

6　Coal Industry Act 1994 Sch 10 para 3(1).

7　Coal Industry Act 1994 Sch 10 para 3(3).

8　Coal Industry Act 1994 Sch 10 para 3(4). Any question arising under Sch 10 para 3(3) or Sch 10 para 3(4) must be referred to and determined by the High Court: Sch 10 para 3(5). On such a reference, the High Court has power to dispense with the required consent either without conditions or limitations or subject to any such conditions or limitations as are mentioned in Sch 10 para 3(4): Sch 10 para 3(6). In determining any question referred to it under these provisions, the High Court must have regard primarily to the safety and efficient working of the undertaking in question: Sch 10 para 3(7).

9　As to restructuring schemes see PARA 72.

10　Ie by virtue of the Coal Act 1938 s 33(6) (repealed).

11　Coal Industry Act 1994 Sch 10 para 3(8).

## 181. Damage arising from exercise of right.

The provisions of the Coal Industry Act 1994 which deal with the right to withdraw support from land[1] do not include provisions for compensation[2]. Liabilities in connection with any damage caused by the withdrawal of support are governed by the general statutory provisions relating to subsidence damage by coal mining[3].

1　Ie the Coal Industry Act 1994 s 38: see PARA 176.

2　As to claims for compensation in relation to statutory rights to withdraw support see PARA 248.

3　As to subsidence damage by coal mining see PARA 200 et seq. As to the meaning of 'subsidence damage' see PARA 203.

# (4) Subsidence Damage

## (i) Common Law

## 182. Nature of the action for damage.

At common law, if the surface[1] subsides and is injured by the removal of the supporting strata, the owner of the surface, if entitled to the right of support[2], may bring a claim against the owner of the minerals[3] or other person who removed the strata[4] for the damage sustained by the subsidence, even though on the supposition that the surface and the minerals belong to the same owner the mining operations may not have been conducted negligently or contrary to the custom of the district[5]. Although it is not clear what is the true category of such a claim[6], it is not founded on negligence, but arises from the invasion of the right of the surface owner[7].

1　As to the meaning of 'surface' see PARA 17.

2    As to the general principles of the right of support see PARA 114 et seq. As to the withdrawal of
     support for the purpose of coal-mining operations see the Coal Industry Act 1994 ss 38–41; and
     PARA 176 et seq.
3    As to the meaning of 'minerals' see PARA 10.
4    As to the persons liable for wrongful withdrawal of support see PARAS 190–193.
5    *Humphries v Brogden* (1850) 12 QB 739 at 744 per Lord Campbell CJ; and see *Bankart v
     Houghton* (1860) 27 Beav 425 at 433, obiter, per Romilly MR. As to the damage caused by the
     withdrawal of support in connection with coal-mining operations see the Coal Mining Subsidence
     Act 1991; and PARA 200 et seq.
6    *Graff Bros Estates Ltd v Rimrose Brook Joint Sewerage Board* [1953] 2 QB 318 at 324, 325,
     [1953] 2 All ER 631 at 633, CA, per Singleton LJ.
7    *Brown v Robins* (1859) 4 H & N 186 at 193 per Martin B; and see *British Coal Corpn v Ellistown
     Pipes Ltd (Hepworth Building Products)* [1994] RVR 81, CA. As to the effect of statutes of
     limitation see generally LIMITATION PERIODS vol 68 (2016) PARA 901 et seq. As to actions by
     and against personal representatives see WILLS AND INTESTACY vol 103 (2016) PARA 1271 et
     seq.

## 183.   The cause of action.

The damage, not the withdrawal of support, is the cause of action, and no right
of the surface[1] owner is infringed unless and until subsidence results[2]. The mine[3]
owner may remove every atom of the minerals[4] so long as the soil above does not
fall; there is, therefore, no interference with the surface owner's right of enjoyment
of his land, and no cause of action on his part, unless and until actual damage
results from the removal of the minerals[5]. If, however, the condition of the surface
owner's land is altered by subsidence, substantial in amount, so as to interfere
with his ordinary enjoyment of his land, he may bring a claim without proof of
pecuniary loss[6].

Each fresh and independent subsidence gives rise to a new cause of action, and
it is no answer to the surface owner's claim for compensation to say that he has
already brought a claim and obtained compensation for previous damage, even
though the subsidence results from the same excavation[7].

A subsidence which is merely a stage in a continuous process can also constitute
a distinct cause of action. There is no distinction in this respect between a case
where the subsidence has gone on continuously and a case where it has taken
place by fits and starts[8].

1    As to the meaning of 'surface' see PARA 17.
2    See *Darley Main Colliery Co v Mitchell* (1886) 11 App Cas 127 at 133, HL, per Lord Halsbury.
3    As to the meaning of 'mine' see PARA 3.
4    As to the meaning of 'minerals' see PARA 10.
5    See *Backhouse v Bonomi* (1861) 9 HL Cas 503; *Darley Main Colliery Co v Mitchell* (1886) 11 App
     Cas 127, HL; *West Leigh Colliery Co Ltd v Tunnicliffe and Hampson Ltd* [1908] AC 27 at 29,
     HL, per Lord Macnaghten. A mine owner who removes the minerals and substitutes artificial
     support incurs no liability if there is no subsidence: *Rowbotham v Wilson* (1857) 8 E & B 123 at
     157, obiter, per Cresswell J (dissenting) (affd on other grounds (1860) 8 HL Cas 348); *Darley
     Main Colliery Co v Mitchell* at 133–134, HL, per Lord Halsbury. As to the liability of successive
     owners see PARA 191.
6    *Mitchell v Darley Main Colliery Co* (1884) 14 QBD 125 at 137–138, CA, per Bowen LJ (affd
     (1886) 11 App Cas 127, HL); *A-G v Conduit Colliery Co* [1895] 1 QB 301 at 310–314, DC, per
     Collins J. If and so far as *Smith v Thackerah* (1866) as reported in 35 LJCP 276 lays down a
     contrary rule, it must be regarded as overruled by the authorities cited earlier in this note, but it
     may perhaps be distinguished as a case in which damage not measurable in money was treated as
     negligible and consequently disregarded on the de minimis principle: see *A-G v Conduit Colliery
     Co* at 313 per Collins J.

7   *Darley Main Colliery Co v Mitchell* (1886) 11 App Cas 127, HL. There is nothing in this result
    which conflicts with the ordinary principle that all damages incident to one cause of action must
    be recovered once and for ever; the application of the principle is that all damages resulting from
    the same subsidence must be recovered in one and the same claim: *Darley Main Colliery Co v
    Mitchell* at 132–133 per Lord Halsbury. As to when time begins to run under the Limitation Act
    1980 see LIMITATION PERIODS vol 68 (2016) PARA 920 et seq.
8   *Crumbie v Wallsend Local Board* [1891] 1 QB 503, CA.

## 184.   Effect of other workings.

To establish liability at common law on the part of a mine[1] owner whose
operations have contributed to or caused damage by subsidence, it is necessary to
show that he has infringed a legal right of the party who has suffered injury. Thus
if land whose stability has been diminished by undermining subsides in
consequence of the mining operations of a neighbouring proprietor, the
neighbouring proprietor is under no liability if his land did not afford support to
his neighbour's land before any mining took place and the right of support has not
been acquired against him for the land in its altered state[2]. This is so even if no
subsidence would have resulted but for the operations of the neighbouring
proprietor, and the principle may also apply if the mine owner whose operations
have caused damage is a mere trespasser[3]. However, the mine owner will be liable
for the whole damage arising from his workings if his land in fact afforded
support to the neighbouring land in its natural state, even though the extent of the
damage has been increased by former workings of another person or the injured
party himself[4].

1   As to the meaning of 'mine' see PARA 3.
2   *Partridge v Scott* (1838) 3 M & W 220; *Birmingham Corpn v Allen* (1877) 6 ChD 284, CA.
3   *Darley Main Colliery Co v Mitchell* (1886) 11 App Cas 127 at 146, HL, per Lord Bramwell.
4   See *Brown v Robins* (1859) 4 H & N 186; *Hunt v Peake* (1860) John 705; *Manley v Burn* [1916]
    2 KB 121, CA.

## 185.   Defective construction of buildings.

The nature of the soil may affect the right of action, but defective construction
of buildings apparently does not. Damages may be awarded for injury to buildings
erected on undermined ground, even though the buildings have not been
constructed of sufficient solidity considering the nature of the ground, if a right of
support has been acquired for the land in its altered state[1]. Defective construction
of buildings may nevertheless affect the measure of damages[2].

1   *Richards v Jenkins* (1868) 17 WR 30; and see *Aynsley v Bedlington Coal Co Ltd* (1918) 87 LJKB
    1031 at 1035, CA, per Pickford LJ, and at 1037, obiter, per Scrutton LJ.
2   See *Jones v Consolidated Anthracite Collieries and Lord Dynevor* [1916] 1 KB 123 at 137 per
    Scrutton J.

## 186.   Measure of damages.

In accordance with general principles, the measure of damages is prima facie
the diminution attributable to the subsidence in the value of the land to the
claimant or, in the case of a claimant in possession with full ownership, the cost
of reasonable reinstatement[1]. Certain consequential loss may also be recovered[2].
In estimating the diminution in value no allowance may be made for prospective
injury from future subsidence, even subsidence from the same excavation; the
prospective damage gives rise to no cause of action, and it cannot be rendered
actionable by tacking it onto a claim which is admittedly actionable[3].

Injury to buildings will generally be included in the damage, and will be so if
a right of support has been acquired for the buildings. The principle is not limited,
however, to the acquired right of support: where the natural right exists, the value

of buildings may be recovered if their weight has in no way contributed to the subsidence[4]. Nevertheless the value of a house may not be recoverable if it has fallen by its own weight[5].

1   *Tunnicliffe and Hampson Ltd v West Leigh Colliery Co Ltd* [1905] 2 Ch 390. As to damages generally see DAMAGES.

2   As to the recovery of consequential loss see PARA 187.

3   *West Leigh Colliery Co Ltd v Tunnicliffe and Hampson Ltd* [1908] AC 27, HL. As to prospective injury as a possible element in equitable damages see *Barbagallo v J F Catelan Pty Ltd* [1986] 1 Qd R 245 at 250–252, Qd SC, per Thomas J (withdrawal of support case); and DAMAGES vol 29 (2014) PARA 618.

4   *Brown v Robins* (1859) 4 H & N 186; *Hamer v Knowles* (1861) 6 H & N 454; and see *Aynsley v Bedlington Coal Co Ltd* (1918) 87 LJKB 1031 at 1035, CA, per Pickford LJ, and at 1037, obiter, per Scrutton LJ.

5   *Wilde v Minsterley* (1639) 2 Roll Abr 564, Trespass (I); Com Dig, Action upon the Case for a Nuisance (A); *Palmer v Fleshees* (1663) 1 Sid 167; *Wyatt v Harrison* (1832) 3 B & Ad 871 at 876. In *Woodall v Hingley* (1866) 14 LT 167 at 168, Martin B gave his opinion that if a house is built upon loose sandy soil and the house is damaged in consequence partly of the bad soil on which it was built and partly of the mining operations of a neighbour in his own land, no action is maintainable against the neighbour; but see PARA 184.

## 187.   Consequential damage.

In addition to damages for depreciation in the value of buildings, consequential damages may also be recovered for injury by loss of profit in trade[1]. Where the right of support is an acquired right, allowance may also be made in respect of loss through a house being rendered uninhabitable[2]. The right to recover consequential damages may be excluded by an express covenant of indemnity against any physical damage that may be caused[3].

1   *Stroyan v Knowles* (1861) 6 H & N 454. As to the rules governing the measure of damages in tort generally see DAMAGES vol 29 (2014) PARA 408 et seq.

2   *Markham v Paget* [1908] 1 Ch 697.

3   See *Butterley Co Ltd v New Hucknall Colliery Co Ltd* [1910] AC 381 at 392, HL, per Lord Atkinson.

## 188.   Purchaser's rights in respect of subsequent subsidence.

Where land containing old workings is sold and subsidence occurs after the sale, the purchaser takes the property at his own risk if there is no fraud or concealment and the fact of the existence of the workings is known to the purchaser at the date of the purchase. If subsidence ensues, it is the necessary consequence of the condition of the property at the time of the purchase[1].

1   See *Spoor v Green* (1874) LR 9 Exch 99 at 108 per Cleasby B, and at 111 per Bramwell B. The statement in the headnote to this decision that the principle of *Backhouse v Bonomi* (1861) 9 HL Cas 503 (see PARA 183) has no application in the case of subsidence caused by a trespasser appears to be incorrect. As to the extent of a vendor's duty to disclose latent defects see CONVEYANCING vol 23 (2016) PARA 61.

## 189.   Remedies for disturbance.

In the case of damage by subsidence, the remedy is usually in tort, but there may also be a remedy in contract or for breach of a qualification or condition attached to the right to withdraw support. Instruments of severance frequently contain express provision for payment of compensation for surface[1] damage. It is a question of construction whether that provision extends to damage by subsidence; if it does, and the instrument does not confer upon the mine[2] owner the right to let down the surface, the remedy provided is cumulative[3]. If, on the other hand, the instrument gives a right to withdraw support, the remedy, if any, lies either in contract or for breach of a qualification or condition attached to the right to withdraw support[4].

The right to recover damages by a civil claim may be replaced by a statutory remedy[5].

1   As to the meaning of 'surface' see PARA 17.
2   As to the meaning of 'mine' see PARA 3.
3   *Harris v Ryding* (1839) 5 M & W 60; *Smart v Morton* (1855) 5 E & B 30; and see PARA 132.
4   *Aspden v Seddon* (1876) 1 Ex D 496, CA; *Chamber Colliery Co Ltd v Twyerould* (1893) [1915] 1 Ch 268n, HL; and see *Tito v Waddell (No 2)* [1977] Ch 106 at 296–299, [1977] 3 All ER 129 at 286–289 per Megarry V-C. It is a question of construction of the instrument of severance whether the obligation to pay compensation amounts to a qualification or condition attached to the right to withdraw support, or alternatively whether the obligation is an independent obligation for breach of which an action lies in contract: see *Tito v Waddell (No 2)* at 297, 302, and at 287, 291. See also PARA 195.
5   As to the statutory remedies for subsidence damage caused by withdrawal of support in connection with coal-mining operations see the Coal Mining Subsidence Act 1991; and PARA 209 et seq. Other statutory remedies may be by relevant local legislation: see eg the Manchester Ship Canal (Bridgewater Canal) Act 1907, which authorises the working of mines and minerals under and adjacent to a certain part of the Bridgewater Canal. The Manchester Ship Canal (Bridgewater Canal) Act 1907 was amended to take account of the restructuring of the coal industry under the Coal Industry Act 1994 by the Manchester Ship Canal (Bridgewater Canal) Act 1907 (Amendment) Order 1996, SI 1996/1484. As to the restructuring of the coal industry under privatisation see PARAS 50, 51 et seq.

### 190. Persons liable for withdrawal of support.

If the withdrawal of the support is wrongful, the person who has made the excavation is, in general, the only person liable. As between the lessor and the lessee of mines[1], it is the lessee who is primarily liable, but circumstances may exist which render the lessor jointly or solely liable. Thus if a lessee acts under the authority of his lessor, both are liable for wrongful withdrawal of support[2].

1   As to the meaning of 'mine' see PARA 3.
2   *Siddons v Short* (1877) 2 CPD 572; and see *Davis v Treharne* (1881) 6 App Cas 460, HL.

### 191. Liability of successive owners.

Where subsidence occurs after the original wrongdoer has gone out of possession, a later occupier is not, in general, liable in respect of it; for, although the cause of action is not complete until subsidence occurs[1], neither is it constituted without the original excavation or omission to substitute artificial support[2]. A later occupier who has made no excavation is under no duty to substitute artificial support for that withdrawn by his predecessor, nor is any liability imposed upon him merely by virtue of his occupation of the mine[3].

1   See PARA 183.
2   See *Darley Main Colliery Co v Mitchell* (1886) 11 App Cas 127, HL.
3   *Greenwell v Low Beechburn Coal Co* [1897] 2 QB 165; followed in *Hall v Duke of Norfolk* [1900] 2 Ch 493; cf *Manley v Burn* [1916] 2 KB 121, CA.

### 192. Liability of trustees and contractors.

A trustee who works a mine[1] forming part of his testator's estate is personally liable for the damage caused by subsidence to the land of an adjoining owner; but if the mine is carried on for the benefit of the trust estate and the subsidence results from a reasonable and proper course of working, he will be entitled to be indemnified out of the estate, and the adjoining owner is entitled to be paid directly from the trust estate[2].

Contractors, as well as principals, are liable for damage caused by the wrongful withdrawal of support[3].

1 As to the meaning of 'mine' see PARA 3.
2 *Re Raybould, Raybould v Turner* [1900] 1 Ch 199. As to a trustee's right of indemnity see generally TRUSTS AND POWERS vol 98 (2013) PARA 342 et seq.
3 *Dalton v Angus & Co* (1881) 6 App Cas 740, HL; *Jordeson v Sutton, Southcoates and Drypool Gas Co* [1898] 2 Ch 614 at 626, 627 per North J (affd [1899] 2 Ch 217, CA).

## 193. Liability of licensees and licensors.

A licensee who wrongfully withdraws support is alone liable if the licence under which he works is irrevocable; but if the licence is revocable the licensor is also liable if he knew that injury would result from the licensee's workings and he has failed to prevent the injury by revoking the licence[1].

1 *Atkinson v King* (1878) 2 LR Ir 320 (Ir CA). As to the licensing of coal-mining operations see PARA 89 et seq. As to the meaning of 'coal-mining operations' see PARA 51.

## 194. Covenants for title and quiet enjoyment.

If an owner of land grants a lease of mines[1] with power to let down the surface[2], then subsequently transfers the surface to another, reserving the mines without power to let down the surface, with a covenant for title, the prior lease is a breach of the covenant[3]. Similarly, an owner of land grants a lease of mines with power to let down the surface, then subsequently leases the surface, reserving the mines without power to let down the surface, it is possible that the lessee of the surface may recover damages against his lessor for breach of a covenant for quiet enjoyment[4].

1 As to the meaning of 'mine' see PARA 3.
2 As to the meaning of 'surface' see PARA 17.
3 *Taylor v Shafto* (1867) 8 B & S 228, Ex Ch. The old covenants for title are not deemed to be included in any conveyance or transfer made on or after 1 July 1995 following the repeal of the Law of Property Act 1925 s 76 by the Law of Property (Miscellaneous Provisions) Act 1994 ss 10(1), 21(2), (3), Sch 2. Where a transfer of the surface is expressed to be made with full title guarantee in the circumstances described in the text, there will probably be breach of the covenant implied by the Law of Property (Miscellaneous Provisions) Act 1994 s 3(1)(b) (ie that the property is free from all other rights exercisable by third parties). Similarly if made with limited title guarantee there will probably be a breach of s 3(1)(a). See CONVEYANCING vol 23 (2016) PARA 181.
4 See *Markham v Paget* [1908] 1 Ch 697. In *Jones v Consolidated Anthracite Collieries Ltd and Lord Dynevor* [1916] 1 KB 123 at 136, 137, Scrutton J left the question open, and an examination of the authorities convinced him that the precise nature and limits of acts of interference not going to title and possession, which would constitute a breach of the covenant, were far from being accurately defined. In *Dennett v Atherton* (1872) LR 7 QB 316 at 327, Willes J considered that there would be no breach of the covenant if a seller or lessor had worked out mines and the purchaser or lessee were to build a house which subsided into old workings.
  As to covenants for quiet enjoyment see PARA 341.

## 195. Effect of compensation provision.

A provision for compensation annexed to a power to let down the surface[1] may, according to the construction of the instrument, be treated as a condition which qualifies the right to work and so binds the person exercising that right[2]. Thus a covenant to make compensation for damage done in working so as to let down the surface has been treated not as comprising a burden running with the land but as an inherent qualification of the right to work with the effect of letting down the surface. What is in form a covenant may appear from the whole of the provisions of the instrument to be intended also to operate as a condition[3]. On the other hand, a covenant seems to be the more appropriate form of provision where there is no power to let down. In such circumstances, a condition has been treated as a covenant[4].

1   As to the meaning of 'surface' see PARA 17.
2   *Aspden v Seddon* (1876) 1 Ex D 496, CA; *Westhoughton UDC v Wigan Coal and Iron Co Ltd* [1919] 1 Ch 159 at 174–175, CA, per Duke LJ; and see *Tito v Waddell (No 2)* [1977] Ch 106 at 296–299, 302, [1977] 3 All ER 129 at 286–289, 291 per Megarry V-C.
3   *Chamber Colliery Co Ltd v Twyerould* (1893) [1915] 1 Ch 268n at 272n, HL, per Lord Watson; and see *Tito v Waddell (No 2)* [1977] Ch 106 at 298, 302, [1977] 3 All ER 129 at 287, 291 per Megarry V-C.
4   *Jones v Consolidated Anthracite Collieries Ltd and Lord Dynevor* [1916] 1 KB 123.

### 196.   Compensation covenant runs with the land.

A covenant to pay compensation for damage by subsidence runs with the land; it is not merely collateral, but affects the nature and value of the land[1]. A covenant by a mining lessee with the owner or owners, occupier or occupiers, for the time being of the surface[2] is effectual, even though the surface owner at the date of the demise is not named a party to the deed; it will be treated as a covenant with the surface owner at that date and, by virtue of the statutory right of persons who are not parties to an instrument to take the benefit of covenants respecting land[3], will enure for the benefit of his successors in title[4].

1   *Norval v Pascoe* (1864) 34 LJ Ch 82; *Dyson v Forster* [1909] AC 98, HL; and see LANDLORD AND TENANT vol 62 (2016) PARA 450. The assignment of the covenant does not by itself carry with it the right to compensation for damage accrued before the assignment: *Snowdon v Ecclesiastical Comrs for England* [1935] Ch 181.
2   As to the meaning of 'surface' see PARA 17.
3   Ie by virtue of the Law of Property Act 1925 s 56(1). As to deeds and their execution generally see DEEDS AND OTHER INSTRUMENTS vol 32 (2012) PARA 227
4   *Dyson v Forster* [1909] AC 98, HL; affg sub nom *Forster v Elvet Colliery Co Ltd* [1908] 1 KB 629, CA. As to whether a clause which exempts the mine owner from liability for injury by subsidence runs with the land see *Rowbotham v Wilson* (1860) 8 HL Cas 348 (affg (1857) 8 E & B 123); cf *Richards v Harper* (1866) LR 1 Exch 199. As to the meaning of 'mine' see PARA 3.

### 197.   Right to injunction.

The wrongful withdrawal of support will in general entitle the injured party to an injunction[1] to restrain the defendant from further working the mines[2] so as to let down the surface[3]. However, a mandatory injunction to carry out works to restore support may be refused if it is not possible to identify the steps the defendant should take, or if the costs to the defendant are likely to be disproportionate[4]. An injunction to restrain working may prescribe no limits within which the workings are restrained[5], and whilst in form it may presuppose the possibility of working the mines without letting down the surface[6]; nonetheless in practice, an injunction, in effect, frequently renders the mines or some part of them unworkable in a commercial sense. Where the claimant, however, is clearly entitled to the right of support, an injunction will not be refused merely on the ground that the effectual working of the mines will be rendered impracticable[7]. Where no claim of right is set up by the defendant, an injunction will not be granted, if the mining operations have been concluded[8].

Injunctions have, in general, been granted where subsidence has already occurred and damage resulted. If the subsidence is substantial it is not necessary that pecuniary loss should be shown[9], and it is usually no ground for declining to grant an injunction that pecuniary compensation will be a sufficient remedy[10], or that the loss to the surface owner is trifling[11]. However, an injunction is a discretionary remedy and it will be refused if it would be oppressive to grant an injunction[12]. As a good working rule an injunction will usually be refused if: (1) the injury to the claimant's legal rights is small; (2) it is capable of being estimated in money; (3) it can be adequately compensated by a small money payment; and (4) it would be oppressive to the defendant to grant an injunction[13]. Instead damages in substitution for an injunction may be given. Damages may be awarded in substitution for an injunction if it would be oppressive to grant an injunction even if the compensation payable will be substantial, where the claimant has made it clear that he is seeking a money payment[14]. An award of damages may reflect the fair and reasonable price which the claimant could have negotiated for an agreement to withdraw support[15]. Moreover, if the defendant wrongfully threatens to withdraw support, an injunction may be granted even though no subsidence has taken place[16]. Subsidence is recognised to be the inevitable result of mining operations in many cases, and accordingly, if it is shown that subsidence will result from the operations of the mine owner, the court will interfere for the purpose of preventing irreparable damage[17].

An interim injunction will not be granted, if serious injury may result from the suspension of the mining operations[18].

1   As to the right to an injunction generally see CIVIL PROCEDURE vol 12 (2015) PARA 1098 et seq.
2   As to the meaning of 'mine' see PARA 3.
3   See *Proud v Bates* (1865) 34 LJ Ch 406; *Dugdale v Robertson* (1857) 3 K & J 695 at 696, 701; *Hunt v Peake* (1860) John 705 (land artificially burdened); *Trinidad Asphalt Co v Ambard* [1899] AC 594, PC (land in natural state). As to the meaning of 'surface' see PARA 17.
4   See *Redland Bricks Ltd v Morris* [1970] AC 652, [1969] 2 All ER 576, HL.
5   See *Elliot v North Eastern Rly Co* (1863) 10 HL Cas 333 at 358 per Lord Chelmsford.
6   See *Butterley Co Ltd v New Hucknall Colliery Co Ltd* [1909] 1 Ch 37 at 47, CA, per Cozens-Hardy MR; affd [1910] AC 381, HL.
7   See *Wakefield v Duke of Buccleuch* (1867) LR 4 Eq 613 at 638 per Malins V-C (affd sub nom *Duke of Buccleuch v Wakefield* (1870) LR 4 HL 377); *Earl of Westmoreland v New Sharlston Colliery Co Ltd* (1898) 79 LT 716 at 722 per North J (affd (1899) 80 LT 846, CA; sub nom *New Sharlston Collieries Co Ltd v Earl of Westmorland* [1904] 2 Ch 443n, HL). See also PARA 113.
8   *Jordeson v Sutton, Southcoates and Drypool Gas Co* [1898] 2 Ch 614 at 628 per North J (affd [1899] 2 Ch 217, CA); *A-G v Conduit Colliery Co* [1895] 1 QB 301 at 311, DC, per Collins J.
9   See *A-G v Conduit Colliery Co* [1895] 1 QB 301 at 311, DC, per Collins J.
10   *Siddons v Short* (1877) 2 CPD 572 at 577 per Grove J.
11   *Trinidad Asphalt Co v Ambard* [1899] AC 594, PC.
12   *Jaggard v Sawyer* [1995] 2 All ER 189, [1995] 1 WLR 269, CA; *Gafford v Graham* (1998) 77 P&CR 73, [1999] 3 EGLR 75, CA.
13   *Shelfer v City of London Electric Lighting Co* [1895] 1 Ch 287, CA; *Jaggard v Sawyer* [1995] 2 All ER 189, [1995] 1 WLR 269, CA.
14   *Gafford v Graham* (1998) 77 P&CR 73, [1999] 3 EGLR 75, CA.
15   *Jaggard v Sawyer* [1995] 2 All ER 189, [1995] 1 WLR 269, CA; *A-G v Blake (Jonathan Cape Ltd, third party)* [2001] 1 AC 268, [2000] 4 All ER 385, HL; *Amec Developments Ltd v Jury's Hotel Management (UK) Ltd* (2000) 82 P&CR 22, [2001] 1 EGLR 81.
16   *Siddons v Short* (1877) 2 CPD 572.
17   See *Birmingham Corpn v Allen* (1877) 6 ChD 284 at 288 per Jessel MR; affd 6 ChD 284 at 290, CA. See also PARA 129.
18   See *Hilton v Earl Granville* (1841) Cr & Ph 283 at 297 per Lord Cottenham LC; *Wheatley v Westminster Brymbo Coal Co* (1869) LR 9 Eq 538 at 551 per Malins V-C.

## 198. Liberty to inspect mines and plans.

Liberty to inspect mines[1] and the working plans may be obtained on interim application if the claimant makes out a prima facie case that his right of support has been infringed[2]. However, power to order inspection lies with the arbitrator, not with the court, where there is provision for arbitration[3].

1   As to the meaning of 'mine' see PARA 3.
2   See *Wall v Dunn* (1876) 1 Seton's Judgments and Orders (7 Edn) 563, 564; *Baynton v Leonard*

(1853) 1 Seton's Judgments and Orders (7 Edn) 565; and PARA 40.

3   *Barnett v Aldridge Colliery* (1887) 4 TLR 16; and see *Vasso v Vasso* [1983] 3 All ER 211, [1983] 1 WLR 838 (affd sub nom *The Andria* [1984] QB 477, [1984] 1 All ER 1126). See also the Arbitration Act 1996 s 38(4); and ARBITRATION vol 2 (2017) PARA 548.

## (ii)  Statutory Compensation

### A.    SUBSIDENCE DAMAGE BY BRINE PUMPING

**199.  Compensation for subsidence damage by brine pumping.**
In districts where brine pumping was carried on, it was often impossible to identify the particular operations which caused or contributed to subsidence[1]. In addition to local provisions in Cheshire[2] (where the industry was historically of particular importance), a more general means of providing compensation for damage was provided by the Brine Pumping (Compensation for Subsidence) Act 1891 which, now that brine pumping is no longer an active concern[3], has been repealed.

1   Where the particular operations could be identified an action for damage caused by the unauthorised withdrawal of support could be brought in the usual way: eg see *Lotus Ltd v British Soda Co Ltd* [1972] Ch 123, [1971] 1 All ER 265.
2   The Cheshire Brine Subsidence Compensation Board was constituted and operates under the Cheshire Brine Pumping (Compensation for Subsidence) Acts 1952 and 1964 and deals with claims for damage caused by brine pumping within a single compensation defined Cheshire Brine Subsidence Compensation District. See also the Non-metropolitan Counties (Local Statutory Provisions) Order 1986, SI 1986/1133.
3   The Lion Salt Works in Marston, the last recorded open pan block salt producing works producing salt from natural brine, finally closed in 1986.

### B.    SUBSIDENCE DAMAGE BY COAL MINING

## (A)   Introduction

**200.  Historical background.**
By the Coal-Mining (Subsidence) Act 1950[1] (now repealed) and the subordinate legislation made under it, obligations were placed on the National Coal Board (later renamed the British Coal Corporation)[2] to carry out repairs or to make payments in respect of subsidence damage to dwelling-houses caused by coal mining, and power was given to the Corporation to execute works for the prevention or reduction of such damage[3]. The principal object of the legislation was to remedy the perceived injustices resulting from the fact that in many areas of the country, as a result of previous dealings in the surface land and the mineral rights, coal-mining operators had the right to remove support without incurring any liability to the surface owner for damage thereby caused[4]. The type of damage and classes of property protected were extended by the Coal-Mining Subsidence Act 1957. Distinct rights to compensation or repair existed under the Coal Industry Act 1975, which conferred on the Corporation a new statutory right to withdraw support in extension of, and replacement for, rights under earlier legislation[5].

The statutory framework for compensation for subsidence damage caused by the withdrawal of support from land in connection with coal-mining operations is now contained in the Coal Mining Subsidence Act 1991[6], which was passed to repeal and re-enact with amendments the Coal-Mining (Subsidence) Act 1957 and certain repealed provisions of the Coal Industry Act 1975[7]. As a result of the restructuring of the coal industry under privatisation[8], it is no longer the British

Coal Corporation which owes obligations concerning compensation for subsidence damage, but the responsible person in relation to the damage[9].

1   The Coal-Mining (Subsidence) Act 1950 (which did not apply to damage occurring after 31 July 1957: see s 18(2) (repealed)) preceded the Coal-Mining (Subsidence) Act 1957 (repealed).

2   See PARA 49.

3   See the Coal-Mining (Subsidence) Act 1950 ss 1–8 (repealed).

4   See the *Report of the Royal Commission on Mining Subsidence* (Cmd 2899) (1927); and 185 HC Official Report (6th series), 4 February 1991, col 69.

5   See PARA 176 et seq.

6   See the Coal Mining Subsidence Act 1991 s 1; and PARA 201 et seq. The Coal Mining Subsidence Act 1991 derived from recommendations of the Waddilove Committee, which was appointed by the government to review the operation of the Coal-Mining (Subsidence) Act 1957 (now repealed) and other aspects of subsidence compensation. Most of the committee's recommendations were accepted by the government in its response published in October 1987: see *The Repair and Compensation System for Coal Mining Subsidence Damage* (Cm 235) (1987).

7   Coal Mining Subsidence Act 1991, long title. Apart from the process of consolidation, many of the innovations in the Coal Mining Subsidence Act 1991 were intended to put the previous practice of the British Coal Corporation, which went beyond strict legal obligations, onto a statutory footing: see 185 HC Official Report (6th series), 4 February 1991, cols 69–70. This had been one of the recommendations of the Waddilove Committee. As to the British Coal Corporation see PARAS 49–50.

8   See PARAS 50, 51 et seq.

9   As to the responsible person see PARA 204.

### 201. The Coal Mining Subsidence Act 1991.

The main purpose of the Coal Mining Subsidence Act 1991[1] is to place obligations on the responsible person[2] to take remedial action[3] in respect of subsidence damage to which the Act applies[4]. Remedial action may take the form of the execution of remedial works[5], payments in lieu[6] or depreciation payments[7], subject to provisions as to the determination of the appropriate remedial action in a particular case[8]. The responsible person is also under a duty to make payments in respect of emergency works executed by other persons[9].

Additional remedies include provision for cases where dwelling-houses are rendered uninhabitable, and compensation for inconvenience during works[10], provision for agricultural losses[11], provision for the purchase of property affected by blight[12], compensation for consequential losses of small firms[13], and for damage to moveable property[14], and compensation for death or disablement[15]. Special provisions apply in the case of ancient monuments and listed buildings[16], ecclesiastical property[17] and property belonging to protected tenants[18].

The Coal Mining Subsidence Act 1991 also includes provisions to deal with cases where further damage is likely[19]. It empowers responsible persons to execute preventive measures in respect of buildings, structures or works[20] and enables drainage authorities to require the execution of such works[21]. It contains provision for the avoidance of double claims[22], for the reimbursement of successful claimants' expenses[23], for the resolution of disputes[24] and for notices, information and reports[25].

The Coal Mining Subsidence Act 1991 preserves a distinct right to compensation in certain cases where special terms and conditions as to compensation remain applicable to damage caused by the working of coal in the exercise of statutory rights to withdraw support[26].

The Coal Industry Act 1994[27], in addition to adapting the Coal Mining Subsidence Act 1991 to the requirements of the privatised coal industry[28], contains additional provisions relating to responsible persons[29], a subsidence adviser[30], and the resolution of disputes[31]. It also creates offences relating to the provision of subsidence information[32].

1 Coal Mining Subsidence Act 1991 s 54(1). The Coal Mining Subsidence Act 1991 came into force on 30 November 1991: see s 54(2); and the Coal Mining Subsidence Act 1991 (Commencement) Order 1991, SI 1991/2508. The Coal Mining Subsidence Act 1991 does not apply to Northern Ireland: s 54(4). The Coal Mining Subsidence Act 1991 makes various transitional provisions, savings and repeals: see ss 53, 54(3), Sch 7 (amended by the Coal Industry Act 1994 Sch 9 para 41(5)); Coal Mining Subsidence Act 1991 Sch 8. In particular it repeals the Coal-Mining (Subsidence) Act 1957 (see the Coal Mining Subsidence Act 1991 Sch 8) and makes special provision where, before 30 November 1991, a notice or claim has been made in respect of subsidence damage under the Coal-Mining (Subsidence) Act 1957 (see the Coal Mining Subsidence Act 1991 Sch 7 paras 1, 2)).

2 As to the responsible person see PARA 204.
3 As to remedial action see PARA 209.
4 As to the meaning of 'subsidence damage' see PARA 203.
5 See PARA 212.
6 See PARAS 214–216.
7 See PARAS 217–220.
8 See PARA 211.
9 See PARA 221.
10 See PARAS 228–231.
11 See PARAS 232–234.
12 See PARAS 235–236.
13 See PARA 237.
14 See PARA 238.
15 See PARA 239.
16 See PARA 225. As to the protection of ancient monuments generally see NATIONAL CULTURAL HERITAGE vol 77 (2016) PARA 1006 et seq. As to listed buildings generally see PLANNING vol 83 (2018) PARA 1181 et seq.
17 See PARA 226.
18 See PARA 227.
19 See PARAS 222–224.
20 See PARA 240.
21 See PARA 241 et seq.
22 See PARA 245.
23 See PARA 247.
24 See PARAS 249–250.
25 See PARAS 251–253.
26 See PARA 248.
27 See PARA 51 et seq.
28 As to the restructuring of the coal industry under privatisation see PARAS 50, 51 et seq.
29 See PARA 207.
30 See PARA 208.
31 See PARAS 249–250.
32 See PARA 254.

## 202. The Secretary of State's power to make regulations or orders.

Any power of the Secretary of State[1] to make regulations or orders under the Coal Mining Subsidence Act 1991[2] is exercisable by statutory instrument[3] and includes power to make different provision for different cases or classes of case[4], and to make such supplementary, incidental, consequential or transitional provisions as the Secretary of State considers necessary or expedient[5].

1 As to the Secretary of State see PARA 2. The Coal Mining Subsidence Act 1991 refers to the possibility of the Secretary of State and the Minister of Agriculture, Fisheries and Food acting jointly (see the Coal Mining Subsidence Act 1991 s 50(3)), but the Ministry of Agriculture,

Fisheries and Food has been dissolved and the minister's functions have been transferred to the Secretary of State for Environment, Food and Rural Affairs (see the Ministry of Agriculture, Fisheries and Food (Dissolution) Order 2002, SI 2002/794; and PARA 2).

    As to regulations made in relation to land drainage systems see the Coal Mining Subsidence Act 1991 s 36(7); and PARAS 241–243.

2   See the Coal Mining Subsidence Act 1991 (Commencement) Order 1991, SI 1991/2508 (see PARA 201); the Coal Mining Subsidence (Notices and Claims) Regulations 1991, SI 1991/2509 (see PARAS 210, 214, 229, 232); the Coal Mining Subsidence (Preventive Measures and Rates of Interest) Order 1991, SI 1991/2510 (see PARA 217); the Coal Mining Subsidence (Subsidence Adviser) Regulations 2004, SI 2004/2241 (see PARA 208); the Coal Mining Subsidence (Blight and Compensation for Inconvenience During Works) Regulations 1994, SI 1994/2564 (see PARAS 231, 235); the Coal Mining Subsidence (Provision of Information) Regulations 1994, SI 1994/2565 (see PARAS 207, 251); the Coal Mining Subsidence (Arbitration Schemes) Regulations 1994, SI 1994/2566 (see PARA 250); and the Coal Mining Subsidence (Land Drainage) Regulations 1994, SI 1994/3064 (see PARAS 242–243).

3   A statutory instrument containing any regulations or order under the Coal Mining Subsidence Act 1991 (other than an order under s 54(2) bringing the Coal Mining Subsidence Act 1991 into force: see PARA 202) is subject to annulment in pursuance of a resolution of either House of Parliament: s 50(2).

4   Coal Mining Subsidence Act 1991 s 50(1)(a).

5   Coal Mining Subsidence Act 1991 s 50(1)(b). As to the exercise of any power to make subordinate legislation under the Coal Mining Subsidence Act 1991 before the restructuring date (ie 31 October 1994: see PARA 50) see the Coal Industry Act 1994 s 67(7), Sch 10 para 13(3).

## *(B)*    *Subsidence*

### 203.    Subsidence damage.

Subsidence damage is any damage[1] to land, or to any buildings[2], structures[3] or works on, in or over it, caused by the withdrawal of support[4] from land in connection with[5] lawful coal-mining operations[6]. References in the Coal Mining Subsidence Act 1991 to subsidence damage do not apply to damage caused in connection with the working and getting of coal[7] and other minerals[8] (1) where the working and getting of the coal was ancillary to the working of the other minerals; or (2) where the coal was worked or gotten by virtue of the grant of a gale in the Forest of Dean or any other part of the Hundred of St Briavels in Gloucester[9]. Nor do such references apply to damage occurring underground in a mine[10] of coal[11].

Where in any proceedings[12] the question arises whether any damage to property is subsidence damage, and it is shown that the nature of the damage and the circumstances are such as to indicate that the damage may be such, the onus is on the responsible person[13] to show that the damage is not subsidence damage[14].

1   An alteration of the level or gradient of any land not otherwise damaged which does not affect its fitness for use for the purposes for which, immediately before the alteration occurred, it was used, or might reasonably have been expected to be used, is not regarded as damage for these purposes: Coal Mining Subsidence Act 1991 s 1(2).

2   'Building' is not defined in the Coal Mining Subsidence Act 1991; but see *Stevens v Gourley* (1859) 7 CBNS 99 at 112; *Cheshire County Council v Woodward* [1962] 2 QB 126, [1962] 1 All ER 517.

3   'Structure' includes any works providing passage or hard standing for persons, animals or vehicles (including railway or tramway vehicles and aircraft): Coal Mining Subsidence Act 1991 s 52(1). 'Works' includes sewers, drains, pipes, cables, wires and any other apparatus: s 52(1).

4   Withdrawal of support is not necessarily confined to active operations and may include a passive withdrawal caused by the natural movement of infill downwards into the unfilled part of a shaft: see *British Coal Corpn v Netherlee Trustees* 1995 SLT 1038, Inner House. As to the statutory right to withdraw support from land in relation to coal mining see PARA 176 et seq.

5   The words 'in connection with' may have a wider meaning than 'caused by' or 'resulting from': see *British Coal Corpn v Netherlee Trustees* 1995 SLT 1038, Inner House.

6   Coal Mining Subsidence Act 1991 ss 1(1), 52(1). In so far as s 1 relates to operations carried on

at any time on or after the restructuring date (ie 31 October 1994: see PARA 50), 'lawful coal-mining operations' means any coal-mining operations to which the Coal Industry Act 1994 s 25 (see PARA 89) applies (including operations carried on in contravention of s 25(1) and those that are actionable apart from the Coal Mining Subsidence Act 1991) which: (1) are carried on by a person who is for the time being a licensed operator; or (2) are carried on by a person who has been such a licensed operator and in continuation of operations begun by that person before he ceased to be such an operator: s 1(3) (substituted by the Coal Industry Act 1994 s 42(1)). However, for these purposes any operations carried on or begun by any person as a person who is for the time being authorised to carry on coal-mining operations on behalf of a person who is or has been a licensed operator are to be treated as carried on or begun by the latter person, whether or not the authorisation extends to the operations in question: Coal Mining Subsidence Act 1991 s 1(3) (as so substituted). As to the meaning of 'coal-mining operations' see PARA 51; and as to the meaning of 'licensed operator' see PARA 58.

In relation to operations carried on before the restructuring date, the provision contained in s 1 (as originally enacted) is important as preserving liability for historic subsidence liabilities. In this case, 'lawful coal-mining operations' means the lawful working and getting of coal, or of coal and other minerals worked with coal, or the lawful getting of any product from coal in the course of working it: s 1(3) (as originally enacted).

7   As to the meaning of 'coal' see PARA 48 (definition applied by the Coal Mining Subsidence Act 1991 s 52(1)). As to the Coal Commission see PARA 48.
8   As to the meaning of 'minerals' see PARA 10.
9   Coal Mining Subsidence Act 1991 s 1(4)(a). As to mining in Gloucestershire see PARA 607 et seq.
10  As to the meaning of 'mine' see PARA 3 (definition applied by the Coal Mining Subsidence Act 1991 s 1(4)(b)).
11  Coal Mining Subsidence Act 1991 s 1(4)(b).
12  Ie under the Coal Mining Subsidence Act 1991: see s 40(2). As to the determination of disputes see PARAS 249–250.
13  As to the responsible person see PARA 204.
14  Coal Mining Subsidence Act 1991 s 40(2). This provision applies for the purpose of determining questions under the Coal Industry Act 1994 s 47(1) (see PARAS 249–250) as it applies for determining questions under the Coal Mining Subsidence Act 1991: Coal Industry Act 1994 s 47(3).

## 204.  Persons responsible for subsidence.

The responsible person[1], in relation to any subsidence damage[2], is:

(1)     the person with responsibility for subsidence affecting the land which has been damaged or the damaged part of it[3]; or

(2)     in the case of damage to other property, the person with responsibility for subsidence affecting the land where that property or the damaged part of it was situated at the time of the damage[4].

Where the land is for the time being within the area of responsibility[5] of any person as the holder[6] of a licence under Part II of the Coal Industry Act 1994[7], the person with responsibility for subsidence affecting that land is the licence holder[8]. In any other case, the Coal Authority has responsibility for subsidence[9].

A person is the responsible person in relation to any subsidence damage whether that damage was caused or occurred before or after the time when he became the person with responsibility for subsidence affecting the land in question[10]. Accordingly, where[11] any person becomes the person with responsibility for subsidence affecting any land (the 'successor'), all the rights and liabilities[12] of the successor's predecessor as the person with such responsibility (the 'predecessor'[13]) are transferred, by virtue only of his becoming the person with responsibility, to the successor; and anything which has been done under or for any of the purposes of the Coal Mining Subsidence Act 1991 or regulations made under it by or in relation to the predecessor, or is deemed to have been so done, is deemed[14] to have been done by or in relation to the successor[15]. It is the duty of the person who becomes[16] the person with responsibility affecting any land to take all reasonable steps to secure that the change in the person with that responsibility does not result in any undue delay in the performance of any obligations falling by virtue of that change to be performed by that person[17].

1　In the Coal Mining Subsidence Act 1991, the provisions relating to subsidence damage refers throughout to the British Coal Corporation (as to which see PARAS 49–50). However, except where the Coal Industry Act 1994 s 43(8), Sch 6 otherwise provides, the Coal Mining Subsidence Act 1991 and the regulations under it which were in force immediately before the restructuring date (ie 31 October 1994: see PARA 50) have effect since that date with the substitution, in relation to any subsidence damage, for references to the Corporation of references to the person who is the responsible person in relation to that damage: Coal Industry Act 1994 s 43(1). Note that this provision does not apply to the references to the Corporation in the Coal Mining Subsidence Act 1991 s 53(1), Sch 7 (transitional provisions) so far as it has effect in relation to times before the restructuring date: Coal Industry Act 1994 Sch 6 para 12. As to the restructuring of the British Coal Corporation's undertaking see PARA 71 et seq.
2　As to the meaning of 'subsidence damage' see PARA 203.
3　Coal Industry Act 1994 s 43(2)(a). Section 43(2) is subject to ss 43(3)–(8), 44: s 43(2).
4　Coal Industry Act 1994 s 43(2)(b).
5　As to the area of responsibility see PARA 205.
6　As to the meaning of 'holder' see PARA 93.
7　Ie the Coal Industry Act 1994 Pt II (ss 25–36): see PARA 89 et seq.
8　Coal Industry Act 1994 s 43(3)(a).
9　Coal Industry Act 1994 s 43(3)(b). As to the Coal Authority see PARA 52 et seq.
10　Coal Industry Act 1994 s 43(4).
11　Ie by virtue of any designation or of any transfer of rights and obligations or of the operation of any such provision as is mentioned in the Coal Industry Act 1994 s 37(3) (see PARA 205): see s 43(5).
12　Ie under the Coal Mining Subsidence Act 1991 or under any regulations made under it or the Coal Industry Act 1994 Pt II: see s 43(5). As to the meaning of 'liability' see PARA 51.
13　The provisions of the Coal Industry Act 1994 s 43(5), (6) have effect in relation to the coming into force of s 43(1) on the restructuring date (ie 31 October 1994: see PARA 50) as they have effect in relation to any other transfer of rights and obligations but as if the references to the predecessor were references to the British Coal Corporation: s 43(7). As to the British Coal Corporation see PARAS 49–50.
14　Ie so far as necessary for that purpose and for the purposes of the continuation by or against the successor of any proceedings under or for the purposes of the Coal Mining Subsidence Act 1991 or those regulations: see the Coal Industry Act 1994 s 43(5).
15　Coal Industry Act 1994 s 43(5).
16　Ie under the Coal Industry Act 1994 s 43(5).
17　Coal Industry Act 1994 s 43(6).

## 205.　Areas of responsibility.

A licence under Part II of the Coal Industry Act 1994[1] may designate, in relation to its holder[2], the area which is to be treated[3] as that person's area of responsibility[4]. An area so designated may comprise:

(1)　the whole or any one or more parts of the area where the operations to which the licence relates are to be carried on[5]; or

(2)　the whole or any parts of that area together with such other areas appearing to the Coal Authority[6] to be capable of being affected by those operations as may be described in the licence[7].

An area designated as an area of responsibility, except so far as it may be modified in accordance with any condition contained in the licence[8], continues to be treated[9] as the area of responsibility of the holder of the licence in question until such time as may be determined, in accordance with the provisions of the licence, to be the time for responsibilities in respect of the designated area to revert (subject to any further designation of the whole or any part of that area) to the Coal Authority[10].

1  Ie the Coal Industry Act 1994 Pt II (ss 25–36): see PARA 89 et seq.
2  As to the meaning of 'holder' see PARA 93.
3  Ie for the purposes of the Coal Industry Act 1994 Pt III (ss 37–56): see s 37(1).
4  Coal Industry Act 1994 s 37(1).
5  Coal Industry Act 1994 s 37(2)(a).
6  As to the Coal Authority see PARA 52 et seq.
7  Coal Industry Act 1994 s 37(2)(b).
8  The conditions included in a licence may provide for the modification from time to time of the area of responsibility of the holder of the licence: Coal Industry Act 1994 s 37(4).
9  Ie for the purposes of the Coal Industry Act 1994: see s 37(3).
10  Coal Industry Act 1994 s 37(3). For these purposes it is immaterial that the authorisation contained in the licence in question is revoked or otherwise ceases to have effect before the time so determined: s 37(5).

## 206. Cases where there is more than one responsible person.

Where, in the case of any subsidence damage[1], the area of responsibility[2] of any person as holder[3] of a licence under Part II of the Coal Industry Act 1994[4] includes only part of the damaged land[5] or, as the case may be, of the land where the damaged property[6] was situated, then the responsible persons in relation to that damage are that person, together with every other person within whose area of responsibility any part of that land is situated, and if any part of that land is not situated within the area of responsibility of any person, the Coal Authority[7]; and the obligations and liabilities[8] of the responsible person are imposed jointly and severally on those persons[9].

The rules relating to the transfer of rights and liabilities[10] which apply where one person succeeds to the position of another as responsible person are modified where a person ceases at any time to be the person with responsibility for subsidence affecting any land but continues, after that time, to be the person with responsibility for subsidence affecting other land[11]; and both the predecessor and the successor are responsible persons in relation to any subsidence damage to which any of the predecessor's rights or liabilities relate[12]. In any such case, the rights and liabilities of the predecessor, so far as they relate to subsidence damage in relation to which the predecessor continues to be a responsible person, continue to be vested in the predecessor, as well as being vested in the successor[13]. The general rules as to the transfer of rights and liabilities do not authorise the continuation against the successor of any proceedings[14] which have been begun, or are deemed to have been begun, against the predecessor, and may be continued against the predecessor[15].

These provisions[16], so far as they relate to obligations, liabilities or rights of responsible persons, also apply as respects obligations, liabilities or rights[17] of persons who would be responsible persons if subsidence damage occurred[18].

1  As to the meaning of 'subsidence damage' see PARA 203.
2  As to the area of responsibility see PARA 205.
3  As to the meaning of 'holder' see PARA 93.
4  Ie the Coal Industry Act 1994 Pt II (ss 25–36): see PARA 89 et seq.
5  This reference to the damaged land is a reference, where only part of the land has been damaged, to the damaged part of that land: Coal Industry Act 1994 s 44(4).
6  This reference to the damaged property is a reference, where only part of the property has been damaged, to the damaged part of that property: Coal Industry Act 1994 s 44(4).
7  See the Coal Industry Act 1994 s 44(1)(a). As to the Coal Authority see PARA 52 et seq.
8  Ie by virtue of the Coal Industry Act 1994 s 43 (see PARA 204): see s 44(1).
9  See the Coal Industry Act 1994 s 44(1)(b).

10 Ie those contained in Coal Industry Act 1994 s 43(5) (see PARA 204): see s 44(2).
11 Coal Industry Act 1994 s 44(2)(a).
12 Coal Industry Act 1994 s 44(2)(b).
13 Coal Industry Act 1994 s 44(3)(a).
14 Ie under or for the purposes of the Coal Mining Subsidence Act 1991: see the Coal Industry Act 1994 s 44(3)(b).
15 Coal Industry Act 1994 s 44(3)(b). This provision is without prejudice to any rules of court in accordance with which the successor may be joined as a party to any proceedings in respect of any such rights or liabilities as are mentioned in s 44(3)(a): s 44(3) proviso.
16 Ie the Coal Industry Act 1994 s 44: see s 43(8), Sch 6 para 9.
17 Ie those arising under modifications made to the Coal Mining Subsidence Act 1991 by the Coal Industry Act 1994 Sch 6 paras 6, 8: Sch 6 para 9.
18 Coal Industry Act 1994 Sch 6 para 9. For that purpose, references in s 44 to subsidence damage are to be construed accordingly: Sch 6 para 9.

## 207. Information to be provided by responsible persons.

The Secretary of State[1] may make provision by regulations[2] imposing requirements on a person with responsibility for subsidence affecting any land[3] to:

(1)      furnish information, on request[4], to the owner[5] or occupier of any part of that land[6];

(2)      furnish information to the Coal Authority[7] about any such request for information relating to, or to the possibility of, subsidence damage[8] as is made otherwise than by the owner or occupier of any part of that land[9];

(3)      notify a person who has made a request for information that it has been forwarded to the Authority[10]; and

(4)      ensure that certain forms and documents accompany the information furnished[11].

Such regulations may contain such provision as the Secretary of State thinks fit with respect to the descriptions of information to which any request made for the purposes of any such regulations is to be confined, and the particulars to be included in, or omitted from, information so furnished[12].

1   As to the Secretary of State see PARA 2.
2   See the Coal Mining Subsidence (Provision of Information) Regulations 1994, SI 1994/2565. The provisions of the Coal Mining Subsidence Act 1991 dealing with the Secretary of State's power to make regulations and orders (see s 50; and PARA 202) apply in relation to the power to make regulations under the Coal Industry Act 1994 s 45 as they apply in relation to that power under the Coal Mining Subsidence Act 1991: Coal Industry Act 1994 s 45(3).
3   As to the responsible person see PARA 204.
4   'Request' means a request in writing: Coal Mining Subsidence Act 1991 s 52(1).
5   'Owner', in relation to any real property in England and Wales, means the lessee under the ground lease if it is held on such a lease, and the owner of the fee simple if it is not: Coal Mining Subsidence Act 1991 s 52(1) (definition applied by the Coal Industry Act 1994 s 45(3)). 'Ground lease' means a lease for building purposes at a rent (or, where the rent varies, at a maximum rent) which does not substantially exceed the rent which a tenant might reasonably have been expected, at the date when the lease was granted, to pay for the land comprised in the lease, excluding any buildings, for a term equal to the term created by the lease: Coal Mining Subsidence Act 1991 s 52(1) (definition as so applied).
6   See the Coal Industry Act 1994 s 45(1)(a); and the Coal Mining Subsidence (Provision of Information) Regulations 1994, SI 1994/2565, regs 4, 5.
     Where a request is made of a person with responsibility which satisfies the requirements in heads (a)–(d), that person must, within 14 days beginning with the date on which the request is received, furnish in writing to the person who made the request the information in heads (1)–(4), unless not more than 30 days before that request was made, a similar request was made on behalf of the same person to the same person with responsibility who responded: reg 4(1), (2). The requirements are:

(1)    the full name and address of the person with responsibility referred to in head (d) (or where an employee or agent of the person with responsibility is appointed to represent him in his dealings with the inquirer in relation to subsidence damage, the name of that employee or agent) (reg 5(1)(a), (2)(a));

(2)    the place or places of business at which that person may be contacted during normal business hours (or where an employee or agent of the person with responsibility is appointed to represent him in his dealings with the inquirer in relation to subsidence damage, the employee's or agent's place of business at which he may be contacted during normal business hours) (reg 5(1)(b), (2)(b));

(3)    any telephone or facsimile transmission number for communicating with that person at every such place (or where an employee or agent of the person with responsibility is appointed to represent him in his dealings with the inquirer in relation to subsidence damage, the employee's or agent's telephone or facsimile transmission number) (reg 5(1)(c), (2)(b)); and

(4)    a copy of the document known as 'Coal Mining Subsidence Damage – a Guide to Claimants' Rights' as for the time being issued by the Secretary of State (as to whom see PARA 2) (Coal Mining Subsidence (Provision of Information) Regulations 1994, SI 1994/2565, reg 5(3)).

A request satisfies the requirements if it:

(a)    is a request for information relating to, or to the possibility of, subsidence damage (reg 4(3)(a));

(b)    is accompanied by the provision of the address of the person making the request (reg 4(3)(b));

(c)    is made by, or on behalf of, a person appearing to be the owner or occupier of any land (reg 4(3)(c)); and

(d)    is made of a person with responsibility for subsidence affecting the whole or any part of the land appearing to be owned or occupied by the person by, or on whose behalf, the request is made (reg 4(3)(d)).

'Person with responsibility' means, in relation to any land, the person who would be the responsible person in relation to any subsidence damage to that land if such damage were to result from any underground coal-mining operations: reg 1(2). 'Address' means, in the case of a body corporate, the address of its registered or principal office; and in the case of any other person, the address of his usual place of business: reg 1(2).

7    As to the Coal Authority see PARA 52 et seq.

8    As to the meaning of 'subsidence damage' see PARA 203.

9    See the Coal Industry Act 1994 s 45(1)(b); and the Coal Mining Subsidence (Provision of Information) Regulations 1994, SI 1994/2565, regs 6, 7. Where a request is made of a person with responsibility which complies with reg 4(3)(a), (b) but not (d) (reg 6(2)), that person must, within 14 days beginning with the date on which he received it:

(1)    notify the Authority of the request (reg 6(1)(a));

(2)    furnish the Authority in writing with the following information:

    (a)    the name and address of the person making the request as supplied by that person (regs 6(1)(b), 7(a));

    (b)    details of any telephone or facsimile transmission number supplied by the person making the request (regs 6(1)(b), 7(b));

    (c)    details of the request including whether it was expressed to relate to actual subsidence damage, the possibility of such damage or otherwise (regs 6(1)(b), 7(c)); and

    (d)    such documents as the person making the request has furnished to the person of whom the request is made, including copies of any correspondence furnished by him (regs 6(1)(b), 7(d)); and

(3)    notify the person making the request that the Authority has been informed of it (reg 6(1)(c)).

A request satisfies the requirements of reg 7 (whether it is made orally or in writing) if it complies with reg 4(3)(a) and (b) but does not comply with reg 4(3)(d): reg 6(2).

10    Coal Industry Act 1994 s 45(1)(c).

11    See the Coal Industry Act 1994 s 45(1)(d); and the Coal Mining Subsidence (Provision of Information) Regulations 1994, SI 1994/2565, regs 5, 7.

12    See the Coal Industry Act 1994 s 45(2).

## 208. The subsidence adviser.

The Secretary of State[1] may by regulations[2] make such provision as he considers necessary or expedient (1) for the appointment of an independent person known as 'the subsidence adviser' to carry out, in prescribed[3] cases, specified functions[4]; and (2) for regulating and facilitating the carrying out of those functions by the subsidence adviser[5]. These functions are:

(a)    the provision of advice and assistance to persons[6] in connection with the making of complaints, or the taking of any other steps, in relation to any matter arising under the Coal Mining Subsidence Act 1991 or certain questions[7] which may be referred to the appropriate tribunal[8];

(b)    the making to persons with responsibility for subsidence affecting land of recommendations as to the manner in which they conduct themselves where such a matter has arisen or any such question falls to be determined[9];

(c)    the making of reports dealing generally with the way in which persons with responsibility for subsidence affecting land conduct themselves where such matters arise or such questions fall to be determined[10]; and

(d)    the making of reports about the carrying out by the subsidence adviser of his functions[11].

Such regulations may also require the subsidence adviser to publish his recommendations and reports[12], and to give persons concerned with any matter being handled by him opportunities for making representations and objections[13]. The Coal Authority[14] must furnish the subsidence adviser with all the information and assistance he reasonably requires in any case in which the Authority is the person with responsibility for subsidence affecting the land in question[15].

The Secretary of State may by regulations make provision for the expenses incurred by the subsidence adviser in carrying out his functions, and his remuneration, to be met, in whole or in part, by some or all of the persons with responsibility for subsidence affecting land or in another prescribed manner[16]. Provision may be made for any matter to which the regulations relate to be determined by the Authority[17]. Provision may also be made, where any expenses are to be met by the Authority in accordance with the regulations, for amounts to be recoverable by the Authority from other persons with responsibility for subsidence affecting land[18].

1    As to the Secretary of State see PARA 2.
2    See the Coal Mining Subsidence (Subsidence Adviser) Regulations 2004, SI 2004/2241. As to the Secretary of State's power to make regulations or orders see PARA 202.
3    For these purposes, 'prescribed' means prescribed by regulations under the Coal Industry Act 1994 s 46, and the Coal Mining Subsidence Act 1991 s 50 (see PARA 202) applies in relation to the powers to make regulations under the Coal Industry Act 1994 s 46 as it applies in relation to any power of the Secretary of State to make regulations under the Coal Mining Subsidence Act 1991: Coal Industry Act 1994 s 46(7). The supplementary, incidental and transitional provision that may be contained, by virtue of s 46(7), in regulations under s 46 may include transitional provision in relation to matters arising under the Coal Mining Subsidence Act 1991 at times before the restructuring date (ie 31 October 1994: see PARA 50): Coal Industry Act 1994 s 46(8).
4    Coal Industry Act 1994 s 46(1)(a). The functions referred to are those specified in the Coal Industry Act 1994 s 46(2): see s 46(1)(a).
5    Coal Industry Act 1994 s 46(1)(b).
6    Ie other than those with responsibility for subsidence affecting land: see Coal Industry Act 1994 s 46(2)(a).
7    Ie those which fall within the Coal Industry Act 1994 s 47(1) (see PARA 249): see s 46(2)(a).
8    Coal Industry Act 1994 s 46(2)(a).
9    Coal Industry Act 1994 s 46(2)(b).
10   Coal Industry Act 1994 s 46(2)(c).

11 Coal Industry Act 1994 s 46(2)(d).
12 Coal Industry Act 1994 s 46(3)(a).
13 Coal Industry Act 1994 s 46(3)(b).
14 As to the Coal Authority see PARA 52 et seq.
15 Coal Industry Act 1994 s 46(4).
16 Coal Industry Act 1994 s 46(5).
17 See the Coal Industry Act 1994 s 46(6)(a).
18 See the Coal Industry Act 1994 s 46(6)(b).

## (C) Remedial Action

### (a) In General

**209. The duty to take remedial action.**
The responsible person[1] is under a duty, in respect of subsidence damage[2] to any property, to take remedial action of one or more of the following kinds[3]:
(1) the execution of remedial works[4];
(2) the making of payments[5] in respect of the cost of remedial works executed by some other person[6]; and
(3) the making of a payment[7] in respect of the depreciation in the value of the damaged property[8].

Where emergency works are executed by any other person, the responsible person is also under a duty[9] to make a payment[10] in respect of the cost of those works[11].

1 As to the responsible person see PARA 204.
2 As to the meaning of 'subsidence damage' see PARA 203.
3 Coal Mining Subsidence Act 1991 s 2(1). This is subject to the provisions of Pt II (ss 2–21): see s 2(1). References in the Coal Mining Subsidence Act 1991, in relation to any subsidence damage, to the responsible person's remedial obligation are references to their obligation under s 2(1): ss 2(3), 52(1).
4 Coal Mining Subsidence Act 1991 s 2(2)(a). The remedial works referred to are those executed in accordance with s 7 (see PARA 213): s 2(2)(a). As to the schedule of remedial works see PARA 212.
5 Ie payments in lieu under the Coal Mining Subsidence Act 1991 s 8 (see PARA 216) or s 9 (see PARA 215): see s 2(2)(b).
6 Coal Mining Subsidence Act 1991 s 2(2)(b).
7 Ie depreciation payments under the Coal Mining Subsidence Act 1991 s 10 (see PARA 219) or s 11 (see PARA 218): see s 2(2)(c).
8 Coal Mining Subsidence Act 1991 s 2(2)(c).
9 This is subject to the provisions of the Coal Mining Subsidence Act 1991 Pt II: see s 2(4).
10 Ie in accordance with the Coal Mining Subsidence Act 1991 s 12 (see PARA 221): see s 2(4).
11 Coal Mining Subsidence Act 1991 s 2(4).

**210. Notice of subsidence damage.**
The statutory remedies[1] are not available in respect of subsidence damage[2] to any property unless the owner[3] of the property or some other person who is liable to make good the damage in whole or in part has given to the responsible person[4] the required notice[5] with respect to the damage within the required period[6], and has afforded such person reasonable facilities to inspect the property, so far as he was in a position to do so[7]. The required notice with respect to any subsidence damage is a notice stating that the damage has occurred and containing prescribed particulars[8].

As soon as reasonably practicable after receiving a damage notice or, where he receives two or more such notices in respect of the same damage, after receiving the first of them, the responsible person must give to the claimant[9], and to any other person interested[10], a notice indicating whether or not he agrees that he has a remedial obligation[11] in respect of the whole or any part of the damage specified in the damage notice[12]. Where the responsible person gives such a notice[13] indicating his agreement that he has such an obligation, he must also give to the claimant, and to any other person interested, a notice (1) stating the kind of remedial action available for meeting that obligation and, if more than one, which of them the responsible person proposes to take[14]; and (2) in the case of a notice stating that the responsible person proposes to execute remedial works with respect to any damage, informing the claimant or that person that, if he makes a request[15], the responsible person may elect to make a payment in lieu[16] instead of executing the works[17]. Where the responsible person accedes to such a request, he must give to the claimant and any other person interested a revised notice[18] stating that he proposes to elect to make a payment in lieu instead of executing the works[19].

Where a damage notice[20] is received by a person with responsibility for subsidence affecting any land, and that person is neither the Coal Authority[21] nor the person who is or would be the responsible person in relation to the damage with respect to which the notice is given, the person who has received the notice must, as soon as reasonably practicable after receiving it, forward the notice to the Authority[22]. Where a damage notice is received by the Authority[23], and the Authority is not itself the person who is or would be the responsible person in relation to the damage with respect to which the notice is given, the Authority must, as soon as reasonably practicable after receiving it, forward the notice to the person appearing to the Authority to be the person who is or would be the responsible person in relation to that damage[24].

1 Ie the remedies under the Coal Mining Subsidence Act 1991 s 2(1) or s 2(4) (see PARA 209): see s 3(1).

2 As to the meaning of 'subsidence damage' see PARA 203.

3 As to the meaning of 'owner' see PARA 207.

4 As to the responsible person see PARA 204.

5 'Notice' means notice in writing; and 'notify' is to be construed accordingly: Coal Mining Subsidence Act 1991 s 52(1). References, in relation to any damage, to a notice affecting the required remedial action in respect of the damage are references to: (1) any notice of proposed remedial action with respect to that damage; and (2) any notice with respect to a decision by the British Coal Corporation to make or revoke an election to take in respect of that damage any remedial action other than that indicated in any such notice mentioned in head (1): s 52(2). As to notices see PARA 251 et seq. The provisions of the Coal Industry Act 1994 s 63 (see PARA 110) apply also to the service of documents under the Coal Mining Subsidence Act 1991: s 51 (substituted by the Coal Industry Act 1994 s 67(1), Sch 9 para 41(3)). As to the British Coal Corporation see PARAS 49–50.

6 The period allowed for giving a notice with respect to any subsidence damage is six years beginning with the first date on which any person entitled to give the notice had the knowledge required for founding a claim in respect of the damage: Coal Mining Subsidence Act 1991 s 3(3). For these purposes the knowledge required for founding a claim in respect of any subsidence damage is knowledge (1) that the damage has occurred; and (2) that the nature of the damage and the circumstances are such as to indicate that the damage may be subsidence damage: s 3(4). A person's knowledge includes knowledge which he might reasonably have been expected to acquire from: (a) any facts which were observable or ascertainable by him; and (b) any facts which would have been ascertainable by him with the help of any expert advice which it was reasonable for him to seek: s 3(4), (5). 'Claim' means a claim in writing: s 52(1).

7 Coal Mining Subsidence Act 1991 s 3(1).

8 Coal Mining Subsidence Act 1991 s 3(2). 'Prescribed' means prescribed by regulations made by the Secretary of State: s 52(1). As to the Secretary of State see PARA 2; and as to the Secretary of State's power to make regulations or orders see PARA 202. References in the Coal Mining Subsidence Act 1991, in relation to any subsidence damage, to a damage notice are references to such a notice with

respect to the damage given within the period allowed: s 3(2). As to the prescribed particulars see the Coal Mining Subsidence (Notices and Claims) Regulations 1991, SI 1991/2509, regs 1, 2, Sch 1.

9 'Claimant', in relation to any subsidence damage, means the person who gave or, as the case may be, was the first person to give a damage notice to the responsible person in respect of the damage, and includes any successor in title of his: Coal Mining Subsidence Act 1991 ss 3(6), 52(1).

10 'Any other person interested', in relation to any subsidence damage and any time, means any person other than the claimant who, not less than seven days before that time, gave such a notice to the responsible person in respect of the damage, and includes any successor in title of any such person: Coal Mining Subsidence Act 1991 ss 3(6), 52(1).

11 As to the meaning of 'remedial obligation' see PARA 209.

12 Coal Mining Subsidence Act 1991 s 4(1).

13 Ie under the Coal Mining Subsidence Act 1991 s 4(1).

14 Coal Mining Subsidence Act 1991 s 4(2)(a).

15 Ie a request informing the responsible person that the person making the request wishes to execute the remedial works in question himself or to have them executed on his behalf by a person specified in the request: see the Coal Mining Subsidence Act 1991 ss 4(2), 8(3). As to the meaning of 'request' see PARA 207. As to the meaning of 'works' see PARA 203.

16 As to payments in lieu see PARAS 214–216.

17 Coal Mining Subsidence Act 1991 s 4(2)(b).

18 Ie under the Coal Mining Subsidence Act 1991 s 4(2).

19 Coal Mining Subsidence Act 1991 s 4(3).

20 See the Coal Industry Act 1994 s 43(8), Sch 6 para 1(4).

21 As to the Coal Authority see PARA 52 et seq.

22 Coal Industry Act 1994 Sch 6 para 1(1).

23 Ie whether as a result of being forwarded under the Coal Industry Act 1994 Sch 6 para 1(1) or otherwise: see Sch 6 para 1(2).

24 Coal Industry Act 1994 Sch 6 para 1(2). The person to whom a notice is forwarded under Sch 6 para 1 is deemed for the purposes of the Coal Mining Subsidence Act 1991: (1) to have been given that notice by the person whose notice it is; and (2) to have received the notice within the period allowed by the Coal Mining Subsidence Act 1991 s 3 if it was or is deemed to have been so received by the person who forwarded it: Coal Industry Act 1994 Sch 6 para 1(3).

## 211. Determination of appropriate remedial action.

Where the responsible person[1] has given a notice of proposed remedial action[2] with respect to any damage, he must meet his remedial obligation[3] in respect of that damage by taking the appropriate remedial action[4], and not in any other way[5]. The appropriate remedial action in relation to any damage is that stated in the notice of proposed remedial action with respect to that damage[6]. Where the responsible person has power to elect to make a discretionary payment in lieu[7] or a discretionary depreciation payment[8] in respect of any damage, and he has not exercised that power by stating in the notice of proposed remedial action that he proposes to make such a payment, he may exercise that power at any time subsequent to the date of that notice, but only with the agreement of the claimant[9] and any other person interested[10]. Where, after the date of that notice, the responsible person elects to take remedial action other than that stated in the notice[11], so long as the election is effective the appropriate remedial action in relation to that damage is the substituted action[12].

1 As to the responsible person see PARA 204.

2 References, in relation to any damage, to a notice of proposed remedial action are references to a notice under the Coal Mining Subsidence Act 1991 s 4(2) (whether as originally given or as revised under s 4(3)) (see PARA 210): s 4(4). As to the meaning of 'notice' see PARA 210. As to notices see PARA 251 et seq.

3 As to the meaning of 'remedial obligation' see PARA 209.

4 As to the duty to take remedial action see PARA 209.

5 Coal Mining Subsidence Act 1991 s 5(1). This does not apply where a responsible person has made an obligatory payment in lieu under s 9 (see PARA 215) or an obligatory depreciation payment under s 11 (see PARA 218): s 5(1).

6  Coal Mining Subsidence Act 1991 s 5(2). This is subject to s 5(4), (6): see s 5(2).
7  Ie under the Coal Mining Subsidence Act 1991 s 8 (see PARA 216): s 5(3).
8  Ie under the Coal Mining Subsidence Act 1991 s 10 (see PARA 219): s 5(3).
9  As to the meaning of 'claimant' see PARA 210.
10  Coal Mining Subsidence Act 1991 s 5(3). As to the meaning of 'any other person interested' see PARA 210.
11  This action is called the 'substituted action': Coal Mining Subsidence Act 1991 s 5(4).
12  Coal Mining Subsidence Act 1991 s 5(4). An election by the responsible person under either s 8 or s 10 may at any time be revoked by the responsible person, but only with the agreement of the claimant and any other person interested: s 5(5). Where the responsible person revokes such an election made in respect of any damage by a notice of proposed remedial action, s 5 applies as if the execution of remedial works had been specified in that notice as the responsible person's proposed remedial action with respect to that damage: s 5(6).

### 212. Schedule of remedial works.

At the same time as the responsible person[1] gives a notice of proposed remedial action[2] with respect to any damage (other than a notice stating that the only kind of action available for meeting his remedial obligation[3] is the making of an obligatory payment in lieu[4] or an obligatory depreciation payment[5]) he must send to the claimant[6] and any other person interested a schedule of remedial works which meets the following requirements[7].

The schedule of remedial works must specify: (1) the works which the responsible person considers to be remedial works in relation to the damage, that is to say, such works[8] as are necessary in order to make good the damage, so far as it is reasonably practicable to do so, to the reasonable satisfaction of the claimant and any other person interested[9]; and (2) in the case of each item of those works, the amount of the cost which the responsible person considers it would be reasonable for any person to incur in order to secure that the work is executed[10]. The responsible person must send with a schedule of remedial works a notice stating that, if any other party does not agree that the remedial action to be taken by the responsible person in respect of any damage should be determined by reference, where relevant, to the works and costs specified in the schedule, he should notify the responsible person within the period of 28 days beginning with the date of his receipt of the schedule[11]. If any other party gives such a notification within that period and he and the responsible person do not agree the schedule, with or without modifications, before the end of the next succeeding period of 28 days, the matter may be referred to the appropriate tribunal, which may determine the works and costs to be specified in the schedule[12].

The schedule comes into effect (a) if no other party gives such a notification to the responsible person, at the end of the 28 day period from the receipt of the schedule[13]; and (b) in any other case, on the date on which the schedule is agreed or determined[14]. The schedule may be varied by agreement between the parties or determined[15] by the appropriate tribunal[16]. Where any party by a notice given to the other party or parties requests[17] a variation of the schedule, and the requested variation is not agreed between both or all parties, with or without modifications, before the end of the period of 28 days beginning with the date of the notice, the matter may be referred to the appropriate tribunal, which may determine whether the schedule is to have effect subject to the variation[18]. On and after the date on which the schedule relating to any damage first comes into effect only the works specified in it are regarded as remedial works in relation to the damage[19].

1  As to the responsible person see PARA 204.
2  As to notices of proposed remedial action see PARA 211. As to the meaning of 'notice' see PARA 210. As to notices see PARA 251 et seq.

3  As to the meaning of 'remedial obligation' see PARA 209.
4  Ie under the Coal Mining Subsidence Act 1991 s 9 (see PARA 215): see s 6(1).
5  Ie under the Coal Mining Subsidence Act 1991 s 11 (see PARA 218): see s 6(1).
6  As to the meaning of 'claimant' see PARA 210. The claimant and any other person interested are together referred to as 'the other parties': see the Coal Mining Subsidence Act 1991 s 6(1). As to the meaning of 'any other person interested' see PARA 210.
7  Coal Mining Subsidence Act 1991 s 6(1). References, in relation to any subsidence damage, to the schedule of remedial works are references to the schedule of remedial works under s 6 relating to the damage, as that schedule has effect for the time being: ss 6(8), 52(1). As to the meaning of 'subsidence damage' see PARA 203; and as to the meaning of 'works' see PARA 203.
8  Such works include works of redecoration: see the Coal Mining Subsidence Act 1991 s 6(1).
9  Coal Mining Subsidence Act 1991 ss 6(2)(a), 52(1).
10  Coal Mining Subsidence Act 1991 ss 6(2)(b), 52(1).
11  Coal Mining Subsidence Act 1991 s 6(3).
12  Coal Mining Subsidence Act 1991 s 6(4) (amended by SI 2009/1307).
13  See the Coal Mining Subsidence Act 1991 s 6(3), (5)(a)(i).
14  See the Coal Mining Subsidence Act 1991 s 6(4), (5)(a)(ii).
15  Ie determined under the Coal Mining Subsidence Act 1991 s 6(6): see s 6(5)(b).
16  Coal Mining Subsidence Act 1991 s 6(5)(b).
17  As to the meaning of 'request' see PARA 207.
18  Coal Mining Subsidence Act 1991 s 6(6) (amended by SI 2009/1307).
19  See the Coal Mining Subsidence Act 1991 ss 6(7), 52(1).

### 213.  Execution of remedial works.

Where the responsible person[1] is under an obligation to execute remedial works[2] in respect of any damage, he must execute them as soon as reasonably practicable after the date on which a schedule of remedial works[3] first comes into effect in relation to the damage[4]. The responsible person, if so requested by the claimant[5] or any other person interested[6] at any time before the remedial works are completed, must give him adequate information, in writing, with respect to any of those works still remaining to be executed[7].

1  As to the responsible person see PARA 204.
2  Ie the remedial works specified in the Coal Mining Subsidence Act 1991 s 6(2): see PARA 212. As to the meaning of 'works' see PARA 203.
3  As to the schedule of remedial works see PARA 212.
4  Coal Mining Subsidence Act 1991 s 7(1), (2).
5  As to the meaning of 'claimant' see PARA 210.
6  As to the meaning of 'any other person interested' see PARA 210.
7  Coal Mining Subsidence Act 1991 s 7(3).

### 214.  Payments in lieu of remedial of works.

The responsible person[1] is not required to make any payment in lieu[2] in respect of any works[3] executed by any other person in connection with any property unless that person (1) has given to the responsible person the required notice[4] with respect to the works[5]; and (2) has afforded the responsible person reasonable facilities to inspect the property, so far as he was in a position to do so[6].

The responsible person may make advance payments in respect of any proposed expenditure[7] qualifying for a payment in lieu[8]. However, such an advance payment may only be made if the responsible person is satisfied that it will be applied in meeting the expenditure in question[9], and the responsible person may not unreasonably refuse any request[10] to make an advance payment received from the person or persons by whom the cost of executing the works in question is to be incurred[11].

Any payment in lieu (including an advance payment) must be made to the person or persons by whom the cost of executing the works in question is (or is to be) incurred[12]. If there are two or more such persons, the payment must be apportioned between them either in such manner as may be determined by agreement or, in default of agreement, in shares corresponding to their respective shares in the cost[13]. With the exception of advance payments[14], before the expenditure in question is incurred, any payment in lieu must be made as soon as reasonably practicable after the expenditure in respect of which it is required to be made has been incurred[15].

1　As to the responsible person see PARA 204.
2　References to payments in lieu are references to payments in accordance with the Coal Mining Subsidence Act 1991 s 8 (see PARA 216) or s 9 (see PARA 215): ss 2(5)(a), 52(1).
3　As to the meaning of 'works' see PARA 203.
4　The required notice with respect to any works is a notice which contains adequate particulars of the works; and, except in such circumstances as may be prescribed, is given at the prescribed interval before the works are begun: Coal Mining Subsidence Act 1991 s 13(2). As to the meaning of 'notice' see PARA 210. As to notices see PARA 251 et seq. As to the meaning of 'prescribed' see PARA 210. As to the prescribed interval see the Coal Mining Subsidence (Notices and Claims) Regulations 1991, SI 1991/2509, reg 3.
5　Coal Mining Subsidence Act 1991 s 13(1)(a).
6　Coal Mining Subsidence Act 1991 s 13(1)(b).
7　For the purposes of the Coal Mining Subsidence Act 1991 s 13(3), proposed expenditure is expenditure qualifying for a payment in lieu if it is expenditure of a description in respect of which a payment in lieu would be required if it had been incurred: s 13(4).
8　Coal Mining Subsidence Act 1991 s 13(3).
9　Coal Mining Subsidence Act 1991 s 13(5)(a). An advance payment is to be regarded as made in accordance with s 8 (see PARA 216) or s 9 (see PARA 215) which requires the payment in lieu on account of which it is made: s 13(5)(b).
10　As to the meaning of 'request' see PARA 207.
11　Coal Mining Subsidence Act 1991 s 13(6).
12　Coal Mining Subsidence Act 1991 s 13(7).
13　Coal Mining Subsidence Act 1991 s 13(7).
14　See the Coal Mining Subsidence Act 1991 s 13(3).
15　Coal Mining Subsidence Act 1991 s 13(8).

### 215.　Obligatory payments in lieu.

The responsible person[1] must meet his remedial obligation[2] in respect of any damage by making an obligatory payment in lieu[3]:

(1)　where the damaged property is a highway maintainable at the public expense in England and Wales[4];

(2)　where the execution of remedial works[5] falls within a duty with respect to the damaged property which, in connection with the maintenance of public services, is imposed by virtue of any enactment on (a) a government department[6]; (b) a local authority[7]; or (c) statutory undertakers[8];

(3)　where it is certified by the Secretary of State[9] on an application made to him by any other person or of his own motion, that in his opinion it is not in the public interest that the responsible person should himself execute the remedial works[10].

The payment required in respect of any damage is equal to the cost reasonably incurred by any person in executing remedial works[11]. However, where remedial works are executed after the end of the period of three years beginning with the date of the claimant's[12] damage notice[13], the amount of such payment must not exceed the cost which might reasonably have been expected to have been incurred in executing those works if they had been executed immediately before the end of that period[14].

1　As to the responsible person see PARA 204.

2  As to the meaning of 'remedial obligation' see PARA 209.
3  Coal Mining Subsidence Act 1991 s 9(1).
4  Coal Mining Subsidence Act 1991 s 9(2)(a). As to highways maintainable at the public expense see HIGHWAYS, STREETS AND BRIDGES vol 55 (2012) PARA 252 et seq.
5  Ie the remedial works specified in the Coal Mining Subsidence Act 1991 s 6(2): see PARA 212. As to the meaning of 'works' see PARA 203.
6  Coal Mining Subsidence Act 1991 s 9(2)(b)(i).
7  Coal Mining Subsidence Act 1991 s 9(2)(b)(ii).
8  Coal Mining Subsidence Act 1991 s 9(2)(b)(iii). 'Statutory undertakers' means: (1) any persons authorised by any enactment to carry on any railway, light railway, tramway, road transport, water transport, canal, inland navigation, dock, harbour, pier or lighthouse undertaking or any undertaking for the supply of hydraulic power; and (2) any licence holder within the meaning of the Electricity Act 1989 (see ENERGY AND CLIMATE CHANGE vol 43 (2011) PARAS 508, 524 et seq); (3) any public gas supplier (see ENERGY AND CLIMATE CHANGE vol 42 (2011) PARA 264); (4) any water or sewerage undertaker (see WATER AND WATERWAYS vol 100 (2018) PARA 505); (5) the Environment Agency (see ENVIRONMENTAL QUALITY AND PUBLIC HEALTH vol 45 (2010) PARA 68 et seq; WATER AND WATERWAYS vol 100 (2018) PARA 23); (6) the Natural Resources Body for Wales (see OPEN SPACES vol 78 (2018) PARA561); (7) any electronic communications code operator, any former public telecommunications operator (see TELECOMMUNICATIONS vol 97 (2015) PARA 168); (8) any universal service provider in connection with the provision of a universal postal service (see POSTAL SERVICES); (9) the Civil Aviation Authority (see AVIATION vol 2 (2017) PARA 752 et seq); (10) any person who holds a licence under the Transport Act 2000 Pt I Ch I (ss 1–40) (to the extent that the person is carrying out activities authorised by the licence) (see AVIATION vol 2 (2017) PARA 863 et seq); and (11) any relevant airport operator within the meaning of the Airports Act 1986 Pt V (ss 57–62) (see AVIATION vol 2 (2017) PARA 913): Coal Mining Subsidence Act 1991 s 52(1) (definition amended by the Gas Act 1995 s 16(1), Sch 4 para 2(2)(l); SI 1996/593; and SI 2001/1149). In head (8), 'universal service provider' has the same meaning as in the Postal Services Act 2011 Pt 3 (ss 27–67) (see POSTAL SERVICES); and any reference to the provision of a universal postal service is to be construed in accordance with Pt 3: Coal Mining Subsidence Act 1991 s 52(1) (definition added by SI 2001/1149; amended by the Postal Services Act 2011 Sch 12 Pt 3 para 135; amd SI 2013/755).
9  As to the Secretary of State see PARA 2.
10  Coal Mining Subsidence Act 1991 s 9(2)(c).
11  Coal Mining Subsidence Act 1991 s 9(3).
12  As to the meaning of 'claimant' see PARA 210.
13  As to the meaning of 'damage notice' see PARA 210. As to the meaning of 'notice' see PARA 210. As to notices see PARA 251 et seq.
14  Coal Mining Subsidence Act 1991 s 9(4). As to the reckoning of this period while a stop notice is in force see s 16(5)(d); and PARA 222. As to the meaning of 'stop notice' see PARA 222.

## 216. Discretionary payments in lieu.

The responsible person[1] may elect to make payments in respect of the cost of remedial works[2] instead of executing such works himself in any of the following cases[3].

Where the responsible person receives the necessary request[4] from the claimant[5] or any other person interested[6], he may elect to make, in respect of the cost incurred by another person in executing any of the remedial works, a payment equal to the aggregate amount of the costs specified in the schedule of remedial works[7]. Where it is proposed to merge the execution of other works in connection with the damaged property with the execution of remedial works, or it is proposed to redevelop the damaged property instead of executing remedial works, the responsible person may elect to make a payment equal to any sums from time to time shown to have been expended by any other person in executing the merged works or the redevelopment works, up to an aggregate amount not exceeding the total scheduled cost[8]. Where, in the case of any property affected by subsidence damage[9], immediately before that damage became evident the property was in a state of disrepair and it is not practicable to execute remedial works without including additional works which would not be necessary but for the disrepair[10] and the total scheduled cost is at least 20 per cent[11] higher than it would have been if the costs of the works attributable to the disrepair had not been included, then the responsible person may elect to make in respect of the cost incurred by any other person in executing remedial works a payment equal to the amount by which the total scheduled cost exceeds the aggregate amount of the costs specified in the schedule of works in respect of the works attributable to the disrepair[12].

The responsible person may not unreasonably refuse a request to make an election to make a payment[13]. He is to be regarded as acting unreasonably in refusing any request[14] which is received before he has begun to execute remedial works[15], except where: (1) he has acceded to another such request made by another person; (2) the execution of remedial works by a person other than the responsible person would significantly impede the discharge of his remedial obligation[16] in respect of one or more neighbouring properties; or (3) if the damage has rendered the property structurally unsound, the execution of such works by the person by whom the request was made or, as the case may be, by the person specified in the request would be unlikely to restore the structural integrity of the property, and (in any case) as soon as reasonably practicable after receiving the request, the responsible person gives notice[17] to that effect to the person by whom the request was made[18]. Nor is the responsible person to be regarded as acting unreasonably in refusing any request[19] which is received after he has begun to execute remedial works[20].

An election under these provisions, and any revocation of such an election, must be made by a notice given to the claimant and any other person interested[21].

1   As to the responsible person see PARA 204.
2   Ie the remedial works specified in the Coal Mining Subsidence Act 1991 s 6(2): see PARA 212. As to the meaning of 'works' see PARA 203.
3   Coal Mining Subsidence Act 1991 s 8(1).
4   For this purpose, the necessary request is a request informing the responsible person that the person making the request wishes to execute the remedial works in question himself or to have them executed on his behalf by a person specified in the request: Coal Mining Subsidence Act 1991 s 8(3). The responsible person may not unreasonably refuse any request complying with s 8(3) to make an election under s 8(2): s 8(7)(a). As to the meaning of 'request' see PARA 207.
5   As to the meaning of 'claimant' see PARA 210.
6   As to the meaning of 'any other person interested' see PARA 210.
7   Coal Mining Subsidence Act 1991 s 8(2). As to the schedule of remedial works see PARA 212.
8   Coal Mining Subsidence Act 1991 s 8(4). The total scheduled cost is the aggregate of the costs specified in the schedule of works: see s 8(4). The responsible person may not unreasonably refuse any request received from the claimant or any other person interested to make an election under this provision: s 8(7)(b). Where the responsible person has elected to make a payment in respect of a dwelling-house under s 8(4), he is entitled to recover as a civil debt from the owner of the dwelling-house any amount by which the responsible person's expenditure under Sch 5 (see PARA 229) in connection with the dwelling-house exceeds what it would have been if remedial works only had been executed: Sch 5 para 7. As to the relief for temporary dispossession see PARA 229. 'Dwelling-house', in relation to England and Wales, means any building or part of a building used wholly or partly as a private dwelling, together with any yard, garden, outhouses and appurtenances belonging to or usually enjoyed with that building or part: s 52(1).
9   As to the meaning of 'subsidence damage' see PARA 203.
10 These works are termed 'the works attributable to the disrepair': see the Coal Mining Subsidence Act 1991 s 8(5).
11 The Secretary of State may by order substitute for this percentage (whether as originally enacted or as previously amended) such other percentage as he thinks fit: Coal Mining Subsidence Act 1991 s 8(12). At the date at which this volume states the law no such order had been made. As to the Secretary of State see PARA 2; and as to the Secretary of State's power to make regulations or orders see PARA 202.

12 Coal Mining Subsidence Act 1991 s 8(5). In any such case the schedule of remedial works must distinguish the works attributable to the disrepair from the works which would be necessary apart from the disrepair: s 8(6).

13 See the Coal Mining Subsidence Act 1991 s 8(7).

14 Ie a request falling within the Coal Mining Subsidence Act 1991 s 8(7)(a) to make an election to make, in respect of costs incurred by another person in executing any remedial works, a payment equal to the amount of the costs specified in relation to those works in the schedule of remedial works: see s 8(8).

15 Coal Mining Subsidence Act 1991 s 8(8). The reference to remedial works in s 8(8) does not include any remedial works begun before the further damage becomes evident: see s 18(3)(g); and PARA 224.

16 As to the meaning of 'remedial obligation' see PARA 209.

17 As to the meaning of 'notice' see PARA 210. As to notices see PARA 251 et seq.

18 Coal Mining Subsidence Act 1991 s 8(9).

19 Ie a request falling within the Coal Mining Subsidence Act 1991 s 8(7): see s 8(10).

20 Coal Mining Subsidence Act 1991 s 8(10). The reference to remedial works in s 8(10) does not include any remedial works begun before the further damage becomes evident: see s 18(3)(g); and PARA 224.

21 Coal Mining Subsidence Act 1991 s 8(11).

## 217. Depreciation payments.

The responsible person[1] may elect to make, and in certain circumstances must make, a depreciation payment[2] instead of executing remedial works[3] or making any payment in lieu[4]. However, the responsible person may not make a depreciation payment[5] in respect of subsidence damage[6] to a dwelling-house[7], except after consultation with the local authority[8] in whose area the dwelling-house is situated[9]. The responsible person may not make a depreciation payment in respect of subsidence damage to any property other than a dwelling-house, where that property is of a prescribed description[10], except after consultation with the Minister of the Crown or other person as may be so prescribed in relation to that description of property[11].

A depreciation payment must be made as soon as reasonably practicable after the obligation to make it arises[12]. Provision is made for determining the unit of property to be taken into account[13] and for determining the basis of the valuation[14] and the amount of any depreciation in the value of any such unit in respect of which a depreciation payment falls to be made[15]. Interest is payable on outstanding depreciation payments[16].

1 As to the responsible person see PARA 204.

2 References to depreciation payments are references to payments in accordance with the Coal Mining Subsidence Act 1991 s 10 (see PARA 219) or s 11 (see PARA 218): see ss 2(5)(b), 52(1).

3 Ie the remedial works specified in the Coal Mining Subsidence Act 1991 s 6(2): see PARA 212. As to the meaning of 'works' see PARA 203.

4 As to payments in lieu see PARAS 214–216.

5 Ie other than a payment under the Coal Mining Subsidence Act 1991 s 11(3) (see PARA 218): see s 14(1).

6 As to the meaning of 'subsidence damage' see PARA 203.

7 As to the meaning of 'dwelling-house' see PARA 216.

8 Ie within the meaning of the Housing Act 1985 (see HOUSING vol 56 (2017) PARA 12): see the Coal Mining Subsidence Act 1991 s 14(1).

9 Coal Mining Subsidence Act 1991 s 14(1).

10 Ie prescribed for the purposes of the Coal Mining Subsidence Act 1991 s 14(2): see s 14(2). At the date at which this volume states the law no such regulations had been made. As to the meaning of 'prescribed' see PARA 210. As to the Secretary of State see PARA 2; and as to the Secretary of State's power to make regulations or orders see PARA 202.

11 Coal Mining Subsidence Act 1991 s 14(2).

12 Coal Mining Subsidence Act 1991 s 14(3).

13 The unit of property to be taken into account for any purposes of the Coal Mining Subsidence Act 1991 s 10 or s 11 is:

(1)     where any property affected constitutes or is comprised in a dwelling-house, that dwelling-house (s 14(4), Sch 1 para 1(1)(a));

(2)     where any property affected, other than property to which head (1) applies, is situated in England and Wales and is a relevant non-domestic hereditament for the purposes of the Local Government Finance Act 1988 Pt III (ss 41–67), that hereditament (Coal Mining Subsidence Act 1991 Sch 1 para 1(1)(b));

(3)     in any other case, such unit consisting of or comprising any property affected as may be equitable in all the circumstances of the case (Sch 1 para 1(1)(d)).

If it is equitable in all the circumstances of the case to do so, two or more units of property, or a unit of property part only of which is property affected, may in either case be treated for those purposes either as a single unit of property, or as consisting of such separate units of property as may be equitable in those circumstances: Sch 1 para 1(2). For these purposes, a reference to property affected is a reference to property which has been affected by subsidence damage: Sch 1 para 1(3).

14 For any purposes of the Coal Mining Subsidence Act 1991 s 10 or s 11, the value of a unit of property at any time is taken to be the amount which it might be expected to realise in the state in which it is at that time on a sale effected at that time: Sch 1 para 2(1). In the case of property comprising land or buildings, such a sale is a sale of the fee simple in the open market and with vacant possession, subject to (1) any restrictive covenant, easement, quasi-easement or other right inuring for the benefit of other land; (2) any public right of way, right of common or other right inuring for the benefit of the public or any section of the public; and (3) any restriction imposed by or under any enactment, to which the property is subject at the time of the sale, but free from any other incumbrance: Sch 1 para 2(2). In the case of property comprising land or buildings, the value is to be determined without regard to any liability of the property to become subject after the time of the sale to any restriction by virtue of any enactment other than a demolition or closing order made under housing clearance powers, or where the property is situated in England and Wales, the declaration of an area to be a clearance area under such powers: Sch 1 para 2(3). 'Housing clearance powers' means the Housing Act 1985 Pt IX (ss 264–323) (see HOUSING vol 56 (2017) PARA 621 et seq): Coal Mining Subsidence Act 1991 s 52(1). Provision may be made by regulations made by the Secretary of State for ascertaining the value of a unit of property consisting of or comprising property of a kind not normally the subject of sales in the open market: see Sch 1 para 2(4). At the date at which this volume states the law no such regulations had been made. In determining the value of any property which has been affected by subsidence damage, any right to a depreciation payment in respect of that damage is to be disregarded: Sch 1 para 2(5).

15 For the purposes of the Coal Mining Subsidence Act 1991 s 10 or s 11 the amount of the depreciation in the value of a unit of property caused by any subsidence damage is taken to be the amount by which the value of the property at the relevant time is less than what would have been its value at that time if it had not been affected by the damage: Sch 1 para 3(1). For these purposes the relevant time:

(1)     in relation to the determination of the amount of a discretionary depreciation payment under s 10 is the time immediately after the date on which the responsible person gives to the claimant a notice of proposed remedial action with respect to the damage (Sch 1 para 3(2)(a));

(2)     in relation to the determination of the amount of an obligatory depreciation payment under s 11(1) is whichever is the later of the time mentioned in head (1) and the time immediately after (a) the service of the notice to treat; (b) the making of the demolition or closing order; or (c) where the property is situated in England and Wales, the declaration of the area to be a clearance area, by virtue of which the obligation to make the payment arises (Sch 1 para 3(2)(b)); and

(3)     in relation to the determination of the amount of a depreciation payment under s 11(3) (obligation to make a depreciation payment in respect of depreciation continuing after completion of remedial works), is the time immediately after the completion of the remedial works (Sch 1 para 3(2)(c)).

16 So much of any depreciation payment as for the time being remains unpaid by the responsible person carries interest at the applicable rate (if any) in respect of any period falling (1) after the relevant time in relation to that payment; and (2) before the whole amount and any accrued interest is paid: Coal Mining Subsidence Act 1991 Sch 1 para 4(1). However, any period of delay in determining the amount of any such payment which is attributable to unreasonable conduct on the part of the claimant or any other person interested is to be disregarded: Sch 1 para 4(2). References, in relation to any interest payable by the responsible person, to the applicable rate are

references to such rate as may from time to time be prescribed by order made by the Secretary of State; and such an order may (a) apply different rates in relation to different periods; (b) include provision for a nil rate to apply in relation to any period; and (c) fix any rate by specifying it or by applying any rate for the time being applicable for any other purpose (whether statutory or otherwise): s 52(3). At the date at which this volume states the law, the applicable rate is the rate for the time being prescribed under the Land Compensation Act 1961 s 32 (see COMPULSORY ACQUISITION OF LAND vol 18 (2009) PARA 641): Coal Mining Subsidence (Preventive Measures and Rates of Interest) Order 1991, SI 1991/2510, arts 1, 3.

## 218. Obligatory depreciation payments.

Where in the case of any dwelling-house[1] affected by subsidence damage[2], at any time before the completion of remedial works[3] or, in certain other cases[4] at any time before all sums in respect of which the responsible person[5] is liable to make payments have been expended (1) a notice to treat[6] for the compulsory purchase of the dwelling-house under housing clearance powers[7] is served in such circumstances that the compulsory purchase will be attributable to the damage; or (2) a demolition or closing order is made[8] in respect of the dwelling-house under housing clearance powers in such circumstances that the making of the order is so attributable, the responsible person must make a payment equal to the amount of the depreciation in the value of the dwelling-house caused by the damage[9].

Where in the case of any property affected by subsidence damage remedial works have been executed, but there is a depreciation in the value of the property caused by any damage the making good of which to the reasonable satisfaction of the claimant[10] and any other person interested[11] was not reasonably practicable, the responsible person must make in respect of the property a payment equal to the amount of that depreciation[12].

1 As to the meaning of 'dwelling-house' see PARA 216.
2 As to the meaning of 'subsidence damage' see PARA 203.
3 Ie the remedial works specified in the Coal Mining Subsidence Act 1991 s 6(2): see PARA 212. As to the meaning of 'works' see PARA 203.
4 Ie in a case falling within the Coal Mining Subsidence Act 1991 s 8(4) (see PARA 216): see s 11(1).
5 As to the responsible person see PARA 204.
6 References in the Coal Mining Subsidence Act 1991 s 10 (see PARA 219) or s 11 to the service of a notice to treat are references to the service of such a notice under the Compulsory Purchase Act 1965 s 5 (see COMPULSORY ACQUISITION OF LAND vol 18 (2009) PARA 616): Coal Mining Subsidence Act 1991 s 10(5). As to the meaning of 'notice' see PARA 210. As to notices see PARA 251 et seq.
7 As to the meaning of 'housing clearance powers' see PARA 217.
8 This reference to the making of a demolition or closing order in respect of the dwelling-house includes, in relation to England and Wales, a reference to an area in which the dwelling-house is situated being declared to be a clearance area: Coal Mining Subsidence Act 1991 s 11(4).
9 Coal Mining Subsidence Act 1991 s 11(1). This provision applies without prejudice to any expenditure or liability of the responsible person under s 7 (see PARA 213) or s 8 (see PARA 216) in respect of works already executed, and where the responsible person makes a payment under s 11(1) no further action is required of him under Pt II (ss 2–21) in pursuance of his remedial obligation in respect of the dwelling-house: s 11(2). As to the meaning of 'remedial obligation' see PARA 209.
10 As to the meaning of 'claimant' see PARA 210.
11 As to the meaning of 'any other person interested' see PARA 210.
12 Coal Mining Subsidence Act 1991 s 11(3).

## 219. Discretionary depreciation payments.

The responsible person may elect to make a payment equal to the amount of the depreciation in the value of the damaged property caused by the damage (known as the 'depreciation amount')[1] instead of executing any remedial works[2] or making any payment in lieu[3] where[4]:

(1)     the aggregate amount of the costs specified in the schedule of remedial works[5] exceeds the depreciation amount by at least 20 per cent[6];

(2)     the property is not a dwelling-house[7] and the responsible person and the person or persons to whom any payment would fall to be made agree that such a payment should be made[8];

(3)     the property is a dwelling-house and it appears that a notice to treat[9] is likely to be served for the compulsory purchase of the dwelling-house under housing clearance powers[10] in such circumstances that the compulsory purchase will be attributable to the subsidence damage[11].

An election to make a discretionary depreciation payment, and any revocation of such an election, must be made by a notice given to the claimant[12] and any other person interested[13].

1   As to the responsible person see PARA 204. As to discretionary depreciation payments see *Langley v Coal Authority* [2003] EWCA Civ 204, [2005] RVR 111, [2003] All ER (D) 297 (Feb).
2   Ie the remedial works specified in the Coal Mining Subsidence Act 1991 s 6(2): see PARA 212. As to the meaning of 'works' see PARA 203.
3   As to payments in lieu see PARAS 214–216.
4   See the Coal Mining Subsidence Act 1991 s 10(1).
5   As to the schedule of remedial works see PARA 212.
6   Coal Mining Subsidence Act 1991 s 10(2)(a). The Secretary of State may by order substitute for this percentage (whether as originally enacted or as previously amended) such other percentage as he thinks fit; and such an order may provide for different percentages to apply in relation to different descriptions of property: s 10(3). At the date at which this volume states the law no such order had been made. As to the Secretary of State see PARA 2; and as to the Secretary of State's power to make regulations or orders see PARA 202.
7   As to the meaning of 'dwelling-house' see PARA 216.
8   Coal Mining Subsidence Act 1991 s 10(2)(b).
9   As to the service of a notice to treat see PARA 218. As to the meaning of 'notice' see PARA 210. As to notices see PARA 251 et seq.
10  As to the meaning of 'housing clearance powers' see PARA 217.
11  Coal Mining Subsidence Act 1991 s 10(2)(c) (amended by the Coal Industry Act 1994 ss 43, 67, Sch 6 para 3(1), Sch 11 Pt II). As to the meaning of 'subsidence damage' see PARA 203.
12  As to the meaning of 'claimant' see PARA 210.
13  Coal Mining Subsidence Act 1991 s 10(4). As to the meaning of 'any other person interested' see PARA 210.

## 220. Recipients of depreciation payments.

A depreciation payment[1] must be made to the person who is for the time being the owner[2] of the property in question, except in the following circumstances[3]. If any other person is liable to make good the whole of the damage to which the payment relates, the payment must be made to him[4]. If any other person is liable to make good any part of that damage, such part of the amount of the payment must be paid to him as bears to the whole of that amount the same proportion as the scheduled cost of works[5] for which he is responsible bears to the total scheduled cost[6].

Provision is made for determining the persons who are to receive depreciation payments in special cases[7]. Where the interest in the property of any person to whom[8] the whole or part of a depreciation payment would fall to be made was subject to a mortgage at the relevant time[9], the payment or that part of the payment must be paid to the mortgagee[10]. The Secretary of State[11] may by regulations make provision as to the person to whom a depreciation payment or any part of it is to be paid in cases where the interest in the property of a person to whom[12] the whole or part of the payment would fall to be paid was at the relevant time subject to a rentcharge[13]. Where, in the case of property situated in

England or Wales, the interest in the property of the person to whom[14] the whole or part of a depreciation payment would fall to be paid is subject to a settlement or otherwise held in such manner that the person entitled to the interest would not be competent to give an effective discharge for the proceeds of a sale of the interest, that payment or that part of that payment must be paid to the person competent to give such a discharge[15]. Where the interest in the property of the person to whom the whole or part of a depreciation payment falls to be paid, or the proceeds of sale of that interest, are the subject of a devise or bequest, that devise or bequest is to be treated as including that payment or that part of that payment[16]. Where the interest in the property of the person to whom the whole or part of a depreciation payment falls to be paid is the subject of a contract of sale made before the relevant time or a notice to treat[17] served before that time under an enactment authorising the compulsory acquisition of the interest, that payment or that part of that payment must be held by that person in trust for the purchaser unless the contract is rescinded or the notice ceases to have effect[18].

1  As to depreciation payments see PARAS 217–219.
2  As to the meaning of 'owner' see PARA 207.
3  Coal Mining Subsidence Act 1991 s 15(1).
4  Coal Mining Subsidence Act 1991 s 15(2).
5  This reference to the scheduled cost of works for which the other person is responsible is a reference to the aggregate amount of the costs specified in the schedule of remedial works in respect of works required for making good the part of the damage which he is liable to make good: Coal Mining Subsidence Act 1991 s 15(4)(a). As to the schedule of remedial works see PARA 212. As to the meaning of 'works' see PARA 203.
6  Coal Mining Subsidence Act 1991 s 15(3). This reference to the total scheduled cost is a reference to the aggregate amount of all costs specified in the schedule of remedial works: s 15(4)(b).
7  See the Coal Mining Subsidence Act 1991 s 15(5), Sch 2. References in s 15, Sch 2 to a depreciation payment or part of such a payment include any interest payable in respect of that payment or that part in accordance with Sch 1 (see PARA 217): see s 15(5).
8  Ie apart from the Coal Mining Subsidence Act 1991 Sch 2 para 1 or Sch 2 para 4: see Sch 2 para 1(1).
9  Ie the time when the subsidence damage became evident: see the Coal Mining Subsidence Act 1991 Sch 2 para 1(1). As to the meaning of 'subsidence damage' see PARA 203.
10 Coal Mining Subsidence Act 1991 Sch 2 para 1(1) (amended by the Coal Industry Act 1994 ss 43(8), 67(8), Sch 6 para 11, Sch 11 Pt II). The mortgagee is liable to account for such a payment as if it had been proceeds of sale of the mortgaged interest arising under a power of sale exercised by the mortgagee at the relevant time, except that the mortgagee is not entitled to credit for any costs incurred by him in connection with the claiming, ascertainment, apportionment or making of the payment: Coal Mining Subsidence Act 1991 Sch 2 para 1(2). If at the time when the depreciation payment is made the debt secured by the mortgage (other than any part of it representing costs for which the mortgagee would not be entitled to credit) has been paid in full, the depreciation payment is to be disposed of as if the interest had not been subject to the mortgage: Sch 2 para 2(1), (2). As to the situation where the interest was subject to two or more successive mortgages see Sch 2 para 2(1), (3). Schedule 2 para 1 has effect in any case, as regards any mortgage, subject to any agreement between the mortgagee and the person who apart from that mortgage would have been entitled to receive the depreciation payment or part of that payment: Sch 2 para 2(1), (4). As to mortgages generally see MORTGAGE vol 77 (2016) PARA 101 et seq.
11 As to the Secretary of State see PARA 2.
12 Ie apart from the Coal Mining Subsidence Act 1991 Sch 2 para 2 or Sch 2 para 4: see Sch 2 para 3(1).
13 Coal Mining Subsidence Act 1991 Sch 2 para 3(1). At the date at which this volume states the law no such regulations had been made. As to the Secretary of State's power to make regulations or orders see PARA 202. For these purposes, 'rentcharge' means, in relation to property situated in England and Wales, any annual or other periodic sum charged on or issuing out of land, except rent reserved by a lease or tenancy and any sum payable by way of interest: Sch 2 para 3(2)(a). As to rentcharges generally see REAL PROPERTY AND REGISTRATION vol 87 (2017) PARA 1033 et seq.

14 Ie apart from the Coal Mining Subsidence Act 1991 Sch 2 para 4(1): see Sch 2 para 4(1).
15 Coal Mining Subsidence Act 1991 Sch 2 para 4(1). Note that as from 1 January 1997 no new settlements can be created under the Settled Land Act 1925. As to the phasing out of strict settlements and the introduction of the 'trust of land' see the Trusts of Land and Appointment of Trustees Act 1996 s 2(1); and PARA 282.
16 Coal Mining Subsidence Act 1991 Sch 2 para 5. As to devises and bequests generally see WILLS AND INTESTACY vol 102 (2016) PARA 183.
17 As to the service of a notice to treat see PARA 218. As to the meaning of 'notice' see PARA 210. As to notices see PARA 251 et seq.
18 Coal Mining Subsidence Act 1991 Sch 2 para 6(1). Any lien upon that interest to which that person is entitled by virtue of the contract extends to that payment or that part of that payment: Sch 2 para 6(2).

### 221. Payments in respect of emergency works.

Where emergency works[1] are executed by any other person, the responsible person[2] is under a duty[3] to make a payment[4] in respect of the cost of those works[5]. Emergency works are works urgently and reasonably required in order that the damaged property may continue to be used for the purposes for which it was used immediately before the damage became evident, or in order to prevent the property being affected by further subsidence damage[6]. The required payment is equal to the cost reasonably incurred by any person other than the responsible person in executing those works[7]. However, the responsible person is not required to make any payment in respect of any emergency works executed by any other person in connection with any property unless that person (1) has given to the responsible person as soon as was reasonably practicable in all the circumstances a notice[8] containing adequate particulars of those works[9]; and (2) has afforded the responsible person reasonable facilities to inspect the property, so far as he was in a position to do so[10]. The responsible person is also not required to make such a payment if the emergency works are executed after he has elected[11] to make a depreciation payment[12] in respect of the damaged property[13].

Any payment in respect of emergency works must be made to the person or persons by whom the cost of executing the works in question is (or is to be) incurred[14].

1 As to the meaning of 'works' see PARA 203.
2 As to the responsible person see PARA 204.
3 This is subject to the provisions of the Coal Mining Subsidence Act 1991 Pt II (ss 2–21): see s 2(4).
4 Ie in accordance with the Coal Mining Subsidence Act 1991 s 12: see s 2(4).
5 Coal Mining Subsidence Act 1991 s 2(4).
6 See the Coal Mining Subsidence Act 1991 s 12(1). As to the meaning of 'subsidence damage' see PARA 203.
7 See the Coal Mining Subsidence Act 1991 s 12(1).
8 As to the meaning of 'notice' see PARA 210. As to notices see PARA 251 et seq.
9 Coal Mining Subsidence Act 1991 s 12(2)(a)(i).
10 Coal Mining Subsidence Act 1991 s 12(2)(a)(ii).
11 Ie under the Coal Mining Subsidence Act 1991 s 10 (see PARA 219): see s 12(2)(b).
12 As to depreciation payments see PARAS 217–220.
13 Coal Mining Subsidence Act 1991 s 12(2)(b).
14 Coal Mining Subsidence Act 1991 s 12(3). If there are two or more such persons, the payment must be apportioned between them in such manner as may be determined by agreement or, in default of agreement, in shares corresponding to their respective shares in the cost: s 12(3).

### 222. Stop notices where further damage is likely to occur.

Where at any time (1) a damage notice[1] has been given to the responsible person[2] in respect of subsidence damage[3] to any property; and (2) it appears to be probable that further subsidence damage will occur to that property within the period of 18 months beginning with that time, the following provisions apply, and the responsible person must as soon as reasonably practicable after receiving such a notice, consider whether the condition in head (2) above is satisfied[4].

The responsible person may give to the claimant[5] and any other person interested[6] a notice to the effect that, except for emergency works[7] and such other works as may be specified in the notice (known as 'excepted works'), the responsible person will neither execute any works for making good the damage while the notice remains in force nor make any payments in respect of such works executed while the notice remains in force[8]. Such a notice in relation to any damage is a 'stop notice'[9]. The responsible person must specify in such a notice such works[10] (if any) as are required in order to render the damaged property reasonably fit to be used for the purposes for which it was used immediately before the damage became evident[11].

Where the responsible person gives a stop notice to any person with respect to any damage:

(a)     the responsible person's remedial obligation[12] to that person in respect of the damage is subject to the terms of that notice[13];

(b)     any notice affecting the required remedial action[14] in respect of the damage given by the responsible person before the stop notice is given ceases to have effect, except in so far as it relates to excepted works[15];

(c)     any schedule of remedial works[16] relating to the damage sent to that person before the stop notice is given does not take effect or, as the case may be, ceases to have effect, except in so far as it relates to excepted works and related costs[17];

(d)     any period during which the stop notice is in force is to be disregarded in reckoning the period allowed for making a claim for obligatory payments in lieu[18], except in relation to any excepted works[19]; and

(e)     so long as the stop notice is in force the responsible person is not required to give any notice of proposed remedial action[20] in respect of the damage or to send to that person any schedule of remedial works, except so far as any such notice or schedule is required for the purposes of excepted works[21].

A stop notice given to any person with respect to any damage has no effect unless it is given within the period of three months[22] beginning with the relevant time[23], or such longer period beginning with that time as may be agreed between the responsible person and that person[24].

1   As to the meaning of 'damage notice' see PARA 210. As to the meaning of 'notice' see PARA 210. As to notices see PARA 251 et seq.
2   As to the responsible person see PARA 204.
3   As to the meaning of 'subsidence damage' see PARA 203.
4   Coal Mining Subsidence Act 1991 s 16(1) (amended by the Coal Industry Act 1994 ss 43(8), 67(8), Sch 6 para 3, Sch 11 Pt II).
5   As to the meaning of 'claimant' see PARA 210.
6   As to the meaning of 'any other person interested' see PARA 210.
7   As to the meaning of 'emergency works' see PARA 221; and as to the meaning of 'works' see PARA 203.
8   Coal Mining Subsidence Act 1991 s 16(2).
9   See the Coal Mining Subsidence Act 1991 s 16(4), 52(1).
10  Ie not being emergency works or works the execution of which is not reasonably practicable in all the circumstances of the case: see the Coal Mining Subsidence Act 1991 s 16(3).
11  Coal Mining Subsidence Act 1991 s 16(3).
12  As to the meaning of 'remedial obligation' see PARA 209.
13  Coal Mining Subsidence Act 1991 s 16(5)(a).

14 As to remedial action see PARA 209.
15 Coal Mining Subsidence Act 1991 s 16(5)(b).
16 As to the schedule of remedial works see PARA 212.
17 Coal Mining Subsidence Act 1991 s 16(5)(c).
18 Ie the period mentioned in the Coal Mining Subsidence Act 1991 s 9(4) (see PARA 215). As to payments in lieu see PARAS 214–216. As to the meaning of 'claim' see PARA 210.
19 Coal Mining Subsidence Act 1991 s 16(5)(d).
20 As to the meaning of 'notice of proposed remedial action' see PARA 211.
21 Coal Mining Subsidence Act 1991 s 16(5)(e). In the case excepted from head (e) in the text, the provisions of Pt II (ss 2–21) apply as if:
  (1)    the responsible person's remedial obligation in respect of the damage were limited to such part of the damage as can be remedied or alleviated by the excepted works (s 16(5)(f)(i)); and
  (2)    references to such works as are necessary in order to make good the damage to that person's reasonable satisfaction were references to the excepted works (s 16(5)(f)(ii)).
22 The Secretary of State may by order substitute for this period (whether as originally enacted or as previously amended) such other period as he thinks fit: Coal Mining Subsidence Act 1991 s 16(8). At the date at which this volume states the law no such order had been made. As to the Secretary of State see PARA 2; and as to the Secretary of State's power to make regulations or orders see PARA 202.
23 For this purpose, 'the relevant time' means: (1) the time when it first appears to be probable that further subsidence damage will occur to the property within the next succeeding period of 18 months; or (2) any later time when it first appears that any such damage will be substantially more serious than appeared at that earlier time: Coal Mining Subsidence Act 1991 s 16(7) (amended by the Coal Industry Act 1994 ss 43(8), 67(8), Sch 6 para 3, Sch 11 Pt II).
24 Coal Mining Subsidence Act 1991 s 16(6).

### 223.   Revocation and review of stop notices.

The responsible person[1] is under a duty to revoke a stop notice[2] relating to any damage to any property if:

  (1)    at any time, it no longer appears to be probable that further damage will occur to that property within the period of 18 months beginning with that time[3]; or

  (2)    at any time after the end of the period of three years[4] beginning with the relevant date[5], the claimant[6] and any other person interested[7] request the responsible person to revoke it[8].

Where a stop notice has been given with respect to any damage, the responsible person must consider, initially not later than 12 months after the date on which the notice was given and subsequently at intervals not exceeding 12 months, whether to revoke it[9]. Where a stop notice given to any person with respect to any damage is revoked a fresh notice of proposed remedial action[10] relating to the damage (or to so much of it as has not been made good by any emergency works[11] or any excepted works[12]) must be given by the responsible person to that person as soon as reasonably practicable after the date of the revocation[13]. Any such notice of proposed remedial action which is effective immediately before that date ceases to have effect on the giving of the fresh notice[14] and any schedule of remedial works[15] relating to the damage which is effective immediately before that date also ceases to have effect when the schedule of remedial works sent[16] in connection with the fresh notice of proposed remedial action comes into effect[17].

1   As to the responsible person see PARA 204.
2   As to the meaning of 'stop notice' see PARA 222. As to the meaning of 'notice' see PARA 210. As to notices see PARA 251 et seq.
3   Coal Mining Subsidence Act 1991 s 17(1)(a) (amended by the Coal Industry Act 1994 ss 43(8), 67(8), Sch 6 para 3, Sch 11 Pt II).

4  The Secretary of State may by order substitute for this period (whether as originally enacted or as previously amended) such other period as he thinks fit: Coal Mining Subsidence Act 1991 s 17(5). At the date at which this volume states the law no such order had been made. As to the Secretary of State see PARA 2; and as to the Secretary of State's power to make regulations or orders see PARA 202.

5  For these purposes, the 'relevant date', in relation to a stop notice, means: (1) the date on which the stop notice was given; or (2) where one or more previous stop notices had been given in respect of the whole or any part of the damage, the date on which that notice or, as the case may be, the first of those notices was given: Coal Mining Subsidence Act 1991 s 17(4).

6  As to the meaning of 'claimant' see PARA 210.

7  As to the meaning of 'any other person interested' see PARA 210.

8  Coal Mining Subsidence Act 1991 s 17(1)(b).

9  Coal Mining Subsidence Act 1991 s 17(2). On any occasion when in pursuance of s 17(2) the responsible person considers whether to revoke a stop notice he must give notice of his decision to the person to whom the stop notice was given as soon as he has made it: s 17(6).

10  As to the meaning of 'notice of proposed remedial action' see PARA 211.

11  As to the meaning of 'emergency works' see PARA 221.

12  Ie within the meaning of the Coal Mining Subsidence Act 1991 s 16 (see PARA 222): see s 17(3)(a).

13  Coal Mining Subsidence Act 1991 s 17(3)(a).

14  Coal Mining Subsidence Act 1991 s 17(3)(b).

15  As to the schedule of remedial works see PARA 212.

16  Ie under the Coal Mining Subsidence Act 1991 s 6(1) (see PARA 212): see s 17(3)(c).

17  Coal Mining Subsidence Act 1991 s 17(3)(c).

## 224. The effect of further damage.

Where a damage notice[1] has been given to the responsible person[2] in respect of subsidence damage[3] to any property and further subsidence damage to that property becomes evident in certain circumstances[4], the original damage and the further damage are to be treated as one and a fresh damage notice will only be required if, before the further damage becomes evident, the responsible person has elected[5] to make a payment in lieu[6] instead of executing any remedial works[7]. Any notice affecting the required remedial action[8] in respect of the original damage given before the further damage becomes evident ceases to have effect[9]. Where a fresh damage notice is not required, a fresh notice of proposed remedial action[10] relating to the combined damage must be given by the responsible person to the claimant[11] and any other person interested[12] as soon as reasonably practicable after the further damage becomes evident[13]. Any schedule of remedial works[14] relating to the original damage sent to the claimant or any other person interested before the further damage becomes evident does not take effect or, as the case may be, ceases to have effect[15]. Any stop notice[16] given to any person with respect to the original damage has effect in relation to the combined damage as if there were specified in it as excepted works such works (if any) as may be specified by the responsible person[17]. The responsible person, the claimant and any other person interested may agree that certain effects of further damage do not apply or are to be modified[18].

These provisions are without prejudice to any liability of the responsible person in respect of the cost of any works executed before the further damage becomes evident[19].

1  As to the meaning of 'damage notice' see PARA 210. As to the meaning of 'notice' see PARA 210. As to notices see PARA 251 et seq.

2  As to the responsible person see PARA 204.

3  As to the meaning of 'subsidence damage' see PARA 203.

4  Coal Mining Subsidence Act 1991 s 18(1). The circumstances referred to in the text are that:
    (1)    the further damage becomes evident before the completion of remedial works or, in a

case falling within s 8(4) (see PARA 216), before all sums in respect of which the responsible person is liable to make payments have been expended (s 18(2)(a)); and

(2)    at the time when it becomes evident, the responsible person has neither elected under s 10 (see PARA 219) nor become liable under s 11(1) (see PARA 218) to make a depreciation payment in respect of the damaged property (s 18(2)(b)).

As to depreciation payments see PARAS 217–220.

5  Ie under the Coal Mining Subsidence Act 1991 s 8 (see PARA 216): see s 18(3)(a).

6  As to payments in lieu see PARAS 214–216.

7  Coal Mining Subsidence Act 1991 s 18(3)(a).

8  As to remedial action see PARA 209.

9  Coal Mining Subsidence Act 1991 s 18(3)(b). Accordingly, Pt II (ss 2–21) applies as if that notice had not been given: s 18(3)(b).

10  As to the meaning of 'notice of proposed remedial action' see PARA 211.

11  As to the meaning of 'claimant' see PARA 210.

12  As to the meaning of 'any other person interested' see PARA 210.

13  Coal Mining Subsidence Act 1991 s 18(3)(c).

14  As to the schedule of remedial works see PARA 212.

15  Coal Mining Subsidence Act 1991 s 18(3)(d). If the aggregate amount of the costs specified in a fresh schedule of remedial works does not exceed the aggregate amount of the costs specified in any schedule of remedial works to which s 18(3)(d) applies by more than 20% (or such percentage as the Secretary of State may by order substitute as he thinks fit: see s 18(8)), s 6(3), (4) (see PARA 212) does not apply and s 6(5)(a) has effect as if for s 6(5)(a)(i), (ii) there were substituted a reference to the date on which the schedule is sent to the claimant or any other person interested: s 18(3)(e), (4).

16  As to the meaning of 'stop notice' see PARA 222.

17  Coal Mining Subsidence Act 1991 s 18(3)(f). The responsible person must specify in such a notice such works (if any) as are required in order to render the damaged property reasonably fit to be used for the purposes for which it was used immediately before the original damage became evident, not being emergency works, or works the execution of which is not reasonably practicable in all the circumstances of the case: s 18(5). Note that the references to remedial works in s 8(8), (10) (see PARA 216) do not include any remedial works begun before the further damage becomes evident: s 18(3)(g).

18  Ie they may agree: (1) that the Coal Mining Subsidence Act 1991 s 18(3)(a)–(e) does not apply; and (2) that any such notice or schedule as is mentioned in s 18(3)(b) or s 18(3)(d) has effect in relation to the combined damage with such modifications as may be so agreed: see s 18(6).

19  Coal Mining Subsidence Act 1991 s 18(7).

## (b)   Special Cases

## 225. Ancient monuments and listed buildings.

Where certain ancient monuments[1] and listed buildings[2] are affected by subsidence damage[3] and the character of the property as one of historic, architectural, archaeological or other special interest is or may be affected by that damage, then in so far as it is reasonably practicable and in the public interest so to restore the property to its former condition[4] as to maintain its character as one of special interest, the statutory provisions relating to remedial action[5] have effect with modifications[6]. Any question arising[7] as to whether or how far it is reasonably practicable or in the public interest to restore any such property is to be determined by the Secretary of State[8].

1  Ie any property which (1) is for the time being included in the Schedule of monuments compiled and maintained under the Ancient Monuments and Archaeological Areas Act 1979 s 1 (see NATIONAL CULTURAL HERITAGE vol 77 (2016) PARA 1014 et seq); and (2) has been notified to the responsible person by the Secretary of State as an ancient monument within the meaning of the Ancient Monuments and Archaeological Areas Act 1979 for the time being under the care of the Secretary of State: Coal Mining Subsidence Act 1991 s 19(1)(a), (b). As to the responsible person see PARA 204. As to the Secretary of State see PARA 2. As to ancient monuments generally see NATIONAL CULTURAL HERITAGE vol 77 (2016) PARA 1006 et seq.

2  Ie any property which is a listed building within the meaning of the Planning (Listed Buildings and Conservation Areas) Act 1990 s 1 (see PLANNING vol 83 (2018) PARA 1181) and is not of a description specified in an order made by the Secretary of State: Coal Mining Subsidence Act 1991 s 19(1)(c).

3  As to the meaning of 'subsidence damage' see PARA 203.

4  For these purposes, 'former condition', in relation to any property, means a condition comparable to its condition immediately before the subsidence damage occurred: Coal Mining Subsidence Act 1991 s 19(4).

5  Ie under the Coal Mining Subsidence Act 1991 Pt II (ss 2–21): see s 19(2). As to remedial action see PARA 209.

6  Coal Mining Subsidence Act 1991 s 19(2). The provisions of Pt II apply in relation to the damage as if s 6(2)(a) (see PARA 212) defined 'remedial works' as such works as are necessary for the purpose of so restoring the property, and as if s 10 (see PARA 219) were omitted: s 19(2).

7  Ie by virtue of the Coal Mining Subsidence Act 1991 s 19(2): see s 19(3).

8  Coal Mining Subsidence Act 1991 s 19(3).

## 226. Ecclesiastical property etc.

The diocesan board of finance for the diocese in which the land is situated[1] is entitled, in addition to any other person entitled, to give a damage notice[2] in respect of subsidence damage[3] to any ecclesiastical property[4], and where any other such person is the claimant[5], the diocesan board of finance for the diocese in which the land is situated is to be treated as another person interested[6] whether or not it gives such a notice[7]. Any depreciation payment[8] in respect of ecclesiastical property which would otherwise fall to be made to the owner[9] of the property is to be made to the diocesan board of finance for the diocese in which the land is situated[10] and applied by it for the purposes for which the proceeds of a sale of the property by agreement would be applicable under any enactment or Measure authorising, or disposing of the proceeds of, such a sale[11]. Where a depreciation payment, in relation to any property other than ecclesiastical property would otherwise fall to be made to a person whose interest in the property is held for religious purposes, and a request[12] for payment is made to the responsible person[13] by or on behalf of the representative body[14], the payment must be made to that body[15].

1  As diocesan boards of finance see ECCLESIASTICAL LAW vol 34 (2011) PARA 241 et seq.

2  As to the meaning of 'damage notice' see PARA 210.

3  As to the meaning of 'subsidence damage' see PARA 203.

4  For this purpose, 'ecclesiastical property' means property in England belonging to any ecclesiastical benefice of the Church of England, or being or forming part of a church subject to the jurisdiction of a bishop of any diocese of the Church of England or the site of such a church, or being or forming part of a burial ground subject to such jurisdiction: Coal Mining Subsidence Act 1991 s 20(4) (amended by the Church of England (Miscellaneous Provisions) Measure 2006 Sch 5 para 29(1)).

5  As to the meaning of 'claimant' see PARA 210.

6  As to the meaning of 'any other person interested' see PARA 210.

7  Coal Mining Subsidence Act 1991 s 20(1) (amended by the Church of England (Miscellaneous Provisions) Measure 2006 Sch 5 para 29(1)). As to preventive works on ecclesiastical property see PARA 240.

8  Ie under the Coal Mining Subsidence Act 1991 s 10 (see PARA 219) or s 11 (see PARA 218): see s 20(2). As to depreciation payments see PARAS 217–220.

9  As to the meaning of 'owner' see PARA 207.

10  Coal Mining Subsidence Act 1991 s 20(2)(a) (amended by the Church of England (Miscellaneous Provisions) Measure 2006 Sch 5 para 29(1)).

11  Coal Mining Subsidence Act 1991 s 20(2)(b) (amended by the Church of England (Miscellaneous Provisions) Measure 2006 Sch 5 para 29(1)).

12  As to the meaning of 'request' see PARA 207.

13  As to the responsible person see PARA 204.

14 'The representative body', in relation to property of any description held for religious purposes, means the body of persons (if any) which, in relation to that property or property of that description, has been notified to the responsible person by the Secretary of State, after consultation with such persons and organisations as he may think appropriate: Coal Mining Subsidence Act 1991 s 20(4). As to the Secretary of State see PARA 2.

15 Coal Mining Subsidence Act 1991 s 20(3).

## 227. Property belonging to protected tenants.

Where property belonging to a protected tenant[1] is affected by subsidence damage and neither he nor any other person would be liable to make good the damage in whole or in part[2], then subject to certain restrictions, he is to be treated as a person liable to make good that damage either in whole or in part[3].

Where in the case of any damaged property it is claimed that a person who[4] is neither the owner[5] of, nor liable to make good in whole or in part the damage to, the property falls to be treated as so liable by virtue of the provision described above, and a damage notice is given in respect of the property, whether by that or any other person, that person is not to be treated as so liable except where[6]:

(1)      it is agreed between the person in question and his landlord before the end of the period of one month beginning with the first giving of a damage notice in respect of the property, or it is determined in proceedings[7] begun before the end of that period, that he is a protected tenant and the property belongs to him[8]; and

(2)      notice[9] of that agreement or of the beginning of those proceedings has been given to the responsible person[10] before the end of that period[11].

1    For the purposes of the Coal Mining Subsidence Act 1991 s 21, Sch 3, property affected by subsidence damage belongs to a protected tenant if he would have been entitled under any enactment contained in the relevant Act or Acts to remove the property, or to be paid compensation in respect of it by his landlord, if his tenancy had terminated immediately before the damage occurred: s 21(2). As to the meaning of 'subsidence damage' see PARA 203. For these purposes, 'protected tenant' means a person who is: (1) a tenant for the purposes of the Landlord and Tenant Act 1927 Pt I (ss 1–17) (see LANDLORD AND TENANT) or the Agricultural Holdings Act 1986 (see AGRICULTURAL LAND vol 1 (2008) PARA 323); or (2) a tenant under a farm business tenancy within the meaning of the Agricultural Tenancies Act 1995 (see AGRICULTURAL LAND vol 1 (2008) PARA 302): Coal Mining Subsidence Act 1991 s 21(3)(a), (aa) (added by the Agricultural Tenancies Act 1995 s 40, Schedule para 36). References, in relation to a protected tenant, to the relevant Act or Acts are to be construed accordingly: Coal Mining Subsidence Act 1991 s 21(3).
     Any question arising in relation to any property as to whether or not any person is a protected tenant is to be determined as if it had arisen under the relevant Act or Acts: Sch 3 para 1(4). Where the liability of the responsible person to comply with any statutory requirement relating to remedial action (see Pt II (ss 2–21)) in consequence of the giving of a damage notice depends on the determination of the question whether or not a person falls to be treated as liable, the responsible person is not to be required to comply with that requirement until it is established whether or not that person falls to be so treated: Sch 3 para 2(3). As to the meaning of 'damage notice' see PARA 210. As to the meaning of 'notice' see PARA 210. As to notices see PARA 251 et seq.

2    Ie apart from the provisions of the Coal Mining Subsidence Act 1991 Sch 3: see s 21(1).

3    Coal Mining Subsidence Act 1991 s 21(1), Sch 3 para 1(1). The protected tenant is liable to meet such part of the cost of making good the whole of the damage as is given by the formula set out in Sch 3 para 1(3) if, by reason of any other enactment contained in the relevant Act or Acts, compensation in respect of the damaged property would have been payable to the protected tenant of less than the amount provided for by whichever of the following enactments would otherwise have been applicable: (1) the Landlord and Tenant Act 1927 s 1(1); (2) the Agricultural Holdings Act 1986 s 66(1), Sch 9 Pt I para 2(1); and (3) the Agricultural Tenancies Act 1995 s 20: Coal Mining Subsidence Act 1991 Sch 3 para 1(1), (2) (amended by the Agricultural Tenancies Act 1995 Schedule para 37). As to the enactments mentioned in heads (1)–(3) see AGRICULTURAL LAND. As to the formula for calculating the cost of making good the damage see the Coal Mining Subsidence Act 1991 Sch 3 para 1(3).

Any question arising as to the amount of any compensation which would have been payable to the protected tenant under the relevant Act or Acts is to be determined as if it had arisen under the relevant Act or Acts: Sch 3 para 1(4).

4   Ie apart from the provisions of Coal Mining Subsidence Act 1991 Sch 3: see Sch 3 para 2(1).

5   As to the meaning of 'owner' see PARA 207.

6   Coal Mining Subsidence Act 1991 Sch 3 para 2(1).

7   Ie proceedings by virtue of the Coal Mining Subsidence Act 1991 Sch 3 para 1(4): see Sch 3 para 2(2)(a). Proceedings to determine by arbitration whether or not a person is a protected tenant by virtue of the Agricultural Holdings Act 1986 are deemed to be begun when either (1) an arbitrator has been appointed by agreement between that person and his landlord; or (2) an application for the appointment of an arbitrator has been made by that person or his landlord to the President of the Royal Institution of Chartered Surveyors or, as the case may be, the Secretary of State: Coal Mining Subsidence Act 1991 Sch 3 para 2(4). As to arbitration generally see ARBITRATION vol 2 (2017) PARA 501 et seq.

8   Coal Mining Subsidence Act 1991 Sch 3 para 2(2)(a).

9   As to the meaning of 'notice' see PARA 210. As to notices see PARA 251 et seq.

10  As to the responsible person see PARA 204.

11  Coal Mining Subsidence Act 1991 Sch 3 para 2(2)(b).

### (c)   Dwelling-houses Rendered Uninhabitable

**228.   Home loss payments.**
Where a dwelling-house[1] is affected by subsidence damage[2], a person displaced[3] from it is entitled in certain circumstances to receive a home loss payment from the responsible person[4] if:

(1)    by reason of deterioration due to the subsidence damage in the condition of the dwelling-house, it cannot reasonably be rendered fit to be used as such[5]; and

(2)    the dwelling-house is not used as such by or with the authority of the person who immediately before the deterioration in its condition was entitled to possession of it[6].

A person is not entitled to a home loss payment unless, throughout the period of one year ending with the date of displacement, he has been in occupation of the dwelling-house (or a substantial part of it) as his only or main residence, and he has been in such occupation by virtue of a specified interest or right[7]. A person is also not entitled to a home loss payment so long as any application made by him to challenge the validity of a notice[8] given by the responsible person has neither been determined nor withdrawn[9]. The responsible person is not liable to make such a payment except on a claim[10] made by the person entitled to it giving such particulars as the responsible person may reasonably require to determine whether the payment should be made and, if so, its amount[11]. Provision is made for the calculation of the amount of the home loss payment[12].

Where a person is entitled to such a payment, it must be made within the period of three months beginning with the date on which the claim is made[13]. Where a person ('the deceased') entitled to a home loss payment dies without having claimed it, a claim may be made, by a person[14] who, throughout a period of not less than one year ending with the date of displacement of the deceased, has resided in the dwelling-house (or a substantial part of it) as his only or main residence, and is entitled to benefit by virtue of testamentary dispositions taking effect on, or the law of intestate succession or the right of survivorship between joint tenants as applied to, the death of the deceased[15]. Where there are two or more persons entitled to make a claim to a home loss payment in respect of the same dwelling-house[16] the payment to be made on each claim is equal to the whole amount of the home loss payment divided by the number of such persons[17].

1   As to the meaning of 'dwelling-house' see PARA 216. Where the claimant has successively been in occupation of different dwelling-houses in the same building, being dwelling-houses consisting of a room or rooms not constructed or structurally adapted for use as a separate dwelling, the Coal Mining Subsidence Act 1991 s 22(1), Sch 4 paras 1(2), 3(3)–(5) have effect as if those dwelling-houses were the same dwelling-house: Sch 4 para 3(6). As to the meaning of 'the claimant' see PARA 210.

2   As to the meaning of 'subsidence damage' see PARA 203.

3   The provisions of the Coal Mining Subsidence Act 1991 Sch 4 do not apply in any case where the displacement occurred before 30 November 1991: s 53(1), Sch 7 para 3(1)(a).

4   Coal Mining Subsidence Act 1991 s 22(1), Sch 4 para 1(1). As to the responsible person see PARA 204.

5   Coal Mining Subsidence Act 1991 s 22(2)(a).

6   Coal Mining Subsidence Act 1991 s 22(2)(b).

7   Coal Mining Subsidence Act 1991 Sch 4 para 1(2). However, if those conditions are satisfied on the date of displacement, a discretionary payment may be made to him of an amount not exceeding that to which he would have been entitled if he had satisfied those conditions throughout that period: Sch 4 para 1(2). As to the calculation of the period see Sch 4 para 3(3), (4).

     The specified interests and rights mentioned in the text are:

     (1)    any interest in the dwelling-house (Sch 4 para 1(4)(a));

     (2)    a right to occupy the dwelling-house as a statutory tenant within the meaning of the Rent Act 1977 or under a restricted contract within the meaning of that Act or a contract which would be such a contract if the contract or dwelling-house were not excluded by s 19(4) or s 19(5)(b) (s 19 repealed in relation to contracts entered into after 15 January 1989) (Coal Mining Subsidence Act 1991 Sch 4 para 1(4)(b));

     (3)    a right to occupy the dwelling-house under a licence to which the Housing Act 1985 Pt IV (ss 79–117) (secure tenancies), or the Housing Act 1996 Pt V Ch I (ss 124–143) (introductory tenancies) applies (Coal Mining Subsidence Act 1991 Sch 4 para 1(4)(d) (amended by SI 1997/74));

     (4)    a right to occupy the dwelling-house under a contract of employment (Coal Mining Subsidence Act 1991 Sch 4 para 1(4)(e)).

     Where an interest in a dwelling-house is vested in trustees (other than a sole tenant for life within the meaning of the Settled Land Act 1925) and a person beneficially entitled (whether directly or derivatively) under the trust is entitled or permitted by reason of his interest to occupy the dwelling-house, he is to be treated for these purposes as occupying it by virtue of an interest in the dwelling-house: Coal Mining Subsidence Act 1991 Sch 4 para 1(5). As to the phasing out of strict settlements and the introduction of the 'trust of land' see the Trusts of Land and Appointment of Trustees Act 1996 s 2(1); and PARA 282.

8   Ie an application under the Coal Mining Subsidence Act 1991 s 23(1), Sch 5 para 3(3) to challenge the validity of a notice given by the responsible person under Sch 5 para 3(1)(b) (see PARA 229): see Sch 4 para 1(3).

9   Coal Mining Subsidence Act 1991 Sch 4 para 1(3).

10   As to the meaning of 'claim' see PARA 210.

11   Coal Mining Subsidence Act 1991 Sch 4 para 3(1).

12   See the Coal Mining Subsidence Act 1991 Sch 4 para 2. Where a person who on the date of displacement is occupying, or is treated for the purposes of Sch 4 para 1 as occupying, the dwelling-house by virtue of an 'owner's interest' (ie the interest of a person who is an owner as defined in the Acquisition of Land Act 1981 s 7 (see COMPULSORY ACQUISITION OF LAND vol 18 (2009) PARA 560): Coal Mining Subsidence Act 1991 Sch 4 para 2(5)), the amount of the home loss payment is the aggregate of:

     (1)     10% of the value of his interest in the dwelling-house or, as the case may be, the interest in the dwelling-house vested in trustees, subject to a maximum of £15,000 and a minimum of £1,500 (Sch 4 para 2(1)(a)); and

     (2)    his reasonable expenses in removing from the dwelling-house (Sch 4 para 2(1)(b)).

     In the case of any other person, the amount of the home loss payment is the aggregate of £1,500 and his reasonable expenses in removing from the dwelling-house: Sch 4 para 2(2). References to the value of an interest in the dwelling-house are to be taken to be a reference to the value of that interest immediately before the deterioration in the condition of the dwelling-house:

see s 14(4), Sch 1 para 2, Sch 4 para 2(4). The Secretary of State may from time to time by regulations prescribe a different maximum or minimum for the purposes of head (1) and a different amount for the purposes of head (2): Sch 4 para 2(3). At the date at which this volume states the law no such regulations had been made. As to the Secretary of State see PARA 2; and as to the Secretary of State's power to make regulations or orders see PARA 202.

13 Coal Mining Subsidence Act 1991 Sch 4 para 3(2).

14 The person must not be under the age of 18 years: see the Coal Mining Subsidence Act 1991 Sch 4 para 3(5).

15 Coal Mining Subsidence Act 1991 Sch 4 para 3(5). As to testamentary dispositions and intestate succession see WILLS AND INTESTACY vol 102 (2016) PARAS 1 et seq, 477 et seq. As to survivorship between joint tenants see REAL PROPERTY AND REGISTRATION vol 87 (2017) PARA 202; WILLS AND INTESTACY vol 102 (2016) PARA 29.

16 Ie whether by virtue of joint occupation or of Coal Mining Subsidence Act 1991 Sch 4 para 3(5): see Sch 4 para 3(7).

17 Coal Mining Subsidence Act 1991 Sch 4 para 3(7).

## 229. Relief for temporary dispossession.

Where a dwelling-house[1] is affected by subsidence damage[2], a person temporarily dispossessed[3] of the dwelling-house has a right to certain relief as respects any period during which[4]:

(1)     by reason of deterioration due to the subsidence damage in the condition of the dwelling-house, and having regard to the time which will be required to remedy that deterioration, the dwelling-house is not in a reasonably fit state for it to be used as such[5]; and

(2)     the dwelling-house is not used as such by or with the authority of the person who immediately before the deterioration in its condition was entitled to possession of it[6].

In the case of any resident[7], the responsible person[8], so long as the period of dispossession[9] lasts, is under an obligation at all times[10]:

(a)     to make available alternative living accommodation which is of a standard comparable to the general standard of the housing accommodation under the management of the local authority[11] and is otherwise reasonable having regard to all the circumstances, including the probable duration of the period of dispossession[12]; or

(b)     to pay to the resident the amount, if any, by which the aggregate expenditure reasonably incurred by him by way of rent[13], food, living accommodation, heating, light and other household expenses exceeds what it would have been if the subsidence damage had not occurred and he had continued to reside in the dwelling-house[14].

The responsible person is not under any such obligation in respect of any part of the period of dispossession during which, irrespective of the subsidence damage, the resident in question would not have been residing at the dwelling-house[15]. Where the responsible person is under an obligation under head (a) or head (b) above[16], he is also under an obligation to pay the resident's reasonable expenses in removing from the dwelling-house of which he is temporarily dispossessed[17], and to pay him any expenses reasonably incurred by him in consequence of the temporary dispossession[18].

Subject to certain exceptions[19], the responsible person's obligations under head (a) and head (b) above cease towards any resident notwithstanding that the period of dispossession has not expired (i) if the occupier[20] has ceased (otherwise than by reason of his death) to be entitled to possession of the dwelling-house or, as the case may be, of the site of it[21]; or (ii) on the expiration of a period of six months from the service by the responsible person on the resident in question of notice[22] of the responsible person's opinion that the period of dispossession will continue indefinitely or will be unreasonably long[23], or that the resident in question will not resume residence at the dwelling-house or on its site at the expiration of that period[24].

The responsible person is not under any obligation by virtue of head (a) or head (b) above unless either the owner or the occupier of the dwelling-house is a resident and (A) has given notice to the responsible person, within the prescribed time and containing prescribed particulars[25], that in his opinion that by reason of deterioration due to the subsidence damage in the condition of the dwelling-house, and having regard to the time required to remedy that deterioration, the house is not in a reasonably fit state for it to be used as such[26]; and (B) has afforded the responsible person reasonable facilities to inspect the dwelling-house so far as he was in a position to afford such facilities[27].

Where the responsible person has made alternative living accommodation available to a resident[28], the responsible person is entitled to possession of that accommodation in certain circumstances[29]. He is also entitled to recover as a civil debt from the resident in question any amount by which the aggregate expenditure incurred by him by way of rent is less than it would have been if the subsidence damage had not occurred and he had continued to reside in the dwelling-house[30], but the responsible person is not entitled to recover an amount in excess of that which would have been payable by way of rent for the alternative living accommodation if it had been provided by the local authority[31].

Where no damage notice has been given in respect of the dwelling-house, or the responsible person has elected to make a discretionary payment in lieu[32] or a discretionary depreciation payment[33] or is obliged to make a depreciation payment[34], the responsible person may exercise in the name of the occupier any right with respect to the repair of the dwelling-house exercisable by the occupier against anyone other than the responsible person[36].

1   As to the meaning of 'dwelling-house' see PARA 216.
2   As to the meaning of 'subsidence damage' see PARA 203.
3   The Coal Mining Subsidence Act 1991 s 23(1), Sch 5 does not apply in any case where the period of dispossession began before 30 November 1991 (s 53(1), Sch 7 para 3(1)(b)), and nothing in the Coal Mining Subsidence Act 1991 affects the operation of the Coal-Mining (Subsidence) Act 1957 (repealed) in relation to any case where the period of dispossession began before that date (Coal Mining Subsidence Act 1991 Sch 7 para 3(2)(a)).
4   Coal Mining Subsidence Act 1991 s 23(1).
5   Coal Mining Subsidence Act 1991 s 23(2)(a).
6   Coal Mining Subsidence Act 1991 s 23(2)(b).
7   For these purposes, 'resident' means any person ordinarily resident in the dwelling-house during the period immediately preceding the deterioration in its condition: Coal Mining Subsidence Act 1991 Sch 5 para 1.
8   As to the responsible person see PARA 204.
9   For these purposes, the 'period of dispossession' means the period during which the requirements of the Coal Mining Subsidence Act 1991 s 23(2) are satisfied: Sch 5 para 1.
10   Subject to the Coal Mining Subsidence Act 1991 Sch 5 para 4(2), (3), and without prejudice to his liability under Sch 5 para 2(1) in respect of any part of the period of dispossession falling before the making of his election, the responsible person may elect which of the two courses open to him set out in head (a) and head (b) in the text he will for the time being adopt in any particular case: Sch 5 para 2(3).
11   For these purposes, the 'local authority' means the local authority within the meaning of the Housing Act 1985 (see HOUSING vol 56 (2017) PARA 12) in whose area the dwelling-house is situated: Coal Mining Subsidence Act 1991 Sch 5 para 1.
12   Coal Mining Subsidence Act 1991 Sch 5 para 2(1)(a).

13 For these purposes, 'rent' includes any mortgage interest, interest on a heritable security, service charges or water charges payable in respect of a dwelling-house and any community charges payable in respect of periods of residence in, or periods of having an interest in, a dwelling-house: Coal Mining Subsidence Act 1991 Sch 5 para 1. Note that no person is subject to a community charge in England and Wales in respect of any day falling after 31 March 1993: see the Local Government Finance Act 1992 s 100(1), (2)(a); and LOCAL GOVERNMENT FINANCE vol 70 (2018) PARA 344. For financial years from 1 April 1993, residents of chargeable dwellings in England and Wales are liable to pay council tax in accordance with the provisions of Pt I (ss 1–69): see LOCAL GOVERNMENT FINANCE vol 70 (2018) PARA 348 et seq.

14 Coal Mining Subsidence Act 1991 Sch 5 para 2(1)(b).

15 Coal Mining Subsidence Act 1991 Sch 5 para 2(2).

16 Ie under the Coal Mining Subsidence Act 1991 Sch 5 para 2(1).

17 Coal Mining Subsidence Act 1991 Sch 5 para 2(4)(a).

18 Coal Mining Subsidence Act 1991 Sch 5 para 2(4)(b).

19 See the Coal Mining Subsidence Act 1991 Sch 5 para 3(2), (3).

20 For these purposes, 'occupier' means the person who immediately before the deterioration in the condition of the dwelling-house was entitled to possession of it: Coal Mining Subsidence Act 1991 Sch 5 para 1.

21 Coal Mining Subsidence Act 1991 Sch 5 para 3(1)(a).

22 Any person upon whom such a notice is served may apply to the county court, which, if satisfied that there are not reasonable grounds for the opinion of the responsible person, may declare the notice to be of no effect: Coal Mining Subsidence Act 1991 Sch 5 para 3(3). As to the meaning of 'notice' see PARA 210. As to notices see PARA 251 et seq.

23 Coal Mining Subsidence Act 1991 Sch 5 para 3(1)(b)(i). Where a damage notice (as to which see PARA 210) has been given in respect of the dwelling-house, the responsible person is not entitled under Sch 5 para 3(1)(b)(i) to give a notice: (1) unless the responsible person has elected to make a payment under s 8 (see PARA 216) or s 10 (see PARA 219) or is obliged to make a payment under s 11(1) (see PARA 218) (Sch 5 para 3(2)(a)); or (2) while a notice under s 16(2) (see PARA 222) is in force with respect to the dwelling-house (Sch 5 para 3(2)(b)).

24 Coal Mining Subsidence Act 1991 Sch 5 para 3(1)(b)(ii).

25 See the Coal Mining Subsidence (Notices and Claims) Regulations 1991, SI 1991/2509, reg 4, Sch 2.

26 See the Coal Mining Subsidence Act 1991 s 23(2)(a), Sch 5 para 4(1)(a)8.

27 See the Coal Mining Subsidence Act 1991 Sch 5 para 4(1)(b). As soon as reasonably practicable after receiving such a notice the responsible person must give to that person notice (1) as to whether or not he agrees with that person's opinion; and (2) if he so agrees, as to the manner in which he proposes to discharge his obligations under heads (a) and (b) in the text, and where it appears appropriate to the responsible person to do so, he may serve a separate notice on any other resident: Sch 5 para 4(2). In giving such a notice, the responsible person must not unreasonably refuse any request from a resident to adopt in his case such of the alternatives set out in heads (a) and (b) in the text as is specified in the request: Sch 5 para 4(3). Where the responsible person has given notice to any resident of an intention to adopt either of these alternatives, he must not adopt the other alternative without his consent, which must not be unreasonably withheld: Sch 5 para 4(4).

28 Ie under head (a) in the text.

29 Coal Mining Subsidence Act 1991 Sch 5 para 5(1). In a case falling within head (ii) in the text the responsible person is entitled to possession of the accommodation at the expiration of the period of six months mentioned there: Sch 5 para 5(2)(a). The responsible person is entitled to the possession of the accommodation without prejudice to any of his obligations under head (a) or head (b) in the text or to the provisions of Sch 5 para 4(4) at any time not less than one month after the responsible person has given notice to the resident in question of his intention to take possession (Sch 5 para 5(2)(b)), and where such notice is given the responsible person's obligations under head (a) and head (b) in the text continue until the expiration of the month mentioned in Sch 5 para 5(2)(b), or such longer period as may be specified in the notice, notwithstanding that the period of dispossession may have expired (Sch 5 para 5(3)).

30 Coal Mining Subsidence Act 1991 Sch 5 para 5(4). The responsible person is under an obligation to pay to the resident in question:

    (1)    any amount by which the aggregate expenditure incurred by him by way of rent is greater than it would have been if the subsidence damage had not occurred and he had continued to reside in the dwelling-house (Sch 5 para 5(5)(a)); and

(2)      any amount by which he shows that the aggregate expenditure reasonably incurred by him by way of food, living accommodation (other than rent), heating, light and other household expenses is greater than it would have been in those circumstances (Sch 5 para 5(5)(b)).

In any case where the responsible person is entitled to recover an amount by virtue of Sch 5 para 5(4), and is under an obligation to pay an amount by virtue of head (2), the two amounts are be set off one against the other and extinguished or reduced accordingly: Sch 5 para 5(6).

31   Coal Mining Subsidence Act 1991 Sch 5 para 5(7).
32   See the Coal Mining Subsidence Act 1991 s 8; and PARA 216.
33   See the Coal Mining Subsidence Act 1991 s 10; and PARA 219.
34   See the Coal Mining Subsidence Act 1991 s 11(1); and PARA 218.
36   Coal Mining Subsidence Act 1991 Sch 5 para 6(1), (2). This right is exercisable during any period while the responsible person is under an obligation by virtue of head (a) and head (b) in the text: see Sch 5 para 6(2).

## 230. Care of vacant dwelling-houses.

Where (1) by reason of deterioration due to the subsidence damage[1] in the condition of the dwelling-house[2], and having regard to the time which will be required to remedy that deterioration, the dwelling-house is not in a reasonably fit state for it to be used as such, and it is not used as such by or with the authority of the person who immediately before the deterioration in its condition was entitled to possession of it[3]; and (2) notice[4] of that fact is given to the responsible person[5] by the occupier[6], the responsible person must take reasonable steps for (a) preventing or minimising the risk of the house or its contents suffering loss or damage while it is unoccupied; and (b) inspecting the house for the purpose of discovering whether any such loss or damage has occurred[7]. The steps which it may be reasonable to take include, in particular, steps for keeping the dwelling-house weatherproof and secure against persons seeking to enter it as trespassers[8]. However, this ceases to apply on the occurrence of certain specified events[9] notwithstanding that the statutory requirements continue to be satisfied[10].

Where the responsible person requests permission from the occupier to remove and place in storage at the responsible person's own expense any of the contents of the dwelling-house, the responsible person is not liable[11] for any loss or damage to any of those contents as respects which such permission is unreasonably refused[12].

1   As to the meaning of 'subsidence damage' see PARA 203.
2   As to the meaning of 'dwelling-house' see PARA 216.
3   See the Coal Mining Subsidence Act 1991 s 23(2); and PARA 229.
4   As to the meaning of 'notice' see PARA 210. As to notices see PARA 251 et seq.
5   As to the responsible person see PARA 204.
6   Ie the person who immediately before the deterioration in the condition of the dwelling-house was entitled to possession of it: see the Coal Mining Subsidence Act 1991 s 24(1).
7   See the Coal Mining Subsidence Act 1991 s 24(1), (3). Any claim arising out of a breach of the duty imposed by s 24(3) is to be determined by the county court in England and Wales: s 24(5). Nothing in s 24 affects any liability of the responsible person arising apart from the provisions of s 24: s 24(6).
8   See the Coal Mining Subsidence Act 1991 s 24(3).
9   The specified events are that: (1) the occupier has ceased (otherwise than by reason of his death) to be entitled to possession of the dwelling-house or, as the case may be, of its site; or (2) the expiration of a period of six months from the service by the responsible person on the resident of notice of its opinion that the period of dispossession will continue indefinitely or will be unreasonably long, or that the resident will not resume residence at the expiration of that period: see the Coal Mining Subsidence Act 1991 s 23(1), Sch 5 para 3(1); and PARA 229.
10   Coal Mining Subsidence Act 1991 s 24(2).
11   Ie by virtue of the Coal Mining Subsidence Act 1991 s 24(3): see s 24(4).
12   Coal Mining Subsidence Act 1991 s 24(4).

## 231. Compensation for inconvenience during works.

The Secretary of State[1] may, after consultation with the responsible person[2], make regulations[3] requiring the payment by the responsible person of compensation for any inconvenience or disturbance which may be caused, as a result of the responsible person executing the remedial works[4], to persons residing in dwelling-houses affected by subsidence damage[5]. In particular, a person is entitled to claim compensation if:

(1)    he is the owner[6] of, or any other person liable to make good in whole or in part the damage to, a dwelling-house which has been affected by subsidence damage[7];

(2)    a schedule of remedial works has come into effect in relation to that damage and the remedial works specified in it have been, or are being, carried out by or on behalf of the responsible person[8];

(3)    the total cost of the remedial works specified in the schedule of remedial works at the time the person makes a claim exceeds £3,000[9];

(4)    the remedial works were not, or have not been, completed within six months[10] from the date of their commencement[11]; and

(5)    the person has resided in the dwelling-house for a total period of six months during the time from the commencement of the remedial works[12].

The responsible person[13] must pay to any person entitled to such compensation:

(a)    10% of the total cost of the remedial works specified in the schedule of remedial works[14] at the time those works are completed[15]; and

(b)    interest on that sum at the applicable rate[16] for the period commencing on the date on which the person claimed compensation and expiring on the date on which he received it[17].

A claim for compensation must be made to the responsible person in writing after the expiry of six months from the date of commencement of the remedial works[18].

1   As to the Secretary of State see PARA 2; and as to the Secretary of State's power to make regulations or orders see PARA 202.

2   As to the responsible person see PARA 204.

3   The Coal Mining Subsidence (Blight and Compensation for Inconvenience During Works) Regulations 1994, SI 1994/2564, make provision with respect to: (1) the making of claims for compensation under the regulations; (2) the descriptions of persons who may make a claim for such compensation; (3) the matters in respect of which, and any circumstances in which, such compensation is or is not to be payable; and (4) the sums, or the method of determining the sums, payable by way of such compensation: see the Coal Mining Subsidence Act 1991 s 25(2)(a)–(d); the Coal Mining Subsidence (Blight and Compensation for Inconvenience During Works) Regulations 1994, SI 1994/2564, regs 5–7. As to the meaning of 'claim' see PARA 210.

4   Ie the remedial works specified in the Coal Mining Subsidence Act 1991 s 6(2): see PARA 212. As to the meaning of 'works' see PARA 203.

5   Coal Mining Subsidence Act 1991 s 25(1). As to meaning of 'subsidence damage' see PARA 203.

6   As to the meaning of 'owner' see PARA 207.

7   Coal Mining Subsidence (Blight and Compensation for Inconvenience During Works) Regulations 1994, SI 1994/2564, reg 6(1)(a).

8   Coal Mining Subsidence (Blight and Compensation for Inconvenience During Works) Regulations 1994, SI 1994/2564, reg 6(1)(b).

9   Coal Mining Subsidence (Blight and Compensation for Inconvenience During Works) Regulations 1994, SI 1994/2564, reg 6(1)(c).

10  Any period during which the carrying out of remedial works has ceased (1) at the request of the owner of, or any other person interested in, the dwelling-house; (2) on account of any conduct on the part of any person residing in the dwelling-house; or (3) in accordance with a stop notice, must

not be counted in the determination of any period of six months for the purposes of heads (4)–(5) in the text or the Coal Mining Subsidence (Blight and Compensation for Inconvenience During Works) Regulations 1994, SI 1994/2564, reg 7(2): reg 6(2). As to the meaning of 'stop notice' see PARA 222. As to the meaning of 'notice' see PARA 210. As to notices see PARA 251 et seq.

11 Coal Mining Subsidence (Blight and Compensation for Inconvenience During Works) Regulations 1994, SI 1994/2564, reg 6(1)(d).

12 Coal Mining Subsidence (Blight and Compensation for Inconvenience During Works) Regulations 1994, SI 1994/2564, reg 6(1)(e). Where a person has made a claim for compensation, there must not be counted for the purpose of determining the period of residence in the dwelling-house in question of any other person for the purpose of head (5) in the text any period before the completion of the remedial works to which the claim of the first person referred to above relates during which the other person resides in the dwelling-house: reg 6(3).

13 For these purposes, 'the responsible person' means, in relation to subsidence damage to a dwelling-house, the person who, by virtue of the Coal Industry Act 1994 s 43 (see PARA 204) or s 44 (see PARA 206) is the responsible person in relation to that damage: Coal Mining Subsidence (Blight and Compensation for Inconvenience During Works) Regulations 1994, SI 1994/2564, reg 5.

14 As to the schedule of remedial works see PARA 212.

15 Coal Mining Subsidence (Blight and Compensation for Inconvenience During Works) Regulations 1994, SI 1994/2564, reg 7(1)(a).

16 As to the applicable rate see PARA 217.

17 Coal Mining Subsidence (Blight and Compensation for Inconvenience During Works) Regulations 1994, SI 1994/2564, reg 7(1)(b).

18 Coal Mining Subsidence (Blight and Compensation for Inconvenience During Works) Regulations 1994, SI 1994/2564, reg 7(2).

## (d) Agricultural Losses

### 232. Farm loss payments.

Where land constituting or included in an agricultural unit[1] is affected by subsidence damage[2], an occupier displaced[3] from the land has a right in certain circumstances, to receive a farm loss payment if, by reason of deterioration due to the damage in the condition of the land, the land cannot profitably be used for agricultural purposes[4]. If any person in occupation of the agricultural unit who has an owner's interest[5] is displaced from the whole, or a sufficient part[6], of the land affected by the subsidence damage and, not more than three years after the date of displacement, he begins to farm a new agricultural unit elsewhere in Great Britain[7], he is entitled to receive a farm loss payment from the responsible person[8].

No farm loss payment may be made to any person unless, on the date on which he begins to farm the new unit, he is in occupation of the whole of that unit in right of a freehold interest in it or a tenancy of it, not having been entitled to any such interest or tenancy before the date of displacement[9]. The responsible person is not liable to make a farm loss payment except on a claim[10] made by the person entitled to it before the end of the period of one year beginning with the date on which he begins to farm the new unit[11].

The amount of any farm loss payment is equal to the average annual profit[12] derived from the use for agricultural purposes of the agricultural land comprised in the land affected[13], but where the value of the agricultural land comprised in the land affected exceeds the value of the agricultural land comprised in the new unit, the amount of the farm loss payment is reduced proportionately[14].

A claim for farm loss payment must be made in the prescribed form, and contain the prescribed particulars[15]. Where a person dies before the expiration of the period for making a claim and would have been entitled to such a payment if he had made a claim within that period, a claim may be made, before the expiration of that period, by his personal representative[16].

Special provisions apply where the land is occupied for the purposes of a partnership firm[17].

1  'Agricultural unit', in relation to England and Wales, has the meaning given by the Town and Country Planning Act 1990 s 171(1) (see PLANNING vol 83 (2018) PARA 1105); 'agriculture', 'agricultural' and 'agricultural land', in relation to England and Wales, have the meanings given by the Agriculture Act 1947 s 109 (see AGRICULTURAL LAND AND ALLOTMENTS vol 1 (2017) PARA 424): Coal Mining Subsidence Act 1991 s 52(1).

2  As to the meaning of 'subsidence damage' see PARA 203.

3  The Coal Mining Subsidence Act 1991 s 26, Sch 6 does not apply in any case where the displacement occurred before 30 November 1991: s 53(1), Sch 7 para 3(1)(a).

4  See the Coal Mining Subsidence Act 1991 s 26, Sch 6.

5  For these purposes, 'owner's interest' means a freehold interest or a tenancy where his interest is as tenant for a year or from year to year or a greater interest: Coal Mining Subsidence Act 1991 Sch 6 para 1(2).

6  'Sufficient part' means not less than 0.5 hectares or such area as the Secretary of State may by order specify: Coal Mining Subsidence Act 1991 Sch 6 para 1(2). As to the Secretary of State see PARA 2; and as to the Secretary of State's power to make regulations or orders see PARA 202.

7  As to the meaning of 'Great Britain' see PARA 48.

8  Coal Mining Subsidence Act 1991 Sch 6 para 1(1). As to the responsible person see PARA 204.
   A farm loss payment carries interest at the applicable rate (if any) from the date of displacement until payment but any period of delay in determining the amount of any such payment which is attributable to unreasonable conduct on the part of that person is to be disregarded: Sch 6 para 3(5) (amended by the Coal Industry Act 1994 s 67(1), Sch 9 para 41(4)). As to the applicable rate see PARA 217.

9  Coal Mining Subsidence Act 1991 Sch 6 para 1(3). No farm loss payment may be made to any person who is entitled to a payment under s 28 (see PARA 234) in respect of land which consists of or includes the land from which he was displaced: Sch 6 para 1(4).

10  As to the meaning of 'claim' see PARA 210.

11  See the Coal Mining Subsidence Act 1991 Sch 6 paras 1(1), 3(1).

12  The profit is computed by reference to the profits for the three years ending with the date of displacement or, if the person concerned has then been in occupation for a shorter period, that period: see the Coal Mining Subsidence Act 1991 Sch 6 para 2(1).

13  See the Coal Mining Subsidence Act 1991 Sch 6 para 2(1), (2). In calculating the profits a sum equal to the rent that might reasonably be expected to be payable in respect of the agricultural land comprised in the land affected if it were let for agricultural purposes to a tenant responsible for rates, repairs and other outgoings must be deducted; and that deduction must be made whether or not the land is in fact let and, if it is, must be made to the exclusion of any deduction for the rent actually payable: Sch 6 para 2(3).

14  Coal Mining Subsidence Act 1991 Sch 6 para 2(4). For these purposes, the value of any land is to be determined:
   (1)   on the basis of its value as land used solely for agriculture (Sch 6 para 2(5)(a));
   (2)   by reference to the condition of the land and its surroundings and to prices current (a) in the case of the land comprised in the land affected, on the date of displacement; (b) in the case of land comprised in the new unit, on the date on which the person concerned begins to farm the new unit (Sch 6 para 2(5)(b)); and
   (3)   without regard to the principal dwelling, if any, comprised in the same agricultural unit as that land (Sch 6 para 2(5)(c)).
   Schedule 1 para 2 (see PARA 217) applies for the purpose of determining the value of any land for the purposes of Sch 6 para 2(4) as it applies for the purpose of determining the value of a unit of property at any time for the purposes of s 10 (see PARA 219) or s 11 (see PARA 218): Sch 6 para 2(6).

15  See the Coal Mining Subsidence Act 1991 Sch 6 para 3(2); and the Coal Mining Subsidence (Notices and Claims) Regulations 1991, SI 1991/2509, reg 5, Sch 3.

16  Coal Mining Subsidence Act 1991 Sch 6 para 3(4).

17  Where the agricultural unit containing the land affected is occupied for the purposes of a partnership firm the Coal Mining Subsidence Act 1991 Sch 6 paras 1, 2 have effect in relation to the firm and not the partners individually (any interest of a partner in the land acquired being treated as an interest of the firm) except that the requirements in Sch 6 para 1 as to the new unit are to be treated as complied with in relation to the firm as soon as they are complied with by any one of the persons who were members of the firm: Sch 6 para 3(3).

**233. Crop loss payments.**

Where at any time land constituting or included in an agricultural unit[1] is affected by subsidence damage[2], for each year[3] or part of a year falling within the period beginning with that time and ending with the discharge by the responsible person[4] of his remedial obligation[5] with respect to the damage, the responsible person is under an obligation to make to the occupier[6] of the unit a payment for the loss of return from crops of the amount given by the specified formula[7]. Similarly, for each year or part of a year falling within that period, the responsible person is under an obligation to make to the occupier of the unit a payment for the loss of yield from land used for pasture of the amount given by another specified formula[8].

The responsible person is not liable to make a crop loss payment except on a claim[9] made by the person entitled to it within the period of 12 months beginning with the end of the year or part of a year to which the payment relates[10]. Where such a claim is made, the responsible person may, by notice[11] given to any person who is entitled to give a damage notice[12] in respect of the subsidence damage, elect to treat that claim as if it were also such a notice given by that person in respect of that damage[13].

A crop loss payment carries interest at the applicable rate (if any) from the date of the claim on which the payment is made until payment but any period of delay in determining the amount of any such payment which is attributable to unreasonable conduct on the part of that person is disregarded[14].

1   As to the meaning of 'agricultural unit' see PARA 232.
2   As to the meaning of 'subsidence damage' see PARA 203.
3   'Year' means a calendar year: Coal Mining Subsidence Act 1991 s 27(8). Section 27 does not apply as respects any calendar year or part of such a year falling before 30 November 1991: s 53(1), Sch 7 para 3(1)(c).
4   As to the responsible person see PARA 204.
5   As to the meaning of 'remedial obligation' see PARA 209.
6   In relation to any agricultural activity carried on land constituting or included in an agricultural unit, the person having the right to carry it on is to be treated as the occupier of that unit: Coal Mining Subsidence Act 1991 s 27(8).
7   Coal Mining Subsidence Act 1991 s 27(1), (2). As to the specified formula see s 27(2). The following are to be disregarded for the purposes of s 27(2):
    (1)    any crops which would normally have been harvested before the subsidence damage became evident (s 27(4)(a));
    (2)    any crops which were or would have been sown or planted after an election by the responsible person under s 10 (see PARA 219) to make a depreciation payment in respect of the damage (s 27(4)(b)); and
    (3)    if all reasonable steps have not been taken to protect them, any crops grown in a greenhouse affected by the damage (s 27(4)(c)).
    'Greenhouse' includes any building or structure designed to afford protection from the weather or to secure the retention of heat: s 27(8).
8   Coal Mining Subsidence Act 1991 s 27(3). As to the specified formula see s 27(3). Any use of land for pasture which was or would have been so used after an election by the responsible person under s 10 (see PARA 219) to make a depreciation payment in respect of the damage is to be disregarded for the purposes of s 27(3): see s 27(4).
9   As to the meaning of 'claim' see PARA 210.
10  Coal Mining Subsidence Act 1991 s 27(5).
11  As to the meaning of 'notice' see PARA 210. As to notices see PARA 251 et seq.
12  As to the meaning of 'damage notice' see PARA 210.
13  Coal Mining Subsidence Act 1991 s 27(6).
14  Coal Mining Subsidence Act 1991 s 27(7) (amended by the Coal Industry Act 1994 s 67(1), Sch 9 para 41(1)). As to the applicable rate see PARA 217.

## 234. Payments for tenant farmers.

Where the responsible person[1] makes a depreciation payment[2] to the owner[3] of any agricultural land[4] which is subject to a tenancy, he must also make a payment to the tenant of the amount given by the specified formula[5]. Where the responsible person makes such a payment to a tenant who has been displaced from the whole or a sufficient part[6] of the land affected by the subsidence damage[7], he must also make a payment to him equal to the compensation which would have been payable to him for any loss or injury sustained by him on the assumptions that:

(1)    the land had been compulsorily acquired at the relevant time[8];
(2)    the tenant had no greater interest in the land than as tenant for a year or from year to year[9];
(3)    the land had not been affected by the subsidence damage[10]; and
(4)    the displacement had been caused by the compulsory acquisition[11].

1  As to the responsible person see PARA 204.
2  As to depreciation payments see PARAS 217–220.
3  As to the meaning of 'owner' see PARA 207.
4  As to the meaning of 'agricultural land' see PARA 232.
5  Coal Mining Subsidence Act 1991 s 28(1). As to the specified formula see s 28(1).
    Schedule 1 para 2 (see PARA 217) applies for the purpose of determining the value mentioned in s 28(1) as it applies for the purpose of determining the value of a unit of property at any time for the purposes of s 10 (see PARA 219) or s 11 (see PARA 218); and Sch 1 para 4 (interest on depreciation payments) applies in relation to any payment under s 28 as if the payment were a depreciation payment, and as if the relevant time in relation to the payment were the time immediately after the making of the claim: s 28(4).
6  For these purposes, 'sufficient part' means not less than 0.5 hectares or such area as the Secretary of State may by order specify: Coal Mining Subsidence Act 1991 s 28(5). As to the Secretary of State see PARA 2; and as to the Secretary of State's power to make regulations or orders see PARA 202.
7  As to the meaning of 'subsidence damage' see PARA 203.
8  Coal Mining Subsidence Act 1991 s 28(2)(a), (3)(a). For these purposes, the 'relevant time' means the relevant time for the purposes of s 14(4), Sch 1 para 3 (see PARA 217): s 28(5). Any reference to compensation is a reference to compensation under the Compulsory Purchase Act 1965 s 20 (see COMPULSORY ACQUISITION OF LAND vol 18 (2009) PARA 699 et seq): Coal Mining Subsidence Act 1991 s 28(5).
9  Coal Mining Subsidence Act 1991 s 28(2)(a), (3)(b).
10  Coal Mining Subsidence Act 1991 s 28(2)(a), (3)(c).
11  Coal Mining Subsidence Act 1991 s 28(2)(b).

### (e)    Blighted Property

## 235. Property affected by blight.

The Secretary of State[1] may, after consultation with the responsible person[2], make regulations[3] with respect to the action to be taken by the responsible person for alleviating cases of hardship suffered as a result of property being blighted by subsidence damage[4] or the possibility of such damage[5]. The action which may be required is: (1) the purchase of any blighted property at a price equivalent to its unblighted value[6]; or (2) the payment of an amount equivalent to the difference between the value of any such property and its unblighted value[7]. Regulations may make provision as to:

(a)    the making of claims[8] under the regulations and the descriptions of persons who may make them[9];

(b)     the descriptions of property in respect of which such claims may be made and the circumstances in which such property is to be regarded as blighted for the purposes of the regulations[10];

(c)     the circumstances in which action is or is not required to be taken (including the circumstances in which a person is to be regarded as suffering hardship)[11];

(d)     the determination of the value or unblighted value of any blighted property[12].

1   As to the Secretary of State see PARA 2.
2   As to the responsible person see PARA 204.
3   See the Coal Mining Subsidence (Blight and Compensation for Inconvenience During Works) Regulations 1994, SI 1994/2564; and PARA 236. As to the Secretary of State's power to make regulations or orders see PARA 202.
4   As to the meaning of 'subsidence damage' see PARA 203.
5   Coal Mining Subsidence Act 1991 s 29(1).
6   Coal Mining Subsidence Act 1991 s 29(2)(a). For these purposes, 'unblighted value' in relation to any blighted property, means the value which it would have if it were not blighted: s 29(4). As to the obligation to purchase a blighted dwelling see PARA 236.
7   Coal Mining Subsidence Act 1991 29(2)(b).
8   As to the meaning of 'claim' see PARA 210.
9   Coal Mining Subsidence Act 1991 s 29(3)(a).
10 Coal Mining Subsidence Act 1991 s 29(3)(b). As to the circumstances in which a property is blighted see PARA 236.
11 Coal Mining Subsidence Act 1991 s 29(3)(c). As to the circumstances in which action is required to be taken see PARA 236.
12 Coal Mining Subsidence Act 1991 s 29(3)(d); and see PARA 236.

### 236. Purchase of blighted dwelling-houses.

Where a dwelling-house is blighted[1] the owner[2] is entitled to require the responsible person[3] to purchase his interest in it if:

(1)     the owner has made reasonable endeavours to sell his interest in it[4];

(2)     because the dwelling-house is blighted, the owner has been unable to sell his interest in it except at a price which is substantially lower than that for which it might reasonably have been expected to be sold if it was not blighted[5]; and

(3)     the principal reason for the proposed sale is a change in the owner's personal or family circumstances such as would be likely to cause any reasonable owner to decide to sell the owner's interest in the dwelling-house[6].

Where the owner of a blighted dwelling-house is entitled to require the responsible person to purchase his interest in it, the responsible person must, on the owner making a written request to him, forthwith proceed to purchase the owner's interest in the dwelling-house at its unblighted value[7] at the date the request was made[8].

1   As to the meaning of 'dwelling-house' see PARA 216. A dwelling-house is blighted for these purposes if:
     (1)    it has been affected by subsidence damage and either a stop notice in respect of that damage is in force or there is a reasonable probability that such a notice will be given (Coal Mining Subsidence (Blight and Compensation for Inconvenience During Works) Regulations 1994, SI 1994/2564, reg 2(2)(a)); or
     (2)    there is a reasonable probability that the dwelling-house will be affected by subsidence damage within nine months and that a stop notice will be given in respect of that damage (reg 2(2)(b)).
    As to the meaning of 'subsidence damage' see PARA 203. As to the meaning of 'stop notice' see PARA 222; and as to meaning of 'notice' see PARA 210. As to notices see PARA 251 et seq.

2 As to the meaning of 'owner' see PARA 207.
3 As to the responsible person see PARA 204. For these purposes, unless the context otherwise requires, the 'responsible person' means, in relation to a dwelling-house: (1) where it has been affected by subsidence damage, the person who, by virtue of the Coal Industry Act 1994 s 43 (see PARA 204) or s 44 (see PARA 206) is the responsible person in relation to that damage; (2) where there is a reasonable probability of subsidence damage as mentioned in the Coal Mining Subsidence (Blight and Compensation for Inconvenience During Works) Regulations 1994, SI 1994/2564, reg 2(2)(b), the person who would be the person referred to in head (1) in relation to that damage if it did occur: reg 2(1).
4 See the Coal Mining Subsidence (Blight and Compensation for Inconvenience During Works) Regulations 1994, SI 1994/2564, reg 3(1), (2)(a).
5 See the Coal Mining Subsidence (Blight and Compensation for Inconvenience During Works) Regulations 1994, SI 1994/2564, reg 3(1), (2)(b).
6 See the Coal Mining Subsidence (Blight and Compensation for Inconvenience During Works) Regulations 1994, SI 1994/2564, reg 3(1), (2)(c).
7 For these purposes, 'unblighted value' means, in relation to an interest in a dwelling-house, the price for which that interest could reasonably be expected to be sold if the dwelling-house was not affected, or there was no reasonable probability that it would be affected, by subsidence damage to which a stop notice applies or would apply: Coal Mining Subsidence (Blight and Compensation for Inconvenience During Works) Regulations 1994, SI 1994/2564, reg 2(1).
8 Coal Mining Subsidence (Blight and Compensation for Inconvenience During Works) Regulations 1994, SI 1994/2564, reg 4.

### (f) Losses to Small Firms

**237. Compensation for consequential losses to small firms.**
Where at any time any property, which is used wholly or partly for the purposes of a small firm[1], and as respects which one or more notices of the possibility of subsidence damage[2] have been or should have been given to the owner[3] or occupier[4], is affected by subsidence damage, special provisions apply for the period beginning with that time and ending with the discharge by the responsible person of his remedial obligation[5] with respect to the damage[6].

For each year[7] or part of a year which falls within that period, and in which any consequential loss[8] resulting from the damage is suffered by the firm, the responsible person is under an obligation to make a payment to the firm of such amount as would have been payable to the firm by way of damages in respect of that loss if the damage had been attributable to the negligence of the responsible person[9]. In determining the amount of such a payment regard must be had to the rules of law relating to remoteness and the mitigation of losses[10].

The responsible person is not liable to make a compensation payment unless, as soon as reasonably practicable after the first time (1) when the firm suffers any consequential loss resulting from the damage; or (2) if later, when the firm has the required knowledge[11], the firm gives notice of the loss to the responsible person[12]. Where such a notice is given, the responsible person may, by notice given to any person who is entitled to give a damage notice[13] in respect of the subsidence damage, elect to treat the notice as if it were also a damage notice given by that person in respect of that damage[14]. The responsible person is not liable to make a compensation payment except on a claim[15] made by the firm within the period of 12 months beginning with the end of the year or part of a year to which the payment relates[16].

1 Houses built by a building company for the purposes of sale are not, pending sale, property which is used wholly or partly for the purposes of the company within the meaning of this provision: see *Collins (Pontefract) Ltd v British Coal Corpn* (1996) 73 P & CR 102, Lands Tribunal; affd (1997) 76 P & CR 219, CA.
   'Small firm' means any person who, at the time when the property is affected by subsidence

damage (as to the meaning of which see PARA 203), is carrying on a business and the number of employees employed by him, added to the number of employees employed by any associated employer of his, does not exceed 20: Coal Mining Subsidence Act 1991 s 30(7), (8). The Secretary of State may by order substitute for the number of employees specified in s 30(8) (whether as originally enacted or as previously amended) such other number of employees as he thinks fit: s 30(9). At the date at which this volume states the law no such order had been made. As to the Secretary of State see PARA 2; and as to the Secretary of State's power to make regulations or orders see PARA 202. 'Employee' has the same meaning as in the Employment Rights Act 1996; and 'associated employer' is to be construed in accordance with s 231: Coal Mining Subsidence Act 1991 s 30(7) (amended by the Employment Rights Act 1996 s 240, Sch 1 para 49). As to employment generally see EMPLOYMENT.

2  Ie notices under the Coal Mining Subsidence Act 1991 s 46 (see PARA 251). As to the meaning of 'notice' see PARA 210. As to notices see PARA 251 et seq.
3  As to the meaning of 'owner' see PARA 207.
4  Ie under the Coal Mining Subsidence Act 1991 s 46(1) (see PARA 251): see s 30(1).
5  As to the meaning of 'remedial obligation' see PARA 209.
6  Coal Mining Subsidence Act 1991 s 30(1) (amended by the Coal Industry Act 1994 s 67(8), Sch 11 Pt II).
7  For these purposes, 'year' means a calendar year: Coal Mining Subsidence Act 1991 s 30(7).
8  'Consequential loss' does not include: (1) any loss for which provision is made by the Coal Mining Subsidence Act 1991 s 27(2) or s 27(3) (see PARA 233); or (2) any loss resulting from subsidence damage as respects which the responsible person's remedial obligation is excluded by s 33(3) (see PARA 240): s 30(7) (amended by the Coal Industry Act 1994 Sch 11 Pt II).
9  Coal Mining Subsidence Act 1991 s 30(2). As to the principles of negligence generally see NEGLIGENCE.
10  Coal Mining Subsidence Act 1991 s 30(2). As to the rules of remoteness and mitigation of loss see DAMAGES vol 29 (2014) PARAS 378 et seq, 409 et seq.
11  Ie the knowledge mentioned in the Coal Mining Subsidence Act 1991 s 3(4) read with s 3(5) (see PARA 210): see s 30(3).
12  Coal Mining Subsidence Act 1991 s 30(3).
13  As to the meaning of 'damage notice' see PARA 210.
14  Coal Mining Subsidence Act 1991 s 30(4).
15  As to the meaning of 'claim' see PARA 210.
16  Coal Mining Subsidence Act 1991 s 30(5). A payment carries interest at the applicable rate (if any) from the date of the claim on which the payment is made until payment but any period of delay in determining the amount of any such payment which is attributable to unreasonable conduct on the part of that firm is disregarded: s 30(6) (amended by the Coal Industry Act 1994 s 67(1), Sch 9 para 41(2)). As to the applicable rate see PARA 217.

## (g)  Moveable Property

### 238.  Compensation for damage to moveable property.

Where damage is caused[1] to any moveable property[2] by the happening of subsidence damage[3], the responsible person[4] is liable to pay to any person having an interest in the property such amount by way of compensation as would have been payable to that person by way of damages if:

(1)  the damage to the moveable property had been attributable to the negligence of the responsible person[5]; and

(2)  liability for any consequential loss resulting from the damage were excluded[6].

Compensation is nonetheless payable in respect of consequential loss where the claim[7] is made by a small firm[8] where (a) the moveable property was used wholly or partly for the purposes of the firm; and (b) the property affected by subsidence damage was property as respects which one or more notices had been or should have been given[9] that there was a risk of land being affected by subsidence damage[10]. In determining the amount of such a payment as is payable regard must be had to the rules of law relating to remoteness and the mitigation of losses[11].

The responsible person is not liable to pay compensation to any person in respect of damage to any moveable property where (i) at the time when it was damaged, the property was on any land in circumstances such that its presence constituted a trespass to that land; or (ii) the damage was wholly attributable to the fault[12] of that person or any person in lawful possession of the property, and if the damage was partly attributable to the fault of that person or any person in lawful possession of the property, the liability of the responsible person is reduced proportionately[13].

1   The provisions relating to compensation for damage to moveable property do not apply in any case where the injury was caused before 30 November 1991: Coal Mining Subsidence Act 1991 s 53(1), Sch 7 para 3(1)(d).
2   For these purposes, 'moveable property' means, in relation to England and Wales, any chattel personal other than a thing in action or money: Coal Mining Subsidence Act 1991 s 31(4). As to personal property generally see PERSONAL PROPERTY.
3   As to the meaning of 'subsidence damage' see PARA 203.
4   As to the responsible person see PARA 204.
5   Coal Mining Subsidence Act 1991 s 31(1)(a). As to negligence generally see NEGLIGENCE.
6   Coal Mining Subsidence Act 1991 s 31(1)(b).
7   As to the meaning of 'claim' see PARA 210.
8   For these purposes, 'small firm' has the meaning which would be given by the Coal Mining Subsidence Act 1991 s 30(7) (see PARA 237) if the reference to the time when the property is affected by subsidence damage were a reference to the time when damage is caused to the moveable property: s 31(4).
9   Ie under the Coal Mining Subsidence Act 1991 s 46(1) (see PARA 251): see s 31(2).
10  Coal Mining Subsidence Act 1991 s 31(2) (amended by the Coal Industry Act 1994 s 67(8), Sch 11 Pt II).
11  Coal Mining Subsidence Act 1991 s 31(2). As to the rules of remoteness and mitigation of loss see DAMAGES vol 29 (2014) PARAS 378 et seq, 409 et seq.
12  For these purposes, 'fault' includes any act or omission which would, if the damage to the moveable property had been caused by the negligence of the responsible person, have constituted fault for the purposes of the Law Reform (Contributory Negligence) Act 1945: Coal Mining Subsidence Act 1991 s 31(4). As to contributory negligence see NEGLIGENCE vol 78 (2018) PARA 75 et seq.
13  Coal Mining Subsidence Act 1991 s 31(3).

### (h)   Death or Disablement

### 239.  Compensation for death or disablement.

If, as the result of an injury caused by the happening of subsidence damage[1], any person dies or is disabled (whether permanently or temporarily), and no other action[2] to recover damages is maintainable in respect of the death or disablement, the responsible person[3] is liable to pay damages[4]. The responsible person is liable, in the case of a death, to pay the like damages, recoverable in the like manner and within the like time[5], as would have been payable if:

(1)   the death had been attributable to the negligence of the responsible person[6]; and

(2)   the persons by or on behalf of whom an action could have been brought against the responsible person for damages in respect of the death if it had been so attributable included any person who at the time of the death was, or but for the injury would have been, wholly or partly maintained by the deceased[7]; and

(3)   the damages were claimed under the Fatal Accidents Act 1976[8].

In a case of disablement, the responsible person is liable to pay the like damages, recoverable in the like manner and within the like time, as would have been payable if the disablement had been attributable to the negligence of the responsible person[9]. However, no liability attaches to the responsible person in respect of the death or disablement of any person as a result of an injury if at the time when that person incurred the injury he was on any land as a trespasser, or the injury was wholly attributable to the fault[10] of that person[11].

1 As to the meaning of 'subsidence damage' see PARA 203.
2 Ie apart from under the Coal Mining Subsidence Act 1991 s 32: see s 32(1). It would therefore seem that this provision does not prevent another claim being brought under s 32 in the alternative.
3 As to the responsible person see PARA 204.
4 See the Coal Mining Subsidence Act 1991 s 32(1). The provisions relating to compensation for death or disablement do not apply in any case where the injury was caused before 30 November 1991 (s 53(1), Sch 7 para 3(1)(d)), and nothing in the Coal Mining Subsidence Act 1991 affects the operation of the Coal-Mining (Subsidence) Act 1957 s 12 (repealed) in relation to any case where the injury was caused before that date (Coal Mining Subsidence Act 1991 Sch 7 para 3(2)(b)).
5 It seems clear that the effect of the wording of this provision is that proceedings are to be brought before the ordinary courts by way of derogation from the provisions of the Coal Mining Subsidence Act 1991 s 40 (see PARA 249) and the Coal Industry Act 1994 s 47 (see PARAS 249–250), under which disputes as to subsidence matters fall in general to be referred to and determined by the Lands Tribunal or under arbitration. Accordingly, proceedings under the Coal Mining Subsidence Act 1991 s 32 must be brought in the County Court (or the High Court if the value of the claim is £50,000 or more): see the High Court and County Court Jurisdiction Order 1991, SI 1991/724, art 5 (amended by SI 1999/1014; and SI 2009//577).
6 Coal Mining Subsidence Act 1991 s 32(2)(a). As to negligence generally see NEGLIGENCE.
7 Coal Mining Subsidence Act 1991 s 32(2)(b).
8 Coal Mining Subsidence Act 1991 s 32(2)(c).
9 Coal Mining Subsidence Act 1991 s 32(3).
10 For these purposes, 'fault' includes any act or omission which would, if the death or disablement had been caused by the negligence of the responsible person, have constituted fault for the purposes of the Law Reform (Contributory Negligence) Act 1945: Coal Mining Subsidence Act 1991 s 32(5). As to contributory negligence see NEGLIGENCE vol 78 (2018) PARA 75 et seq.
11 Coal Mining Subsidence Act 1991 s 32(4). If the injury was partly attributable to the fault of that person the liability of the responsible person is reduced proportionately: s 32(4).

## (D) Preventive and other Measures

### (a) Existing Buildings, Structures or Works

**240. Existing buildings, structures or works.**
Where it appears (1) that subsidence damage[1] is likely to occur to any building, structure[2] or works[3] for the time being on, in or over any land; and (2) that the execution of preventive works on that property (or on that property and some other property which would benefit from those preventive works) would prevent the occurrence or reduce the extent of such damage[4], the responsible person[5] may:

(a) with the consent of all persons who are owners[6] of any property[7] on which the preventive works would fall to be executed, or who would be liable to make good in whole or in part subsidence damage to any of that property, execute the preventive works[8]; or

(b) on undertaking to pay any cost reasonably incurred in the execution of the preventive works, request their execution by the owner of the property on which they would fall to be executed or any other person who would be liable as mentioned in head (a) above in respect of that property[9].

If any person unreasonably withholds his consent to the execution of preventive works by the responsible person, or unreasonably fails to comply with any request to execute such works made by the responsible person[10], and subsidence damage subsequently occurs to the property, then:

(i)      if the damage could have been prevented by the execution of the preventive works, the responsible person is not required to take any remedial action[11] in respect of that damage[12];

(ii)     if the extent of the damage could have been reduced by the execution of the preventive works, the responsible person is not required to take any remedial action which would not have been required if the preventive works had been executed[13]; and

(iii)    if the property is a dwelling-house[14], the person concerned is not entitled, in respect of the damage, to give a notice[15] for relief for temporary dispossession or to receive relief[16] for temporary dispossession[17].

1    As to the meaning of 'subsidence damage' see PARA 203.
2    As to the meaning of 'structure' see PARA 203.
3    As to the meaning of 'works' see PARA 203.
4    Coal Mining Subsidence Act 1991 s 33(1) (amended by the Coal Industry Act 1994 ss 43(8), 67(8), Sch 6 para 3(1), Sch 11 Pt II). As to relevant transitional provisions see the Coal Mining Subsidence Act 1991 s 53(1), Sch 7 para 4.
5    As to the responsible person see PARA 204.
6    As to the meaning of 'owner' see PARA 207.
7    Where any such property is ecclesiastical property (as to the meaning of which see PARA 226) the Diocesan Board of Finance for the diocese in which the land is situated is included among the persons whose consent is required: Coal Mining Subsidence Act 1991 s 33(7) (amended by the Church of England (Miscellaneous Provisions) Measure 2006 Sch 5 para 29(2)). As to diocesan boards of finance see ECCLESIASTICAL LAW vol 34 (2011) PARA 241 et seq. Where different consents are required in respect of different parts of any property, those different parts are to be treated as different properties: s 33(4).
8    Coal Mining Subsidence Act 1991 s 33(2)(a).
9    Coal Mining Subsidence Act 1991 s 33(2)(b).
10   The withholding by any person of consent to the execution of preventive works on any property by the responsible person, and the failure to comply with any request to execute such works made by the responsible person, are not to be regarded as unreasonable in a case to which the Coal Mining Subsidence Act 1991 s 9 (see PARA 215) applies: s 33(6).
11   As to remedial action see PARA 209.
12   Coal Mining Subsidence Act 1991 s 33(3)(a). Heads (i)–(ii) in the text do not apply in the case of a failure to comply with a request to execute preventive works if the failure is the result of an express refusal to comply or permit compliance by one or more, but not both or all, of two or more persons whose compliance or permission is necessary: s 33(5).
13   Coal Mining Subsidence Act 1991 s 33(3)(b).
14   As to the meaning of 'dwelling-house' see PARA 216.
15   Ie a notice under the Coal Mining Subsidence Act 1991 s 23(1), Sch 5 para 4 (see PARA 229): see s 33(3)(c). As to the meaning of 'notice' see PARA 210. As to notices see PARA 251 et seq.
16   Ie under the Coal Mining Subsidence Act 1991 Sch 5: see s 33(3)(c).
17   Coal Mining Subsidence Act 1991 s 33(3)(c).

## (b)    Land Drainage Systems

**241. Remedial measures to be taken.**

In any area in England and Wales outside the Doncaster Drainage Area[1], the responsible person[2] must from time to time carry out to the reasonable satisfaction of the appropriate drainage authority[3], and in accordance with such arrangements as to timing as may be agreed or determined[4], such measures for remedying, mitigating or preventing any deterioration in a land drainage system[5], by reason of subsidence damage[6] which has occurred or appears likely to occur, as may be reasonably required by the appropriate drainage authority[7].

The responsible person may elect not to carry out such measures himself, but to make a payment to the appropriate drainage authority equal to the cost reasonably incurred by the authority in carrying out the measures, or if the authority proposes to merge the carrying out of the measures with the execution of other works, the responsible person may make payments equal to any sums from time to time shown to have been expended by the authority in carrying out the merged operations up to the appropriate amount[8]. Where it is agreed or determined to be appropriate, the responsible person's liability for the cost of any recurring measures may be discharged by a lump sum payment agreed or determined to represent the capital amount of that cost[9].

Provisions relating to stop notices[10] apply where a damage notice[11] has been given to the responsible person in respect of any property, and he is of the opinion with respect to all or any of the permanent works which would otherwise fall to be executed in connection with the property that the necessity for those works or the nature or manner of their execution is likely to be so affected by operations[12] as to make it unreasonable that those works should be executed for the time being[13].

The responsible person has the same powers of surveying and entering on any land, and of doing anything there, as are conferred on the appropriate drainage authority by the enactments relating to land drainage[14].

Regulations[15] may make provision with respect to the procedure to be followed by the responsible person and by the appropriate drainage authority in giving effect to these land drainage measures[16], and for the determination of questions arising between the responsible person and the authority[17].

1   For these purposes, 'the Doncaster Drainage Area' has the same meaning as in the Doncaster Area Drainage Act 1929 (see PARA 244): Coal Mining Subsidence Act 1991 s 36(8). As to relevant transitional provisions see s 53(1), Sch 7 para 6. As to land drainage generally see WATER AND WATERWAYS vol 101 (2018) PARA 845 et seq. As to the Doncaster Drainage District see PARA 244.
2   As to the responsible person see PARA 204.
3   For these purposes, 'the appropriate drainage authority' means:
    (1)    in a case where the measures would fall to be carried out either in connection with a main river, or outside any internal drainage
           (a)    in relation to measures to be carried out wholly in England, the Environment Agency;
           (b)    in relation to measures to be carried out wholly in Wales, the Natural Resources Body for Wales;
           (c)    in relation to measures to be carried out partly in England and partly in Wales, either of those bodies
    (2)    in any other case, the internal drainage board in whose district the measures would fall to be carried out: Coal Mining Subsidence Act 1991 s 36(8) (amended by virtue of SI 1996/593; and SI 2013/755).
    As to the Environment Agency see ENVIRONMENTAL QUALITY AND PUBLIC HEALTH vol 45 (2010) PARA 68 et seq; WATER AND WATERWAYS vol 101 (2018) PARA 846. 'Main river' means a main river for the purposes of the Water Resources Act 1991 Pt IV (ss 105–113) (see WATER AND WATERWAYS vol 101 (2018) PARA 846): Coal Mining Subsidence Act 1991 s 36(8) (amended by the Water Consolidation (Consequential Provisions) Act 1991 s 2, Sch 1 para 59).
4   For these purposes, 'agreed or determined' means agreed between the responsible person and the appropriate drainage authority or, in default of such agreement, determined in the manner provided by regulations: Coal Mining Subsidence Act 1991 s 36(8).
5   For these purposes, 'land drainage system' means a drainage system maintainable by a drainage authority: Coal Mining Subsidence Act 1991 s 36(8).

6  As to the meaning of 'subsidence damage' see PARA 203.

7  Coal Mining Subsidence Act 1991 s 36(1).

8  Coal Mining Subsidence Act 1991 s 36(2). For these purposes, 'the appropriate amount' means such aggregate amount as may be agreed or determined to be reasonable in all the circumstances, having regard to the expenditure which would have been incurred by the responsible person or by the authority in carrying out the measures: s 36(2). The responsible person in a case where the measures fall to be carried out in connection with property comprised in a main river, must make the appropriate election, and in any other case, must not unreasonably refuse any request to make that election received from the appropriate drainage authority: s 36(3). However, the responsible person is not deemed to act unreasonably in refusing any such request received after he has begun to carry out the measures: s 36(3) proviso.

9  Coal Mining Subsidence Act 1991 s 36(4).

10  See the Coal Mining Subsidence Act 1991 s 16(1)–(5); and PARA 222. As to the meaning of 'stop notice' see PARA 222. As to the meaning of 'notice' see PARA 210. As to notices see PARA 251 et seq.

11  As to the meaning of 'damage notice' see PARA 210.

12  Ie under the Coal Mining Subsidence Act 1991 s 36 or under the Doncaster Area Drainage Act 1929 Pt II (ss 9–12): see the Coal Mining Subsidence Act 1991 s 36(5).

13  Coal Mining Subsidence Act 1991 s 36(5). In its application to any stop notice so given, s 17(1) (see PARA 223) has effect as if it referred to the responsible person no longer being of the opinion that the necessity for the works or the nature or manner of their execution is likely to be so affected by operations as to make it unreasonable that those works should be executed for the time being: s 36(5).

14  Coal Mining Subsidence Act 1991 s 36(6). However, this does not apply in relation to any land occupied by or on behalf of the Crown: s 36(6) proviso.

15  As to the regulations made see the Coal Mining Subsidence (Land Drainage) Regulations 1994, SI 1994/3064; and PARAS 242–243. As to the power to make regulations or orders see PARA 202.

16  Coal Mining Subsidence Act 1991 s 36(7)(a).

17  Coal Mining Subsidence Act 1991 s 36(7)(b).

## 242. Determination of questions relating to land drainage.

In default of agreement, any land drainage question[1] arising between the responsible person[2] and the appropriate drainage authority[3] is to be referred to and determined by an arbitrator agreed for that purpose or, in default of such agreement, appointed by the President of the Institute of Civil Engineers[4].

Where either the appropriate drainage authority or the responsible person so requests[5], any question as to the reasonableness of any requirement to carry out remedial measures[6], or the timing of those measures, must be referred to and determined by the Secretary of State[7]. Before the determination is made[8], every party must be allowed a reasonable opportunity to make representations[9]. Where, after the determination, the Secretary of State is satisfied on an application[10] made by any party to that determination that fresh evidence has become available which: (1) could not reasonably have been discovered before such determination; and (2) renders it desirable for that determination to be reconsidered, he must, after giving notice in writing to every party and allowing every such party a reasonable opportunity to make representations, make a further determination[11].

1  Ie under the Coal Mining Subsidence Act 1991 s 36: see PARA 241.

2  For these purposes, 'the responsible person' means: (1) in relation to subsidence damage that has occurred, the person who, by virtue of the Coal Industry Act 1994 s 43 (see PARA 204) and s 44 (see PARA 206), is the responsible person in relation to that damage; and (2) in relation to such subsidence damage as appears likely to occur, the person who would be the person referred to in head (1) in relation to that damage if it did occur: Coal Mining Subsidence (Land Drainage) Regulations 1994, SI 1994/3064, reg 1(2). As to the meaning of 'subsidence damage' see PARA 203.

3  As to the meaning of 'appropriate drainage authority' see PARA 241.

4  See the Coal Mining Subsidence (Land Drainage) Regulations 1994, SI 1994/3064, regs 2, 4(1). As to arbitration generally see ARBITRATION vol 2 (2017) PARA 501 et seq.

5   The person making such a request must:
   (1)    make the request in writing (Coal Mining Subsidence (Land Drainage) Regulations 1994, SI 1994/3064, reg 3(2)(i));
   (2)    specify in the request the questions to be determined (reg 3(2)(ii));
   (3)    supply copies of the request to every other party to the determination (reg 3(2)(iii)); and
   (4)    comply with such other requirements (whether general or specific in nature) as to the form and manner in which the questions may be submitted, and the period within which they may be submitted, as the Secretary of State may specify by notice (reg 3(2)(iv)).
    As to the Secretary of State see PARA 2. The Coal Mining Subsidence (Land Drainage) Regulations 1994, SI 1994/3064, reg 3 refers to the possibility of the Secretary of State and the Minister of Agriculture, Fisheries and Food acting jointly, but the Ministry of Agriculture, Fisheries and Food has been dissolved and the minister's functions have been transferred to the Secretary of State for Environment, Food and Rural Affairs (see the Ministry of Agriculture, Fisheries and Food (Dissolution) Order 2002, SI 2002/794; and PARA 2).
6   See the Coal Mining Subsidence Act 1991 s 36(1), (2); and PARA 241.
7   Coal Mining Subsidence (Land Drainage) Regulations 1994, SI 1994/3064, reg 3(1).
8   Ie under the Coal Mining Subsidence (Land Drainage) Regulations 1994, SI 1994/3064, reg 3(1): see reg 3(3). A determination is final: see reg 3(4).
9   Coal Mining Subsidence (Land Drainage) Regulations 1994, SI 1994/3064, reg 3(3).
10   A party making such an application must:
   (1)    make the application in writing (Coal Mining Subsidence (Land Drainage) Regulations 1994, SI 1994/3064, reg 3(6)(i));
   (2)    specify particulars of the fresh evidence (reg 3(6)(ii)); and
   (3)    supply copies of the application to every other party to the determination (reg 3(6)(iii)).
11   Coal Mining Subsidence (Land Drainage) Regulations 1994, SI 1994/3064, reg 3(5).

## 243. Election by the responsible person.

After being informed by the appropriate drainage authority[1] of the remedial measures[2] that the responsible person[3] is required to carry out, the responsible person must, as soon as reasonably practicable in the circumstances, give notice in writing to that authority stating that he has elected either to carry out such measures himself or to make a payment[4] to the authority[5]. However, where the responsible person and the appropriate drainage authority have not agreed upon the remedial measures, or any question regarding (1) the form which such measures are to take; (2) the timing of such measures; or (3) the reasonableness of such measures, has been referred to arbitration or the Secretary of State[6], the requirement to give notice[7] does not apply until agreement has been reached or the question determined[8]. An election to carry out remedial measures or to make a payment is binding on the responsible person, unless the appropriate drainage authority agrees otherwise[9]. Where the responsible person has made an election to make a payment, the appropriate drainage authority must:

  (a)    give notice in writing to him specifying particulars of the remedial measures which it intends to carry out or, where it is its intention to merge the carrying out of the measures with the execution of other works[10], particulars of such works, not less than 28 days before the measures or the works are begun[11]; and

  (b)    so far as it is within the authority's power to do so, afford the responsible person reasonable facilities for inspecting the area in which the measures or the works are to be carried out[12].

1   As to the meaning of 'appropriate drainage authority' see PARA 241.
2   Ie in accordance with the Coal Mining Subsidence Act 1991 s 36(1) (see PARA 241): see the Coal Mining Subsidence (Land Drainage) Regulation 1994, SI 1994/3064, reg 5(1).
3   As to the responsible person see PARAS 204, 206, 242.
4   Ie in pursuance of the Coal Mining Subsidence Act 1991 s 36(2) (see PARA 241): see the Coal Mining Subsidence (Land Drainage) Regulations 1994, SI 1994/3064, reg 5(1).

5　Coal Mining Subsidence (Land Drainage) Regulations 1994, SI 1994/3064, reg 5(1). Where, after remedial measures have been agreed or determined, those measures are varied, every such variation is deemed to revoke any notice under reg 5(1), and the responsible person must give a further notice under reg 5(1): see reg 6(1). However, this provision does not relieve the responsible person from liability to make any payment to the appropriate drainage authority in respect of such measures as have been carried out by that authority before any such variation: reg 6(2).

6　As to the Secretary of State see PARA 2. The Coal Mining Subsidence (Land Drainage) Regulations 1994, SI 1994/3064, refer to the possibility of the Secretary of State and the Minister of Agriculture, Fisheries and Food acting jointly, but the Ministry of Agriculture, Fisheries and Food has been dissolved and the minister's functions have been transferred to the Secretary of State for Environment, Food and Rural Affairs (see the Ministry of Agriculture, Fisheries and Food (Dissolution) Order 2002, SI 2002/794; and PARA 2).

7　Ie in accordance with the Coal Mining Subsidence (Land Drainage) Regulations 1994, SI 1994/3064, reg 5(1): see reg 5(2).

8　Coal Mining Subsidence (Land Drainage) Regulations 1994, SI 1994/3064, reg 5(2).

9　Coal Mining Subsidence (Land Drainage) Regulations 1994, SI 1994/3064, reg 5(3).

10　Ie in accordance with the Coal Mining Subsidence Act 1991 s 36(2) (see PARA 241): see the Coal Mining Subsidence (Land Drainage) Regulations 1994, SI 1994/3064, reg 5(4)(i).

11　Coal Mining Subsidence (Land Drainage) Regulations 1994, SI 1994/3064, reg 5(4)(i).

12　Coal Mining Subsidence (Land Drainage) Regulations 1994, SI 1994/3064, reg 5(4)(ii).

## 244. The Doncaster Drainage District.

The Doncaster Area Drainage Acts 1929 and 1933 imposed obligations on mine owners[1] to establish and maintain funds for the maintenance of drainage works constructed under the Acts, and to undertake certain works and liabilities consequent on the subsidence of land in the neighbourhood of the River Don by mining operations. In 1947 an Order in Council[2] was made discharging any right conferred or obligation imposed by these Acts on mine owners working or proposing to work minerals under land situated within the Doncaster Drainage District[3] or on the Catchment Board of the River Ouse (Yorks) Catchment Area[4] or the Catchment Board of the River Trent Catchment Area[5] in respect of any mine which by virtue of the Coal Industry Nationalisation Act 1946 vested in the National Coal Board[6] (later renamed the British Coal Corporation)[7].

Certain obligations imposed by the Doncaster Area Drainage Act 1929[8] do not apply to such coal mines[9] in respect of which interests have vested[10] in the Coal Authority[11]. However, where such a mine has at the date of vesting permanently ceased to be worked or at any time thereafter permanently ceases to be worked, the Coal Authority must maintain in proper condition any drainage works at any time constructed under the Doncaster Area Drainage Act 1929[12] in respect of that mine[13]. The Coal Authority may[14] require any of such drainage works to be transferred to the Environment Agency on such terms and conditions as may be agreed between the Coal Authority and the Environment Agency[15]. If any dispute arises between the Coal Authority and the Environment Agency as to whether or not any mine has permanently ceased to be worked, or the terms and conditions subject to which any such drainage works are to vest in the Environment Agency, the matter is to be determined by arbitration[16]. The transferred drainage works vest in and become the property of the Environment Agency on the expiry of six months from the date when agreement as to the terms and conditions was reached or, in the event of a dispute which is referred to arbitration, from the date of the award of the arbitrator[17]. On vesting, the obligation of the Coal Authority to maintain those works ceases[18].

1　'Mine owner' means the owner, lessee or other persons entitled to work and get minerals; and 'minerals' means all minerals and substances in or under land, obtainable whether by underground or by surface working: Doncaster Area Drainage Act 1929 s 33.

2　Ie the Coal Industry Nationalisation (Doncaster Drainage) Order 1947, SR & O 1947/651.

3   See the Doncaster Area Drainage Act 1929 s 1.
4   The catchment board was dissolved by the Yorkshire Ouse River Board Constitution Order 1950, SI 1950/64. The functions and responsibilities of catchment boards are now vested in the Environment Agency: see WATER AND WATERWAYS vol 101 (2018) PARA 845. As to land drainage generally see WATER AND WATERWAYS vol 101 (2018) PARA 845 et seq. As to the Environment Agency see ENVIRONMENTAL QUALITY AND PUBLIC HEALTH vol 45 (2010) PARA 68 et seq; WATER AND WATERWAYS vol 100 (2018) PARA 23.
5   The catchment board was dissolved by the Trent River Board Constitution Order 1950, SI 1950/2041.
6   See the Coal Industry Nationalisation Act 1946 s 45(1), (3)–(5) (repealed); and the Coal Industry Nationalisation (Doncaster Drainage) Order 1947, SR & O 1947/651, art 2(1). The order contained also supplemental provisions consequent on the nationalisation of the coal-mining industry: see arts 2(2)–(6), 3–6. As to the nationalisation of the coal-mining industry see PARA 49.
7   See PARA 49.
8   Ie the obligations on mine owners to establish funds for maintenance of works imposed by the Doncaster Area Drainage Act 1929 s 10.
9   As to the meaning of 'coal mine' see PARA 3.
10  Ie by virtue of the Coal Industry Act 1994 s 7(3): see PARA 66.
11  Doncaster Area Drainage Act 1929 s 10(6) (amended by SI 1994/3062).
12  Ie under the Doncaster Area Drainage Act 1929 s 9.
13  Doncaster Area Drainage Act 1929 s 10A(1) (s 10A added by SI 1994/3062).
14  Ie by notice served on the Environment Agency: see the Doncaster Area Drainage Act 1929 s 10A(2); and the Environment Act 1995 (Consequential Amendments) Regulations 1996, SI 1996/593, reg 2, Sch 1.
15  Doncaster Area Drainage Act 1929 s 10A(2).
16  Doncaster Area Drainage Act 1929 s 10A(3), (4). As to arbitration generally see ARBITRATION vol 2 (2017) PARA 501 et seq.
17  Doncaster Area Drainage Act 1929 s 10A(5).
18  Doncaster Area Drainage Act 1929 s 10A(5).

*(E)    Supplementary Provisions*

(a)    Claims

## 245.   Avoidance of double claims.

A person entitled to give a damage notice[1] in respect of subsidence damage[2] to any property is not entitled to proceed at the same time in respect of the same damage to that property with both (1) such a notice; and (2) a claim[3] against the person with responsibility for subsidence affecting any land[4] for damages or compensation arising apart from the Coal Mining Subsidence Act 1991, although he may elect which notice or claim he will proceed with for the time being[5]. Where any person proceeds with one such original notice or claim he is not entitled to proceed with the other unless it is determined, whether by agreement or otherwise, that he is entitled to none of the relief claimed by the original notice or claim, or that notice or claim is withdrawn before it is determined[6].

1   As to the meaning of 'damage notice' see PARA 210. As to the meaning of 'notice' see PARA 210. As to notices see PARA 251 et seq.
2   As to the meaning of 'subsidence damage' see PARA 203.
3   As to the meaning of 'claim' see PARA 210.
4   See the Coal Industry Act 1994 s 43(8), Sch 6 para 7. As to the responsible person see PARA 204.
5   Coal Mining Subsidence Act 1991 s 37(1).
6   Coal Mining Subsidence Act 1991 s 37(2). Where two or more persons are entitled to give a damage notice under Pt II (ss 2–21) in respect of the same subsidence damage to any property, s 37(1), (2) applies as if any election made by any one of them to proceed with such a notice had also been made by the other or others of them: s 37(3).

## 246. Agreements as to the working of minerals or the leaving of minerals unworked.

The provisions of the Coal Mining Subsidence Act 1991 and of any other enactment[1] making provision with respect to rights and liabilities between the person with responsibility for subsidence affecting any land[2] and any government department, local authority or statutory undertakers[3] in respect of the working of minerals[4] under or adjacent to any property, or the leaving of minerals unworked for the support of any property[5], have effect subject to the terms of any agreement with respect to such rights and liabilities which has been entered into between the responsible person and the department, authority or undertakers otherwise than in connection with a disposition of an interest in land and is for the time being subsisting[6].

1 See PARA 189.
2 See the Coal Industry Act 1994 s 43(8), Sch 6 para 7. As to the responsible person see PARA 204.
3 As to the meaning of 'statutory undertakers' see PARA 215.
4 As to the meaning of 'minerals' see PARA 10.
5 As to the right of support see PARA 114 et seq.
6 Coal Mining Subsidence Act 1991 s 37(4). Without prejudice to s 37(4), the provisions of the Coal Mining Subsidence Act 1991 and the Coal Industry Act 1994 relating to any person who is the responsible person in relation to any subsidence damage, or who would be the responsible person if any such damage occurred, do not affect any rights or obligations in connection with that damage that arise (1) under a restructuring scheme; (2) under the conditions of any licence under Pt II (ss 25–36); or (3) apart from the Coal Industry Act 1994, as between different persons who are or have been at any time licensed operators, or as between the Coal Authority and any one or more such persons: s 67(7), Sch 10 para 13(2). As to restructuring schemes see PARA 72. As to the Coal Authority see PARA 52 et seq.

## 247. Reimbursement of a successful claimant's expenses.

Where the person with responsibility for subsidence affecting any land[1] takes any remedial action[2], or makes any payment to, or makes any living accommodation available to, any person[3], he must also pay any costs or expenses reasonably incurred by the claimant[4] or any other person interested[5] or by the person in question (1) for the preparation and prosecution of his damage notice[6] or claim[7]; or (2) in the case of costs or expenses incurred by the claimant before the subsidence damage[8] became evident, with a view to the possible preparation and prosecution of his damage notice[9]. These provisions, however, do not apply to:

(a) costs and expenses incurred by the claimant or any other person interested (i) in securing or attempting to secure the agreement or consent of any other person to the exercise by the person with responsibility for subsidence affecting any land of certain powers[10] under the Coal Mining Subsidence Act 1991[11]; or (ii) in pursuing an application[12] to the county court regarding the unreasonable withholding of consent[13];

(b) costs or expenses incurred by the claimant or any other person interested more than four years[14] before the giving of his damage notice[15];

(c) costs or expenses incurred in or in connection with any proceedings before any tribunal, court or other person if an order for their payment has been or could have been made by that tribunal, court or other person[16].

1 See the Coal Industry Act 1994 s 43(8), Sch 6 para 7. As to the responsible person see PARA 204.
2 As to remedial action see PARA 209.

3   Ie under the Coal Mining Subsidence Act 1991 Pt III (ss 22–36): see s 38(1).
4   As to the meaning of 'claimant' see PARA 210.
5   As to the meaning of 'any other person interested' see PARA 210.
6   As to the meaning of 'damage notice' see PARA 210. As to the meaning of 'notice' see PARA 210. As to notices see PARA 251 et seq.
7   As to the meaning of 'claim' see PARA 210.
8   As to the meaning of 'subsidence damage' see PARA 203.
9   Coal Mining Subsidence Act 1991 s 38(1), (2).
10   Ie those mentioned in the Coal Mining Subsidence Act 1991 s 41(1)(a) (see PARA 249): see s 38(3)(a).
11   Coal Mining Subsidence Act 1991 s 38(3)(a).
12   Ie under the Coal Mining Subsidence Act 1991 s 41(2) (see PARA 249): see s 38(3)(b).
13   Coal Mining Subsidence Act 1991 s 38(3)(b).
14   The Secretary of State may by order substitute for this period (whether as originally enacted or as previously amended) such other period as he thinks fit, or direct that the Coal Mining Subsidence Act 1991 s 38(4) is not to apply in such circumstances as may be specified in the order: s 38(6). At the date at which this volume states the law no such order had been made. As to the Secretary of State see PARA 2; and as to the Secretary of State's power to make regulations or orders see PARA 202.
15   Coal Mining Subsidence Act 1991 s 38(4).
16   Coal Mining Subsidence Act 1991 s 38(5).

## 248.   Claim for compensation in relation to statutory rights to withdraw support.

In any case where (1) immediately before 1 September 1975[1] the National Coal Board[2] had a right[3] to withdraw support from any land[4]; and (2) after that date that land has been damaged by the working of coal[5] in the exercise of the right to withdraw support conferred by the Coal Industry Act 1975[6] or the Coal Industry Act 1994[7], any person interested in that land may claim compensation for that damage in accordance with the terms and conditions which were applicable before that date[8]. No person is entitled both to receive compensation for damage under these provisions and to receive compensation for that damage, or have that damage made good under Part II[9] of the Coal Mining Subsidence Act 1991[10].

1   Ie the commencement of the Coal Industry Act 1975: see s 8. As to the historical background to the coal-mining subsidence legislation see PARA 200.
2   The National Coal Board later became known as the British Coal Corporation: see PARA 49. As to the British Coal Corporation see PARAS 49–50.
3   Ie by virtue of the Coal Act 1938 s 4, Sch 2 para 5 (repealed) which related to cases where the surface and the mine were separately held on 1 January 1939.
4   As to the statutory right to withdraw support from land in relation to coal mining see PARA 176 et seq.
5   As to the meaning of 'coal' see PARA 48 (definition applied by the Coal Mining Subsidence Act 1991 s 52(1)).
6   Ie by the Coal Industry Act 1975 s 2 (repealed).
7   Ie by the Coal Industry Act 1994 s 38 (see PARA 176).
8   Coal Mining Subsidence Act 1991 s 53(1), Sch 7 para 2(1). See also PARA 182 et seq.
9   Ie the Coal Mining Subsidence Act 1991 Pt II (ss 2–21): see PARA 209 et seq.
10   Coal Mining Subsidence Act 1991 Sch 7 para 2(2).

### (b)   Disputes and Complaints

## 249.   Reference of disputes.

In general[1], and subject to provisions as to arbitration[2], any question arising under the Coal Mining Subsidence Act 1991 falls, in default of agreement, to be referred to and determined by the Upper Tribunal[3]. Such questions may include:

(1)    any question as to who is the person with responsibility[4] for subsidence affecting particular land[5];

(2)    the question whether there has been a contravention of any subsidence requirement[6]; and

(3)    the question how any such contravention is to be remedied[7].

The tribunal, court, or other person by whom any question is to be heard or determined under the Coal Mining Subsidence Act 1991 may make such orders as may be necessary to give effect to its or his determination, and in particular may by order require any person with responsibility for subsidence affecting any land[8] to carry out any obligations imposed upon him by the Coal Mining Subsidence Act 1991 within such period as the tribunal, court or person may direct[9], and award damages in respect of any failure of the person with responsibility for subsidence affecting any land[10] to carry out any such obligations[11]. When a question[12] is referred to the Upper Tribunal or to arbitration[13], the powers of the tribunal or arbitrator include[14]:

(a)    power to have such regard as may appear appropriate to any recommendations or report[15] of the subsidence adviser[16];

(b)    power by order to require a person with responsibility for subsidence affecting land to take such steps for remedying any contravention of a subsidence requirement as that tribunal or arbitrator may direct[17]; and

(c)    power to award such compensation not exceeding £5,000[18] in respect of any inconvenience caused to a person by a contravention of a subsidence requirement which does not otherwise[19] fall to be compensated for[20].

No question as to whether any person with responsibility for subsidence affecting any land[21] is in breach of his remedial obligation[22] in respect of any subsidence damage[23] may be heard and determined by any tribunal, court or other person unless the necessary reference is made or the necessary proceedings are instituted, before the end of: (i) the period of three years beginning with the earliest date on which the responsible person is in breach of his remedial obligation; or (ii) the period of six years beginning with the first date on which any person entitled to give a damage notice had the knowledge required for funding a claim in respect of that damage[24], whichever period expires last[25].

Where the agreement or consent of two or more persons is required for the person with responsibility for subsidence affecting any land[26] to exercise certain powers under the Coal Mining Subsidence Act 1991[27] and that responsible person has reached agreement with or obtained the consent of one or more, but not both or all of those persons[28], and if on an application made by them or by the responsible person it appears to a county court that any person whose agreement or consent is required has withheld his agreement or consent unreasonably, the court may order that the power in question is to apply as if the responsible person had reached agreement with or obtained the consent of that person[29].

If the occupier of any premises refuses to afford the person with responsibility for subsidence affecting any land[30] such facilities as he may require to enter upon, inspect and execute works, then a magistrates court, on a complaint[31] made by the responsible person, may confer such powers to enter, inspect and execute works on the premises as may appear to the court to be necessary, and the court may order the occupier to permit the exercise of these powers[32].

1    Ie except as provided otherwise by or under the Coal Mining Subsidence Act 1991 (eg under s 32: see PARA 239): see s 40(1).

2    See PARA 250.

3    Coal Mining Subsidence Act 1991 ss 40(1), 52(1) (s 40(1) amended by SI 2009/1307; Coal Mining Subsidence Act 1991 s 52(1) definition added by SI 2009/1309; Coal Industry Act 1994 s 47(10) (definition added by SI 2009/1309)). As to the Upper Tribunal generally see COURTS AND TRIBUNALS vol 24 (2010) PARA 883 et seq. As to procedure see the Tribunal Procedure (Upper Tribunal) (Lands Chamber) Rules 2010, SI 2010/2600; and COMPULSORY ACQUISITION OF LAND.

4    As to the responsible person see PARA 204.

5    Coal Industry Act 1994 s 47(1)(a) (amended by SI 2009/1307).

6    Coal Industry Act 1994 s 47(1)(b). References to a contravention of a subsidence requirement mean a contravention by the responsible person of:

       (1)     any requirements imposed on him by or under the Coal Mining Subsidence Act 1991 or by any regulations under the Coal Industry Act 1994 s 45 (see PARA 207) (s 47(9)(a));

       (2)     the requirement under s 43(6) (see PARA 204) (s 47(9)(b));

       (3)     the requirement under s 43(8), Sch 6 para 1 to forward a damage notice to the Coal Authority as soon as practicable after receiving it (s 47(9)(c));

       (4)     the requirement to comply with an order under s 47(4)(b) or the Coal Mining Subsidence Act 1991 s 40(3)(a) (Coal Industry Act 1994 s 47(9)(d) (amended by SI 2009/1307)).

   As to the meaning of 'damage notice' see PARA 210. As to the meaning of 'notice' see PARA 210. As to notices see PARA 251 et seq. As to the Coal Authority see PARA 52 et seq.

7    Coal Industry Act 1994 s 47(1)(c).

8    Coal Industry Act 1994 s 43(8), Sch 6 para 7.

9    Coal Mining Subsidence Act 1991 s 40(3)(a).

10    Coal Industry Act 1994 Sch 6 para 7.

11    Coal Mining Subsidence Act 1991 s 40(3)(b). As to the power of the Lands Tribunal to award interest on a sum awarded as compensation for subsidence damage see *Knibb v National Coal Board* [1987] QB 906, [1986] 3 All ER 644, CA; *British Coal Corpn v Gwent County Council* (1995) 71 P & CR 482, CA.

12    Ie a question falling within the Coal Industry Act 1994 s 47(1): see s 47(4).

13    See PARA 250.

14    Ie in addition to the incidental power conferred by the Coal Industry Act 1994 s 47(3) and the Coal Mining Subsidence Act 1991 s 40(3): see the Coal Industry Act 1994 s 47(4).

15    Ie made by virtue of regulations made under Coal Industry Act 1994 s 46 (see PARA 208): see s 47(4)(a).

16    Coal Industry Act 1994 s 47(4)(a) (amended by SI 2009/1307). As to the subsidence adviser see PARA 208.

17    Coal Industry Act 1994 s 47(4)(b).

18    Or such higher amount as may be substituted by an order made by the Secretary of State: Coal Industry Act 1994 s 47(6). At the date at which this volume states the law no such order had been made. The Coal Mining Subsidence Act 1991 s 50 (see PARA 202) applies to the power to make orders under this provision as it applies to any power to make regulations or orders under that Act: see the Coal Industry Act 1994 s 47(10), (11). As to the Secretary of State see PARA 2.

19    Ie apart from the Coal Industry Act 1994 s 47(4)(c).

20    Coal Industry Act 1994 s 47(4)(c).

21    Coal Industry Act 1994 Sch 6 para 7.

22    As to the meaning of 'remedial obligation' see PARA 209.

23    As to the meaning of 'subsidence damage' see PARA 203.

24    See the Coal Mining Subsidence Act 1991 s 3; and PARA 210.

25    Coal Mining Subsidence Act 1991 s 44(1), (2). Any period during which the responsible person's obligation is subject to the terms of a stop notice (as to the meaning of which see PARA 222) is to be disregarded: s 44(3).

26    Coal Industry Act 1994 Sch 6 para 7.

27    Ie the powers conferred under the Coal Mining Subsidence Act 1991 s 5(3), (5) (see PARA 211), s 10(2)(b) (see PARA 219), or s 33(2)(a) (see PARA 240): s 41(1)(a).

28    Coal Mining Subsidence Act 1991 s 41(1)(b).

29    Coal Mining Subsidence Act 1991 s 41(2). The provisions of the Coal Mining Subsidence Act 1991 s 38(2) relating to the reimbursement of a claimant's expenses (see PARA 248) do not apply to costs or expenses relating to securing or attempting to secure consent as mentioned in s 41(1)(a) or in pursuing an application under s 41(2): see s 38(3).

30    Coal Industry Act 1994 Sch 6 para 7.

31    As to magistrates' courts generally and the procedure by way of complaint see MAGISTRATES.

32 Coal Mining Subsidence Act 1991 s 42(1). However, this provision does not extend to premises occupied by or on behalf of the Crown: s 42(2).

## 250. Arbitration.

The Secretary of State[1] may make provision by regulations[2] as he considers appropriate:

(1)    for establishing procedures to facilitate the making[3] of references to arbitration[4] of questions arising under the Coal Mining Subsidence Act 1991 or under the Coal Industry Act 1994[5] relating to subsidence matters[6];

(2)    for enabling such questions to be referred to and determined by arbitration in cases where they would fall to be determined by the Upper Tribunal[7] on account of the failure by a person who is (or who asserts he is) the person with responsibility for subsidence affecting land[8] to agree to the arbitration or any other method of determining the question[9]; and

(3)    for regulating the conduct of such arbitrations[10].

There are two established arbitration schemes:

(a)    the Householders[11] Arbitration Scheme for the determination of questions arising between responsible persons and householders[12];

(b)    the General Arbitration Scheme for the determination of other questions[13].

Disputes are to be determined by a single arbitrator appointed by the Arbitration Body[14]. Any question concerning the arbitration procedure is to be determined according to the law of the place where the arbitration is held[15], and subject to this, the dispute is to be determined according to the law for the time being in force in England and Wales as the parties may agree or, in default of agreement, as determined by the arbitrator[16].

The Secretary of State also may by regulations provide for the expenses of maintaining procedures to be met in whole or in part by some or all of the persons with responsibility for subsidence affecting land or in other ways[17], and also provide for one or more of the parties to a reference[18] to be required to pay, or make a contribution towards, the costs or other expenses incurred in relation to that reference by any person[19].

Regulations under these provisions may provide for prescribed matters to be determined[20] by the Coal Authority[21] and for the recovery by that Authority of expenses so incurred from other persons with responsibility for subsidence affecting land[22].

1   As to the Secretary of State see PARA 2.
2   See the Coal Mining Subsidence (Arbitration Schemes) Regulations 1994, SI 1994/2566. The Coal Mining Subsidence Act 1991 s 50 (see PARA 202) applies to the power to make regulations under these provisions as it applies to any power to make regulations or orders under that Act: Coal Industry Act 1994 s 47(10). As to the Secretary of State's power to make regulations or orders see PARA 202.
3   Ie by agreement or in accordance with regulations under head (2) in the text: see the Coal Industry Act 1994 s 47(2)(a).
4   Ie such arbitration as may be prescribed by regulations under the Coal Industry Act 1994 s 47: s 47(2)(a), (10). As to arbitration generally see ARBITRATION vol 2 (2017) PARA 501 et seq.
5   The questions referred to in PARA 249 heads (1)–(3).
6   Coal Industry Act 1994 s 47(2)(a). The Coal Mining Subsidence (Arbitration Schemes) Regulations 1994, SI 1994/2566, apply to questions referred to in the Coal Industry Act 1994 s 47(1) and to any question under the Coal Mining Subsidence Act 1991 other than those arising under s 32 (see PARA 239) or s 36 (see PARA 241): see the Coal Mining Subsidence (Arbitration Schemes) Regulations 1994, SI 1994/2566, reg 2. The Arbitration Act 1996 Pt I (ss 1–84) applies

(subject to ss 95–98) to arbitrations under these provisions: see s 94; and ARBITRATION vol 2 (2017) PARA 501 et seq.
7    As to the Upper Tribunal see COURTS AND TRIBUNALS vol 24 (2010) PARA 883 et seq.
8    As to the responsible person see PARA 204.
9    Coal Industry Act 1994 s 47(2)(b), 47(10) (definition added by SI 2009/1307).
10   Coal Industry Act 1994 s 47(2)(c).
11   'Householder' means a person who occupies a dwelling-house and who either is the owner of it or is liable to make good any damage to it in whole or part: Coal Mining Subsidence (Arbitration Schemes) Regulations 1994, SI 1994/2566, reg 1(2).
12   See the Coal Mining Subsidence (Arbitration Schemes) Regulations 1994, SI 1994/2566, reg 3(1), Sch 1.
13   See the Coal Mining Subsidence (Arbitration Schemes) Regulations 1994, SI 1994/2566, reg 3(2), Sch 2.
14   See the Coal Mining Subsidence (Arbitration Schemes) Regulations 1994, SI 1994/2566, regs 4, 7.
15   See the Coal Mining Subsidence (Arbitration Schemes) Regulations 1994, SI 1994/2566, reg 6(1).
16   See the Coal Mining Subsidence (Arbitration Schemes) Regulations 1994, SI 1994/2566, reg 6(2).
17   Coal Industry Act 1994 s 47(7)(a); and see the Coal Mining Subsidence (Arbitration Schemes) Regulations 1994, SI 1994/2566, reg 8 which makes provision as to the costs of the Arbitration Body.
18   Ie a reference in accordance with the regulations: see the Coal Industry Act 1994 s 47(7)(b).
19   Coal Industry Act 1994 s 47(7)(b). As to the costs of arbitration proceedings see the Coal Mining Subsidence (Arbitration Schemes) Regulations 1994, SI 1994/2566, reg 5, Schs 1, 2.
20   Ie in such manner and by reference to such factors as may be described in the regulations: see the Coal Industry Act 1994 s 47(8)(a).
21   As to the Coal Authority see PARA 52 et seq.
22   Coal Industry Act 1994 s 47(8)(b). As to the apportionment of the costs of the Arbitration Body amongst responsible persons and for the recovery by the Authority of the amounts so apportioned see the Coal Mining Subsidence (Arbitration Schemes) Regulations 1994, SI 1994/2566, reg 8.

(c)   Notices, Information and Reports

**251.   Notices to owners and occupiers of property.**
Where it is proposed to carry on any underground coal-mining operations[1], the responsible person[2] must give to the owners or occupiers[3] of any land which might be affected by subsidence as a result of the operations notice[4] there is a risk of their land being so affected[5]; and must also give notice that he has done so to any organisation appearing to be representative of those owners or occupiers[6]. Where notice that there is a risk of the land being affected by subsidence has been given, the responsible person must give notice to the owners or occupiers of any of the following facts:
(1)      any decision not to proceed with the proposed operations[7];
(2)      anything which gives the responsible person reason to believe that there is no longer any risk of the land being affected by subsidence[8]; and
(3)      the discontinuance of any operations which have been carried on[9].
The responsible person must[10] from time to time, until notice is given of any of the facts in heads (1) to (3) above, give notice to the owners or occupiers reminding them of any risk there may be of the land being, or having been, affected by subsidence[11]. Failure to give a required notice is an offence[12].
The Secretary of State[13] may by regulations[14] make provision as to the contents and form of the notices[15], the times at which and the manner in which they are to be given[16], and any information, forms and documents which are to accompany them[17].

1    As to the position where underground coal-mining operations proposed to be carried on after 30 November 1991 can be regarded as a continuation of operations carried on before that date, see the Coal Mining Subsidence Act 1991 s 53(1), Sch 7 para 7.

2   Ie the person who would be the responsible person in relation to any subsidence damage to that land if such damage were to result from the operations: see the Coal Industry Act 1994 s 43(8), Sch 6 para 8. As to the responsible person see PARA 204.

3   For these purposes, references, in relation to any land, to the owners or occupiers include references to any person who is the owner or occupier of any part of the land or is liable to make good in whole or in part any subsidence damage affecting the land: Coal Mining Subsidence Act 1991 s 46(8)(b). As to the meaning of 'owner' see PARA 207; and as to the meaning of 'subsidence damage' see PARA 203. References to land include references to any buildings, structures or works on, in or over land: s 46(8)(a). As to the meaning of 'structure' and as to the meaning of 'works' see PARA 203.

4   As to the meaning of 'notice' see PARA 210.

5   Coal Mining Subsidence Act 1991 s 46(1)(a).

6   Coal Mining Subsidence Act 1991 s 46(1)(b).

7   Coal Mining Subsidence Act 1991 s 46(3)(a).

8   Coal Mining Subsidence Act 1991 s 46(3)(b).

9   Coal Mining Subsidence Act 1991 s 46(3)(c).

10  Ie where a notice has been given under the Coal Mining Subsidence Act 1991 s 46(1)(a): see s 46(4).

11  Coal Mining Subsidence Act 1991 s 46(4). If no other time for giving a notice under s 46(4) is prescribed by regulations under s 46(5)(b), the responsible person must give the notice within the period of one year beginning with the date on which the most recent notice under s 46 was given: s 46(6).

12  See the Coal Industry Act 1994 s 48(5), (6); and PARA 254.

13  As to the Secretary of State see PARA 2.

14  See the Coal Mining Subsidence (Provision of Information) Regulations 1994, SI 1994/2565. As to the Secretary of State's power to make regulations or orders see PARA 202. The Coal Mining Subsidence Act 1991 provides that in the event that no other manner for giving notice is prescribed the responsible person must take all reasonably practicable steps for bringing the notice to the attention of the person to whom it is to be given: s 46(7).

15  Coal Mining Subsidence Act 1991 s 46(5)(a). The regulations made under s 46 provide that every notice given to the owners or occupiers of any land in accordance with s 46(1)(a) or s 46(4) must be accompanied by the following information:

   (1)   the full name and address of the person with responsibility giving the notice (Coal Mining Subsidence (Provision of Information) Regulations 1994, SI 1994/2565, reg 2(1)(a));

   (2)   the place or places of business at which that person may be contacted during normal business hours, and any telephone or facsimile transmission number for communicating with him at every such place (reg 2(1)(b)); and

   (3)   a copy of the document known as '*Coal Mining Subsidence Damage – a Guide to Claimants' Rights*' as for the time being issued by the Secretary of State (Coal Mining Subsidence (Provision of Information) Regulations 1994, SI 1994/2565, reg 2(1)(c)).

   Where an employee or agent of the person with responsibility is appointed to represent him in his dealings with the owner or occupier in relation to subsidence damage to the land (a) the information to be furnished must include the name of that employee or agent (reg 2(2)(a)); and (b) head (2) has effect with the substitution for references to the person with responsibility of references to that employee or agent (reg 2(2)(b)).

16  Coal Mining Subsidence Act 1991 s 46(5)(b). When, on a person other than the British Coal Corporation (as to which see PARAS 49–50) becoming a person with responsibility in relation to any land a notice under s 46(1) or s 46(4) has been given to any owner or occupier of the land less than 12 months before the happening of that event, and since the giving of that notice no notice has fallen to be given under heads (1)–(3) in the text, the person with responsibility must, within the period of 3 months commencing with the date of his becoming that person, give to the owners or occupiers of the land any notice falling to be given under s 46(3), or if no such notice falls to be given, notice under s 46(4): Coal Mining Subsidence (Provision of Information) Regulations 1994, SI 1994/2565, reg 3(1), (2).

17  Coal Mining Subsidence Act 1991 s 46(5)(c) (amended by the Coal Industry Act 1994 s 45(4)).

## 252. Notices to local authorities.

Where it is proposed to carry on any underground coal-mining operations[1], the responsible person[2] must give notice[3] of the operations to any local authority[4] whose area includes land which may be affected by subsidence as a result of the operations[5]. Where any underground coal-mining operations are being carried on, the responsible person must give notice of such facts as may be prescribed[6] to any local authority whose area includes land which has been or may be affected by subsidence as a result of the operations[7]. Failure to give a required notice is an offence[8].

The Secretary of State[9] may make provision by regulations[10] as to the contents and form of such notices[11], the times at which they are to be given[12], and any information, forms and documents which are to accompany them[13].

Each local authority must secure that copies of all notices and other information received by it[14] are made available, at all reasonable times, for inspection by the public free of charge, and must also provide facilities for obtaining copies of such documents on payment of a reasonable fee[15].

1   As to the position where underground coal-mining operations proposed to be carried on after 30 November 1991 can be regarded as a continuation of operations carried on before that date, see the Coal Mining Subsidence Act 1991 s 53(1), Sch 7 para 7.
2   Ie the person who would be the responsible person in relation to any subsidence damage to that land if such damage were to result from the operations: see the Coal Industry Act 1994 s 43(8), Sch 6 para 8. As to the responsible person see PARA 204. As to the meaning of 'subsidence damage' see PARA 203.
3   As to the meaning of 'notice' see PARA 210.
4   For these purposes, 'local authority' means: (1) in relation to England the council of a district or non-metropolitan county; and (2) in relation to Wales, the council of a county or county borough: Coal Mining Subsidence Act 1991 s 47(6) (amended by the Local Government (Wales) Act 1994 s 66(6), (8), Sch 16 para 91, Sch 18).
5   Coal Mining Subsidence Act 1991 s 47(1).
6   As to the meaning of 'prescribed' see PARA 210.
7   Coal Mining Subsidence Act 1991 s 47(2).
8   See the Coal Industry Act 1994 s 48(5), (6); and PARA 254.
9   As to the Secretary of State see PARA 2.
10  At the date at which this volume states the law no such regulations had been made. As to the Secretary of State's power to make regulations or orders see PARA 202.
11  Coal Mining Subsidence Act 1991 s 47(4)(a).
12  Coal Mining Subsidence Act 1991 s 47(4)(b).
13  Coal Mining Subsidence Act 1991 s 47(4)(c) (amended by the Coal Industry Act 1994 s 45(4)).
14  Ie under the Coal Mining Subsidence Act 1991 s 47: see s 47(5)(a).
15  Coal Mining Subsidence Act 1991 s 47(5)(b).

### 253. Reports on the operation of the Coal Mining Subsidence Act 1991.

The Secretary of State[1] may give directions to the Coal Authority[2] requiring it, on or before a specified date or at specified intervals, to make a report to him on the operation of the Coal Mining Subsidence Act 1991 during any specified period or periods[3]. The Secretary of State's directions may specify the matters to be dealt with, and any particular information to be given, in the report and the form in which the report is to be made[4]. He may also require the Authority to publish the report[5]. The Secretary of State must lay a copy of every such report received by him before Parliament[6].

1   As to the Secretary of State see PARA 2.
2   See the Coal Industry Act 1994 s 43(8), Sch 6 para 10. As to the Coal Authority see PARA 52 et seq.
3   Coal Mining Subsidence Act 1991 s 49(1) (amended by the Coal Industry Act 1994 s 43(8), Sch 6 para 10).
4   Coal Mining Subsidence Act 1991 s 49(2)(a).
5   Coal Mining Subsidence Act 1991 s 49(2)(b) (amended by the Coal Industry Act 1994 s 43(8), Sch 6 para 10).
6   Coal Mining Subsidence Act 1991 s 49(3).

**254. Offences with respect to subsidence information.**

It is an offence for any person[1] for specified purposes[2] in relation to the Coal Mining Subsidence Act 1991:

(1)     to furnish any other person with any information which he knows to be false in a material particular[3];

(2)     recklessly to furnish any other person with any information which is false in a material particular[4]; or

(3)     to withhold any information from any person with intent to deceive[5].

A licensed operator[6] is guilty of an offence if he:

(a)     furnishes the Coal Authority[7] with any information which he knows to be false in a material particular[8];

(b)     recklessly furnishes the Authority with any subsidence information[9] which is false in a material particular[10]; or

(c)     with intent to deceive, withholds any subsidence information from the Authority[11].

Any person who fails to give any notice which he is required to give to property owners[12] and local authorities[13] in accordance with the statutory requirements[14] is guilty of an offence[15]. A person guilty of an offence under these provisions is liable, on summary conviction, to a fine not exceeding the statutory maximum[16] and, on conviction on indictment, to a fine[17].

1   This includes a body of persons corporate or unincorporate: Interpretation Act 1978 s 5, Sch 1. As to offences by bodies corporate under the Coal Industry Act 1994 see PARA 111.

2   A person is guilty of an offence if he engages in the conduct mentioned in heads (1)–(3) in the text for the purposes of:

    (1)     obtaining for himself or any other person any benefit under the Coal Mining Subsidence Act 1991 (Coal Industry Act 1994 s 48(1)(a)); or

    (2)     facilitating the temporary or permanent avoidance, by himself or any other person, of the whole or any part of:

        (a)     any obligation under the Coal Mining Subsidence Act 1991 (Coal Industry Act 1994 s 48(1)(b)(i));

        (b)     any other requirement mentioned in the Coal Industry Act 1994 s 47(9)(a)–(c) (see PARA 249); or

        (c)     any liability for contravention of any such obligation or requirement (s 48(1)(b)(iii)).

    As to the meaning of 'contravention' see PARA 54.

3   Coal Industry Act 1994 s 48(2)(a).

4   Coal Industry Act 1994 s 48(2)(b). As to recklessness generally see CRIMINAL LAW vol 25 (2016) PARA 11.

5   Coal Industry Act 1994 s 48(2)(c).

6   As to the meaning of 'licensed operator' see PARA 58.

7   As to the Coal Authority see PARA 52 et seq.

8   Coal Industry Act 1994 s 48(3)(a).

9   'Subsidence information', in relation to a person who is or has been a licensed operator, means information relating to the extent of the existing or potential liabilities of that person in respect of subsidence damage: Coal Industry Act 1994 s 48(4). As to the meaning of 'subsidence damage' see PARA 203 (definition applied by s 65(1)).

10  Coal Industry Act 1994 s 48(3)(b).

11  Coal Industry Act 1994 s 48(3)(c).

12  Ie in accordance with the Coal Mining Subsidence Act 1991 s 46 (see PARA 251): see the Coal Industry Act 1994 s 48(5).

13  Ie in accordance with the Coal Mining Subsidence Act 1991 s 47 (see PARA 252): see the Coal Industry Act 1994 s 48(5).

14  As to the requirement to give notices to property owners see PARA 251; and as to the requirement to give notices to local authorities see PARA 252.

15 Coal Industry Act 1994 s 48(5). In any proceedings against a person for an offence by virtue of s 48(5) it is a defence for that person to show that he took such steps as were reasonable to avoid commission of the offence: s 48(6).
16 Coal Industry Act 1994 s 48(7)(a). As to the statutory maximum see SENTENCING vol 92 (2015) PARA 176.
17 Coal Industry Act 1994 s 48(7)(b).

## (5) Rights of Way

### 255. General principles.

A person may construct a road through his own mine[1] by virtue of his right of property in the mine; and for this purpose the term 'mine' in an exception is not restricted to the mineral stratum, but includes a layer of the adjoining soil sufficient for working the excepted mine in a proper manner[2].

Rights of way may also exist as rights in another's land appurtenant to a mine[3]. In such a case the dominant owner is not entitled as against the servient owner to the exclusive use of the right of way[4], and it appears that the servient owner may make alterations in the way provided he does not obstruct it[5].

Common law provisions are supplemented by statutory provisions whereby a mine operator may have conferred on him rights of way, whether on the surface or (as appropriate) underground[6].

1  As to the meaning of 'mine' see PARA 3.
2  *Batten Pooll v Kennedy* [1907] 1 Ch 256; following *Proud v Bates* (1865) 34 LJ Ch 406; *Duke of Hamilton v Graham* (1871) LR 2 Sc & Div 166; *Eardley v Granville* (1876) 3 ChD 826; and distinguishing *Ramsay v Blair* (1876) 1 App Cas 701, HL.
3  As to the principles governing rights of way generally see REAL PROPERTY AND REGISTRATION.
4  See *R v Jolliffe* (1787) 2 Term Rep 90 at 95 per Buller J.
5  *Bradburn v Morris, Morris v Bradburn* (1876) 3 ChD 812 at 821, CA, per James LJ, and at 823 per Mellish LJ.
6  As to rights of airway, shaftway or surface or underground wayleave see the Mines (Working Facilities and Support) Act 1966 (see PARAS 380–395), which applies to all minerals. As to the meaning of 'minerals' see PARA 10. As to additional rights in relation to underground land for the purposes of coal-mining operations see the Coal Industry Act 1994 s 51; and PARA 396. As to the meaning of 'coal-mining operations' see PARA 51. As to the authorisation of, and facilities for, opencast working of coal see the Opencast Coal Act 1958 Pt I (ss 4–16); and PARA 424 et seq.

### 256. General wayleave.

A general grant[1] of wayleave, in connection with mines[2], but undefined in position, will authorise the construction and use of such a way as is necessary, having regard to the surrounding circumstances of the case or the requirements of the grantee[3]. Thus a right of wayleave may authorise a framed wagon-way, if it is necessary for the carriage of coals[4]; and the term 'sufficient wayleave' may authorise the construction of a fenced railway, if this is necessary to enable the minerals[5] to be worked at a reasonable profit[6].

1  As to the creation of rights of way by express grant see REAL PROPERTY AND REGISTRATION vol 87 (2017) PARA 750.
2  As to the meaning of 'mine' see PARA 3.
3  See *Farrow v Vansittart* (1839) 1 Ry & Can Cas 602 at 609.
4  *Senhouse v Christian* (1787) 1 Term Rep 560.
5  As to the meaning of 'minerals' see PARA 10.
6  *Dand v Kingscote* (1840) 6 M & W 174. The right, under a Canal Act passed before the introduction of locomotive engines, to make railways or roads to convey coals to the canal authorised the construction of railways for the use of locomotive engines: *Bishop v North* (1843) 11 M & W 418.

## 257. Particular wayleave.

If the purposes for which the way is to be used are defined in the grant, the user is restricted to these purposes[1]. Thus a right of wagon-way[2] or a mere right of passage[3] will not authorise the construction and use of a tramway or railway; and a grant for all purposes except the carriage of minerals[4], or for agricultural purposes[5] or other purposes not including mining purposes[6], will not authorise the carriage of minerals. A right of way for minerals cannot be used for other purposes[7], and a right for the carriage of minerals from a particular mine[8] does not authorise the carriage of foreign minerals[9], nor, if a terminus is defined, carriage beyond that terminus[10]. It is a question of construction whether a wayleave is limited to the carriage of minerals from a particular mine[11].

1 *Duke of Hamilton v Graham* (1871) LR 2 Sc & Div 166 at 169 per Lord Hatherley LC; and see REAL PROPERTY AND REGISTRATION.
2 *Farrow v Vansittart* (1839) 1 Ry & Can Cas 602 at 609; *Re Bidder and North Staffordshire Rly Co* (1878) 4 QBD 412 at 429, CA, per Bramwell LJ (affd sub nom *Elliot v North Staffordshire Rly Co* [1881] WN 52, HL).
3 *Duke of Beaufort v Bates* (1862) 3 De GF & J 381 at 392 per Turner LJ; *Neath Canal Co v Ynisarwed Resolven Colliery Co* (1875) 10 Ch App 450.
4 *Marquis of Stafford v Coyney* (1827) 7 B & C 257. As to the meaning of 'minerals' see PARA 10.
5 *Bradburn v Morris, Morris v Bradburn* (1876) 3 ChD 812, CA.
6 *Cowling v Higginson* (1838) 4 M & W 245.
7 *Durham and Sunderland Rly Co v Walker* (1842) 2 QB 940, Ex Ch; *Meynell v Surtees* (1854) 3 Sm & G 101 at 117–118 per Stuart V-C; *Farrow v Vansittart* (1839) 1 Ry & Can Cas 602.
8 As to the meaning of 'mine' see PARA 3.
9 *Dand v Kingscote* (1840) 6 M & W 174; *Durham and Sunderland Rly Co v Walker* (1842) 2 QB 940, Ex Ch; *Midgley v Richardson* (1845) 14 M & W 595.
10 See *James v Cochrane* (1853) 8 Exch 556 at 573 et seq, Ex Ch, per Coleridge J.
11 The grant was held to be general in *Re Bidder and North Staffordshire Rly Co* (1878) 4 QBD 412, CA (affd sub nom *Elliot v North Staffordshire Rly Co* [1881] WN 52, HL); *James v Cochrane* (1853) 8 Exch 556, Ex Ch; *Bowes v Lord Ravensworth* (1855) 15 CB 512; *Proud v Bates* (1865) 34 LJ Ch 406. Where land is granted for the purpose of constructing and using a mineral railway, then, according to the terms of the grant, the land may be used for any other purpose not inconsistent with its use as a mineral railway: *Attwood v Llay Main Collieries Ltd* [1926] Ch 444.

## 258. Direction of way.

When it arises by implication of law[1], the right of way must be exercised in some convenient direction[2]. Under an express grant the direction is in general defined, and no material deviation may be made from the defined route, although the deviation may be sanctioned by acquiescence[3]. Where no definite route is prescribed the road may be constructed in the most convenient direction for getting to the mines[4]; the shortest practicable route need not be chosen[5].

1 As to the creation of rights of way by implication of law see REAL PROPERTY AND REGISTRATION vol 87 (2017) PARA 878.
2 *Staple v Heydon* (1703) 6 Mod Rep 1 at 3.
3 *Mold v Wheatcroft* (1859) 27 Beav 510. As to the right to deviate by reason of obstruction see REAL PROPERTY AND REGISTRATION vol 87 (2017) PARA 840.
4 As to the meaning of 'mine' see PARA 3.
5 *Richards v Richards* (1859) John 255.

## 259. User of prescriptive right of way.

Where a right of way is acquired by prescription[1] the burden on the servient tenement may not be increased by more onerous user or by the construction of a more onerous way[2]; but, while user for a particular purpose will not in general justify a user for other purposes or for a different object[3], user for a variety of purposes may be evidence of a right of user for all purposes[4].

1   As to the creation of rights of way by prescription see REAL PROPERTY AND REGISTRATION vol 87 (2017) PARA 803.
2   *Marquis of Stafford v Coyney* (1827) 7 B & C 257.
3   *Cowling v Higginson* (1838) 4 M & W 245; *Bradburn v Morris, Morris v Bradburn* (1876) 3 ChD 812, CA. As to particular wayleave see PARA 257.
4   *Wimbledon and Putney Commons Conservators v Dixon* (1875) 1 ChD 362, CA.

## 260. Obstruction and wrongful user.

The obstruction of a private right of way will give rise to a claim for damages[1]. The dominant owner is also entitled to an injunction[2] and, if necessary, to a mandatory injunction[3].

If a right of way is wrongly claimed an injunction will in general be granted to restrain the future user[4]; and if rails have been wrongfully laid[5], or an aperture is made in adjoining land[6] for the carriage of minerals[7], an injunction will be granted to compel the wrongdoer to remove the rails or to stop up the aperture; but not if the wrongdoer merely uses an aperture wrongfully made by another person, although he will be compelled to allow the injured party access to enable him to stop it up[8].

1   *Bell v Midland Rly Co* (1861) 10 CBNS 287; *Mold v Wheatcroft* (1859) 27 Beav 510 at 521 per Romilly MR; and see REAL PROPERTY AND REGISTRATION. As to damages generally see DAMAGES.
2   *Newmarch v Brandling* (1818) 3 Swan 99. As to the principles upon which injunctions are granted see CIVIL PROCEDURE vol 12 (2015) PARA 1098 et seq.
3   See *Bradburn v Morris, Morris v Bradburn* (1876) 3 ChD 812, CA; and CIVIL PROCEDURE vol 12 (2015) PARA 1102 et seq.
4   *Powell v Aiken* (1858) 4 K & J 343; *Wright v Pitt* (1870) LR 12 Eq 408 at 417 per Malins V-C; *Phillips v Homfray, Fothergill v Phillips* (1871) 6 Ch App 770; *Wimbledon and Putney Commons Conservators v Dixon* (1875) 1 ChD 362, CA; *Eardley v Granville* (1876) 3 ChD 826 at 832 per Jessel MR.
5   *Neath Canal Co v Ynisarwed Resolven Colliery Co* (1875) 10 Ch App 450.
6   *Powell v Aiken* (1858) 4 K & J 343.
7   As to the meaning of 'minerals' see PARA 10.
8   *Powell v Aiken* (1858) 4 K & J 343.

## 261. Trespass.

If a mine[1] owner carries minerals[2] through land in which he has neither a right of property nor a right of way, he commits a trespass in respect of which a claim for damages will lie[3]. Similarly, if he uses a way of a kind unauthorised by his grant[4], or in a direction which is unauthorised[5], or for improper purposes[6] such as for the carriage of foreign minerals, he may be liable in damages[7].

1   As to the meaning of 'mine' see PARA 3.
2   As to the meaning of 'minerals' see PARA 10.
3   *Monmouth Canal Co v Harford* (1834) 1 Cr M & R 614.
4   *Neath Canal Co v Ynisarwed Resolven Colliery Co* (1875) 10 Ch App 450.
5   *Senhouse v Christian* (1787) 1 Term Rep 560; *Abson v Fenton* (1823) 1 B & C 195; *Dand v Kingscote* (1840) 6 M & W 174 at 198, 199 per Parke B.
6   *Howell v King* (1674) 1 Mod Rep 190; *Marquis of Stafford v Coyney* (1827) 7 B & C 257; *Dand v Kingscote* (1840) 6 M & W 174 at 195 per Parke B; *Midgley v Richardson* (1845) 14 M & W 595; *Powell v Vickerman* (1887) 3 TLR 358.
7   These principles do not apply to a way which exists by virtue of a right of property: see *Batten Pooll v Kennedy* [1907] 1 Ch 256.

## 262. Measure of damages or compensation.

The measure of damages for the trespass on another's land by the carriage of minerals[1] is the value of the land for the purposes for which it is used; compensation is measured by wayleave rent in respect of the minerals carried[2], and the rate, if any, used in the neighbourhood is adopted as a convenient measure[3].

In the case of rights granted compulsorily under the Opencast Coal Act 1958 special provisions as to compensation apply[4]. Special provisions also apply to compensation for the grant of rights under the Mines (Working Facilities and Support) Act 1966[5].

1  As to the meaning of 'minerals' see PARA 10.
2  See *Martin v Porter* (1839) 5 M & W 351; *Powell v Aiken* (1858) 4 K & J 343; *Hilton v Woods* (1867) LR 4 Eq 432; *Jegon v Vivian* (1871) 6 Ch App 742; *Phillips v Homfray, Fothergill v Phillips* (1871) 6 Ch App 770; *A-G v Tomline* (1880) 15 ChD 150, CA; and DAMAGES vol 29 (2014) PARA 421.
3  *Whitwham v Westminster Brymbo Coal and Coke Co* [1896] 2 Ch 538, CA.
4  Compensation is assessed in accordance with the Opencast Coal Act 1958 Pt II (ss 17–36): see PARA 461 et seq.
5  Compensation is determined by the court, in accordance with the Mines (Working Facilities and Support) Act 1966 s 8: see PARA 394.

# (6) Rights as to Water

## (i) Use of Water

## 263. Natural watercourses.

The natural right enjoyed by a riparian proprietor[1] to use the water of a stream cannot be granted to a non-riparian proprietor[2]; and a lessee of mines[3] under land adjoining a stream is not, as regards the user of the water in the stream, a riparian proprietor[4]. The reasonable use of the stream to which a riparian proprietor is entitled includes the abstraction of reasonable quantities for the purpose of working machinery connected with his mines[5]; and his proprietary rights relate to water flowing on the surface of the land or below it[6] provided that the water flows in a known and defined channel[7]. However, the abstraction of water from any source of supply is subject to statutory control[8].

A riparian proprietor is not bound to submit to a greatly increased flow of water caused by the discharge into the stream of water raised from mines by artificial means[9]. Nor is a mine owner entitled by working the minerals[10] under a river to cause subsidence of the bed so as sensibly to interfere with the flow to a lower riparian tenement[11]; still less is he entitled to tap the bed of the river and divert the water through his own workings into those of his neighbour[12].

1  As to the natural rights of a riparian owner to use water see generally WATER AND WATERWAYS vol 100 (2018) PARA 128 et seq.
2  *Ormerod v Todmorden Joint Stock Mill Co Ltd* (1883) 11 QBD 155, CA; *Stockport Waterworks Co v Potter* (1864) 3 H & C 300 at 326 per Pollock CB; and see *Attwood v Llay Main Collieries Ltd* [1926] Ch 444.
3  As to the meaning of 'mine' see PARA 3.
4  *Insole v James* (1856) 1 H & N 243.
5  See *Attwood v Llay Main Collieries Ltd* [1926] Ch 444; and WATER AND WATERWAYS vol 100 (2018) PARA 142.
6  *Black v Ballymena Township Comrs* (1886) 17 LR Ir 459; *Chasemore v Richards* (1859) 7 HL Cas

349; and see WATER AND WATERWAYS vol 100 (2018) PARA 116.

7   *Grand Junction Canal Co v Shugar* (1871) 6 Ch App 483; *Acton v Blundell* (1843) 12 M & W 324, Ex Ch; *English v Metropolitan Water Board* [1907] 1 KB 588; *Blackrod UDC v John Crankshaw & Co Ltd* (1913) 136 LT Jo 239; and see further REAL PROPERTY AND REGISTRATION.

8   Ie under the Water Resources Act 1991 Pt II Ch II (ss 24–72): see WATER AND WATERWAYS vol 100 (2018) PARA 502. As to the meaning of 'source of supply' see the Water Resources Act 1991 s 221(1); and WATER AND WATERWAYS vol 100 (2018) PARA 338.

9   *John Young & Co v Bankier Distillery Co* [1893] AC 691, HL.

10  As to the meaning of 'minerals' see PARA 10.

11  *Elwell v Crowther* (1862) 31 Beav 163. Rights to alter and divert streams for mining purposes are conferred by the Inclosure Act 1859 s 3.

12  *Crompton v Lea* (1874) LR 19 Eq 115.

## 264. Artificial watercourses.

There may be a right to conduct water in an artificial channel over adjoining land[1], in which event a party through whose land the water flows prima facie may abstract[2] or divert the water without liability to other owners through whose land it flows[3]. If the water is discharged for a temporary and particular purpose, such as for the draining of mines[4] or by tapping a natural source for mining purposes, no right to the uninterrupted use of the stream will be acquired by persons through whose land it flows[5]; but if the stream was originally intended to have a permanent flow, or if the party by whom it was caused to flow has abandoned, without intention to resume, the works by which the flow was caused, and given up all right to and control over the stream, rights may be acquired by prescription both as against the person from whose land the stream issues and any person through whose land it flows, similar to the rights existing in natural streams ex jure naturae[6].

1   This right must exist as an easement. As to the creation of such a right see REAL PROPERTY AND REGISTRATION vol 87 (2017) PARA 731 et seq.

2   As to statutory control of the abstraction of water see PARA 263.

3   *Wood v Waud* (1849) 3 Exch 748; *Nuttall v Bracewell* (1866) LR 2 Exch 1 at 14 per Channell B; and see WATER AND WATERWAYS vol 100 (2018) PARA 139.

4   As to the meaning of 'mine' see PARA 3.

5   *Arkwright v Gell* (1839) 5 M & W 203; *Gaved v Martyn* (1865) 19 CBNS 732; *Chamber Colliery Co v Hopwood* (1886) 32 ChD 549, CA; *Burrows v Lang* [1901] 2 Ch 502.

6   *Gaved v Martyn* (1865) 19 CBNS 732 at 759 per Erle CJ; *Ivimey v Stocker* (1866) 1 Ch App 396; *Baily & Co v Clark, Son and Morland* [1902] 1 Ch 649, CA; *Whitmores (Edenbridge) Ltd v Stanford* [1909] 1 Ch 427; cf *Ennor v Barwell* (1860) 2 Giff 410 at 419–421 per Stuart V-C (on appeal 1 De GF & J 529).

## 265. Remedies for infringement of rights.

A claim in damages lies if the natural or acquired rights of a riparian proprietor are infringed[1], and an injunction will generally be given to restrain the continuance of the injury[2], even if no actual damage is proved[3]. If a prima facie case is shown, inspection of the neighbour's property may be obtained on interim application[4]. The infringement of rights in an artificial watercourse also gives rise to the right to damages and to an injunction[5], but if the aggrieved party allows his neighbour to incur expenditure the right to an injunction may be lost, and an injunction will not readily be granted if the result would be to cause inconvenience or injury in the working of a mine[6].

1   *Bastard v Smith* (1838) 2 Mood & R 129 (natural rights); *Pennington v Brinsop Hall Coal Co* (1877) 5 ChD 769 at 773, 774 per Fry J. As to the rights of a riparian proprietor see WATER AND WATERWAYS vol 100 (2018) PARA 128 et seq.

2   *Ennor v Barwell* (1860) 2 Giff 410; on appeal 1 De GF & J 529.

3  *Pennington v Brinsop Hall Coal Co* (1877) 5 ChD 769. For remedies in respect of the infringement of riparian rights see generally WATER AND WATERWAYS vol 100 (2018) PARA 147. As to the remedy of injunction see CIVIL PROCEDURE vol 12 (2015) PARA 1098 et seq.
4  See *Ennor v Barwell* (1860) 1 De GF & J 529; and cf *Bradford Corpn v Ferrand* [1902] 2 Ch 655, DC. See PARA 38.
5  *Gaved v Martyn* (1865) 19 CBNS 732; *Ivimey v Stocker* (1866) 1 Ch App 396.
6  *Birmingham Canal Co v Lloyd* (1812) 18 Ves 515; and see CIVIL PROCEDURE vol 12 (2015) PARA 586. As to the meaning of 'mine' see PARA 3.

## 266. Percolating water.

As there is no natural right in respect of water flowing in an undefined channel[1], a mine[2] owner who, in carrying on mining operations in the usual manner, drains away water from adjacent and superjacent land so that the wells and springs become dry is under no liability in respect of such drainage[3]; but the right to prevent the abstraction or diversion of water which percolates through the soil may be acquired by grant; thus a person who has conveyed land containing wells may be precluded from abstracting the water which supplies the wells, and damages may be recovered for the infringement of that right[4].

1  As to rights of water in natural watercourses see PARA 263.
2  As to the meaning of 'mine' see PARA 3.
3  *Acton v Blundell* (1843) 12 M & W 324, Ex Ch; *Ballacorkish Silver, Lead and Copper Mining Co Ltd v Harrison* (1873) LR 5 PC 49; and see *Langbrook Properties Ltd v Surrey County Council* [1969] 3 All ER 1424, [1970] 1 WLR 161. As to percolating water generally see REAL PROPERTY AND REGISTRATION vol 87 (2017) PARA 927; ENVIRONMENTAL QUALITY AND PUBLIC HEALTH vol 45 (2010) PARA 272. As to statutory control of the abstraction of water see PARA 263. As to brine pumped to the surface, obtained by the dissolution of rock salt underground the source of which cannot be definitely ascertained see *Salt Union Ltd v Brunner, Mond & Co* [1906] 2 KB 822.
4  *Whitehead v Parks* (1858) 2 H & N 870.

## (ii) Discharge of Water

## 267. Right to permit percolation.

Incident to property in land there is a right to permit water naturally present to flow or percolate under the action of gravitation to land or underground strata at a lower level[1], in which case the only remedy of the lower owner is to protect himself by the retention or erection of barriers[2]. However, prima facie there is no right on the part of the upper owner to be an active agent in discharging water into land at a lower level by interference with the action of gravitation, or by conducting the water through artificial channels constructed for that purpose[3].

1  As to the right to permit percolation see generally WATER AND WATERWAYS. See also *Smith v Kenrick* (1849) 7 CB 515; *John Young & Co v Bankier Distillery Co* [1893] AC 691 at 697, HL, per Lord Watson, and at 701 per Lord Shand.
2  See *Smith v Kenrick* (1849) 7 CB 515; *Baird v Williamson* (1863) 15 CBNS 376 at 392 per Erle CJ.
3  See *Gaved v Martyn* (1865) 19 CBNS 732 at 758, obiter, per Erle CJ; *Roberts v Rose* (1865) LR 1 Exch 82, Ex Ch; *Baird v Williamson* (1863) 15 CBNS 376; *Lomax v Stott* (1870) 39 LJ Ch 834.

## 268. Percolation caused by working mines.

The occupier of a mine[1] is entitled to get all the minerals[2] in his mine in a skilful and usual course of working[3], and legitimate operations conducted for that purpose do not impose a liability upon the owner of mines lying at a higher level, if the result[4] is to permit the escape of water which collects in the workings, or even if the natural flow is increased. Thus the removal of a stratum which results in the inundation of a lower mine by an accumulation of water above the stratum[5], or the construction between two parallel inclined seams of a passage for the carriage of minerals which incidentally allows water to flow along it[6], or working in a proper manner which results in surface cracks and allows surface water to enter[7], or getting the minerals by quarrying where that is the usual mode of working in the district[8], or damming up water by a barrier so that water accumulates and overflows into an adjacent mine[9], or increasing the natural flow by vigorous working[10], does not impose liability upon the owner of an upper mine in respect of injury caused to the adjoining mine owner by the inflow of water resulting from the respective operations. It is essential, however, that the mining operations should be ordinary, reasonable and proper. Operations which result in the flooding of a mine and are of no advantage to the owner of that mine are not ordinary, reasonable or proper[11].

1   As to the meaning of 'mine' see PARA 3.
2   As the meaning of 'minerals' see PARA 10.
3   As to the relationships between operators of coal mines whose operations interact with each other see PARA 95.
4   It is in any case a precondition of liability that the escape of water should have been caused or permitted by the defendant's working: *Westhoughton Coal and Cannel Co Ltd v Wigan Coal Corpn Ltd* [1939] Ch 800, [1939] 3 All ER 579, CA.
5   *Smith v Kenrick* (1849) 7 CB 515; *Hurdman v North Eastern Rly Co* (1878) 3 CPD 168 at 174, CA, per Cotton LJ.
6   *Baird v Williamson* (1863) 15 CBNS 376.
7   *Wilson v Waddell* (1876) 2 App Cas 95, HL.
8   See *Smith v Fletcher* (1874) LR 9 Exch 64, Ex Ch; affd sub nom *Fletcher v Smith* (1877) 2 App Cas 781, HL.
9   *Lomax v Stott* (1870) 39 LJ Ch 834.
10   *Scots Mines Co v Leadhills Mines Co* (1859) 34 LTOS 34, HL.
11   *Crompton v Lea* (1874) LR 19 Eq 115. Whether particular mining operations are ordinary, reasonable and proper is a question of fact in each case: *Crompton v Lea*.

### 269. Liability in case of trespass.

A mine[1] owner who trespasses on an adjoining mine and pierces a barrier[2] is liable in respect of the injury caused by the inflow of water[3]; but the damage is consequential on the original trespass and must be recovered once for all; there is no continuing nuisance and a subsequent trespasser cannot be sued in respect of further damage[4].

1   As to the meaning of 'mine' see PARA 3.
2   As to the relationships between operators of coal mines whose operations interact with each other see PARA 95.
3   *Firmstone v Wheeley* (1844) 2 Dow & L 203; *Clegg v Dearden* (1848) 12 QB 576; *Smith v Kenrick* (1849) 7 CB 515.
4   *Clegg v Dearden* (1848) 12 QB 576; *Smith v Kenrick* (1849) 7 CB 515. However, as to liability for allowing an existing nuisance to continue see *Leakey v National Trust for Places of Historic Interest or Natural Beauty* [1980] QB 485, [1980] 1 All ER 17, CA; and NUISANCE vol 78 (2018) PARA 182.

### 270. Diversion of water.

The diversion of the flow of water within the limits of the mine[1] owner's own property does not render him liable if the burden upon the lower owner is not increased by it[2], but it is otherwise if the result of the operations is to increase the volume of the discharge or to alter its direction[3].

1   As to the meaning of 'mine' see PARA 3.
2   *West Cumberland Iron and Steel Co v Kenyon* (1879) 11 ChD 782, CA.

3 See *Smith v Kenrick* (1849) 7 CB 515; *Rylands v Fletcher* (1868) LR 3 HL 330; *West Cumberland Iron and Steel Co v Kenyon* (1879) 11 ChD 782 at 785–790, CA. However, see also *Leakey v National Trust for Places of Historic Interest or Natural Beauty* [1980] QB 485, [1980] 1 All ER 17, CA; and NUISANCE vol 78 (2018) PARA 118.

## 271.  Pumping.

A mine[1] owner is not, prima facie, entitled to pump up water from his mine and discharge it into a stream in which his neighbour has riparian rights[2], or to conduct water to a mine at a lower level by artificial pipes[3] or channels[4]. He will be liable for the damage caused if he pumps up water from a lower part of his mine and allows it to descend by gravitation into the adjoining mine[5], or conducts water to a weak spot in his neighbour's boundary[6].

1 As to the meaning of 'mine' see PARA 3.
2 *John Young & Co v Bankier Distillery Co* [1893] AC 691, HL. As to statutory control of the abstraction of water see PARA 263. As to statutory control of the discharge of water see ENVIRONMENTAL QUALITY AND PUBLIC HEALTH vol 45 (2010) PARA 288 et seq. As to the relationships between operators of coal mines whose operations interact with each other see PARA 95.
3 *Lomax v Stott* (1870) 39 LJ Ch 834; cf *Westhoughton Coal and Cannel Co Ltd v Wigan Coal Corpn Ltd* [1939] Ch 800, [1939] 3 All ER 579, CA.
4 *Baird v Williamson* (1863) 15 CBNS 376 at 390, 391 per Erle CJ; *Phillips v Homfray, Fothergill v Phillips* (1871) 6 Ch App 770 at 781 per Lord Hatherley LC.
5 *Baird v Williamson* (1863) 15 CBNS 376 at 391 per Erle CJ.
6 *Westminster Brymbo Coal and Coke Co v Clayton* (1867) 36 LJ Ch 476 at 478 per Wood V-C.

## 272.  Landowner's liability.

Prima facie a person is liable for all the damage which may result from the escape of water which he has collected[1] and retained upon his land for his own purposes. Thus he is liable if water which he has collected and retained breaks into a subjacent mine[2]. His liability does not depend upon any question of negligence or unusual or unreasonable user[3]. However, the right to discharge water into a neighbour's mine may be acquired as an easement[4] by grant, by prescription or by statute[5], whether the water does or does not originate in the land of the dominant owner[6].

1 It is otherwise where the accumulation is due to natural causes: *Rouse v Gravelworks Ltd* [1940] 1 KB 489, [1940] 1 All ER 26, CA.
2 See *Rylands v Fletcher* (1868) LR 3 HL 330; and NUISANCE vol 78 (2010) PARA 147 et seq, 186, 197. As to the meaning of 'mine' see PARA 3.
3 *Rylands v Fletcher* (1868) LR 3 HL 330 at 340–342 per Lord Cranworth.
4 See REAL PROPERTY AND REGISTRATION.
5 Mining easements in respect of water are provided for by the Railways Clauses Consolidation Act 1845 s 80 (see PARA 135); the Waterworks Clauses Act 1847 s 24 (repealed, but the repeal does not affect statutes which have incorporated this provision in so far as it has not been superseded by the Water Act 1945 s 32, Sch 3 (largely repealed, with savings, by the Water Act 1989 s 190(3), Sch 27) or by any later enactment); the Water Act 1945 Sch 3 para 15 (repealed with savings); the Inclosure Act 1859 s 3; the Acquisition of Land Act 1981 s 3, Sch 2 para 5(1) (see PARA 166); and the Water Industry Act 1991 s 188, Sch 14 para 3(1) (see WATER AND WATERWAYS vol 101 (2018) PARA 761).
6 As to discharge into 'controlled waters' see ENVIRONMENTAL QUALITY AND PUBLIC HEALTH vol 45 (2010) PARA 299 et seq.

## (iii) Water Conservation

### 273. Mining operations which may affect water conservation.

Where a person proposes to construct or extend a boring for the purpose of searching for or extracting minerals[1], he must, before he begins to construct or extend the boring, give to the appropriate agency a notice[2] of his intention in the prescribed form[3].

1  As to the meaning of 'minerals' see PARA 10.
2  As to the service of documents see the Water Resources Act 1991 s 220; and WATER AND WATERWAYS vol 100 (2018) PARA 29.
3  Water Resources Act 1991 s 199(1) (amended by the Environment Act 1995 s 120(1), Sch 22 para 128; and SI 2013/755). The notice required by the Water Resources Act 1991 s 199(1) must be given in such form as the appropriate agency determines: Water Resources (Abstraction and Impounding) Regulations 2006, SI 2006/641, reg 29 (amended by SI 2013/755). As to notice etc of mining operations which may affect water conservation see WATER AND WATERWAYS vol 100 (2018) PARA 344.

## (7) Rights as to Air

### 274. Underground ventilation.

Prima facie a mine[1] owner has no right to ventilate his own mine by making an aperture into or an airway through his neighbour's mine[2], and apparently he may not ventilate his mine by sending his air into his neighbour's mine or by drawing air from that mine into his own, even though he makes no airway through or into his neighbour's mine for the purpose. If, however, through the operation of natural causes, or in consequence of his neighbour's acts, the mine owner's mine is ventilated by the passage of air from his mine to his neighbour's mine, or in the opposite direction, no cause of action accrues to the neighbouring owner: his only remedy is to block up the aperture[3].

If a mine owner wrongfully ventilates his mine by driving a passage through or into his neighbour's land, prima facie his neighbour will be entitled to a mandatory injunction to compel the wrongdoer to stop up the aperture[4]. Where the wrongdoer is succeeded in possession by a person who is privy to him in title and who continues to use the airway, then, although a mandatory injunction will not be issued against the subsequent occupier, the court will order that the aggrieved person be permitted to have access to the aperture for the purpose of closing it, and an injunction will be issued against the continuance of the user of the air-course[5].

The measure of damages in respect of the wrongful user of a neighbouring mine for the purpose of ventilation is the diminution, if any, in the value of the neighbouring mine plus such a sum as represents a reasonable payment for the user so enjoyed[6]. Damages will, therefore, be assessed upon the basis of the quantity of minerals[7] which the wrongdoer has gotten from his own mine and which has been made accessible by the ventilation through his neighbour's land, and may be awarded in the form of an air-leave rent or royalty on such quantity[8].

1  As to the meaning of 'mine' see PARA 3.
2  *Powell v Aiken* (1858) 4 K & J 343; *Bowser v Maclean* (1860) 2 De GF & J 415.
3  *Powell v Aiken* (1858) 4 K & J 343; and see *Jegon v Vivian* (1871) 6 Ch App 742 at 759 per Lord Hatherley LC; *Phillips v Homfray, Fothergill v Phillips* (1871) 6 Ch App 770 at 781 per Lord Hatherley LC; *Powell v Vickerman* (1887) 3 TLR 358. As to the relationships between operators of coal mines whose operations interact with each other see PARA 95.
4  *Powell v Aiken* (1858) 4 K & J 343 at 356 per Page Wood V-C; and see *Phillips v Homfray,*

*Fothergill v Phillips* (1871) 6 Ch App 770 at 776. As to mandatory injunctions generally see CIVIL PROCEDURE vol 12 (2015) PARA 1102 et seq.
5   *Powell v Aiken* (1858) 4 K & J 343 at 356–357 per Page Wood V-C.
6   See *Whitwham v Westminster Brymbo Coal and Coke Co* [1896] 2 Ch 538, CA; and DAMAGES vol 29 (2014) PARAS 334, 408, 421.
7   As to the meaning of 'minerals' see PARA 10.
8   *Bowser v Maclean* (1860) 2 De GF & J 415; *Phillips v Homfray, Fothergill v Phillips* (1871) 6 Ch App 770.

## 275.   Easements of air.

A right to ventilate a mine[1] by means of a passage into or through a neighbour's land may exist as an easement, and may be created by grant, by implication of law or by prescription[2]. A right to the passage of air not flowing through a defined channel may be the subject of express grant or covenant, but cannot be claimed by prescription[3]. A right to cut an airway may also be created by statute[4].

1   As to the meaning of 'mine' see PARA 3.
2   See REAL PROPERTY AND REGISTRATION.
3   See REAL PROPERTY AND REGISTRATION.
4   Eg under the mining codes, which restrict the right to work minerals lying below railway and water undertakings: see PARA 166.

## 276.   Nuisance at common law.

The emission of smoke, fumes or noxious vapours in such circumstances that the value of neighbouring property is diminished, or the beneficial use of that property interfered with, constitutes an actionable nuisance at common law[1] for which damages may be recovered[2], and the commission of which will, in general, be restrained by injunction[3]. The person primarily liable in respect of a nuisance is the person who has created it[4] or authorised its creation[5], but in certain circumstances the occupier of premises from which a nuisance has emanated may also be liable[6].

1   *St Helen's Smelting Co v Tipping* (1865) 11 HL Cas 642; and see generally NUISANCE vol 78 (2018) PARAS 123, 126, 127. The escape of noxious fumes may also attract the principle of *Rylands v Fletcher* (1868) LR 3 HL 330: see NUISANCE vol 78 (2018) PARA 147 et seq, 186, 197.
2   See generally DAMAGES vol 29 (2014) PARAS 409, 425.
3   *Walter v Selfe* (1851) 4 De G & Sm 315; and see CIVIL PROCEDURE vol 12 (2015) PARA 1155; NUISANCE.
4   *Thompson v Gibson* (1841) 7 M & W 456. See generally NUISANCE vol 78 (2018) PARA 182.
5   *Harris v James* (1876) 45 LJQB 545; cf *Rich v Basterfield* (1847) 4 CB 783.
6   *White v Jameson* (1874) LR 18 Eq 303.

## 277.   Statutory controls on emissions of smoke etc.

The owner[1] of a mine[2] or quarry[3] to which provisions of the Clean Air Act 1993 apply[4] must employ all practicable means[5] for preventing combustion of refuse deposited from the mine or quarry; and for preventing or minimising the emission of smoke[6] and fumes[7] from such refuse; and if he fails to do so, he is guilty of an offence[8]. A person[9] guilty of such an offence[10] is liable on summary conviction to a fine not exceeding level 5 on the standard scale[11]; or to cumulative penalties on continuance[12].

1   As to the meaning of 'owner' see PARA 521 (definition applied by the Clean Air Act 1993 s 42(6)).
2   As to the meaning of 'mine' see PARA 3 (definition applied by Clean Air Act 1993 s 42(6)).
3   As to the meaning of 'quarry' see PARA 4.
4   Ie the provisions of the Clean Air Act 1993 s 42. Section 42 applies to any mine or quarry from which coal or shale has been, is being or is to be got: s 42(1).

5   'Practicable means' includes the provision and maintenance of plant and its proper use: Clean Air Act 1993 s 64(1).
6   'Smoke' includes soot, ash, grit and gritty particles emitted in smoke: Clean Air Act 1993 s 64(1).
7   'Fumes' means any airborne solid matter smaller than dust: Clean Air Act 1993 s 64(1).
8   Clean Air Act 1993 s 42(2). Neither the provisions of the Environmental Protection Act 1990 Pt III (ss 79–84) nor any provision of the Clean Air Act 1993 Pts 1–III (ss 1–29) apply in relation to smoke, grit or dust from the combustion of refuse deposited from any mine or quarry to which s 42 applies: s 42(4). The Secretary of State may, by regulations, apply all or any of the provisions of s 42(4) to fumes or prescribed gases or both as they apply to grit and dust: see s 47(1)(a). Section 42(2)–(4) does not apply to any deposit of refuse deposited from a mine or quarry before 5 July 1956 (the date of the passing of the Clean Air Act 1956) if at that date the deposit was no longer in use as such and was not under the control of the owner of the mine or quarry: Clean Air Act 1993 s 67(2), Sch 5 para 10. As to the Secretary of State see PARA 2.
9   'Person' includes a body of persons corporate or unincorporate: see the Interpretation Act 1978 s 5, Sch 1.
10   Ie an offence under the Clean Air Act 1993 s 42(2): see s 42(3).
11   Clean Air Act 1993 s 42(3)(a). As to the standard scale see SENTENCING vol 92 (2015) PARA 176.
12   Clean Air Act 1993 s 42(3)(b). This is in accordance with the Clean Air Act 1993 s 50: see s 42(3).

# (8) Surface Rights on Disposition

### 278. Express and implied rights of working.

Upon the severance of mines[1] from the surface, whether by grant or exception, working powers and liberties are usually expressly granted or reserved[2], but in the absence of express provision there is incident, by implication of law, to the ownership of mines a power to get and carry away the minerals[3], and on the same principle an express power will give rise to an implication of all incidental liberties necessary for the exercise of the power[4]. An implied liberty will not be curtailed by the terms of an express power which may be exercisable to a greater extent or for a longer period[5], but it will be curtailed if the express power is in such terms as necessarily restrict the implied liberty[6]. An implied liberty may be available if the grant of the express liberty is invalid[7].

Prima facie there is incident to the ownership of mines, subject to planning legislation[8], power on the part of the mine owner to enter upon the surface[9], to dig pits and get the minerals[10], to drive shafts vertically through an upper seam[11], or to make underground communications through a vertical barrier separating excepted mines[12]. However, the power to win and work will not be implied if the process, as in the case of quarrying, will be destructive of or permanently injurious to the surface[13]. Such a power will only be conferred if the instrument of severance grants the liberty in clear and unambiguous language[14].

1   As to the meaning of 'mine' see PARA 3.
2   Provision is made for powers of working and incidental liberties in connection with minerals by various public general Acts, namely in the case of inclosures (see the Inclosure Act 1859; and COMMONS vol 13 (2017) PARA 319 et seq); in favour of the Duke of Cornwall and his lessees in respect of mines in the assessionable manors of the Duchy and mines under the foreshore in the Duchy (see CROWN AND CROWN PROCEEDINGS vol 29 (2014) PARA 161); in favour of the Crown and persons claiming under it in respect of mines under the sea adjacent to Cornwall (see CROWN AND CROWN PROCEEDINGS vol 29 (2014) PARAS 182–183); in favour of the Crown in respect of the foreshore or adjacent land (see CROWN AND CROWN PROCEEDINGS vol 29 (2014) PARAS 137–138); and in favour of persons licensed under the Coal Industry Act 1994 Pt II (ss 25–36) (see PARA 89 et seq). See *Honeywell Cotton Spinning Co v Marland* [1875] WN 46. A to the position where land is granted for building purposes excepting the minerals see *Robinson v Milne* (1884) 53 LJ Ch 1070; and BUILDING CONTRACTS vol 6 (2018) PARA 287. As to the meaning of 'minerals' see PARA 10.

3  Cf Shep Touch (8 Edn) 89, 100; *Earl of Cardigan v Armitage* (1823) 2 B & C 197 at 207 per Bayley J; *Durham and Sunderland Rly Co v Walker* (1842) 2 QB 940 at 968, Ex Ch, per Tindal CJ; *Re Wilson Syndicate Conveyance, Wilson v Shorrock* [1938] 3 All ER 599 at 603 per Bennett J. See, to the contrary, *Harris v Ryding* (1839) 5 M & W 60 at 65 per Lord Abinger CB. As to easements created by implication of law see REAL PROPERTY AND REGISTRATION.

4  *Dand v Kingscote* (1840) 6 M & W 174 at 196 per Parke B. The limitation to such implied or incidental powers, and the manner in which express powers must be exercised, are discussed in dealing with leases: see PARA 325 et seq.

5  *Stukeley v Butler* (1614) Hob 168; *Earl of Cardigan v Armitage* (1823) 2 B & C 197 at 211 per Bayley J; cf *Hodgson v Field* (1806) 7 East 613.

6  *Re Wilson Syndicate Conveyance, Wilson v Shorrock* [1938] 3 All ER 599, where express power for getting minerals by underground working was held to exclude implied power to destroy the surface.

7  *Whidborne v Ecclesiastical Comrs for England* (1877) 7 ChD 375 at 381.

8  See PARA 352; and PLANNING.

9  For the measure of compensation where there is express power to occupy and use surface land subject to the payment of compensation see *Mordue v Dean and Chapter of Durham* (1873) LR 8 CP 336.

10 *Earl of Cardigan v Armitage* (1823) 2 B & C 197 at 207 per Bayley J; *Durham and Sunderland Rly Co v Walker* (1842) 2 QB 940 at 968, Ex Ch, per Tindal CJ. See, to the contrary, *Harris v Ryding* (1839) 5 M & W 60 at 65 per Lord Abinger CB.

11 *Goold v Great Western Deep Coal Co* (1865) 2 De GJ & Sm 600.

12 *Re Lord Gerard and London and North Western Rly Co* [1895] 1 QB 459 at 466, CA, per Lord Esher MR, and at 471 per Rigby LJ.

13 *Bell v Wilson* (1866) 1 Ch App 303; *Hext v Gill* (1872) 7 Ch App 699 at 714 per Mellish LJ; *Whidborne v Ecclesiastical Comrs for England* (1877) 7 ChD 375 at 379–381 per Hall V-C; *Midland Rly Co v Miles* (1886) 33 ChD 632 at 647 per Stirling J; and see *General Accident Fire and Life Assurance Corpn Ltd v British Gypsum Ltd* [1967] 3 All ER 40, [1967] 1 WLR 1215.

14 *Hext v Gill* (1872) 7 Ch App 699 at 714, 717–718 per Mellish LJ. See *A-G v Welsh Granite Co* (1887) 35 WR 617, CA; and cf *Re Wilson Syndicate Conveyance, Wilson v Shorrock* [1938] 3 All ER 599.

## 279.  Implication of ancillary powers.

An express liberty to dig pits implies prima facie a right, subject to planning regulation[1], to fix on the surface machinery necessary for draining the mines and raising the minerals[2]. Similarly, it has been held that a liberty with employees, carriages and horses to enter and carry away the minerals may authorise the construction of a railway[3], and liberty to make a sough or drain carries with it liberty to make sough pits for its repair[4]. To an express right of working is probably incidental the right to deposit minerals and spoil on the surface[5], or, in the case of a quarry, to deposit spoil upon the grantor's adjoining land[6]; and an express right to work implies a power, so far as it is necessary for winning and getting the minerals, to remove overlying strata and intermixed minerals[7] but not to appropriate intermixed minerals or minerals in overlying strata[8] unless they are of the nature of spoil[9]. Refuse produced in refining the minerals gotten may be sold by the lessee, but refuse or spoil, if abandoned, becomes part of the freehold[10].

1  See PARA 352 et seq; and PLANNING.

2  *Dand v Kingscote* (1840) 6 M & W 174 at 196 per Parke B. As to the express and implied powers, in leases, to bore and sink see PARA 325 et seq. As to the meaning of 'mine' see PARA 3; and as to the meaning of 'minerals' see PARA 10.

3  *Earl of Antrim v Dobbs* (1891) 30 LR Ir 424.

4  *Hodgson v Field* (1806) 7 East 613.

5  *Earl of Cardigan v Armitage* (1823) 2 B & C 197 at 211 per Bayley J; *Marshall v Borrowdale Plumbago Mines and Manufacturing Co Ltd* (1892) 8 TLR 275.

6  *Middleton v Clarence* (1877) IR 11 CL 499.

7  *Robinson v Milne* (1884) 53 LJ Ch 1070 at 1074 per North J.

8   *Rogers v Brenton* (1847) 10 QB 26 at 56 per Lord Denman CJ (intermixed minerals); *Goold v Great Western Deep Coal Co* (1865) 2 De GJ & Sm 600 at 608 per Lord Westbury (overlying strata).
9   *Robinson v Milne* (1884) 53 LJ Ch 1070.
10  *Boileau v Heath* [1898] 2 Ch 301.

## 280.   Spoilbanks.

If there is express power in a lease to deposit spoil, the spoilbanks belong to the lessee[1]. Where spoil from a colliery is wrongfully deposited on land, the measure of damages in respect of land actually used is the diminution, if any, in the value of that land plus such a sum as represents a reasonable payment for the user of it[2].

1   *Robinson v Milne* (1884) 53 LJ Ch 1070. As to powers in leases see PARA 325 et seq.
2   *Whitwham v Westminster Brymbo Coal and Coke Co* [1896] 2 Ch 538, CA.

## 281.   Liability to fence workings.

Prima facie it is the duty of a mine[1] owner properly to fence a shaft sunk through the surface in the exercise of a liberty, whether express or implied; failure in this respect renders him liable in respect of injuries to cattle of the surface owner which fall through the shaft[2].

1   As to the meaning of 'mine' see PARA 3.
2   *Williams v Groucott* (1863) 4 B & S 149; and see BOUNDARIES vol 4 (2011) PARA 352. As to the duty to fence an abandoned mine see PARA 534.

# 5. DISPOSITION

## (1) Powers of Disposition

### (i) Powers of Absolute Disposition

**282. Limited owners.**

In relation to an estate in fee simple, persons other than the beneficial owner of the land and minerals[1] may have a power to dispose absolutely of land and minerals. These powers include those of the tenant for life of settled land[2], trustees[3], personal representatives[4], mortgagees[5] and persons having an interest in land subject to compulsory acquisition[6].

If the land and minerals are partnership property, a disposition of them is governed by the law of partnership[7]. If the person otherwise entitled to dispose of the land is under a disability by reason of minority or mental disorder, his power of disposition may be restricted[8].

1   As to the meaning of 'minerals' see PARA 10.
2   Prior to 1 January 1997 a tenant for life of settled land might sell or exchange the settled land or any part of it or any easement, right or privilege of any kind over or in relation to the land: see the Settled Land Act 1925 s 38(i), (iii). He might deal with the surface and minerals separately: see s 50. See SETTLEMENTS. However, as from 1 January 1997 the Trusts of Land and Appointment of Trustees Act 1996 introduced, in place of strict settlements, a new system of holding land on trust with the imposition of the 'trust of land': see ss 1(2), 4, 27(2); and the Trusts of Land and Appointment of Trustees Act 1996 (Commencement) Order 1996, SI 1996/2974. Accordingly, no settlement created after the 1 January 1997 is a settlement for the purposes of the Settled Land Act 1925; and no settlement is to be deemed to be made under the Settled Land Act 1925 after 1 January 1997: see the Trusts of Land and Appointment of Trustees Act 1996 s 2(1); and the Trusts of Land and Appointment of Trustees Act 1996 (Commencement) Order 1996, SI 1996/2974. For the purpose of exercising their functions as trustees, the trustees of land have in relation to the land subject to the trust all the powers of an absolute owner: Trusts of Land and Appointment of Trustees Act 1996 s 6(1). 'Trustees of land' means trustees of a trust of land: s 1(1)(b). As to the phasing out of strict settlements under the Settled Land Act 1925 see the Trusts of Land and Appointment of Trustees Act 1996 s 2, Sch 1; REAL PROPERTY AND REGISTRATION vol 87 (2017) PARA 102 et seq; SETTLEMENTS.
3   Eg prior to 1 January 1997 under the Settled Land Act 1925 ss 23(1), 26(1) and the Law of Property Act 1925 s 28(1) (repealed), and on or after 1 January 1997 under the Trusts of Land and Appointment of Trustees Act 1996 s 6(1), (3): see REAL PROPERTY AND REGISTRATION vol 87 (2017) PARAS 104, 1056; SETTLEMENTS; TRUSTS AND POWERS vol 98 (2013) PARA 476. As to the law relating to trustees generally see TRUSTS AND POWERS vol 98 (2013) PARA 1 et seq.
4   See the Administration of Estates Act 1925 s 39(1)(iii); the Trusts of Land and Appointment of Trustees Act 1996 s 18; and WILLS AND INTESTACY vol 103 (2016) PARAS 1019, 1021.
5   See the Law of Property Act 1925 s 101(1), (2); and MORTGAGE vol 77 (2016) PARA 101 et seq.
6   See the Lands Clauses Consolidation Act 1845 s 6; the Compulsory Purchase Act 1965 s 3; and COMPULSORY ACQUISITION OF LAND vol 18 (2009) PARA 550 et seq.
7   See PARTNERSHIP.
8   See CHILDREN AND YOUNG PERSONS vol 9 (2017) PARA 30 et seq; SETTLEMENTS.

**283. Co-owners.**

Where persons are co-owners of a mine[1], the trustees in whom the mine is vested[2], apart from their powers of sale[3], may partition the property[4]. In the case of persons who are co-owners of the mine and partners in the mine, or in the mine and the working[5], a sale by one owner of his share, without the consent of the others[6], is probably a ground of dissolution of the partnership[7].

1   As to co-owners see PARA 364. As to the meaning of 'mine' see PARA 3.

2 See PARA 364.

3 See SETTLEMENTS. As to the introduction of the 'trust of land' see the Trusts of Land and Appointment of Trustees Act 1996 s 2(1); and PARA 282.

4 Ie prior to 1 January 1997 this was with the consent of the co-owners of full age interested in possession: see the Law of Property Act 1925 s 28(3) (repealed); and see *Crawshay v Maule* (1818) 1 Swan 495 at 518 per Lord Eldon LC. On or after 1 January 1997 the trustees of land may, where beneficiaries of full age are absolutely entitled in undivided shares to land subject to the trust, partition the land, or any part of it, and provide (by way of mortgage or otherwise) for the payment of any equality money: see the Trusts of Land and Appointment of Trustees Act 1996 s 7; and REAL PROPERTY AND REGISTRATION vol 87 (2017) PARA 230. As to the meaning of 'trustees of land' see PARA 282.

5 As to such co-owners see PARA 365.

6 See PARA 366.

7 As to the grounds of dissolution of the partnership see PARTNERSHIP vol 79 (2014) PARA 173 et seq.

## 284. The Crown.

The Crown Estate Commissioners[1] have certain powers of sale and other disposal of mines and minerals comprised in land which is the property of the Crown[2].

Subject to certain formalities, mines and minerals which form part of the private estates of the Crown may be disposed of by sale or gift, or by will or other testamentary disposition, as freely in all respects as by an ordinary subject[3] but a purchaser from the Crown is not entitled to covenants for title[4].

1 As to the constitution, composition and functions of the Crown Estate Commissioners see the Crown Estate Act 1961 s 1; and CROWN AND CROWN PROCEEDINGS vol 29 (2014) PARA 192 et seq.

2 As to their powers of sale and other disposal see generally CROWN AND CROWN PROCEEDINGS vol 29 (2014) PARA 204. As to the meaning of 'mines and minerals' see PARA 10; as to the meaning of 'mine' see PARA 3.

3 As to the sovereign's right to dispose of private estates see generally CROWN AND CROWN PROCEEDINGS vol 29 (2014) PARA 273.

4 As to covenants for title see generally CROWN AND CROWN PROCEEDINGS vol 29 (2014) PARA 207.

## 285. The Duchy of Cornwall.

The Duke of Cornwall may, either by way of absolute sale or for a limited period, dispose of any mines[1], minerals[2] or rights of entry or other rights in respect of mines and minerals forming part of the possessions of the Duchy. The disposition may be made subject to any reservations or exceptions[3]. He may also exchange mines or minerals in accordance with the provisions of the Inclosure Acts[4].

1 As to the meaning of 'mine' see PARA 3.

2 As to the meaning of 'minerals' see PARA 10.

3 As to the power to alienate Duchy land see generally CROWN AND CROWN PROCEEDINGS vol 29 (2014) PARA 242. When there is no Duke of Cornwall, the Duchy is vested in the Sovereign: see generally CROWN AND CROWN PROCEEDINGS vol 29 (2014) PARA 33.

4 As to inclosure of land generally see COMMONS vol 13 (2017) PARA 318 et seq. As to the Inclosure Acts generally see COMMONS vol 13 (2017) PARA 319 et seq.

## 286. Ecclesiastical corporations.

With certain exceptions[1], all ecclesiastical corporations, both aggregate and sole, may, with the approval of the Church Commissioners[2], sell, exchange, lease or otherwise dispose of any mines or minerals the property of the corporation[3]. Diocesan boards of finance have similar powers in relation to mines and minerals vested in them[4].

1 As to the exceptions see the Ecclesiastical Leasing Act 1842 s 1, incorporated by reference in the Ecclesiastical Leasing Act 1858 s 1; and ECCLESIASTICAL LAW vol 34 (2011) PARA 927.

2 As to the Church Commissioners see ECCLESIASTICAL LAW vol 34 (2011) PARA 66 et seq.

3 See the Ecclesiastical Leasing Act 1858 s 1; and ECCLESIASTICAL LAW vol 34 (2011) PARA 927. The Ecclesiastical Leasing Acts 1842 and 1858 no longer apply to incumbents: see the Endowments and Glebe Measure 1976 s 47(3), Sch 7. As to the meaning of 'mine' see PARA 3; and as to the meaning of 'minerals' see PARA 10.

4 As to the transfer to diocesan boards of finance see the Endowments and Glebe Measure 1976 ss 20, 45(1); and ECCLESIASTICAL LAW vol 34 (2011) PARA 692.

### (ii) Powers of Leasing

### 287. General principles.

In relation to an estate in fee simple, a person other than the beneficial owner of the land and minerals[1] may have a power to lease land and minerals. Such a power may subsist as a common law power[2], or it may be conferred by statute[3]. If the person otherwise entitled to grant a lease of the land is under a disability by reason of minority or mental disorder, his power of leasing may be restricted[4]. There are also special rules governing the granting of leases by certain persons and bodies[5].

1 As to the meaning of 'minerals' see PARA 10.

2 See PARA 288.

3 See PARA 289.

4 As to the capacity of persons under disability to grant leases generally see CHILDREN AND YOUNG PERSONS vol 9 (2017) PARA 49; LANDLORD AND TENANT vol 62 (2016) PARA 67 et seq; SETTLEMENTS.

5 Eg ecclesiastical corporations (see PARA 286); trustees (see PARA 290); universities and colleges (see PARA 291); charities (see PARA 292); the Crown and the Duke of Cornwall (see PARA 293); and mortgagees (see MORTGAGE vol 77 (2016) PARA 101 et seq).

### 288. Common law power of leasing.

A limited owner has a common law power to make a demise for a term not exceeding the duration of his own estate[1]. Every power of appointment over, or power to convey or charge land or any interest in it, whether created by a statute or other instrument or implied by law, and whether created before or after the commencement of the Law of Property Act 1925 (not being a power vested in a legal mortgagee or an estate owner in right of his estate and exercisable by him or by another person in his name and on his behalf), operates only in equity[2]. Subject to this statutory restriction, powers of leasing may be created by instrument or implied by law. In particular, where there was an agreement that a settlement relating to land is to contain all usual powers, it appears that a power for the tenant for life to grant mining leases may be included[3]. As from 1 January 1997 no new settlements can be created under the Settled Land Act 1925[4].

1 See LANDLORD AND TENANT vol 62 (2016) PARA 67 et seq.

2 See the Law of Property Act 1925 s 1(7); and TRUSTS AND POWERS vol 98 (2013) PARA 41.

3 *Hill v Hill* (1834) 6 Sim 136 at 145 per Shadwell V-C in relation to powers in a strict settlement; and see TRUSTS AND POWERS vol 98 (2013) PARA 291; SETTLEMENTS. A grant of a mining lease by a tenant for life would have normally been made under the statutory power: see PARA 289.

4 As to the phasing out of strict settlements and the introduction of the 'trust of land' see the Trusts of Land and Appointment of Trustees Act 1996 s 2(1); and PARA 282.

## 289. Statutory powers of leasing.

Under the Settled Land Act 1925, a tenant for life, or person having the powers of a tenant for life, might grant mining leases[1] of mines[2], open or new, for a term not exceeding 100 years; and the court could, with respect to the district in which any settled land is situated, enlarge this power in certain circumstances[3].

As from 1 January 1997 no new settlements can be created under the Settled Land Act 1925[4]. The Trusts of Land and Appointment of Trustees Act 1996 introduces a new unitary system of holding land on trust. For the purpose of exercising their functions as trustees, the trustees of land[5] have in relation to the land subject to the trust all the powers of an absolute owner[6]. The trustees of land may, by power of attorney, delegate to any beneficiary[7] or beneficiaries of full age and beneficially entitled to an interest in possession in land subject to the trust any of their functions as trustees which relate to the land[8]. A beneficiary to whom such powers are delegated can therefore grant mining leases[9].

1　For the purposes of the Settled Land Act 1925, 'mining lease' means a lease for any mining purposes or purposes connected therewith, and includes a grant or licence for any mining purposes: see s 117(1)(xv); and PARA 319.
2　As to the meaning of 'mine' see PARA 3.
3　See the Settled Land Act 1925 s 20, ss 41, 42, 45, 46, 117(1)(xv); and SETTLEMENTS. The tenant for life could deal with the surface and the minerals separately: see s 50. As to the powers of a tenant for life generally see SETTLEMENTS.
4　As to the phasing out of strict settlements and the introduction of the 'trust of land' see the Trusts of Land and Appointment of Trustees Act 1996 s 2(1); and PARA 282.
5　As to the meaning of 'trustees of land' see PARA 282.
6　Trusts of Land and Appointment of Trustees Act 1996 s 6(1).
7　For these purposes 'beneficiary', in relation to a trust, means any person who under the trust has an interest in property subject to the trust (including a person who has such an interest as a trustee or a personal representative) (Trusts of Land and Appointment of Trustees Act 1996 s 22(1)); references to a beneficiary who is beneficially entitled do not include a beneficiary who has an interest in property subject to the trust only by reason of being a trustee or personal representative (s 22(2)); and a person who is a beneficiary only by reason of being an annuitant is not to be regarded as entitled to an interest in possession in land subject to the trust (s 22(3)).
8　Trusts of Land and Appointment of Trustees Act 1996 s 9(1). As to the functions of trustees of land and their powers of delegation see ss 6, 8–11; and REAL PROPERTY AND REGISTRATION vol 87 (2017) PARA 104; TRUSTS AND POWERS vol 98 (2013) PARAS 428, 474 et seq. As to the powers of a beneficiary under a trust of land generally see SETTLEMENTS.
9　See REAL PROPERTY AND REGISTRATION vol 87 (2017) PARA 104; TRUSTS AND POWERS vol 98 (2013) PARA 474 et seq.

## 290. Trustees and personal representatives.

In certain cases trustees and personal representatives could have exercised the powers to grant mining leases[1] conferred on a tenant for life[2] under the Settled Land Act 1925[3]. Trustees authorised by statute to grant mining leases of separate properties, held upon different trusts, may not grant one lease of both properties[4].

As from 1 January 1997 no new settlements can be created under the Settled Land Act 1925[5].

1　As to the meaning of 'mining lease' see PARA 289.
2　As to the statutory powers of leasing see PARA 289.
3　See the Settled Land Act 1925 ss 23(1), 26(1); the Law of Property Act 1925 s 28(1) (repealed); the Administration of Estates Act 1925 s 39(1); and SETTLEMENTS; TRUSTS AND POWERS vol 98 (2013) PARA 1 et seq; WILLS AND INTESTACY vol 103 (2016) PARAS 1019, 1021. Before 1926, trustees had no power to grant mining leases unless expressly authorised to do so, and apart from statute, the court could not assist them (even where the legal estate was vested in such trustees and such leases would be beneficial to the beneficiaries): see *Wood v Patteson* (1847) 10 Beav 541. See also TRUSTS AND POWERS vol 98 (2013) PARA 1 et seq. As to express powers of leasing see

generally TRUSTS AND POWERS vol 98 (2013) PARA 486 et seq. Accordingly, prima facie, a trust for sale did not authorise trustees to grant mining leases (*Jervoise v Clarke* (1821) Madd & G 96); nor did a general power to lease authorise the grant of a lease of unopened mines (*Clegg v Rowland* (1866) LR 2 Eq 160; *Re Baskerville, Baskerville v Baskerville* [1910] 2 Ch 329; *Re Harter, Harter v Harter* [1913] WN 104), although it was not necessary that a power to authorise such a grant should refer expressly to unopened mines (*Daly v Beckett* (1857) 24 Beav 114; *Re Barker, Wallis v Barker* (1903) 88 LT 685). It was a question of construction in each case: see *Leigh v Earl of Balcarres* (1848) 6 CB 847.

4   *Tolson v Sheard* (1877) 5 ChD 19, CA.
5   As to the phasing out of strict settlements and the introduction of the 'trust of land' see the Trusts of Land and Appointment of Trustees Act 1996 s 2(1); and PARA 282. As to the statutory powers of leasing see PARA 289.

## 291.   University and college estates.

The universities of Oxford, Cambridge and Durham, and the colleges or halls in them, and the colleges of Winchester and Eton[1], may lease any land[2] belonging to the university or college in question, or any easement, right, or privilege of any kind, over or in relation to the land, for any purpose whatever, whether involving waste or not, for any term not exceeding, in the case of a mining lease, 60 years[3]. Any such lease must conform to conditions similar to those imposed in respect of mining leases granted by a tenant for life[4], and the leasing power extends to the making of a lease for giving effect to a covenant for renewal, and a lease for confirming a previous void or voidable lease[5]. The provisions as to rent are identical in effect with those applicable to mining leases granted under the powers of the Settled Land Act 1925[6] by tenants for life[7]. Where a lease for a longer term or on other conditions is necessary by reason of local conditions, such a lease may be granted with ministerial authority[8]. Powers of accepting surrenders in respect of mines and minerals are also exercisable subject to conditions similar to those affecting tenants for life[9]. The surface and minerals may be dealt with separately[10].

As from 1 January 1997 no new settlements can be created under the Settled Land Act 1925[11].

1   See the Universities and College Estates Act 1925 s 1; and EDUCATION vol 36 (2015) PARA 1329.
2   'Land' includes, inter alia, mines and minerals, whether or not held apart from the surface: see the Universities and College Estates Act 1925 s 43(iv); and EDUCATION vol 36 (2015) PARA 1329.
3   See the Universities and College Estates Act 1925 s 6(ii).
4   As to regulations respecting leases generally see the Universities and College Estates Act 1925 s 7; cf the Settled Land Act 1925 s 42; and SETTLEMENTS.
5   See the Universities and College Estates Act 1925 s 8.
6   As to regulations respecting mining leases see the Settled Land Act 1925 s 45; and SETTLEMENTS.
7   As to regulations respecting mining leases see the Universities and College Estates Act 1925 s 10 (amended by SI 1978/443).
8   See the Universities and College Estates Act 1925 s 11. The Universities and College Estates Act 1925 refers to the Minister of Agriculture, Fisheries and Food, but the Ministry of Agriculture, Fisheries and Food has been dissolved and the minister's functions have been transferred to the Secretary of State for Environment, Food and Rural Affairs (see the Ministry of Agriculture, Fisheries and Food (Dissolution) Order 2002, SI 2002/794; and PARA 2).
9   See the Universities and College Estates Act 1925 s 13 (amended by the Universities and College Estates Act 1964 ss 2–3, Sch 1 Pt II para 4). Cf the Settled Land Act 1925 s 52; and SETTLEMENTS. As to the meaning of 'mines and minerals' see PARA 10.
10  See the Universities and College Estates Act 1925 s 22. The Universities and College Estates Act 1925 also contains provisions similar to those affecting tenants for life as to the power to compromise claims (s 17 (amended by the Universities and College Estates Act 1964 ss 2–3, Sch 1 Pt I para 3)), the power to vary leases (Universities and College Estates Act 1925 s 18), and the power to grant options (s 23 (amended by the Universities and College Estates Act 1964 ss 2–3, Sch 1 Pt I para 4, Pt II para 9)). As to the application of mineral rents see s 12. As to the powers of tenants for life see SETTLEMENTS.

11 As to the phasing out of strict settlements and the introduction of the 'trust of land' see the Trusts of Land and Appointment of Trustees Act 1996 s 2(1); and PARA 282.

## 292. Land held on charitable, ecclesiastical or public trusts.

Trustees in whom land is vested on charitable, ecclesiastical or public trusts have, in reference to that land, the powers of leasing conferred by the Trusts of Land and Appointment of Trustees Act 1996[1] subject to statutory controls over the trustees[2].

1  See SETTLEMENTS; TRUSTS AND POWERS vol 98 (2013) PARA 1 et seq. As to powers of leasing by charities generally see CHARITIES vol 8 (2015) PARA 401 et seq. Prior to 1 January 1997, trustees in whom land is vested on charitable, ecclesiastical or public trusts had, in reference to that land, the powers of leasing conferred by the Settled Land Act 1925 upon a tenant for life: see s 29(1) (repealed). Those powers were only exercisable subject to such consents or orders, if any, being obtained as would, if the Settled Land Act 1925 had not been passed, have been requisite if the lease had been made under an express power conferred by the instrument creating the trust: see s 29(2) (repealed). Before the disposition of charity land was regulated by statute, trustees of charity land had a general power of granting leases of such land, governed by the same general principles as applied to sales: see eg *A-G v Warren* (1818) 2 Swan 291 at 302–303 per Plumer MR. It is not clear whether the statutory powers superseded this general power, but it was not safe for purchasers to rely on the general power as authorising a transaction: see CHARITIES vol 8 (2015) PARA 408 et seq.
2  For example, as to the restrictions on dispositions of charity land see the Charities Act 1993 s 36; and CHARITIES vol 8 (2015) PARA 401 et seq.

## 293. The Crown and the Duchy of Cornwall.

The Crown Estate Commissioners[1] have powers of leasing mines and minerals belonging to the Crown[2]. Subject to certain formalities, mines and minerals which form part of the private estates of the Crown may be leased as freely as by an ordinary subject[3].

The Duke of Cornwall may grant a mining lease of Duchy land for any term of years[4].

1  As to the constitution, composition and functions of the Crown Estate Commissioners see the Crown Estate Act 1961 s 1; and CROWN AND CROWN PROCEEDINGS vol 29 (2014) PARA 192 et seq.
2  As to their powers of leasing generally see CROWN AND CROWN PROCEEDINGS vol 29 (2014) PARA 204. As to the meaning of 'mines and minerals' see PARA 10; and as to the meaning of 'mine' see PARA 3. The Commissioners must not grant a lease of land of the Crown Estate, or of any right or privilege over or in relation to any such land, for a term ending more than 150 years from the date of the lease, and every such lease granted by them must be made to take effect in possession not later than 12 months after its date or in reversion after an existing lease having at that date not more than 21 years to run: Crown Estate Act 1961 s 3(2) (amended by the Miscellaneous Financial Provisions Act 1983 s 5). See generally CROWN AND CROWN PROCEEDINGS vol 29 (2014) PARA 204.
3  As to the sovereign's right to dispose of private estates see generally CROWN AND CROWN PROCEEDINGS vol 29 (2014) PARA 271.
4  See the Duchy of Cornwall Management Act 1863 s 21 (amended by the Duchy of Cornwall Management Act 1982 s 5(a)); the Duchy of Cornwall Management Act 1863 s 37; and CROWN AND CROWN PROCEEDINGS vol 29 (2014) PARA 248. When there is no Duke of Cornwall, the Duchy is vested in the Sovereign: see generally CROWN AND CROWN PROCEEDINGS vol 29 (2014) PARA 33.

## (2) Dispositions other than Leases

### (i) Contracts for Sale

**294. General rules and requirements.**

The rules of law applicable to contracts for the sale or demise of land[1] apply generally to contracts concerning mines, quarries and unsevered minerals, for the mines and minerals are part and parcel of the land[2].

The statutory requirements[3], relating to contracts for the sale or other disposition of an interest in land[4] apply equally to a contract for the sale of a mine or quarry, or of a share of a mine or quarry[5], or for a right to enter upon land and dig for and take minerals[6], but not to an agreement relating to a mine unless it concerns an interest in the mine itself[7], or, as a rule, to a partnership agreement[8], unless it amounts to a contract for the sale of an interest in the land[9].

1   As to the rules of law applicable to contracts for the sale or demise of land generally see LANDLORD AND TENANT vol 62 (2016) PARA 2; CONVEYANCING vol 23 (2016) PARA 1 et seq.
2   See *Wilkinson v Proud* (1843) 11 M & W 33; *Williamson v Wootton* (1855) 3 Drew 210 at 213 per Kindersley V-C; *Kerr v Pawson* (1858) 25 Beav 394 at 406 per Romilly MR. As to the registration of estate contracts see REAL PROPERTY AND REGISTRATION vol 87 (2017) PARA 672. As to the meaning of 'mine' see PARA 3; and as to the meaning of 'minerals' see PARA 10.
3   Ie the Law of Property (Miscellaneous Provisions) Act 1989 s 2, which requires contracts for the sale or other disposition of an interest in land to be made in writing and signed by all the parties to the contract: see CONVEYANCING vol 23 (2016) PARA 27.
4   See the Law of Property (Miscellaneous Provisions) Act 1989 s 2; *McCausland v Duncan Lawrie Ltd* [1996] 4 All ER 995, [1997] 1 WLR 38, CA; and CONTRACT; CONVEYANCING vol 23 (2016) PARA 27.
5   *Boyce v Green* (1826) Batt 608.
6   *Smart v Jones* (1864) 15 CBNS 717.
7   *Cheadle v Proctor* (1868) 19 LT 289.
8   *Forster v Hale* (1800) 5 Ves 308 at 314 per Lord Loughborough LC; and see PARTNERSHIP.
9   *Caddick v Skidmore* (1857) 2 De G & J 52.

**295. Contracts passing mines and minerals.**

A contract for the sale of freehold land includes the mines and minerals under that land unless expressly excepted[1]; but if land is taken compulsorily by a railway authority[2], or for waterworks and sewers[3], the mines and minerals are not acquired unless expressly purchased and conveyed. A railway authority need not acquire the surface and minerals at the same time[4].

1   *Williamson v Wootton* (1855) 3 Drew 210 at 213 per Kindersley V-C; *Hayford v Criddle* (1855) 22 Beav 477 at 480 per Romilly MR; *Kerr v Pawson* (1858) 25 Beav 394 at 406 per Romilly MR. As to the meaning of 'mines and minerals' see PARA 10; and as to the meaning of 'mine' see PARA 3. As to the presumption arising from surface ownership see PARA 18; and CONVEYANCING vol 23 (2016) PARA 1 et seq.
2   As to the working of mines lying under or near a railway see the Railways Clauses Consolidation Act 1845 ss 77–85; PARA 142 et seq; *Re Metropolitan District Rly Co and Cotton's Trustees* (1881) 45 LT 103, CA. Minerals do not impliedly pass with the surface: see PARA 142. A mining code based on that applicable to railways under the Railways Clauses Consolidation Act 1845 ss 77–85 may be incorporated in a compulsory purchase order: see the Acquisition of Land Act 1981 s 3, Sch 2; and PARA 135. The railways code is also incorporated under the Transport and Works Act 1992 by virtue of the Transport and Works (Model Clauses for Railways and Tramways) Order 2006, SI 2006/1954: see PARA 135; and RAILWAYS AND TRAMWAYS vol 86 (2017) PARAS 313–314, 314. As to the incorporation of the Railways Clauses Consolidation Act 1845 in local acts and compulsory purchase orders of provisions excluding minerals see COMPULSORY ACQUISITION OF LAND vol 18 (2009) PARA 515.

3   See the Water Industry Act 1991 s 188, Sch 14; the Water Resources Act 1991 s 182, Sch 23; and
    WATER AND WATERWAYS vol 101 (2018) PARA 758 et seq.
        In the case of the compulsory acquisition of land by virtue of the Water Industry Act 1991 or
    the Water Resources Act 1991 (see WATER AND WATERWAYS vol 101 (2018) PARAS 719–720),
    the provisions of the Water Industry Act 1991 Sch 14 or, as the case may be, the Water Resources
    Act 1991 Sch 23, have effect instead of the Acquisition of Land Act 1981 s 3, Sch 2: see the Water
    Industry Act 1991 s 188; and the Water Resources Act 1991 s 182 (amended by the Environment
    Act 1995 s 120(1), Sch 22 para 128).
4   *Errington v Metropolitan District Rly Co* (1882) 19 ChD 559, CA.

## 296.  Effect of absence of title to minerals.

If the vendor under a contract for the sale of freehold land has no title to the
mines and minerals[1], he cannot enforce the contract if he has agreed to show good
title[2], even if he is willing to or the court could compensate the purchaser[3]. This
is so even where no evidence is given of the existence in the land of minerals of any
value[4], for the objection to the title is valid unless it is shown that there is no
subject matter for the reservation to act upon, or that all right to exercise it has
ceased[5]. If the vendor cannot make a title by the date for completion he cannot
maintain an action for damages for breach of contract, even where he has
subsequently acquired the right to the minerals for a nominal sum[6].

1   As to the meaning of 'mines and minerals' see PARA 10; and as to the meaning of 'mine' see PARA
    3.
2   *Upperton v Nickolson* (1871) 6 Ch App 436 (where land formerly copyhold); *Pretty v Solly* (1859)
    26 Beav 606; *Bellamy v Debenham* [1891] 1 Ch 412, CA; and see *McGrory v Alderdale Estate Co
    Ltd* [1918] AC 503, HL.
3   *Re Hargreaves and Thompson's Contract* (1886) 32 ChD 454 at 455, CA; see *Re Davis and Cavey*
    (1888) 40 ChD 601; *Re Wilsons and Stevens' Contract* [1894] 3 Ch 546. As to compensation for
    failure to make title see PARA 298.
4   *Barton v Downes* (1842) Fl & K 505 at 506; *Martin v Cotter* (1846) 3 Jo & Lat 496, agreeing,
    at 509 per Sugden LC, with the law laid down in *Lyddall v Weston* (1739) 2 Atk 19 at 20 per Lord
    Hardwicke.
5   *Martin v Cotter* (1846) 3 Jo & Lat 496 at 509 per Sugden LC; *Ramsden v Hurst* (1858) 27 LJ Ch
    482. As to cesser of the right to work minerals see PARAS 8, 30–31; and *Seaman v Vawdrey* (1810)
    16 Ves 390 at 392 per Grant MR.
6   *Bellamy v Debenham* [1891] 1 Ch 412, CA; and see *Brickles v Snell* [1916] 2 AC 599.

## 297.  Effect of vendor's knowledge of absence of title.

A vendor who contracts to sell land by a description which includes minerals[1],
knowing that he has no title to them, cannot avoid the contract under a power to
rescind if an objection to the title is insisted on which he is unable or, on the
ground of expense, declines to remove or comply with; for the court will consider
his conduct in applying the condition[2]. A vendor of land sold as containing
minerals has, however, been allowed to rescind where the title to minerals under
part of the land has been the subject of an objection the removal of which would
have involved a long and expensive inquiry[3].

1   As to the meaning of 'minerals' see PARA 10.
2   *Re Jackson and Haden's Contract* [1906] 1 Ch 412, CA; and see *Procter v Pugh* [1921] 2 Ch 256,
    (1921) 127 LT 126; *Re Des Reaux and Setchfields's Contract* [1926] Ch 178, (1925) 134 LT 623;
    and CONVEYANCING vol 23 (2016) PARA 463.
3   See *Mawson v Fletcher* (1870) 6 Ch App 91, where the contract for sale included a condition that
    if any objection or requisition should be delivered and persisted in, the vendor should be at liberty
    to rescind the contract on returning to the purchaser his deposit, without interest or expenses.

## 298.  Compensation for failure to make title.

If a vendor has no title to the mines and minerals[1], a purchaser of land may be
entitled to compensation under a clause in the contract providing that errors in the

particulars are to be the subject of compensation[2]; and compensation has been obtained by purchasers in cases in which a provision of the contract was not relied on[3]; but a purchaser cannot obtain compensation if he has gone into possession and has not objected to the title within the time named by the contract[4]. Compensation may be given to a purchaser by reason of misrepresentation on the vendor's part[5].

1 As to the meaning of 'mines and minerals' see PARA 10; and as to the meaning of 'mine' see PARA 3.
2 *Re Jackson and Haden's Contract* [1906] 1 Ch 412, CA (where the vendor had no right to rescind on the ground of an objection to the title under the contract); see *Baines v Tweddle* [1959] Ch 679, [1959] 2 All ER 724, CA; and CONVEYANCING vol 23 (2016) PARAS 278, 463 et seq.
3 *Seaman v Vawdrey* (1810) 16 Ves 390; *Ramsden v Hurst* (1858) 27 LJ Ch 482; cf *Smithson v Powell, Powell v Smithson* (1852) 20 LTOS 105; *Re Bunbury's Estate* (1867) 1 IR Eq 458.
4 *Smithson v Powell, Powell v Smithson* (1852) 20 LTOS 105 (where no compensation awarded).
5 *Powell v Elliot* (1875) 10 Ch App 424. As to misrepresentation see MISREPRESENTATION.

### 299. Rights of purchaser taking with notice.

Mining contracts, whether by way of sale or of demise, do not usually import any guarantee of the existence or value of minerals[1]. If land is sold as containing minerals, and the purchaser enters into the contract with knowledge that the minerals have been partly worked, it is his business to ascertain the extent of the working[2]. Further, when mines[3] are not in the occupation of the vendor, a purchaser of land takes with notice of the rights of those in possession[4], and if the contract is for the sale of what was formerly copyhold land, the purchaser cannot object to the title on the ground that the right to minerals is in the lord[5]; but it seems that notice that the land sold is enfranchised copyhold is not sufficient to affect a purchaser with notice that the vendor has no title to the mines and minerals[6].

1 *Jefferys v Fairs* (1876) 4 ChD 448 at 452 per Bacon V-C. As to the meaning of 'minerals' see PARA 10.
2 *Colby v Gadsden* (1865) 34 Beav 416 at 421 per Romilly MR; and see *Jennings v Broughton* (1853) 5 De GM & G 126.
3 As to the meaning of 'mine' see PARA 3.
4 *Holmes v Powell* (1856) 8 De GM & G 572. As to the liability of registered land to overriding interests see the Land Registration Act 2002 ss 11, 12, 28, 29, Sch 1 paras 2, 7, 8, 9, Sch 3 paras 2, 7, 8, 9 in particular; and REAL PROPERTY AND REGISTRATION vol 87 (2017) PARAS 351 et seq, 451.
5 *Hayford v Criddle* (1855) 22 Beav 477 at 480 per Romilly MR. As to copyhold see CUSTOM AND USAGE vol 32 (2012) PARA 42.
6 See *Bellamy v Debenham* [1891] 1 Ch 412 at 420, CA, per Lindley LJ; and *Kerr v Pawson* (1858) 25 Beav 394. As to a sale of settled land comprising enfranchised copyholds see SETTLEMENTS. As to the lord's right to the minerals see CUSTOM AND USAGE vol 32 (2012) PARA 112; REAL PROPERTY AND REGISTRATION vol 87 (2017) PARA 40. As to the meaning of 'mines and minerals' see PARA 10.

### 300. Implied terms of the contract of sale.

A contract for the sale or other disposition of an interest in land can only be made in writing and only by incorporating all the terms which the parties have expressly agreed in one document or, where contracts are exchanged, in each. The terms may be incorporated in a document either by being set out in it or by reference to some other document[1].

It appears that in a contract for a sale of mines[2] for working, time is of the essence of the contract even if not expressly stated to be so[3]. In the absence of express provision to the contrary, a purchaser of mines is entitled to the profits from the date on which he pays the purchase money[4].

A purchaser who goes into possession and works a mine before conveyance may be ordered on interim application to pay the purchase money into court[5].

1  See the Law of Property (Miscellaneous Provisions) Act 1989 s 2(1), (2); *McCausland v Duncan Lawrie Ltd* [1996] 4 All ER 995, [1997] 1 WLR 38, CA; and REAL PROPERTY AND REGISTRATION vol 87 (2017) PARA 975.
2  As to the meaning of 'mine' see PARA 3.
3  *Green v Sevin* (1879) 13 ChD 589 at 594, obiter, per Fry J; and see *Macbryde v Weekes* (1856) 22 Beav 533. It seems that notice may be given fixing a reasonable time for completion if no time is named in the contract: *Macbryde v Weekes*.
4  See PARA 362. It was held in *Wren v Kirton* (1803) 8 Ves 502 and in *Williams v Attenborough* (1823) Turn & R 70 at 73 per Lord Eldon LC, that the purchaser was entitled to profits from the commencement of the month in which he paid the purchase money, but these decisions do not appear to be good law.
5  *Buck v Lodge* (1812) 18 Ves 450. As to how far taking possession is an acceptance by the purchaser of the vendor's title see CONVEYANCING vol 23 (2016) PARA 1 et seq.

### 301.  Purchaser's duty of disclosure.

A purchaser of land need not disclose to the vendor his knowledge of the existence[1] or value[2] of minerals[3] in the land unless he is in a fiduciary position towards the vendor[4]. If, however, a purchaser has wrongfully worked minerals under the land he must disclose the working to the vendor before contracting to buy, failing which the vendor will be entitled to refuse to complete the contract[5]. Any attempt by the purchaser to mislead or hurry the vendor may be a ground for refusing specific performance of the contract[6], or may give rise to a claim for damages[7]. It is uncertain whether a tenant for life buying from the trustees of the settlement was bound to make disclosure[8].

As from 1 January 1997 no new settlements can be created under the Settled Land Act 1925[9].

1  *Fox v Mackreth* (1788) 2 Bro CC 400 at 420 per Lord Thurlow LC; *Turner v Harvey* (1821) Jac 169 at 178 per Lord Eldon LC.
2  *Walters v Morgan* (1861) 3 De GF & J 718; *Phillips v Homfray, Fothergill v Phillips* (1871) 6 Ch App 770 at 779 per Lord Hatherley LC.
3  As to the meaning of 'minerals' see PARA 10.
4  *Luddy's Trustee v Peard* (1886) 33 ChD 500 at 520, obiter, per Kay J. A sale under an execution of an insolvent partner's share in a mine to his co-partners will be set aside if the purchasers have concealed matters affecting the value of the property: *Perens v Johnson, Johnson v Perens* (1857) 3 Sm & G 419.
5  *Phillips v Homfray, Fothergill v Phillips* (1871) 6 Ch App 770.
6  *Turner v Harvey* (1821) Jac 169 at 178 per Lord Eldon LC; *Walters v Morgan* (1861) 3 De GF & J 718 at 723 per Lord Campbell LC.
7  As to damages for misrepresentation see the Misrepresentation Act 1967 s 2; and MISREPRESENTATION vol 76 (2013) PARA 788 et seq.
8  *Dicconson v Talbot* (1870) 6 Ch App 32.
9  As to the phasing out of strict settlements and the introduction of the 'trust of land' see the Trusts of Land and Appointment of Trustees Act 1996 s 2(1); and PARA 282.

### 302.  Specific performance.

A contract for the sale or lease of a mine[1] will be specifically enforced, if fairly entered into, even if the mine is worthless, or on the ground of the purchaser's ignorance of mining matters, or hardship that might be caused to the purchaser[2], but the court will not order specific performance of a contract for the sale or lease of mineral property if its terms[3] or the subject matter[4] are insufficiently defined. However, a description is sufficient if the subject matter is ascertainable, even where the boundaries of the property are not defined in the contract[5]. If possession has been taken under the contract, a lesser certainty of description will suffice[6].

The court will specifically enforce a contract to grant a wayleave[7], but if the grant would be useless to the defendant[8], or the contract has been entered into by the defendant under a material mistake[9], the claimant will be left to his remedy in damages[10].

1   As to the meaning of 'mine' see PARA 3.
2   *Haywood v Cope* (1858) 25 Beav 140; *Jefferys v Fairs* (1876) 4 ChD 448. Pending the hearing of a claim for specific performance there is jurisdiction to restrain a defendant in possession from allowing the mine to be drowned out: *Strelley v Pearson* (1880) 15 ChD 113. As to the power in interim remedies to order the preservation of relevant property see CPR 25.1(1)(c)(i), (d), (l), 25.3, CPR PD 25A–*Interim Injunctions* paras 2.1–4.5. As to the remedy of specific performance generally see SPECIFIC PERFORMANCE vol 95 (2017) PARA 501 et seq.
3   *Williamson v Wootton* (1855) 3 Drew 210.
4   *Price v Griffith* (1851) 1 De GM & G 80; *Lancaster v De Trafford* (1862) 31 LJ Ch 554; *Davis v Shepherd* (1866) 1 Ch App 410; and see *Low Moor Co v Stanley Coal Co* (1875) 33 LT 436.
5   *Haywood v Cope* (1858) 25 Beav 140.
6   *Parker v Taswell* (1858) 2 De G & J 559 at 571 per Lord Chelmsford LC.
7   — *v White* (circa 1709) 3 Swan 108n; *Ricketts v Bell* (1847) 1 De G & Sm 335.
8   — *v White* (circa 1709) 3 Swan 108n.
9   As to what mistakes are material see MISTAKE.
10   *Ricketts v Bell* (1847) 1 De G & Sm 335.

### 303. Contracts not specifically enforceable.

The court will not normally grant specific performance of a contract to sell minerals to be obtained from a mine[1], for this is a contract for the sale of chattels[2] and would involve the superintendence by the court of the working of the mine[3]. Similarly, in the normal course the breach of a contract to sell chattels will not be restrained by mandatory injunction[4]. For the same reasons a contract to work a quarry will not be specifically enforced[5].

The right to specific performance of a contract may be barred by laches[6]. Delay is not a bar while both parties are insisting on the performance of the contract[7], but after they are at arm's length a short delay may be sufficient[8]. There is an expectation of the court for persons to be unusually vigilant and active in asserting any right to specific performance in matters relating to commodities fluctuating from day to day in market price[9]. The purchaser should give notice of repudiation and abandonment if he has been in possession of the mine and intends to rely on delay as a defence[10].

Misrepresentation[11] or concealment[12] by the vendor may be a ground for refusing specific performance, but if the purchaser, with knowledge of the misrepresentation, gives notice to the vendor requiring him to complete, he cannot afterwards avail himself of this defence[13].

1   *Pollard v Clayton* (1855) 1 K & J 462. As to specific performance of a contract see generally SPECIFIC PERFORMANCE vol 95 (2017) PARA 501 et seq. As to the meaning of 'minerals' see PARA 10; and as to the meaning of 'mine' see PARA 3.
2   *Fothergill v Rowland* (1873) LR 17 Eq 132 at 139 per Jessel MR.
3   *Pollard v Clayton* (1855) 1 K & J 462; and see *Wheatley v Westminster Brymbo Coal Co* (1869) LR 9 Eq 538 at 551, 552 per Malins V-C; *Co-operative Insurance Society Ltd v Argyll Stores (Holdings) Ltd* [1998] AC 1, [1997] 3 All ER 297, HL (a covenant in a lease of retail premises to keep open for trade during the usual hours of business was not, other than in exceptional circumstances, specifically enforceable, since it was the settled practice of the court not to make an order requiring a person to carry on a business).
4   *Fothergill v Rowland* (1873) LR 17 Eq 132; and see CIVIL PROCEDURE vol 12 (2015) PARAS 1083 et seq, 463, 465. See also *Co-operative Insurance Society Ltd v Argyll Stores (Holdings) Ltd* [1998] AC 1, [1997] 3 All ER 297, HL.

5　*Booth v Pollard* (1840) 4 Y & C Ex 61.
6　*Walker v Jeffreys* (1842) 1 Hare 341; *Eads v Williams* (1854) 4 De GM & G 674 at 691 per Lord Cranworth LC; *Sharp v Wright* (1859) 28 Beav 150; *Huxham v Llewellyn* (1873) 21 WR 570; *Glasbrook v Richardson* (1874) 23 WR 51.
7　*Colby v Gadsden* (1865) 34 Beav 416 at 418 per Romilly MR.
8　*Huxham v Llewellyn* (1873) 21 WR 570; *Glasbrook v Richardson* (1874) 23 WR 51.
9　*Pollard v Clayton* (1855) 1 K & J 462.
10　*Haywood v Cope* (1858) 25 Beav 140 at 150 per Romilly MR.
11　*Higgins v Samels* (1862) 2 John & H 460; *Colby v Gadsden* (1867) 15 WR 1185. See also MISREPRESENTATION vol 76 (2013) PARA 784.
12　*Haywood v Cope* (1858) 25 Beav 140 at 147 per Romilly MR. As to setting aside the contract see PARA 304.
13　*Macbryde v Weekes* (1856) 22 Beav 533 at 538 per Romilly MR; and see *British and Commonwealth Holdings plc v Quadrex Holdings Inc* [1989] QB 842, [1989] 3 All ER 492, CA.

## 304.　Fraud, misrepresentation and mistake.

The contract will be set aside if induced by fraud[1] or material misrepresentation[2]; but if the purchaser has tested the accuracy of the vendor's statements he cannot avoid the contract[3], and, even though induced by misrepresentation, a contract will not be set aside if the position of the parties has been so altered that they cannot be restored to their former position[4]. Furthermore, if the purchaser requires the vendor to complete he cannot then set up as a defence to a claim for specific performance a misrepresentation of the vendor of which he was aware at the time of giving notice[5]. In addition, or as an alternative, to the right to rescission, a purchaser who has been induced to enter into the contract as a result of fraud or material misrepresentation may be entitled to damages[6].

Mutual mistake is a good ground for a claim for rescission of the contract[7], but the mere existence of faults in the mine is not a good ground[8].

The burden of proof in a claim for rescission of a contract relating to mines is on the party claiming it[9], and he should institute proceedings at once, for his right to relief is quickly barred by laches[10].

A receiver and manager of a colliery may be appointed until the hearing of a claim for rescission[11].

1　*Attwood v Small* (1838) 6 Cl & Fin 232, HL; *Phosphate Sewage Co v Hartmont* (1877) 5 ChD 394, CA; *Erlanger v New Sombrero Phosphate Co* (1878) 3 App Cas 1218, HL; applied in *O'Sullivan v Management Agency and Music Ltd* [1985] QB 428, [1985] 3 All ER 351, CA. When a mine is sold by the court the biddings will not be opened except on the ground of fraud or improper conduct in the management of the sale: see the Sale of Land by Auction Act 1867 s 7; *Delves v Delves* (1875) LR 20 Eq 77; and CONVEYANCING vol 23 (2016) PARAS 122, 398, 458.As to the meaning of 'mine' see PARA 3.
2　*Jennings v Broughton* (1853) 17 Beav 234 at 238 per Romilly MR (affd (1854) 5 De GM & G 126); *Lagunas Nitrate Co v Lagunas Syndicate* [1899] 2 Ch 392, CA; applied in *O'Sullivan v Management Agency and Music Ltd* [1985] QB 428, [1985] 3 All ER 351, CA. See also MISREPRESENTATION vol 76 (2013) PARA 773 et seq.
3　*Attwood v Small* (1838) 6 Cl & Fin 232, HL; *Jennings v Broughton* (1853) 17 Beav 234 (affd (1854) 5 De GM & G 126); *Haywood v Cope* (1858) 25 Beav 140 at 148 per Romilly MR.
4　*Lagunas Nitrate Co v Lagunas Syndicate* [1899] 2 Ch 392 at 423, 433, CA, per Lindley MR; and see MISREPRESENTATION vol 76 (2013) PARA 829 et seq.
5　*Macbryde v Weekes* (1856) 22 Beav 533; and see *British and Commonwealth Holdings plc v Quadrex Holdings Inc* [1989] QB 842, [1989] 3 All ER 492, CA.
6　As to damages for misrepresentation see the Misrepresentation Act 1967 s 2; and MISREPRESENTATION vol 76 (2013) PARA 788 et seq.
7　*Davis v Shepherd* (1866) 1 Ch App 410 at 419 per Turner LJ; and see MISTAKE vol 77 (2016) PARA 48 et seq.

8  *Ridgway v Sneyd* (1854) Kay 627 at 635 per Page Wood V-C. It has been suggested that an exaggerated account of a mine's prospects is not a good ground for rescission (see *Jennings v Broughton* (1853) 17 Beav 234; affd (1854) 5 De GM & G 126), but it seems that this may no longer be the case (see MISREPRESENTATION vol 76 (2013) PARAS 713–714).

9  *Jennings v Broughton* (1853) 17 Beav 234; affd (1854) 5 De GM & G 126.

10  *Ernest v Vivian* (1863) 33 LJ Ch 513; *Erlanger v New Sombrero Phosphate Co* (1878) 3 App Cas 1218, HL; *Lagunas Nitrate Co v Lagunas Syndicate* [1899] 2 Ch 392, CA. As to the defence of laches see EQUITABLE JURISDICTION vol 47 (2014) PARA 253.

11  *Gibbs v David* (1875) LR 20 Eq 373.

## (ii) Conveyances on Sale; Mortgages

### 305. Effect of conveyance of land on ownership of minerals.

All mines and minerals[1], whether their ownership is severed from the ownership of the surface of the land or not, lie in grant, and are conveyed by deed[2]. Unless they are expressly excepted or circumstances exist to rebut the presumption, a conveyance of land passes the mines and minerals in it[3]. If, however, the ownership of the mines and minerals has been previously severed from the ownership of the land, the title to them remains unaffected by such a conveyance[4]. In various cases conveyances of land taken in the exercise of compulsory powers[5] are deemed not to include the minerals, except such parts of them as are necessary to be dug or carried away or used in the construction of the works, unless the minerals are expressly conveyed[6]. In such cases, however, the purchaser acquires the whole soil except the minerals[7].

A conveyance of a manor passes mines, minerals and quarries reputed or known as part, parcel or member of the manor[8]. A conveyance by the Crown as lord of a manor of minerals found within the commons, wastes or marshes within the manor passes minerals under the foreshore of a river[9].

A conveyance of land adjoining a railway or a canal does not pass any part of the minerals under the railway[10] or canal, even if those minerals are vested in the person conveying as the presumption of ownership *usque ad medium filum viae* does not apply[11].

1  As to the meaning of 'mines and minerals' see PARA 10.

2  See the Law of Property Act 1925 ss 51(1), 52(1), 205(1)(ix); and DEEDS AND OTHER INSTRUMENTS vol 32 (2012) PARA 214. Prior to the passing of the Real Property Act 1845 ss 2, 3 (both repealed), open mines were corporeal hereditaments and lay in livery: Shep Touch (8 Edn) 96. There was some doubt whether unopened mines were corporeal or incorporeal hereditaments: *Wilkinson v Proud* (1843) 11 M & W 33 at 35; *Carlyon v Lovering* (1857) 1 H & N 784 at 799 per Watson B. As to the registration of title to minerals see PARA 316.

3  *Harris v Ryding* (1839) 5 M & W 60 at 73 per Alderson B; *Spoor v Green* (1874) LR 9 Exch 99 at 107 per Cleasby B; *Earl of Jersey v Neath Poor Law Union Guardians* (1889) 22 QBD 555 at 558, CA, per Lord Esher MR.

4  *Denison v Holiday* (1858) 3 H & N 670.

5  For this purpose a voluntary conveyance made in contemplation of compulsory powers is treated as indistinguishable from a conveyance taken in exercise of such powers: *Elliot v North Eastern Rly Co* (1863) 10 HL Cas 333 at 352 per Lord Chelmsford. See PARA 137.

6  See the Railways Clauses Consolidation Act 1845 ss 77–85; PARA 142 et seq; the Water Industry Act 1991 s 188, Sch 14; the Water Resources Act 1991 s 182, Sch 23; WATER AND WATERWAYS vol 101 (2018) PARA 758 et seq; and cf the Acquisition of Land Act 1981 s 3, Sch 2 para 2(2); and see PARA 142. The purchaser may become entitled to a conveyance of the minerals if they are expressly named in the notice to treat: *Errington v Metropolitan District Rly Co* (1882) 19 ChD 559 at 569, CA, per Jessel MR, and at 573 per Brett LJ. As to the construction of a conveyance to a railway authority from which mines and minerals are excepted by the operation of the Railways Clauses Consolidation Act 1845 s 77 see *Midland Rly Co and Kettering, Thrapston and Huntington Rly Co v Robinson* (1889) 15 App Cas 19, HL.

7   *Pountney v Clayton* (1883) 11 QBD 820 at 833, CA, per Brett MR; *Ruabon Brick and Terra Cotta Co v Great Western Rly Co* [1893] 1 Ch 427 at 457, CA, per Bowen LJ; *Re Lord Gerard and London and North Western Rly Co* [1895] 1 QB 459, CA.
8   See the Law of Property Act 1925 s 62(3); and CUSTOM AND USAGE. As to the effect of general words apart from the Law of Property Act 1925 see *A-G v Ewelme Hospital* (1853) 17 Beav 366 at 386 per Romilly MR. Mines severed from a manor cannot be reunited so as to become parcel of it: see *Revell v Jodrell* (1788) 2 Term Rep 415 at 419, 424.
9   *A-G v Hanmer* (1858) 27 LJ Ch 837 (on appeal (1859) 4 De G & J 205); and see *Ecroyd v Coulthard* [1898] 2 Ch 358 at 367, CA, per Lindley MR; and CUSTOM AND USAGE.
10  *Thompson v Hickman* [1907] 1 Ch 550.
11  *Chamber Colliery Co Ltd v Rochdale Canal Co* [1895] AC 564, HL; and see PARA 22.

## 306. Conveyance of land excepting the minerals.

Mines and minerals[1] may be excepted from a conveyance of land, and are properly the subject of an exception and not of a reservation[2]. Consequently, as the property in the excepted mines and minerals remains in the same ownership[3], words of limitation were never necessary[4]. It is a question of construction whether in any particular case the words used amount to an exception of mines or minerals[5] or to a regrant of a right to work[6]. The exception of minerals out of land conveyed, which is of no advantage unless a right to work them is added, necessarily implies the existence of a power to recover the minerals and of the right of working[7]. Nevertheless, if land is sold for a specific purpose and minerals are expressly excepted in the conveyance, the minerals may still be removed by the purchaser so far as may be necessary to enable the land to be employed for the purpose for which it was sold[8].

1   As to the meaning of 'mines and minerals' see PARA 10; and as to the meaning of 'mine' see PARA 3.
2   *Earl of Cardigan v Armitage* (1823) 2 B & C 197; *Doe d Douglas v Lock* (1835) 2 Ad & El 705; *Proud v Bates* (1865) 34 LJ Ch 406; *Duke of Hamilton v Graham* (1871) LR 2 Sc & Div 166; *Eardley v Granville* (1876) 3 ChD 826 at 834 per Jessel MR; *Batten Pooll v Kennedy* [1907] 1 Ch 256. As to the distinction between exceptions and reservations and the effect of an exception of minerals see DEEDS AND OTHER INSTRUMENTS vol 32 (2012) PARAS 438–439.
3   See *Fernando v De Silva* (1912) 107 LT 670 at 671, PC.
4   See Shep Touch (8 Edn) 100. As to conveyances after 1925 see the Law of Property Act 1925 s 60(1).
5   *Duke of Hamilton v Dunlop* (1885) 10 App Cas 813, HL.
6   *Duke of Sutherland v Heathcote* [1892] 1 Ch 475, CA; *Chetham v Williamson* (1804) 4 East 469; *Lord Mountjoy and Earl of Huntington's Case* (1583) Godb 17.
7   *Borys v Canadian Pacific Rly Co* [1953] AC 217 at 227, 228, 232, [1953] 1 All ER 451 at 457–458, 460, PC; *Rowbotham v Wilson* (1860) 8 HL Cas 348 at 360 per Lord Wensleydale; *Ramsay v Blair* (1876) 1 App Cas 701 at 705, HL, per Lord Hatherley. As to reservations see DEEDS AND OTHER INSTRUMENTS vol 32 (2012) PARA 440.
8   *Robinson v Milne* (1884) 53 LJ Ch 1070. See also *Earl of Jersey v Neath Poor Law Union Guardians* (1889) 22 QBD 555, CA; *Glasgow Corpn v Farie* (1888) 13 App Cas 657, HL.

## 307. Effect of covenants in conveyance.

Where a conveyance contained a covenant to pay, for all coal found under certain land, £40 per acre, and to pay a yearly sum of £40 until the total amount was paid, 'found' was construed to mean 'ascertained to be', and the finding of coal was held not to be a condition precedent to the payment[1].

A covenant for quiet enjoyment contained in a conveyance of land not excepting mines and minerals[2] is not broken if the surface of the land subsides owing to the minerals having been worked out before the date of the grant[3].

A rentcharge reserved in respect of minerals raised from property at any time is not void as a perpetuity[4].

1   *Jowett v Spencer* (1847) 1 Exch 647.

2 As to the meaning of 'mines and minerals' see PARA 10; and as to the meaning of 'mine' see PARA 3.

3 *Spoor v Green* (1874) LR 9 Exch 99. A covenant for quiet enjoyment contained in a grant of land excepting the minerals with power to work is broken if the surface of the land subsides owing to workings subsequent to the grant, under a lease giving power to let down the surface, made before the grant: *Taylor v Shafto* (1867) 8 B & S 228, Ex Ch. See also *Dennett v Atherton* (1872) LR 7 QB 316, Ex Ch; *Re Griffiths, Griffiths v Riggs* (1917) 61 Sol Jo 268. As to the operation of this covenant see generally LANDLORD AND TENANT vol 62 (2016) PARA 404 et seq; CONVEYANCING vol 23 (2016) PARA 1 et seq. As to subsidence damage see PARA 182 et seq.

4 *Morgan v Davey* (1883) Cab & El 114; and see PERPETUITIES AND ACCUMULATIONS vol 80 (2013) PARA 6.

## 308. Mortgages.

Mortgages of mineral property are subject to the general law of mortgage, which is dealt with elsewhere in this work[1]. A mortgage of such property usually contains special provisions[2], and the mortgagee's power of securing the appointment of a manager or receiver is peculiarly appropriate to this class of security[3].

1 As to the law of mortgage see MORTGAGE vol 77 (2016) PARA 101 et seq.

2 Eg a power in the mortgagee to work the mine in case of default. As to the provisions usually included in mortgages of mineral property see MORTGAGE vol 77 (2016) PARA 180.

3 See MORTGAGE vol 77 (2016) PARA 101 et seq; RECEIVERS.

### (iii) Enfranchisement and Inclosure

## 309. Enfranchisement.

In the case of a common law enfranchisement[1], the mines and minerals[2], unless expressly excepted, passed to the tenant as part of the freehold[3]. In the case of an enfranchisement under the Copyhold Act 1894[4], the rights of the lord or tenant in any mines or minerals in or under the enfranchised land were not affected by the enfranchisement unless with the express consent in writing of the lord or tenant entitled to them[5]; and the enfranchisement effected by the Law of Property Act 1922[6] did not affect the lord's or tenant's rights to mines and minerals or rights of working them[7].

1 Prior to 1926 enfranchisement could be effected both at common law and under a number of statutes repealed and consolidated by the Copyhold Act 1894 (itself repealed by the Statute Law (Repeals) Act 1969): see REAL PROPERTY AND REGISTRATION vol 87 (2017) PARA 35 et seq. As to the right to work coal in former copyhold land see PARA 397 et seq.

2 As to the ownership of mines and minerals in or under manorial land see CUSTOM AND USAGE. As to the meaning of 'mines and minerals' see PARA 10; and as to the meaning of 'mine' see PARA 3.

3 See Scriven on Copyholds (7th Edn) 306–307.

4 The Copyhold Act 1894 was repealed by the Statute Law (Repeals) Act 1969.

5 Copyhold Act 1894 s 23(1) (repealed).

6 As to the enfranchisement of copyholds see the Law of Property Act 1922 s 128, Sch 12 (both repealed); and REAL PROPERTY AND REGISTRATION vol 87 (2017) PARA 36 et seq.

7 Law of Property Act 1922 s 128(2), Sch 12 para 5 (both repealed).

## 310. General effect of inclosure.

The minerals[1] under the waste of a manor are the property of the lord by virtue of his ownership of the soil; but his power of dealing with them is restricted by the rights enjoyed by the commoners over the surface[2]. The commoners' rights are extinguished by inclosure, and subject to any limitations resulting from the terms of inclosure, the lord may then sell, lease or deal with the minerals as he pleases[3].

1   As to the meaning of 'minerals' see PARA 10.
2   See COMMONS vol 13 (2017) PARA 465 et seq; CUSTOM AND USAGE.
3   As to inclosure generally see COMMONS vol 13 (2017) PARA 318 et seq. This is subject to the statutory vesting of unworked coal in the Coal Authority (see PARAS 50, 66). Coal-mining operations are required to be licensed under the Coal Industry Act 1994 Pt II (ss 35–36): see PARA 89 et seq. As to the meaning of 'coal-mining operations' see PARA 51. As to the Coal Authority see PARA 52 et seq.

## 311.   Inclosure by the lord.

The lord, as owner of the soil[1], may inclose as against common of pasture[2]; but, except by virtue of a special custom[3], which to be reasonable must involve leaving a sufficiency for the commoners[4], he may not inclose against common of turbary or estovers[5], or a right to dig sand or gravel[6] or to get stone[7], unless the place inclosed is such that the right of the commoner is incapable of exercise there[8]. However, the carrying out of certain works on common land without the consent of the appropriate national authority is now prohibited[9].

1   *Folkard v Hemmett* (1776) 5 Term Rep 417n.
2   As to common of pasture see COMMONS vol 13 (2017) PARA 332 et seq.
3   *Arlett v Ellis* (1827) 7 B & C 346; *Lascelles v Lord Onslow* (1877) 2 QBD 433, DC; and see COMMONS vol 13 (2017) PARAS 462, 469.
4   *Lascelles v Lord Onslow* (1877) 2 QBD 433, DC; and see *Bateson v Green* (1793) 5 Term Rep 411; *Arlett v Ellis* (1827) 7 B & C 346 at 369 per Bayley J.
5   *Lascelles v Lord Onslow* (1877) 2 QBD 433, DC; *Duberley v Page* (1788) 2 Term Rep 391; *Grant v Gunner* (1809) 1 Taunt 435. As to common of turbary and common of estovers see COMMONS vol 13 (2017) PARAS 356–359.
6   *Duberley v Page* (1788) 2 Term Rep 391.
7   *Heath v Deane* [1905] 2 Ch 86 at 93 per Joyce J.
8   *Peardon v Underhill* (1850) 16 QB 120. As to these restrictions on inclosure generally and the restrictions contained in the Commons Act 2006 see COMMONS vol 13 (2017) PARA 470.
9   See the Commons Act 2006 s 39; and COMMONS vol 13 (2017) PARA 462.

## 312.   Inclosure under private Acts.

As the whole of a waste could not generally be inclosed[1], and the usual statutory procedure is inapplicable to common fields, recourse was formerly had for that purpose to private Acts of Parliament under which the land to be inclosed was allotted to the persons having interests in the land in severalty. Under such Acts, in the absence of provisions as to the mines and minerals, these prima facie pass to the allottees as part of the soil[2]. The mines and minerals may, however, be reserved to the lord either expressly[3] or by implication[4]. Whether any and what minerals[5], under what land[6] and with what powers of working[7] are reserved are questions depending for their solution upon the true construction of the particular Act under which the inclosure is made.

1   See PARA 311.
2   *Townley v Gibson* (1788) 2 Term Rep 701, where an exception of royalties and manorial rights was held insufficient to prevent the minerals passing to the allottees. As to the meaning of 'mines and minerals' see PARA 10; and as to the meaning of 'mine' see PARA 3.
3   See eg the Acts referred to in *Ewart v Graham* (1859) 7 HL Cas 331; *Robinson v Wray* (1866) LR 1 CP 490; *Butterknowle Colliery Co Ltd v Bishop Auckland Industrial Co-operative Co* [1906] AC 305, HL.
4   *Micklethwait v Winter* (1851) 6 Exch 644.
5   As to the meaning of an exception of mines and minerals in an Inclosure Act see *Earl of Rosse v Wainman* (1845) 14 M & W 859 (affd sub nom *Wainman v Earl of Rosse* (1848) 2 Exch 800); *Micklethwait v Winter* (1851) 6 Exch 644; *A-G v Welsh Granite Co* (1887) 35 WR 617, CA; cf

*North British Rly Co v Budhill Coal and Sandstone Co* [1910] AC 116, HL; *Thomson v St Catharine's College, Cambridge* [1919] AC 468, HL (overruling (on the construction of the same Act) *Master and Fellows of St Catharine's College, Cambridge v Greensmith* [1912] 2 Ch 280; and *St Catharine's College, Cambridge v Rosse* [1916] 1 Ch 73, CA); and see PARA 19.

6   *Pretty v Solly* (1859) 26 Beav 606; *Wakefield v Duke of Buccleuch* (1867) LR 4 Eq 613 (affd sub nom *Duke of Buccleuch v Wakefield* (1870) LR 4 HL 377) (mines under allotments).

7   *Midgley v Richardson* (1845) 14 M & W 595; *Bowes v Lord Ravensworth* (1855) 15 CB 512; *Hayles v Pease & Partners Ltd* [1899] 1 Ch 567.

### 313. Inclosure by the appropriate national authority.

An application to the appropriate national authority[1] for a provisional order for the inclosure or regulation of a common[2] comprised a statement as to the mines[3], minerals[4], and valuable strata, if any, under the common[5]. The provisional order itself, among other matters relating to rights in the soil and minerals[6], contained provisions as to entry on the surface of land allotted for the purpose of working, and as to compensation for surface damage[7] where the minerals were reserved to the lord[8]. If mineral property or other rights are vested in persons other than the lord of the manor and are likely to be affected by the order, such provisions and reservations as are required to be inserted by the Inclosure Acts 1845 to 1868 or as appear to the appropriate national authority proper, must be inserted[9].

If the provisional order stated that the lord's right and interest had been estimated exclusively of his right and interest in the mines, minerals, stone and other substrata, he was entitled, on written request, to have reserved or awarded to him reasonable rights of working, which could be awarded either subject or not to compensation for damage occasioned to the surface[10]. The rights of working could be made exercisable in respect of minerals belonging to the lord situated under land other than the land allotted, whether or not within the manor[11].

1   Ie the Secretary of State or where functions have been transferred in relation to Wales, the Welsh Ministers: see PARA 2.

2   It is considered that the Inclosure Act 1845 and its amending Acts, under which such a provisional order may be made, may be regarded as obsolete, but inclosure under the Acts is discussed briefly in view of its possible effect on existing titles or on disputed registrations under the Commons Registration Act 1965. See further COMMONS.

3   As to the meaning of 'mine' see PARA 3.

4   As to the meaning of 'minerals' see PARA 10.

5   See the Commons Act 1876 s 10 (amended by the Local Government Act 1894 s 21(1); and the Local Government Act 1972 s 179(3)). As to the procedure for inclosure and regulation see COMMONS vol 13 (2017) PARA 488 et seq.

6   See COMMONS vol 13 (2017) PARA 364 et seq.

7   See *Allaway v Wagstaff* (1859) 4 H & N 681, decided on the construction of the Dean Forest (Mines) Act 1838 s 68. As to mining and quarrying in Gloucestershire see PARA 607 et seq.

8   As to provisional orders to specify the rights reserved as to mines etc and the compensation to be made for surface damage etc see the Inclosure Act 1859 s 1 (repealed). The compensation could be payable wholly by the lord or other owner of minerals or wholly by the owners of allotments, or partly by one and partly by the others: see s 2 (repealed). As to powers to work mines etc see s 3. As to allotments to provide materials for the repair of roads see COMMONS vol 13 (2017) PARA 320.

9   See COMMONS vol 13 (2017) PARA 323.

10   See the Inclosure Act 1845 s 76 (repealed).

11   See the Inclosure Commissioners Act 1851 s 9 (repealed).

### 314. Minerals in regulated pasture.

If any part of the land dealt with on inclosure was converted into regulated pasture, the mines[1] under the part so converted could with the consent of the lord and a majority in value of the other persons interested be reserved to the lord, and the mines under the parts allotted in severalty became the property of the persons entitled to the allotments[2]. If not so dealt with, the mines beneath the regulated pasture vested in the persons having rights in them in proportion to their shares[3].

1  As to the meaning of 'mine' see PARA 3.
2  See the Inclosure Act 1845 s 97 (repealed). As to the conversion of land into regulated pasture see COMMONS vol 13 (2017) PARA 321.
3  See Inclosure Act 1845 s 11; and COMMONS vol 13 (2017) PARA 321.

### 315.  Minerals unaffected by inclosure.

The rights and property in mines and minerals[1] which had been severed from the surface before the inclosure, and all incidental rights, remained unaffected by the inclosure if not compensated for; and mines leased before the inclosure were also unaffected[2]. Minerals under inclosures of more than 20 years' standing were not adversely affected by any inclosure proceedings[3].

1  As to the meaning of 'mines and minerals' see PARA 10; and as to the meaning of 'mine' see PARA 3.
2  See the Inclosure Act 1845 s 98.
3  See the Inclosure Act 1847 s 3 (repealed).

## (iv)  Registration

### 316.  Registration of title to mines and minerals.

The title to mines and minerals[1] the ownership of which is severed from that of the land[2] in which they are situated may be registered[3], but registration is not compulsory[4]. Mines and minerals may also be registered as parcel of the land under which they are situated either by implication as included in the expression 'land'[5], or by express entry on the register[6]. Mines and minerals under registered land may be severed from the surface either by registered transfer or by an unregistered instrument[7].

Application for the registration of mines and minerals severed from the land is made and proceeded with in the same manner as in the case of other hereditaments, subject to modifications; and plans necessary for identifying the mines and minerals together with particulars of working rights are required[8]. The conveyance of mines and minerals the title to which is registered is effected by the use of transfers in the specified form[9].

1  As to the meaning of 'mines and minerals' see PARA 10.
2  'Land' includes, inter alia, mines and minerals, whether or not held with the surface: see the Land Registration Act 2002 s 132(1).
3  As to registration of title to land generally see REAL PROPERTY AND REGISTRATION vol 87 (2017) PARA 231 et seq.
4  Certain rights in mines and minerals are 'overriding interests' under the Land Registration Act 2002: see s 11(4)(a), (b); and REAL PROPERTY AND REGISTRATION vol 87 (2017) PARA 351. Those interests include: (1) an interest in any coal or coal mine, the rights attached to any such interest and the rights of any person under the Coal Industry Act 1994 s 38, s 49 or s 51 (Land Registration Act 2002 s 11, Sch 1 para 7); (2) in the case of land to which title was registered before 1898, rights to mines and minerals (and incidental rights) created before 1898 (Sch 1 para 8); and (3) in the case of land to which title was registered between 1898 and 1925 inclusive, rights to mines and minerals (and incidental rights) created before the date of registration of the title (Sch 1 para 9). See REAL PROPERTY AND REGISTRATION vol 87 (2017) PARA 389.
5  See the Land Registration Act 2002 s 132(1).
6  The proprietor of land who is also the proprietor of the mines and minerals may be expressly registered as such proprietor by a note to that effect in the register. No indemnity is payable on account of any mines or minerals or the existence of any right to work or get mines or minerals, unless it is noted on the register that the title includes the mines or minerals: see Land Registration

Act 2002 s 103, Sch 8 para 2; and REAL PROPERTY AND REGISTRATION vol 87 (2017) PARA 498.
7　See REAL PROPERTY AND REGISTRATION vol 87 (2017) PARA 902.
8　See REAL PROPERTY AND REGISTRATION vol 87 (2017) PARA 348.
9　See REAL PROPERTY AND REGISTRATION vol 87 (2017) PARA 430.

### 317. Registration of land charges.

Charges affecting mines and minerals[1], whether or not severed from the surface, may be registered under the Land Charges Act 1972 and the Local Land Charges Act 1975 in the same way as charges which affect non-mineral land[2]. The law relating to such charges is discussed elsewhere in this work[3].

1　As to the meaning of 'mines and minerals' see PARA 10; and as to the meaning of 'mine' see PARA 3.
2　See the Land Charges Act 1972 s 17(1); the Local Land Charges Act 1975 s 16(1) ('land' includes mines and minerals, whether or not severed from the surface); and REAL PROPERTY AND REGISTRATION vol 87 (2017) PARA 6.
3　See REAL PROPERTY AND REGISTRATION vol 87 (2017) PARA 641 et seq.

## (3) Leases

### (i) In General

### 318. Nature of mining lease.

A lease[1] may be granted of land or any part of land, and since minerals are a part of the land[2] it follows that a lease can be granted of the surface of the land and the minerals below, or of the surface alone[3], or of the minerals alone[4]. It has been said that a contract for the working and getting of minerals, although for convenience called a mining lease, is not in reality a lease at all in the sense in which one speaks of an agricultural lease, and that such a contract, properly considered, is really a sale of a portion of the land at a price payable by instalments, that is, by way of rent or royalty, spread over a number of years[5].

1　As to leases generally see LANDLORD AND TENANT vol 62 (2016) PARA 67 et seq.
2　See PARA 17. As to the meaning of 'minerals' see PARA 10.
3　See eg *Masters v Green* (1888) 20 QBD 807 at 808, DC, per Field J.
4　*Jegon v Vivian* (1865) LR 1 CP 9 at 18; on appeal sub nom *Vivian v Jegon* (1868) LR 3 HL 285; and see LANDLORD AND TENANT vol 62 (2016) PARA 17 et seq..
5　See *Gowan v Christie* (1873) LR 2 Sc & Div 273 at 284, HL, per Lord Cairns; *Coltness Iron Co v Black* (1881) 6 App Cas 315 at 335, HL, per Lord Blackburn; *Re Aldam's Settled Estate* [1902] 2 Ch 46 at 56, CA, per Collins MR; *Earl Fitzwilliam's Collieries Co v Phillips* [1943] AC 570 at 582, [1943] 2 All ER 346 at 350, HL, per Lord Wright.

### 319. Statutory definitions of 'mining lease'.

In the Law of Property Act 1925, 'mining lease' means a lease for mining purposes, that is, the searching for, winning[1], working, getting, making merchantable, carrying away or disposing of mines and minerals[2], or connected purposes, and includes a grant or licence[3] for mining purposes[4]; and 'lease' includes an underlease or other tenancy[5].

In the Settled Land Act 1925[6] and the Landlord and Tenant Act 1927, 'mining lease' means a lease[7] for any mining purpose or connected purposes, and 'mining purposes' includes the sinking and searching for, winning, working, getting, making merchantable, smelting or otherwise converting or working for the purposes of any manufacture, carrying away and disposing of mines and minerals[8], in or under land[9], and the erection of buildings, and the execution of engineering and other works suitable for those purposes[10].

'Mining lease' is also defined for the purposes of the Opencast Coal Act 1958[11], whilst 'coal-mining lease'[12], 'lease'[13] and 'mine of coal'[14] were all defined for the purposes of the Coal Act 1938.

1 See *Lewis v Fothergill* (1869) 5 Ch App 103 at 111 per Lord Hatherley LC; *Lord Rokeby v Elliot* (1879) 13 ChD 277 at 279, CA (revsd sub nom *Elliot v Lord Rokeby* (1881) 7 App Cas 43, HL, without affecting this point).
2 As to the meaning of 'mines and minerals' in the Law of Property Act 1925 see PARA 10.
3 As to licences see PARA 346 et seq.
4 See the Law of Property Act 1925 s 205(1)(xiv).
5 See the Law of Property Act 1925 s 205(1)(xxiii).
6 This definition enables a tenant for life, in a proper case, to grant a lease of a right to let down or damage the surface: *Sitwell v Earl of Londesborough* [1905] 1 Ch 460; cf *IRC v Joicey (No 2)* [1913] 2 KB 580, CA (release by copyholder of right to support not a lease of a right to work minerals).
7 In the Settled Land Act 1925, 'lease' includes an agreement for a lease (see s 117(1)(x)); and in the Landlord and Tenant Act 1927, 'lease' means a lease, underlease or other tenancy, assignment operating as a lease or underlease, or an agreement for such lease, underlease, tenancy or assignment (see s 25(1)).
8 As to the meaning of 'mines and minerals' in the Settled Land Act 1925 see PARA 10.
9 Ie in the Settled Land Act 1925, the settled land or any other land: see s 117(1)(xv).
10 See the Settled Land Act 1925 s 117(1)(xv); and the Landlord and Tenant Act 1927 s 25(1). This definition of 'mining lease' is applied for the purposes of the Landlord and Tenant Act 1954 Pt II (ss 23–46) by s 46. Part II (which provides for security of tenure for business, professional and other tenants) does not apply to a tenancy created by a mining lease: s 43(1)(b). See further LANDLORD AND TENANT vol 64 (2016) PARA 1599 et seq..
11 See the Opencast Coal Act 1958 s 51(1); and PARA 439.
12 'Coal-mining lease' means in relation to any coal a lease that confers a right to work and carry away that coal, and means in relation to any mine of coal a lease that confers a right to use it for a coal-mining purpose: see the Coal Act 1938 s 44 (repealed with savings).
13 'Lease' includes a licence (whether personal or by way of profit à prendre) that confers a right to work and carry away coal or a right to use a mine of coal for a coal-mining purpose: see the Coal Act 1938 s 44 (repealed with savings).
14 See the Coal Act 1938 s 44 (repealed with savings); and PARA 48.

## 320. Rents and royalties.

An agreement for a lease usually contains stipulations as to the dead rents[1] and other rents and royalties to be reserved by, and the covenants and provisions to be inserted in, the lease, but the omission to provide for the payment of a dead rent does not render the agreement so inequitable as to be unenforceable[2].

Rent and royalties are true rents in the sense that they are incident to the reversion[3], but periodical payments under a lease of mines for a specific period may amount to personal debts only[4].

A lessee who goes into possession and works minerals before completion of the lease may be ordered on interim application to pay into court the amount of royalties due in respect of minerals raised[5].

1 As to the meaning of 'dead rent' see PARA 330.
2 *Walters v Morgan* (1861) 3 De GF & J 718.
3 *Barrs v Lea* (1864) 33 LJ Ch 437.
4 *Lord Hatherton v Bradburne* (1843) 13 Sim 599; and see *Re Smith (a lunatic)* (1874) 10 Ch App 79 at 86 per James LJ. As to the meaning of 'mine' see PARA 3.
5 *Lewis v James* (1886) 32 ChD 326, CA. As to the meaning of 'minerals' see PARA 10.

## 321. Usual provisions in leases.

The statutory formalities regarding the disposition of an interest in land will apply to a contract for a mining lease[1]. In a contract for a lease for working a mine², time is of the essence of the contract even if not expressly stated to be so³. Mining leases usually contain clauses providing for the reference of disputes to arbitration⁴ or determination by an expert where the value of the minerals gotten is in dispute.

1 See the Law of Property (Miscellaneous Provisions) Act 1989 s 2; and REAL PROPERTY AND REGISTRATION vol 87 (2017) PARA 975.
2 As to the meaning of 'mine' see PARA 3.
3 *Macbryde v Weekes* (1856) 22 Beav 533; *Green v Sevin* (1879) 13 ChD 589 at 594, obiter, per Fry J. Notice may be given fixing a time for completion if no time is named in the contract: *Macbryde v Weekes.*
4 As to the effect of such a clause see *Willesford v Watson* (1873) 8 Ch App 473. As to arbitration generally see ARBITRATION vol 2 (2017) PARA 501 et seq. As to the meaning of 'minerals' see PARA 10.

## (ii) Property Demised; Consideration

### A. PARCELS

### 322. Parcels in agreement for lease.

Unless the minerals¹ intended to be included in an agreement for a lease² are properly defined in it, the agreement will be unenforceable. Uncertainty may arise either from an imperfect enumeration of the minerals to be dealt with³ or an indefinite description of the area under which they are situated⁴. A description by name of the area is sufficient if the boundaries can be ascertained⁵. An agreement for the lease of a particular vein is not void merely because the vein cannot be found⁶.

1 As to the meaning of 'minerals' see PARA 10.
2 As to leases, agreements for leases and their costs see LANDLORD AND TENANT vol 62 (2016) PARA 67 et seq.
3 *Price v Griffith* (1851) 1 De GM & G 80 (agreement to lease 'coals etc').
4 *Lancaster v De Trafford* (1862) 31 LJ Ch 554 (description of ironstone as situate under lands at Patricroft, Patricroft being a district without defined boundaries); *Davis v Shepherd* (1866) 1 Ch App 410 (agreement defined the minerals by reference to the supposed line of a fault and approximate acreage, but the fault did not run in the direction supposed, and would have included a larger area: agreement held to be unenforceable).
5 *Haywood v Cope* (1858) 25 Beav 140.
6 *Jefferys v Fairs* (1876) 4 ChD 448. As to the meaning of 'vein' see PARA 14.

### 323. Parcels in lease.

Mines and minerals¹ included in a demise are usually described by reference to the surface under which they lie. Faults crossing a mineral area form natural boundaries between different mines, and are sometimes used to define the extent of the demise by reference to a line drawn on a plan showing the position or supposed position of the fault². When a plan is indorsed on or annexed to the lease and referred to in it, the plan ought to be looked at as part of the description³. If there is any discrepancy between the plan and description, the description, if clear, will prevail⁴, but endeavour should be made to reconcile any apparent discrepancy⁵. Where the superficial limits of demised mines are ascertained it is sometimes a question of construction what seams or veins are included in the demise⁶, or as to the extent of the demise where the description contains technical expressions which have a definite meaning according to local usage⁷.

1 As to the meaning of 'mines and minerals' see PARA 10; and as to the meaning of 'mine' see PARA 3.

2  *Davis v Shepherd* (1866) 1 Ch App 410.
3  *Lyle v Richards* (1866) LR 1 HL 222.
4  See *Taylor v Parry* (1840) 9 LJCP 298; and DEEDS AND OTHER INSTRUMENTS vol 32 (2012) PARA 430. As to the application of the rule *falsa demonstratio non nocet* see DEEDS AND OTHER INSTRUMENTS vol 32 (2012) PARA 428.
5  *Brain v Harris* (1855) 10 Exch 908.
6  *Carr v Benson* (1868) 3 Ch App 524, CA (where the meaning of a grant was interpreted by reference to a concurrent licence); *Dugdale v Robertson* (1857) 3 K & J 695 (which restricted any right to mine under certain defined lands).
7  *Clayton v Gregson* (1836) 5 Ad & El 302; and see CUSTOM AND USAGE vol 32 (2012) PARAS 52, 65 et seq.

## 324. Exceptions and reservations.

It is usual in mining leases to make certain exceptions and reservations[1] in favour of the lessor. These are intended either for the protection of the demised mines or the surface land and buildings on it, or for the preservation of the lessor's right to work excepted mines[2]. Sometimes there is an exception from the liberty to work, in which case the part of the mine so excepted remains subject to the demise[3]. Thus a covenant to work mines and get the minerals[4] until the whole are worked, except pillars and barriers which the lessor may require to be left unworked, operates as a partial exemption from the covenant to work, and the lessee retains an interest in the pillars and barriers entitling him to compensation on compulsory acquisition[5]. There is an implied reservation to the lessor of the right to descend the lessee's shafts for the purpose of inspecting the demised mines and the lessee's workings in them[6].

1  As to the difference between an exception and a reservation see DEEDS AND OTHER INSTRUMENTS vol 32 (2012) PARA 438.
2  As to the meaning of 'mine' see PARA 3.
3  *Dugdale v Robertson* (1857) 3 K & J 695; *Mostyn v Lancaster* (1883) 23 ChD 583, CA.
4  As to the meaning of 'minerals' see PARA 10.
5  *Swindell v Birmingham Canal Co* (1860) 9 CBNS 241.
6  *Lewis v Marsh* (1849) 8 Hare 97.

### B.  RIGHTS OF WORKING

## 325. General principles.

A lease of mines or minerals includes by implication a right to get out or enjoy all minerals[1] except coal[2]. The incidental power, however, warrants nothing beyond what is strictly necessary for the convenient working of the minerals (which does not include the surface)[3], and it is usual in a mining lease to grant express liberty to work and to do such other things as, in the particular instance, are contemplated as being desirable for that purpose. An implied power is not restricted by the grant of an express power which is exercisable to a greater extent or for a longer period[4]; but if the express power is restrictive of that which would otherwise be implied the grantee is limited to the exercise of the express power[5]. Express powers must be exercised in good faith in a reasonable course of working[6].

1  *Rowbotham v Wilson* (1860) 8 HL Cas 348 at 360 per Lord Wensleydale; *Ramsay v Blair* (1876) 1 App Cas 701 at 703, HL, per Lord Chelmsford; *Borys v Canadian Pacific Rly Co* [1953] AC 217, [1953] 1 All ER 451, PC. As to powers of working where mines are included in leases of land see PARA 368 et seq. As to surface rights generally see PARA 278 et seq. As to the meaning of 'mine' see PARA 3; and as to the meaning of 'minerals' see PARA 10.
2  Unworked coal is vested in the coal authority which has power to dispose of it: see PARAS 52, 58. Coal-mining operations are required to be licensed under the Coal Industry Act 1994 Pt II (ss 25–36): see PARA 89 et seq. As to the meaning of 'coal-mining operations' see PARA 51. As to the

Coal Authority see PARA 52 et seq.
3   *Earl of Cardigan v Armitage* (1823) 2 B & C 197 at 211; *Lord Darcy v Askwith* (1618) Hob 234; *Marshall v Borrowdale Plumbago Mines and Manufacturing Co Ltd* (1892) 8 TLR 275.
4   *Earl of Cardigan v Armitage* (1823) 2 B & C 197; *Hodgson v Field* (1806) 7 East 613; and see *Whidborne v Ecclesiastical Comrs for England* (1877) 7 ChD 375; and DEEDS AND OTHER INSTRUMENTS vol 32 (2012) PARA 384.
5   *Re Wilson Syndicate Conveyance, Wilson v Shorrock* [1938] 3 All ER 599 (working restricted to underground working); *General Accident Fire and Life Assurance Corpn Ltd v British Gypsum Ltd* [1967] 3 All ER 40, [1967] 1 WLR 1215 ('win' included searching for minerals but construction of deed confined searching to underground searching); and see PARA 278.
6   *Honeywell Cotton Spinning Co v Marland* [1875] WN 46.

## 326. Shafts.

If minerals[1] cannot be got otherwise, the owner or lessee of the minerals may bore in a reasonable way through the lessor's land and minerals not included in the demise in order to reach them, and it does not matter whether the barrier is horizontal or vertical[2].

The grant of an express liberty to sink pits or shafts[3] imposes no obligation on the lessee to sink, even though at the time the lease was granted he did not own any adjoining mines[4], or although it appears from the lease that all parties contemplated that a shaft would be sunk[5], or that working by instroke is less advantageous[6], or that the lease contains a covenant that the mines will be delivered up at the end of the term in such a state that the working may be continued by the reversioner[7]. However, if the lease contains a covenant to work, and the mine cannot be worked otherwise, the lessee is bound to sink a shaft[8], and in some cases a covenant to work in a proper and workmanlike manner may impose a similar liability[9]. A proper and workmanlike manner may not mean the best possible mode of working for the lessor, but it means in such a manner as shall not be simply an attempt to get out of the earth as much mineral as can be got for the particular purpose of the lessee, regardless of any ordinary or workmanlike proceeding[10]. If the lessee enters into an absolute covenant to sink a shaft, performance will not be excused because it would be useless or unprofitable[11]. It is, of course, otherwise if the covenant is made subject to a qualification which excuses performance[12]. The measure of damages for breach of a covenant to sink a shaft is the sum which the lessor must expend in sinking where the lessor can go onto the soil[13]. Where the lessor cannot go onto the soil the damages are either the amount the lessee would have expended in sinking the pit or where the lessee covenanted to pay the lessor a sum if minerals were found when the pit was sunk, that sum[14].

Liberty to sink a pit creates an interest in the land in respect of which compensation is payable when the surface is taken in the exercise of compulsory powers[15].

A lessee of minerals who sinks a shaft in land of which the surface is occupied by another must keep the shaft properly fenced[16].

1   As to the meaning of 'minerals' see PARA 10.
2   *Re Lord Gerard and London and North Western Rly Co* [1895] 1 QB 459 at 466, CA, per Lord Esher MR; cf *Goold v Great Western Deep Coal Co* (1865) 2 De GJ & Sm 600; and see also *Harris v Ryding* (1839) 5 M & W 60.
3   As to what this power impliedly includes see PARA 180.
4   *Jegon v Vivian* (1871) 6 Ch App 742. As to the meaning of 'mine' see PARA 3.
5   *James v Cochrane* (1853) 8 Exch 556, Ex Ch; *Jegon v Vivian* (1871) 6 Ch App 742.
6   *Wheatley v Westminster Brymbo Coal Co* (1869) LR 9 Eq 538. As to instroke see PARA 327.
7   *Lewis v Fothergill* (1869) 5 Ch App 103; and see *Jegon v Vivian* (1871) 6 Ch App 742.
8   *James v Cochrane* (1852) 7 Exch 170 at 178, obiter, per Parke B; affd (1853) 8 Exch 556, Ex Ch.

9   *Lewis v Fothergill* (1869) 5 Ch App 103 (working the coal by instroke was held under the circumstances to be working in a proper and workmanlike manner).
10  *Lewis v Fothergill* (1869) 5 Ch App 103 at 108 per Lord Hatherley LC.
11  *Jervis v Tomkinson* (1856) 1 H & N 195.
12  *Hanson v Boothman* (1810) 13 East 22.
13  *Pell v Shearman* (1855) 10 Exch 766 at 769 per Parke B.
14  See *Pell v Shearman* (1855) 10 Exch 766.
15  *Re Masters and Great Western Rly Co* [1901] 2 KB 84, CA; and see COMPULSORY ACQUISITION OF LAND.
16  *Williams v Groucott* (1863) 4 B & S 149; and see PARA 281.

### 327.   Instroke.

'Instroke' means liberty to work a demised mine[1] from an adjoining mine. In the absence of express stipulation a lessee is not bound to sink a shaft from the surface, but may work by instroke[2], and may make use, for that purpose, of apertures lawfully made in any barrier which he has covenanted to leave between the demised mine and adjoining mines[3].

1   As to the meaning of 'mine' see PARA 3.
2   *Whalley v Ramage* (1862) 10 WR 315; *Lewis v Fothergill* (1869) 5 Ch App 103; *Jegon v Vivian* (1871) 6 Ch App 742; and see PARA 326.
3   *James v Cochrane* (1853) 8 Exch 556, Ex Ch (where there was liberty to create the apertures in the barrier).

### 328.   Outstroke.

'Outstroke' means liberty to work an adjoining mine[1] from the demised mine. Whether or not a lessee may work by outstroke depends on the extent of the demise. If access to the adjoining mine, sufficient for the purpose of working, can be obtained without entry on property not included in the lease, or without unwarranted user of any rights of way, the lessee may work by outstroke without express liberty to do so. In many cases the lease only grants to the lessee rights of way over the surface and through the shaft for the purpose of working the demised mine, and in such cases the lessee cannot work by outstroke, as he cannot use rights of way for purposes other than those for which they are granted[2].

1   As to the meaning of 'mine' see PARA 3.
2   As to the rights of the lessee in the cubical space occupied or formerly occupied by minerals see PARA 369. As to user of rights of way see PARA 255 et seq. As to the meaning of 'minerals' see PARA 10.

### 329.   Right to withdraw support.

If it is intended that the lessee is to be entitled to work so as to withdraw support from the surface, the lease should grant express liberty so to work[1]. The mere fact of giving a right to sink pits and to work and get minerals is not sufficient to deprive the surface owner of his common law right of support[2]. To displace this common law right permission to withdraw support must be given expressly or by necessary implication[3]. Cases of express permission present no difficulty; but the question whether or not permission is given by implication must be decided by consideration of the whole of the lease and of the state of knowledge at the time when, and the circumstances in which, it was made, as to whether according to the local practice the minerals could be got without subsidence, of which oral evidence may be given[4]. The test is whether the introduction of a clause to the effect that the mines[5] must be worked so as not to let down the surface would or would not be inconsistent with the actual demise: if it would not, then the surface cannot be let down[6].

1   The right to withdraw support may, however, arise by implication: see PARA 128 et seq.

2   *Davis v Treharne* (1881) 6 App Cas 460, HL; *Butterknowle Colliery Co v Bishop Auckland Industrial Co-operative Co* [1906] AC 305 at 313, HL, per Lord Macnaghten. As to the right of support see further PARA 114 et seq. As to the meaning of 'minerals' see PARA 10.

3   *Davis v Treharne* (1881) 6 App Cas 460, HL; *Butterley Co Ltd v New Hucknall Colliery Co Ltd* [1910] AC 381, HL. See further PARA 127 et seq.

4   *Butterley Co Ltd v New Hucknall Colliery Co Ltd* [1910] AC 381, HL; *Locker-Lampson v Staveley Coal and Iron Co Ltd* (1908) 25 TLR 136.

5   As to the meaning of 'mine' see PARA 3.

6   *Butterknowle Colliery Co v Bishop Auckland Industrial Co-operative Co* [1906] AC 305 at 309, HL, per Lord Loreburn LC. For cases in which it has been held that an implied right is granted see *Butterley Co Ltd v New Hucknall Colliery Co Ltd* [1910] AC 381, HL; *Locker-Lampson v Staveley Coal and Iron Co Ltd* (1908) 25 TLR 136; *Smith v Darby* (1872) LR 7 QB 716; *Shafto v Johnson* (1863) 8 B & S 252n; *Brewer v Rhymney Iron Co* [1910] 1 Ch 766; and see PARA 127 et seq. It is submitted that little reliance can be placed on the cases decided before *Davis v Treharne* (1881) 6 App Cas 460, HL. As to the right of a tenant for life to grant a lease of the right to let down the surface see *Sitwell v Earl of Londesborough* [1905] 1 Ch 460.

C.    CONSIDERATION

### 330. Dead rent.

It is usual in mining leases to reserve both a fixed annual rent (otherwise known as a 'dead rent', 'minimum rent' or 'certain rent') and royalties varying with the amount of minerals worked[1]. The object of the fixed rent is to ensure that the lessee will work the mine[2]; but it is sometimes ineffective for that purpose[3]. Another function of the fixed rent is to ensure a definite minimum income to the lessor in respect of the demise.

If a fixed rent is reserved, it is payable until the expiration of the term even though the mine is not worked[4], or is exhausted during the currency of the term[5], or is not worth working[6], or is difficult or unprofitable to work owing to faults[7] or accidents[8], or even if the demised seam proves to be non-existent[9].

Where a fixed rent is reserved to commence from the time when a certain quantity of minerals has been got and the lessee covenants to get that quantity without delay, the commencement of the payment will not be delayed should the lessee fraudulently fail to complete the getting of the quantity[10].

1   See *Mitchell v Mosley* [1914] 1 Ch 438, CA. Rent and royalties to be rendered in kind may be reserved: see *R v Earl of Pomfret* (1816) 5 M & S 139; *Re Moody and Yates' Contract* (1885) 30 ChD 344 at 346, 347, CA, per Brett MR. As to the use of the terms 'rent' and 'royalty' to denote payments in respect of coal see *Greville-Nugent v Mackenzie* [1900] AC 83 at 87, 88, HL, per the Earl of Halsbury LC. As to the taxation of mining rents and royalties generally see INCOME TAXATION vol 58 (2014) PARA 124. As to the meaning of 'minerals' see PARA 10.

2   *Jegon v Vivian* (1865) LR 1 CP 9 at 34 per Erle CJ (subsequent proceedings *Jegon v Vivian* (1871) 6 Ch App 742 at 758 per Lord Hatherley LC); *Re Aldam's Settled Estate* [1902] 2 Ch 46 at 60, CA, per Stirling LJ. As to the meaning of 'mine' see PARA 3.

3   See *Glassbrook Bros Ltd v Leyson* [1933] 2 KB 91 at 119, CA, per Slesser LJ, and at 123 per Romer LJ. See also *McDonald v Kent Coal Co Ltd* [1943] 3 WWR 207 (Can).

4   *Jegon v Vivian* (1871) 6 Ch App 742 at 757 per Lord Hatherley LC; *Jones v Reynolds* (1836) 7 C & P 335.

5   *R v Bedworth Inhabitants* (1807) 8 East 387; *Marquis of Bute v Thompson* (1844) 13 M & W 487.

6   *Haywood v Cope* (1858) 25 Beav 140 at 149 per Romilly MR; *Strelley v Pearson* (1880) 15 ChD 113.

7   *Mellers v Duke of Devonshire* (1852) 16 Beav 252; *Ridgway v Sneyd* (1854) Kay 627.

8   *Phillips v Jones* (1839) 9 Sim 519.

9  *Jefferys v Fairs* (1876) 4 ChD 448. Possibly if the seam demised were found to have been previously worked out it would be treated as a case of mutual mistake (*Ridgway v Sneyd* (1854) Kay 627 at 635 per Page Wood V-C), and thus as a ground for rescinding the lease (*Solle v Butcher* [1950] 1 KB 671, [1949] 2 All ER 1107, CA). However, as to the validity of an agreement for a lease of a particular vein even though it cannot be found see PARA 322.

10  *Green v Sparrow* (1725) 3 Swan 408n.

### 331.  Royalties.

A royalty, in the sense in which the word is used in connection with mining leases, is a payment to the lessor proportionate to the amount of the demised mineral worked within a specified period[1]. A royalty is a true rent[2], and as such may be apportioned[3] on a time basis[4]. Usually the royalties are made to merge in the fixed rent by means of a provision that the lessee, without any additional payment, may work, in each period for which a payment of fixed rent is made, so much of the minerals as would, at the royalties reserved, produce a sum equal to the fixed rent.

Reservations of royalties take different forms and, as a lessor may reserve royalties in the form he considers most suitable or advantageous in any particular case, the questions which arise are questions of construction and the decided cases cannot be reduced to any principle generally applicable[5]. Sometimes in colliery leases coal consumed in working was freed from royalty[6].

An average or short workings clause by which overpayments by the lessee in years in which the workings are less than those covered by the minimum or fixed rent are permitted to be recouped in subsequent years in which the workings are sufficient to produce royalties in excess of that minimum[7] confers no right of property in minerals remaining unworked when the lease is determined[8].

1  See *Bridges v Potts* (1864) 17 CBNS 314 at 345 per Willes J. As to the meaning of 'minerals' see PARA 10.

2  *R v Westbrook, R v Everist* (1847) 10 QB 178 at 203; and see *Verdin v Coughtrie (Inspector of Taxes)* [1961] AC 880 at 894, sub nom *Tollemache Settled Estates (Trustees) v Coughtrie (Inspector of Taxes)* [1961] 1 All ER 593 at 596, HL, per Lord Denning; *T and E Homes Ltd v Robinson (Inspector of Taxes)* [1979] 2 All ER 522, [1979] 1 WLR 452, CA.

3  Ie under the Apportionment Act 1870 s 2: see LANDLORD AND TENANT vol 62 (2016) PARA 273.

4  *Coal Commission v Earl Fitzwilliam's Royalties Co* [1942] Ch 365, [1942] 2 All ER 56.

5  *Clifton v Walmesley* (1794) 5 Term Rep 564 (royalty payable on sums for which coal should sell at pit's mouth: construction of covenant held not affected by mistaken conduct of parties). See also *Gerrard v Clifton* (1798) 7 Term Rep 676; *Earl of Shrewsbury v Gould* (1819) 2 B & Ald 487 (lessee's duty to burn lime); *Edwards v Rees* (1836) 7 C & P 340 (royalty payable on money which should arise from sales, no allowance for bad debts); *Bishop v Goodwin* (1845) 14 M & W 260 (covenant to pay royalties quarterly, no average over other quarters of same year); *Buckley v Kenyon* (1808) 10 East 139; *Cartwright v Forman* (1866) 7 B & S 243 (delivery of coal for lessor's use when mine not workable at a profit); *Morley v Yorkshire Lead Mines* [1890] WN 47 (royalty payable on dressed or undressed ore); *Elliot v Lord Rokeby* (1881) 7 App Cas 43, HL (deduction allowed for expenses of winning where several seams); *Mitchell v Mosley* [1914] 1 Ch 438, CA.

6  *Senhouse v Harris* (1862) 5 LT 635.

7  As to the construction of such a clause see *Clayton v Penson* [1878] WN 158.

8  See *Re Fullerton's Will* [1906] 2 Ch 138.

### 332.  Wayleave royalties.

Royalties estimated similarly to royalties on demised minerals[1] are often reserved in respect of minerals worked by way of outstroke[2] from and brought through the demised mine[3] or over surface land[4]. Such minerals are frequently referred to as foreign minerals and such royalties are known as wayleave rents or wayleaves. If a wayleave is used without authority, the measure of damages is the sum which would properly have been payable in royalty if the right of wayleave had been granted[5].

1   As to the meaning of 'minerals' see PARA 10.
2   As to outstroke see PARA 328.
3   *Senhouse v Harris* (1862) 5 LT 635. As to the meaning of 'mine' see PARA 3.
4   *Directors etc of Great Western Rly Co v Rous* (1870) LR 4 HL 650.
5   *Jegon v Vivian* (1871) 6 Ch App 742; *Livingstone v Rawyards Coal Co* (1880) 5 App Cas 25, HL; *Whitwham v Westminster Brymbo Coal and Coke Co* [1896] 2 Ch 538, CA; and see PARA 262.

## (iii) Covenants

### A.   COVENANTS TO PAY RENT, ROYALTIES, TAXES ETC

### 333.   Covenant to pay rent and royalties.

Nearly every mining lease contains a covenant by the lessee for payment of the specified rent and royalties, and sometimes, where the lessee is under an express obligation to refrain from or to do certain acts, a stipulation is inserted for the payment of a penal sum, either fixed in amount or proportionate to the extent to which the obligation is disregarded, as where the lessee is under an obligation to restore the surface at the end of the term to its original condition[1]. Where the covenant is absolute in its terms, a stipulation for the payment of a sum in case of breach does not give the lessee the right to commit the breach on payment of that sum[2].

The benefit of a covenant for the payment of wayleave rent passes with the land over which the wayleave has been granted[3].

1   *Re Earl of Mexborough and Wood* (1882) 47 LT 516, which involved consideration of whether the sum payable was a penalty and therefore unenforceable. It was adjudged not to exceed the amount of damage that would be caused. Such provisions are commonly found in modern day construction or building contracts and the amount payable referred to as 'liquidated damages'. See further BUILDING CONTRACTS.
2   *Forrest v Merry and Cuninghame Ltd* [1909] AC 417, HL.
3   *Lord Hastings v North Eastern Rly Co* [1898] 2 Ch 674; affd [1899] 1 Ch 656, CA; on appeal sub nom *North Eastern Rly Co v Lord Hastings* [1900] AC 260, HL. See the Law of Property Act 1925 s 141 in the case of tenancies granted before 1 January 1996, and the Landlord and Tenant (Covenants) Act 1995 in the case of tenancies granted on or after that date; and LANDLORD AND TENANT vol 62 (2016) PARA 458. As to wayleave rents and royalties see PARA 332.

### 334.   Action for and indemnity against rent and royalties.

No claim may be brought, or distress made, to recover arrears of rent, or damages in respect of arrears of rent, after the expiration of six years from the date on which the arrears became due[1]. In a claim for recovery of rents and royalties, interest may also be claimed[2]. A claim action for an account does not lie against a person entitled in equity who is in possession of the demised property, nor is he liable upon the covenants in the lease[3].

Where the assignee of a lease covenanted with his assignor to pay the rents reserved by the lease so long as he was in possession, and at all times thereafter to indemnify his assignor against the rent payable under the lease, the covenant for indemnity was not restricted to the rents during the period while the assignee was in possession[4].

1   See the Limitation Act 1980 s 19; and LIMITATION PERIODS vol 68 (2016) PARA 1035.
2   *Newton v Nock* (1880) 43 LT 197. See also the Law Reform (Miscellaneous Provisions) Act 1934 s 3; the Senior Courts Act 1981 s 35A; the County Courts Act 1984 s 69; and FINANCIAL INSTITUTIONS vol 48 (2015) PARA 389.

3  *Walters v Northern Coal Mining Co* (1855) 5 De GM & G 629; *Cox v Bishop* (1857) 8 De GM
   & G 815. The decisions to the contrary in *Clavering v Westley* (1735) 3 P Wms 402 and in *Wright
   v Pitt* (1870) LR 12 Eq 408 cannot be relied on: see *Ramage v Womack* [1900] 1 QB 116. See also
   LANDLORD AND TENANT vol 62 (2016) PARA 347. As to the right to an account in equity see
   *Parrott v Palmer* (1834) 3 My & K 632; and EQUITABLE JURISDICTION vol 47 (2014) PARA 49
   et seq.
4  *Crossfield v Morrison* (1849) 7 CB 286. However, such covenants are now restricted by the effect
   of the Landlord and Tenant (Covenants) Act 1995: see LANDLORD AND TENANT.

## 335. Covenant to pay rates, taxes and other assessments.

The lessee usually expressly covenants to pay all rates, taxes and other
assessments[1], and in the absence of an express covenant an undertaking to pay
rates and taxes may be inferred from words in the reddendum importing payment
of rent clear of all taxes etc. Usually the covenant is worded so as to include all
assessments that may be imposed in the future[2]. If the lessee covenants to pay all
rates, taxes and assessments he is only liable for all such payments as are of a
recurring nature, but if such a covenant includes any of the words 'duties',
'outgoings', 'impositions' or 'burdens' he is generally liable for non-recurring
expenses of permanent statutory improvements[3]. However, 'outgoings' has been
held not to include the cost of statutory drainage works carried out by a lessee
under a mining lease where that cost was deductible from the rent under a local
Act[4].

1  As to the taxation of mining concerns and mineral royalties see PARA 357; and INCOME
   TAXATION vol 58 (2014) PARA 124; LANDLORD AND TENANT.
2  See *Duke of Devonshire v Barrow Haematite Steel Co Ltd* (1877) 2 QBD 286, CA; *Chaloner v
   Bolckow* (1878) 3 App Cas 933, HL.
3  See eg *Thompson v Lapworth* (1868) LR 3 CP 149; *Budd v Marshall* (1880) 5 CPD 481, CA; and
   see further LANDLORD AND TENANT vol 62 (2016) PARA 421.
4  *Dalton Main Collieries Ltd v Rossington Main Colliery Co Ltd and Amalgamated Denaby
   Collieries Ltd* [1941] Ch 268, [1941] 1 All ER 544, CA. As to impositions see *Denaby and Cadeby
   Main Collieries Ltd v Brodsworth Main Colliery Co Ltd* [1941] Ch 289n, CA.

### B.  COVENANTS AS TO WORKING THE MINE

## 336. Covenant to work continuously.

Covenants as to working are inserted in a mining lease either to ensure that the
demised mine will be worked continuously, or that it will be worked in a
particular manner[1], or in some cases to effect both objects. A lessee is not bound
to work continuously or at all unless he undertakes to do so[2], and it is often a
difficult question of construction into which of the foregoing classes a particular
covenant falls[3].

If a lessee covenants without qualification to work the demised mine
continuously he is liable for breach of covenant even if the working should prove
difficult and unprofitable or even impossible[4], and even if the dead rent[5] is paid[6],
but a covenant to work continuously or at a certain rate may in some cases be
construed to apply only to the minerals found, so that if none are discovered there
is nothing to which the covenant can apply[7]. Sometimes covenants to work are
qualified so as to save the lessee from useless expense. The extent of these
qualifications is a question of construction[8], extrinsic evidence being admissible to
explain the accepted meaning of the terms used[9].

Specific performance of a covenant to work continuously cannot be obtained,
as the court refuses to supervise the working of a mine[10]. The measure of damages
for breach of a covenant to work is the amount which would in all probability
have been paid to the lessor if the mine had been worked[11]. Where working is

unduly expensive a lessee may be relieved from such a covenant on payment to the lessor of all that he would receive under the lease and surrender of the lease[12].

1   See PARA 337. As to the meaning of 'mine' see PARA 3.
2   *Quarrington v Arthur* (1842) 10 M & W 335 (undertaking to work mine discovered or opened: none were discovered or opened); *Wheatley v Westminster Brymbo Coal Co* (1869) LR 9 Eq 538; *Jegon v Vivian* (1871) 6 Ch App 742. As to the importance of such a covenant see *Glassbrook Bros Ltd v Leyson* [1933] 2 KB 91, CA. A lessee who has not covenanted to work may by agreement with a third person limit his workings to a specified amount: *Forrest v Merry and Cuninghame Ltd* [1909] AC 417, HL.
3   *Walker v Jeffreys* (1842) 1 Hare 341; *Wheatley v Westminster Brymbo Coal Co* (1869) LR 9 Eq 538; *Lord Abinger v Ashton* (1873) LR 17 Eq 358; *Charlesworth v Watson* [1906] AC 14, HL. See also *Doyershoek Asbestos Mine (Pty) Ltd v Estate Snyman* 1956 2 SA 304, SA SC App Div, where the law as stated in the text was considered by Centlivres CJ.
4   *Foley v Addenbrooke* (1844) 13 M & W 174; *Jervis v Tomkinson* (1856) 1 H & N 195; *Lord Clifford v Watts* (1870) LR 5 CP 577 at 588 per Willes J; *Jegon v Vivian* (1871) 6 Ch App 742; *Charlesworth v Watson* [1906] AC 14, HL; *Wigan Coal and Iron Co v Eckersley* (1910) 103 LT 468, HL; and see *Kinsman v Jackson* (1880) 42 LT 80 (on appeal 42 LT 558, CA), where the question was one of construction. Possibly where the mine is drowned without the default of the lessee, the lessee may not be liable for not working: see *Walker v Jeffreys* (1842) 1 Hare 341.
5   As to dead rent see PARA 330.
6   *Whitehead v Bennett* (1861) 9 WR 626; *Simpson v Ingleby* (1872) 27 LT 695.
7   *Lord Clifford v Watts* (1870) LR 5 CP 577. As to the meaning of 'minerals' see PARA 10.
8   *Jones v Shears* (1836) 7 C & P 346; *Foley v Addenbrooke* (1844) 13 M & W 174; *Griffiths v Rigby* (1856) 1 H & N 237; *Lord Abinger v Ashton* (1873) LR 17 Eq 358; *Newton v Nock* (1880) 43 LT 197; cf *Swindell v Birmingham Canal Co* (1860) 9 CBNS 241.
9   *Clayton v Gregson* (1836) 5 Ad & El 302; and see DEEDS AND OTHER INSTRUMENTS vol 32 (2012) PARA 398 et seq.
10  *Pollard v Clayton* (1855) 1 K & J 462; *Wheatley v Westminster Brymbo Coal Co* (1869) LR 9 Eq 538; and see *Lord Abinger v Ashton* (1873) LR 17 Eq 358. As to specific performance generally see SPECIFIC PERFORMANCE vol 95 (2017) PARA 501 et seq.
11  *Watson v Charlesworth* [1905] 1 KB 74, CA; affd sub nom *Charlesworth v Watson* [1906] AC 14, HL.
12  *Smith v Morris* (1788) 2 Bro CC 311; and see *Phillips v Jones* (1839) 9 Sim 519; *Mellers v Duke of Devonshire* (1852) 16 Beav 252; *Ridgway v Sneyd* (1854) Kay 627; *Simpson v Ingleby* (1872) 26 LT 543 (on appeal 27 LT 695). However, relief cannot be obtained from an absolute covenant to pay a minimum rent or to pay for a certain quantity of mineral whether got or not: *Mellers v Duke of Devonshire*. As to the difference between the cases see *Ridgway v Sneyd*.

### 337. Covenant to work in a particular manner.

A covenant to work a mine[1] in a particular way, as in a workmanlike manner or in accordance with the method usually practised in the district[2], does not bind the lessee to work at all, but only to work in the way specified when he does work[3]. However, if stipulations as to the method of working are added to a covenant to work, such stipulations do not detract from the obligation to work, but impose an additional obligation[4].

In the absence of express stipulation, the convenience and business interests of a lessee in pursuing a regular course of working through contiguous areas held under different lessors do not affect his liability under any one of these leases. The lessee's liability must in each case be determined by reference to the lease in question and as if the obligation under the working covenant in that lease alone is upon him, and he is under no obligation to any other lessor[5].

A covenant to work in a particular way will not be enforced by an order for specific performance or by an injunction restraining working in any other way[6], but an injunction may be obtained to restrain a lessee from doing a particular act which he has covenanted not to do[7].

1   As to the meaning of 'mine' see PARA 3.

2　A covenant to employ a particular method of working must be read in conjunction with the other provisions of the lease, and a different method may be adopted where necessary to avoid a breach of such other provisions: *Brewer v Rhymney Iron Co* [1910] 1 Ch 766.

3　*Wheatley v Westminster Brymbo Coal Co* (1869) LR 9 Eq 538; *Jegon v Vivian* (1871) 6 Ch App 742 at 757 per Lord Hatherley; *Lord Abinger v Ashton* (1873) LR 17 Eq 358.

4　*Walker v Jeffreys* (1842) 1 Hare 341; *Jervis v Tomkinson* (1856) 1 H & N 195; *Charlesworth v Watson* [1906] AC 14, HL; and see *Doyershoek Asbestos Mine (Pty) Ltd v Estate Snyman* 1956 2 SA 304, SA SC App Div.

5　*Eckersley v Wigan Coal and Iron Co Ltd* (1910) 102 LT 264 at 269, CA, per Cozens-Hardy MR; on appeal sub nom *Wigan Coal and Iron Co v Eckersley* 103 LT 468, HL.

6　*Wheatley v Westminster Brymbo Coal Co* (1869) LR 9 Eq 538; *Lord Abinger v Ashton* (1873) LR 17 Eq 358; and see *Moore v Ullcoats Mining Co Ltd* [1908] 1 Ch 575 at 585 per Warrington J. As to specific performance generally see SPECIFIC PERFORMANCE vol 95 (2017) PARA 501 et seq.

7　*Anon* (1754) Amb 209; *Wheatley v Westminster Brymbo Coal Co* (1869) LR 9 Eq 538. As to the remedy of injunction generally see CIVIL PROCEDURE vol 12 (2015) PARA 1098 et seq.

## 338.　Covenant to sink shafts or pits.

In the absence of a covenant to that effect, express or implied, there is no obligation upon a lessee to sink a shaft. The mere grant of a liberty to sink a pit or shaft implies no obligation to sink[1]; nor, where the lessee is in a position to work from an adjoining mine[2] and the right to work by instroke[3] is not excluded, will the inference be strengthened by the fact that it was possibly contemplated by the parties that a shaft would be sunk for the purpose of working the demised mine, and that specific liberties are conferred by the lease for that purpose and for raising and carrying away over the surface not only the minerals[4] from the demised mines but also minerals from the land of adjoining owners[5].

If the lease imposes an obligation to work the demised mines, the lessee will be bound to sink a shaft if no other mode of working is possible[6], but no such obligation arises merely from a covenant to deliver up at the end of the term the mines and works in such a condition that the lessor may continue the workings[7].

If a lessee enters into an unqualified covenant to sink a pit, he will be liable in damages if he does not sink it, even if it is known that the sinking will be fruitless[8]. The measure of damages recoverable in ordinary cases for breach of such a covenant is the cost to the lessor of sinking the pit[9]. If a covenant imposes an obligation to proceed to search for and sink for minerals as far as practicable, the lessee may be absolved from liability if he shows that his efforts and exploratory works were usual and customary in such cases[10].

1　*James v Cochrane* (1852) 7 Exch 170; on appeal (1853) 8 Exch 556, Ex Ch.

2　As to the meaning of 'mine' see PARA 3.

3　As to instroke see PARA 327.

4　As to the meaning of 'minerals' see PARA 10

5　*Jegon v Vivian* (1871) 6 Ch App 742 at 755 per Lord Hatherley LC. See further PARA 326.

6　*James v Cochrane* (1852) 7 Exch 170 at 178 per Pollock CB; on appeal (1853) 8 Exch 556, Ex Ch.

7　*Jegon v Vivian* (1871) 6 Ch App 742 at 756 per Lord Hatherley LC. See further PARA 326.

8　*Jervis v Tomkinson* (1856) 1 H & N 195.

9　*Pell v Shearman* (1855) 10 Exch 766 at 769 per Parke B.

10　*Hanson v Boothman* (1810) 13 East 22.

## 339.　Covenants relating to pillars and barriers.

Under a covenant to leave, at the end of the lease, sufficient pillars for the support of the roof of the mine[1] or the surface, or for the prevention of thrusts and creeps, the duty to leave pillars does not allow the pillars to be removed provided artificial support is substituted. In this respect the lessee's obligation differs from his obligation, if it exists, to support the surface, for in this latter case the lessee may work out the minerals affording support provided artificial support is substituted[2].

A covenant to leave pillars for support will be enforced by injunction[3], and if a lessee works pillars which he has covenanted to leave, he is liable for the damage thereby caused, whether to the surface[4] or to the mine[5]. He must also pay for the minerals contained in the pillars, less the cost of bringing them to the surface, but without any allowance for severing[6]. A covenant to leave barriers may also be enforced by mandatory injunction[7].

If an act is prohibited both by the general law and by covenant the lessor may avail himself of either remedy[8].

1  As to the meaning of 'mine' see PARA 3.
2  See *Hodgson v Moulson* (1865) 18 CBNS 332; *Mostyn v Lancaster, Taylor v Mostyn* (1883) 23 ChD 583, CA; and PARAS 116, 122. As to the meaning of 'minerals' see PARA 10.
3  *Mostyn v Lancaster, Taylor v Mostyn* (1883) 23 ChD 583, CA. Where there is an express contract not to work specified pillars, the right to an injunction is not affected by any question of the safety or the danger of working: *Mostyn v Lancaster, Taylor v Mostyn.*
4  *Hodgson v Moulson* (1865) 18 CBNS 332. A mandatory injunction to restore fences injured by subsidence may be obtained: *Newton v Nock* (1880) 43 LT 197. As to mandatory injunctions generally see CIVIL PROCEDURE vol 12 (2015) PARAS 1099, 1102 et seq.
5  *Taylor v Mostyn* (1886) 33 ChD 226, CA.
6  *Taylor v Mostyn* (1886) 33 ChD 226, CA.
7  Eg if a lessee in breach of an express covenant pierces a barrier, he will be compelled by mandatory injunction to stop up the opening: *Earl of Mexborough v Bower* (1843) 7 Beav 127; affd 2 LTOS 205. Working a barrier is waste: *Marker v Kenrick* (1853) 13 CB 188.
8  *Marker v Kenrick* (1853) 13 CB 188.

C.  OTHER COVENANTS

340.  Usual covenants.

In addition to the covenants to pay rent etc and as to the working of the mine[1], it is usual to insert in mining leases covenants as to repair[2], as to securing the mine[3] against being drowned, as to compensation for surface damage[4], as to inspection of workings by the lessor, and as to the removal of machinery during or at the end of the term. There are also usually covenants dealing with keeping and inspection of accounts, and the means by which minerals gotten are to be weighed and valued.

In the absence of agreement, a lessee is not bound to drain the demised mine, and the fact that the lessor has a right to pass through the mine does not impose an obligation on the lessee to keep it free from water, as there is no derogation from the grant[5]. Even where a lease contains a covenant not to do any act which would tend to the drowning of the mine, the court will not restrain the lessee from removing pumping machinery during the term[6], but a covenant to pump may be enforced by an interim injunction[7], and a covenant not to remove machinery at the end of the term will be enforced by injunction[8].

1  See PARA 333 et seq.
2  The questions arising on covenants to repair are mainly questions of fact or construction: see eg *Foley v Addenbrooke* (1844) 13 M & W 174; *James v Cochrane* (1853) 8 Exch 556, Ex Ch. As to the obligation of a lessee who has covenanted to deliver up in repair see *Lurcott v Wakely and Wheeler* [1911] 1 KB 905, CA; and LANDLORD AND TENANT vol 62 (2016) PARA 329 et seq. A covenant to repair is not specifically enforceable: see *Lord Abinger v Ashton* (1873) LR 17 Eq 358 at 376 per Jessel MR; and SPECIFIC PERFORMANCE vol 95 (2017) PARA 501 et seq.
3  As to the meaning of 'mine' see PARA 3.
4  A covenant to restore damaged surface is not specifically enforceable: *Flint v Brandon* (1803) 8 Ves 159. As to terminal compensation under a compulsory rights order for opencast working of coal

see PARA 475 et seq.

5   *Payne v Rocher Colliery Co* [1887] WN 37. In the absence of stipulation the lessor is entitled to go down the shaft to inspect the demised mine: *Lewis v Marsh* (1849) 8 Hare 97.

6   *Rolleston v New* (1858) 4 K & J 640. The lessee may, however, by removing the machinery render himself liable to an action for damages: *Rolleston v New* at 649 per Page Wood V-C.

7   *Goodrich v Everglyn Coal Co* [1889] WN 152. As to interim injunctions generally see CIVIL PROCEDURE vol 12 (2015) PARAS 581 et seq, 1076, 1101.

8   *Hamilton v Dunsford* (1857) 6 I Ch R 412. Where a lessee covenanted to deliver up at the end of the term machinery with respect to which the lessor could have given notice to purchase at any time during the term, an injunction to restrain a breach was refused as oppression: *Talbot v Ford* (1842) 13 Sim 173.

## 341. Covenant for quiet enjoyment.

If a mining lease contains no express covenant for quiet enjoyment, such a covenant will be implied by the use of the words 'demise' or 'let' or other equivalent words[1]. The working of an upper stratum so as to cause falls in the demised mine is a breach of the covenant[2], but the working of an adjoining mine in a proper manner which unexpectedly causes flooding is not[3].

Not every disappointment which a lessee meets with or experiences in the course of his enjoyment of the demised mines is a disturbance of that enjoyment within the meaning of the covenant for quiet enjoyment, but any substantial interruption of the enjoyment of the demised premises by the lessor or those claiming under him will, in general, be a breach of the covenant[4], because it is to some extent an interference with both the title and the possession[5].

Sometimes an act may be not only a breach of a covenant for quiet enjoyment but also wrongful as a derogation from the lessor's grant[6].

1   *Markham v Paget* [1908] 1 Ch 697; *Mostyn v West Mostyn Coal and Iron Co* (1876) 1 CPD 145 at 152 per Brett J; and see LANDLORD AND TENANT vol 62 (2016) PARA 404 et seq.

2   *Shaw v Stenton* (1858) 2 H & N 858; cf *Mundy v Duke of Rutland* (1883) 23 ChD 81, CA. As to the meaning of 'mine' see PARA 3.

3   *Harrison, Ainslie & Co v Lord Muncaster* [1891] 2 QB 680, CA; and see NUISANCE.

4   *Sanderson v Berwick-upon-Tweed Corpn* (1884) 13 QBD 547, CA.

5   See *Jones v Consolidated Anthracite Collieries Ltd and Lord Dynevor* [1916] 1 KB 123 at 136, 137 per Scrutton J; cf *Morgan v Hunt* (1690) 2 Vent 213; *Spencer v Marriott* (1823) 1 B & C 457; *Dennett v Atherton* (1872) LR 7 QB 316. As to what acts constitute a breach of the covenant for quiet enjoyment see LANDLORD AND TENANT vol 62 (2016) PARA 411.

6   *Markham v Paget* [1908] 1 Ch 697. For a case where workings were restrained as inconsistent with a prior grant see *Earl of Glasgow v Hurlet and Campsie Alum Co* (1850) 3 HL Cas 25. As to the principle that a grantor must not derogate from his grant see DEEDS AND OTHER INSTRUMENTS vol 32 (2012) PARA 258; LANDLORD AND TENANT vol 62 (2016) PARA 414.

## 342. Covenants running with the land.

A covenant contained in a lease of mines and minerals[1] to erect a smelting mill on land not included in the lease has been held to run with the reversion[2], and covenants to make compensation for surface damage have been held to run with the land[3].

1   As to the meaning of 'mines and minerals' see PARA 10 and as to the meaning of 'mine' see PARA 3.

2   *Sampson v Easterby* (1829) 9 B & C 505 at 516; affd sub nom *Easterby v Sampson* (1830) 6 Bing 644, Ex Ch. The basis of the decision seems to have been that, on the facts, the demise of the mines was immediately connected with possession of the smelting mill. See also *Dewar v Goodman* [1909] AC 72, HL; *Ricketts v Churchwardens of Enfield* [1909] 1 Ch 544. As to covenants running with the land generally see REAL PROPERTY AND REGISTRATION vol 87 (2017) PARA 1005 et seq; LANDLORD AND TENANT vol 62 (2016) PARA 462.

3   *Norval v Pascoe* (1864) 34 LJ Ch 82; *Aspden v Seddon, Preston v Seddon* (1876) 1 Ex D 496, CA;
    *Dyson v Forster, Dyson v Seed, Quinn, Morgan etc* [1909] AC 98, HL; *Westhoughton UDC v
    Wigan Coal and Iron Co Ltd* [1919] 1 Ch 159, CA; *Snowdon v Ecclesiastical Comrs for England*
    [1935] Ch 181. A covenant by the lessee with 'the owner or owners, occupier or occupiers for the
    time being' of the surface is effectual even if the surface owners are not parties to the lease, and may
    be enforced by the surface owners at the time of the demise and by their successors in title: *Dyson
    v Forster, Dyson v Seed, Quinn, Morgan etc.*

## (iv)  Distress, Forfeiture and Determination of Tenancy

### 343.  Distress.

Royalties, as well as a fixed or dead rent[1], may be distrained for[2]. An express
power to distrain, extending to chattels in adjoining or neighbouring mines[3] in the
lessee's occupation, does not constitute the lease a bill of sale[4], and is binding upon
assignees of such mines who take with notice[5].

1   As to dead rent see PARA 330.
2   *Daniel v Gracie* (1844) 6 QB 145. As to distress generally see LANDLORD AND TENANT vol 62
    (2016) PARA 282.
3   As to the meaning of 'mine' see PARA 3.
4   *Re Roundwood Colliery Co, Lee v Roundwood Colliery Co* [1897] 1 Ch 373, CA; Bills of Sale Act
    1878 s 6; and see FINANCIAL INSTRUMENTS AND TRANSACTIONS vol 49 (2015) PARAS 431,
    436.
5   *Daniel v Stepney* (1874) LR 9 Exch 185, Ex Ch.

### 344.  Forfeiture.

It is usual to insert in mining leases a power of re-entry, exercisable not only on
non-payment of rent but also on breach of covenant or condition. Sometimes the
power is also made exercisable in case the mine is not worked for a specified
period[1], or in case the lessee becomes bankrupt or makes an arrangement with his
creditors, or, being a company, goes into liquidation, receivership or
administration. If a lease contains, instead of a power of re-entry, a provision that
in certain events the lease is to be void the effect is the same, and the lease, on the
happening of such events, will subsist until the lessor elects to determine[2]. In either
case the demand for possession should be made without undue delay[3], and must
be unequivocal[4].

1   To avoid forfeiture in such case the working must be in good faith (*Doe d Bryan v Bancks* (1821)
    4 B & Ald 401), although the lessees may be given reasonable time for the restitution of the works
    where the lessor has continued to accept dead rent (*Whitehead v Bennett* (1861) 4 LT 818). As to
    the meaning of 'mine' see PARA 3.
2   *Doe d Bryan v Bancks* (1821) 4 B & Ald 401; *Roberts v Davey* (1833) 4 B & Ad 664; *James v
    Young* (1884) 27 ChD 652.
3   *Bowser v Colby* (1841) 1 Hare 109. Where the delay was insufficient to deprive the lessor of the
    right to take proceedings, he was nevertheless compelled to allow the lessee an opportunity of
    putting himself in a position to comply with the covenant the breach of which was complained of:
    *Whitehead v Bennett* (1861) 9 WR 626.
4   *Moore v Ullcoats Mining Co Ltd* [1908] 1 Ch 575; *Muskett v Hill* (1839) 9 LJCP 201. As to the
    necessity of serving notice before re-entry, and as to relief against forfeiture see LANDLORD AND
    TENANT vol 62 (2016) PARA 510 et seq.

### 345.  Determination of tenancy by lessee.

Some mining leases contain a clause empowering the lessee to determine the
tenancy as soon as the minerals are exhausted or in some other event[1]. To
determine the term effectively, all conditions, such as giving notice[2] or the
performance of covenants or otherwise, to which the exercise of the power is
made subject must be strictly observed[3]. A power for the lessee to give notice at

any time authorises him to give a notice expiring during the currency of a year[4]. A power to determine in case of accident is not exercisable on account of an accident happening before the actual date of grant of the lease but subsequent to the date expressed in the lease to be the commencement of the term[5]. If a lessee continues in possession after the expiration of the notice, it is a question of fact whether he has waived the notice and continues to hold over as tenant[6].

Power is frequently conferred upon the lessee to determine the lease if the mines[7] cannot be worked to a profit. Such a provision is generally accompanied by a specification of means for ascertaining by arbitration or by the opinion of experts whether it can be said of a mine at a particular time that it cannot be so worked. For the purposes of such a provision, 'profit' means gain after paying for work and labour and the rent of the mine[8]. In general, the power will only be exercisable if it can be shown that the working of the mine over a considerable period of time will prove unprofitable. A mere temporary loss of profit due to market fluctuations in the price of the produce of the mine will be insufficient to enable the lessee to avail himself of the benefit of the provision[9].

1　As to the construction of 'fairly worked out', 'fairly workable' and 'fairly wrought' see *Jones v Shears* (1836) 7 C & P 346; *Griffiths v Rigby* (1856) 1 H & N 237; *Cartwright v Forman* (1866) 7 B & S 243; *Carr v Benson* (1868) 3 Ch App 524, CA. As to the construction of 'economically viable' see *Nocton Ltd v Water Hall Group plc* [1997] EGCS 97. As to the meaning of 'minerals' see PARA 10.

2　*Cartwright v Forman* (1866) 7 B & S 243.

3　*Grey v Friar* (1854) 4 HL Cas 565. However, a notice that contained a minor misdescription, served to determine a lease has been held to be valid: see *Mannai Investment Co Ltd v Eagle Star Life Assurance Co Ltd* [1997] AC 749, [1997] 3 All ER 352, HL.

4　*Bridges v Potts* (1864) 17 CBNS 314. In such case an apportioned part of the rent is payable for the broken period: see the Apportionment Act 1870 s 2; and LANDLORD AND TENANT vol 62 (2016) PARA 273 et seq. As to the construction of similar powers in leases generally see LANDLORD AND TENANT vol 62 (2016) PARAS 107, 196; LANDLORD AND TENANT vol 64 (2016) PARAS 1184, 1239.

5　*Jervis v Tomkinson* (1856) 1 H & N 195.

6　*Jones v Shears* (1836) 4 Ad & El 832, where the lessees claimed to remain in possession in pursuance of a custom. As to the tacit incorporation of usages in leases see *Tucker v Linger* (1883) 8 App Cas 508, HL; and CUSTOM AND USAGE vol 32 (2012) PARA 53. As to a case dealing with an alleged usage with reference to a quarry see *Vint v Constable* (1871) 25 LT 324.

7　As to the meaning of 'mine' see PARA 3.

8　*Gowan v Christie* (1873) LR 2 Sc & Div 273 at 282, HL, per Lord Cairns.

9　See *Gowan v Christie* (1873) LR 2 Sc & Div 273 at 284, HL, per Lord Cairns.

# (4) Licences

## 346. Licence coupled with grant.

A right to work mines[1] and carry away the minerals[2] won is more than a mere licence[3]. It is a profit à prendre lying in grant[4], which may be limited either for freehold or chattel interests[5], and the estates so created may be devised[6], inherited[7] or assigned[8]. It does not convey any estate in the land or in the mines except the parts[9] severed which become the property of the grantee[10]. Such a licence is irrevocable[11].

A licensee who has entered into possession is liable in a claim for use and occupation[12], and he may if ousted, at any rate where the licence is exclusive[13], bring a claim to recover possession[14].

1　As to the meaning of 'mine' see PARA 3.

2　As to the meaning of 'minerals' see PARA 10.

3   As to the licensing of coal-mining operations by the Coal Authority see PARA 89 et seq. As to the meaning of 'coal-mining operations' see PARA 51. As to the Coal Authority see PARA 52 et seq.
4   *Duke of Sutherland v Heathcote* [1892] 1 Ch 475 at 483–484, CA; see *Watson v Spratley* (1854) 10 Exch 222 at 235 per Martin B; *Re Associated Portland Cement Manufacturers Ltd's Application* [1966] 1 Ch 308 at 323, [1965] 2 All ER 547 at 555 per Buckley J; *Alfred F Beckett Ltd v Lyons* [1967] Ch 449 at 482, [1967] 1 All ER 833 at 851, CA, per Winn LJ; *T and E Homes Ltd v Robinson (Inspector of Taxes)* [1976] 3 All ER 497 at 508, [1976] 1 WLR 1150 at 1160 per Goulding J. As to profits à prendre see REAL PROPERTY AND REGISTRATION vol 87 (2017) PARA 974. An agreement for the sale of sand and gravel to be removed from a parcel of land, although stated to be for the sale of goods, may be a grant of a profit à prendre: *Stratford v Mole and Lea* (1941) 24 TC 20.
5   *Haigh v Jaggar* (1847) 16 M & W 525 (although the court construed the deed to operate as a lease of the mine); *Martyn v Williams* (1857) 1 H & N 817. As to the effect of a grant to a grantee, his executors and administrators, without the mention of any term see *Port v Turton* (1763) 2 Wils 169; *Haigh v Jaggar*; *Low Moor Co v Stanley Coal Co Ltd* (1876) 34 LT 186, CA.
6   *Lord Mountjoy and Earl of Huntington's Case* (1583) Godb 17.
7   *Martyn v Williams* (1857) 1 H & N 817.
8   *Muskett v Hill* (1839) 5 Bing NC 694; *Martyn v Williams* (1857) 1 H & N 817.
9   *Norway v Rowe* (1812) 19 Ves 144 at 158 per Lord Eldon LC; *Roberts v Davey* (1833) 4 B & Ad 664; *London and North Western Rly Co v Ackroyd* (1862) 31 LJ Ch 588 at 591 per Page Wood V-C.
10  *Doe d Hanley v Wood* (1819) 2 B & Ald 724 at 739.
11  *Wood v Manley* (1839) 11 Ad & El 34; and see LANDLORD AND TENANT vol 62 (2016) PARA 13.
12  *Jones v Reynolds* (1836) 7 C & P 335. Merely digging trial pits is not necessarily taking possession: *Jones v Reynolds* at 336 per Coleridge J.
13  *Wilson v Mackreth* (1766) 3 Burr 1824. As to exclusive licences see PARA 350.
14  *Crocker v Fothergill* (1819) 2 B & Ald 652; *Doe d Hanley v Wood* (1819) 2 B & Ald 724 at 739; *Jones v Reynolds* (1836) 4 Ad & El 805.

## 347. Bare licence.

A bare licence which does not amount to a profit à prendre, such as a licence to search for minerals[1], confers upon the grantee no property in the minerals found[2]. The grantee has the right of possession for the purpose of examining the minerals found, and has a right of action against a third person who interferes with that possession[3]. A bare licence, whether granted by deed or not and whether or not for valuable consideration, is prima facie revocable[4], but effect will be given to a term in a contractual licence providing that the licence is not to be revoked[5]. Revocation of a contractual licence in breach of such a term entitles the licensee to damages for breach of contract[6].

1   As to the meaning of 'minerals' see PARA 10.
2   *Re Haven Gold Mining Co* (1882) 20 ChD 151, CA.
3   *Northam v Bowden* (1855) 11 Exch 70.
4   *Wood v Leadbitter* (1845) 13 M & W 838.
5   *Winter Garden Theatre (London) Ltd v Millennium Productions Ltd* [1948] AC 173, [1947] 2 All ER 331, HL. It does not require much to induce a court to read into an agreement of a commercial character, either by construction or by implication, a provision that the arrangements are to be terminable only upon reasonable notice: see *Australian Blue Metal Ltd v Hughes* [1963] AC 74 at 98, [1962] 3 All ER 335 at 341, PC (mining licence held terminable at will). See further CONTRACT.
6   *Smart v Jones* (1864) 15 CBNS 717; *Kerrison v Smith* [1897] 2 QB 445, DC.

## 348. Form of licence.

Mining licences, coupled with a grant, must be created by deed in order to create a legal right[1], and can only be legally transferred by deed[2]; but a licence under hand only[3], or one which is merely oral, may be effectual if the licensee incurs expense in working on the faith of it[4].

Except so far as they differ by the omission of the demised parcels, mining licences which amount to a profit à prendre are usually made in a form similar to mining leases and contain similar covenants and provisions[5]. Covenants, for instance, to pay for surface damage[6] and to repair[7], run with the land in the case of such a licence as in the case of a lease.

Payments reserved in respect of a licence are in the nature of rent[8], but they are not a true rent and cannot be distrained for[9]. It is necessary, therefore, to insert a power of distress. It is also proper and usual to insert a proviso for re-entry[10].

1   *Wood v Leadbitter* (1845) 13 M & W 838; *Doe d Morgan v Powell* (1844) 8 Scott NR 687 at 701 per Tindall CJ, and at 703 per Maule J; *Watson v Spratley* (1854) 10 Exch 222 at 235 per Martin B. However, the court gives effect to equitable doctrines and the revocation of a licence coupled with a grant which should be, but is not, under seal may be restrained: see DEEDS AND OTHER INSTRUMENTS vol 32 (2012) PARA 211; LANDLORD AND TENANT vol 62 (2016) PARA 97.
2   *Harker v Birkbeck* (1764) 3 Burr 1556 at 1563 per Lord Mansfield CJ; *Watson v Spratley* (1854) 10 Exch 222.
3   *Atkinson v King* (1878) 2 LR Ir 320 at 335, Ir CA, per Ball LC.
4   *Harrison v Ames* (1850) 15 LTOS 321.
5   As to the licensing of coal-mining operations by the Coal Authority see PARA 89 et seq. As to the meaning of 'coal-mining operations' see PARA 51. As to the Coal Authority see PARA 52 et seq.
6   *Norval v Pascoe* (1864) 34 LJ Ch 82.
7   *Martyn v Williams* (1857) 1 H & N 817. A claim for damages for breach of covenant does not pass to a purchaser of the land: *Martyn v Williams*. As to the different regimes before and after 1 January 1996 see the Law of Property Act 1925 s 141; and the Landlord and Tenant (Covenants) Act 1995 ss 3(1), 30(4).
8   *Re Brindley, ex p Hankey* (1829) Mont & M 247. See also *Duke of Fife's Trustees v George Wimpey & Co Ltd* 1943 SC 377, Ct of Sess.
9   See *Ward v Day* (1863) 4 B & S 337; *Re Roundwood Colliery Co, Lee v Roundwood Colliery Co* [1897] 1 Ch 373, CA; and LANDLORD AND TENANT vol 62 (2016) PARA 282.
10  *Doe d Hanley v Wood* (1819) 2 B & Ald 724.

## 349. Construction of licences.

It is sometimes a matter of difficulty to decide whether a particular form of words operates to grant a licence or an estate. Each case depends on its own circumstances, and it is impossible to lay down any general rule except that words denoting liberty to work minerals[1], if unexplained by the other parts of the deed, only amount to the grant of a licence[2]. Where the words occur by way of exception or reservation in a grant of land it is important to consider what estate in the minerals the person in whose favour the exception or reservation is intended to operate had before the execution of the grant. If he was legal owner of the minerals, doubtful words are more easily construed as an exception of the minerals[3]. In an instrument granting a licence the use of subsequent expressions which are only appropriate if the instrument operates as a demise of the minerals will not enlarge the words of grant[4]. Instruments may sometimes operate as a demise of the minerals for a term and as a licence for a subsequent term[5]. Difficulties arising from informal agreements can only be solved by a consideration of the circumstances of each case[6].

1   As to the meaning of 'minerals' see PARA 10.
2   *Doe d Hanley v Wood* (1819) 2 B & Ald 724; *Duke of Sutherland v Heathcote* [1892] 1 Ch 475, CA; *Lord Mountjoy and Earl of Huntington's Case* (1583) Godb 17; and see *Hunts Refuse Disposals Ltd v Norfolk Environmental Waste Services Ltd* [1997] 1 EGLR 16, [1997] 03 EG 139, CA (words denoting liberty to deposit waste found to be a licence). See generally LANDLORD AND TENANT vol 62 (2016) PARA 8 et seq. An unenrolled bargain and sale of mines to a person, his executors and administrators, followed by possession was held to create a tenancy at will: *Low Moor Co v Stanley Coal Co Ltd* (1876) 34 LT 186, CA; but see *Haigh v Jaggar* (1847) 16 M & W 525.
3   *Chetham v Williamson* (1804) 4 East 469 (right given to mortgagor held to amount to licence only; in considering the judgment in this case it must be remembered that minerals now lie in grant); *Duke of Hamilton v Dunlop* (1885) 10 App Cas 813, HL (right given to owner; words denoting

liberty only held to amount to exception of minerals on construction of deed as a whole); *Duke of Sutherland v Heathcote* [1892] 1 Ch 475, CA (right given to donees of joint power held to amount to liberty only).

4   *Doe d Hanley v Wood* (1819) 2 B & Ald 724.

5   *Haigh v Jaggar* (1847) 16 M & W 525; *Stanley v Riky* (1893) 31 LR Ir 196, Ir CA.

6   See eg *Re Brindley, ex p Hankey* (1829) Mont & M 247; *Daniel v Gracie* (1844) 6 QB 145; *Re Stroud and East and West India Docks and Birmingham Junction Rly Co* (1849) 8 CB 502. In these cases agreements as to getting earth and making bricks on payment of royalties were held to create tenancies from year to year or at will. In *Atkinson v King* (1878) 2 LR Ir 320, Ir CA, an agreement to allow a man to sink a pit for coal at a royalty was held to create a licence.

## 350. Exclusive licences.

A licence is said to be exclusive if it is expressed to grant to the grantee the sole right to exercise the liberty granted within the defined limits. If it is not clearly so expressed, the grantor may himself exercise the same right and authorise others to do so[1], provided neither he nor they interfere with the operations of the licensee[2], nor deprive him of the benefits of his licence[3]. An exclusive licensee may maintain trespass[4].

1   *Lord Mountjoy and Earl of Huntington's Case* (1583) Godb 17; *Chetham v Williamson* (1804) 4 East 469; *Doe d Hanley v Wood* (1819) 2 B & Ald 724; *Carr v Benson* (1868) 3 Ch App 524, CA; *Duke of Sutherland v Heathcote* [1892] 1 Ch 475, CA.

2   *Duke of Sutherland v Heathcote* [1892] 1 Ch 475, CA; *Roads v Trumpington Overseers* (1870) LR 6 QB 56.

3   *Carr v Benson* (1868) 3 Ch App 524, CA; *Newby v Harrison* (1861) 4 LT 397 (affd 4 LT 424).

4   *Harker v Birkbeck* (1764) 3 Burr 1556. As to his right to recover possession see PARA 348. As to the rights of a non-exclusive licensee who has taken possession see *Doe d Hanley v Wood* (1819) 2 B & Ald 724; and PARA 346. As to what acts constitute taking possession see *Carr v Benson* (1868) 3 Ch App 524, CA; and PARA 346.

## 351. Licensor's remedies.

The licensor's remedies are divisible into those to which he is entitled under the general law and those which he enjoys by virtue of provisions contained in the instrument granting the licence. The remedies under the general law are a claim for an account[1] and, where the licensee has actually exercised the right, a claim for use and occupation[2]. The remedies under provisions in the licence are a claim on the covenant for payment of rent and exercise of the powers of distress if expressly provided for[3], and re-entry[4]. A licence which contains a provision that in certain events it is to be void is not, upon the happening of the prescribed event, void, but voidable at the instance of the licensor[5]. Notice to determine a licence must be definite[6]. Although payments reserved under a licence cannot be distrained for, an attempt to levy a distress may be sufficient evidence of intention to waive a previous forfeiture[7].

1   *Wright v Pitt* (1870) LR 12 Eq 408. As to claims for account generally see EQUITABLE JURISDICTION vol 47 (2014) PARA 49 et seq.

2   *Jones v Reynolds* (1836) 4 Ad & El 805. As to claims for use and occupation generally see LANDLORD AND TENANT vol 62 (2016) PARA 278.

3   *Ward v Day* (1863) 4 B & S 337 at 358 per Blackburn J.

4   As to these provisions see PARA 343 et seq.

5   *Roberts v Davey* (1833) 4 B & Ad 664.

6   *Muskett v Hill* (1839) 5 Bing NC 694.

7   *Ward v Day* (1863) 4 B & S 337.

# 6. RIGHT TO WORK MINERALS

## (1) Mineral Development

### (i) Planning and the Environment

**352. The minerals planning legislation.**
The town and country planning system in respect of the development[1] of land[2] in England and Wales is regulated by statute, principally the Town and Country Planning Act 1990, certain other consolidating Acts[3], and the subordinate legislation made thereunder[4]. These statutes also contain provisions specific to minerals planning[5]. Mineral Planning Guidance Notes ('MPGs') set out the government's policy on minerals and planning issues and provided guidance to local authorities, the minerals industry and others on policies and the operation of the planning system with regard to minerals. However most of these MPGs have now been repealed by the National Planning Policy Framework ('NPPF') which sets out the government's planning policies for England and how these are expected to be applied[6].

Planning permission is required for the carrying out of any development of land[7]. In relation to development consisting of the winning and working of minerals[8] or involving the depositing of mineral waste[9] specified provisions[10] of the Town and Country Planning Act 1990 have effect subject to such adaptations and modifications as may be prescribed[11].

1   As to the meaning of 'development' for the purposes of the Town and Country Planning Act 1990 see s 55(1); and PLANNING vol 81 (2018) PARA 333.
2   As to the meaning of 'land' for the purposes of the Town and Country Planning Act 1990 see s 336(1); and PLANNING vol 81 (2018) PARA 3.
3   Ie the Planning (Listed Buildings and Conservation Areas) Act 1990 (see PLANNING vol 83 (2018) PARA 1165 et seq); the Planning (Hazardous Substances) Act 1990 (see PLANNING vol 83 (2018) PARA 1289 et seq); and the Planning (Consequential Provisions) Act 1990 (see PLANNING). As to the consolidating Acts see PLANNING vol 81 (2018) PARA 3 et seq.
4   As to Departmental circulars and Planning Policy Guidance Notes see PLANNING vol 81 (2018) PARAS 37–38.
5   As to mineral workings, the control of uses relating to minerals, and compensation in respect of restrictions on mineral working etc see PLANNING vol 82 (2018) PARA 654 et seq. As to the temporary stopping up of highways for working of minerals see HIGHWAYS, STREETS AND BRIDGES vol 55 (2012) PARA 822.
      As to the ironstone restoration fund see PARA 580 et seq. As to the suspension of certain public rights of way see PARA 424. As to the environmental duties in connection with planning see PARA 354. As to the obligations to restore land affected by coal-mining operations see PARA 573. As to the review of old mineral permissions and the periodic review of mineral planning permissions see generally PLANNING vol 82 (2018) PARA 662 et seq.
      In relation to minerals, the subordinate legislation includes the Town and Country Planning (Compensation for Restrictions in Mineral Working and Mineral Waste Depositing) Regulations 1997, SI 1997/1111; the Town and Country Planning (General Permitted Development) Order 1995, SI 1995/418; and the Town and Country Planning (Minerals) Regulations 1995, SI 1995/2863 (modification of the provisions of the Town and Country Planning Act 1990 (see generally PLANNING vol 81 (2018) PARA 33)).
      Subject to the provisions of the Town and Country Planning (General Permitted Development) Order 1995, SI 1995/418, and Conservation of Habitats and Species Regulations 2017, SI 2017/1012, regs 75–78 (see PLANNING vol 81 (2018) PARA 362) the Town and Country Planning (General Permitted Development) Order 1995, SI 1995/418, art 3(1) grants planning permission for the classes of development described as permitted development in Sch 2 including: (1) development ancillary to mining operations (see Sch 2 Pt 19); (2) coal mining development by

the Coal Authority and licensed operators (see Sch 2 Pt 20); (3) waste tipping at a mine (see Sch 2 Pt 21); (4) mineral exploration (see Sch 2 Pt 22); and (5) removal of material from mineral working deposits (see Sch 2 Pt 23). See further PLANNING vol 81 (2018) PARAS 359 et seq, 502 et seq. As to the Coal Authority see PARA 52 et seq.

6   Some of the relevant provisions in the NPPF on minerals planning include: (1) provisions about the appropriateness of mineral extraction in Green Belt (see NPPF para 90); (2) provisions about facilitating the sustainable use of minerals (see NPPF paras 142–149); (3) provisions about local plans in relation to minerals (see NPPF para 163). As to the NPPF generally see PLANNING.
    At the date this volume states the law, the following MPGs are still in force: (a) MPG 4: *The Review of Mineral Working Sites*. This covers the review of mineral working sites, including the compensation implications; (b) MPG 8: *Planning and Compensation Act 1991: Interim Development Order Permissions (IDOS) – Statutory Provisions and Procedures*. This sets out the procedures to be followed in applying for registration and for the determination of conditions; (c) MPG 9: *Planning and Compensation Act 1991: Interim Development Order Permissions (IDOS) – Conditions*. This gives advice on the considerations to be taken into account by applicants and mineral planning authorities in preparing and determining the conditions to which registered permissions should be subject; (d) MPG 14: *Environment Act 1995: Review of Mineral Planning Permissions*. This gives advice to mineral planning authorities and the minerals industry on the statutory procedures to be followed and the approach to be adopted to the preparation and consideration of updated planning conditions in the review process. As to the repeal of the MPGs see the NPPF, Annex 3. The Technical Guidance to the NPPF provides additional guidance to local planning authorities to ensure the effective implementation of the planning policy set out in the NPPF.

7   See the Town and Country Planning Act 1990 s 57(1). As to planning permission required for development see s 57; and PLANNING vol 81 (2018) PARA 354; as to the granting of planning permission see s 58; and PLANNING vol 81 (2018) PARA 354; and as to development orders see ss 59–61; and PLANNING vol 81 (2018) PARA 359 et seq. As to development ancillary to mining operations see the Town and Country Planning (General Permitted Development) Order 1995, SI 1995/418, Sch 2 Pt 19. As to the form and content of applications for planning permission see the Town and Country Planning Act 1990 s 62; and PLANNING vol 82 (2018) PARA 420. As to the conditions imposed on a grant, revocation or modification of planning permission for development consisting of the winning and working of minerals see PLANNING vol 82 (2018) PARA 655 et seq. As to old mining permissions see PLANNING vol 82 (2018) PARA 662 et seq; and *R v North Yorkshire County Council, ex p Brown* [1998] 2 CMLR 166, 76 P&CR 433, CA (local authority required to consider an environmental assessment before determining the conditions to which an old mining permission was subject). See also *Leicestershire County Council v Secretary of State for Communities and Local Government* [2007] EWHC 1427 (Admin), [2007] All ER (D) 264 (Jun) (mineral planning authority refused application for planning permission for opencast coal mining on a green field site, pointing to the cumulative environmental impact that would be caused but the Secretary of State's decision to grant conditional planning permission as any adverse impact that might be caused could be mitigated by the imposition of planning conditions, stood).

8   As to the meanings of the 'winning and working of minerals', 'minerals' and 'mineral-working deposit' for the purposes of the Town and Country Planning Act 1990 see s 336(1); and PLANNING vol 81 (2018) PARA 8.

9   As to the meaning of 'depositing of mineral waste' for the purposes of the Town and Country Planning Act 1990 see s 336(1); and PLANNING vol 81 (2018) PARA 8.

10  Ie the provisions specified in the Town and Country Planning Act 1990 Sch 16 Pts I, II: see PLANNING vol 81 (2018) PARA 8.

11  See the Town and Country Planning Act 1990 s 315(1) (amended by the Planning and Compensation Act 1991 s 21, Sch 1 paras 1, 11). As to the power to modify statutory provisions in relation to minerals see PLANNING vol 81 (2018) PARA 8.

## 353.  ROMP applications.

Applications may be made to a relevant mineral planning authority[1] to determine the conditions to which a planning permission is to be subject under provisions relating to (1) the registration of old mining permissions[2]; (2) the review of old mineral planning permissions[3]; or (3) the periodic review of mineral planning permissions[4] ('ROMP applications')[5].

1   As to 'relevant mineral planning authority' see PLANNING vol 82 (2018) PARA 99.

2 See the Planning and Compensation Act 1991 Sch 2; and PLANNING vol 82 (2018) PARA 663
3 See the Environment Act 1995 s 96, Sch 13; and PLANNING vol 82 (2018) PARA 665 et seq. See also *Stancliffe Stone Co Ltd v Peak District National Park Authority* [2005] EWCA Civ 747, [2005] 4 PLR 35, [2006] JPL 247 (The ROMP regime is intended to be a self-contained regime. Therefore, the court should give weight to the opinion of an authority charged with the task of reaching a decision in the course of implementing the old minerals planning permissions review scheme, in the circumstances in which Parliament thought it necessary to provide an appeal process, and where the authority had identified correctly the question that they needed to decide). See also *Wirral Borough Council v Brock plc* [2004] EWCA Civ 1611, [2005] 2 P & CR 318, [2005] JPL 1067; and *R v North Lincolnshire Council, ex p Horticultural and Garden Sales (Humberside) Ltd* (1997) 76 P & CR 363, [1998] Env LR 295.
4 See the Environment Act 1995 Sch 14; and PLANNING vol 82 (2018) PARA 676 et seq. As to planning permission generally see PLANNING.
5 As to ROMPs see PLANNING vol 82 (2018) PARA 99 et seq.

## 354. Environmental duties in connection with planning.

Where a planning authority[1] considers any coal-mining proposals included in an application for planning permission[2], it must have regard to:

(1) the desirability of the preservation of natural beauty, of the conservation of flora and fauna and geological or physiographical features of special interest and of the protection of sites, buildings, structures and objects of architectural, historic or archaeological interest[3]; and

(2) the extent (if any) to which the person by whom the proposals were formulated has complied with certain requirements[4].

1 'Planning authority' means: (1) any local planning authority within the meaning of the Town and Country Planning Act 1990; or (2) the appropriate national authority in the exercise and performance of such of his powers and duties under the Town and Country Planning Act 1990 as relate to the grant of planning permission: see the Coal Industry Act 1994 s 53(4). The appropriate national authority is the Secretary of State or where functions have been transferred in relation to Wales, the Welsh Ministers: see PARA 2. As to local planning authorities see the Town and Country Planning Act 1990 s 1; and PLANNING vol 81 (2018) PARA 160 et seq.
2 Ie coal-mining proposals formulated for inclusion in so much of any application for planning permission as relates to any of the following: (1) the carrying on of any coal-mining operations; (2) the restoration of land used in connection with the carrying on of any coal-mining operations; and (3) the carrying on of any other operations incidental to any coal-mining operations or to the restoration of land which has been so used: Coal Industry Act 1994 s 53(1). For these purposes, 'planning permission', in relation to England and Wales, has the same meaning as in the Town and Country Planning Act 1990 s 336(1) (see PLANNING vol 81 (2018) PARA 162): Coal Industry Act 1994 s 53(4). As to the meaning of 'coal-mining operations' see PARA 51.
3 Coal Industry Act 1994 s 53(2)(a). As to ancient monuments and archaeological areas see generally NATIONAL CULTURAL HERITAGE vol 77 (2016) PARA 1006 et seq.
4 Coal Industry Act 1994 s 53(2)(b). The requirements are: (1) to have regard, in formulating those proposals, to the desirability of the matters mentioned in the Coal Industry Act 1994 s 53(2)(a) (see head (1) in the text); and (2) to formulate proposals (as part of or in addition to the coal-mining proposals) for the adoption of such measures (if any) as it is reasonably practicable for that person to adopt for mitigating any adverse effect of the development to which the coal-mining proposals relate on the natural beauty of any area or on any such flora, fauna, features, sites, buildings, structures or objects as are so mentioned: s 53(3). For these purposes, 'development' in relation to England and Wales, has the same meaning as in the Town and Country Planning Act 1990 s 55 (see PLANNING vol 81 (2018) PARA 333): Coal Industry Act 1994 s 53(4).

## 355. Obligations to restore land affected by coal-mining operations.

The power of the appropriate national authority[1] by a development order[2] to make the planning permission[3] granted by any such order subject to conditions includes power, in relation to any permission to win or work any minerals[4] in a coal mine[5] started before 1 July 1948, to make it a condition of that permission that there is compliance with certain requirements[6] as may be specified or described in the order[7].

These requirements[8] are such as the appropriate national authority thinks fit in relation to: (1) the demolition or removal of any buildings[9], plant, machinery, structures or erections used[10] at any time for or in connection with any previous coal-mining operations[11] at that mine; and (2) the re-instatement, restoration and aftercare of any land[12] used at any time for or in connection with any previous coal-mining operations at that mine[13].

A condition contained in a development order by virtue of these provisions[14] may provide: (a) for the requirements imposed by that condition to include a requirement framed by reference to the opinion or approval of the relevant planning authority[15]; and (b) for that condition to be capable of being modified by agreement with the relevant planning authority[16].

The appropriate national authority's powers[17] to modify a development order must not be exercised at any time after the end of the period of six months beginning with the restructuring date[18], except for purposes which do not, in relation to any coal mine, include any of the following: (i) imposing a requirement which had not previously been imposed in relation to that coal mine; (ii) making a requirement which had been imposed in relation to that coal mine more onerous; and (iii) making provision by reference to any person's opinion or approval so as to confer powers that did not exist before and might be exercised for a purpose falling within head (i) or head (ii) above[19].

1   Ie the Secretary of State or where functions have been transferred in relation to Wales, the Welsh Ministers: see PARA 2.

2   As to the meaning of 'development order' see the Town and Country Planning Act 1990 s 59; and PLANNING vol 81 (2018) PARA 359.

3   As to the meaning of 'planning permission' see the Town and Country Planning Act 1990 s 336(1); and PLANNING vol 81 (2018) PARA 162. As to the granting of planning permission by development order see ss 59–61; and PLANNING vol 81 (2018) PARAS 359, 362.

4   As to the meaning of 'minerals' see PARA 10.

5   As to the meaning of 'coal mine' see PARA 3.

6   Ie the requirements of the Coal Industry Act 1994 s 54(2).

7   Coal Industry Act 1994 s 54(1). This provision is subject to s 54(5).

8   Ie those which fall within the Coal Industry Act 1994 s 54.

9   As to the meaning of 'building' see the Town and Country Planning Act 1990 s 336(1); and PLANNING vol 81 (2018) PARA 3.

10  As to the meaning of 'used' see the Town and Country Planning Act 1990 s 336(1); and PLANNING vol 81 (2018) PARA 337.

11  For these purposes, 'previous coal-mining operations', in relation to the requirements imposed by any condition, means:

(1)    any coal-mining operations carried on by any person before 1 July 1948; or

(2)    any coal-mining operations which:

    (a)    were carried on by any person at any time on or after that date but before the coming into force of that condition; and

    (b)    were operations constituting development for which planning permission was granted by a development order or any corresponding order made, or having effect as if made, under any enactment then in force,

and references in the Coal Industry Act 1994 s 54 to the use of anything in connection with any such operations include references to its use for or in connection with activities carried on in association with, or for purposes connected with, the carrying on of those operations: see s 54(3). As to the meaning of 'coal-mining operations' see PARA 51. As to the meaning of 'enactment' see the Town and Country Planning Act 1990 s 336(1); and PLANNING vol 81 (2018) PARA 3.

12  As to the meaning of 'land' see Town and Country Planning Act 1990 s 336(1); and PLANNING vol 81 (2018) PARA 3.

13  Coal Industry Act 1994 s 54(2). As to treatment of land that is derelict as a result of mining operations see PARA 582.

14 Ie by the Coal Industry Act 1994 s 54.
15 For these purposes, 'relevant planning authority', in relation to England and Wales, means the mineral planning authority within the meaning of the Town and Country Planning Act 1990: see the Coal Industry Act 1994 s 54(7).
16 Coal Industry Act 1994 s 54(4).
17 Ie under the Coal Industry Act 1994 s 54.
18 Ie 31 October 1994: see PARA 50.
19 Coal Industry Act 1994 s 54(5). However, this does not affect the continuing effect after the end of that period of any modification made after the passing of the Coal Industry Act 1994 (ie 5 July 1994) and before the end of that period: s 54(5) proviso. As to the meaning of 'modifications' see PARA 51. Expressions used in s 54 and in the Town and Country Planning Act 1990 have, in the application of the Coal Industry Act 1994 s 54 to England and Wales, the same meanings in s 54 as in the Town and Country Planning Act 1990: see the Coal Industry Act 1994 s 54(6).

### 356. Facilities for United Kingdom Research and Innovation.

Before any person sinks, for the purpose of searching for or getting any minerals[1], a shaft or borehole intended to reach a depth of more than 30.480 metres below the surface, he must give to United Kingdom Research and Innovation ('UKRI') written notice of his intention to do so[2]. He must keep a journal of any such sinking and retain for a period of not less than six months such specimens of the strata passed through as may have been obtained in the course of the sinking, either as cores or fragments, and must allow UKRI or any officer appointed by them[3], to have free access at all reasonable times to any such shaft, borehole or core, to inspect and take copies of the journals of such shafts or boreholes, to inspect all specimens so obtained and kept, and to take representative specimens of any such cores[4].

The owner or manager of every mine must allow UKRI or any officer appointed by it to have free access at all reasonable times to all underground workings, and must supply to UKRI or to any such officer such information and such specimens of seams or strata sunk through or opened out at the mine as may be reasonably required by UKRI[5].

If any person sinking any shaft or borehole, or the owner or manager of any mine fails to comply with any obligation imposed on him by these requirements[6], he is, in respect of each offence, liable on summary conviction to a fine not exceeding level 3 on the standard scale[7]. If the person sinking any shaft or borehole gives notice in writing to UKRI requiring it to treat as confidential any copies of journals or specimens so taken by UKRI or by any officer appointed by it, UKRI must not allow those copies or specimens to be published or shown to any person not being an officer of UKRI, except with the consent of the person sinking such shaft or borehole[8]. If, however, at any time UKRI gives notice to any person from whom such consent is required that, in its opinion, his consent is unreasonably withheld, then that person may, within three months after such notice is given, appeal to the High Court[9]. If at the expiration of that period no such appeal is made, or if after hearing the appeal the High Court does not make an order restraining it from doing so, UKRI may proceed as if such consent had been given[10].

1  As to the meaning of 'minerals' see PARA 10 .
2  See the Mining Industry Act 1926 s 23(1) (amended by the Science and Technology Act 1965 s 3(5), Sch 2; the Higher Education and Research Act 2017 Sch 12 para 2; and SI 1991/2531). As to the Natural Environment Research Council see NATIONAL CULTURAL HERITAGE vol 77 (2016) PARA 966.
3  Any officer appointed by UKRI has the same rights as to the production and inspection of plans, sections and drawings which, by or by virtue of the Mines and Quarries Act 1954 are required to be kept, as are by that Act conferred on inspectors, and that Act applies accordingly: Mining

Industry Act 1926 s 23(5) (substituted by the Mines and Quarries Act 1954 s 188, Sch 4; and amended by the Science and Technology Act 1965 Sch 2; and the Higher Education and Research Act 2017 Sch 12 para 2). As to the powers of inspectors see the Health and Safety at Work etc Act 1974 s 20; and HEALTH AND SAFETY AT WORK vol 52 (2014) PARA 339.

4   See the Mining Industry Act 1926 s 23(1) .

5   Mining Industry Act 1926 s 23(3) (amended by the Mines and Quarries Act 1954 s 188, Sch 4; the Science and Technology Act 1965 Sch 2; and the Higher Education and Research Act 2017 Sch 12 para 2).

6   Ie by the Mining Industry Act 1926 s 23(1)–(3).

7   See the Mining Industry Act 1926 s 23(4) (amended by the Mines and Quarries Act 1954 s 188, Sch 4; and the Criminal Justice Act 1982 ss 38, 46). As to the standard scale see SENTENCING vol 92 (2015) PARA 176.

8   See the Mining Industry Act 1926 s 23(2) (amended by the Science and Technology Act 1965 Sch 2; and the Higher Education and Research Act 2017 Sch 12 para 2).

9   See the Mining Industry Act 1926 s 23(2) proviso (amended by the Railway and Canal Commission (Abolition) Act 1949 s 1(1)(a); the Science and Technology Act 1965 Sch 2; and the Higher Education and Research Act 2017 Sch 12 para 2). As to the High Court procedure see PARA 395.

10  See the Mining Industry Act 1926 s 23(2) proviso.

## (ii) Miscellaneous Provisions

### 357. Taxation.

The taxation of mines, quarries and mineral rights is dealt with elsewhere in this work[1]. The Coal Industry Act 1994 makes specific provision in relation to the taxation effects of restructuring of the coal industry[2], and the financial structure of successor companies[3].

1   As to income tax and corporation tax see INCOME TAXATION vol 58 (2014) PARA 35 et seq; INCOME TAXATION vol 58A (2014) PARA 1018 et seq. As to capital gains tax see CAPITAL GAINS TAXATION. As to value added tax see VALUE ADDED TAX. As to petroleum revenue tax and oil taxation see OIL AND GAS TAXATION vol 78 (2010) PARA 301 et seq. As to profits or gains arising out of land as in the case of mines, quarries and similar concerns see INCOME TAXATION vol 58 (2014) PARA 124. As to exceptions from the charge to tax see INCOME TAXATION vol 58 (2014) PARA 40. As to mineral extraction see INCOME TAXATION vol 58 (2014) PARA 456 et seq. As to balancing charges and balancing allowances see INCOME TAXATION vol 58 (2014) PARA 465 et seq.

2   See the Coal Industry Act 1994 s 21, Sch 4; and PARA 72.

3   See the Coal Industry Act 1994 s 15, Sch 3; and PARA 74.

### 358. Control of prices of minerals.

Prices for the sale of coal[1] used to be subject to the provisions of the former Treaty establishing the European Coal and Steel Community[2], which included powers for the Commission of the European Communities to fix prices[3]. The Commission proposed a gradual transition of the coal and steel trade into the Treaty on the Functioning of the European Union[4]. The rules of this Treaty as well as the procedural rules and other secondary legislation derived from it have applied to the coal and steel trade since 24 July 2002[5].

1   As to the meaning of 'coal' for these purposes see the Treaty establishing the European Coal and Steel Community (Paris, 18 April 1951; TS 16 (1979); Cmnd 7461), Annex I. By virtue of the ECSC Treaty art 97, that Treaty expired on 23 July 2002.

2   See the Treaty establishing the European Coal and Steel Community, arts 60–64 (now expired).

3   See the Treaty establishing the European Coal and Steel Community, art 61 (now expired).

4   Ie the Treaty on the Functioning of the European Union (Rome, 25 March 1957; TS 1 (1973); Cmnd 5179). The Treaty was formerly known as the Treaty establishing the European Community; it has been renamed and its provisions renumbered: see EUROPEAN UNION.

5   See the Treaty on the Functioning of the European Union (Rome, 25 March 1957; TS 1 (1973); Cmnd 5179). As to the control of prices see the Treaty on the Functioning of the European Union, art 173. As to rules on competition see arts 101-109; and COMPETITION vol 18 (2009) PARA 61 et seq. See also Council Regulation (EC) 405/2003 (OJ L 62, 6.3.2003, p 1–3) concerning Community monitoring of imports of hard coal originating in third countries.

### 359.   Mining consultants etc.

The right of freedom of establishment and freedom to provide services in respect of activities of self-employed persons in mining and quarrying[1], in prospecting and drilling for petroleum and natural gas[2] and in the coal trade[3] is provided for by directives of the Council of the European Communities.

1   See EC Council Directive 64/428 (OJ L117, 22.7.64, p 1871; S edn 1963–64 p 151).
2   See EC Council Directive 69/82 (OJ L68, 19.3.69, p 4; S edn 1969(I) p 111).
3   See EC Council Directive 70/522 (OJ L267, 11.12.70, p 14; S edn 1970(III) p 831); and EC Council Directive 70/523 (OJ L267, 11.12.70, p 18; S edn 1970(III) p 835).

## (2)  Rights Apart from Statute

### (i)  Absolute Owners

### 360.   Rights of working.

A tenant in fee simple may work mines[1] and dispose of the produce as he pleases, even though subject to an executory limitation over[2]. So, too, may a tenant in tail in possession, for he may at any time convert his tenancy in tail into an estate in fee simple[3]. Mines belonging to a mentally disordered person who is incapable of managing his property and affairs may be worked by his receiver under the direction of the court[4]; and special rules apply to ecclesiastical property[5]. Statutory companies, although they may be authorised to acquire mines, have no power to work them unless such power is expressly or impliedly conferred on them by the legislature[6].

1   As to the meaning of 'mine' see PARA 3.
2   See *Turner v Wright* (1860) 2 De GF & J 234; *Re Hanbury's Settled Estates* [1913] 2 Ch 357. As to the nature of executory limitations see generally REAL PROPERTY AND REGISTRATION vol 87 (2017) PARA 168.
        On the restructuring date (31 October 1994: see PARA 50) the exclusive right of searching for, boring for, working and getting coal in Great Britain, placed on the British Coal Corporation (formerly the National Coal Board) ceased, and the Corporation's interests in unworked coal and coal mines vested in the Coal Authority: see the Coal Industry Act 1994 s 7(2), (3); and PARA 66. As to the British Coal Corporation see PARAS 49–50; and as to the Coal Authority see PARA 52 et seq. As to the meaning of 'Great Britain' see PARA 48.
3   See *A-G v Duke of Marlborough* (1818) 3 Madd 498 at 532, 535. Under the law before 1926 the guardian of a tenant in tail who was a minor could exercise the right of working incident to the minor's estate: *Lyddal v Clavering* (1741) Amb 371n. As to minors' interests in land generally see CHILDREN AND YOUNG PERSONS vol 9 (2017) PARA 30 et seq.
4   *Ex p Tabbart* (1801) 6 Ves 428; and see MENTAL HEALTH AND CAPACITY.
5   See ECCLESIASTICAL LAW vol 34 (2011) PARA 818 et seq.
6   *Ecclesiastical Comrs for England v North Eastern Rly Co* (1877) 4 ChD 845; *Glasgow Corpn v Farie* (1888) 13 App Cas 657 at 697, HL, per Lord Macnaghten; and see also *A-G v Great Northern Rly Co* (1860) 1 Drew & Sm 154; and CORPORATIONS vol 24 (2010) PARA 424 et seq.

### 361.   Rights where ownership severed.

If the ownership of the mines[1] is severed from that of the surface, the owner of the mines has absolute powers of using as he may think fit the empty space from which minerals[2] have been worked (subject only to any statutory or common law restriction to the contrary)[3]; and, where for the purpose of properly working mines excepted from a grant, roads have been extended into the adjoining strata, such owner is entitled to use the roads for any purpose[4]. If the ownership of minerals only is severed, the owner of the minerals has no power to use the empty space except for the purpose of getting the remaining minerals[5].

1  As to the meaning of 'mine' see PARA 3.
2  As to the meaning of 'minerals' see PARA 10.
3  *Proud v Bates* (1865) 34 LJ Ch 406; *Duke of Hamilton v Graham* (1871) LR 2 Sc & Div 166; *Great Western Rly Co v Cefn Cribbwr Brick Co* [1894] 2 Ch 157 at 165 per Kekewich J.
4  *Batten Pooll v Kennedy* [1907] 1 Ch 256.
5  *Ramsay v Blair* (1876) 1 App Cas 701, HL.

## 362. Rights pending completion of sale.

As the purchaser is in equity the owner of the property comprised in a contract for sale from the date of the contract, the vendor, after the date of the contract, must not do anything to diminish its value[1]. If, therefore, a vendor delays completion and continues to work a mine[2] or quarry[3] for his own benefit, he is liable for so doing[4]. However, if the mine or quarry is open[5], the vendor may continue to work, or, if the property is leased, to receive the royalties, and to retain the proceeds of such working or the royalties, as ordinary rents and profits, during the period between the date of the contract and that fixed for completion[6] in the absence of any contrary stipulation in the contract of sale.

1  *Clarke v Ramuz* [1891] 2 QB 456 at 462, CA, per Kay LJ. See also CONVEYANCING vol 23 (2016) PARAS 59, 193.
2  As to the meaning of 'mine' see PARA 3.
3  As to the meaning of 'quarry' see PARA 4.
4  *Nelson v Bridges* (1839) 2 Beav 239 at 243 per Lord Langdale MR, where the vendor was held liable for the damage sustained by the defendant in his business as a stone dealer; *Brown v Dibbs* (1877) 25 WR 776, PC, where the vendor was held liable for the market value of the coal got, less the cost of severance and conveyance to the place of sale.
5  As to open mines see PARA 5 et seq.
6  *Leppington v Freeman* (1891) 66 LT 357, CA. See also CONVEYANCING vol 23 (2016) PARAS 59, 196. As to the liability of a purchaser who works the minerals before completion see PARA 300.

### (ii) Co-owners

## 363. Possible relations between co-owners.

Persons jointly interested in a mine[1] or quarry[2] may be legally related to each other in three different ways:

(1)   they may be merely co-owners of the property[3]; or
(2)   they may be co-owners of the property and partners in working it[4]; or
(3)   they may form a partnership, the mine or quarry itself being the partnership property[5].

1  As to the meaning of 'mine' see PARA 3.
2  As to the meaning of 'quarry' see PARA 4.
3  See PARA 364.
4  See PARA 365.
5  See PARA 366.

## 364. Co-owners of the property only.

Land held in co-ownership may be the subject either of a joint tenancy or of a tenancy in common. However, the only concurrent interest in land capable of existing at law is a joint tenancy; tenancies in common exist in equity only[1]. Where a legal estate (not being settled land) is held by joint tenants it is held in trust[2], but not so as to sever the joint tenancy in equity[3].

In the case of mines[4] to which persons are entitled as co-owners, each co-owner is entitled to enter and work provided he does not take more than his share or work wastefully[5]. If he takes more than his share he may be made liable in a claim for an account[6], but in such a claim he will be allowed the costs of severing the minerals[7] and bringing them to bank[8]. If there has been actual ouster, the person excluded may recover mesne profits[9]. In case of disagreement a receiver or manager will not be appointed, as this would involve working under the supervision of the court for an indefinite period[10]. In taking an account, one co-owner of a mine or quarry[11] who has worked with the consent of the others will be given allowances for necessaries[12]. Any co-owner may assign his share without the consent of the others[13], but a sale of the legal estate in the mine or any part of it must be carried out by the trustees in whom the legal estate is vested[14]. The trustees have a power to partition[15].

1  See the Law of Property Act 1925 ss 1(6), 34(1), 36(2); and REAL PROPERTY AND REGISTRATION vol 87 (2017) PARAS 43, 205 et seq, 218. The legal estate is held in trust for the persons interested in the land: see s 34(2); and REAL PROPERTY AND REGISTRATION vol 87 (2017) PARA 218.

2  Ie as if the persons beneficially entitled were tenants in common.

3  See the Law of Property Act 1925 s 36(1); and REAL PROPERTY AND REGISTRATION vol 87 (2017) PARA 197.

4  As to the meaning of 'mine' see PARA 3.

5  *Job v Potton* (1875) LR 20 Eq 84. See also *Glyn v Howell* [1909] 1 Ch 666 at 677 per Eve J; *Wilkinson v Haygarth* (1847) 12 QB 837 (on appeal (1848) 12 QB 851, Ex Ch).

6  *Denys v Shuckburgh* (1840) 4 Y & C Ex 42; *Bentley v Bates* (1840) 4 Y & C Ex 182; *Re Smith (a lunatic)* (1874) 10 Ch App 79; *Adair v New River Co Ltd and Metropolitan Water Board* (1908) 25 TLR 193 at 196, CA, per Farwell LJ (affd sub nom *Metropolitan Water Board v Adair and New River Co* (1911) 27 TLR 253, HL).
    On an application for an order under the Trusts of Land and Appointment of Trustees Act 1996 s 14 (see TRUSTS AND POWERS vol 98 (2013) PARA 479) the court may make any such order relating to the exercise by the trustees of any of their functions (including an order relieving them of any obligation to obtain the consent of, or to consult, any person in connection with the exercise of any of their functions), or declaring the nature or extent of a person's interest in property subject to the trust, as the court thinks fit: see s 14(2). As to the rights of a beneficiary under a trust see generally TRUSTS AND POWERS vol 98 (2013) PARA 1 et seq.

7  As to the meaning of 'minerals' see PARA 10.

8  *Roberts v Eberhardt* (1853) Kay 148.

9  *Denys v Shuckburgh* (1840) 4 Y & C Ex 42.

10  *Roberts v Eberhardt* (1853) Kay 148; cf *Jefferys v Smith* (1820) 1 Jac & W 298. If necessary an interim receiver and manager will be appointed where the mine has been worked in partnership and the partnership has been dissolved and the mine ordered to be sold: *Lees v Jones* (1857) 3 Jur NS 954.

11  As to the meaning of 'quarry' see PARA 4.

12  *Scott v Nesbitt* (1808) 14 Ves 438. In this respect the rights of a co-owner of a mine or quarry are more favourable than those of co-owners of other types of property: see *Scott v Nesbitt*.

13  *Bentley v Bates* (1840) 4 Y & C Ex 182 at 186, 191 per Lord Abinger CB.

14  As to the general power of trustees see the Trusts of Land and Appointment of Trustees Act 1996 s 6; and SETTLEMENTS vol 91 (2012) PARA 804. As from 1 January 1997 no new settlements can be created under the Settled Land Act 1925. As to the phasing out of strict settlements and the introduction of the 'trust of land' see the Trusts of Land and Appointment of Trustees Act 1996 s 2(1); and PARA 282.

15  The trustees of land may, where beneficiaries of full age are absolutely entitled in undivided shares to land subject to the trust, partition the land, or any part of it, and provide (by way of mortgage or otherwise) for the payment of any equality money (Trusts of Land and Appointment of Trustees

Act 1996 s 7(1)). See further REAL PROPERTY AND REGISTRATION vol 87 (2017) PARA 230. See also *Re Thomas, Thomas v Thompson* [1930] 1 Ch 194; *Re Brooker, Public Trustee v Young* [1934] Ch 610 (discussing similar provision made by the Law of Property Act 1925 s 28(3) (repealed)). On an application for an order under the Trusts of Land and Appointment of Trustees Act 1996 s 14 (see TRUSTS AND POWERS vol 98 (2013) PARA 479) the court may make an order relieving the trustees of any obligation to obtain the consent of any person in connection with the exercise of any of their functions: see s 14(2). As to the power of the court to authorise dealings with trust property see the Trustee Act 1925 s 57; and *Re Beale's Settlement Trusts, Huggins v Beale* [1932] 2 Ch 15. See further EQUITABLE JURISDICTION vol 47 (2014) PARA 67; REAL PROPERTY AND REGISTRATION; TRUSTS AND POWERS vol 98 (2013) PARA 1 et seq.

### 365. Co-owners of the property and partners in the profits.

All property and rights and interests in property originally brought into the partnership stock or acquired, whether by purchase or otherwise, on account of the firm, or for the purposes and in the course of the partnership business, are called in the Partnership Act 1890 partnership property, and must be held and applied by the partners exclusively for the purposes of the partnership and in accordance with the partnership agreement[1].

However, co-ownership of land does not of itself create a partnership, whether or not the tenants share the profits[2], and where mines[3] are held in co-ownership the co-owners may constitute themselves partners in the business enterprise without the land and minerals[4] becoming partnership property[5].

In such circumstances each partner is entitled to take part in the working so long as he works properly and does not obstruct or interfere with the others[6]; and he may maintain an action for an account against the others without seeking a dissolution[7], but if a dissolution is not sought a receiver or manager will not in general be appointed[8]. However, if dissolution is asked for, a receiver will be appointed on an interim application, provided the applicant shows exclusion or interference[9]. Each partner who has incurred expense in working or preserving the mine is entitled to be recouped out of profits before any division is made[10]. If one partner becomes indebted to the partnership the others will have a lien on his share for the amount of that indebtedness[11]. Each partner may transfer his equitable interest in the mine without the consent of the other owners[12].

If two tenants in common of a mine at their joint expense construct a shaft on land belonging to one of them, money paid by a stranger as wayleave belongs to both[13].

1 Partnership Act 1890 s 20(1); see *Crawshay v Collins* (1808) 15 Ves 218; and PARTNERSHIP vol 79 (2014) PARAS 115, 118.
2 See the Partnership Act 1890 s 2(1); and PARTNERSHIP vol 79 (2014) PARA 9. See also *Fereday v Wightwick* (1829) 1 Russ & M 45 (mines leased and worked as a partnership).
3 As to the meaning of 'mine' see PARA 3.
4 As to the meaning of 'minerals' see PARA 10.
5 *Steward v Blakeway* (1869) 4 Ch App 603; *Davis v Davis* [1894] 1 Ch 393 at 401–402 per North J (although in that case no land was acquired by the partners); and see PARTNERSHIP vol 79 (2014) PARA 117. Where co-owners of an estate or interest in any land, or in Scotland of any heritable estate, not being itself partnership property, are partners as to profits made by the use of that land or estate, and purchase other land or estate out of the profits to be used in like manner, the land or estate so purchased belongs to them, in the absence of an agreement to the contrary, not as partners, but as co-owners for the same respective estates and interests as are held by them in the land or estate first mentioned at the date of the purchase: Partnership Act 1890 s 20(3); and see PARTNERSHIP vol 79 (2014) PARA 117.
6 *Jefferys v Smith* (1820) 1 Jac & W 298; *Roberts v Eberhardt* (1853) Kay 148.
7 *Bentley v Bates* (1840) 4 Y & C Ex 182.
8 See *Roberts v Eberhardt* (1853) Kay 148; and PARTNERSHIP vol 79 (2014) PARA 162; RECEIVERS.

9  *Roberts v Eberhardt* (1853) Kay 148; *Lees v Jones* (1857) 3 Jur NS 954.
10 *Roberts v Eberhardt* (1853) Kay 148.
11 *Fereday v Wightwick* (1829) 1 Russ & M 45; *Crawshay v Maule* (1818) 1 Swan 495.
12 See PARA 366; and *Bentley v Bates* (1840) 4 Y & C Ex 182.
13 *Clegg v Clegg* (1861) 3 Giff 322.

### 366.  Partners in the property and in the profits.

If co-owners are partners both in the mine[1] and in the profits their relations generally are regulated by the law of partnership[2].

Each partner is entitled to take part in the working so long as he acts with due regard to the rights of the other partners[3], and each may bind the others by incurring debts for wages, goods and supplies necessary for carrying on the mine[4], but not by drawing, making, accepting or indorsing bills of exchange or promissory notes[5] (which are not governed by the same rules as ordinary contracts not under seal). A partner is entitled to be repaid money advanced by him for the purpose of carrying on the business[6], but it seems that, in the absence of express authority, a partner in a mining partnership is not entitled to borrow money on the credit of the partnership[7].

All proper expenses in working or preserving the mine ought to be deducted from the profits before any division is made[8], and each partner is liable to contribute in case of loss[9], unless the loss is caused by the improper conduct of some members of the partnership[10].

A partner may transfer his share either absolutely or by way of mortgage, but the rights of the transferee will be those of an equitable part owner, including the right to an account, and not those of a partner[11], unless by express or tacit agreement he is accepted as a partner by the other partners[12]. A mortgagee may enforce his security by foreclosure, and in a claim for foreclosure he may obtain an account as at the date of the issue of the writ, but he may not contest any dealings with capital or profits or object to the management of the mine before that date[13]. If a person who is a mortgagee of a share becomes also a partner, his rights as mortgagee will be modified by the obligations he assumes toward the other partners[14]. Although a purchaser may not be accepted as a partner the purchaser as cestui que trust is personally bound to indemnify the vendor as trustee from the liabilities of the trust property[15].

Any partner in a claim for dissolution, and in some special cases without asking for dissolution[16], is entitled on interim application to the appointment of a receiver and manager if he can show mismanagement or exclusion[17].

1  As to the meaning of 'mine' see PARA 3.
2  As to the law of partnership generally see PARTNERSHIP.
3  *Rowe v Wood* (1822) 2 Jac & W 553; *Roberts v Eberhardt* (1853) Kay 148. As to the duty of partners to render accounts, etc see the Partnership Act 1890 s 28; and PARTNERSHIP vol 79 (2014) PARA 134.
4  *Re German Mining Co, ex p Chippendale* (1853) 4 De GM & G 19. As to the power of partners to bind the firm see the Partnership Act 1890 s 5; and PARTNERSHIP vol 79 (2014) PARA 39.
5  *Ducarrey v Gill* (1830) Mood & M 450; *Bentley v Bates* (1840) 4 Y & C Ex 182 at 191 per Lord Abinger CB; *Thicknesse v Bromilow* (1832) 2 Cr & J 425; *Brown v Byers* (1847) 16 LJ Ex 112; and see *Bottomley v Nuttall* (1858) 5 CBNS 122. A partner who signs a bill on behalf of the partnership is personally liable on it: *Brown v Byers*. As to acquiescence by a partner see *Harrison v Heathorn* (1843) 12 LJCP 282. As to partners bound by acts on behalf of the firm see the Partnership Act 1890 s 6; and PARTNERSHIP vol 79 (2014) PARA 52. As to signature essential to liability see the Bills of Exchange Act 1882 s 23(2).
6  *Re German Mining Co, ex p Chippendale* (1853) 4 De GM & G 19. If one partner becomes indebted to the partnership, the others have a lien on his share for the amount of the debt: see PARA 365.

7 *Burmester v Norris* (1851) 21 LJ Ex 43; *Ducarrey v Gill* (1830) Mood & M 450; *Re German Mining Co, ex p Chippendale* (1853) 4 De GM & G 19; *Brown v Kidger* (1858) 28 LJ Ex 66. These cases all were decided on the principle that borrowing is not strictly necessary for business. It is submitted that the continued application of that principle to a similar case may be considered doubtful considering the significant capital requirements of mining.

8 *Roberts v Eberhardt* (1853) Kay 148.

9 *Re German Mining Co, ex p Chippendale* (1853) 4 De GM & G 19.

10 *Thomas v Atherton* (1878) 10 ChD 185, CA. 'Prima facie, damages given against one partner for a partnership act are to be paid like any other partnership debt, but with this exception, that if the damages were occasioned by the personal misconduct or culpable negligence of one partner, he alone must bear the consequences': *Thomas v Atherton* at 199 per James LJ.

11 *Bentley v Bates* (1840) 4 Y & C Ex 182; *Redmayne v Forster* (1866) LR 2 Eq 467; and see the Partnership Act 1890 s 31; and MORTGAGE vol 77 (2016) PARA 138.

12 See *Jefferys v Smith* (1827) 3 Russ 158; *Crawshay v Maule* (1818) 1 Swan 495.

13 *Redmayne v Forster* (1866) LR 2 Eq 467, where, as the other partners had a right of pre-emption, it was held that they were necessary parties to the action for foreclosure.

14 *Rowe v Wood* (1822) 2 Jac & W 553.

15 *Dodson v Downey* [1901] 2 Ch 620 at 623 per Farwell J.

16 Eg on the ground of danger to the property: see *Sheppard v Oxenford* (1855) 1 K & J 491.

17 *Roberts v Eberhardt* (1853) Kay 148; and see *Hall v Hall* (1850) 3 Mac & G 79 (where the appointment of a receiver and manager was refused). As to powers of the High Court with respect to injunctions and receivers see the Senior Courts Act 1981 s 37; and CIVIL PROCEDURE vol 12 (2015) PARA 1077 et seq; RECEIVERS vol 88 (2012) PARA 13 et seq. As to remedies available in county courts see the County Courts Act 1984 s 38; and COURTS AND TRIBUNALS vol 24 (2010) PARA 768.

## 367. Effect of laches.

Having regard particularly to the speculative nature of mining property, a person claiming to assert an equitable right with regard to such property, as to a share in a renewed lease[1], must apply for relief promptly, otherwise he will be refused on the ground of laches[2]. However, this rule is not applicable if the applicant has been refused information necessary to enable him to decide what course to adopt[3].

Laches is not, however, sufficient to bar a legal right[4]. Abandonment must be shown[5], but abandonment has been presumed from a delay amounting to six years[6].

1 A partner renewing in his own name a lease of the partnership is a trustee of the new lease for the partnership: *Featherstonhaugh v Fenwick* (1810) 17 Ves 298; *Clegg v Fishwick* (1849) 1 Mac & G 294; *Clegg v Edmondson* (1857) 8 De GM & G 787; *Clements v Hall* (1858) 2 De G & J 173; and see PARTNERSHIP vol 79 (2014) PARAS 108, 115 et seq.

2 *Senhouse v Christian* (1795) 19 Beav 356n; *Norway v Rowe* (1812) 19 Ves 144; *Prendergast v Turton* (1841) 1 Y & C Ch Cas 98 (affd (1843) 13 LJ Ch 268); *Clegg v Edmondson* (1857) 8 De GM & G 787; and see *Nelson v Rye* [1996] 2 All ER 186, [1996] 1 WLR 1378. The court is likely to take into account the considerable expenditure involved (*Senhouse v Christian*) even where the mining operation is self-financing (*Clegg v Edmondson*).

3 *Clements v Hall* (1858) 2 De G & J 173.

4 *Clarke and Chapman v Hart* (1858) 6 HL Cas 633; and see *Kershaw v Whelan (No 2)* (1997) 141 Sol Jo LB 37.

5 *Clarke and Chapman v Hart* (1858) 6 HL Cas 633; *Palmer v Moore* [1900] AC 293, PC.

6 *Rule v Jewell* (1881) 18 ChD 660; and see EQUITABLE JURISDICTION vol 47 (2014) PARA 262.

## (iii) Limited Owners

## 368. Working of mines and waste.

The rights of limited owners are governed by the doctrine of waste[1]. Prima facie, working new or unopened mines or quarries[2] is waste, but working open mines is not waste: it is enjoyment of the profits of the estate[3]. The right to commit waste is not incident to the equitable interest of a tenant for life[4] or the estate of a tenant for years[5]. Consequently, in the absence of express provision contained in the instrument under which their interests arise, tenants for life[6] and tenants for years[7] may work open mines, but may not dig in new mines except for the purposes of repairs, improvements or the like[8].

As from 1 January 1997 no new settlements can be created under the Settled Land Act 1925[9].

1 Co Litt 53b. As to waste see generally LANDLORD AND TENANT vol 62 (2016) PARA 324 et seq; SETTLEMENTS vol 91 (2012) PARA 887 et seq.
2 As to whether a mine is open or unopen see *Chaytor v Trotter* (1902) 87 LT 33, CA. As to the meaning of 'mine' see PARA 3; and as to the meaning of 'quarry' see PARA 4. As to open mines see PARA 5 et seq.
3 Co Litt 54b; *Campbell v Wardlaw* (1883) 8 App Cas 641 at 645, HL, per Lord Blackburn, and at 650 per Lord Watson; *Dashwood v Magniac* [1891] 3 Ch 306 at 327, CA, per Chitty J, at 360–361 per Bowen LJ, and at 384–385 per Kay LJ, dissenting.
4 Co Litt 54b; *Whitfield v Bewit* (1724) 2 P Wms 240; *Viner v Vaughan* (1840) 2 Beav 466.
5 Co Litt 54b; *Saunders's Case* (1599) 5 Co Rep 12a; *Clegg v Rowland* (1866) LR 2 Eq 160; *Elias v Snowdon Slate Quarries Co* (1879) 4 App Cas 454, HL. It is immaterial that the term is of great duration: see *Elias v Griffith* (1878) 8 ChD 521, CA.
6 *Saunders's Case* (1599) 5 Co Rep 12a; *Clavering v Clavering* (1726) 2 P Wms 388; *Campbell v Leach* (1775) Amb 740; *Viner v Vaughan* (1840) 2 Beav 466; *Dickin v Hamer* (1860) 1 Drew & Sm 284; *Bagot v Bagot, Legge v Legge* (1863) 32 Beav 509; *Campbell v Wardlaw* (1883) 8 App Cas 641, HL; *Dashwood v Magniac* [1891] 3 Ch 306, CA.
7 *Saunders's Case* (1599) 5 Co Rep 12a; *Astry v Ballard* (1677) 2 Mod Rep 193; *Clegg v Rowland* (1866) LR 2 Eq 160; *Elias v Snowdon Slate Quarries Co* (1879) 4 App Cas 454, HL.
8 Co Litt 53b.
9 As to the phasing out of strict settlements and the introduction of the 'trust of land' see the Trusts of Land and Appointment of Trustees Act 1996 s 2(1); and PARA 282.

## 369. Right to profit from open mines.

In conformity with the principles as to waste[1] a tenant for life is entitled to receive the profits from mines[2] worked under a demise made[3] or contracted to be made[4] by the settlor, or made in exercise of powers given by the settlor[5] (or by the Settled Land Act 1925[6], subject to the statutory limitations), or derived from workings of open mines by the trustees of the settlement[7]. If minerals[8] have been worked in and under land held by a tenant for life or years, or at will, the tenant may use the empty space created by the working in any manner he chooses[9].

Where mines are included in a residuary devise of realty, a tenant for life is entitled to the profits so long as the mines are properly retained unconverted by the trustees[10]. However, if an interest in mines of the nature of personal property, such as shares in a mining company[11], is included in a residuary bequest, it is a question of construction of the will[12] whether the property is to be enjoyed in specie[13] or notionally converted and interest paid upon the value[14].

As from 1 January 1997 no new settlements can be created under the Settled Land Act 1925[15].

1 See PARA 368.
2 As to the meaning of 'mine' see PARA 3.
3 *Spencer v Scurr* (1862) 31 Beav 334; *Miller v Miller* (1872) LR 13 Eq 263.
4 *Re Kemeys-Tynte, Kemeys-Tynte v Kemeys-Tynte* [1892] 2 Ch 211.
5 *Daly v Beckett* (1857) 24 Beav 114; *Re North, Garton v Cumberland* [1909] 1 Ch 625; *Chaytor v Trotter* (1902) 87 LT 33, CA.
6 See the Settled Land Act 1925 s 47; and SETTLEMENTS vol 91 (2012) PARA 744.
7 *Earl Cowley v Wellesley* (1866) LR 1 Eq 656.
8 As to the meaning of 'minerals' see PARA 10.
9 *Lewis v Branthwaite* (1831) 2 B & Ad 437; *Keyse v Powell* (1853) 2 E & B 132; *Milne v Taylor* (1850) 16 LTOS 172.

10  *Re Earl of Darnley, Clifton v Darnley* [1907] 1 Ch 159; *Miller v Miller* (1872) LR 13 Eq 263; and see *Wentworth v Wentworth* [1900] AC 163, PC; *Re Oliver, Wilson v Oliver* [1908] 2 Ch 74 at 78 per Warrington J.
11  *Re Bates, Hodgson v Bates* [1906] WN 191.
12  As to the construction of wills see generally WILLS AND INTESTACY vol 102 (2016) PARA 185 et seq.
13  *Re Bates, Hodgson v Bates* [1906] WN 191 (enjoyment in specie).
14  *Re Woods, Gabellini v Woods* [1904] 2 Ch 4; *Re Chaytor, Chaytor v Horn* [1905] 1 Ch 233. As to the rate of interest, and as to the adjustment of the rights as between tenant for life and remainderman see WILLS AND INTESTACY vol 103 (2016) PARA 1118 et seq. This adjustment does not seem to apply to property as to which a person dies wholly or partially intestate: see the Administration of Estates Act 1925 s 33(5); and WILLS AND INTESTACY vol 103 (2016) PARA 1138.
15  As to the phasing out of strict settlements and the introduction of the 'trust of land' see the Trusts of Land and Appointment of Trustees Act 1996 s 2(1); and PARA 282.

### 370.  Settlement containing special provisions.

The rights of a tenant for life may be varied by the instrument under which he holds from those normally incident to his interest. Thus he may be restrained from working open mines[1], or may, by being a tenant for life without impeachment of waste, be enabled to open new mines[2]. The fact that a settlement contains an express grant of land and mines to the trustees does not enlarge the powers of the tenant for life with regard to mines[3].

As from 1 January 1997 no new settlements can be created under the Settled Land Act 1925[4].

1  *Ferrand v Wilson* (1845) 15 LJ Ch 41. As to the meaning of 'mine' see PARA 3. As to open mines see PARA 5 et seq.
2  *Campbell v Wardlaw* (1883) 8 App Cas 641, HL; *Re Ridge, Hellard v Moody* (1885) 31 ChD 504, CA. But a limited owner, although unimpeachable for waste, may not commit equitable waste: *Bishop of London v Web* (1718) 1 P Wms 527; *Rowe v Wood* (1822) 2 Jac & W 553. See further *Re Hodgkinson, Hodgkinson v Hodgkinson* (1924) 132 LT 526. As to equitable waste see EQUITABLE JURISDICTION vol 47 (2014) PARA 80; SETTLEMENTS vol 91 (2012) PARA 898.
3  *Whitfield v Bewit* (1724) 2 P Wms 240.
4  As to the phasing out of strict settlements and the introduction of the 'trust of land' see the Trusts of Land and Appointment of Trustees Act 1996 s 2(1); and PARA 282. As to the exclusion and restriction of powers see s 8; and TRUSTS AND POWERS vol 98 (2013) PARA 476.

### 371.  Powers of tenant for years.

Similarly, the rights of a tenant for years may be varied by the lease under which he holds. If the lease expressly grants 'all mines' he may work new mines[1]; if it grants land with the mines in it, and the land contains both open and unopened mines, the lessee may only work the opened mines; however, if there are no open mines, he may open new ones[2]. An exception of 'all royalties' in a lease of land does not diminish the tenant's power to work open mines[3]. The rights of a tenant for years may be extended by custom[4], or by the High Court after a preliminary application to the Secretary of State[5] for the purpose[6].

As from 1 January 1997 no new settlements can be created under the Settled Land Act 1925[7].

1  As to the meaning of 'mine' see PARA 3.
2  *Saunders's Case* (1599) 5 Co Rep 12a; *Clegg v Rowland* (1866) LR 2 Eq 160; *Dashwood v Magniac* [1891] 3 Ch 306, CA. As to open mines see PARA 5 et seq.
3  *Brown v Chadwick* (1857) 7 ICLR 101; *Countess of Listowel v Gibbings* (1858) 9 ICLR 223.
4  *Tucker v Linger* (1883) 8 App Cas 508, HL. See generally CUSTOM AND USAGE.
5  As to the Secretary of State see PARA 2.
6  See PARA 380 et seq.

7   As to the phasing out of strict settlements and the introduction of the 'trust of land' see the Trusts
    of Land and Appointment of Trustees Act 1996 s 2(1); and PARA 282.

## 372.  Meliorating waste.

A limited owner may be free from liability if his workings, although technically
waste, have in fact improved the land[1]. A tenant for life may not, however,
deliberately commit waste on the plea that improvement is his object[2].

As from 1 January 1997 no new settlements can be created under the Settled
Land Act 1925[3].

1   See generally *Doherty v Allman* (1878) 3 App Cas 709, HL; LANDLORD AND TENANT vol 62
    (2016) PARA 325; SETTLEMENTS.
2   *Coppinger v Gubbins* (1846) 3 Jo & Lat 397; *Harris v Ekins* (1872) 20 WR 999.
3   As to the phasing out of strict settlements and the introduction of the 'trust of land' see the Trusts
    of Land and Appointment of Trustees Act 1996 s 2(1); and PARA 282.

## 373.  Ownership of minerals improperly worked.

If minerals[1] are improperly worked by a limited owner, the minerals so severed,
or their value, belong to the first person beneficially entitled in fee simple in
possession. If at the time of working there is a person in existence beneficially
entitled in fee simple, the severed minerals immediately become his property[2],
even if his equitable interest is defeasible[3], and even if, between his interest and
that of the person in possession, a life interest without impeachment of waste is
interposed[4]. If at the time of working there is no such person in existence, the
proceeds of the severed minerals are invested and the income accumulated during
the life of the wrongdoer, and after his death the income of the aggregate fund will
be paid to the persons, if any, successively entitled, whether with or without
impeachment of waste, to limited interests in the estate until some person becomes
beneficially entitled to the fee simple in possession[5].

1   As to the meaning of 'minerals' see PARA 10.
2   *Whitfield v Bewit* (1724) 2 P Wms 240; *Bewick v Whitfield* (1734) 3 P Wms 267 at 268; *Bell v
    Wilson* (1866) 1 Ch App 303; *Re Barrington, Gamlen v Lyon* (1886) 33 ChD 523.
3   See *Re Cavendish, Cavendish v Mundy* [1877] WN 198.
4   *Pigot v Bullock* (1792) 1 Ves 479 at 484; *Re Barrington, Gamlen v Lyon* (1886) 33 ChD 523.
5   *Bagot v Bagot, Legge v Legge* (1863) 32 Beav 509; and see *Gresley v Mousley* (1862) 3 De G F
    & J 433.

## 374.  Remedies for improper working.

If minerals[1] are improperly worked, the owner of the severed minerals may
bring a claim for conversion[2] or for an account[3]. A claim for account will lie even
where the claimant is not entitled to an injunction[4], and is also available against
the estate of a deceased wrongdoer[5]. Further, if the claimant has not disentitled
himself by his own conduct[6], the remedy by injunction is available[7], even if the
injury is only threatened[8]. The same remedies are available in the case of equitable
waste[9].

If there is collusion between a limited owner and a remainderman these
remedies may be utilised by trustees to preserve contingent remainders and to
protect the interests of persons not in esse entitled to intermediate interests[10].

The lapse of six years normally operates to bar the remedy[11].

1   As to the meaning of 'minerals' see PARA 10.
2   *Clavering v Clavering* (1729) Mos 219; and see *Re Barrington, Gamlen v Lyon* (1886) 33 ChD
    523. See also the Torts (Interference with Goods) Act 1977; PARA 33; and TORT vol 97 (2015)
    PARA 604 et seq.

3  *Jesus College v Bloom* (1745) Amb 54; *Garth v Cotton* (1753) 3 Atk 751 at 753, 756 per Lord
Hardwicke LC; *Parrott v Palmer* (1834) 3 My & K 632; *Bagot v Bagot, Legge v Legge* (1863) 32
Beav 509; *Wright v Pitt* (1870) LR 12 Eq 408. As to the power to award interest on debts and
damages see the Senior Courts Act 1981 s 35A; the County Courts Act 1984 s 69; COURTS AND
TRIBUNALS vol 24 (2010) PARA 701; and DAMAGES vol 29 (2014) PARA 635. As to the claim for
an account see PARA 33; and EQUITABLE JURISDICTION vol 47 (2014) PARA 49 et seq.
4  See *Jesus College v Bloom* (1745) Amb 54.
5  *Bagot v Bagot, Legge v Legge* (1863) 32 Beav 509. See the Law Reform (Miscellaneous Provisions)
Act 1934 s 1; and WILLS AND INTESTACY vol 103 (2016) PARAS 1212 et seq, 1277 et seq.
6  *Burrowes v Hayes* (1834) Hayes & Jo 597.
7  *Flamang's Case* (circa 1783), cited in *Hanson v Gardiner* (1802) 7 Ves 305 at 308; *Viner v
Vaughan* (1840) 2 Beav 466 at 469 per Lord Langdale MR; *Ferrand v Wilson* (1845) 4 Hare 344
at 388. The court is unwilling to grant an interim injunction in the case of mines actually being
worked: *Clavering v Clavering* (1726) 2 P Wms 388 at 389 per King LC. As to the remedy of
injunction generally see CIVIL PROCEDURE vol 12 (2015) PARA 1098 et seq. See also PARA 36.
8  *Gibson v Smith* (1741) 2 Atk 182.
9  *Bishop of London v Web* (1718) 1 P Wms 527.
10  *Garth v Cotton* (1753) 3 Atk 751.
11  See PARA 45.

### 375. Reversioners and remaindermen.

A reversioner or remainderman is not entitled to work mines[1]. If he does in fact
work them, the tenant for life is probably entitled to have the proceeds invested
and to be paid the income arising from them, but he may, by his conduct, disentitle
himself to any benefit[2].

1  *Dickin v Hamer* (1860) 1 Drew & Sm 284. See also *Doherty v Allman* (1878) 3 App Cas 709 at
734, HL, per Lord Blackburn. As to interests in reversion generally see REAL PROPERTY AND
REGISTRATION vol 87 (2017) PARA 156 et seq. As to the meaning of 'mine' see PARA 3.
2  *Dickin v Hamer* (1860) 1 Drew & Sm 284 at 298 per Kindersley V-C.

### (iv) Fiduciary Owners, Mortgagors and Mortgagees

### 376. Powers of trustees and personal representatives.

If and as long as any person who is entitled to a beneficial interest in possession
affecting land is a minor[1], or any person is contingently entitled to land, the
trustees appointed for the purpose by the settlement[2] may enter into and continue
in possession of the land on his behalf[3]. The trustees manage or superintend the
management of the land, and have full power to continue the working of mines[4],
minerals[5] and quarries[6] which have usually been worked[7]. In dealing with the real
and personal estate of the deceased his personal representatives, for the purposes
of administration or during the minority of any beneficiary or the subsistence of
any life interest or until the period of distribution arrives, have powers of
management[8]. As from 1 January 1997 no new settlements can be created under
the Settled Land Act 1925[9].

Apart from these provisions trustees are not entitled, except in the execution of
powers conferred upon them by the document constituting the trust, to work
mines or quarries[10].

1  As to the age of majority see the Family Law Reform Act 1969 s 1; and CHILDREN AND YOUNG
PERSONS vol 9 (2017) PARA 1.
2  In the case of a strict settlement if no trustees are so appointed, the settlement trustees may act
unless the settlement or court order by which they or their predecessors were appointed expressly
provides to the contrary: Settled Land Act 1925 s 102(1). If there are no settlement trustees, the
court may appoint trustees to act: s 102(1). As to the appointment and retirement of trustees in the
case of a trust of land see the Trusts of Land and Appointment of Trustees Act 1996 ss 19, 20; and
TRUSTS AND POWERS vol 98 (2013) PARAS 285, 286, 337.

3   See the Settled Land Act 1925 s 102(1), (5); and CHILDREN AND YOUNG PERSONS vol 9 (2017)
    PARAS 54–55. As to the general power of trustees in the case of a trust of land see the Trusts of
    Land and Appointment of Trustees Act 1996 s 6; and TRUSTS AND POWERS vol 98 (2013)
    PARA 476.
4   As to the meaning of 'mine' see PARA 3.
5   As to the meaning of 'minerals' see PARA 10.
6   As to the meaning of 'quarry' see PARA 4.
7   See the Settled Land Act 1925 s 102(2)(c). Where a minor is impeachable for waste, the trustees
    must not commit waste: see s 102(2).
8   As to the powers of management see the Administration of Estates Act 1925 s 39; and WILLS AND
    INTESTACY vol 103 (2016) PARA 1019 et seq.
9   As to the phasing out of strict settlements and the introduction of the 'trust of land' see the Trusts
    of Land and Appointment of Trustees Act 1996 s 2(1); and PARA 282.
10  As to the powers of trustees generally see TRUSTS AND POWERS vol 98 (2013) PARA 411 et seq.

### 377. Mortgagors.

A mortgagor in possession may be restrained from committing waste if the security is insufficient[1], and if he opens a new mine or quarry the opening will enure for the benefit of the mortgagee[2].

1   *Farrant v Lovel* (1750) 3 Atk 723; *King v Smith* (1843) 2 Hare 239; and see MORTGAGE vol 77
    (2016) PARA 360.
2   *Elias v Snowdon Slate Quarries Co* (1879) 4 App Cas 454, HL. If the mines are being worked at
    the time when the mortgagee takes possession, he is, it seems, bound to continue the workings in
    the ordinary course: *Rowe v Wood* (1822) 2 Jac & W 553 at 555, 556 per Lord Eldon LC;
    *Gloucester County Bank v Rudry Merthyr Steam and House Coal Colliery Co* [1895] 1 Ch 629,
    CA.

### 378. Mortgagees.

A mortgagee in possession may work open mines[1] but he is not bound to make any greater expenditure on them than would be made by a prudent owner[2]. If the security is insufficient he may open and work new mines, but not otherwise[3], and the burden of showing that the security is insufficient is on the mortgagee[4]. If a mortgagee who is not entitled to do so works mines he will be charged with the gross receipts and disallowed his expenses[5], and he may be charged an occupation rent[6]; and persons working by his authority may be jointly liable with him[7]. If, on the other hand, the working is justified, the mortgagee is chargeable only with the net profits[8]. In any case a mortgagee who opens mines speculates at his own hazard, and cannot throw any part of a loss upon the mortgagor[9].

Whether or not his security is insufficient, a mortgagee in possession will be restrained from working mines wastefully or improperly[10], and, if mismanagement is proved, a receiver or manager may be appointed by the court[11], and the mortgagee may be made liable for damage caused by his improper working[12].

1   See PARA 377. As to the meaning of 'mine' see PARA 3. As to open mines see PARA 5 et seq.
2   *Rowe v Wood* (1822) 2 Jac & W 553. As to his rights in respect of permanent improvements see
    *Tipton Green Colliery Co v Tipton Moat Colliery Co* (1877) 7 Ch D 192.
3   *Millett v Davey* (1862) 31 Beav 470. A mortgagee may, of course, be expressly authorised to work
    by the mortgage deed: see eg *Norton v Cooper* (1854) 5 De GM & G 728.
4   *Millett v Davey* (1862) 31 Beav 470. The fact that interest is in arrear is important in enabling the
    mortgagee to justify his working: *Millett v Davey* at 473 per Romilly MR.
5   *Thorneycroft v Crockett* (1848) 16 Sim 445; *Hood v Easton* (1854) 2 Giff 692.
6   *Thorneycroft v Crockett* (1848) 16 Sim 445.
7   *Hood v Easton* (1854) 2 Giff 692.
8   *Millett v Davey* (1862) 31 Beav 470.
9   *Hughes v Williams* (1806) 12 Ves 493; *Rowe v Wood* (1822) 2 Jac & W 553.
10  *Millett v Davey* (1862) 31 Beav 470; and see MORTGAGE vol 77 (2016) PARA 438 et seq.

11 *Rowe v Wood* (1822) 2 Jac & W 553; and see RECEIVERS vol 88 (2012) PARA 185.
12 *Taylor v Mostyn* (1886) 33 ChD 226, CA, where the mortgagee was also lessee, and was held liable to be charged in the mortgage action for breaches of covenant under the lease.

### (v) Public Authorities

**379. Powers of public authorities to take minerals.**

Highway authorities have the right to dig and gather materials for the purpose of repairing roads out of and from commons, and also in some cases from inclosed land which is not of a strictly private nature[1].

Railway and other authorities[2] have special powers in respect of getting materials for the construction of railways and other works[3]; and water and sewerage authorities and the Environment Agency[4] have similar powers[5].

1 See HIGHWAYS, STREETS AND BRIDGES.
2 See PARA 135.
3 See PARAS 135, 142.
4 As to the Environment Agency see ENVIRONMENTAL QUALITY AND PUBLIC HEALTH vol 45 (2010) PARA 68 et seq; WATER AND WATERWAYS vol 100 (2018) PARA 23.
5 As to mineral rights see the Water Industry Act 1991 s 188, Sch 14; the Water Resources Act 1991 s 182, Sch 23; and WATER AND WATERWAYS vol 101 (2018) PARA 758 et seq.

# (3) Statutory Rights of Working

## (i) Mines (Working Facilities and Support) Act 1966

### A. RIGHTS, RESTRICTIONS AND SAVINGS

**380. The legislation.**

In addition to the rights which exist at common law[1], rights of working minerals[2], including rights to ancillary facilities, are provided for by statute. Thus extensive rights of searching for and working minerals may be granted under the Mines (Working Facilities and Support) Act 1966[3]. There is also power to work minerals under the Atomic Energy Act 1946[4], and power to search, bore for and get petroleum under the Petroleum Act 1998[5]. Special provision was made in relation to coal by the Opencast Coal Act 1958, but powers under the Opencast Coal Act 1958 ceased to be exercisable after 31 December 1999[6] and coal now falls within the general regime for minerals contained in the Mines (Working Facilities and Support) Act 1966.

The right to work minerals is subject to the provisions of the town and country planning legislation[7] and other relevant statutory controls[8].

1 See PARAS 360–379.
2 As to the meaning of 'minerals' see PARA 10.
3 See PARA 381 et seq. The Mines (Working Facilities and Support) Act 1966, which came into force on 10 April 1966 (see s 16(3)), is a consolidating statute. Its provisions were contained previously in the Mines (Working Facilities and Support) Act 1923 Pt I (ss 1–14) (repealed), and various amending enactments, all of which are repealed, subject to savings for transitional purposes: see the Mines (Working Facilities and Support) Act 1966 s 15(1), Sch 1 (repealed).

The scope of the Mines (Working Facilities and Support) Act 1966 was extended by the Mines (Working Facilities and Support) Act 1974 and it has been made subject to various other amendments, including amendments consequential on the restructuring of the coal industry under privatisation by the Coal Industry Act 1994: see PARA 51 et seq.

4   See ENERGY AND CLIMATE CHANGE vol 44 (2011) PARA 848 et seq.
5   Ie the Petroleum 1998 as applied by the Continental Shelf Act 1964. As to petroleum production see ENERGY AND CLIMATE CHANGE vol 44 (2011) PARA 848 et seq.
6   See the Coal Industry Act 1994 s 52(1); and PARA 414. The Opencast Coal Act 1958 has not been repealed, and makes provision (inter alia) for compensation: see PARA 413 et seq.
7   See PARA 352; and PLANNING. As to examples of other statutory provisions relevant to the right to work minerals see PARA 356 (facilities for Natural Environment Research Council); PARA 357 (taxation); PARA 358 (control of prices of minerals); and PARA 359 (mining consultants etc).
8   Eg the Health and Safety at Work etc Act 1974; the Mines and Quarries Act 1954; and the Environmental Protection Act 1990. See also the Deep Sea Mining (Temporary Provisions) Act 1981; and INTERNATIONAL RELATIONS LAW vol 61 (2010) PARA 172 et seq.

## 381. Grant of rights.

Application may be made to the Secretary of State[1] for the grant of certain rights to search for[2] or work[3] minerals[4], or for certain ancillary rights[5]. On such application being referred to the High Court[6], subject to certain statutory provisions[7], the court may confer the rights[8] if it is satisfied that the grant is expedient in the national interest[9].

1   As to the Secretary of State see PARA 2.
2   See PARA 356.
3   In the Mines (Working Facilities and Support) Act 1966 references to working minerals include references to working, carrying away, treating and converting minerals: s 14(1). As to the meaning of 'minerals' see s 14(1); and PARA 10.
4   See PARAS 382–383.
5   See PARA 384.
6   See PARAS 390, 392.
7   Ie those of the Mines (Working Facilities and Support) Act 1966: see PARA 390 et seq.
8   See the Mines (Working Facilities and Support) Act 1966 s 1; and PARAS 382–384.
9   See the Mines (Working Facilities and Support) Act 1966 s 3(1). It has been suggested that 'national interest' may be considered as something which is to be distinguished from the private interest of individuals, and that the expression is akin to the economic doctrine of 'the greatest good of the greatest number': *Consett Iron Co Ltd v Clavering Trustees* (1934) unreported per MacKinnon J (on appeal [1935] 2 KB 42, CA). It is submitted that the expression is synonymous with 'public benefit'. In *A-G v Terry* (1874) 9 Ch App 423 at 427n, 428n, Jessel MR considered that public benefit must involve direct benefit. See also *Re Consett Iron Co Ltd's Application* [1938] 1 All ER 439, sub nom *Consett Iron Co Ltd v Clavering Estates (Durham) Ltd* (1938) 54 TLR 348. It has been suggested that the task delegated to the court is very similar to that which is discharged by the Committee of Parliament considering the expediency of allowing a motion to come up for private legislation: see *Consett Iron Co Ltd v Clavering Trustees*, cited in *Re Consett Iron Co Ltd's Application* at 445 and 352.
    It has been suggested that the potential employment of a number of workers was relevant in considering the national interest: see *Re Consett Iron Co Ltd's Application* at 447 and 352 per Finlay J, and at 450 and 354 per Sir Francis Taylor KC. See also *BP Petroleum Developments Ltd v Ryder* [1987] 2 EGLR 233 at 238–239, [1987] RVR 211 at 214 per Gibson J.
    The question whether a particular thing is in the national interest is a question of the times, and is a question of fact: *Re Amalgamated Anthracite Collieries Ltd's Application* (1927) 43 TLR 672. It would not be in the national interest to risk considerable damage to surface works for the sake of getting a negligible quantity of minerals, and even where the parties can agree on terms of a settlement the public interest must be considered and safeguarded and a fortiori the court cannot be bound by an offer put forward by one of them: *Re Nunnery Colliery Co's Application* (1924) 69 Sol Jo 52; *Re Naylor Benzon Mining Co Ltd* [1950] Ch 567 at 576, [1950] 1 All ER 518 at 524 per Wynn-Parry J. The same applies where rival applicants have agreed to divide an area between them: *Re J and J Charlesworth Ltd and Henry Briggs, Son & Co Ltd* (1926) 43 TLR 100.
    The fact that the danger may exist of minerals being left permanently unworked is relevant only in so far as it relates to the national interest which is itself a question for the court to decide according to the facts of the case: *Re Henry Lowson Ltd's Application* (1930) 144 LT 128. See also *Archibald Russell Ltd v Nether Pollok Ltd* 1938 SC 1; and PARA 392.

As to the national interest generally see *Re Manners Colliery Co Ltd* (1926) 42 TLR 773; *Re Denaby and Cadeby Main Collieries Ltd* (1927) 43 TLR 322; *Re Tilmanstone (Kent) Collieries Ltd* [1928] 1 KB 599, CA; *Re Hamsterley Ganister Co Ltd's Application* (1931) 75 Sol Jo 602; *Re West of England Road Metal Co Ltd* [1936] 2 All ER 1607; *Re Walsall Wood Colliery Co Ltd's Application* [1939] 2 KB 817, [1939] 3 All ER 864; *Re Wolstanton Ltd's Application* [1952] Ch 519 (sub nom *Re National Coal Board's Application* [1952] 1 All ER 678n); *Re National Coal Board's Application* [1958] 2 All ER 351n, [1958] 1 WLR 599; *Re W J King & Sons Ltd's Application* [1976] 1 All ER 770, [1976] 1 WLR 521, CA.

## 382.   General rights in respect of minerals.

A right to search for[1] or work any minerals[2] other than peat cut for purposes other than sale may be conferred on any person, exercisable either by himself or through a lessee[3].

Where the working, or the working in the most efficient and economical manner, of any such minerals is impeded[4] by any restrictions, terms or conditions[5] contained in a mining lease[6], or otherwise binding on the person entitled to work the minerals, a right may be conferred to work the minerals freed wholly or partially from the restrictions or conditions, or to work the minerals on other terms and conditions[7].

No application with respect to the grant of a right under these provisions[8] made in respect of coal[9] may be referred by the Secretary of State[10] to the court[11] unless the Coal Authority[12] has given notice in writing to the Secretary of State that it has no power to grant the right, or any of the rights, for which the application is made[13].

Where there is a danger[14] of any minerals other than coal being left permanently[15] unworked (1) by reason of the necessity for the concurrence[16] of two or more persons[17]; or (2) by reason of the minerals being owned in such small parcels that they cannot be properly or conveniently[18] worked by themselves[19], a right to work the minerals may be conferred on a person having an interest[20] in them or, in the case of minerals owned in small parcels, in minerals adjacent[21] to them, exercisable either by himself or through a lessee[22].

1   See PARA 356.
2   As to references to working minerals see PARA 381. As to the meaning of 'minerals' see PARA 10.
3   Mines (Working Facilities and Support) Act 1966 s 1, Table para 1(1), (2) (Table para 1 substituted by the Mines (Working Facilities and Support) Act 1974 s 1; and amended by the Coal Industry Act 1994 s 67(1), (8), Sch 9 para 10(1)(a), Sch 11 Pt II). This provision, and Table para 2, apply to the granting of a right required by reason of the subsistence either of a retained interest (as defined by the Coal Act 1938 s 5 (repealed)) or of any interest arising under a freeholder's lease (as defined by the Coal Act 1943 s 4 (repealed)) (Mines (Working Facilities and Support) Act 1966 s 13(a)), but they do not apply to minerals within the Coal Act 1938 s 3(4)(b) (repealed) (which refers to minerals other than coal comprised in a coal-mining lease subsisting at the valuation date under that Act (Mines (Working Facilities and Support) Act 1966 s 13(b)). Where the Coal Industry Act 1994 repeals any provisions of the Coal Act 1938, that repeal does not affect so much of the Coal Industry Act 1994 or any other enactment as makes provision by reference to anything within the meaning of the Coal Act 1938: see the Coal Industry Act 1994 s 67(7), Sch 10 para 1.
4   'Impeded' here relates exclusively to something which impedes or obstructs the actual working or carrying away of the minerals, ie the manner of working or carrying away, and does not apply to financial obligations (eg royalties and wayleave rents) imposed by a lease upon the lessee: see *Consett Iron Co Ltd v Clavering Trustees* [1935] 2 KB 42, CA.
5   Restrictions, terms or conditions contained in a mining lease do not here include financial terms, and accordingly there is no jurisdiction to relieve a lessee from his obligations to pay royalties, wayleave rents or any rent imposed by his lease: *Consett Iron Co Ltd v Clavering Trustees* [1935] 2 KB 42, CA. A statutory restriction on working imposed by an Inclosure Act award is within the provision: *Re Walsall Wood Colliery Co Ltd's Application* [1939] 2 KB 817, [1939] 3 All ER 864.
6   'Lease' includes underlease or other tenancy and a licence, and 'lessor' and 'lessee' have corresponding meanings: Mines (Working Facilities and Support) Act 1966 s 14(1).
7   See the Mines (Working Facilities and Support) Act 1966 s 1, Table para 1(3).

8 Ie under the Mines (Working Facilities and Support) Act 1966 s 1, Table para 1.

9 In the mines (Working Facilities and Support) Act 1966, unless the context otherwise requires 'coal' means bituminous coal, cannel coal and anthracite: see s 14(1). In s 4(5), 'coal' does not include lignite or brown coal but (subject to that) does include, together with coal as defined in s 14(1), all other minerals worked or to be worked therewith: see s 4(6) (added by the Coal Industry Act 1994 Sch 9 para 10(3)(b)).

10 As to the Secretary of State see PARA 2.

11 For the purposes of the Mines (Working Facilities and Support) Act 1966, unless the context otherwise requires, 'court' in the application of the Act to England and Wales, means the High Court: see s 14(1).

12 As to the Coal Authority see PARA 52 et seq.

13 See the Mines (Working Facilities and Support) Act 1966 s 4(5) (amended by the Coal Industry Act 1987 s 1(1), (2), Sch 1 para 12; and the Coal Industry Act 1994 s 67(1), Sch 9 para 10(3)(a)).

14 'Danger' has been held to include various factors according to the circumstances of the particular case: see *Re New Hucknall Colliery Co Ltd* (1925) 41 TLR 383 (minerals set out as pillar for support of church; applicants wishing to remove pillar by continuous system of longwall working); *Re Nunnery Colliery Co's Application* (1924) 69 Sol Jo 52. It is suggested that other cases include difficulty in establishing ownership of minerals in numerous small plots (see *Re Walsall Wood Colliery Co Ltd's Application* [1939] 2 KB 817, [1939] 3 All ER 864); trouble and expense of separate negotiations with such numerous owners with the possibility of failure to secure reasonable terms (see eg *Archibald Russell Ltd v Nether Pollok Ltd* 1938 SC 1); surrounding minerals in possession of applicants who are the only persons who can practicably or economically and efficiently work the minerals in question (cf *Re J and J Charlesworth Ltd and Henry Briggs, Son & Co Ltd* (1926) 43 TLR 100).

15 It is submitted that 'permanently' is used here in a merely relative sense, to exclude a temporary suspension of comparatively short duration. See further *Re West of England Road Metal Co Ltd* [1936] 2 All ER 1607.

16 For the purposes of the Mines (Working Facilities and Support) Act 1966 a person whose concurrence is necessary for the exercise of a right is deemed to be a person having power to grant the right, or a person from whom the right must be obtained as the case may be: s 14(2).

17 Ie by reason of the minerals being comprised in or lying under former copyhold land (see PARA 309; and *Re Markham Main Colliery Ltd* (1925) 41 TLR 672), or land subject to a lease (see *Re East Yorkshire Gravel Co Ltd's Application* [1954] 3 All ER 631, [1955] 1 WLR 88), exception, reservation, restriction, covenant or condition, or otherwise (eg by reason of an inclosure award: see *Calstock RDC v Cornwall County Council* (1924) 1 Bamber's Mining Cases 79; *Re Walsall Wood Colliery Co Ltd's Application* [1939] 2 KB 817, [1939] 3 All ER 864) not capable of being worked without the concurrence of two or more persons: see the Mines (Working Facilities and Support) Act 1966 s 1, Table para 2(2)(a). 'Copyhold land' has the same meaning as in the Law of Property Act 1922 (see s 189 (repealed)): Mines (Working Facilities and Support) Act 1966 s 14(1). As to the statutory right to work coal in former copyhold land see PARA 397 et seq.

18 'Properly and conveniently' does not exclude considerations of cost: *Re Tilmanstone (Kent) Collieries Ltd* [1928] 1 KB 599, CA.

19 See the Mines (Working Facilities and Support) Act 1966 s 1, Table para 2(2)(b). Two classes of case may be suggested: (1) an isolated parcel belonging to one owner, which is too small to be worked independently; and (2) a considerable area made up of numerous small parcels, each in different ownership.

20 Ie a proprietary interest: *Re East Yorkshire Gravel Co Ltd's Application* [1954] 3 All ER 631, [1955] 1 WLR 88; cf *Re West of England Road Metal Co Ltd* [1936] 2 All ER 1607. A proprietary interest may be of at least three kinds, that of an owner, a lessee or a licensee with a licence not presently revocable: *Re East Yorkshire Gravel Co Ltd's Application* at 636 and 94 respectively per Harman J.

21 'Adjacent' has in ordinary usage no precise and uniform meaning, but it is not confined to places adjoining and includes those close to or near: see *Wellington Corpn v Lower Hutt Corpn* [1904] AC 773, PC; cf *Re Ecclesiastical Comrs for England's Conveyance* [1936] Ch 430 at 441 per Luxmoore J. See also *Birmingham Corpn v Allen* (1877) 6 ChD 284, CA; *English Clays Lovering Pochin & Co Ltd v Plymouth Corpn* [1974] 2 All ER 239, [1974] 1 WLR 742, CA.

22 See the Mines (Working Facilities and Support) Act 1966 s 1, Table para 2(1), (2). Subject to s 4(5), where the working of any coal, or the working of any coal in the most efficient and economical manner, is impeded by any restrictions, terms or conditions contained in a mining lease, or otherwise binding on the person entitled to work the coal, a right may be conferred to work the coal freed wholly or partially from such restrictions or conditions, or to work the coal on other terms and conditions: see s 1, Table para 3(2) (repealed). Section 1, Table para 3 (repealed) was

repealed by the Coal Industry Act 1994 Sch 9 para 10(1)(b), (2), Sch 11 Pt II, as from 31 October 1994; but where an application to work coal freed from restrictions contained in a mining lease had been made before that date, that application may be continued and disposed of on or after that date as if it were an application under the Mines (Working Facilities and Support) Act 1966 s 1, Table para 1: Coal Industry Act 1994 Sch 9 para 10(2).

### 383. Rights in respect of the adjustment of boundaries.

Where the persons working two adjoining mines[1] have agreed on an adjustment of boundaries between the mines[2] with a view to reducing the amount of minerals[3] to be left unworked between the mines, or to enabling the minerals to be worked[4] more efficiently or economically, and effect cannot be given to the agreement by reason of the failure or refusal of the lessors[5] of the mines or the owners of the surface[6], or any of them, to concur, a right may be conferred on the persons working the mines respectively to work the minerals in accordance with the adjusted boundaries[7]. However, no order may be made under this provision on the ground of any failure or refusal on the part of the Coal Authority[8].

1  As to the meaning of 'mine' see PARA 3.
2  Eg the substitution of a straight boundary for a sinuous boundary.
3  As to the meaning of 'minerals' see PARA 10.
4  As to references to working minerals see PARA 381.
5  As to the meaning of 'lessor' see PARA 382.
6  'Surface' in relation to land includes any buildings, works or things erected, constructed or growing on it: see the Mines (Working Facilities and Support) Act 1966 s 14(1).
7  See the Mines (Working Facilities and Support) Act 1966 s 1, Table para 4(1).
8  See the Mines (Working Facilities and Support) Act 1966 s 1, Table para 4(2) (amended by the Coal Industry Act 1994 s 67(1), Sch 9 para 10(1)(c)). As to the Coal Authority see PARA 52 et seq.

### 384. Ancillary rights.

An ancillary right may be conferred[1] on a person having the right to work minerals[2] who is working or desirous of working the minerals either by himself or through his lessees[3], if the right is required in order that the minerals may be properly and conveniently[4] worked by him, and the proper and efficient working of the minerals is unduly hampered[5] by his inability[6] or failure to obtain that right[7].

In relation to minerals, 'ancillary right' means any facility, right or privilege and, without prejudice to the generality of that provision, includes: (1) a right to let down the surface[8]; (2) a right of airway, shaftway, or surface or underground wayleave[9], or other right for the purpose of access to or conveyance of minerals[10], or the ventilation or drainage of the mines[11]; (3) a right to use and occupy the surface for the erection of washeries, coke ovens, railways, by-product works or brick-making or other works, or of dwellings for persons employed in connection with the working of the minerals or with any such works[12]; (4) a right to obtain a supply of water or other substances in connection with the working of minerals[13]; and (5) a right to dispose of water or other liquid matter obtained from mines or any by-product works[14]. So far as required in order that coal[15] may be properly and conveniently worked, and where the surface has been used for the erection of any works for a coal-mining purpose[16], or of dwellings for persons employed in connection with the working of coal or in connection with any such works for a coal-mining purpose or with any works mentioned in head (3) above, 'ancillary right' also includes a right to use and occupy the works and dwellings for the purposes for which they were erected[17].

An ancillary right may be conferred on a person on whom a right to work minerals is conferred at the same time or at any subsequent time[18].

1  The right may be conferred even where the same right was surrendered by the applicant if the terms of the original grant were unreasonable: *Re Consett Iron Co Ltd's Application* [1938] 1 All ER 439.

2  References in the Mines (Working Facilities and Support) Act 1966 to a right to work minerals include references to any right granted under s 1, Table para 1 or Table para 3(2) (repealed) (see PARA 382): see s 14(3). As to references to working minerals see PARA 381. As to the meaning of 'minerals' see PARA 10.

3  As to the meaning of 'lessee' see PARA 382.

4  As to the meaning of 'properly and conveniently' see PARA 382.

5  Cf PARA 382. See also *Re Consett Iron Co Ltd's Application* [1938] 1 All ER 439, sub nom *Consett Iron Co Ltd v Clavering Estates (Durham) Ltd* (1938) 54 TLR 348. It is not necessary for the applicant to show that he is hampered at the time of the application; potential hampering is sufficient: *Re Wolstanton Ltd's Application* [1952] Ch 519, sub nom *Re National Coal Board's Application* [1952] 1 All ER 678n.

6  See eg the reasons set out in PARA 391.

7  See the Mines (Working Facilities and Support) Act 1966 s 1, Table para 5(1).

8  See the Mines (Working Facilities and Support) Act 1966 ss 2(1)(a), 14(1). As to the meaning of 'surface' see PARA 383. 'Right to let down the surface' includes a right to let down superincumbent or adjacent strata up to and including the surface: s 14(1). As to the statutory right to withdraw support under the Coal Industry Act 1994 see PARA 176 et seq. As to the right to let down the surface which may be conferred see *Re Markham Main Colliery Ltd* (1925) 41 TLR 672; *Re Manners Colliery Co Ltd* (1926) 42 TLR 773. In practically all applications for the right to work, the right to let down the surface is also included. The right is granted subject to payment of compensation for damage resulting from it to persons entitled to it. The High Court has no power, on such an application, to vest land in the applicant, even though a right to work or quarry may in effect amount to a grant of the land itself (*Re West of England Road Metal Co Ltd* [1936] 2 All ER 1607), nor has it power to sanction the extinguishment or diversion of a highway (*Hoddesdon UDC v Broxbourne Sand and Ballast Pits Ltd* [1936] 2 KB 19, [1936] 1 All ER 798) or to grant a declaration that a highway is repairable by the inhabitants at large (*Re Somerville & Co Ltd's Application* [1937] 1 All ER 507).

9  See *Re Markham Main Colliery Ltd* (1925) 41 TLR 672; *Re Consett Iron Co Ltd's Application* [1938] 1 All ER 439. The former Railway and Canal Commission (see PARA 390) normally granted underground wayleaves free of wayleave rent. As to surface wayleaves see *Re Tilmanstone (Kent) Collieries Ltd* [1928] 1 KB 599, CA, where aerial ropeways extended for several miles between a colliery and Dover harbour.

10 As to the construction of the provision stated in the text see generally *Re Tilmanstone (Kent) Collieries Ltd* [1928] 1 KB 599, CA.

11 See the Mines (Working Facilities and Support) Act 1966 s 2(1)(b) (amended by the Petroleum Act 1987 s 27(a)); Mines (Working Facilities and Support) Act 1966 s 14(1).

12 See the Mines (Working Facilities and Support) Act 1966 ss 2(1)(c), 14(1).

13 See the Mines (Working Facilities and Support) Act 1966 ss 2(1)(d), 14(1).

14 See the Mines (Working Facilities and Support) Act 1966 ss 2(1)(e), 14(1).

15 As to the meaning of 'coal' see PARA 382.

16 As to the meaning of 'coal-mining purpose' see the Coal Act 1938 s 44(1) (repealed with savings); and PARA 48definition applied by the Mines (Working Facilities and Support) Act 1966 s 14(1)).

17 See the Mines (Working Facilities and Support) Act 1966 s 2(3). Where such a right is to be granted on the termination of a lease, and a right to erect or use the works or dwellings was comprised in that lease, the High Court, in determining whether any compensation or consideration is to be paid or given in respect of the right to be granted by it and the amount of any compensation, must have regard to the fact that the right comprised in the lease was comprised in it and to the amount of any rent reserved by the lease in respect of it: see s 2(4). As to the meaning of 'lease' see PARA 382.

18 See the Mines (Working Facilities and Support) Act 1966 s 1, Table para 5(2).

### 385.  Effect of grant of right.

A right granted under these provisions[1] does not confer on the grantee any greater or other power than if the right had been granted by a person legally entitled to grant the right, or relieve the grantee from any obligation or liability to which he would have been subject had the right been granted by such a person[2].

1　Ie under the Mines (Working Facilities and Support) Act 1966: see PARA 381 et seq.
2　Mines (Working Facilities and Support) Act 1966 s 10.

### 386.　Grant of rights to persons in fiduciary position.

An order under these provisions[1] may confer rights on a tenant for life or on any person having the statutory powers of a tenant for life[2], or any trustee, personal representative or other person in a fiduciary position; and any such rights so conferred are deemed to form part of the property subject to the settlement or the estate of the deceased person or the property subject to the trust, as the case may be[3].

As from 1 January 1997 no new settlements can be created under the Settled Land Act 1925[4].

1　Ie under the Mines (Working Facilities and Support) Act 1966: see PARA 381 et seq.
2　As to the persons having the statutory powers of a tenant for life see the Settled Land Act 1925 ss 20–26; and SETTLEMENTS vol 91 (2012) PARA 662 et seq.
3　See the Mines (Working Facilities and Support) Act 1966 s 11.
4　As to the phasing out of strict settlements and the introduction of the 'trust of land' see the Trusts of Land and Appointment of Trustees Act 1996 s 2(1); and PARA 282.

### 387.　Restrictions on working minerals required for support.

If any person having an interest in any land is not entitled to support or sufficient support, whether vertical or lateral, for any buildings or works, whether on or below the surface[1], erected or constructed, or intended to be erected or constructed, on or below the surface, and alleges that it is not reasonably practicable to obtain a right to such support by private arrangement for any of the reasons subsequently stated[2], he may send to the Secretary of State[3] an application that such restrictions may be imposed on the working of the minerals[4] under that land and the adjacent land as he may consider necessary to secure sufficient support to the buildings or works[5]. The Secretary of State must consider the application, and unless, after communication with such other parties interested, if any, as he thinks fit, he is of opinion that a prima facie case is not made out, he must refer it to the High Court[6], which, if satisfied as to the statutory requirements and that it is expedient in the national interest[7], may impose the necessary restrictions[8] and, in default of agreement, determine the compensation payable[9]. There are special provisions which relate to coal[10].

1　As to the meaning of 'surface' see PARA 383.
2　See the Mines (Working Facilities and Support) Act 1966 s 3(2); and PARA 391.
3　As to the Secretary of State see PARA 2.
4　As to references to working minerals see PARA 381. As to the meaning of 'minerals' see PARA 10.
5　See the Mines (Working Facilities and Support) Act 1966 s 7(1). The application must set out the circumstances alleged to justify the imposition of the restrictions, and must be in such form, and be accompanied by such information verified in such manner, as the Secretary of State may direct: see s 7(2); and cf PARA 390. The right to apply for restrictions does not apply to railway or canal companies, local authorities or other statutory bodies: see PARA 389.
　　For the purposes of s 7, where any building or work is an ancient monument within the meaning of the Ancient Monuments and Archaeological Areas Act 1979 (see NATIONAL CULTURAL HERITAGE vol 77 (2016) PARA 804), and is, in pursuance of that Act, under the guardianship or protection of the appropriate national authority, or is under the guardianship of a local authority, the appropriate national authority or the local authority, as the case may be, are deemed to be persons entitled to make an application under the Mines (Working Facilities and Support) Act 1966 s 7: see s 7(8) (amended by the Ancient Monuments and Archaeological Areas

Act 1979 s 64(2), (3), Sch 4 para 9, Sch 5; and by virtue of SI 1969/383, 1969/388; and SI 1970/1681). The appropriate national authority is the Secretary of State or where functions have been transferred in relation to Wales, the Welsh Ministers: see PARA 2. As to ancient monuments see generally NATIONAL CULTURAL HERITAGE vol 77 (2016) PARA 1006 et seq. See also the Mines (Working Facilities and Support) Act 1966 s 7A; and PARA 388.

6   See the Mines (Working Facilities and Support) Act 1966 ss 7(3), 14(1). However, see also s 4(3); and PARA 390. Where it is alleged that the right in question cannot be obtained by reason of any person not having the necessary powers of disposition, or having unreasonably refused to grant it or having demanded terms which are unreasonable the Secretary of State must first communicate with that person: see s 7(3) proviso.

7   As to the national interest see PARA 381.

8   Where any such case is referred to the court the court if satisfied that the requirements of the Mines (Working Facilities and Support) Act 1966 s 7 are complied with in the case of the applicant, and that it is expedient in the national interest that restrictions should be imposed, may, by order, impose such restrictions, on such terms and subject to such conditions and for such period, as the court may think just, and upon such order being made the right to enforce the restrictions imposed by the order, subject to the provisions of s 7(5)–(8), vests in the applicant: see s 7(4). However, see also s 5(1); and PARA 392. The restrictions may be either on the quantity or position of the minerals to be worked, or on the methods of working or packing or otherwise such as may be necessary to secure adequate support to the buildings or works or to prevent or minimise damage to them: s 7(6). Regard must be had to the comparative values of the minerals and of the buildings or works or the cost of repairing damage likely to be caused to them by subsidence or to the comparative importance in the national interest of the erection or preservation of the buildings or works and of the working of the minerals: see s 7(7); and *Re Manners Colliery Co Ltd* (1926) 42 TLR 773.

The Coal Industry Act 1994 s 38 (right to withdraw support) (see PARA 176) does not affect any restrictions, terms or conditions applicable to the working of coal by virtue of any order made (whether before or after the restructuring date) under the Mines (Working Facilities and Support) Act 1966 s 1 or s 7 (acquisition of rights to work minerals): see the Coal Industry Act 1994 s 40(2)(a); and PARAS 176 et seq, 391. As to the restructuring date (ie 31 October 1994) see PARA 50.

9   See the Mines (Working Facilities and Support) Act 1966 s 7(5). However, see also s 5(2) (and PARA 392); s 8 (and PARA 394 et seq).

10  See the Mines (Working Facilities and Support) Act 1966 s 7A; and PARA 388.

## 388. Restrictions on working minerals required for support: special provisions relating to coal.

Subject to certain provisions[1], on an application under the Mines (Working Facilities and Support) Act 1966[2], the applicant is not required to pay or give any compensation or consideration[3] in respect of the imposition of restrictions appearing to the court[4] to be justified by the existence of any right to withdraw support to which any person[5] is entitled under the Coal Industry Act 1994[6].

This provision[7] applies in any case where the Coal Industry Act 1994[8] applies to the land in question otherwise than by virtue of the Coal Industry Act 1975[9] only if the application under the Mines (Working Facilities and Support) Act 1966[10] is sent to the Secretary of State before the end of the period of six months beginning with the date on which particulars of the notice relating to the land to which the application relates are first registered by the Coal Authority[11].

1   Ie subject to the Mines (Working Facilities and Support) Act 1966 s 7A(2), (3).

2   Ie on an application under the Mines (Working Facilities and Support) Act 1966 s 7: see PARA 387.

3   As to the requirement to pay or give compensation or consideration see the Mines (Working Facilities and Support) Act 1966 s 8; and PARAS 392, 394.

4   As to the meaning of 'court' see PARA 382. See also PARAS 390, 392.

5   Subject to the provisions of the Coal Industry Act 1994 Pt III (ss 37–56), on and after the restructuring date, any licensed operator is to be entitled, so far as may be reasonably requisite for the carrying on of any coal-mining operations to which s 25 applies, to withdraw support from any land to which s 38 applies: see s 38(1); and PARA 176. As to the restructuring date (ie 31 October 1994) see PARA 50. As to the meaning of 'licensed operator' see PARA 58; and as to the meaning

of 'coal-mining operations' see PARA 51.

6   Ie under the Coal Industry Act 1994 s 38: see the Mines (Working Facilities and Support) Act 1966
    s 7A(1) (s 7A added by the Coal Industry Act 1994 s 67(1), Sch 9 para 10(4)). The Mines (Working
    Facilities and Support) Act 1966 s 7A(1) does not apply in a case where, in accordance with the
    Coal Industry Act 1994 s 38(2)(b), that provision applies to the land in question by virtue of the
    Coal Industry Act 1975 s 2(5)(a) (repealed): see the Mines (Working Facilities and Support) Act
    1966 s 7A(2).
7   Ie the Mines (Working Facilities and Support) Act 1966 s 7A(1).
8   Ie the Coal Industry Act 1994 s 38: see PARA 176.
9   Ie the Coal Industry Act 1975 s 2(5) (repealed).
10  Ie under the Mines (Working Facilities and Support) Act 1966 s 7: see PARA 387.
11  Ie under the Coal Industry Act 1994 s 56: see the Mines (Working Facilities and Support) Act 1966
    s 7A(3). As to the Coal Authority see PARA 52 et seq. As to the registration of rights under the Coal
    Industry Act 1994 s 56 see PARAS 106, 176, 397.

### 389.   Saving for railways, canals, local authorities and statutory bodies.

Nothing in the Mines (Working Facilities and Support) Act 1966 prejudicially
affects: (1) the right under the Railways Clauses Consolidation Act 1845[1], or any
Act modifying that Act[2], or any other Act, whether public general, or local and
private, of any railway or canal company, local authority or other statutory body
to acquire minerals[3] for the purposes of support[4]; or (2) any rights or interests in
minerals which may have been acquired[5] by any such company, authority or
body[6]; or (3) any right of support from minerals[7] to which any such company,
authority or body may be entitled[8]; or (4) any right empowering any such
company, authority or body to acquire the rights to which it is entitled directly or
indirectly under any special Act or order relating to the company, authority or
body or any statute incorporated with it[9]. Nor does it confer on any such
company, authority or body the right to acquire under the Mines (Working
Facilities and Support) Act 1966 any rights to prohibit or restrict the working[10] of
minerals[11].

1   Having regard to the words following the reference to the Act, this includes mining code
    provisions: see PARA 135 et seq.
2   Eg the Mines (Working Facilities and Support) Act 1923 ss 15, 16: see PARA 135 et seq.
3   As to the meaning of 'minerals' see PARA 10.
4   See the Mines (Working Facilities and Support) Act 1966 s 12(1)(a). See also PARA 135 et seq.
5   Eg by implication at common law (see PARA 137), or by purchase of minerals (see PARAS
    145–147), or by payment of compensation under the mining code (see PARA 135 et seq).
6   Mines (Working Facilities and Support) Act 1966 s 12(1)(b).
7   Eg the right of a highway authority to support for the highway: *Hoddeson UDC v Broxbourne
    Sand and Ballast Pits Ltd* [1936] 2 KB 19, [1936] 1 All ER 798.
8   Mines (Working Facilities and Support) Act 1966 s 12(1)(c).
9   Mines (Working Facilities and Support) Act 1966 s 12(1)(d).
10  As to references to the working of minerals see PARA 381.
11  See the Mines (Working Facilities and Support) Act 1966 s 12(1). Notwithstanding anything in s
    12, any restrictions the imposition of which appears to the court to be justified as mentioned in s
    7A(1) (see PARA 388): (1) may be imposed under s 7 on the application of, and so as to vest the
    right to enforce the restrictions in, any such company, authority or body as is mentioned in s 12;
    and (2) may be so imposed on the application of, and so as to vest the right to enforce the
    restrictions in: (a) the Environment Agency, the Natural Resources Body for Wales or any water
    or sewerage undertaker; (b) any gas transporter within the meaning of the Gas Act 1986 Pt I (ss
    1–48); or (c) any company or other body or person carrying on an undertaking primarily for the
    supply of electricity or hydraulic power, for public purposes or to members of the public: see the
    Mines (Working Facilities and Support) Act 1966 s 7A(4) (s 7A added by the Coal Industry Act
    1994 s 67(1), Sch 9 para 10(4); amended by the Gas Act 1995 s 16(1), Sch 4 para 2(2)(c);
    SI 1996/593; and SI 2013/755). As to the meaning of 'court' see PARA 382. As to the Environment
    Agency see ENVIRONMENTAL QUALITY AND PUBLIC HEALTH vol 45 (2010) PARA 68 et seq;
    WATER AND WATERWAYS vol 100 (2018) PARA 23. As to water and sewerage undertakers see

ENVIRONMENTAL QUALITY AND PUBLIC HEALTH vol 46 (2010) PARA 999 et seq; WATER AND WATERWAYS vol 100 (2018) PARA 476. As to the meaning of 'gas transporter' (previously known as a 'public gas transporter') see the Utilities Act 2000 s 76(1) (as substituted and amended), s 76(7); and ENERGY AND CLIMATE CHANGE vol 42 (2011) PARA 264 et seq. As to the supply of electricity see ENERGY AND CLIMATE CHANGE vol 43 (2011) PARA 507.

For the purposes of the Transport Act 1947 Pt II (ss 12–28) (repealed) and the Transport Act 1962 Pt II (ss 31–41), the provision set out in the text is deemed to have been enacted before those Acts: see the Mines (Working Facilities and Support) Act 1966 s 12(2). See further the Transport Act 1947 s 14(3), (4) (repealed) (transfer to the British Transport Commission (now the British Railways Board) of certain rights and liabilities under agreements and statutory provisions); the Transport Act 1962 s 35(1), Sch 6 (distribution of the undertaking of the British Transport Commission); and RAILWAYS AND TRAMWAYS.

B.   OBTAINING A GRANT; COMPENSATION

## 390. Applications for grant of rights.

An application for the grant of working facilities[1] must be sent to the Secretary of State[2], and the applicant for an ancillary right[3] for the purpose of or in connection with working any minerals[4] may be a person either having or applying for the right to work those minerals[5]. The application must set out the circumstances alleged to justify the grant of the right, and must be in such form and accompanied by such information verified in such manner as the Secretary of State may direct[6].

The Secretary of State must consider the application and refer the matter to the High Court[7] unless, after communication with such interested parties, if any, as he may think fit[8], he is of the opinion that a prima facie case is not made out[9].

Where the application relates to a right to obtain a supply of water, or a right to dispose of water or other liquid matter, or any other right which appears to the Secretary of State to affect any local authority[10], the Secretary of State, before referring the matter to the High Court, must send a copy of the application to the local authority in order to enable it to take such steps as it thinks fit for placing its views before the court[11].

1  Ie a grant of a right under the Mines (Working Facilities and Support) Act 1966 s 1: see PARA 381 et seq.
2  As to the Secretary of State see PARA 2.
3  As to ancillary rights see PARA 384.
4  As to references to working minerals see PARA 381. As to references to rights to work minerals see PARA 384. As to the meaning of 'minerals' see PARA 10.
5  See the Mines (Working Facilities and Support) Act 1966 s 4(1).
6  See the Mines (Working Facilities and Support) Act 1966 s 4(2).
7  Under the Mines (Working Facilities and Support) Act 1923 Pt I (ss 1–14) (repealed: see PARA 380) applications were formerly referred to the Railway and Canal Commission, but on the dissolution of that Commission under the Railway and Canal Commission (Abolition) Act 1949 its functions in this regard devolved on the High Court: s 1(1)(a).
8  Where it is alleged that the right in question cannot be obtained by reason of any person not having the necessary powers of disposition, or having unreasonably refused to grant it, or having demanded terms which are unreasonable, the Secretary of State may not refer the application to the court without first communicating with that person: see the Mines (Working Facilities and Support) Act 1966 s 4(3) proviso.
9  See the Mines (Working Facilities and Support) Act 1966 ss 4(3), 14(1). As to the function of the Secretary of State under s 4(3) see *Re W J King & Sons Ltd's Application* [1976] 1 All ER 770 at 777–778, [1976] 1 WLR 521 at 530, 531, CA.
10 It is submitted that the obligation under this provision is operative only where the application appears to affect the local authority directly. Local authorities now have relatively restricted functions in relation to those matters: see WATER AND WATERWAYS vol 100 (2018) PARA 657 et

seq. The rights of local authorities are protected further: see PARA 389. 'Local authority' is not defined for these purposes.
11 See the Mines (Working Facilities and Support) Act 1966 s 4(4).

## 391. Limitation on power to grant rights.

No grant of working facilities[1] is to be made unless the court is satisfied that the grant is expedient in the national interest[2], and unless it is shown that it is not reasonably practicable to obtain the right in question by private arrangement for any of the following reasons:

(1)    that the persons with power to grant the right are numerous or have conflicting interests[3];

(2)    that the persons with power to grant the right, or any of them, cannot be ascertained or cannot be found[4];

(3)    that the persons from whom the right must be obtained, or any of them, have not the necessary powers of disposition[5], whether by reason of defect in title[6], legal disability or otherwise[7];

(4)    that the person with power to grant the right[8] unreasonably refuses to grant it or demands terms which, having regard to the circumstances, are unreasonable[9].

1    Ie a grant under the Mines (Working Facilities and Support) Act 1966 s 1: see PARA 381 et seq.
2    See the Mines (Working Facilities and Support) Act 1966 s 3(1); and PARA 381.
3    See the Mines (Working Facilities and Support) Act 1966 s 3(2)(a). This would apply eg where the minerals underlie numerous small parcels of land in separate ownership: see PARA 382; and *Re Walsall Wood Colliery Co Ltd's Application* [1939] 2 KB 817, [1939] 3 All ER 864.
4    See the Mines (Working Facilities and Support) Act 1966 s 3(2)(b). Head (2) in the text is satisfied if, by reason of the number of small parcels (eg resulting from allotments under an Inclosure Act or award) or otherwise, it is not reasonably practicable to ascertain: (1) who are the owners; or (2) whether the surface owners have or have not the right to support of the surface and so to prohibit the working of the underlying minerals: see *Re Walsall Wood Colliery Co Ltd's Application* [1939] 2 KB 817, [1939] 3 All ER 864.
5    Having regard to the provision relating to estates in land and powers of disposition contained in the Law of Property Act 1925, the Settled Land Act 1925 and kindred statutes (see PARAS 282 et seq, 371 et seq), it is thought that only in very exceptional cases can the difficulty as to want of powers of disposition arise. As to the phasing out of strict settlements and the introduction of the 'trust of land' see the Trusts of Land and Appointment of Trustees Act 1996 s 2(1); and PARA 282.
6    'Defect in title' may include cases where the title is doubtful.
7    See the Mines (Working Facilities and Support) Act 1966 s 3(2)(c). The words 'or otherwise', although they are to be construed ejusdem generis with the words which precede, are nonetheless wide enough to embrace a restriction on disposition imposed by an Inclosure Act award: *Walsall Wood Colliery Co Ltd's Application* [1939] 2 KB 817, [1939] 3 All ER 864.
8    As to references to persons whose concurrence is necessary for the exercise of a right see PARA 382.
9    See the Mines (Working Facilities and Support) Act 1966 s 3(2)(d). In the case of a quarry an application to buy the land is a sufficient compliance with the statutory requirement that an application must be made for a right to work the minerals, since the working of the quarry involves destruction of the surface: *Re West of England Road Metal Co Ltd* [1936] 2 All ER 1607.
         Unreasonableness is a matter of law, and it is a condition precedent to the grant of every application that the High Court should be satisfied that all powers of private arrangement between the parties have been exhausted: see *Glassbrook Bros Ltd v Leyson* [1933] 2 KB 91, CA. In considering the question of reasonableness the court must take into consideration all the circumstances as they exist at the date of the hearing, including the circumstance that the court has formed the view that the national interest lies with one or the other of the competing proposals: *Archibald Russell Ltd v Nether Pollok Ltd* 1938 SC 1. As to the national interest see PARA 381.
         In deciding whether there has been an unreasonable refusal to grant the right applied for, or whether the terms demanded in negotiation are, having regard to the circumstances, unreasonable, the terms granted by the High Court are not to be applied as the test of unreasonableness: see *Glassbrook Bros Ltd v Leyson*. The court's jurisdiction is limited in this respect by the statute, and that jurisdiction cannot be extended by the finding of facts which would confer jurisdiction if there is no evidence to support such findings: see *Bunbury v Fuller* (1853) 9 Exch 111 at 140, Ex Ch,

per Coleridge J; *R v Income Tax Special Purposes Comrs* (1888) 21 QBD 313 at 319, CA, per Lord Esher MR; *Glassbrook Bros Ltd v Leyson* at 107 per Lord Hanworth MR; *R v Fulham, Hammersmith and Kensington Rent Tribunal, ex p Philippe* [1950] 2 All ER 211, DC; *Anisminic Ltd v Foreign Compensation Commission* [1969] 2 AC 147, [1969] 1 All ER 208, HL; *Pearlman v Keepers and Governors of Harrow School* [1979] QB 56, [1979] 1 All ER 365, CA; and see JUDICIAL REVIEW vol 61 (2010) PARAS 610 et seq, 655. The question whether or not there is evidence to support the findings of the court as to unreasonableness is a question of law: see *Shotts Iron Co v Fordyce* [1930] AC 503, HL; *Glassbrook Bros Ltd v Leyson*. It is not unreasonable of the owner of minerals to stipulate that the applicants should enter into a proper covenant to work; such a covenant is not equivalent to the reservation of a minimum rent, for breach of it may entitle the lessor to damages in excess of such rent: see *Glassbrook Bros Ltd v Leyson*; *Jegon v Vivian* (1871) 6 Ch App 742.

## 392. References to the High Court.

Where a matter is referred[1] to the High Court, the court, if satisfied[2] that the requirements of the statute[3] are complied with in the case of the applicant, and that the grant of a right is expedient in the national interest[4], may by order[5] grant the right on such terms[6] and subject to such conditions, and for such period, as the court may think fit[7]. Upon such an order being made, the right specified in the order vests in the applicant, subject to the provisions set out below[8]. Where such a right is granted, the applicant must pay or give, to such persons as the High Court may determine to be entitled to it, such compensation[9] or consideration in respect of the acquisition of the right as, in default of agreement, the court may determine[10].

In determining the duration of any right to be granted, the High Court must have regard (1) to the time reasonably necessary to enable the minerals to be fully worked; and (2) where the applicant's interest in any minerals is an interest as lessee[11], to the duration of such interest[12].

Where the right applied for is a right to let down the surface[13], the High Court, in determining whether the right should be granted, must have regard (a) to the value of the minerals required for the support of any works or buildings or intended works or buildings on or below the surface as compared with the value of the buildings or works, and as to whether the support of the buildings or works or intended buildings or works is in the national interest more important than the working of the minerals[14]; and (b) if there are no such buildings or works, to the extent to which the use of the surface for the purposes for which it is used or is intended to be used will be prejudicially affected by subsidence, and as to whether the support of the surface is in the national interest more important than the working of the minerals required for its support[15].

In determining whether any right should be granted, or the conditions upon which any such right should be granted, the High Court must have regard to all the circumstances of the case[16], and in particular to the extent to which the retention of any minerals is required for the protection of mines or other works from flooding, or for any other mining purpose, and, so far as relevant, to the royalties, covenants and conditions reserved by or contained in the applicant's existing mining lease[17] or leases, if any, or customary in mining leases in the district[18].

The High Court has a complete discretion in awarding costs[19].

1 Ie under the Mines (Working Facilities and Support) Act 1966 s 4: see PARA 390. As to the procedure on such a reference see PARA 395.
2 Ie if upon the evidence before the High Court it comes to the reasonable conclusion that the requirements referred to are complied with: see *R v Bloomsbury Income Tax Comrs, ex p Hooper* [1915] 3 KB 768, DC.

3  Ie the Mines (Working Facilities and Support) Act 1966: see PARA 380 et seq. The right applied for must be within the ambit of the Act. As to rights outside the Mines (Working Facilities and Support) Act 1966 see eg *Consett Iron Co Ltd v Clavering Trustees* [1935] 2 KB 42, CA (application to vary financial terms of existing lease); *Hoddesdon UDC v Broxbourne Sand and Ballast Pits Ltd* [1936] 2 KB 19, [1936] 1 All ER 798 (application to let down public highway, tantamount to its extinguishment); *Re Tilmanstone (Kent) Collieries Ltd* [1928] 1 KB 599, CA, where it was argued unsuccessfully that the grant of a wayleave over the surface of land beyond the boundaries of the mine premises was not within the statute.

4  See the Mines (Working Facilities and Support) Act 1966 s 3(1); and PARA 381.

5  A form of order on an application to work granite, including ancillary rights, is indicated in *Re West of England Road Metal Co Ltd* [1936] 2 All ER 1607 at 1612 per MacKinnon J.

6  'Terms' here does not include 'financial terms': see *Consett Iron Co Ltd v Clavering Trustees* [1935] 2 KB 42, CA; *Re Sherwood Colliery Co Ltd* [1939] 1 All ER 88.

7  See the Mines (Working Facilities and Support) Act 1966 s 5(1). As to the court's responsibility as guardian of the public interest see PARA 381. The Coal Industry Act 1994 s 38 (right to withdraw support) (see PARA 176) does not affect any restrictions, terms or conditions applicable to the working of coal by virtue of any order made (whether before or after the restructuring date) under the Mines (Working Facilities and Support) Act 1966 s 1 or s 7 (acquisition of rights to work minerals): see the Coal Industry Act 1994 s 40(2)(a); and PARAS 176 et seq, 391.

8  Mines (Working Facilities and Support) Act 1966 s 5(1). On an application to assign the rights granted the assignee must be represented in order that they may be accepted by him before the court: *Re Bolsover Colliery Co Ltd's Application* [1940] WN 218.

9  As to compensation see further PARA 394. Compensation will be ordered only in respect of land wholly within the application area; and a local authority or sewerage undertaker will not be entitled to compensation for damage to sewers under the surface of the application area unless it is also the owner of the surface: *Re National Coal Board's Application* [1960] Ch 192, [1959] 3 All ER 58.

10 See the Mines (Working Facilities and Support) Act 1966 s 5(2). It is suggested that the words 'in default of agreement' contemplate that when the court has decided to grant the right applied for and the terms and conditions subject to which the right is granted, the parties concerned are to have the opportunity, if they so desire, to agree the compensation or consideration to be paid or given. As to the principles on the basis of which compensation is to be determined by the court see PARA 394.

11 As to the meaning of 'lessee' see PARA 382.

12 See the Mines (Working Facilities and Support) Act 1966 s 5(3). It has been questioned (but not decided to the contrary) whether there is jurisdiction to grant an anticipatory claim: see *Consett Iron Co Ltd v Clavering Trustees* [1935] 2 KB 42 at 73, CA, per Slesser, LJ; cf *Re West of England Road Metal Co Ltd* [1936] 2 All ER 1607. A refusal to grant a right to work at a distant date is not res judicata but is without prejudice to a future application: *Re Manners Colliery Co Ltd* (1926) 42 TLR 773.

13 Ie a right under the Mines (Working Facilities and Support) Act 1966 s 2(1)(a): see PARA 384. As to the meaning of 'surface' see PARA 383.

14 See the Mines (Working Facilities and Support) Act 1966 s 2(2)(a).

15 See the Mines (Working Facilities and Support) Act 1966 s 2(2)(b). See *Re Wolstanton Ltd's Application* [1952] Ch 519 at 527 per Danckwerts J (sub nom *Re National Coal Board's Application* [1952] 1 All ER 678n): 'I have to weigh against the national interest, which requires the working of these minerals, the prejudicial effect on the property of surface owners likely to be caused by subsidence. The latter is undoubtedly a serious matter to owners of property who are compelled by their circumstances to live or do their business in a mining area, but it may be that, subject to compensation for the pecuniary loss caused to them in respect of their property, they must, by reason of the overwhelming national interest in having the output of coal maintained or increased, submit, as a section only of the community, to the inconvenience which is thereby caused to them'. It is submitted that Danckwerts J's finding of 'overwhelming national interest' in having the output of coal maintained or increased was a reflection of the economic circumstances and political values prevailing at the time, and that it might no longer be sustainable. For a reflection of more recent circumstances and values see the Coal Industry Act 1994 s 2(1)(a) (see PARA 58), which refers to the maintenance and development of 'an economically viable coal-mining industry'. See also *Re Nunnery Colliery Co's Application* (1924) 69 Sol Jo 52.

16 An obligation to pay for damage that might arise in the future from subsidence should be treated as a term or condition on or subject to which a right might be granted under the Mines (Working Facilities and Support) Act 1966 s 5(1), but such a payment should not be regarded as

compensation under s 5(2); therefore the question whether an obligation to make such a payment should be imposed must be determined on the principle enacted by s 5(4), namely by having regard to all the circumstances of the case: *Re National Coal Board's Application* [1960] Ch 192, [1959] 3 All ER 58; not following *Re Beckermet Mining Co Ltd's Application* [1938] 1 All ER 389. On that basis (or indeed even if the true basis is that payment for such damage is compensation within the Mines (Working Facilities and Support) Act 1966 s 5(2)), an objector who owns part of the surface of the application area might be able to obtain compensation for future damage by subsidence, including consequential damage such as loss of profits, and not be limited to a measure confined to covering physical damage to land and buildings: *Re National Coal Board's Application*.

17 As to the meaning of 'lease' see PARA 382.
18 See the Mines (Working Facilities and Support) Act 1966 s 5(4). The royalties, covenants and conditions contained in the applicant's existing mining lease or leases, if any, or customary in mining leases in the district would seem to afford the most cogent evidence as to the terms and conditions of grants as between willing grantor and willing grantee. However, the court is not precluded from awarding compensation or consideration in the form of a lump sum: *Re Associated Portland Cement Manufacturers Ltd's Application* [1966] 1 Ch 308 at 324, [1965] 2 All ER 547 at 554 per Buckley J. As to the granting of facilities under the Petroleum Act 1998 see ENERGY AND CLIMATE CHANGE vol 44 (2011) PARA 1053.
19 *Re National Coal Board's Application* [1960] Ch 192, [1959] 3 All ER 58. If in the case of an application for the grant of a right under the Mines (Working Facilities and Support) Act 1966 s 1, Table para 1 (see PARA 382), or Table para 3(2) (repealed), it is proved to the satisfaction of the court that there is good cause for requiring the applicant to give security for any costs which may be ordered to be paid by him to any person affected by the application, the court has power to make an order that all proceedings upon the application must be stayed until such security for the costs of that person as may be required by the order has been given to the satisfaction of the court, and may order the payment into the Senior Courts of the whole or any part of any sum so required to be paid by way of such security: see s 5(5) (amended by the Constitutional Reform Act 2005 Sch 11 para 4). Contrast an application for ancillary rights made by the holder of a petroleum licence, for which see the Petroleum Act 1998 s 7(4)(c), (d); and ENERGY AND CLIMATE CHANGE vol 44 (2011) PARA 1053.

### 393. Application by more than one applicant.

Where separate applications are made by two or more persons for the right to work the same minerals[1] and are referred to the court[2], the court, in addition to the matters already mentioned[3], must determine which, if any, of the applicants is to be preferred, or whether the right to work one part of the minerals should be granted to one applicant and the right to work another part should be granted to another applicant, having regard to the question as to how the minerals can be most conveniently worked, to the respective rights of the applicants in the surface[4] or adjacent[5] minerals, and generally to all the circumstances of the case[6].

This provision applies, subject to the necessary modifications, to applications, for an ancillary right[7], and so that the ancillary right may be granted to the applicants, or to any two or more of them, jointly[8].

1 As to references to working minerals see PARA 381. As to references to rights to work minerals see PARA 384. As to the meaning of 'minerals' see PARA 10.
2 As to the meaning of 'court' see PARA 382.
3 See PARA 392.
4 As to the meaning of 'surface' see PARA 383.
5 As to the meaning of 'adjacent' see PARA 382.
6 See the Mines (Working Facilities and Support) Act 1966 s 6(1). In *Re J and J Charlesworth Ltd and Henry Briggs, Son & Co Ltd* (1926) 43 TLR 100, the parties agreed to divide the area of coal in question between them, but the Railway and Canal Commission (which then had jurisdiction: see PARA 390) ruled that it was not bound by the agreement and must consider the national interest. Accordingly, it required certain modifications to the agreement. See also *J C Jenkins & Co Ltd v Lancaster's Steam Collieries Ltd* (1924) 1 Bamber's Mining Cases 100.
7 As to ancillary rights see PARA 384.
8 See the Mines (Working Facilities and Support) Act 1966 s 6(2).

**394. Compensation on grant or restriction.**

Where a right by way of working facilities is granted[1] or any restriction on the working of minerals is imposed[2], the High Court may determine the amount and nature of compensation or consideration to be paid or given, and the persons to whom it is to be paid or given, either at the time when it determines whether the right should be granted or the restriction imposed or at any subsequent time[3].

The compensation or consideration in respect of any such right, including the right to enforce restrictions, must be assessed by the High Court on the basis of what would be fair and reasonable between a willing grantor and a willing grantee[4], having regard to the conditions subject to which the right is or is to be granted[5]. Where the person to whom any compensation or consideration is payable cannot be found or ascertained, the compensation or consideration must be paid into court[6].

The High Court may impose as a condition on the grant of any right or the imposition of any restriction that any compensation or consideration payable in respect of it must be paid, or that security to the satisfaction of the court for the payment of it must be given, before the right is commenced to be exercised or the restriction is enforced[7].

1  Ie under the Mines (Working Facilities and Support) Act 1966 s 1: see PARA 381 et seq. As to references to right to work minerals see PARA 384. As to references to working minerals see PARA 381. As to the meaning of 'minerals' see PARA 10.

2  Ie under the Mines (Working Facilities and Support) Act 1966 s 7: see PARA 387.

3  See the Mines (Working Facilities and Support) Act 1966 s 8(1). This provision does not detract from the right of the applicants and the parties concerned to agree between themselves what consideration or compensation should be paid or given: see PARA 392. As to exceptions to the right to compensation see PARAS 388, 392.

4  A willing grantor is a free agent, not required by compulsory powers to grant (see *IRC v Clay* [1914] 3 KB 466 at 473, CA, per Cozens-Hardy MR), one who is prepared to make the grant provided a fair consideration is obtained in all the circumstances of the case; he is not a grantor prepared to grant at any price and on any terms and who is actually at the time wishing to grant; he is not an anxious grantor (*IRC v Clay* at 478 per Pickford LJ). The principles to be applied in determining compensation under the Mines (Working Facilities and Support) Act 1966 s 8, are those which have been applied in determining compensation under the Lands Clauses Consolidation Act 1845 s 63 (see also the Compulsory Purchase Act 1965; and COMPULSORY ACQUISITION OF LAND vol 18 (2009) PARA 810): *BP Petroleum Developments Ltd v Ryder* [1987] 2 EGLR 233, [1987] RVR 211; and see *Re Naylor Benzon Mining Co Ltd* [1950] Ch 567, [1950] 1 All ER 518. These principles are summarised by Peter Gibson J in *BP Developments Ltd v Ryder* at 246 and 229 as follows: 'The grantor must receive consideration or compensation on the basis of the value of what he has lost, not on the basis of the value to the grantee of what he is acquiring. The value is of the rights over land with its existing use and subject to its existing restrictions, but together with all its potentialities; and, subject to not receiving more than he has lost the landowner is entitled to compensation for disturbance and injurious affection as well. The existence of the scheme underlying the compulsory acquisition must be disregarded, but the presence in the market of a purchaser for whom the rights have a special value may be taken into account. The loss of the bargaining power of the landowner through his veto which he enjoyed until compulsory powers are invoked by the making of the application is not a factor to be taken into account'. See, however, the criticism of the reasoning in *BP Petroleum Developments Ltd v Ryder* by Judge Hague QC in *Mercury Communications Ltd v London and India Dock Investments Ltd* [1994] 1 EGLR 229 at 236. The principles upon which a minimum rent may be imposed by way of compensation are discussed in *Re Sherwood Colliery Co Ltd* [1939] 1 All ER 88. A lump sum may be awarded, and in assessing such a sum no deduction on account of income tax need be made: *Re Associated Portland Cement Manufacturers Ltd's Application* [1966] 1 Ch 308, [1965] 2 All ER 547. In apportioning royalties between the tenant and the landlord all special circumstances are taken into account: *Re Markham Main Colliery Ltd* (1925) 41 TLR 672; and see *Re Trusts affecting Compensation Moneys in respect of Coal Holdings, Public Trustee v Manchester Corpn* [1949] Ch 737, [1949] 2 All ER 498.

5    Mines (Working Facilities and Support) Act 1966 s 8(2). In construing s 8(2), the court should
     approach it with the same general attitude and expectation as ordinarily it brought to the
     construction of statutory provisions dealing with compensation for compulsory land acquisition:
     see *Bocardo SA v Star Energy UK Onshore Ltd* [2009] EWCA Civ 579, [2010] Ch 100, [2010] 1
     All ER 26 (affd [2010] UKSC 35, [2011] 1 AC 380, [2010] 3 All ER 975). Special provisions apply
     on the grant of a right under s 2(3): see PARA 384.
6    Mines (Working Facilities and Support) Act 1966 s 8(4). The High Court, in any case where it
     thinks fit, may order the payment into court of the whole or any part of any compensation or
     consideration determined by it, and, pending the determination of the amount of this
     compensation or consideration, may order the payment into court of such sum on account as it
     thinks fit: see s 8(3). Payments into court must be made into the Senior Courts: see s 8(6)(a)
     (amended by the Constitutional Reform Act 2005 Sch 11 Pt 2 para 4(3)).
7    See the Mines (Working Facilities and Support) Act 1966 s 8(5).

## 395. Procedure on applications.

Where, under any provision of the Mines (Working Facilities and Support) Act
1966, the Secretary of State[1] refers any application to the High Court, he must file
a reference signed by him or a person authorised to sign on his behalf in the
Chancery Division of the High Court[2], together with any documents and plans
deposited with him by the applicant in support of his application[3] and within
three days of filing the reference, give notice to the applicant that the reference has
been filed[4].

Within ten days after receipt of that notice[5] the applicant must issue a claim
form which need not be served on any other party[6]. Within seven days after issue
of the claim form the applicant must apply for the claim to be listed for a hearing
before a master and give notice of the hearing date to the Secretary of State[7]. At
the hearing, the master must fix a time within which any notice of objection[8] must
be given[9], fix a date for the further hearing of the claim[10] and give directions about
any advertisement that is to be inserted or notice of the application and hearing
date that is to be given; and what persons are to be served with a copy of the
application or any other document in the proceedings[11].

Any person wishing to oppose the application must, within the time fixed by
the master[12], serve on the applicant a notice of objection[13]. An objector is entitled
to appear in person or by a solicitor or counsel at the further hearing of the claim
and to take such part in the proceedings as the master or judge thinks fit; but if he
does not so appear his notice of objection is of no effect and he is not entitled to
take any part in the proceedings unless the master or judge otherwise orders[14].

Not less than two days before the date set for the further hearing, the applicant
must file at court (1) any notices of objection served on him; (2) a list of objectors,
together with their names and addresses, the names and addresses of their
solicitors, if any; and a summary of their respective grounds of objection[15]. If the
objector does not appear, or is not represented, at the further hearing his notice of
objection will have no effect and he will not be entitled to take any further part
in the proceedings unless the court orders otherwise[16].

At the further hearing the court will give directions about the future conduct of
the claim[17] and adjourn the claim for hearing before the judge in such manner as
he thinks best adapted to secure the just, expeditious and economical disposal of
the proceedings[18].

In so far as they are not inconsistent with the procedure described above the
ordinary rules applicable in the Chancery Division have effect in relation to the
proceedings[19]. Appeals lie, in accordance with the provisions of general
application, to the Court of Appeal and the House of Lords[20].

The Secretary of State and any other government department must give to the
High Court such assistance as the court may require for the purposes of its duties

under the Mines (Working Facilities and Support) Act 1966, and are entitled to appear and be heard at any proceedings on any application before the court under that Act[21].

The provisions above[22] apply, with appropriate modifications, to proceedings in which jurisdiction has been conferred on the High Court by the Railway and Canal Commission (Abolition) Act 1949[23], except to the extent that an Act, a rule or a practice direction, provides otherwise[24].

1 As to the Secretary of State see PARA 2.
2 CPR PD 8A—*Alternative Procedure for Claims* para 15.2, 15.3(1).
3 CPR PD 8A—*Alternative Procedure for Claims* para 15.2, 15.3(2).
4 CPR PD 8A—*Alternative Procedure for Claims* para 15.2, 15.3(3).
5 Ie referred to in CPR PD 8A—*Alternative Procedure for Claims* para 15.3(3).
6 CPR PD 8A—*Alternative Procedure for Claims* para 15.4. The claim form (1) must identify the application under the Mines (Working Facilities and Support) Act 1966 and the remedy sought; and (2) need not be served on any other party: CPR PD 8A para 15.5.
7 CPR PD 8A—*Alternative Procedure for Claims* para 15.6. The applicant must, not less than two days before the date fixed for a hearing, file at court (1) a witness statement in support of the claim, giving details of all persons known to the applicant to be interested in, or affected by, the application; and (2) a draft of any proposed advertisement or notice of the application: CPR PD 8A para 15.7.
8 Ie under CPR PD 8A—*Alternative Procedure for Claims* para 15.9.
9 CPR PD 8A—*Alternative Procedure for Claims* para 15.8(1).
10 CPR PD 8A—*Alternative Procedure for Claims* para 15.8(2).
11 CPR PD 8A—*Alternative Procedure for Claims* para 15.8(3).
12 Ie under CPR PD 8A—*Alternative Procedure for Claims* para 15.8.
13 See CPR PD 8A—*Alternative Procedure for Claims* para 15.9. The notice must state his name and address and that of his solicitor, if any; the grounds of his objection and any alternative methods of effecting the objects of the application which he alleges may be used; and the facts on which he relies: see CPR PD 8A para 15.9(a)–(e). Any document that is required to be served on a person who has given notice of objection may be served by delivering it or sending it by prepaid post where the name and address of a solicitor is stated in the notice of objection, to the solicitor at that address, and in any other case, to the objector at his address stated in the notice of objection: CPR PD 8A para 15.10.
14 CPR PD 8A—*Alternative Procedure for Claims* para 15.11.
15 CPR PD 8A—*Alternative Procedure for Claims* para 15.12.
16 CPR PD 8A—*Alternative Procedure for Claims* para 15.13.
17 Such directions include (1) any further information the applicant is required to give in relation to any of the grounds or facts relied on in support of the application; (2) any further information the objector is required to give in relation to any of the grounds or facts relied on in opposition to the application; (3) whether the applicant may serve a reply to any notice of objection; (4) whether any particular fact should be proved by a witness statement; (5) whether any statements of case or points of claim or defence are to be served: CPR PD 8A—*Alternative Procedure for Claims* para 15.14(1).
18 CPR PD 8A—*Alternative Procedure for Claims* para 15.4(2).
19 As to the ordinary rules applicable in the Chancery Division see CIVIL PROCEDURE vol 11 (2015) PARA 16. The court has no inherent jurisdiction to make an interim order pending final determination of the application, but it is possible that it has such jurisdiction under the Mines (Working Facilities and Support) Act 1966 itself: see *Re W J King & Sons Ltd's Application* [1976] 1 All ER 770 at 778–779, [1976] 1 WLR 521 at 531–532, CA; cf *Re National Coal Board's Application* [1958] 2 All ER 351n, [1958] 1 WLR 599.
20 See COURTS AND TRIBUNALS vol 24 (2010) PARAS 657 et seq, 693–694.
21 See the Mines (Working Facilities and Support) Act 1966 s 9 (amended by virtue of SI 1969/1498; SI 1970/1537; SI 1974/692; SI 1992/1314; and the Coal Industry Act 1994 s 67(8), Sch 11 Pt II).
22 Ie CPR PD 8A—*Alternative Procedure for Claims* paras 15.3–15.14.
23 Ie by the Railway and Canal Commission (Abolition) Act 1949 s 1. Applications were formerly referred to the Railway and Canal Commission, but on the dissolution of that Commission under the Railway and Canal Commission (Abolition) Act 1949 its functions in that regard devolved on the High Court: s 1(1)(a).
24 CPR PD 8A—*Alternative Procedure for Claims* para 14.1.

## (ii) Working Rights for Coal in Relation to Underground Land

**396. Rights for coal in relation to underground land.**
Under the Coal Industry Act 1994[1] a licensed operator[2], or any person authorised[3] to act on his behalf in the carrying on of any of the operations which the operator is authorised to carry on, is entitled at any time on or after the restructuring date to exercise certain rights in relation to any underground land in the area in which the operator in question is authorised to carry on coal-mining operations[5].

The Coal Authority[6] and persons authorised by the Authority to exercise its rights under these provisions are also entitled at any time on or after the restructuring date to exercise those rights in relation to any underground land in relation to which there is not for the time being any person who, as a licensed operator, is authorised to carry on any coal-mining operations to which the licensing requirements apply[7].

The rights which may be so exercised are the rights (1) to enter upon, remove, execute works in, pass through or occupy that land; or (2) to do any acts requisite or convenient for the carrying on of any coal-mining operations[8]. However, the right may only be exercised for certain purposes, that is to say, in relation to a licensed operator or a person authorised to act on his behalf, the carrying on of any coal-mining operations and, in relation to the Authority, any purposes connected with the carrying out of its functions under the Coal Industry Act 1994[9].

Nothing in these provisions authorises:

(a)    any interference with the carrying on of any underground operations carried on otherwise than for purposes connected with any coal-mining operations[10];

(b)    the withdrawal of support from any land[11] or any interference with the surface of any land[12];

(c)    the doing of any act which, apart from these provisions, would be actionable by virtue of (i) any liberty, privilege, easement, advantage or other right annexed to any other land[13]; (ii) any restrictive covenant; or (iii) any statutory prohibition or restriction, which adversely affects the land in question[14]; or

(d)    the doing of any act which, apart from these provisions, would be actionable as a trespass or nuisance[15] and, if done, would be likely to cause actual damage of more than a purely nominal amount[16].

Moreover, nothing in these provisions confers any right to search for, bore for or get any oil or gas which is or becomes absorbed in or adsorbed to any coal[17]; nor is anything in these provisions to be taken to authorise a contravention of the licensing requirements[18] or of any of the conditions of a licence[19].

1    Ie the Coal Industry Act 1994 s 51. These provisions replace the provisions of earlier legislation; the rights conferred by virtue of the Coal Act 1938 s 15 (repealed), the Coal Industry Nationalisation Act 1946 s 8(1) (repealed) and the Control of Pollution Act 1974 s 25 (repealed) (which made provision similar to that made by the Coal Industry Act 1994 s 51, and extended such provision to waste disposal), or by virtue of any of those provisions, are not exercisable at any time on or after the restructuring date (ie 31 October 1994: see PARA 50): see s 51(8).

2    As to the meaning of 'licensed operator' see PARA 58.

3    Ie authorised as mentioned in the Coal Industry Act 1994 s 27(4): see PARA 93.

5    Coal Industry Act 1994 s 51(1). As to the meaning of 'coal-mining operations' see PARA 51.

6    As to the Coal Authority see PARA 52 et seq.

7    Coal Industry Act 1994 s 51(2). This entitlement is subject to the provisions of s 5(6): see PARA

64. As to the licensing requirements see PARA 89 et seq.

8  Coal Industry Act 1994 s 51(3).

9  Coal Industry Act 1994 s 51(4).

10  Coal Industry Act 1994 s 51(5)(a).

11  As to the right under the Coal Industry Act 1994 to withdraw support from land see PARA 176.

12  Coal Industry Act 1994 s 51(5)(b).

13  For these purposes, the reference to a liberty, privilege, easement, advantage or other right being annexed to any land is a reference to its appertaining to that land or any part of it, to its being demised, occupied or enjoyed with that land or any part of it or to its being reputed or known as part or parcel of the land or as appurtenant to the land or any part of it: Coal Industry Act 1994 s 51(6).

14  Coal Industry Act 1994 s 51(5)(c).

15  As to trespass see TORT vol 97 (2015) PARA 525 et seq; and as to nuisance see NUISANCE.

16  Coal Industry Act 1994 s 51(5)(e).

17  Ie any such right as is mentioned in the Coal Industry Act 1994 s 9(1)(b): see PARA 68. As to oil and gas see ENERGY AND CLIMATE CHANGE.

18  Ie the Coal Industry Act 1994 s 25(1): see PARA 89.

19  Coal Industry Act 1994 s 51(7). As to the licensing requirements generally and the conditions of a licence under Pt II (ss 25–36) see PARA 89 et seq.

### (iii)  Statutory Right to Work Coal in Former Copyhold Land

### 397.  Right to work coal in former copyhold land.

Where any coal[1] or coal mine[2] is comprised in or lies under land which was formerly copyhold[3] and a relevant notice specifying the area in which that land is comprised has been given[4] and has come into force or has been published before the restructuring date[5] in accordance with the statutory provisions then in force[6], the relevant person[7] has the like right in relation to that coal or coal mine to carry on coal-mining operations to which the licensing requirements apply[8] as if all retained interests[9] in that coal or mine subsisting on 31 August 1975 were vested in him, notwithstanding that they are by virtue of any enactment in fact vested in another person[10].

There are provisions for compensation and certain other matters where a relevant notice is given or has been published[11].

The publication of a relevant notice does not prevent any person from acquiring by agreement any retained interest in any coal or coal mine comprised in or lying under land in the area to which the notice relates[12].

1  As to the meaning of 'coal' see PARA 51.

2  As to the meaning of 'coal mine' see PARA 3.

3  See CUSTOM AND USAGE; REAL PROPERTY AND REGISTRATION vol 87 (2017) PARA 36 et seq.

4  Ie in accordance with the Coal Industry Act 1994 s 50, which applies with respect to the giving of a notice for the purposes of s 49 at any time on or after the restructuring date: s 50(1). The only person who may give the notice is a person who is authorised by a licence under Pt II (ss 25–36) (see PARA 89 et seq) or by virtue of s 25(3) (see PARA 89) to carry on coal-mining operations in the area specified in the notice: s 50(2). The notice must: (1) indicate the land to which it relates either by reference to a map or in any other manner which, in the circumstances, is sufficient to identify it; (2) identify the person by whom the notice is given and summarise the respects in which the requirements of s 50(2) are satisfied in relation to that person; (3) state that there are proposals to carry on coal-mining operations in relation to any coal or coal mine which may require the exercise in relation to that land of such a right as is mentioned in s 49(1); and (4) invite the owners of retained interests in any coal or coal mine comprised in or lying under the land in the area to which the notice relates to give notice of their interests, within the period which begins with the date of the first publication of the notice and ends six years after the coming into force of the notice, to the person who gave the notice: s 50(3). The notice must be given by being published in the London Gazette, and at least once in each of two successive weeks in newspapers circulating

in the locality where the land to which the notice relates is situated: s 50(4). A notice given for these purposes at any time on or after the restructuring date comes into force when particulars of it are first registered by the Coal Authority in accordance with s 56 (see PARA 106): s 49(6). As to the Coal Authority see PARA 52 et seq. As to the meaning of 'coal-mining operations' see PARA 51.

    The Authority must not enter any notice given for the purposes of s 49 on or after the restructuring date in the register (ie the register maintained under s 56: see PARA 106) unless it is satisfied that the notice has been properly given in accordance with the requirements of the Coal Industry Act 1994: see s 56(3).

5  Ie 31 October 1994: see PARA 50.

6  Ie the Coal Industry Act 1975 s 3 (repealed), which contained provisions equivalent to the provisions of the Coal Industry Act 1994 ss 49, 50. Subject to s 49(1)–(8), the rights conferred on the British Coal Corporation by the Coal Industry Act 1975 s 3 (repealed) are not exercisable at any time on or after the restructuring date: Coal Industry Act 1994 s 49(9). As to the British Coal Corporation see PARAS 49–50.

7  For these purposes, the relevant person, in relation to any relevant notice, is: (1) in the case of a notice given in accordance with the Coal Industry Act 1994 s 50, the person who gave the notice; and (2) in the case of a notice published in accordance with the Coal Industry Act 1975 s 3 (repealed), the British Coal Corporation: Coal Industry Act 1994 s 49(2).

    In so far as:

    (a)     a person other than the relevant person is for the time being a licensed operator in relation to the coal or mine which is comprised in, or lies under, the land comprised in the area specified in a relevant notice; and

    (b)     compensation under s 49, Sch 7 Pt I (see PARA 399) or, in relation to times before the restructuring date, under the Coal Industry Act 1975 s 3(4) (repealed) either has become due in respect of any retained interest affected by that notice and has been paid in full or would have become due in respect of such an interest but for an agreement under the Coal Industry Act 1994 Sch 7 para 8 (see PARA 399) or the Coal Industry Act 1975 s 3, Sch 2 para 8 (repealed),

the person mentioned in head (a) is entitled (instead of the relevant person) to exercise the relevant person's rights by virtue of the Coal Industry Act 1994 s 49(1): s 49(3). As to the meaning of 'licensed operator' see PARA 58. In the case of any licensed operator who is entitled by virtue of s 49 to carry on any coal-mining operations in relation to any coal or coal mine, the rights comprised in his entitlement are also exercisable by any person authorised as mentioned in s 27(4) (see PARA 93) to act on his behalf in the carrying on of any of the operations which the operator is authorised to carry on: s 49(4).

8  Ie the Coal Industry Act 1994 s 25: see PARA 89.

9  As to the meaning of 'retained interest' see PARA 48 (definition applied by the Coal Industry Act 1994 s 49(8)). However, all retained interests except those which are interests in coal or a mine of coal in or under land formerly copyhold have vested in the Corporation: see PARAS 49–50.

10  Coal Industry Act 1994 s 49(1). Nothing in these provisions confers any such right as is mentioned in s 9(1)(b) (see PARA 68) or is to be taken to authorise a contravention of s 25(1) (see PARA 89) or any of the conditions of a licence under Pt II (see PARA 89 et seq); and the rights that are conferred on the Corporation by these provisions have effect subject to any transfer of those rights, in accordance with any restructuring scheme, to any other person: s 49(5). As to restructuring schemes see PARA 72.

11  See the Coal Industry Act 1994 s 49(7), Sch 7; and PARAS 398–400.

    Where notice of a retained interest was given before the restructuring date by virtue of the Coal Industry Act 1975 s 3 (repealed), certain provisions of the Coal Industry Act 1975 continue to have effect instead of the corresponding provisions of the Coal Industry Act 1994 Sch 7: see Sch 7 para 12.

12  See the Coal Industry Act 1994 Sch 7 para 10. However, at any time after an acceptance notice (see PARA 398) has been served in respect of a retained interest, the person who served it ceases to be entitled to acquire by agreement that interest or any other retained interest in any coal or coal mine comprised in or lying under any of the land in which the accepted interest subsists: Sch 7 para 8(3). This does not prejudice the making of agreements with respect to compensation (see PARA 399): see Sch 7 para 8(3).

## 398. Claims in respect of retained interests.

At any time after the restructuring date[1] and in pursuance of an invitation contained in a relevant notice[2], the claimant of compensation may give a retained interest[3] notice[4]. The claimant must furnish, together with the retained interest notice, adequate proof of his title to the interest at the time when he gives the notice[5].

Where any of the British Coal Corporation's[6] rights in relation to any land[7] have been transferred in accordance with a restructuring scheme[8] to any other person (1) the persons to whom a retained interest notice relating to that land may be given for these purposes are the Corporation, the Coal Authority[9] or that other person; and (2) a retained interest notice given to the Corporation or the Authority must be forwarded by the Corporation or Authority, as soon as reasonably practicable after being received, to that other person and is to be treated for these purposes as if given to that other person when it was given to the Corporation or Authority[10].

Within the period of three months beginning with the date on which the person to whom it is given receives a retained interest notice, or within such longer period as may be agreed between that person and the claimant, that person must serve on the claimant either an acceptance notice in the prescribed form[11] accepting the claimant's title to the retained interest and acknowledging that compensation is payable[12] or a rejection notice rejecting the claimant's retained interest notice[13]. Where a person serves an acceptance notice or a rejection notice, he must at the same time send a copy of that notice to the Authority[14]. A person who fails to comply with any of these requirements as to the service of notices, or as to the sending of a copy of any notice to the Authority is guilty of an offence[15].

Where, after the receipt by any person of a retained interest notice, an acceptance notice is served in respect of the retained interest concerned, the service of that acceptance notice is a valid ground for the service of a rejection notice in respect of any other retained interest which is received by any person after the service of that acceptance notice and relates to any of the land in which the accepted interest subsists[16].

As soon as practicable after any person has served an acceptance notice on a claimant, that person must pay to the claimant any reasonable legal expenses incurred by the claimant for the purposes of establishing his ownership of the retained interest to which the acceptance notice relates and giving the retained interest notice by virtue of which the acceptance notice came to be served[17].

A claimant who has served a retained interest notice relating to any land and who is aggrieved by the service on him of a rejection notice relating to his retained interest notice[18] may, within the period of three months beginning with the date of service of the rejection notice, make an application to the county court for an order directing the withdrawal of the rejection notice and the service of an acceptance notice in respect of the retained interest which he claims[19].

On such an application, the court may direct that, in addition to the applicant and the person who served the rejection notice, the Authority and any person other than the claimant who has given a retained interest notice relating to the whole or any part of the relevant land is to be made a party to the application unless, in the case of a person other than the claimant who has given a retained interest notice (a) a rejection notice has already been served in respect of that retained interest notice; and (b) the time within which that person might have made an application under these provisions in respect of that rejection notice has expired without such an application having been made[20].

The court must determine whether the applicant or any other party to the application who contests the applicant's claim or any other person (whether a party to the application or not) on whom an acceptance notice relating to the whole or any part of relevant land has been served was, at the time when he gave his retained interest notice, entitled to a retained interest in the whole or any part of the relevant land; and the court must order service (if it has not already been done) of an acceptance notice or, if more than one of them were so entitled to a retained interest in the same piece of land, on that one of them whose retained interest notice was given first[21].

1  Ie 31 October 1994: see PARA 50.
2  As to the relevant notice see PARA 397.
3  As to the meaning of 'retained interest' see PARA 48 (definition applied by the Coal Industry Act 1994 s 49(8)).
4  See the Coal Industry Act 1994 s 49, Sch 7 para 1(1), (2).
5  Coal Industry Act 1994 Sch 7 para 2.
6  As to the British Coal Corporation see PARAS 49–50.
7  Ie under the Coal Industry Act 1994 s 49: see PARA 397.
8  As to restructuring schemes see PARA 72.
9  As to the Coal Authority see PARA 52 et seq.
10  Coal Industry Act 1994 Sch 7 para 1(3).
11  For these purposes, 'prescribed' means prescribed by regulations made by the Secretary of State by statutory instrument; and a statutory instrument containing regulations under this provision is subject to annulment in pursuance of a resolution of either House of Parliament: Coal Industry Act 1994 Sch 7 para 3(7). As to the form prescribed see the Coal Industry (Retained Copyhold Interests) Regulations 1994, SI 1994/2562. As to the Secretary of State see PARA 2.
12  Ie that an obligation under the Coal Industry Act 1994 Sch 7 Pt I to pay compensation in respect of the retained interest has arisen or will arise if the right in question is exercised: see Sch 7 para 3.
13  See the Coal Industry Act 1994 Sch 7 para 3(1), (2). A rejection notice must specify the ground or grounds on which the claimant's retained interest notice is rejected and, where the matters specified concern only a part of the land to which the retained interest notice relates, must identify the part in question: Sch 7 para 3(5).
14  Coal Industry Act 1994 Sch 7 para 3(3).
15  Coal Industry Act 1994 Sch 7 para 3(4). Such a person is liable, on summary conviction, to a fine not exceeding level 3 on the standard scale: Sch 7 para 3(4). As to the standard scale see SENTENCING vol 92 (2015) PARA 176.
16  Coal Industry Act 1994 Sch 7 para 3(6).
17  Coal Industry Act 1994 Sch 7 para 4.
18  Ie other than a rejection notice served in pursuance of an order under the Coal Industry Act 1994 Sch 7 para 5.
19  Coal Industry Act 1994 Sch 7 para 5(1).
20  Coal Industry Act 1994 Sch 7 para 5(2).
21  Coal Industry Act 1994 Sch 7 para 5(3). An order under Sch 7 para 5(3) may contain such provisions as the court considers appropriate (1) for securing that every party to the application other than (a) the person to whom the retained interest notice in question was given; and (b) any person on whom an acceptance notice has been or is ordered to be served, is or has been served with a rejection notice; and (2) where it appears to the court that an acceptance notice has been served which should not have been served, for securing (a) that the notice is cancelled; and (b) that the person who served the notice brings the cancellation to the attention of the person who, if the notice had not been cancelled, would have been the person with an actual or contingent entitlement to compensation under Sch 7 Pt I in respect of the accepted interest: Sch 7 para 5(4). If, in accordance with this provision, the court orders the cancellation of an acceptance notice, it must be conclusively presumed for the purposes of s 49 and s 50 (see PARA 397) and for the purposes of Sch 7 (except Sch 7 para 5) that the person on whom the acceptance notice was served did not have a retained interest in the relevant land at the time when he served his retained interest notice and that a rejection notice was served in respect of that retained interest notice: Sch 7 para 5(5). As to contingent entitlement to compensation see PARA 399.
    Nothing in Sch 7 para 4 affects the power of the court on an application under Sch 7 para 5 (or in any subsequent proceedings) to make such order as to costs as it thinks fit; and any such order may make such modifications, if any, of a person's obligation under Sch 7 para 4 as appear to the court to be just in the light of other provisions as to costs which are contained in the order: Sch 7 para 5(6).

## 399.   Compensation in respect of retained interests.

Where any person has begun to exercise any right[1] in relation to any coal[2] or coal mine[3] comprised in or lying under any land in which a retained interest[4] subsists, and a right to compensation has not arisen under this provision in respect of the exercise of the right by a person whose right it was previously, then the person who has begun to exercise the right must pay compensation in respect of that interest[5]. Compensation is to be calculated by reference to the consideration which, on the date on which the exercise of the right began, would have been appropriate, as between a willing grantor and a willing grantee, on a conveyance of that interest[6] to the person who exercises that right[7]. Where compensation is due to any person, any reasonable valuation expenses incurred by him for the purpose of ascertaining the value, at the date referred to, of the retained interest to which the compensation relates must be paid to him in addition to the compensation[8]. Any dispute as to the amount of any compensation or as to the amount of any valuation expenses to be paid must be determined by the Upper Tribunal[9].

The person having the right to receive compensation in respect of a retained interest to which an acceptance notice[10] relates is the person on whom that notice was served, notwithstanding that he may not own the retained interest at the time when the compensation becomes due; and accordingly that right devolves on his death and may be assigned in like manner as the right of a creditor under an unsecured debt[11].

If, at the time when compensation becomes due in respect of a retained interest, any compensation is paid in good faith to the person who produces the acceptance notice relating to that interest, the surrender of that notice by way of receipt for the compensation constitutes an adequate discharge to the person paying the compensation of his liability to pay that compensation, without any further proof that the person producing the acceptance notice is entitled to receive the compensation[12].

If at any time after an acceptance notice has been served in respect of a retained interest, and before the date on which compensation becomes due in respect of that interest, any person ('the relevant person') enters into an agreement in that behalf with another person (being the person with the contingent entitlement to any such compensation) then, on payment to that other person of such consideration as may be agreed, the relevant person is relieved of any contingent liability under these provisions in respect of that retained interest[13].

Where any person makes a payment of compensation under these provisions[14] or enters into an agreement relieving him of contingent liability[15], he must, as soon as reasonably practicable after making the payment or entering into the agreement, send particulars of the payment or agreement to the Coal Authority[16].

A person who fails to comply with any of the requirements as to the sending of any particulars to the Authority is guilty of an offence[17].

1  Ie any right which is a right of his under the Coal Industry Act 1994 s 49(1): see PARA 397.
2  As to the meaning of 'coal' see PARA 51.
3  As to the meaning of 'coal mine' see PARA 3.
4  As to the meaning of 'retained interest' see PARA 48 (definition applied by the Coal Industry Act 1994 s 49(8)).
5  Coal Industry Act 1994 s 49, Sch 7 para 6(1). Where a person who has become liable for any compensation under this provision ceases to be a person who is entitled to exercise the right in question, his so ceasing affects neither his liability nor the amount of the compensation: Sch 7 para 6(3). However, Sch 7 para 6(3) is subject to so much of any restructuring scheme as makes provision for the transfer to any other person, as from the restructuring date (ie 31 October 1994:

see PARA 50) or any subsequent date, of any of the British Coal Corporation's liabilities (ie by virtue of Sch 7 para 6): see Sch 7 para 6(6). As to restructuring schemes see PARA 72. As to the British Coal Corporation see PARAS 49–50.

6   Ie so far as it subsists in the land subject to the right: see the Coal Industry Act 1994 Sch 7 para 6(2).

7   Coal Industry Act 1994 Sch 7 para 6(2).

8   See the Coal Industry Act 1994 Sch 7 para 6(4).

9   Coal Industry Act 1994 Sch 7 para 6(5) (amended by SI 2009/1307). The powers of the Upper Tribunal by virtue of this provision in respect of the costs of proceedings before the tribunal are not prejudiced by Sch 7 para 6(4): see Sch 7 para 6(6) (amended by SI 2009/1307). As to the Upper Tribunal see COURTS AND TRIBUNALS vol 24 (2010) PARA 883.

10  As to acceptance notices see PARA 398.

11  Coal Industry Act 1994 Sch 7 para 7(2). Subject to Sch 7 para 5 (see PARA 398), it must be conclusively presumed that a person on whom a rejection notice has been served has neither an actual nor, as the case may be, a contingent entitlement to compensation under these provisions in respect of the interest to which the notice relates: Sch 7 para 7(1). As to rejection notices see PARA 398.

    References, in relation to any right under s 49(1) (see PARA 397), to a person with a contingent entitlement to compensation under Sch 7 Pt I are references to any person who would be entitled to any such compensation if the person with that right began to exercise it: Sch 7 para 6(7).

12  Coal Industry Act 1994 Sch 7 para 7(3).

13  Coal Industry Act 1994 Sch 7 para 8(1). Where any such agreement is entered into, Sch 7 para 7(3) applies in relation to the payment of the consideration agreed as it applies in relation to a payment of compensation at the time referred to in that provision: Sch 7 para 8(2).

14  Ie under the Coal Industry Act 1994 Sch 7 Pt I.

15  Ie an agreement for the purposes of the Coal Industry Act 1994 Sch 7 para 8.

16  Coal Industry Act 1994 Sch 7 para 9(1). As to the Coal Authority see PARA 52 et seq.

    The particulars to be sent to the Authority include particulars identifying: (1) the person to whom the payment is made or, as the case may be, the parties to the agreement; and (2) the interest in respect of which the payment is made or, as the case may be, in respect of which the contingent liability extinguished by the agreement arose: Sch 7 para 9(2).

    As to registration of this information see s 56; and PARA 106.

17  Coal Industry Act 1994 Sch 7 para 9(3). Such a person is liable, on summary conviction, to a fine not exceeding level 3 on the standard scale: Sch 7 para 9(3). As to the standard scale see SENTENCING vol 92 (2015) PARA 176.

## 400.   Prior rights.

If (1) the British Coal Corporation[1] was, on 31 August 1975, entitled[2] to work any coal[3] or to use any coal mine[4] in which a retained interest[5] subsisted at that time; (2) that entitlement has continued throughout the period since that date as an entitlement of the Corporation or, at different times, of the Corporation and a person to whom the Corporation's rights have been transferred in accordance with a restructuring scheme[6]; and (3) the Corporation or such person was still so entitled, then the provisions relating to the working of coal in or under land which was formerly copyhold[7] would not apply with respect to that coal or coal mine or to any retained interest in it except in relation to matters unconnected with the exercise of that entitlement[8]. Where, on or after the restructuring date[9], a notice which is given for the purposes of those provisions specifies any area and at the time when the notice was published the above conditions[10] were satisfied in relation to any coal or coal mine comprised in or lying under land in that area, then so much of that land as consists of that coal or coal mine is deemed to be excluded from that area[11]. If notice of a retained interest is given[12] at a time when the above conditions[13] were satisfied in relation to any coal or coal mine comprised in or lying under the land in which that interest subsists, then for the purpose of determining the amount of any compensation under these provisions that interest so far as it relates to that coal or mine must be treated as no longer subsisting[14].

1   As to the British Coal Corporation see PARAS 49–50.
2   Ie by virtue of an order under the Mines (Working Facilities and Support) Act 1966 s 1 (see PARAS 381–384) or by any agreement: see the Coal Industry Act 1994 s 49, Sch 7 para 11(1).
3   As to the meaning of 'coal' see PARA 51.
4   As to the meaning of 'coal mine' see PARA 3.
5   As to the meaning of 'retained interest' see PARA 48 (definition applied by the Coal Industry Act 1994 s 49(8)).
6   As to restructuring schemes see PARA 72.
7   Ie the Coal Industry Act 1994 s 49: see PARA 397. As to copyhold see CUSTOM AND USAGE; REAL PROPERTY AND REGISTRATION vol 87 (2017) PARA 36 et seq.
8   Coal Industry Act 1994 Sch 7 para 11(1).
9   Ie 31 October 1994: see PARA 50.
10  See heads (1)–(3) in the text.
11  Coal Industry Act 1994 Sch 7 para 11(2).
12  Ie in pursuance of an invitation to give notice of retained interests (see PARA 397): see the Coal Industry Act 1994 Sch 7 para 11(3), (4).
13  See heads (1)–(3) in the text.
14  Coal Industry Act 1994 Sch 7 para 11(3).

## (iv) Deep Sea Mining

### 401. Prohibition of unlicensed deep sea mining.

Before the conclusion of the United Nations Convention of the Law of the Sea[1], several states enacted legislation and entered into international agreements for the avoidance of conflicts over deep sea mining areas[2]. In 1981, the United Kingdom enacted the Deep Sea Mining Act 1981 to make provision for deep sea mining operations[3].

A person[4] may not:

(1)     explore for mineral resources[5] of any description in any area of the deep sea bed[6] unless the person holds an exploration licence[7] which is in force or is the agent or employee of the holder of such a licence (acting in that capacity) and the licence relates to mineral resources of that description and to that area of the deep sea bed[8];

(2)     exploit mineral resources of any description in any area of the deep sea bed unless the person holds an exploitation licence[9] which is in force or is the agent or employee of the holder of such a licence (acting in that capacity, and the licence relates to mineral resources of that description and to that area of the deep sea bed[10].

A person who contravenes heads (1) and (2) is guilty of an offence[11].

1   Ie the United Nations Convention on the Law of the Sea (New York, 10 December 1982; TS 81 (1999); Cmnd 4524).
2   Eg the Agreement Concerning Interim Arrangements Relating to Polymetallic Nodules of the Deep Sea Bed (Washington, 2 September 1982; TS 46 (1982); Cmnd 8685); Provisional Understanding on Deep Sea Matters (Geneva, 3 August 1984; TS 24 (1985); Cmnd 9536).
3   Deep Sea Mining Act 1981 preamble, s 18(1). The Deep Sea Mining Act 1981 was previously known as the Deep Sea Mining (Temporary Provisions) Act 1981 and was renamed by the Deep Sea Mining Act 2014 Schedule para 16. The Deep Sea Mining Act 1981 applies to Northern Ireland: s 18(7). Her Majesty may by Order in Council direct that any of the provisions of the Deep Sea Mining Act 1981 are to extend, with such modifications (if any) as may be specified in the order, to the Channel Islands, the Isle of Man or any colony: s 18(6). In exercise of this power the following orders have been made: Deep Sea Mining (Temporary Provisions) Act 1981 (Guernsey) Order 1997, SI 1997/2978; Deep Sea Mining (Temporary Provisions) Act 1981 (Jersey) Order 1997, SI 1997/2979; Deep Sea Mining Act 1981 (Isle of Man) Order 2015, SI 2015/2012.

4    The Deep Sea Mining Act 1981 s 1 applies to any person who is a United Kingdom national, a
     Scottish firm or a body incorporated under the law of any part of the United Kingdom and is
     resident in any part of the United Kingdom: see the Deep Sea Mining Act 1981 s 1(1), (4). 'United
     Kingdom national' means (1) a British citizen, a British overseas territories citizen, a British
     National (Overseas) or a British Overseas citizen; (2) a person who under the British Nationality
     Act 1981 is a British subject; or (3) a British protected person (within the meaning of that Act): s
     1(6) (amended by the British Nationality Act 1981 s 52(6); the British Overseas Territories Act
     2002 s 2(3);and SI 1986/984). In any proceedings, a certificate issued by the Secretary of State or
     the Scottish Ministers certifying that an area of the sea bed is beyond the limits of national
     jurisdiction of the United Kingdom or any other State] shall be conclusive as to that fact; and any
     document purporting to be such a certificate shall be received in evidence and shall, unless the
     contrary is proved, be deemed to be such a certificate: s 1(7) (amended by the Deep Sea Mining Act
     2014 Schedule para 2).
5    'Mineral resource' means a solid, liquid or gaseous mineral resource: Deep Sea Mining Act 1981
     s 1(6).
6    'Deep sea bed' means the area of the sea bed situated beyond the limits of national jurisdiction of
     the United Kingdom or any other state: Deep Sea Mining Act 1981 ss 1(6), 17 (definition
     substituted by the Deep Sea Mining Act 2014 Schedule para 14). As to the meaning of 'United
     Kingdom' see PARA 48.
7    'Exploration', in relation to mineral resources of any area of the deep sea bed, means the
     investigation of that area of the deep sea bed for the purpose of ascertaining whether or not the
     mineral resources of that area of the deep sea bed can be commercially exploited: Deep Sea Mining
     Act 1981 s 17. 'Exploration licence" has the meaning given by s 2 (see PARA 402): s 17 (definition
     substituted by the Deep Sea Mining Act 2014 Schedule para 14).
8    Deep Sea Mining Act 1981 s 1(1) (s 1(1), (2) substituted, s 1(2A) added by Deep Sea Mining Act
     2014 Schedule para 2). The Deep Sea Mining Act 1981 s 1(1), (2) are subject to s 3A: s 1(2A). A
     person to whom s 1 applies is not prohibited by s 1 from prospecting for mineral resources in any
     area of the deep sea bed if that person does so in accordance with the terms of a notification of
     prospecting given by that person to the International Seabed Authority under the Convention and
     recorded by the Authority as complying with the requirements of the Convention: s 3A(1) (s 3A
     added by the Deep Sea Mining Act 2014 Schedule para 4). Where a person to whom Deep Sea
     Mining Act 1981 s 1 holds a contract for exploration granted by the Authority or is the agent or
     employee of the holder of such a contract (acting in that capacity), that person is not prohibited
     by that section from exploring for any of the description of mineral resources to which the contract
     relates in any area of the deep sea bed in respect of which the contract is in force: s 3A(2). Where
     a person to whom s 1 applies holds a contract for exploitation granted by the Authority or is the
     agent or employee of the holder of such a contract (acting in that capacity), that person is not
     prohibited by that section from exploiting any of the description of mineral resources to which the
     contract relates in any area of the deep sea bed in respect of which the contract is in force: s 3A(3).
9    Exploitation' means commercial exploitation: Deep Sea Mining Act 1981 s 17. 'Exploitation
     licence' has the meaning given by s 2: s 17.
10   Deep Sea Mining Act 1981 s 1(2).
11   Deep Sea Mining Act 1981 s 1(3). Deep Sea Mining Act 1981 s 1(3). A person guilty of such an
     offence is liable, on conviction on indictment, to a fine; or, on summary conviction, to a fine not
     exceeding the statutory maximum: s 1(3)(a), (b). As to the supplementary provisions relating to
     offences under the Deep Sea Mining Act 1981 see PARA 411. As to the statutory maximum see
     SENTENCING vol 92 (2015) PARA 176. The application of s 1 may be extended by Order in
     Council see s 1(5).

## 402.   Exploration and exploitation licences.

The Secretary of State may, on payment of such a fee[1] as may with the consent
of the Treasury be prescribed[2], grant to such persons as he thinks fit licences for
the exploration[3] or exploitation[4] licences, except where the Scottish Ministers
have power to grant the exploration or exploitation licence in question[5]. An
exploration or an exploitation licence may be granted for such period as the
Secretary of State thinks fit and must not come into force before the date on which
a corresponding contract comes into force[6]. An exploration or exploitation licence
may contain such terms and conditions as the Secretary of State thinks fit: (1)
relating to the safety, health or welfare of persons employed in the licensed
operations[7] or in the ancillary operations[8]; (2) relating to the processing or other

treatment of any mineral resources[9] extracted in pursuance of the licence which is carried out by or on behalf of the licensee[10] on any ship[11]; (3) relating to the disposal of any waste material resulting from such processing or other treatment[12]; (4) requiring plans, returns, accounts or other records with respect to any matter connected with the licensed mineral resource and the licensed area or licensed operations or ancillary operations, to be provided to the Secretary of State[13]; (5) requiring samples of the licensed mineral resource discovered in or extracted from the licensed area, or assays of such samples, to be provided to the Secretary of State[14]; (6) requiring any exploration for or exploitation of the licensed mineral resource in the licensed area to be diligently carried out[15]; (7) requiring the licensee to comply with such provisions of the United Nations Convention on the Law of the Sea and the Agreement relating to the Implementation of Part XI of the United Nations Convention on the Law of the Sea of December 1982, interpreted in accordance with Article 2 of the Agreement, as are applicable to contractors[16]; (8) requiring compliance with any other rules, regulations and procedures issued or adopted by the International Seabed Authority, as are applicable to contractors[17]; (9) requiring compliance with a corresponding contract[18]; (10) requiring compliance with any plan of work authorised by a corresponding contract;[19] (11) requiring payment to the Secretary of State of such sums as may with the consent of the Treasury be prescribed at such times as may be prescribed[20]; and (12) permitting the transfer of the licence in prescribed cases or with the written consent of the Secretary of State[21]. Where the Secretary of State has granted an exploration licence he must not grant an exploitation licence which relates to any part of the licensed area in relation to the exploration licence and to any of the mineral resources to which that licence relates unless the exploitation licence is granted to the holder of the exploration licence or with that person's written consent[22].It is the duty of the licensee to exercise his rights under the licence with reasonable regard to the interests of other persons in their exercise of the freedom of the high seas[23].

1   As to the fee payable for the grant of an exploration licence see the Deep Sea Mining (Exploration Licences) (Applications) Regulations 1982, SI 1982/58, reg 3. As to the additional fees payable see the Deep Sea Mining (Exploration Licences) Regulations 1984, SI 1984/1230, reg 5. As to the Secretary of State see PARA 2.

2   'Prescribed' means prescribed by regulations under the Deep Sea Mining Act 1981 s 12: s 17. As to the power to make regulations prescribing anything required or authorised to be prescribed under this Act in relation to an exploration or exploitation licence granted or to be granted by the Secretary of State or generally for carrying the Deep Sea Mining Act 1981: see s 12.

3   As to the meaning of 'exploration' see PARA 401. 'Exploration licence' means a licence under the Deep Sea Mining Act 1981 s 2 authorising the licensee to explore for mineral resources of a description specified in the licence in an area so specified: ss 2(1), 17 (substituted by the Deep Sea Mining Act 2014 Schedule para 3).

4   As to the meaning of 'exploitation' see PARA 401. 'Exploitation licence' means a licence under the Deep Sea Mining Act 1981 authorising the licensee to exploit mineral resources of a description specified in the licence in an area so specified;: Deep Sea Mining Act 1981 ss 2(1), 17.

5   See the Deep Sea Mining Act 1981 s 2(2) (amended by the Deep Sea Mining Act 2014 Schedule para 3). Nothing in the Food and Environment Protection Act 1985 Pt II (deposits in the sea) (see ENVIRONMENTAL QUALITY AND PUBLIC HEALTH vol 45 (2010) PARA 525) or the Marine and Coastal Access Act 2009 (Pt 4) (marine licensing) (see WATER AND WATERWAYS vol 100PARA 81) applies to anything done in pursuance of an exploration or exploitation licence or a contract granted by the Authority: see the Deep Sea Mining Act 1981 s 16 (substituted by the Deep Sea Mining Act 2014 Schedule para 14).

6   Deep Sea Mining Act 1981 s 2(3) (substituted by the Deep Sea Mining Act 2014 Schedule para 3).

7   'Licensed operations' means any activities which the licensee may carry on by virtue of his licence: Deep Sea Mining Act 1981 s 17.

8　Deep Sea Mining Act 1981 s 2(3A)(a) (s 2(3A) added by the Deep Sea Mining Act 1981 s 17). 'Ancillary operations', in relation to any licensed operations, means any activity carried on by or on behalf of the licensee which is ancillary to the licensed operations (including the processing and transportation of any substances recovered): s 17.

9　As to the meaning of 'mineral resources' see PARA 401.

10　'Licensee' means the holder of an exploration or exploitation licence: Deep Sea Mining Act 1981 s 17.

11　Deep Sea Mining Act 1981 s 2(3A)(b).

12　Deep Sea Mining Act 1981 s 2(3A)(c).

13　Deep Sea Mining Act 1981 s 2(3A(d).

14　Deep Sea Mining Act 1981 s 2(3A)(e).

15　Deep Sea Mining Act 1981 s 2(3A)(f).

16　Deep Sea Mining Act 1981 s 2(3A)(g).

17　Deep Sea Mining Act 1981 s 2(3A)(h).

18　Deep Sea Mining Act 1981 s 2(3A)(i).

19　Deep Sea Mining Act 1981 s 2(3A)(j).

20　Deep Sea Mining Act 1981 s 2(3A)(k).

21　Deep Sea Mining Act 1981 s 2(3A)(m).

22　Deep Sea Mining Act 1981 s 2(5) (substituted by the Deep Mining Act 2014 Schedule para 3).

23　Deep Sea Mining Act 1981 s 7.

## 403.　Contracts granted by the International Seabed Authority.

The Secretary of State must not grant an exploration[1] or exploitation licence[2] which relates to any area of the deep sea bed[3] in respect of which a contract granted by the International Seabed Authority is in force and any description of mineral resources[4] to which the contract relates.[5].

1　As to the meaning of 'exploration' see PARA 401. As to the meaning of 'exploration licence' see PARA 402.

2　As to the meaning of 'exploitation' see PARA 401. As to the meaning of 'exploitation licence' see PARA 402. As to the Secretary of State see PARA 2

3　As to the meaning of 'deep sea bed' see PARA 401.

4　As to the meaning of 'mineral resources' see PARA 401.

5　Deep Sea Mining Act 1981 s 3(1) (s 3 substituted by the Deep Sea Mining Act 2014 Schedule para 4). The Deep Sea Mining Act 1981 s 3 does not apply where the contract is a corresponding contract in relation to a licence previously granted by the Secretary of State: s 3(2). For the purposes of any proceedings a contract granted by the Authority may be proved by the production of a copy of the contract certified to be a true copy by an official of the Authority; and any document purporting to be such a copy is to be received in evidence and is to be deemed to be such a contract unless the contrary is proved: s 3(3).

## 404.　Prevention of interference with licensed operations.

A person to whom the prohibition of unlicensed deep sea mining[1] applies must not intentionally interfere with any operations carried on in pursuance of: (1) a contract granted by the International Seabed Authority; or (2) an exploration[2] or exploitation licence[3]. Any person who contravenes this provision is guilty of an offence[4].

1　Ie the prohibition in the Deep Sea Mining Act 1981 s 1: see PARA 401.

2　As to the meaning of 'exploration licence' see PARA 402.

3　Deep Sea Mining Act 1981 s 4(1) (amended by the Deep Sea Mining Act 2014 Schedule para 5). As to the meaning of 'exploitation licence' see PARA 402.

4　Deep Sea Mining Act 1981 s 4(2). A person guilty of such an offence is liable, on conviction on indictment, to a fine; or, on summary conviction, to a fine not exceeding the statutory maximum: s 4(2)(a), (b). As to the statutory maximum see SENTENCING vol 92 (2015) PARA 176. As to the supplementary provisions relating to offences under the Deep Sea Mining Act 1981 see PARA 411.

### 405. Protection of the marine environment.

In determining whether to grant an exploration[1] or exploitation licence[2] the Secretary of State must have regard to the need to protect (so far as reasonably practicable) marine creatures, plants and other organisms and their habitat from any harmful effects which might result from any activities to be authorised by the licence[3]. The Secretary of State must consider any representations made to him concerning such effects[4].

1  As to the meaning of 'exploration licence' see PARA 402.
2  As to the meaning of 'exploitation licence' see PARA 402.
3  See the Deep Sea Mining Act 1981 s 5(1) (amended by the Deep Sea Mining Act 2014 Schedule para 6). Without prejudice to s 2(3A) (see PARA 402), any exploration or exploitation licence granted by the Secretary of State must contain such terms and conditions as he considers necessary or expedient to avoid or minimise any such harmful effects: see s 5(2). As to the Secretary of State see PARA 2.
4  See the Deep Sea Mining Act 1981 s 5(1).

### 406. Variation and revocation of licences.

The Secretary of State[1] may vary or revoke any exploration[2] or exploitation licence[3] where the variation or revocation is in his opinion required (1) to ensure the safety, health or welfare of persons engaged in any of the licensed operations[4] or ancillary operations[5]; or (2) to protect any marine creatures, plants or other organisms or their habitat[6]; or (3) in pursuance of foreign discriminatory action[7]; or (4) to avoid a conflict with any obligation of the United Kingdom arising out of any international agreement in force for the United Kingdom[8]. The Secretary of State may vary or revoke any exploration or exploitation licence in any case, with the consent of the licensee[9]. The Secretary of State may revoke an exploration or exploitation licence in any case where a term or condition of the licence or any regulation made under the Deep Sea Mining Act 1981 has not been complied with[10].

1  As to the Secretary of State see PARA 2.
2  As to the meaning of 'exploration licence' see PARA 402.
3  As to the meaning of 'exploitation licence' see PARA 402.
4  As to the meaning of 'licensed operation' see PARA 402.
5  See the Deep Sea Mining Act 1981 s 6(1)(a)(i), (3) (s 6(3) added by the Deep Sea Mining Act 2014 Schedule para 7).. As to the meaning of 'ancillary operations' see PARA 402.
6  Deep Sea Mining Act 1981 s 6(1)(a)(ii).
7  Deep Sea Mining Act 1981 s 6(1)(a)(iii). As to foreign discriminatory action see PARA 407.
8  Deep Sea Mining Act 1981 s 6(1)(a)(iv). As to the meaning of 'United Kingdom' see PARA 48
9  Deep Sea Mining Act 1981 s 6(1)(b). As to the meaning of 'licensee' see PARA 402.
10 See the Deep Sea Mining Act 1981 s 6(2), (3).

### 407. Foreign discriminatory action.

Where any ship[1] which is registered in a country of which the government[2], in the opinion of the Secretary of State, has adopted or is proposing to adopt discriminatory measures or practices prohibiting or otherwise restricting the use, in connection with any deep sea bed mining operations[3], of ships registered in the United Kingdom[4], the Secretary of State may include in any exploration[5] or exploitation licence[6], either on granting the licence or by a subsequent variation, such terms and conditions as he considers expedient for prohibiting or otherwise restricting the use in connection with the licensed operations[7] or any ancillary operations[8] of any ship[9].

1  'Ship' includes every description of vessel used in navigation: Deep Sea Mining Act 1981 s 17.

2   Or an agency or authority of the government: Deep Sea Mining Act 1981 s 8(1) ( s 8(1), (2), (4) amended by the Deep Sea Mining Act 2014 Schedule para 8). In the Deep Sea Mining Act 1981 s 8, references to an agency or authority of a government include references to any undertaking appearing to the Secretary of State to be, or to be acting on behalf of, an undertaking which is in effect owned or controlled (directly or indirectly) by a state other than the United Kingdom: See s 8(4). As to the Secretary of State see PARA 2. As to the meaning of 'United Kingdom' see PARA 48.

3   As to the meaning of 'deep sea bed mining operations' see PARA 402.

4   See the Deep Sea Mining Act 1981 s 8(1). The Secretary of State may by order extend s 8 to ships which are registered in any country of which the government (or any agency or authority of the government), in his opinion, has adopted or is proposing to adopt discriminatory measures or practices prohibiting or otherwise restricting the use in connection with any deep sea bed mining operations of ships registered in the Channel Islands, the Isle of Man or any colony. s 8(3).

5   As to the meaning of 'exploration licence' see PARA 402.

6   As to the meaning of 'exploitation licence' see PARA 402.

7   As to the meaning of 'licensed operation' see PARA 402.

8   As to the meaning of 'ancillary operations' see PARA 402.

9   Deep Sea Mining Act 1981 s 8(2). This provision does not prejudice the Secretary of State's ability to include the terms and conditions listed under s 2(3A): s 8(2).

## 408. Enforcement of decisions of the Seabed Disputes Chamber and arbitration awards.

A decision of the Seabed Disputes Chamber of the International Tribunal for the Law of the Sea in relation to certain disputes[1] may be registered in the High Court or the Court of Session ('the registering court') in such manner as may be prescribed by rules of court[2]. Where a decision is registered under these provisions, it is to be treated for the following purposes as if it had been originally given by the registering court and had (where relevant) been entered: (1) its force and effect for the purposes of enforcement; (2) the powers of the registering court in relation to its enforcement; (3) the taking of proceedings for or with respect to its enforcement[3]. The debt resulting from the registration is to carry interest as if the decision were a judgment of the registering court and the debt had become due on the date of registration[4]. The reasonable costs and expenses of and incidental to its registration are to be recoverable as if they were sums recoverable under the decision[5].

An award made in disputes concerning interpretation or application of contracts[6] is to be treated[7] as a New York Convention award[8], whether or not (in either case) it would be so treated apart from this provision[9].

1   Ie of a type described in the United Nations Convention on the Law of the Sea, art 187(c), (d) or (e): Deep Sea Mining Act 1981 s 8A(1) ( s 8A— 8C added by the Deep Sea Mining Act 2014 Schedule para 9).

2   Deep Sea Mining Act 1981 s 8A(1).

3   Deep Sea Mining Act 1981 s 8A(2). Section 8A(2) is subject to any provision made by rules of court as to the manner in which and conditions subject to which a decision registered under s 8A may be enforced: s 8A(6). As to proof and admissibility of the Seabed Disputes Chamber see s 8B.

4   See the Deep Sea Mining Act 1981 s 8A(3).

5   See the Deep Sea Mining Act 1981 s 8A(4). Costs or expenses recoverable by virtue of s 8A(4) are to carry interest as if they were the subject of an order for costs and expenses made by the registering court on the date of registration: s 8A(5).

6   Ie in pursuance of the United Nations Convention on the Law of the Sea, art 188(2)(a)

7   Ie for the purposes of the Arbitration Act 1996 Pt 3 (recognition and enforcement of certain foreign awards)

8   ARBITRATION vol 2 (2017) PARA 589

9   See the Deep Sea Mining Act 1981 s 8C.

## 409. Inspectors.

The Secretary of State[1] may appoint as inspectors to discharge such functions as may be prescribed[2] and generally to assist him in the execution of the Deep Sea Mining Act 1981 such persons appearing to him to be qualified for the purpose as he considers appropriate from time to time[3].

1　As to the Secretary of State see PARA 2.
2　As to the meaning of 'prescribed' see PARA 402.
3　See the Deep Sea Mining Act 1981 s 11(1) (amended by the Deep Sea Mining Act 2014 Schedule para 11). The Secretary of State may make to or in respect of any inspector appointed under s 11(1) such payments by way of remuneration or otherwise as the Secretary of State may determine with the approval of the Minister for the Civil Service: Deep Sea Mining Act 1981 s 11(2). As to the Minister for the Civil Service see CONSTITUTIONAL AND ADMINISTRATIVE LAW vol 20 (2014) PARAS 234, 285 et seq.

## 410. Disclosure of information.

A person must not disclose any information which he has received in pursuance of the Deep Sea Mining Act 1981 and which relates to any other person except: (1) with the written consent of that other person[1]; or (2) to the Treasury, the Commissioners of Customs and Excise or the Secretary of State[2]; or (3) with a view to the institution of or otherwise for the purposes of any criminal proceedings under this Act or regulations made under this Act[3]; or (4) in accordance with regulations made under the Deep Sea Mining Act 1981[4]; or (5) to the International Seabed Authority[5]. Any person who discloses any information in contravention this provision is to be guilty of an offence[6].

1　See the Deep Sea Mining Act 1981 s 13(1)(a).
2　Deep Sea Mining Act 1981 s 13(1)(b). As to the Treasury see CONSTITUTIONAL AND ADMINISTRATIVE LAW vol 20 (2014) PARA 262 et seq. As to the Commissioners of Customs and Excise see INCOME TAXATION vol 58 (2014) PARA 33. As to the Secretary of State see PARA 2.
3　Deep Sea Mining Act 1981 s 13(1)(c).
4　Deep Sea Mining Act 1981 s 13(1)(d).
5　Deep Sea Mining Act 1981 s 13(1)(e) (substituted by the Deep Sea Mining Act 2014 Schedule para 13).
6　Deep Sea Mining Act 1981 s 13(2). Any person guilty of such an offence is liable, on conviction on indictment, to imprisonment for a term not exceeding two years or to a fine or to both (s 13(2)(a)) or, on summary conviction, to a fine not exceeding the statutory maximum (s 13(2)(b)). As to the statutory maximum see SENTENCING vol 92 (2015) PARA 176. As to the supplementary provisions relating to offences under the Deep Sea Mining Act 1981 see PARA 411.

## 411. Supplementary provisions relating to offences.

Proceedings for an offence under the Deep Sea Mining Act 1981 or under regulations made under the Act may be taken, and the offence may for incidental purposes be treated as having been committed, in any place in the United Kingdom[1]. A person may be guilty of an offence under regulations made under the Deep Sea Mining Act 1981 whether or not he is a British citizen, a British overseas territories citizen, a British National (Overseas) or a British Overseas citizen or, in the case of a body corporate, it is incorporated under the law of any part of the United Kingdom[2]. Where an offence has been committed by a body corporate and is proved to have been committed with the consent or connivance of, or to be attributable to any neglect on the part of, a director[3], manager, secretary or other similar officer of the body corporate or any person who was purporting to act in any such capacity, he as well as the body corporate is guilty of that offence and is liable to be proceeded against and punished accordingly[4]. In any proceedings for an offence of failing to comply with any provision of the Deep Sea Mining Act

1981 or of regulations made under the Act, it is a defence to prove that the accused used all due diligence to comply with that provision[5].

1 Deep Sea Mining Act 1981 s 14(1). Proceedings for such an offence are not to be instituted in England and Wales or Northern Ireland except: (1) in the case of proceedings in England and Wales, by or with the consent of the Director of Public Prosecutions; or (2) in the case of proceedings in Northern Ireland, by or with the consent of the Director of Public Prosecutions for Northern Ireland; or (3) in any case, by the Secretary of State or a person authorised by him in that behalf: s 14(2). As to the meaning of 'United Kingdom' see PARA 48. As to the Director of Public Prosecutions see CRIMINAL PROCEDURE vol 27 (2015) PARAS 25, 30 et seq. As to the Secretary of State see PARA 2.
2 Deep Sea Mining Act 1981 s 14(3) (amended by the British Overseas Territories Act 2002 s 2(3); and SI 1986/948).
3 For these purposes, 'director', in relation to a body corporate which (1) is established by or under any enactment for the purpose of carrying on under public ownership any industry or part of an industry or undertaking; and (2) is a body whose affairs are managed by its members, means a member of the body corporate: Deep Sea Mining Act 1981 s 14(4).
4 Deep Sea Mining Act 1981 s 14(4).
5 Deep Sea Mining Act 1981 s 14(5).

## 412. Civil liability for breach of statutory duty.

Breach of a duty imposed on any person by a provision of certain regulations made in pursuance of the Deep Sea Mining Act 1981[1] is actionable so far, and only so far, as the breach causes personal injury[2]. A defence to a charge which is available by virtue of the supplementary provisions relating to offences under the Deep Sea Mining Act 1981[3] or by virtue of regulations made under that Act is not a defence in any civil proceedings[4].

1 Ie regulations which state that the Deep Sea Mining Act 1981 s 15(1) applies to such a breach: see s 15(1).
2 Deep Sea Mining Act 1981 s 15(1). References in the Fatal Accidents Act 1976 s 1 to a wrongful act, neglect or default, include references to any such breach which is so actionable: Deep Sea Mining Act 1981 s 15(1). As to the Fatal Accidents Act 1976 see NEGLIGENCE vol 78 (2010) PARA 25 et seq. 'Personal injury' includes any disease, any impairment of a person's physical or mental condition and any fatal injury: s 15(4). Nothing in s 15(1) is to prejudice any action which lies apart from these provisions: s 15(2).
3 Ie the Deep Sea Mining Act 1981 s 14(5): see PARA 411.
4 Deep Sea Mining Act 1981 s 15(3).

# 7. OPENCAST WORKING OF COAL

## (1) Introduction

### (i) The Opencast Coal Act 1958

**413. Introduction.**

Before the Opencast Coal Act 1958[1] came into operation[2], power to take possession of and to use land for the purpose of opencast coal mining[3] was conferred by the Defence (General) Regulations 1939[4]. These emergency powers were revoked[5] and replaced by the comprehensive scheme of the Opencast Coal Act 1958[6]. Provisions of the Coal Industry Act 1975 which required opencast operations by the British Coal Corporation[7] to be authorised and provided for the grant of planning permission for such operations by ministerial direction, have been repealed[8]; and the Act was modified to take account of the restructuring of the coal industry under privatisation by the Coal Industry Act 1994. Although the government found it unsatisfactory for the coal industry to have access to special procedures not available in relation to other minerals, procedures under the Opencast Coal Act 1958 continued to be available for a transitional period[9]. However, certain powers contained in the Opencast Coal Act 1958 (namely, the power to make a compulsory rights order[10], the power to make an order suspending a right of way[11], the power to make orders conferring rights for the purposes of drainage or water supply[12], and the power to make a direction designating land for prospecting[13]) have not been exercisable since 31 December 1999[14]. The Opencast Coal Act 1958 has not been repealed, and many of its provisions, particularly those relating to compensation[15], continue to have some relevance.

1   The Opencast Coal Act 1958 does not extend to Northern Ireland: s 53(3).
2   Ie on 30 September 1958: see the Opencast Coal Act 1958 s 53(2) (repealed).
3   As to whether an opencast working is a mine see PARA 3.
4   See the Defence (General) Regulations 1939, SR & O 1939/927, regs 51, 51A (revoked).
5   As to the transitional provisions to which this was subject see the Requisitioned Land and War Works Act 1945 ss 28(2), 30(1) (repealed); the Land Powers (Defence) Act 1958 s 1(2); and the Opencast Coal Act 1958 s 48 (repealed), Sch 10 paras 5, 42 (repealed). Any reference in the Opencast Coal Act 1958 to an enactment must be construed as a reference to that enactment as amended by or under any other enactment: s 51(9).
6   See PARA 414 et seq.
7   As to the British Coal Corporation see PARAS 49–50.
8   See the Opencast Coal Act 1958 ss 1, 2 (both repealed). The repeal of ss 1, 2 did not affect a direction given under s 2 before the day on which the repeal of that section came into operation, and any repeal by the Housing and Planning Act 1986 of an enactment relating to directions under the Opencast Coal Act 1958 s 2 has no effect in relation to directions whose effect is continued by the Housing and Planning Act 1986 s 39(1): see s 39(1), (2). Section 39 came into force on 11 December 1987: see the Housing and Planning Act 1986 (Commencement No 9) Order 1987, SI 1987/1939.
9   In 1993, the Minister for Energy announced that the government found it unsatisfactory for the coal industry to have access to special procedures (such as those governing the compulsory acquisition of rights to explore for and work opencast coal under the Opencast Coal Act 1958) which were not generally available: see 233 HC Official Report (6th series), 2 December 1993, written answers col 735. It was intended that there should be a review of the powers, available in relation to minerals generally, contained in the Mines (Working Facilities and Support) Act 1966, and that any new powers available in respect of opencast coal after 31 December 1999 should form part of a new general regime for all minerals: see eg the Department of Trade and Industry

Press Release P/93/719 (2 December 1993); and the Department of Trade and Industry consultative document entitled *Review of Mining Legislation – The Compulsory Acquisition of Rights Over Land for Mineral Development* (February 1995). As to the regime for minerals generally under the Mines (Working Facilities and Support) Act 1966 see PARA 380 et seq.

10 See PARA 431 et seq.

11 See PARA 424 et seq.

12 See PARA 430.

13 See PARAS 420–421.

14 See the Coal Industry Act 1994 s 52(1); and PARA 414.

15 See PARA 461 et seq.

## 414. Powers under the Opencast Coal Act 1958.

Under the Opencast Coal Act 1958, for the purpose of facilitating the working of coal by opencast operations, the Coal Authority[1] had power, by means of a compulsory rights order made by the Authority and confirmed by the appropriate national authority[2], to confer[3] temporary rights of occupation and use of any land[4] on which the applicant for the order desired to work coal[5] by such operations or to carry out operations incidental to such working[6]. When such an order has been made, compensation in respect of it is payable[7].

There was also a power to suspend certain public rights of way[8], to acquire rights for the purposes of drainage and water supply[9], and to designate land for the purpose of prospecting[10].

The powers mentioned above have not been exercisable since 31 December 1999[11].

The Opencast Coal Act 1958 also makes particular provision as to agricultural tenancies in England and Wales[12]. The provisions of the Opencast Coal Act 1958 apply to certain special cases subject to modification[13], and there are powers to modify the Act itself by regulations in order to adapt it to special circumstances[14].

1 As to the Coal Authority see PARA 52 et seq.

2 Ie the Secretary of State or where functions have been transferred in relation to Wales, the Welsh Ministers: see PARA 2.

3 Ie in accordance with the provisions of the Opencast Coal Act 1958 Pt I (ss 4–16): see s 4(1); and PARA 431.

4 'Land' includes land covered by water: Opencast Coal Act 1958 s 51(1).

5 'Coal' means bituminous coal, cannel coal and anthracite: Opencast Coal Act 1958 s 51(1).

6 See the Opencast Coal Act 1958 s 4(1) (substituted by the Coal Industry Act 1975 s 4(1); amended by the Housing and Planning Act 1986 Sch 8 para 2(1); and the Coal Industry Act 1994 Sch 8 para 2(1)). As to compulsory rights orders see PARA 431 et seq. As to the period for which a compulsory rights order may have effect see PARA 432.

7 See the Opencast Coal Act 1958 Pt II (ss 17–36); and PARA 461 et seq. As to types of compensation payable see PARA 461 et seq.

8 As to the suspension of public rights of way see PARA 424.

9 As to rights as to drainage or water supply see PARA 430.

10 As to entry on land for the purpose of prospecting see PARA 420–421.

11 See the Coal Industry Act 1994 s 52(1). See also PARA 413. Section 52(1) provides that the following powers under the Opencast Coal Act 1958 are not exercisable at any time after 31 December 1999: (1) the power to make a compulsory rights order (see PARA 431); (2) the power under s 15 (see PARA 424 et seq) to make an order suspending a right of way; and (3) the power to make an order under s 16 (orders conferring rights for the purposes of drainage or water supply) (see PARA 430), and the Secretary of State may not, at any time after that date, give a direction designating any land for the purposes of s 39(2) (rights of entry) (see PARA 420) except on an application made to him before that date by the Coal Authority. As to the regime for minerals generally under the Mines (Working Facilities and Support) Act 1966 see PARA 380 et seq.

Subject to the Coal Industry Act 1994 s 52(1) and to any transfers in accordance with a restructuring scheme of any rights or liabilities under the Opencast Coal Act 1958, the Opencast

Coal Act 1958 has effect on and after the restructuring date (ie 31 October 1994: see PARA 50) with the amendments specified in the Coal Industry Act 1994 s 52(2), Sch 8 (which as well as making other minor amendments of the Opencast Coal Act 1958, makes the modifications, in relation to the period before 31 December 1999, which are requisite for enabling orders under the Opencast Coal Act 1958 to be made in favour of persons other than the British Coal Corporation): Coal Industry Act 1994 s 52(2). As to restructuring schemes see PARA 72. As to the meaning of 'modifications' see PARA 51.

Section 52(1) is without prejudice to the effect after 31 December 1999 of anything done under the Opencast Coal Act 1958 on or before that date or generally to the operation of the Opencast Coal Act 1958 in relation to anything so done: Coal Industry Act 1994 s 52(3).

12 See eg PARA 428 et seq.

13 Eg with respect to matters arising between landlords and tenants, mortgagees and mortgagors, and in respect of mining leases or orders conferring working rights (see PARA 444 et seq), with respect to tenancies of allotments (see PARAS 460, 500–502), and with respect to land held for religious purposes (see PARA 515).

14 See eg the Opencast Coal Act 1958 s 34, Sch 6 para 29.

## 415. Application to Crown land.

In general, the Opencast Coal Act 1958 applies in relation to land[1] in which there is a Crown or Duchy interest[2] as it applies to land in which there is no such interest[3]. However, subject to any express provision in the Opencast Coal Act 1958 to the contrary[4], the provisions of the Act do not apply to any land in which there is a Crown or Duchy interest, but no private interest[5] other than any interest belonging to the Coal Authority[6].

1 As to the meaning of 'land' see PARA 414.

2 'Crown or Duchy interest' means an interest belonging to Her Majesty in right of the Crown or of the Duchy of Lancaster, or belonging to the Duchy of Cornwall, or belonging to a government department, or held in trust for Her Majesty for the purposes of a government department: Opencast Coal Act 1958 s 44(4). As to Crown land generally see CROWN AND CROWN PROCEEDINGS vol 29 (2014) PARAS 114 et seq, 192 et seq.

3 See the Opencast Coal Act 1958 s 44(1), which applies with necessary modifications in relation to land which is subject to a right restrictive of its use, being a right the benefit of which is annexed to land in which there is a Crown or Duchy interest, or, not being so annexed, belongs to Her Majesty in right of the Crown or of the Duchy of Lancaster, or belongs to the Duchy of Cornwall, or belongs to a government department, or is held in trust for Her Majesty for the purposes of a government department, as it applies in relation to land in which there is a Crown or Duchy interest: see s 44(5).

4 See eg the Opencast Coal Act 1958 s 44(5) proviso, which excludes the exception.

5 'Private interest' means an interest which is not a Crown or Duchy interest: Opencast Coal Act 1958 s 44(4).

6 Opencast Coal Act 1958 s 44(1) proviso (amended by the Coal Industry Act 1987 s 1(2), Sch 1 para 7(c); and the Coal Industry Act 1994 s 52(2), Sch 8 paras 1, 33(a)). As to the Coal Authority see PARA 52 et seq.

## 416. Protection from compulsory purchase.

Where a compulsory purchase order[1] has been submitted or prepared, and the land[2] comprised in the order includes land in respect of which opencast planning permission[3] has been granted and is for the time being occupied by a relevant person[4] for the purpose of carrying on the permitted activities[5], and within the time limited for making objections to the order, that relevant person gives notice of that fact to the appropriate national authority[6] to whom the order has been submitted, or by whom it has been prepared, as the case may be, specifying the land in respect of which the permission was granted and which is so occupied[7], the compulsory purchase order must not be confirmed or made so as to authorise the compulsory purchase of any of the land specified in that notice, unless the appropriate national authority is satisfied that it can be purchased without serious detriment to the permitted activities[8].

1　Ie a compulsory purchase order within the meaning of the Acquisition of Land Act 1981: see generally COMPULSORY ACQUISITION OF LAND.

2　As to the meaning of 'land' see PARA 414.

3　'Opencast planning permission' means planning permission which permits the working of coal by opencast operations or the carrying out of operations incidental to such working: Opencast Coal Act 1958 s 51(1) (definition added by the Housing and Planning Act 1986 s 39(3), Sch 8 Pt I para 13(a); and amended by the Coal Industry Act 1987 s 1(2), Sch 1 para 7(c); and the Coal Industry Act 1994 s 52(2), Sch 8 paras 1, 36(1)(a)).

　　Where opencast planning permission has been granted, the Communications Act 2003 Sch 3A Pt 10 (the electronic communications code) which provides a procedure for certain cases where works involve the alteration of electronic communications apparatus) applies for the purposes of any permitted activities to the person with the benefit of that permission: Opencast Coal Act 1958 s 45(2) (substituted by the Telecommunications Act 1984 s 109, Sch 4 para 38; and amended by the Housing and Planning Act 1986 s 39(3), Sch 8 Pt I para 12; the Coal Industry Act 1994 s 52(2), Sch 8 para 34; the Communications Act 2003 Sch 17 para 27(1); and the Digital Economy Act 2017 Sch 3 para 5). As to the electronic communications code see the Telecommunications Act 1984 Sch 4 para 1; and TELECOMMUNICATIONS vol 97 (2015) PARA 155 et seq.

4　'Relevant person' means any licensed operator within the meaning of the Coal Industry Act 1994 or any person who is certified by the Coal Authority as a person whose application to that Authority for a licence under Pt II (ss 25–36) is pending: Opencast Coal Act 1958 s 38 (definition added by the Coal Industry Act 1994 Sch 8 paras 1, 28(c)). As to the meaning of 'licensed operator' see PARA 58. As to the Coal Authority see PARA 52 et seq.

5　Opencast Coal Act 1958 s 38(a) (amended by the Housing and Planning Act 1986 Sch 8 Pt I para 9; the Coal Industry Act 1987 Sch 1 para 7(c); and the Coal Industry Act 1994 Sch 8 para 28(a), (b)). 'Permitted activities' means: (1) the working of coal by opencast operations pursuant to opencast planning permission and the carrying out of operations incidental to such working; and (2) the carrying out of any conditions subject to which opencast planning permission has been granted: Opencast Coal Act 1958 s 51(1) (definition added by the Housing and Planning Act 1986 Sch 8 Pt I para 13(b)).

　　Any reference in the Opencast Coal Act 1958 to the working of coal by opencast operations includes a reference to the getting and winning of coal worked by such operations, and to the carrying away of any such coal from the land on which it has been worked (s 51(5)) and any reference to the working of coal or other minerals on any land, or to the carrying out of any other operations on any land, must be construed as including a reference to the working of the coal or other minerals, or the carrying out of those operations, as the case may be, in or under that land (s 51(6)). Waste heaps and other deposits resulting from the working of minerals must be taken to form part of the land on which they are situated, if apart from s 51(7) they would not be taken to form part thereof, and any reference to the working of minerals on, in or under land, or to underground or surface working, must be construed accordingly: see s 51(7).

6　Ie the Secretary of State or where functions have been transferred in relation to Wales, the Welsh Ministers: see PARA 2.

7　Ie occupied as mentioned in the Opencast Coal Act 1958 s 38(a): see s 38(b) (amended by the Housing and Planning Act 1986 Sch 8 Pt I para 9; the Coal Industry Act 1987 Sch 1 para 7(c); and the Coal Industry Act 1994 Sch 8 para 28(a), (b)).

8　See the Opencast Coal Act 1958 s 38 (amended by the Housing and Planning Act 1986 Sch 8 Pt I para 9; the Coal Industry Act 1987 Sch 1 para 7(c); and the Coal Industry Act 1994 Sch 8 paras 1, 28(a), (b), (c); and by virtue of the Minister of Technology Order 1969, SI 1969/1498, arts 2(1), 5(6); and the Secretary of State for Trade and Industry Order 1970, SI 1970/1537, arts 2(2), 7(4)).

## (ii) Administration and Notices

### 417. Powers of the appropriate national authority and the Coal Authority.

The appropriate national authority[1] has a general power to make regulations in accordance with the provisions of the Opencast Coal Act 1958[2]. His confirmation was required for compulsory rights orders[3], orders suspending certain public rights of way[4], and orders conferring rights for the purposes of drainage or water supply[5]. He also had the power to give a direction designating land in relation to the powers of prospecting conferred by the Act[6]. Any expenses incurred for the purposes of the Opencast Coal Act 1958 by the appropriate national authority are payable out of the moneys provided by Parliament[7].

The Coal Authority[8] had the power to make compulsory rights orders[9], orders suspending certain public rights of way[10], and orders conferring rights for the purposes of drainage or water supply[11]. The Authority also had the power to apply to the appropriate national authority for a direction designating land in relation to the powers of prospecting conferred by the Act[12], and the power to authorise in writing persons to exercise such powers in relation to land so designated[13].

The powers to make compulsory rights orders, orders suspending public rights of way, orders conferring rights for the purposes of drainage or water supply, and directions designating land for prospecting, have not been exercisable since 31 December 1999[14].

1   Ie the Secretary of State or where functions have been transferred in relation to Wales, the Welsh Ministers: see PARA 2.
2   See the Opencast Coal Act 1958 s 49(1); and PARA 418.
3   See the Opencast Coal Act 1958 s 4(1); and PARA 431.
4   See the Opencast Coal Act 1958 s 15; and PARAS 424–425.
5   See the Opencast Coal Act 1958 s 16; and PARA 430.
6   See the Opencast Coal Act 1958 s 39(1); and PARAS 420–421.
7   Opencast Coal Act 1958 s 50.
8   As to the Coal Authority see PARA 52 et seq.
9   See the Opencast Coal Act 1958 s 4(1); and PARA 431.
10  See the Opencast Coal Act 1958 s 15; and PARAS 424–425.
11  See the Opencast Coal Act 1958 s 16; and PARA 430.
12  See the Opencast Coal Act 1958 s 39(1); and PARAS 420–421.
13  See the Opencast Coal Act 1958 s 39(2); and PARA 420.
14  See PARA 414.

### 418.  Subordinate legislation.

The appropriate national authority[1] may make regulations prescribing anything authorised or required to be prescribed for the purposes of any provision of the Opencast Coal Act 1958, or for the purposes of any enactment applied by or incorporated with it, except any provision whereby anything is expressly authorised or required to be prescribed by some other Minister of the Crown or government department[2].

Any power to make regulations or orders[3] under the Opencast Coal Act 1958 is exercisable by statutory instrument; and any instrument containing any such regulations or orders is subject to annulment in pursuance of a resolution of either House of Parliament[4].

1   Ie the Secretary of State or where functions have been transferred in relation to Wales, the Welsh Ministers: see PARA 2.
2   Opencast Coal Act 1958 s 49(1). Subject to the provisions of s 49, any power conferred by the Opencast Coal Act 1958 to make an order or give any directions includes power, subject to the like provisions and conditions, to vary or revoke the order or directions by a subsequent order or subsequent directions, as the case may be: s 49(4).
    A compulsory rights order must not be varied by extending the period for which it is to have effect: s 49(5). However, where the period specified in the order is less than 20 years, s 49(5) does not prevent the variation of the order by the extension of that period, if the period as extended does not exceed 20 years: see s 49(5) proviso (amended by the Coal Industry Act 1975 s 4(2), Sch 3 para 8). As to compulsory rights orders see PARA 431 et seq. The power to make compulsory rights orders has not been exercisable since 31 December 1999: see PARA 414. As to the duration, variation and revocation of compulsory rights orders see PARA 432.

A compulsory rights order may, by notice to the person entitled to the rights conferred by the order, be revoked at any time by the Coal Authority (as to which see PARA 52 et seq), if it is satisfied that that person has consented to the revocation; or by the Secretary of State, if he is satisfied that that person has contravened, or is contravening, any of the provisions of the order or any requirement otherwise imposed on that person by or under the Opencast Coal Act 1958: s 49(4A) (added by the Coal Industry Act 1994 s 52(2), Sch 8 para 35).

Where, in the case of any compulsory rights order made or confirmed at any time on or after the restructuring date (ie 31 October 1994: see PARA 50), it appears to the Coal Authority: (1) that the order would not have been made or confirmed, or would not have extended to certain interests or rights, if a person to whom a relevant offer was made had accepted it; (2) that that person has, since the making of the order, made a written offer to the person entitled to the rights conferred by it ('the operator') to enter into an agreement on the terms of the relevant offer; (3) that the written offer was made either at a time before the specification of a date in relation to the order as the date of entry or at a time more than 28 days before any date so specified; (4) that the person making the offer will enter into an agreement with the operator on those terms if the order is revoked or varied under the Opencast Coal Act 1958 s 49(4B); and (5) that the circumstances (apart from the expiration or rejection of the relevant offer and the making and confirmation of the order) are not such as to make it unreasonable for the operator to be required to treat the terms of the relevant offer as still available for acceptance, that Authority may, by notice to the operator and subject to such conditions as it thinks fit, either revoke the order or vary it by limiting it so that it does not extend to the interests and rights of the person who is offering to be bound by an agreement on the terms he previously failed to accept: s 49(4B) (added by the Coal Industry Act 1994 Sch 8 para 35).

For this purpose, 'relevant offer', in relation to a compulsory rights order, means any offer which was made by the applicant for the order to a person who is one of the persons directly concerned; and was an offer as to the terms on which the applicant was willing (instead of requiring rights as against that person to be conferred by a compulsory rights order) to enter into an agreement with that person: Opencast Coal Act 1958 s 49(4C) (added by the Coal Industry Act 1994 Sch 8 para 35).

The provisions of the Opencast Coal Act 1958 s 49(4) do not affect the revocation of an order made by virtue of s 15 (suspension of rights of way: see PARAS 424–425) where, in accordance with s 15(4), the appropriate national authority is required to revoke the order: s 49(6).

3   Ie orders under Opencast Coal Act 1958 s 26(5); s 28(5); and s 35(8): see s 49(3).
4   Opencast Coal Act 1958 s 49(2), (3). As to the annulment of statutory instruments by Parliament generally see STATUTES AND LEGISLATIVE PROCESS vol 96 (2012) PARA 1049.

## 419. Inquiries.

Certain provisions[1] which relate to local inquiries have effect in relation to any inquiry held under the Opencast Coal Act 1958 in relation to land in England or Wales[2].

1   Ie the provisions of the Local Government Act 1972 s 250(2)–(5): see LOCAL GOVERNMENT vol 69 (2018) PARA 861.
2   See the Opencast Coal Act 1958 s 47(2) (amended by the Local Government Act 1972 s 272(2); and the Acquisition of Land Act 1981 s 34, Sch 6 Pt I).

## 420. Entry on land.

Where it appears to the appropriate national authority[1] to be expedient that any land[2] should be prospected: (1) for the purpose of ascertaining whether it contains coal[3] suitable for working by opencast operations[4], and, if so, what quantity of such coal it contains, and how the coal in question could best be so worked; or (2) for the purpose of ascertaining whether the land would be suitable for use for any purposes connected with the working of coal on any adjacent land by opencast operations, including purposes of access and of restoring land affected by the working of coal by such operations, the Secretary of State may on the application of the Coal Authority[5] give a direction[6] designating that land as land in relation to which, during such period as may be specified in the direction, certain powers[7] are to be exercisable, subject to such conditions, if any, as may be specified in the direction[8]. However, this power to make directions has not been exercisable since 31 December 1999[9].

Subject to certain provisions[10], during any period for which, by virtue of such a direction, powers[11] are exercisable in relation to land designated in the direction, and subject to compliance with any conditions specified in the direction, any person authorised in writing by the Coal Authority may, at any reasonable time, for either of the purposes mentioned in head (1) or head (2) above[12]: (a) enter upon that land, or upon any other land to which entry is required for obtaining access to that land; (b) carry out on the designated land such operations as may be requisite, in relation to that land, for either of the purposes mentioned in head (1) or head (2) above; and (c) remove from the designated land any samples of minerals[13] or of other substances obtained by carrying out any such operations, and dispose of any such samples as the Coal Authority may think fit to authorise him to dispose of[14].

Where, in the exercise of such powers conferred, it is proposed to enter upon any land and carry out any operations there involving the excavation of the land, or the making of borings therein (i) the power to carry out those operations is not exercisable unless the notice[15] included notice of the intention to carry out those operations; and (ii) if the land in question is held by the persons carrying on a statutory undertaking[16], or by an internal drainage board, and those persons or that board object to the proposed operations on the ground that the carrying out of the operations would be seriously detrimental to the carrying on of their undertaking or, in the case of an internal drainage board, to the performance of their functions, the operations must not be carried out except with the consent of the appropriate minister[17].

Subject to the provisions of the Opencast Coal Act 1958[18], any person authorised in writing by the Authority may, at any reasonable time, enter upon and survey any land, whether comprised in a direction[19] or not (A) for any purpose in connection with, or preparatory to, an application for opencast planning permission or the making or confirmation of any order[20]; or (B) where opencast planning permission has been granted, for any purpose in connection with, or preparatory to, the carrying on of any of the permitted activities or the performance of any functions prescribed[21], not being a purpose for which a right of entry is exercisable apart from this head[22]; or (C) for the purpose of estimating value, or assessing loss, in connection with any claim for compensation under the Act[23]; or (D) for the purpose of affixing[24] on land any notice[25].

1   Ie the Secretary of State or where functions have been transferred in relation to Wales, the Welsh Ministers: see PARA 2.

2   As to the meaning of 'land' see PARA 414. Nothing in the Opencast Coal Act 1958 s 39 authorises any person to enter upon any land which is covered by buildings: s 39(4).

3   As to the meaning of 'coal' see PARA 414.

4   As to references to working coal by opencast operations see PARA 416. As to references to working coal see PARA 416.

5   As to the Coal Authority see PARA 52 et seq.

6   As to the power to give directions see PARA 418.

7   Ie the powers conferred by the Opencast Coal Act 1958 s 39(2).

8   See the Opencast Coal Act 1958 s 39(1) (amended by the Coal Industry Act 1994 s 52(2), Sch 8 paras 1, 29(1)). Any authorisation by the Coal Authority of any person for the purposes of the exercise of the powers conferred by the Opencast Coal Act 1958 s 39, and any conditions of such an authorisation, may be revoked or varied by that Authority at any time: s 39(7B) (added by the Coal Industry Act 1994 Sch 8 para 29(5)).

Except with the consent of the appropriate authority the powers conferred by the Opencast Coal Act 1958 s 39 are not exercisable in relation to land in which for the time being there is a Crown or Duchy interest (as to the meaning of which see PARA 415), but nothing in s 44 (see PARA 415) affects the validity or operation of an order, or the exercise of any power, as against any person having, in or over the land in question, any interest or right other than a Crown or Duchy interest: see s 44(2) proviso.

For the purposes of s 44, 'the appropriate authority' means:

(1)   in relation to land belonging to Her Majesty in right of the Crown and forming part of the Crown Estate, the Crown Estate Commissioners, and, in relation to any other land belonging to Her Majesty in right of the Crown, the government department having the management of the land (s 44(4)(a));

(2)   in relation to land belonging to Her Majesty in right of the Duchy of Lancaster, the Chancellor of the Duchy (s 44(4)(b));

(3)   in relation to land belonging to the Duchy of Cornwall, such person as the Duke of Cornwall, or the possessor for the time being of that Duchy, appoints (s 44(4)(c)); and

(4)   in relation to land belonging to a government department or held in trust for Her Majesty for the purposes of a government department, that department (s 44(4)(d)).

If any question arises as to what authority is the appropriate authority in relation to any land, that question is to be referred to the Treasury, whose decision is final: s 44(4). As to the Treasury see CONSTITUTIONAL AND ADMINISTRATIVE LAW vol 20 (2014) PARAS 262–265.

9   See the Coal Industry Act 1994 s 52(1); and PARA 414.

10   Ie subject to the Opencast Coal Act 1958 s 39(3)–(10).

11   Ie the powers conferred by the Opencast Coal Act 1958 s 39(2).

12   Ie mentioned in the Opencast Coal Act 1958 s 39(1).

13   As to the meaning of 'minerals' see PARA 10.

14   Opencast Coal Act 1958 s 39(2) (amended by the Coal Industry Act 1994 Sch 8 para 29(2), (3)). However, nothing in the Opencast Coal Act 1958 s 39(2) is to be construed as authorising any interference with the exercise of a public right of way, or any contravention of a prohibition or restriction imposed by or under an enactment (whether contained in a public general Act or in any other Act): s 39(2) proviso.

15   Ie under the Opencast Coal Act 1958 s 39(5): see PARA 421.

16   'Statutory undertakers' and 'statutory undertaking' have the same meanings as in the Town and Country Planning Act 1990 s 262 (see PLANNING vol 83 (2018) PARA 1072) (but excluding a universal service provider within the meaning of the Postal Services Act 2011 Pt 3 (ss 27-67) (see POSTAL SERVICES) and his undertaking): Opencast Coal Act 1958 s 51(1) (definition amended by the Planning (Consequential Provisions) Act 1990 Sch 3 para 3; the Postal Services Act 2011 Sch 12 para 80; and SI 2001/1149); see PLANNING.

17   See the Opencast Coal Act 1958 s 39(6) (amended by the Water Act 1989 s 190, Sch 25 para 26). As to who is the 'appropriate minister' see the Opencast Coal Act 1958 s 51(1) (substituted by SI 1976/1775; amended by the Gas Act 1986 s 67(4), Sch 9 Pt I; the Electricity Act 1989 s 112(4), Sch 18; the Water Act 1989 s 190(1), (3), Sch 25 para 26(5), Sch 27 Pt I; SI 1979/571; SI 1981/238; SI 1983/1127; SI 1992/1314, SI 2001/1149; and by virtue of SI 1997/2971, SI 2001/2568 (itself amended by SI 2002/2626)); and see the Water Act 1989 s 190(1), Sch 25 para 1(9), (10)(i) (Sch 25 para 1(9) amended by virtue of SI 1996/593); the Gas Act 1995 s 16(1), Sch 4 para 2(10)(a); and the Electricity Act 1989 s 112(1), Sch 16 para 3(1)(b) (amended by SI 1992/1314). As to the transfer of the function of 'the appropriate Minister' under the Opencast Coal Act 1958 s 39(6) in relation to Wales see the National Assembly for Wales (Transfer of Functions) Order 1999, SI 1999/672 Sch 1 (amended by SI 2013/755).

18   Ie the Opencast Coal Act 1958 s 39(4)–(10).

19   Ie a direction under the Opencast Coal Act 1958 s 39(1).

20   Opencast Coal Act 1958 s 39(3)(a). The orders referred to in the text are those under Pt I (ss 4–16). As to the meaning of 'opencast planning permission' see PARA 416.

21   Ie any functions under the Opencast Coal Act 1958 Pt I. As to the meaning of 'permitted activities' see PARA 416.

22   Opencast Coal Act 1958 s 39(3)(b).

23   Opencast Coal Act 1958 s 39(3)(c).

24   Ie in accordance with the Opencast Coal Act 1958 s 15A(5)(c) or any of the provisions of Sch 2 or Sch 9. Any reference in the Opencast Coal Act 1958 s 39 to Pt I, or to Sch 2, includes a reference to the provisions of any enactment as applied by Pt I, or by Sch 2, as the case may be: see s 39(10) (amended by the Housing and Planning Act 1986 Sch 12 Pt II).

25   Opencast Coal Act 1958 s 39(3)(d) (amended by the Housing and Planning Act 1986 s 39(3), Sch 8 Pt I para 10; and the Coal Industry Act 1994 Sch 8 para 29(3), (4)).

## 421. Incidents of power of entry.

Any power conferred on a person by virtue of the provisions as to entry on land[1] is exercisable by him either alone or with other persons, and is exercisable together with any vehicles, apparatus, materials or animals required for the purpose for which the power is exercised[2]. A person authorised under those provisions to enter upon any land must, if so required, produce evidence of his authority before entering it, or while remaining there, and must not[3] demand admission as of right to any land which is occupied unless 42 days' notice of the intended entry has been given to the occupier and to the owner of the land[4].

Any person who wilfully[5] obstructs[6] a person acting in the exercise of any such power of entry is liable on summary conviction to a fine not exceeding level 1 on the standard scale[7].

Where, in the exercise of any such power of entry any damage is caused to land or chattels, any person interested in the land or chattels is entitled to compensation in respect of that damage from the Coal Authority[8]; and where, in consequence of the exercise of any such power, any person is disturbed in his enjoyment of any land or chattels, he is entitled to compensation from the Authority in respect of that disturbance[9].

1   Ie by virtue of the Opencast Coal Act 1958 s 39: see PARA 420. The power to make directions designating land and conferring power to enter land has not been exercisable since 31 December 1999: see PARA 414.

2   See the Opencast Coal Act 1958 s 39(9).

3   Ie subject to the Opencast Coal Act 1958 s 39(6)–(10).

4   See the Opencast Coal Act 1958 s 39(5). However, this provision, in so far as it relates to the giving of notice, does not apply where entry is required only for the purpose of affixing on land any notice in accordance with s 15A(5)(c) or any of the provisions of Sch 2 or Sch 9: see s 39(5) proviso (amended by the Housing and Planning Act 1986 s 39(3), Sch 8 Pt I para 11; and the Coal Industry Act 1994 s 52(2), Sch 8 para 29(4)).

     'Owner', in relation to land, subject to the Opencast Coal Act 1958 s 51(2), means the estate owner in respect of the fee simple thereof: s 51(1). In relation to any land which is subject to a long tenancy, 'owner' means the person entitled to that tenancy, so however that for the purposes of the Opencast Coal Act 1958 s 51(2) a long tenancy, which is in reversion expectant (whether immediately or not) upon the termination of another long tenancy, is to be disregarded: s 51(2). For this purpose, 'long tenancy' means a tenancy granted for a term of years certain, being a term of ninety-nine years or more, whether subsequently extended (by act of the parties or by virtue of any enactment) or not: s 51(2).

5   As to the meaning of 'wilfully' generally see CRIMINAL LAW vol 25 (2016) PARA 8.

6   As to the meaning of 'obstructs' in various contexts see eg *Hinchliffe v Sheldon* [1955] 3 All ER 406, [1955] 1 WLR 1207, DC; *Evans v Lloyd* [1962] 2 QB 471, [1962] 1 All ER 239, DC; *Rice v Connolly* [1966] 2 QB 414, [1966] 2 All ER 649, DC; *Dibble v Ingleton* [1972] 1 QB 480, sub nom *Ingleton v Dibble* [1972] 1 All ER 275, DC; *Willmott v Atack* [1977] QB 498, [1976] 3 All ER 794, DC; and CRIMINAL LAW vol 26 (2016) PARA 799.

7   See the Opencast Coal Act 1958 s 39(8) (amended by the Criminal Justice Act 1982 ss 38, 46). As to the standard scale see SENTENCING vol 92 (2015) PARA 176.

8   As to the Coal Authority see PARA 52 et seq.

9   Opencast Coal Act 1958 s 39(7) (amended by the Coal Industry Act 1994 Sch 8 paras 1, 29(3)). The persons who may be authorised by the Coal Authority to exercise the powers conferred by the Opencast Coal Act 1958 s 39 must include any person who proposes to exercise those powers for the purposes and on behalf of any person who is or has applied to become a licensed operator within the meaning of the Coal Industry Act 1994; but where (1) any person does exercise powers under the Opencast Coal Act 1958 s 39 for the purposes of such a person; and (2) his written authority specifies that person and states that he is authorised to exercise those powers for the purposes and on behalf of that person, s 39(7) has effect as if the references to the Coal Authority were references to the specified person: see s 39(7A) (s 39(7A), (7B) added by the Coal Industry Act

1994 Sch 8 paras 1, 29(5)). Any authorisation by the Coal Authority of any person for the purposes of the exercise of the powers conferred by s 39, and any conditions of such an authorisation, may be revoked or varied by that Authority at any time: s 39(7B). As to the meaning of 'licensed operator' see PARA 58.

## 422. Notices.

Subject to certain provisions[1], any notice or other document required or authorised to be served or given under the Opencast Coal Act 1958, or under any enactment applied by or incorporated with that Act, may be served or given either: (1) by delivering it to the person on whom it is to be served, or to whom it is to be given[2]; or (2) by leaving it at the usual or last known place of abode of that person or, in a case where an address for service has been given by that person, at that address[3]; or (3) by sending it in a prepaid registered letter or by the recorded delivery service, addressed to that person at his usual or last known place of abode, or, in a case in which an address for service has been given by him, at that address[4]; or (4) in the case of an incorporated company or body, by delivering it to the secretary or clerk of the company or body at its registered or principal office, or sending it in a prepaid registered letter or by the recorded delivery service, addressed to that officer at that office[5].

Where the notice or document is required or authorised to be served on any person as having an interest in land, and the name of that person cannot be ascertained after reasonable inquiry, or where the notice or document is required or authorised to be served on any person as an occupier of land, the notice must be deemed to be duly served if: (a) being addressed to him either by name or by the description of 'the owner' or 'the occupier' as the case may be, of the land (describing it), it is delivered or sent in the manner prescribed[6]; or (b) being so addressed, it is sent in a prepaid registered letter or by the recorded delivery service to the land in question and is not returned to the person by whom or on whose behalf it is sent, or is delivered to some person on that land or is affixed conspicuously to some object on that land[7].

Where the notice or other document is required to be served on or given to all persons having interests, or interests of a specified description, in any land, or being occupiers of any land, and it appears to the person required or authorised to serve or give the notice or other document that any part of that land is unoccupied, the notice or other document is deemed to be duly served on all persons having interests, or the relevant interests, as the case may be, in that part of the land and on any occupiers of that part of the land (other than a person who has given an address for the service of the notice on him) if it is addressed to 'the owners and any occupiers' of that part of the land (describing it) and is affixed conspicuously to some object on the land[8].

1 Ie subject to the provisions of the Opencast Coal Act 1958 s 47, Sch 9. The provisions of Sch 9 have effect as to the service of notices under the Act: s 47(1).
2 Opencast Coal Act 1958 Sch 9 para 1(a).
3 Opencast Coal Act 1958 Sch 9 para 1(b).
4 Opencast Coal Act 1958 Sch 9 para 1(c); Recorded Delivery Service Act 1962 s 1(2), Schedule para 1.
5 Opencast Coal Act 1958 Sch 9 para 1(d); Recorded Delivery Service Act 1962 Schedule para 1. As to proof of delivery see generally CIVIL PROCEDURE vol 12 (2015) PARA 1004.
6 Ie prescribed by the Opencast Coal Act 1958 Sch 9 para 1: see Sch 9 para 2(a).
7 Opencast Coal Act 1958 Sch 9 para 2(b); Recorded Delivery Service Act 1962 Schedule para 1.
8 Opencast Coal Act 1958 Sch 9 para 3(1). However, this provision does not apply to any notice required to be served or given under the provisions of the Acquisition of Land Act 1981 as applied,

in relation to compulsory rights orders, by the Opencast Coal Act 1958 s 4 (see PARA 442): see Sch 9 para 3(2) (amended by the Acquisition of Land Act 1981 s 34, Sch 4 para 11(6); and the Housing and Planning Act 1986 s 39(4), Sch 12 Pt II).

The Opencast Coal Act 1958 Sch 9 paras 1–3 do not apply to any notice for which a method of service is prescribed by regulations under the Act, except in so far as any of those provisions are applied by those regulations: see Sch 9 para 4.

## (2) Opencast Planning Permission and Ancillary Rights

### (i) Powers and Prohibitions

### 423. Planning permission.

Opencast working is subject to general planning procedures, which are set out elsewhere in this work[1].

1   As to permitted coal mining development see the Town and Country Planning (General Permitted Development) Order 1995, SI 1995/418, art 3, Sch 2 Pts 19–23; and PLANNING vol 81 (2018) PARA 363 et seq. As to the meaning of 'opencast planning permission' see PARA 416.

### 424. Suspension of public rights of way.

Where any person applies for opencast planning permission[1], and over any part of the land[2] to which the application relates there subsists a public right of way[3], not being a right enjoyed by vehicular traffic[4], that person may also apply to the Coal Authority[5] for an order suspending the public right of way[6]. However, the power to make such an order has not been exercisable since 31 December 1999[7].

The Authority could not make an order unless: (1) opencast planning permission had been applied for or granted; and (2) it was satisfied that the applicant was a licensed operator within the meaning of the Coal Industry Act 1994 or a person whose application to the Authority for a licence[8] was pending; and had complied with the statutory requirements[9] before submitting the application; and (3) it was also satisfied that a suitable alternative way would be made available by the applicant, whether on land comprised in the opencast planning permission or on other land, for use by the public during the period for which the order remained in force; or that the provision of such an alternative way was not required[10].

An order[11] could be made either in accordance with the application or subject to such modifications as the Authority might determine[12].

1   As to the meaning of 'opencast planning permission' see PARA 416.
2   As to the meaning of 'land' see PARA 414.
3   As to statutory provisions as to the stopping up or diversion of highways see generally HIGHWAYS, STREETS AND BRIDGES vol 55 (2012) PARAS 816–818.
4   See, however, the definitions of 'bridleway' and 'footway' in the Highways Act 1980 s 329(1): see HIGHWAYS, STREETS AND BRIDGES vol 55 (2012) PARAS 68, 842.
5   Applications were previously made to the Secretary of State: see the Opencast Coal Act 1958 s 15 (as originally enacted). An application to the Secretary of State for an order under s 15 which was pending immediately before the restructuring date has effect on and after that date as if made to the Coal Authority and does not require the confirmation of the Secretary of State: Coal Industry Act 1994 s 67(7), Sch 10 para 9(3), (4). As to the Secretary of State see PARA 2. As to the Coal Authority see PARA 52 et seq.
6   Opencast Coal Act 1958 s 15(1) (s 15 substituted and s 15A added by the Housing and Planning Act 1986 s 39(3), Sch 8 Pt I para 6; and the Opencast Coal Act 1958 s 15(1) amended by the Coal Industry Act 1987 s 1(2), Sch 1 para 7(c); and the Coal Industry Act 1994 s 52(2), Sch 8 paras 1, 12(1), (2)). As to the position where the original applicant is succeeded by a successor see the Opencast Coal Act 1958 s 15(3A), (3B) (s 15(3A), (3B) both added by the Coal Industry Act 1994

Sch 8 paras 1, 12(3)). 'Successor', in relation to an applicant for an order under any provision of the Opencast Coal Act 1958, means any person, whether or not the immediate successor of the applicant, who: (1) in accordance with the provisions of any licence granted to the applicant under the Coal Industry Act 1994 Pt II (ss 25–36), succeeds to any entitlement of that applicant under that licence to work any coal by opencast operations; or (2) becomes entitled by virtue of the grant of a new licence under Pt II to work by such operations any coal which the applicant was previously entitled so to work as a licensed operator within the meaning of that Act: Opencast Coal Act 1958 s 51(1) (definition added by the Coal Industry Act 1994 Sch 8 paras 1, 36(1)(b)).

7  See the Coal Industry Act 1994 s 52(1); and PARA 414.

8  Ie under the Coal Industry Act 1994 Pt II: see the Opencast Coal Act 1958 s 15(2). As to the meaning of 'licensed operator' see PARA 58.

9  Ie the requirement that notice should be given before submission of an application for an order under the Opencast Coal Act 1958 s 15, identifying the right of way and stating: (1) that it was proposed to apply for a suspension order in connection with the working of coal by opencast operations; (2) whether the applicant proposed to make available any alternative way and, if so, what the alternative was; and (3) that opencast planning permission had been applied for, or, as the case may be, had been granted: see s 15A(1) (amended by the Coal Industry Act 1987 Sch 1 para 7(c); and the Coal Industry Act 1994 s 67(7), (8), Sch 8 paras 1, 13(1), Sch 11 Pt II). As to the working of coal by opencast operations see PARA 416. As to the meaning of 'coal' see PARA 414. As to the prescribed forms for the purposes of these provisions see the Opencast Coal (Compulsory Rights, Drainage and Rights of Way) (Forms) Regulations 1994, SI 1994/3097, reg 4, Schedule Forms 6–8.
An order under the Opencast Coal Act 1958 s 15 could not be made except where conditions for the making of the order were imposed or other provision was included in the order for securing the reconstruction of the way on the restoration of the land over which the right of way subsisted immediately before the order was made: s 15(5) (amended by the Coal Industry Act 1994 Sch 8 paras 1, 12(5)). See also PARA 427. 'Restoration', in relation to land, includes rehabilitation; and 'restore' is to be construed accordingly: Opencast Coal Act 1958 s 51(1).

10  See the Opencast Coal Act 1958 s 15(2) (amended by the Coal Industry Act 1987 Sch 1 para 7(c); and the Coal Industry Act 1994 Sch 8 paras 1, 12(1), (2)). In connection with the provision of such a suitable alternative way as is referred to in the Opencast Coal Act 1958 s 15(2), see further s 15(6) (as so substituted; and amended by the Planning (Consequential Provisions) Act 1990 s 4, Sch 2 para 5(b)).

11  Ie an order under the Opencast Coal Act 1958 s 15: see s 15A(9).

12  See the Opencast Coal Act 1958 s 15A(9) (amended by the Coal Industry Act 1994 Sch 8 para 13(10), Sch 11 Pt II). This did not prejudice the Secretary of State's power to make further modifications when confirming the order: see s 15A(9); and PARA 426.

## 425. Procedure on application.

As soon as reasonably practicable after making an order[1] the Coal Authority[2] had to submit it to the appropriate national authority[3] for confirmation and publish a notice in the prescribed form identifying the right of way in question and stating:

(1)    that the Authority had made an order that would suspend the right of way in connection with the working of coal by opencast operations[4] and had submitted the order for confirmation to the appropriate national authority[5];

(2)    whether the applicant for the order was to make any alternative way available and, if so, what the alternative was[6];

(3)    that opencast planning permission[7] had been applied for or, as the case may be, granted[8]; and

(4)    that objections to the confirmation of the order could be made in writing to the appropriate national authority within a specified time[9].

Detailed provision was made as to the manner of publication, and the giving of information[10].

The appropriate national authority could not confirm an order unless he was satisfied that: (a) the required notice had been published and the prescribed requirements had been satisfied; (b) the period for the making of objections had expired; and (c) the opencast planning permission had been granted[11]. The appropriate national authority could cause a public local inquiry to be held before determining whether to confirm an order[12], and he had to consider all objections to the application and the report of the person who held the inquiry before determining whether to confirm the order[13].

1  Ie an order under the Opencast Coal Act 1958 s 15: see s 15A(1A).
2  As to the Coal Authority see PARA 52 et seq.
3  Ie the Secretary of State or where functions have been transferred in relation to Wales, the Welsh Ministers: see PARA 2.
4  As to the working of coal by opencast operations see PARA 416. As to the meaning of 'coal' see PARA 414.
5  Opencast Coal Act 1958 s 15A(1A)(a) (s 15A added by the Housing and Planning Act 1986 s 39(3), Sch 8 Pt I para 6; and the Opencast Coal Act 1958 s 15A(1A) added by the Coal Industry Act 1994 s 52(2), Sch 8 para 13(2), (4)).
6  Opencast Coal Act 1958 s 15A(1A)(b).
7  As to the meaning of 'opencast planning permission' see PARA 416.
8  Opencast Coal Act 1958 s 15A(1A)(c).
9  Opencast Coal Act 1958 s 15A(1A)(d). As to the period for the making of objections see s 15A(3).
10 See the Opencast Coal Act 1958 s 15A(2), (4) (s 15A(2), (4) amended by the Coal Industry Act 1994 Sch 8 para 13(3), (5)). See also the Opencast Coal Act 1958 s 15A(5) (s 15A(5) amended by the Local Government (Wales) Act 1994 s 66(6), (8), Sch 16 para 14, Sch 18; and the Coal Industry Act 1994 Sch 8 para 13(6), (11)).
11 See the Opencast Coal Act 1958 s 15A(2A) (added by the Coal Industry Act 1994 Sch 8 para 13(2), (4)). A confirmed order did not have effect until notice of it had been given by the person on whose application the order was made: see the Opencast Coal Act 1958 s 15A(10), (11) (s 15A(10) amended by the Coal Industry Act 1994 Sch 8 para 13(6), (11); and the Opencast Coal Act 1958 s 15A(11) amended by the Coal Industry Act 1994 Sch 8 para 13(9), (12)).
12 See the Opencast Coal Act 1958 s 15A(7) (amended by the Coal Industry Act 1994 Sch 8 para 13(8)).
13 Opencast Coal Act 1958 s 15A(8) ( amended by the Coal Industry Act 1994 Sch 8 para 13(9), (12)).

## 426. Effect of order suspending rights of way.

An order[1] does not have effect unless confirmed by the appropriate national authority[2]; and where it has been confirmed, has effect (with such modifications as the appropriate national authority may have determined in confirming it) so as to suspend the right of way to which it relates with effect[3] from such date as may be determined by the appropriate national authority and specified in the order as confirmed[4].

Where, in pursuance of an order[5], a public right of way is suspended, and, immediately before the date on which that order became operative, there was under, in, upon, over, along or across the way to which the order relates, an electronic communications apparatus[6] kept installed for the purposes of an electronic communications code[7], the operator of that system has the same rights in respect of that apparatus as if the order had not become operative[8].

1  Ie an order under the Opencast Coal Act 1958 s 15: see s 15(3).
2  Ie the Secretary of State or where functions have been transferred in relation to Wales, the Welsh Ministers: see PARA 2.
3  Ie subject to the Opencast Coal Act 1958 s 15A(10), (11): s 15(3).
4  See the Opencast Coal Act 1958 s 15(3) (s 15 substituted by the Housing and Planning Act 1986 s 39(3), Sch 8 Pt I para 6; and the Opencast Coal Act 1958 s 15(3) further substituted by the Coal Industry Act 1994 s 52(2), Sch 8 paras 1, 12(3)).
5  Ie an order under the Opencast Coal Act 1958 s 15 (as substituted and amended): see s 45(3).
6  As to the meaning of 'electronic communications apparatus' see the Telecommunications Act 1984 s 109, Sch 4 para 1; and TELECOMMUNICATIONS vol 97 (2015) PARAS 52, 168, 179.
7  As to the meaning of 'electronic communications code' see the Telecommunications Act 1984 Sch 4 para 1; and TELECOMMUNICATIONS vol 97 (2015) PARAS 53, 179.

8  Opencast Coal Act 1958 s 45(3) (amended by the Coal Industry Act 1975 s 7(4), Sch 5; the Telecommunications Act 1984 Sch 4 para 38(4), Sch 5 para 45; and the Communications Act 2003 Sch 17 para 27(1)). However, the Opencast Coal Act 1958 s 45(3) has effect without prejudice to the provisions of s 45(2): see s 45(3) proviso.

### 427. Revocation of order suspending certain public rights of way.

Where an order suspending public rights of way has been made[1] the appropriate national authority[2] must revoke it: (1) if no permitted activities[3] have been carried on pursuant to the opencast planning permission[4] on the land[5] over which the right of way subsisted, and he is satisfied that there is no early prospect of such activities being so carried on[6]; or (2) as soon after such permitted activities have been so carried on as he is satisfied that it is no longer necessary for the fulfilment for the purpose of carrying on such permitted activities that the right of way should be suspended[7]; or (3) he is satisfied that it is appropriate to do so on account of any failure on the part of the person on whose application the order was made to comply with any of the prescribed requirements[8]. Provision is made for the reconstruction of the way on the restoration[9] of the land over which the right of way subsisted immediately before the order was made[10].

1  Ie an order under the Opencast Coal Act 1958 s 15. The power to make such orders has not been exercisable since 31 December 1999: see PARA 414.
2  Ie the Secretary of State or where functions have been transferred in relation to Wales, the Welsh Ministers: see PARA 2.
3  As to the meaning of 'permitted activities' see PARA 416.
4  As to the meaning of 'opencast planning permission' see PARA 416.
5  As to the meaning of 'land' see PARA 414.
6  See the Opencast Coal Act 1958 s 15(4)(a) (s 15 substituted by the Housing and Planning Act 1986 s 39(3), Sch 8 Pt I para 6).
7  See the Opencast Coal Act 1958 s 15(4)(b).
8  See the Opencast Coal Act 1958 s 15(4)(c) (amended by the Coal Industry Act 1994 s 52(2), Sch 8 paras 1, 12(4)). The prescribed requirements referred to in the text are any of the requirements of the Opencast Coal Act 1958 s 15A(10) (see PARA 425): s 15(4)(c) (as so substituted and amended).
9  As to the meaning of 'restoration' see PARA 424.
10 See the Opencast Coal Act 1958 s 15(5) (amended by the Coal Industry Act 1994 Sch 8 paras 1, 12(5)). See also PARA 424.
    For the purposes of the Opencast Coal Act 1958 s 15(5) (as substituted and amended), a local planning authority may enter into an agreement with any applicant for an order under s 15 as to the steps to be taken by that person or any of his successors for securing the reconstruction of the way in question; and such an agreement has effect, so far as it relates to steps to be taken by any successor of the applicant, as if that successor had been a party to it and was bound by it to the same extent as the applicant: s 15(5A) (s 15(5A) added by the Coal Industry Act 1994 Sch 8 paras 1, 12(6).
    'Local planning authority' and 'local authority' have the meanings assigned by the Town and Country Planning Act 1990 s 336(1) (see PLANNING vol 81 (2018) PARAS 3–4): Opencast Coal Act 1958 s 51(1) (definition amended by virtue of the Planning (Consequential Provisions) Act 1990 Sch 3 para 3). As to the meaning of 'successor' see PARA 424.

### (ii) Particular Effects of Grants of Opencast Planning Permission

### 428. Provisions as to agricultural tenancies in England and Wales.

Where opencast planning permission[1] has been granted subject to a restoration[2] condition and to an aftercare condition in which the use specified is use for agriculture[3] or use for forestry, and immediately before that permission is granted, any of the land[4] comprised therein consists of an agricultural holding held under a tenancy in relation to which the Agricultural Holdings Act 1986 applies or part of such an agricultural holding, whether any of that land is comprised in a compulsory rights order[5] or not, special provisions apply for the purposes of that Act[6].

The tenant of the holding is not to be taken to have failed to fulfil his responsibilities to farm in accordance with the rules of good husbandry[7]: (1) by reason of his having permitted any of the land comprised in the opencast planning permission to be occupied for the purpose of carrying on any of the permitted activities[8], or by reason of any other thing done or omitted by him for facilitating the use of any of that land for that purpose[9]; (2) where any of that land is comprised in a compulsory rights order, by reason of the occupation or use of any of that land in the exercise of rights conferred by the order, in so far as that occupation or use was not permitted or facilitated by the tenant as mentioned in head (1) above[10].

Nothing done or omitted by the tenant or by the landlord of the holding by way of permitting any of the land in respect of which opencast planning permission has been granted to be occupied for the purpose of carrying on any of the permitted activities, or by way of facilitating the use of any of that land for that purpose, is to be taken to be a breach of any term or condition of the tenancy, either on the part of the tenant or on the part of the landlord[11].

On a reference to arbitration under the Agricultural Holdings Act 1986[12] with respect to the rent which should be properly payable for the holding, in respect of any period for which the person with the benefit of the opencast planning permission is in occupation of the holding, or of any part thereof, for the purpose of carrying on any of the permitted activities, the arbitrator must not take into account any increase or diminution in the rental value of the holding in so far as that increase or diminution is attributable to the occupation of the holding, or of that part of the holding, by that person for the purpose of carrying on any of the permitted activities[13].

1   As to the meaning of 'opencast planning permission' see PARA 416.
2   As to the meaning of 'restoration' see PARA 424.
3   For these purposes, 'agriculture' has the same meaning as in the Agriculture Act 1947 s 109(3) (see AGRICULTURAL LAND AND ALLOTMENTS vol 1 (2017) PARA 424), and 'agricultural' (except in the expressions 'agricultural holding' and 'agricultural land') is construed accordingly: Opencast Coal Act 1958 s 51(1). 'Agricultural holding' has the meaning assigned to it by the Agricultural Holdings Act 1986 s 1(1) (see AGRICULTURAL LAND AND ALLOTMENTS vol 1 (2017) PARA 423): Opencast Coal Act 1958 s 51(1) (definition amended by the Agricultural Holdings Act 1986 s 100, Sch 14 para 31(b)).
4   As to the meaning of 'land' see PARA 414.
5   As to compulsory rights orders see the Opencast Coal Act 1958 s 4; and PARA 431 et seq. The power to make such orders has not been exercisable since 31 December 1999: see PARA 414.
6   See the Opencast Coal Act 1958 s 14(1) (s 14 substituted by the Housing and Planning Act 1986 s 39(3), Sch 8 Pt I para 5; Opencast Coal Act 1958 s 14(1) amended by the Agricultural Tenancies Act 1995 s 40, Schedule para 13(2), (3)). The Opencast Coal Act 1958 s 14(1) is without prejudice to the provisions of Pt III (ss 37–53) as to matters arising between landlords and tenants in consequence of compulsory rights orders: see s 14(1) (as so substituted). For the purposes of the Agricultural Holdings Act 1986 the holding is not to be taken to have ceased to be an agricultural holding; and where only part of the holding is comprised in opencast planning permission, that part is not to be taken to have ceased to form part of an agricultural holding, by reason only that, while occupied or used for the permitted activities, the land is not being used for agriculture within the meaning of that Act: see the Opencast Coal Act 1958 s 14(2) (s 14 as so substituted; s 14(2) amended by the Agricultural Tenancies Act 1995 Schedule para 13(2), (3)).
7   As to such rules see the Agriculture Act 1947 s 11 (applied by the Agricultural Holdings Act 1986 s 96(3)); and AGRICULTURAL PRODUCTION AND MARKETING vol 1 (2017) PARA 12.
8   As to the meaning of 'permitted activities' see PARA 416.
9   Opencast Coal Act 1958 s 14(3)(a).

10　Opencast Coal Act 1958 s 14(3)(b).

11　Opencast Coal Act 1958 s 14(4). For the purposes of the Agricultural Holdings Act 1986 s 27(1)–(3) ( Tribunal's consent to operation of notice to quit) the condition specified in s 27(3)(f) is not treated as satisfied if the use for the purpose for which the landlord proposes to terminate the tenancy is the use of the land for carrying on any of the permitted activities: see the Opencast Coal Act 1958 s 14(5) (amended by SI 2013/1036).

12　Ie the Agricultural Holdings Act 1986 s 12: see the Opencast Coal Act 1958 s 14(6).

13　See the Opencast Coal Act 1958 s 14(6) (amended by the Coal Industry Act 1994 s 52(2), Sch 8 para 10). For the purpose of the operation of the Agricultural Holdings Act 1986 s 13 (increases of rent for landlord's improvements) in relation to improvements carried out on the holding, in a case where the improvements have been affected by anything done for the purpose of carrying on any of the permitted activities, the increase (if any) of the rental value of the holding attributable to the carrying out of the improvements is assessed as if it had not been done: Opencast Coal Act 1958 s 14(7). Section 14 does not extend to Scotland: s 14(8) (as so substituted).

## 429.　Provisions as to farm business tenancies.

Without prejudice to the provisions of the Opencast Coal Act 1958[1] as to matters arising between landlords and tenants in consequence of compulsory rights orders[2], where opencast planning permission[3] has been granted subject to a restoration[4] condition and, immediately before that permission is granted, any of the land[5] comprised therein consists of the holding[6] or part of the holding held under a farm business tenancy[7], whether any of that land is comprised in a compulsory rights order or not, special provisions apply for the purposes of the Agricultural Tenancies Act 1995[8].

For the purposes of the Agricultural Tenancies Act 1995[9], the land is to be taken, while it is occupied or used for the permitted activities[10], to be used for the purposes for which it was used immediately before it was occupied or used for the permitted activities[11].

For the purposes of the Agricultural Tenancies Act 1995, nothing done or omitted by the tenant or by the landlord under the tenancy by way of permitting any of the land in respect of which opencast planning permission has been granted to be occupied for the purpose of carrying on any of the permitted activities, or by way of facilitating the use of any of that land for that purpose, is to be taken to be a breach of any term or condition of the tenancy, either on the part of the tenant or on the part of the landlord[12].

1　Ie the Opencast Coal Act 1958 Pt III (ss 37–53): see s 14B.

2　As to compulsory rights orders see the Opencast Coal Act 1958 s 4; and PARA 431 et seq. The power to make such orders has not been exercisable since 31 December 1999: see PARA 414.

3　As to the meaning of 'opencast planning permission' see PARA 416.

4　As to the meaning of 'restoration' see PARA 424.

5　As to the meaning of 'land' see PARA 414.

6　For the purposes of the Opencast Coal Act 1958 s 14B, 'holding', in relation to a farm business tenancy, has the same meaning as in the Agricultural Tenancies Act 1995 s 38(1) (see AGRICULTURAL LAND AND ALLOTMENTS vol 1 (2017) PARA 402): Opencast Coal Act 1958 s 14B(5).

7　For these purposes, 'farm business tenancy' has the same meaning as in the Agricultural Tenancies Act 1995 s 1 (see AGRICULTURAL LAND AND ALLOTMENTS vol 1 (2017) PARA 402): Opencast Coal Act 1958 s 51(1) (definition added by the Agricultural Tenancies Act 1995 s 40, Schedule para 19(b)).

8　See the Opencast Coal Act 1958 s 14B(1) (s 14B added by the Agricultural Tenancies Act 1995 Schedule para 14).

9　Ie the Agricultural Tenancies Act 1995 s 1 (see AGRICULTURAL LAND AND ALLOTMENTS vol 1 (2017) PARA 402): see the Opencast Coal Act 1958 s 14B(2).

10　As to the meaning of 'permitted activities' see PARA 416.

11　Opencast Coal Act 1958 s 14B(2).

12　Opencast Coal Act 1958 s 14B(3). In determining, under the Agricultural Tenancies Act 1995 s

13(1), (2) (see AGRICULTURAL LAND AND ALLOTMENTS vol 1 (2017) PARA 409), the rent which should be properly payable for the holding, in respect of any period for which the person with the benefit of the opencast planning permission is in occupation of the holding, or of any part thereof, for the purpose of carrying on any of the permitted activities, the arbitrator is to disregard any increase or diminution in the rental value of the holding in so far as that increase or diminution is attributable to the occupation of the holding, or of that part of the holding, by that person for the purpose of carrying on any of the permitted activities: Opencast Coal Act 1958 s 14B(4). Section 14B does not extend to Scotland: s 14B(6).

### 430. Rights as to drainage or water supply.

For the purposes of draining land[1], or bringing a supply of water to land, in respect of which opencast planning permission[2] has been applied for or granted, the Coal Authority[3], on an application[4], may, by means of an order made by it and confirmed by the appropriate national authority[5], confer on the person with the benefit of the permission[6] a right[7] to place drainage works[8], or water pipes, on any other land, whether above or below ground, and to use, repair and maintain those works, or pipes, without purchasing any other interest in that land[9]. However, the power to make such an order has not been exercisable since 31 December 1999[10].

The Authority could not make such an order except on the application of a person who:

(1) was the person with the benefit of the opencast planning permission or, where the permission had been applied for but had not been granted, the person who would have the benefit of that permission[11];

(2) satisfied the Authority that he was either a licensed operator[12] or a person whose application to the Authority for a licence[13] was pending[14]; and

(3) satisfied the Authority that he had served notice[15] in the prescribed[16] form of the application for the order on every owner[17], lessee and occupier of the other land (except tenants for a month or any period of less than a month)[18],

and an order made before the opencast planning permission had been granted was not to be confirmed until after it had been granted[19].

The order had to specify the land (being the whole or part of the land in respect of which the planning permission had been applied for or granted) for the benefit of which the right was to be conferred[20].

An order made under these provisions is a local land charge[21].

1 As to the meaning of 'land' see PARA 414. Except with the consent of the appropriate authority no order is to be made under the Opencast Coal Act 1958 s 16 in respect of any land in which for the time being there is a Crown or Duchy interest (as to the meaning of which see PARA 415): s 44(2)(b). However, this does not affect the validity or operation of an order, or the exercise of any power, as against any person having, in or over the land in question, any interest or right other than a Crown or Duchy interest: s 44(2) proviso.

2 As to the meaning of 'opencast planning permission' see PARA 416.

3 Applications were previously made to the Secretary of State: see the Opencast Coal Act 1958 s 16 (as originally enacted). An application to the Secretary of State for an order under s 16 (as originally enacted) which is pending immediately before the restructuring date (ie 31 October 1994: see PARA 50) has effect on and after that date as if made to the Coal Authority: Coal Industry Act 1994 s 67(7), Sch 10 para 9(3). This does not affect the operation of the Opencast Coal Act 1958 in relation to any such order made before the restructuring date: Coal Industry Act 1994 Sch 10 para 9(5). As to the Coal Authority see PARA 52 et seq.

4 Ie on an application in accordance with the Opencast Coal Act 1958 s 16(2A): see s 16(1), (2). As to the position where the original applicant is succeeded by a successor see s 16(4B), (4C) (added by the Coal Industry Act 1994 Sch 8 para 14(2), (6), (9)). As to the meaning of 'successor' see PARA 424.

5 Ie the Secretary of State or where functions have been transferred in relation to Wales, the Welsh

Ministers: see PARA 2.

6 References in relation to any opencast planning permission, to the person with the benefit of that permission are to be construed as a reference to any person who: (1) is able, on account of his having all such interests or rights as (apart from that permission) he requires for the purpose, to carry out any of the permitted activities; or (2) would be so able if the rights which he had and was entitled to exercise included any such right as he has applied for, or is entitled to apply for, under the Opencast Coal Act 1958 or any right which has been conferred on him under the Opencast Coal Act 1958 but has not yet become exercisable: s 51(1A) (added by the Coal Industry Act 1994 s 52(2), Sch 8 para 36(2)).

7 Any right conferred by an order under the Opencast Coal Act 1958 s 16 is exercisable by, or by any person authorised by: (1) a person who: (a) is for the time being in occupation of the land specified in accordance with s 16(3) in the order; (b) is the person on whom the right was conferred; and (c) was in occupation of that land when it was conferred; or (2) a person who is for the time being in occupation of the land by virtue of the transfer to him either: (a) by, or with the written approval of, the Coal Authority; or (b) in any other case described in the order, of any interest or right which, at the time when the right was conferred under s 16, was vested in a person who became entitled to exercise it by virtue of head (1): s 16(4) (substituted by the Coal Industry Act 1994 Sch 8 para 14(4)). A right conferred by an order under the Opencast Coal Act 1958 s 16 (whether or not conferred while the person on whom it was conferred was in occupation of the land) is, in the case of land in England and Wales, treated as an easement appurtenant in perpetuity to that land: see s 16(4) (as so substituted).

　　For the purposes of any such order conferring rights exercisable on any land in England and Wales: (i) the Acquisition of Land Act 1981 Pts II–IV (ss 10–27) apply as they would apply in relation to a compulsory rights order in which that land is comprised, and s 29 applies accordingly but with the omission of s 29(4), (5); and (ii) the Compulsory Purchase Act 1965 has effect as if the conferring of those rights were the compulsory acquisition of those rights by the person on whom they are conferred; and references (whatever the terms used) to the land comprised in the compulsory purchase order were construed, where the context so requires, as references to the land on which the works or pipes are to be placed, and references to the obtaining or taking possession of the first mentioned land were construed as references to the exercise of the right: see the Opencast Coal Act 1958 s 16(4A) (added by the Acquisition of Land Act 1981 s 34, Sch 4 para 11(4); and amended by the Coal Industry Act 1994 Sch 8 para 14(5)).

8 For the purposes of the Opencast Coal Act 1958 s 16, 'drainage works' includes any pipes or other works for draining land and any works accessory to such works; and (1) any right to maintain drainage works or water pipes in pursuance of an order made by virtue of s 16 includes the right to remove those works or pipes, whether for the purpose of replacing them by other drainage works or water pipes or otherwise; and (2) any right to maintain drainage works on any land in pursuance of such an order, if the order so provides, includes a right to discharge water from those works on to that land: s 16(7).

9 See the Opencast Coal Act 1958 s 16(1), (2) (amended by the Housing and Planning Act 1986 s 39(3), Sch 8 Pt I para 7; and the Coal Industry Act 1994 Sch 8 para 14(1)). Nothing in the Opencast Coal Act 1958 s 16 is to be construed as authorising any interference with the exercise of a public right of way, or any contravention of a prohibition or restriction imposed by or under any enactment (whether contained in a public general Act or in any other Act): see s 16(8).

10 See the Coal Industry Act 1994 s 52(1); and PARA 414.

11 Coal Industry Act 1994 s 16(2A)(a) (s 16(2A) added by the Coal Industry Act 1994 Sch 8 para 14(2), (6), (9)).

12 Ie within the meaning of the Coal Industry Act 1994: see the Opencast Coal Act 1958 s 16(2A)(b).

13 Ie a licence under the Coal Industry Act 1994 Pt II (ss 25–36) (see PARA 89 et seq): see the Opencast Coal Act 1958 s 16(2A)(b).

14 Coal Industry Act 1994 s 16(2A)(b).

15 The Acquisition of Land Act 1981 s 12(2), (3) (statutory tenants etc and ecclesiastical property) (see COMPULSORY ACQUISITION OF LAND vol 18 (2009) PARA 560) has effect in relation to the service of a notice under the Opencast Coal Act 1958 s 16 as respects any land in England and Wales as they have effect in relation to the service of a notice under the Acquisition of Land Act 1981 s 12: see the Opencast Coal Act 1958 s 16(7A) (added by the Coal Industry Act 1994 Sch 8 para 14(2), (6), (9)).

16 'Prescribed' means prescribed by regulations made under the Opencast Coal Act 1958: s 51(1).

17 As to the meaning of 'owner' see PARA 421.

18 Coal Industry Act 1994 s 16(2A)(c).

19 See the Opencast Coal Act 1958 s 16(2A).

20 See the Opencast Coal Act 1958 s 16(3) (amended by the Coal Industry Act 1994 Sch 8 para 14(3); and the Housing and Planning Act 1986 Sch 8 Pt I para 7).

21 The provisions of the Opencast Coal Act 1958 s 11 apply in relation to an order made and confirmed under s 16 as they apply in relation to a compulsory rights order: see s 16(6) (amended by the Coal Industry Act 1994 Sch 8 para 14(8)). See further PARA 431. As to land charges generally see REAL PROPERTY AND REGISTRATION vol 87 (2017) PARA 641 et seq.

# (3) Acquisition of Temporary Rights of Use and Occupation

## (i) Compulsory Rights Orders

### 431. Nature of compulsory rights order.

For the purpose of facilitating the working of coal by opencast operations[1], the Coal Authority[2] has power, by means of a compulsory rights order[3] made by the Authority and confirmed by the appropriate national authority[4], to confer[5] temporary[6] rights of occupation and use of the whole, or such part as, subject to the confirmation of the appropriate national authority, the Authority thinks fit, of any land[7] on which the applicant for the order desires to work coal by such operations or to carry out operations incidental to such working[8]. However, the power to make such an order has not been exercisable since 31 December 1999[9].

The Authority could not make a compulsory rights order except on the application of a person who satisfied the Authority that: (1) he was either a licensed operator[10] or a person whose application to that Authority for a licence[11] was pending[12]; and (2) he had served notice in the prescribed[13] form of the application for the order on every person known to him to be a person who would, in relation to the order applied for, be directly concerned[14].

Subject to certain provisions[15], the rights conferred by an order made on such an application[16] were conferred on the applicant and his successors[17] so as to be exercisable for the purposes only of: (a) operations which the applicant or, as the case may be, any such successor is authorised to carry out by virtue of being a licensed operator[18]; and (b) operations which are incidental to operations falling within head (a) above, including operations carried out at times when the authorisation for the operations falling within head (a) is not in force[19].

Certain classes of rights are not affected by a compulsory rights order[20], and such an order may be expressed to extend to certain classes of right only[21]. Further, certain types of property are exempt from inclusion in a compulsory rights order[22].

A compulsory rights an order is subject to certain requirements in relation to opencast planning permission[23].

Compulsory rights orders are local land charges[24], and records must be made relating to the land comprised in those orders[25].

1 As to the meaning of 'coal' see PARA 414. As to references to working coal by opencast operations see PARA 416.

2 As to the Coal Authority see PARA 52 et seq.

3 As to the prescribed form in connection with a compulsory rights order see the Opencast Coal (Compulsory Rights, Drainage and Rights of Way) (Forms) Regulations 1994, SI 1994/3097, reg 3, Form 2.

4 Ie the Secretary of State or, where functions have been transferred in relation to Wales, the Welsh Ministers: see PARA 2.

5 Ie confer in accordance with the provisions of the Opencast Coal Act 1958 Pt I (ss 4–16): see s 4(1).

6 As to the duration of compulsory rights orders see PARA 432.

7   As to the meaning of 'land' see PARA 414. Except with the consent of the appropriate authority, no compulsory rights order could be made in respect of any land in which for the time being there is a Crown or Duchy interest (as to the meaning of which see PARA 415): Opencast Coal Act 1958 s 44(2)(a). However, this does not affect the validity or operation of an order, or the exercise of any power, as against any person having, in or over the land in question, any interest or right other than a Crown or Duchy interest: s 44(2) proviso. Where a compulsory rights order has been made, with the consent of the appropriate authority, in respect of land in which there is a Crown or Duchy interest, that interest, in so far as the order confers rights exercisable as against all persons directly concerned, is treated as not being the interest of a person directly concerned, and no compensation is payable under Pt II (ss 17–36) in respect of that interest: s 44(3) (amended by the Coal Industry Act 1994 ss 52(2), 67(8), Sch 8 para 33, Sch 11 Pt II).

Notwithstanding anything in the Opencast Coal Act 1958 Pt I, none of the rights or powers conferred by Pt I or by any order made under Pt I authorises any interference with any electronic communications apparatus kept installed for the purposes of an electronic communications code network or includes any right or power to require any such apparatus to be altered: see s 45(1) (amended by the Telecommunications Act 1984 Sch 4 para 38; and the Communications Act 2003 Sch 17 para 27(1)). As to the meanings of 'electronic communications apparatus' and 'electronic communications code network see the Telecommunications Act 1984 s 109, Sch 4 para 1; and TELECOMMUNICATIONS vol 97 (2015) PARAS 53, 168.

Paragraph 108(2) of the electronic communications code (alteration of apparatus to include moving, removal or replacement of apparatus) applies for the purposes of the Opencast Coal Act 1958 s 45(1) as it applies for the purposes of that code: s 45(4) (substituted by the Telecommunications Act 1984 Sch 4 para 38, Sch 5 para 4; and amended by the Communications Act 2003 Sch 17 para 27(1)); the Digital Economy Act 2017 Sch 3 para 5(3); and SI 2017/1285).

8   Opencast Coal Act 1958 s 4(1) (substituted by the Coal Industry Act 1975 s 4; amended by the Housing and Planning Act 1986 s 39(3), Sch 8 Pt I para 2; and the Coal Industry Act 1994 Sch 8 para 2(1)); Opencast Coal Act 1958 s 51(1). Cf the provisions of the Mines (Working Facilities and Support) Act 1966 s 3(2); and PARA 391.

Where any compulsory rights order was made under the Opencast Coal Act 1958 before the restructuring date (ie 31 October 1994: see PARA 50) and was awaiting confirmation on that date, that order could be confirmed on or after that date in accordance with the Opencast Coal Act 1958 as if it had been made by the Authority on the application of the British Coal Corporation: Coal Industry Act 1994 Sch 10 para 9(1). The rights conferred on the Corporation by any compulsory rights order made under the Opencast Coal Act 1958 before the restructuring date have effect on and after that date as if conferred on the Corporation and its successors (within the meaning of that Act) so as to be exercisable for the purposes only of: (1) operations which the Corporation or, as the case may be, any such successor is authorised to carry out by virtue of being a licensed operator; and (2) operations which are incidental to operations falling within head (1) (including operations carried out at times when the authorisation for the operations falling within head (1) is not in force): Coal Industry Act 1994 Sch 10 para 9(2). As to the British Coal Corporation see PARAS 49–50.

9   See the Coal Industry Act 1994 s 52(1); and PARA 414.

10  As to the meaning of 'licensed operator' see PARA 58 (definition applied by the Opencast Coal Act 1958 s 4(1A)).

11  Ie a licence under the Coal Industry Act 1994 Pt II (ss 25–36): see the Opencast Coal Act 1958 s 4(1A).

12  See the Opencast Coal Act 1958 s 4(1A)(a) (s 4(1A) added by the Coal Industry Act 1994 Sch 8 para 2(2)).

13  As to the meaning of 'prescribed' see PARA 430.

14  See the Opencast Coal Act 1958 s 4(1A)(b). In the Opencast Coal Act 1958, subject to the provisions of ss 7–53, 'persons directly concerned', in relation to a compulsory rights order, means persons who for the time being have any interest in any of the land comprised in the order, or have, apart from the order, a right to occupy any of that land, or are entitled to any right restrictive of the use of any of that land: see s 5(6) (amended by the Coal Industry Act 1975 s 4(2), Sch 3 para 2); Opencast Coal Act 1958 s 51(1) (amended by the Coal Industry Act 1975 Sch 3 para 9).

15  Ie subject to the provisions of the Opencast Coal Act 1958 s 5: see s 4(1B).

16  Ie an application as is mentioned in the Opencast Coal Act 1958 s 4(1A): see s 4(1B).

17  As to the meaning of 'successor' see PARA 424.

18  Opencast Coal Act 1958 s 4(1B)(a) (s 4(1B) added by the Coal Industry Act 1994 Sch 8 para 2(2)).

19  Opencast Coal Act 1958 s 4(1B)(b).

20  See PARA 438.

21 See PARA 439.

22 See PARA 440.

23 As to the requirements in relation to opencast planning permission see PARA 441.

24 Opencast Coal Act 1958 s 11(1) (substituted by the Local Land Charges Act 1975 s 17(2), Sch 1). Any rules made under the Local Land Charges Act 1975 s 14 for the purposes of the Opencast Coal Act 1958 s 11 must include provision for cancelling the registration of a compulsory rights order if the Secretary of State decides not to confirm the order, or if the order is revoked, or at the end of the period for which it has effect; and for varying the registration of such an order if the order as confirmed by the Secretary of State differs from the order as made, or if the order is subsequently varied: s 11(3) (amended by the Local Land Charges Act 1975 s 19(1), Schs 1, 2). See also the Local Land Charges Rules 2018, SI 2018/273. As to land charges generally see REAL PROPERTY AND REGISTRATION vol 87 (2017) PARA 641 et seq.

25 See PARA 462.

## 432. Duration, variation and revocation of compulsory rights order.

The period for which a compulsory rights order has effect is a period beginning with the date on which the order becomes operative[1], and of such duration, not exceeding 20 years, as may be specified in the order[2].

Such an order may not be varied by extending the period for which it is to have effect[3], provided that where the period specified in the order is less than 20 years, this provision[4] does not prevent the variation of the order by the extension of that period, if the period as extended does not exceed 20 years[5].

1 This date is referred to in the Opencast Coal Act 1958 s 4(2) as 'the operative date': s 51(1).

2 Opencast Coal Act 1958 s 4(2) (substituted by the Coal Industry Act 1975 s 4(1)). The Opencast Coal Act 1958 s 4(2) is subject to the provisions of Pt III (ss 37–53) as to the variation of orders: see s 4(2) (as so substituted). The power to make compulsory rights orders has not been exercisable since 31 December 1999: see PARA 414.

3 Opencast Coal Act 1958 s 49(5).

4 Ie the Opencast Coal Act 1958 s 49(5): see s 49(5) proviso.

5 See the Opencast Coal Act 1958 s 49(5) proviso (substituted by Coal Industry Act 1975 s 4(2), Sch 3 para 8). Note that the power to make compulsory rights orders is not exercisable after 31 December 1999: see s 52(1); and PARA 414.

## 433. Effect of compulsory rights order.

As from the date of entry[1], and during the period (referred to as 'the period of occupation') for which, on and after that date, a compulsory rights order has effect[2], it confers upon the person entitled to the rights conferred by the order[3], and upon persons authorised by that person, the like rights to occupy the land comprised in the order, and to exclude other persons from it, as if that person had acquired a freehold interest in the entirety of that land with vacant possession and free from incumbrances of any description[4].

In addition, a compulsory rights order confers upon the person entitled to the rights conferred by the order, and upon persons authorised by that person, the right during the period of occupation, as against all persons directly concerned[5], to carry out, on or in relation to any of the land comprised in the order, all such operations as may appear to that person, in relation to the opencast planning permission referred to in the order, to be requisite for, or incidental to, the permitted activities[6]. Such an order also confers rights of working minerals (other than coal), and rights relating to timber, crops and chattels[7].

1 'The date of entry' is the date on which the rights conferred by the order are to become exercisable and which is specified in the notice referred to in the Opencast Coal Act 1958 s 5(2) (see PARA 443): see s 5(2); s 51(1).

2 Opencast Coal Act 1958 s 5(4); s 51(1) (amended by the Coal Industry Act 1975 s 4(2), Sch 3 para 9). As to compulsory rights orders see the Opencast Coal Act 1958 s 4; and PARA 431 et seq. The power to make such orders has not been exercisable since 31 December 1999: see PARA 414.

3   Subject to the Opencast Coal Act 1958 s 5(5B), the rights conferred by a compulsory rights order:
    (1) are exercisable by a successor of the original applicant for the order only where the Coal
    Authority has transferred to that successor the entitlement to exercise the rights conferred by the
    order; but (2) where the Authority has so transferred them, are not, at any time after the transfer,
    exercisable by any person in his capacity as the original applicant or as a previous successor of that
    applicant; and references in the Opencast Coal Act 1958 to the person entitled to the rights
    conferred by a compulsory rights order are references to the person who is for the time being the
    person by whom those rights are exercisable in accordance with s 4(1B) and s 5: s 5(5A) (added
    by the Coal Industry Act 1994 s 52(2), Sch 8 para 3(3)).
        Where at any time after an application for a compulsory rights order has been made and before
    any order made on that application is confirmed (a) any person becomes the successor of the
    original applicant for the order and notifies that fact (i) if no order has been made on the
    application, to the Coal Authority, or (ii) if such an order has been made, to the appropriate
    national authority; and (b) the Authority or, as the case may be, the appropriate national authority
    decides to proceed in relation to the application or order in accordance with the Opencast Coal Act
    1958 s 5(5B), the provisions of the Act and of any enactment applied by the Act have effect as if
    the application had been made by that person, as if he had the same right to make it as the original
    applicant and as if anything done for the purposes of the application by or in relation to the
    original applicant or a previous successor had been done by or in relation to that person: s 5(5B)
    (added by the Coal Industry Act 1994 Sch 8 para 3(3)).
        The Coal Authority or, as the case may be, the appropriate national authority (A) is to make
    a transfer under the Opencast Coal Act 1958 s 5(5A) by giving written notice of the transfer to
    each of the persons who, in consequence of the transfer, is to cease to be, or is to become, entitled
    to the rights conferred by the order; (B) may by notice to the successor make any modifications of
    a compulsory rights order which are necessary in consequence only of the making of a transfer
    under s 5(5A); and (C) may make a decision to proceed in accordance with s 5(5B) subject to
    compliance by the successor giving the notification with such conditions as that Authority or the
    appropriate national authority thinks fit: s 5(5C) (added by the Coal Industry Act 1994 Sch 8 para
    3(3)). As to the Coal Authority see PARA 52 et seq. The appropriate national authority is the
    Secretary of State or where functions have been transferred in relation to Wales, the Welsh
    Ministers: see PARA 2.
4   See the Opencast Coal Act 1958 s 5(1) (amended by the Coal Industry Act 1975 s 4(2), Sch 3 para
    2); the Opencast Coal Act 1958 s 5(4) (amended by the Coal Industry Act 1994 Sch 8 para 3(1),
    (2)). In relation to a compulsory rights order which provides that its operation is limited to
    particular interests or rights (see PARA 439), the Opencast Coal Act 1958 s 5(4), has effect as if for
    the words from 'confer upon the person entitled to the rights conferred by the order' to the words
    'exclude other persons therefrom' there were substituted the words 'as against all persons directly
    concerned (defined for this purpose in PARA 439), confer upon the person entitled to the rights
    conferred by the order, and upon persons authorised by that person, the like right to exclude
    persons from the land comprised in the order': s 8(3)(b) (amended by the Coal Industry Act 1975
    s 5(3), Sch 5; and the Coal Industry Act 1994 Sch 8 paras 1, 5).
5   As to the meaning of 'persons directly concerned' see PARA 431. As to Crown and Duchy interests,
    however, see PARA 431. As to the meaning of 'persons directly concerned' where the order is
    limited to particular interests or rights see PARA 439.
6   Opencast Coal Act 1958 s 5(5) (amended by the Coal Industry Act 1975 s 4(2), Sch 3 para 2; the
    Housing and Planning Act 1986 s 39(3), Sch 8 Pt I para 3; and the Coal Industry Act 1994 Sch 8
    para 3(2)). As to the meaning of 'opencast planning permission' see PARA 416. As to the meaning
    of 'permitted activities' see PARA 416. As to the making available of alternative rights of way in
    lieu of suspended rights of way see PARA 424. As to limitations see PARAS 438–440.
7   See PARAS 434–437.

## 434.  Rights of working minerals other than coal.

A compulsory rights order[1] confers upon the person entitled to the rights
conferred by the order[2], and upon persons authorised by that person, the right to
get and carry away any minerals[3] worked in the exercise of rights conferred by the
order, in so far as any such minerals are not already the property of that person;
and any minerals got and carried away by virtue of this provision[4], and removed

from the land[5] comprised in the order, become the property of the person entitled to the rights conferred by the order[6].

1    As to compulsory rights orders see the Opencast Coal Act 1958 s 4; and PARA 431 et seq. The power to make such orders has not been exercisable since 31 December 1999: see PARA 414.
2    See PARA 433.
3    As to the meaning of 'minerals' see PARA 10. As to these purposes, 'minerals' does not include coal unless it is coal that is not vested in the Coal Authority: see PARAS 50, 66. As to the Coal Authority see PARA 52 et seq.
4    Ie the Opencast Coal Act 1958 s 10(1).
5    As to the meaning of 'land' see PARA 414.
6    See the Opencast Coal Act 1958 s 10(1)(amended by the Coal Industry Act 1994 s 52(2), Sch 8 para 6).

### 435. Rights concerning timber.

Where, in the exercise of rights conferred by a compulsory rights order[1], any trees are felled, or any buildings, fences, sheds or other fixtures or structures are dismantled, the order confers upon the person entitled to the rights conferred by the order[2], and upon persons authorised by that person, the right to carry away and dispose of the timber, or, as the case may be, of any resulting materials; and any timber or minerals[3] carried away by virtue of this provision[4], and removed from the land[5] comprised in the order, become the property of the person entitled to the rights conferred by the order[6].

1    As to compulsory rights orders see the Opencast Coal Act 1958 s 4; and PARA 431 et seq. The power to make such orders has not been exercisable since 31 December 1999: see PARA 414.
2    See PARA 433.
3    As to the meaning of 'minerals' see PARA 10.
4    Ie the Opencast Coal Act 1958 s 10(2).
5    As to the meaning of 'land' see PARA 414.
6    See the Opencast Coal Act 1958 s 10(2) (amended by the Coal Industry Act 1994 s 52(2), Sch 8 para 6).

### 436. Rights concerning crops.

Where on the date of entry[1] any crops were growing on any of the land[2] comprised in a compulsory rights order[3], or any crops are grown on any of that land during the period of occupation[4], the order confers upon the person entitled to the rights conferred by the order, and upon persons authorised by that person, the right during the period of occupation to harvest or lift crops and to remove or otherwise dispose of them; and any crops harvested or lifted by virtue of this provision[5] becomes the property of the person entitled to the rights conferred by the order[6].

1    As to the meaning of 'the date of entry' see PARAS 433, PARA 443.
2    As to the meaning of 'land' see PARA 414.
3    As to compulsory rights orders see the Opencast Coal Act 1958 s 4; and PARA 431 et seq. The power to make such orders has not been exercisable since 31 December 1999: see PARA 414.
4    As to the meaning of 'period of occupation' see PARA 433.
5    Ie the Opencast Coal Act 1958 s 10(3).
6    See the Opencast Coal Act 1958 s 10(3) (amended by Coal Industry Act 1994 s 52(2), Sch 8 para 6).

### 437. Right to remove chattels.

At any time on or after the operative date[1] of a compulsory rights order[2], the person entitled to the rights conferred by the order may serve notice[3] on the person who is for the time being entitled to possession of any chattel[4] which is on, under or over any of the land[5] comprised in the order, requiring him to remove it from that land within such period, not being less than 56 days from the date of service of the notice, as may be specified in the notice[6].

If the person on whom a notice is so served fails to comply with the notice within the period specified in it, the person who served the notice may cause the chattel to which the notice relates to be removed from the land comprised in the order, or to be removed from one part of that land to another part of it, and is not liable for any loss or damage attributable to the removal except any such loss or damage which is shown to be due to failure to exercise reasonable care[7]. Where any person causes a chattel to be so removed[8], that person may dispose of the chattel, by sale, destruction or otherwise, as that person may think fit, unless before the end of the period of three months beginning with the date of the removal the person for the time being entitled to possession of the chattel claims it from the person who caused the chattel to be removed and takes all reasonable steps for accepting custody of it[9].

Where a chattel is sold in the exercise of the powers so conferred, the person who makes the sale must pay the proceeds of sale to the person who was entitled to possession of the chattel immediately before the sale, and the receipt of that person is a sufficient discharge to the person who makes the sale for those proceeds[10].

1  As to the meaning of 'the operative date' see PARA 432.
2  As to compulsory rights orders see the Opencast Coal Act 1958 s 4; and PARA 431 et seq. The power to make such orders has not been exercisable since 31 December 1999: see PARA 414.
3  As to the service of notices see PARA 422.
4  For the purposes of the Opencast Coal Act 1958 s 12, 'chattel' includes apparatus of any description, whether above or below the surface of the land: s 12(5).
5  As to the meaning of 'land' see PARA 414.
6  Opencast Coal Act 1958 s 12(1) (amended by the Coal Industry Act 1994 s 52(2), Sch 8 para 8(1)). The Opencast Coal Act 1958 s 12(1) does not apply to any apparatus belonging to statutory undertakers and used by those undertakers for the purposes of their undertaking or belonging to an internal drainage board and used by that board for the purposes of their functions: s 12(1) proviso (amended by the Water Act 1989 s 190, Sch 25 para 26). As to the meaning of 'statutory undertakers' see PARA 420. 'Functions' includes powers and duties, and references to the performance of functions are to be construed accordingly: Opencast Coal Act 1958 s 51(1).
7  See the Opencast Coal Act 1958 s 12(2) (amended by the Coal Industry Act 1994 Sch 8 para 8(2), (4), (5)). Where the person who has served a notice under the Opencast Coal Act 1958 s 12(1) ceases, without exercising any power under s 12(2), to be the person entitled to the rights under the compulsory rights order, that notice ceases to have effect for the purposes of s 12: see s 12(2A) (added by the Coal Industry Act 1994 Sch 8 para 8(3)).
8  Ie removed under the Opencast Coal Act 1958 s 12(2): see s 12(3).
9  See the Opencast Coal Act 1958 s 12(3) (amended by the Coal Industry Act 1994 Sch 8 para 8(2), (4), (5)).
10  See the Opencast Coal Act 1958 s 12(4) (amended by the Coal Industry Act 1994 Sch 8 para 8(2), (4), (5)).

### 438. General limitations on compulsory rights orders.

Nothing in the provisions of the Opencast Coal Act 1958 relating to the effect of opencast site orders[1] is to be construed as authorising any interference with the exercise of a public right of way[2].

The rights conferred by a compulsory rights order[3] to carry out operations upon the land[4] comprised in the order[5] do not affect any of the following rights[6] (but this is without prejudice to the operation of the right[7] to exclusive occupation[8]):

(1)    any right of support for any land not comprised in the order, or for any building or structure on any such land, or any right of action of any person in so far as it arises from the withdrawal of support to which he is entitled for any such land, building or structure[9];

(2)    any rights of any statutory water undertakers[10] under any public general Act, or under any byelaw made by virtue of such an Act, or under any local enactment[11], in so far as (apart from the Opencast Coal Act 1958), the Act, byelaw or enactment restricts, or enables the undertakers to restrict, the working of coal[12] or other minerals[13], or the doing of any other act, on land comprised in the order[14];

(3)    any rights of any statutory undertakers[15], or of any internal drainage board[16] in respect of any apparatus on, under or over land comprised in the order, being apparatus in respect of which, at any time since the granting of the opencast planning permission[17] referred to in the order, the person entitled to the rights conferred by the compulsory rights order has been entitled to serve a notice under the provisions of the Town and Country Planning Act 1990, applied by the Opencast Coal Act 1958[18];

(4)    the rights conferred by any agreement to which the person entitled to the rights conferred by the compulsory rights order is or is deemed to be a party and which is and for the time being in force whereby (apart from the Opencast Coal Act 1958) that person is required to leave any coal unworked[19];

(5)    any rights of the body carrying on a railway, canal, inland navigation, harbour or dock undertaking (not being rights falling within heads (1) to (3) above) under any enactment (whether contained in a public general Act or in any other Act) in so far as (apart from the Opencast Coal Act 1958) the enactment would operate so as either to restrict, or enable that body to restrict, the working of coal or other minerals on land comprised in the order which is adjacent to a railway, waterway, harbour, dock or other works situated on land not comprised in the order, being works vested in that body or works which they have any right or duty to maintain[20], or to require, or enable that body to require, coal or other minerals on land comprised in the order to be left unworked for the protection or support of such a railway, waterway, harbour, dock or other works[21]; and

(6)    any right of action of a person who is not a person directly concerned[22], or any right of action of a person directly concerned in so far as it arises otherwise than by virtue of his being entitled to an interest in or right over land, or in so far as it arises by virtue of his being entitled to an interest in, or right over, land not comprised in the order[23].

1   Ie in the Opencast Coal Act 1958 s 5 (see PARA 433): see s 7(6).

2   Opencast Coal Act 1958 s 7(6) (amended by the Coal Industry Act 1975 ss 4(2), 7(4), Sch 3 para 4, Sch 5). This is without prejudice to the Opencast Coal Act 1958 s 7(1)–(5): see s 7(6). As to the suspension of certain public rights of way see PARAS 426–429.

3   As to compulsory rights orders see the Opencast Coal Act 1958 s 4; and PARA 433 et seq. The power to make such orders has not been exercisable since 31 December 1999: see PARA 414.

4   As to the meaning of 'land' see PARA 414.

5   See the Opencast Coal Act 1958 s 5(5); and PARA 433 et seq.

6   Opencast Coal Act 1958 s 7(1) (amended by the Coal Industry Act 1975 Sch 3 para 4(1), (2), Sch 5).

7   Ie in the Opencast Coal Act 1958 s 5(4) (see PARA 433): s 7(5). As to rights of occupation see PARA

433.

8   Opencast Coal Act 1958 s 7(5) (amended by the Coal Industry Act 1975 Sch 3 para 4, Sch 5).

9   Opencast Coal Act 1958 s 7(2)(a). As to rights of support generally see PARA 114 et seq.

10   For the purposes of the Opencast Coal Act 1958 s 7, in England, 'statutory water undertakers' means, the Environment Agency, a water undertaker or a sewerage undertaker and in Wales, the Natural Resources Body for Wales, a water undertaker or a sewerage undertaker: see s 7(8) (substituted by the Coal Industry Act 1994 s 52(2), Sch 8 para 4(c); and amended by the Environment Act 1995 s 120, Sch 22 para 5(1); and SI 2013/755). As to the Environment Agency see ENVIRONMENTAL QUALITY AND PUBLIC HEALTH vol 45 (2010) PARA 68 et seq; WATER AND WATERWAYS vol 100 (2018) PARA 23.

11   For the purposes of the Opencast Coal Act 1958 s 7, 'local enactment', means any local statutory provision within the meaning of the Water Industry Act 1991: Opencast Coal Act 1958 s 7(8).

12   As to the meaning of 'coal' see PARA 414.

13   As to the meaning of 'minerals' see PARA 10. As to the working of coal or other minerals see PARA 416.

14   Opencast Coal Act 1958 s 7(2)(b) (amended by the Water Act 1989 s 190, Sch 25 para 26, Sch 27 Pt I).

15   As to the meaning of 'statutory undertakers' see PARA 420.

16   As to internal drainage boards see the Land Drainage Act 1991; and WATER AND WATERWAYS vol 101 (2018) PARA 844.

17   As to the meaning of 'opencast planning permission' see PARA 416.

18   Opencast Coal Act 1958 s 7(2)(c) (amended by the Water Act 1989 s 190, Sch 25 para 26, Sch 27 Pt I; and the Coal Industry Act 1994 Sch 8 para 4(a)). The provisions of the Town and Country Planning Act 1990 are applied by the Opencast Coal Act 1958 s 13 (repealed): see s 7(2)(c).

19   Opencast Coal Act 1958 s 7(3)(a) (amended by the Coal Industry Act 1975 s 7(4), Sch 5; and the Coal Industry Act 1994 Sch 8 para 4(b)).

20   Opencast Coal Act 1958 s 7(3)(b)(i). These provisions clearly refer to the mining codes; see further PARA 135 et seq.

21   Opencast Coal Act 1958 s 7(3)(b)(ii).

22   See the Opencast Coal Act 1958 s 7(4)(a). As to the meaning of 'person directly concerned' see PARA 431. A person is not to be taken to be a person directly concerned in relation to a compulsory rights order by reason only that he is entitled to the rights specified in s 7(2), (3): see s 7(7) (amended by the Coal Industry Act 1975 Sch 3 para 4, Sch 5).

23   See the Opencast Coal Act 1958 s 7(4)(b), which is modified in the case of limited compulsory rights orders by s 8(3)(c): see PARA 439.

### 439. Particular limitation of compulsory rights orders.

A compulsory rights order[1] may provide that its operation is to be limited so as to extend only to such one or more interests or rights as may be specified in the order[2]. The interests or rights which may be so specified are: (1) an easement or similar right[3] in respect of the whole or part of the land comprised in the order[4]; (2) a right restrictive of the use of the whole or part of that land[5]; and (3) the interest or rights created or conferred by a mining lease[6] or order conferring working rights[7] in respect of minerals[8] in or under that land or part of it[9].

1   As to compulsory rights orders see the Opencast Coal Act 1958 s 4; and PARA 431 et seq. The power to make such orders has not been exercisable since 31 December 1999: see PARA 414.

2   Opencast Coal Act 1958 s 8(1) (amended by the Coal Industry Act 1975 ss 4(2), 7(4), Sch 3 para 5(1), Sch 5). In relation to a compulsory rights order which provides that its operation is to be limited as mentioned in the Opencast Coal Act 1958 s 8(1): (1) 'persons directly concerned' means persons who for the time being are entitled to any interest or right specified in the order, and does not include any other person (s 8(3)(a)); and (2) s 5(4) (see PARA 433) and s 7(4)(b) (see PARAS 438, 440) have effect subject to modifications (see s 8(3)(b), (c) (s 8(3)(b) amended by the Coal Industry Act 1975 ss 4(2), 7(4), Sch 3 para 5(1), Sch 5; and the Coal Industry Act 1994 s 52, Sch 8 para 5)). Cf PARA 433.

3   'Similar right', where the reference is to an easement or similar right in relation to land, means any of the following: any right to take game or fish or other sporting right exercisable in respect of that land, any right to fell and remove trees, any right to take timber or other wood, water, turf or other materials from it, any right to work minerals on it (otherwise than by virtue of a mining lease or of an order conferring working rights, and any right to depasture cattle or other animals on it

(Opencast Coal Act 1958 s 51(3)), except any such sporting or other right which subsists only as a right incidental to the ownership of the land or to some other interest in it or to a right to occupy it (s 51(3)(a)), or which is exercisable by virtue of a licence granted otherwise than for valuable consideration (s 51(3)(b)). Any right over land which constitutes an easement or similar right in relation to it, if apart from s 51(3) it would not constitute an interest in that land, is to be treated for this purpose as constituting an interest in it: s 51(3).

4   See the Opencast Coal Act 1958 s 8(2)(a).
5   See the Opencast Coal Act 1958 s 8(2)(b).
6   'Mining lease' means a lease for the purpose of working and getting minerals, whether by underground or by surface working; and in this definition 'lease' includes an underlease and an agreement for a lease or underlease and a tenancy agreement, and also includes a licence, but does not include an option to take a lease, underlease or tenancy agreement, and does not include a mortgage: Opencast Coal Act 1958 s 51(1). 'Mortgage' includes any charge or lien on property for securing money or money's worth, and 'mortgagee' and 'mortgagor' are construed accordingly: s 51(1).
7   'Order conferring working rights' means an order made under the Mines (Working Facilities and Support) Act 1966 (see PARA 380 et seq): Opencast Coal Act 1958 s 51(1) (amended by the Mines (Working Facilities and Support) Act 1966 s 15(4)).
8   As to the meaning of 'minerals' see PARA 10.
9   See the Opencast Coal Act 1958 s 8(2)(c).

## 440.   Property not to be included in compulsory rights orders.

A compulsory rights order[1] cannot comprise any part of a building which, at the time when the order was made, was wholly or partly occupied as a dwelling house[2], nor may it comprise any part of the land adjacent to such a building which, at that time, was occupied together with the whole or part of that building and either was within 50 yards from a part of that building[3] or, provided it was not agricultural land[4], formed part of a garden, yard, court or forecourt belonging to that building[5].

No compulsory rights order could be made so as to comprise any land which was or had been comprised in a previous compulsory rights order as confirmed by the appropriate national authority[6] other than a previous order which, as so confirmed, was a limited order[7]. Nor could a compulsory rights order, as confirmed by the appropriate national authority, comprise any land of which possession had previously been taken in the exercise of emergency powers[8], and which had at any time been retained in the exercise of those powers for the purpose of working coal on that land, or on contiguous land, by opencast operations[9] and had before the confirmation of the order ceased to be so retained[10]. Exceptionally, a compulsory rights order may include such land if, at the time of confirming the order, the appropriate national authority was satisfied that there were special circumstances existing at that time, or special circumstances relating to the land in question, which justified its inclusion in the order[11].

1   As to compulsory rights orders see the Opencast Coal Act 1958 s 4; and PARA 431 et seq. The power to make such orders has not been exercisable since 31 December 1999: see PARA 414.
2   'Dwelling house' is not defined in the Opencast Coal Act 1958, but see eg *Lewin v End* [1906] AC 299 at 304, HL, where Lord Atkinson defined a dwelling house as a house in which people actually live or which is physically capable of being used for human habitation; *Macmillan & Co Ltd v Rees* [1946] 1 All ER 675, CA, where it was held that premises are not to be regarded as a dwelling house by reason only of their use for meals or for sleeping at night. See also *Lewin v End* at 302 per Lord Loreburn LC; *Re 1–4, White Row Cottages, Bewerley* [1991] Ch 441 at 446, 447, [1991] 4 All ER 50 at 53, 54 per Mummery J; and *Batey (Inspector of Taxes) v Wakefield* [1982] 1 All ER 61 at 63, 64, [1981] STC 521 at 523, 524, CA, per Fox LJ.
3   See the Opencast Coal Act 1958 s 9(1)(a).
4   'Agricultural land' means land used for agriculture which is so used for the purposes of a trade or business: Opencast Coal Act 1958 s 51(1).
5   See the Opencast Coal Act 1958 s 9(1)(b).

6 Ie the Secretary of State or where functions have been transferred in relation to Wales, the Welsh Ministers: see PARA 2.
7 See the Opencast Coal Act 1958 s 9(3). As to the confirmation of compulsory rights orders see PARA 431. As to limited orders see PARA 439
8 See the Opencast Coal Act 1958 s 9(4)(a) (s 9(4) amended by the Coal Industry Act 1975 Sch 3 para 6). 'Emergency powers' means any powers exercisable by virtue of the Defence (General) Regulations 1939, SR & O 1939/927 (revoked), or by virtue of the Requisitioned Land and War Works Act 1945 or by virtue of the prerogative of the Crown: Opencast Coal Act 1958 s 51(1).
9 See the Opencast Coal Act 1958 s 9(4)(b).
10 See the Opencast Coal Act 1958 s 9(4)(c).
11 See the Opencast Coal Act 1958 s 9(4).

## (ii) Procedure

**441. Requirements in relation to opencast planning permission.**
A compulsory rights order[1] could only be made if opencast planning permission[2] had been applied for or granted in respect of the land[3] comprised in the order or was deemed to have been granted in respect of it[4]. Where such an order was made before opencast planning permission had been granted, the appropriate national authority[5] could not confirm[6] it unless such permission in respect of that land had first been granted[7]. Where such an order was made in a case where opencast planning permission had been granted or was deemed to have been granted, the order, as from the time when it was made, must include a reference to the permission[8].

If opencast planning permission is granted in respect of land comprised in such an order and the appropriate national authority subsequently confirms the order, the order as confirmed must include a reference to the permission[9]. No such order, as confirmed, may extend to any land which is not comprised in the permission referred to in the order[10].

1 As to compulsory rights orders see the Opencast Coal Act 1958 s 4; and PARA 431 et seq. The power to make such orders has not been exercisable since 31 December 1999: see PARA 414.
2 As to the meaning of 'opencast planning permission' see PARA 416.
3 As to the meaning of 'land' see PARA 414.
4 Opencast Coal Act 1958 s 4(6) (s 4(6), (6A)–(6D) substituted by the Housing and Planning Act 1986 s 39(3), Sch 8 Pt I para 2(2)).
5 Ie the Secretary of State or where functions have been transferred in relation to Wales, the Welsh Ministers: see PARA 2.
6 As to confirmation see PARA 431.
7 See the Opencast Coal Act 1958 s 4(6A) .
8 See the Opencast Coal Act 1958 s 4(6B).
9 See the Opencast Coal Act 1958 s 4(6C).
10 See the Opencast Coal Act 1958 s 4(6D).

**442. Procedure for making compulsory rights order.**
The procedure for making a compulsory rights order[1] by the Coal Authority[2] was similar to that to be followed by a local authority making a compulsory purchase order in accordance with the standard authorisation procedure[3]. The Lands Clauses Acts and the Compulsory Purchase Act 1965[4] do not apply to the compulsory acquisition of rights by virtue of a compulsory rights order, or to the taking or retention of possession of land in the exercise of such rights[5].

The compulsory rights order had to be in the prescribed form[6] and describe the land to which it applies by reference to a map[7]. Before submitting the order to the appropriate national authority, the Authority had to publish a notice[8]: (1) stating that the order had been made and was about to be submitted for confirmation; (2)

describing the land and stating the purpose for which the land was required; (3) naming a place within the locality where a copy of the order and map referred to could be inspected; and (4) specifying the time (not being less than 21 days from the first publication of the notice) within which, and the manner in which, objections to the order could be made[9].

The Authority had to: (a) serve on all persons who at the time when notice of the order was first published[10] were known to the Authority to be persons directly concerned[11] a notice in the prescribed form[12] stating the effect of the order and that it was about to be submitted for confirmation, and specifying the time (not being less than 21 days from service of the notice) within which, and the manner in which, objections could be made[13]; and (b) affix conspicuously to some conspicuous object or objects on the land comprised in the order a notice or notices containing the particulars specified in head (a) above[14].

The same provisions applied, subject to modifications, to the confirmation of a compulsory rights order, and the hearing or disregarding of objections, as apply in the case of compulsory purchase orders under the standard authorisation procedure[15]. Except where the appropriate national authority was proceeding concurrently with respect to an application for opencast planning permission[16] and a compulsory rights order, he could disregard an objection to such an order if he was satisfied that it related to the question whether opencast planning permission should be, or should have been, granted and either it related exclusively to that question, or in so far as it related to other matters, they consisted entirely of matters which could be dealt with in the assessment of compensation[17].

Unless all persons interested consented, the order as confirmed by the appropriate national authority did not confer on the Authority rights of occupation and use of any land which the order would not have conferred if it had been confirmed without modification[18], and notice had to be published and served after confirmation in the same manner as in the case of compulsory purchase orders and in the form prescribed[19]. In some circumstances, the power to confirm an order may be exercised by the Authority[20].

The provisions applicable to the purchase of certain descriptions of land by means of a compulsory purchase order[21] applied with modifications to the acquisition of compulsory rights in respect of that land by means of a compulsory rights order[22], as did the provisions regarding the validity and date of operation of compulsory purchase orders and certificates[23].

1    As to compulsory rights orders see the Opencast Coal Act 1958 s 4; and PARA 431 et seq. The power to make such orders has not been exercisable since 31 December 1999: see PARA 414.
2    As to the Coal Authority see PARA 52 et seq.
3    The provisions of the Acquisition of Land Act 1981 Pt II (ss 10–15), Pt III (ss 16–22) and Pt IV (ss 23–27) apply (with modifications) to compulsory rights orders, subject to s 29: Opencast Coal Act 1958 s 4(4A) (added by the Acquisition of Land Act 1981 s 34, Sch 4 para 11(2)); and see the Acquisition of Land Act 1981 s 29(1). The Acquisition of Land Act 1981 Pts II, III, IV apply with the substitution of references to compulsory rights orders for references to compulsory purchase orders, of references to the Coal Authority for references to the acquiring authority, of references to the appropriate national authority for references to the confirming authority, and of references to operating so as to confer temporary rights of occupation and use of land for references to authorising the compulsory purchase of land: see s 29(2) (amended by the Coal Industry Act 1994 s 67(1), (8), Sch 9 para 27(2), Sch 11 Pt II). As to compulsory purchase generally see COMPULSORY ACQUISITION OF LAND. The appropriate national authority is the Secretary of State or where functions have been transferred in relation to Wales, the Welsh Ministers: see PARA 2.

4   As to the Lands Clauses Acts and the Compulsory Purchase Act 1965 generally see COMPULSORY
    ACQUISITION OF LAND.
5   Opencast Coal Act 1958 s 4(7) (amended by the Acquisition of Land Act 1981 Sch 4 para 11(3)).
6   Anything which, by the Acquisition of Land Act 1981 Pt II or Pt III, or Sch 1 or Sch 3, is required
    or authorised to be prescribed is prescribed by regulations made by the appropriate national
    authority by statutory instrument: see s 7(2). In the application of the Acquisition of Land Act
    1981 to compulsory rights orders 'prescribed' means prescribed by regulations under the Opencast
    Coal Act 1958: Acquisition of Land Act 1981 s 29(10). As to the prescribed form in connection
    with compulsory rights orders see the Opencast Coal (Compulsory Rights, Drainage and Rights of
    Way) (Forms) Regulations 1994, SI 1994/3097, reg 3, Form 2.
7   Acquisition of Land Act 1981 s 10(2).
8   Ie in the prescribed form: see the Opencast Coal (Compulsory Rights, Drainage and Rights of
    Way) (Forms) Regulations 1994, SI 1994/3097, reg 3, Form 3.
9   See the Acquisition of Land Act 1981 ss 10(3), 11(1), (2).
10  Ie published under the Acquisition of Land Act 1981 s 11: see s 29(4).
11  As to the meaning of 'persons directly concerned' see PARAS 431, PARA 439 (definition applied by
    the Acquisition of Land Act 1981 s 29(11) (substituted by the Housing and Planning Act 1986 s
    39(3), Sch 8 Pt II para 18)).
12  See the Opencast Coal (Compulsory Rights, Drainage and Rights of Way) (Forms) Regulations
    1994, SI 1994/3097, reg 3, Form 4.
13  Acquisition of Land Act 1981 s 12(1)(a) (substituted by s 29(4)).
14  Acquisition of Land Act 1981 s 12(1)(b).
15  See the Acquisition of Land Act 1981 s 29(5). As to the procedure for confirming an order see s
    13, which applied with the substitution of a reference to any person who, in relation to the order,
    was a person directly concerned for any reference to any owner, lessee or occupier: see s 29(5).
16  As to the meaning of 'opencast planning permission' see PARA 416 (definition applied by the
    Acquisition of Land Act 1981 s 29(11) (substituted by the Housing and Planning Act 1986 Sch 8
    Pt II para 18)).
17  Acquisition of Land Act 1981 s 29(6) (amended by the Housing and Planning Act 1986 Sch 8 Pt
    II para 18). This provision is without prejudice to the operation of the Acquisition of Land Act
    1981 s 13: see s 29(6).
18  See the Acquisition of Land Act 1981 s 14 . As to land not originally included in the order see s
    14; and COMPULSORY ACQUISITION OF LAND vol 18 (2009) PARA 569.
19  See the Acquisition of Land Act 1981 s 15. As to notices after confirmation of the order see s 15;
    and COMPULSORY ACQUISITION OF LAND vol 18 (2009) PARA 571. As to the prescribed form
    see the Opencast Coal (Compulsory Rights, Drainage and Rights of Way) (Forms) Regulations
    1994, SI 1994/3097, reg 3, Form 3.
20  See the Acquisition of Land Act 1981 s 14A (added by the Planning and Compulsory Purchase Act
    2004 s 102(1), (2)).
21  Ie the provisions of the Acquisition of Land Act 1981 Pt III: see generally COMPULSORY
    ACQUISITION OF LAND.
22  The Acquisition of Land Act 1981 s 19 (see COMPULSORY ACQUISITION OF LAND vol 18
    (2009) PARAS 531, 604) applied as if any reference to giving other land in exchange were
    construed as a reference to making other land available during the period for which the
    compulsory rights order is to have effect; the provisions of s 19 as to the vesting of land, and as
    to its being made subject to the like rights, trusts and incidents as the land purchased, applied with
    the necessary modifications, and s 19(3)(b) did not apply: see s 29(7). The prescribed form for the
    purposes of s 22 in connection with compulsory rights orders, is the Opencast Coal (Compulsory
    Rights, Drainage and Rights of Way) (Forms) Regulations 1994, SI 1994/3097, reg 3, Form 5.
23  Ie the provisions of the Acquisition of Land Act 1981 Pt IV (see generally COMPULSORY
    ACQUISITION OF LAND). As to the application of s 23 (see COMPULSORY ACQUISITION OF
    LAND vol 18 (2009) PARA 610 et seq) see the Acquisition of Land Act 1981 s 29(8). Section 26
    (see COMPULSORY ACQUISITION OF LAND vol 18 (2009) PARA 602 et seq) applied subject to
    the modification that the date on which the compulsory rights order became operative was to be
    the date mentioned in s 26(1) or such later date, not being more than one year after confirmation
    of the order, as might be determined by the Secretary of State and specified in the order as
    confirmed: see s 29(9).

**443. Notification and challenge of compulsory rights order.**
The person on whose application a compulsory rights order[1] was made had to publish, serve and affix notices specifying the date on which the rights conferred by the order were to become exercisable[2].

Any person who, in relation to the order referred to in such a notice, was a person directly concerned[3] and who claimed that any of the relevant requirements[4] had not been complied with, could, at any time not later than the end of the period of six weeks beginning with the date of the first publication of that notice, make an application to the High Court[5].

Where, on determining such an application, the court was satisfied that any of the relevant requirements had not been complied with, and that the interests of the applicant had been substantially prejudiced[6] by the failure to comply with them, the court could, by an order made either generally or with respect to so much of the land comprised in the compulsory rights order as might be specified in the order[7], declare that the rights which (if all the relevant requirements had been complied with) would have been conferred by the order had not become exercisable, and direct that the order was to cease to have effect as from a specified date[8].

Subject to such an application or to any proceedings on or in consequence of it, where the first publication of a notice was effected[9], all the requisite notices of the order referred to in that notice were deemed to have been published, served and affixed[10], and to have specified the date specified in that notice[11]; that date is deemed for all purposes to be a date satisfying the prescribed requirements[12]; and the exercise of any rights by virtue of the order may not be questioned in any legal proceedings whatsoever on the ground that any of the relevant requirements have not been complied with[13].

1 As to compulsory rights orders see the Opencast Coal Act 1958 s 4; and PARA 431 et seq. The power to make such orders has not been exercisable since 31 December 1999: see PARA 414.
2 Opencast Coal Act 1958 s 5(2) (amended by the Coal Industry Act 1994 Sch 8 para 3(1), (2)); Opencast Coal Act 1958 Sch 2 para 13(1)–(5) (Sch 2 para 13 amended by Coal Industry Act 1994 s 52(2), Sch 8 paras 1, 39). See also PARA 433. As to the service of notices see PARA 422.
   The date referred to in the text is known as 'the date of entry' being the date: (1) not less than 56 days after the first publication of a notice specifying that date; and (2) not more than six months after the operative date: s 5(2). As to the meaning of 'not less than 56 days' see *McQueen v Jackson* [1903] 2 KB 163; *Re Hector Whaling Ltd* [1936] Ch 208; cf *Schnabel v Allard* [1967] 1 QB 627, [1966] 3 All ER 816, CA. 'Months' means calendar months: Interpretation Act 1978 ss 5, 22(1), Sch 1, Sch 2 para 4(1)(a) (amended by the Family Law Reform Act 1987 s 33(1), (4), Sch 2 para 74, Sch 4); and see eg *Stewart v Chapman* [1951] 2 KB 792, [1951] 2 All ER 613, DC; *Cartwright v MacCormack (Trafalgar Insurance Co Ltd, Third Parties)* [1963] 1 All ER 11, [1963] 1 WLR 18, CA.
3 As to the meaning of 'person directly concerned' see PARA 431.
4 In the Opencast Coal Act 1958 Sch 2 Pt II, 'the relevant requirements' means the requirements of s 5(2), Sch 2 para 13: Sch 2 para 16.
5 Opencast Coal Act 1958 Sch 2 para 14(1). On any such application, the court could by interim order direct, either generally or in relation to any part of the land comprised in the compulsory rights order, that such rights (if any) as were conferred by the order were not to be exercised until the final determination of the proceedings: Sch 2 para 14(2).
6 As to the meaning of 'substantially prejudiced' see COMPULSORY ACQUISITION OF LAND vol 18 (2009) PARA 614.
7 Ie in the order under the Opencast Coal Act 1958 Sch 2 para 14(3). As to the meaning of 'land' see PARA 414.
8 Opencast Coal Act 1958 Sch 2 para 14(3).
9 Ie effected in accordance with the Opencast Coal Act 1958 Sch 2 para 13(2): see Sch 2 para 15.
10 Ie in accordance with the requirements of the Opencast Coal Act 1958 Sch 2 para 13: see Sch 2 para 15.
11 Opencast Coal Act 1958 Sch 2 para 15(a).

12 Opencast Coal Act 1958 Sch 2 para 15(b). The requirements referred to in the text are those of s 5(2).
13 Opencast Coal Act 1958 Sch 2 para 15(c). As to the effect of such a provision see COMPULSORY ACQUISITION OF LAND.

### (iii) Particular Consequences of Compulsory Rights Orders

A. PROTECTION OF TENANCIES AND MORTGAGES

## 444. Breaches of terms and conditions during occupation.

Where a compulsory rights order[1] is in operation or land[2] is occupied or used in the exercise of rights conferred by such an order, and the land comprised in the order is subject to a tenancy[3] or mortgage[4], the rights of the parties to the tenancy or mortgage are modified[5]. Where any obligation or restriction imposed by the terms and conditions of the tenancy or mortgage would, apart from the Opencast Coal Act 1958, fall to be performed or observed by any such party at a time within the period of occupation[6], and in consequence of the rights conferred by the order, or of anything done in the exercise of those rights, that obligation or restriction cannot be so performed or observed at that time[7], the failure to perform or observe it at that time is deemed not to be a breach of any of the terms and conditions of the tenancy or mortgage[8].

1  As to compulsory rights orders see the Opencast Coal Act 1958 s 4; and PARA 431 et seq. The power to make such orders has not been exercisable since 31 December 1999: see PARA 414.
2  As to the meaning of 'land' see PARA 414.
3  'Tenancy' has the meaning assigned to it by the Landlord and Tenant Act 1954 s 69(1) (see LANDLORD AND TENANT vol 64 (2016) PARA 1597): Opencast Coal Act 1958 s 51(1).
4  As to the meaning of 'mortgage' see PARA 439.
5  See the Opencast Coal Act 1958 s 37, Sch 7 paras 14, 15.
6  Opencast Coal Act 1958 Sch 7 para 14(a). As to the meaning of 'the period of occupation' see PARA 433.
7  Opencast Coal Act 1958 Sch 7 para 14(b).
8  Opencast Coal Act 1958 Sch 7 para 14. These provisions are without prejudice to Sch 7 para 4 or Sch para 12, including those provisions as applied in relation to mortgages by Sch 7 para 7 or Sch 7 para 13: Sch 7 para 16.

## 445. Breaches of terms and conditions after occupation.

Where at any time while any land[1] is comprised in a compulsory rights order[2] it is subject to a tenancy[3] or mortgage[4] which continues until after the end of the period of occupation[5], and at any time within 12 months after the end of that period proceedings are brought to enforce a right of re-entry, forfeiture or foreclosure, or a right to damages or any other remedy, in respect of any failure after the end of that period to comply with any of the terms and conditions of the tenancy or mortgage, the person against whom the proceedings are brought may apply in those proceedings for relief[6].

If the court is satisfied that the failure to comply was attributable to a change in the state of the land resulting from its occupation and use in the exercise of rights conferred by the order it may grant such relief, in respect of the matters to which the proceedings relate, as it considers reasonable in the circumstances[7].

1  As to the meaning of 'land' see PARA 414.
2  As to compulsory rights orders see the Opencast Coal Act 1958 s 4; and PARA 431 et seq. The power to make such orders has not been exercisable since 31 December 1999: see PARA 414.
3  As to the meaning of 'tenancy' see PARA 444.
4  As to the meaning of 'mortgage' see PARA 439.

5 As to the meaning of 'the period of occupation' see PARA 433.
6 Opencast Coal Act 1958 s 37, Sch 7 para 15(1).
7 Opencast Coal Act 1958 Sch 7 para 15(2). These provisions are without prejudice to those referred to in PARA 444: Sch 7 para 16.

B.   ADJUSTMENTS IN RESPECT OF AGRICULTURAL HOLDINGS AND FARM BUSINESS TENANCIES

## (A)   Agricultural Holdings

### 446.   Long-term improvements and special system of farming.

Where (1) the land comprised in a compulsory rights order[1] consists of or includes land which immediately before the date of entry[2] constituted or formed part of an agricultural holding held under a tenancy[3] in relation to which the Agricultural Holdings Act 1986 applies[4] and before that date long-term improvements qualifying for compensation[5] had been carried out on that land, or a special system of farming qualifying for compensation had been adopted[6]; and (2) the tenancy under which the tenant could have claimed compensation, or a subsequent tenancy under which the tenant has retained or succeeded to the relevant right to compensation, terminates on or after the date of entry, but before the end of the period of occupation[7], without being succeeded by another such subsequent tenancy[8], the provisions of the Agricultural Holdings Act 1986 as to compensation for long-term improvements[9] and for a special system of farming[10] apply with modifications[11] to that tenancy[12].

1 As to compulsory rights orders see the Opencast Coal Act 1958 s 4; and PARA 431 et seq. The power to make such orders has not been exercisable since 31 December 1999: see PARA 414.
2 As to the meaning of 'the date of entry' see PARAS 433, PARA 443.
3 As to the meaning of 'tenancy' see PARA 444.
4 Opencast Coal Act 1958 s 24(1)(a) (amended by the Agricultural Tenancies Act 1995 s 40, Schedule para 15(1), (2)); Opencast Coal Act 1958 s 37, Sch 7 para 1(1)(a).
5 See the Opencast Coal Act 1958 s 24(7)(a); s 24(9); and PARA 481.
6 Opencast Coal Act 1958 s 24(1)(b) (amended by the Agricultural Holdings Act 1986 s 100, Sch 14 para 26); Opencast Coal Act 1958 Sch 7 para 1(1)(a). See s 24(7)(b); and PARA 481.
7 As to the meaning of 'the period of occupation' see PARA 433.
8 Opencast Coal Act 1958 Sch 7 para 1(1)(b).
9 See AGRICULTURAL LAND AND ALLOTMENTS vol 1 (2017) PARAS 533–538.
10 See AGRICULTURAL LAND AND ALLOTMENTS vol 1 (2017) PARAS 548–549.
11 The provisions referred to in the text apply, in relation to the tenancy, as if, at the termination of the tenancy, the land in question were in the state in which it was immediately before the date of entry (Opencast Coal Act 1958 Sch 7 para 1(2)(a)), and, if the tenant quitted the holding before the termination of his tenancy, they apply as if he had quitted on its termination (Sch 7 para 1(2)(b)). See also PARA 462.
12 Opencast Coal Act 1958 Sch 7 para 1(1), (2) (amended by the Agricultural Holdings Act 1986 Sch 14 para 33). The Opencast Coal Act 1958 s 24(5) (see PARA 481) applies for the purposes of Sch 7 para 1(1), as it applies for the purposes mentioned in s 24(5); and s 24(6) (see PARA 481) applies in relation to Sch 7 para 1(2) as it applies in relation to s 24(2): Sch 7 para 1(3).

### 447.   Position where the land has been restored.

Where land[1] comprised in an agricultural holding[2] held under a tenancy[3] in relation to which the Agricultural Holdings Act 1986 applies is comprised in a compulsory rights order[4], whether any other land is comprised in the holding, or comprised in the order, or not, and (1) before the date of entry[5] long-term improvements qualifying for compensation[6], or a special system of farming qualifying for compensation[7], had been carried out or adopted on the land[8]; (2) the benefit of the improvements or the increased value attributable to the special system has been replaced or regained, on the restoration[9] of the land, by works, or the continuous adoption of a new system of farming, of comparable benefit to the land[10]; and (3) but for that restoration certain provisions of the Agricultural Holdings Act 1986[11] as to compensation for long-term improvements and for a special system of farming would have applied[12], those provisions have effect in relation to those works or that new system as if those works had been carried out, or that system adopted, by the person who carried out or adopted the previous improvements or system[13].

1   As to the meaning of 'land' see PARA 414.
2   As to the meaning of 'agricultural holding' see PARA 428.
3   As to the meaning of 'tenancy' see PARA 444.
4   As to compulsory rights orders see the Opencast Coal Act 1958 s 4; and PARA 431 et seq. The power to make such orders has not been exercisable since 31 December 1999: see PARA 414.
5   As to the meaning of 'the date of entry' see PARAS 433, PARA 443.
6   See PARA 446.
7   See PARA 446.
8   Opencast Coal Act 1958 s 37, Sch 7 para 2(1)(a) (amended by the Agricultural Holdings Act 1986 s 100, Sch 14 para 33; and the Agricultural Tenancies Act 1995 s 40, Schedule para 20(3)). The references in the Opencast Coal Act 1958 Sch 7 para 2(1)(a) to the Agricultural Holdings Act 1986 include references to the Agricultural Holdings Act 1948: Opencast Coal Act 1958 Sch 7 para 2(3A) (added by the Agricultural Holdings Act 1986 Sch 14 para 33).
9   As to the meaning of 'restoration' see PARA 424.
10  Opencast Coal Act 1958 Sch 7 para 2(1)(b).
11  The provisions referred to are those mentioned in the Opencast Coal Act 1958 s 24(2), as extended by s 24(6): Sch 7 para 2(1)(b). See also PARA 446.
12  Ie would have applied as mentioned in the Opencast Coal Act 1958 s 24(3) (see PARA 481): Sch 7 para 2(1)(b).
13  Opencast Coal Act 1958 Sch 7 para 2(1) (Sch 7 para 2(2) amended by the Agricultural Holdings Act 1986 Sch 14 para 33). For these purposes, the Opencast Coal Act 1958 s 24(7), (8) (see PARA 481) applies as it applies for the purposes of s 24: Sch 7 para 2(3).

### 448. Compensation for expenses.

Where a tenant is entitled to compensation for long-term improvements or for a special system of farming[1], and (1) after the end of the period of occupation[2] expenses are incurred in replacing the benefit of the improvements by other long-term improvements of comparable benefit to the land, or in regaining the increased value attributable to that system of farming by the continuous adoption of a special system of farming of comparable benefit to the land[3]; and (2) the person incurring those expenses, whether he is the landlord or not, is entitled to compensation[4] in respect of them under the Opencast Coal Act 1958[5], the provisions of the Agricultural Holdings Act 1986[6] apply as if the works in respect of which those expenses are incurred were improvements carried out by the landlord at the request of the tenant[7], if they would not otherwise constitute such improvements[8].

1   Ie by virtue of the Opencast Coal Act 1958 s 24 (see PARA 481): see s 37, Sch 7 para 3(1).
2   As to the meaning of 'the period of occupation' see PARA 433. The power to make compulsory rights orders conferring rights to occupy land has not been exercisable since 31 December 1999: see PARA 414.
3   Opencast Coal Act 1958 Sch 7 para 3(1)(a).
4   Ie compensation under the Opencast Coal Act 1958 s 22 (see PARA 476): see Sch 7 para 3(1)(b).
5   Opencast Coal Act 1958 Sch 7 para 3(1)(b).
6   See AGRICULTURAL LAND AND ALLOTMENTS vol 1 (2017) PARA 421 et seq.
7   See AGRICULTURAL LAND AND ALLOTMENTS vol 1 (2017) PARA 440.

8   Opencast Coal Act 1958 Sch 7 para 3(1) (amended by the Agricultural Holdings Act 1986 s 100, Sch 14 para 33). The Opencast Coal Act 1958 s 14(8) does not affect the operation of the Agricultural Holdings Act 1986 s 13, in so far as s 13 applies in accordance with the Opencast Coal Act 1958 Sch 7 para 3(1): Sch 7 para 3(2) (amended by the Agricultural Holdings Act 1986 Sch 14 para 33).

### 449.   Variation of terms of tenancy or mortgage.

Where, immediately before the operative date[1] of a compulsory rights order[2], any of the land comprised in the order consisted of or included an agricultural holding[3] or part of an agricultural holding[4], and the tenancy[5] relating to that holding continues until after the end of the period of occupation[6], the landlord or the tenant of the holding may, by notice in writing served[7] on his tenant or landlord, demand a reference to arbitration under the Agricultural Holdings Act 1986[8] of the question whether any of the terms and conditions of the contract of tenancy, including any term or condition relating to rent, should be varied in consequence of any change in the state of the land resulting from the occupation or use of the land in the exercise of rights conferred by the order[9].

On such a reference the arbitrator must determine what variations, if any, should be made and the date, which must not be earlier than the end of the period of occupation, from which they are to take effect or to be treated as having taken effect, and as from that date the contract of tenancy has effect, or must be treated as having had effect, subject to those variations[10].

These provisions as to variations of tenancies apply to mortgages[11] with necessary modifications[12].

1   As to the meaning of 'the operative date' see PARA 432.
2   As to compulsory rights orders see the Opencast Coal Act 1958 s 4; and PARA 431 et seq. The power to make such orders has not been exercisable since 31 December 1999: see PARA 414.
3   As to the meaning of 'agricultural holding' see PARA 428. For the purposes of the Opencast Coal Act 1958 s 37, Sch 7 para 4, 'agricultural holding' does not include an agricultural holding held under a farm business tenancy: Sch 7 para 4(7) (added by the Agricultural Tenancies Act 1995 s 40, Schedule para 20(6)).
4   Opencast Coal Act 1958 Sch 7 para 4(1)(a).
5   As to the meaning of 'tenancy' see PARA 444.
6   Opencast Coal Act 1958 Sch 7 para 4(1)(b). As to the meaning of 'the period of occupation' see PARA 433.
7   As to the service of notices see PARA 422.
8   The Agricultural Holdings Act 1986 s 84 applies to such a reference: Opencast Coal Act 1958 Sch 7 para 4(4) (amended by the Agricultural Holdings Act 1986 s 100, Sch 14 para 33).
9   Opencast Coal Act 1958 Sch 7 para 4(2) (amended by the Agricultural Holdings Act 1986 Sch 14 para 33).
10  Opencast Coal Act 1958 Sch 7 para 4(3). The provisions of Sch 7 para 4 do not affect any right of the landlord or tenant, or the jurisdiction of the arbitrator, under the Agricultural Holdings Act 1986 s 12 or s 13 (including s 13 as applied by the Opencast Coal Act 1958 Sch 7 para 3); but where there is a reference to arbitration under either of those sections and under Sch 7 para 4, in respect of the same holding, and it appears to the arbitrator that the reference relates wholly or mainly to the consequences of the occupation or use of the land in the exercise of rights conferred by the order, he may direct that proceedings on the two references be taken concurrently: Sch 7 para 4(5), (6) (amended by the Agricultural Holdings Act 1986 Sch 14 para 33).
11  As to the meaning of 'mortgage' see PARA 439.
12  The provisions of the Opencast Coal Act 1958 Sch 7 para 4(1)–(6) apply in relation to mortgages as they apply in relation to contracts of tenancy, as if any reference in Sch 7 para 4(1)–(6) to such a contract, or to a tenancy, were a reference to a mortgage, and any reference to land consisting of or including an agricultural holding or part of an agricultural holding were a reference to agricultural land subject to a mortgage but not comprised in a farm business tenancy, and any reference to a landlord or to a tenant were a reference to a mortgagee or to a mortgagor, as the case may be: Sch 7 para 7 (amended by the Agricultural Tenancies Act 1995 Schedule para 20(10)).

## 450. Removal of fixtures and buildings.

Where the land comprised in a compulsory rights order[1] consists of or includes the whole or part of an agricultural holding[2] held under a tenancy[3] in relation to which the Agricultural Holdings Act 1986 applies, the requirement[4] to remove fixtures and buildings has effect in relation to the holding subject to modifications[5].

1 As to compulsory rights orders see the Opencast Coal Act 1958 s 4; and PARA 431 et seq. The power to make such orders has not been exercisable since 31 December 1999: see PARA 414. As to the meaning of 'land' see PARA 414.
2 As to the meaning of 'agricultural holding' see PARA 428.
3 As to the meaning of 'tenancy' see PARA 444.
4 Ie the Agricultural Holdings Act 1986 s 10 (see the Opencast Coal Act 1958 Sch 7 para 5(1)) (including the Agricultural Holdings Act 1986 s 10 as extended by s 79(3) in relation to market gardens: see the Opencast Coal Act 1958 Sch 7 para 5(5) (amended by the Agricultural Holdings Act 1986 Sch 14 para 33)). See AGRICULTURAL LAND AND ALLOTMENTS vol 1 (2017) PARA 436.
5 Opencast Coal Act 1958 Sch 7 para 5(1) (amended by the Agricultural Holdings Act 1986 s 100, Sch 14 para 33; and the Agricultural Tenancies Act 1995 s 40, Schedule para 20(8)). The modifications are: (1) that only 14 days' notice need be given by the tenant on or after the operative date of the order in respect of a fixture or building on a part of the holding which is within the land comprised in the order (Opencast Coal Act 1958 Sch 7 para 5(2) (amended by the Agricultural Holdings Act 1986 Sch 14 para 33)) (cf the Agricultural Holdings Act 1986 s 10(3)(b)); and (2) where the tenant has given a notice under s 10(3), or under s 10(3) as modified by the Opencast Coal Act 1958 Sch 7 para 5(2), and that notice is given on or after the operative date of the order, or, if given before, expires on or after that date (whether or not the landlord has given a counter-notice before that date), the Agricultural Holdings Act 1986 s 10(4) does not apply to the fixture or building (Opencast Coal Act 1958 Sch 7 para 5(3) (amended by the Agricultural Holdings Act 1986 Sch 14 para 33); Opencast Coal Act 1958 Sch 7 para 5(4)). As to the meaning of 'the operative date' see PARA 432.

### (B) Farm Business Tenancies

## 451. Tenant's improvements.

Where (1) any part of the land[1] comprised in a compulsory rights order[2] was held, immediately before the date of entry[3], under a farm business tenancy[4]; (2) there have been provided in relation to the former tenant's improvements in respect of which, immediately before that date, the tenant had a prospective right to compensation[5] on quitting the holding on the termination of the tenancy[6]; and (3) the farm business tenancy at the end of which the tenant could have claimed compensation for tenant's improvements terminates on or after the date of entry, but before the end of the period of occupation[7], without being succeeded by another such subsequent tenancy[8], the provisions of the Agricultural Tenancies Act 1995[9] apply with modifications to that tenancy[10].

1 As to the meaning of 'land' see PARA 414.
2 As to compulsory rights orders see the Opencast Coal Act 1958 s 4; and PARA 431 et seq. The power to make such orders has not been exercisable since 31 December 1999: see PARA 414.
3 As to the meaning of 'the date of entry' see PARAS 433, PARA 443.
4 Opencast Coal Act 1958 s 25A(1)(a) (s 25A added by the Agricultural Tenancies Act 1995 s 40, Schedule para 16); Opencast Coal Act 1958 Sch 7 para 1A(1)(a) (Sch 7 para 1A added by the Agricultural Tenancies Act 1995 Schedule para 20(2)). As to the meaning of 'farm business tenancy' see PARA 429.
5 Ie under the Agricultural Tenancies Act 1995 s 16 (see AGRICULTURAL LAND AND ALLOTMENTS vol 1 (2017) PARA 411): see the Opencast Coal Act 1958 s 25A(1)(b); Sch 7 para 1A(1)(b).
6 Opencast Coal Act 1958 s 25A(1)(b); Sch 7 para 1A(1)(b).
7 As to the meaning of 'the period of occupation' see PARA 433.

8   Opencast Coal Act 1958 Sch 7 para 1A(1).
9   Ie the provisions of the Agricultural Tenancies Act 1995 Pt III (ss 15–27) (see AGRICULTURAL LAND AND ALLOTMENTS vol 1 (2017) PARAS 410–419): see the Opencast Coal Act 1958 Sch 7 para 1A(2).
10   Opencast Coal Act 1958 Sch 7 para 1A(2). The Agricultural Tenancies Act 1995 Pt III applies in relation to the tenancy mentioned in the Opencast Coal Act 1958 Sch 7 para 1A(1) as if, at the termination of that tenancy, the land in question were in the state in which it was immediately before the date of entry; and if the tenant under that tenancy quitted the holding before the termination of his tenancy, the Agricultural Tenancies Act 1995 Pt III applies as if he had quitted the holding on the termination of his tenancy: Opencast Coal Act 1958 Sch 7 para 1A(2).
      For the purposes of Sch 7 para 1A(2), 'holding', in relation to a farm business tenancy, and 'termination', in relation to a tenancy, have the same meanings as in the Agricultural Tenancies Act 1995 s 38(1) (see AGRICULTURAL LAND AND ALLOTMENTS vol 1 (2017) PARAS 402, 405): Opencast Coal Act 1958 Sch 7 para 1A(3).

## 452. Position where the land has been restored.

Where land[1] comprised in a farm business tenancy[2] is comprised in a compulsory rights order[3], whether any other land is comprised in the holding, or comprised in the order, or not, and (1) before the date of entry[4] there had been provided in relation to the land in question tenant's improvements ('the former tenant's improvements') in respect of which, immediately before that date, the tenant had a prospective right to compensation[5] on quitting the holding on the termination of the tenancy[6]; and (2) at the end of the period of occupation[7] the circumstances are such that the Agricultural Tenancies Act 1995[8] would have applied[9] but for the fact that the benefit of the former tenant's improvements has been replaced, on the restoration[10] of the land, by other improvements ('the new improvements') of comparable benefit to the land[11], the Agricultural Tenancies Act 1995[12] has effect in relation to the new improvements as if those improvements were tenant's improvements[13].

1   As to the meaning of 'land' see PARA 414.
2   As to the meaning of 'farm business tenancy' see PARA 429.
3   As to compulsory rights orders see the Opencast Coal Act 1958 s 4; and PARA 431 et seq. The power to make such orders has not been exercisable since 31 December 1999: see PARA 414.
4   As to the meaning of 'the date of entry' see PARAS 433, PARA 443.
5   Ie compensation under the Agricultural Tenancies Act 1995 s 16 (see AGRICULTURAL LAND AND ALLOTMENTS vol 1 (2017) PARA 411): see the Opencast Coal Act 1958 Sch 7 para 2A(1).
6   Opencast Coal Act 1958 Sch 7 para 2A(1)(a) (Sch 7 para 2A added by the Agricultural Tenancies Act 1995 s 40, Schedule para 20(4)).
7   As to the meaning of 'the period of occupation' see PARA 433.
8   Ie the Agricultural Tenancies Act 1995 Pt III (ss 15–27) (see AGRICULTURAL LAND AND ALLOTMENTS vol 1 (2017) PARAS 410–419): see the Opencast Coal Act 1958 Sch 7 para 2A(1)(b).
9   Ie as mentioned in the Opencast Coal Act 1958 s 25A(3), (4): see Sch 7 para 2A(1)(b).
10   As to the meaning of 'restoration' see PARA 424.
11   Opencast Coal Act 1958 Sch 7 para 2A(1)(b).
12   Ie the Agricultural Tenancies Act 1995 Pt III (see AGRICULTURAL LAND AND ALLOTMENTS vol 1 (2017) PARAS 410–419): see the Opencast Coal Act 1958 Sch 7 para 2A(2).
13   Opencast Coal Act 1958 Sch 7 para 2A(2). Section 25A(2), (6) applies for the purposes of Sch 7 para 2A as it applies for the purposes of s 25A: Sch 7 para 2A(3).

## 453. Compensation for expenses.

Where a tenant is entitled to compensation[1] for tenant's improvements[2] and (1) after the end of the period of occupation[3] expenses are incurred in replacing the benefit of the tenant's improvements by other improvements of comparable benefit to the land[4]; and (2) the person incurring those expenses, whether he is the landlord or not, is entitled to compensation in respect of those expenses[5], the

Agricultural Tenancies Act 1995[6] applies as if the works in respect of which those expenses are incurred were not tenant's improvements, if apart from this provision[7] they would constitute such improvements[8].

1   Ie by virtue of the Opencast Coal Act 1958 s 25A (see PARA 451): see Sch 7 para 3A.
2   Ie as mentioned in the Opencast Coal Act 1958 s 25A: see Sch 7 para 3A.
3   As to the meaning of 'the period of occupation' see PARA 433. The power to make compulsory rights orders conferring rights to occupy land has not been exercisable since 31 December 1999: see PARA 414.
4   Opencast Coal Act 1958 Sch 7 para 3A(a) (added by the Agricultural Tenancies Act 1995 s 40, Schedule para 20(5)). As to the meaning of 'land' see PARA 414.
5   Ie compensation under the Opencast Coal Act 1958 s 22 (see PARA 476): see Sch 7 para 3A.
6   Ie the Agricultural Tenancies Act 1995 s 13 (see AGRICULTURAL LAND AND ALLOTMENTS vol 1 (2017) PARA 409): see the Opencast Coal Act 1958 Sch 7 para 3A.
7   Ie the Opencast Coal Act 1958 Sch 7 para 3A.
8   Opencast Coal Act 1958 Sch 7 para 3A(b) (added by the Agricultural Tenancies Act 1995 s 40, Schedule para 20(5)).

### 454.   Variation of terms of tenancy or mortgage.

Where (1) immediately before the operative date[1] of a compulsory rights order[2], any of the land[3] comprised in the order was subject to a farm business tenancy[4]; and (2) that tenancy continues until after the end of the period of occupation[5], the landlord or tenant under the tenancy may, by notice in writing served on his tenant or landlord, demand a reference to arbitration of the question whether any of the terms and conditions of the tenancy, including any term or condition relating to rent, should be varied in consequence of any change in the state of the land resulting from the occupation or use of the land in the exercise of rights conferred by the order[6].

On such a reference, the arbitrator must determine what variations, if any, should be made in the terms and conditions of the tenancy, and the date, not being earlier than the end of the period of occupation, from which any such variations are to take effect or are to be treated as having taken effect; and as from that date the tenancy has effect, or, as the case may be, is treated as having had effect, subject to any variations determined by the arbitrator under this provision[7].

These provisions as to variations of tenancies apply to mortgages[8] with necessary modifications[9].

1   As to the meaning of 'the operative date' see PARA 432.
2   As to compulsory rights orders see the Opencast Coal Act 1958 s 4; and PARA 431 et seq. The power to make such orders has not been exercisable since 31 December 1999: see PARA 414.
3   As to the meaning of 'land' see PARA 414.
4   As to the meaning of 'farm business tenancy' see PARA 429.
5   Opencast Coal Act 1958 s 37, Sch 7 para 4A(1) (Sch 7 para 4A added by the Agricultural Tenancies Act 1995 s 40, Schedule para 20(7)). As to the meaning of 'the period of occupation' see PARA 433.
6   Opencast Coal Act 1958 Sch 7 para 4A(2). The Agricultural Tenancies Act 1995 s 28(3) applies in relation to a notice under the Opencast Coal Act 1958 Sch 7 para 4A(2) as it applies in relation to a notice under the Agricultural Tenancies Act 1995 s 28(2) (see AGRICULTURAL LAND AND ALLOTMENTS vol 1 (2017) PARA 420): Opencast Coal Act 1958 Sch 7 para 4A(2).
7   Opencast Coal Act 1958 Sch 7 para 4A(3). The provisions of Sch 7 para 4A do not affect any right of the landlord or the tenant, or the jurisdiction of the arbitrator, under the Agricultural Tenancies Act 1995 Pt II (ss 9–14) (see AGRICULTURAL LAND AND ALLOTMENTS vol 1 (2017) PARAS 406–409); but where there is a reference by virtue of the Opencast Coal Act 1958 Sch 7 para 4A and a reference under the Agricultural Tenancies Act 1995 Pt II in respect of the same tenancy, and it appears to the arbitrator that the reference under Pt II relates wholly or mainly to

the consequences of the occupation or use of the land in the exercise of rights conferred by the order, he may direct that proceedings on the two references are to be taken concurrently: Opencast Coal Act 1958 Sch 7 para 4A(4).

8   As to the meaning of 'mortgage' see PARA 439.

9   The provisions of the Opencast Coal Act 1958 Sch 7 para 4A apply in relation to mortgages of land comprised in farm business tenancies as they apply in relation to such tenancies, as if any reference in Sch 7 para 4A to such a tenancy were a reference to such a mortgage, and any reference to a landlord or to a tenant were a reference to a mortgagee or to a mortgagor, as the case may be: Sch 7 para 7A (added by the Agricultural Tenancies Act 1995 Schedule para 20(11)).

### C.   NON-AGRICULTURAL LAND ADJUSTMENTS

### 455.   Compensation for improvements.

Where (1) the land comprised in a compulsory rights order[1] consists of or includes land which immediately before the date of entry[2] constituted or formed part of a holding to which the provisions of the Landlord and Tenant Act 1927 relating to compensation for improvements and goodwill on the termination of business tenancies[3] apply[4], and on which before that date improvements qualifying for compensation[5] had been carried out[6]; and (2) the tenancy[7] under which the tenant could have claimed compensation for the improvements[8] terminates on or after the date of entry but before the end of the period of occupation[9], those provisions as to compensation for improvements apply, in relation to that tenancy, as if at its termination[10] the land in question were in the state in which it was immediately before the date of entry[11]. If the tenant quitted the holding before the termination of his tenancy, those provisions apply as if he had quitted the holding on its termination[12].

1   As to compulsory rights orders see the Opencast Coal Act 1958 s 4; and PARA 431 et seq. The power to make such orders has not been exercisable since 31 December 1999: see PARA 414. As to the meaning of 'land' see PARA 414.

2   As to the meaning of 'the date of entry' see PARAS 433, PARA 443.

3   Ie the Landlord and Tenant Act 1927 Pt I (ss 1–17): see LANDLORD AND TENANT vol 64 (2016) PARA 1679.

4   Opencast Coal Act 1958 ss 30(1)(a), 37, Sch 7 para 8(1)(a).

5   See the Landlord and Tenant Act 1927 s 1; s 2; and LANDLORD AND TENANT vol 64 (2016) PARA 1683.

6   Opencast Coal Act 1958 s 30(1)(b), Sch 7 para 8(1)(a).

7   As to the meaning of 'tenancy' see PARA 444.

8   In the Opencast Coal Act 1958 Sch 7 Pt II, 'improvement' includes the erection of a building: Sch 7 para 8(4).

9   Opencast Coal Act 1958 Sch 7 para 8(1)(b). As to the meaning of 'the period of occupation' see PARA 433.

10   'Termination', in relation to a tenancy, means the cesser of the tenancy, whether by effluxion of time or for any other reasons: Opencast Coal Act 1958 s 51(1).

11   Opencast Coal Act 1958 Sch 7 para 8(2)(a).

12   Opencast Coal Act 1958 Sch 7 para 8(2)(b). For these purposes, s 30(5) (see PARA 490) applies with the substitution, for references to s 30(2), of references to Sch 7 para 8(2): Sch 7 para 8(3).

### 456.   Position where the land has been restored.

Where land[1] comprised in a holding to which the provisions of the Landlord and Tenant Act 1927 relating to compensation for improvements and goodwill on the termination of business tenancies[2] apply is comprised in a compulsory rights order[3], whether any other land is comprised in the holding, or comprised in the order, or not, and (1) the tenancy[4] under which that holding was held immediately before the operative date[5] continues until after the end of the period of occupation[6]; (2) before the operative date improvements[7] had been carried out on the land in question[8]; and (3) at the end of the period of occupation the circumstances are such that compensation[9] would be payable in respect of those improvements but for the fact that their benefit has been replaced, on the restoration[10] of the land, by works of comparable benefit to the land[11], those provisions as to compensation for improvements apply to those works as if they had been carried out by the person who carried out the previous improvements[12].

1  As to the meaning of 'land' see PARA 414.
2  Ie the Landlord and Tenant Act 1927 Pt I (ss 1–17): see LANDLORD AND TENANT vol 64 (2016) PARA 1679 et seq.
3  As to compulsory rights orders see the Opencast Coal Act 1958 s 4; and PARA 431 et seq. The power to make such orders has not been exercisable since 31 December 1999: see PARA 414.
4  As to the meaning of 'tenancy' see PARA 444.
5  As to the meaning of 'the operative date' see PARA 432.
6  Opencast Coal Act 1958 s 37, Sch 7 para 9(1)(a). As to the meaning of 'the period of occupation' see PARA 433.
7  As to the meaning of 'improvements' see PARA 455.
8  Opencast Coal Act 1958 Sch 7 para 9(1)(b).
9  Ie under the Opencast Coal Act 1958 s 30: see PARA 490.
10  As to the meaning of 'restoration' see PARA 424.
11  Opencast Coal Act 1958 Sch 7 para 9(1)(c).
12  Opencast Coal Act 1958 Sch 7 para 9(2).

## 457.  Variation of terms of tenancy or mortgage.

Where, immediately before the operative date[1] of a compulsory rights order[2], any of the land[3] comprised in the order was subject to a tenancy[4], but was not comprised in a tenancy in relation to which the Agricultural Holdings Act 1986 applies or in a farm business tenancy[5], and the tenancy continues until after the end of the period of occupation[6], the landlord or the tenant of the holding may, by notice in writing served[7] on his tenant or landlord, demand a reference to the court[8] of the question whether any of the terms and conditions of the contract of tenancy, including any term or condition as to rent, should be varied in consequence of any change in the state of the holding resulting from the occupation or use of the land in the exercise of rights conferred by the compulsory rights order[9].

On such a reference the court must determine what variations, if any, should be made, and the date, which must not be earlier than the end of the period of occupation, from which they are to take effect or to be treated as having taken effect; and as from that date the contract of tenancy has effect, or is to be treated as having had effect, subject to those variations[10].

These provisions as to the variation of terms of tenancies[11] apply with necessary modifications to mortgages[12].

1  As to the meaning of 'the operative date' see PARA 432.
2  As to compulsory rights orders see the Opencast Coal Act 1958 s 4; and PARA 431 et seq. The power to make such orders has not been exercisable since 31 December 1999: see PARA 414.
3  As to the meaning of 'land' see PARA 414.
4  As to the meaning of 'tenancy' see PARA 444.
5  Opencast Coal Act 1958 s 37, Sch 7 para 12(1)(a) (amended by the Agricultural Tenancies Act 1995 s 40, Schedule para 20(12)). As to the meaning of 'farm business tenancy' see PARA 429.
6  Opencast Coal Act 1958 Sch 7 para 12(1)(b). As to the meaning of 'the period of occupation' see PARA 433.
7  As to the service of notices see PARA 422.
8  'The court' means the court exercising the jurisdiction conferred on the tribunal by the Landlord and Tenant Act 1927 Pt I (ss 1–17), in accordance with the Landlord and Tenant Act 1954 s 63 (see LANDLORD AND TENANT vol 63 (2016) PARA 969), the provisions of which apply to references under the Opencast Coal Act 1958 Sch 7 para 12: Sch 7 para 12(4).

9    Opencast Coal Act 1958 Sch 7 para 12(2).

10   Opencast Coal Act 1958 Sch 7 para 12(3).

11   Ie the Opencast Coal Act 1958 Sch 7 para 12: see Sch 7 para 13.

12   The provisions of the Opencast Coal Act 1958 Sch 7 para 12 apply in relation to mortgages as they apply in relation to contracts of tenancy, as if any reference to such a contract, or to a tenancy, other than a reference to a tenancy in relation to which the Agricultural Holdings Act 1986 applies or a farm business tenancy, were a reference to a mortgage, and any reference to a landlord or to a tenant were a reference to a mortgagee or to a mortgagor, as the case may be: Opencast Coal Act 1958 Sch 7 para 13 (amended by the Agricultural Tenancies Act 1995 Schedule para 20(13)). As to the meaning of 'mortgage' see PARA 439.

D.    MINING LEASES

## 458. Restrictions on rent and royalties.

Where the land comprised in a compulsory rights order[1] consists of or includes land which, immediately before the operative date[2] of the order, was subject to a mining lease[3] or order conferring working rights[4] the benefit of which is held for the purposes of a mineral undertaking, the provisions of the lease or order are modified as follows[5]. The provisions of the lease or order have effect subject to the limitation that the aggregate amount of the rent, royalties and other sums payable by the mineral operator[6] by virtue of the lease or order for any year[7] which is either the year beginning with the operative date of the compulsory rights order[8], or a year beginning with the anniversary of that date and falling within the period of occupation[9], must not exceed the aggregate amount of the rent, royalties and other sums that would have been payable by the mineral operator under the lease or order for that year if the compulsory rights order had not been made, and he had exercised the relevant rights and facilities[10] in the manner in which, and to the extent to which, he might reasonably have been expected to exercise them in those circumstances[11].

1   As to compulsory rights orders see the Opencast Coal Act 1958 s 4; and PARA 431 et seq. The power to make such orders has not been exercisable since 31 December 1999: see PARA 414. As to the meaning of 'land' see PARA 414.

2   As to the meaning of 'the operative date' see PARA 432.

3   As to the meaning of 'mining lease' see PARA 439. As to mining leases generally see PARA 318 et seq.

4   As to the meaning of 'order conferring working rights' see PARA 439. As to such orders generally see PARA 380 et seq.

5   Opencast Coal Act 1958 s 37, Sch 7 para 17(1). 'Mineral undertaking' means an undertaking for the working and getting of minerals, whether by underground or surface working: s 51(1). As to the meaning of 'minerals' see PARA 10.

6   For these purposes, 'mineral operator' means: (1) in relation to land which, immediately before the operative date of the order in question, is subject to a mining lease or order conferring working rights held for the purpose of a mineral undertaking, the person for the time being entitled to the benefit of that lease or order (Opencast Coal Act 1958 s 33(1)(a), (2), Sch 5 para 1(2)(a), Sch 7 para 17(2)); and (2) in relation to land which, immediately before that date, is land in which the interest of the owner of the land or of any stratum of it (whether on or below the surface) is held for the purposes of such an undertaking, the person for the time being entitled to that interest (s 33(1)(b), Sch 5 para 1(2)(b), Sch 7 para 17(2)).

7   'Year' means any period of 12 months: Opencast Coal Act 1958 s 51(1).

8   Opencast Coal Act 1958 Sch 7 para 18(a).

9   Opencast Coal Act 1958 Sch 7 para 18(b). As to the meaning of 'the period of occupation' see PARA 433.

10   For these purposes, 'the relevant rights and facilities', in relation to a mineral undertaking, means all rights and facilities for the time being available to the person carrying it on for the purpose of working, getting, carrying away, using, treating, converting and disposing of minerals, whether on land comprised in the compulsory rights order in question or elsewhere: Opencast Coal Act 1958

Sch 5 para 1(3), Sch 7 para 17(2). As to references to working minerals on land see PARA 416.
11 Opencast Coal Act 1958 Sch 7 para 18.

### E. BUSINESS TENANCIES

### 459. Application of the Landlord and Tenant Act 1954.

Where any of the land comprised in a compulsory rights order[1] is land which, immediately before the operative date[2] of the order, was subject to a tenancy[3] to which the provisions of the Landlord and Tenant Act 1954 relating to business tenancies[4] apply[5], then, as from that date and so long thereafter as the tenancy continues and the order continues to have effect, so much of that land as is comprised in the tenancy[6] and immediately before that date was occupied by the tenant for the purposes of the relevant business[7], or for those and other purposes, or was occupied by a person employed by the tenant for those purposes[8], is to be treated for the purposes of those provisions as if it were so occupied[9] even if for the time being it is not[10].

1  As to compulsory rights orders see the Opencast Coal Act 1958 s 4; and PARA 431 et seq. The power to make such orders has not been exercisable since 31 December 1999: see PARA 414. As to the meaning of 'land' see PARA 414.
2  As to the meaning of 'the operative date' see PARA 432.
3  As to the meaning of 'tenancy' see PARA 444.
4  Ie the Landlord and Tenant Act 1954 Pt II (ss 23–46): see LANDLORD AND TENANT vol 64 (2016) PARA 1597.
5  Opencast Coal Act 1958 s 37, Sch 7 para 19(1).
6  Opencast Coal Act 1958 Sch 7 para 20(1)(a).
7  'The relevant business' means the business by reason of which, immediately before the operative date, the tenancy was one to which the Landlord and Tenant Act 1954 Pt II applied: Opencast Coal Act 1958 Sch 7 para 20(2). 'Business' includes a trade, profession and employment, and any activity carried on by a body of persons, whether corporate or unincorporate: Landlord and Tenant Act 1954 s 23(2); applied by the Opencast Coal Act 1958 Sch 7 para 19(2).
8  Opencast Coal Act 1958 Sch 7 para 20(1)(b).
9  Opencast Coal Act 1958 Sch 7 para 20(1). As to further adjustments relating to business tenancies see Sch 7 paras 21–24; and LANDLORD AND TENANT vol 64 (2016) PARAS 1668–1670.
10  Opencast Coal Act 1958 Sch 7 para 20(1)(c).

### F. ALLOTMENTS

### 460. Termination of allotment tenancy.

Where the land comprised in a compulsory rights order[1] consists of or includes any land which, immediately before the operative date[2] of the order, was occupied, with or without other land, under an allotment tenancy[3], that tenancy, if not previously terminated, terminated on the date of entry[4].

1  As to compulsory rights orders see the Opencast Coal Act 1958 s 4; and PARA 431 et seq. The power to make such orders has not been exercisable since 31 December 1999: see PARA 414. As to the meaning of 'land' see PARA 414.
2  As to the meaning of 'the operative date' see PARA 432.
3  'Allotment tenancy' means a tenancy under which land is occupied by the tenant and is either land let under that tenancy for use by the tenant as an allotment garden, or an allotment other than an allotment garden: Opencast Coal Act 1958 s 41(1), Sch 8 para 1(1). 'Allotment' has the meaning assigned to it by the Allotments Act 1922 s 3(7), and 'allotment garden' has the meaning assigned to it by s 22(1) (see AGRICULTURAL LAND AND ALLOTMENTS vol 1 (2017) PARA 649): Opencast Coal Act 1958 s 41(2). Land used by a tenant as an allotment garden is presumed to have been let for such use by him: Allotments Act 1922 s 22(4); applied by the Opencast Coal Act 1958 Sch 8 para 1(2).

4    Opencast Coal Act 1958 Sch 8 para 2. As to the meaning of 'the date of entry' see PARAS 433, PARA 443. As to compensation see PARAS 500–502.

## (4) Compensation for Compulsory Rights Orders

### (i) In General

**461. Types of compensation payable.**

The Opencast Coal Act 1958 contains elaborate provisions with regard to the compensation payable in respect of the occupation and use of land pursuant to a compulsory rights order[1]. No such compensation is payable by any person unless a claim for it is duly made to that person[2]. A person entitled to the rights conferred by a compulsory rights order must, for the purpose of facilitating the assessment of compensation, cause records to be made of the condition of the land in question[3]. These compensation provisions[4] relate to compensation in respect of minerals[5], agricultural land[6], non-agricultural land[7], easements and rights[8], and depreciation[9]. Provision is also made for certain special cases[10].

1    See the Opencast Coal Act 1958 Pt II (ss 17–36). As to compulsory rights orders see s 4; and PARA 431 et seq. The power to make such orders has not been exercisable since 31 December 1999: see PARA 414.
2    See the Opencast Coal Act 1958 s 40(1); and PARA 509.
3    See the Opencast Coal Act 1958 s 36(1); and PARA 462.
4    See PARA 462 et seq.
5    See PARA 464 et seq.
6    See PARA 472 et seq.
7    See PARAS 488–490.
8    See PARA 491 et seq.
9    See PARAS 494–496.
10   Ie compensation in respect of concurrent and limited compulsory rights orders (see PARAS 497–498), compensation in respect of woodlands (see PARA 499), allotments (see PARAS 500–502), restricted lettings, easements and similar rights (see PARA 503), and the apportionment of compensation (see PARA 504 et seq).

**462. Records.**

In the case of any compulsory rights order[1], where any person duly published, served and affixed notices[2], he also had to cause a record[3] to be made of the condition[4] of all the land comprised in the order[5], and, except in the case of a limited compulsory rights order[6], of any other land forming, in relation to that order, part of a holding[7].

In the case of any compulsory rights order other than a limited order, the person entitled immediately before the end of the period of occupation[8] to the rights conferred by the order must, at the end of that period, cause a record to be made of the condition, as at the end of that period, of all the land comprised in the order[9].

Any record of the condition of land made under these provisions must be made in pursuance of a comprehensive survey of the land, in so far as such a survey can be carried out by inspection and without any operations involving the excavation of land or the making of borings, and must include all such particulars of the land and of things in or on it as are reasonably required for recording the results of such a survey[10].

If any person fails to cause any record to be made or served in accordance with any requirement imposed on him[11]: (1) his obligation to comply with that requirement is enforceable by the Coal Authority[12] as if it were a duty owed by that person to that Authority; and (2) without prejudice to its rights by virtue of head (1) above, that Authority may itself cause the record to be made and served in accordance with that requirement and may recover any expenses reasonably incurred in doing so from the person in contravention of that requirement[13].

1   As to compulsory rights orders see the Opencast Coal Act 1958 s 4; and PARA 431 et seq. The power to make such orders has not been exercisable since 31 December 1999: see PARA 414.
2   Ie under the Opencast Coal Act 1958 s 5(2): see PARA 443.
3   For the purpose of facilitating the assessment of compensation under the Opencast Coal Act 1958 Pt II (ss 17–36), a person entitled to the rights conferred by a compulsory rights order is to cause records to be made in accordance with the provisions of s 36: s 36(1) (amended by the Coal Industry Act 1994 s 52(2), Sch 8 paras 1, 27(1)).
4   Ie the condition as on the date of entry. As to the meaning of 'the date of entry' see PARAS 433, PARA 443. For the purposes of any provision of the Opencast Coal Act 1958, in so far as it relates to the state or condition in which land was at a time specified in that provision, regard must be had to all matters relevant to that state or condition at that time, including, without prejudice to the generality of the foregoing, the characteristics of the soil, whether on or below the surface, the presence of any minerals in or under the land, the growth of trees, hedges or other vegetation, and any buildings, structures, apparatus or other works which were on, in, under or over the land at that time; and any reference in any provision of the Opencast Coal Act 1958 to the state or condition in which land would have been, or might reasonably have been expected to be, in circumstances specified in that provision is to be construed accordingly: s 51(4). As to the meaning of 'land' see PARA 414.
5   Opencast Coal Act 1958 s 36(2)(a) (amended by the Coal Industry Act 1975 ss 4(2), 7(4), Sch 3 para 7, Sch 5; and the Coal Industry Act 1994 Sch 8 para 27(2)).
6   Opencast Coal Act 1958 s 36(2) proviso (amended by the Coal Industry Act 1975 Sch 3 para 7, Sch 5). As to limited orders see PARA 439.
7   Opencast Coal Act 1958 s 36(2)(b) (amended by the Coal Industry Act 1975 Sch 3 para 7, Sch 5; and the Coal Industry Act 1994 Sch 8 para 27(2)). A holding for this purpose is one to which the Opencast Coal Act 1958 s 17 or s 29 applies: see s 36(2)(b); and PARAS 472–473, 488.
8   As to the meaning of 'the period of occupation' see PARA 433.
9   Opencast Coal Act 1958 s 36(3) (amended by the Coal Industry Act 1994 Sch 8 para 27).
10  Opencast Coal Act 1958 s 36(4). With respect to professional and other fees incurred by persons in obtaining advice or conducting negotiations with regard to any record made under s 36, the appropriate national authority may make regulations requiring persons required to make such records, within such limits (whether as to descriptions of fees, or as to amount, or otherwise) and subject to such conditions as may be prescribed, to pay fees so incurred: s 36(9) (amended by the Coal Industry Act 1994 Sch 8 para 27); and see the Opencast Coal (Fees) Regulations 1960, SI 1960/194 (amended by the Decimal Currency Act 1969 s 10(1), Coal Industry Act 1987 s 1(3) (repealed); and SI 2009/1307). This provision applies provided that no regulations under the Opencast Coal Act 1958 s 36 apply to any fees in so far as they form part of the costs of an arbitration under s 36 or affect any power of an arbitrator with respect to any such costs: s 36(9) proviso. The appropriate national authority is the Secretary of State or where functions have been transferred in relation to Wales, the Welsh Ministers: see PARA 2. As to regulation-making powers generally see PARA 418.
11  Ie imposed by the Opencast Coal Act 1958 s 36: see s 36(9A).
12  As to the Coal Authority see PARA 52 et seq.
13  Opencast Coal Act 1958 s 36(9A) (added by the Coal Industry Act 1994 Sch 8 para 27(7)).

### 463. Service of and objection to records.

Where any person has caused a record to be made[1] he must within a specified time[2] serve[3], on every person who is then known to him to be a person directly concerned[4], a notice in the prescribed form[5] together with a copy of the record[6].

If any such person so served gives notice[7] of objection to the person who served the record, within 21 days after the date on which the copy was sent to him, requiring the record to be amended in one or more respects specified in the notice, then if all the persons whose agreement is requisite[8] agree on an amendment of the record (whether the amendment is that specified in the notice of objection or another amendment in substitution for it), the person who served the record must cause the record to be amended accordingly[9]. If no such agreement is reached, and the objection is not withdrawn, the matter in dispute must be determined by arbitration[10].

1   Ie under the Opencast Coal Act 1958 s 36: see s 36(5); and PARA 462.
2   In the case of a record made under the Opencast Coal Act 1958 s 36(2) the time is 21 days after the date of entry (s 36(5)(a)); in the case of a record made under s 36(3) it is 21 days after the end of the period of occupation (s 36(5)(b)). As to the meaning of 'the date of entry' see PARAS 433, PARA 443; and as to the meaning of 'the period of occupation' see PARA 433.
3   As to the service of notices see PARA 422.
4   As to the meaning of 'person directly concerned' see PARA 431.
5   Forms of notices are prescribed by the Opencast Coal (Notice of Record) Regulations 1958, SI 1958/2121, reg 3, Schedule.
6   Opencast Coal Act 1958 s 36(5) (amended by the Coal Industry Act 1994 Sch 8 paras 1, 27).
7   As to the giving of notices see PARA 422.
8   Ie the person who served the record, the person who gave the notice of objection and all other persons to whom copies of the record were sent under the Opencast Coal Act 1958 s 36: s 36(7) (amended by the Coal Industry Act 1994 Sch 8 paras 1, 27).
9   Opencast Coal Act 1958 s 36(6)(a) (amended by the Coal Industry Act 1994 Sch 8 para 27).
10  Opencast Coal Act 1958 s 36(6)(b). The reference is to a single arbitrator appointed by the person who served the record and the person who gave the notice of objection in consequence of which the dispute arose (s 36(8)(a) (amended by the Coal Industry Act 1994 Sch 8 para 27)); and, except in relation to that appointment, the persons who served the record, the persons who gave the notice of objection and all other persons to whom copies of the record were sent under the Opencast Coal Act 1958 s 36 are to be parties to the reference (Opencast Coal Act 1958 s 36(8)(b)). As to references to arbitration see ARBITRATION vol 2 (2017) PARA 501 et seq.

## (ii)  Compensation in Respect of Minerals

### 464.  Annual compensation; in general.

Where the land comprised in a compulsory rights order[1] consists of or includes land which, immediately before the operative date[2] of the order, was subject to a mining lease[3] or order conferring working rights[4] the benefit of which is held for the purposes of a mineral undertaking[5], or was land in which the interest of the owner[6] of the land or of any stratum, whether on or below the surface, is held for the purposes of a mineral undertaking, the provisions of the Opencast Coal Act 1958 relating to compensation[7] in respect of minerals[8] have effect[9].

1   As to compulsory rights orders see the Opencast Coal Act 1958 s 4; and PARA 431 et seq. The power to make such orders has not been exercisable since 31 December 1999: see PARA 414. As to the meaning of 'land' see PARA 414.
2   As to the meaning of 'the operative date' see PARA 432.
3   As to the meaning of 'mining lease' see PARA 439.
4   As to the meaning of 'order conferring working rights' see PARA 439.
5   As to the meaning of 'mineral undertaking' see PARA 458
6   As to the meaning of 'owner' see PARA 421.
7   The provisions referred to are those of the Opencast Coal Act 1958 Sch 5 (see PARA 465 et seq), which have effect in relation to land comprised in a compulsory rights order in the circumstances specified in the text; and any reference in Sch 5 to land to which that Schedule applies is a reference to land which, immediately before the operative date of the order, fell within s 33(1)(a) or s 33(1)(b): Sch 5 para 1(1).
8   As to the meaning of 'minerals' see PARA 10.
9   Opencast Coal Act 1958 s 33(1). The provisions of Pt II (ss 17–36), other than s 33, have effect subject to the provisions of Sch 5 in cases falling within that Schedule: s 33(2).

## 465. Annual compensation payable to mineral operator.

For the year[1] beginning with the operative date[2] of the compulsory rights order[3], and for each subsequent year which begins with an anniversary of that date and falls within the period of occupation[4], the following must be assessed:

(1)    the profit or loss which a person carrying on the relevant undertaking[5] might reasonably have been expected to make for that year by the exercise of the relevant rights and facilities[6] if the order had not been made[7]; and

(2)    the profit or loss which such a person might reasonably have been expected to make for that year by the exercise of those rights and facilities in the circumstances existing in that year[8].

Where, in any one year, both those assessments show a profit, but the assessment under head (2) above shows a smaller profit than that under head (1), the mineral operator[9] is entitled to compensation for that year of an amount equal to the difference[10]. Where the assessment under head (1) above shows a profit and that under head (2) above shows a loss, the amount of the loss is added to the amount of that profit, and the mineral operator is entitled to compensation for that year of an amount equal to the sum of those amounts[11]. Where both assessments show a loss, but that under head (2) above shows a greater loss than that under head (1) above, the mineral operator is entitled to compensation for that year of an amount equal to the difference[12].

1   As to the meaning of 'year' see PARA 458.
2   As to the meaning of 'the operative date' see PARA 432.
3   As to compulsory rights orders see the Opencast Coal Act 1958 s 4; and PARA 431 et seq. The power to make such orders has not been exercisable since 31 December 1999: see PARA 414.
4   As to the meaning of 'the period of occupation' see PARA 433.
5   'Relevant undertaking' means the mineral undertaking of the mineral operator: Opencast Coal Act 1958 s 33(1), Sch 5 para 1(2). As to the meaning of 'mineral undertaking' see PARA 458; and as to the meaning of 'mineral operator' see PARA 458.
6   As to the meaning of 'relevant rights and facilities' see PARA 458. Any reference in Opencast Coal Act 1958 Sch 5 to the exercise of those rights and facilities in the manner in which they might reasonably have been expected to be exercised in circumstances there mentioned is to be construed as including a reference to the exercise of those rights and facilities to the extent to which they might reasonably have been expected to be exercised in those circumstances: Sch 5 para 1(4).
7   Opencast Coal Act 1958 Sch 5 para 3(a).
8   Opencast Coal Act 1958 Sch 5 para 3(b).
9   As to the meaning of 'mineral operator' see PARA 458.
10  Opencast Coal Act 1958 Sch 5 para 4(1). Any entitlement to compensation under Sch 5 is an entitlement to compensation from, in the case of compensation under Sch 5 para 4 or Sch 5 para 12, the persons who, for the whole or any part of the year in question, have been entitled to the rights conferred by the order: Sch 5 para 2(1)(a) (Sch 5 para 2 substituted by the Coal Industry Act 1994 s 52(2), Sch 8 para 41). The Opencast Coal Act 1958 Sch 5 para 2(1)(a) has effect subject, where different persons have been entitled to the rights conferred by an order for different parts of the year, to any apportionment under s 35(3): Sch 5 para 2(2) (as so substituted).
      The provisions of Sch 6 paras 8, 9 have effect (with the necessary modifications) in relation to any compensation payable under Sch 5 para 4, and to any compensation received by virtue of Sch 5 para 5 or Sch 5 para 6 as those provisions have effect in relation to compensation to which a person is entitled by virtue of s 17, and to compensation received by virtue of s 26 or s 27: s 34, Sch 6 para 10.
      Where a person is entitled to compensation for any year in respect of a holding by virtue of s 17, then in so far as it is shown that reasonable opportunities were open to him (apart from the occupation and use of any part of the holding not comprised in the order) to mitigate any loss of profit from the holding by augmenting his income for that year in other ways, and those opportunities would not have been open to him if he had continued to be in occupation of the entirety of the holding, the amount of any profit assessed for that year under s 19(1) (repealed) is reduced by the amount by which he has augmented his income for that year by availing himself of those opportunities, or by which he might reasonably have been expected to augment his income

for that year if he had availed himself of those opportunities, as the case may be: Sch 6 para 8(1). For the purposes of Sch 6 para 8 no account is taken of any opportunities of which the person in question has not availed himself (notwithstanding that they were opportunities of the kind described in Sch 6 para 8(1)) in so far as they would have involved his engaging (whether as an employed person or otherwise) in a substantially different occupation from that in which he was engaged during the period preceding the operative date of the order: Sch 6 para 8(2). Section 19(8)(a) (repealed), Sch 6 para 7 (repealed) apply for the purposes of Sch 6 para 8 as they apply for the purposes of s 19 (repealed): Sch 6 para 8(3).

Where a person is entitled to compensation for any year in respect of a holding by virtue of s 17 and he has received any compensation by virtue of s 26 in respect of any improvements carried out on land comprised in that holding, being improvements of a description specified in Sch 4 Pt I or Pt VI, or by virtue of s 27 in respect of a forced sale of any property kept on or used for the purposes of that holding, or removed from that holding, as the case may be, the amount of any profit assessed for that year under s 19(1) (repealed) is reduced by the amount of the income from that compensation which is attributable to that year: Sch 6 para 9(1). For the purposes of Sch 6 para 9(1), the income from any compensation which is attributable to any year in a case where the compensation is shown to have been invested by the recipient thereof is taken to be the amount of income accruing in respect of that year from the property representing the compensation and, in any other case, is taken to be an amount equal to the income which would have accrued for that year from property representing the compensation if it had been invested in securities bearing interest at the rate for the time being in force for the purposes of s 35: Sch 6 para 9(2). In Sch 6 para 9 any reference to Sch 4 Pt I or Pt VI includes a reference to that Part as varied by any order made under s 26 or s 28: Sch 6 para 9(3). In Sch 6 paras 8, 9, references to s 17; s 19 (repealed); and s 27 include references to the provisions of those sections as applied by s 29: Sch 6 para 11 (amended by virtue of the Coal Industry Act 1994 s 67(8), Sch 11 Pt III).

By the Coal Industry Act 1994 s 52(2), Sch 8 paras 1, 42(3), (6), the Opencast Coal Act 1958 Sch 6 paras 8, 9 (other than as applied by Sch 6 para 10 to compensation under Sch 5) ceased to have effect on the restructuring date (ie 31 October 1994: see PARA 50), except in relation to any compulsory rights order confirmed before that date: see the Coal Industry Act 1994 Sch 8 paras 1, 42(3), (6).

In the Opencast Coal Act 1958 Sch 6 paras 8–31 any reference to a holding, in relation to any provisions of Pt II (ss 17–36), includes a reference to land which, in accordance with any of Sch 6 paras 1–5 is to be treated as if it were a separate holding for the purposes of those provisions: Sch 6 para 6.

11  Opencast Coal Act 1958 Sch 5 para 4(2).
12  Opencast Coal Act 1958 Sch 5 para 4(3).

### 466. Initial compensation payable to mineral operator.

For the year[1] beginning with the operative date[2] of the compulsory rights order[3], the mineral operator[4], in addition to any annual compensation[5], was entitled to compensation of an amount equal to the amount of any expenses[6] reasonably incurred by him which were directly attributable to his being required to vacate land comprised in the order[7].

If, in consequence of the confirmation[8] of the compulsory rights order, the mineral operator incurs a loss in respect of a forced sale of any livestock, vehicles, plant, equipment or other chattels kept on land comprised in the order, or used on any such land for the purposes of the relevant undertaking[9], the mineral operator is entitled, subject to his having given the person potentially liable the required notice and afforded him facilities for inspection[10], to compensation of an amount equal to that loss[11].

1  As to the meaning of 'year' see PARA 458.
2  As to the meaning of 'the operative date' see PARA 432.
3  As to compulsory rights orders see the Opencast Coal Act 1958 s 4; and PARA 431 et seq. The power to make such orders has not been exercisable since 31 December 1999: see PARA 414.
4  As to the meaning of 'mineral operator' see PARA 458.
5  As to annual compensation see PARA 465.

6  These expenses included any expenses reasonably incurred by the mineral operator in procuring
   the cancellation or modification of a contract in force immediately before the operative date, in so
   far as it was (1) a contract for the supply of goods or the rendering of services which would have
   been required by him for the purposes of the relevant undertaking (as to the meaning of which see
   PARA 465) if the order had not been made, but in consequence of the order are not required for
   those purposes (Opencast Coal Act 1958 s 33(1), Sch 5 para 5(2)(a)); or (2) a contract for the
   supply by him of minerals (as to the meaning of which see PARA 10) or other goods which but for
   the order would have been supplied by him, directly or indirectly, by means of operations on land
   comprised in the order, and, in consequence of the order, cannot be so supplied (Sch 5 para
   5(2)(b)). As to the distinction between a contract for services and a contract of service see generally
   EMPLOYMENT vol 39 (2014) PARA 1 et seq.
7  Opencast Coal Act 1958 Sch 5 para 5(1). As to compensation see PARA 465. As to the meaning
   of 'land' see PARA 414.
8  See PARA 442.
9  As to the meaning of 'relevant undertaking' see PARA 465.
10 A person was not entitled to such compensation in respect of a forced sale unless he had given to
   the person potentially liable not less than ten days' notice of the intended sale, and had, before the
   sale, afforded to the person to whom the notice was given, or any person designated for the
   purpose by him, reasonable facilities to inspect the property intended to be sold, in so far as he was
   in a position to afford such facilities: Opencast Coal Act 1958 s 27(3) (amended by the Coal
   Industry Act 1994 s 52(2), Sch 8 para 21(3)), applied by the Opencast Coal Act 1958 Sch 5 para
   6(2). See PARA 487.
11 Opencast Coal Act 1958 Sch 5 para 6(1). As to compensation see PARA 465. Any entitlement to
   compensation under Sch 5 is an entitlement to compensation from, in the case of compensation
   under Sch 5 para 5, the person on whose application that order is made (Sch 5 para 2(1)(b) (Sch 5
   para 2 substituted by the Coal Industry Act 1994 Sch 8 para 41)); in the case of compensation
   under the Opencast Coal Act 1958 Sch 5 para 6, the person by whom the compensation would be
   payable if it were compensation under s 27 (Sch 5 para 2(1)(c) (as so substituted)).

## 467. Terminal compensation payable to mineral operator.

Where land[1] which attracts the operation of the provisions of the Opencast
Coal Act 1958 relating to compensation in respect of minerals[2] continues after the
end of the period of occupation[3] to be subject to a mining lease[4] or order
conferring working rights[5] or to be held by the owner[6] for the purposes of a
mineral undertaking[7], then for each year after the period of occupation[8] the
following must be assessed:

(1)     the current value, as at the end of the period of occupation, of the
        expectation of making a profit for that year assessed with regard to the
        effect of the compulsory rights order[9]; and

(2)     the current value, as at the end of that period, of the expectation of
        making a profit for that year assessed as if the compulsory rights order
        had not been made[10].

If the aggregate of the values assessed under head (1) above is less than the
aggregate of the values assessed under head (2) above, the mineral operator[11] is
entitled to compensation of an amount equal to the difference[12].

1  As to the meaning of 'land' see PARA 414.
2  Ie the provisions of the Opencast Coal Act 1958 s 33(1), Sch 5: see Sch 5 para 7(1). As to the
   meaning of 'minerals' see PARA 10.
3  As to the meaning of 'the period of occupation' see PARA 433.
4  As to the meaning of 'mining lease' see PARA 439.
5  As to the meaning of 'order conferring working rights' see PARA 439.
6  As to the meaning of 'owner' see PARA 421.
7  Ie continues to be land falling within the Opencast Coal Act 1958 s 33(1)(a) or s 33(1)(b) (see
   PARA 464): s 33(1), Sch 5 para 7(1). As to the meaning of 'mineral undertaking' see PARA 458.
8  'Year after the period of occupation' means a year (as to the meaning of which see PARA 458)
   which is either the year beginning with the end of the period of occupation or a year beginning with
   the anniversary of the end of that period: Opencast Coal Act 1958 Sch 5 para 7(4).

9　Opencast Coal Act 1958 Sch 5 para 8(1)(a). The profit to be assessed is that which a person carrying on the relevant undertaking might reasonably be expected to make by the exercise of the relevant rights and facilities (see PARA 458) as they subsist at the end of the period of occupation, and in the circumstances existing at the end of that period, on the assumption that, during that period, he had exercised them, so far as was reasonably practicable (see HEALTH AND SAFETY AT WORK vol 52 (2014) PARA 381), having regard to the effect of the compulsory rights order, in such manner as in the circumstances he might reasonably have been expected to exercise them (see PARA 465): Sch 5 para 7(3). As to the meaning of 'relevant undertaking' see PARA 465. As to compulsory rights orders see s 4; and PARA 431 et seq. The power to make such orders has not been exercisable since 31 December 1999: see PARA 414.

10　Opencast Coal Act 1958 Sch 5 para 8(1)(b). The profit to be assessed is that which a person carrying on the relevant undertaking might reasonably have been expected to make by the exercise of the relevant rights and facilities as they might reasonably have been expected to subsist at the end of the period of occupation, and in the circumstances which might reasonably have been expected to exist at the end of that period, if (1) the compulsory rights order had not been made (Sch 5 para 7(2)(a)); and (2) during the period of occupation, the person carrying on the relevant undertaking had exercised the relevant rights and facilities in the manner in which, had that order not been made, he might reasonably have been expected to exercise them (Sch 5 para 7(2)(b)).

11　As to the meaning of 'mineral operator' see PARA 458.

12　Opencast Coal Act 1958 Sch 5 para 8(2). Any entitlement to compensation under Sch 5 is an entitlement to compensation from, in the case of compensation under Sch 5 para 7, 8, 9, 10 or 13, the person who immediately before the end of the period of occupation is the person entitled to the rights conferred by the order: Sch 5 para 2(1)(d) (Sch 5 para 2 substituted by the Coal Industry Act 1994 s 52(2), Sch 8 para 41).

## 468. Terminal compensation where mining lease has minimum rent provision.

Where land[1] which attracts the operation of the provisions of the Opencast Coal Act 1958 relating to compensation in respect of minerals[2] continues after the end of the period of occupation[3] to be subject to a mining lease[4] or an order conferring working rights[5] the benefit of which is held for the purposes of a mineral undertaking[6], and the lease or order contains a provision as to minimum rent[7], the following must be assessed:

(1)　the capital equivalent[8], as at the end of that period, of the aggregate minimum rent liabilities[9] assessed with regard to the effect of the compulsory rights order[10]; and

(2)　the capital equivalent, as at the end of that period, of those liabilities assessed as if that order had not been made[11].

If the capital equivalent under head (1) above is greater than that under head (2) above, the mineral operator is entitled to compensation of an amount equal to the difference[12].

1　As to the meaning of 'land' see PARA 414.

2　Ie the provisions of the Opencast Coal Act 1958 s 33(1), Sch 5: see Sch 5 paras 1(1), 9(1), (5). As to the meaning of 'minerals' see PARA 10.

3　As to the meaning of 'the period of occupation' see PARA 433.

4　As to the meaning of 'mining lease' see PARA 439.

5　As to the meaning of 'order conferring working rights' see PARA 439.

6　As to the meaning of 'mineral undertaking' see PARA 458.

7　Opencast Coal Act 1958 Sch 5 paras 1(1), 9(1), (5). In this context 'rent' includes yearly or other rent, and any toll, duty, royalty or other annual or periodical payment in the nature of rent, whether payable in money or money's worth or otherwise: Sch 5 para 9(6).

8　The capital equivalent of the aggregate minimum rent liabilities for any year is to be taken to be the amount of a fund which, if set aside for the purpose at the end of the period of occupation, would afford a sufficient, but not more than sufficient, indemnity against those liabilities as so assessed: Opencast Coal Act 1958 Sch 5 para 10(3). As to the meaning of 'year' see PARA 458.

9　Any reference to a minimum rent liability for any year is a reference to the difference between the rent payable for that year under the lease or order and the rent which would have been so payable if there had been no provision as to minimum rent: Opencast Coal Act 1958 Sch 5 para 9(4), (5).

10 Opencast Coal Act 1958 Sch 5 para 10(1)(a). For each year after the period of occupation there must be assessed, in the circumstances existing at the end of that period, the minimum rent liability, if any, which the mineral operator might reasonably be expected to incur under that mining lease or order, on the assumption that, during that period, he had exercised the relevant rights and facilities, so far as was reasonably practicable, having regard to the effect of the compulsory rights order, in such manner as in the circumstances he might have reasonably been expected to exercise them: Sch 5 para 9(3), (5). See also PARA 465. As to the meaning of 'year after the period of occupation' see PARA 467; as to the meaning of 'relevant rights and facilities' see PARA 458; and as to the meaning of 'mineral operator' see PARA 458. As to compulsory rights orders see s 4; and PARA 431 et seq. The power to make such orders has not been exercisable since 31 December 1999: see PARA 414.

11 Opencast Coal Act 1958 Sch 5 para 10(1)(b). For each year after the period of occupation there must be assessed the minimum rent liability, if any, that the mineral operator might reasonably have been expected to incur under that mining lease or order if (1) the compulsory rights order had not been made (Sch 5 para 9(2)(a)); and (2) during the period of occupation he had exercised the relevant rights and facilities in the manner in which, had that order not been made, he might reasonably have been expected to exercise them (Sch 5 para 9(2)(b)).

12 Opencast Coal Act 1958 Sch 5 para 10(2). Any entitlement to compensation under Sch 5 is an entitlement to compensation from, in the case of compensation under Sch 5 paras 7, 8, 9, 10 or 13, the person who immediately before the end of the period of occupation is the person entitled to the rights conferred by the order: Sch 5 para 2(1)(d) (Sch 5 para 2 substituted by the Coal Industry Act 1994 s 52(2), Sch 8 para 41).

**469. Annual compensation payable to owner other than mineral operator.**
Where there is land[1] which attracts the operation of the provisions of the Opencast Coal Act 1958 relating to compensation in respect of minerals[2], and the interest[3] of the owner[4] of that land, or a stratum of it, is held by a person other than the mineral operator[5], there must be assessed for the year[6] beginning with the operative date[7] of the compulsory rights order[8], and for each subsequent year, the aggregate amount of the rent, royalties and other sums to which the owner[9] might reasonably have been expected to be entitled for that year in respect of that interest, and in respect of any interest of his in any other relevant land[10]: (1) if the compulsory rights order had not been made[11]; and (2) having regard to that order[12].

For any year in which the assessment under head (2) above is less than that under head (1) above, the owner of the separate interest is entitled to compensation of an amount equal to the difference[13].

1 As to the meaning of 'land' see PARA 414.
2 Ie the provisions of the Opencast Coal Act 1958 s 33(1), Sch 5: see Sch 5 para 11(1).
3 This interest is referred to in the Opencast Coal Act 1958 Sch 5 paras 12, 13 as 'the separate interest': see Sch 5 para 11(2). Any reference in those paragraphs to the owner of the separate interest is a reference to the person for the time being entitled to that interest: Sch 5 para 11(2).
4 As to the meaning of 'owner' see PARA 421.
5 Opencast Coal Act 1958 Sch 5 para 11(1). As to the meaning of 'mineral operator' see PARA 458.
6 As to the meaning of 'year' see PARA 458.
7 As to the meaning of 'the operative date' see PARA 432.
8 As to compulsory rights orders see the Opencast Coal Act 1958 s 4; and PARA 431 et seq. The power to make such orders has not been exercisable since 31 December 1999: see PARA 414.
9 Ie the owner of the separate interest.
10 'Other relevant land' means land, other than the land in which the separate interest subsists, which is land in which the mineral operator has an interest held for the purposes of the relevant undertaking: Opencast Coal Act 1958 Sch 5 para 12(4). As to the meaning of 'relevant undertaking' see PARA 465.
11 Opencast Coal Act 1958 Sch 5 para 12(1)(a). The assessment must be made as if the person carrying on the relevant undertaking had exercised the relevant rights and facilities in the manner in which, in those circumstances, he might reasonably have been expected to exercise them: Sch 5 para 12(1)(b). See also PARA 465. As to the meaning of 'relevant rights and facilities' see PARA 458.

12 Opencast Coal Act 1958 Sch 5 para 12(2). The assessment must be made on the assumption that the person carrying on the relevant undertaking exercised the relevant rights and facilities during that year, so far as was reasonably practicable, having regard to the effect of the compulsory rights order, in such manner as in those circumstances he might reasonably have been expected to exercise them: Sch 5 para 12(2).

13 Opencast Coal Act 1958 Sch 5 para 12(3). Any entitlement to compensation under Sch 5 is an entitlement to compensation from, in the case of compensation under Sch 5 para 4 or Sch 5 para 12, the persons who, for the whole or any part of the year in question, have been entitled to the rights conferred by the order: Sch 5 para 2(1)(a) (Sch 5 para 2 substituted by the Coal Industry Act 1994 s 52(2), Sch 8 para 41). The Opencast Coal Act 1958 Sch 5 para 2(1)(a) has effect subject, where different persons have been entitled to the rights conferred by an order for different parts of the year, to any apportionment under s 35(3): Sch 5 para 2(2) (as so substituted).

## 470. Terminal compensation payable to owner other than mineral operator.

There must be assessed the market value which, at the end of the period of occupation[1], the separate interest[2] might reasonably have been expected to have: (1) if the compulsory rights order had not been made[3]; and (2) in the circumstances existing at the end of the period of occupation having regard to that order[4].

If the value under head (2) above is less than that under head (1) above the owner of the separate interest is entitled to compensation of an amount equal to the difference[5].

1 As to the meaning of 'the period of occupation' see PARA 433.

2 As to the separate interest see PARA 469.

3 Opencast Coal Act 1958 s 33(1), Sch 5 para 13(1)(a). This assessment must be made on the same assumptions as are stated in PARA 469: Sch 5 para 13(1)(b). As to compulsory rights orders see s 4; and PARA 431 et seq. The power to make such orders has not been exercisable since 31 December 1999: see PARA 414.

4 Opencast Coal Act 1958 Sch 5 para 13(2). This assessment must be made on the assumption that during the period of occupation the person carrying on the relevant undertaking exercised the relevant rights and facilities as stated in PARA 469: Sch 5 para 13(2). As to the meaning of 'relevant rights and facilities' see PARA 458.

5 Opencast Coal Act 1958 Sch 5 para 13(3). Any entitlement to compensation under Sch 5 is an entitlement to compensation from, in the case of compensation under Sch 5 paras 7, 8, 9, 10 or 13, the person who immediately before the end of the period of occupation is the person entitled to the rights conferred by the order: Sch 5 para 2(1)(d) (Sch 5 para 2 substituted by the Coal Industry Act 1994 s 52(2), Sch 8 para 41).

## 471. Compensation in respect of disposable minerals.

Where the operator exercises any right of his by virtue of a compulsory rights order[1] to get any minerals[2] other than coal[3]; and the land[4] where the right is exercised was not comprised in that order in the specified circumstances[5], the person who, apart from the compulsory rights order and the statutory right to get any minerals other than coal[6], would have been entitled to the minerals is entitled[7] to compensation from the operator of an amount equal to 12.5 per cent of the market value[8] of the minerals at the time when the right is exercised[9].

Where more than one person is entitled to such compensation, the amount of compensation mentioned above is apportioned between them according to the values of the interests or rights in respect of which each of them would have been entitled to, or to a share of, the minerals[10].

As soon as reasonably practicable, after the end of every period of 12 months during which any person has exercised such a right[11], that person must give written notice[12] to every person appearing to him to be a person entitled to such compensation in respect of any exercise by him during that period of that right[13].

1 As to compulsory rights orders see the Opencast Coal Act 1958 s 4; and PARA 431 et seq. The

power to make such orders has not been exercisable since 31 December 1999: see PARA 414.

Section 31A does not apply where the right in question is exercisable by virtue of a compulsory rights order confirmed before the restructuring date (ie 31 October 1994: see PARA 50): Coal Industry Act 1994 s 52(2), Sch 8 para 24(2).

2  As to the meaning of 'minerals' see PARA 10.
3  Ie by virtue of the Opencast Coal Act 1958 s 10(1): see s 31A(1)(a) (s 31A added by the Coal Industry Act 1994 Sch 8 para 24). As to the meaning of 'coal' see PARA 414.
4  As to the meaning of 'land' see PARA 414.
5  Ie specified in the Opencast Coal Act 1958 s 33(1) (see PARA 464): see s 31A(1)(b).
6  Ie the Opencast Coal Act 1958 s 10(1): see s 31A(2).
7  Ie is entitled subject to the provisions of the Opencast Coal Act 1958 s 31A(3)–(7): see s 31A(2).
8  Where, in the case of any minerals, it would be reasonable for steps for making them saleable or for enhancing their value to be taken on the land between the time when those minerals are got and any sale of the minerals by the operator from the land, it is assumed, for the purpose of determining the market value of those minerals as at the time mentioned in the Opencast Coal Act 1958 s 31A(2), that the minerals were in the same condition at the time so mentioned as they would have been had those steps already been taken: s 31A(3).

   Any question for the purposes of s 31A(3) as to the extent to which it would be reasonable for any steps to be taken in relation to any minerals is determined as at the time mentioned in s 31A(3)(a) and on the assumption that it is not reasonable for steps to be taken where the total cost to the operator of taking those steps is equal to or more than the difference between (1) what would be the market value of the minerals for the purposes of s 31A(2) if it were reasonable for those steps to be taken; and (2) what would be their market value for those purposes if it were not; and for this purpose, where the minerals would not be saleable without the taking of those steps, the market value referred to in head (2) is taken to be nil: s 31A(4).
9  Opencast Coal Act 1958 s 31A(2).
10 Opencast Coal Act 1958 s 31A(5).
11 Ie as is mentioned in the Opencast Coal Act 1958 s 31A(1): see s 31A(6).
12 Such a notice must describe the minerals in respect of which the entitlement to compensation of the person given the notice arises; and state the amount appearing to the person giving the notice to be the amount which for the purposes of the Opencast Coal Act 1958 s 31A(2), is to be taken to be the market value of those minerals as at the time when the right in question was exercised in relation to those minerals: s 31A(7). As to the service of notices see PARA 422.
13 Opencast Coal Act 1958 s 31A(6). As to the meaning of 'reasonably practicable' see HEALTH AND SAFETY AT WORK vol 52 (2014) PARA 381.

### (iii) Agricultural Land

A.  ANNUAL COMPENSATION

## 472. Meaning of 'holding'.

For the purposes of the compensation provisions of the Opencast Coal Act 1958[1], where land, immediately before the operative date[2] of a compulsory rights order, was occupied as a unit[3] and was so occupied wholly or mainly[4] for the purposes of agriculture[5] carried on by way of a trade or business[6], the entirety[7] of that land (excluding the coal[8] and any other minerals[9] vested in the Coal Authority[10] or the person entitled to rights conferred by the order) is taken, in relation to that compulsory rights order, to constitute a holding[11].

1  Ie the Opencast Coal Act 1958 Pt II (ss 17–36): see s 17(2). Where a compulsory rights order is, with the consent of the appropriate authority, made in respect of land in which there is a Crown or Duchy interest (as to the meaning of which see PARA 415), that interest, in so far as the order confers rights exercisable as against all persons directly concerned, is treated as not being the interest of a person directly concerned, and no compensation is payable under Pt II in respect of that interest: s 44(3) (amended by the Coal Industry Act 1994 ss 52(2), 67(8), Sch 8 para 33, Sch 11 Pt II). See also PARA 415. As to the meaning of 'appropriate authority' see PARA 420; and as to the meaning of 'land' see PARA 414. As to compulsory rights orders see the Opencast Coal Act 1958 s 4; and PARA 431 et seq. The power to make such orders has not been exercisable since

31 December 1999: see PARA 414.
2   As to the meaning of 'the operative date' see PARA 432.
3   Opencast Coal Act 1958 s 17(2)(a). Where at any time on or after the operative date and before the end of the period of occupation (as to the meaning of which see PARA 433) an act or event occurs by which different persons become entitled to occupy different parts of the holding, or would be so entitled if the order had not been made, as from the occurrence of that act or event each such part must be treated as if it were a separate holding (s 34, Sch 6 para 1(1), (2) (amended by the Coal Industry Act 1994 Sch 8 paras 1, 42(1), (2), (6))) but no compensation is payable by virtue of the Opencast Coal Act 1958 s 17 in respect of land so treated which does not include any of the land comprised in the compulsory rights order (Sch 6 para 1(2) proviso). Where at any such time a new tenancy is created comprising the holding or any part of it, that tenancy must be disregarded for the purposes of s 17; s 18; Sch 6 para 1: Sch 6 para 2 (amended by the Coal Industry Act 1994 Sch 8 paras 1, 42(1), (2), (6)).
      The Opencast Coal Act 1958 Sch 6 paras 1(2), 2 do not apply in relation to any compulsory rights order confirmed before the restructuring date (ie 31 October 1994: see PARA 50): see the Coal Industry Act 1994 Sch 8 paras 1, 42(1), (2), (6); and PARAS 473–474, 480, 504–507.
4   'Wholly or mainly' appears to have no uniform meaning, but it would seem that if more than one-half of the holding in question is occupied for the purposes of agriculture, the holding is wholly or mainly so occupied: see *Miller v Ottilie (Owners)* [1944] KB 188, [1944] 1 All ER 277, CA; *Berthelemy v Neale* [1952] 1 All ER 437, CA. See also *Glasgow Corpn v Johnstone* [1965] AC 609, [1965] 1 All ER 730, HL; *Wynn v Skegness UDC* [1966] 3 All ER 336, [1967] 1 WLR 52. The word 'mainly' probably means 'more than half'; cf *Fawcett Properties Ltd v Buckingham County Council* [1961] AC 636 at 669, [1960] 3 All ER 503 at 512, HL, per Lord Morton of Henryton.
5   As to the meaning of 'agriculture' see PARA 428.
6   Opencast Coal Act 1958 s 17(2)(b). Cf the Agricultural Holdings Act 1948 s 1(2) (repealed); the Agricultural Holdings Act 1986 s 1(4); and AGRICULTURAL LAND AND ALLOTMENTS vol 1 (2017) PARA 424.
7   Where the land comprised in a compulsory rights order consists of or includes land of which, immediately before the operative date of the order, the surface is occupied by one person and any of the subjacent strata by another, those subjacent strata are not to be treated as constituting a holding to which the Opencast Coal Act 1958 s 17, s 21 or s 29 applies: s 33(1), Sch 5 para 15(1). Where for any year compensation would be payable under s 17 in respect of a holding, but it may reasonably be assumed that part of the holding would have been prevented from being used in the same way and with the same standard of efficiency as in the period preceding the operative date of the order if the order had not been made, and the person carrying on the relevant undertaking had exercised the relevant rights and facilities in the manner in which, in those circumstances, he might reasonably have been expected to exercise them (see PARA 465), the provisions of s 18; and s 19 (repealed) apply in relation to that year as if that part of the holding were not comprised in the holding, and any reference to the entirety of the holding in s 18; and s 19 (repealed) is to be construed accordingly: Sch 5 para 14(1), (2). As to the meaning of 'year' see PARA 458; as to the meaning of 'relevant undertaking' see PARA 465 and as to the meaning of 'relevant rights and facilities' see PARA 458.
8   As to the meaning of 'coal' see PARA 414.
9   As to the meaning of 'minerals' see PARA 10.
10  As to the Coal Authority see PARA 52 et seq.
11  Opencast Coal Act 1958 s 17(2) (amended by the Coal Industry Act 1994 Sch 8 para 15(3)).

## 473. Annual compensation generally.

Where a compulsory rights order[1] comprises the whole or part of a holding[2], compensation is payable in respect of that holding for the year[3] beginning with the operative date[4], and for each subsequent year which begins with an anniversary of that date and falls wholly or partly within the period of occupation[5].

Subject (where different persons have been entitled to the rights for different parts of the year) to any apportionment[6], the liability to pay such compensation falls on the persons who, for the whole or any part of the year in question, have been entitled to the rights conferred by the order[7].

The compensation payable for any year in respect of a holding[8] is a sum equal to the annual borrowing cost for that year of the market value of the rights conferred by the compulsory rights order in relation to the holding[9].

Subject to certain provisions[10], the person entitled to any compensation payable for any year[11] in respect of a holding is the person who in respect of so much, if any, of the holding as is not comprised in the compulsory rights order, is for the time being entitled to occupy[12] that part of the holding, and in respect of so much of the holding as is comprised in the order, would be entitled for the time being to occupy it if the order had not been made[13].

Where the period for which a compulsory rights order is to have effect is extended[14] under the Opencast Coal Act 1958, the provisions as to annual compensation[15] have effect in relation to the additional period as if the rights conferred for that period had been conferred by a new compulsory rights order[16].

1  As to compulsory rights orders see the Opencast Coal Act 1958 s 4; and PARA 431 et seq. The power to make such orders has not been exercisable since 31 December 1999: see PARA 414.
2  Ie to which the Opencast Coal Act 1958 s 17 applies: see s 17(1). As to the meaning of 'holding' see PARA 472.
3  As to the meaning of 'year' see PARA 458.
4  Opencast Coal Act 1958 s 17(1)(a) (amended by the Coal Industry Act 1994 ss 52(2), 67(8), Sch 8 para 15(1), Sch 11 Pt II). As to the meaning of 'the operative date' see PARA 432. As to terminal compensation see PARA 475. As to additional compensation on re-occupation see PARA 480. As to the time when compensation payable under the Opencast Coal Act 1958 s 17 (or under s 17 as applied by s 29) accrues due see PARA 510. As to claims for compensation see PARA 509. As to the provisions for compensation in relation to certain restricted lettings, easements and similar rights see PARAS 491, 503.
5  Opencast Coal Act 1958 s 17(1)(b). As to the meaning of 'the period of occupation' see PARA 433.
6  Ie under the Opencast Coal Act 1958 s 35(3): see s 17(1A) .
7  Opencast Coal Act 1958 s 17(1A) (added by the Coal Industry Act 1994 Sch 8 para 15(2)).
8  Ie a holding to which the Opencast Coal Act 1958 s 17 applies: see s 18(1).
9  Opencast Coal Act 1958 s 18(1) (s 18 substituted by the Coal Industry Act 1994 Sch 8 para 16). Subject to the Opencast Coal Act 1958 s 35(2), any such compensation payable by virtue of s 17 is considered as accruing due from day to day and is apportionable in respect of time accordingly: s 35(3).
    Section 18 applies in relation to any compulsory rights order confirmed on or after the restructuring date (ie 31 October 1994: see PARA 50): see the Coal Industry Act 1994 Sch 8 para 16. On and after the restructuring date compensation payable under the Opencast Coal Act 1958 is payable in respect of any compulsory rights order made before that date as if the British Coal Corporation were the person on whose application that order was made: Coal Industry Act 1994 s 67(7), Sch 10 para 9(6). As to the British Coal Corporation see PARAS 49–50.
    The Opencast Coal Act 1958 ss 19, 20 were repealed by the Coal Industry Act 1994 Sch 8 paras 1, 17, Sch 11 Pt III, with effect in relation to any compulsory rights order confirmed on or after the restructuring date (ie 31 October 1994: see PARA 50).
10  Ie subject to the Opencast Coal Act 1958 s 17(3A): see s 17(3).
11  Ie by virtue of the Opencast Coal Act 1958 s 17: see s 17(3).
12  Any agreement for the letting of land or the grant of a licence in respect of land, where, before the agreement was entered into, the letting or grant was approved under the Agricultural Holdings Act 1986 s 2 or the Agricultural Holdings Act 1948 s 2 (repealed) (see AGRICULTURAL LAND AND ALLOTMENTS vol 1 (2017) PARA 427) (each of which relates to the effect of certain lettings and licences to occupy agricultural land, but excepts lettings and licences approved under that provision from the operation of that provision) are treated for the purposes of the Opencast Coal Act 1958 s 17 as conferring a right to occupy the land to which the agreement relates, if apart from s 34, Sch 6 para 24 it would not be treated as conferring such a right: Sch 6 para 24 (amended by the Agricultural Holdings Act 1986 s 100, Sch 14 para 32).
    For the purposes of the Opencast Coal Act 1958 Pt II (ss 17–36), in its application to land in which there is an interest which is subject to a mortgage (as to the meaning of which see PARA 439), a mortgagee is not to be taken to be entitled to occupy that land, or to be the person who, but for a compulsory rights order, would be entitled to occupy it, unless (1) the interest which is subject to the mortgage is the interest of the person who, apart from the mortgage, is entitled to

occupy that land, or who would, but for the order, be entitled to occupy it (s 43(1)(a)); and (2) the mortgagee is, to the extent of the interest comprised in the mortgage, and subject to the rights conferred by the order, in possession of the land or of its rents and profits (s 43(1)(b)). If, in those circumstances, a mortgagee is the person entitled to any annual compensation under Pt II (ie such compensation as is mentioned in s 35(2): s 43(7); and see PARA 510), any such compensation paid to him must be applied by him in or towards the satisfaction of interest arising under the mortgage, and, in so far as not so applied, must be applied towards the reduction of the principal debt secured by the mortgage: s 43(2).

13  Opencast Coal Act 1958 s 17(3) (amended by the Coal Industry Act 1994 Sch 8 para 15(4), Sch 11 Pt II).

Where (1) any compensation is payable for any year by virtue of the Opencast Coal Act 1958 s 17 in respect of any holding; and (2) the amount of that compensation falls to be calculated in accordance with s 18 by reference to the market value of rights which, if the compulsory rights order were not in force, could not be conferred for that year or any part of it except by or with the consent of one or more persons who are included in the persons directly concerned but do not fall within s 17(3), the entitlement to that compensation is apportioned, according to the extent to which those rights could not be conferred for that year or part of a year without their participation or consent, between those persons and any person falling within s 17(3): s 17(3A) (s 17(3A)–(3C) added by the Coal Industry Act 1994 Sch 8 para 15(5)).

Subject to the Opencast Coal Act 1958 s 17(3C), the persons entitled under s 17(3A) to a share of any compensation includes persons whose participation in or consent to the conferring of any right would be required if the right were conferred at some time after the beginning of the year or part of a year in question; and any apportionment under s 17(3A) is to take account of the length of the period for which any person is, during that year or part of a year, a person without whose participation or consent any right could not be conferred: s 17(3B).

No person is entitled under s 17(3A) to any share of any compensation in respect of any such easement or right as might give rise to an entitlement to compensation under s 31: s 17(3C).

These provisions do not apply in relation to any compulsory rights order confirmed before the restructuring date (ie 31 October 1994: see PARA 50): see the Coal Industry Act 1994 Sch 8 paras 1, 15(5)–(7), Sch 11 Pt III.

14  As to the variation and extension of orders see the Opencast Coal Act 1958 s 49(4), (5); and PARA 418.

15  Ie the Opencast Coal Act 1958 s 17; and s 18: see s 18(6).

16  Opencast Coal Act 1958 s 18(6) (s 18 substituted by the Coal Industry Act 1994 Sch 8 para 16).

## 474.  Calculation of annual compensation.

The compensation payable for any year[1] in respect of a holding to which the Opencast Coal Act 1958[2] applies is a sum equal to the annual borrowing cost for that year of the market value[3] of the rights conferred by the compulsory rights order[4] in relation to the holding[5].

In calculating for these purposes[6] the fair market price[7] for the grant of any rights, due allowance is to be made for any entitlement to compensation which may arise[8], under any of the provisions of the Act[9].

Nothing in the provisions of the Opencast Coal Act 1958 relating to annual compensation or its calculation[10] confers any entitlement to compensation in respect of the annual borrowing cost of any amount representing the value of any person's interest in coal[11], or any amount representing the value of any opportunity arising by virtue of an interest or right in or in relation to any land[12] to obtain or make use of any rights to win, work or get any coal[13].

1  As to the meaning of 'year' see PARA 458.
2  Ie the Opencast Coal Act 1958 s 17: see s 18(1). As to the meaning of 'holding' see PARA 472.
3  For the purposes of the Opencast Coal Act 1958 s 18, the market value of any rights conferred by a compulsory rights order is equal to the amount which, as at the date of entry, would (apart from the order) represent the fair market price, as between willing and independent parties, for the grant of those rights by a person entitled to grant them and for the period for which the order is to have effect: s 18(2). As to the meaning of 'the date of entry' see PARAS 433, PARA 443.
4  As to compulsory rights orders see Opencast Coal Act 1958 s 4; and PARA 431 et seq. The power to make such orders has not been exercisable since 31 December 1999: see PARA 414.

5 Opencast Coal Act 1958 s 18(1) (s 18 substituted by the Coal Industry Act 1994 s 52(8), Sch 8 para 16). The Opencast Coal Act 1958 s 18 applies in relation to compulsory rights orders confirmed on or after the restructuring date (ie 31 October 1994: see PARA 50): see the Coal Industry Act 1994 Sch 8 paras 1, 16; and PARA 473.

The Opencast Coal Act 1958 s 18 (as originally enacted) and ss 19, 20 (prior to their repeal) (additional annual compensation and special compensation for cost of removal) provided for compensation for a compulsory rights order by reference to annual value, and for additional annual compensation and for compensation for the cost of removal. Sections 19, 20 (both repealed) do not have effect in relation to any compulsory rights order confirmed on or after the restructuring date (ie 31 October 1994: see PARA 50): Coal Industry Act 1994 s 67(8), Sch 8 paras 1, 17, Sch 11 Pt III.

6 Ie the purposes of the Opencast Coal Act 1958 s 18: see s 18(3).
7 For the purposes of the Opencast Coal Act 1958 s 18, the annual borrowing cost for any year of any amount ('the market price') is the aggregate sum which would fall to be paid in that year by way of payments of interest and re-payments of capital if the market price had been borrowed on the date of entry on terms which: (1) required interest to be paid and capital to be repaid by way of the relevant number of equal annual instalments; and (2) provided for interest on outstanding capital to become due immediately before the time for the payment of each instalment, at an annual rate equal, as at the entry date, to the rate prescribed under s 35(8) (see PARA 510): s 18(4). 'The relevant number' means the number of years for which, when it was confirmed, the compulsory rights order was to have effect: s 18(4) (as so substituted).

As to market value see COMPULSORY ACQUISITION OF LAND vol 18 (2009) PARA 797 et seq.
8 Ie otherwise than by virtue of the Opencast Coal Act 1958 s 17: see s 18(3).
9 Opencast Coal Act 1958 s 18(3).
10 Ie nothing in the Opencast Coal Act 1958 s 17 or s 18: see s 18(5).
11 As to the meaning of 'coal' see PARA 414.
12 As to the meaning of 'land' see PARA 414.
13 Opencast Coal Act 1958 s 18(5).

B.   TERMINAL COMPENSATION

### 475. Terminal compensation; in general.

Where a compulsory rights order[1] comprises the whole or part of a holding[2], the Opencast Coal Act 1958[3] has effect as to compensation payable in respect of that holding by the person (called the 'final operator'[4]) who immediately before the end of the period of occupation is the person entitled to the rights conferred by the order[5].

Compensation payable in respect of a holding under these provisions consists of either or both of the following: (1) compensation by way of payment of cost of works[6]; and (2) compensation by reference to the diminution in value of the holding[7].

1 As to compulsory rights orders see the Opencast Coal Act 1958 s 4; and PARA 431 et seq. The power to make such orders has not been exercisable since 31 December 1999: see PARA 414.
2 Ie a holding to which the Opencast Coal Act 1958 s 21 applies: see s 21(1). As to the meaning of 'holding' see PARA 472. Section 17(2) (see PARA 472) has effect in relation to s 21 as it has effect in relation to s 17, and references to a holding to which s 21 applies are construed accordingly: s 21(2).

Where the land comprised in a compulsory rights order consists of or includes land of which, at the end of the period of occupation, the surface is owned by one person and any of the subjacent strata by another, the subjacent strata are not to be treated as constituting or forming part of a holding to which s 21 applies, or a holding in respect of which s 21 has effect as applied by s 29: s 33(1), Sch 5 para 15(2). See also PARA 472. As to the meaning of 'the period of occupation' see PARA 433. Where a compulsory rights order comprises the whole or part of a holding to which s 21 applies, and at the end of the period of occupation one person is the owner of part of the holding and another person the owner of another part (s 34, Sch 6 para 4(1)), then for the purposes of ss 21–23 each of those parts is to be treated as if it were a separate holding to which s 21 applied

(Sch 6 para 4(2)); but no compensation is payable by virtue of ss 21–23 in respect of land thus treated as a separate holding which does not include any of the land comprised in the order (Sch 6 para 4 proviso). See further PARA 504.

3    Ie the provisions of the Opencast Coal Act 1958 ss 21–23: see s 21(1).

4    For the purposes of the Opencast Coal Act 1958 s 22(3), Sch 3, the 'final operator' means the person who immediately before the end of the period of occupation is the person entitled to the rights conferred by the order: Sch 3 para 1 (definition added by the Coal Industry Act 1994 s 52(2), Sch 8 paras 1, 40(1)(a)). As to the meaning of 'the period of occupation' see PARA 433.

5    Opencast Coal Act 1958 s 21(1) (amended by the Coal Industry Act 1994 Sch 8 para 18).

6    Opencast Coal Act 1958 s 21(3)(a). As to cost of works see PARA 476.

7    Opencast Coal Act 1958 s 21(3)(b). As to compensation for diminished value see PARA 479. As to provisions for additional compensation on reoccupation see PARA 480.

## 476. Cost of works.

If at the end of the period of occupation[1] any land[2] forming part of the holding[3] and comprised in the compulsory rights order[4] has not been restored[5] to the condition[6] in which it was immediately before the date of entry[7], and after the end of that period expenses are reasonably incurred by any person in respect of work carried out, over and above the ordinary maintenance and use of the land, for the purpose of further restoring that land to or towards that condition or a substantially similar condition[8], compensation is payable[9] of an amount equal to those expenses[10]. Expenses are not treated as having been reasonably incurred if the work was begun more than 15 years after the end of the period of occupation[11] except in the case of work required for making good damage caused by the settlement of soil replaced in the course of restoring the land or any other damage to the land caused by subsidence which is attributable to anything done in the exercise of rights conferred by the compulsory rights order in question[12]. Where it is shown that the expenses incurred in carrying out any work exceeded the reasonable cost of the work, having regard to the prices of materials and rates of remuneration for services current at the time when the work is carried out[13], any claim for compensation in respect of those expenses is to be disallowed to the extent of the excess[14].

1    As to the meaning of 'the period of occupation' see PARA 433.

2    As to the meaning of 'land' see PARA 414.

3    As to the meaning of 'holding' see PARA 472.

4    As to compulsory rights orders see the Opencast Coal Act 1958 s 4; and PARA 431 et seq. The power to make such orders has not been exercisable since 31 December 1999: see PARA 414.

5    As to the meaning of 'restore' see PARA 424.

6    See PARA 462.

7    Opencast Coal Act 1958 s 22(1)(a). As to the meaning of 'the date of entry' see PARAS 433, PARA 443.

8    Opencast Coal Act 1958 s 22(1)(b). Where an agricultural holding held under a tenancy in relation to which the Agricultural Holdings Act 1986 applies, or a holding under a farm business tenancy, consists of or includes land which was comprised in a compulsory rights order, and after the end of the period of occupation the landlord proposes to carry out any such work as is mentioned in the Opencast Coal Act 1958 s 22(1)(b), the landlord or any person authorised by him may at all reasonable times enter upon the holding for the purpose of carrying out that work: s 37, Sch 7 para 6(1) (amended by the Agricultural Tenancies Act 1995 s 40, Schedule para 20(9)(a)). Nothing in the Opencast Coal Act 1958 Sch 7 para 6(1) affects any right exercisable by virtue of the Agricultural Holdings Act 1986 s 23 (which confers rights of entry for certain purposes): Opencast Coal Act 1958 Sch 7 para 6(2) (amended by the Agricultural Holdings Act 1986 s 100, Sch 14 para 33). In the Opencast Coal Act 1958 Sch 7 para 6(1), 'holding', in relation to a farm business tenancy, has the same meaning as in the Agricultural Tenancies Act 1995 (see AGRICULTURAL LAND AND ALLOTMENTS vol 1 (2017) PARA 402): Opencast Coal Act 1958 Sch 7 para 6(2A) (added by the Agricultural Tenancies Act 1995 Schedule para 20(9)(b)).

Where a holding to which the Landlord and Tenant Act 1927 Pt I (ss 1–17) applies consists of or includes land which was comprised in a compulsory rights order, and after the end of the period of occupation the landlord proposes to carry out any such work as is mentioned in the Opencast Coal Act 1958 s 22(1)(b), the landlord or any person authorised by him may at all reasonable times enter upon the holding for the purpose of carrying out that work: Sch 7 para 11(1). Nothing in Sch 7 para 11(1) affects any right exercisable by virtue of the Landlord and Tenant Act 1927 s 10 (which confers rights of entry for certain purposes): Opencast Coal Act 1958 Sch 7 para 11(2).

9 Compensation is payable from time to time as the expenses are incurred to the person who incurs them: Opencast Coal Act 1958 s 22(2)(a), (b).

10 Opencast Coal Act 1958 s 22(1), (2)(b). The provisions of Sch 3 have effect with regard to such compensation: s 22(3); and see PARAS 477–478. Such compensation is not payable in respect of work carried out on land that forms part of the holding and is land to which Sch 5 applies (see PARA 464): s 33(1), Sch 5 para 14(3).

11 Opencast Coal Act 1958 s 22(3), Sch 3 para 11(1).

12 Opencast Coal Act 1958 Sch 3 para 11(2). As to subsidence damage see PARA 182 et seq.

13 This reasonable cost is referred to in the Opencast Coal Act 1958 Sch 3 as 'the proper cost': Sch 3 para 1.

14 Opencast Coal Act 1958 Sch 3 para 12. Except in so far as objection is made to any work on the grounds mentioned in Sch 3 para 4(c) (see PARA 477), expenses incurred in carrying out any work may not be disallowed, wholly or in part, on the ground that the proper cost of that work, or of that work together with any other work, is greater than any increase attributable to it in the value of the land: Sch 3 para 13(1).

### 477. Procedure for obtaining cost of works compensation.

The final operator[1] is not required to pay compensation[2] in respect of expenses incurred in carrying out any work unless: (1) not less than the prescribed[3] length of time before the work was begun, the person incurring the expenses gave to the final operator notice in writing[4] containing adequate particulars of the work, together with a statement of the time when it was proposed to carry out the work and an estimate of the cost of the work[5]; and (2) at all reasonable times after the service of that notice, that person afforded to the final operator reasonable facilities to inspect the land[6] to which the notice related, in so far as he was in a position to afford such facilities[7].

Where such a notice has been given, the final operator, within the prescribed time after the giving of that notice, may serve on the applicant a counter-notice[8], stating that he objects: (a) to the work specified in the applicant's notice, or to such one or more items as may be specified in the counter-notice[9]; and (b) on such one or more grounds as may be specified in the counter-notice[10]. If more than one notice is given in respect of the same land, and the current notice specifies similar work to that specified in a previous notice the specified grounds are modified[11].

Where a notice has been given[12], and the applicant has incurred expenses in carrying out any of the work specified in that notice, and claims compensation in respect of those expenses, if the final operator has not served a counter-notice[13] in respect of that notice, he is not entitled to object to that claim on any of the specified grounds[14]; if the final operator has served such a counter-notice, he is not entitled to object to that claim on any of the specified grounds[15], except in so far as the claim relates to items which were specified in the counter-notice and the objection is on grounds which were so specified in relation to those items[16].

1 As to the meaning of 'final operator' see PARA 475.

2 'Compensation' means compensation under the Opencast Coal Act 1958 s 22 (see PARA 476): s 22(3), Sch 3 para 1.

3 As to the meaning of 'prescribed' see PARA 430.

4 The notice must be given not less than 56 days before the work, particulars of which are set out in the notice, is begun, by delivering it at or sending it in a prepaid registered letter or by the recorded delivery service to either the principal office of the final operator or such other office of

the final operator as it has notified in writing to the person giving the notice as an office at which such a notice may be served: Opencast Coal (Notice of Work) Regulations 1958, SI 1958/1649, reg 3 (amended by SI 1962/1696; and by virtue of the Coal Industry Act 1994 s 52(2), Sch 8 paras 1, 40).

5   Opencast Coal Act 1958 Sch 3 para 2(1)(a) (amended by the Coal Industry Act 1994 Sch 8 paras 1, 40). As to cost of works see PARA 476.

6   As to the meaning of 'land' see PARA 414.

7   Opencast Coal Act 1958 Sch 3 para 2(1)(b). The person giving such a notice is referred to in Sch 3 as 'the applicant': Sch 3 para 2(2).

8   The counter-notice must be served within 42 days after the notice has been given: Opencast Coal (Notice of Work) Regulations 1958, SI 1958/1649, reg 4 (amended by virtue of the Coal Industry Act 1994 Sch 8 paras 1, 40). As to the service of notices see PARA 422.

9   Opencast Coal Act 1958 Sch 3 para 3(a) (amended by the Coal Industry Act 1994 Sch 8 para 40).

10  Opencast Coal Act 1958 Sch 3 para 3(b). The specified grounds are:

    (1)     that the work could not reasonably be regarded as work falling within s 22(1)(b) (see PARA 476) (Sch 3 para 4(a));

    (2)     that the work is likely to be ineffective, or is by its nature unsuitable to the land in question, or is proposed to be carried out in an unsuitable way (Sch 3 para 4(b));

    (3)     that the estimated cost of the work (arrived at by agreement or by reference to the Upper Tribunal (Sch 3 paras 1, 6 (Sch 3 para 1 amended by SI 2009/1307)) is grossly disproportionate to any prospective increase attributable to the work in the value of the land (Sch 3 para 4(c));

    (4)     that the work, in a case where the former use (ie the use immediately before the operative date of the order (Sch 3 para 1)) of the land in question was agricultural, would not be appropriate to the use of that land for agriculture (as to the meaning of which see PARA 428) or, in any other case, would not be appropriate to the use of that land for its former use (Sch 3 para 4(d));

    (5)     that the work would not be required but for dilapidation, deterioration or damage which has occurred since the end of the period of occupation and is attributable to default on the part of the owner or of an occupier of the land (Sch 3 para 4(e));

    (6)     that the work, if carried out at the time specified in the applicant's notice, would be premature (Sch 3 para 4(f));

    (7)     that the work, if carried out at that time, would not have been carried out at the first reasonable opportunity after the end of the period of occupation, or within a reasonable time after that opportunity arose (Sch 3 para 4(g)).

The reference to default in head (5) is to be construed in accordance with Sch 3 para 7: Sch 3 para 7(1).

In relation to agricultural land, the reference to default on the part of the owner is construed as a reference to failure on his part to manage the land in accordance with the rules of good estate management, and the reference to default on the part of an occupier of the land is construed as a reference to failure on the part of such an occupier to fulfil his responsibilities to farm the land in accordance with the rules of good husbandry: Sch 3 para 7(2). In relation to any other land, the reference to default on the part of the owner is construed as a reference to failure on his part to deal with the land in a proper and due course of management, and the reference to default on the part of an occupier of the land is construed as a reference to failure on the part of such an occupier to maintain and use the land in a reasonable manner: Sch 3 para 7(3). The Agriculture Act 1947 ss 10, 11 (which prescribe tests for determining good estate management and good husbandry) apply for the purposes of the Opencast Coal Act 1958 Sch 3 para 7(2): Sch 3 para 7(4).

Subject to Sch 3 para 13(1) (see PARA 476), nothing in Sch 3 is to be construed as precluding the final operator from maintaining any objection to a claim for compensation, in so far as the objection is on any grounds other than those mentioned in Sch 3 para 4: Sch 3 para 13(2) (amended by the Coal Industry Act 1994 Sch 8 paras 1, 40).

11  Thus for the Opencast Coal Act 1958 Sch 3 para 4(c) there is substituted the ground that the aggregate cost of that work and of all relevant work specified in previous notices relating to the same land is grossly disproportionate to the aggregate increase attributable to all such work in the value of the land: Sch 3 para 5(1). Consequential amendments in the procedure for obtaining compensation in such circumstances are contained in Sch 3 para 5(2)–(6).

In Sch 3 para 4(c) (as substituted by Sch 3 para 5(1)) the reference to the aggregate cost of the new work and of all other relevant work specified in previous notices relating to the same land is a reference to the aggregate of the estimated cost of the new work (Sch 3 para 5(2)(a)), and the estimated cost of any similar work specified in any previous notice given by the applicant which is still outstanding on the relevant date (Sch 3 para 5(2)(b)), and the proper cost of any similar work specified in any previous notice given by the applicant in respect of which a claim for compensation has been allowed before the relevant date or is still outstanding on that date (Sch 3 para 5(2)(c)). In Sch 3 para 4(c) (as substituted by Sch 3 para 5(1)) the reference to the aggregate increase attributable to all such work as is therein mentioned in the value of the land is a reference to the aggregate of the prospective increase in that value attributable to the new work (Sch 3 para 5(3)(a)), and the prospective increase in that value attributable to any similar work specified in any previous notice given by the applicant which is still outstanding on the relevant date (Sch 3 para 5(3)(b)), and the increase in that value attributable to any similar work specified in any previous notice given by the applicant in respect of which a claim for compensation has been allowed before the relevant date or is still outstanding on that date (Sch 3 para 5(3)(c)). For these purposes: (1) a previous notice specifying similar work is taken to be outstanding on the relevant date if such a notice has been given before the relevant date and has not been withdrawn, and either the final operator has not before that date served a counter-notice objecting to that work, or, if the final operator has served such a counter-notice, that objection has before that date been withdrawn or determined by the Upper Tribunal not to be well-founded, and no claim for compensation has before the relevant date been made in respect of expenses incurred in carrying out that work (Sch 3 para 5(4)(a) (Sch 3 para 5(4), (5) amended by the Coal Industry Act 1994 Sch 8 paras 1, 40)); (2) a claim for compensation in respect of any work is taken to have been allowed before the relevant date if before that date a claim for compensation has been made in respect of expenses incurred in carrying out that work, and it has been agreed by the final operator, or determined by the Upper Tribunal, that compensation is payable in respect of those expenses, whether the amount of compensation so agreed or determined to be payable was the amount claimed or a different amount (Opencast Coal Act 1958 Sch 3 para 5(4)(b)); (3) a claim for compensation in respect of any work is taken to be still outstanding on the relevant date if at that date a claim for compensation has been made in respect of expenses incurred in carrying out that work, and that claim has not been withdrawn, and it has not been determined by the Upper Tribunal that no compensation is payable in respect of those expenses, but it has not been agreed by the final operator or determined by the Tribunal, that compensation is payable in respect of those expenses (Sch 3 para 5(4)(c)).

In Sch 3 para 5, 'similar work', in relation to the new work, means work directed to the same aspect of restoration as the new work; 'previous notice', in relation to the current notice, means a notice given under Sch 3 para 2 before the date on which the current notice was given; and 'the relevant date', in relation to the current notice, means the date on which the final operator serves a counter-notice objecting to the new work, or the date on which the time for serving such a counter-notice expires, whichever is the earlier: Sch 3 para 5(5). In Sch 3 paras 6–13 (except where the contrary is expressly provided) any reference to Sch 3 para 4(c), in relation to work to which Sch 3 para 4 applies in accordance with Sch 3 para 5(1), is construed as a reference to Sch 3 para 4(c) (as substituted by Sch 3 para 5(1)), and any reference in Sch 3 to the grounds mentioned in Sch 3 para 4 is construed accordingly: Sch 3 para 5(6).

12  Ie under the Opencast Coal Act 1958 Sch 3 para 2: see Sch 3 para 8).
13  Ie under the Opencast Coal Act 1958 Sch 3 para 3: see Sch 3 para 8(a).
14  Opencast Coal Act 1958 Sch 3 para 8(a) (Sch 3 para 8(a), (b) amended by the Coal Industry Act 1994 Sch 8 paras 1, 40). The grounds referred to are those set out in the Opencast Coal Act 1958 Sch 3 para 4. See, however, Sch 3 para 13(2).
15  The grounds referred to are those set out in the Opencast Coal Act 1958 Sch 3 para 4.
16  Opencast Coal Act 1958 Sch 3 para 8(b).

## 478. Determination of objections.

Where a notice has been given[1], and the final operator[2] has served a counter-notice objecting to the work specified in the notice, or to one or more items in it, the applicant, before beginning to carry out any item to which such an objection relates, may require the question whether the objection is well-founded to be referred to the Upper Tribunal[3]. If on such a reference the Upper Tribunal determines that the objection is not well-founded, and the applicant incurs expenses in carrying out any of the work to which the objection relates and claims compensation in respect of those expenses, then[4] the final operator is not entitled to object to that claim on any of the grounds which were the grounds of that objection[5].

1  Ie under the Opencast Coal Act 1958 s 22, Sch 3 para 2 (see PARA 477): see Sch 3 para 9(1).
2  As to the meaning of the 'final operator' see PARA 475.

3   Opencast Coal Act 1958 Sch 3 paras 1, 9(1) (Sch 3 para 1 amended by SI 2009/1307; Opencast Coal Act 1958 Sch 3 para 9 amended by the Coal Industry Act 1994 s 52(2), Sch 8 paras 1, 40). As to the Upper Tribunal see COURTS AND TRIBUNALS vol 24 (2010) PARA 883.

4   Ie in addition to any grounds on which the final operator is precluded by the Opencast Coal Act 1958 Sch 3 para 8 from objecting to that claim: see Sch 3 para 9(2).

5   Opencast Coal Act 1958 Sch 3 para 9(2). If on such a reference the Tribunal determines that the objection is well-founded, and the applicant incurs expenses in carrying out any of the work to which the objection relates, and claims compensation in respect of those expenses: (1) if the objection was on the grounds mentioned in any of Sch 3 para 4(a), (b), (c), (d), (e) (see PARA 477), no compensation is payable in respect of those expenses; (2) if the objection was on the grounds mentioned in Sch 3 para 4(f) (see PARA 477), no compensation is payable in respect of those expenses by virtue of the notice referred to in Sch 3 para 9(1)), but without prejudice to the service of a further notice under Sch 3 para 2 in respect of the work in question; (3) if the objection was on the grounds mentioned in Sch 3 para 4(g) (see PARA 477), the expenses are disallowed by virtue of this provision in so far as (but no further than) they were greater than they would have been if the work to which the objection related had been carried out at the first reasonable opportunity after the end of the period of occupation: Sch 3 para 9(3).

If, in a case where such a notice has been given, and the final operator has served a counter-notice objecting to the work specified in the notice, or to one or more items in it: (a) the applicant incurs expenses in carrying out work to which the objection relates, without having required the question whether the objection is well-founded to be referred to the Tribunal, and claims compensation in respect of those expenses; (b) on a reference to the Tribunal with respect to that claim the final operator maintains the objection; and (c) on that reference the Tribunal determines that the objection is well-founded, heads (1)–(3) apply (subject to the provisions of Sch 3 para 10)) as they apply in the circumstances mentioned in Sch 3 para 9(3): Sch 3 para 10(1) (amended by the Coal Industry Act 1994 Sch 8 paras 1, 40).

Where the objection was on the grounds mentioned in the Opencast Coal Act 1958 Sch 3 para 4(c) (see PARA 477) (otherwise than in a case falling within Sch 3 para 5) so much of Sch 3 para 10(1) as relates to the maintenance of the objection, and to a determination that the objection is well-founded, applies as if, in Sch 3 para 4(c), the reference to the estimated cost of the work were a reference to the proper cost of the work: Sch 3 para 10(2).

Where the objection was on the grounds mentioned in Sch 3 para 4(c) (as substituted by Sch 3 para 5(1): see PARA 477), so much of Sch 3 para 10(1) as relates to the maintenance of the objection, and to a determination that the objection is well-founded, applies as if, in Sch 3 para 5, any reference to the relevant date were a reference to the date on which the question whether compensation is payable in respect of expenses incurred in carrying out the new work (within the meaning of Sch 3 para 5) falls to be determined by the Tribunal, and the objection had been formulated accordingly: Sch 3 para 10(3).

## 479. Compensation for diminished value.

In the case of an agricultural holding[1] the following values must be computed: (1) where the entirety of the holding is comprised in the compulsory rights order[2], the value at the end of the period of occupation[3] of a freehold interest in the holding[4]; (2) where part of the holding is not comprised in the order, the value such an interest would have at the end of the period of occupation if that part of the holding were in the state[5] in which it was immediately before the date of entry[6], the remainder of the holding being taken to be in the state in which it is at the end of the period of occupation[7]; (3) in either case, the value which a freehold interest in the holding would have at the end of the period of occupation if the entirety of the holding were in the state in which it was immediately before the date of entry[8].

If the value of a freehold interest in the holding computed as in head (1) or head (2) above, as the case may be, but with the benefit of any prospective right to compensation by way of payment of cost of works[9] in respect of the holding, is less than the value of such an interest computed as in head (3) above, compensation is payable to the owner of the holding at the end of the period of occupation of an amount equal to the difference[10].

1   Ie a holding to which the Opencast Coal Act 1958 s 17(2) (see PARA 463, PARA 475) applies: see s 23(1).

2   As to compulsory rights orders see the Opencast Coal Act 1958 s 4; and PARA 431 et seq. The power to make such orders has not been exercisable since 31 December 1999: see PARA 414.

3   As to the meaning of 'the period of occupation' see PARA 433.

4   Opencast Coal Act 1958 s 23(2)(a). In computing value as mentioned in s 23(2)(a), (b) or (c), it must be assumed that a freehold interest in the holding is, in the circumstances, being offered for sale in the open market by a willing seller immediately after the end of the period of occupation, with vacant possession and free of incumbrances, other than any easement or similar right, any right restrictive of the use of land, and any mining lease or order conferring working rights affecting the holding or any part of it at that time: s 23(4). As to the meaning of 'similar right' see PARA 439; and as to the meaning of 'order conferring working rights' see PARA 439.
      'Incumbrance', in relation to any land, includes any interest in or right over that land (including any such right inuring for the benefit of the public or of a section of it): s 51(1).
      In the case of property of a kind not normally the subject of sales in the open market, the appropriate national authority may make regulations providing for value to be ascertained by reference to such matters as may be specified in the regulations: s 34, Sch 6 para 14. At the date at which this volume states the law no such regulations had been made. As to regulation-making powers generally see PARA 418. The appropriate national authority is the Secretary of State or where functions have been transferred in relation to Wales, the Welsh Ministers: see PARA 2.

5   See PARA 462.

6   As to the meaning of 'the date of entry' see PARAS 433, PARA 443.

7   Opencast Coal Act 1958 s 23(2)(b).

8   Opencast Coal Act 1958 s 23(2)(c).

9   As to cost of works compensation see PARA 476.

10  Opencast Coal Act 1958 s 23(1), (3). If the entirety of the holding consists of land to which Sch 5 applies (see PARA 464), no such compensation is payable: s 33(1), Sch 5 para 14(4). As to terminal compensation in such a case see PARAS 467–470. If only part of the holding consists of land to which Sch 5 applies, s 23 has effect in relation to the holding; but s 23(2), (4) applies as if that land did not form part of the holding, and any reference in s 23 to values computed in accordance with s 23(2)(a)–(c) is to be construed accordingly: Sch 5 para 14(5).

C.   ADDITIONAL COMPENSATION ON RE-OCCUPATION

**480. Additional compensation on re-occupation of holding.**

With a view to furthering the resumption of agriculture[1] on land[2] formerly comprised in a compulsory rights order[3], a person is entitled to additional compensation[4] in respect of a holding[5] qualifying for compensation in respect of agricultural land if he is in occupation of the holding[6] at the end of the period of occupation[7] or if he enters into occupation[8] of the holding at or after the end of that period, provided that he is occupying the holding, or enters into such occupation, wholly or mainly for the purposes of agriculture carried on by way of a trade or business[9].

Such additional compensation is payable by the person who immediately before the end of the period of occupation is the person entitled to the rights conferred by the order[10] and subject to certain provisions[11], is an amount equal to the annual compensation payable in respect of that holding[12] for the last 12 months[13] of the period of occupation[14].

1   As to the meaning of 'agriculture' see PARA 428.

2   As to the meaning of 'land' see PARA 414.

3   As to compulsory rights orders see the Opencast Coal Act 1958 s 4; and PARA 431 et seq. The power to make such orders has not been exercisable since 31 December 1999: see PARA 414.

4   Ie compensation under the Opencast Coal Act 1958 s 23A: see s 23A(1).

5   Ie a holding to which the Opencast Coal Act 1958 s 21 (see PARA 475) applies: see s 23A(1). As

to the meaning of 'holding' see PARA 472.

6   Where a compulsory rights order comprises the whole or part of a holding qualifying for compensation in respect of agricultural land, and at the end of the period of occupation one person is entitled to occupy part and another person to occupy another part of that holding, each of those parts is to be treated for the purposes of the Opencast Coal Act 1958 s 23A as if it were a separate holding so qualifying for compensation: s 34, Sch 6 para 4A (added by the Coal Industry Act 1975 s 6(3)).

7   As to the meaning of 'the period of occupation' see PARA 433.

8   The additional compensation on reoccupation is not payable to a person unless he is either (1) the person who, immediately before the operative date (as to the meaning of which see PARA 432) of the compulsory rights order, was entitled to occupy the holding (referred to in the Opencast Coal Act 1958 s 23A(2) as 'the original occupier'); or (2) a person who, before the end of the period of occupation, became entitled to the relevant interest in the holding in accordance with the disposition of the original occupier's estate effected by his will or codicil, or by intestacy, or by a combination of his will or codicil and intestacy: s 23A(2), (3) (s 23A added by the Coal Industry Act 1975 s 6(1)). For this purpose, 'the relevant interest' means the interest by which the person in question became entitled to occupy the holding, or would have become so entitled if the compulsory rights order had not been made; and 'will' includes a codicil: Opencast Coal Act 1958 s 23A(3). See also PARA 487.

9   Opencast Coal Act 1958 s 23A(1).

10   As to the payment of compensation see PARA 512.

11   Ie subject to the provisions of the Opencast Coal Act 1958 s 23A(5)–(7): see s 23A(4).

12   Ie compensation payable under the Opencast Coal Act 1958 s 17 (see PARA 473): see s 23A(4).
      Where the person entitled, immediately after the end of the period of occupation, to occupy the holding ceases, before he enters into occupation, to be entitled to occupy some part of it, his entry into the part which he remains entitled to occupy is to be treated for the purposes of s 23A(1) as entry into occupation of the holding (s 23A(6)(a)), but the additional compensation payable to him on reoccupation is such proportion of the compensation which would have been payable had he remained entitled to enter into occupation of the whole of the holding as is properly attributable to the part which he remains entitled to occupy (s 23A(6)(b)). Where these provisions apply and, immediately before the end of the period of occupation, only part of the holding concerned (called 'the compensatable portion') was comprised in the compulsory rights order, then (1) if the part of the holding which the person concerned ceased to be entitled to occupy comprises the whole of the compensatable portion, no additional compensation on reoccupation is payable to him (s 23A(7)(a)); (2) if the person concerned remains entitled to occupy the whole of the compensatable portion, such additional compensation payable to him is not to be reduced under s 23A(6)(b) (s 23A(7)(b)); and (3) in any other case, for the purpose of determining the proportion of the compensation properly attributable to any part of the holding under s 23A(6)(b), the holding is to be treated as consisting of the compensatable portion only (s 23A(7)(c)).

13   Subject to the provisions of the Opencast Coal Act 1958 s 23A(6), (7), in any case where the compensation last payable in respect of a holding under s 17 was in fact payable by reference to a period of less than 12 months, the compensation payable in respect of that holding by virtue of s 23A is an amount equal to the compensation which was so payable under s 17 multiplied by the fraction of which the numerator is 365 and the denominator is the number of days in the period by reference to which the compensation was so payable under that section: s 23A(5) (amended by the Coal Industry Act 1994 s 52(2), Sch 8 paras 1, 19(1)).

14   Opencast Coal Act 1958 s 23A(4) (amended by the Coal Industry Act 1994 Sch 8 paras 1, 19(1)). The Opencast Coal Act 1958 s 23A(4), (5) does not apply in relation to any compulsory rights order confirmed before the restructuring date (ie 31 October 1994: see PARA 50): see the Coal Industry Act 1994 Sch 8 para 19(1), (2).

### D.   TENANTS' RIGHTS

## 481.   Compensation for long-term improvements etc in relation to agricultural holdings.

Special provisions apply where the land[1] comprised in a compulsory rights order[2] consists of or includes land ('the tenant's land') which, immediately before the date of entry[3], constituted or formed part of an agricultural holding held under a tenancy in relation to which the Agricultural Holdings Act 1986 applies[4], and which is land on which, before that date, there had been carried out long-term improvements[5] qualifying for compensation under that Act[6], or there had been adopted a special system of farming so qualifying[7] for compensation[8].

If at the end of the period of occupation[9] the tenant's land has lost the benefit[10] of any of the improvements, or of the special system of farming, and that land is subject to the same tenancy as immediately before the date of entry, or is subject to a subsequent tenancy[11] under which the tenant has retained or succeeded to the relevant right to compensation, and the tenancy under which that land is then held continues after the end of the period of occupation, the provisions of the Agricultural Holdings Act 1986 as to compensation for long-term improvements[12] and for a special system of farming[13] apply subject to modification[14]. In such a case, deductions may fall to be made from the compensation in question[15].

1  As to the meaning of 'land' see PARA 414.
2  As to compulsory rights orders see the Opencast Coal Act 1958 s 4; and PARA 431 et seq. The power to make such orders has not been exercisable since 31 December 1999: see PARA 414.
3  As to the meaning of 'the date of entry' see PARAS 433, PARA 443.
4  Opencast Coal Act 1958 s 24(1)(a) (amended by the Agricultural Tenancies Act 1995 s 40, Schedule para 15(1), (2)). As to the meaning of 'agricultural holding' see PARA 428.
5  'Long-term improvement' means any improvement of a description specified in the Agricultural Holdings Act 1986 s 64(4), Sch 7 Pt I or Pt II (see AGRICULTURAL LAND AND ALLOTMENTS vol 1 (2017) PARA 529): Opencast Coal Act 1958 s 24(9) (amended by the Agricultural Holdings Act 1986 s 100, Sch 14 para 26).
6  Any reference to long-term improvements qualifying for compensation under the Agricultural Holdings Act 1986 is a reference to long-term improvements in respect of which, immediately before the date of entry, a tenant of the agricultural holding in question had a prospective right to compensation under the Agricultural Holdings Act 1986 on quitting the holding on the termination of his tenancy: Opencast Coal Act 1958 s 24(7)(a) (amended by the Agricultural Holdings Act 1986 Sch 14 para 26). As to the meaning of 'termination' see PARA 455. In determining whether the conditions specified in the Opencast Coal Act 1958 s 24(7)(a) or s 24(7)(b) are fulfilled, no account is to be taken of any provision of the Agricultural Holdings Act 1986 by which a right to compensation is conditional on the making of a claim or the giving of notice of intention to claim, or is liable to be affected by the service of a notice by the landlord: Opencast Coal Act 1958 s 24(8) (amended by the Agricultural Holdings Act 1986 Sch 14 para 26). As to adjustments between landlords and tenants see PARA 446 et seq.
    The references to the Agricultural Holdings Act 1986 in the Opencast Coal Act 1958 s 24(8) include references to the Agricultural Holdings Act 1948 (repealed): Opencast Coal Act 1958 s 24(9A) (added by the Agricultural Holdings Act 1986 Sch 14 para 26).
7  Any reference to a special system of farming (as to which see AGRICULTURAL LAND AND ALLOTMENTS vol 1 (2017) PARAS 548–549) qualifying for compensation under the Agricultural Holdings Act 1986 is a reference to a system of farming in respect of which, immediately before the date of entry, a tenant of the agricultural holding in question had a prospective right to compensation under s 70 on quitting the holding on the termination of his tenancy: Opencast Coal Act 1958 s 24(7)(b) (amended by the Agricultural Holdings Act 1986 Sch 14 para 26).
    The references to the Agricultural Holdings Act 1986 in the Opencast Coal Act 1958 s 24(7) include references to the Agricultural Holdings Act 1948 (repealed): Opencast Coal Act 1958 s 24(9A) (added by the Agricultural Holdings Act 1986 Sch 14 para 26). The reference to the Agricultural Holdings Act 1986 s 70 in the Opencast Coal Act 1958 s 24(7)(b) includes a reference to the Agricultural Holdings Act 1948 s 56 (repealed): Opencast Coal Act 1958 s 24(9A).
8  Opencast Coal Act 1958 s 24(1)(b) (amended by the Agricultural Holdings Act 1986 Sch 14 para 26). The references to the Agricultural Holdings Act 1986 in the Opencast Coal Act 1958 s 24(1)(b) include references to the Agricultural Holdings Act 1948 (repealed): Opencast Coal Act 1958 s 24(9A).
9  As to the meaning of 'the period of occupation' see PARA 433.
10 The tenant's land is to be taken to have lost the benefit of a long-term improvement if that benefit has been lost, wholly or in part, without being replaced by another long-term improvement of comparable benefit to the land (Opencast Coal Act 1958 s 24(4)(a)); and the land is to be taken to have lost the benefit of a special system of farming if the increased value attributable to that system has been lost, wholly or in part, without being regained by the continuous adoption of a system of comparable benefit to the land (s 24(4)(b)).

11 The tenant's land is taken to be subject to such a subsequent tenancy if either (1) by virtue of the Agricultural Holdings Act 1986 s 69(1) or Sch 9 para 5(1) (which relate respectively to improvements made during one of a series of tenancies) (see AGRICULTURAL LAND AND ALLOTMENTS vol 1 (2017) PARA 531), the same tenant would have the like right to compensation in right of the subsequent tenancy as he would have had in right of the previous tenancy (Opencast Coal Act 1958 s 24(5)(a) (amended by the Agricultural Holdings Act 1986 Sch 14 para 26)); or (2) by virtue of the Agricultural Holdings Act 1986 s 69(2), s 69(3) or Sch 9 Pt I para 5(2) (which relate respectively to improvements paid for by an incoming tenant) (see AGRICULTURAL LAND AND ALLOTMENTS vol 1 (2017) PARA 531), the tenant under the subsequent tenancy would have the like right to compensation as the tenant would have had under the previous tenancy (Opencast Coal Act 1958 s 24(5)(b) (amended by the Agricultural Holdings Act 1986 Sch 14 para 26)).

12 See AGRICULTURAL LAND AND ALLOTMENTS vol 1 (2017) PARA 533 et seq. The provisions of the Agricultural Holdings Act 1986 referred to in the Opencast Coal Act 1958 s 24(2) are taken to include any provisions of the Agricultural Holdings Act 1986 as to the making of claims for any such compensation as is mentioned in the Opencast Coal Act 1958 s 24(2), as to the calculation of any such compensation and the settlement or determination of such claims, as to the recovery of any such compensation, and as to any other matters incidental to it (s 24(6) (amended by the Agricultural Holdings Act 1986 Sch 14 para 26)); provided that any provisions of the Agricultural Holdings Act 1986 as to the giving of notice of intention to make a claim applies with the modification that the time for giving such a notice is any time not later than three months after the end of the period of occupation; and s 83(4) (which relates to the time for settling such claims) applies with the substitution, for the reference to eight months from the termination of the tenancy, of a reference to eight months from the end of the period of occupation: Opencast Coal Act 1958 s 24(6) proviso (amended by the Agricultural Holdings Act 1984 s 10(1), Sch 3 para 29).

13 See AGRICULTURAL LAND AND ALLOTMENTS vol 1 (2017) PARAS 548–549.

14 Opencast Coal Act 1958 s 24(2) (amended by the Agricultural Holdings Act 1986 Sch 14 para 26). The provisions of the Agricultural Holdings Act 1986 referred to in the text apply as if (1) the tenant's land were in the state (see PARA 462) in which it was immediately before the date of entry (Opencast Coal Act 1958 s 24(3)(a) (amended by the Agricultural Holdings Act 1986 Sch 14 para 26)); and (2) the tenancy under which that land is held at the end of the period of occupation had terminated immediately after the end of that period and the tenant had then quitted the holding (Opencast Coal Act 1958 s 24(3)(b)).

If, however, in a case where long-term improvements qualifying for compensation under the Agricultural Holdings Act 1986 had been carried out on the tenant's land, if the tenant's land has lost the benefit of some of those improvements, but has not lost the benefit of all of them, the provisions of the Agricultural Holdings Act 1986 referred to in the text apply as mentioned in the Opencast Coal Act 1958 s 24(3)(a), (b), but as if the improvements of which the tenant's land has not lost the benefit had not been long-term improvements qualifying for compensation under the Agricultural Holdings Act 1986: Opencast Coal Act 1958 s 24(3) proviso.

The references to compensation under the Agricultural Holdings Act 1986 in the Opencast Coal Act 1958 s 24(3) include references to the Agricultural Holdings Act 1948 (repealed): Opencast Coal Act 1958 s 24(9A) (added by the Agricultural Holdings Act 1986 Sch 14 para 26).

15 See PARA 482.

## 482. Deductions from compensation in relation to agricultural holdings.

Where a tenant of an agricultural holding[1] is entitled to compensation[2] in respect of land[3] constituting or forming part of that holding, there must be deducted from the amount of that compensation[4], the amount of any compensation which would have been recoverable from the tenant by the landlord in respect of compensation for dilapidation, deterioration or damage for which the tenant is responsible[5], or in respect of compensation for general reduction in the value of the holding due to the tenant's failure to fulfil his responsibilities[6], if the tenancy[7] under which that land was held immediately before the date of entry[8] had terminated immediately before that date and the tenant had then quitted the holding on the termination of his tenancy[9].

1 As to the meaning of 'agricultural holding' see PARA 428.
2 Ie compensation under the Opencast Coal Act 1958 s 24 (see PARA 481): see s 25(1).
3 As to the meaning of 'land' see PARA 414.
4 Ie calculated apart from the Opencast Coal Act 1958 s 25(1).

5   Ie under the Agricultural Holdings Act 1986 s 71: see AGRICULTURAL LAND AND ALLOTMENTS vol 1 (2017) PARAS 553–554.
6   Ie under the Agricultural Holdings Act 1986 s 72: see AGRICULTURAL LAND AND ALLOTMENTS vol 1 (2017) PARAS 557–559.
7   As to the meaning of 'tenancy' see PARA 444.
8   As to the meaning of 'the date of entry' see PARAS 433, PARA 443.
9   Opencast Coal Act 1958 s 25(1) (amended by the Agricultural Holdings Act 1986 s 100, Sch 14 para 27).
   For this purpose (1) no account is to be taken of any dilapidation or deterioration of, or damage to, any part of the holding which was not comprised in the compulsory rights order, or of any reduction in the value of any such part of the holding (Opencast Coal Act 1958 s 25(1) proviso); and (2) any provision of the Agricultural Holdings Act 1986, whereby any right to compensation is conditional upon the making of a claim, or the giving of notice of intention to make a claim, is to be disregarded (Opencast Coal Act 1958 s 25(2) (amended by the Agricultural Holdings Act 1986 Sch 14 para 27)).
   In the Opencast Coal Act 1958 s 25 references to the Agricultural Holdings Act 1986 and to ss 71, 72 include respectively references to the Agricultural Holdings Act 1948 and to ss 57, 58 (repealed): Opencast Coal Act 1958 s 25(2A) (added by the Agricultural Holdings Act 1986 Sch 14 para 27).

### E.   COMPENSATION FOR SHORT-TERM AGRICULTURAL IMPROVEMENTS

## 483.   Provisions as to compensation.

Where, in the exercise of rights conferred by a compulsory rights order[1], any person occupies any land[2] which, immediately before the date of entry[3], was agricultural land[4] and was not comprised in a farm business tenancy[5], compensation is payable[6] by that person in respect of any improvements[7] or other such matters[8] in relation to that land[9].

Compensation is not payable[10] where a person's occupation of any land, in exercise of rights conferred by a compulsory rights order, is confined to replacing in occupation a person previously entitled to exercise the rights conferred by that order[11].

Where such compensation is payable in respect of any improvements or other matters, the compensation is to be of an amount equal to the amount of the compensation which would have been payable in respect of those improvements or matters under the Agricultural Holdings Act 1986[12] if: (1) where the land in question did not form part of an agricultural holding immediately before that date of entry, it had formed part of such a holding immediately before that date[13]; and (2) in any case, the tenancy of the agricultural holding comprising that land had terminated on the date of entry and the tenant had then quitted the holding[14].

1   As to compulsory rights orders see the Opencast Coal Act 1958 s 4; and PARA 431 et seq. The power to make such orders has not been exercisable since 31 December 1999: see PARA 414.
2   As to the meaning of 'land' see PARA 414.
3   As to the meaning of 'the date of entry' see PARAS 433, PARA 443.
4   As to the meaning of 'agricultural land' see PARA 440.
5   As to the meaning of 'farm business tenancy' see PARA 429.
6   The person entitled to any compensation so payable in the case of land which, immediately before the date of entry, was occupied by a tenant, is that tenant (Opencast Coal Act 1958 s 26(4)(a)); and in any other case, is the person who was the owner of the land immediately before the date of entry (s 26(4)(b)). As to the meaning of 'owner' see PARA 421.
7   See the Opencast Coal Act 1958 s 26(2)(a). The improvements referred to in the text are those of the following descriptions which had been carried out on the land before the date of entry: mole drainage and works to secure its efficient functioning; protection of fruit trees against animals; chalking of land; clay burning; liming of land; application to land of purchased (including artificial) manure; and consumption on the land of corn (whether or not produced there) or of cake or other feeding stuff not produced there, by horses, cattle, sheep or pigs, or by poultry folded on the land as part of a system of farming practised there: s 26(2)(a), Sch 4 Pt I.

If, by virtue of the power conferred by the Agricultural Holdings Act 1986 s 91, the provisions of Sch 8 are varied, the appropriate national authority may by order make such corresponding variations in the provisions of the Opencast Coal Act 1958 Sch 4 Pts I, II, III as he may consider appropriate: s 26(5) (amended by the Agricultural Holdings Act 1986 s 100, Sch 14 para 28). See also PARA 486. The appropriate national authority is the Secretary of State or where functions have been transferred in relation to Wales, the Welsh Ministers: see PARA 2.

8   Ie matters of the following descriptions which applied to the land immediately before the date of entry: growing crops, and severed or harvested crops and produce, grown on the land in the year ending with that date; seeds sown and cultivations, fallows and acts of husbandry performed there at the tenant's expense; pasture laid down with clover, grass, lucerne, sainfoin or other seeds, being either pasture paid for by the tenant on entering on the land or laid down at his expense otherwise than under an obligation imposed on him by written agreement to lay it down to replace temporary pasture which was there when he entered on the land and for which he did not pay; and acclimatisation, hefting or settlement of hill sheep on hill land: Opencast Coal Act 1958 s 26(2)(b), Sch 4 Pt II. If immediately before the date of entry the land was not occupied by the tenant these descriptions are modified by omitting, in the description of seeds sown, the reference to the tenant's expense, and, in the description of pasture, the words 'being either' to the end of that description: s 26(2) proviso, Sch 4 Pt III.
9   Opencast Coal Act 1958 s 26(1) (amended by the Coal Industry Act 1994 s 52(2), Sch 8 para 20(1); and the Agricultural Tenancies Act 1995 s 40, Schedule para 17(2)).
10  Ie by virtue of the Opencast Coal Act 1958 s 26: see s 26(1A).
11  Opencast Coal Act 1958 s 26(1A) (added by the Coal Industry Act 1994 Sch 8 para 20(2)).
12  As to such compensation see AGRICULTURAL LAND AND ALLOTMENTS vol 1 (2017) PARAS 539.
13  Opencast Coal Act 1958 s 26(3)(a) (s 26(3) amended by the Coal Industry Act 1994 s 67(8), Sch 8 para 20(3), Sch 11 Pt II; and the Agricultural Holdings Act 1986 Sch 14 para 28). As to the meaning of 'agricultural holding' see PARA 428.
14  Opencast Coal Act 1958 s 26(3)(b). The reference in s 26(3) to the Agricultural Holdings Act 1986 includes a reference to the Agricultural Holdings Act 1948 (repealed): Opencast Coal Act 1958 s 26(5A) (added by the Agricultural Holdings Act 1986 Sch 14 para 28).

## 484.   Terminal compensation.

The provisions of the Opencast Coal Act 1958 relating to terminal compensation[1] apply, with modifications[2], where compensation for short-term agricultural improvements and related matters[3] is payable, and the land in relation to which that compensation is payable constitutes or forms part of a holding qualifying for annual compensation under the Act[4].

1   Ie the Opencast Coal Act 1958 ss 21–23: see PARA 475 et seq.
2   The modifications are that the Opencast Coal Act 1958 s 22 applies as if any reference to the condition in which the land was immediately before the date of entry were, where applicable, a reference to the condition in which that land would have been, immediately before that date, if the improvements or other matters in question had not been carried out, or had not applied to that land (s 34, Sch 6 para 16(2)); and that s 23 applies as if, for the value mentioned in s 23(2)(c), there were substituted the value (computed as prescribed in s 23(4)) which, at the end of the period of occupation, a freehold interest in the holding would have if (1) those improvements or other matters had not been carried out, or had not applied to the land in question (Sch 6 para 16(3)(a), (4)); but (2) in all other respects the entirety of the holding were in the state in which it was immediately before the date of entry (Sch 6 para 16(3)(b), (4)).
3   Ie compensation under the Opencast Coal Act 1958 s 26: see PARA 483.
4   Opencast Coal Act 1958 Sch 6 para 16(1). The holding referred to is one to which s 21 applies: see PARA 475.

## 485.   Farm business tenancies: tenant's right to compensation for improvements etc.

Where (1) any part of the land[1] comprised in a compulsory rights order[2] was held, immediately before the date of entry[3], under a farm business tenancy[4]; (2) there have been provided in relation to the land which is both so comprised and so held ('the tenant's land') tenant's improvements[5] in respect of which, immediately before that date, the tenant had a prospective right to compensation[6] on quitting the holding[7] on the termination[8] of the tenancy[9]; (3) at the end of the period of occupation[10], the tenant's land has lost the benefit of any such improvement[11]; and (4) immediately after the end of that period, the tenant's land is comprised in the same tenancy as immediately before the date of entry, or is comprised in a subsequent farm business tenancy at the end of which the tenant is not deprived[12], of his right to compensation[13] in respect of any tenant's improvement[14] provided during the earlier tenancy in relation to the tenant's land[15], the Agricultural Tenancies Act 1995[16] applies[17] as if the tenant's land were in the state in which it was immediately before the date of entry, and the tenancy under which that land is held at the end of the period of occupation had terminated immediately after the end of that period and the tenant had then quitted the holding[18].

1 As to the meaning of 'land' see PARA 414.
2 As to compulsory rights orders see the Opencast Coal Act 1958 s 4; and PARA 431 et seq. The power to make such orders has not been exercisable since 31 December 1999: see PARA 414.
3 As to the meaning of 'the date of entry' see PARAS 433, PARA 443.
4 Opencast Coal Act 1958 s 25A(1)(a) (s 25A added by the Agricultural Tenancies Act 1995 s 40, Schedule para 16). As to the meaning of 'farm business tenancy' see PARA 429.
5 In the Opencast Coal Act 1958 s 25A, 'tenant's improvement' has the same meaning as in the Agricultural Tenancies Act 1995 s 15 (see AGRICULTURAL LAND AND ALLOTMENTS vol 1 (2017) PARA 410): Opencast Coal Act 1958 s 25A(6).
6 Ie compensation under the Agricultural Tenancies Act 1995 s 16 (see AGRICULTURAL LAND AND ALLOTMENTS vol 1 (2017) PARA 411): see the Opencast Coal Act 1958 s 25A(1)(b).
7 In the Opencast Coal Act 1958 s 25A, 'holding', in relation to a farm business tenancy, has the same meaning as in the Agricultural Tenancies Act 1995 s 38(1) (see AGRICULTURAL LAND AND ALLOTMENTS vol 1 (2017) PARA 402): Opencast Coal Act 1958 s 25A(6).
8 In the Opencast Coal Act 1958 s 25A, 'termination', in relation to a tenancy, has the same meaning as in the Agricultural Tenancies Act 1995 s 38(1) (see AGRICULTURAL LAND AND ALLOTMENTS vol 1 (2017) PARA 405): Opencast Coal Act 1958 s 25A(6).
9 Opencast Coal Act 1958 s 25A(1)(b).
10 As to the meaning of 'the period of occupation' see PARA 433.
11 Opencast Coal Act 1958 s 25A(1)(c).
12 Ie by virtue of the Agricultural Tenancies Act 1995 s 23(3) (see AGRICULTURAL LAND AND ALLOTMENTS vol 1 (2017) PARA 415): see the Opencast Coal Act 1958 s 25A(1)(d). For the purposes of s 25A(1), the Agricultural Tenancies Act 1995 s 22(2) (which requires notice to be given of the intention to make a claim: see AGRICULTURAL LAND AND ALLOTMENTS vol 1 (2017) PARA 418) is disregarded: Opencast Coal Act 1958 s 25A(2).
   For the purposes of s 25A(1), (4), the tenant's land is taken to have lost the benefit of a tenant's improvement if the benefit of that improvement has been lost, wholly or in part, without being replaced by another improvement of comparable benefit to the land: s 25A(5).
13 Ie compensation under the Agricultural Tenancies Act 1995 s 16 (see AGRICULTURAL LAND AND ALLOTMENTS vol 1 (2017) PARA 411): see the Opencast Coal Act 1958 s 25A(1)(d).
14 In the Opencast Coal Act 1958 s 25A, references to the provision of a tenant's improvement have the same meaning as in the Agricultural Tenancies Act 1995 s 15 (see AGRICULTURAL LAND AND ALLOTMENTS vol 1 (2017) PARA 411): Opencast Coal Act 1958 s 25A(6).
15 Opencast Coal Act 1958 s 25A(1)(d).
16 Ie the Agricultural Tenancies Act 1995 Pt III (ss 15–27) (see AGRICULTURAL LAND AND ALLOTMENTS vol 1 (2017) PARA 410 et seq): see the Opencast Coal Act 1958 s 25A(3).
17 Ie subject to the Opencast Coal Act 1958 s 25A(4), which provides that where the tenant's land has lost the benefit of some tenant's improvements but has not lost the benefit of all of them, the Agricultural Tenancies Act 1995 Pt III applies as mentioned in the Opencast Coal Act 1958 s 25A(3), but as if the improvements of which the tenant's land has not lost the benefit had not been tenant's improvements (see s 25A(4)).
18 Opencast Coal Act 1958 s 25A(3).

## 486.   Compensation for short-term improvements etc.

Where the land[1] comprised in a compulsory rights order[2] consists of or includes land which, immediately before the date of entry[3], was agricultural land[4] used as a market garden[5], and was not comprised in a farm business tenancy[6], the provisions of the Opencast Coal Act 1958 in respect of compensation for short-term improvements and related matters[7] have effect, subject to modifications[8] in relation to that land[9].

1   As to the meaning of 'land' see PARA 414.
2   As to compulsory rights orders see the Opencast Coal Act 1958 s 4; and PARA 431 et seq. The power to make such orders has not been exercisable since 31 December 1999: see PARA 414.
3   As to the meaning of 'the date of entry' see PARAS 433, PARA 443.
4   As to the meaning of 'agricultural land' see PARA 440.
5   'Market garden' is not defined in the Opencast Coal Act 1958; see, however, AGRICULTURAL LAND AND ALLOTMENTS vol 1 (2017) PARA 424.
6   Opencast Coal Act 1958 s 28(1) (amended by the Agricultural Tenancies Act 1995 s 40, Schedule para 18(2)). As to the meaning of 'farm business tenancy' see PARA 429.
7   Ie the provisions of the Opencast Coal Act 1958 s 26 (see PARA 483): see s 28(2).
8   Unless, immediately before the date of entry, the land was occupied by a tenant, Opencast Coal Act 1958 s 26 has effect as if the following descriptions of improvements were included among those specified in Sch 4 Pt I (see PARA 483): planting of standard or other fruit trees or fruit bushes permanently set out, or of strawberry plants, or of asparagus, rhubarb and other vegetable crops which continue productive for two years or more; and the erection, alteration or enlargement of buildings for the purpose of the trade or business of a market gardener: s 28(2), Sch 4 Pt VI.
       Where the land in question, immediately before the date of entry, was occupied by a tenant, s 28(2) does not apply to any improvements of a description specified in Sch 4 Pt VI unless they are improvements in respect of which the Agricultural Holdings Act 1986 s 79(2)–(5) (which relates to market gardens) (see AGRICULTURAL LAND AND ALLOTMENTS vol 1 (2017) PARA561 et seq) has effect, whether by virtue of an agreement or of a direction given under s 80(2): Opencast Coal Act 1958 s 28(3) (amended by the Agricultural Holdings Act 1986 s 100, Sch 14 para 30).
       If, by virtue of the power conferred by the Agricultural Holdings Act 1986 s 91, the provisions of Sch 10 are varied, the appropriate national authority may by order make such corresponding variations in the provisions of the Opencast Coal Act 1958 Sch 4 Pt VI as he may consider appropriate: s 28(5) (amended by the Agricultural Holdings Act 1986 Sch 14 para 30). The appropriate national authority is the Secretary of State or where functions have been transferred in relation to Wales, the Welsh Ministers: see PARA 2.
9   Opencast Coal Act 1958 s 28(1), (2). In relation to land falling within s 28(1), any reference in the preceding provisions of Pt II (ss 17–36) to rights under the Agricultural Holdings Act 1986 s 10 (see AGRICULTURAL LAND AND ALLOTMENTS vol 1 (2017) PARA 436) includes a reference to rights under s 10 as extended by s 79(3) (see AGRICULTURAL LAND AND ALLOTMENTS vol 1 (2017) PARA 565): Opencast Coal Act 1958 s 28(4) (amended by the Agricultural Holdings Act 1986 Sch 14 para 30).

## 487.   Compensation for loss in respect of a forced sale.

Where, in consequence of the confirmation of a compulsory rights order[1], a person incurs a loss in respect of a forced sale of any property consisting of: (1) livestock, vehicles, plant, equipment or other chattels which are kept on a holding[2], or which are used for the purposes of such a holding; or (2) a fixture or building, not falling within head (1) above, which he has removed from such a holding[3], he is entitled[4] to compensation from the person on whose application the compulsory rights order was made of an amount equal to that loss[5].

This does not apply except where the person incurring the loss is the person who is for the time being entitled to occupy so much of the holding as is comprised in the order, or would be entitled for the time being to occupy it if the order had not been made[6].

Where, in the case of any sale in respect of which compensation is payable[7], a person other than the person who applied for the order is entitled, on the effective date[8] of the sale, to the rights conferred by the compulsory rights order, that compensation is payable by the person entitled to those rights, instead of by the person who applied for the order[9].

A person is not entitled to such compensation in respect of a forced sale unless he has given to the person potentially liable[10] not less than ten days' notice[11] of the intended sale, and has, before the sale, afforded to the person to whom the notice was given, or any person designated for the purpose by him, reasonable facilities to inspect the property intended to be sold, in so far as he was in a position to afford such facilities[12].

1  As to compulsory rights orders see the Opencast Coal Act 1958 s 4; and PARA 431 et seq. The power to make such orders has not been exercisable since 31 December 1999: see PARA 414.
2  Ie a holding to which, when the order becomes operative, the Opencast Coal Act 1958 s 17 applies: see s 27(1).
3  Ie in pursuance of the Agricultural Holdings Act 1986 s 10 (see AGRICULTURAL LAND AND ALLOTMENTS vol 1 (2017) PARA 436): see the Opencast Coal Act 1958 s 27(1).
4  Ie subject to the provisions of the Opencast Coal Act 1958 s 27(2)–(5): see s 27(1).
5  Opencast Coal Act 1958 s 27(1) (amended by the Agricultural Holdings Act 1986 s 100, Sch 14 para 29; and the Coal Industry Act 1994 s 52(2), Sch 8 para 21(1)).
6  Opencast Coal Act 1958 s 27(2). In relation to land comprised in a compulsory rights order, any reference to the person who would be entitled to occupy that land if the order had not been made is to be construed, in relation to any time before the date of entry as a reference to the person who is for the time being entitled to occupy that land: s 51(8). As to the meaning of 'the date of entry' see PARAS 433 , PARA 443.
7  Ie compensation payable under the Opencast Coal Act 1958 s 27: s 27(2A).
8  'Effective date', in relation to a sale, means the date on which the property sold becomes the property of the purchaser: Opencast Coal Act 1958 s 27(5) (added by the Coal Industry Act 1994 Sch 8 para 21(2), (4)).
9  Opencast Coal Act 1958 s 27(2A) (added by the Coal Industry Act 1994 Sch 8 para 21(2), (4)).
10  'The person potentially liable', in relation to a notice relating to a sale, means the person on whom the liability to pay the compensation will fall on the effective date of the sale if the person entitled to the rights conferred by the compulsory rights order in question does not change before that date: Opencast Coal Act 1958 s 27(5).
11  As to the giving of notices see PARA 422.
12  Opencast Coal Act 1958 s 27(3) (amended by the Coal Industry Act 1994 Sch 8 para 21(3)).

## (iv) Non-agricultural Land

### 488. Meaning of 'holding'.

Where land[1], immediately before the operative date[2] of a compulsory rights order[3], was occupied as a unit, but was not so occupied wholly or mainly for the purposes of agriculture[4] carried on by way of a trade or business, the entirety of that land (excluding the coal[5] and any other minerals[6] vested in the Coal Authority[7] or any licensed operator[8]) constitutes a holding to which the compensation provisions of the Opencast Coal Act 1958 relating to non-agricultural land[9] apply[10].

1  As to the meaning of 'land' see PARA 414.
2  As to the meaning of 'the operative date' see PARA 432.
3  As to compulsory rights orders see the Opencast Coal Act 1958 s 4; and PARA 431 et seq. The power to make such orders has not been exercisable since 31 December 1999: see PARA 414.
4  As to the meaning of 'agriculture' see PARA 428. See also the Opencast Coal Act 1958 s 17(2); and PARA 472.

5  As to the meaning of 'coal' see PARA 414.
6  As to the meaning of 'minerals' see PARA 10.
7  As to the Coal Authority see PARA 52 et seq.
8  Ie a 'licensed operator' within the meaning of the Coal Industry Act 1994 (see PARA 58): see the Opencast Coal Act 1958 s 29(1).
9  Ie the provisions of the Opencast Coal Act 1958 s 29 (see PARA 489): see s 29(1).
10  Opencast Coal Act 1958 s 29(1) (amended by the Coal Industry Act 1994 s 52(2), Sch 8 para 22(1)).

### 489. Types of compensation payable.

Annual compensation[1], and compensation in respect of forced sales[2] are payable by and to the same persons[3] and in the same manner as in the case of agricultural land[4]. Terminal compensation[5] is also payable as in the case of agricultural land[6], but special rules apply to compensation for non-agricultural tenants' improvements[7].

1  Ie compensation payable under the Opencast Coal Act 1958 s 17 or s 18: see PARA 474.
2  Ie compensation payable under the Opencast Coal Act 1958 s 27: see PARA 487. For this purpose the provisions of s 27 have effect as if in s 27(1) for the reference to such a fixture or building as is there mentioned there were substituted a reference to any trade or other fixture (not falling within s 27(1)(a)) which the person in question has lawfully removed from the holding: s 29(2) proviso.
3  See the Opencast Coal Act 1958 s 17(3)–(3B); and PARA 473; applied by s 29(2) (amended by the Coal Industry Act 1994 s 52(2), Sch 8 paras 1, 22(2)).
4  See the Opencast Coal Act 1958 s 17(1), (1A), (3)–(3B) (see PARA 473); s 18 (see PARA 474); s 27 (see 478; applied by s 29(2)). As to the application of s 29 to the case of a holding held in divided ownership see s 34, Sch 6 paras 1–4 (see PARAS 472, PARA 475); applied by Sch 6 para 5. As to the application of s 29 to land the strata of which are in different ownership see s 33(1), Sch 5 para 15 (see PARAS 472, PARA 475). See also Sch 5 para 14(1), (2) (see PARA 472), Sch 6 para 11.
5  Ie compensation under the Opencast Coal Act 1958 ss 21–23: see PARA 475 et seq.
6  Opencast Coal Act 1958 s 21(1); ss 21(3), 22, 23; applied by s 29(3). The provisions of Sch 5 para 14(3)–(5) have effect for this purpose: Sch 5 para 14(6) (see PARAS 476, PARA 479). Where a compulsory rights order comprises the whole or part of a holding to which s 29 applies, and after the end of the period of occupation the tenant carries out improvements, and, in respect of expenses incurred in carrying out those improvements, is entitled to compensation under s 22 as applied by s 29, those improvements are to be treated for the purposes of the Landlord and Tenant Act 1927 and of the Landlord and Tenant Act 1954 Pt II (ss 23–46) as if they had been carried out by the landlord: Opencast Coal Act 1958 s 37, Sch 7 para 10. The provisions of the Opencast Coal Act 1958 relating to additional compensation do not have effect on or after the restructuring date (ie 31 October 1994: see PARA 50): see PARA 474.
7  See PARA 490.

### 490. Compensation for non-agricultural tenants' improvements.

Where the land[1] comprised in a compulsory rights order[2] consists of or includes land ('the tenant's land') which, immediately before the date of entry[3], constituted or formed part of a holding to which the provisions of the Landlord and Tenant Act 1927 relating to compensation for improvements and goodwill on the termination of business tenancies[4] apply[5] and which was land on which, before that date, there had been carried out improvements[6] qualifying for compensation under that Act[7], then if at the end of the period of occupation[8] the land has lost the benefit[9] of any of the improvements and is subject to the same tenancy[10] as immediately before the date of entry, and that tenancy continues until after the end of the period of occupation, those provisions apply[11] on the basis of certain assumptions[12].

1  As to the meaning of 'land' see PARA 414.
2  As to compulsory rights orders see the Opencast Coal Act 1958 s 4; and PARA 431 et seq. The power to make such orders has not been exercisable since 31 December 1999: see PARA 414.

3   As to the meaning of 'the date of entry' see PARAS 433, PARA 443.
4   Ie the Landlord and Tenant Act 1927 Pt I (ss 1–17) (see LANDLORD AND TENANT vol 64 (2016) PARA 1679 et seq): see the Opencast Coal Act 1958 s 30(1)(a).
5   Opencast Coal Act 1958 s 30(1)(a).
6   'Improvement' includes the erection of a building: Opencast Coal Act 1958 s 30(8).
7   Opencast Coal Act 1958 s 30(1)(b). The improvements referred to are those in respect of which, immediately before the date of entry, the tenant of the holding in question had a prospective right to compensation under the Landlord and Tenant Act 1927 on quitting the holding on the termination of his tenancy: Opencast Coal Act 1958 s 30(6). As to the meaning of 'termination' see PARA 455. In determining whether these conditions are fulfilled no account is to be taken of any provision in the Landlord and Tenant Act 1927 by which a right to compensation is conditional upon the making of a claim, or is liable to be affected by the service of a notice by the landlord: Opencast Coal Act 1958 s 30(7).
8   As to the meaning of 'the period of occupation' see PARA 433.
9   The land is taken to have lost the benefit of an improvement if the benefit of that improvement has been lost, wholly or in part, without being replaced by another improvement of comparable benefit to the land: Opencast Coal Act 1958 s 30(4).
10  As to the meaning of 'tenancy' see PARA 444.
11  Those provisions are to be taken to include any provisions of the Landlord and Tenant Act 1927 as to the making of claims, the calculation of compensation and the determination of claims, the recovery of compensation, and as to any other incidental matters (Opencast Coal Act 1958 s 30(5)), but the time for making a claim is not later than three months after the end of the period of occupation (s 30(5) proviso).
12  Opencast Coal Act 1958 s 30(2). Thus the Landlord and Tenant Act 1927 applies as if (1) the land were in the state in which it was immediately before the date of entry (Opencast Coal Act 1958 s 30(3)(a)); (2) the tenancy under which that land is held at the end of the period of occupation had terminated immediately after the end of that period and the tenant had then quitted the holding (s 30(3)(b)); and (3) it were established that, after the termination of that tenancy, there was no intention to demolish or make structural alterations in any premises on the land or any part of such premises or to change the use of that land or any premises upon it (s 30(3)(c)). If the land has lost the benefit of some, but not all, of the improvements in question the Landlord and Tenant Act 1927 applies as before described, but as if the improvements of which the land has not lost the benefit had not been improvements qualifying for compensation under that Act: Opencast Coal Act 1958 s 30(3) proviso.

## (v) Compensation for Easements and Rights

### 491. In general.

Where, by reason of a compulsory rights order[1] or of anything done in the exercise of rights conferred by such an order, the exercise of an easement[2] or similar right[3] over any land[4] comprised in the order, or of any right restrictive of the use of any such land, is prevented or injuriously affected, annual[5] and terminal[6] compensation is payable in respect of it[7].

1   As to compulsory rights orders see the Opencast Coal Act 1958 s 4; and PARA 431 et seq. The power to make such orders has not been exercisable since 31 December 1999: see PARA 414.
2   An easement or other right consisting of such a right as is mentioned in the Opencast Coal Act 1958 s 7(2) or s 7(3) (see PARA 438) is, however, excepted from the application of s 31: s 31(1) proviso. As to easements generally see REAL PROPERTY AND REGISTRATION vol 87 (2017) PARA 731 et seq. In two instances rights which are not strictly easements are notionally treated as such for the purpose of s 31(2) (see PARA 492). These are:
    (1)   where the whole or part of the land comprised in a compulsory rights order is subject to a right of the kind mentioned in s 34, Sch 6 para 20(a) (see PARA 503), and in any year in which that right subsists, being a year such as is mentioned in s 31(2) (see PARA 492), the exercise of that right is prevented or injuriously affected by reason of the order or of anything done in the exercise of rights conferred by the order (Sch 6 para 23); and
    (2)   where the whole or part of a holding to which s 17 (see PARA 472) applies consists of land occupied under a letting or licence approver the Agricultural Holdings Act 1986 s

2 or the Agricultural Holdings Act 1948 s 2 (repealed) (see AGRICULTURAL LAND AND
ALLOTMENTS vol 1 (2017) PARA 427), and

(a)    by the agreement under which the land was let or the licence granted a right to
use the land for specified purposes was reserved to the lessor or grantor (Opencast
Coal Act 1958 Sch 6 para 25(a) (amended by the Agricultural Holdings Act 1986
s 100, Sch 14 para 32));

(b)    the exercise of that right is prevented or injuriously affected by reason of the
compulsory rights order or of anything done in the exercise of rights conferred by
the order (Opencast Coal Act 1958 Sch 6 para 25(b)); and

(c)    that right does not constitute an easement or similar right (Sch 6 para 25(c)).

As to the meaning of 'land' see PARA 414.

3   As to the meaning of 'similar right' see PARA 439.

4   The provisions of the Opencast Coal Act 1958 s 44(1)–(4) (which relate to Crown land: see PARAS
415, 431, PARA 472) apply, with necessary modifications, in relation to land which is subject to
a right restricting its use, being a right the benefit of which is annexed to land in which there is a
Crown or Duchy interest (as to the meaning of which see PARA 415) or, not being so annexed,
belongs to Her Majesty in right of the Crown or of the Duchy of Lancaster, or belongs to the
Duchy of Cornwall, or belongs to a government department, or is held in trust for Her Majesty for
the purposes of a government department, as those provisions apply in relation to land in which
there is a Crown or Duchy interest: s 44(5). Those provisions apply in particular as if s 44(1)
proviso were omitted, and as if in s 44(4)(a)–(d) (see PARA 420) any reference to land belonging
as therein mentioned were a reference to a right the benefit of which belongs, or is annexed to land
belonging, as therein mentioned: s 44(5) proviso.

5   See PARA 492.

6   See PARA 493.

7   Opencast Coal Act 1958 s 31(1).

## 492.   Annual compensation.

For the year[1] beginning with the operative date[2] of the compulsory rights
order[3], and for each subsequent year which begins with an anniversary of that
date and falls wholly or partly within the period of occupation[4], the person for the
time being entitled to the easement or right in question[5] is entitled to
compensation of an amount equal to the loss, if any, suffered by him by reason
that the exercise of the easement or right is prevented or injuriously affected[6].

1   As to the meaning of 'year' see PARA 458.

2   As to the meaning of 'the operative date' see PARA 432.

3   As to compulsory rights orders see the Opencast Coal Act 1958 s 4; and PARA 431 et seq. The
power to make such orders has not been exercisable since 31 December 1999: see PARA 414.

4   As to the meaning of 'the period of occupation' see PARA 433.

5   As to easements generally see REAL PROPERTY AND REGISTRATION vol 87 (2017) PARA 731 et
seq. In relation to common or waste land the appropriate national authority (ie the Secretary of
State or where functions have been transferred in relation to Wales, the Welsh Ministers: see PARA
2) may make regulations modifying the Opencast Coal Act 1958 s 31(1)–(4) in order to secure an
apportionment of compensation among the persons entitled: see s 31(5). At the date at which this
volume states the law no such regulations had been made. As to regulation-making powers
generally see PARA 418.

6   Opencast Coal Act 1958 s 31(2) (amended by the Coal Industry Act 1994 ss 52(2), 67(8), Sch 8
paras 1, 23(1), Sch 11 Pt II).
Subject (where different persons have been entitled to the rights for different parts of the year)
to any apportionment under the Opencast Coal Act 1958 s 35(3) (see PARA 473), the liability to
pay compensation under s 31(2) falls on the persons who, for the whole or any part of the year in
question, have been entitled to the rights conferred by the order: s 31(2A) (added by the Coal
Industry Act 1994 Sch 8 para 23(2)).

## 493.   Terminal compensation.

Where, after the end of the period of occupation[1], the exercise of the easement[2]
or right continues to be prevented or injuriously affected by reason of anything

done during that period in the exercise of rights conferred by the compulsory rights order[3], terminal compensation is payable[4].

If the easement or right is appurtenant to, or the benefit of it is in any other way annexed to, any land[5], the owner[6] of that land at the end of the period of occupation is entitled to compensation from the person who immediately before the end of the period of occupation is the person entitled to the rights conferred by the order of an amount equal to the diminution, if any, in the value of that land[7], in so far as the diminution is attributable to the fact that the exercise of the easement or right is prevented or injuriously affected[8]. In any other case, the person who at the end of that period is entitled to the right in question is entitled to compensation from the person who immediately before the end of the period of occupation is the person entitled to the rights conferred by the order of an amount equal to the market value which the right would then have if its exercise were not prevented or affected, reduced by the amount of any market value which the right actually has at the end of that period[9].

1   As to the meaning of 'the period of occupation' see PARA 433.
2   As to easements generally see REAL PROPERTY AND REGISTRATION vol 87 (2017) PARA 731 et seq.
3   As to compulsory rights orders see the Opencast Coal Act 1958 s 4; and PARA 431 et seq. The power to make such orders has not been exercisable since 31 December 1999: see PARA 414.
4   Opencast Coal Act 1958 s 31(3) (amended by the Coal Industry Act 1994 s 52(2), Sch 8 paras 1, 23(3)). See also PARA 492.
5   As to the meaning of 'land' see PARA 414.
6   As to the meaning of 'owner' see PARA 421.
7   The value of the land is taken to have been diminished if, and to the extent to which, the value of a freehold interest in that land at the end of the period of occupation is less than the value which such an interest would then have if the land comprised in the order, over which the easement or right is exercisable, were in the state in which it was immediately before the date of entry; and for the purpose of computing those values the Opencast Coal Act 1958 s 23(4) (see PARA 479) applies with the substitution, for references to the holding, of references to the land to which the benefit of the easement or right is annexed: s 31(4). As to the meaning of 'the date of entry' see PARAS 433, PARA 443.
8   Opencast Coal Act 1958 s 31(3)(a).
9   Opencast Coal Act 1958 s 31(3)(b). Where property is of a kind not normally subject to sale in the open market, and compensation is to be assessed by reference to the value which the property would have if so sold, the appropriate national authority may make regulations providing for the ascertainment of the value of the property: s 34, Sch 6 para 14. At the date at which this volume states the law no such regulations had been made. The appropriate national authority is the Secretary of State or where functions have been transferred in relation to Wales, the Welsh Ministers: see PARA 2.

### (vi) Compensation for Depreciation of other Land

**494. Compensation for depreciation of other land; in general.**
When a compulsory rights order[1] was made, and immediately before the operative date[2] of the order the person who was the owner[3] of the whole or part of the land[4] comprised in the order held an interest in other land not forming part of the land comprised in the order, or of any holding qualifying for compensation under the Opencast Coal Act 1958[5], annual[6] and terminal[7] compensation is payable in respect of any depreciation in value of that other land[8].

1   As to compulsory rights orders see the Opencast Coal Act 1958 s 4; and PARA 431 et seq. The power to make such orders has not been exercisable since 31 December 1999: see PARA 414.
2   As to the meaning of 'the operative date' see PARA 432.
3   As to the meaning of 'owner' see PARA 421.

4   As to the meaning of 'land' see PARA 414.
5   The holding referred to is one to which the Opencast Coal Act 1958 s 17 or s 29 (see PARAS 472, 488) applies: see s 32(1).
6   See PARA 495.
7   See PARA 496.
8   Opencast Coal Act 1958 s 32(1).

### 495. Annual compensation.

Where a compulsory rights order[1] has become operative, and in the case of any land[2] which, in relation to that order, is land[3] to which the Opencast Coal Act 1958[4] applies it is shown that for any year[5] (being either the year beginning with the operative date[6] of the order, or a year beginning with an anniversary of that date and falling wholly or partly within the period of occupation[7]) the annual value[8] of the relevant land is less than the annual value of that land would have been if the land comprised in the order had not included any of the owner's land comprised in the order[9], and all the owner's land comprised in the order had remained in the state[10] in which it was immediately before the operative date, the person who is for the time being the owner of the relevant land is entitled to compensation for that year of an amount equal to the difference[11].

No annual compensation is payable for any year for which the interest of the owner of the other land is held subject to, and with the benefit of, a tenancy which was subsisting immediately before the operative date of the order, unless the rent payable for that year is subject to a liability to be reduced in consequence of the order or of anything done in the exercise of rights conferred by the order[12], or is a rent which has been so reduced in pursuance of such a liability[13]. Nor is any such compensation payable for any year for which the owner of the other land is entitled to annual compensation in respect of a right restrictive of the use of land[14], being a right which fulfils certain conditions[15].

1   As to compulsory rights orders see the Opencast Coal Act 1958 s 4; and PARA 431 et seq. The power to make such orders has not been exercisable since 31 December 1999: see PARA 414.
2   As to the meaning of 'land' see PARA 414.
3   Ie in the Opencast Coal Act 1958 s 32(2), (3) referred to as 'the relevant land': see s 32(2).
4   Ie the Opencast Coal Act 1958 s 32: see s 32(2).
5   As to the meaning of 'year' see PARA 458. For the position where a person is the owner of the other land for part only of a year see PARAS 504–508.
6   As to the meaning of 'the operative date' see PARA 432.
7   As to the meaning of 'the period of occupation' see PARA 433.
8   The annual value of any land for any year is taken to be an amount equal to the annual rent at which, immediately before the beginning of that year, that land, in the appropriate circumstances, might reasonably have been expected to be let from year to year under a contract of tenancy whereby the tenant undertook to pay all usual tenant's rates and taxes and to bear the cost of the repairs and insurance and the other expenses, if any, necessary to maintain the land in a state to command that rent, and not to carry out any operations on the land, or to make any change in the use of it, for which permission would be required under the Town and Country Planning Act 1990 Pt III (ss 55–106) (see PLANNING vol 81 (2018) PARA 333 et seq) or the Town and Country Planning (Scotland) Act 1997 Pt III (ss 26–75), except any operations for which such permission has been granted and is in force immediately before the beginning of that year: Opencast Coal Act 1958 s 32(2B) (added by the Coal Industry Act 1994 s 52(2), Sch 8 para 25(2); and amended by the Planning (Consequential Provisions) (Scotland) Act 1997 s 4, Sch 2 para 5(4)). The appropriate circumstances in determining the annual value of the relevant land for any year is taken to be the actual circumstances existing immediately before the beginning of that year, and in determining what would have been the annual value of the relevant land in the circumstances specified in the Opencast Coal Act 1958 s 32(2B)(a), (b) is taken to be the circumstances specified in s 32(2B)(a), (b): s 32(3) (amended by the Coal Industry Act 1994 Sch 8 para 25(3)). In either case the relevant land is assumed to have been available for letting with vacant possession immediately before the beginning of the year in question: Opencast Coal Act 1958 s 32(3) proviso.

Where any land to which s 32 applies in relation to a compulsory rights order is (1) land which, immediately before the operative date of the order, was used for a purpose for which land would not normally be let from year to year; or (2) land in respect of which, immediately before the operative date, there was in force permission granted under the Town and Country Planning Act 1990 Pt III (see PLANNING) for the land to be used for such a purpose, the Opencast Coal Act 1958 s 32(3) does not apply, and for the purposes of s 32(2) annual value is determined in accordance with regulations made by the appropriate national authority under Sch 6 para 13: s 34, Sch 6 para 13(1); and see the Opencast Coal (Annual Value in Special Cases) Regulations 1959, SI 1959/981 (amended by SI 1960/402; SI 1960/1248; SI 1960/2394; and SI 1961/1620). The appropriate national authority is the Secretary of State or where functions have been transferred in relation to Wales, the Welsh Ministers: see PARA 2.

9 Any reference to the owner's land comprised in the order is a reference to so much of the land comprised in the order as, immediately before the operative date, was land in which the interest of the owner was held by the person who was then the owner of the relevant land: Opencast Coal Act 1958 s 32(7)(a)(i). As to the meaning of 'owner' see PARA 421.

10 See PARA 462.

11 Opencast Coal Act 1958 s 32(2) (amended by the Coal Industry Act 1994 s 67(8), Sch 8 para 25(1), Sch 11 Pt II). Subject (where different persons have been entitled to the rights for different parts of the year) to any apportionment under the Opencast Coal Act 1958 s 35(3) (see PARA 473), the liability to pay compensation under s 32(2) falls on the persons who, for the whole or any part of the year in question, have been entitled to the rights conferred by the order: s 32(2A) (added by the Coal Industry Act 1994 Sch 8 para 25(2)). As to the persons entitled to the rights conferred by the order see PARA 433.

Where under the Opencast Coal Act 1958 s 32(2) a person is entitled to compensation as the owner of any land, and his interest in that land is subject to a mortgage (as to the meaning of which see PARA 439) and the mortgagee is, to the extent of that interest, in possession of the land or of the rents and profits, the compensation is paid to the mortgagee, and is paid or applied by him as mentioned in s 43(2) (see PARA 473): s 43(3) (amended by the Coal Industry Act 1994 Sch 8 para 32, Sch 11 Pt II).

12 Ie if by the terms of the tenancy or any enactment the tenant is entitled to require that rent to be so reduced, or is entitled to require the question whether the rent should be so reduced, or generally what rent should be payable under the tenancy, to be referred to arbitration or to any court or tribunal: Opencast Coal Act 1958 Sch 6 para 17(2).

13 Opencast Coal Act 1958 Sch 6 paras 17(1), 19. The reference to a rent which has been so reduced is to be construed in accordance with Sch 6 para 17(2): Sch 6 para 19.

14 See the Opencast Coal Act 1958 s 31(2); and PARA 492.

15 Opencast Coal Act 1958 Sch 6 paras 18(1), 19. The right is restrictive of the use of the whole or part of the land comprised in the order: Sch 6 para 18(2)(a). The benefit of the right must be annexed to the other land, or to that land together with further land, or be exercisable by the owner of that land: Sch 6 para 18(2)(b). The exercise of the right, in relation to any land comprised in the order, could (apart from the order) have prevented that land from being used for the activities which, in relation to the opencast planning permission referred to in the order, constitute the permitted activities: Sch 6 para 18(2)(c) (amended by the Housing and Planning Act 1986 s 39(3), Sch 8 Pt I para 16).

## 496. Terminal compensation.

For the purpose of assessing terminal compensation two values must be computed. These are: (1) the value[1], at the end of the period of occupation, of the owner's interest in the relevant land, assessed on the assumption that, in so far as any of the owner's land comprised in the compulsory rights order[2] has not then been restored to the condition[3] in which it was immediately before the date of entry[4], all restorative work[5] will be carried out on that land in due course[6]; and (2) the value which, at the end of the period of occupation, the owner's interest in the relevant land would have if the entirety of the owner's land comprised in the order were in the state in which it was immediately before the date of entry[7].

If the value under head (1) above is less than that under head (2) above, the person who at the end of the period of occupation is entitled to the owner's interest in the relevant land is entitled to compensation from the person who immediately before the end of the period of occupation is the person entitled to the rights conferred by the order, and that compensation is of an amount equal to the difference[8].

1   In computing this value it must be assumed that the owner's interest in the relevant land is in the circumstances being offered for sale subject to any incumbrances to which that interest is subject at the end of the period of occupation: Opencast Coal Act 1958 s 32(6). As to the meaning of 'incumbrance' see PARA 479. As to the meaning of 'the period of occupation' see PARA 433. 'The relevant land' means the land to which s 32 (see PARA 494) applies (s 32(2)), and 'the owner's interest in the relevant land' means the interest in that land which constitutes the interest of the owner of it (s 32(4)). As to the meaning of 'land' see PARA 414. As to the meaning of 'owner' see PARA 421.
2   Ie so much of the land comprised in the order as, immediately before the operative date, was land in which the owner's interest was held by the person then entitled to the owner's interest in the relevant land: Opencast Coal Act 1958 s 32(7)(a)(ii). As to the meaning of 'the operative date' see PARA 432. As to compulsory rights orders see s 4; and PARA 431 et seq. The power to make such orders has not been exercisable since 31 December 1999: see PARA 414.
3   See PARA 462.
4   As to the meaning of 'the date of entry' see PARAS 433, PARA 443.
5   Ie work qualifying for compensation under the Opencast Coal Act 1958 s 22 (see PARA 476) which is work for the purpose of further restoring that land to or towards the condition in which it was immediately before the date of entry, or a condition substantially similar to it, being work in respect of which, so far as the nature of the work is concerned, expenses would be treated as reasonably incurred for the purposes of s 22(1): s 32(7)(b). As to the meaning of 'restore' see PARA 424.
6   Opencast Coal Act 1958 s 32(5)(a). 'In due course' means at the first reasonable opportunity after the end of the period of occupation, or within a reasonable time after that opportunity arises: s 32(7)(c).
7   Opencast Coal Act 1958 s 32(5)(b).
8   Opencast Coal Act 1958 s 32(4) (amended by the Coal Industry Act 1994 s 52(2), Sch 8 para 25(4)).

## (vii) Special Cases

### A.   CONCURRENT AND LIMITED COMPULSORY RIGHTS ORDERS

**497. Concurrent compulsory rights orders.**
The appropriate national authority[1] may by regulations[2] make provision for modifying or adapting any of the provisions of the Opencast Coal Act 1958 relating to compensation in respect of compulsory rights orders[3] in their application to land[4] which (1) constitutes or forms part of the land comprised in such an order, or, in relation to such an order, forms part of a holding qualifying for compensation[5], or is other land in the same ownership qualifying[6] for compensation[7]; and (2) at any time after the operative date[8] of that order, and before the end of the period of occupation[9], constitutes or forms part of the land comprised in another such order, or, in relation to another such order, forms part of a holding qualifying for compensation[10], or is other land in the same ownership qualifying[11] for compensation[12].

1   Ie the Secretary of State or where functions have been transferred in relation to Wales, the Welsh Ministers: see PARA 2.
2   See the Opencast Coal (Concurrent Orders and Requisitions) Regulations 1959, SI 1959/980, regs 1–3, 5. As to regulation-making powers generally see PARA 418.
3   As to compulsory rights orders see the Opencast Coal Act 1958 s 4; and PARA 431 et seq. The power to make such orders has not been exercisable since 31 December 1999: see PARA 414.
4   As to the meaning of 'land' see PARA 414.

5  Ie a holding to which the Opencast Coal Act 1958 s 17 or s 29 (see PARAS 463, 479) applies: see
   s 34, Sch 6 para 29(a).
6  Ie under the Opencast Coal Act 1958 s 32 (see PARA 494 et seq): see Sch 6 para 29(a).
7  Opencast Coal Act 1958 Sch 6 para 29(a).
8  As to the meaning of 'the operative date' see PARA 432.
9  As to the meaning of 'the period of occupation' see PARA 433.
10 Ie a holding to which the Opencast Coal Act 1958 s 17 or s 29 (see PARAS 472, 488) applies: see
   Sch 6 para 29(b).
11 Ie under the Opencast Coal Act 1958 s 32 (see PARA 494 et seq): see Sch 6 para 29(b).
12 Opencast Coal Act 1958 Sch 6 para 29(b).

## 498. Limited compulsory rights orders.

Subject to two exceptions, the compensation provisions of the Opencast Coal
Act 1958 do not have effect in relation to limited compulsory rights orders[1]. These
exceptions are: (1) that in so far as the operation of such an order extends to an
easement or similar right[2] in respect of the whole or part of the land[3] comprised
in the order, or to a right restrictive of the use of the whole or part of that land,
the provisions of the Opencast Coal Act 1958 with regard to compensation for
easements or similar rights[4] have effect with respect to that easement or right, but
not with respect to any easement or right to which the operation of the order does
not extend[5]; and (2) that in so far as the operation of such an order extends to the
interests or rights created or conferred by a mining lease[6] or order conferring
working rights[7] in respect of minerals[8] in or under the land comprised in the order
or part of it, the provisions of the Opencast Coal Act 1958 relating to
compensation for minerals[9] have effect with respect to that interest or those rights,
but not with respect to any interest or rights created or conferred by a mining lease
or order to which the compulsory rights order does not extend[10].

1  Opencast Coal Act 1958 s 34, Sch 6 para 30(1), (4). A limited compulsory rights order is one
   falling within s 8(1): see PARA 439. As to compulsory rights orders see s 4; and PARA 431 et seq.
   The power to make such orders has not been exercisable since 31 December 1999: see PARA 414.
2  See PARA 491. As to the meaning of 'similar right' see PARA 439. As to easements generally see
   REAL PROPERTY AND REGISTRATION vol 87 (2017) PARA 731 et seq.
3  See PARA 491. As to the meaning of 'land' see PARA 414.
4  Ie the provisions of the Opencast Coal Act 1958 s 31 (see PARAS 491–493): see Sch 6 para 30(2).
   For the purposes of s 31, s 23(4) (see PARA 479) continues to apply: Sch 6 para 30(4).
5  Opencast Coal Act 1958 Sch 6 para 30(2).
6  As to the meaning of 'mining lease' see PARA 439.
7  As to the meaning of 'order conferring working rights' see PARA 439.
8  As to the meaning of 'minerals' see PARA 10.
9  Ie the provisions of the Opencast Coal Act 1958 s 33, Sch 5 (see PARA 464 et seq): see Sch 6 para
   30(3).
10 Opencast Coal Act 1958 Sch 6 para 30(3).

### B.   WOODLANDS

## 499. Modification or adaptation of compensation provisions.

The appropriate national authority[1] may by regulations[2] make provision for
modifying or adapting any of the provisions of the Opencast Coal Act 1958
relating to compensation in their application to land[3] which immediately before
the operative date[4] of a compulsory rights order[5], or the date of entry[6] under such
an order, was used as woodlands, or as woodlands of a particular description
specified in the regulations[7].

1  Ie the Secretary of State or where functions have been transferred in relation to Wales, the Welsh
   Ministers: see PARA 2.

2  At the date at which this volume states the law no such regulations had been made. As to regulation-making powers generally see PARA 418.
3  As to the meaning of 'land' see PARA 414.
4  As to the meaning of 'the operative date' see PARA 432 .
5  As to compulsory rights orders see the Opencast Coal Act 1958 s 4; and PARA 431 et seq. The power to make such orders has not been exercisable since 31 December 1999: see PARA 414.
6  As to the meaning of 'the date of entry' see PARAS 433, PARA 443.
7  Opencast Coal Act 1958 s 34, Sch 6 para 15. The compensation provisions affected by Sch 6 para 15 are only those enacted in respect of compulsory rights orders.

### C.  ALLOTMENTS

## 500.  Terminal compensation.

On the statutory termination[1] of an allotment tenancy[2], the tenant under that tenancy is not entitled to any compensation from his landlord by virtue of the Small Holdings and Allotments Act 1908 or the Allotments Act 1922 or the Allotments Act 1950, or by virtue of any other enactment relating to allotments[3], but the provisions of the Opencast Coal Act 1958[4] have effect as to compensation payable by the person on whose application the compulsory rights order was made to the tenant in respect of the termination of that tenancy[5].

Such compensation is of an amount equal to one year's rent under the tenancy[6] together with the amount of the compensation, if any, to which, under specified enactments[7], the tenant would have been entitled from his landlord, on quitting the land on the termination of his tenancy, if the tenancy had been terminated by the landlord as from the date of entry[8], and, in the case of an allotment garden[9], the tenancy had been so terminated by re-entry[10]. Compensation accrues due on the date of entry[11].

1  The right to compensation under the Opencast Coal Act 1958 s 41(1), Sch 8 para 3 does not arise unless the allotment tenancy is determined by Sch 8 para 2 (see PARA 460), when the rights under a compulsory rights order become exercisable. As to the meaning of 'termination' see PARA 455. As to compulsory rights orders see s 4; and PARA 431 et seq. The power to make such orders has not been exercisable since 31 December 1999: see PARA 414.
2  Ie by virtue of Opencast Coal Act 1958 Sch 8 para 2: see Sch 8 para 3(1). As to the meaning of 'allotment tenancy' see PARA 460.
3  For such legislation see generally AGRICULTURAL LAND AND ALLOTMENTS vol 1 (2017) PARA 649 et seq. As to compensation see AGRICULTURAL LAND AND ALLOTMENTS vol 1 (2017) PARA 705 et seq.
4  Ie the provisions of the Opencast Coal Act 1958 Sch 8 para 3: see Sch 8 para 3(1).
5  Opencast Coal Act 1958 Sch 8 para 3(1) (amended by the Coal Industry Act 1994 s 52(2), Sch 8 para 43). As to the effect of a compulsory rights order upon an allotment tenancy see PARA 460.
6  Opencast Coal Act 1958 Sch 8 para 3(4). For this purpose the rate of the rent is taken to be that at which it was payable immediately before the date on which the compulsory rights order was made, or, if the tenancy was not then subsisting, such rate as would have represented a reasonable rent in relation to that tenancy if the order had not been made: Sch 8 para 3(4). As to the meaning of 'year' see PARA 458.
7  The specified enactments are: the Allotments Act 1922 ss 2, 3; 5 (see AGRICULTURAL LAND AND ALLOTMENTS vol 1 (2017) PARA 706 et seq); and the Small Holdings and Allotments Act 1908 s 47 (see AGRICULTURAL LAND AND ALLOTMENTS). In determining the amount of such compensation, no account is to be taken of any sum due to the landlord from the tenant, or of any right which the landlord would have had, under the Allotments Act 1950 or otherwise, to deduct any sum so due: Opencast Coal Act 1958 Sch 8 para 4 (amended by the Coal Industry Act 1994 s 67(8), Sch 8 para 43, Sch 11 Pt II). Where the land which, immediately before the operative date of the compulsory rights order, was occupied under a tenancy which constitutes a holding to which the Opencast Coal Act 1958 s 29 applies (see PARA 488), ss 22, 23 (see PARAS 476–479) apply in relation to that holding subject to modifications: Sch 8 para 9(1). These are that s 22 applies as if any reference in it to the condition in which the land was immediately before the date of entry were

a reference to the condition in which the land would have been then, if the matters qualifying for compensation had not existed (Sch 8 para 9(2)), these latter matters being those in respect of which compensation is payable as stated in the text to this note (see Sch 8 para 9(4)); and that s 23(2)(c) applies as if for the value there mentioned there were substituted the value which, at the end of the period of occupation, a freehold interest in the holding would have if it were then in the state in which it might reasonably have been expected to be, immediately before the date of entry, if the matters qualifying for compensation had not existed (Sch 8 para 9(3)).

8   Opencast Coal Act 1958 Sch 8 para 3(2)(a), (3).
9   As to the meaning of 'allotment garden' see PARA 460.
10   Opencast Coal Act 1958 Sch 8 para 3(2)(b), (3). The re-entry referred to is that mentioned in the Allotments Act 1922 s 2(2): see AGRICULTURAL LAND AND ALLOTMENTS vol 1 (2017) PARA 706.
11   Opencast Coal Act 1958 Sch 8 para 6(1). Section 35(7), (8) (see PARAS 510–511) applies in relation to any compensation payable under Sch 8 as it applies in relation to any such compensation as is referred to in s 35(7): Sch 8 para 6(3) (amended by the Coal Industry Act 1994 Sch 8 para 43, Sch 11 Pt II).

## 501. Compensation for forced sale.

Where, in consequence of the confirmation of a compulsory rights order[1], the tenant under an allotment tenancy[2] incurs a loss in respect of a forced sale of any trees, bushes, structures, improvements or other property which, in pursuance of statutory powers[3], he has removed from the land comprised in the tenancy, he is entitled, subject to certain provisions[4], to compensation of an amount equal to that loss[5]. Such compensation accrues due on the effective date[6] of the sale, or, if that date was before the operative date[7] of the order, is to be treated as having accrued due on the effective date of the sale[8].

1   As to compulsory rights orders see the Opencast Coal Act 1958 s 4; and PARA 431 et seq. As to their confirmation see PARA 442. The power to make such orders has not been exercisable since 31 December 1999: see PARA 414.
2   As to the meaning of 'allotment tenancy' see PARA 460.
3   Ie in pursuance of the Allotments Act 1922 s 4 or s 5, or of the Small Holdings and Allotments Act 1908 s 47(4) (see AGRICULTURAL LAND AND ALLOTMENTS vol 1 (2017) PARAS 712, 740): Opencast Coal Act 1958 s 41(1), Sch 8 para 5(1).
4   Ie subject to Opencast Coal Act 1958 Sch 8 para 5(1A)–(3): see Sch 8 para 5(1). Section 27(3) (see PARA 487) applies for the purposes of Sch 8 para 5 as it applies for the purposes of s 27: Sch 8 para 5(2).
5   Opencast Coal Act 1958 Sch 8 para 5(1) (amended by the Coal Industry Act 1994 ss 52(2), 67(8), Sch 8 para 43(3), Sch 11 Pt II). Compensation under the Opencast Coal Act 1958 Sch 8 para 5 is payable by the person by whom it would be payable if it were compensation under s 27: Sch 8 para 5(1A) (added by the Coal Industry Act 1994 Sch 8 para 43(3), Sch 11 Pt II). The provisions of the Opencast Coal Act 1958 Sch 8 para 5(1); Sch 8 para 5(2) have effect without prejudice to any right to compensation under s 27 (as applied by s 29), but compensation is not payable under Sch 8 para 5, in respect of a forced sale if compensation in respect of it is payable under s 27 (as so applied): Sch 8 para 5(3).
6   'Effective date', in relation to a sale, means the date on which the property sold becomes the property of the purchaser: Opencast Coal Act 1958 s 35(9) (applied by Sch 8 para 6(3) (amended by the Coal Industry Act 1994, ss 52, 67, Sch 8 para 43(2), (4), Sch 11 Pt II)).
7   As to the meaning of 'the operative date' see PARA 432.
8   Opencast Coal Act 1958 Sch 8 para 6(2).

## 502. Determination of disputes.

Any dispute as to a right to compensation under the provisions of the Opencast Coal Act 1958 relating to allotment tenancies[1], or as to the amount of any such compensation, or as to a right to compensation[2], in respect of a holding consisting exclusively of land[3] occupied under an allotment tenancy, or as to the amount of any such compensation, is determined[4] by a valuation[5] made by a person appointed in default of agreement by the county court having jurisdiction in the place where the land in question is situated, on an application in writing made for the purpose by the person claiming the compensation or by the person from whom it is claimed[6].

1  Ie the provisions of the Opencast Coal Act 1958 s 41, Sch 8: see Sch 8 para 7. As to the meaning of 'allotment tenancy' see PARA 460.
2  Ie compensation under the Opencast Coal Act 1958 s 17 (as applied by s 29): see Sch 8 para 7. Section 29 is concerned with compensation where the holding was not occupied wholly or mainly for the purposes of agriculture carried on by way of a trade or business: see PARA 488.
3  As to the meaning of 'land' see PARA 414
4  Ie notwithstanding anything in the Opencast Coal Act 1958 s 40(3) (see PARA 509): see Sch 8 para 7.
5  The Allotments Act 1922 s 6(2) (which relates to the charges of the valuer for a valuation under s 6) applies in relation to a valuation under the Opencast Coal Act 1958 Sch 8 para 7 as it applies in relation to a valuation under the Allotments Act 1922 s 6 (see AGRICULTURAL LAND AND ALLOTMENTS vol 1 (2017) PARA 713), with the substitution, for the reference to the landlord, of a reference to the person from whom the compensation under the Opencast Coal Act 1958 Sch 8 is claimed: see Sch 8 para 8 (amended by the Coal Industry Act 1994 s 52(2), Sch 8 para 43(1), (6)).
6  Opencast Coal Act 1958 Sch 8 para 7 (amended by the Coal Industry Act 1994 s 67(8), Sch 8 para 43(5), Sch 11 Pt II; and the Crime and Courts Act 2013 Sch 9 para 22); and see the Courts Act 1971 s 56(1), Sch 8 Pt I para 2; and COURTS AND TRIBUNALS vol 24 (2010) PARAS 721, 725. As to claims for compensation see also PARA 509.

### D.  COMPENSATION FOR RESTRICTED LETTINGS, EASEMENTS AND SIMILAR RIGHTS

### 503.  Rights to be disregarded.

For the purposes of certain of the compensation provisions of the Opencast Coal Act 1958[1] (1) any right conferred by a letting of land[2], or a licence to occupy land, in pursuance of an agreement made, whether the agreement expressly so provides or not, in contemplation of the use of the land only for grazing or mowing during some specified period of the year[3]; and (2) any easement or similar right[4] over land[5], is to be disregarded, and in relation to any land which is subject to any such right, those provisions apply as if that right had not been conferred, reserved or otherwise acquired[6].

1  Ie the Opencast Coal Act 1958 s 17(2), (3) (see PARAS 472–473); s 21(2) (see PARA 475); s 29(1) (see PARA 488); and s 17(3) (as applied by s 29(2) (see PARA 489)): see s 34, Sch 6 para 21.
2  As to the meaning of 'land' see PARA 414.
3  See the Opencast Coal Act 1958 Sch 6 para 20(a) (amended by the Agricultural Holdings Act 1986 s 100, Sch 14 para 32). As to the meaning of 'year' see PARA 458.
4  See PARA 491. As to the meaning of 'similar right' see PARA 439. As to easements generally see REAL PROPERTY AND REGISTRATION vol 87 (2017) PARA 731 et seq.
5  Opencast Coal Act 1958 Sch 6 para 20(b).
6  Opencast Coal Act 1958 Sch 6 para 21.

### E.  APPORTIONMENT OF COMPENSATION

### 504.  Changes in right of occupation.

Where an act or event occurs by which one person becomes the person who is for the time being entitled to occupy part of a holding[1] or who would be so entitled if a compulsory rights order[2] had not been made, and another person becomes the person who is for the time being entitled to occupy another part of that holding, or who would be so entitled if the order had not been made, and that act or event occurs during the course of the year[3] beginning with the operative date[4] of the order in question, or in the course of a year beginning with an anniversary of that date, the compensation provisions of the Opencast Coal Act

1958[5] apply subject to qualification[6]. The qualification is that those provisions apply (1) in relation to the entirety of the holding, with respect to the part of that year ending with that act or event; and (2) in relation to each of the separate holdings[7], with respect to the part of that year after that act or event, as if any reference in those provisions to a year included a reference both to the part of that year ending with that act or event and to the part of that year after that act or event[8].

1  Ie a holding to which the Opencast Coal Act 1958 s 17 (see PARA 472) applies: see s 34, Sch 6 para 26(1).
2  As to compulsory rights orders see the Opencast Coal Act 1958 s 4; and PARA 431 et seq. The power to make such orders has not been exercisable since 31 December 1999: see PARA 414.
3  As to the meaning of 'year' see PARA 458.
4  As to the meaning of 'the operative date' see PARA 432.
5  Ie the provisions of the Opencast Coal Act 1958 Pt II (ss 17–36), Sch 6, other than Sch 6 para 26(1): see Sch 6 para 26(1).
6  Opencast Coal Act 1958 Sch 6 para 26(1).
7  See the Opencast Coal Act 1958 Sch 6 para 1(2); Sch 6 para 5; and PARA 472.
8  Opencast Coal Act 1958 Sch 6 para 26(1). The provisions of Sch 6 para 26 do not apply in relation to any compensation the entitlement to which is apportioned in accordance with s 17(3A) (see PARA 473): Sch 6 para 26(5) (added by the Coal Industry Act 1994 s 52(2), Sch 8 paras 1, 42(4), (6)). The Opencast Coal Act 1958 Sch 6 para 26(5) does not apply in relation to any compulsory rights order confirmed before the restructuring date (ie 31 October 1994: see PARA 50): Coal Industry Act 1994 Sch 8 para 42(4), (6).

## 505. Changes in right of compensation.

Where, in consequence of any act or event[1] occurring on or after the operative date[2] of a compulsory rights order[3] and before the end of the period of occupation[4], one person would be entitled to compensation for any year[5] in respect of a holding[6] if that act or event had occurred before the beginning of that year, and another person would be entitled to compensation for that year in respect of the holding if that act or event had occurred after the end of that year, the compensation provisions of the Opencast Coal Act 1958[7] apply as if any reference to a year included a reference both to the part of that year ending with that act or event and to the part of that year after that act or event[8].

1  Ie other than such an act or event as is mentioned in the Opencast Coal Act 1958 s 34, Sch 6 para 26(1) (see PARA 504): Sch 6 para 26(2).
2  As to the meaning of 'the operative date' see PARA 432.
3  As to compulsory rights orders see the Opencast Coal Act 1958 s 4; and PARA 431 et seq. The power to make such orders has not been exercisable since 31 December 1999: see PARA 414.
4  As to the meaning of 'the period of occupation' see PARA 433.
5  As to the meaning of 'year' see PARA 458.
6  As to the meaning of 'holding' see PARAS 472, 488.
7  Ie the provisions of the Opencast Coal Act 1958 Pt II (ss 17–36), Sch 6, other than Sch 6 para 26(2): Sch 6 para 26(2), which has effect, with necessary modifications, in relation to compensation under Sch 5 para 4, 5 or 12 (see PARAS 465–466, 469): Sch 6 para 27.
8  Opencast Coal Act 1958 Sch 6 para 26(2). As to the application of Sch 6 para 26 see PARA 504.

## 506. Compulsory rights order having effect for part of a year.

For the purposes of the application of the compensation provisions of the Opencast Coal Act 1958[1] to a compulsory rights order[2] which has effect only for part of a year[3], or for one or more complete years followed by part of another year, any reference in those provisions to a year is to be construed as including a reference to that part of a year[4].

1   The provisions referred to are those of the Opencast Coal Act 1958 Pt II (ss 17–36), Sch 6, other than Sch 6 para 26(3), which has effect, with necessary modifications, in relation to compensation under Sch 5 paras 4, 5 or 12 (see PARAS 465, 466, 469): s 34, Sch 6 para 27.

2   As to compulsory rights orders see the Opencast Coal Act 1958 s 4; and PARA 431 et seq. The power to make such orders has not been exercisable since 31 December 1999: see PARA 414.

3   As to the meaning of 'year' see PARA 458.

4   Opencast Coal Act 1958 Sch 6 para 26(3). As to the application of Sch 6 para 26 see PARA 504.

### 507. Apportionment of annual value.

Where any of the compensation provisions of the Opencast Coal Act 1958[1] are applied to a part of a year[2], any reference to annual value, or to any other amount which is required to be assessed by reference to a year, is to be construed as a reference to so much of the annual value for that year, or of the amount in question assessed by reference to that year, as, on a rateable apportionment of that value or amount as between different parts of that year, is properly attributable to that part of that year[3].

1   The provisions referred to are those of the Opencast Coal Act 1958 Pt II (ss 17–36), Sch 6: s 34, Sch 6 para 26(4), which has effect, with necessary modifications, in relation to compensation under Sch 5 para 4, 5 or 12 (see PARAS 465–466, 469): Sch 6 para 27.

2   Ie in accordance with the Opencast Coal Act 1958 Sch 6 para 26(1)–(3): see PARAS 504–506. As to the meaning of 'year' see PARA 458.

3   Opencast Coal Act 1958 Sch 6 para 26(4). As to the application of Sch 6 para 26 see PARA 504.

### 508. Compensation for depreciation of other land.

Where compensation is payable in respect of depreciation in the value of other land[1] held in the same ownership[2], and a person is the owner[3] of that other land for part, but not the whole, of a year[4], the relevant provision[5] applies as if any reference to a year included a reference to that part of a year[6].

1   As to the meaning of 'year' see PARA 458.

2   Ie under the Opencast Coal Act 1958 s 32 (see PARAS 494–496): see s 34, Sch 6 para 28(1).

3   As to the meaning of 'owner' see PARA 421.

4   As to the meaning of 'year' see PARA 458.

5   Ie the Opencast Coal Act 1958 s 32(2) (see PARA 495): see Sch 6 para 28(1).

6   Opencast Coal Act 1958 Sch 6 para 28(1), (2). Schedule 6 para 28(1) has effect without prejudice to the operation of Sch 6 para 26(3): Sch 6 para 28(2). Schedule 6 para 26(4) has effect in relation to Sch 6 para 28(1) as it has effect in relation to Sch 6 para 26(1)–(3) (see PARAS 504–506): Sch 6 para 28(2).

## (5) Claims and Payments

### 509. Claims.

Compensation under the Opencast Coal Act 1958 is not payable by any person unless a claim for it is duly made to that person[1]. The procedure for making claims[2] for compensation under the Opencast Coal Act 1958, other than claims for compensation under certain enactments applied by that Act[3], is prescribed[4] by regulations[5]. Generally, the Upper Tribunal[6] must determine any dispute (1) as to a right to compensation from any person, or as to the amount of any such compensation[7]; (2) as to a right to the payment of any fees by virtue of regulations[8], or as to the amount of the fees payable in any case by virtue of any such regulations[9]; or (3) as to the amount of the quarterly payments payable[10] in respect of certain types of compensation[11].

1 Opencast Coal Act 1958 s 40(1) (amended by the Coal Industry Act 1994 s 52(2), Sch 8 para 30).
2 A claim is a condition precedent to the payment of compensation: see PARA 461.
3 Ie compensation payable in accordance with any enactment applied by the Opencast Coal Act 1958 s 13 (repealed) or s 16 (see PARA 430) or any sum payable in accordance with any enactment applied by s 45 (see PARA 416): s 40(4). As to the determination of disputes see also PARA 502.
4 As to the meaning of 'prescribed' see PARA 430.
5 See the Opencast Coal Act 1958 s 40(2), which prescribes the matters for which such regulations may provide. Regulations made under s 40 by the appropriate national authority may: (1) require claims for compensation under the Opencast Coal Act 1958 to be made in such form, and within such time, as may be prescribed by the regulations (s 40(2)(a)); (2) require a claimant to provide such evidence in support of the claim, and such information as to the interest of the claimant in land to which the claim relates, and as to the interests of other persons which are known to the claimant, as may be so prescribed (s 40(2)(b)); (3) include provisions as to professional and other fees incurred by claimants in preparing and supporting claims for compensation under the Act, requiring any person, within such limits (whether as to descriptions of fees, or as to amount, or otherwise) and subject to such conditions as may be prescribed, to pay fees so incurred (s 40(2)(c) (amended by the Coal Industry Act 1994 Sch 8 para 30)). No such regulations, in so far as they are made under the Opencast Coal Act 1958 s 40(2)(c), apply to the costs of any proceedings before a court or tribunal, or affect any power of a court or tribunal with respect to any such costs: s 40(2) proviso. The appropriate national authority is the Secretary of State or where functions have been transferred in relation to Wales, the Welsh Ministers: see PARA 2. As to the meaning of 'land' see PARA 414.
   As to regulation-making powers generally see PARA 418. See the Opencast Coal (Claims) Regulations 1959, SI 1959/1146 (amended by the Coal Industry Act 1987, s 1(3)); and the Opencast Coal (Fees) Regulations 1960, SI 1960/194 (amended by the Decimal Currency Act 1969 s 10(1), Coal Industry Act 1987 s 1(3); and SI 2009/1307). Claims must be made in accordance with the appropriate forms set out in the Opencast Coal (Claims) Regulations 1959, SI 1959/1146, Sch 1 (reg 3(1), (2)), modified as necessary in certain circumstances (reg 3(1) proviso), within the appropriate time-limits laid down in Sch 2 (reg 4), which there is discretion to enlarge in proper cases (reg 4 proviso). If any person so requires, a claimant for compensation is to provide proper proofs of title and other necessary evidence: see reg 5, Sch 3.
6 As to the Upper Tribunal see COURTS AND TRIBUNALS vol 24 (2010) PARA 883.
7 Opencast Coal Act 1958 s 40(3)(a) (s 40(3) amended by SI 2009/1307; Opencast Coal Act 1958 s 40(3)(a) amended by Coal Industry Act 1994 Sch 8 para 30). As to an exception see PARA 490 .
8 Ie regulations made under the Opencast Coal Act 1958 s 40 or under s 36 (see PARA 462): see s 40(3)(b).
9 Opencast Coal Act 1958 s 40(3)(b).
10 Ie in accordance with the Opencast Coal Act 1958 s 35(2) (see PARA 510): see s 40(3)(c).
11 Opencast Coal Act 1958 s 40(3)(c). The types of compensation referred to in the text are those mentioned in s 35(2) (see PARA 510: see s 40(3)(c).

## 510. Payment of annual compensation.

Annual compensation[1] payable under the Opencast Coal Act 1958 accrues due from day to day and is apportionable in respect of time accordingly[2]. In respect of such compensation every person potentially liable for the compensation[3] must, on account of any compensation that may become payable by him at the end of the year, make such quarterly payments[4] as may be reasonable in the circumstances[5] but, subject to this, the requirement to make payments will not arise until after the end of the year for which the compensation is payable[6]. Where interest is payable the rate is such as the Treasury may by order prescribe[7].

1 Ie compensation payable under the Opencast Coal Act 1958 s 17 (see PARA 472 et seq) (or s 17 as applied by s 29 (see PARA 488)); s 31(2) (see PARA 492); s 32(2) (see PARA 495); or Sch 5 para 4, 5 or 12 (see PARAS 465–466, 469): see s 35(2).
2 Opencast Coal Act 1958 s 35(3).

3 References to a 'person potentially liable to compensation', in relation to any time during a year at the end of which compensation may become payable under the Opencast Coal Act 1958, are references to the person on whom the liability to pay the compensation will fall at the end of the year if the person entitled to the rights conferred by the compulsory rights order in question does not change before the end of the year: s 35(9) (definition added by the Coal Industry Act 1994 s 52(2), Sch 8 para 26(5)). As to the meaning of 'year' see PARA 458. As to compulsory rights orders see the Opencast Coal Act 1958 s 4; and PARA 431 et seq. The power to make such orders has not been exercisable since 31 December 1999: see PARA 414.

4 'Quarterly payments' means payments calculated by reference to the usual quarter days: Opencast Coal Act 1958 s 35(9).

5 Opencast Coal Act 1958 s 35(1) (amended by the Coal Industry Act 1994 Sch 8 para 26(1)); Opencast Coal Act 1958 s 35(2)(a) (amended by the Coal Industry Act 1994 Sch 8 para 26(2)).

6 Opencast Coal Act 1958 s 35(1), (2)(b). If the amount of the compensation payable for any year by any person to another exceeds the aggregate amount of the quarterly payments made on that account during that year, the balance is payable together with interest on the amount of the balance from the end of that year to the date of payment: s 35(1), (2)(c). If the aggregate amount of the compensation paid for any year by any person to another in respect of any such compensation (excluding any amount paid on account of interest) exceeds the principal amount of the compensation payable for that year by that person to that other person, the person who paid it (without prejudice to any right of recovery apart from s 35(2)) is entitled to deduct the amount of the overpayment from any compensation payable by him to that person for any subsequent year: s 35(1), (2)(d).

7 Opencast Coal Act 1958 s 35(8). At the date at which this volume states the law the rate is 4% per annum less than the base rate quoted from time to time by the Committee of London Clearing Bankers or, where there is for the time being more than one such rate, the rate which, when the base rate quoted by each bank is ranked in a descending sequence of seven, is fourth in the sequence: see the Opencast Coal (Rate of Interest on Compensation) Order 1992, SI 1992/46 (amended by SI 2001/3649). As to the Treasury see CONSTITUTIONAL AND ADMINISTRATIVE LAW vol 20 (2014) PARAS 262–265.

### 511. Payment of terminal compensation.

Terminal compensation[1] payable under the Opencast Coal Act 1958 accrues due at the end of the period of occupation[2], and, if not paid within 30 days of that date, is payable together with interest[3] from that date to the date of payment[4].

1 Ie compensation payable under the Opencast Coal Act 1958 s 23 (see PARA 479) (or s 23 as applied by s 29 (see PARA 488)); s 31(3) (see PARA 493); s 32(4) (see PARA 496); or Sch 5 para 8, 10 or 13 (see PARAS 467–468, 470): s 35(4).

2 Opencast Coal Act 1958 s 35(4). As to the meaning of 'the period of occupation' see PARA 433.

3 As to interest see PARA 510.

4 Opencast Coal Act 1958 s 35(7) (amended by the Coal Industry Act 1994 ss 52(2), 67(8), Sch 8 para 26(4), Sch 11 Pt II).

### 512. Payment of additional compensation on reoccupation.

Additional compensation payable under the Opencast Coal Act 1958 on the reoccupation of a holding qualifying for compensation as agricultural land[1] accrues due on the date when the person entitled to compensation[2] enters into occupation, if after the end of the period of occupation[3], and at the end of the period of occupation in any other case[4]. If the compensation is not paid within the period of 30 days beginning with the date on which it accrues due, it is payable together with interest[5] from that date until the date of payment[6].

1 Ie compensation payable under the Opencast Coal Act 1958 s 23A (see PARA 480): see the Opencast Coal Act 1958 s 35(4A) .

2 See PARA 480.

3 As to the meaning of 'the period of occupation' see PARA 433.

4 Opencast Coal Act 1958 s 35(4A) (added by the Coal Industry Act 1975 s 6(2)).

5 As to interest see PARA 510.

6 Opencast Coal Act 1958 s 35(7) (amended by the Coal Industry Act 1994 ss 52(2), 67(8), Sch 8 para 26(4), Sch 11 Pt II).

**513. Payment of compensation for improvements and forced sales.**

Compensation for short-term improvements[1] payable under the Opencast Coal Act 1958 accrues due at the beginning of the period of occupation[2]; and compensation payable in respect of forced sales[3] accrues due on the effective date[4] of the sale or, if that date was before the operative date[5] of the order, is to be treated as having accrued due on the effective date of the sale[6]. In each case, if the compensation is not paid within the period of 30 days beginning with the date on which it accrues due, it is payable together with interest[7] from that date until the date of payment[8].

1  Ie compensation under the Opencast Coal Act 1958 s 26 (see PARA 483): see s 35(5).
2  Opencast Coal Act 1958 s 35(5). As to the meaning of 'the period of occupation' see PARA 433.
3  Ie compensation under the Opencast Coal Act 1958 s 27 (or under s 27 as applied by s 29 (see PARA 487)): see s 35(6).
4  As to the meaning of 'the effective date' see PARA 501.
5  As to the meaning of 'the operative date' see PARA 432.
6  Opencast Coal Act 1958 s 35(6).
7  As to interest see PARA 510.
8  Opencast Coal Act 1958 s 35(7) (amended by the Coal Industry Act 1994 ss 52(2), 67(8), Sch 8 para 26(4), Sch 11 Pt II).

**514. Payment of compensation in respect of disposable minerals.**

Any compensation payable in respect of disposable minerals[1] accrues due at the end of the year[2] in which the right in question is exercised[3]. If the compensation is not paid within the period of 30 days beginning with the date on which it accrues due, it is payable together with interest[4] from that date until the date of payment[5].

1  Ie compensation payable under the Opencast Coal Act 1958 s 31A (see PARA 471): see s 35(6A). As to the meaning of 'minerals' see PARA 10.
2  As to the meaning of 'year' see PARA 458.
3  Opencast Coal Act 1958 s 35(6A) (added by the Coal Industry Act 1994 s 52(2), Sch 8 para 26(3)).
4  As to interest see PARA 510.
5  Opencast Coal Act 1958 s 35(7) (amended by the Coal Industry Act 1994 s 67(8), Sch 8 para 26(4), Sch 11 Pt II).

**515. Payment where land is held for religious purposes.**

Where any compensation, other than compensation by way of payment for the cost of works[1], is payable by any person ('the person liable') under the Opencast Coal Act 1958, and that compensation would otherwise be payable to a person in right of an interest in land held by him for religious purposes[2], then (1) if the land is ecclesiastical property[3], the compensation is to be paid to the Diocesan Board of Finance for the diocese in which the land is situated[4]; and (2) in other cases, if the person liable is so requested by or on behalf of a body of persons notified to him by the appropriate national authority[5], after consultation with such persons or organisations as he may think appropriate, as the appropriate representative body, the person liable must pay the compensation to that body[6].

1  Ie compensation under the Opencast Coal Act 1958 s 22 (see PARA 478): s 42(1) proviso.
2  Opencast Coal Act 1958 s 42(1) (amended by Coal Industry Act 1994 s 52(2), Sch 8 paras 1, 31). As to the meaning of 'land' see PARA 414.
3  'Ecclesiastical property' means property belonging to an ecclesiastical benefice of the Church of England, or being or forming part of a church subject to the jurisdiction of a bishop of a diocese of the Church of England or the site of such a church, or being or forming part of a burial ground subject to such jurisdiction: Opencast Coal Act 1958 s 42(7) (amended by the Church of England (Miscellaneous Provisions) Measure 2006 Sch 5 para 6). Where any ecclesiastical property is

vested in the incumbent of a benefice which is vacant, it is treated for the purposes of these purposes as being vested in the Diocesan Board of Finance for the diocese in which the land is situated: s 42(6) (substituted by the Church of England (Miscellaneous Provisions) Measure 2006 Sch 5 para 6(c)). As to diocesan boards of finance see ECCLESIASTICAL LAW vol 34 (2011) PARA 241 et seq.

4   Opencast Coal Act 1958 s 42(2) (amended by the Church of England (Miscellaneous Provisions) Measure 2006 Sch 5 para 6).

5   Ie the Secretary of State or where functions have been transferred in relation to Wales, the Welsh Ministers: see PARA 2.

6   Opencast Coal Act 1958 s 42(4) (amended by Coal Industry Act 1994 Sch 8 paras 1, 31). Where, apart from the Opencast Coal Act 1958 s 42, compensation would be payable to a person as the owner of land, and (1) by virtue of s 42(2) or s 42(4), the compensation is payable to the Diocesan Board of Finance for the diocese in which the land is situated or a representative body; and (2) by virtue of the operation in relation to that land of s 24 or s 30, compensation is recoverable from him by another person, the Diocesan Board of Finance for the diocese in which the land is situated or representative body must indemnify him against any liability in respect of that compensation, and for that purpose may apply any money or securities held by them: s 42(5) (amended by the Church of England (Miscellaneous Provisions) Measure 2006 Sch 5 para 6).

## 516.   Payment where land is subject to mortgage or settlement.

Where any compensation, other than annual compensation[1] or compensation by way of payment of the cost of works[2], payable under the Opencast Coal Act 1958 is payable in right of an interest in land[3] which is subject to a mortgage[4], any mortgagee of the interest may make a claim for the compensation[5] and the compensation is payable to the mortgagee[6] or, where there is more than one mortgagee, to the first mortgagee[7]. Where any such compensation is payable in right of an interest in land which is subject to a settlement, or is otherwise held in such a manner that the person entitled to that interest would not be competent to give an effective discharge for the proceeds of a sale of it, that compensation must be paid to the person who would be competent to give such a discharge[8].

1   In this context 'annual compensation' means any such compensation as is mentioned in the Opencast Coal Act 1958 s 35(2) (see PARA 510): s 43(7). For the circumstances in which a mortgagee is entitled to annual compensation, and as to the application of compensation money paid to a mortgagee so entitled see PARA 473. As to the payment of compensation for depreciation of other land to a mortgagee when the interest is subject to a mortgage and the mortgagee is in possession see PARA 495. As to mortgage generally see MORTGAGE vol 77 (2016) PARA 101 et seq.

2   Ie compensation under the Opencast Coal Act 1958 s 22 (see PARA 476): see s 43(4).

3   As to the meaning of 'land' see PARA 414.

4   As to the meaning of 'mortgage' see PARA

5   Opencast Coal Act 1958 s 43(4)(a) (amended by the Coal Industry Act 1994 ss 52(2), 67(8), Sch 8 para 32, Sch 11 Pt II). Such a claim does not, however, prejudice the making of a claim by the person entitled to the interest: Opencast Coal Act 1958 s 43(4)(a).

6   Where compensation is so payable and compensation is recoverable from the mortgagee by another person by virtue of the Opencast Coal Act 1958 s 24 or s 30 (see PARAS 481, 490), the mortgagee must apply the compensation paid to him in the first place in or towards the payment of the compensation so recoverable, and any balance must be applied as if it were proceeds of sale: s 43(5).

7   Opencast Coal Act 1958 s 43(4)(b). Subject to s 43(5), compensation so paid must be applied by the mortgagee as if it were proceeds of sale: s 43(4)(b).

8   Opencast Coal Act 1958 s 43(6) (amended by the Coal Industry Act 1994 Sch 8 para 32, Sch 11 Pt II).

# 8. REGULATION OF MINES AND QUARRIES IN GENERAL

## (1) Common Law Obligations

### 517. Nuisance.

The general principles of the law of nuisance[1] apply to the use of land as a mine[2] or quarry[3], to the use of premises as part of a mine or quarry and to the operations, or the consequences of operations, carried on there. Examples of nuisance are the emission of dust[4] or noxious fumes[5], the discharge of effluents so as to pollute a river[6], the creation of noise and vibration so as materially to interfere with comfort[7], and the projection of debris by blasting[8]. The emission of smoke or fumes and the lack of proper fencing of abandoned and disused mines and quarries are in certain circumstances statutory nuisances[9], and noise emitted from premises so as to be prejudicial to health or a nuisance constitutes a statutory nuisance under the Environmental Protection Act 1990[10].

The escape of dangerous matter from land upon which it has been brought or collected in circumstances which amounts to an unnatural use of the land may impose on the occupier of the land liability[11] in nuisance for the damage done by the escape[12].

1   See generally NUISANCE.
2   As to the meaning of 'mine' see PARA 3.
3   As to the meaning of 'quarry' see PARA 4.
4   *Pwllbach Colliery Co Ltd v Woodman* [1915] AC 634, HL.
5   *St Helen's Smelting Co v Tipping* (1865) 11 HL Cas 642; *Cooke v Forbes* (1867) LR 5 Eq 166; *Salvin v North Brancepeth Coal Co* (1874) 9 Ch App 705.
6   See eg *Stockport Waterworks Co v Potter* (1861) 7 H & N 160; *Pride of Derby and Derbyshire Angling Association Ltd v British Celanese Ltd* [1953] Ch 149, [1953] 1 All ER 179, CA; and ENVIRONMENTAL QUALITY AND PUBLIC HEALTH vol 45 (2010) PARA 270 et seq.
7   *Crump v Lambert* (1867) LR 3 Eq 409; affd 17 LT 133.
8   *A-G (on the relation of Glamorgan County Council and Portardawe RDC) v PYA Quarries Ltd* [1957] 2 QB 169, [1957] 1 All ER 894, CA (projectiles, dust, vibration).
9   See PARAS 276–277; and NUISANCE vol 78 (2018) PARA 155 et seq. As to the control of major accidents involving dangerous substances see the Control of Major Accident Hazards Regulations 1999, SI 1999/743; and HEALTH AND SAFETY AT WORK vol 53 (2014) PARA 629 et seq et seq. As to emissions generally see also ENVIRONMENTAL QUALITY AND PUBLIC HEALTH vol 45 (2010) PARA 1 et seq; ENVIRONMENTAL QUALITY AND PUBLIC HEALTH vol 46 (2010) PARA 576 et seq.
10   See the Environmental Protection Act 1990 s 79; and NUISANCE vol 78 (2018) PARA 115.
11   Ie under the principle in *Rylands v Fletcher* (1868) LR 3 HL 330: see NUISANCE vol 78 (2018) PARA 147 et seq.
12   *Western Engraving Co v Film Laboratories Ltd* [1936] 1 All ER 106, CA (escape of water brought to factory in large quantities); *Read v J Lyons & Co Ltd* [1947] AC 156, [1946] 2 All ER 471, HL.

### 518. Negligence.

At common law an employer of workers at a mine[1] or quarry[2] owes to each worker a duty to take reasonable care for his safety in all the circumstances of the case so as not to expose him to unnecessary risk[3]. Similarly, the occupier of a mine or quarry owes the common duty of care to those lawfully visiting the premises under the Occupiers' Liability Act 1957[4].

1   As to the meaning of 'mine' see PARA 3.
2   As to the meaning of 'quarry' see PARA 4.
3   See HEALTH AND SAFETY AT WORK vol 52 (2014) PARA 376 et seq.
4   See HEALTH AND SAFETY AT WORK vol 52 (2014) PARA 376 et seq. As to the common duty of care see NEGLIGENCE vol 78 (2018) PARA 32. As to the duty owed to persons other than visitors

see the Occupiers' Liability Act 1984; and NEGLIGENCE vol 78 (2018) PARA 40. As to occupiers'
liability generally see NEGLIGENCE vol 78 (2018) PARA 29 et seq.

## 519. Breach of statutory duty.

Where a person whom the provisions of the mines and quarries legislation are
designed to protect suffers injury by reason of a breach of any such provision
creating a duty towards him, he may recover damages in a civil action for breach
of statutory duty[1], subject to the common law and statutory defences which are
available to the owner[2].

No provision of the Mines and Quarries Acts 1954 or of the subordinate
legislation made under it, is to be construed as derogating from the legal duties[3]
owed by an employer to his employees[4]. The owner of a mine or quarry may be
liable both in negligence and for breach of statutory duty[5].

1 See HEALTH AND SAFETY AT WORK vol 52 (2014) PARA 380. As to the civil right of action for
   breach of statutory duty generally see TORT vol 97 (2015) PARA 500 et seq.
2 See HEALTH AND SAFETY AT WORK vol 52 (2014) PARA 382; HEALTH AND SAFETY AT WORK
   vol 53 (2014) PARA 814.
3 Ie any rule of law with respect to the duties owed by employers to their employees including, in
   particular, without prejudice to that generality, the duty to provide a safe system of working:
   Mines and Quarries Act 1954 s 193 (amended by SI 1999/2024),. As to the duties of employers
   at mines see the Management of Health and Safety at Mines Regulations 1993, SI 1993/1897, regs
   6, 7, Sch 1; PARA 536; and HEALTH AND SAFETY AT WORK vol 53 (2014) PARA 703. As to the
   duties of employers at quarries and persons entitled to work quarries see the Quarries Regulations
   1999, SI 1999/2024, regs 6, 41; PARA 538; and HEALTH AND SAFETY AT WORK vol 53 (2014)
   PARAS 793, 797.
4 Mines and Quarries Act 1954 s 193.
      The owner of a mine is not absolved from liability to pay damages in respect of a
   contravention, in relation to the mine, by a person employed by him of: (1) a provision of the
   Mines and Quarries Act 1954, of an order made under it or of regulations; or (2) a prohibition,
   restriction or requirement imposed by a notice served under or by virtue of the Act by an inspector,
   by reason only that the provision contravened was one which expressly imposed on that person or
   on persons of a class to which, at the time of the contravention, he belonged, a duty or requirement
   or expressly prohibited that person, or persons of such a class or all persons from doing a specified
   act or, as the case may be, that the prohibition, restriction or requirement was expressly imposed
   on that person or that that person was, in pursuance of the Act or regulations, appointed by a
   person other than the owner: s 159 (amended by SI 1999/2024). As to the meaning of 'mine' see
   PARA 3.
5 See *National Coal Board v England* [1954] AC 403, [1954] 1 All ER 546, HL; and HEALTH AND
   SAFETY AT WORK vol 52 (2014) PARA 379.

# (2) Statutory Regulation

## (i) In General

## 520. General application of the legislation.

Safety, health and welfare in mines[1] and quarries[2] are regulated by the Mines
and Quarries Acts 1954 and Mines and Quarries (Tips) Act 1969[3], the Health and
Safety at Work etc Act 1974 and subordinate legislation made under those Acts[4],
particularly the Quarries Regulations 1999[5] and the Mines Regulations 2014[6].
Health and safety legislation is to be found elsewhere in this work[6].

The Mines and Quarries Act 1954 regulated the management and control of
mines although much of the legislation relating to mines and quarries is now
contained in regulations and is to be found elsewhere in this work[7]. The Quarries

Regulations 1999 make provision for ensuring safety at excavations and tips associated with quarries[9]. The Mines and Quarries (Tips) Act 1969 details the measures in relation to the prevention of public danger from disused tips in relation to both mines and quarries[10].

The Mines and Quarries Act 1954 applies to all mines, including those belonging to the Crown or a government department or held in trust for the Crown for the purposes of a government department[11], and including training mines[12].

1 As to the meaning of 'mine' see PARA 3.
2 As to the meaning of 'quarry' see PARA 4.
3 As to management of health and safety in mines see now the Mines Regulations 2014, SI 2014/3248. As to health and safety requirements in quarries see now the Quarries Regulations 1999, SI 1999/2024.
4 See HEALTH AND SAFETY AT WORK vol 52 (2014) PARA 313. As to the power to make and revoke rules under the Mines and Quarries Act 1954 see ss 173, 174 (amended by SI 1974/2013). Regulations made under repealed provisions of the Mines and Quarries Acts 1954 and 1969 but continued in force by health and safety regulations may apply to all mines and quarries, to any class of mines or quarries or to a particular mine or quarry: see HEALTH AND SAFETY AT WORK vol 52 (2014) PARA 313. Some of them grant exemptions from their provisions, or provide for the grant of exemption by the Health and Safety Executive or an authorised inspector: see HEALTH AND SAFETY AT WORK vol 52 (2014) PARA 313. 'Inspector' means an inspector appointed by the Health and Safety Executive under the Health and Safety at Work etc Act 1974 s 19; and references to the inspector for the district are references, as respects a mine, to the inspector so appointed for carrying into effect the provisions of the Mines and Quarries Acts 1954 and 1969 in the district in which the mine is situated: Mines and Quarries Act 1954 s 182(1) (definition amended by SI 1974/2013; and SI 1999/2024). As to the Health and Safety Executive and inspectors see HEALTH AND SAFETY AT WORK vol 52 (2014) PARAS 326 et seq, 338 et seq. As to exemptions from the Quarries Regulations 1999, SI 1999/2024, see reg 46; PARA 524; and HEALTH AND SAFETY AT WORK vol 53 (2014) PARA 792.
5 Ie the Quarries Regulations 1999, SI 1999/2024, made under the Health and Safety at Work etc Act 1974 s 15(1), s 15(2), (3)(a), (5)(b), s 82(3)(a), Sch 3 paras 1(1), (2), 3(1), (2), 6, 8, 9, 12, 14, 15(1), 16, 18, 20, 21(b). The regulations impose requirements with respect to health and safety in quarries and supersede certain requirements formerly imposed by or under the Mines and Quarries Act 1954, the Mines and Quarries (Tips) Act 1969 and certain health and safety regulations. The Quarries Regulations 1999, SI 1999/2024, make a number of amendments to the earlier legislation to restrict its application to mines (see PARAS 519, 521 et seq), although the Mines and Quarries (Tips) Act 1969 Pt II (ss 11–36) continues to apply to both mines and quarries (see PARA 558 et seq). The Quarries Regulations 1999, SI 1999/2024, give effect in relation to quarries to EC Council Directive 92/104 (OJ L404, 31.12.92, p 10) concerning minimum requirements for improving the health and safety protection for workers in surface and underground material.
   Save where the contrary intention appears, the Quarries Regulations 1999, SI 1999/2024, generally apply to all quarries where persons work: reg 4(1). However, they do not apply to:
   (1)   any quarry at which there has been no extraction or preparation for sale of minerals within the previous 12 months (reg 4(2)(a));
   (2)   any quarry in relation to which notice of abandonment or ceasing of operations has been given in accordance with reg 45(1) (see PARAS 529, 530, 532; and HEALTH AND SAFETY AT WORK vol 53 (2014) PARA 792) to the Health and Safety Executive, provided that the quarry is no longer being used for the extraction or preparation for sale of minerals (reg 4(2)(b)); or
   (3)   any part of a quarry which is being used exclusively by a person for a work activity unconnected with the extraction of minerals, or the preparation for sale of minerals, provided that any work activities with a view to abandoning that quarry or for the purpose of preventing the flow from that quarry into an adjacent quarry of water or material that flows when wet are not being carried on at that quarry (reg 4(2)(c), (3)).
   The regulations apply to a self-employed person as they apply to an employer and as if that self-employed person were both an employer and a person at work: reg 4(4). For these purposes, 'minerals' includes stone, slate, clay, gravel, sand and any other natural deposits except peat: reg 2(1). 'Preparation for sale' includes the crushing, screening, washing, drying and bagging of minerals: reg 2(1).

As to exemptions from the Quarries Regulations 1999, SI 1999/2024, see reg 46; PARA 524; and HEALTH AND SAFETY AT WORK vol 53 (2014) PARA 792.

6 Ie the Mines Regulations 2014, SI 2014/3248 made under the Health and Safety at Work etc Act 1974 s 15(1), s 15(2), s 15(3)(a), s 15(4)(a), s 15(5), and s 15(8), 18(2)(za), (a), s 80(1), s 82(3)(a) and Sch 3 paras 1(1), (2), 3, 6(1), 8, 9, 10, 11, 13(1) and (3), 14, 16, 18(a), 20, 21 (a), b). The regulations consolidate and modernise the law on health and safety in mines in Great Britain and repeals the majority of extant provisions of the Mines and Quarries Act 1954 and all of Part 1 of the Mines and Quarries (Tips) Act 1969. Except where a contrary intention appears, the Mines Regulations 2014, SI 2014/3248 apply to all mines: reg 4(1). Subject to reg 69 (plans of abandoned mines), these Regulations do not apply to abandoned mines: reg 4(2). The Mines Regulations 2014, SI 2014/3248, apply to a tip if: (1) the tip is on premises which are deemed to form part of a mine under reg 3 (see PARA 3); or (2) the tip is not on such premises but the mine with which it is associated has not been abandoned and the premises on which the tip is situated continue to be occupied exclusively by the owner of that mine: reg 4(3). If a tip is not, apart from reg 4, deemed to form part of a mine under reg 3 by reason only that part, but not the whole, of the premises on which the tip is situated is occupied exclusively by the owner of the mine, the tip is deemed to be one to which these Regulations apply and the premises on which it is situated are deemed to form part of the mine with which it is associated: see reg 4(4)-(7). Pt 8 (regs 60–67) applies to a tip on premises which are occupied exclusively by the owner of an abandoned mine and which are used for depositing refuse from another mine as if the person who is in control of the tip were the mine operator: reg 4(8).

6 See HEALTH AND SAFETY AT WORK.

7 The Mines Regulations 2014, SI 2014/3248, provide for the management and administration of health and safety of mines, and the Quarries Regulations 1999, SI 1999/2024, impose requirements with respect to health and safety in quarries: see HEALTH AND SAFETY AT WORK vol 53 (2014) PARAS 702 et seq, 792 et seq.

9 See the Quarries Regulations 1999, SI 1999/2024, Pt VI (regs 30–38); and PARA 548 et seq.

10 See the Mines and Quarries (Tips) Act 1969 Pt II (ss 11–36); and PARA 558 et seq.

11 Mines and Quarries Act 1954 s 179 (amended by the Quarries Regulations 1999, SI 1999/2024, Sch 2 Pt II). Any expenses incurred under or by virtue of the Mines and Quarries Act 1954 by the Secretary of State are to be defrayed out of moneys provided by Parliament and any sums received by him under or by virtue of the Mines and Quarries Act 1954 are to be paid into the Exchequer: s 178. As to the Secretary of State see PARA 2.

12 See the Mines and Quarries Act 1954 s 183. A training mine is an excavation or series of excavations made for training purposes, ie for the purposes of instructing or training below ground persons in, or in any work connected with, mining minerals: see the Mines and Quarries Act 1954 s 183. As to the meaning of 'minerals' for these purposes see PARA 10.

## 521. Meanings of 'owner' and 'operator'.

For the purposes of the Mines and Quarries Act 1954[1], the owner of a mine[2] is the person for the time being entitled to work it[3], and a liquidator, receiver or manager who carries on the business of an owner is an additional owner[4].

For the purposes of the Quarries Regulations 1999[5], the operator in relation to a quarry[6] means the person in overall control of the working of the quarry[7].

1 As to these Acts see PARA 520.

2 As to the meaning of 'mine' see PARA 3.

3 Mines and Quarries Act 1954 s 181(1) (amended by SI 1999/2024).

4 Mines and Quarries Act 1954 s 181(4). Any other person authorised to carry on the owner's business by an order of a court of competent jurisdiction is also an additional owner: Mines and Quarries Act 1954 s 181(4).

5 Ie the Quarries Regulations 1999, SI 1999/2024.

6 As to the meaning of 'quarry' see PARA 4.

7 Quarries Regulations 1999, SI 1999/2024, reg 2(1). The regulations impose various duties on the operator: see HEALTH AND SAFETY AT WORK vol 53 (2014) PARA 793.

## 522. Working of mines and quarries.

A mine[1] ise treated as being worked at any time when there are persons at work below ground or plant or equipment is in operation at the mine to maintain the safety of that mine or of any other mine or the operation of driving a shaft[2] or outlet is being undertaken at the mine[3].

In general[4], the Quarries Regulations 1999[5] apply to all quarries[6] where people work[7].

1   As to the meaning of 'mine' see PARA 3.
2   As to the meaning of 'shaft' see PARA 3.
3   Mines and Quarries Act 1954 s 182(3)(a) (substituted by SI 2014/3248).
4   Ie except where a contrary intention appears, and subject to the Quarries Regulations 1999, SI 1999/2024, reg 4(2) (see PARA 520; and HEALTH AND SAFETY AT WORK vol 53 (2014) PARA 792).
5   Ie the Quarries Regulations 1999, SI 1999/2024.
6   As to the meaning of 'quarry' see PARA 4.
7   See the Quarries Regulations 1999, SI 1999/2024, reg 4(1); and PARA 520.

### (ii)  Central Administration of the Mining Industry

**523.  Health and safety regulations.**
The Secretary of State[1] has power under the Health and Safety at Work etc Act 1974 to make health and safety regulations[2] for the general purposes of the health, safety and welfare provisions[3] of that Act[4]. Without prejudice to the generality of this power, these regulations may for any of those general purposes make provision for specified purposes[5].

The power to make health and safety regulations[8] includes power, in relation to any requirement of any such regulations that a person carrying on coal-mining operations[9] is to be a participant in a mine rescue team[10] approved by the Secretary of State, to provide: (1) for approval to be given or withdrawn from any scheme only after such consultation as may be specified or described in the regulations; and (2) for the approved schemes to be confined to those which appear to the Secretary of State to be such as to secure that it is reasonably practicable for every licensed operator[11] who is required to do so to participate, on reasonable terms, in an approved scheme[12].

The power to make health and safety regulations, the purposes for which such regulations may be made and the procedure for making them are all dealt with elsewhere in this work[13].

1   As to the Secretary of State see PARA 2.
2   As to such regulations see HEALTH AND SAFETY AT WORK vol 52 (2014) PARAS 388–389. These regulations include the Mines Regulations 2014, SI 2014/3248, and the Quarries Regulations 1999, SI 1999/2024 (see PARA 520).
3   Ie for the purposes of the Health and Safety at Work etc Act 1974 Pt I (ss 1–54): see HEALTH AND SAFETY AT WORK vol 52 (2014) PARA 384 et seq.
4   See the Health and Safety at Work etc Act 1974 s 15(1); and HEALTH AND SAFETY AT WORK vol 52 (2014) PARAS 302, 319, 388.
5   See HEALTH AND SAFETY AT WORK vol 52 (2014) PARA 388. The purposes specified include repealing or modifying the existing statutory provisions: see HEALTH AND SAFETY AT WORK vol 52 (2014) PARA 389.
8   Ie regulations under the Health and Safety at Work etc Act 1974 s 15 (see HEALTH AND SAFETY AT WORK vol 52 (2014) PARAS 388–389): see the Coal Industry Act 1994 s 55(3).
9   As to the meaning of 'coal-mining operations' see PARA 51.
10  References to a mine rescue team are references to any scheme or other arrangements the participants in which are entitled, in an emergency, to the services of persons with the expertise and equipment required for rescuing individuals from underground: Coal Industry Act 1994 s 55(2).
11  As to the meaning of 'licensed operator' see PARA 58.

12  Coal Industry Act 1994 s 55(1). As to rescue organisation at mines see HEALTH AND SAFETY AT WORK vol 53 (2014) PARA 785.
13  See generally HEALTH AND SAFETY AT WORK.

### 524. Powers as to exemptions, consents etc.

Any power conferred on the Health and Safety Executive[1] or an authorised inspector[2] by the Mines and Quarries Acts 1954 and 1969[3], by regulations under them[4], or by certain health and safety regulations[5], to grant, give or impose an exemption, consent, approval, authority, direction, requirement, prohibition or restriction, or to make a determination, is to be construed as including power to vary or revoke the same, in the like manner and subject to the same conditions, if any[6]. Subject to any express provision of the Acts or of such regulations, any exemption, consent, approval or authority granted by the Health and Safety Executive or an inspector may be for a limited or unlimited period, and may be absolute or conditional[7].

1  As to the Health and Safety Executive see HEALTH AND SAFETY AT WORK vol 52 (2014) PARA 326 et seq.
2  As to the meaning of 'inspector' see PARA 520; and HEALTH AND SAFETY AT WORK vol 52 (2014) PARA 338.
3  As to these Acts see PARA 520.
4  Ie under the Mines and Quarries Act 1954 s 141: see HEALTH AND SAFETY AT WORK vol 52 (2014) PARA 313.
5  Ie health and safety regulations which expressly apply to all mines, any class of mines or a particular mine: Mines and Quarries Act 1954 s 176(1) (s 176(1), (2) amended by SI 1974/2013; and the Mines and Quarries Act 1954 s 176(1) further amended by SI 1999/2024. As to health and safety regulations applying to mines see the Mines Regulations 2014, SI 2014/3248; PARA 525 et seq; and HEALTH AND SAFETY AT WORK vol 53 (2014) PARA 702 et seq. As to health and safety regulations applying to quarries see the Quarries Regulations 1999, SI 1999/2024; PARA 525 et seq; and HEALTH AND SAFETY AT WORK vol 53 (2014) PARA 792 et seq. As to the meaning of 'mine' see PARA 3; and as to the meaning of 'quarry' see PARA 4.
6  Mines and Quarries Act 1954 s 176(1)
7  Mines and Quarries Act 1954 s 176(2).
  The Health and Safety Executive may, by a certificate in writing, exempt any mine, part of a mine or class of mines, any person or class of persons, any plant or equipment or class of plant or equipment, or any operation or class of operations from all or any of the requirements and prohibitions in the Mines Regulations 2014, SI 2014/3248 and any such exemption may be granted subject to conditions and to a limit of time and may be revoked at any time by a certificate in writing: see reg 70(1)-(3). The Executive may not grant an exemption unless it is satisfied that the health and safety of persons who are likely to be affected by the exemption will not be prejudiced in consequence of it, having regard to the circumstances of the case and in particular to the conditions (if any) it proposes to attach to the exemption and any other requirements imposed by or under any enactment which apply to the case: reg 70(4).
  Similarly the Health and Safety Executive may, by a certificate in writing, exempt any quarry, part of a quarry or class of quarries, any person or class of persons, any plant or class of plant or any operation or class of operations from all or any of the prohibitions and requirements of the Quarries Regulations 1999, SI 1999/2024, and any such exemption may be granted subject to conditions and to a limit of time and may be revoked at any time by a certificate in writing: reg 46(1). However, the Health and Safety Executive must not grant any such exemption unless, having regard to the circumstances of the case and in particular to: (i) the conditions, if any, it proposes to attach to the exemption; and (ii) any other requirements imposed by or under any enactment which apply to the case, it is satisfied that the health and safety of persons who are likely to be affected by the exemption will not be prejudiced in consequence of it: reg 46(2).
  See further HEALTH AND SAFETY AT WORK.

## (iii)  Records, Returns and Information

### 525.  Record keeping.

Records of appointments in relation to mines[1] and quarries[2] must be made in the appropriate form and retained for a minimum period[3].

1  As to the meaning of 'mine' see PARA 3.
2  As to the meaning of 'quarry' see PARA 4.
3  In relation to mines see the Mines Regulations 2014, SI 2014/3248, reg 68. In relation to quarries see the Quarries Regulations 1999, SI 1999/2024, reg 44. See further HEALTH AND SAFETY AT WORK vol 52 (2014) PARA 356; HEALTH AND SAFETY AT WORK vol 53 (2014) PARA 793.

### 526  Plans of abandoned mines.

Where the mine operator[1] gives a notice of abandonment, the mine operator must, within three months of the date on which the mine is abandoned or the tip is closed, send to the Health and Safety Executive[2], or a body approved by it, an accurate plan of that mine or tip[3] (as the case may be)[4]. Where a plan has been sent to the Executive or a body so approved, that plan must be retained by the Executive or that body in accordance with arrangements approved by the Executive[5].

1  As to the meaning of 'mine operator' see PARA 528. As to the meaning of 'mine' see PARA 3.
2  As to the Health and Safety Executive see HEALTH AND SAFETY AT WORK vol 52 (2014) PARA 326 et seq.
3  As to the meaning of 'tip' see PARA 542.
4  Mines Regulations 2014, SI 2014/3248, reg 69(1).
5  Mines Regulations 2014, SI 2014/3248, reg 69(2).

### 527.  Information.

The Health and Safety Executive[1] has power, exercisable with the consent of the Secretary of State[2], to obtain from any person information which the Executive or an enforcing authority[3] needs for the discharge of its functions[4]. This power is discussed elsewhere in this work[5].

1  As to the Health and Safety Executive see HEALTH AND SAFETY AT WORK vol 52 (2014) PARA 326 et seq.
2  As to the Secretary of State see PARA 2.
3  As to the meaning of 'enforcing authority' see HEALTH AND SAFETY AT WORK vol 52 (2014) PARA 322.
4  See the Health and Safety at Work etc Act 1974 s 27(1); and HEALTH AND SAFETY AT WORK vol 52 (2014) PARA 334.
5  See HEALTH AND SAFETY AT WORK vol 52 (2014) PARA 332 et seq.

### 528.  Instructions, rules and schemes.

The mine[1] operator must ensure that copies of all current instructions, rules and schemes[2] are given to any person at work at the mine upon whom they impose duties and are comprehensible to all persons at work at the mine to whom they apply[3].

It is the duty of the operator[4] of a quarry[5] to ensure that copies of all current instructions, rules and schemes[6] are kept at the quarry and are given to any person at work at the quarry upon whom they impose duties and that they are comprehensible to all such persons to whom they apply[7].

1 'Mine operator' means: (1) in relation to a mine, the person who is in control of the operation of the mine; and (2) in relation to a mine which is to be constructed or operated, the person who proposes to control its operation or (if that person is not known) the person who in the course of a trade, business or other undertaking carried on by that person has commissioned its design and construction: Mines Regulations 2014, SI 2014/3248, reg 2(1). As to the meaning of 'mine' see PARA 3.
2 Ie made under the Mines Regulations 2014, SI 2014/3248.
3 See the Mines Regulations 2014, SI 2014/3248, reg 12(1)(b); and HEALTH AND SAFETY AT WORK vol 53 (2014) PARA 703.
4 As to the meaning of 'operator' at a quarry see PARA 521.
5 As to the meaning of 'quarry' see PARA 4.
6 Ie made under the Quarries Regulations 1999, SI 1999/2024.
7 See the Quarries Regulations 1999, SI 1999/2024, reg 10(1)(b); and HEALTH AND SAFETY AT WORK vol 53 (2014) PARA 793

### 529. Notification of information at mine or quarry.

The mine operator[1] must notify specified information including the name and address of the mine, the owner and the mine operator to the Health and Safety Executive in writing[2].

For quarries[3] specified information[4] must be notified in writing to the Health and Safety Executive[5]. The health and safety document[6] and all the information notified in it must be made available to each employer of persons at work at the quarry and to all persons at work at the quarry[7].

1 As to the meaning of 'mine operator' see PARA 528. As to the meaning of 'mine' see PARA 3.
2 See the Mines Regulations 2014, SI 2014/3248, reg 6(1), (2); and HEALTH AND SAFETY AT WORK vol 53 (2014) PARA 706
3 As to the meaning of 'quarry' see PARA 4.
4 See the Quarries Regulations 1999, SI 1999/2024, reg 45(2); PARAS 530, 532; and HEALTH AND SAFETY AT WORK vol 53 (2014) PARA 792 et seq.
5 See the Quarries Regulations 1999, SI 1999/2024, reg 45; and HEALTH AND SAFETY AT WORK vol 53 (2014) PARA 792. As to the Health and Safety Executive see HEALTH AND SAFETY AT WORK vol 52 (2014) PARA 326 et seq.
6 Ie the document required by the Quarries Regulations 1999, SI 1999/2024, reg 7: see PARA 538; and HEALTH AND SAFETY AT WORK vol 53 (2014) PARA 793.
7 See the Quarries Regulations 1999, SI 1999/2024, reg 7(3)(b); PARA 538; and HEALTH AND SAFETY AT WORK vol 53 (2014) PARA 793.

### 530. Notification of change of operator etc.

Where there is any change in the name, address and location of a mine[1] or any change in the name, address or location of the mine operator, the mine operator must notify the Health and Safety Executive within 28 days[2].

The operator[3] of a quarry[4] must notify the Health and Safety Executive in writing within 14 days of certain events[5] including the appointment or change of the operator of such quarry[6].

The operator[7] must ensure that written notice of the appointment or a change of the operator of a quarry[8] is given within 14 days to the Health and Safety Executive[9].

1 As to the meaning of 'mine' see PARA 3.
2 See the Mines Regulations 2014, SI 2014/3248, reg 6 (3), (4)(a), (b); and HEALTH AND SAFETY AT WORK vol 53 (2014) PARA 703. As to the meaning of 'mine operator' see PARA 528. As to the Health and Safety Executive see HEALTH AND SAFETY AT WORK vol 52 (2014) PARA 326 et seq.
3 As to the meaning of 'operator' at a quarry see PARA 521.

4   As to the meaning of 'quarry' see PARA 4.
5   See the Quarries Regulations 1999, SI 1999/2024, reg 45; and HEALTH AND SAFETY AT WORK vol 53 (2014) PARA 792.
6   See the Quarries Regulations 1999, SI 1999/2024, reg 45(2)(c); and HEALTH AND SAFETY AT WORK vol 53 (2014) PARA 792.
7   As to the meaning of 'operator' at a quarry see PARA 521.
8   As to the meaning of 'quarry' see PARA 4.
9   See the Quarries Regulations 1999, SI 1999/2024, reg 45(1), (2)(c); PARA 532; and HEALTH AND SAFETY AT WORK vol 53 (2014) PARA 792 et seq.

## 531. Service of documents.

The provisions of the Health and Safety at Work etc Act 1974 as to service of notices and other documents[1], which are dealt with elsewhere in this work[2], apply to notices and other documents required or authorised to be served, sent or given under the Mines and Quarries Acts 1954 and 1969[3] or the subordinate legislation under them[4].

1   See the Health and Safety at Work etc Act 1974 s 46.
2   See HEALTH AND SAFETY AT WORK vol 52 (2014) PARA 351.
3   As to these Acts see PARA 520.
4   See the Health and Safety at Work etc Act 1974 ss 46, 53(1), Sch 1; and HEALTH AND SAFETY AT WORK.

## 532. Notification of beginning and ending of mining and quarrying operations.

The mine operator[1] must notify the Health and Safety Executive[2] in writing of the use of a mine for a purpose other than the extraction of mineral, within 28 days of that event occurring[3].

Where a mine has been abandoned, and also where a seam, vein system, shaft or outlet ceases to be used or has been abandoned, the owner must notify the Health and Safety Executive of the event within 28 days of its occurrence[4].

The operator[5] of a quarry[6] must ensure that, within 14 days of any the following events, written notice is given to the Health and Safety Executive: (1) the beginning of operations for the purpose of opening a quarry; (2) the abandonment of or ceasing of operations at a quarry[7]; and (3) the appointment or change of the operator of a quarry[8].

1   As to the meaning of 'mine operator' see PARA 528. As to the meaning of 'mine' see PARA 3.
2   As to the Health and Safety Executive see HEALTH AND SAFETY AT WORK vol 52 (2014) PARA 326 et seq.
3   See the Mines Regulations 2014, SI 2014/3248, reg 6(4)(c); and HEALTH AND SAFETY AT WORK vol 53 (2014) PARA 703As to the meaning of 'owner' see PARA 521.
4   See the Mines Regulations 2014, SI 2014/3248, reg 6(4)(d). In the case of a mine which was in existence or under construction on 6 April 2015 (ie the date of coming into force of the regulations), notification under the Mines and Quarries Act 1954 s 139(1) (repealed) or under the Management and Administration of Safety and Health at Mines Regulations 1993, SI 1993/1897, reg 7 is deemed to be notification under reg 6(1): reg 6(5). As to the duty to inform the appropriate agency of the abandonment of mines see PARA 533. Under the terms of the document required to be prepared by the Coal Authority and the Health and Safety Executive (see the Coal Industry Act 1994 s 4(1); and PARA 60) the Health and Safety Executive informs the Coal Authority of, inter alia, information it receives of the start or the cessation of coal-mining operations or the abandonment of a mine or coal quarry: see PARA 60. As to the Coal Authority see PARA 52 et seq.
5   As to the meaning of 'operator' at a quarry see PARA 521.
6   As to the meaning of 'quarry' see PARA 4.

7 Without prejudice to the duty to give notice under the Quarries Regulations 1999, SI 1999/2024, reg 45(1) in respect of an event in head (2) in the text, the operator of every quarry of coal must, within three months of the date on which the quarry of coal is abandoned, send to the Health and Safety Executive, or a body approved by it, an accurate plan of that quarry, and where such a plan has been so sent, that plan must be retained by the Executive or that body in accordance with arrangements approved by the Executive: see reg 45(3), (4); and HEALTH AND SAFETY AT WORK vol 53 (2014) PARA 792.

8 See the Quarries Regulations 1999, SI 1999/2024, reg 45(1), (2); and HEALTH AND SAFETY AT WORK vol 53 (2014) PARA 792.

### 533. Duty to inform the appropriate agency of abandonment of mines.

If, in the case of any mine[1], there is to be an abandonment at any time after the expiration of the initial period[2], it is the duty of the operator of the mine to give notice[3] of the proposed abandonment to the appropriate agency[4] at least six months before the abandonment takes effect[5]. For these purposes, 'abandonment', in relation to a mine, includes[6]:

(1)   the discontinuance of any or all of the operations for the removal of water from the mine[7];

(2)   the cessation of working of any relevant seam, vein or vein system[8];

(3)   the cessation of use of any shaft or outlet of the mine[9];

(4)   in the case of a mine in which activities other than mining activities are carried on (whether or not mining activities are also carried on in the mine): (a) the discontinuance of some or all of those other activities in the mine; and (b) any substantial change in the operations for the removal of water from the mine[10].

A notice of abandonment[11] must contain such information (if any) as is prescribed[12] for the purpose, which may include information about the operator's opinion as to any consequences of the abandonment[13]. A person who fails to give the required notice is guilty of an offence and liable, on summary conviction, to a fine not exceeding the statutory maximum[14]; and on conviction on indictment, to a fine[15]. A person is not guilty of such an offence if: (i) the abandonment happens in an emergency in order to avoid danger to life or health[16]; and (ii) notice of the abandonment, containing such information as may be prescribed, is given as soon as reasonably practicable after the abandonment has happened[17]. Where the operator of a mine is the official receiver acting in a compulsory capacity, he is not guilty of an offence by reason of any failure to give the required notice if, as soon as reasonably practicable (whether before or after the abandonment), he gives to the Environment Agency notice of the abandonment or proposed abandonment, containing such information as may be prescribed[18].

Where the Environment Agency receives notice or otherwise learns of an abandonment or proposed abandonment in the case of any mine, and considers that, in consequence of the abandonment or proposed abandonment taking effect, any land has or is likely to become contaminated land[19], it is the duty of the Environment Agency to inform the local authority[20] in whose area that land is situated of the abandonment or proposed abandonment[21].

1   As to the meaning of 'mine' see PARA 3 (definition applied by the Water Resources Act 1991 s 91A(2) (ss 91A, 91B both added by the Environment Act 1995 s 58)).

2   'The initial period' means the period of six months beginning with the day on which the Water Resources Act 1991 s 91B(1) comes into force: s 91B(8). In so far as power is conferred on the Secretary of State to make regulations or orders, give directions or issue guidance or make provision with respect to the exercise of any such power, the Environment Act 1995 s 58 came into force on 21 September 1995 (see the Environment Act 1995 s 125(3); and the Environment Act 1995 (Commencement No 1) Order 1995, SI 1995/1983); otherwise it came into force on 1 July 1998 (see the Environment Act 1995 (Commencement No 11) Order 1998, SI 1998/604). As to the

Secretary of State see PARA 2.

3   Where a person gives notice under the Water Resources Act 1991 s 91B(1), he must publish prescribed particulars of, or relating to, the notice in one or more local newspapers circulating in the locality where the mine is situated: s 91B(6). The prescribed particulars for the purposes of s 91B(6) are: (1) the name and address of the mine; (2) the name and address of the operator; (3) the nature of each abandonment or proposed abandonment, specifying (if relevant) the appropriate provisions under s 91A(1)(a) (see heads (1)–(4)); (4) the date or dates of each abandonment proposed abandonment; (5) the address at which notice under s 91B(1), (4)(b) or (5) may be inspected; and (6) the provisions of s 91B under which the notice has been served: Mines (Notice of Abandonment) Regulations 1998, SI 1998/892, reg 3, Sch 2..

4   As to the Environment Agency see ENVIRONMENTAL QUALITY AND PUBLIC HEALTH vol 45 (2010) PARA 68 et seq; WATER AND WATERWAYS vol 100 (2018) PARA 23.

5   Water Resources Act 1991 s 91B(1) (amended by SI 2013/755). The information to be included in a notice to the Environment Agency and the Natural Resources Body for Wales under s 91B(1) is as follows:

    (1)      the name and address of the operator and, if different, the owner of the mine (Mines (Notice of Abandonment) Regulations 1998, SI 1998/892, reg 2, Sch 1 para 1(1) (reg 2 amended by SI 2013/755));

    (2)      details of any changes to the names and addresses referred to in head (1) likely to occur before the latest date for any abandonment specified in the notice (Sch 1 para 1(2));

    (3)      the nature and date of each proposed abandonment, specifying (if relevant) the appropriate provision or provisions under the Water Resources Act 1991 s 91A(1)(a) (see heads (1)–(4) in the text1) (Mines (Notice of Abandonment) Regulations 1998, SI 1998/892, Sch 1 para 1(3));

    (4)      the name and address of the mine, including an Ordnance Survey National Grid reference for its address (Sch 1 para 1(4));

    (5)      a description and schematic drawing showing the area, extent and depth below the surface of: (a) the mine; (b) where not all of the mine is to be abandoned, that part which it is proposed to abandon; (c) any relevant seam, vein or vein system; and (d) any shaft or outlet of the mine (Sch 1 para 1(5));

    (6)      the volume of water discharged to the surface from the mine, and from any part of the mine, to be abandoned, for the two years prior to the date of the notice (Sch 1 para 1(6));

    (7)      the latest information available to the operator on the extent and chemical composition of underground water in the worked areas of the mine (Sch 1 para 1(7));

    (8)      the projected volume of water discharged to the surface from the mine, and from any part of the mine, to be abandoned for the period from the date of the notice to the date of each abandonment specified in it (Sch 1 para 1(8));

    (9)      proposals for the monitoring of groundwater levels and the chemical composition of water in the worked areas of the mine from the date of the notice to the date of each abandonment specified in it (Sch 1 para 1(9));

    (10)      proposals to: (a) treat, lessen or prevent the discharge of water from the mine; or (b) treat water in the mine (Sch 1 para 1(10));

    (11)      the operator's opinion as to the likelihood of any of the following matters occurring as a consequence of the abandonment: (a) the flooding of any worked areas, such areas to be shown on a plan or a schematic drawing identifying the location and extent of such workings; (b) the migration of water to any other mine (whether or not abandoned) and the name of any such mine; (c) the recovery levels of ground water within the mine workings being reached and the period of time within which those levels will be reached; and (d) the discharge of water on to land or into surface water, and the location and chemical composition of any such discharge, together with the information on which the opinion is based (Sch 1 para 1(11));

    (12)      the operator's opinion as to the volume of water likely to be discharged to the surface from the mine to be abandoned, and from any part of that mine, for a period of at least two years from the date of the last abandonment specified in the notice, together with the information on which the opinion is based (Sch 1 para 1(12)).

6   'Abandonment' does not include any disclaimer under the Insolvency Act 1986 s 178 or s 315 (power of liquidator, or trustee of a bankrupt's estate, to disclaim onerous property) (see BANKRUPTCY AND INDIVIDUAL INSOLVENCY vol 5 (2013) PARA 490 et seq) by the official receiver acting in a compulsory capacity: Water Resources Act 1991 s 91A(1)(b). 'The official receiver' has the same meaning as it has in the Insolvency Act 1986 by virtue of s 399(1) (see

BANKRUPTCY AND INDIVIDUAL INSOLVENCY vol 5 (2013) PARA 35): Water Resources Act 1991 s 91A(2). 'Acting in a compulsory capacity', in the case of the official receiver, means acting as: (1) liquidator of a company; (2) receiver or manager of a bankrupt's estate, pursuant to the Insolvency Act 1986 s 287 (see BANKRUPTCY AND INDIVIDUAL INSOLVENCY vol 5 (2013) PARA 221 et seq); (3) trustee of a bankrupt's estate; (4) liquidator of an insolvent partnership; (5) trustee of an insolvent partnership; (6) trustee, or receiver or manager, of the insolvent estate of a deceased person: Water Resources Act 1991 s 91A(2).

7  Water Resources Act 1991 s 91A(1)(a)(i).

8  Water Resources Act 1991 s 91A(1)(a)(ii). 'Relevant seam, vein or vein system', in the case of any mine, means any seam, vein or vein system for the purpose of, or in connection with, whose working any excavation constituting or comprised in the mine was made: s 91A(2).

9  Water Resources Act 1991 s 91A(1)(a)(iii).

10  Water Resources Act 1991 s 91A(1)(a)(iv).

11  Ie under the Water Resources Act 1991 s 91A(1).

12  'Prescribed' means prescribed in regulations; and 'regulations' means regulations made by the Secretary of State: Water Resources Act 1991 s 91A(2). As to the information to be contained in a notice of abandonment, or proposed abandonment and the particulars to be published in a local newspaper, see the Mines (Notice of Abandonment) Regulations 1998, SI 1998/892.

13  Water Resources Act 1991 s 91B(2).

14  As to the statutory maximum see SENTENCING vol 92 (2015) PARA 176.

15  Water Resources Act 1991 s 91B(3).

16  Water Resources Act 1991 s 91B(4)(a).

17  Water Resources Act 1991 s 91B(4)(b). The information to be included in a notice to the Environment Agency under s 91B(4)(b) is as follows:

(1)    the name and address of the operator and, if different, the owner of the mine (Mines (Notice of Abandonment) Regulations 1998, SI 1998/892, Sch 1 paras 1(1), 2(1));

(2)    the nature and date of each abandonment, specifying (if relevant) the appropriate provision or provisions under the Water Resources Act 1991 s 91A(1)(a) (see heads (1)–(4) in the text) (Mines (Notice of Abandonment) Regulations 1998, SI 1998/892, Sch 1 paras 1(3), 2(1));

(3)    the name and address of the mine, including an Ordnance Survey National Grid Reference for its address (Sch 1 paras 1(4), 2(1));

(4)    a description and schematic drawing showing the area, extent and depth below the surface of: (a) the mine; (b) where not all of the mine has been abandoned, that part which has been abandoned; (c) any relevant seam, vein or vein system; and (d) any shaft or outlet of the mine (Sch 1 paras 1(5), 2(1));

(5)    the volume of water discharged to the surface from the mine, and from any part of the mine abandoned for the two years prior to the date of the notice (Sch 1 paras 1(6), 2(1));

(6)    the latest information available to the operator on the extent and chemical composition of underground water in the worked areas of the mine (Sch 1 para 1(7));

(7)    proposals to: (a) treat, lessen or prevent the discharge of water from the mine; or (b) treat water in the mine (Sch 1 para 1(10));

(8)    the operator's opinion as to the likelihood of any of the following matters occurring as a consequence of the abandonment: (a) the flooding of any worked areas, such areas to be shown on a plan or a schematic drawing identifying the location and extent of such workings; (b) the migration of water to any other mine (whether or not abandoned) and the name of any such mine; (c) the recovery levels of ground water within the mine workings being reached and the period of time within which those levels will be reached; and (d) the discharge of water on to land or into surface water, and the location and chemical composition of any such discharge, together with the information on which the opinion is based (Sch 1 para 1(11));

(9)    the operator's opinion as to the volume of water likely to be discharged to the surface from the mine abandoned, and from any part of that mine, for a period of at least two years from the date of the last abandonment specified in the notice, together with the information on which the opinion is based (Sch 1 paras 1(12), 2(1));

(10)   the nature of the emergency which necessitated the abandonment under the Water Resources Act 1991 s 91B(4)(a) (Mines (Notice of Abandonment) Regulations 1998, SI 1998/892, Sch 1 para 2(2)).

Where a person gives notice under the Water Resources Act 1991 s 91B(4)(b), he must publish prescribed particulars of, or relating to, the notice in one or more local newspapers circulating in the locality where the mine is situated: s 91B(6).

18   Water Resources Act 1991 s 91B(5). The information to be included in a notice to the Environment Agency under s 91B(5), where the notice is given after the abandonment, is as follows:

     (1)     the name and address of the operator and, if different, the owner of the mine (Mines (Notice of Abandonment) Regulations 1998, SI 1998/892, Sch 1 paras 1(1), 3(1));

     (2)     the nature and date of each abandonment, specifying (if relevant) the appropriate provision or provisions under the Water Resources Act 1991 s 91A(1)(a) (see heads (1)–(4) in the text) (Mines (Notice of Abandonment) Regulations 1998, SI 1998/892, Sch 1 paras 1(3), 3(1));

     (3)     the name and address of the mine, including an Ordnance Survey National Grid reference for its address (Sch 1 paras 1(4), 3(1));

     (4)     a description and schematic drawing showing the area, extent and depth below the surface of: (a) the mine; (b) where not all of the mine has been abandoned, that part which has been abandoned; (c) any relevant seam, vein or vein system; and (d) any shaft or outlet of the mine (Sch 1 paras 1(5), 3(1));

     (5)     the volume of water discharged to the surface from the mine abandoned, and from any part of that mine, for the two years prior to the date of the notice (Sch 1 paras 1(6), 3(1));

     (6)     the latest information available to the operator on the extent and chemical composition of underground water in the worked areas of the mine (Sch 1 paras 1(7), 3(1));

     (7)     proposals to: (a) treat, lessen or prevent the discharge of water from the mine; or (b) treat water in the mine (Sch 1 paras 1(10), 3(1));

     (8)     the operator's opinion as to the likelihood of any of the following matters occurring as a consequence of the abandonment: (a) the flooding of any worked areas, such areas to be shown on a plan or a schematic drawing identifying the location and extent of such workings; (b) the migration of water to any other mine (whether or not abandoned) and the name of any such mine; (c) the recovery levels of ground water within the mine workings being reached and the period of time within which those levels will be reached; and (d) the discharge of water on to land or into surface water, and the location and chemical composition of any such discharge, together with the information on which the opinion is based (Sch 1 paras 1(11), 3(1));

     (9)     the operator's opinion as to the volume of water likely to be discharged to the surface from the mine, and from any part of the mine abandoned, for a period of at least two years from the date of the last abandonment specified in the notice, together with the information on which the opinion is based (Sch 1 paras 1(12), 3(1));

     (10)    such information as demonstrates that the operator is a person to whom the Water Resources Act 1991 s 91B(5) applies (Mines (Notice of Abandonment) Regulations 1998, SI 1998/892, Sch 1 para 3(2)).

     Where a person gives notice under the Water Resources Act 1991 s 91B(5), he must publish prescribed particulars of, or relating to, the notice in one or more local newspapers circulating in the locality where the mine is situated: s 91B(6).

19   Ie within the meaning of the Environmental Protection Act 1990 Pt IIA (ss 78A–78YC). As to contaminated land see ENVIRONMENTAL QUALITY AND PUBLIC HEALTH vol 46 (2010) PARA 760 et seq.

20   'Local authority' means: (1) any unitary authority; (2) any district council, so far as it is not a unitary authority; (3) the Common Council of the City of London and, as respects the Temples, the Sub-Treasurer of the Inner Temple and the Under-Treasurer of the Middle Temple respectively: Water Resources Act 1991 s 91B(8). 'Unitary authority' means: (a) the council of a county, so far as it is the council of an area for which there are no district councils; (b) the council of any district comprised in an area for which there is no county council; (c) the council of a London borough; (d) the council of a county borough in Wales: s 91B(8).

21   Water Resources Act 1991 s 91B(7).

## 534.   Fencing of abandoned mines and quarries.

It is the duty of the owner[1] of every mine[2] which has been abandoned or which has not been worked[3] for a period of 12 months to secure that the surface entrance to every shaft[4] or outlet is provided with an efficient inclosure, barrier, plug or other device to prevent persons from accidentally falling down the shaft or entering the outlet, and that the device provided is properly maintained[5]. This requirement does not, however, apply to mines which are not mines of coal, stratified ironstone, shale or fireclay and have not been worked[6] since 9 August 1872[7].

Certain shafts or outlets of mines not provided with the above safeguards and certain quarries[8] constituting a danger to the public are deemed[9] to be statutory nuisances[10] and persons other than the owner of the mine or quarry may recover from the owner expenses incurred in connection with the abatement of such nuisances[11].

1  As to the meaning of 'owner' see PARA 521.
2  As to the meaning of 'mine' see PARA 3.
3  As to the working of mines see PARA 522.
4  As to the meaning of 'shaft' see PARA 3.
5  Mines and Quarries Act 1954 s 151(1). This provision is expressly excepted from 'the existing statutory provisions' listed in the Health and Safety at Work etc Act 1974 s 53(1), Sch 1; thus it cannot be modified or repealed by health and safety regulations: see HEALTH AND SAFETY AT WORK. As to the proceedings and penalty for an offence relating to the fencing of abandoned mines and quarries see the Mines and Quarries Act 1954 ss 155, 163(1), 164 (all repealed, save in respect of contravention of s 151). As to the meaning of 'maintained' see PARA 538.
6  Ie for the purpose of getting minerals (as to the meaning of which see PARA 10) or products of them: see the Mines and Quarries Act 1954 s 151(1) proviso.
7  Mines and Quarries Act 1954 s 151(1) proviso.
8  As to the meaning of 'quarry' see PARA 4.
9  Ie for the purposes of the Environmental Protection Act 1990 Pt III (ss 79–84), Sch 3: see NUISANCE vol 78 (2018) PARA 155 et seq.
10  See the Mines and Quarries Act 1954 s 151(2) (s 151(2), (3) amended by the Environmental Protection Act 1990 s 162(1), Sch 15 para 5); and NUISANCE vol 78 (2018) PARA 156.
11  See the Mines and Quarries Act 1954 s 151(3); and NUISANCE vol 78 (2018) PARA 156.

## (iv)  Management and Control of Mines and Quarries

### A.    APPOINTMENT OF MANAGERS

**535.  Appointment of managers and operators.**
With a view to securing the health and safety of persons at work at the mine, the mine operator[1] must: (1) establish a management structure which enables the mine to be operated in accordance with the relevant statutory provisions; (2) make a record of the management structure and the extent of the authority and duties of persons in that structure; (3) appoint a competent individual to be responsible for the overall management of the mine, provided that where the mine operator is an individual and is competent, the mine operator may discharge the functions of that competent individual[2]; (4) ensure that when, for whatever reason, the individual appointed in accordance with head (3) is not readily available, a competent individual is nominated as a substitute to hold the authority and perform the duties of the first named individual; (5) ensure that a competent individual is present at and in charge of the operation of the mine at all times when persons are working at the mine; and (6) ensure that sufficient competent individuals are appointed to the management structure to manage the mine safely[3]. The mine operator must ensure that the management structure is reviewed regularly and revised where necessary and in particular if the mine undergoes significant changes, extensions or conversions[4]. The mine operator must ensure that each person who forms part of the management structure is provided with a copy of those parts of the health and safety document which describe that person's authority and duties[5].

The mine operator must ensure that no person undertakes any work at the mine unless the person either is competent to do that work or does so under the instruction and supervision of some other person who is competent to give instruction in, and to supervise, the doing of that work and no work is undertaken at the mine unless a sufficient number of persons are present who have the requisite competence to perform the tasks assigned to them[5].

The person entitled to work a quarry[6] must not permit another person to be the operator[7] of the quarry unless that person is suitable and has sufficient resources to be able to operate the quarry safely[8].

1   As to the meaning of 'mine operator' see PARA 528.
2   The reference to a competent individual in charge in head (3) is a reference to that individual in charge subject to the overall control exercised by the mine operator: Mines Regulations 2014, SI 2014/3248, reg 10(5).
3   Mines Regulations 2014, SI 2014/3248, reg 10(1) and HEALTH AND SAFETY AT WORK (2014) PARA 702. Without prejudice to the generality of reg 10(1), the management structure must be established to provide in particular that all persons working in the mine come under the authority of a competent person in the management structure who has a duty to exercise such supervision as is appropriate to ensure the health and safety of those persons and of all others who may be affected by their activities: reg 10(2).
4   Mines Regulations 2014, SI 2014/3248, reg 10(3).
5   Mines Regulations 2014, SI 2014/3248, reg 10(4).
5   Mines Regulations 2014, SI 2014/3248, reg 11.
6   As to the meaning of 'quarry' see PARA 4.
7   As to the meaning of 'operator' at a quarry see PARA 521.
8   See the Quarries Regulations 1999, SI 1999/2024, reg 5 et seq; PARA 538; and HEALTH AND SAFETY AT WORK vol 53 (2014) PARA 793.

B.    POWERS AND DUTIES OF OWNERS, MANAGERS AND OPERATORS

### 536.   Duties of mine owners.

The owner[1] of a mine[2] must not appoint another person to be the mine operator[3] unless that person is suitable and has sufficient resources to be able to operate the mine safely[4].

Where the owner of a mine appoints another person to be the mine operator: (1) the owner must provide the mine operator with any relevant information that is available, or that becomes available, about circumstances that might affect the health and safety of persons at the mine[5]; (2) a written statement of that appointment must be signed by the owner and the mine operator and a copy must be provided to the mine operator[6].

The owner must keep the record, and the mine operator must keep the copy, referred to in paragraph (2) for the duration of the appointment[7].

1   As to the meaning of 'owner' see PARA 521.
2   As to the meaning of 'mine' see PARA 3.
3   As to the meaning of 'mine operator' see PARA 528.
4   Mines Regulations 2014, SI 2014/3248, reg 5(1); and HEALTH AND SAFETY AT WORK vol 53 (2014) PARA 703.
5   Mines Regulations 2014, SI 2014/3248, reg 5(2).
6   Mines Regulations 2014, SI 2014/3248, reg 5(3).
7   Mines Regulations 2014, SI 2014/3248, reg 5(4).

### 537.   Powers and duties of mine operators.

The mine operator[1] must take the necessary measures to ensure, so far as is reasonably practicable, that the mine and its equipment are designed, constructed, equipped, commissioned, operated and maintained in such a way that persons at work can perform the work assigned to them without endangering their own health and safety or the health and safety of others[2].

The mine operator must coordinate all measures relating to the health and safety of persons at work at the mine and their implementation[3]. The mine operator must ensure that, in the event of the abandonment or ceasing of operations at a mine, the mine is left, so far as is reasonably practicable, in a safe condition[4].

The mine operator must ensure that no work is carried out at the mine unless a 'health and safety document' has been prepared which demonstrates that the risks to which persons at the mine are exposed have been assessed and that adequate measures have been and will continue to be taken to safeguard the health and safety of persons at the mine[5].

The mine operator must ensure that rules are in place at the mine with a view to securing the health and safety of persons at the mine; and the safe use of equipment. The mine operator must ensure, so far as is reasonably practicable, that any instructions, rules and schemes made are followed or complied with, by persons at work at the mine[6].

The mine operator must make arrangements for the systematic inspection of all parts of the mine below ground where people work or pass or which otherwise could have an effect on the health and safety of persons at work at the mine[7].

The mine operator must ensure that a record is kept of every person below ground at the mine[8].

He must ensure that: (1) danger areas are clearly identified; (2) there is a suitable barrier or enclosure to prevent, so far as is reasonably practicable, inadvertent entry by any unauthorised person to a danger area; and (3) where any person is authorised to enter the danger area, appropriate measures are taken to protect that person's health and safety[9]. The mine operator also has duties relating to the control of major hazards at the mine. He must implement a fire protection plan[9] and must have in place certain arrangements in mines likely to experience explosive atmospheres[10].

The mine operator must also ensure explosives are transported, stored, handled and used safely and securely[11].

He must also ensure that good ground control measures are taken as are necessary to keep secure every place in the mine where persons work or pass[12].

The mine operator has also duties in relation to inrushes of gas, water or other materials that flow when wet must be prevented[13], shafts and winding apparatus[14], transport systems[15], ventilation[16], the mine environment[17], lighting[18], exits[19] and surveyors and plans[20].

Every employer of persons at work at a mine and every person at work at a mine must co-operate with the mine operator to the extent necessary to enable the mine operator to comply with the relevant statutory provisions[21].

1   'Mine operator' means: (1) in relation to a mine, the person who is in control of the operation of the mine; and (2) in relation to a mine which is to be constructed or operated, the person who proposes to control its operation or (if that person is not known) the person who in the course of a trade, business or other undertaking carried on by that person has commissioned its design and construction: Mines Regulations 2014, SI 2014/3248, reg 2(1). As to the meaning of 'mine' see PARA 3.

2   Mines Regulations 2014, SI 2014/3248, reg 7(1); and HEALTH AND SAFETY AT WORK vol 53 (2014) PARA 704.

3   Mines Regulations 2014, SI 2014/3248, reg 7(2).

4   Mines Regulations 2014, SI 2014/3248, reg 7(3).

5   See the Mines Regulations 2014, SI 2014/3248, reg 9. As to permits to work where it is shown by the health and safety document that a measure to carry out hazardous operations and operations which are usually straightforward but which may interact with other activities to cause serious hazards is necessary see reg 13.

6  See the Mines Regulations 2014, SI 2014/3248, reg 12. Rules required by reg 12 must include rules (in these Regulations referred to as 'tips rules') for the purpose of ensuring the safe construction and operation of tips: see reg 66; and PARA 546.
7  See the Mines Regulations 2014, SI 2014/3248, reg 14. As to the maintenance and inspection of equipment see reg 15.
8  See the Mines Regulations 2014, SI 2014/3248, reg 16.
9  See the Mines Regulations 2014, SI 2014/3248, reg 17.
9  See the Mines Regulations 2014, SI 2014/3248, regs 19, 20.
10 See the Mines Regulations 2014, SI 2014/3248, regs 21–26.
11 See the Mines Regulations 2014, SI 2014/3248, regs 27–31.
12 See the Mines Regulations 2014, SI 2014/3248, reg 32, Sch 1; and HEALTH AND SAFETY vol 53 (2014) PARA 737.
13 See the Mines Regulations 2014, SI 2014/3248, regs 33–35; and HEALTH AND SAFETY vol 53 (2014) PARA 742.
14 See the Mines Regulations 2014, SI 2014/3248, regs 36–40.
15 See the Mines Regulations 2014, SI 2014/3248, regs 41, 42; and HEALTH AND SAFETY vol 53 (2014) PARA 728.
16 See the Mines Regulations 2014, SI 2014/3248, reg 43.
17 See the Mines Regulations 2014, SI 2014/3248, regs 44, 45; and HEALTH AND SAFETY vol 53 (2014) PARA 744.
18 See the Mines Regulations 2014, SI 2014/3248, regs 46, 47.
19 See the Mines Regulations 2014, SI 2014/3248, reg 48–57.
20 See the Mines Regulations 2014, SI 2014/3248, regs 58, 59.
21 Mines Regulations 2014, SI 2014/3248, reg 8. As to the power of safety representatives to report imminent risks see reg 18.

**538.  Powers and duties of operators of quarries.**
The person entitled to work a quarry[1] must not permit another person to be the operator[2] of the quarry unless that person is suitable and has sufficient resources to be able to operate the quarry safely[3]. The operator has a general duty to take the measures necessary to ensure, so far as reasonably practicable, that its quarry and its plant are designed, constructed, equipped, commissioned, operated and maintained[4] in such a way that persons at work can perform the work assigned to them without endangering their own or others' health and safety[5].

There are a number of specific duties in regard to health and safety in quarries[6]. The quarry operator must ensure that no work is carried out at the quarry unless a health and safety document[7] has been prepared, kept up to date and made available to employers and to all persons at work at the quarry and that the relevant measures identified in the document are taken and any plans followed[8]. Related to this is the operator's duty to establish the required management structure to enable the quarry to be operated in accordance with the health and safety document; to make the appropriate records and appointments; to review or revise the management structure; and to ensure that each person in the management structure is provided with a copy of the relevant parts of the health and safety document[9]. The operator must ensure that persons undertaking work at the quarry have the required training and competence[10]. He must ensure that rules are in place at the quarry for securing the health and safety of persons at the quarry and the safe use of equipment[11]. He must ensure that the required reviews of health and safety measures are carried out[12]. The operator also has extensive duties in regard to the systematic inspection[13], maintenance and testing of the quarry, its buildings and plant, and the preparation of the required written reports[14]. The operator has further duties in regard to the design, construction, maintenance and precautions of benches and haul roads[15]; rules to control the risks to persons at the quarry arising from the use of vehicles[16] at the quarry[17];

escape and rescue facilities at the quarry[18]; and barriers discouraging trespass around the boundary of the quarry[19].

The quarry operator must ensure that a number of additional health and safety requirements[20] are complied with as appropriate having regard to the features of the quarry, the nature and circumstances of the work carried on there or to a specific risk[21]. These requirements relate to permits to work (including carrying out hazardous operations or operations that may cause serious hazards), safety drills, fire and explosion hazards, control of harmful and explosive atmospheres, danger areas and lighting[22].

The operator has further duties[23] relating to explosives[24] at a quarry[25]. These duties include such matters as safe and secure storage, transport and use, the appointment of explosive supervisors, the drawing up of suitable shotfiring[26] rules and specifications, the supervision of shotfiring and taking specified steps in the case of misfires[27]. There are a number of prohibited activities in relation to explosives[28].

The operator must make arrangements to promote health, safety and welfare measures and check the effectiveness of such measures through the appointment of a committee with powers of inspection[29].

1   As to the meaning of 'quarry' see PARA 4.

2   As to the meaning of 'operator' at a quarry see PARA 521.

3   See the Quarries Regulations 1999, SI 1999/2024, reg 5(1); and HEALTH AND SAFETY AT WORK vol 53 (2014) PARA 793 et seq. There are certain related requirements in regard to the records that must be made and kept: see reg 5(2)–(4).

4   'Maintained' with respect to the quarry and its plant means maintained, where necessary to secure the health and safety of any person, in an efficient state, in efficient working order and in good repair; and 'maintenance' is to be construed accordingly: Quarries Regulations 1999, SI 1999/2024, reg 2(1).

5   See the Quarries Regulations 1999, SI 1999/2024, reg 6(1); and HEALTH AND SAFETY AT WORK vol 53 (2014) PARA 793. As to related duties see reg 6(2)–(4).

6   See generally the Quarries Regulations 1999, SI 1999/2024; and HEALTH AND SAFETY AT WORK vol 53 (2014) PARA 792 et seq.

7   The health and safety document is the document required in accordance with the Quarries Regulations 1999, SI 1999/2024, reg 7: reg 2(1). The document must:

   (1)   demonstrate that the risks to which persons at work at the quarry are exposed have been assessed in accordance with the Management of Health and Safety at Work Regulations 1999, SI 1999/3242, reg 3 (see HEALTH AND SAFETY AT WORK vol 52 (2014) PARA 393) (Quarries Regulations 1999, SI 1999/2024, reg 7(1)(a) (amended by SI 1999/3242));

   (2)   demonstrate that adequate measures, including measures concerning the design, use and maintenance of the quarry and of its plant, will be taken to safeguard the health and safety of persons at the quarry, and in the area immediately surrounding the quarry who are directly affected by the activities of the quarry (Quarries Regulations 1999, SI 1999/2024, reg 7(1)(b));

   (3)   include a statement of how the measures referred to in head (2) will be co-ordinated (reg 7(1)(c));

   (4)   give details of the management structure (see reg 8; and HEALTH AND SAFETY AT WORK vol 53 (2014) PARA 793) and sets out the authority and duties of each person in the management structure (reg 7(1)(d)); and

   (5)   record the following information:

      (a)   the rules required by reg 10(1)(a) (reg 7(1)(e)(i));

      (b)   the arrangements for the review of safety measures in accordance with reg 11 (reg 7(1)(e)(ii));

      (c)   details of the inspection, maintenance and testing schemes prepared in accordance with reg 12 (reg 7(1)(e)(iii));

      (d)   the rules made under reg 14 controlling risks from vehicles (reg 7(1)(e)(iv));

      (e)   details of the permit to work system required by reg 18 (reg 7(1)(e)(v));

      (f)   the shotfiring rules required by reg 25(2) (reg 7(1)(e)(vi));

    (g)    the excavations and tips rules required by reg 31 (see PARA 552) (reg 7(1)(e)(vii));

    (h)    the conclusions of any appraisal or assessment of an excavation or tip undertaken in accordance with reg 32 (see PARA 553) (reg 7(1)(e)(viii)); and

    (i)    the arrangements for health surveillance required by reg 43 (reg 7(1)(e)(ix)).

In addition to the matters referred to heads (1)–(5), the health and safety document must where appropriate also include:

    (i)    a plan detailing the equipment and measures required to protect persons at work at the quarry from the risk of explosion (reg 7(2)(a));

    (ii)    where toxic gases are or may be present in the atmosphere at the quarry in such concentration that the atmosphere may be harmful to the health of persons at work, a plan detailing the protective equipment and measures required to protect persons at work at the quarry from the harmful atmosphere (reg 7(2)(b)); and

    (iii)    a diagram of the quarry indicating those areas to which the regulations do not apply by virtue of reg 4(2)(c) (see PARA 520) (reg 7(2)(c)).

8  See the Quarries Regulations 1999, SI 1999/2024, reg 7(1), (3), (4); and HEALTH AND SAFETY AT WORK vol 53 (2014) PARA 793.

9  See the Quarries Regulations 1999, SI 1999/2024, reg 8; and HEALTH AND SAFETY AT WORK vol 53 (2014) PARA 793. Note that each person in the management structure must carry out the duties assigned to him in the health and safety document for the protection of the health and safety of persons at work at the quarry: see reg 7(5).

10  See the Quarries Regulations 1999, SI 1999/2024, reg 9; and HEALTH AND SAFETY AT WORK vol 53 (2014) PARA 793.

11  See the Quarries Regulations 1999, SI 1999/2024, reg 10; and HEALTH AND SAFETY AT WORK vol 53 (2014) PARA 793. The operator also has a related duty to ensure that copies of all instructions, rules and schemes are kept at the quarry, are given to all relevant workers and are comprehensible to them and that they are complied with: see PARA 528.

12  See the Quarries Regulations 1999, SI 1999/2024, reg 11; and HEALTH AND SAFETY AT WORK vol 53 (2014) PARA 793.

13  'Inspection' means such visual or more rigorous inspection by a competent person as is appropriate for the purpose: Quarries Regulations 1999, SI 1999/2024, reg 12(3). 'Competent' in relation to a person means a person with sufficient training, experience, knowledge and other qualities to enable him properly to undertake the duties assigned to him; and 'competence' is to be construed accordingly: reg 2(1).

14  See the Quarries Regulations 1999, SI 1999/2024, reg 12; and HEALTH AND SAFETY AT WORK vol 53 (2014) PARA 794.

15  See the Quarries Regulations 1999, SI 1999/2024, reg 13; and HEALTH AND SAFETY AT WORK vol 53 (2014) PARA 794.

16  'Vehicle' means any mechanically propelled vehicle (including mechanically propelled plant): Quarries Regulations 1999, SI 1999/2024, reg 2(1).

17  See the Quarries Regulations 1999, SI 1999/2024, reg 14; and HEALTH AND SAFETY AT WORK vol 53 (2014) PARA 794.

18  See the Quarries Regulations 1999, SI 1999/2024, reg 15; and HEALTH AND SAFETY AT WORK vol 53 (2014) PARA 794.

19  See the Quarries Regulations 1999, SI 1999/2024, reg 16; and HEALTH AND SAFETY AT WORK vol 53 (2014) PARA 794.

20  Ie under the Quarries Regulations 1999, SI 1999/2024, Pt IV (regs 17–23).

21  See the Quarries Regulations 1999, SI 1999/2024, reg 17 and HEALTH AND SAFETY AT WORK vol 53 (2014) PARA 795.

22  See the Quarries Regulations 1999, SI 1999/2024, regs 18–23; and HEALTH AND SAFETY AT WORK vol 53 (2014) PARA 795.

23  Ie under the Quarries Regulations 1999, SI 1999/2024, Pt V (regs 24–29).

24  'Explosives' means explosive articles or explosive substances; 'explosive article' means an article containing one or more explosive substances; and 'explosive substance' means: (1) a solid or liquid substance; or (2) a mixture of solid or liquid substances or both, which is capable by chemical reaction in itself of producing gas at such a temperature and pressure and at such a speed as could cause damage to surroundings or which is designed to produce an effect by heat, light, sound, gas or smoke or a combination of these as a result of non-detonative self-sustaining exothermic chemical reactions: Quarries Regulations 1999, SI 1999/2024, reg 2(1) (definitions substituted by SI 2002/2174).

25  See the Quarries Regulations 1999, SI 1999/2024, reg 24; and HEALTH AND SAFETY AT WORK vol 53 (2014) PARA 796.

26  A 'shotfirer' means a person appointed pursuant to the Quarries Regulations 1999, SI 1999/2024, reg 25(2)(a)(ii) (see HEALTH AND SAFETY AT WORK vol 53 (2014) PARA 796) to be responsible for shotfiring operations: reg 2(1). 'Shotfiring operations' includes: (1) checking to ensure that the blasting specification is still appropriate for the site conditions at the time the blasting is to take place; (2) mixing explosives; (3) priming a cartridge; (4) charging and stemming a shothole; (5) linking or connecting a round of shots; (6) withdrawal and sheltering of persons; (7) inspecting and testing a shotfiring circuit; (8) firing a shot; and (9) checking for misfires: reg 2(1). 'Misfire' means an occurrence in relation to the firing of shots where: (a) testing before firing reveals broken continuity which cannot be rectified; or (b) a shot or any part of a shot fails to explode when an attempt is made to fire it: reg 2(1).

27  See the Quarries Regulations 1999, SI 1999/2024, regs 25–26, 28; and HEALTH AND SAFETY AT WORK vol 53 (2014) PARA 796.

28  See the Quarries Regulations 1999, SI 1999/2024, reg 29; and HEALTH AND SAFETY AT WORK vol 53 (2014) PARA 796.

29  See the Quarries Regulations 1999, SI 1999/2024, reg 40; and HEALTH AND SAFETY AT WORK vol 53 (2014) PARA 797. As to the duty of every employer and person at work to co-operate with the operator to enable him to comply with the relevant statutory provisions see reg 39; and HEALTH AND SAFETY AT WORK vol 53 (2014) PARA 797. As to the duties of an employer not to employ anyone at a quarry unless there is an operator and to comply with the relevant statutory provisions see reg 41; and HEALTH AND SAFETY AT WORK vol 53 (2014) PARA 797. As to the obligation of every person at work at a quarry to carry out the duties allocated to him taking into consideration his and others' health and safety, and to comply with the operator's rules made under reg 10: see reg 42; and HEALTH AND SAFETY AT WORK vol 53 (2014) PARA 797. As to the duty of every employer to ensure, where health surveillance under the Management of Health and Safety at Work Regulations 1999, SI 1999/3242, reg 6 (see PARA 536; and HEALTH AND SAFETY AT WORK vol 52 (2014) PARA 399) is required in respect of any work to which a person is to assigned, that the surveillance commences before the person starts the work see the Quarries Regulations 1999, SI 1999/2024, reg 43; and HEALTH AND SAFETY AT WORK vol 53 (2014) PARA 797.

## (v) General Welfare

### 539. Sanitary conveniences.

In relation to any workplace that is a quarry[1] or located below ground at a mine[2], there is a requirement that sanitary conveniences[3] must be, so far as is reasonably practicable, at readily accessible places[4].

Regulations make provision regarding the location, construction, equipment, cleaning and use of such sanitary conveniences[5].

1  As to the meaning of 'quarry' see PARA 4.
2  As to the meaning of 'mine' see PARA 3.
3  ie provided under the Workplace (Health, Safety and Welfare) Regulations 1992, SI 1992/3004, reg 20: see HEALTH AND SAFETY AT WORK vol 52 (2014) PARA 438.
4  See the Workplace (Health, Safety and Welfare) Regulations 1992, SI 1992/3004, regs 3(7) (reg 3 substituted by SI 2014/3248).
5  In respect of mines of coal, stratified ironstone, shale and fireclay, provision for the location, construction, equipment, cleaning and use of such conveniences is made by the Coal and Other Mines (Sanitary Conveniences) Regulations 1956 (contained in the Coal and Other Mines (Sanitary Conveniences) Order 1956, SI 1956/1776, Schedule (amended by the Employment Act 1989 s 9, Sch 2 Pt II)). It is an offence for a person to relieve his bowels otherwise than in a sanitary convenience: Coal and Other Mines (Sanitary Conveniences) Regulations 1956, reg 5(1); cf *Senior v Brodsworth Main Colliery Co Ltd* (1917) 86 LJKB 1387, CA. With respect to other mines see the Miscellaneous Mines (General) Regulations 1956, reg 73 (amended by the Employment Act 1989 Sch 2 Pt II). The Miscellaneous Mines (General) Regulations 1956 are contained in the Miscellaneous Mines Order 1956, SI 1956/1778, Sch 1 (amended by the Employment Act 1989

Sch 2 Pt II; and by SI 1983/994; SI 1993/302; SI 1993/1897). Both sets of regulations took effect as if made under the Mines and Quarries Act 1954 s 141 (repealed so far as relevant), but continue in force by virtue of the Mines and Quarries Acts 1954 to 1971 (Repeals and Modifications) Regulations 1974, SI 1974/2013, reg 7(3): see HEALTH AND SAFETY AT WORK vol 52 (2014) PARA 313. Note that the Workplace (Health, Safety and Welfare) Regulations 1992, SI 1992/3004 (see HEALTH AND SAFETY AT WORK vol 52 (2014) PARA 420 et seq) do not apply to a workplace located below ground at a mine: see reg 3(1)(c) (substituted by SI 1995/2036).

### 540. Drinking water, washing and changing.

Regulations[1] require the provision and maintenance, at certain mines[2], of suitable accommodation for changing and drying clothes and for taking meals[3].

1  See the Miscellaneous Mines (General) Regulations 1956, reg 72 (contained in the Miscellaneous Mines Order 1956, SI 1956/1778, Sch 1); and PARA 539.
2  Ie mines other than of coal, stratified ironstone, shale or fireclay: see the Miscellaneous Mines (General) Regulations 1956, reg 1.
3  Miscellaneous Mines (General) Regulations 1956, reg 72. Health and safety regulations may now be made for these purposes: see generally HEALTH AND SAFETY AT WORK. Note that the Workplace (Health, Safety and Welfare) Regulations 1992, SI 1992/3004 (see HEALTH AND SAFETY AT WORK vol 52 (2014) PARA 420 et seq) do not apply to a workplace located below ground at a mine: see reg 3(1)(c) (substituted by SI 1995/2036).

### 541. Care of animals.

The employment of horses at mines of coal, stratified ironstone, shale and fireclay is governed by regulations[1], which: (1) prohibit the taking below ground of any horse[2] which is less than four years old, or blind, or which has not been certified as free from glanders[3]; (2) provide for periodical veterinary examinations[4]; (3) restrict the carrying of horses on vehicles[5] and prohibit the riding of them below ground[6]; (4) lay down the maximum hours of work[7]; (5) require the appointment, and specify the duties, of horse-keepers[8]; (6) impose requirements as to stabling[9]; and (7) make general provision for the health and welfare of horses at rest and at work[10].

1  See the Coal and Other Mines (Horses) Regulations 1956 (contained in the Coal and Other Mines (Horses) Order 1956, SI 1956/1777), which took effect as if made under the Mines and Quarries Act 1954 s 141 (repealed so far as relevant), but continue in force by virtue of the Mines and Quarries Acts 1954 to 1971 (Repeals and Modifications) Regulations 1974, SI 1974/2013, reg 7(3): see HEALTH AND SAFETY AT WORK vol 52 (2014) PARA 313. Requirements with respect to the management of animals may now be imposed by health and safety regulations: see generally HEALTH AND SAFETY AT WORK vol 52 (2014) PARA 388.
2  'Horse' includes pony, mule and donkey: Coal and Other Mines (Horses) Regulations 1956, reg 16(1).
3  See the Coal and Other Mines (Horses) Regulations 1956, reg 3.
4  See the Coal and Other Mines (Horses) Regulations 1956, reg 4.
5  See the Coal and Other Mines (Horses) Regulations 1956, reg 5.
6  See the Coal and Other Mines (Horses) Regulations 1956, reg 6.
7  See the Coal and Other Mines (Horses) Regulations 1956, reg 7.
8  See the Coal and Other Mines (Horses) Regulations 1956, regs 8–10.
9  See the Coal and Other Mines (Horses) Regulations 1956, regs 11–12.
10  See the Coal and Other Mines (Horses) Regulations 1956, regs 13–15.

## (vi)  Tips

**542.  General duty to ensure safety of tips.**

The mine operator[1] must ensure that tips[2] are designed, constructed, operated and maintained so as to ensure that instability or movement, which is likely to give rise to a risk to the health and safety of any person is avoided.[3].

1   As to the meaning of 'mine operator' see PARA 528.
2   'Tip' means an accumulation or deposit of any refuse from a mine (whether in a solid or liquid state or in solution or suspension) other than an accumulation or deposit situated underground, and includes, but is not limited to overburden dumps, backfill, spoil heaps, stock piles and lagoons and any wall or other structure that retains or confines a tip: Mines Regulations 2014, SI 2014/3248, reg 2. Subject to reg 4(8), from the date of a notice of abandonment of a mine any tip that is deemed to form part of that mine (in this regulation referred to as an 'abandoned tip') ceases to be a tip to which these Regulations apply: see reg 67(1). Despite reg 67(1), reg 68 see PARA 525) continues to apply in relation to every report or record made in relation to an abandoned tip: reg 67(2). As to the application to the Mines Regulations 2014, SI 2014/3248 to tips see PARA 520.
3   Mines Regulations 2014, SI 2014/3248, reg 60.

**543.  Appraisal of tips.**

The mine operator[1] must ensure that: (1) a suitable appraisal of all existing or proposed tips[2] at the mine is undertaken by a competent person in order to determine whether any such tip is or, in the case of a proposed tip, would be, a significant hazard; (2) any significant findings made during the appraisal are recorded; and (3) the record is made available to each employer of persons at the mine[3].

Where the person undertaking the appraisal concludes that the tip represents a significant hazard, the mine operator must ensure that a geotechnical assessment[4] is carried out in accordance with certain requirements[5] as soon as is reasonably practicable[6].

Where the geotechnical specialist concludes[7] that a tip represents a significant hazard by way of instability or movement ('notifiable tip'), the mine operator must ensure that the tip is subject to a further geotechnical assessment at least every two years[8]. The mine operator must ensure that a geotechnical assessment is undertaken as soon as is reasonably practicable where, in relation to a notifiable tip, there is: (a) any reason to suspect that there has been or will be a significant change to the matters to which the geotechnical assessment relates or any neighbouring land which may be affected by movement by or instability of the tip; or (b) any reason to doubt the validity of the conclusion of the current assessment[9].

The mine operator must ensure that sufficient records are kept of the nature, quantity and location of all substances accumulated or deposited at a notifiable tip to enable an accurate assessment of the stability of that tip to be made[10].

1   As to the meaning of 'mine operator' see PARA 528.
2   As to the meaning of 'tip' see PARA 542.
3   Mines Regulations 2014, SI 2014/3248, reg 61(1). Where the person undertaking the appraisal concludes that the tip presents no significant hazard, the mine operator must ensure that a competent person carries out further appraisals (1) at appropriate intervals; (2) whenever there is any reason to suspect that there has been or will be a significant change to the matters to which the appraisal relates or any neighbouring land which may be affected by movement by or instability of the tip to which the appraisal relates; and (3) whenever there is any reason to doubt the validity of the conclusion of the current appraisal: reg 61(2).

4   'Geotechnical assessment' means an assessment carried out by a geotechnical specialist identifying and assessing all factors liable to affect the stability and safety of a proposed or existing tip; 'geotechnical specialist" means a person who is suitably qualified and competent to perform a geotechnical analysis to determine the hazard and risk arising from the tip being assessed: Mines Regulations 2014, SI 2014/3248, reg 62(1).
5   Ie in accordance with the Mines Regulations 2014, SI 2014/3248, reg 62.
6   Mines Regulations 2014, SI 2014/3248, reg 61. As to geotechnical assessments see reg 62, Sch 2.
7   Ie under the Mines Regulations 2014, SI 2014/3248, reg 62(3)(a).
8   Mines Regulations 2014, SI 2014/3248, reg 63(1).
9   Mines Regulations 2014, SI 2014/3248, reg 63(2).
10  Mines Regulations 2014, SI 2014/3248, reg 64.

## 544. Notification of tips.

The mine operator[1] must give not less than 30 days' notice in writing to the Health and Safety Executive[2] (or such other period as the Executive may permit) of the mine operator's intention to commence or continue (as appropriate) operations in relation to any: (1) proposed tip[3] which it is reasonable to expect will be a significant hazard[4]; or (2) notifiable tip[5] other than a notifiable tip which was a classified tip[6] and in respect of which notice has been given[7].

A brief description of the tip, including its location, size and the material to be excavated or tipped must be included in any notice[8]. In relation to a tip falling within head (2), the geotechnical specialist's conclusions[9] must also be included in the notice[10].

Where a geotechnical specialist[11] concludes during the geotechnical assessment[12] of a notifiable tip that the tip no longer presents a significant hazard by way of instability or movement, the mine operator must give notice in writing of that conclusion and the reasons for that conclusion to the Executive within two months of the geotechnical assessment[13].

1   As to the meaning of 'mine operator' see PARA 528.
2   As to the Health and Safety Executive see HEALTH AND SAFETY AT WORK vol 52 (2014) PARA 326 et seq.
3   As to the meaning of 'tip' see PARA 542.
4   In the case of tips falling within head (1), notice must be given before the commencement of operations: Mines Regulations 2014, SI 2014/3248, reg 65(3)(a).
5   As to the meaning of 'notifiable tip' see PARA 543.
6   Ie within the meaning of the Mines and Quarries (Tips) Regulations 1971, SI 1971/1377: see PARA 545 et seq.
7   Mines Regulations 2014, SI 2014/3248, reg 65(1). The text refers to notice in accordance with the Mines and Quarries (Tips) Regulations 1971, SI 1971/1377, reg 8(1): Mines Regulations 2014, SI 2014/3248, reg 65(1). Head (2) does not apply to a tip in relation to which notice of intention to commence operations has been given previously: reg 65(2). In the case of tips falling within head (2), notice must be given as soon as possible after the date on which the mine operator receives the geotechnical assessment: Mines Regulations 2014, SI 2014/3248, reg 65(3)(b). Where tipping operations from a mine are to be begun on premises which at that time are not the site of a tip to which Pt I applies, the owner must also, and within a similar period, give notice to the district inspector of whether or not the resulting tip is intended to be a classified tip, and if the notice states that the resulting tip is intended to be a classified tip, it is thereupon treated as such: Mines and Quarries (Tips) Regulations 1971, SI 1971/1377, reg 8(1), (4) (reg 8(1), (2), (4) amended by SI 1999/2024). Where the owner has given such notice that the resulting tip is not to be a classified tip, the inspector may at any time before tipping operations are begun for the purpose of ensuring the safety of the tip or for securing that the site is satisfactory by notice served on the owner direct that the tip is to be treated as a classified tip: Mines and Quarries (Tips) Regulations 1971, SI 1971/1377, reg 8(2). The owner may require a reference upon such a notice: reg 8(3).
8   Mines Regulations 2014, SI 2014/3248, reg 65(4)(a).
9   Ie under the Mines Regulations 2014, SI 2014/3248, reg 62(3).
10  Mines Regulations 2014, SI 2014/3248, reg 65(4)(b).
11  As to the meaning 'geotechnical specialist' see PARA 543 .

12 As to the meaning 'geotechnical assessment' see PARA 543.
13 Mines Regulations 2014, SI 2014/3248, reg 65(5).

### 545. General management of tips.

Subject to a power of exemption[1], comprehensive provisions govern the drainage[2], supervision[3] and inspection[4] of tips to which the security provisions of the Mines and Quarries (Tips) Act 1969[5] apply and the appointment of competent persons for these purposes[6]. There are special provisions relating to classified tips[7], according to whether they are active[8] or closed[9], and provision is also made as to the conduct of employees at tips to which those provisions apply[10].

1 Ie subject to the power of an authorised inspector to exempt:
    (1)    in the case of an active tip, the mine with which it is associated or any part of it, including the tip; or
    (2)    in the case of a closed tip, the tip or any part of it,
    from any provision of the regulations where he considers that its application is inappropriate or that the exemption will not prejudice the security of the tip: Mines and Quarries (Tips) Regulations 1971, SI 1971/1377, reg 3 (amended by SI 1999/2024). As to the meaning of 'tip' see PARA 543. As to the meanings of 'active tip' and 'closed tip' see PARA 543; and as to the meaning of 'mine' see PARA 3.
2 Tipping operations from every mine must be carried out in such a way as to secure that the operations and the tip resulting from them do not cause an accumulation of water in under or near the tip which may make the tip insecure: Mines and Quarries (Tips) Regulations 1971, SI 1971/1377, reg 4(1) (amended by SI 1999/2024). Every active and closed tip must be kept efficiently drained: Mines and Quarries (Tips) Regulations 1971, SI 1971/1377, reg 4(2). As to the meaning of 'tipping operations' see PARA 543 .
3 See the Mines and Quarries (Tips) Regulations 1971, SI 1971/1377, regs 5, 6 (amended by SI 1999/2024).
4 See the Mines and Quarries (Tips) Regulations 1971, SI 1971/1377, regs 5(3), 6, 11, 17 (regs 6, 11 and 17 amended by SI 1999/2024).
5 Ie the Mines and Quarries (Tips) Act 1969 Pt I (ss 1–10). As to tips to which the provisions apply see PARA 543.
6 See the Mines and Quarries (Tips) Regulations 1971, SI 1971/1377, regs 5(1), 11, 12, 14, 17, 18 (regs 11, 12, 14, 17, 18 amended by SI 1999/2024).
7 As to the meaning of 'classified tip' see PARA 543 .
8 As to the provisions relating to active classified tips see the Mines and Quarries (Tips) Regulations 1971, SI 1971/1377, Pt III (regs 9–16) (amended by SI 1999/2024).
9 As to the provisions relating to closed classified tips see the Mines and Quarries (Tips) Regulations 1971, SI 1971/1377, Pt IV (regs 17–20) (amended by SI 1999/2024). As to the resumption of tipping operations at closed tips see the Mines and Quarries (Tips) Regulations 1971, SI 1971/1377, Pt V (regs 21–23) (amended by SI 1999/2024).
10 See the Mines and Quarries (Tips) Regulations 1971, SI 1971/1377, reg 27.

### 546. Rules as to operation of tips.

Rules in place[1] must include rules (in these Regulations referred to as 'tips rules') for the purpose of ensuring the safe construction and operation of tips[2]. Tips rules must in particular specify: (1) the manner in which the activities[3] are to be carried out; (2) the nature and extent of supervision of such activities; and (3) the precautions to be taken during such activities to ensure the health and safety of any person and the safety and stability of a tip[4].

Tipping rules are to be made in the case of every mine or quarry with which is associated[5] an active classified tip[6] with respect to tipping operations on that tip and the nature of the refuse to be deposited on that tip[7].

1 Ie as required by the Mines Regulations 2014, SI 2014/3248, reg 12: see PARA 528.
2 Mines Regulations 2014, SI 2014/3248, reg 66(1). As to the meaning of 'tip' see PARA 542 .
3 Ie referred to in the Mines Regulations 2014, SI 2014/3248, reg 66(1).
4 Mines Regulations 2014, SI 2014/3248, reg 66(2).
5 As to the mine with which a tip is associated see PARA 544. As to the meaning of 'mine' see PARA

    3 (definition applied by the Mines and Quarries (Tips) Act 1969 s 1(3)(a)).
6   As to the meaning of 'active tip' see PARA 543. As to the meaning of 'classified tip' see PARA 543.
7   See the Mines and Quarries (Tips) Regulations 1971, SI 1971/1377, regs 10, 23.

### 547. Plans and sections of tips.

Provision may be made by regulations[1] requiring that the person having responsibility for every active or closed tip[2] of a prescribed class or description must keep at the office at the mine with which the tip is associated[3], or other place approved by an authorised inspector[4].

1   See the Mines and Quarries (Tips) Regulations 1971, SI 1971/1377, reg 9 (amended by SI 1999/2024) (procedure before beginning of tipping operations at active classified tips); reg 13 (amended by SI 1999/2024) (plans, sections and maps in connection with active classified tips); regs 19, 20 (both amended by SI 1999/2024) (plans, sections and maps in connection with closed classified tips); reg 21 (amended by SI 1999/2024) (procedure before resumption of tipping operations at closed tips); and regs 24, 25 (both amended by SI 1999/2024) (transmission of plans etc relating to tips ceasing to be associated with a mine or quarry). As to the meaning of 'tipping operations' see PARA 543. As to the meaning of 'classified tip' see PARA 543 .
2   As to the meanings of 'active tip' and 'closed tip' see PARA 543.
3   As to the mine with which a tip is associated see PARA 544. As to the meaning of 'mine' see PARA 3 (definition applied by the Mines and Quarries (Tips) Act 1969 s 1(3)(a)).
4   See the Mines and Quarries (Tips) Regulations 1971, SI 1971/1377, reg 13 (amended by SI 1999/2024). The following are required to be kept: (1) plans and sections of active classified tips to show the extent of the tip up to a date not more than 15 months past or such other date as an inspector may require; (2) plans to show the premises on which the tip is situated and neighbouring land within 250 metres of the boundaries of those premises; and (3) sections to show any variation in the thickness or character of strata which may affect the security of the tip: reg 13(c). As to the requirement to keep reports, directions and maps see reg 13(a), (b), (d). The Mines and Quarries (Tips) Regulations 1971, SI 1971/1377, reg 24 requires that within three months of the abandonment of a mine the owner must send to the district inspector: (1) all such plans, drawings and sections relating to tips associated with the mine as were required to be kept by virtue of the Mines and Quarries (Tips) Act 1969 s 6 (see PARA 547) (Mines and Quarries (Tips) Regulations 1971, SI 1971/1377, reg 24(a) (regs 24, 25 amended by the SI 1999/2024)); (2) all such other plans relating to such tips as were required to be kept by the Mines and Quarries (Tips) Regulations 1971, SI 1971/1377 (reg 24(b)); (3) all such reports or records relating to such tips as were required to be kept by virtue of regs 13, 14(b), 20 (see PARAS 545, 547) (reg 24(c)). Similarly, before an owner of a mine with which a tip is associated parts with exclusive occupation of the whole of the premises on which the tip is situated, he must send the district inspector all such plans, drawings, sections, reports and records (or accurate copies of them) relating to the tip as mentioned in reg 24: reg 25. As to the meaning of 'inspector' see PARA 520 (definition applied by the Mines and Quarries (Tips) Act 1969 s 1(3)(a)). As to inspectors see HEALTH AND SAFETY AT WORK vol 52 (2014) PARA 388 et seq.

B.   SAFETY OF EXCAVATIONS AND TIPS AT QUARRIES

### 548. The legislation.

Provisions[1] about the safety of excavations[2] and tips[3] associated with quarries[4] are contained in the Quarries Regulations 1999[5].

1   See PARA 549 et seq.
2   As to the meaning of 'excavation' see PARA 4 .
3   As to the meaning of 'tip' see PARA 4 .
4   As to the meaning of 'quarry' see PARA 4.
5   Ie the Quarries Regulations 1999, SI 1999/2024, which are made under the Health and Safety at Work etc Act 1974 (see PARA 520; and HEALTH AND SAFETY AT WORK vol 52 (2014) PARA 313).

## 549. General duty of operator.

The operator[1] of a quarry[2] must ensure that excavations[3] and tips[4] are designed, constructed, operated and maintained[5] so as to ensure that instability or movement, which is likely to give rise to a risk to the health and safety of any person, is avoided[6]. In addition to this general duty the operator has a number of specific duties relating to excavations and tips[7].

1   As to the meaning of 'operator' see PARA 521.
2   As to the meaning of 'quarry' see PARA 4.
3   As to the meaning of 'excavation' see PARA 4 .
4   As to the meaning of 'tip' see PARA 4.
5   As to the meaning of 'maintained' see PARA 538 .
6   Quarries Regulations 1999, SI 1999/2024, reg 30.
7   See PARA 550 et seq.

## 550. Duty to keep record of substances tipped.

The operator[1] of a quarry[2] must ensure that sufficient records are kept of the nature, quantity and location of all substances accumulated or deposited at a notifiable tip[3] to enable an accurate assessment of the stability of that tip to be made[4].

1   As to the meaning of 'operator' see PARA 521.
2   As to the meaning of 'quarry' see PARA 4.
3   As to notifiable tips see the Quarries Regulations 1999, SI 1999/2024, reg 34; and PARA 556.
4   Quarries Regulations 1999, SI 1999/2024, reg 36.

## 551. Notification requirements.

In relation to any:
(1)     proposed excavation[1] or tip[2] which it is reasonable to expect will be a significant hazard[3];
(2)     notifiable excavation[4]; or
(3)     notifiable tip[5] other than a notifiable tip which was a classified tip[6], and in respect of which the relevant notice has been given[7],
the operator[8] of a quarry[9] must[10] give not less than 30 days' notice[11] (or such shorter period as the Health and Safety Executive[12] may permit) to the Health and Safety Executive of his intention to commence or, in relation to excavations and tips falling within heads (2) and (3) above, continue, operations[13].

The following information must be included in any notice given by the operator in accordance with the above requirements[14]:
(a)     a brief description of the excavation or tip, including its location, size, and the material to be excavated or tipped[15]; and
(b)     in relation to excavations and tips falling within heads (2) and (3) above, the conclusions reached by the geotechnical specialist[16] carrying out the geotechnical assessment[17].

Where the conclusion reached by a geotechnical specialist during the geotechnical assessment of an excavation or tip which has been subject to a geotechnical assessment at least every two years[18] is that the excavation or tip no longer presents a significant hazard by way of instability or movement, the operator must give notice of that conclusion and the reasons for that conclusion to the Health and Safety Executive within two months of the geotechnical assessment[19].

1   As to the meaning of 'excavation' see PARA 4 .
2   As to the meaning of 'tip' see PARA 4 .

3   Quarries Regulations 1999, SI 1999/2024, reg 37(1)(a). 'Hazard' in relation to an excavation or tip means having the potential to cause harm to the health and safety of any person: reg 2(1).
4   Quarries Regulations 1999, SI 1999/2024, reg 37(1)(b). As to notifiable excavations see reg 34; and PARA 556.
5   As to notifiable tips see reg 34; and PARA 556.
6   Ie within the meaning of the Mines and Quarries (Tips) Regulations 1971, SI 1971/1377, reg 2(1) (see PARA 543).
7   Quarries Regulations 1999, SI 1999/2024, reg 37(1)(c). The notice referred to in the text is that given under the Mines and Quarries (Tips) Regulations 1971, SI 1971/1377, reg 8(1) (see PARA 544).
8   As to the meaning of 'operator' see PARA 521.
9   As to the meaning of 'quarry' see PARA 4.
10  This is subject to the Quarries Regulations 1999, SI 1999/2024, reg 37(2), which provides that heads (2) and (3) in the text do not apply to an excavation or tip in relation to which notice of intention to commence operations has previously been given.
11  The 30 days' notice referred to must be given: in the case of excavations and tips falling within head (1) in the text, before the commencement of operations; and in the case of excavations and tips falling within heads (2) and (3) in the text, as soon as possible after the date on which the operator is notified of the geotechnical specialist's conclusions, reached in accordance with the Quarries Regulations 1999, SI 1999/2024, reg 33(1)(b) (see PARA 555): reg 37(3).
12  As to the Health and Safety Executive see HEALTH AND SAFETY AT WORK vol 52 (2014) PARA 326 et seq.
13  Quarries Regulations 1999, SI 1999/2024, reg 37(1).
14  Ie in accordance with the Quarries Regulations 1999, SI 1999/2024, reg 37(1).
15  Quarries Regulations 1999, SI 1999/2024, reg 37(4)(a).
16  As to the meaning of 'geotechnical specialist' see PARA 555 .
17  Quarries Regulations 1999, SI 1999/2024, reg 37(4)(b). The conclusions referred to in the text are those reached in accordance with reg 33(1)(b),(c) and (d) (see PARA 555). As to geotechnical assessments see PARA 555.
18  Ie in accordance with Quarries Regulations 1999, SI 1999/2024, reg 34(1) (see PARA 556).
19  Quarries Regulations 1999, SI 1999/2024, reg 37(5).

## 552.   Excavations and tips rules.

The operator[1] of a quarry[2] must ensure that suitable and sufficient rules (the 'excavations and tips rules') are made to ensure the safe construction and operation of excavations[3] and tips[4]. Such rules must in particular specify the following matters:

(1)     the manner in which such activities are to be carried out[5];
(2)     the nature and extent of supervision of such activities[6]; and
(3)     the precautions to be taken during such activities to ensure the health and safety of any person and the safety and stability of the excavation or tip[7].

1   As to the meaning of 'operator' see PARA 521.
2   As to the meaning of 'quarry' see PARA 4.
3   As to the meaning of 'excavation' see PARA 4 .
4   Quarries Regulations 1999, SI 1999/2024, regs 2(1), 31. As to the meaning of 'tip' see PARA 4 .
5   Quarries Regulations 1999, SI 1999/2024, reg 31(a).
6   Quarries Regulations 1999, SI 1999/2024, reg 31(b).
7   Quarries Regulations 1999, SI 1999/2024, reg 31(c).

## 553.   Appraisal of excavations and tips.

The operator[1] must ensure that a suitable and sufficient appraisal of all proposed or existing excavations[2] or tips[3] at the quarry[4] is undertaken by a competent[5] person in order to determine whether any such excavation or tip is a significant hazard[6].

The operator must ensure that:

(1)      any significant findings made during an appraisal, any conclusions reached[7], and the reasons for those conclusions, are recorded by the competent person undertaking the appraisal[8];

(2)      the competent person signs and dates any such record[9]; and

(3)      the record made in accordance with head (1) above is made available to each employer of persons at work at the quarry and to all persons at work at the quarry[10].

Where the conclusion reached by the competent person following an appraisal[11] is that the excavation or tip presents no significant hazard, the operator must ensure that a competent person carries out further such appraisals:

(a)      at appropriate intervals[12];

(b)      whenever there is any reason to suspect that there has been or will be a significant change to the matters to which the appraisal relates, or any neighbouring land which may be affected by movement by or instability of the excavation or tip to which the appraisal relates[13]; and

(c)      whenever there is any reason to doubt the validity of the conclusion of the current appraisal[14].

Where the conclusion reached by the competent person following an appraisal[15] is that the excavation or tip represents a significant hazard, the operator must ensure that a geotechnical assessment is carried out[16] as soon as is reasonably practicable[17].

1   As to the meaning of 'operator' see PARA 521.
2   As to the meaning of 'excavation' see PARA 4.
3   As to the meaning of 'tip' see PARA 4 .
4   As to the meaning of 'quarry' see PARA 4.
5   As to the meaning of 'competent' see PARA 538 .
6   Quarries Regulations 1999, SI 1999/2024, reg 32(1). As to the meaning of 'hazard' see PARA 551. As to the operator's duties in relation to excavations and tips which are and are not significant hazards see regs 34, 35; and PARAS 556 and 560.
7   Ie any conclusions reached in accordance with the Quarries Regulations 1999, SI 1999/2024, reg 32(1).
8   Quarries Regulations 1999, SI 1999/2024, reg 32(2)(a).
9   Quarries Regulations 1999, SI 1999/2024, reg 32(2)(b).
10   Quarries Regulations 1999, SI 1999/2024, reg 32(2)(c).
11   Ie an appraisal made pursuant to the Quarries Regulations 1999, SI 1999/2024, reg 32(1).
12   Quarries Regulations 1999, SI 1999/2024, reg 32(3)(a).
13   Quarries Regulations 1999, SI 1999/2024, reg 32(3)(b).
14   Quarries Regulations 1999, SI 1999/2024, reg 32(3)(c).
15   Ie an appraisal pursuant to the Quarries Regulations 1999, SI 1999/2024, reg 32(1).
16   Ie a geotechnical assessment in accordance with the Quarries Regulations 1999, SI 1999/2024, reg 33 (see PARA 555).
17   Quarries Regulations 1999, SI 1999/2024, reg 32(4). Where, at the coming into force of these regulations (1 January 2000: but see reg 1), a report has been obtained in accordance with the Mines and Quarries (Tips) Regulations 1971, SI 1971/1377, regs 9(2)(a), 12(1) or 18(1) (see PARAS 543, 545, 547) and is less than two years old, that report is treated as a geotechnical assessment for the purpose of the Quarries Regulations 1999, SI 1999/2024, reg 32(4) and remains valid for a maximum of two years from the date when it was first made: reg 38.

## 554. Operator's duties in relation to geotechnical assessments.

The operator[1] of a quarry[2] must ensure that:

(1)      any significant findings made during a geotechnical assessment[3] and any conclusions reached[4], and the reasons for those conclusions, are recorded by the geotechnical specialist[5] undertaking the assessment[6]; and

(2)     such geotechnical specialist signs and dates any such record and records his professional qualifications on it[7].

The operator must ensure that any information available to him which may be relevant for the purposes of a geotechnical assessment is made available to the geotechnical specialist undertaking that assessment[8].

The operator must also ensure that any remedial works identified during the geotechnical assessment[9] are completed by the date specified[10].

1   As to the meaning of 'operator' see PARA 521.
2   As to the meaning of 'quarry' see PARA 4.
3   As to geotechnical assessments see PARA 555. As to the operator's duty to ensure that a geotechnical assessment is carried out see PARA 553.
4   Ie reached in accordance with the Quarries Regulations 1999, SI 1999/2024, reg 33(1)(b), (c) or (d) (see PARA 555).
5   As to the meaning of 'geotechnical specialist' see PARA 555 .
6   Quarries Regulations 1999, SI 1999/2024, reg 33(2)(a).
7   Quarries Regulations 1999, SI 1999/2024, reg 33(2)(b).
8   Quarries Regulations 1999, SI 1999/2024, reg 33(3).
9   Ie under the Quarries Regulations 1999, SI 1999/2024, reg 33(1)(c) (see PARA 555 head (3)).
10  Quarries Regulations 1999, SI 1999/2024, reg 33(4) (amended by SI 2002/2174).

### 555. Geotechnical assessments.

For the purposes of the Quarries Regulations 1999[1], a 'geotechnical assessment' means an assessment carried out by a geotechnical specialist[2] identifying and assessing all factors liable to affect the stability and safety of a proposed or existing excavation[3] or tip[4] It includes:

(1)     preparation by or under the supervision of the geotechnical specialist or, as appropriate, consideration by the geotechnical specialist, of the documents and particulars specified below[5];

(2)     the conclusion of the geotechnical specialist as to the safety and stability of the proposed or existing excavation or tip being assessed, including his conclusions as to whether such excavation or tip represents a significant hazard[6] by way of instability or movement[7];

(3)     where appropriate, the conclusion of the geotechnical specialist as to whether any remedial work is required in relation to the excavation or tip being assessed and the date by which such work should be completed[8];

(4)     where appropriate, the conclusion of the geotechnical specialist as to the date by which the next geotechnical assessment should take place[9]; and

(5)     consideration by the geotechnical specialist of the excavations and tips rules[10].

The documents and particulars referred to in head (1) above are as follows:

(a)     site survey[11];
(b)     site investigation[12];
(c)     cross-sections based on site investigation[13];
(d)     plans based on site investigation[14];
(e)     assumptions made before analysis[15];
(f)     findings of analysis[16];
(g)     design coming out of analysis[17]; and
(h)     requirements during and after construction[18].

1   Ie the Quarries Regulations 1999, SI 1999/2024.

2  'Geotechnical specialist' means a chartered engineer or chartered geologist who has: (1) three or more years' relevant experience in soil mechanics, rock mechanics or excavation engineering; and (2) is competent to perform a geotechnical analysis to determine the hazard and risk arising from the excavation or tip being assessed: Quarries Regulations 1999, SI 1999/2024, reg 2(1). As to the meaning of 'competent' see PARA 538.

3  As to the meaning of 'excavation' see PARA 4 .

4  Quarries Regulations 1999, SI 1999/2024, reg 33(1). As to the meaning of 'tip' see PARA 4.

5  Quarries Regulations 1999, SI 1999/2024, reg 33(1)(a). The documents and particulars are those specified in Sch 1: see heads (a)–(h) in the text.

6  As to the meaning of 'hazard' see PARA 551 . As to the operator's duties in relation to excavations and tips which are and are not significant hazards see the Quarries Regulations 1999, SI 1999/2024, regs 34–35; and PARAS 556, 557.

7  Quarries Regulations 1999, SI 1999/2024, reg 33(1)(b).

8  Quarries Regulations 1999, SI 1999/2024, reg 33(1)(c).

9  Quarries Regulations 1999, SI 1999/2024, reg 33(1)(d).

10  Quarries Regulations 1999, SI 1999/2024, reg 33(1)(e). As to the excavations and tips rules see PARA 552.

11  Quarries Regulations 1999, SI 1999/2024, reg 33(1)(a), Sch 1 para 1(a). The site survey is an accurate plan which should be prepared on a scale not less detailed than 1:2500 showing:

    (1)    the boundaries of the quarry or premises upon which the excavation or tip or proposed excavation or tip is or is to be situated (Sch 1 para 1(a));

    (2)    the site of the excavation or tip or proposed excavation or tip (Sch 1 para 1(b));

    (3)    any contiguous land or structures which might be affected by the excavation or tip or proposed excavation or tip (Sch 1 para 1(c)); and

    (4)    all mine workings (whether abandoned or not), buried quarry workings, known cave systems, active or former landslips, springs, artesian wells, watercourses and other natural or man-made features including tunnel pipes or culverts which might affect the safety of the excavation or tip or proposed excavation or tip or which might be relevant for the purpose of determining whether excavation or tipping operations can be carried out safely (Sch 1 para 1(d)),

which plan must be contoured to Ordnance Datum Newlyn at a vertical interval not greater than five metres and orientated to and correlated with the Ordnance Survey National Grid and marked with squares corresponding to the 100 metre squares shown on Ordnance Survey sheets on the scale of 1:2500 (Sch 1 para 1).

12  Quarries Regulations 1999, SI 1999/2024, Sch 1 para 2. The site investigation is a record of all relevant site investigation information including surveys, tests, boreholes and groundwater measurements made for the purpose of the geotechnical assessment together with the results of any testing including the strength of materials within and beneath the tip or within the excavated slope, and the record must include any known historical information relevant to the site investigation: Sch 1 para 2.

13  Quarries Regulations 1999, SI 1999/2024, Sch 1 para 3. These are sufficient accurate cross-sections on a scale not less detailed than 1:1250 of the site of the excavation or tip or proposed excavation or tip showing the existing ground surface and all relevant superficial materials and bedrock underlying the site and:

    (1)    any variation in the thickness, level or character of the superficial deposits and bedrock materials based on the site investigation (Sch 1 para 3(a)); and

    (2)    the position of any surface whether natural or manmade which may affect the safety of the excavation or tip or proposed excavation or tip (Sch 1 para 3(a)).

14  Quarries Regulations 1999, SI 1999/2024, Sch 1 para 4. These are plans showing the position of all boreholes, wells and trial pits used in the site investigation and the location and levels of all materials and surfaces which may affect the safety of the excavation or tip or proposed excavation or tip: Sch 1 para 4.

15  Quarries Regulations 1999, SI 1999/2024, Sch 1 para 5. This is a record of any assumptions relevant to the assessment of ground conditions relating to the safety of the excavation or tip made by the geotechnical specialist including a record of any relevant information which was not available when undertaking the assessment: Sch 1 para 5.

16  Quarries Regulations 1999, SI 1999/2024, Sch 1 para 6. This is a record of the calculations carried out in order to determine the safety of the excavation or tip, including any variables or parameters used in those calculations and the reasons for using them and the findings of those calculations expressed as the factor of safety or the probability of failure or other recognised basis of assessing stability: Sch 1 para 6.

17 Quarries Regulations 1999, SI 1999/2024, Sch 1 para 7. This is an accurate plan on a scale not less detailed than 1:2500 recording:

(1)     in relation to tips or proposed tips, the design of the tip, including the area of land covered or to be covered, the gradients of that land, the designed contours at vertical intervals of not more than two metres, the side slopes and boundaries of the tip and the designed position and nature of construction of any wall or other structure retaining or confining the tip (Sch 1 para 7(a)); and

(2)     in relation to excavations or proposed excavations, the design of the excavation, including the height or proposed height of the slope, the position and width of any benches and representative contours of the excavation at vertical intervals of not more than five metres (Sch 1 para 7(a)).

18 Quarries Regulations 1999, SI 1999/2024, Sch 1 para 8. This is a record of the nature and extent of inspection, supervision and safety measures necessary to ensure the safety of the excavation or tip and a specification of necessary engineering works and safety measures; and a record of the action to be taken regarding defects specified in the report: Sch 1 para 8.

## 556. Operator's duties in relation to further geotechnical assessment of excavations and tips which are a significant hazard.

Where the conclusion recorded by a geotechnical specialist[1] as to the safety and stability of the proposed or existing excavation[2] or tip[3] being assessed[4] following a geotechnical assessment[5] is that the excavation or tip represents a significant hazard[6] by way of instability or movement, the operator[7] of a quarry[8] must ensure[9] that the excavation or tip is subject to a further geotechnical assessment at least every two years[10]. Such excavations and tips are known as 'notifiable excavations' and 'notifiable tips' respectively[11].

Where, in relation to such an excavation or tip, there is any reason:

(1)     to suspect that there has been or will be a significant change to the matters to which the geotechnical assessment relates, or any neighbouring land which may be affected by movement by or instability of the excavation or tip[12]; or

(2)     to doubt the validity of the conclusion of the current assessment[13],

the operator must ensure that a further geotechnical assessment is undertaken as soon as is reasonably practicable[14].

1  As to the meaning of 'geotechnical specialist' see PARA 555.
2  As to the meaning of 'excavation' see PARA 4 .
3  As to the meaning of 'tip' see PARA 4 .
4  Ie under the Quarries Regulations 1999, SI 1999/2024, reg 33(1)(b) (see PARA 555 head (2)).
5  As to geotechnical assessments see PARA 555.
6  As to the meaning of 'hazard' see PARA 551 .
7  As to the meaning of 'operator' see PARA 521.
8  As to the meaning of 'quarry' see PARA 4.
9  Ie subject to the Quarries Regulations 1999, SI 1999/2024, reg 33(1)(d) (see PARA 555 head (4)).
10 Quarries Regulations 1999, SI 1999/2024, reg 34(1). As to the operator's duties in relation to excavations and tips which are not a significant hazard see reg 35; and PARA 557.
11 Quarries Regulations 1999, SI 1999/2024, regs 2(1), 34(3).
12 Quarries Regulations 1999, SI 1999/2024, reg 34(2)(a).
13 Quarries Regulations 1999, SI 1999/2024, reg 34(2)(b).
14 Quarries Regulations 1999, SI 1999/2024, reg 34(2). This is without prejudice to reg 34(1).

## 557. Operator's duties in relation to excavations and tips which are not a significant hazard.

Where the conclusion reached by a geotechnical specialist[1] as to the safety and stability of the proposed or existing excavation[2] or tip[3] being assessed[4] following a geotechnical assessment[5] is that it presents no significant hazard[6], the operator[7] must ensure that:

(1)    the geotechnical specialist specifies the frequency with which appraisals[8] are to be conducted in order to ensure the continued safety and stability of the excavation or tip[9]; and

(2)    a record of that specification is made[10].

1   As to the meaning of 'geotechnical specialist' see PARA 555 .
2   As to the meaning of 'excavation' see PARA 4 .
3   As to the meaning of 'tip' see PARA 4.
4   Ie in accordance with the Quarries Regulations 1999, SI 1999/2024, reg 33(1)(b) (see PARA 555 head (2)).
5   As to geotechnical assessments see PARA 555.
6   As to the meaning of 'hazard' see PARA 551 .
7   As to the meaning of 'operator' see PARA 521.
8   Ie appraisals pursuant to the Quarries Regulations 1999, SI 1999/2024, reg 32 (see PARA 553).
9   Quarries Regulations 1999, SI 1999/2024, reg 35(a).
10  Quarries Regulations 1999, SI 1999/2024, reg 35(b). As to the operator's duties in relation to excavations and tips which are a significant hazard see reg 34; and PARA 556.

### C.    PREVENTION OF PUBLIC DANGER FROM DISUSED TIPS IN MINES AND QUARRIES

### (A)   Disused Tips

**558.  The legislation.**

For the purpose of ensuring that disused tips[1] do not, by reason of instability[2], constitute a danger to members of the public, local authorities[3] have the functions conferred on them by the disused tip provisions[4] of the Mines and Quarries (Tips) Act 1969[5].

In the application of those provisions of the Mines and Quarries (Tips) Act 1969, specified provisions of the Public Health Act 1936[6] apply as if the disused tip provisions were contained in the Public Health Act 1936 and as if any reference in the Public Health Act 1936 to a local authority were to a local authority within the meaning of the disused tip provisions[7].

1   For the purposes of the Mines and Quarries (Tips) Act 1969 Pt II (ss 11–36), 'disused tip' is a tip other than one to which the Quarries Regulations 1999, SI 1999/2024 or the Mines Regulations 2014, SI 2014/3248 apply: ss 11(2), 36(1) (s 11(2) substituted by SI 2014/3248). 'Tip' means an accumulation or deposit of refuse from a mine or quarry (whether in a solid state or in solution or suspension) other than an accumulation or deposit situated underground, and where any wall or other structure retains or confines a tip then, whether or not that wall or structure is itself composed of refuse, it is deemed to form part of the tip for the purposes of the Mines and Quarries (Tips) Act 1969 Pt II: s 11(3A) (added by SI 2014/3248). As to the power conferred by the disused tip provisions of the Mines and Quarries (Tips) Act 1969 to make regulation see s 29.
2   For the purposes of the Mines and Quarries (Tips) Act 1969 Pt II, a disused tip is to be treated as unstable if and only if there is, or there is reasonable ground for believing that there is likely to be, such a movement of the refuse which makes up the tip as to cause a significant increase in the area of land covered by the tip: s 36(2).
3   In the Mines and Quarries (Tips) Act 1969 Pt II, 'local authority' in England means the council of a county, metropolitan district or London borough, the Common Council of the City of London or the Council of the Isles of Scilly; and in Wales means the council of a county or county borough: ss 11(3), 36(1) (s 11(3) amended by the Local Government Act 1972 s 272(1), Sch 30; the Local Government Act 1985 s 16, Sch 8 para 27; and the Local Government (Wales) Act 1994 s 66(6), Sch 16 para 34). As to areas and authorities in England and Wales see LOCAL GOVERNMENT vol 69 (2018) PARA 36 et seq.
4   Ie the Mines and Quarries (Tips) Act 1969 Pt II.
5   Mines and Quarries (Tips) Act 1969 s 11(1). In the Mines and Quarries (Tips) Act 1969 Pt II, any reference to a section or subsection not otherwise identified is a reference to that section of the Mines and Quarries (Tips) Act 1969 or to that subsection of the section in which the reference

occurs; and any reference to any other enactment is to be taken as referring to that enactment as amended by or under any other enactment: s 36(5), (6). Part II does not extend to Northern Ireland: s 38(5).

6   Ie the Public Health Act 1936 s 275 (power of local authority to execute work on behalf of owners); s 304 (judges and justices not to be disqualified by liability to rates); s 305 (protection of members and officers of local authorities from personal liability); and s 341 (power to apply provisions of the Act to Crown property). See further ENVIRONMENTAL QUALITY AND PUBLIC HEALTH vol 45 (2010) PARA 1 et seq.

7   Mines and Quarries (Tips) Act 1969 s 33 (amended by the Local Government (Miscellaneous Provisions) Act 1976 s 81(1), Sch 2).

## 559. Information as to disused tips.

For the purpose of enabling a local authority[1] to assess whether a disused tip[2] wholly or partly within its area is stable[3] and whether any instability of the tip is or is likely to constitute a danger to members of the public, the local authority may, by notice served[4] on the owner[5] of the tip or on any other person who it has reason to believe may be able to assist it, require him, within a specified time[6], to produce to the authority such document[7] within his possession[8] or control as may be specified[9].

Any person who without reasonable excuse fails to comply with such a notice[10] is liable on summary conviction to a fine not exceeding level 3 on the standard scale[11]. Any person who, in pursuance of such a notice, with intent to deceive, produces any document or information which is false in a material particular, or knowingly or recklessly makes a statement which is similarly false, is liable on summary conviction to a fine not exceeding the prescribed sum, or on conviction on indictment, to imprisonment for a term not exceeding two years or to a fine or both[12].

1   As to the meaning of 'local authority' see PARA 558 .

2   As to the meaning of 'disused tip' see PARA 558.

3   As to stability see PARA 558 .

4   As to the service of documents see PARA 577.

5   'Owner', in relation to a disused tip, means the person who has a legal estate in the land on which the tip is situated which: (1) is either the fee simple or a tenancy for a specific term which has not less than one year unexpired and is not a mortgage term (Mines and Quarries (Tips) Act 1969 s 36(3)(a)(i)); and (2) is not in reversion expectant on the termination of such a tenancy (s 36(3)(a)(ii)). As to legal estates in land see REAL PROPERTY AND REGISTRATION vol 87 (2017) PARA 5. As to mortgage generally see MORTGAGE vol 77 (2016) PARA 101 et seq.

6   Ie such time, not being less than 14 days, as may be specified in the notice: see the Mines and Quarries (Tips) Act 1969 s 12(1).

7   Ie whether in the form of maps, surveys, plans, records of work or otherwise and whether relating to the tip itself or the land on which it is situated: see the Mines and Quarries (Tips) Act 1969 s 12(1).

8   As to what constitutes possession of a document see CIVIL PROCEDURE vol 12 (2015) PARA 621; PERSONAL PROPERTY vol 80 (2013) PARA 834 et seq.

9   Mines and Quarries (Tips) Act 1969 s 12(1). Certain local authority functions under the Mines and Quarries (Tips) Act 1969 are 'relevant functions' for the purposes of the Regulatory Enforcement and Sanctions Act 2008 s 4, Sch 3: see LOCAL GOVERNMENT vol 69 (2018) PARA 816.

10   Ie a notice under the Mines and Quarries (Tips) Act 1969 s 12: see s 12(2).

11   Mines and Quarries (Tips) Act 1969 s 12(2) (amended by the Criminal Justice Act 1982 ss 37, 38, 46). As to the standard scale see SENTENCING vol 92 (2015) PARA 176.

12   Mines and Quarries (Tips) Act 1969 s 12(2) (amended by the Magistrates' Courts Act 1980 s 32(2)). As to forgery see CRIMINAL LAW vol 25 (2016) PARA 404 et seq. As to the prescribed sum see SENTENCING vol 92 (2015) PARA 176.

**560. Right of entry to carry out exploratory tests etc.**
Subject to certain provisions[1], a person duly authorised in writing[2] by a local authority[3] may at any reasonable time enter upon the land on which a disused tip[4] is situated, or upon any neighbouring land, for the purpose of: (1) investigating whether any instability[5] of the tip might constitute a danger to members of the public[6]; (2) carrying out operations[7], referred to as 'exploratory tests'[8], to determine whether the tip is unstable[9]; and (3) inspecting any operations being carried out on that land where those operations may affect the stability of the tip[10]. However, a person so authorised must not demand admission as of right to any occupied land unless at least 48 hours' written notice has been given to the occupier[11].

If it is shown[12] to the satisfaction of a justice of the peace that admission has been refused to any land which any person is entitled to enter under these provisions, that a refusal is apprehended, or that the occupier is temporarily absent, and that there is reasonable ground for entry for the purpose for which entry is required, the justice may by warrant[13] authorise entry, if need be by force[14].

If a local authority has reasonable ground for believing that a disused tip is unstable and that possible danger to members of the public requires an immediate entry on to any such land as is referred to above[15] for one or more of the purposes specified[16], a person duly authorised in writing by the local authority may make such entry at any time and without giving notice or obtaining a warrant[17].

Any person who wilfully obstructs[18] a person exercising these powers is liable on summary conviction to a fine not exceeding level 3 on the standard scale[19].

1   Ie the Mines and Quarries (Tips) Act 1969 s 13(2)–(6): see s 13(1).
2   The person authorised must, if required, produce evidence of his authority and may take on to the land such other persons and such equipment as may be necessary: Mines and Quarries (Tips) Act 1969 s 13(5). Certain local authority functions under the Mines and Quarries (Tips) Act 1969 are 'relevant functions' for the purposes of the Regulatory Enforcement and Sanctions Act 2008 s 4, Sch 3: see LOCAL GOVERNMENT vol 69 (2018) PARA 816.
3   As to the meaning of 'local authority' see PARA 558 .
4   As to the meaning of 'disused tip' see PARA 558 .
5   As to instability see PARA 558 .
6   Mines and Quarries (Tips) Act 1969 s 13(1)(a).
7   'Operations' includes surveys and tests as well as tipping operations and building, engineering, mining and other operations: Mines and Quarries (Tips) Act 1969 s 36(1). As to the meaning of 'tipping operations' see PARA 543 .
8   Mines and Quarries (Tips) Act 1969 ss 13(1)(b), 36(1).
9   Mines and Quarries (Tips) Act 1969 s 13(1)(b).
10  Mines and Quarries (Tips) Act 1969 s 13(1)(c).
11  Mines and Quarries (Tips) Act 1969 s 13(1).
12  Ie on sworn information in writing: see the Mines and Quarries (Tips) Act 1969 s 13(2). As to informations see MAGISTRATES vol 71 (2013) PARA 522.
13  As to justices' warrants generally see MAGISTRATES.
14  Mines and Quarries (Tips) Act 1969 s 13(2). A warrant must not be issued on the ground of a refusal or apprehended refusal unless notice of the application for a warrant has been given to the occupier: s 13(2). The warrant continues in force until the purpose for which entry is required has been satisfied: s 13(3).
15  Ie the land on which the tip is situated, or any neighbouring land: see the Mines and Quarries (Tips) Act 1969 s 13(1).
16  As to the purposes for which entry may be required see heads (1)–(3) in the text.
17  Mines and Quarries (Tips) Act 1969 s 13(4).
18  As to the meaning of 'wilfully' generally see CRIMINAL LAW vol 25 (2016) PARA 8. As to the meaning of 'obstructs' in various contexts see eg *Hinchliffe v Sheldon* [1955] 3 All ER 406, [1955] 1 WLR 1207, DC; *Evans v Lloyd* [1962] 2 QB 471, [1962] 1 All ER 239, DC; *Rice v Connolly* [1966] 2 QB 414, [1966] 2 All ER 649, DC; *Dibble v Ingleton* [1972] 1 QB 480, [1972] 1 All ER

275, DC; *Willmott v Atack* [1977] QB 498, [1976] 3 All ER 794, DC; and CRIMINAL LAW vol 26 (2016) PARA 799.

19 Mines and Quarries (Tips) Act 1969 s 13(6). As to the standard scale see SENTENCING vol 92 (2015) PARA 176.

## (B) Remedial Operations, Compensation and Contribution

### 561. Notice requiring remedial operations.

If it appears to a local authority[1] that a disused tip[2] situated wholly or partly within its area is unstable[3] and for that reason constitutes or is likely to constitute a danger to members of the public, the authority may by notice in the prescribed form[4] served[5] on the owner[6] require him to carry out, within a specified period[7], such remedial operations[8] as may be specified in the notice[9]. The notice may require such operations to be carried out on the tip itself, on the land on which it is situated or on any neighbouring land in the occupation of the owner of the tip or in which he has, otherwise than as a mortgagee, an estate or interest superior to that of the occupier[10]. The local authority must, within a specified period[11], serve copies of the notice on certain other persons[12].

An owner on whom such a notice is served by a local authority may, within a specified period[13], serve a counter-notice in the prescribed form[14] requiring the local authority to exercise its powers to carry out remedial operations itself[15]. The local authority's notice and the copies of it are thereupon deemed never to have been served[16] and the local authority must, as soon as reasonably practicable, exercise its powers to carry out remedial operations itself[17]. The local authority must serve a copy of the counter-notice on every person on whom it served a copy of the notice[18].

1   As to the meaning of 'local authority' see PARA 558 .
2   As to the meaning of 'disused tip' see PARA 558 .
3   As to instability see PARA 558 .
4   Ie in a form prescribed by regulations made by the Secretary of State: Mines and Quarries (Tips) Act 1969 s 36(1). The Mines and Quarries (Tips) Act 1969 refers to the Minister of Housing and Local Government as the appropriate minister (see s 36(4)); as to the transfer of functions to the Secretary of State see PARA 2.
     No such notice may be served where the land on which the tip is situated is ecclesiastical property: see PARA 578.
5   As to the service of notices see PARA 577.
6   As to the meaning of 'owner' see PARA 559 .
7   Ie within such period as may be specified in the notice and beginning not earlier than 21 days after the date of service of the notice: Mines and Quarries (Tips) Act 1969 s 14(1).
8   In the Mines and Quarries (Tips) Act 1969 Pt II (ss 11–36), 'remedial operations', in relation to a disused tip, means operations which, in the opinion of the local authority concerned, are necessary to ensure the stability of the tip: ss 14(2), 36(1). As to the meaning of 'operations' see PARA 560.
9   Mines and Quarries (Tips) Act 1969 s 14(1). Certain local authority functions under the Mines and Quarries (Tips) Act 1969 are 'relevant functions' for the purposes of the Regulatory Enforcement and Sanctions Act 2008 s 4, Sch 3: see LOCAL GOVERNMENT vol 69 (2018) PARA 816.
10   Mines and Quarries (Tips) Act 1969 s 14(3).
11   Ie within the period of seven days beginning with the day on which the notice was served: see the Mines and Quarries (Tips) Act 1969 s 14(4).
12   See the Mines and Quarries (Tips) Act 1969 s 14(4). The persons on whom copies of the notice to the owner must be served are:
     (1)      any other person who is in occupation of the whole or part of the land on which remedial operations are required to be carried out and any other person who, to the knowledge of the local authority, has an estate or interest, otherwise than as a mortgagee, in that land (s 14(4)(a));

(2)   any other person who, to its knowledge, either has an estate or interest, otherwise than as a mortgagee, in the land on which the tip is situated, or had such an estate or interest at any time within the period of 12 years immediately preceding the date of service of the notice on the owner (s 14(4)(b));

(3)   any other person who, to its knowledge, has an interest in, including a right to acquire, all or any of the material comprised in the tip (s 14(4)(c));

(4)   any other person who, to its knowledge, has at any time within the period referred to in head (2) used the tip for the purpose of the deposit of refuse from a mine or quarry (s 14(4)(d)); and

(5)   any other person who it has reason to believe has, at any time within that period, caused or contributed to the instability of the tip by the carrying out of any operations on the tip, on the land on which it is situated or on neighbouring land or by failing to take any steps which he might reasonably have taken to prevent the tip from becoming unstable (s 14(4)(e)).

13  Ie the period of 21 days beginning with the day on which the notice was served: see the Mines and Quarries (Tips) Act 1969 s 14(5).
14  As to the form of notice see the Disused Mine and Quarry Tips (Prescribed Forms) Regulations 1969, SI 1969/807, reg 3(b), Schedule, Form 2.
15  Mines and Quarries (Tips) Act 1969 s 14(5). As to these powers see s 17; and PARA 565.
16  See the Mines and Quarries (Tips) Act 1969 s 14(5)(b).
17  See the Mines and Quarries (Tips) Act 1969 s 14(5)(c).
18  See the Mines and Quarries (Tips) Act 1969 s 14(5)(a).

## 562.  Effect of notice requiring remedial operations.

If, without reasonable excuse, the owner[1] of a disused tip[2] on whom is served a notice[3] requiring remedial operations[4] fails to carry out those operations within the period specified[5] or any extension of that period[6], he is liable on summary conviction to a fine not exceeding level 5 on the standard scale[7].

Where any such notice requires the owner of a disused tip to carry out remedial operations on any land not in his occupation but in which he has an estate or interest superior to that of the occupier[8], then, as against the occupier and any other person having an estate or interest in the land, the owner has the right to enter on to the land to carry out the remedial operations and any consequential works of reinstatement and to take with him such other persons and such equipment as may be necessary[9].

Where, in the course of carrying out remedial operations specified in such a notice, material which is not the property of the owner is removed from the tip, the owner may sell the material but must account to its owner for the proceeds of sale; but this does not prevent the owner of a disused tip from setting off[10] the proceeds of sale or any part of them against any sum which under the statutory provisions[11] he is entitled to recover from the owner of the material[12].

1  As to the meaning of 'owner' see PARA 559 .
2  As to the meaning of 'disused tip' see PARA 558 .
3  As to the notice see PARA 561.
4  As to the meaning of 'remedial operations' see PARA 561.
5  Ie within such period as may be specified in the notice and beginning not earlier than 21 days after the date of service of the notice: Mines and Quarries (Tips) Act 1969 s 14(1).
6  Ie under the Mines and Quarries (Tips) Act 1969 s 15(3) or s 15(4): see PARA 563.
7  Mines and Quarries (Tips) Act 1969 s 14(8) (amended by the Criminal Justice Act 1982 ss 37, 38, 46). As to the standard scale see SENTENCING vol 92 (2015) PARA 176.
8  See PARA 559 .
9  Mines and Quarries (Tips) Act 1969 s 14(6).
10  As to rights of set-off generally see CIVIL PROCEDURE vol 11 (2015) PARA 382 et seq.
11  Ie provisions of the Mines and Quarries (Tips) Act 1969 Pt II (ss 11–36) subsequent to s 14(7): see s 21; and PARA 570.
12  Mines and Quarries (Tips) Act 1969 s 14(7). See further PARA 565 .

## 563.   Appeals against notices requiring remedial operations.

A person on whom is served a notice[1] or copy of a notice[2] requiring remedial operations[3] may apply[4] to the court[5], within a specified period[6] and on specified grounds[7], for an order varying or cancelling the notice[8].

The specified grounds are: (1) that there is no reasonable ground for believing that the tip is unstable[9] or that, by reason of instability it constitutes or is likely to constitute a danger to members of the public[10]; (2) that the remedial operations specified in the notice are more extensive than is necessary to secure the safety of members of the public[11]; (3) that the stability of the tip could be secured by operations[12] different, in whole or in part, from the remedial operations specified and that the owner[13] is prepared to undertake those alternative operations[14]; (4) that the owner or some other person has already begun, or has contracted for a third person to begin, operations different, in whole or in part, from the remedial operations specified and that those alternative operations will ensure the stability of the tip[15]; (5) that the time within which the remedial operations specified are to be carried out is not reasonably sufficient for the purpose[16]; (6) that there is some defect or error in, or in connection with the notice[17].

If the court is satisfied that any such ground is made out, it may make an order varying or cancelling the notice[18]. Where the court varies the notice, the notice and any copy[19] are deemed always to have had effect as so varied[20].

1   As to the notice see PARA 561.
2   See PARA 561 .
3   As to the meaning of 'remedial operations' see PARA 561 .
4   As to the cancellation of such a notice by the local authority, notwithstanding that an application has been made under this provision see PARA 564. As to the meaning of 'local authority' see PARA 558 .
5   'The court' means the High Court or the county court: Mines and Quarries (Tips) Act 1969 s 28 (substituted by SI 1991/724; and amended by the Crime and Courts Act 2013 Sch 9 Pt 3 para 52).
6   Ie the period of 21 days beginning with the date of service of the notice on the owner: see the Mines and Quarries (Tips) Act 1969 s 15(1).
7   See the Mines and Quarries (Tips) Act 1969 s 15(1)(a)–(f).
8   See the Mines and Quarries (Tips) Act 1969 s 15(1).
9   As to instability see PARA 558 .
10  Mines and Quarries (Tips) Act 1969 s 15(1)(a).
11  Mines and Quarries (Tips) Act 1969 s 15(1)(b).
12  As to the meaning of 'operations' see PARA 560 .
13  As to the meaning of 'owner' see PARA 559 .
14  Mines and Quarries (Tips) Act 1969 s 15(1)(c).
15  Mines and Quarries (Tips) Act 1969 s 15(1)(d).
16  Mines and Quarries (Tips) Act 1969 s 15(1)(e).
17  Mines and Quarries (Tips) Act 1969 s 15(1)(f). So far, however, as an application is on the ground mentioned in head (6) in the text, the court must dismiss the application if it is satisfied that the defect or error concerned was not material: s 15(2).
18  Mines and Quarries (Tips) Act 1969 s 15(3). Where an application for variation or cancellation is made to the court and not withdrawn, the period specified in the notice for remedial operations to be carried out does not expire until the application is finally determined; and where the court is not satisfied that the ground, or any of the grounds, of the application are made out, it may nevertheless by order extend the period specified in the notice for remedial operations to be carried out: s 15(4). The period of notice referred to is within such period as may be specified in the notice and beginning not earlier than 21 days after the date of service of the notice: Mines and Quarries (Tips) Act 1969 s 14(1).
19  Ie a copy served under the Mines and Quarries (Tips) Act 1969 s 14(4) (see PARA 561 ): see s 15(3).
20  Mines and Quarries (Tips) Act 1969 s 15(3).

**564. Cancellation of notice requiring remedial operations.**

Where a local authority[1] has served on the owner[2] of a disused tip[3] a notice requiring remedial operations[4] then, notwithstanding that an application may have been made to the court for variation or cancellation[5], or that the owner may have begun to carry out the operations, and whether or not the period specified[6] for carrying out the operations has expired, the local authority may at any time before the completion of the remedial operations cancel the notice by a further notice[7] served[8] on the owner[9]. Upon such cancellation the owner is no longer required to carry out the remedial operations, but the cancellation does not affect the right of the local authority to serve a further notice requiring remedial operations[10].

Where a local authority has cancelled a notice requiring remedial operations, the owner may apply to the court[11] for an order directing the local authority to reimburse to him the whole, or such part as the court thinks fit, of: (1) any expenditure incurred by him in consequence of the service of that notice[12]; and (2) any expenditure[13] incurred by him which is attributable to the cancellation[14]. In determining whether to make such an order[15] or the extent of such reimbursement, the court must have regard to all the circumstances and, in particular, to the grounds of cancellation and to whether the local authority has served, or intends to serve, a further notice requiring remedial operations, or whether the local authority intends to carry out remedial operations itself[16].

1   As to the meaning of 'local authority' see PARA 558 .
2   As to the meaning of 'owner' see PARA 559 .
3   As to the meaning of 'disused tip' see PARA 558 .
4   As to the notice see PARA 561. As to the meaning of 'remedial operations' see PARA 561 .
5   See PARA 563.
6   Ie specified in the notice: see PARA 561.
7   The notice must be in the prescribed form (see PARA 561 ): see the Disused Mine and Quarry Tips (Prescribed Forms) Regulations 1969, SI 1969/807, reg 3(c), Schedule, Form 3.
8   As to the service of notices see PARA 577.
9   Mines and Quarries (Tips) Act 1969 s 16(1). The local authority must serve a copy of the notice of cancellation on every person on whom it served a copy of the notice requiring remedial works under s 14 (see PARA 561 ): s 16(2).
10  See the Mines and Quarries (Tips) Act 1969 s 16(3).
11  As to the meaning of 'the court' see PARA 563 .
12  Mines and Quarries (Tips) Act 1969 s 16(4)(a).
13  Ie whether relating to the reinstatement of any land, the cancellation of any contract or otherwise: see the Mines and Quarries (Tips) Act 1969 s 16(4)(b).
14  Mines and Quarries (Tips) Act 1969 s 16(4)(b).
15  Ie under the Mines and Quarries (Tips) Act 1969 s 16(4): see s 16(5).
16  Mines and Quarries (Tips) Act 1969 s 16(5). As to the carrying out of remedial operations by local authorities see PARA 565.

**565. Remedial operations etc by local authorities.**

Where a local authority[1] considers that circumstances exist which would empower it to serve a notice requiring remedial operations[2] then, instead of serving such a notice, the authority may itself carry out remedial operations and any works of reinstatement reasonably necessary in consequence of those remedial operations[3].

Where it proposes to carry out remedial operations under these provisions it must, within the specified period[4], serve notice[5] of its intention on the owner of the disused tip concerned specifying the nature and extent of the operations and of any consequential works of reinstatement which it proposes to carry out[6]. If, however, the local authority has reasonable ground for believing that a disused tip is unstable[7] and that possible danger to members of the public requires the immediate carrying out of remedial operations, it may begin operations forthwith, notwithstanding that the required notice has not been given[8]; but if no such notice has been served when the remedial operations are begun, then, as soon thereafter as reasonably practicable, the local authority must serve notice[9] on the owner of the tip of the commencement of the operations, specifying the nature and extent of the operations and of any consequential works of reinstatement which it proposes to carry out[10].

A local authority may sell any material removed from a disused tip in the course of remedial operations carried out by it under these provisions and must account to the owner of the material for the proceeds of sale; but this does not prevent the local authority from setting off[11] the proceeds of sale or any part of them against any sum which under the statutory provisions[12] the authority is entitled to recover from the owner of the material[13].

1   As to the meaning of 'local authority' see PARA 558 .
2   See the Mines and Quarries (Tips) Act 1969 s 14(1); and PARA 561. As to the meaning of 'remedial operations' see PARA 561 . As to the service of notices see PARA 577.
3   Mines and Quarries (Tips) Act 1969 s 17(1). Certain local authority functions under the Mines and Quarries (Tips) Act 1969 are 'relevant functions' for the purposes of the Regulatory Enforcement and Sanctions Act 2008 s 4, Sch 3: see LOCAL GOVERNMENT vol 69 (2018) PARA 816.
4   Ie not less than 21 days before the operations are begun: see the Mines and Quarries (Tips) Act 1969 s 17(2). As to the meaning of 'operations' see PARA 560 .
5   The notice must be in the prescribed form (see PARA 561 ): Mines and Quarries (Tips) Act 1969 s 17(4). As to the form of notice see the Disused Mine and Quarry Tips (Prescribed Forms) Regulations 1969, SI 1969/807, reg 3(d), Schedule, Form 4. Concurrently with the service of the notice on the owner of the disused tip, or as soon thereafter as is reasonably practicable, a copy must be served on the persons referred to in PARA 561 , with references there to the notice being construed for this purpose as references to the notice mentioned in the text to this note: Mines and Quarries (Tips) Act 1969 s 17(5). Notice, in the prescribed form, of remedial operations must be served on those persons where a local authority is the owner of a disused tip situated wholly or partly within its area: see s 17(7), Sch 2 paras 1, 2. As to the form of notice see the Disused Mine and Quarry Tips (Prescribed Forms) Regulations 1969, SI 1969/807, reg 3(f), Schedule, Form 6. As to the meaning of 'owner' see PARA 559. As to the meaning of 'disused tip' see PARA 558 .
6   Mines and Quarries (Tips) Act 1969 s 17(2).
7   As to instability see PARA 558.
8   Ie notwithstanding that no notice has been served as mentioned in the Mines and Quarries (Tips) Act 1969 s 17(2) or that less than 21 days has elapsed since the service of such a notice: see s 17(3).
9   The notice must be in the prescribed form: Mines and Quarries (Tips) Act 1969 s 17(4). For the form of notice see the Disused Mine and Quarry Tips (Prescribed Forms) Regulations 1969, SI 1969/807, reg 3(e), Schedule, Form 5.
10   Mines and Quarries (Tips) Act 1969 s 17(3).
11   As to rights of set-off generally see CIVIL PROCEDURE vol 11 (2015) PARA 382 et seq.
12   Ie the provisions of the Mines and Quarries (Tips) Act 1969 Pt II (ss 11–36) subsequent to s 17(6): see s 17(6). See also s 21; and PARA 570.
13   Mines and Quarries (Tips) Act 1969 s 17(6). See also s 14(7); and PARA 562. Section 14(7) applies, with modifications, where a local authority has served notice of a determination to carry out remedial operations in relation to a disused tip of which it is the owner and which is situated wholly or partly within its area: see s 17(7), Sch 2 paras 1, 3(a).

## 566. Right of entry to carry out remedial operations etc.

Where a local authority[1] has served notice[2] of its intention to carry out remedial operations[3] in relation to a disused tip[4], or where the circumstances are such that the authority may begin such operations without notice[5], a person duly authorised in writing[6] by the authority may at any reasonable time enter upon the land on which the disused tip is situated, or upon any neighbouring land, for any purpose connected with the remedial operations or consequential works of reinstatement;

but a person so authorised must not demand admission as of right to any occupied land unless 24 hours' written notice has been given to the occupier[7].

If it is shown to the satisfaction of a justice of the peace[8] on sworn information in writing that: (1) admission to any land which any person is entitled to enter has been refused, or that a refusal is apprehended, or that the occupier is temporarily absent; and (2) there is reasonable ground for entry on to the land for the purpose for which entry is required, the justice may by warrant authorise that person to enter the land if need be by force[9]. However, a warrant is not to be issued on the ground that entry has been refused or that a refusal of entry is apprehended unless the justice is satisfied that notice in writing of the intention to apply for a warrant has been given to the occupier[10]. Where the circumstances are such that the local authority may begin remedial operations without notice[11], the right of entry under these provisions may be exercised without notice or warrant[12].

Any person who wilfully obstructs[13] a person exercising these powers is liable on summary conviction to a fine not exceeding level 3 on the standard scale[14].

1   As to the meaning of 'local authority' see PARA 558 .
2   As to the service of notices see PARA 577.
3   As to the meaning of 'remedial operations' see PARA 561 .
4   Ie under the Mines and Quarries (Tips) Act 1969 s 17(2) (see PARA 565): see s 18(1). As to the meaning of 'disued tip' see PARA 558.
5   See the Mines and Quarries (Tips) Act 1969 s 17(3); and PARA 565.
6   The person authorised must, if required, produce evidence of his authority and may take on to the land such other persons and such equipment as may be necessary: Mines and Quarries (Tips) Act 1969 s 18(5). Certain local authority functions under the Mines and Quarries (Tips) Act 1969 are 'relevant functions' for the purposes of the Regulatory Enforcement and Sanctions Act 2008 s 4, Sch 3: see LOCAL GOVERNMENT vol 69 (2018) PARA 816. Certain persons or indorsements mentioned in these paragraphs are specified for the purposes of Regulatory Enforcement and Sanctions Act 2008 s 37, Schs 5, 6 (meaning of 'regulator' for the purposes of imposing civil sanctions): see CONSTITUTIONAL AND ADMINISTRATIVE LAW vol 20 (2014) PARA 331.
7   Mines and Quarries (Tips) Act 1969 s 18(1). Section 18 applies also where a local authority has served notice of a determination to carry out remedial operations in relation to a disused tip of which it is the owner and which is situated wholly or partly within its area: s 17(7), Sch 2 paras 1, 3(b).
8   As to justices of the peace see generally MAGISTRATES.
9   Mines and Quarries (Tips) Act 1969 s 18(2). Every warrant granted under s 18(2) continues in force until the purpose for which the entry is required has been satisfied: s 18(3).
10   Mines and Quarries (Tips) Act 1969 s 18(2).
11   See the Mines and Quarries (Tips) Act 1969 s 17(3); and PARA 565.
12   Mines and Quarries (Tips) Act 1969 s 18(4).
13   As to the meaning of 'wilfully' generally see CRIMINAL LAW vol 25 (2016) PARA 8. As to the meaning of 'obstructs' in various contexts see eg *Hinchliffe v Sheldon* [1955] 3 All ER 406, [1955] 1 WLR 1207, DC; *Evans v Lloyd* [1962] 2 QB 471, [1962] 1 All ER 239, DC; *Rice v Connolly* [1966] 2 QB 414, [1966] 2 All ER 649, DC; *Dibble v Ingleton* [1972] 1 QB 480, [1972] 1 All ER 275, DC; *Willmott v Atack* [1977] QB 498, [1976] 3 All ER 794, DC; and CRIMINAL LAW vol 26 (2016) PARA 799.
14   Mines and Quarries (Tips) Act 1969 s 18(6) (amended by the Criminal Justice Act 1982 ss 35, 37, 38, 46). As to the standard scale see SENTENCING vol 92 (2015) PARA 176.

### 567. Compensation for damage or disturbance.

Subject to certain provisions[1], where, as a result of exploratory tests[2] or remedial operations[3], any land on which entry is made for the purpose of those tests or operations[4] is damaged, or any person is disturbed in his enjoyment of any land, then any person interested in the damaged land or, as the case may be, disturbed in his enjoyment of any land is entitled to recover compensation[5]. The compensation is recoverable from the local authority or, in the case of damage or disturbance resulting from remedial operations by the owner of the disused tip, from him[6].

Any dispute arising on a claim for compensation is to be determined by the court[7].

1   Ie the Mines and Quarries (Tips) Act 1969 s 20(2)–(6): see s 20(1).
2   As to exploratory tests see PARA 560.
3   Ie remedial operations carried out by the owner in pursuance of a notice under the Mines and Quarries (Tips) Act 1969 s 14 (see PARA 561), or by the local authority under s 17(2) (see PARA 565): see s 20(1). As to the meaning of 'remedial operations' see PARA 561 ; as to the meaning of owner see PARA 559; and as to the meaning of 'local authority' see PARA 558. Section 20(1)–(3) applies in relation to damage or disturbance resulting from works of reinstatement consequential upon any remedial operations, and references to remedial operations include references to such works: s 20(4). The provisions apply also where remedial operations are carried out by a local authority in relation to a tip of which it is the owner and which is situated wholly or partly within its area: s 17(7), Sch 2 para 5. Certain local authority functions under the Mines and Quarries (Tips) Act 1969 are 'relevant functions' for the purposes of the Regulatory Enforcement and Sanctions Act 2008 s 4, Sch 3: see LOCAL GOVERNMENT vol 69 (2018) PARA 816.
4   See PARAS 560, 566.
5   Mines and Quarries (Tips) Act 1969 s 20(1). This provision does not entitle the owner of a disused tip to compensation for damage or disturbance resulting from remedial operations by him or any other person who was the owner of the disused tip when the remedial operations were carried out: s 20(3). As to the meaning of 'disused tip' see PARA 558. As to compensation in respect of ecclesiastical property see PARA 578.
6   Mines and Quarries (Tips) Act 1969 s 20(2). These provisions have effect subject to the subsequent provisions of Pt II (ss 11–36): s 20(2).
7   Mines and Quarries (Tips) Act 1969 s 20(5). As to the meaning of 'the court' see PARA 563.

### 568.   Claims for compensation by owners and contributories.

Special provisions[1] have effect in certain circumstances[2] in relation to any claim for compensation for damage or disturbance[3] by the owner of a disused tip or by a contributory[4]. Where these provisions apply to the owner of a disused tip, then until the expiry of 12 months beginning with the date on which remedial operations by the local authority were completed, the owner is not in general[5] entitled to enforce his claim otherwise than by way of set-off[6] against any sum demanded from him by the local authority[7] in respect of expenses and related matters referable to exploratory tests and remedial operations[8]. Similarly, where these provisions apply to a contributory, then until the expiry of the relevant period[9] the contributory is not in general[10] entitled to enforce his claim otherwise than by way of set-off against any sum demanded from him by the owner of the disused tip[11] or by the local authority[12] by way of contribution[13].

The time within which an owner or contributory to whom the above provisions apply may bring proceedings to recover the whole or any part of the compensation to which his claim refers is, in general, six years from the expiry of the period of 12 months[14] referred to above in relation to an owner or, as the case may be, of the relevant period in relation to a contributory[15].

1   Ie the Mines and Quarries (Tips) Act 1969 s 20(6), Sch 3.
2   Mines and Quarries (Tips) Act 1969 Sch 3 applies to the owner of a disused tip if: (1) a local authority has carried out remedial operations in relation to that tip (see PARA 565) or has carried out any exploratory tests which gave rise to the remedial operations (Sch 3 para 1(1)(a)); (2) the owner has served on the local authority a claim for compensation under s 20 (see PARA 567) in respect of damage or disturbance resulting from those exploratory tests or remedial operations (Sch 3 para 1(1)(b)); and (3) either no order for contribution has been made under s 19 (see PARA 569) in respect of the expenses otherwise falling to be borne by the owner in respect of those tests or operations or one or more such orders have been made but the specified percentage (as to which

see PARA 569) or, as the case may be, the aggregate of the specified percentages is less than 100 (Sch 3 para 1(1)(c)). As to the meaning of 'owner' see PARA 559; as to the meaning of 'disused tip' see PARA 558; as to the meaning of 'local authority' see PARA 558; and as to the meaning of 'remedial operations' see PARA 561. As to exploratory tests see PARA 560. In Sch 3 any reference to remedial operations includes a reference to works of reinstatement consequential on those remedial operations: Sch 3 para 4.

Schedule 3 applies to a contributory if: (a) the expenses in respect of which a contribution may be claimed by the owner under s 21 (see PARA 570) or by the local authority under s 23 (see PARA 572) include expenses incurred in carrying out remedial operations or exploratory tests which gave rise to the remedial operations or to the service of a notice requiring the owner to carry out remedial operations (see PARA 561) (Sch 3 para 1(2)(a)); and (b) the contributory has served on the owner of the disused tip or, as the case may be, the local authority concerned a claim for compensation under s 20 (see PARA 567) in respect of damage or disturbance resulting from those exploratory tests or remedial operations (Sch 3 para 1(2)(b)). Schedule 3 para 1(2) applies subject to modifications where a local authority carries out remedial operations on a disused tip of which it is the owner: see Sch 3 para 5(a). As to the meaning of 'contributory' see PARA 569. Certain local authority functions under the Mines and Quarries (Tips) Act 1969 are 'relevant functions' for the purposes of the Regulatory Enforcement and Sanctions Act 2008 s 4, Sch 3: see LOCAL GOVERNMENT vol 69 (2018) PARA 816.

3   See PARA 567.
4   Mines and Quarries (Tips) Act 1969 s 20(6).
5   Where a demand under the Mines and Quarries (Tips) Act 1969 s 23(4) (see PARA 572) in respect of expenditure on exploratory tests or remedial operations (see PARA 572) is served by the local authority concerned on the owner of a disused tip to whom the provisions of Sch 3 apply and the amount recoverable by virtue of that demand, having regard to any application made by the owner to the court for variation or cancellation, is less than the amount of the owner's claim for compensation against the local authority, Sch 3 para 2(1), does not apply to any proceedings brought by the owner to recover the balance of that compensation from the local authority: Sch 3 para 2(2).
6   As to rights of set-off generally see CIVIL PROCEDURE vol 11 (2015) PARA 382 et seq.
7   See PARA 572.
8   Mines and Quarries (Tips) Act 1969 Sch 3 para 2(1).
9   The relevant period is: (1) in relation to a claim by a contributory for compensation recoverable from the owner, the period of 12 months beginning with the date of the completion by the owner of the remedial operations in relation to the tip (Mines and Quarries (Tips) Act 1969 Sch 3 para 3(3)(a)); (2) in relation to a claim by a contributory for compensation recoverable from a local authority where the expenses in respect of which a contribution may be claimed by him from the local authority are such as are mentioned in s 23(1) (see PARA 572), the period of 12 months beginning with the date of completion of the remedial operations referred to in s 23 (Sch 3 para 3(3)(b)); and (3) in relation to such a claim as is mentioned in head (2) where the expenses in respect of which a contribution may be claimed by the contributory from the local authority are such as are mentioned in s 23(3) (see PARA 572), the period of 12 months beginning with the date of completion of the exploratory tests referred to in s 23 (Sch 3 para 3(3)(c)). In relation to head (2), Sch 3 para 3(2) applies also, subject to modifications, where a local authority carries out remedial operations in relation to a tip situated wholly or partly within its area and of which it is the owner: Sch 3 para 5(c).
10  Where a demand for contribution under the Mines and Quarries (Tips) Act 1969 s 21 (see PARA 570) or s 23 (see PARA 572) in respect of the expenses referred to in Sch 3 para 1(2)(a) is served on a contributory to whom the provisions of Sch 3 apply, and the amount recoverable by virtue of that demand, having regard to any application made by the contributory to the court for variation (see PARAS 571, 573) or cancellation (see PARA 565), is less than the amount of the contributory's claim for compensation against the person or local authority making the demand, Sch 3 para 3(1) does not apply to any proceedings brought by the contributory to recover the balance of that compensation from that person or local authority: Sch 3 para 3(2). This also applies, subject to modifications, where a local authority carries out remedial operations in relation to a tip situated wholly or partly within its area and of which it is the owner: Sch 3 para 5(a), (b).
11  As to demands by the owner see PARA 570.
12  As to demands by the local authority see PARA 572.

13 Mines and Quarries (Tips) Act 1969 Sch 3 para 3(1). This also applies, subject to modifications, where a local authority carries out remedial operations in relation to a tip situated wholly or partly within its area and of which it is the owner: Sch 3 para 5(a).

14 In any case referred to in the Mines and Quarries (Tips) Act 1969 Sch 3 para 2(2) or Sch 3 para 2(3) the time is six years from the date of service of the demand there referred to: Sch 3 para 6(1)(b).

15 Mines and Quarries (Tips) Act 1969 Sch 3 para 6(1)(a). Schedule 3 para 6(1) is to be construed as one with the Limitation Act 1980 Pt I (ss 1–27) (see LIMITATION PERIODS): Mines and Quarries (Tips) Act 1969 Sch 3 para 6(2) (amended by the Limitation Act 1980 s 40(2), Sch 3).

## 569. Contribution orders.

Where the local authority[1] has served on the owner[2] of a disused tip[3] a notice requiring remedial operations[4] or a notice that the authority will carry out remedial operations[5] and an application to the court[6] is made within a specified period[7], the court may order that a contribution towards the expenses otherwise falling to be borne by the owner[8] as a result of the remedial operations is to be made by any one or more of other specified persons[9] on whom notice of the application has been served[10]. Such an application may be made by the owner and, in the case of a notice that the local authority will carry out remedial operations[11], the local authority[12].

A 'contributory' is the person to whom the order above relates to[13] and on whom the notice of application has been served namely:

(1) any person who at the date of service of the notice relating to remedial operations[14] had an estate or interest, otherwise than as a mortgagee[15], in the land on which the tip is situated and any person who had such an estate or interest at any time within the period of 12 years immediately preceding that date[16];

(2) any other person who has, at any time within that period, used the tip for the deposit of refuse from a mine or quarry[17]; and

(3) any other person who, in the court's opinion, has at any time within that period caused or contributed to the instability[18] of the tip by the carrying out of any operations[19] on the tip, on the land on which it is situated or on neighbouring land or by failing to take any steps which he might reasonably have taken to prevent the tip from becoming unstable[20].

An order made under these provisions must specify the amount of the contribution to be made by the person to whom it relates as a percentage, called 'the specified percentage'[21] (which, if the court thinks appropriate, may be 100 per cent) of the total amount in respect of which a contribution can be claimed[22]. In determining whether to make an order requiring any person to make a contribution or the amount of any contribution the court must have regard to all the circumstances of the case and, in particular to:

(a) the extent to which that person has, by act or omission, contributed to the instability of the tip[23];

(b) the extent to which he has used the tip for the deposit of refuse[24];

(c) the nature and extent of any estate or interest which he had, at the date of service of the notice[25] relating to remedial operations, in the land on which the tip is situated[26];

(d) in the case of a person who had such an estate or interest but disposed of it before that date, whether he did so to evade any liability[27] in connection with the tip[28]; and

(e)    the terms of any covenant, agreement or statutory provision affecting the rights and obligations in relation to that tip of that person and its owner[29].

1    As to the meaning of 'local authority' see PARA 558.
2    As to the meaning of 'owner' see PARA 559.
3    As to the meaning of 'disused tip' see PARA 558.
4    As to the meaning of 'remedial operations' see PARA 561. As to such a notice see PARA 561. As to the service of notices see PARA 577.
5    See PARA 565. Where a local authority has served notice of a determination to carry out remedial operations in relation to a disused tip of which it is the owner and which is situated wholly or partly within its area, then, at any time within the period of three months beginning with the date of commencement of those operations, the local authority may apply under the Mines and Quarries (Tips) Act 1969 s 19; and for that purpose s 19 has effect subject to modifications: see s 17(7), Sch 2 paras 1, 4. Certain local authority functions under the Mines and Quarries (Tips) Act 1969 are 'relevant functions' for the purposes of the Regulatory Enforcement and Sanctions Act 2008 s 4, Sch 3: see LOCAL GOVERNMENT vol 69 (2018) PARA 816.
6    As to the meaning of 'the court' see PARA 563.
7    The application is of no effect unless it is made within the following period: (1) where it relates to a notice under the Mines and Quarries (Tips) Act 1969 s 14 requiring remedial operations (see PARA 561) and there is no appeal under s 15 against that notice (see PARA 563), the period of three months beginning with the date of service of that notice on the owner (s 19(3)(a)); (2) where it relates to such a notice and there is an appeal against that notice, the period beginning with the date of service of that notice and ending three months after the date on which the appeal is withdrawn or finally determined (s 19(3)(b)); and (3) where it relates to a notice under s 17 that the local authority will carry out remedial operations (see PARA 565), the period of three months beginning with the date of service of that notice on the owner (s 19(3)(c)).
8    As to the right of a local authority to recover expenses from the owner see PARA 572.
9    As to the specified persons see heads (1)–(3) in the text.
10   Mines and Quarries (Tips) Act 1969 s 19(1).
11   See the Mines and Quarries (Tips) Act 1969 s 17; and PARA 565.
12   See the Mines and Quarries (Tips) Act 1969 s 19(2).
13   See the Mines and Quarries (Tips) Act 1969 ss 19(6), 36(1).
14   Ie a notice under the Mines and Quarries (Tips) Act 1969 s 14 (see PARA 561) requiring remedial operations or a notice under s 17 (see PARA 565) that the local authority will carry out remedial operations: see s 19(1)(a).
15   As to estates and interests of mortgagees see MORTGAGE vol 77 (2016) PARA 101 et seq.
16   Mines and Quarries (Tips) Act 1969 s 19(1)(a).
17   Mines and Quarries (Tips) Act 1969 s 19(1)(b). As to the meaning of 'mine' see PARA 3; and as to the meaning of 'quarry' see PARA 4, 520 (definitions applied by s 1(3)(a)).
18   As to instability see PARA 558.
19   As to the meaning of 'operations' see PARA 560.
20   Mines and Quarries (Tips) Act 1969 s 19(1)(c).
21   Mines and Quarries (Tips) Act 1969 ss 19(6), 36(1).
22   Mines and Quarries (Tips) Act 1969 s 19(5).
23   Mines and Quarries (Tips) Act 1969 s 19(4)(a).
24   Mines and Quarries (Tips) Act 1969 s 19(4)(b).
25   Ie under the Mines and Quarries (Tips) Act 1969 s 14 or s 17: see s 19(4)(c).
26   Mines and Quarries (Tips) Act 1969 s 19(4)(c).
27   Ie whether under the Mines and Quarries (Tips) Act 1969 Pt II (ss 11–36) or otherwise: see s 19(4)(d).
28   Mines and Quarries (Tips) Act 1969 s 19(4)(d).
29   Mines and Quarries (Tips) Act 1969 s 19(4)(e).

### 570. Recovery from contributories of owner's expenses.

Subject to certain provisions[1], where remedial operations[2] have been carried out by the owner[3] of a disused tip[4] in compliance with a notice requiring such operations[5], and an order for contribution towards the owner's expenses has been made[6], the owner is entitled to recover from the contributory[7] the specified percentage[8] of the aggregate[9] of: (1) the expenses reasonably incurred by the owner in the remedial operations and any works of reinstatement reasonably necessary in consequence of those operations[10]; (2) the amount of any compensation for damage or disturbance[11] referable to those operations or works which is recoverable, or has been recovered[12], from the owner[13]; and (3) the amount of any such compensation in respect of which the owner could himself have made a claim[14] if the operations, and any such works, had been carried out by the local authority[15].

No contribution is recoverable under these provisions unless a demand for it, containing specified particulars[16], is served[17] on the contributory[18].

Where remedial operations have been carried out as mentioned above[19] and the notice requiring such operations has been cancelled by the local authority[20], these provisions[21] and related provisions as to appeals[22] have effect subject to modifications[23].

1   Ie the Mines and Quarries (Tips) Act 1969 s 21(2)–(4): see s 21(1).
2   As to the meaning of 'remedial operations' see PARA 561.
3   As to the meaning of 'owner' see PARA 559.
4   As to the meaning of 'disused tip' see PARA 558.
5   As to such notices see the Mines and Quarries (Tips) Act 1969 s 14; and PARA 561.
6   As to such orders see the Mines and Quarries (Tips) Act 1969 s 19; and PARA 569.
7   As to the meaning of 'contributory' see PARA 569.
8   As to the meaning of 'the specified percentage' see PARA 569.
9   Mines and Quarries (Tips) Act 1969 s 21(1). Certain local authority functions under the Mines and Quarries (Tips) Act 1969 are 'relevant functions' for the purposes of the Regulatory Enforcement and Sanctions Act 2008 s 4, Sch 3: see LOCAL GOVERNMENT vol 69 (2018) PARA 816.
10   Mines and Quarries (Tips) Act 1969 s 21(2)(a).
11   Ie any such compensation as is mentioned in the Mines and Quarries (Tips) Act 1969 s 20(2)(b) (see PARA 567): see s 21(2)(b).
12   Ie in pursuance of a claim under the Mines and Quarries (Tips) Act 1969 s 20 (see PARAS 567–568): see s 21(2)(b).
13   Mines and Quarries (Tips) Act 1969 s 21(2)(b).
14   Ie under the Mines and Quarries (Tips) Act 1969 s 20 (see PARAS 567–568): see s 21(2)(c).
15   Mines and Quarries (Tips) Act 1969 s 21(2)(c). As to the meaning of 'local authority' see PARA 558. Similar provisions have effect where: (1) a local authority has carried out remedial operations in relation to a tip situated wholly or partly within its area and of which it is the owner; and (2) an order has been made under s 19 (see PARA 569) requiring any person to make a contribution towards the expenses otherwise falling to be borne by the local authority as such owner: see s 17(7), Sch 2 paras 1, 6(1). Section 23(5), which deals with the payment of interest and payment by instalments (see PARA 572) applies to any sum so recoverable: see Sch 2 para 6(3).
16   The demand must specify, in addition to the sum claimed by way of contribution, the total amount in respect of which contribution is claimed (Mines and Quarries (Tips) Act 1969 s 21(3)(a)) and the separate amounts which comprise that total, distinguished by reference to s 21(2)(a)–(c) (see heads (1)–(3) in the text) (s 21(3)(b)).
17   As to the service of notices see PARA 577.
18   Mines and Quarries (Tips) Act 1969 s 21(3). See also Sch 2 paras 1, 6(2).
19   Ie by the owner of a disused tip in compliance with a notice under the Mines and Quarries (Tips) Act 1969 s 14: see s 21(4).
20   See PARA 564.
21   Ie the provisions of the Mines and Quarries (Tips) Act 1969 s 21.
22   See the Mines and Quarries (Tips) Act 1969 s 22; and PARA 571.
23   See the Mines and Quarries (Tips) Act 1969 s 21(4), Sch 4. Schedule 4 contains modifications as to references to remedial operations (Sch 4 paras 1, 2), the determination of the expenses reasonably incurred by the owner in carrying out remedial operations and works of reinstatement (Sch 4 paras 1, 3), and the particulars to be given in demands for payment (Sch 4 paras 1, 4(a), (b)).

## 571. Appeals against demands for recovery of owner's expenses.

A contributory[1] may apply to the court[2], within a specified period[3] and on specified grounds[4], for variation of a demand for recovery of the contribution[5] in respect of the owner's expenses; and if the court is satisfied that the ground, or any of the grounds, of the application is made out, it may make an order reducing the amount recoverable by the owner to such amount as the court thinks fit[6].

Subject to this right of appeal and to modifications which apply where the notice requiring remedial operations has been cancelled by the local authority[7], such a demand is final and conclusive[8].

1  As to the meaning of 'contributory' see PARA 569.
2  As to the meaning of 'the court' see PARA 563.
3  Ie the period of six weeks beginning with the date of service of the demand on the contributory: see the Mines and Quarries (Tips) Act 1969 s 22(1).
4  The grounds are that:
   (1)  the amount of the expenses incurred by the owner in the remedial operations was greater than was reasonable (Mines and Quarries (Tips) Act 1969 s 22(1)(a));
   (2)  the amount of the expenses incurred by the owner in works of reinstatement was greater than was reasonably necessary to reinstate the land in consequence of the remedial operations (s 22(1)(b));
   (3)  because the time taken by the owner in remedial operations or any consequential works of reinstatement was unreasonably long, compensation under s 20 in respect of damage or disturbance (see PARA 567) is greater than it would otherwise have been (s 22(1)(c));
   (4)  the amount of any compensation in respect of damage or disturbance is greater than necessary to compensate the person concerned (s 22(1)(d));
   (5)  the amount specified in the demand as being referable to s 21(2)(c) (see PARA 570 head (3)) is greater than the compensation which could have been claimed by the owner in the circumstances specified in head (3) (s 22(1)(e));
   (6)  the amount claimed in the demand is greater than the specified percentage (as to which see PARA 569) of the amount determined under s 21(2) as the aggregate of the expenses and amounts mentioned in PARA 570 heads (1)–(3) (s 22(1)(f)).
   As to the meaning of 'owner' see PARA 559; and as to the meaning of 'remedial operations' see PARA 561. Certain local authority functions under the Mines and Quarries (Tips) Act 1969 are 'relevant functions' for the purposes of the Regulatory Enforcement and Sanctions Act 2008 s 4, Sch 3: see LOCAL GOVERNMENT vol 69 (2018) PARA 816.
5  Ie under the Mines and Quarries (Tips) Act 1969 s 21(3) (see PARA 570): see s 22(1).
6  Mines and Quarries (Tips) Act 1969 s 22(2). Similar provisions have effect in the circumstances mentioned in PARA 570: see s 17(7), Sch 2 paras 1, 6(4). Section 24(4), which deals with circumstances in which the court may make an order (see PARA 573), applies in relation to an application made in such circumstances; and, subject to the right to make such an application, the demand of the local authority for contribution is final and conclusive: Sch 2 paras 1, 6(5). As to the meaning of 'local authority' see PARA 558.
7  See the Mines and Quarries (Tips) Act 1969 s 21(4), Sch 4; and PARA 570. Schedule 4 contains modifications as to references to remedial operations (Sch 4 paras 1, 2), the determination of the expenses reasonably incurred by the owner in carrying out remedial operations and works of reinstatement (Sch 4 paras 1, 3), and the grounds for an application to the court (Sch 4 paras 1, 4(c)).
8  Mines and Quarries (Tips) Act 1969 s 22(3).

### (C)  Recovery of Expenses; Grants

## 572. Right of local authority to recover expenses.

Subject to certain provisions[1], where a local authority[2] has carried out remedial operations[3] in relation to a disused tip[4], the authority is entitled to recover from the owner[5] of the tip: (1) the expenses reasonably incurred by the authority in any exploratory tests[6] which gave rise to the remedial operations[7]; (2) the expenses so incurred in the remedial operations and any works of reinstatement reasonably necessary in consequence of those operations[8]; and (3) the amount of any compensation for damage or disturbance[9] referable to those tests, operations or works which is recoverable, or has been recovered[10], from the local authority[11].

Subject to certain provisions[12], where a local authority has carried out, in relation to a disused tip, exploratory tests which resulted in the service of a notice requiring remedial operations, the authority is entitled to recover from the owner: (a) the expenses reasonably incurred by the authority in carrying out those tests[13]; (b) such sum, not exceeding 5 per cent of the expenses referred to in head (a) above, as the authority thinks fit in respect of its establishment charges[14]; and (c) the amount of any compensation for damage or disturbance referable to those tests which is recoverable, or has been recovered, from the local authority[15].

Where a contribution order[16] has been made requiring any person to contribute towards the expenses otherwise falling to be borne by the owner of a disused tip as a result of the remedial operations referred to above[17], the local authority is entitled to recover from the contributory[18] the specified percentage[19] of the amount recoverable[20] from the owner[21], and the amount recoverable from the owner is reduced accordingly[22].

No sum is recoverable under these provisions unless a demand for it, containing specified particulars[23], is served[24] on the owner or, as the case may be, the contributory concerned[25].

Together with any sum recoverable by a local authority from the owner of a disused tip or from a contributory, the local authority is entitled to recover interest from the date of service on him of the demand until the total amount recoverable from that person is paid, at such reasonable rate as the authority may determine[26]. With the agreement of the local authority, any sum so recoverable may be paid in such instalments as may be agreed[27].

1   Ie the Mines and Quarries (Tips) Act 1969 ss 23(2)–(6), 24, 25: see s 23(1).
2   As to the meaning of 'local authority' see PARA 558.
3   As to the meaning of 'remedial operations' see PARA 561.
4   Ie under the Mines and Quarries (Tips) Act 1969 s 17 (see PARA 565): see s 23(1). As to the meaning of 'disused tip' see PARA 558.
5   As to the meaning of 'owner' see PARA 559. For these purposes, the owner of the disused tip is the person who was the owner at the date of the commencement of the remedial operations: Mines and Quarries (Tips) Act 1969 s 23(6)(a). Certain local authority functions under the Mines and Quarries (Tips) Act 1969 are 'relevant functions' for the purposes of the Regulatory Enforcement and Sanctions Act 2008 s 4, Sch 3: see LOCAL GOVERNMENT vol 69 (2018) PARA 816.
6   As to exploratory tests see PARA 560.
7   Mines and Quarries (Tips) Act 1969 s 23(1)(a). For the purposes of s 23, exploratory tests relating to a disused tip are deemed to give rise to remedial operations in relation to that tip or, as the case may be, to result in the service of a notice requiring remedial operations if, within the period of six months after the completion of the tests, the local authority began those operations or served the notice requiring remedial operations: s 23(6)(b).
8   Mines and Quarries (Tips) Act 1969 s 23(1)(b).
9   Ie any compensation such as is mentioned in the Mines and Quarries (Tips) Act 1969 s 20(2) (see PARA 567): see s 23(1)(d).
10   Ie in pursuance of a claim under the Mines and Quarries (Tips) Act 1969 s 20 (see PARAS 567–568): see s 23(1)(d).
11   Mines and Quarries (Tips) Act 1969 s 23(1)(d).
12   Ie the Mines and Quarries (Tips) Act 1969 ss 23(3)–(6), 24: see s 23(2).
13   Mines and Quarries (Tips) Act 1969 s 23(2)(a).
14   Mines and Quarries (Tips) Act 1969 s 23(2)(b).
15   Mines and Quarries (Tips) Act 1969 s 23(2)(c).
16   Ie an order under the Mines and Quarries (Tips) Act 1969 s 19 (see PARA 569): see s 23(3).
17   Ie in the Mines and Quarries (Tips) Act 1969 s 23(1) or s 23(2): see s 23(3).
18   As to the meaning of 'contributory' see PARA 569.
19   As to the meaning of 'the specified percentage' see PARA 569.

20 Ie disregarding the reduction referred to in the Mines and Quarries (Tips) Act 1969 s 23(3)(b).
21 Mines and Quarries (Tips) Act 1969 s 23(3)(a).
22 Mines and Quarries (Tips) Act 1969 s 23(3)(b).
23 The demand must specify, in addition to the sum claimed by the local authority: (1) in the case of a demand served on a contributory, the total amount in respect of which the contribution is claimed (Mines and Quarries (Tips) Act 1969 s 23(4)(a)); (2) in the case of a demand served on the owner, the sums, if any, which the local authority is entitled to recover from any contributory or contributories (s 23(4)(b)); and (3) in either case, the separate amounts which comprise the total amount recoverable by the local authority, distinguished by reference to s 23(1)(a)–(d) (see heads (1)–(3) in the text) or, as the case may be s 23(2)(a)–(c) (see heads (a)–(c) in the text) (s 23(4)(c)).
24 As to the service of documents see PARA 577.
25 Mines and Quarries (Tips) Act 1969 s 23(4).
26 Mines and Quarries (Tips) Act 1969 s 23(5) (amended by the Local Government, Planning and Land Act 1980 s 1(6), Sch 6 para 12).
27 Mines and Quarries (Tips) Act 1969 s 23(5).

## 573. Appeals against demands by local authorities.

An owner[1] of a disused tip[2], or a contributory[3], on whom was served a demand by a local authority[4] for recovery of expenses[5] may apply to the court[6] within a specified period[7] and on specified grounds[8] for variation or cancellation of the demand[9]. If on such an application the court is satisfied that any ground is made out, it may make an order either cancelling the demand or reducing the amount recoverable from the person concerned to such amount as it thinks fit[10]. Subject to this right of appeal, such a demand is final and conclusive[11].

1  As to the meaning of 'owner' see PARA 559.
2  As to the meaning of 'disused tip' see PARA 558.
3  As to the meaning of 'contributory' see PARA 569.
4  As to the meaning of 'local authority' see PARA 558.
5  Ie a demand under the Mines and Quarries (Tips) Act 1969 s 23(4) (see PARA 572): see s 24(1).
6  As to the meaning of 'the court' see PARA 563.
7  Ie the period of six weeks beginning with the date of the service of the demand on the owner or contributory: see the Mines and Quarries (Tips) Act 1969 s 24(1).
8  Where the demand is made in a case falling within the Mines and Quarries (Tips) Act 1969 s 23(1), where the local authority has carried out remedial operations, the grounds are:
   (1)    that the amount of the expenses incurred by it in the exploratory tests or remedial operations was greater than was reasonable (s 24(2)(a));
   (2)    that the amount of the expenses incurred by it in works of reinstatement was greater than was reasonably necessary to reinstate the land in consequence of the remedial operations (s 24(2)(b));
   (3)    that at the time the remedial operations were begun, there was no reasonable ground for believing that the tip was unstable (see PARA 558) or that, by reason of instability, the tip constituted, or was likely to constitute, a danger to members of the public (s 24(2)(c));
   (4)    that the remedial operations were more extensive than was necessary to secure the safety of members of the public (s 24(2)(d));
   (5)    that because the time taken by the local authority in the exploratory tests or remedial operations or any consequential works of reinstatement was unreasonably long, compensation under s 20 in respect of damage or disturbance (see PARA 567) is greater than it would otherwise have been (s 24(2)(e));
   (6)    that the amount of any compensation in respect of damage or disturbance is greater than necessary to compensate the person concerned (s 24(2)(f));
   (7)    that in the case of a demand served on a contributory, the amount claimed in the demand is greater than the specified percentage (as to which see PARA 569) of the amount determined under s 23(1) (see PARA 572) (s 24(2)(g));
   (8)    that in the case of a demand served on the owner, the amount claimed in the demand does not give proper allowance for any sum which the local authority is entitled to recover from a contributory (s 24(2)(h)).

Where the demand is made in a case falling within s 23(2) where the local authority has carried out exploratory tests which resulted in a notice requiring remedial operations, five grounds are specified, corresponding with those in heads (1), (5)–(8), but with the substitution, for the reference in head (7) to s 23(1), of a reference to s 23(2): see s 24(3)(a)–(e). As to exploratory tests see PARA 560. As to the meaning of 'remedial operations' see PARA 561.

9    See the Mines and Quarries (Tips) Act 1969 s 24(1).
10   Mines and Quarries (Tips) Act 1969 s 24(4).
11   Mines and Quarries (Tips) Act 1969 s 24(5).

## 574. Grants towards local authority expenditure.

The appropriate national authority[1] may, with Treasury consent, make grants to a local authority[2] towards expenditure incurred by the local authority in or in connection with remedial operations[3], any previous exploratory tests[4] and any consequential works of reinstatement[5]. Such grants are to be of such amounts and payable at such times and subject to such conditions as the appropriate national authority may determine, either generally or in the case of any particular local authority or grant[6]; and they may be made either as periodical grants in respect of costs incurred or treated as incurred in respect of borrowings by the authority to defray qualifying expenditure, or as capital grants in respect of such expenditure or in substitution for such periodical grants[7].

Where such a grant is made the appropriate national authority may, after consultation with the local authority, direct that, having regard to the amount of the grant, the total amount recoverable[8] from the owner[9] of the tip and any contributories[10] in respect of remedial operations carried out by the authority[11] is to be limited to an amount specified in the direction[12], and the amount so recoverable is then limited accordingly[13].

1    The Mines and Quarries (Tips) Act 1969 refers to the Minister of Housing and Local Government as the appropriate minister (see s 36(4)); as to the transfer of functions to the Secretary of State see PARA 2. The appropriate national authority is the Secretary of State or where functions have been transferred in relation to Wales, the Welsh Ministers: see PARA 2.
2    As to the meaning of 'local authority' see PARA 558. Where, by virtue of the Local Government Act 1972 Pt VI (ss 101–109) (see LOCAL GOVERNMENT vol 69 (2018) PARA 399 et seq), a district council incurs any such expenditure as is referred to in the Mines and Quarries (Tips) Act 1969 s 25(1), grants under s 25 may be made to that council and references to a local authority are to be construed accordingly: s 25(6) (added by the Local Government Act 1972 s 251(2), Sch 29 para 28). Certain local authority functions under the Mines and Quarries (Tips) Act 1969 are 'relevant functions' for the purposes of the Regulatory Enforcement and Sanctions Act 2008 s 4, Sch 3: see LOCAL GOVERNMENT vol 69 (2018) PARA 816.
3    As to the meaning of 'remedial operations' see PARA 561.
4    As to exploratory tests see PARA 560.
5    Mines and Quarries (Tips) Act 1969 s 25(1). Sums required for the payment of such grants are to be defrayed out of money provided by Parliament (s 37(a)), as is any increase attributable to the Mines and Quarries (Tips) Act 1969 in the sums payable out of money so provided under any other enactment (s 37(b)).
6    Mines and Quarries (Tips) Act 1969 s 25(2).
7    Mines and Quarries (Tips) Act 1969 s 25(3). As to grants generally to local authorities see LOCAL GOVERNMENT FINANCE vol 70 (2018) PARA 29 et seq.
8    Ie under the Mines and Quarries (Tips) Act 1969 s 23 (see PARA 572): see s 25(4).
9    As to the meaning of 'owner' see PARA 559.
10   As to the meaning of 'contributory' see PARA 569.
11   See the Mines and Quarries (Tips) Act 1969 s 23(1)(a)–(d) (s 23(1)(c) repealed by the Local Government Act 1972 s 42(2), Sch 8); and PARA 572.
12   Mines and Quarries (Tips) Act 1969 s 25(4). Where (1) a local authority has carried out remedial operations in relation to a tip situated wholly or partly within its area and of which it is the owner (see s 17(7), Sch 2 paras 1, 7(1)(a)); (2) an order has been made under s 19 (see PARA 569) (Sch 2 para 7(1)(b)); and (3) a grant has been made under s 25 and the Secretary of State proposes to give

a direction under s 25(4) (Sch 2 para 7(1)(c)), the provisions of s 25(4) and Sch 2 para 6 have effect subject to modifications: see Sch 2 paras 1, 7(1), (2).

13 See the Mines and Quarries (Tips) Act 1969 s 25(5). In such a case ss 23(3), (4), 24(2) have effect subject to consequential modifications: see s 25(5)(a)–(e).

### (D) Miscellaneous and Supplemental

### 575. Penalties for obstructing remedial operations and damaging works.

Any person who wilfully[1] prevents or interferes with exploratory tests[2] or remedial operations[3] is liable on summary conviction to a fine not exceeding level 3 on the standard scale[4]. Any person who wilfully damages or otherwise interferes with works completed in the course of remedial operations for the purpose of ensuring the stability of a disused tip[5] is liable similarly to a fine not exceeding level 5 on the standard scale[6].

1 As to the meaning of 'wilfully' generally see CRIMINAL LAW vol 25 (2016) PARA 8.
2 As to exploratory tests see PARA 560.
3 As to the meaning of 'remedial operations' see PARA 561.
4 Mines and Quarries (Tips) Act 1969 s 26(1) (s 26(1), (2) amended by the Criminal Justice Act 1982 ss 37, 38, 46). As to the standard scale see SENTENCING vol 92 (2015) PARA 176.
5 As to the meaning of 'disused tip' see PARA 558. As to stability see PARA 558.
6 Mines and Quarries (Tips) Act 1969 s 26(2).

### 576. Offences generally.

Proceedings for an offence under the disused tip provisions of the Mines and Quarries (Tips) Act 1969[1] may not be instituted except by a local authority[2] or by or with the consent of the Director of Public Prosecutions[3]. Where such an offence committed by a body corporate[4] is proved to have been committed with the consent or connivance of, or to be attributable to any neglect on the part of, a director[5], manager, secretary or similar officer of that body, or any person purporting to act in any such capacity, he, as well as the body corporate, is guilty of the offence, and is liable to be proceeded against and punished accordingly[6].

1 Ie the Mines and Quarries (Tips) Act 1969 Pt II (ss 11–36).
2 As to the meaning of 'local authority' see PARA 558.
3 Mines and Quarries (Tips) Act 1969 s 27(1). As to the office and functions of the Director of Public Prosecutions see CRIMINAL PROCEDURE vol 27 (2015) PARAS 25, 30 et seq.
4 As to the criminal responsibility of corporations see CORPORATIONS vol 24 (2010) PARAS 482–483.
5 'Director', in relation to a body corporate established by or under any enactment for the purpose of carrying on under national ownership any industry or part of an industry or undertaking, being a body corporate whose affairs are managed by its members, means a member of that body corporate: Mines and Quarries (Tips) Act 1969 s 27(3).
6 Mines and Quarries (Tips) Act 1969 s 27(2).

### 577. Service of documents.

Any document required or authorised[1] to be given or served under the disused tip provisions of the Mines and Quarries (Tips) Act 1969[2] may either be delivered to the person to whom it is to be given or on whom it is to be served, left at his proper address[3] or sent to him by post[4]. Any document required or authorised to be given to or served on a body corporate is duly given or served if given to or served on the secretary or clerk of that body[5].

If the name or address of any owner, lessee or occupier of land to or on whom any document is to be so given or served cannot be ascertained after reasonable inquiry but there is on that land an occupied building, the document may be addressed to the person to or on whom it is to be given or served by the description of 'owner', 'lessee' or 'occupier' of the land (describing it) and either delivering it to some responsible person in the building or sending it by post in a letter similarly addressed[6].

1   In relation to any document required or authorised by the Mines and Quarries (Tips) Act 1969 Pt II (ss 11–36) to be given or served by a local authority, s 30(1)–(4) has effect in place of the Local Government Act 1972 s 233 (service of notices by local authority) (see LOCAL GOVERNMENT vol 69 (2018) PARA 648), but does not affect the operation in relation to such a document of s 234 (authentication of documents) (see LOCAL GOVERNMENT vol 69 (2018) PARA 646): Mines and Quarries (Tips) Act 1969 s 30(5) (amended by the Local Government Act 1972 s 272(2)); Interpretation Act 1978 s 17(2)(a). As to the meaning of 'local authority' see PARA 558.

2   Ie the Mines and Quarries Act 1969 Pt II.

3   For the purposes of the Mines and Quarries Act 1969 s 30 and the application to it of the Interpretation Act 1978 s 7 (references to service by post), the proper address of any person to or on whom any document is to be given or served is, in the case of the secretary or clerk of a body corporate, that of the registered or principal office of that body, and in any other case is the last known address of the person to be served; but where under agreed arrangements the person to be served has given an address for service in the United Kingdom that is his proper address: Mines and Quarries (Tips) Act 1969 s 30(3) (amended by the Interpretation Act 1978 s 25(2)); Interpretation Act 1978 s 17(2)(a). As to the meaning of 'United Kingdom' see PARA 48.

4   Mines and Quarries (Tips) Act 1969 s 30(1). As to service by post see further the Interpretation Act 1978 s 7; and STATUTES AND LEGISLATIVE PROCESS vol 96 (2012) PARA 1219. As to the service of documents in connection with ecclesiastical property see PARA 578.

5   Mines and Quarries (Tips) Act 1969 s 30(2).

6   Mines and Quarries (Tips) Act 1969 s 30(4).

## 578. Ecclesiastical property.

No notice requiring remedial operations[1] may be served in respect of a disused tip[2] if the land on which the tip concerned is situated is ecclesiastical property[3], but this does not affect the powers of a local authority[4] to carry out remedial operations itself[5].

Where under the disused tip provisions of the Mines and Quarries (Tips) Act 1969[6] a document is required or authorised to be given to, or served on, any person as occupier of, or owner of an estate or interest in, any land which is ecclesiastical property, a copy must be given to or served on the Diocesan Board of Finance for the diocese in which the land is situated[7].

Any compensation for damage or disturbance[8] payable to a person by virtue of his having an estate in fee simple in any land must, if the land is ecclesiastical property and the fee simple is vested in any person other than the Diocesan Board of Finance for the diocese in which the land is situated, be paid to it instead of to that person[9].

1   Ie a notice under the Mines and Quarries (Tips) Act 1969 s 14 (see PARA 561). As to the meaning of 'remedial operations' see PARA 561.

2   As to the meaning of 'disused tip' see PARA 558.

3   'Ecclesiastical property' means land belonging to an ecclesiastical benefice of the Church of England, or being or forming part of a church subject to the jurisdiction of the bishop of any diocese of the Church of England or the site of such a church, or being or forming part of a burial ground so subject: Mines and Quarries (Tips) Act 1969 s 31(7). 'Benefice' means an ecclesiastical benefice of the Church of England: s 31(7). Where any ecclesiastical property is vested in the incumbent of a benefice which is vacant, it is to be treated for the purposes of Pt II (ss 11–36) as being vested in the Diocesan Board of Finance for the diocese in which the land is situated (s 31(5)(a) (s 31(5) amended by the Church of England (Miscellaneous Provisions) Measure 2006 Sch 5 para 16)); and where by virtue of this provision the diocesan board of finance for the diocese in which the land is situated is the owner of land belonging to an ecclesiastical benefice and by virtue of its ownership is liable to pay any sum under Pt II either as owner of a disused tip or as a contributory, its liability must be met from, and is not to exceed the total of, the sums held by it for that benefice (Mines and Quarries (Tips) Act 1969 s 31(5)(b)). As to the meaning of 'disused tip' see PARA 558; and as to the meaning of 'contributory' see PARA 569. As to diocesan boards

of finance generally see ECCLESIASTICAL LAW vol 34 (2011) PARA 241 et seq. Where s 31(5) does not apply but a liability to pay any sum under Pt II falls on any person, either as owner of a disused tip or as a contributory, by virtue of there being vested in him the fee simple in land belonging to an ecclesiastical benefice, the diocesan board of finance for the diocese in which the land is situated may apply any sums held by them for that benefice in discharging the whole or any part of that liability: s 31(6).

4   As to the meaning of 'local authority' see PARA 558.
5   Mines and Quarries (Tips) Act 1969 s 31(1). As to the powers of local authorities to carry out remedial operations see s 17; and PARA 565.
6   Ie under the Mines and Quarries (Tips) Act 1969 Pt II.
7   Mines and Quarries (Tips) Act 1969 s 31(2) (amended by the Church of England (Miscellaneous Provisions) Measure 2006 Sch 5 para 16).
8   As to such compensation see the Mines and Quarries (Tips) Act 1969 s 20; and PARA 567.
9   Mines and Quarries (Tips) Act 1969 s 31(3) (amended by the Church of England (Miscellaneous Provisions) Measure 2006 Sch 5 para 16). Any sums so paid to the Diocesan Board of Finance for the diocese in which the land is situated with reference to any land must, if the land is not consecrated, be applied by them for the purposes for which the proceeds of a sale by agreement of the fee simple would be applicable under any enactment or Measure authorising such a sale and, if the land is consecrated, be applied by it in such manner as they may determine: s 31(4) (amended by the Church of England (Miscellaneous Provisions) Measure 2006 Sch 5 para 16).

## 579.   Raising money in special cases.

In particular cases concerning limited owners, university and college estates and the duchies of Lancaster and Cornwall special provisions have effect with respect to the raising of money for the payment of certain types of expenditure, known as 'relevant expenditure'[1], under the disused tip provisions[2] of the Mines and Quarries (Tips) Act 1969[3].

1   'Relevant expenditure' means: (1) expenses incurred in remedial operations in pursuance of a notice under the Mines and Quarries (Tips) Act 1969 s 14 requiring such operations (see PARA 561) and in any consequential works of reinstatement (s 32(1)(a)); (2) compensation recoverable under s 20 for damage and disturbance (see PARA 567) and referable to any such remedial operations or works of reinstatement (s 32(1)(b)); and (3) sums recoverable under s 21, s 23 or Sch 2 para 6 from contributories (see PARA 570) or by local authorities (see PARA 572) (s 32(1)(c)). As to the meaning of 'remedial operations' see PARA 561; and as to the meaning of 'local authority' see PARA 558.
2   Ie the Mines and Quarries (Tips) Act 1969 Pt II (ss 11–36).
3   See the Mines and Quarries (Tips) Act 1969 s 32(1). The special provisions are as follows:
    (1)   the purposes authorised for the application of capital money by the Settled Land Act 1925 s 73 (see SETTLEMENTS vol 91 (2012) PARA 709) and by the Universities and College Estates Act 1925 s 26 (see EDUCATION vol 36 (2015) PARA 1329) must include the payment of any relevant expenditure (Mines and Quarries (Tips) Act 1969 s 32(2)(a) (s 32(2)(a), (b) amended by the Trusts of Land and Appointment of Trustees Act 1996 s 25(2), Sch 4));
    (2)   the purposes authorised by the Settled Land Act 1925 s 71 (see SETTLEMENTS vol 91 (2012) PARAS 721, 750, 751), and by the Universities and College Estates Act 1925 s 30 (see EDUCATION vol 36 (2015) PARA 1329), as purposes for which money may be raised by mortgage must include the payment of any relevant expenditure (Mines and Quarries (Tips) Act 1969 s 32(2)(b));
    (3)   the purposes authorised by the Duchy of Lancaster Act 1817 s 25 for the application of money arising by the sale of annuities include the payment of relevant expenditure in relation to property belonging to the Crown in right of the Duchy of Lancaster (Mines and Quarries (Tips) Act 1969 s 32(2)(c); Statute Law (Repeals) Act 1977 s 3, Sch 3 (repealed));
    (4)   the purposes authorised by the Duchy of Cornwall Management Act 1863 s 8 for the advancement of parts of gross sums include the payment of relevant expenditure in relation to property belonging to the Crown in right of the Duchy of Cornwall (Mines and Quarries (Tips) Act 1969 s 32(2)(d)).

As to the Duchy of Lancaster and the Duchy of Cornwall see CROWN AND CROWN PROCEEDINGS vol 29 (2014) PARAS 214 et seq, 232 et seq.

# 9. RESTORATION IN THE IRONSTONE DISTRICT

### 580. The legislation.

Provision for the restoration of land within the ironstone district[1] which was used for the working of ironstone by opencast operations was made by the Mineral Workings Act 1951[2] and the Mineral Workings Act 1971[3].

The Mineral Workings Act 1985 deals with residual financial arrangements[4], and arrangements affecting agricultural land[5] and forestry[6]. There are also provisions conferring powers of entry[7] and powers to carry out works[8] on former mining land, which are exercisable in connection with the powers of local authorities to carry out work to reclaim or improve derelict land[9].

1　'Ironstone' mainly denotes a sedimentary rock containing iron carbonate or iron silicate. 'The ironstone district' is the district comprising the counties of Leicestershire, Northamptonshire, Warwickshire; the county of Lincolnshire other than the districts of Boston and South Holland; the county of Oxfordshire other than so much of it as was immediately before 1 April 1974 comprised in the royal county of Berkshire; in the county of Humberside, the districts of Cleethorpes, Glanford, Grimsby and Scunthorpe and part of the district of Boothferry (ie the parishes of Amcotts, Belton, Crowle, Eastoft, Epworth, Garthorpe, Haxey, Keadby with Althorpe, Luddington, Owston Ferry, West Butterwick and Wroot); and the district of Peterborough other than the parishes of Orton Longueville, Orton Waterville, Stanground North and Thorney: see the Mineral Workings Act 1985 s 9, Sch 1. Note that the former county of Humberside now consists of the county of East Riding of Yorkshire, the city of Kingston upon Hull and the unitary authorities of North Lincolnshire and North East Lincolnshire.
2　The Mineral Workings Act 1951 is mainly repealed: see the Mineral Workings Act 1985 ss 1, 10, Sch 2; and the Planning (Consequential Provisions) Act 1990 s 3, Sch 1 Pt II. Provisions of the Mineral Workings Act 1951 relating to the modification of payments in lieu of restoration under ironstone leases remain in force: see PARA 581. The Mineral Workings Act 1951 does not extend to Northern Ireland: s 43(1), (2).
3　The Mineral Workings Act 1971 is repealed by the Mineral Workings Act 1985 s 1, Sch 2.
4　See the Mineral Workings Act 1985 s 3, 6; and FORESTRY vol 52 (2014) PARA 48.
5　See the Mineral Workings Act 1985 s 4.
6　See the Mineral Workings Act 1985 s 5.
7　See the Mineral Workings Act 1985 s 7; and PARA 583.
8　See the Mineral Workings Act 1985 s 8; and PARA 584.
9　Ie under the National Parks and Access to the Countryside Act 1949: see OPEN SPACES AND COUNTRYSIDE vol 78 (2018) PARA 432. See, in particular, the power under the National Parks and Access to the Countryside Act 1949 s 89; and PARA 582.

### 581.　Modification of payments in lieu of restoration under ironstone leases.

Where any ironstone comprised in a mining lease made before 1 August 1951[1] is worked by opencast operations in accordance with planning permission[2], then if:

(1)　the lease contains provisions requiring or enabling the lessee to pay a specified sum in lieu of compliance with any obligation relating to the restoration of the land or by way of liquidated damages for breach of such an obligation, or to return the land after restoration or upon payment of a specified sum in lieu of restoration; and

(2)　the planning permission is subject to conditions regulating the manner in which the land is to be dealt with after working, but not requiring its restoration in the manner or to the extent specified in the lease, and those conditions are complied with,

the sum payable by the lessee under the lease in respect of that land must be reduced to such extent, if any, as may be just having regard to any benefit accruing to the lessor, or any person deriving title from him, in consequence of compliance with those conditions[3].

Any question whether any and if so what reduction falls to be made under these provisions in the sums payable under a lease must, in default of agreement between the parties, be determined by arbitration[4].

1   Ie the commencement of the Mineral Workings Act 1951: see s 28(1). These provisions apply in relation to a conveyance of ironstone or a conveyance of land subject to an exception of ironstone as they apply in relation to a mining lease, and as if for references to the lessee and to the lessor there were substituted respectively references to the person entitled to the ironstone by virtue of the conveyance or exception and to the person entitled to the surface of the land: s 28(4). As to the meanings of 'land' and of 'lease' for these purposes see the Town and Country Planning Act 1990; and PLANNING vol 81 (2018) PARAS 3, 161 (definitions applied by the Mineral Workings Act 1951 s 41 (amended by the Mineral Workings Act 1985 ss 1, 6(4), 10, Sch 2; and the Planning (Consequential Provisions) Act 1990 s 4, Sch 2 para 2)).

2   As to the meaning of 'planning permission' see the Town and Country Planning Act 1990; and PLANNING vol 81 (2018) PARA 162 (definition applied by the Mineral Workings Act 1951 s 41). As to planning permission generally see PLANNING vol 81 (2018) PARA 333 et seq.

3   Mineral Workings Act 1951 s 28(1). For the purpose of calculating the amount of any reduction, the value of any benefit accruing in consequence of compliance with any conditions must be ascertained by reference to prices of land current at the time when the sum to be reduced is payable; but if that sum is less than the sum which would represent the value of the land at that time if it were restored to the extent contemplated in the lease, the value of the benefit must be reduced proportionately: s 28(3).

4   Mineral Workings Act 1951 s 28(2). As to arbitration generally see ARBITRATION vol 2 (2017) PARA 501 et seq.

# 10. RECLAIMING OR IMPROVING FORMER MINING LAND

## 582. Treatment of derelict land.

Where it appears to a local authority[1] that any land[2] in its area is derelict, neglected or unsightly or likely to become so by reason of actual or apprehended collapse of the surface as the result of the carrying out of relevant operations[3] which have ceased to be carried out, it may carry out, for the purpose of reclaiming or improving that land or of enabling it to be brought into use, such works on that land or any other land as appear to it expedient[4].

The powers mentioned above may be exercised by an authority either on land belonging to it or with the consent of all persons interested therein on other land; and in relation to such other land these powers include power to make arrangements whereby the work is carried out, on such terms as may be provided under the arrangements, by a person other than the authority[5]. Where a local authority exercises its powers over land not belonging to it, the management of the land, so far as related to anything done by the authority, may be undertaken either by the authority or by the person interested in the land as may be agreed between them and on such terms as may be so agreed[6].

A local authority may acquire land compulsorily for the purpose of any of these functions[7].

These provisions apply to Crown land[8] if the appropriate authority[9] consents to their application[10].

1   'Local authority', for these purposes, means a local planning authority, a county council not being a local planning authority, or a district council: National Parks and Access to the Countryside Act 1949 s 89(7) (added by the Local Authorities (Land) Act 1963 s 6(4); and amended by the Local Government Act 1972 Sch 17 para 38, Sch 30).

2   'Land' includes land covered by water: National Parks and Access to the Countryside Act 1949 s 114(1).

3   'Relevant operations' means underground mining operations other than operations for the purpose of the working and getting of coal, or of coal and other minerals worked with coal, or for the purpose of getting any product from coal in the course of working and getting coal: National Parks and Access to the Countryside Act 1949 s 89(2) (substituted by the Derelict Land Act 1982 s 3(1)). As to a local authority's power to enter and work on former mining land see the Mineral Workings Act 1985 ss 7, 8; and PARAS 583, 584. As to mining generally see PARA 48 et seq.

4   National Parks and Access to the Countryside Act 1949 s 89(2). As to obligations to restore land affected by coal-mining operations see PARA 355.

5   See the National Parks and Access to the Countryside Act 1949 s 89(3). However, nothing in s 89(1)–(3) authorises the doing of any act in contravention of any enactment: s 89(4) (amended by the Local Authorities (Land) Act 1963 s 6(2); and the Countryside Act 1968 Sch 5).

6   See the National Parks and Access to the Countryside Act 1949 s 89(6) (amended by the Local Authorities (Land) Act 1963 s 6(1)).

7   National Parks and Access to the Countryside Act 1949 s 89(5) (amended by the Local Authorities (Land) Act 1963 s 6(1)). As to compulsory acquisition of land generally see COMPULSORY ACQUISITION OF LAND.

8   As to Crown land generally see CROWN AND CROWN PROCEEDINGS vol 29 (2014) PARAS 114 et seq, 192 et seq.

9   'The appropriate authority', in relation to any Crown land, means (1) in the case of land belonging to Her Majesty in right of the Crown, the Commissioners of Crown Lands (reconstituted as the Crown Estate Commissioners) (see CROWN AND CROWN PROCEEDINGS vol 29 (2014) PARA 192 et seq) or other government department having the management of the land in question; (2) in the case of land belonging to Her Majesty in right of the Duchy of Lancaster, the Chancellor of the Duchy; (3) in the case of land belonging to the Duchy of Cornwall, such person as the Duke of Cornwall or the possessor for the time being of the Duchy of Cornwall appoints; and (4) in the case of land belonging to a government department or held in trust for Her Majesty for the purpose of a government department, that department: National Parks and Access to the Countryside Act

1949 s 101(11)(a)–(d) (amended by virtue of the Crown Estate Act 1961 s 1; and the Interpretation Act 1978 Sch 1). Questions of doubt as to who is the appropriate authority in a particular case must be determined by the Treasury: National Parks and Access to the Countryside Act 1949 s 101(11).

10 National Parks and Access to the Countryside Act 1949 s 101(7). However, an interest in Crown land may be acquired for the purposes of s 89 only with the consent of the appropriate authority; and if any land affected by the arrangements under s 89(3) or an agreement under s 89(6) becomes Crown land, the arrangements or agreement cease to apply to the land unless the appropriate authority consents to the continued application to it of the arrangements or agreement: s 101(7)(a), (b).

### 583. Power to enter former mining land.

The following provisions apply where a local authority has carried out, is carrying out or is considering whether to carry out works[1] on any land for the purpose of (1) reclaiming or improving land under which relevant operations[2] have been, but are no longer being, carried out; or (2) enabling it to be brought into use[3].

A person duly authorised in writing by the authority may at any reasonable time enter such land[4] in order to (a) carry out the works referred to; (b) survey the land for the purpose of ascertaining the effect on it of the works; (c) survey the land for the purpose of ascertaining the location, extent and state of mine workings produced by relevant operations, the state of the land, the risk of collapse of its surface, the likely extent of collapse, and the nature and extent of any works which may be necessary to prevent collapse or to deal with a collapse which has occurred[5].

A person may not demand admission to any land as of right unless at least ten clear days' notice[6] in writing of the intended entry has been given to every person who is an owner[7] or occupier, or the entry is authorised by a warrant[8]. A person duly authorised to enter any land must, if so required, produce evidence of his authority before so entering and may take with him on to the land such other persons and such equipment as may be necessary[9].

Any person who intentionally obstructs a person entitled to enter land is guilty of an offence and liable on summary conviction to a fine not exceeding level 3 on the standard scale[10].

Where, in consequence of an exercise of the power to enter land, any damage is caused to land or chattels, or any loss occurs to chattels, the local authority authorising the entry must pay compensation in respect of the damage or loss to every person interested in the land or chattels[11]. Where, in consequence of an exercise of such power, any person is disturbed in his enjoyment of land or chattels, the local authority authorising the entry must pay compensation in respect of the disturbance to that person[12].

1 Ie works under the National Parks and Access to the Countryside Act 1949 s 89(2) (see PARA 582): see the Mineral Workings Act 1985 s 7(1).

2 As to the meaning of 'relevant operations' see PARA 582 (definition applied by Mineral Workings Act 1985 s 7(2)).

3 Mineral Workings Act 1985 s 7(1).

4 Ie the land first mentioned in the Mineral Workings Act 1985 s 7(1): see s 7(3).

5 Mineral Workings Act 1985 s 7(3). The power to survey land includes power to search and bore for the purpose of ascertaining the nature of its subsoil: s 7(4).

6 Such notice must specify the purpose for which entry is required and, in a case where entry is sought for the purpose of carrying out works, must indicate as far as is practicable the nature of the intended works: Mineral Workings Act 1985 s 7(6).

7  'Owner', in relation to any land, means a person, other than a mortgagee not in possession, who is for the time being entitled to dispose of the fee simple of the land, whether in possession or in reversion, and also includes a person holding, or entitled to the rents and profits of, the land under a lease or agreement: Mineral Workings Act 1985 s 7(14).

8  Mineral Workings Act 1985 s 7(5). If it is shown to the satisfaction of a justice of the peace on sworn information in writing (1) that a person entitled to enter land under s 7 is not or will not be able to gain admission to the land, or that any owner or occupier who has not been given notice under s 7(5) is one who has not been identified or (though identified) has not been traced after reasonable inquiry by the authority; and (2) that there is reasonable ground for entering the land for the purpose for which entry is required, the justice may by warrant under his hand authorise that person to enter the land, if need be by force: s 7(7). However, such a warrant must not be granted on the ground that a person is not or will not be able to gain admission unless the justice is satisfied that the authority has taken reasonable steps to notify every person who is an owner or occupier of the intention to apply for a warrant: s 7(7). Every warrant granted under s 7 continues in force until the purpose for which entry is required has been satisfied: s 7(8).

9  Mineral Workings Act 1985 s 7(9).

10  Mineral Workings Act 1985 s 7(10) (amended by the Statute Law (Repeals) Act 1993). As to the standard scale see SENTENCING vol 92 (2015) PARA 176.

11  Mineral Workings Act 1985 s 7(11). Any dispute about a right to compensation or about its amount must be referred to and determined by the Upper Tribunal; and the Land Compensation Act 1961 s 4 (see COMPULSORY ACQUISITION OF LAND vol 18 (2009) PARAS 716, 717) applies in relation to the determination of any such dispute: Mineral Workings Act 1985 s 7(13) (amended by SI 2009/1307).

12  Mineral Workings Act 1985 s 7(12). See also s 7(13).

## 584.  Works on former mining land.

The following provisions apply where a local authority[1] proposes to carry out works on any land for the purposes of (1) reclaiming or improving land under which relevant operations[2] have been, but are no longer being, carried out; or (2) enabling it to be brought into use[3].

If the following conditions are fulfilled, the authority may carry out the works without the consent of persons interested in the land[4], notwithstanding the provision[5] requiring such consent[6]. The conditions are that (a) in the authority's opinion the surface of the land under which the relevant operations have been carried out has collapsed or is in imminent danger of collapse; (b) in the authority's opinion the works are necessary as a matter of urgency because in its opinion there is, or is likely to be, a risk of death or injury to persons or damage to other land or property; and (c) any person who has not given his required consent[7] has, in the authority's opinion, withheld consent unreasonably or has not been identified or (though identified) has not been traced after reasonable inquiry by the authority[8].

The authority must not carry out the works[9] without the consent of interested persons unless it gives notice that it proposes to do so to any person who, after reasonable inquiry by the authority, appears to it to be interested in the land on which it proposes to carry out the works and has been traced[10]. Where such a notice has been given, a person interested in the land may (whether or not he has been given such notice) apply to the Secretary of State (not less than ten clear days before the date stated in the notice as the date when the authority proposes to start the works) for a decision whether or not the works may be carried out without the consent of all persons interested in the land[11]. When such an application is made, the Secretary of State must notify the authority as soon as practicable, and the works[12] must not be carried out without the consent of persons interested in the land unless he indicates that he has decided that they may be so carried out[13].

Where in consequence of the carrying out of works[14] without the consent of persons interested in the land any damage is caused to land or chattels, or any depreciation in the value of an interest in land occurs, or any loss occurs in relation to chattels, the authority must pay compensation in respect of the damage, depreciation or loss to every person interested in the land[15]. Where in consequence of the carrying out of such works any person is disturbed in his enjoyment of land or chattels, the authority must pay compensation in respect of the disturbance to that person[16].

1  Ie under the National Parks and Access to the Countryside Act 1949 s 89(2) (see PARA 582): see the Mineral Workings Act 1985 s 8(1).
2  As to the meaning of 'relevant operations' see PARA 582 (definition applied by the Mineral Workings Act 1985 s 8(1)).
3  Mineral Workings Act 1985 s 8(1).
4  Ie the land first mentioned in Mineral Workings Act 1985 s 8(1): see s 8(2).
5  Ie the National Parks and Access to the Countryside Act 1949 s 89(3) (see PARA 582): see the Mineral Workings Act 1985 s 8(2).
6  Mineral Workings Act 1985 s 8(2).
7  Ie required by National Parks and Access to the Countryside Act 1949 s 89(3): see the Mineral Workings Act 1985 s 8(3).
8  Mineral Workings Act 1985 s 8(3).
9  Ie the works as mentioned in Mineral Workings Act 1985 s 8(2).
10  Mineral Workings Act 1985 s 8(4). A notice under s 8(4) must state when the authority proposes to start the works and must contain such other information, be in such form, and be given in such manner and at such time before it is proposed to start the works, as may be prescribed by regulations made by the Secretary of State: see s 8(5), (12), (13); and see the Mining Dereliction (Compulsory Works) (Procedure) Regulations 1985, SI 1985/814. As to the Secretary of State see PARA 2.
11  Mineral Workings Act 1985 s 8(6). Regulations made by the Secretary of State may prescribe the manner of making applications under s 8(6), the grounds on which they may be made, the procedure for reaching and indicating decisions on them, and such other matters relating to them as the Secretary of State thinks expedient: s 8(8); and see the Mining Dereliction (Compulsory Works) (Procedure) Regulations 1985, SI 1985/814.
12  Ie the works as mentioned in the Mineral Workings Act 1985 s 8(2): see s 8(7).
13  Mineral Workings Act 1985 s 8(7).
14  Ie the works as mentioned in Mineral Workings Act 1985 s 8(2): see s 8(9).
15  Mineral Workings Act 1985 s 8(9). Any dispute about a right to compensation or about its amount must be referred to and determined by the Upper Tribunal; and the Land Compensation Act 1961 s 4 (see COMPULSORY ACQUISITION OF LAND vol 18 (2009) PARAS 716, 717) applies in relation to the determination of any such dispute: Mineral Workings Act 1985 s 8(11) (amended by SI 2009/1307).
16  Mineral Workings Act 1985 s 8(10).

# 11. LOCAL RIGHTS AND CUSTOMS

## (1) In General

### 585. Manorial land.

Apart from the Forest of Dean and certain other mining districts[1], customary rights of working are mainly of importance in connection with manorial land[2]. If either lord or tenant is entitled to work mines[3] or quarries[4] in former copyhold land[5] or in former customary freehold land[6], it is by virtue of a special custom[7]. The tenant may only work mines or quarries in the waste if so entitled by custom, and the right of the lord of a manor to work mines or quarries in the waste may be varied by custom from that which he would enjoy under the general law[8]. If either lord[9] or tenant[10] exceeds his rights he may be restrained by injunction[11].

The customary right of a tenant to dig mines in his copyhold could be enjoyed without stint[12], but a custom to dig without stint in the waste is bad[13].

1 As to customary rights in these districts see PARAS 587 et seq, 594 et seq, 611 et seq.
2 See CUSTOM AND USAGE vol 32 (2012) PARA 44.
3 As to the meaning of 'mine' see PARA 3.
4 As to the meaning of 'quarry' see PARA 4.
5 As to rights to work coal in former copyhold land see PARA 397. As to the abolition of copyhold tenure and the enfranchisement of copyhold land see CUSTOM AND USAGE vol 32 (2012) PARA 43; REAL PROPERTY AND REGISTRATION vol 87 (2017) PARA 36 et seq.
6 See eg *Duke of Portland v Hill* (1866) LR 2 Eq 765.
7 See CUSTOM AND USAGE vol 32 (2012) PARA 44 et seq.
8 See COMMONS vol 13 (2017) PARA 462; CUSTOM AND USAGE vol 32 (2012) PARA 115.
9 *Place v Jackson* (1824) 4 Dow & Ry KB 318.
10 *Dean and Chapter of Ely v Warren* (1741) 2 Atk 189 at 190 per Lord Hardwicke LC.
11 As to injunctions generally see CIVIL PROCEDURE vol 12 (2015) PARA 1098 et seq.
12 *Marquis of Salisbury v Gladstone* (1861) 9 HL Cas 692.
13 *Lady Wilson v Willes* (1806) 7 East 121.

### 586. Proof of custom.

Customary rights in respect of minerals[1] are proved in the same manner as other customary rights[2]. Evidence of a custom in one manor cannot be given to establish the existence of a similar custom in another manor[3], except possibly in the case of manors whose physical characteristics are similar, such as manors situate in the fen country or in mining districts[4]. Evidence of a custom to commit one sort of waste, such as cutting trees, is not evidence of a custom to commit another sort of waste, such as digging mines[5], although a custom to dig one sort of mineral may be evidence of a right to dig another[6].

1 As to the meaning of 'minerals' see PARA 10.
2 See CUSTOM AND USAGE vol 32 (2012) PARA 26.
3 *Marquis of Anglesey v Lord Hatherton* (1842) 10 M & W 218.
4 *Dean and Chapter of Ely v Warren* (1741) 2 Atk 189. See also *Marquis of Anglesey v Lord Hatherton* (1842) 10 M & W 218 at 237 per Lord Abinger CB (discussing exceptions to the general rule).
5 *Bishop of Winchester v Knight* (1717) 1 P Wms 406 at 407 per Lord Cowper LC; *Parrott v Palmer* (1834) 3 My & K 632 at 637 per Lord Brougham LC. As to the meaning of 'mine' see PARA 3.
6 *Bishop of Winchester v Knight* (1717) 1 P Wms 406 at 407 per Lord Cowper LC.

# (2) Tin Bounding in Cornwall and Devon

## (i) Cornwall

### 587. Tin mining in Cornwall.

Tin was worked in Cornwall from ancient times. Those engaged in tin mining[1] developed a body of stannary customs[2] which were regulated by their Convocation[3], and enforced by their own court[4]. There were also statutory provisions relating to the stannaries[5], but these have largely been repealed as no working tin mines now remain in Cornwall.

1   Originally, mining companies subject to the stannaries jurisdiction were unincorporated cost-book companies with unlimited liability. By 1920 all the cost-book companies had disappeared, having been either dissolved or converted into registered companies. Provisions in the Companies Act 1948 relating to such companies have been repealed as obsolete: see the Companies Consolidation (Consequential Provisions) Act 1985 ss 28, 29, Sch 1 (now repealed). The Stannaries Act 1869 and the Stannaries Act 1887 (both Acts now repealed) contained provisions as to the regulation of mining companies in the stannaries.

2   The customs were recognised in a Charter, 33 Edw I, which was granted to the tinners of Cornwall in 1305. A copy of the Charter appears in Pearce *The Laws and Customs of the Stannaries* (1725); and see also *Vice v Thomas* (1842) Smirke's Report 1.

3   The Convocation last met in 1753. It appears that on occasion the Convocation made new laws, as well as affirming old customs: *Rogers v Brenton* (1847) 10 QB 26 at 31.

    Legislation passed by the Convocation and giving effect to the Cornwall mining customs is contained in Pearce *The Laws and Customs of the Stannaries* (1725) Pt I; and in *The Laws of the Stannaries of Cornwall*, an anonymous collection published by order of the Convocation in Truro in 1752 which has also appeared in a second edition, cited in this title as *Laws of the Stannaries* (2nd Edn, 1824).

4   See PARA 589.

5   See eg the Stannaries Act 1836; the Stannaries Act 1855; the Stannaries Act 1869; the Stannaries Act 1887; and the Stannaries Court (Abolition) Act 1896. These Acts are largely repealed, although certain provisions of the Stannaries Act 1836 and the Stannaries Act 1855 relating to the former stannaries jurisdiction continue to have effect: see PARA 589; and COURTS AND TRIBUNALS vol 24 (2010) PARA 764.

### 588. The custom of tin bounding.

The ownership of a mine[1] is vested prima facie in the owner of the freehold[2]. This right of ownership is, however, modified by the custom of tin bounding. The custom has fallen into disuse, but it has never been abrogated. Under the custom, if a tin mine[3] lay within waste land or certain inclosed land[4] and was not worked by the surface owner, a tinner[5] could claim and, if various conditions were met[6], be granted tin bounds[7]. The grant carried the exclusive right to search for and work all tin and tin ore within the bounds, subject to a payment to the owner of the soil[8].

Laws passed by the Convocation[9] included detailed provisions as to the rights, duties and liabilities of tin bounders[10].

1   As to the meaning of 'mine' see PARA 3.

2   *Rogers v Brenton* (1847) 10 QB 26 at 50 per Lord Denman CJ; and see PARA 18. As to royal mines see CROWN AND CROWN PROCEEDINGS vol 29 (2014) PARA 132 et seq.

3   The custom applied only to tin. The tinner was not entitled to other minerals found in the course of working: *Rogers v Brenton* (1847) 10 QB 26 at 56 per Lord Denman CJ. As to customs generally see CUSTOM AND USAGE vol 32 (2012) PARA 1. As to the meaning of 'minerals' see PARA 10.

4   Ie inclosed land in which the custom was exercised before inclosure and which either was the property of an individual or formed part of any of the 17 assessionable manors: *Laws of the*

*Stannaries* (2nd Edn, 1824) p 34. As to the assessionable manors see CROWN AND CROWN PROCEEDINGS vol 29 (2014) PARAS 139–140.

5   Ie a person employing himself in tin mining: *Rogers v Brenton* (1847) 10 QB 26 at 50 per Lord Denman CJ; and see *Laws of the Stannaries* (2nd Edn, 1824) p 35.

6   As to the conditions see *Laws of the Stannaries* (2nd Edn, 1824) pp 56, 94.

7   *Rogers v Brenton* (1847) 10 QB 26; *Ivimey v Stocker* (1865) 2 Drew & Sm 537 at 542 per Kindersley V-C (revsd on other points (1866) 1 Ch App 396); *Rowe v Brenton* (1828) 8 B & C 737, reported at length in Concanen's Report 1; and see *Vice v Thomas* (1842) 4 Y & C Ex 538, reported at length in Smirke's Report 1.

8   *Laws of the Stannaries* (2nd Edn, 1824) p 34. In the absence of any special custom, the payment was one-fifteenth of the mineral worked: *Laws of the Stannaries* (2nd Edn, 1824) p 34. For an example of a special custom to render a share other than one-fifteenth see *Rowe v Brenton* (1828) 8 B & C 737 at 755 per Parke J. The lord was liable to be rated in respect of his share: see eg *Crease v Sawle* (1842) 2 QB 862. It was held that a tinner was not exempt from paying rates by reason of a claim under the tinners' charters to exemption from taxes: *Trull v Restormel Borough Council* [1994] RVR 122.

9   See PARA 587.

10   See eg *Laws of the Stannaries* (2nd Edn, 1824) p 20 (omission to renew bounds), p 57 (marking and renewal of bounds), pp 59–60 (rights of co-adventurers), pp 91–92 (neglect to work), p 104 (rights as to water) and pp 105–106 (obstruction of streams). A tin bounder was required to work bona fide, but not necessarily without intermission: *Rogers v Brenton* (1847) 10 QB 26.

## 589. The Stannaries Court.

The court of the Cornish tin miners, known as the Stannaries Court[1], had jurisdiction both at common law and in equity[2]. The court has ceased to exist and the jurisdiction is now exercisable by the county courts of Cornwall[3].

1   The full name of the court was the Court of the Vice-Warden of the Stannaries: see the Stannaries Court (Abolition) Act 1896 s 1(1); and COURTS AND TRIBUNALS vol 24 (2010) PARA 764.

2   The jurisdiction extended to: (1) actions between miners (except in relation to land or where judgment of life or limb was exacted), whether or not the cause of the action arose out of the working of mines within the stannaries; and (2) actions between miners and strangers, but only in relation to matters arising out of mining within the stannaries, unless the stranger consented and submitted to the jurisdiction: see the Charter, 33 Edw I, which was granted to the tinners of Cornwall in 1305 (see PARA 587). See also *R v East Powder Justices, ex p Lampshire* [1979] QB 616 at 625, [1979] 2 All ER 329 at 334, DC, per Robert Goff J. The former criminal jurisdiction of the Stannaries Court had been in abeyance for several centuries, and did not survive the abolition of the court and the transfer of its civil jurisdiction to the county courts of Cornwall): *R v East Powder Justices, ex p Lampshire* at 625–626 and 334–335, DC, per Robert Goff J. See also *Trull v Restormel Borough Council* [1994] RVR 122. As to the meaning of 'mine' see PARA 3.

3   See the Stannaries Court (Abolition) Act 1896 s 1; the Order dated 16 December 1896, SR & O 1896/1106; and COURTS AND TRIBUNALS vol 24 (2010) PARA 764.

### (ii) Devon

## 590. Tin mining in Devon.

Tin was worked in Devon from early times, but generally on a small scale. As in Cornwall, there developed a body of stannary customs[1] with a Convocation to regulate them[2]. The jurisdiction of the former Stannaries Court was extended to Devon by statute[3].

1   The Devon customs were recognised in 1305 in a Charter, 33 Edw I, in terms similar to those applicable to the tinners of Cornwall (see PARA 587). The text of the Devon Charter is contained in Pearce *The Laws and Customs of the Stannaries* (1725).

2   The last recorded session of the Devon Convocation was in 1703. Legislation giving effect to the Devon mining customs is set out in Pearce *The Laws and Customs of the Stannaries* (1725) Pt II.

3   Stannaries Act 1855 s 32 (repealed); and see the Stannaries Act 1869 s 2 (repealed). As to the Stannaries Court, and its abolition, see PARA 589; and COURTS AND TRIBUNALS vol 24 (2010) PARA 764.

**591. The custom of tin bounding in Devon.**

The custom of tin bounding in Devon was generally similar to that in Cornwall[1]. It fell into disuse in the eighteenth century but has not been abrogated. Under the Devon custom a tinner could work tin existing in any land in the county other than meadows, orchards, gardens, houses or grain or corn land, or certain woods or groves[2]. He could also work tin in the excepted lands with the consent of the owner and occupier; and if such consent was given, the owner and occupier were entitled to a share of the produce[3]. Tin bounds were required to be renewed yearly[4].

1   As to the custom in Cornwall see PARA 588. As to customs generally see CUSTOM AND USAGE vol 32 (2012) PARA 1 et seq.
2   Pearce *The Laws and Customs of the Stannaries* (1725) p 248. The woods and groves referred to were those where the working would necessitate the overthrowing of 20 timber trees of 20 years' growth: Pearce *The Laws and Customs of the Stannaries* (1725) p 248.
3   Pearce *The Laws and Customs of the Stannaries* (1725) p 249.
4   See Pearce *The Laws and Customs of the Stannaries* (1725) p 200.

# (3) Lead Mining in Derbyshire

## (i) In General

**592. Districts.**

In Derbyshire lead is principally found in two districts, the Hundred of High Peak, in which there is a district called the King's Field or King's Fee, comprising seven liberties or districts[1], and an adjoining district, the Wapentake of Wirksworth, also comprising a district called the King's Field, with eight manors or liberties[2].

Mining operations specifically directed at lead appear to be at an end in Derbyshire, but some lead ore can be recovered in the course of working other minerals[3].

1   Ie Castleton, Bradwell, Hucklow, Winster, Monyash, Taddington and Upper Haddon: see the High Peak Mining Customs and Mineral Courts Act 1851, preamble.
2   Ie Crich, Ashford, Stoney Middleton and Eyam, Hartington, Litton, Peak Forest, Tideswell and Youlgreave: see the Derbyshire Mining Customs and Mineral Courts Act 1852, preamble.
3   Eg minerals such as fluorspar, barite and calcite. As to the meaning of 'minerals' see PARA 10.

**593. Ownership of property.**

The King's Field was originally Crown property in the right of the Duchy of Lancaster[1], and with other districts was from time immemorial subject to customs by which any subject of the realm was entitled to search and mine for lead on payment of certain mineral duties[2]. Notwithstanding the apparent ending of mining for lead[3], the customs have not been abrogated.

According to the districts in which the mines[4] are situated, the mineral duties belong to the Crown, its lessees or private owners[5]. The land enclosing the mines belongs to private persons, the grants of the soil operating subject to the customary duties and rights[6].

1   As to the Duchy of Lancaster generally see CROWN AND CROWN PROCEEDINGS vol 29 (2014) PARA 214 et seq.
2   See the High Peak Mining Customs and Mineral Courts Act 1851, preamble; and the Derbyshire Mining Customs and Mineral Courts Act 1852, preamble. See also *Wake v Redfearn* (1880) 43 LT 123, DC. As to mineral duties see PARA 606. As to the meaning of 'minerals' see PARA 10. As to

customs generally see CUSTOM AND USAGE vol 32 (2012) PARA 1.

3   See PARA 592.

4   As to the meaning of 'mine' see PARA 3.

5   See the High Peak Mining Customs and Mineral Courts Act 1851, preamble; and the Derbyshire Mining Customs and Mineral Courts Act 1852, preamble. See also *Wake v Hall* (1883) 8 App Cas 195 at 211, HL, per Lord FitzGerald.

6   See the High Peak Mining Customs and Mineral Courts Act 1851, preamble; and the Derbyshire Mining Customs and Mineral Courts Act 1852, preamble. See also *Wake v Hall* (1883) 8 App Cas 195 at 211, HL, per Lord FitzGerald.

## 594.   Source and proof of custom.

The mineral laws and customs are defined and regulated by statute[1] and special courts called the Barmote Courts exist to administer them[2].

To prove a custom with respect to rights of miners in one manor in Derbyshire, evidence of customs in an adjoining manor is admissible[3]. The rights and customs exercisable by the miners are of an onerous character with regard to the landowners and must be construed strictly[4].

1   The High Peak Mining Customs and Mineral Courts Act 1851 defines the customs in the King's Field and other parts of the High Peak, while the Derbyshire Mining Customs and Mineral Courts Act 1852 defines the customs in the Wapentake of Wirksworth and eight manors. As to the districts concerned see PARA 592. New customs and rules were defined in 1859 under the power in the High Peak Mining Customs and Mineral Courts Act 1851 s 56: see PARA 595. The objects of the Acts of 1851 and 1852 are substantially the same, namely, settling the customs of each district and establishing and regulating the jurisdiction of the local courts, but each district has its independent local customs and rights and its distinct courts, juries and officers: see *Wake v Redfearn* (1880) 43 LT 123 at 125, DC, per Cockburn CJ. As to cases on customs decided before the passing of these Acts see *Beresford v Bacon* (1685) 2 Lut 1317; *Linn-Regis Corpn v Taylor* (1684) 3 Lev 160; *Rowls v Gells* (1776) 2 Cowp 451; *A-G v Wall* (1760) 4 Bro Parl Cas 665.

2   See PARAS 595–596.

3   *Dean and Chapter of Ely v Warren* (1741) 2 Atk 189; *Marquis of Anglesey v Lord Hatherton* (1842) 10 M & W 218 at 237 per Lord Abinger CB; and see *Rowe v Brenton* (1828) 8 B & C 737 at 758 per Parke J. See also PARA 583.

4   *Wake v Redfearn* (1880) 43 LT 123 at 126, DC, per Cockburn CJ.

## 595.   The Barmote Courts of High Peak.

The Great Barmote[1] Courts and the Small Barmote Courts of High Peak are ancient courts[2] with jurisdiction relating to mining rights and civil pleas relating to those rights in the liberties of the King's Field[3] and other parts of the Hundred of High Peak in Derbyshire where Her Majesty is entitled to mineral duties[4].

The courts are regulated by statute[5], and are courts of record[6]. The judge is the steward (who is appointed by the Crown[7]) or the deputy steward[8]. The officers of the courts are the barmaster and deputy barmasters[9]; and there is also a grand jury. Two Great Barmote Courts are directed to be held at Monyash during the year, and Small Barmote Courts at places fixed by the steward as may be required[10]. There is detailed provision as to the jurisdiction of the courts[11].

There is a power to make new rules and customs, with the approval of the Chancellor of the Duchy of Lancaster, for the regulation of the working and carrying on of the mines within the district, for the guidance and protection of the mines, for regulating the practice and proceedings of the Great and Small Barmote Courts and of views and other proceedings, and for the execution of any process of these courts[12].

The procedure as to the grant of new trials, setting aside judgments, and stay of proceedings is similar to that of the High Court, and the issue of subpoenas (which may be served in any part of England), execution and other procedural matters are regulated by statute[13].

1  Barmote is derived from 'bargh mote'. 'Bargh' is 'a mine whereout of metalls are digged': Robertson *Phraseologie Generalis* (1693) p 207. The privileges of the miners in High Peak are defined and regulated by statute: see PARA 594. As to the meaning of 'mine' see PARA 3.

2  The future of the Barmote Courts of High Peak, and also of the Barmote Courts of Wirksworth and adjacent liberties, has been discussed by the Law Commission: see *Jurisdiction of Certain Ancient Courts* (Law Com no 72) (1976). The Law Commission recommended the abolition of various obsolete courts; but on the principle that jurisdictions which were not obsolete should be preserved, the recommendations did not include any of the Barmote Courts.

3  As to these liberties see PARA 592.

4  As to mineral duties see PARA 606. As to the meaning of 'minerals' see PARA 10.

5  Ie the High Peak Mining Customs and Mineral Courts Act 1851.

6  See the High Peak Mining Customs and Mineral Courts Act 1851 s 15.

7  Ie under the seal of the Duchy of Lancaster: see the High Peak Mining Customs and Mineral Courts Act 1851 s 3. The steward must be a barrister of five years' standing or a solicitor of seven years' standing: see s 3. As to the seal of the Duchy of Lancaster see CROWN AND CROWN PROCEEDINGS vol 29 (2014) PARA 217.

8  See the High Peak Mining Customs and Mineral Courts Act 1851 ss 3–5, 15.

9  See the High Peak Mining Customs and Mineral Courts Act 1851 ss 9–12. The barmasters and deputy barmasters have various administrative functions: see eg ss 13, 14, 25, Sch 1 arts 3–5, 7–10, 19. See also PARA 600 et seq.

10  See the High Peak Mining Customs and Mineral Courts Act 1851 s 6.

11  The principal statutory business of the Great Barmote Court is the swearing in of a grand jury: see the High Peak Mining Customs and Mineral Courts Act 1851 s 7. The jurisdiction of the Small Barmote Courts includes actions of title, trespass and debt: see ss 7, 16, Sch 1. It extends to a person who, although mining for a mineral other than lead ore, and therefore not ipso facto a miner under the High Peak Mining Customs and Mineral Courts Act 1851, nevertheless in the course of such mining in fact takes lead ore: *R v Sanders* [1917] 2 KB 390, DC; and see PARA 592.

   Provision is made as to the procedure for initiating actions: see the High Peak Mining Customs and Mineral Courts Act 1851 ss 24, 25, 51. Actions are tried summarily, leaving questions of fact to be determined by the jury; and the judgment is enforceable by warrant: see s 24. The jurisdiction is not exclusive: see s 55. Causes may be removed by quashing order on judicial review: see ss 29, 52. As to quashing orders (previously certiorari) see JUDICIAL REVIEW vol 61 (2010) PARA 693 et seq.

12  See the High Peak Mining Customs and Mineral Courts Act 1851 s 56. These rules and customs were given effect by an order of the Chancellor of the Duchy of Lancaster dated 30 May 1859 approving the customs, articles, rules and orders made on 5 April 1859 by the steward and grand jury at a Great Barmote Court. The order is printed in SR & O Rev 1948 vol X p 1005. As to the Chancellor of the Duchy of Lancaster see CROWN AND CROWN PROCEEDINGS vol 29 (2014) PARA 214 et seq.

13  See the High Peak Mining Customs and Mineral Courts Act 1851 ss 27, 31–33.

## 596. The Barmote Courts of Wirksworth and adjacent liberties.

The Barmote Courts of Wirksworth and adjacent liberties are similar to those of High Peak[1]. They also are regulated by statute[2], and are courts of record[3]. The jurisdiction over the King's Field in the Wapentake of Wirksworth is vested in the Wirksworth Barmote Court, and separate courts exist for five adjacent manors or liberties in private ownership[4]. The steward for the Wirksworth Barmote Court is appointed by the Crown[5] and the stewards for the private liberties are appointed by the persons entitled to the first estate of freehold in the mineral duties payable in the appropriate liberty[6]. Provisions as to the qualification of stewards[7] and as to jurisdiction and procedure[8] and quashing orders[9] are similar to those in the case of the Barmote Courts of High Peak[10]. There are certain rules and customs[11], but there is no power to formulate new rules and customs.

1  See PARA 595. As to the continued existence of the Barmote Courts see PARA 595.

2  Ie the Derbyshire Mining Customs and Mineral Courts Act 1852.

3   See the Derbyshire Mining Customs and Mineral Courts Act 1852 s 24.

4   Ie (1) Ashford, Hartington, Peak Forest and Tideswell; (2) Crich; (3) Stoney Middleton and Eyam; (4) Youlgreave; and (5) Litton: see the Derbyshire Mining Customs and Mineral Courts Act 1852 ss 12–14.

5   Ie under the seal of the Duchy of Lancaster: see the Derbyshire Mining Customs and Mineral Courts Act 1852 s 3. As to the seal of the Duchy of Lancaster see CROWN AND CROWN PROCEEDINGS vol 29 (2014) PARA 217.

6   See the Derbyshire Mining Customs and Mineral Courts Act 1852 ss 3, 4. In default the Chancellor of the Duchy of Lancaster may appoint them: see s 8. As to mineral duties see PARA 606. As to the person entitled to the mineral duties see PARA 593. As to the meaning of 'minerals' see PARA 10. As to the Chancellor of the Duchy of Lancaster see CROWN AND CROWN PROCEEDINGS vol 29 (2014) PARA 214 et seq.

7   See the Derbyshire Mining Customs and Mineral Courts Act 1852 ss 3, 4.

8   See the Derbyshire Mining Customs and Mineral Courts Act 1852 s 16.

9   See the Derbyshire Mining Customs and Mineral Courts Act 1852 ss 38, 60. As to quashing orders (formerly certiorari) see JUDICIAL REVIEW vol 61 (2010) PARA 693 et seq.

10   See PARA 595.

11   Ie those scheduled to the Act regulating the courts: see the Derbyshire Mining Customs and Mineral Courts Act 1852 Sch 1.

## (ii) Rights of Mining

### 597. Right to search for ore.

Every subject of the realm[1] may by the local customs enter and search for lead ore in any part of the land where the custom prevails[2], under the obligation of making good any damage done if no vein of ore is found[3].

1   This includes the owner of the soil in which the mine is situate (*Wake v Hall* (1880) 7 QBD 295 at 298, CA, per Lord Selborne LC; affd (1883) 8 App Cas 195, HL) or a lessee from the Crown of mineral rights (*Arkwright v Evans* (1880) 49 LJMC 82 at 86, DC, per Lord Coleridge CJ); but anyone may contract himself out of his customary rights (*Wright v Pitt* (1870) LR 12 Eq 408 at 416 per Malins V-C). A landowner has no greater nor better right to work mines under his land than any other person; and if he works them at all, he can only do so upon the customary terms and on payment of the customary royalties: *Wake v Hall*. A person who mines for minerals other than lead ore is not ipso facto a miner within the High Peak Mining Customs and Mineral Courts Act 1851, but he becomes a miner if in fact he takes lead ore: *R v Sanders* [1917] 2 KB 390, DC. As to the meaning of 'mine' see PARA 3. As to the meaning of 'minerals' see PARA 10. As to customs generally see CUSTOM AND USAGE vol 32 (2012) PARA 1.

2   Churches, burial grounds, dwelling houses, orchards, gardens and highways are excepted; but, subject to certain conditions and obligations, the miner may also follow a vein or search for lead ore under the excepted places: see the High Peak Mining Customs and Mineral Courts Act 1851 Sch 1 art 1; and the Derbyshire Mining Customs and Mineral Courts Act 1852 Sch 1 art 1. As to the meaning of 'vein' see PARA 3.

3   High Peak Mining Customs and Mineral Courts Act 1851 Sch 1 art 1; Derbyshire Mining Customs and Mineral Courts Act 1852 Sch 1 art 1. See also *Gilbert v Tomison* (1824) 4 Dow & Ry KB 222; *R v Sanders* [1917] 2 KB 390, DC.

### 598. Relations between miner and landowner.

The rights of landowner and miner are correlative. There is no privity of title between them. The miner is entitled to the use of the land in order to get lead and, while the mine is being worked, to various other easements and rights, but he has no absolute right in perpetuity[1]. In the High Peak district, the landowner is entitled to all that remains when the lead has been extracted and to the full property in the land when the mine is abandoned[2].

1   *Wake v Hall* (1883) 8 App Cas 195 at 206, HL, per Lord Watson, at 209 per Lord Bramwell, and at 214–215 per Lord FitzGerald. As to the meaning of 'mine' see PARA 3.

2  High Peak Mining Customs and Mineral Courts Act 1851 Sch 1 art 2. See also *Wake v Redfearn* (1880) 43 LT 123 at 126, DC, per Cockburn CJ; *Stokes v Arkwright* (1897) 66 LJQB 845; *Duke of Devonshire v Stokes* (1897) 76 LT 424, DC. The customs in the other districts differ slightly: see the Derbyshire Mining Customs and Mineral Courts Act 1852 Sch 1 art 2.

## 599. Meers.

In the High Peak district[1], when a person discovers a new vein[2] he is entitled to two strips of land called 'meers', varying in area according to the district[3], along the vein, one on each side of the point where the vein was discovered[4]. A third meer, which the barmaster may set out at either extremity of the two meers, belongs to the owner of the mineral duties[5].

When the first two meers are freed[6], the finder may claim the subsequent meers at either extremity[7]. If the third meer is not worked by the owner of the mineral duties, the finder of the original vein may purchase the meer at a price fixed by the steward or barmaster and the grand jury, or may work through it, reserving the ore found there, less expenses, for the owner of the mineral duties[8].

1  In the other districts the custom varies slightly: see the Derbyshire Mining Customs and Mineral Courts Act 1852 Sch 1 arts 10, 11, 18. See also *Rowls v Gells* (1776) 2 Cowp 451.
2  As to the meaning of 'vein' see PARA 3.
3  See the High Peak Mining Customs and Mineral Courts Act 1851 Sch 1 art 18; and the Derbyshire Mining Customs and Mineral Courts Act 1852 Sch 1 art 18. Thus a meer in the Peak Forest measures 32 yards, in Wirksworth 29 yards, and in Youlgreave 28 yards.
4  See the High Peak Mining Customs and Mineral Courts Act 1851 Sch 1 arts 10, 11, 18. The point is known as the 'founder': s 2.
5  High Peak Mining Customs and Mineral Courts Act 1851 Sch 1 art 10. As to mineral duties see PARA 606. As to the person entitled to the mineral duties see PARA 593. As to the meaning of 'minerals' see PARA 10.
6  As to freeing see PARA 600.
7  High Peak Mining Customs and Mineral Courts Act 1851 Sch 1 art 10; Derbyshire Mining Customs and Mineral Courts Act 1852 Sch 1 art 10. Under these provisions the finder is not entitled to more than 50 subsequent meers in each vein.
8  High Peak Mining Customs and Mineral Courts Act 1851 Sch 1 art 10; Derbyshire Mining Customs and Mineral Courts Act 1852 Sch 1 art 10. See also the rules set out in the order of the Chancellor of the Duchy of Lancaster dated 30 May 1859 (see PARA 595) r 6. See further *Wake v Hall* (1880) 7 QBD 295 at 298, CA, per Lord Selborne LC; affd (1883) 8 App Cas 195, HL.

## 600. Setting out meers.

One of the duties of the barmaster[1] is, in the presence of two of the grand jury, to measure and set out meers[2], this operation being called the 'gift'[3], and to record gifts in the barmaster's book[4].

A meer may not be set out until ore has been raised and the first customary payment[5] has been made to the owner of the mineral duties[6]. This is called 'freeing' the mine[7]. Similar payments must be made for every third and subsequent meer reached by the miner[8]. No ore may be sold or disposed of before being measured by a barmaster[9].

1  As to other duties of the barmaster see eg PARA 595.
2  High Peak Mining Customs and Mineral Courts Act 1851 Sch 1 art 10; Derbyshire Mining Customs and Mineral Courts Act 1852 Sch 1 art 10.
3  High Peak Mining Customs and Mineral Courts Act 1851 s 2; Derbyshire Mining Customs and Mineral Courts Act 1852 s 2.
4  High Peak Mining Customs and Mineral Courts Act 1851 Sch 1 art 10; Derbyshire Mining Customs and Mineral Courts Act 1852 Sch 1 art 10.
5  High Peak Mining Customs and Mineral Courts Act 1851 Sch 1 art 3; Derbyshire Mining Customs and Mineral Courts Act 1852 Sch 1 art 3. The payment consists of ore in a dish of a specified measurement: see the High Peak Mining Customs and Mineral Courts Act 1851 Sch 1 art 3; and the Derbyshire Mining Customs and Mineral Courts Act 1852 Sch 1 art 3.

6　High Peak Mining Customs and Mineral Courts Act 1851 Sch 1 art 11; Derbyshire Mining Customs and Mineral Courts Act 1852 Sch 1 art 11. If less than a meer is taken, only a proportionate payment need be made: High Peak Mining Customs and Mineral Courts Act 1851 Sch 1 art 18; Derbyshire Mining Customs and Mineral Courts Act 1852 Sch 1 art 18. As to mineral duties see PARA 606. As to the person entitled to the mineral duties see PARA 593. As to the meaning of 'minerals' see PARA 10.

7　As to the meaning of 'mine' see PARA 3.

8　High Peak Mining Customs and Mineral Courts Act 1851 Sch 1 art 11; Derbyshire Mining Customs and Mineral Courts Act 1852 Sch 1 art 11.

9　High Peak Mining Customs and Mineral Courts Act 1851 Sch 1 art 8; Derbyshire Mining Customs and Mineral Courts Act 1852 Sch 1 art 8.

## 601.　Forfeiture.

The penalty for working a mine before it is freed[1], or for committing a trespass[2] in the third meer[3], is forfeiture of the mine to the owner of the mineral duties[4], enforceable by proceedings in the Small Barmote Court in the name of the barmaster[5]. The non-working of a mine or vein for no sufficient reason is also a cause of forfeiture, upon which it may be given by the barmaster to any person willing to work it[6].

Where a person has shares in a mine and refuses to join the owners of the other shares in working it, or to pay his proportion of the expenses, he is liable to forfeit his share to the other co-owners[7].

1　As to freeing see PARA 600. As to the meaning of 'mine' see PARA 3.

2　As to trespass see the High Peak Mining Customs and Mineral Courts Act 1851 Sch 1 art 16; and the Derbyshire Mining Customs and Mineral Courts Act 1852 Sch 1 art 16. As to 'views' to ascertain whether a trespass has been committed, and recovery of ore from trespassers, see the High Peak Mining Customs and Mineral Courts Act 1851 Sch 1 arts 22–25, 28; and the Derbyshire Mining Customs and Mineral Courts Act 1852 Sch 1 arts 23–26, 29. See also the rules set out in the order of the Chancellor of the Duchy of Lancaster dated 30 May 1859 (see PARA 595) r 11. As to trespass generally see TORT vol 97 (2015) PARA 525 et seq.

3　As to the third meer see PARA 599.

4　As to mineral duties see PARA 606. As to the person entitled to the mineral duties see PARA 593. As to the meaning of 'minerals' see PARA 10.

5　High Peak Mining Customs and Mineral Courts Act 1851 Sch 1 art 12; Derbyshire Mining Customs and Mineral Courts Act 1852 Sch 1 art 12. As to Small Barmote Courts see *R v Sanders* [1917] 2 KB 390, DC; and PARA 595.

6　High Peak Mining Customs and Mineral Courts Act 1851 Sch 1 art 19; Derbyshire Mining Customs and Mineral Courts Act 1852 Sch 1 art 19. See also the rules set out in the order of the Chancellor of the Duchy of Lancaster dated 30 May 1859 (see PARA 595) r 7. See further *Wake v Hall* (1880) 7 QBD 295 at 299, CA, per Lord Selborne LC; affd (1883) 8 App Cas 195, HL.

7　High Peak Mining Customs and Mineral Courts Act 1851 Sch 1 art 20; Derbyshire Mining Customs and Mineral Courts Act 1852 Sch 1 art 21. See also the rules set out in the order of the Chancellor of the Duchy of Lancaster dated 30 May 1859 (see PARA 595) rr 8, 10.

## 602.　Incidental rights.

While his mine[1] is being worked, and without paying compensation to the landowner or occupier, the miner is entitled to a right of way (limited to purposes and persons connected with the mine) from the mine to the nearest highway, and also to the nearest stream, spring or natural pond, and to take water from it[2].

Similarly, without payment of compensation to the landowner or occupier, he is entitled to the exclusive use of such surface land as is thought necessary by the barmaster for the purposes of working the mine[3], but he is not entitled to use surface land in one district for mining purposes incidental to mining in another district[4].

Buildings necessary for the purposes of the mine may be erected on the surface, and modern appliances may be used for working the lead[5]. Buildings and machinery may be removed by the miner or compensation claimed where a mine is forfeited for not being worked[6]. Conversely, a landowner may require a miner, on abandoning his mine, to remove his buildings and restore the surface[7].

Persons who relieve or unwater a mine are entitled by custom, so long as the relief continues, to such portion of the ore gotten as the barmaster determines, recoverable, according to value, in the High Court or county court[8].

1   As to the meaning of 'mine' see PARA 3.
2   High Peak Mining Customs and Mineral Courts Act 1851 Sch 1 art 4; Derbyshire Mining Customs and Mineral Courts Act 1852 Sch 1 art 4 (under which the right as to water relates only to a running stream, not being ornamental water or a private fishery). These rights must be marked out by the barmaster and two of the grand jury: High Peak Mining Customs and Mineral Courts Act 1851 Sch 1 art 4; Derbyshire Mining Customs and Mineral Courts Act 1852 Sch 1 art 4. See also *Wake v Hall* (1880) 7 QBD 295 at 298, CA, per Lord Selborne LC; affd (1883) 8 App Cas 195, HL.
3   High Peak Mining Customs and Mineral Courts Act 1851 Sch 1 art 5; Derbyshire Mining Customs and Mineral Courts Act 1852 Sch 1 art 5 (under which certain payments must be made for the use of cultivated land).
4   *Wake v Redfearn* (1880) 43 LT 123, DC. It is doubtful whether a miner may use surface land in the same district as that in which he is mining, where it is not immediately over the lead vein actually being worked: *Wake v Redfearn* at 127 per Manisty J.
5   High Peak Mining Customs and Mineral Courts Act 1851 Sch 1 art 5; Derbyshire Mining Customs and Mineral Courts Act 1852 Sch 1 art 5. See also *Wake v Hall* (1883) 8 App Cas 195 at 212, HL, per Lord FitzGerald.
6   *Wake v Hall* (1880) 7 QBD 295 at 303, CA, per Lord Selborne LC; affd (1883) 8 App Cas 195, HL. As to forfeiture see PARA 601.
7   *Wake v Hall* (1883) 8 App Cas 195 at 209–210, HL, per Lord Bramwell; cf *A-G to Prince of Wales v Collom* [1916] 2 KB 193.
8   High Peak Mining Customs and Mineral Courts Act 1851 Sch 1 art 26; Derbyshire Mining Customs and Mineral Courts Act 1852 Sch 1 art 27. See also *Arkwright v Gell* (1839) 5 M & W 203 at 228–229 per Lord Abinger CB.

### 603. Fences.

A mine[1] which is being worked must be fenced by the miner[2], but if the mine has been abandoned the landowner must fence it[3].

1   As to the meaning of 'mine' see PARA 3.
2   High Peak Mining Customs and Mineral Courts Act 1851 Sch 1 art 5; Derbyshire Mining Customs and Mineral Courts Act 1852 Sch 1 art 5. See also *Sybray v White* (1836) 1 M & W 435.
3   *Arkwright v Evans* (1880) 49 LJMC 82 at 87, DC(CP), per Lord Coleridge CJ; *Duke of Devonshire v Stokes* (1897) 76 LT 424, DC; *Stokes v Arkwright* (1897) 66 LJQB 845. See further PARASBOUNDARIES vol 4 (2011) PARA 350 et seq.

### 604. Title to mines.

Gifts from the barmaster[1] are deemed the origin of title, even if the mine was worked prior to the gift[2]. Where priority of title is disputed, the longest continued ownership (which is a question of fact for the jury) prevails[3]. Questions of title and all disputes arising in the working of mines are determinable in the Small Barmote Court[4].

1   See PARA 600.
2   As to the meaning of 'mine' see PARA 3.
3   High Peak Mining Customs and Mineral Courts Act 1851 Sch 1 art 15; Derbyshire Mining Customs and Mineral Courts Act 1852 Sch 1 art 15. As to the consolidation of titles see the High Peak Mining Customs and Mineral Courts Act 1851 Sch 1 art 27; and the Derbyshire Mining Customs and Mineral Courts Act 1852 Sch 1 art 28.

4　High Peak Mining Customs and Mineral Courts Act 1851 Sch 1 art 16; Derbyshire Mining Customs and Mineral Courts Act 1852 Sch 1 art 16. As to the title to veins which cross or approach one another, but are parted by a 'rither' more than 3 feet or in certain cases 6 feet thick, see the High Peak Mining Customs and Mineral Courts Act 1851 Sch 1 arts 13, 14; and the Derbyshire Mining Customs and Mineral Courts Act 1852 Sch 1 arts 13, 14. As to the Small Barmote Courts see PARA 595.

## 605. Transfer of mines.

A simple entry in the barmaster's book is sufficient to effect a transfer of an interest in mines or veins in the High Peak[1]. Interests in mines or veins in other districts may be transferred by transferor and transferee executing a transfer in a specified form, but an entry of such transfer must be made in the barmaster's book[2].

An entry must also be made, in the case of the bankruptcy of any person entitled to a mine or vein in that district, of the appointment of his trustee[3], and of the material parts of the probate of a will by which any such mine or vein is devised[4].

1　High Peak Mining Customs and Mineral Courts Act 1851 Sch 1 art 6. As to the meanings of 'mine' and of 'vein' see PARA 3.
2　Derbyshire Mining Customs and Mineral Courts Act 1852 Sch 1 art 6. See also the rules set out in the order of the Chancellor of the Duchy of Lancaster dated 30 May 1859 (see PARA 595) r 2.
3　See also the rules set out in the order of the Chancellor of the Duchy of Lancaster dated 30 May 1859 (see PARA 595) r 3.
4　See also the rules set out in the order of the Chancellor of the Duchy of Lancaster dated 30 May 1859 (see PARA 595) r 4.

### (iii) Mineral Duties

## 606. Lot and cope.

The mineral duties payable by the miners to the owners of such duties[1] are 'lot' and 'cope'. Lot is a duty rendered in kind[2]; cope is a money payment[3]. The duty of lot is taken by the barmaster when the ore is measured[4], and payment of cope is recoverable, if necessary, by action in the county court or the Small Barmote Court[5].

1　As to the person entitled to the mineral duties see PARA 593. As to the meaning of 'minerals' see PARA 10.
2　Ie either one-thirteenth or one-ninth part of the ore raised, according to the district: see the High Peak Mining Customs and Mineral Courts Act 1851 Sch 1 art 9; and the Derbyshire Mining Customs and Mineral Courts Act 1852 Sch 1 art 9.
3　The amount of the payment varies according to the district, and is payable for every load of ore measured by the barmaster: see the High Peak Mining Customs and Mineral Courts Act 1851 Sch 1 art 9; the Derbyshire Mining Customs and Mineral Courts Act 1852 Sch 1 art 9; and the Decimal Currency Act 1969 s 10. As to the measurement of loads see the High Peak Mining Customs and Mineral Courts Act 1851 Sch 1 arts 3, 7; and the Derbyshire Mining Customs and Mineral Courts Act 1852 Sch 1 arts 3, 7.
4　High Peak Mining Customs and Mineral Courts Act 1851 Sch 1 art 9; Derbyshire Mining Customs and Mineral Courts Act 1852 Sch 1 art 9. See also *A-G v Wall* (1760) 4 Bro Parl Cas 665.
5　High Peak Mining Customs and Mineral Courts Act 1851 Sch 1 art 9; Derbyshire Mining Customs and Mineral Courts Act 1852 Sch 1 art 9. See also *Duke of Devonshire v Stokes* (1897) 76 LT 424 at 425. As to the Small Barmote Courts see PARA 595.

# (4) Mining and Quarrying in Gloucestershire

## (i) In General

### 607. Ownership of mines and the surface.

The Gloucestershire customs are exercisable in that part of the county lying to the west of the Severn known as the Hundred of St Briavels[1], which includes the Forest of Dean[2] and certain other districts[3].

The surface of the Forest of Dean, with the exception of certain legalised encroachments[4], belongs to the Crown[5], and the surface of the remainder of the hundred belongs partly to the Crown and partly to private owners[6].

Mines[7], other than coal mines[8], in and under the Forest of Dean and the other districts included in the hundred[9] belong to the Crown[10]. Interests in mines in the Forest of Dean and those other districts are subject to the rights of the free miners[11] under the customs[12].

1 See *Fourth Report of the Forest of Dean Commissioners* (1831), which is set out in Wood's Laws of the Dean Forest at 88.
2 The boundaries of the Forest of Dean were finally settled by the Delimitation of Forests Act 1640 and the Dean Forest Act 1667 (both repealed). See further *Second Report of the Forest of Dean Commissioners* (1831), which is set out in Wood's Laws of the Dean Forest at 82. For a map see *Report of the Forest of Dean Committee* (Cmnd 686) (1958).
3 In addition to the Forest of Dean, the hundred includes the parishes of Hewelsfield, St Briavels, Newland, Staunton, English Bicknor, Ruardean, Mitcheldean, Abinghall, Flaxley and Little Dean, parts of the parishes of Westbury-on-Severn, Lea and Newnham, the Manor of Rodley, and the district called Hinder's Lane and Dockham: see Wood's Laws of the Dean Forest at 4.
4 See Wood's Laws of the Dean Forest at 5–6.
5 Dean Forest (Mines) Act 1838, preamble (repealed); Wood's Laws of the Dean Forest at 5–6. See further PARA 606.
6 Dean Forest (Mines) Act 1838, preamble (repealed); Wood's Laws of the Dean Forest at 7.
7 As to the meaning of 'mine' see PARA 3.
8 As to the privatisation of the coal industry see PARAS 3, 50 et seq. See also PARA 609.
9 It is possible that Noxon Park, Kidnalls and Sneyd Woods and Mailscot may be excepted: see *Fourth Report of the Forest of Dean Commissioners* (1831), which is set out in Wood's Laws of the Dean Forest at 88.
10 Dean Forest (Mines) Act 1838, preamble (repealed); Wood's Laws of the Dean Forest at 5–7. See also PARA 609.
11 All male persons, born and abiding within the Hundred of St Briavels, of the age of 21 years and upwards, who have worked for a year and a day in a coal or iron mine within the hundred are free miners (see the Dean Forest (Mines) Act 1838 s 14), provided they are registered as such (see s 21; and PARA 609. For this purpose, it is sufficient that the mine in which such person worked was an opencast mine; it is not necessary that he should have worked in an underground mine: see *Jones v Piggott* (25 March 1996, unreported), Gloucester Crown Court.
     Persons who fulfil similar requirements with regard to stone quarries are also called 'free miners' (see the Dean Forest (Mines) Act 1838 s 15), but their rights are confined to stone quarries (see ss 15, 23). As to the meaning of 'quarry' see PARA 4. As to leases of quarries see PARA 620.
12 See PARA 608 et seq.

### 608. Customary rights.

The customs are of immemorial antiquity, but were uncertain and undefined until they were regulated by statute[1] and by certain awards made by Commissioners under statutory powers[2].

1 See the Dean Forest Act 1819; the Dean Forest (Mines) Act 1838; the Dean Forest Act 1861; the Dean Forest (Mines) Act 1871; the Dean Forest (Mines) Act 1904; and the Dean Forest Act 1906.
2 Three separate awards were made in 1841 by the Dean Forest Mining Commissioners appointed under the Dean Forest (Mines) Act 1838, relating respectively to coal mines, iron mines, and quarries. These awards, which are set out in Wood's Laws of the Dean Forest at 199 et seq, defined

the existing gales, and the galees at the time were confirmed in their possessions (see the Dean Forest (Mines) Act 1838 s 27 (amended by the Statute Law (Repeals) Act 1969); and the First Schedule to each of the awards). The Second Schedule to each of these awards contains a series of regulations with regard to the class of undertakings dealt with in the award. An award was made by the Commissioners under the Dean Forest (Mines) Act 1871 modifying and explaining certain clauses in the awards of coal and iron mines made in 1841. This award is set out in Wood's Laws of the Dean Forest at 365. After the making of the awards, the previous customs ceased to be valid except so far as confirmed by the Dean Forest (Mines) Act 1838 or by the awards: s 31 (repealed). As to the meaning of 'mine' see PARA 3; as to the meaning of 'quarry' see PARA 4; and as to the meaning of 'gale' see PARA 610.

## 609. The gaveller and deputy gaveller.

The officer who represents the Crown in its dealings with the free miners[1] is known as the gaveller, an office now vested in the Forestry Commissioners[2]. The gaveller or deputy gaveller[3] is required to keep a register of free miners[4]; and no one, unless registered, is accounted a free miner[5].

1   As to the meaning of 'free miner' see PARA 607.
2   The office was formerly vested in the Commissioners of Woods, Forests, Land Revenues, Works and Buildings (subsequently the Commissioners of Crown Lands and now the Crown Estate Commissioners: see CROWN AND CROWN PROCEEDINGS vol 29 (2014) PARA 194): see the Dean Forest (Mines) Act 1838 s 13 (repealed); and the Crown Lands Act 1851 s 2 (repealed). The estate, interest, rights, powers and liabilities of the Crown and the Commissioners of Crown Lands in the Forest of Dean or as Lord of the Manor of St Briavels, or the Hundred of St Briavels, and certain other manors, or in or in connection with any mines or minerals (other than mines royal) appertaining or reputed to appertain to the lordship of any such manor were transferred to and vested in the Forestry Commissioners by the Forestry (Transfer of Woods) Order 1924, SR & O 1924/386 (now lapsed): see FORESTRY vol 52 (2014) PARA 1. Thus the office of gaveller vested in the Forestry Commissioners together with all the powers, rights and authorities belonging or appertaining to that office, and all such powers, rights and authorities may be exercised either by the Forestry Commissioners or by the deputy gaveller appointed by them, and any instrument required by any Act to be made by the gaveller may be made under the seal of the Forestry Commissioners: see art 5. As to mines royal see CROWN AND CROWN PROCEEDINGS vol 29 (2014) PARA 132 et seq.
    On 15 June 1945 all land then vested in the Forestry Commissioners vested in the Minister of Agriculture and Fisheries: see the Forestry Act 1945 s 4 (repealed); and FORESTRY vol 52 (2014) PARA 2. The Minister of Agriculture and Fisheries became the Minister of Agriculture, Fisheries and Food (see the Transfer of Functions (Ministry of Food) Order 1955, SI 1955/554), but that ministry has been dissolved and the minister's functions have been transferred to the Secretary of State for Environment, Food and Rural Affairs (see the Ministry of Agriculture, Fisheries and Food (Dissolution) Order 2002, SI 2002/794; and PARA 2). In exercising their functions, the Forestry Commissioners must comply with ministerial directions: see FORESTRY vol 52 (2014) PARA 44. As to the minister's powers of disposal of land vested in him see FORESTRY vol 52 (2014) PARA 45. The minister has specific powers to grant licences for certain mining purposes: see the Dean Forest (Mines) Act 1838 s 65 (amended by the Statute Law (Repeals) Act 1969); and the Dean Forest Act 1861 s 15.
    On 1 July 1942 the interest of the Forestry Commissioners in the coal and mines of coal in the Forest of Dean, or other part of the Hundred of St Briavels in respect of which the privileges of free miners were exercisable, vested in the Coal Commission, subject to the provisions of the Dean Forest (Mines) Act 1838 and of any other Dean Forest enactment, and to all interests subsisting or to be created by virtue thereof: Coal Act 1938 s 43(1), (2) (repealed). As to the Coal Commission see PARA 48. The interests in unworked coal and in mines of coal, of colliery concerns (which did not include individuals working coal by virtue of a grant of gales in the Forest of Dean or in any other part of the Hundred of St Briavels: see the Coal Industry Nationalisation Act 1946 s 63(2) (repealed)) and of the Coal Commission were, on 1 January 1947, vested in the National Coal Board, later renamed the British Coal Corporation; and those interests in unworked coal and coal mines have now passed to the Coal Authority: see generally PARAS 48–50. As to the Coal Authority see PARA 52 et seq.

However, all powers conferred by the Dean Forest enactments that were vested in the Forestry Commissioners immediately before 1 July 1942 continued to be exercisable by them; and rent payable to the Commissioners, attributable to the interest transferred, continues to be recoverable by them, but must be paid by them to the Coal Authority, which must pay the Commissioners sums equal to any expenses incurred in the exercise of those powers: see the Coal Act 1938 s 43(6) (repealed with savings); and the Coal Industry Act 1994 s 67(7), Sch 10 para 5.

3 The Forestry Commissioners have power to appoint a deputy gaveller: see the Forestry (Transfer of Woods) Order 1924, SR & O 1924/386, art 5. In practice, it is the deputy gaveller who exercises the functions; and references in this title to the gaveller include references to the deputy gaveller.

4 See the Dean Forest (Mines) Act 1838 ss 16, 17 (both amended by the Statute Law (Repeals) Act 1969).

5 See the Dean Forest (Mines) Act 1838 s 21. The gaveller or deputy gaveller may refuse to register any person who does not produce satisfactory evidence of his claim: see s 17. In case of such refusal there is an appeal to the Crown Court within four months of such refusal: see ss 19, 20 (both amended by the Statute Law (Repeals) Act 1969); and the Courts Act 1971 s 56(1), Sch 8. Registration is proved by an extract from the register signed by the gaveller or deputy gaveller: see the Dean Forest (Mines) Act 1838 s 22 (amended by the Statute Law (Repeals) Act 1969).

## (ii) Gales

### 610. Nature of a gale.

A free miner[1] of coal or iron has the right to require a grant to himself[2] of specified veins of coal or iron in a specified situation[3]. The grant, as also the subject matter of the grant, is known as a 'gale'[4]. No gale may be made of any inclosed land belonging to the Crown[5]. Grants of gales are made in accordance with the order of application[6]. The gaveller[7] is not bound to grant a gale if he is of opinion that it would interfere with an existing gale[8] or that, from its proposed situation or extent, it is not adapted for obtaining the mineral in the best manner[9].

1 As to the meaning of 'free miner' see PARA 607.
2 Grants of coal and iron may only be made to free miners: Dean Forest (Mines) Act 1838 s 23.
3 The application must specify the veins and situation of the proposed grant: Award of Coal Mines 1841 Sch 2 r 11; Award of Iron Mines 1841 Sch 2 r 11. These awards are set out in Wood's Laws of the Dean Forest at 199 and 272. See also PARA 608.
   Only the Crown has the right to make such grants: *A-G v Mathias* (1858) 4 K & J 579.
4 See *Great Western (Forest of Dean) Collieries Co Ltd v Trafalgar Colliery Co Ltd* (1887) 3 TLR 724 at 725 per Kekewich J.
5 See the Dean Forest (Mines) Act 1838 s 64.
6 See the Dean Forest (Mines) Act 1838 s 60; the Dean Forest (Mines) Act 1904 s 7 (both amended by the Statute Law (Repeals) Act 1969); and the Dean Forest Act 1906 s 2.
7 As to the gaveller see PARA 609; and as to the exercise of his functions by the deputy gaveller see PARA 609.
8 A valid application for a gale cannot be made unless the gale is empty at the time: *James v Young* (1884) 27 ChD 652.
9 Dean Forest (Mines) Act 1838 s 62. As to the meaning of 'minerals' see PARA 10.

### 611. Extent of the gale.

The extent of the gale[1] is determined by the gaveller[2], and in setting out the metes and bounds the gaveller must have regard to the probable cost of winning the mineral[3] and the quantity of mineral likely to be obtained[4]. Every grant of a gale must specify the extent of the gale[5].

1 As to the meaning of 'gale' see PARA 610.
2 As to the gaveller see PARA 609; and as to the exercise of his functions by the deputy gaveller see PARA 609.
3 As to the meaning of 'minerals' see PARA 10.
4 Dean Forest (Mines) Act 1838 s 56 (amended by the Statute Law (Repeals) Act 1969; and the Statute Law (Repeals) Act 1978); Award of Coal Mines 1841 Sch 2 r 11; Award of Iron Mines 1841 Sch 2 r 11. These awards are set out in Wood's Laws of the Dean Forest at 199 and 272. See

also PARA 608.
5    See the Dean Forest (Mines) Act 1838 s 56.

## 612. Grant of a gale.

The grant of a gale[1] is made subject to any special rules and regulations thought necessary by the gaveller[2], and provides for the working of a minimum quantity of mineral in each year[3], with liberty to make up short workings in any subsequent year[4]. An underlying seam may be galed even if an upper seam has been previously galed and the upper seam may be sunk through by the galee of the lower seam[5]. A free miner[6] is not entitled to the grant of more than three gales at any one time, or to a fresh grant until one or more of the three existing gales is exhausted[7], unless he surrenders a gale as not containing sufficient mineral to be workable[8]. To be effectual, the grant must be enrolled in the books of the gaveller or deputy gaveller, and a copy is given to the free miner[9].

The general licensing requirements[10] apply in the Forest of Dean and the Hundred of St Briavels as they apply in other areas[11].

The statutory rights to withdraw support from land[12] in connection with the working of coal or coal mines[13] do not apply to land in respect of which the privileges of free miners are exercisable[14]. Nor do the provisions relating to subsidence damage[15] which apply elsewhere in Great Britain[16] apply in the Forest of Dean and the Hundred of St Briavels[17].

1    As to the meaning of 'gale' see PARA 610.
2    Dean Forest (Mines) Act 1838 s 56 (amended by the Statute Law (Repeals) Act 1969; and the Statute Law (Repeals) Act 1978). The special rules must not be inconsistent with the Commissioners' general rules: Dean Forest (Mines) Act 1838 s 56. As to the gaveller see PARA 609; and as to the exercise of his functions by the deputy gaveller see PARA 609.
3    Award of Coal Mines 1841 Sch 2 r 13; Award of Iron Mines 1841 Sch 2 r 13. These awards are set out in Wood's Laws of the Dean Forest at 199 and 272. See also PARA 608. As to the meaning of 'minerals' see PARA 10.
4    Award of Coal Mines 1841 Sch 2 r 14; Award of Iron Mines 1841 Sch 2 r 14; Award of Forest of Dean Mining Commissioners 1871 para 3. The award of 1871 is set out in Wood's Laws of the Dean Forest at 365. See also PARA 608.
5    *Goold v Great Western Deep Coal Co* (1865) 2 De GJ & Sm 600.
6    As to the meaning of 'free miner' see PARA 607.
7    Dean Forest (Mines) Act 1838 s 61.
8    *Ellway v Davis* (1873) LR 16 Eq 294; and see *James v R* (1877) 5 ChD 153, CA.
9    Dean Forest (Mines) Act 1838 s 57 (amended by the Statute Law (Repeals) Act 1969).
10   As to the licensing of coal-mining operations see PARA 89 et seq.
11   However, the Coal Authority makes available a simplified form of licence for use in the Forest of Dean and the Hundred of St Briavels, which recognises the requirement for a licence but also the special customs (see PARAS 607 et seq, 617 et seq) which exist in that area. As to the areas included in the Forest of Dean and the Hundred of St Briavels see PARA 607. As to the Coal Authority see PARA 52 et seq.
12   Ie under the Coal Industry Act 1994 s 38: see PARA 176.
13   As to the meaning of 'mine' see PARA 3.
14   See the Coal Industry Act 1994 s 40(4); and PARA 179.
15   As to subsidence damage see PARA 182 et seq. As to subsidence damage by coal mining see PARA 200 et seq.
16   As to the meaning of 'Great Britain' see PARA 48.
17   See the Coal Mining Subsidence Act 1991 s 1(4)(a); and PARA 203 heads (1), (2).

## 613. Effect of grant of a gale.

The right granted by a gale[1] of coal or iron mines[2] is of the nature of real estate limited to the galee, his heirs and assigns, but conditional upon the due payment of the rents, royalties and dues reserved[3], and due performance and observance of the rules and regulations for the time being in force[4] and contained in the awards[5] and any special rules and regulations contained in the grant[6]. Non-compliance by the miner in any of these respects will render the gale liable to forfeiture[7] although the specific remedy of forfeiture does not bar an action for damages[8]. Forfeiture is complete on service of notice, without actual entry by the gaveller or his deputy[9].

1  As to the meaning of 'gale' see PARA 610. As to the grant of a gale see PARA 612.
2  As to the meaning of 'mine' see PARA 3.
3  As to rents and royalties see PARA 619.
4  Dean Forest Act 1861 s 1; and see PARA 608. It seems that non-domestic rates are payable in relation to active gales: see *Morgan v Crawshay* (1871) LR 5 HL 304; and LOCAL GOVERNMENT FINANCE.
5  See the Dean Forest (Mines) Act 1838 s 29.
6  See the Dean Forest (Mines) Act 1838 s 56 (amended by the Statute Law (Repeals) Act 1969; and the Statute Law (Repeals) Act 1978).
7  Dean Forest (Mines) Act 1838 s 29. As to relief by the court, which cannot be granted after the expiration of six months, see *Re Brain* (1874) LR 18 Eq 389.
8  *Ross v Rugge-Price* (1876) 1 Ex D 269; *Brain v Thomas* (1881) 50 LJQB 662, CA.
9  *Ex p Young and Grindell* (1880) 50 LJ Ch 221; *James v Young* (1884) 27 ChD 652. As to the gaveller see PARA 609; and as to the exercise of his functions by the deputy gaveller see PARA 609.

## 614. Transfer of gales.

Gales[1] may be transferred either inter vivos or by will to any person or persons[2]. A memorial in statutory form[3] of every transfer by deed must be registered in the books of the gaveller[4] within three months from its date[5], or such extended period as the Forestry Commissioners[6] for reasonable cause allow[7], and if not so registered is void[8]. Registration may be refused if rent is unpaid[9] or if the deed effecting a transfer subsequent to one which took place by will or descent does not contain a recital of the circumstances under which devolution by will or descent took place[10]. A memorandum of the entry is indorsed on the original certificate of the grant of the gale[11] or on the last preceding transfer[12]. The transfer of a gale does not automatically transfer a licence under Part II of the Coal Industry Act 1994[13]. The licence must be the subject of a separate transfer, which is subject to the normal requirements of the Coal Authority in that regard[14].

1  As to the meaning of 'gale' see PARA 610.
2  See the Dean Forest (Mines) Act 1838 s 23.
3  See the Dean Forest Act 1861 s 10, Schedule.
4  As to the gaveller see PARA 609; and as to the exercise of his functions by the deputy gaveller see PARA 609.
5  Dean Forest (Mines) Act 1838 s 58; and see also the Dean Forest Act 1861 s 11.
6  See PARA 609. As to the Forestry Commissioners generally see FORESTRY vol 52 (2014) PARA 37 et seq.
7  Dean Forest (Mines) Act 1838 s 59.
8  Dean Forest Act 1861 s 14.
9  Dean Forest Act 1861 s 9.
10  Dean Forest Act 1861 s 11.
11  Dean Forest (Mines) Act 1838 s 58. As to the grant of a gale see PARA 612.
12  Dean Forest Act 1861 s 11.
13  Ie under the Coal Industry Act 1994 Pt II (ss 25–36): see PARA 89 et seq.
14  See PARA 89 et seq. As to the Coal Authority see PARA 52 et seq.

## 615. Inclosed land.

Where mines[1] situated under inclosed land outside the Forest of Dean[2] belonging to private persons are galed[3], the surface owner is entitled to half the profits[4], and any owner of inclosed land is entitled to compensation assessed by the gaveller[5] or deputy gaveller for surface damage[6]. No steam engine or dwelling house may be erected on inclosed land without the consent of the owner[7].

1   As to the meaning of 'mine' see PARA 3.
2   As to the boundaries of the Forest of Dean, and the area in which the Gloucestershire customs are exercisable, see PARA 607.
3   As to the meaning of 'gale' see PARA 610.
4   Dean Forest (Mines) Act 1838 s 67.
5   As to the gaveller see PARA 609; and as to the exercise of his functions by the deputy gaveller see PARA 609.
6   Dean Forest (Mines) Act 1838 s 68 (amended by the Statute Law (Repeals) Act 1969). The compensation may consist of a gross or an annual sum: Dean Forest Act 1861 s 16.
     The statutory provisions do not extend to damage by subsidence, as a galee has no power to let down the surface: *Allaway v Wagstaff* (1859) 4 H & N 681. See also the Coal Mining Subsidence Act 1991 s 1(4)(a); and PARA 203 heads (1), (2).
7   Dean Forest (Mines) Act 1838 s 69.

### 616. Working of gales.

A galee must commence to open the mine[1] within five years of the date of the grant of the gale[2], but in case of accident or other unforeseen impediment the gaveller[3] may give an extension of time[4].

In working a gale general regulations must be complied with[5]. The mine must be worked in a workmanlike manner[6]; proper accounts and plans must be kept, which the gaveller or deputy gaveller is at liberty to inspect[7]; pits and level mounds must be in situations determined by the gaveller or his deputy[8]; the gaveller and his deputy and their agents have power to enter and inspect the mine[9]; and the person working coal must leave such barriers as may be directed by the gaveller or his deputy[10]. In one respect the obligations of a person working a gale are more onerous than those imposed by the general law: a person working a gale drained by a steam engine and situate near and to the rise of another must pump so as to prevent water flowing from one mine into the other[11]. On the abandonment or disuse of a gale the surface must be restored[12].

The duty of performing and observing the rules and regulations is a personal obligation on the person for the time being in possession or receipt of the proceeds of the gale, whether as owner, lessee or underlessee[13].

1   As to the meaning of 'mine' see PARA 3.
2   As to the meaning of 'gale' see PARA 610. As to the grant of a gale see PARA 612
3   As to the gaveller see PARA 609; and as to the exercise of his functions by the deputy gaveller see PARA 609.
4   Award of Forest of Dean Mining Commissioners 1871 para 2. This award is set out in Wood's Laws of the Dean Forest at 365. See also PARA 608.
5   Dean Forest (Mines) Act 1838 s 29.
6   Award of Coal Mines 1841 Sch 2 r 9; Award of Iron Mines 1841 Sch 2 r 9. These awards are set out in Wood's Laws of the Dean Forest at 199 and 272. See also PARA 608.
7   Award of Coal Mines 1841 Sch 2 r 16; Award of Iron Mines 1841 Sch 2 r 16.
8   Award of Coal Mines 1841 Sch 2 r 10; Award of Iron Mines 1841 Sch 2 r 10.
9   Dean Forest (Mines) Act 1838 s 53 (amended by the Statute Law (Repeals) Act 1969); Award of Coal Mines 1841 Sch 2 r 17; Award of Iron Mines 1841 Sch 2 r 17.
10 Award of Coal Mines 1841 Sch 2 r 18. The gaveller may permit the working of coal in any barrier on such terms as he thinks fit: Dean Forest Act 1861 s 24.
11 Award of Coal Mines 1841 Sch 2 r 19; Award of Iron Mines 1841 Sch 2 r 18. See also PARA 614.
12 Award of Coal Mines 1841 Sch 2 r 12; Award of Iron Mines 1841 Sch 2 r 12.
13 Dean Forest Act 1861 s 4.

## 617.   Surrender of gales.

A gale[1] or part of a gale may be surrendered on giving notice to the gaveller[2]. A galee whose gale is drained by a steam engine or other machinery, and lies to the rise of another, must give to the gaveller or deputy gaveller, and also to the owner of the gale lying to the deep, three months' notice of his intention to discontinue working his engine[3].

1   As to the meaning of 'gale' see PARA 610.
2   Award of Coal Mines 1841 Sch 2 r 6; Award of Iron Mines 1841 Sch 2 r 6; Dean Forest Act 1861 s 19. The awards are set out in Wood's Laws of the Dean Forest at 199 and 272. See also PARA 608 2. As to the gaveller see PARA 609; and as to the exercise of his functions by the deputy gaveller see PARA 609.
      The gaveller has power to accept a surrender of part only of a gale (Dean Forest (Mines) Act 1871 s 33); and, on such terms as he thinks fit, a surrender other than by notice (Dean Forest Act 1861 s 20).
3   Award of Coal Mines 1841 Sch 2 r 8; Award of Iron Mines 1841 Sch 2 r 8.

## 618.   Amalgamation, subdivision and rearrangement of gales.

Whenever the gaveller[1] thinks it desirable so to do, having regard to the proper opening or working of any gale[2] and to any representation made by any galee, he may by order in writing under his hand amalgamate, subdivide or otherwise rearrange the area of either any gales in hand or any existing gales[3].

1   As to the gaveller see PARA 609; and as to the exercise of his functions by the deputy gaveller see PARA 609.
2   As to the meaning of 'gale' see PARA 610.
3   Dean Forest (Mines) Act 1904 s 1(1). However, this provision applies only to specified gales: see s 10(1), Schedule.
      An order may not be made in respect of any existing gales without the consent of the galees, except where any gale is so situated that it cannot be separately worked without great injury or detriment to any adjoining or contiguous gale, or without greatly impeding the proper and effectual working of any of the beds or veins of coal within the Hundred of St Briavels which require the use of expensive pits, engines or machinery, or where the gale is so small or otherwise of such a character that it cannot properly or economically be developed and worked as a separate mine: s 1(3). Any such order must be advertised in at least two local newspapers (s 2); and the order takes effect, in respect of existing gales, as if it were a grant of new gales and must be enrolled accordingly (s 3(1)). In addition to any terms and conditions which may be specified in the grant, the order may contain such terms and conditions, including a provision requiring the payment of any sum or compensation by one galee to another, as the gaveller may think proper and as may be agreed to by the galees concerned or, in specified circumstances, determined by arbitration: s 3(2). As to the grant of a gale see PARA 612. As to the areas included in the Hundred of St Briavels see PARA 607.

### (iii)   Rents and Royalties

## 619.   Rules relating to payment.

Galeage rents[1] and royalties are usually due to the Crown in respect of each gale[2], and are payable by the person in possession or receipt of the proceeds of the gale, whether as owner, lessee or otherwise[3]. Every grant of a gale must specify the dead rents and royalties[4], and in case of dispute the amount is determined by arbitration[5]. The rents and royalties of any gale may be revised every 21 years (or, in the case of certain gales[6], 63 years[7]), reckoning from 24 June next following the grant[8], and in case of dispute the amount of the revised rents and royalties must be fixed by arbitration[9]. The rents and royalties are recoverable by distress[10] or in an action[11] by the gaveller[12].

1 'Galeage rents' include dead rents which the Commissioners under the Dean Forest (Mines) Act 1838 had power to award: *Lord Seymour v Morrell* (1851) 17 LTOS 139. Dead rents and royalties may also be reserved on making subsequent grants: Dean Forest (Mines) Act 1838 s 56 (amended by the Statute Law (Repeals) Act 1969; and the Statute Law (Repeals) Act 1978). Galeage rents are payable on 31 December, and royalties on 30 June and 31 December in each year: Dean Forest (Mines) Act 1871 s 35. No galeage rent is payable, in the case of coal mines, for the first two years, and in the case of iron mines for the first four years, after the grant of the gale, unless the minerals are actually wrought: Award of Coal Mines 1841 Sch 2 r 5; Award of Iron Mines 1841 Sch 2 r 5. These awards are set out in Wood's Laws of the Dean Forest at 199 and 272. See also PARA 608. As to the meaning of 'mine' see PARA 3; as to the meaning of 'minerals' see PARA 10; and as to the meaning of 'gale' see PARA 610. As to the grant of a gale see PARA 612.
2 As to the ancient rights of the Crown to share the profits of a gale see *Fourth Report of the Dean Forest Commissioners* (1831), which is set out in Wood's Laws of the Dean Forest at 88. See also *Doe d Thomson v Pearce* (1812) Peake Add Cas 242; *A-G v Jackson* (1846) 5 Hare 355 at 362–363 per Wigram V-C. See further PARA 609.
3 Dean Forest Act 1861 s 4.
4 Dean Forest (Mines) Act 1838 s 56. A parol agreement to pay a larger rent than that specified is not enforceable: *A-G v Jackson* (1846) 5 Hare 355 at 362–363 per Wigram V-C.
5 Dean Forest (Mines) Act 1838 s 56. As to arbitration see ss 47–49; the Dean Forest Act 1861 s 8; and the Dean Forest (Mines) Act 1871 s 37.
6 Ie gales to which the Dean Forest (Mines) Act 1904 applies: see ss 4, 10(1), Schedule.
7 Dean Forest (Mines) Act 1904 s 4.
8 See the Dean Forest (Mines) Act 1838 s 27 (amended by the Statute Law (Repeals) Act 1969); the Dean Forest (Mines) Act 1838 s 46; and the Dean Forest Act 1861 s 7.
9 See the Dean Forest (Mines) Act 1838 ss 27, 47, 48; the Dean Forest Act 1861 s 8; and the Dean Forest (Mines) Act 1871 s 37.
10 See the Dean Forest Act 1819 s 7 (amended by the Statute Law (Repeals) Act 1971); the Dean Forest (Mines) Act 1838 s 52; the Dean Forest Act 1861 s 4; and the Dean Forest (Mines) Act 1871 s 36.
11 Dean Forest Act 1819 s 8 (amended by the Statute Law (Repeals) Act 1971). As to proceedings by action for account see *A-G v Jackson* (1846) 5 Hare 355 at 368 per Wigram V-C.
12 *Lord Seymour v Morrell* (1851) 17 LTOS 139. As to the gaveller see PARA 609; and as to the exercise of his functions by the deputy gaveller see PARA 609.

## (iv) Quarries

### 620–700. Leases of quarries.

Free miners[1] in quarries[2] are eligible to have leases granted to them[3]. A renewal of a quarry lease may be made to a person not a free miner[4]. Lessees working quarries must observe certain general rules and regulations[5].

1 As to the meaning of 'free miner' see PARA 607.
2 As to the meaning of 'quarry' see PARA 4.
3 Dean Forest (Mines) Act 1838 s 23. As to the power to grant leases see PARA 609; and FORESTRY vol 52 (2014) PARA 45. There is no provision for quarries corresponding to the right of a free miner of coal or iron to require a gale to be granted to him (cf PARA 610). As to confirmation of gales of quarries existing prior to statutory regulation see the Dean Forest (Mines) Act 1838 s 27 (amended by the Statute Law (Repeals) Act 1969); and the Award of Quarries 1841, which is set out in Wood's Laws of the Dean Forest at 291. See also PARA 608.
4 Dean Forest (Mines) Act 1871 s 34.
5 See the Dean Forest (Mines) Act 1838 s 29; the Dean Forest Act 1861 ss 18, 19; and the Award of Quarries 1841 Sch 2.

# MISREPRESENTATION

# 1. ACTIONABLE MISREPRESENTATION

## (1) Introduction to actionable misrepresentation

**701. Misrepresentation as a ground for the rescission of a contract or the award of damages.**

A misrepresentation is a positive statement of fact or law[1], which is made or adopted by a party to a contract and is untrue. It may be made fraudulently, carelessly or innocently[2]. Where one person ('the representor')[3] makes a misrepresentation[4] to another ('the representee')[5] which has the object and result of inducing the representee to enter into a contract or other binding transaction with him, the representee may generally[6] elect to regard the contract as rescinded[7].

In these circumstances the representee may invoke the aid of the court, which may confirm by declaration his entitlement so to regard the contract, and grant him such other relief as may flow directly from the fact of rescission, for example, the return of money paid or chattels delivered by him pursuant to the terms of the contract[8]. Alternatively, the representee may set up his entitlement to regard the contract as rescinded by way of defence in any proceedings brought against him in order to enforce its terms[9].

At common law, the relief afforded by the court to a representee as such does not extend to the award of damages for loss suffered by him in consequence of entering into a contract or other binding transaction unless he can further show that the false representation was made fraudulently or negligently[10]. By statute, however, if a person enters into a contract after a misrepresentation has been made to him and as a result suffers loss, he may be awarded damages despite the absence of fraud on the part of the representor, although the representor has a defence if he proves that he had reasonable ground to believe and did believe that the facts represented were true[11].

It seems that where the misrepresentations are not fraudulent (or where they do not give rise to a claim for damages for negligence at common law or under the Misrepresentation Act 1967[12]), the representee may recover an indemnity appropriate to relieve him from consequences and obligations of the contract that is set aside[13].

Misrepresentation in these contexts must be distinguished from mistake (in its legal sense)[14], from mere non-disclosure[15] and from breach of warranty or any other representation assuming the form of a promise or contractual engagement[16].

1   As to misrepresentations of law see PARA 710.
2   As to what constitutes an innocent misrepresentation, which may include one made through negligence see PARA 762.
3   As to who is a representor see PARAS 724–732.
4   As to what constitutes a representation see PARA 702 et seq. As to falsity see PARA 740 et seq.
5   As to who is a representee see PARAS 733–739.
6   As to the conditions of the right to rescind see PARA 813 et seq. As to the defences available in claims based upon misrepresentation, and the circumstances which may preclude the representee from treating the contract as rescinded, see PARAS 801–803, 824–833.
7   See PARA 780 et seq.
8   As to claims for rescission see PARA 811 et seq.
9   As to the circumstances in which misrepresentation may be set up as a defence see PARAS 784, 787.
10 As to claims for damages see PARA 788 et seq. As to fraudulent misrepresentation see PARA 754 et seq. As to negligent misrepresentation see PARA 797 et seq; and NEGLIGENCE vol 78 (2018) PARA 13.

11  See the Misrepresentation Act 1967 s 2(1); and PARAS 800, 810. There may be civil liability for
    misrepresentations under certain statutes: see eg the Financial Services and Markets Act 2000 s 90;
    and COMPANIES vol 14 (2016) PARA 298; the Companies Act 2006 s 463; and COMPANIES vol
    15 (2016) PARA 949; the Landlord and Tenant Act 1954 ss 14A, 37A; and LANDLORD AND
    TENANT vol 64 (2016) PARA 1653; LANDLORD AND TENANT vol 63 (2016) PARA 1003; the
    Rent Act 1977 s 102; and LANDLORD AND TENANT vol 63 (2016) PARA 785; the Housing Act
    1988 s 12; and LANDLORD AND TENANT vol 63 (2016) PARA 925; and the Leasehold Reform Act
    1967 s 20(5); and LANDLORD AND TENANT vol 64 (2016) PARA 1216. See also liability for
    misleading actions under the Consumer Protection from Unfair Trading Regulations 2008,
    SI 2008/1277, Pt 4A (regs 27A-27L) (see CONSUMER PROTECTION vol 21 (2016) PARA 433 et
    seq.
12  See PARA 797-800.
13  See *Newbigging v Adam* (1886) 34 ChD 582 at 589, 594, 596, CA. In this case, in upholding an
    order to indemnify the plaintiff against debts, claims and demands to which he might be liable by
    virtue of having entered into the partnership agreement which was set aside, it was said: 'it is not
    giving damages in consequence of deceit, it is working out the proper result of setting aside a
    contract in consequence of misrepresentation': *Newbigging v Adam* at 589 per Cotton LJ.
14  Ie the misapprehension or misconception of some fact or point of law material to a transaction, by
    both parties or by one party only, where the misapprehension or misconception has not been
    induced by any misrepresentation by either party: see MISTAKE. As to errors for which it is
    possible to say that the representor has assumed responsibility see *Aneco Reinsurance
    Underwriting Ltd (in liquidation) v Johnson & Higgins Ltd* [2001] UKHL 51, [2001] 2 All ER
    (Comm) 929, [2002] 1 Lloyd's Rep 157.
15  As to the duty of disclosure in particular cases see eg AGENCY vol 1 (2017) PARAS 90-91 (duty
    owed by agent to principal); INSURANCE vol 60 (2018) PARA 28 et seq (disclosure to insurers). As
    to the extent of the duty owed by one partner to another see eg *Cassels v Stewart* (1881) 6 App
    Cas 64, HL; and PARTNERSHIP vol 79 (2014) PARA 105 et seq. As to the duty of disclosure owed
    by a solicitor to his client see eg *Nocton v Lord Ashburton* [1914] AC 932 at 964-965, HL, per
    Lord Dunedin; and LEGAL PROFESSIONS vol 66 (2015) PARA 596 et seq. As to the duty owed by
    a trustee in dealings with beneficiaries see TRUSTS AND POWERS vol 98 (2013) PARA 387 et seq.
        Although mere silence or inaction does not in general amount to a misrepresentation, silence
    or inaction may contribute to establish a misrepresentation: see PARAS 747-750. As to the
    circumstances in which silence or inaction may create an estoppel see ESTOPPEL vol 47 (2014)
    PARA 362.
16  As to the distinction between mere representations and statements which are intended to have
    contractual force see PARA 703. As to promises see PARA 706. See also CONTRACT vol 22 (2012)
    PARA 353.

# (2) The Representation

## (i) What Constitutes a Representation

### 702. Constituent elements.

A representation is a statement made by a representor[1] to a representee[2] and
relating by way of affirmation, denial, description or otherwise to a matter of fact.
The statement may be oral or in writing or arise by implication from words or
conduct[3]. The representor and the representee must be distinct from one another
in substance as well as in name; where the persons claiming to have been deceived
by a statement are in effect the same as those who are alleged to have made it,
there is no representation which the law can recognise[4].

In general, the matter of fact to which the statement relates must be a matter
of present or past fact[5], but there are difficulties in applying this principle to
certain classes of statements. Thus, if a person makes a statement relating to his
own or some other person's intention[6], or containing a promise or forecast as to

the future with possible implications as to the present[7], or relating to his own or some other person's opinion, belief or other condition of mind[8], or to a matter of law[9], or to a document[10], or containing laudatory generalities or exaggeration[11], questions may arise whether, and in what sense, and to what extent a representation is contained in or to be implied from the statement.

1   As to who is a representor see PARAS 724–732.
2   As to who is a representee see PARAS 733–739.
3   As to how representations may be made see PARAS 715–722. See also PARAS 708, 747–750.
4   *Re Ambrose Lake Tin and Copper Mining Co, ex p Taylor, ex p Moss* (1880) 14 ChD 390 at 396–397, CA.
5   See eg *Yorkshire Insurance Co Ltd v Craine* [1922] 2 AC 541 at 553, PC. As to the position where the statement is one of law see PARA 710.
6   As to statements of intention see PARAS 704–705.
7   As to promises and forecasts see PARAS 706–707.
8   As to statements of opinion, belief or information see PARAS 708–709.
9   As to statements of law see PARA 710.
10  As to statements as to documents see PARAS 711–712.
11  As to exaggeration and puff see PARAS 713–714.

## 703.   Distinction between representation and contractual term.

A representation must be distinguished from a statement which, while relating to a matter of fact, is intended by the parties to have contractual force and is a contractual term[1]. However, where a person has entered into a contract after a misrepresentation has been made to him, then, if otherwise he would be entitled to rescind the contract without alleging fraud[2], he is entitled to rescind notwithstanding that the misrepresentation has become a term of the contract or the contract has been performed[3]. Furthermore, in appropriate circumstances the same statement may form the basis of claims either for damages for breach of contract or for damages in tort for negligently making the statement[4].

1   *Pawson v Watson* (1778) 2 Cowp 785 at 788, 790; *Langridge v Levy* (1837) 2 M & W 519 (affd sub nom *Levy v Langridge* (1838) 4 M & W 337, Ex Ch); *Behn v Burness* (1863) 3 B & S 751, Ex Ch; *Thomson v Weems* (1884) 9 App Cas 671, HL; *Schawel v Reade* [1913] 2 IR 81, HL; *Heilbut Symons & Co v Buckleton* [1913] AC 30, HL; *Harrison v Knowles and Foster* [1918] 1 KB 608 at 610, CA, per Scrutton LJ; *Pennsylvania Shipping Co v Compagnia Nationale de Navigation* [1936] 2 All ER 1167 at 1171 per Branson J; *Leaf v International Galleries* [1950] 2 KB 86, [1950] 1 All ER 693, CA; *Routledge v McKay* [1954] 1 All ER 855, [1954] 1 WLR 615, CA; *Hornal v Neuberger Products Ltd* [1957] 1 QB 247, [1956] 3 All ER 970, CA; *Oscar Chess Ltd v Williams* [1957] 1 All ER 325, [1957] 1 WLR 370, CA; *Dick Bentley Productions Ltd v Harold Smith (Motors) Ltd* [1965] 2 All ER 65, [1965] 1 WLR 623, CA; *Esso Petroleum Co Ltd v Mardon* [1976] QB 801, [1976] 2 All ER 5, CA. See also *Sycamore Bidco Ltd v Breslin* [2012] EWHC 3443 (Ch) at [200]–[211], [2012] All ER (D) 17 (Dec) (true construction of contract in question prevented warranties in contract from being representations).
    The circumstance that the party making the statement assumes to assert a fact of which the other party is ignorant is not conclusive of the question whether a statement amounts to a warranty: *Heilbut Symons & Co v Buckleton* at 50–51 per Lord Moulton, disapproving a dictum in *De Lassalle v Guildford* [1901] 2 KB 215 at 221, CA, per AL Smith MR.
    As to the warranty of authority implied where any person purports to do any act or make any contract on behalf of a principal see PARA 725; and AGENCY vol 1 (2017) PARAS 161–162. As to conditions and warranties generally see CONTRACT vol 22 (2012) PARAS 556–557. See also eg ANIMALS vol 2 (2017) PARA 24 et seq (warranties on sale of animals); AUCTION vol 4 (2011) PARAS 11, 49 (authority of auctioneer to warrant; oral statements by auctioneers); INSURANCE vol 60 (2018) PARAS 91, 217 et seq (special meaning of 'warranty' in insurance law; warranties; marine insurance); LANDLORD AND TENANT vol 62 (2016) PARAS 308–309 (warranty of fitness). As to conditions and warranties on the sale of goods see SALE OF GOODS AND SUPPLY OF SERVICES vol 91 (2012) PARA 63 et seq.

2 As to rescission for misrepresentation see PARA 811 et seq. In the case of innocent misrepresentation the court may in certain circumstances award damages in lieu of ordering rescission: see the Misrepresentation Act 1967 s 2(2); and PARA 832.

3 See the Misrepresentation Act 1967 s 1; and PARA 816.

4 See *Esso Petroleum Co Ltd v Mardon* [1976] QB 801, [1976] 2 All ER 5, CA.

### (ii) Statements of Intention

## 704. Effect of statement of representor's intention.

A statement of intention is not a representation as to the matter said to be intended, because that belongs to the future and is not a matter of present or past fact[1]. On the other hand, a statement of intention involves a representation as to the existence of the intention which is itself a present fact[2]. However, the difficulty of proving the non-existence of the intention diminishes the value of such representations[3]. The mere circumstance that the expressed intention is not fulfilled does not by itself establish the non-existence of the intention at the time when it was expressed[4], although the non-fulfilment of the intention may be some evidence, strong or weak according to the circumstances of the individual case, that the intention never existed at all[5].

Many examples can be given of a person's statement of his own intention being treated as a representation that he has the intention[6].

1 *Inntrepreneur Pub Co (CPC) v Sweeney* [2002] EWHC 1060 (Ch), [2002] 2 EGLR 132 at 142–144.

2 *Edgington v Fitzmaurice* (1885) 29 ChD 459 at 483, CA, per Bowen LJ; *Angus v Clifford* [1891] 2 Ch 449 at 470, CA, per Bowen LJ.
   The purchasing of goods has been said to be an implied representation of a then present intention of paying for them: *Re Shackleton, ex p Whittaker* (1875) 10 Ch App 446 at 449–450 per Mellish LJ. See also *Re Eastgate, ex p Ward* [1905] 1 KB 465; and *BS & N Ltd (BVI) v Micado Shipping Ltd (Malta), The Seaflower* [2000] 2 All ER (Comm) 169 at 175, [2000] 2 Lloyd's Rep 37 at 42. See also *East v Maurer* [1991] 2 All ER 733, [1991] 1 WLR 461, CA.

3 Cf *Edgington v Fitzmaurice* (1885) 29 ChD 459 at 483, CA. A statement of intention is generally not longstanding: *Limit No 2 Ltd v Axa Versicherung AG* [2008] EWCA Civ 1231, [2009] Lloyd's Rep IR 396, [2008] All ER (D) 115 (Nov) (representation as to intention no longer operative after gap of 19 months).

4 *Benham v United Guarantee and Life Assurance Co* (1852) 7 Exch 744 at 752–753; *Jorden v Money* (1854) 5 HL Cas 185; *Bold v Hutchinson* (1855) 5 De GM & G 558 at 565 ('if a person merely says 'I will leave my daughter £10,000', it does not amount to a misrepresentation if he does not leave her that sum'); *Beattie v Lord Ebury* (1872) 7 Ch App 777 at 804.

5 *Clydesdale Bank Ltd v Paton* [1896] AC 381 at 386–388, 395, HL.

6 Eg statements that the representor was prepared to lend, or pay, or hand over money (*Ramshire v Bolton* (1869) LR 8 Eq 294; *Blake v Albion Life Assurance Society* (1878) 4 CPD 94 at 106; *Babcock v Lawson* (1880) 5 QBD 284, CA); statements as to the objects to which the subscriptions to an issue of shares or debentures of a company were intended to be applied (*Re Deposit and General Life Assurance Co, Ayre's Case* (1858) 25 Beav 513 at 524; *Edgington v Fitzmaurice* (1885) 29 ChD 459 at 479–480, 482–483, CA; *Aaron's Reefs v Twiss* [1896] AC 273 at 283–285, 286, HL); a statement of an intention to relinquish business in favour of the representor's son (*Biddle and Loyd v Levy* (1815) 1 Stark 20); an expression of intention to make a lane giving access to property sold and a new street (*Beaumont v Dukes* (1822) Jac 422 at 424); a statement as to an intended mode of keeping accounts (*Benham v United Guarantee and Life Assurance Co* (1852) 7 Exch 744); a statement of the use which the representor intended to make of demised premises (*Feret v Hill* (1854) 15 CB 207); a statement that the representor had power to stop the sale of certain goods under an execution, and would stop it (*Cooper v Joel* (1859) 1 De GF & J 240); a statement that a company intended to commence operations with a certain number of steamships of a certain type (*Hallows v Fernie* (1868) 3 Ch App 467); a statement that a company was minded to take a third of a certain insurance risk (*Traill v Baring* (1864) 4 De GJ & Sm 318); a statement that the representor was minded to extricate the representee from difficulties and losses, and to act as his friend and benefactor (*Curtis v Bottomley* (1911) Times, 1 August, CA); a brochure stating the intention to develop a time-share resort (*Buxton v Birches Time Share*

*Resort Ltd* [1991] 2 NZLR 641, NZ CA); a statement by the vendor's solicitor that the transaction would be called off if the purchaser did not exchange contracts at once (*Goff v Gauthier* (1991) 62 P & CR 388); a statement that the vendor of a business did not intend to work for a competitor (*East v Maurer* [1991] 2 All ER 733, [1991] 1 WLR 461, CA). See also *Kingscroft Insurance Co Ltd v Nissan Fire & Marine Insurance Co Ltd* [2000] 1 All ER (Comm) 272, [1999] Lloyd's Rep IR 603 (when a person proposes terms of contract to another he normally makes a representation about his intention and ability to perform).

As to who is a representor see PARAS 724–732. As to who is a representee see PARAS 733–739.

## 705. Statements of other persons' intentions.

A statement of another person's intention is a representation of the existence of the intention[1]. It may be construed as such a representation, and not as a guarantee, even when accompanied or fortified by such expressions as 'we do not hesitate to guarantee'[2], if they can fairly be regarded as mere figurative forms of vernacular speech.

1  *Hamar v Alexander* (1806) 2 Bos & PNR 241; *Barley v Walford* (1846) 9 QB 197 (statement that persons, entitled to registered design, intended to proceed against the plaintiff for infringement); *Re Hull and London Life Assurance Co and Hull and London Fire Insurance Co, Gibson's Case, Kemp's Case, Hudson's Case* (1858) 2 De G & J 275 (statement that two named persons would execute a deed of settlement); *Hallows v Fernie* (1868) 3 Ch App 467 (statement that certain persons had consented to become directors of company treated as a statement of fact). See also *R v Gordon* (1889) 23 QBD 354 at 360; *Smelter Corpn of Ireland Ltd v O'Driscoll* [1977] IR 305.
   For statutory restrictions on the bringing of claims upon representations as to credit see PARA 803.
2  *Gerhard v Bates* (1853) 2 E & B 476 at 482 per Coleridge J. See also *Hamar v Alexander* (1806) 2 Bos & PNR 241 ('I durst be bound for him').

### (iii)  Promises and Forecasts

## 706. Promises.

A promise that something will or will not be done or occur in the future is in itself not a statement of a matter of present or past fact and therefore not a representation[1]. However, it may happen that language which contains promissory expressions can be shown, nevertheless, to have been intended as a statement of an existing intention[2]. Conversely, although a party used words expressive of intention, it may be apparent from other expressions or the surrounding circumstances that what was really meant, and the other party understood to be conveyed, was a promise or offer and nothing else[3].

1  *Re Robinson, ex p Burrell* (1876) 1 ChD 537 at 552, CA (it is always necessary to distinguish, when an alleged ground of false representation is set up, between a representation of an existing fact and a promise to do something in the future). A promise, even though it does not amount to a representation, may have legal effect in other ways, for instance if it forms part of a contract or is embodied in a deed: as to the effect of a deed see DEEDS AND OTHER INSTRUMENTS vol 32 (2012) PARA 257 et seq.
2  *Clydesdale Bank Ltd v Paton* [1896] AC 381 at 394, HL (what is in form a promise may be in another aspect a representation). Cf *Denton v Great Northern Rly Co* (1856) 5 E & B 860. See also *Convent Hospital Ltd v Eberlin & Partners* (1989) 23 ConLR 112, CA (statement in a bill of quantities against the entry for a bond was not a representation that a bond could be obtained for that price but a statement of the price which would be charged for the provision of the bond).
3  *Hammersley v Baron De Biel* (1845) 12 Cl & Fin 45.

## 707. Forecasts.

Mere general and indefinite anticipations of the future success or prosperity of any business or undertaking are not representations in any sense[1], but a statement of expectation is a statement that the party does actually expect as stated[2], and is therefore a representation. Moreover, a statement of expectation or a statement in the future tense may impliedly say something as to the existing position and so import an implied representation[3].

Where a person who has special knowledge or skill makes representations to another by way of advice, information or opinion, with the intention of inducing the other to enter into a contract with him, he is under a duty to use reasonable care to see that the advice, information or opinion is reliable; and if he fails in that duty he will be liable for damages for negligence[4].

1 *Bellairs v Tucker* (1884) 13 QBD 562, DC. See also *Beaumont v Dukes* (1822) Jac 422 at 424.
2 *Re Metropolitan Coal Consumers' Association Ltd, Karberg's Case* [1892] 3 Ch 1 at 11, CA.
3 *Willes v Glover* (1804) 1 Bos & PNR 14 at 16 (statement by a shipper that he 'thinks the captain will sail to-morrow' imports that he knows the ship to be in such a condition as to give a just expectation of her sailing at that time); *Gerhard v Bates* (1853) 2 E & B 476 at 490 (defendant, knowing a company to be a bubble company, and that no dividend would ever be paid upon the shares, fraudulently pretended to guarantee to the bearer of shares a minimum annual dividend of 33%); *Mathias v Yetts* (1882) 46 LT 497 at 503, CA. See also *Re Pacaya Rubber and Produce Co Ltd, Burn's Application* [1914] 1 Ch 542 at 549 per Astbury J (where a statement which was in itself merely an estimate of future profit was held to amount to a confirmation of an intended picture of an equipped and immediately workable property); and *Thomas Witter Ltd v TBP Industries Ltd* [1996] 2 All ER 573 at 594–595 per Jacob J (where representation as to basis of the forecast given). See also *FoodCo Uk LLP (t/a Muffin Break) v Henry Boot Developments Ltd* [2010] EWHC 358 (Ch) at [196] et seq.
4 See *Esso Petroleum Co Ltd v Mardon* [1976] QB 801, [1976] 2 All ER 5, CA, where the plaintiffs had let a filling station to the defendant after a careless forecast of its potential throughput and were held liable on a counterclaim both in tort for negligent representation and in contract on a warranty that the forecast was reliable. They were not held to have warranted that the forecast would prove correct; that would have imposed liability for loss of expected profits. As to negligent statements see NEGLIGENCE vol 78 (2018) PARA 13.

## (iv) Statements of Opinion, Belief or Information

### 708. Statements as representations of existence of opinion, belief or information.

If a person makes a statement of his opinion, belief or information, there is a representation that he has that opinion, belief or information[1]. What has been previously said as to statements of intention[2] and statements of expectation[3] is mutatis mutandis applicable in this connection. There may be difficulty in proving such a statement false because it is necessary to prove the non-existence of the opinion, belief or information rather than merely its incorrectness[4]. Similarly, where the facts were equally well known to both parties, there may be difficulty in proving that one party was induced to enter into a transaction by the other party's expression of opinion[5]. A statement of some other person's opinion or belief is a representation that he has that opinion or belief[6].

1 *Edgington v Fitzmaurice* (1885) 29 ChD 459 at 483, CA; *Angus v Clifford* [1891] 2 Ch 449 at 470, CA; *Smith v Land and House Property Corpn* (1884) 28 ChD 7 at 15, CA; *Bisset v Wilkinson* [1927] AC 177 at 182, PC; *Brown v Raphael* [1958] Ch 636, [1958] 2 All ER 79, CA. As to reasonable reliance on any (untrue) statement see *Caparo Industries plc v Dickman* [1990] 2 AC 605, [1990] 1 All ER 568; *Aneco Reinsurance Underwriting Ltd (in liquidation) v Johnson & Higgins Ltd* [2001] UKHL 51, [2001] 2 All ER (Comm) 929, [2002] 1 Lloyd's Rep 157. See also *BFG Bank AG v Brown & Mumford Ltd* [1997] PNLR 202, [1996] EGCS 169, CA (high possibility of obtaining planning permission). Cf *Hummingbird Motors Ltd v Hobbs* [1986] RTR 276, CA; and *IFE Fund SA v Goldman Sachs International* [2006] EWHC 2887 (Comm) at [57]–[60], [2007] 1 Lloyd's Rep 264 at [57]–[60], [2006] All ER (D) 268 (Nov) (distinguishing *Hummingbird Motors Ltd v Hobbs*).
2 See PARA 704.
3 See PARA 707.

4   *New Brunswick and Canada Rly and Land Co v Coneybeare* (1862) 9 HL Cas 711 at 729
    (statement of opinion of directors in prospectus that there was no probability of a rival railway line
    being constructed, not falsified by subsequent construction of such a line); *Melbourne Banking
    Corpn v Brougham* (1882) 7 App Cas 307 at 319–320, PC (bank's valuation of a security held not
    to be a misrepresentation merely because it turned out to be incorrect, there being no proof that
    the valuation was made otherwise than in good faith); *Bisset v Wilkinson* [1927] AC 177, PC
    (similar decision as to a statement of the carrying capacity of a sheep farm); *H & JM Bennett
    (Potatoes) Ltd v Secretary of State for Scotland* 1990 SLT 189, HL.
5   See *Smith v Land and House Property Corpn* (1884) 28 ChD 7 at 15–16, CA, per Bowen LJ. Cf
    *Cassa di Risparmio della Repubblica di San Marino SpA v Barclays Bank Ltd* [2011] EWHC 484
    (Comm), [2011] NLJR 437, [2011] All ER (D) 189 (Mar): where the facts were not equally well
    known to both sides, a statement of opinion by one who knew the facts best might carry with it
    a further implication of fact, namely that the representor by expressing that opinion had impliedly
    stated that he believed that facts existed which reasonably justified it.
        Whether any, and if so, what, representation was made has to be judged objectively according
    to the impact that whatever is said may be expected to have had on a reasonable representee in the
    position, and with the known characteristics, of the actual representee: *MCI WorldCom
    International Inc v Primus Telecommunications Inc* [2004] EWCA Civ 957 at [30], [2004] 2 All
    ER (Comm) 833 at [30]; applied in *Mabanga v Ophir Energy plc* [2012] EWHC 1589 (QB),
    [2012] All ER (D) 85 (Jun).
6   *Re Roberts, Roberts v Roberts* [1905] 1 Ch 704, CA (opinion of counsel); *Re Mount Morgan
    (West) Gold Mine Ltd, ex p West* (1887) 56 LT 622 at 624 (report of expert cited in company
    prospectus). As to misrepresentation in offer documents generally see COMPANIES vol 15A (2016)
    PARA 1259 et seq.

### 709.   Statements as representations of facts other than existence of opinion.

If a person who has only an opinion or information as to a matter chooses to
state it as a fact, the statement is a representation of the matter stated and the
falsity of the representation is established by proof that the matter is not as stated,
even though the representor may have genuinely held the opinion or believed the
information[1]. Sometimes a statement which is apparently in the form of an
opinion, or uses words tending to suggest that it is only an opinion, may be held
to contain or imply a statement of fact, and even from an expression of opinion
there may be an implication that the speaker knows facts which justify the opinion
or at least knows no facts showing it to be unjustified[2].

1   *A-G v Ray* (1874) 9 Ch App 397 at 405; *Hart v Swaine* (1877) 7 ChD 42; *Brownlie v Campbell*
    (1880) 5 App Cas 925 at 936, 945, 953, HL; *Pritty v Child* (1902) 71 LJKB 512, DC. As to who
    is a representor see PARAS 724–732.
2   *Willes v Glover* (1804) 1 Bos & PNR 14 (see PARA 707); *Jones v Keene* (1841) 2 Mood & R 348;
    *Smith v Land and House Property Corpn* (1884) 28 ChD 7 at 15, CA, per Bowen LJ, and at 17
    per Fry LJ (statement that a person was a most desirable tenant); *Ferguson v Wilson* (1904) 6 F 779
    at 783, Ct of Sess; *Bisset v Wilkinson* [1927] AC 177 at 182, PC (where the actual statement in
    question was held to be merely of an opinion honestly held); *Brown v Raphael* [1958] Ch 636,
    [1958] 2 All ER 79, CA (reversion in trust fund set aside to pay annuity sold subject to death duties
    which might become payable; statement in particulars of sale that annuitant was believed to have
    no aggregable estate; representation of reasonable grounds for belief). As to reasonable reliance on
    any (untrue) statement see *Caparo Industries plc v Dickman* [1990] 2 AC 605, [1990] 1 All ER
    568; *Aneco Reinsurance Underwriting Ltd (in liquidation) v Johnson & Higgins Ltd* [2001]
    UKHL 51, [2001] 2 All ER (Comm) 929, [2002] 1 Lloyd's Rep 157.

### (v)  Statements of Law

### 710.   Representation may include a statement of law.

Previously, a mere statement of law (for example, an abstract proposition of
law or a legal inference from facts separately stated or known to both parties)
would not be a representation of what was stated[1]. However, it has been held that
such a rule no longer forms part of English law[2].

Despite this, the distinction between misrepresentations of law and fact remains relevant. A statement of mixed fact and law (for example, a statement as to private rights such as the nature of rights under a will[3] or a lease[4], the ownership of a fishery[5], the priority of stock[6], the borrowing powers of a company[7] or the existence of incumbrances in shares[8]) is a representation of what is stated[9]. This was the principle of division between those statements involving law which constituted representations and those which did not, but the line was not clearly drawn in all the decided cases[10]. It was not clear on which side of the line statements as to the applicability of an enactment to given facts should be placed: one view was that the applicability of an enactment to given facts is a matter of law[11], and the other view was that the conclusion on which the applicability of the enactment depended was a conclusion on a matter of fact[12].

A fraudulent misstatement of law has the effect of a misrepresentation[13]. This may be explained on the basis that a statement of law implies a representation that the maker of the statement has a belief or opinion that it is correct, and, if he does not have such belief or opinion, the implied representation is false and fraudulent.

1   *Directors etc of Midland Great Western Rly Co of Ireland v Johnson* (1858) 6 HL Cas 798 at 811; *Eaglesfield v Marquis of Londonderry* (1876) 4 ChD 693 at 709, CA; *Harse v Pearl Life Assurance Co* [1904] 1 KB 558, CA; *London County Territorial and Auxiliary Forces Association v Nichols* [1949] 1 KB 35 at 50, [1948] 2 All ER 432 at 435, CA, per Scott LJ; *Kai Nam v Ma Kam Chan* [1956] AC 358 at 367, [1956] 1 All ER 783n at 784, PC.

2   See *Kleinwort Benson Ltd v Lincoln City Council* [1999] 2 AC 349, [1998] 4 All ER 513, HL. *Kleinwort Benson Ltd v Lincoln City Council* was decided in the context of a claim for restitution of money paid under a mistake of law, however, in *Brennan v Burdon* [2004] EWCA Civ 1017 at [10], [2005] QB 303 at [10], [2004] 3 WLR 1321 at [10], the Court of Appeal stated that *Kleinwort Benson Ltd v Lincoln City Council* 'now permeates the law of contract'. In *Pankhania v Hackney London Borough Council* [2002] EWHC 2441 (Ch) at [58], [2002] NPC 123 at [58] it was held that the 'misrepresentation of law' rule had not survived the decision in *Kleinwort Benson Ltd v Lincoln City Council*. See MISTAKE vol 77 (2016) PARA 11.

3   *Reynell v Sprye* (1852) 1 De GM & G 660 at 707.

4   *Jones v Edney* (1812) 3 Camp 285.

5   *Cooper v Phibbs* (1867) LR 2 HL 149 at 170.

6   *Eaglesfield v Marquis of Londonderry* (1876) 4 ChD 693 at 714, CA.

7   *West London Commercial Bank v Kitson* (1884) 13 QBD 360 at 363, CA (distinguishing *Rashdall v Ford* (1866) LR 2 Eq 750; and dicta in *Beattie v Lord Ebury* (1872) 7 Ch App 777 at 800).

8   *MacKenzie v Royal Bank of Canada* [1934] AC 468 at 475–476, PC.

9   See ESTOPPEL vol 47 (2014) PARA 381. Cf *Mandeville v GLC* (1982) Times, 28 January (statement by council relating to the right of tenants to buy council houses, made against a background of prospective legislation which was still the subject of debate, was held not to be a representation).

10  As to decisions which appear to be anomalous, in so far as statements as to private rights were held to be mere statements of law and not to constitute representations, see *Rashdall v Ford* (1866) LR 2 Eq 750 (statement that company would shortly have power to issue debentures); *Beattie v Lord Ebury* (1872) 7 Ch App 777 at 800 (assertion by implication that company directors had power to overdraw company's account would be merely a misstatement of law; *Siveyer v Allison* [1935] 2 KB 403 at 406 per Greaves-Lord J (statement by married man that he could obtain decree of nullity). As to representations as to the effect of a document see PARA 712.

11  See *London County Territorial and Auxiliary Forces Association v Nichols* [1949] 1 KB 35 at 50, [1948] 2 All ER 432 at 435, CA, per Scott LJ; *Kai Nam v Ma Kam Chan* [1956] AC 358 at 367, [1956] 1 All ER 783 at 784, PC; *Solle v Butcher* [1950] 1 KB 671 at 703, [1949] 2 All ER 1107 at 1126, CA, per Jenkins LJ (a dissenting judgment). All these cases were concerned with the rent restrictions legislation. See also ESTOPPEL vol 47 (2014) PARA 310.

12  See *Solle v Butcher* [1950] 1 KB 671 at 686–687, [1949] 2 All ER 1107 at 1115–1116, CA, per Bucknill LJ, and at 695 and 1121 per Denning LJ.

13 *British Workman's and General Assurance Co Ltd v Cunliffe* (1902) 18 TLR 502, CA; *Harse v Pearl Life Assurance Co* [1904] 1 KB 558, CA; *Kettlewell v Refuge Assurance Co* [1908] 1 KB 545, CA (affd sub nom *Refuge Assurance Co Ltd v Kettlewell* [1909] AC 243, HL); *Tofts v Pearl Life Assurance Co Ltd* [1915] 1 KB 189, CA; *Hughes v Liverpool Victoria Legal Friendly Society* [1916] 2 KB 482, CA; *Byrne v Rudd* [1920] 2 IR 12, Ir CA.

## (vi) Statements as to Documents

### 711. Statements as to the existence of a document.

Statements as to the existence or non-existence of a document are representations, and it seems that a statement that a person derives power from a document (for example, that a company derives power from its special Act) is a statement that such a document exists[1].

1 *West London Commercial Bank v Kitson* (1884) 13 QBD 360 at 363, CA, per Bowen LJ; *Cemp Properties (UK) Ltd v Dentsply Research and Development Corpn* [1989] 2 EGLR 192, [1989] 35 EG 99 (statement that certain documents were not available for inspection).

### 712. Statements as to the wording or effect of a document.

Statements as to the actual wording or tenor of a document[1], as to the object or effect of a document[2], or as to the class, character or description of a document[3], are all statements of fact and as such are representations[4].

1 *Thoroughgood's Case* (1584) 2 Co Rep 9a; *Anon* (1684) Skin 159; *Beadles v Burch* (1839) 10 Sim 332 at 333; *Clapham v Shillito* (1844) 7 Beav 146; *Billage v Southee* (1852) 9 Hare 534; *Mahomed Kala Mea v Harperink* (1908) 25 TLR 180, PC.
2 *Hirschfeld v London, Brighton and South Coast Rly Co* (1876) 2 QBD 1; *Arkwright v Newbold* (1881) 17 ChD 301 at 318, CA; *Re Mount Morgan (West) Gold Mine Ltd, ex p West* (1887) 56 LT 622 at 624; *Stewart v Kennedy (No 2)* (1890) 15 App Cas 108, HL; *Components' Tube Co v Naylor* [1900] 2 IR 1; *Re Roberts, Roberts v Roberts* [1905] 1 Ch 704, CA; *Mahomed Kala Mea v Harperink* (1908) 25 TLR 180, PC; *Moss & Co Ltd v Swansea Corpn* (1910) 74 JP 351; *Atlantic Lines and Navigation Co Inc v Hallam Ltd, The Lucy* [1983] 1 Lloyd's Rep 188 (delivery of head charter to sub-charterer involved representation as to its effect).
3 *Thoroughgood's Case* (1584) 2 Co Rep 9a; *Edwards v Brown* (1831) 1 Cr & J 307; *Kennedy v Green* (1834) 3 My & K 699; *Hoghton v Hoghton* (1852) 15 Beav 278; *Curson v Belworthy* (1852) 3 HL Cas 742 at 753; *Lewellin v Cobbold* (1853) 1 Sm & G 376; *Lee v Angus* (1866) 15 LT 380 (affd (1868) 7 Ch App 80n); *Foster v Mackinnon* (1869) LR 4 CP 704; *Hunter v Walters* (1871) 7 Ch App 75; *National Provincial Bank of England v Jackson* (1886) 33 ChD 1, CA; *King v Smith* [1900] 2 Ch 425; *Bagot v Chapman* [1907] 2 Ch 222; *Howatson v Webb* [1908] 1 Ch 1, CA; *Carlisle and Cumberland Banking Co v Bragg* [1911] 1 KB 489, CA (overruled on other grounds by *Saunders (Executrix of the Estate of Rose Maud Gallie) v Anglia Building Society* [1971] AC 1004, [1970] 3 All ER 961, HL); *Paul and Vincent Ltd v O'Reilly* (1913) 49 ILT 89; *Re Leighton's Conveyance* [1936] 1 All ER 667.
4 As to the effect of misrepresentation as to the character, class or nature of an instrument where the execution of that instrument has been thereby induced see PARAS 780–782.

## (vii) Exaggeration, Puff Etc

### 713. When exaggeration is not representation.

Mere praise by a person of his own goods, inventions, projects, undertakings, or other marketable commodities or rights, if confined to indiscriminate puffing and pushing, and not related to particulars, is not representation[1].

1 See *Fenton v Browne* (1807) 14 Ves 144 (leasehold property described as 'nearly equal to freehold'); *Scott v Hanson* (1829) 1 Russ & M 128 (14 acres of land described as 'uncommonly rich water meadowland'; as to 12 of the acres, which were not 'uncommonly rich', there was no misrepresentation, but as to the other two, which were not water meadowland at all, there was); *Neeley v Lock* (1838) 8 C & P 527 ('warm protestations' of a person's influence and power); *Jennings v Broughton* (1854) 5 De GM & G 126 (prospectus painted in 'glowing and exaggerated

colours'); *R v Watson* (1857) 4 Jur NS 14, CCR (mere 'exaggeration of the prisoner's prosperity' held not to be a false pretence); *Dimmock v Hallett* (1866) 2 Ch App 21 (description of farms as 'fertile and improvable at a moderate cost' held mere laudatory phraseology; but statements as to their tenancy and occupation treated as statements of fact); *Cargill v Bower* (1878) 10 ChD 502 (sanguine anticipations in a prospectus); *McKeown v Boudard-Peveril Gear Co* (1896) 65 LJ Ch 735, CA (puff in a prospectus). The principle embodied in these cases is that the mere recommendation of goods by the seller imposes no liability upon him.

As to misrepresentation in offer documents generally see COMPANIES vol 15A (2016) PARA 1259 et seq.

## 714. When exaggeration is a representation.

Where instead of basing the exaggeration or puffing upon facts separately stated (in which case each of the two things stands on its own footing, and whereas the one is not a representation at all, the other is wholly so), the representor[1] intermingles it with facts, punctuates it by details or quantifies it by figures, the whole of the compound statement is deemed a representation. Thus, if the statement gives rise to a claim where the facts are proved to have been misstated, it is no defence to allege that the facts were buried under a mass of indefinite and flattering generalities[2].

1  As to who is a representor see PARAS 724–732.
2  *Directors etc of Central Rly Co of Venezuela v Kisch* (1867) LR 2 HL 99 at 113, where, although it was recognised that some high colouring and even exaggeration is to be expected in a prospectus, the statements went far beyond mere colouring. See also *Bile Beans Manufacturing Co v Davidson* (1906) 8 F 1181, Ct of Sess (although mere puffing and exaggeration, however gross, of the merits and virtues of a remedy do not constitute representations, it is otherwise where statements are made as to imaginary discoveries of imaginary new ingredients in the drug sold). Cf *Scott v Hanson* (1829) 1 Russ & M 128; *Dimmock v Hallett* (1866) 2 Ch App 21 (in these cases, the statement was separated into elements that amounted to representation and those that were mere puff: see PARA 713). As to misrepresentation in offer documents generally see COMPANIES vol 15A (2016) PARA 1259 et seq.

# (3) How Representations May Be Made

## (i) Express Representations

## 715. Representations in writing, plans etc.

The usual permanent symbols by which a representation is conveyed are words and figures written or printed or produced by any other equivalent means; but plans and drawings[1], maps[2], pictures and photographs[3], and the like, may effectively serve the same purpose.

1  *Beaumont v Dukes* (1822) Jac 422; *Denny v Hancock* (1870) 6 Ch App 1 at 11–14; *Re Arnold, Arnold v Arnold* (1880) 14 ChD 270 at 282, 284, CA (all these were cases in which plans of property sold played an important part in the representation). See also *S Pearson & Son Ltd v Dublin Corpn* [1907] AC 351, HL (representation contained in, inter alia, plans and drawings prepared by the defendants' engineer). As to the rules of construction to be applied when a plan is attached to or indorsed on a deed see DEEDS AND OTHER INSTRUMENTS vol 32 (2012) PARA 430.
2  *Re Mount Morgan (West) Gold Mine Ltd, ex p West* (1887) 56 LT 622 (map accompanying a prospectus). As to misrepresentation in offer documents generally see COMPANIES vol 15A (2016) PARA 1259 et seq.
3  *Newman v Pinto* (1887) 57 LT 31, CA (deceptive pictures or emblematic designs); *Slingsby v Bradford Patent Truck and Trolley Co* [1906] WN 51, CA ('sketches' of buildings alleged to be 'photographed').

## 716. Representations by speech, gestures or demeanour.

Speech is the most common method for the communication of a statement not in writing, but gestures and demeanour may be used in addition to or as an alternative to spoken language[1].

1  See *Walters v Morgan* (1861) 3 De GF & J 718 at 724 per Lord Campbell LC ('a nod or a wink, or a shake of the head, or a smile' may constitute a representation, throwing upon a purchaser a duty of disclosure which otherwise would not arise); *Turner v Green* [1895] 2 Ch 205 at 209 per Chitty J; cf *Webb v Rorke* (1806) 2 Sch & Lef 661 at 668. As to implied representations by acts or conduct see PARAS 717–722.

## (ii) Representations Implied from Conduct

## 717. Representations implied from conduct (including silence).

Representations may be implied from such statements as statements of existing intention, opinion or belief[1], or from absolute representations coupled with silence as to matters which it was the duty of the representor not to suppress[2]. Representations may also be implied from acts and conduct[3].

1  See PARA 708.
2  Generally, mere non-disclosure is not sufficient, but a partial non-disclosure may amount to a misrepresentation: see PARA 747 et seq. As to who is a representor see PARAS 724–732.
3  The participation of a pop group in an advertising campaign is a representation by conduct of the group's intention not to break up during the term of the contract: *Spice Girls Ltd v Aprilia World Service BV* [2002] EWCA Civ 15, [2002] EMLR 510. See also PARAS 718–722.

## 718. Acts and conduct in sales and purchases.

In contracts of sale, or delivery of property pursuant to a contractual or other obligation, the following implications from acts and conduct may be made: (1) the purchaser of goods by the mere act of purchasing them is deemed to represent that he has the present intention of paying for them[1]; (2) he who assumes to sell property impliedly represents that it exists and has some value[2]; (3) he who delivers or hands over or produces documents in certain circumstances may be held impliedly to represent thereby that they are genuine[3]; and (4) the seller of an article presenting a certain appearance to the purchaser is deemed to represent that the article is in fact what it purports to be, and that there has been no concealment or covering up of defects or other device or manoeuvre whereby the outward appearance of the article is made to deceive[4].

Conversely, a buyer of property who by acts and conduct conceals the merits, or depreciates the value, of that which is offered to him for sale is as much guilty of implied misrepresentation as the seller who, by the like means, conceals its faults[5]. In the case of sales of a marketable commodity, any person who rigs the market or makes a market in the shares or other commodity by procuring persons to enter into pretended bargains in such market at fictitious prices is making a false representation by acts and conduct that the bargains and prices are real[6].

1  See PARA 704.
2  *Colt v Woollaston* (1723) 2 P Wms 154 at 156–157; *Richardson v Silvester* (1873) LR 9 QB 34; *Ajello v Worsley* [1898] 1 Ch 274.
3  *Edinburgh United Breweries v Molleson* [1894] AC 96 at 111, HL, where the handing over of books which the purchaser was entitled to have examined by an accountant as a condition of the sale of a business was held to be an implied representation that they were genuine; *Marnham v Weaver* (1899) 80 LT 412, where the putting forward as security of fictitious leases from the party to himself under an assumed name was held to be an implied misrepresentation of their genuineness. Cf *Gage v Beauchamp* (1920) 36 TLR 253, where supplying for payment a report of a survey of a ship was held to be merely a contract to supply a document and not to raise a

warranty of its accuracy. See also *Boyd and Forrest v Glasgow and South Western Rly Co*, as reported in 1912 SC 93 at 96, 100, 104–105, HL; and subsequent proceedings as reported in 1915 SC 20 at 27–28, HL (contractors undertook to construct a railway on the faith of a purported journal of borings made along the proposed line on behalf of a railway company; in compiling the journal the company's engineer had in good faith altered the reports of the persons who made the borings; it was held that the company was not guilty of fraud or misrepresentation). In *Sony KK v Saray Electronics (London) Ltd* [1983] FSR 302, CA, it was held arguable that a dealer who sells well-known branded electrical goods represents that he is in a position to provide a manufacturer's guarantee. In *Whife v Michael Cullen & Partners* [1993] EGCS 193, CA, there was held to be a triable issue whether a lease with deliberately complex and obscure clauses was a misrepresentation.

4   *Jones v Bowden* (1813) 4 Taunt 847 (sale of sea-damaged pimento by bulk samples, which showed no damage, this being only apparent on unpacking, and sending out advertisements of the sale too late to enable purchasers to inspect; sellers' acts and conduct treated as an implied representation that the pimento was sound); *Lovell v Hicks* (1836) 2 Y & C Ex 46 at 53–55 (sale of an invention for baking bread without the use of spirit or ferment, where the seller gave a demonstration which appeared to satisfy the description, but in the conduct of which spirit and a special ferment had been secretly introduced; acts held to have been one of the means whereby a misrepresentation of the nature and capacity of the invention had been made); *Ormrod v Huth* (1845) 14 M & W 651, Ex Ch (a case of 'false packing', of which, however, the defendant was not proved to have known); *Horsfall v Thomas* (1862) 1 H & C 90 (where it was alleged, but without sufficient proof, that a defect in a cannon had been covered up); *Fitzpatrick v Kelly* (1873) LR 8 QB 337 at 342 per Quain J (when a person asks for butter and the tradesman, without more, sells him an article which seems to be butter, the representation is that the article is butter, that is, unadulterated butter). See FOOD AND DRINK vol 51 (2013) PARA 754; SALE OF GOODS AND SUPPLY OF SERVICES. See also *Gill v M'Dowell* [1903] 2 IR 463 (hermaphrodite beast sent to a sale of bullocks and heifers; the sending was an implied representation that the animal was either a bullock or a heifer; in this case the animal was described as a sort of living lie); *Patterson v Landsberg & Son* (1905) 7 F 675 at 681, Ct of Sess, per Lord Kyllachy (appearance of age presented by articles sold; silence of seller as to the fact that the articles were modern and equivocal language and conduct of seller amounted in themselves to representation that they were in fact antiques). As to falsity by omission, silence or inaction see PARAS 747–750. As to representations by conduct for the purposes of estoppel see ESTOPPEL vol 47 (2014) PARA 307. As to terms implied into contracts for the sale of goods by description see SALE OF GOODS AND SUPPLY OF SERVICES vol 91 (2012) PARA 73 et seq.

5   *Walsham v Stainton* (1863) 1 De GJ & Sm 678 at 689–690 (implied misrepresentation of value of shares by manipulating accounts). As to omission, silence or inaction see PARAS 747–750.

6   *National Exchange Co of Glasgow v Drew and Dick* (1855) 2 Macq 103, HL; *Scott v Brown, Doering, McNab & Co* [1892] 2 QB 724, CA (conspiracy to rig market by misrepresenting value of shares). In the later case, citing *R v De Berenger* (1814) 3 M & S 67 (conspiracy by false rumours), it was said that there was no substantial distinction between false rumours and false and fictitious acts: see *Scott v Brown, Doering, McNab & Co* at 730 per Lopes LJ. A purchaser, induced to purchase shares from either of the parties to the proceedings by means of a fictitious premium created by those parties solely for the purpose of inducing such purchaser to buy, could have successfully sued either or both for a false and fraudulent misrepresentation: *Scott v Brown, Doering, McNab & Co* at 734 per AL Smith LJ. As to the criminal offence of conspiracy see CRIMINAL LAW vol 25 (2016) PARA 78 et seq.

## 719.   Implied representation that transaction is legal.

Some transactions may be carried out in either a lawful or an unlawful manner. Since the law presumes against illegality, the mere fact that a person enters into a transaction may raise an inference that he represents that all the conditions necessary for the legality of the transaction exist.

Thus a shipment of goods may constitute a representation by the shipper to the shipowner that the goods are not being shipped on an illegal voyage[1]. It is possible that the sending of an animal to a public market may amount to a representation that it is not suffering from an infectious disease[2]. It seems that, in company matters, the declaration and payment of a dividend may be equivalent to a statement that profits have been earned out of which alone such dividend can lawfully be paid[3]; and the issue or delivery of fully-paid shares, where there has been no filed contract, raises the inference of a representation that cash has been paid for them, for otherwise such issue or delivery would be unlawful[4]. Similarly, a representation as to a company's profits may involve a representation that the profits have been lawfully earned[5]. On the other hand, if the act in question is such that it infringes no statute, and is not illegal at common law, no such inference arises. Thus the mere act of trading is not an implied representation that the trader is of full age, because it is not generally unlawful for a minor to trade[6]; nor is the mere advertisement of an article, with the descriptive words 'trade mark' added, an implied representation that the party has registered the trade mark, for it is not necessarily illegal to use an unregistered mark[7].

1  *Mitchell, Cotts & Co v Steel Bros & Co Ltd* [1916] 2 KB 610 at 614 per Atkin J.
2  See ANIMALS vol 2 (2017) PARA 24.
3  This would seem to be so on the principle of the *Bloomenthal v Ford* cited below. The question was referred to, but not decided, in *Jackson v Turquand* (1869) LR 4 HL 305 at 308–309 per Lord Hatherley LC, and at 315 per Lord Westbury. However, in an earlier case, the view was expressed that a payment of dividends is an implied declaration to the world by acts and deeds that the company has made profits which justify such a dividend: see *Burnes v Pennell* (1849) 2 HL Cas 497 at 524–525 per Lord Campbell, and at 531 per Lord Brougham. See also *R v Lord Kylsant* [1932] 1 KB 442 at 448–449, CCA, per Avory J.
4  *Bloomenthal v Ford* [1897] AC 156 at 163–164, HL, per Lord Halsbury LC, and at 169 per Lord Herschell. This was an estoppel case, but, since a representation by conduct for the purpose of estoppel in pais is exactly what a representation by conduct is for the purposes of the law of misrepresentation, the authority is in point. As to estoppel in pais see ESTOPPEL vol 47 (2014) PARA 346 et seq. See also COMPANIES vol 14 (2016) PARA 398.
5  *Briess v Woolley* [1954] AC 333, [1954] 1 All ER 909, HL (profits earned by contravening terms of government licence).
6  *Re Jones, ex p Jones* (1881) 18 ChD 109 at 121, 125, CA. See CHILDREN AND YOUNG PERSONS vol 9 (2017) PARAS 20, 23.
7  See *Sen Sen Co v Britten* [1899] 1 Ch 692; and TRADE MARKS AND TRADE NAMES vol 97A (2014) PARAS 85, 131.

**720.  Implied representations that representor is acting in a certain character.**
Where a person, in the course of a transaction, assumes a certain character by conducting himself as if he possessed it, he is deemed to represent by such conduct that he does in fact fill that character. Thus, by the acts of sending bought and sold notes to the other party, and guaranteeing the performance of the contract, a person represents to the other party that he has a principal[1]; and the cases of what is usually treated as implied warranty of authority by an agent[2] may be, and occasionally have been, treated as cases of implied representations[3]. Similarly, although a distinction normally exists between mere non-disclosure and misrepresentation[4], non-disclosure is in certain cases capable of being regarded as a representation (inferred from the conduct of the party in entering into and carrying through a particular transaction) that the transaction, so far as he knows, is of the usual and normal type, and that he has withheld nothing which, if revealed, would show it to be otherwise[5].

1  *Wilson v Short* (1848) 6 Hare 366. See also *Montefiori v Montefiori* (1762) 1 Wm Bl 363.
2  See AGENCY vol 1 (2017) PARA 161. As to the distinction between a representation and a warranty see PARA 703.
3  See eg *Polhill v Walter* (1832) 3 B & Ad 114.
4  See PARA 701.
5  See PARA 747 et seq.

**721.  Personation by acts.**
Personation by acts or conduct is as much representation, even though no word is said, as an assumption of an alias by direct statement[1]. By acts and conduct,

without language, a person may represent that he is associated as agent or partner with a third person, when he is not[2], or conversely that he has no connection with a third person, when he is so connected or is in fact that person[3].

1 *R v Barnard* (1837) 7 C & P 784 (defendant appearing in cap and gown would in itself have been pregnant evidence from which the court should infer that he pretended he was a member of a university). As to statutory offences of impersonation see eg the Police Act 1996 s 90; and POLICE AND INVESTIGATORY POWERS vol 84 (2013) PARA 44.
2 *Higgons v Burton* (1857) 26 LJ Ex 342; *Hardman v Booth* (1863) 1 H & C 803; *Cundy v Lindsay* (1878) 3 App Cas 459, HL. See also *British Sky Broadcasting Group plc v Sky Home Services Ltd* [2006] EWHC 3165 (Ch), [2007] 3 All ER 1066 (where the failure of traders to correct customers' mistaken belief that they were connected with a competitor constituted misrepresentation by conduct) (appeal on costs [2008] EWCA Civ 1101, [2008] All ER (D) 314 (Oct)).
3 *Moens v Heyworth* (1842) 10 M & W 147 at 156–158; *Blake v Albion Life Assurance Society* (1878) 4 CPD 94; *Marnham v Weaver* (1899) 80 LT 412.

**722. Maintenance of deception by acts or conduct.**

Acts or conduct may be employed as a means of maintaining, by periodically repeated representations, a deception once initiated. For instance, by regularly transmitting to the supposed mortgagee sums of money exactly equivalent to the interest which would fall due on the mortgage, if it had been effected[1], or by producing (without handing over) the title deeds of the property supposed to be in mortgage[2], a person who has been entrusted with money to lend on such mortgage is making so many implied representations that the mortgage has been effected and is a subsisting security.

1 *Blair v Bromley* (1847) 2 Ph 354; *Moore v Knight* [1891] 1 Ch 547; *Thorne v Heard and Marsh* [1895] AC 495 at 506, HL.
2 *Re Murray, Dickson v Murray* (1887) 57 LT 223.

# (4) Parties to a Representation

## (i) Liability or Entitlement to Relief

**723. Persons liable or entitled to relief.**

In any proceeding in which misrepresentation is set up, the only person liable is the representor[1], or a person whom the law deems to be the representor, and the only person entitled to relief is the representee[2], or a person whom the law deems to be the representee, subject to the rules as to the transmission or devolution of such liability and title respectively, by reason of death, insolvency, assignment and the like[3].

1 As to who is a representor see PARAS 724–732.
2 As to who is a representee see PARAS 733–739.
3 As to misrepresentation as a defence against an assignee from the representor see PARA 787; as to the parties to a claim for deceit see PARAS 793–796; and as to the parties to a claim for rescission see PARAS 817–820.

## (ii) The Representor

**724. The representor.**

The following is a general statement of the rules for determining which persons are deemed to be representors. In the first place, only the person who actually made the representation is liable for its consequences, unless it was made on behalf of a principal or partner, in which case the principal or partner is deemed the representor, or one of the two representors, as the case may be[1]. Secondly, an agent who has a co-agent, or who is a sub-agent, does not, merely as such, make the co-agent or the intermediate agent, as the case may be, liable as a principal[2]. Thirdly, where it is necessary to establish fraud, an innocent principal is liable for the fraud of his agent, and for this purpose it makes no difference that the principal is a corporation[3]. Lastly, all who concur in making any false representation are jointly responsible, and, if it was fraudulent also, are jointly and severally responsible, to the representee for the consequences[4].

1  See PARA 725. In claims in tort based on negligent misrepresentation, the representor's liability depends on whether he owed a duty of care to the representee, which may in turn depend largely on whether he ought to have foreseen that the statement would be acted on by the representee: see eg *Yianni v Edwin Evans & Sons* [1982] QB 438, [1981] 3 All ER 592; *Smith v Eric S Bush* [1990] 1 AC 831, [1989] All ER 514, HL. An accountancy firm, engaged by company directors to help in the preparation of a share prospectus, does not owe a duty of care to third party shareholders for negligent misstatements which appear in the prospectus: *Abbott v Strong* [1998] 2 BCLC 420. See also PARA 733. As to negligent misrepresentation see PARAS 762–763, 797–800, 813. For the circumstances in which a person (X) can be liable for passing on information produced by another (Y) to someone (Z) with whom he (X) hopes to contract, see *Webster v Liddington* [2014] EWCA Civ 560, [2015] 1 All ER (Comm) 427.
2  See PARAS 726–727.
3  See PARAS 725, 796.
4  See PARAS 730–731. As to who is a representee see PARAS 733–739.

## 725. Principal liable for misrepresentation of agent.

Any person by whose express or implied authority a representation was made is accountable to the representee[1], if it should turn out to be false, and a claim for damages may be brought against the principal or the agent or against both[2]. Where the claim is solely for rescission or analogous relief, the remedy is against the principal only, for the contract is made with him and not with the agent[3], although it is possible to proceed against both the principal and the agent for damages and against the principal only for rescission[4].

1  As to who is a representee see PARAS 733–739.
2  See *Kingsnorth Trust Ltd v Bell* [1986] 1 All ER 423, [1986] 1 WLR 119, CA. See also AGENCY vol 1 (2017) PARA 136. The finding of agency in this case should be considered in the light of *Barclays Bank plc v O'Brien* [1994] 1 AC 180, [1993] 4 All ER 417, HL, but this does not affect the principle that the principal is liable if the representor is in truth an agent. As to responsibility for the fraud of an agent see PARA 796.

   An agent is not liable under the Misrepresentation Act 1967 s 2(1) (see PARA 800) because there is no contract between the agent and the representee: *Resolute Maritime Inc v Nippon Kaiji Kyokai, The Skopas* [1983] 2 All ER 1, [1983] 1 WLR 857.

   An agent who innocently misrepresents that he has authority to act for a principal may be liable to the representee for breach of warranty of authority: see AGENCY vol 1 (2017) PARAS 161–162.

   As to the various classes of agents see AGENCY vol 1 (2017) PARA 11 et seq. As to partners see PARTNERSHIP. As to estoppel by representation see ESTOPPEL vol 47 (2014) PARA 355 et seq.

   As to a claim for damages see PARA 788 et seq.
3  *Eaglesfield v Marquis of Londonderry* (1878) 26 WR 540 at 541, HL, per Lord Blackburn.
4  *Goldrei, Foucard & Son v Sinclair and Russian Chamber of Commerce in London* [1918] 1 KB 180, CA. As to claims for rescission see PARA 811 et seq.

## 726. Position of co-agents.

One co-agent is not liable to the representee[1] for the misrepresentation of another unless he has expressly authorised or tacitly permitted it[2], or the co-agents are partners[3].

1   As to who is a representee see PARAS 733–739.
2   *Cargill v Bower* (1878) 10 ChD 502 at 513–514; *Weir v Bell* (1878) 3 Ex D 238 at 245, 247–248, 250, CA; *Re Denham & Co* (1883) 25 ChD 752 at 764–765.
3   See the Partnership Act 1890 s 6; and AGENCY vol 1 (2017) PARA 28; PARTNERSHIP vol 79 (2014) PARAS 39, 42–43, 52.

## 727. Principal and sub-agent.

A sub-agent may render the ultimate principal liable if the proved circumstances of the case are such that the ultimate principal and the intermediate agent must be deemed to have intended and agreed that the latter should, or might, appoint a substitute for the purpose of discharging in his stead, and on behalf of the former, duties involving the making of representations of the character of that sued upon[1].

1   *De Bussche v Alt* (1878) 8 ChD 286 at 310–311, CA.

## 728. When authority to make representation is implied.

A person is deemed to have the implied authority of another person to make a representation which is made in the course and within the scope of his employment by that other person or, in the case of a partnership, of the partnership business or undertaking[1]. In applying this rule, the nature of the service, employment, business or undertaking must first be proved; and the question then is whether making representations at all is within the class of acts incidental to it[2]. If it is, the further inquiry may become necessary whether the particular representation sued upon belongs to the class of representations which the alleged employee, agent or partner is, by virtue of his employment service or the nature of the partnership business or adventure, employed or authorised to make[3]. If the answer to both these questions is in the affirmative, the principal is a representor and liable as such; if the answer to either is in the negative, he is not[4]. If the misrepresentation is within the scope of the agent's employment, the principal is a representor, even though the misrepresentation is proved by the principal to have been in fact made both with the object and result of serving the agent's private ends only[5].

1   See *Barwick v English Stock Joint Bank* (1867) LR 2 Exch 259 at 266, Ex Ch; *Lloyd v Grace Smith & Co* [1912] AC 716, HL. See also AGENCY vol 1 (2017) PARAS 123, 136, 152–153. As to the implied authority of partners see PARTNERSHIP vol 79 (2014) PARA 39 et seq.
2   See AGENCY vol 1 (2008) PARA 38; and PARTNERSHIP vol 79 (2014) PARA 42.
3   For a useful classification of the kinds of acts which, according to the doctrine of implied authority, will render a company liable for misrepresentation in a prospectus see *Lynde v Anglo-Italian Hemp Spinning Co* [1896] 1 Ch 178 at 182–183 per Romer J. For an explanation of this classification see *Collins v Associated Greyhounds Racecourses Ltd* [1930] 1 Ch 1 at 22 per Luxmoore J (on appeal [1930] 1 Ch 1 at 24, CA); and COMPANIES vol 15A (2016) PARA 1260. As to the various classes of agents see AGENCY vol 1 (2017) PARA 11 et seq. As to misrepresentation in offer documents generally see COMPANIES vol 15A (2016) PARA 1259 et seq.
4   Implied authority was not established in the following cases: *Burnes v Pennell* (1849) 2 HL Cas 497 at 519–520; *Wheelton v Hardisty* (1857) 8 E & B 232 at 260, 268–274, 301–302, Ex Ch; *Re Northumberland and Durham District Banking Co, ex p Bigge* (1858) 28 LJ Ch 50; *Re Liverpool Borough Bank, Duranty's Case* (1858) 26 Beav 268; *Re National Patent Steam Fuel Co, ex p Worth* (1859) 28 LJ Ch 589; *Re Royal British Bank, ex p Frowd* (1861) 30 LJ Ch 322; *New Brunswick and Canada Rly and Land Co v Coneybeare* (1862) 9 HL Cas 711; *Newlands v National Employers' Accident Association Ltd* (1885) 54 LJQB 428 at 430–431, CA; *Lynde v*

*Anglo-Italian Hemp Spinning Co* [1896] 1 Ch 178 at 184–185; *Biggar v Rock Life Assurance Co* [1902] 1 KB 516 at 524–525 per Wright J; *Hoole v Speak* [1904] 2 Ch 732; *M'Millan v Accident Insurance Co* 1907 SC 484; *Hindle v Brown* (1908) 98 LT 791, CA; *Terrill v Parker and Thomas* (1915) 32 TLR 48.

However, in *Gordon v Selico Co Ltd* [1986] 1 EGLR 71, 18 HLR 219, CA, where a contractor made a fraudulent misrepresentation by deliberately covering up evidence of dry rot, both the lessors and the management company were implicated in the fraud because the principal shareholder of the management company was aware of the cover up and the lessors had invested the management agents with ostensible, if not actual, authority to make representations to prospective purchasers or lessees as to the condition of the premises.

5   See AGENCY vol 1 (2017) PARA 136.

### 729. Ratification and estoppel.

Either for the purposes of proceedings to rescind a contract or for the purposes of a claim for damages[1], a person may become liable as principal for the misrepresentation of another by adoption or ratification[2], and by estoppel[3].

1   As to claims for rescission see PARA 811 et seq; and as to claims for damages see PARA 788 et seq.
2   See *Hoole v Speak* [1904] 2 Ch 732 at 735–736 per Kekewich J, where the law is correctly stated as to contract, but the statement that a principal cannot ratify his agent's tort is incorrect: see AGENCY vol 1 (2017) PARA 58 et seq; COMPANIES vol 15A (2016) PARA 1274.
3   *Wright v Crookes* (1840) 1 Scott NR 685 at 698–699. See also AGENCY vol 1 (2017) PARA 25; and as to estoppel generally see ESTOPPEL.

### 730. Liability of joint representors in proceedings for rescission.

It seems that where two or more persons contract with another person and the contract is induced by misrepresentation made by them or on their behalf, they are jointly and severally liable to repay to the representee[1] any money declared to be repayable to him and to pay any indemnity granted to him by way of ancillary relief, in proceedings brought by him for the rescission of the contract[2]. In such a case, it seems that if one of the representors pays the whole or more than his proportionate share of the money repayable or payable to the representee, he is entitled to contribution against the other representors[3].

1   As to who is a representee see PARAS 733–739.
2   See eg the order in *Newbigging v Adam* (1886) 34 ChD 582 at 584, CA; varied on appeal sub nom *Adam v Newbigging* (1888) 13 App Cas 308, HL. As to claims for rescission see PARA 811 et seq.
3   See eg *Re Direct Birmingham, Oxford, Reading and Brighton Rly Co, Spottiswoode's Case, Amsinck's Case* (1855) 6 De GM & G 345. As to contribution see RESTITUTION vol 88 (2012) PARA 480 et seq.

### 731. Liability of joint representors in proceedings for damages.

Where a misrepresentation is made by more than one person, and is made fraudulently, then, in a claim for damages, all those who concurred in the fraud are, as in the case of any other tort, both jointly and severally answerable to the representee[1] for the whole amount of the damages[2]. A judgment recovered against one such representor is not a bar to a claim against any other representor[3]. Each of the representors may recover contribution from any of the others to an amount which the court considers just and equitable, having regard to the extent of that person's responsibility for the damage in question[4].

1   As to who is a representee see PARAS 733–739.
2   *Cullen v Thomson's Trustees and Kerr* (1862) 4 Macq 424 at 432–433, HL; *Swift v Winterbotham* (1873) LR 8 QB 244 at 254 (revsd sub nom *Swift v Jewsbury* (1874) LR 9 QB 301, Ex Ch, but this statement of the law unimpeached); *Phosphate Sewage Co v Hartmont* (1877) 5 ChD 394 at 456, CA; *Re Collie, ex p Adamson* (1878) 8 ChD 807 at 819–820, CA. See also *Thomas Saunders*

*Partnership v Harvey* (1989) 30 ConLR 103 (company made a fraudulent representation in the process of obtaining a sub-contract; company went into liquidation; it was held that the managing director who was the author of the letter containing the misrepresentation and who knew it was untrue was personally liable). See generally TORT vol 97 (2015) PARA 447 et seq.

3 See the Civil Liability (Contribution) Act 1978 s 3; and DAMAGES vol 29 (2014) PARA 620; TORT vol 97 (2015) PARA 449.

4 See the Civil Liability (Contribution) Act 1978 ss 1, 2; and DAMAGES vol 29 (2014) PARAS 622, 624; TORT vol 97 (2015) PARA 451 et seq. As to the effect of the running of time upon a right to claim for contribution see LIMITATION PERIODS vol 68 (2016) PARAS 1006–1007. As to the approach to damages where some, but not all, of the representors have acted fraudulently see *Nationwide Building Society v Dunlop Haywards (DHL) Ltd* [2009] EWHC 254 (Comm), [2009] 2 All ER (Comm) 715, [2010] 1 WLR 258.

## 732. Burden of proof as to representor.

The burden is on the representee[1] of establishing that the representation was made by the person alleged to be the representor or, where he is not alleged to have personally made it, with his authority[2]. Where either personal representation or express authority is relied on by the representee, the questions whether the alleged representation was made, and whether express authority was given, are questions of fact[3], subject to the question of law whether there is any evidence in support of either allegation. Where implied authority is relied on, it is necessary that the circumstances proved or admitted to exist should be such that the existence of an agency is capable of being inferred from them[4]; subject to this, it is a question of fact what the nature and terms of the employment or business were in the particular case, or what were the duties of the alleged agent[5], but it is a question of law whether from the proved or admitted facts in relation to these matters the authority is to be implied[6].

1 As to who is a representee see PARAS 733–739.
2 See eg *Lynde v Anglo-Italian Hemp Spinning Co* [1896] 1 Ch 178 at 184–185; *Newlands v National Employers' Accident Association Ltd* (1885) 54 LJQB 428, CA; *Barnett v South London Tramways Co* (1887) 18 QBD 815, CA.
3 See eg *Ludgater v Love* (1881) 44 LT 694, CA, where it was left to the jury to say whether the vendor's son had in fact made the alleged representation and whether the vendor had authorised his son to make the representation.
4 See *Thorne v Heard and Marsh* [1895] AC 495 at 502, HL. As to implied authority see AGENCY vol 1 (2017) PARA 37 et seq.
5 In *Newlands v National Employers' Accident Association Ltd* (1885) 54 LJQB 428 at 430–431, CA, it was pointed out that no 'practice or regular course of business' had been established by evidence to support the allegation that the secretary had authority to make a statement of the kind which he had made, and that, in the absence of such evidence, it was a conclusion of law that no such implication of authority could be made. In *British Mutual Banking Co Ltd v Charnwood Forest Rly Co* (1887) 18 QBD 714 at 716–719, CA, the jury found that the company secretary had been held out as a person to answer inquiries, but the Court of Appeal held that, from the whole of the proved and found facts, no authority could be inferred in law. So in *Banbury v Bank of Montreal* [1918] AC 626, HL, it was held that there was no evidence before the members of the jury on which they could, as reasonable men, find that a branch manager of a bank had authority to give, on behalf of the bank, advice to the representee as to his investments. As to implied authority see AGENCY vol 1 (2017) PARA 37 et seq.
6 *Mackay v Commercial Bank of New Brunswick* (1874) LR 5 PC 394 at 415–416. As to implied authority see AGENCY vol 1 (2017) PARA 37 et seq.

### (iii) The Representee

## 733. The representee.

A representee in law includes: (1) any person to whom the representation was physically and directly made, or any principal or partner of such person; (2) any specific person, not coming within the description in head (1) above, but whom the representor[1], either actually or in contemplation of law, intended the representation to reach and influence; and (3) any individual member of the public, or of a class, who has acted upon a representation addressed to the public or the class[2].

1  As to who is a representor see PARAS 724–732.
2  These three categories of representee are included in the comprehensive proposition laid down in *Swift v Winterbotham* (1873) LR 8 QB 244 at 253 per Lord Cockburn CJ; on appeal sub nom *Swift v Jewsbury* (1874) LR 9 QB 301, Ex Ch. As to representations made to a class see PARA 739.
    In tort cases, a person may be liable to a third person for a statement made to another person and for another purpose if he knows the statement is likely to be relied on by that third person: see *Smith v Eric S Bush* [1990] 1 AC 831, [1989] All ER 514, HL (valuer who valued a house for a building society for the purposes of a mortgage application may be liable to the intending purchaser of the house). See also PARA 724.

## 734.  Person to whom representation made or his principal or partner.

If a representation is made individually and exclusively to one particular person, with no other person in contemplation, the person to whom the representation is made is obviously the sole representee. It is equally plain that if the representation is made to one person with knowledge on the part of the representor[1] that the person to whom it is made is merely the agent of a particular principal (or of someone who, although undisclosed at the time, turns out to be that principal) for the purpose of receiving and transmitting the representation to the principal, the only representee is the principal, the person to whom the representation is made being the mere messenger or medium through whom the representation is conveyed[2].

On the other hand the representation may be made to one person through another but with the intention that the person through whom the representation is conveyed will also be influenced and act on it, as where the representor knows or believes that the two persons in question are partners or joint-contractors or associates in the business which it is to bring about; in such a case either or each of the persons in question, if either or each acts on the faith of the representation, is deemed a representee[3].

1  As to who is a representor see PARAS 724–732.
2  See eg *Haycraft v Creasy* (1801) 2 East 92; *Gilbert v Endean* (1878) 9 ChD 259, CA.
3  See also PARA 735. It was the case that, generally speaking, in cases of marine insurance, a representation to the first underwriter extended to the others: *Barber v Fletcher* (1779) 1 Doug KB 305 at 306 per Lord Mansfield CJ.

## 735.  Person to whom representation is intended to be passed on.

A second class of case arises where one person makes a representation to another person, either with an express direction or authority to repeat it to a third person, or with intent that it should come to the third person's notice and be acted upon by him. Such an intent is presumed in law on proof of the fact that the representor[1] contemplated at the time that the person to whom the representation was made would pass it on to the third person for him to act upon[2], or subsequently, but before the third person acted upon it, knew that the person to whom it was made had in fact so passed it on to the third person for that purpose[3]. In any such case the third person is a representee[4]. The person to whom the representation was made may also be a representee, depending on all the circumstances of the individual case[5].

1  As to who is a representor see PARAS 724–732.

2　See *Langridge v Levy* (1837) 2 M & W 519 at 520–521, 530–532 (affd sub nom *Levy v Langridge* (1838) 4 M & W 337, Ex Ch), where the plaintiff's father, to whom the representation concerning the gun sold to him was personally made, expressly informed the defendant that the gun was intended for use by the plaintiff as well as by the father himself; *Swift v Winterbotham* (1873) LR 8 QB 244 (varied sub nom *Swift v Jewsbury* (1874) LR 9 QB 301, Ex Ch, but not on the ground that the plaintiff was not in law a representee), where it was proved that the nature of banking business was such that it must have been within the contemplation of the defendant when the representation was made that it would or might be communicated to the customer of the bank on whose behalf it was sought, namely the plaintiff. Cf *Hosegood v Bull* (1876) 36 LT 617, where a bank manager's letter was held not to have been intended to be communicated to the plaintiff; *Parsons v Barclay & Co Ltd and Goddard* (1910) 103 LT 196, CA, a similar case of a banker's confidential report, where the misrepresentation was held not to be such as would found an action for deceit; *Robinson v National Bank of Scotland* 1916 SC 154, HL, a case of a bank manager's letter to another bank containing statements meant to influence such persons as should be interested in the subject matter of the letter, applied in *Hedley Byrne & Co Ltd v Heller & Partners Ltd* [1964] AC 465, [1963] 2 All ER 575, HL. See also *Fortune v Young* 1918 SC 1, Ct of Sess (letter testifying to financial position of a proposed tenant, not addressed to anyone, but written in order that it should be shown to the landlord and his factor); *Gross v Lewis Hillman Ltd* [1970] Ch 445, [1969] 3 All ER 1476, CA (misrepresentation regarding property sued upon by the assignees of the representee). As to statutory restrictions on claims upon representations as to credit see PARA 803.

3　*Pilmore v Hood* (1838) 5 Bing NC 97 at 105–106, 108–109.

4　See the cases cited above; and PARA 734.

5　In general, if the representation is made to one person for the sole purpose of his passing it on as a mere distributing agent to another, the person to whom it is made is not a representee (see PARA 734); but, if it is intended that the person to whom the representation is made should act upon it himself as well as pass it on (see eg *Langridge v Levy* (1837) 2 M & W 519; affd sub nom *Levy v Landgridge* (1838) 4 M & W 337, Ex Ch), both that person and the person to whom it is intended that the representation should be passed on are representees.

## 736. Members of public or particular section of the community.

If a representation is addressed to the public at large or to some section of the community in order to induce members of it to take a particular course, for example, to apply for or purchase shares in a company[1], to give value for a bill of exchange[2], to bid at an auction[3], to apply for a situation[4] or to travel by a particular train[5], and a member of the public or person belonging to the section of the community in question is induced by the representation to take the course in question, that member or person is entitled to all such rights as he would have been entitled to if the representation had been addressed to him individually[6].

1　As to misrepresentation in offer documents generally see COMPANIES vol 15A (2016) PARA 1259 et seq. It has been held that the fact that a company report is marked with a direction that it is for the use of shareholders only does not necessarily prevent it from constituting a representation to the public: *Re Royal British Bank, ex p Brockwell* (1857) 26 LJ Ch 855 at 859, 862. As to the principle that a contract made for the purpose of committing a fraud on the public cannot be enforced see CONTRACT vol 22 (2012) PARA 424 et seq.

2　*Polhill v Walter* (1832) 3 B & Ad 114; *West London Commercial Bank v Kitson* (1884) 13 QBD 360, CA (bills accepted fraudulently). As to the liability of an agent see FINANCIAL INSTRUMENTS AND TRANSACTIONS vol 49 (2015) PARA 260.

3　*Robinson v Wall* (1847) 2 Ph 372 at 374–375 (property advertised to be sold at auction without reserve; secret agreement for bidding on behalf of vendor; specific performance against purchaser not granted).

4　*R v Silverlock* [1894] 2 QB 766, CCR (where, in an indictment for obtaining a cheque by false pretences, a count which averred that a fraudulent newspaper advertisement for a housekeeper was a false pretence to Her Majesty's subjects was held to be good, although it did not allege that the false pretence was made to a particular person).

5　*Denton v Great Northern Rly Co* (1856) 5 E & B 860 (where an intending passenger was held to be entitled to recover for damage sustained as a result of the cancellation of a train mentioned in a railway timetable).

6    The principle is the same as that on which it has been held that, although a contract cannot be made with the world, an offer can be made to the public in general, which, when any person accepts the offer by acting upon it, becomes a contract with that person: *Carlill v Carbolic Smoke Ball Co* [1893] 1 QB 256 at 262, 268–269, CA; and see CONTRACT vol 22 (2012) PARA 240.

## 737.  Burden of proof as to representee.

It is incumbent on the party who asserts a right to relief in respect of a misrepresentation to allege, and, having so alleged, to prove, that he was the representee, or one of the representees[1]. The question whether the party claiming relief in respect of any misrepresentation was or was not a representee is a question of fact, and the subject, therefore, of evidence[2]; but the question whether there is any evidence of this fact, and also all questions which may arise whether, on the proved and admitted facts of the case, the representation was made to the alleged representee, are questions of law[3].

1    In *Behn v Kemble* (1859) 7 CBNS 260, the omission to aver that any representation was made to the plaintiff was one of several omissions which made a count in the declaration bad. As to proof see generally the cases cited in PARAS 733–736; and PARAS 738–739.
2    Such evidence was given in *Swift v Winterbotham* (1873) LR 8 QB 244; on appeal sub nom *Swift v Jewsbury* (1874) LR 9 QB 301, Ex Ch (banking practice). See also *Bedford v Bagshaw* (1859) 4 H & N 538; and PARA 739.
3    See *Gerhard v Bates* (1853) 2 E & B 476; *Bedford v Bagshaw* (1859) 4 H & N 538; *Swift v Winterbotham* (1873) LR 8 QB 244 (on appeal sub nom *Swift v Jewsbury* (1874) LR 9 QB 301, Ex Ch); *R v Aspinall* (1876) 2 QBD 48, CA; *R v Silverlock* [1894] 2 QB 766, CCR; *Andrews v Mockford* [1896] 1 QB 372, CA; *Salaman v Warner* (1891) 65 LT 132, CA.

## 738.  Proof where representation transmitted indirectly to alleged representee.

Where the alleged representee is an individual to whom the representation was not made directly, but passed on through a third person, proof is required of the representor's[1] intention (actual or presumptive) to influence and mislead him by the transmission of the representation through that channel[2].

1    As to who is a representor see PARAS 724–732.
2    *Longmeid v Holliday* (1851) 6 Exch 761 at 766; *Collins v Cave* (1860) 6 H & N 131 at 134, Ex Ch; *Barry v Croskey* (1861) 2 John & H 1 at 23–24; *Le Lievre v Gould* [1893] 1 QB 491 at 497–499, 502, CA, where it was said that *Cann v Willson* (1888) 39 ChD 39 (in which a contrary view had been expressed) was no longer law; *Edinburgh United Breweries Ltd v Molleson* [1894] AC 96 at 109–112, 114, HL. It has been pointed out, in discussing *Levy v Langridge* (1838) 4 M & W 337, Ex Ch (see PARA 735 ), that if a friend of the father or son had used the gun with the permission of either of them, or a stranger, without such permission, had used it, such a person would not have had a cause of action as a representee: see *Blakemore v Bristol and Exeter Rly Co* (1858) 8 E & B 1035 at 1052–1053; *Barry v Croskey* at 17–18, 24. It has been held to be an indictable offence to conspire to raise the price of public funds by false rumours: see *R v De Berenger* (1814) 3 M & S 67; *R v Aspinall* (1876) 2 QBD 48, CA. However, doubts have been expressed whether those who purchased funds on the faith of rumours could have been deemed representees in civil proceedings against the defendant: see *Barry v Croskey* at 18–19 per Wood V-C; *Andrews v Mockford* [1896] 1 QB 372 at 384–385, CA, per Rigby LJ. As to indictable conspiracy see CRIMINAL LAW vol 25 (2016) PARA 90. As to the circumstances in which a conspiracy gives rise to a civil right of action see generally TORT vol 97 (2015) PARA 712 et seq.

## 739.  Proof where representation made to class.

Where the representation is made to a class of which the alleged representee claims to be a member, it must be clearly established that the representee was one of the persons to whom the representor[1] contemplated that the representation should be made[2]. If it is found that, although a certain class of persons was intended to be deceived by the representation, that class was not the particular class to which the representee belongs, but a different or a smaller one, the burden of proof is not discharged; as, for instance, where a person claims to have been induced to purchase shares in the market by a document the primary function of which is to induce, not purchases in the market, but applications for allotment[3], or vice versa[4], or where a company complains of fraudulent statements made by its officers or agents, not to it, but to the public[5], or where a member of the public, as such, claims to have sustained injury in consequence of a misrepresentation addressed to a more limited class of which he is not a member[6].

1 As to who is a representor see PARAS 724–732.
2 *Bedford v Bagshaw* (1859) 4 H & N 538 at 548 per Pollock CB and Bramwell B, where the defendants had obtained a quotation of shares by misrepresentation and the plaintiff, having purchased shares in reliance on the quotation, was held entitled to recover. See, however, the criticism of the application of the principles to the facts of this particular case in *Peek v Gurney* (1873) LR 6 HL 377 at 396–397 per Lord Chelmsford.
3 As to the principle that the function of an offer document is normally exhausted when the shares are issued see COMPANIES vol 15A (2016) PARA 1273. As to misrepresentation in offer documents generally see COMPANIES vol 15A (2016) PARA 1259 et seq.
4 *Re National Patent Steam Fuel Co, ex p Worth* (1859) 28 LJ Ch 589.
5 *Vigers v Pike* (1842) 8 Cl & Fin 562 at 646–647, HL; *Overend & Gurney Co v Gibb* (1872) LR 5 HL 480 at 501; *Re Ambrose Lake Tin and Copper Mining Co, ex p Taylor, ex p Moss* (1880) 14 ChD 390 at 397, 399, CA.
6 *Blakemore v Bristol and Exeter Rly Co* (1858) 8 E & B 1035.

# (5) Misrepresentation

## (i) Falsity

### 740. What constitutes falsity.

A representation is deemed to have been false, and therefore a misrepresentation, if it was at the material date[1] false in substance and in fact. For the purpose of determining whether there has or has not been a misrepresentation at all, the representor's[2] knowledge, belief or other state of mind is immaterial[3], save in cases where the representation relates to the representor's state of mind, although his state of mind is of the utmost importance for the purpose of considering whether the misrepresentation was fraudulent[4].

1 As to the relevant date of falsity see PARAS 752–753.
2 As to who is a representor see PARAS 724–732.
3 Cf *R v Aspinall* (1876) 2 QBD 48 at 57, CA (although the defendant had a criminal intent and believed his statement was false, if in fact by chance the statement was not incorrect, the charge was not supported).
4 As to fraudulent misrepresentation see PARA 754 et seq.

### 741. Standard for determining falsity.

The standard by which the truth or falsity of a representation is to be judged is that if material circumstances are incorrectly stated, that is to say, if the discrepancy between the facts as represented and the actual facts is such as would be considered material by a reasonable representee[1], the representation is false; if otherwise, it is not. Another way of stating the rule is to say that substantial falsity is, on the one hand, necessary, and, on the other, adequate, to establish a misrepresentation[2]. It results from the foregoing statement that where the entire representation is a faithful picture or transcript of the essential facts, no falsity is established, even though there may have been any number of inaccuracies in unimportant details[3]. Conversely, if the general impression conveyed is false, the most punctilious and scrupulous accuracy in immaterial minutiae will not render the representation true[4].

1   As to who is a representee see PARAS 733–739.

2   The two forms of stating the rule were combined, as regards marine insurance, in the Marine Insurance Act 1906 s 20(4), which provided that a representation as to a matter of fact is true, if it be substantially correct, that is to say, if the difference between what is represented and what is actually correct would not be considered material by a prudent insurer. The Marine Insurance Act 1906 s 20 was repealed by the Insurance Act 2015 which now requires the insured under a non-commercial insurance contract to make to the insurer a fair presentation of the risk, in which every material misrepresentation as to a matter of fact must be substantially correct (s 3(3)(c)). This will be satisfied if a prudent insurer would not consider the difference between what is represented and what is actually correct to be material (s 7(5)). See further INSURANCE.

3   See *Pawson v Watson* (1778) 2 Cowp 785 at 788–790, where Lord Mansfield CJ insists on the distinction, in this respect, between a representation, where substantial falsity must be proved, and a warranty, where exact correspondence between the word and the fact is the very thing contracted for, and where, therefore, literal deviation constitutes a breach. Cf the observations in *Thomson v Weems* (1884) 9 App Cas 671 at 683–684, 689, HL; *Hambrough v Mutual Life Insurance Co of New York* (1895) 72 LT 140 at 141–142, CA. Illustrations of inaccuracies held or found to be not substantial or material are to be found in *Dobson v Sotheby* (1827) Mood & M 90 at 92; *Adamson v Evitt* (1830) 2 Russ & M 66 at 72; *Bartlett v Salmon* (1855) 6 De GM & G 33 at 42; *Denton v Macneil* (1866) LR 2 Eq 352; *Bear v Stevenson* (1874) 30 LT 177, PC; *McKeown v Boudard-Peveril Gear Co* (1896) 65 LJ Ch 735 at 736–737, CA; *Seddon v North Eastern Salt Co Ltd* [1905] 1 Ch 326 at 335.

4   See *Arnison v Smith* (1889) 41 ChD 348 at 370–373, CA; *Aaron's Reefs Ltd v Twiss* [1896] AC 273 at 281, HL.

## 742. Burden of proof of falsity.

Since in every form of proceeding based on misrepresentation a misrepresentation of some kind must be established, it follows that the burden of alleging and proving that degree of falsity which is required for the representation to be a misrepresentation rests, in every case, on the party who sets it up[1].

1   *Vernon v Keys* (1810) 12 East 632 (affd (1812) 4 Taunt 488, Ex Ch) (judgment arrested because no unequivocal falsehood averred); *Hallows v Fernie* (1868) 3 Ch App 467 at 477 (the precise representation must be distinctly stated); *Bodger v Nicholls* (1873) 28 LT 441 (no proof that the animal was not sound, even assuming an implied representation that it was); *Melbourne Banking Corpn v Brougham* (1882) 7 App Cas 307 at 314–315, PC; *Smith v Chadwick* (1884) 9 App Cas 187 at 190–192, HL; *Goldstein v Salvation Army Assurance Society* [1917] 2 KB 291 at 294 per Rowlatt J.

## 743. Questions of law and fact.

If the representation is contained in a document, or if, when orally made, its terms are admitted or proved, and there are no surrounding circumstances of such a nature as to suggest an artificial or special meaning, or the possibility of several meanings, the question of what sense should be attributed to it is a question of law to this extent, that it is for the court to say whether it is capable of the meaning alleged, or, on the other hand, whether it admits of any interpretation other than that alleged[1]. Subject to this principle, every question as to the sense which the representation in fact bore, or would have conveyed in the context in which it was made to the mind of the representee[2], is an issue of fact, as to which (in the case of a suggested special sense, at all events) evidence is admissible, and may even be necessary[3].

1   *Bellairs v Tucker* (1884) 13 QBD 562 at 575, DC; *Moore v Explosives Co Ltd* (1887) 56 LJQB 235, CA. See PARAS 710, 765.

2   As to who is a representee see PARAS 733–739.

3   *Woodhouse v Swift* (1836) 7 C & P 310; *Foster v Mentor Life Assurance Co* (1854) 3 E & B 48
    at 71–74, 77–81; *Clarke v Dickson* (1859) 6 CBNS 453 at 469–471; *Charlton v Hay* (1875) 32
    LT 96; *Smith v Chadwick* (1884) 9 App Cas 187 at 195, HL. As to evidence being admissible and
    necessary see *Sen Sen Co v Britten* [1899] 1 Ch 692 at 696 per Stirling J; *Re Carvino Trade Mark*
    [1911] 2 Ch 572 at 581, CA. See further PARA 765.

## (ii)  Construction of Representation

**744.  General principles of construction of representation.**
Whether there is a representation and its nature must be judged objectively
according to the impact that whatever is said may be expected to have on a
reasonable representee in the position and with the known characteristics of the
actual representee[1]. This is consistent with the basic principle of contractual
interpretation which relies on ascertaining the meaning which the document
would convey to a reasonable person having all the background knowledge which
would reasonably have been available to the parties in the situation in which they
were at the time of the contract[2]. In determining whether there has been an
express representation, and to what effect, the court considers what a reasonable
person would have understood from the words used in the context in which they
were used[3]. In determining what, if any, implied representation has been made, the
court has to perform a similar task, except that it has to consider what a
reasonable person would have inferred was being implicitly represented by the
representor's words and conduct in their context[4].

1   *MCI Worldcom International Inc v Primus Telecommunications Inc* [2004] EWCA Civ 957 at
    [30], [2004] 2 All ER (Comm) 833 at [30] per Mance LJ. See also *Raiffeisen Zentralbank
    Osterreich AG v Royal Bank of Scotland plc* [2010] EWHC 1392 (Comm) at [81]–[82], [2011] 1
    Lloyd's Rep 123 at [81]–[82], [2010] All ER (D) 111 (Jun).
2   See *Investors Compensation Scheme Ltd v West Bromwich Building Society, Investors
    Compensation Scheme Ltd v Hopkin & Sons (a firm), Alford v West Bromwich Building Society,
    Armitage v West Bromwich Building Society* [1998] 1 All ER 98 at 114, [1998] 1 WLR 896 at 912
    applied in *MCI Worldcom International Inc v Primus Telecommunications Inc* [2004] EWCA Civ
    957 at [30], [2004] 2 All ER (Comm) 833 at [30] by Mance LJ. As to interpretation of contracts
    generally see CONTRACT vol 22 (2012) PARA 357 et seq.
3   *IFE Fund SA v Goldman Sachs International* [2006] EWHC 2887 (Comm) at [50], [2007] 1
    Lloyd's Rep 264 at [50], [2006] All ER (D) 268 (Nov). See also *Raiffeisen Zentralbank Osterreich
    AG v Royal Bank of Scotland plc* [2010] EWHC 1392 (Comm) at [81]–[82], [2011] 1 Lloyd's Rep
    123 at [81]–[82], [2010] All ER (D) 111 (Jun).
4   *IFE Fund SA v Goldman Sachs International* [2006] EWHC 2887 (Comm) at [50], [2007] 1
    Lloyd's Rep 264 at [50], [2006] All ER (D) 268 (Nov). See also *Raiffeisen Zentralbank Osterreich
    AG v Royal Bank of Scotland plc* [2010] EWHC 1392 (Comm) at [81]–[82], [2011] 1 Lloyd's Rep
    123 at [81]–[82], [2010] All ER (D) 111 (Jun).

**745.  Unambiguous representations.**
If according to the ordinary rules of construction[1] a representation was
reasonably and naturally capable of bearing only one meaning, its truth or falsity
must normally be determined on the assumption that it bore that meaning[2]. In
general a representee[3] cannot establish falsity by putting an unnatural or strained
interpretation on the words used, although he may prove that in fact he so
understood them[4]; nor can a representor[5] escape liability by showing that he
intended his representation to bear some meaning other than the only meaning
which it was naturally capable of bearing[6].

However, there may be exceptional cases in which a representee can prove that
the representation, although true in the natural sense of the words used, was both
understood, and intended by the representor to be understood, in a sense other
than that which it naturally bears[7], or the representor can show that the

representation, although untrue in its natural meaning, was understood in some other meaning by the representee so that the representee was not deceived.

1  As to these rules in their application to written documents see DEEDS AND OTHER INSTRUMENTS vol 32 (2012) PARA 364 et seq.
2  See eg *Smith v Chadwick* (1884) 9 App Cas 187 at 190, HL, per the Earl of Selborne LC, and at 202 per Lord Bramwell.
3  As to who is a representee see PARAS 733–739.
4  *Schroeder v Mendl* (1877) 37 LT 452 at 453, CA, per Bramwell LJ. See also *Hallows v Fernie* (1868) 3 Ch App 467 at 476 (ambiguous representation).
5  As to who is a representor see PARAS 724–732.
6  See *Arnison v Smith* (1889) 41 ChD 348 at 368, CA. See also *Greenwood v Leather Shod Wheel Co* [1900] 1 Ch 421 at 434, CA (liability for misstatements in prospectuses); and COMPANIES vol 15A (2016) PARA 1262. As to misrepresentation in offer documents generally see COMPANIES vol 15A (2016) PARA 1259 et seq.
7  See eg *Moens v Heyworth* (1842) 10 M & W 147 at 158–159 per Alderson B (a true statement which is intended to be disbelieved may be a lie; *Piggott v Stratton* (1859) 1 De GF & J 33 at 50 (representation literally true, but intended to be understood as conveying more than its literal meaning).

## 746. Ambiguous representations.

Where the representation genuinely and reasonably can have more than one meaning, the representee[1] must show in which of the possible senses he understood it, and that in that sense it was false[2]. Where he is able so to do, the fact that it might have been understood in a different sense, which was not false, will not avail the representor[3]. Furthermore, the use of an ambiguous representation may be indicative of fraud on the part of the representor where it can be shown that the ambiguity was employed for the purpose of misleading the representee; so that, where it has in fact misled the representee, the representee may successfully maintain a claim for deceit, notwithstanding the fact that the representation might have been construed in a sense which was not false[4].

1  As to who is a representee see PARAS 733–739.
2  *Smith v Chadwick* (1884) 9 App Cas 187, HL. See also *Vernon v Keys* (1810) 12 East 632 at 636 per Lord Ellenborough CJ (affd (1812) 4 Taunt 488, Ex Ch); *Hallows v Fernie* (1868) 3 Ch App 467 at 487 per Lord Chelmsford LC; *Arkwright v Newbold* (1881) 17 ChD 301 at 324, CA, per Cotton LJ; *Capel & Co v Sim's Ships Compositions Co Ltd* (1888) 58 LT 807 at 808 per Kekewich J; *Bonham-Carter v SITU Ventures Ltd* [2012] EWHC 3589 (Ch) at [119], [2012] All ER (D) 209 (Dec). As to similar rules applicable to the doctrine of estoppel by representation see ESTOPPEL vol 47 (2014) PARA 307.
3  As to who is a representor see PARAS 724–732.
4  *Smith v Chadwick* (1884) 9 App Cas 187 at 201, HL, per Lord Blackburn ('if, with intent to lead the plaintiff to act upon it, they put forth a statement which they know may bear two meanings, one of which is false to their knowledge, and thereby the plaintiff, putting that meaning upon it, is misled, I do not think they could escape by saying he ought to have put the other. If they palter with him, in a double sense, it may be that they lie like truth, but I think they lie, and it is a fraud'); *Low v Bouverie* [1891] 3 Ch 82 at 113, CA, per Kay LJ. See also *Lee v Jones* (1864) 17 CBNS 482 at 496; *Goose v Wilson, Sandford & Co* [2001] Lloyd's Rep PN 189, [2000] All ER (D) 324, CA. As to claims for deceit see PARA 788 et seq.

## (iii)  Falsity by Omission, Silence or Inaction

## 747. When silence constitutes falsity.

There are two main classes of case in which reticence may contribute to establish a misrepresentation: (1) where known material qualifications of an absolute statement are omitted[1]; and (2) where the circumstances raise a duty on the representor[2] to state certain matters, if they exist, and where, therefore, the representee[3] is entitled as against the representor to infer their non-existence from the representor's silence as to them[4].

1  See PARA 748.
2  As to who is a representor see PARAS 724–732.
3  As to who is a representee see PARAS 733–739.
4  See PARAS 749–750. As to the corresponding rules which apply in relation to estoppel by representation see ESTOPPEL vol 47 (2014) PARA 307.

### 748. Omission of qualifications.

Any omission from a statement of reference to qualifying or supplementary facts and circumstances, such as to make what is stated so one-sided, or so absolute, a version of the entirety of the facts as to amount to a travesty, and not an accurate summary, is enough to establish a misrepresentation[1]. A statement which omits such matters is a lie in one of its most dangerous and insidious forms[2]. However, mere incompleteness is not a factor in misrepresentation; it must always be proved clearly that it rendered what was stated fallacious and false[3].

1  *Oakes v Turquand and Harding* (1867) LR 2 HL 325 at 342 per Lord Chelmsford; *Peek v Gurney* (1873) LR 6 HL 377 at 403 per Lord Cairns, where the process in question is characterised as 'such a partial and fragmentary statement of fact as that the withholding of that which is not stated makes that which is stated absolutely false'; *Arkwright v Newbold* (1881) 17 ChD 301 at 318, CA. See also *R v Lord Kylsant* [1932] 1 KB 442, CCA; *R v Bishirgian* [1936] 1 All ER 586, 25 Cr App Rep 176, CCA; *Curtis v Chemical Cleaning and Dyeing Co Ltd* [1951] 1 KB 805, [1951] 1 All ER 631, CA; *Clinicare Ltd v Orchard Homes and Developments Ltd* [2004] EWHC 1694 (QB), [2004] All ER (D) 244 (Jul).
   As to the general principles of construction of a representation see PARA 744. The rules of construction have been applied rigorously to: (1) cases of sales and purchases (*Coverley v Burrell* (1821) 5 B & Ald 257; *Brandling v Plummer* (1854) 2 Drew 427; *Dimmock v Hallett* (1866) 2 Ch App 21; *Denny v Hancock* (1870) 6 Ch App 1; *Jones v Rimmer* (1880) 14 ChD 588 at 591, CA; *Nottingham Patent Brick and Tile Co v Butler* (1886) 16 QBD 778, CA; *Re Davis and Cavey* (1888) 40 ChD 601 at 605; *Hepworth v Pickles* [1900] 1 Ch 108 at 111–112; *Baker v Moss* (1902) 66 JP 360; *Mahomed Kala Mea v Harperink* (1908) 25 TLR 180, PC); (2) offer documents of companies (see COMPANIES vol 15A (2016) PARA 1259 et seq); (3) cases of representation as to the credit and dealings of a third person (*Tapp v Lee* (1803) 3 Bos & P 367; *Ames v Milward* (1818) 8 Taunt 637; *Lee v Jones* (1864) 17 CBNS 482 at 498); and (4) compromises (*Brooke v Lord Mostyn* (1864) 2 De GJ & Sm 373 (revsd, without affecting the law as laid down in the court below, sub nom *Mostyn v Brooke* (1866) LR 4 HL 304); *Gilbert v Endean* (1878) 9 ChD 259 at 268, 270, CA). See also eg *Re Mount Morgan (West) Gold Mine Ltd, ex p West* (1887) 56 LT 622 at 624 (document quoted in prospectus; omission of important qualification upon statement quoted). As to statements as to the effect of documents see PARAS 711–712.
2  See *Tapp v Lee* (1803) 3 Bos & P 367 at 371 per Chambre J; *Foster v Charles* (1830) 6 Bing 396 at 403 per Park J.
3  *Re Coal Economising Gas Co, Gover's Case* (1875) 1 ChD 182 at 199, CA, per Brett J; *McKeown v Boudard-Peveril Gear Co* (1896) 65 LJ Ch 735 at 736, CA, per Rigby LJ; *Re Christineville Rubber Estates Ltd* (1911) 28 TLR 38.

### 749. When non-disclosure involves misrepresentation.

There is another type of reticence or inaction which may, in certain circumstances, and where certain relations exist between the parties, amount to a representation of the non-existence of the matters as to which silence has been observed. Where a person has said something to another, a duty may at once arise to say more, and if he fails to discharge this duty his reticence from that point becomes an implied misrepresentation, although complete silence throughout the transaction would not have amounted to, or have afforded any evidence of, misrepresentation, or even of actionable non-disclosure[1]. This duty may arise in the case of a continuing representation[2]. There are other cases where, in the course of the negotiations, the representor lets fall something which, whether he so intended or not, he at once perceives, or ought to perceive, to be exercising a delusive influence on the representee's mind, and where, by not correcting the delusion, he is deemed to confirm and perpetuate it, and so to misrepresent[3].

Again, in certain circumstances raising a duty to declare the whole truth, a misrepresentation may be made by silence, if the representor fails to contradict a statement, erroneous to his knowledge, which has been made to him by the representee, or which he knows to have been made by, or to, the representee to, or by, a third person. Standing by, and inaction and reticence, in such circumstances may amount either to a tacit adoption by the person keeping silence of another's misrepresentation as his own, or a tacit confirmation of another's error as truth[4].

Lastly, there are certain cases which are usually classed as belonging rather to the province of non-disclosure, pure and simple, than to that of misrepresentation proper, which, nevertheless, have been regarded as illustrations of positive, though implied, misrepresentation[5].

1   *Stikeman v Dawson* (1847) 1 De G & Sm 90 at 104; *Walters v Morgan* (1861) 3 De GF & J 718 at 723–724; *Central Rly Co of Venezuela (Directors etc) v Kisch* (1867) LR 2 HL 99 at 114 (the suppression of a fact will often amount to a misrepresentation); *Davies v London and Provincial Marine Insurance Co* (1878) 8 ChD 469 at 475 per Fry J (in relation to contracts other than contracts requiring good faith as a matter of law, the duty of disclosure may arise from circumstances which occur during the negotiation, eg the subsequent discovery by the representor that what he had originally stated was false at the time, or the supervening of facts rendering false what was originally true); *Arkwright v Newbold* (1880) 17 ChD 301 at 310–311 per Fry J (revsd on appeal on the facts of the case (1881) 17 ChD 301 at 313, CA); *Coaks v Boswell* (1886) 11 App Cas 232 at 236, HL, per Lord Selborne LC (party impliedly undertakes or professes to communicate facts as to which he has been silent, if he makes some other communication which, without the addition of those facts, would be necessarily, or naturally and probably, misleading); *Seaton v Heath* [1899] 1 QB 782 at 792, CA (revsd sub nom *Seaton v Burnand* [1900] AC 135, HL, but not on any ground affecting the proposition that misrepresentation may undoubtedly be made by concealment). See also *With v O'Flanagan* [1936] Ch 575, [1936] 1 All ER 727, CA (there is a duty to communicate a change of circumstances during negotiations); *Geest plc v Fyffes plc* [1999] 1 All ER (Comm) 672 (the potential beneficiary of an indemnity contract is under a duty not to make implied misrepresentations; a surety is not entitled to assume that the beneficiary informed him of the true state of facts as he had made specific requests for information of the beneficiary). If non-disclosure is fraudulent, damages can be awarded on the basis of the tort of deceit: *HIH Casualty and General Insurance Ltd v Chase Manhattan Bank* [2001] EWCA Civ 1250, [2001] 2 Lloyd's Rep 483 at 163; affd on this point [2003] UKHL 6, [2003] 1 All ER (Comm) 349, [2003] Lloyd's Rep IR 230.
     As to where a representor corrects a misrepresentation see PARA 801. As to who is a representor see PARAS 724–732.

2   As to continuing representations see PARA 753. As to the circumstances in which failure to discharge the duty may amount to fraud see PARA 759.

3   *Nicholson v Hooper* (1838) 4 My & Cr 179 at 185–186. As to who is a representee see PARAS 733–739.

4   *Pilmore v Hood* (1838) 5 Bing NC 97 at 107; *North British Insurance Co v Lloyd* (1854) 10 Exch 523 at 529 (one who knows that a false statement is being made to the representee by a third person, and allows it in silence, is himself misrepresenting); *Hardman v Booth* (1863) 1 H & C 803; *Cundy v Lindsay* (1878) 3 App Cas 459 at 465 per Lord Cairns LC (mistake in addressing letters left uncorrected by recipient, although it indicated that the persons who sent the letters believed themselves to be dealing with a person other than the recipient).

5   *Hamilton v Watson* (1845) 12 Cl & Fin 109 at 119, HL; *Lee v Jones* (1864) 17 CBNS 482 at 500, 503–504; *Phillips v Foxall* (1872) LR 7 QB 666 at 679 (these were all suretyship cases). See also *Evans v Edmonds* (1853) 13 CB 777 at 784–785 (separation deed); *Cavendish-Bentinck v Fenn* (1887) 12 App Cas 652 at 671 per Lord Macnaghten (concealment by agent for purchaser of his interest in property to be purchased would have amounted to representation that he had no interest). There are similar rules in connection with the law relating to representation by estoppel:

see ESTOPPEL. As to whether non-disclosure, where there is a duty to disclose, may result in damages see PARA 750.

## 750. When silence is not misrepresentation.

Except as already stated[1], mere silence or inaction, however morally reprehensible it may be[2], neither constitutes, nor is equivalent or contributory to, misrepresentation.

In a case where a positive duty of disclosure exists by reason of the particular relationship of the parties, or the fact that the transaction is uberrimae fidei, the transaction may be voidable on the ground of non-disclosure even though the non-disclosure does not amount to misrepresentation[3]. It has been held previously that mere non-disclosure does not give a right to damages. However, it may now be that where there is a duty to disclose, non-disclosure is tantamount to an implied representation and may result in damages[4].

Where the circumstances are such that no such positive duty of disclosure exists, silence which does not make what is stated false[5], or tacit acquiescence in the self-deception of another, if nothing is said or done either to create or foster the delusion, does not amount to misrepresentation[6]. However, the dropping of a single word or the making of a single gesture in such a case may amount to evidence of a misrepresentation[7].

1　See PARAS 747–749.
2　As to the distinction between the ethical and the legal standard see *Fox v Mackreth* (1791) 2 Cox Eq Cas 320, HL; *Smith v Hughes* (1871) LR 6 QB 597 at 603–604, 607; *Marnham v Weaver* (1899) 80 LT 412 at 413.
3　As to the cases in which such a duty exists see PARA 701.
4　See *Conlon v Simms* [2006] EWHC 401 (Ch) at [201] et seq, [2006] 2 All ER 1024 at [201] et seq, [2006] All ER (D) 134 (Mar); affd [2006] EWCA Civ 1749 at [129]–[130], [2007] 3 All ER 802 at [129]–[130], [2008] 1 WLR 484 at [129]–[130].
5　See PARA 749.
6　This principle, that silence as to matters which there is no duty to disclose can never be an implied representation, is expressed, applied or illustrated in a variety of forms: see eg *Fox v Mackreth* (1791) 2 Cox Eq Cas 320 at 321, HL (by way of illustration, the case was cited of a purchase of land, the purchaser knowing of a mine under it; in such a case he is under no obligation to disclose this fact to the vendor); *Turner v Harvey* (1821) Jac 169 at 178 per Lord Eldon LC (the 'mine' illustration figures again here); *Keates v Earl Cadogan* (1851) 10 CB 591; *Horsfall v Thomas* (1862) 1 H & C 90 at 100; *Ranger v Great Western Rly Co* (1854) 5 HL Cas 72 at 86–87 (nature of material to be excavated by contractor); *Phillips v Homfray* (1871) 6 Ch App 770 at 779 (illustration of purchase of picture by expert from one ignorant of its artistic value); *Smith v Hughes* (1871) LR 6 QB 597 at 603–604, 607, 610–611 (non-correction of a self-induced delusion of purchaser is not misrepresentation by vendor; the 'mine' illustration figures again here); *Coaks v Boswell* (1886) 11 App Cas 232 at 235–236, HL; *Marnham v Weaver* (1899) 80 LT 412 at 412–413 (if a third person knows of, but is not a party to, a deceit and owes no legal duty to the party deceived, he does not render himself liable to that party if he merely preserves silence); *Royal Bank of Scotland v Greenshields* 1914 SC 259, Ct of Sess; cf *Bell v Lever Bros Ltd* [1932] AC 161 at 227, HL, per Lord Atkin.
　　The opinion of Lord Ellenborough CJ in the nisi prius case of *Hill v Gray* (1816) 1 Stark 434, if correctly and fully reported, is directly contrary to the principle described above. Although never formally overruled, this case has been disapproved (see *Keates v Earl Cadogan* at 600 per Jervis CJ; *Peek v Gurney* (1873) LR 6 HL 377 at 390–391 per Lord Chelmsford LC), and cannot now be accepted as law.
7　See *Turner v Harvey* (1821) Jac 169 at 178 per Lord Eldon LC; *Walters v Morgan* (1861) 3 De GF & J 718 at 723–724; *Thompson v Lambert* (1868) 17 WR 111 at 113; *Phillips v Homfray* (1871) 6 Ch App 770 at 777–780; *Marnham v Weaver* (1899) 80 LT 412, where the party charged was not a mere passive spectator of the deceit practised by another, but actively assisted in it.

## (iv) Representation Composed of Several Statements

**751. Construction of complex representation.**

Where the representation was compounded of several statements contained in one document (such as a prospectus or particulars of sale), or in a number of documents, or was made at one interview or series of interviews, the general rule of construction is that all the statements or documents must be considered in their entirety and in their bearing on one another, the primary object being to ascertain whether the conjoint effect of the whole complex representation is true or false of the whole of the facts[1].

However, this general rule is subject to the qualification that if one out of the several statements or documents, not inseparably nor necessarily bound up with the others, has a clear and definite meaning by itself, and in that meaning is false or true, the representee[2] or representor[3], as the case may be, is entitled to rely on this falsity or truth respectively, and it is no answer, in the former case, to say that if the representee had examined the other statements and documents he might have discovered something which would have led him to the truth, or, in the latter, to point to the imperfection and incompleteness of some other statement which does not purport to do more than refer to the true statement, such as an index or marginal note[4].

1   Illustrations of the rule in its application to a number of statements contained in one document, such as a prospectus, are *Cargill v Bower* (1878) 10 ChD 502 at 516; *Re Metropolitan Coal Consumers' Association Ltd, Wainwright's Case* (1890) 63 LT 429, CA; *Aaron's Reefs v Twiss* [1896] AC 273 at 281, HL, per Lord Halsbury LC; *Components' Tube Co v Naylor* [1900] 2 IR 1, where one of the questions held to have been properly left to the jury was whether the prospectus as a whole was substantially misleading and calculated to deceive; *Mair v Rio Grande Rubber Estates Ltd* [1913] AC 853, HL (prospectus and report set out in it); *Re Pacaya Rubber and Produce Co Ltd, Burns' Application* [1914] 1 Ch 542 (similar case); *R v Lord Kylsant* [1932] 1 KB 442, CCA; *R v Bishirgian* [1936] 1 All ER 586, CCA; *Atlantic Estates plc v Ezekiel* [1991] 2 EGLR 202 CA (particulars in auction catalogue). As to misrepresentation in offer documents generally see COMPANIES vol 15A (2016) PARA 1259 et seq.

     In the following cases the rule was applied to the interpretation of the conjoint effect of a number of documents: *Denny v Hancock* (1870) 6 Ch App 1 (particulars of sale and plan); *Cargill v Bower* (prospectus and relative documents); *Re Arnold, Arnold v Arnold* (1880) 14 ChD 270, CA (particulars of sale and plan); *Drincqbier v Wood* [1899] 1 Ch 393 (prospectus and covering letter); *Andrews v Mockford* [1896] 1 QB 372, CA (prospectus and a following telegram published in the financial papers to strengthen the effect of the prospectus); *Oelkers v Ellis* [1914] 2 KB 139 at 147–148 (bundle of correspondence). As to a number of statements in particulars of sale see *Brandling v Plummer* (1854) 2 Drew 427 at 430–431. In all these cases, except *Cargill v Bower*, the result of the examination of the entirety of the representations or documents was to show either that the whole was as false as each part, and each part as false as the whole, or that statements which, severally and separatim, were true, produced nevertheless, when taken together, a totally false impression. In *Cargill v Bower*, on the other hand, statements and documents, inaccurate or incomplete when construed singly, were held, in their conjoint effect, to be a substantially true transcript of the facts. So also in *Bartlett v Salmon* (1855) 6 De GM & G 33 at 42.

2   As to who is a representee see PARAS 733–739.

3   As to who is a representor see PARAS 724–732.

4   *Re Arnold, Arnold v Arnold* (1880) 14 ChD 270 at 282, 284, CA, is an example of the former type of case; and *Moore v Explosives Co* (1887) 56 LJQB 235, CA, illustrates the latter. As to the former see further PARA 801.

## (v) Relevant Date of Falsity

### 752. When falsity must have existed.

The representation must be shown to have been false at the date when the representee[1] altered his position because of it[2].

1 As to who is a representee see PARAS 733–739.
2 *Briess v Woolley* [1954] AC 333 at 354, [1954] 1 All ER 909 at 918, HL, per Lord Tucker.

### 753. Continuing representations.

Where there is an appreciable interval between the date when the representation is made and the date when the representee[1] alters his position on the faith of the representation, and the representation relates to an existing state of things, the representor[2] is deemed to be repeating his representation at every successive moment during the interval unless he withdraws or modifies it by timely notice to the representee in the meantime[3]. It follows that if, during the intervening period, events happen by reason of which the representation is not substantially in accordance with the facts existing at the time when the representee acts upon it, though it was in accordance with the facts existing when it was made, a misrepresentation is established[4]. The circumstances in which such a misrepresentation will amount to a fraudulent misrepresentation are considered elsewhere[5]. Conversely, where a representation which was false when made becomes, in virtue of supervening facts, true when acted upon, there is no falsity at the only material date, and therefore no misrepresentation[6].

1 As to who is a representee see PARAS 733–739.
2 As to who is a representor see PARAS 724–732.
3 *Briess v Woolley* [1954] AC 333 at 354, [1954] 1 All ER 909 at 918, HL, per Lord Tucker. See also *Smith v Kay* (1859) 7 HL Cas 750 at 769 (allegation of misrepresentation at time when representee executed a bond held to be supported by evidence of misrepresentation made before that time, the misrepresentation being a continuing misrepresentation). As to the representor's right to revoke or modify his representation at any time during the period before the representee acts on it see *Holland v Manchester and Liverpool District Banking Co Ltd* (1909) 25 TLR 386 (erroneous entry in pass-book can be set right by banker at any time before customer draws upon supposed balance, but unless and until so corrected, is a continuing representation).
   Similar principles are applicable to representations for the purpose of estoppel (see ESTOPPEL vol 47 (2014) PARA 355 et seq); and, in cases of contract, to a continuing offer (see *Carlill v Carbolic Smoke Ball Co* [1893] 1 QB 256 at 262, CA, per Lindley LJ; and CONTRACT vol 22 (2012) PARA 240). As to the duty to communicate a change of circumstances during negotiations see PARAS 749, 759. As to where a representor corrects a misrepresentation see PARA 801.
4 *Turner v Harvey* (1821) Jac 169; *Re Scottish Petroleum Co, Anderson's Case* (1881) 17 ChD 373 at 377, distinguishing *Hallows v Fernie* (1868) 3 Ch App 467; *Re Scottish Petroleum Co* (1883) 23 ChD 413 at 432, 435, 438, CA; *Whurr v Devenish* (1904) 20 TLR 385, where a horse was offered for sale by auction, and described as the representor's property, but during the progress of the auction was sold privately, notwithstanding which the representor authorised the auction sale to go on; *With v O'Flanagan* [1936] Ch 575, [1936] 1 All ER 727, CA; *Spice Girls Ltd v Aprilia World Service BV* [2002] EWCA Civ 15, [2002] EMLR 510. See also *HB Nickerson & Sons Ltd v Wooldridge* (1980) 115 DLR (3d) 97, NS CA (Canadian employer failing to advise potential employee of change in Canadian regulations requiring substantial Canadian experience for professional qualifications); *Jones v Dumbrell* [1981] VR 199. Cf the insurance cases where there is a material alteration in the health of the assured before completion of the contract: see INSURANCE vol 60 (2018) PARA 88.
   On the other hand, the representation, even though it continues during the whole of the interval between the making of the representation and the alteration of the representee's position, does not last beyond it. The retirement of directors (described as such in a prospectus) after allotment could not make the prospectus false even as a continuing representation: see *Hallows v Fernie* at 472. As to misrepresentation in offer documents generally see COMPANIES vol 15A (2016) PARA 1259 et seq. A representation made as a matter of inducement to enter into a contract

is, depending on the facts of the individual case, to be treated as a continuing representation: *Cramaso LLP v Ogilvie-Grant (Earl of Seafield)* [2014] UKSC 9, [2014] AC 1093, [2014] 1 All ER (Comm) 830.

The obligation to correct the representation subsequently discovered to be false applies only to the representor: *AIC Ltd v ITS Testing Services (UK) Ltd; The Kriti Palm* [2006] EWCA Civ 1601, [2007] 1 All ER (Comm) 667, [2007] 1 Lloyd's Rep 555.

5   See PARA 754 et seq.

6   *Ship v Crosskill* (1870) LR 10 Eq 73 at 85–86; cf *Tofts v Pearl Life Assurance Co Ltd* [1915] 1 KB 189 at 194, CA.

## (6)  Fraudulent Misrepresentation

### 754.  Significance of fraudulent misrepresentation.

Although innocent misrepresentation[1] constitutes a ground for the rescission[2] of a contract or other binding transaction into which the representee[3] has been induced to enter by the misrepresentation, and a defence in any proceedings brought against him to enforce the contract or transaction, a person complaining of having been misled by a misrepresentation to his injury cannot recover damages[4] from the representor[5] in respect of the injury suffered unless he can show that: (1) the representation was not only false but fraudulent[6]; or (2) it was negligent[7]; or (3) it was made by another party to the contract who is unable to prove that he had reasonable ground to believe and did believe that the facts represented were true[8].

Untruth in fact does not of itself necessarily import a dishonest mind[9]. Something more must be shown in order to render a misrepresentation fraudulent[10].

1   As to when a misrepresentation is innocent see PARA 761.

2   As to claims for rescission see PARA 811 et seq.

3   As to who is a representee see PARAS 733–739.

4   As to a claim for damages see PARA 789 et seq.

5   As to who is a representor see PARAS 724–732.

6   See PARAS 701, 755–760. As to claims for deceit see PARA 788 et seq.

7   See *Hedley Byrne & Co Ltd v Heller & Partners Ltd* [1964] AC 465, [1963] 2 All ER 575, HL; PARAS 762, 797–799; and NEGLIGENCE vol 78 (2018) PARA 13. As to the liability of a director for company's negligent misstatement or misrepresentation see *Williams v Natural Life Health Foods Ltd* [1998] 2 All ER 577, [1998] 1 WLR 830, HL; COMPANIES vol 14 (2016) PARA 633; and NEGLIGENCE vol 78 (2018) PARA 15.

8   See the Misrepresentation Act 1967 s 2(1); and PARA 800.

9   Every deceit comprehends a lie, but deceit is more than a lie: *Pasley v Freeman* (1789) 3 Term Rep 51 at 56 per Buller J. Conversely, an intention to deceive does not necessarily involve that the statement made was untrue in fact: see PARAS 740–743.

10  *Derry v Peek* (1889) 14 App Cas 337 at 359, HL, per Lord Herschell. As to the elements in a representation which will render it fraudulent see PARA 756.

### 755.  Meaning of 'fraud'.

'Fraud', in connection with representations upon which it is sought to base a claim for deceit, has the same meaning in both a court of law and a court of equity[1]. In this connection there is no distinction between legal and equitable fraud[2], or between legal fraud and moral fraud[3], and no such thing as imputed or constructive fraud, if and so far as these expressions serve to suggest that any statement may be construed as fraudulent for the purposes of founding a claim for deceit, although the statement is not characterised by actual fraud, as the law has defined it[4] for this purpose.

1   See *Nocton v Lord Ashburton* [1914] AC 932 at 953–954, HL, per Viscount Haldane LC. As to claims for deceit see PARA 788 et seq.

2   *Le Lievre v Gould* [1893] 1 QB 491 at 498, CA; cf *Derry v Peek* (1889) 14 App Cas 337, HL; *Tharp v Tharp* [1916] 1 Ch 142 at 151 per Neville J. The term 'legal fraud' appears to have been first used in *Haycraft v Creasy* (1801) 2 East 92 at 103.

3   *Weir v Bell* (1878) 3 Ex D 238 at 243, CA; *Derry v Peek* (1889) 14 App Cas 337 at 346, 359–380, HL; *Nocton v Lord Ashburton* [1914] AC 932 at 954, HL, per Viscount Haldane LC. However, there are certain cases in which equity affords a remedy other than a claim for deceit and which, although classified in equity as cases of fraud, do not necessarily import the element of dolus malus, such as cases arising out of breach of special duty: see *Nocton v Lord Ashburton* at 952–956 per Viscount Haldane LC; *Robinson v National Bank of Scotland* 1916 SC 154, HL. See also EQUITABLE JURISDICTION vol 47 (2014) PARA 12 et seq. As to liability for careless statements see *Hedley Byrne & Co Ltd v Heller & Partners Ltd* [1964] AC 465, [1963] 2 All ER 575, HL; PARAS 762–763, 797–799; and NEGLIGENCE vol 78 (2018) PARA 13. As to the liability of a director for company's negligent misstatement or misrepresentation see *Williams v Natural Life Health Foods Ltd* [1998] 2 All ER 577, [1998] 1 WLR 830, HL; COMPANIES vol 14 (2016) PARA 633; and NEGLIGENCE vol 78 (2018) PARA 15.

4   See PARA 756.

## 756. What constitutes fraud.

Not only is a misrepresentation fraudulent if it was known or believed by the representor[1] to be false when made, but mere non-belief in the truth is also indicative of fraud[2]. Thus whenever a person makes a false statement which he does not actually and honestly believe to be true, for purposes of civil liability that statement is as fraudulent as if he had stated that which he did not know to be true, or knew or believed to be false[3]. Proof of absence of actual and honest belief is all that is necessary to satisfy the requirements of the law, whether the representation has been made recklessly or deliberately; indifference or recklessness on the part of the representor as to the truth or falsity of the representation[4] affords merely an instance of absence of such a belief.

A representor will not, however, be fraudulent if he believed the statement to be true in the sense in which he understood it, provided that was a meaning which might reasonably be attached to it, even though the court later holds that the statement objectively bears another meaning, which the representor did not believe[5].

1   As to who is a representor see PARAS 724–732.

2   *Taylor v Ashton* (1843) 11 M & W 401 at 415 per Parke B ('it is not necessary to show that the defendants knew the fact to be untrue, if they stated a fact which was untrue for a fraudulent purpose, they at the same time not believing that fact to be true, in that case it would be both a legal and moral fraud'. For the second 'untrue', the report has 'true'; but this seems to be a clerical error and was so treated in *Derry v Peek* (1889) 14 App Cas 337 at 367, HL, per Lord Herschell).

    This proposition has been reasserted in a variety of forms and in a variety of circumstances: see eg *Evans v Edmonds* (1853) 13 CB 777 at 786; *Rawlins v Wickham* (1858) 3 De G & J 304 at 316–317; *Behn v Burness* (1863) 3 B & S 751 at 753, Ex Ch; *Reese River Silver Mining Co v Smith* (1869) LR 4 HL 64 at 79–80 per Lord Cairns (explained in *Derry v Peek* at 370–371 per Lord Herschell); *Hart v Swaine* (1877) 7 ChD 42 at 46–47; *Arkwright v Newbold* (1881) 17 ChD 301 at 320, CA; *Leddell v McDougal* (1881) 29 WR 403, CA; *Edgington v Fitzmaurice* (1885) 29 ChD 459 at 465–466, 480–482, CA; *Derry v Peek* at 374; *Angus v Clifford* [1891] 2 Ch 449 at 471, CA; *Pritty v Child* (1902) 71 LJKB 512 at 514 per Channell J.

3   See *Derry v Peek* (1889) 14 App Cas 337 at 374, HL, per Lord Herschell (fraud is proved when it is shown that a false representation has been made: (1) knowingly; or (2) without belief in its truth; or (3) recklessly, careless whether it be true or false; the third case being but an instance of the second). See also *AIC Ltd v ITS Testing Services (UK) Ltd, The Kriti Palm* [2006] EWCA Civ 1601 at [253], [2007] 1 All ER (Comm) 667 at [253], [2007] 1 Lloyd's Rep 555 at [253]; *Cheltenham Borough Council v Laird* [2009] EWHC 1253 (QB), [2009] IRLR 621. See also

*Standard Chartered Bank v Pakistan National Shipping Corpn (No 2)* [2000] 1 Lloyd's Rep 218, [2000] 1 All ER (Comm) 1, CA (revsd on another point [2002] UKHL 43, [2003] 1 AC 959, [2002] 2 All ER (Comm) 931) (it is not necessary, for the tort of deceit to be made out, to show that the maker of the false representation has been 'dishonest' in the sense that the word is used in criminal law; the necessary intention is that the false statement should be acted upon by the person to whom it was addressed) See *Otkritie International Investment Management Ltd v Urumov* [2014] EWHC 191 (Comm), [2014] All ER (D) 111 (Feb) (financial trader made false representations to financial companies knowing that they were false).

4   See eg *Behn v Burness* (1863) 3 B & S 751 at 753, Ex Ch; *Arkwright v Newbold* (1881) 17 ChD 301 at 320, CA; *Edgington v Fitzmaurice* (1885) 29 ChD 459 at 465–466, 480–482, CA; *Angus v Clifford* [1891] 2 Ch 449 at 471, CA; *Heilbut, Symons & Co v Buckleton* [1913] AC 30 at 49, HL, per Moulton LJ.

5   *Akerhielm v De Mare* [1959] AC 789, [1959] 3 All ER 485, PC; *Gross v Lewis Hillman Ltd* [1970] Ch 445, [1969] 3 All ER 1476, CA.

## 757.   Standard of proof and questions of law and fact.

In determining whether a representation was made fraudulently, the standard of proof applicable is the civil standard of balance of probability and not the criminal standard of proof beyond reasonable doubt, but the degree of probability required to establish proof may vary according to the gravity of the allegation to be proved[1]. The question whether there is any evidence to support an allegation that a representation made was fraudulent is a question of law[2]. Subject to this, the question whether a false representation was actually fraudulent is, in every case, a question of fact[3].

1   *Hornal v Neuberger Products Ltd* [1957] 1 QB 247, [1956] 3 All ER 970, CA. As to the civil standard of proof see CIVIL PROCEDURE vol 12 (2015) PARA 708.

   The fact that fraud is a very serious allegation may be relevant to the inherent probabilities of its occurrence, but it does not affect the standard of proof: *Cheltenham Borough Council v Laird* [2009] EWHC 1253 (QB) at [311], [2009] IRLR 621 at [311].

2   See eg *Ludgater v Love* (1881) 44 LT 694, CA; *Smith v Chadwick* (1884) 9 App Cas 187 at 193, HL.

3   See eg *Barwick v English Joint Stock Bank* (1867) LR 2 Exch 259 at 264, Ex Ch; *Ludgater v Love* (1881) 44 LT 694 at 695, CA, per Brett LJ (in the course of counsel's argument); *Smith v Chadwick* (1884) 9 App Cas 187 at 193, HL.

## 758.   Irrelevancy of representor's motive.

It follows from the meaning of fraudulent misrepresentation[1] that, given absence of actual and honest belief by the representor[2] in the truth of the misrepresentation, his motive in making the misrepresentation is wholly irrelevant[3]. It may be that he intended to injure the representee[4] without benefiting himself, or to benefit himself without injuring the representee[5]; it may be that he did not intend to do either, but solely to benefit a third person[6], or even the representee himself[7], or otherwise to do right[8]. Lastly, he may have acted with no intelligible or rational motive whatsoever and told a lie from mere caprice, mischievousness or stupidity[9]. In all these cases, provided that there was an absence of actual and honest belief in the truth of his assertion, the misrepresentation is accounted fraudulent, and no proof of any wicked or other intention (other than an intention to induce) on the part of the representor is required by the law; or if it is necessary to establish an intention to deceive or injure, that intention is immediately and irrebuttably presumed in law from the mere act of making the misrepresentation without such belief[10].

1   See PARAS 755–756.

2   As to who is a representor see PARAS 724–732.

3	*Stone v Compton* (1838) 5 Bing NC 142 at 155–156; *Crawshay v Thompson* (1842) 4 Man & G
	357 at 382; *Milne v Marwood* (1855) 15 CB 778 at 783; *Denton v Great Northern Rly Co* (1856)
	5 E & B 860; *Peek v Gurney* (1873) LR 6 HL 377 at 409–410; *Arnison v Smith* (1889) 41 ChD
	348 at 368, 372–373, CA; *Derry v Peek* (1889) 14 App Cas 337 at 374, HL; *United Motor Finance
	Co v Addison & Co Ltd* [1937] 1 All ER 425, PC. There must, of course, be an intention to induce:
	see PARA 771 et seq.
4	As to who is a representee see PARAS 733–739.
5	*Evans v Edmonds* (1853) 13 CB 777 at 786; *Armstrong v Jackson* [1917] 2 KB 822 at 827 per
	McCardie J; *Janvier v Sweeney* [1919] 2 KB 316, CA.
6	*Pasley v Freeman* (1789) 3 Term Rep 51 at 58 per Buller J (if A by fraud and deceit cheats B out
	of £1,000, it makes no difference to B whether A, or any other person, pockets that £1,000). See
	also *Foster v Charles* (1830) 7 Bing 105 at 106–107; *Polhill v Walter* (1832) 3 B & Ad 114 at
	123–124; *Leddell v McDougal* (1881) 29 WR 403, CA.
7	*Leddell v McDougal* (1881) 29 WR 403, CA; *Smith v Chadwick* (1884) 9 App Cas 187 at 201,
	HL.
8	*Foster v Charles* (1830) 7 Bing 105 at 107; *Re McCallum, McCallum v McCallum* [1901] 1 Ch 143
	at 163–164, CA; *KBC Bank v Industrial Steels (UK) Ltd* [2001] 1 All ER (Comm) 409 at [31].
9	See eg *Wilkinson v Downton* [1897] 2 QB 57 (so-called 'practical joke' giving rise to tortious
	liability). See also *Richardson v Silvester* (1873) LR 9 QB 34, where particulars of claim alleging
	that the defendant advertised for letting a farm which he knew he had no power to let and which
	he knew was not to be let, and that on the faith of the advertisement the plaintiff incurred expense,
	were held sufficient to disclose a cause of action for deceit, even though they did not allege that the
	defendant's act was done with an intention to injure the plaintiff. As to claims for deceit see PARA
	788 et seq.
10	*Foster v Charles* (1830) 6 Bing 396 at 403; *Corbett v Brown* (1831) 8 Bing 33 at 37; *Crawshay
	v Thompson* (1842) 4 Man & G 357; *Smith v Chadwick* (1884) 9 App Cas 187 at 190, HL; *Coaks
	v Boswell* (1886) 11 App Cas 232 at 236, HL; *Arnison v Smith* (1889) 41 ChD 348 at 372, CA;
	*Wilkinson v Downton* [1897] 2 QB 57 at 59. See also *Eco3 Capital Ltd v Ludsin Overseas Ltd*
	[2013] EWCA Civ 413, [2013] All ER (D) 172 (Apr) at [78] ('intention to deceive' is not a separate
	or free standing element of the tort of deceit but merely another way of describing the mental
	element of the tort).

## 759. Representation subsequently discovered by representor to be false.

Where a representation is a continuing one[1], and between the time when it was
made and the time when the representee[2] altered his position on the faith of it,
either: (1) the representor[3] discovers that his original statement which, when he
made it, he honestly believed to be true, was false; or (2) supervening events
render, to the knowledge of the representor, his statement no longer true, a duty
to disclose the changed situation to the representee may arise[4]. In such cases the
mere fact that the statement may have been innocently made, though false, or true
when made, will not, it seems, prevent the representee from establishing fraud
where he can show that the representor dishonestly[5] failed to discharge the duty
of disclosing the change in the situation[6].

1	See PARA 753.
2	As to who is a representee see PARAS 733–739.
3	As to who is a representor see PARAS 724–732.
4	See *Adamson v Jarvis* (1827) 4 Bing 66 at 74; *Jarrett v Kennedy* (1848) 6 CB 319 at 323; *Reynell
	v Sprye* (1852) 1 De GM & G 660 at 709; *Denton v Great Northern Rly Co* (1856) 5 E & B 860
	at 866–867; *Traill v Baring* (1864) 4 De GJ & Sm 318 at 329; *Davies v London and Provincial
	Marine Insurance Co* (1878) 8 ChD 469 at 475; *Brownlie v Campbell* (1880) 5 App Cas 925 at
	950, HL; *With v O'Flanagan* [1936] Ch 575 at 580–585, [1936] 1 All ER 727 at 732–736, CA,
	per Lord Wright MR. It seems that the duty to disclose must be discharged in unambiguous
	language: see *Arnison v Smith* (1889) 41 ChD 348 at 370–373, CA (error in prospectus not
	covered by subsequent ambiguous circular). As to misrepresentation in offer documents generally
	see COMPANIES vol 15A (2016) PARA 1259 et seq.
5	Ie not through mere inadvertence or through failure to realise the duty resting upon him: see *With
	v O'Flanagan* [1936] Ch 575 at 584, [1936] 1 All ER 727 at 735, CA, per Lord Wright MR,
	criticising dicta in *Brownlie v Campbell* (1880) 5 App Cas 925 at 950, HL, per Lord Blackburn;
	see also *FoodCo UK LLP (t/a Muffin Break) v Henry Boot Developments Ltd* [2010] EWHC 358

(Ch) at [214]. For fraud to be established, the representor must realise the significance of the change in the facts or that he has already made a false statement: *Abu Dhabi Investment Co v H Clarkson & Co Ltd* [2007] EWHC 1267 (Comm) at [232], [2007] All ER (D) 448 (May). Before the court embarks on the inquiry as to whether a representor remembers his earlier statement there must be some basis for supposing that the representor may have forgotten it: *Windsor and District Housing Association v Hewitt* [2011] EWCA Civ 735 at [18].

6   See eg *Adamson v Jarvis* (1827) 4 Bing 66 at 74; *Denton v Great Northern Rly Co* (1856) 5 E & B 860 at 866–867; *With v O'Flanagan* [1936] Ch 575 at 584–585, [1936] 1 All ER 727 at 735, CA, per Lord Wright MR; *Bradford Third Equitable Benefit Building Society v Borders* [1941] 2 All ER 205 at 220, HL, per Wright LJ; but cf *Arkwright v Newbold* (1881) 17 ChD 301, CA, where Cotton LJ at 325 doubted, and James LJ at 329 dissented from, the view that the persons issuing a prospectus were liable to a claim for deceit because they did not mention a fact coming to their knowledge before an allotment of shares which falsified a statement in the prospectus. See also *Manifest Shipping & Co Ltd v Uni-Polaris Insurance Co Ltd and La Réunion Européene, The Star Sea* [1997] 1 Lloyd's Rep 360, CA; affd [2001] UKHL 1, [2003] 1 AC 469, [2001] 1 All ER 743. As to claims for deceit see PARA 788 et seq; and COMPANIES vol 15A (2016) PARAS 1270–1275.

A representation, honestly made at the time of its making, but subsequently discovered to be false, may impose the obligation on its maker to correct the falsehood, if it is still timely to do so, but that obligation applies only to the representor: *AIC Ltd v ITS Testing Services (UK) Ltd, The Kriti Palm* [2006] EWCA Civ 1601, [2007] 1 All ER (Comm) 667, [2007] 1 Lloyd's Rep 555.

**760. Possible defence to claim for fraudulent misrepresentation.**

Contributory negligence is not a defence to claims for fraudulent misrepresentation[1]. However, where it is alleged that a representee[2] who is the victim of fraud is disabled from suing because he is himself involved in illegality, the court may take into account the relative moral culpability of the parties[3].

1   *Standard Chartered Bank v Pakistan National Shipping Corpn (No 2)* [2002] UKHL 43 at [18], [2003] 1 AC 959 at [18], [2003] 1 All ER 173 at [18]; applied in *GE Commercial Finance Ltd v Gee* [2005] EWHC 2056 (QB), [2006] 1 Lloyd's Rep 337. See also *Alliance and Leicester Building Society v Edgestop Ltd* [1994] 2 All ER 38, [1993] 1 WLR 1462; and *Corporacion Nacional del Cobre de Chile v Sogemin Metals Ltd* [1997] 2 All ER 917, [1997] 1 WLR 1396 (bribery).

However, damages for misrepresentation under the Misrepresentation Act 1967 s 2(1) (see PARA 800) may be reduced for contributory negligence: see PARA 810. As to contributory negligence generally see NEGLIGENCE vol 78 (2018) PARA 75 et seq. As to the liability of a director for company's negligent misstatement or misrepresentation see *Williams v Natural Life Health Foods Ltd* [1998] 2 All ER 577, [1998] 1 WLR 830, HL; COMPANIES vol 14 (2016) PARA 633; and NEGLIGENCE vol 78 (2018) PARA 15.

2   As to who is a representee see PARAS 733–739.

3   *Saunders v Edwards* [1987] 2 All ER 651, [1987] 1 WLR 1116, CA (defendant sold the lease of a flat to the plaintiffs and fraudulently represented that it included a roof garden; defendant argued unsuccessfully that the plaintiffs were disabled from suing because they had agreed to an apportionment of the price between the flat and chattels which exaggerated the value of the latter so as to minimise liability to stamp duty). For the rationale of the illegality doctrine see now *Patel v Mirza* [2016] UKSC 42, [2017] AC 467, [2017] 1 All ER 191.

# (7) Innocent Misrepresentation

**761. Misrepresentation innocent if made with honest belief in its truth.**

A misrepresentation must be either fraudulent or innocent[1]. It cannot be both. Fraud and innocence, like falsity and truth, are mutually exclusive categories. It follows from the definition of a fraudulent misrepresentation as a misrepresentation made in the absence of actual honest belief in its truth[2], that: (1) the essential characteristic of an innocent misrepresentation is the presence of such actual honest belief[3]; and (2) nothing more than this absence, or presence, is required to constitute fraud or innocence respectively.

1 Innocent misrepresentations include those made through negligence: see PARAS 762–763.
2 See PARAS 755–756.
3 *Collins v Evans* (1844) 5 QB 820 at 827, 830, Ex Ch; *Derry v Peek* (1889) 14 App Cas 337 at 374–376, HL, per Lord Herschell; *Angus v Clifford* [1891] 2 Ch 449 at 463–464, CA, per Bowen LJ; *Low v Bouverie* [1891] 3 Ch 82 at 105, CA; *Le Lievre v Gould* [1893] 1 QB 491 at 503, CA; *Glasgow and South Western Rly Co v Boyd and Forrest* as reported in 1912 SC 93, HL. See also *Economides v Commercial Union Assurance Co plc* [1998] QB 587, [1997] 3 All ER 636, CA as to the duty of good faith in insurance contracts where insured's misstatement based on honest belief; and *Sykes v Taylor-Rose* [2004] EWCA Civ 299, [2004] All ER (D) 468 (Feb).

## 762. Effect of negligence in establishing liability.

It used to be thought that negligent misrepresentation, as distinct from fraudulent misrepresentation[1], did not give rise to a cause of action at common law or in equity in the absence of breach of fiduciary or contractual duty towards the claimant[2]. However, it is now clear that such a cause of action may arise both at common law[3] and under the Misrepresentation Act 1967[4].

Thus there are now two classes of 'innocent misrepresentation'[5]: (1) those made without fault, which give rise to the remedy of rescission[6]; and (2) those made through negligence, which give rise to the remedies both of rescission and of damages[7].

1 As to fraudulent misrepresentation see PARA 754 et seq.
2 See *Le Lievre v Gould* [1893] 1 QB 491, CA; *Candler v Crane, Christmas & Co* [1951] 2 KB 164, [1951] 1 All ER 426, CA.
3 See *Hedley Byrne & Co Ltd v Heller & Partners Ltd* [1964] AC 465, [1963] 2 All ER 575, HL. See also PARAS 797–799; and for a discussion of this and later authorities see NEGLIGENCE vol 78 (2018) PARA 13. As to the liability of a director for company's negligent misstatement or misrepresentation see *Williams v Natural Life Health Foods Ltd* [1998] 2 All ER 577, [1998] 1 WLR 830, HL; COMPANIES vol 14 (2016) PARA 633; and NEGLIGENCE vol 78 (2018) PARA 15.
4 Ie under the Misrepresentation Act 1967 s 2(1): see PARA 800.
5 'Innocent' in this context means 'not fraudulent'.
6 As to rescission see PARA 811 et seq. As to the availability of damages in lieu of rescission see the Misrepresentation Act 1967 s 2(2); and PARA 832.
7 As to claims for damages see PARA 788 et seq. The Consumer Insurance (Disclosure and Representations) Act 2012 s 2 makes provision about disclosure and representations by a consumer to an insurer before a consumer insurance contract is entered into or varied and provides that the consumer has a duty to take reasonable care not to make a misrepresentation to the insurer; the Act provides a special remedial regime in Sch 1; and INSURANCE vol 60 (2018) PARA 29, 32, 137 et seq. For the different regime applicable to non-consumer insurance contracts, see Insurance Act 2015 Pt 2 (duty of fair presentation) and Sch 1 (remedies, distinguishing deliberate or reckless breaches from other breaches); and see INSURANCE vol 60 (2018), PARA 36.

## 763. Effect of negligence or incompetence in forming belief.

A misrepresentation which is founded on a belief in its truth, if that belief really existed, and was genuinely and honestly entertained, is not deprived of its character of innocence by reason of the mere fact that the belief resulted from want of care, skill or competence, or lapse of memory[1], even though such conduct, in other aspects, may have been of a most culpable character[2]. Negligence is not dishonesty[3]. It has been said that although negligence does not amount to fraud, it may constitute evidence of it[4]; and there may be cases in which the want of care is such that the tribunal appointed to determine the question of fact would be justified in preferring the alternative hypothesis of want of honesty[5]. Nevertheless, carelessness or stupidity in arriving at a genuine conviction must be distinguished from that moral recklessness or callousness which prompts the putting forward of a misrepresentation as to which the representor has no belief at all[6]. Similarly, absence of reasonable grounds for the representor's belief, if in fact it was a real and genuine belief, does not of itself constitute or indicate fraud[7], although there may be cases where the alleged belief must have been based on grounds so utterly preposterous as to compel the inference that in fact it never did exist[8]. On the same principle, actual failure to recollect a fact, where omission would render the representation false, does not of itself render it fraudulent[9].

1   See *Bell v Lever Bros Ltd* [1932] AC 161, HL.
2   This was the case in *Arkwright v Newbold* (1881) 17 ChD 301, CA (the successful defendant being on that account deprived of his costs); and, to some extent, in *Derry v Peek* (1889) 14 App Cas 337 at 376, HL, per Lord Herschell.
3   *Evans v Bicknell* (1801) 6 Ves 174 at 188, 191–192 per Lord Eldon LC; *Taylor v Ashton* (1843) 11 M & W 401 at 415; *Dickson v Reuter's Telegram Co* (1877) 3 CPD 1 at 6, CA; *Derry v Peek* (1889) 14 App Cas 337 at 361, HL; *Angus v Clifford* [1891] 2 Ch 449 at 462–468, CA; *Thiodon v Tindall* (1891) 65 LT 343, DC; *Le Lievre v Gould* [1893] 1 QB 491 at 501, CA; *Robinson v National Bank of Scotland* 1916 SC 154, HL. As to liability for careless statements see *Hedley Byrne & Co Ltd v Heller & Partners Ltd* [1964] AC 465, [1963] 2 All ER 575, HL; *Esso Petroleum Co Ltd v Mardon* [1976] QB 801, [1976] 2 All ER 5, CA; and NEGLIGENCE vol 78 (2018) PARA 13. As to the liability of a director for company's negligent misstatement or misrepresentation see *Williams v Natural Life Health Foods Ltd* [1998] 2 All ER 577, [1998] 1 WLR 830, HL; COMPANIES vol 14 (2016) PARA 633; and NEGLIGENCE vol 78 (2018) PARA 15.
4   See eg *Evans v Bicknell* (1801) 6 Ves 174 at 190–191 per Lord Eldon LC; *Derry v Peek* (1889) 14 App Cas 337 at 369, HL, per Lord Herschell.
5   *Western Bank of Scotland v Addie* (1867) LR 1 Sc & Div 145 at 168, HL, per Lord Cranworth; *Le Lievre v Gould* [1893] 1 QB 491 at 500, CA, per Bowen LJ.
6   See *Derry v Peek* (1889) 14 App Cas 337 at 361, HL, per Lord Herschell; *Le Lievre v Gould* [1893] 1 QB 491 at 501, CA, per Bowen LJ. See also PARA 756. As to who is a representor see PARAS 724–732.
7   *Derry v Peek* (1889) 14 App Cas 337, HL. The decision in this case was acted upon and applied in *Glasier v Rolls* (1889) 42 ChD 436, CA, and has been acted upon in numerous subsequent cases. As regards prospectuses of companies, the law as laid down in *Derry v Peek* has been modified by statutory provisions rendering directors and others liable to pay compensation for misstatements in offer documents even though they are not fraudulent: see COMPANIES vol 15A (2016) PARA 1259 et seq.
8   *Derry v Peek* (1889) 14 App Cas 337 at 369, HL, per Lord Herschell (a consideration of the grounds of belief is no doubt an important aid in ascertaining whether the belief was really entertained). See also *Thomas Witter Ltd v TBP Industries Ltd* [1996] 2 All ER 573 at 586–587 per Jacob J.
9   *Bain v Fothergill* (1874) LR 7 HL 158 at 212; *Mathias v Yetts* (1882) 46 LT 497 at 506, CA; *Low v Bouverie* [1891] 3 Ch 82 at 101, 106, CA.
    The opinions expressed in *Burrowes v Lock* (1805) 10 Ves 470 and in *Slim v Croucher* (1860) 1 De GF & J 518 are inconsistent with *Derry v Peek* (1889) 14 App Cas 337, HL. However, *Burrowes v Lock* can be supported on the ground of estoppel: *Low v Bouverie* at 102; *Nocton v Lord Ashburton* [1914] AC 932 at 952, HL, per Viscount Haldane LC. The view has been expressed that *Slim v Croucher*, in which the assertion was that a valid lease would be granted in the future, cannot any longer be regarded as having been rightly decided (see *Low v Bouverie*); but the circumstances were unusual, and it may be that the decision can be supported on the ground that the defendant warranted by implication that he had power to grant a valid lease (see *Nocton v Lord Ashburton* at 951 per Viscount Haldane LC).
    Where the misrepresentation is only the subject of rescission proceedings, in circumstances where fraud is irrelevant and honesty no answer (see PARA 813), the fact that the omitted matter had escaped the representor's memory is no answer: *Mathias v Yetts* at 502, 504. So also if a person chooses to state a thing as an absolute fact within his own knowledge when he has no clear recollection on the point, he makes a false representation: *Brownlie v Campbell* (1880) 5 App Cas 925 at 936, 945, 953, HL; and see PARA 709.

# (8) Materiality and Inducement

## (i) Materiality and Inducement Distinguished

**764. Distinction between materiality and inducement.**

No misrepresentation, however gross or fraudulent, draws with it any civil consequences unless it was material and was intended to, and did, influence the mind of the representee[1] so as to affect his conduct. Inducement in fact and materiality[2] are distinct and separate matters, and in any form of proceedings for misrepresentation it is necessary to establish both[3]. A court may infer inducement from materiality[4], although such an inference is rebuttable[5].

Actual inducement must be shown, irrespective of materiality. In other words, however probable it may have been in any case that the misrepresentation alleged would influence a normal person to take just the steps which the representee did, yet, if in fact he was not so influenced, he has no cause of action[6].

1   As to who is a representee see PARAS 733–739.
2   Ie a tendency to induce: see PARA 767 et seq.
3   *Smith v Chadwick* (1884) 9 App Cas 187 at 190, HL, per Lord Selborne LC. See also *Pan Atlantic Insurance Co Ltd v Pine Top Insurance Co Ltd* [1995] 1 AC 501, [1994] 3 All ER 581, HL (in which the requirement for both inducement and materiality in misrepresentation cases was extended to non-disclosure cases).
    An express warranty or condition eliminates all questions both of inducement and materiality: see *Pawson v Watson* (1778) 2 Cowp 785 at 788–790; *Attwood v Small* (1838) 6 Cl & Fin 232 at 444, HL; *Thomson v Weems* (1884) 9 App Cas 671 at 683–684, 689, HL; *Hambrough v Mutual Life Insurance Co of New York* (1895) 72 LT 140, CA; *Paxman v Union Assurance Society Ltd* (1923) 39 TLR 424 at 426 per McCardie J. See also INSURANCE.
4   *Mathias v Yetts* (1882) 46 LT 497 at 502, 505, 507, CA; *Smith v Chadwick* (1882) 20 ChD 27 at 44–45, CA; affd (1884) 9 App Cas 187 at 196, HL. See also *Redgrave v Hurd* (1881) 20 ChD 1 at 21, CA where Jessel MR overstated it as a rebuttable presumption of law; it has been since established that it is only an inference of fact: see *Smith v Chadwick* (1884) 9 App Cas 187 at 197; *Smith v Land and House Property Corpn* (1884) 28 ChD 7 at 16, CA; *Pan Atlantic Insurance Co Ltd v Pine Top Insurance Co Ltd* [1995] 1 AC 501 at 570, [1994] 3 All ER 581 at 637, HL; *County NatWest Bank Ltd v Barton* [2002] 4 All ER 494n, sub nom *Barton v County NatWest Bank Ltd* [1999] Lloyd's Rep Bank 408 at [54]–[55], [1999] 33 LS Gaz R 31 at [54]–[55], CA; *Dadourian Group International Inc v Simms* [2009] EWCA Civ 169 at [99], [101], [2009] 1 Lloyd's Rep 601 at [99], [101]; *Hayward v Zurich Insurance Co Plc* [2016] UKSC 48, [2017] AC 142, [2016] 4 All ER 628 at [29]..
5   *Redgrave v Hurd* (1881) 20 ChD 1 at 24, CA; *Mathias v Yetts* (1882) 46 LT 497 at 505 CA; *County NatWest Bank Ltd v Barton* [2002] 4 All ER 494n, [1999] 33 LS Gaz R 31 at [58], CA.
6   See eg *Shrewsbury v Blount* (1841) 2 Man & G 475 (where, the jury having found that the plaintiff did not purchase shares in consequence of certain representations, the court declined to interfere); *Smith v Chadwick* (1884) 9 App Cas 187 at 194, HL (in this case, the statement that a particular person was a director of the company might have influenced persons to take shares, but the plaintiff admitted that in fact it had not influenced him).

**765. Questions of law and fact.**

It is a question of law whether any representation is capable of being construed as material[1], and also whether there is any evidence of actual inducement[2]. Subject to these questions being answered in the affirmative, both inducement and materiality are prima facie issues of fact[3], and neither can be presumed as a matter of law[4]. However, inducement may be inferred in law from proved materiality[5].

1   See also PARA 743. In *Beachey v Brown* (1860) EB & E 796, it was held on demurrer that a certain fact, the concealment of which was complained of, was not material. Cf *Smith v Chadwick* (1882) 20 ChD 27 at 45, CA, per Jessel MR (the misstatement may be so trivial that a court will be of opinion that it could not have affected the plaintiff's mind at all); *Bloomenthal v Ford* [1897] AC 156 at 162, HL, per Lord Halsbury LC ('a statement may be made so preposterous in its nature

that nobody could believe that anyone was misled'). In *Gordon v Street* [1899] 2 QB 641, CA, the question whether the misrepresentation of the plaintiff's identity under cover of an alias was capable of being considered material by a jury was debated as a question of law. See also *Aneco Reinsurance Underwriting Ltd (in liquidation) v Johnson & Higgins Ltd* [2001] UKHL 51, [2002] 1 Lloyd's Rep 157.

2    As to the general principle in claims tried with a jury that it is for the judge to decide, as a question of law, whether there is any issue of fact to go to the jury see CIVIL PROCEDURE vol 12 (2015) PARA 1072.

3    As to inducement see in particular *Andrews v Mockford* [1896] 1 QB 372, CA, where two of the questions left to the jury on the trial related to the issue of inducement, the issue of materiality being separately left to it. See also *Clapham v Shillito* (1844) 7 Beav 146; and as to the distinction between inducement and materiality see PARA 764. As to materiality being an issue of fact see eg *Flinn v Headlam* (1829) 9 B & C 693, where the question was left to the jury. In the following cases a judge, sitting without a jury, determined the issue of materiality as a fact: *Re Universal Non-Tariff Fire Insurance Co, Forbes & Co's Claim* (1875) LR 19 Eq 485 at 493–494, 496; *Capel & Co v Sim's Ships Compositions Co Ltd* (1888) 58 LT 807 at 809–810; *Whurr v Devenish* (1904) 20 TLR 385.

4    See PARA 764. As to inducement see *Arnison v Smith* (1889) 41 ChD 348 at 374, CA, per Lord Halsbury LC. As to inducement for the purposes of estoppel by representation see similar observations in *Bloomenthal v Ford* [1897] AC 156 at 162, HL, per Lord Halsbury LC. As to materiality see *Bevan v Adams* (1870) 22 LT 795, where, the judge having taken upon himself to withdraw the question from the jury and to hold that the representation could not be material, the court ordered a new trial.

5    As to an inference of inducement see PARA 764.

## 766. Matters relevant in determining questions of fact.

In determining, as a fact, whether any representation was of a nature to induce, or did induce, the representee[1] to alter his position, all the circumstances must be considered[2], including, among others, the character of the document in which the representation is contained[3], the nature of the transaction or business into which it is alleged that the representee was induced to enter, and the representee's general or particular experience, whether arising from his profession or trade or otherwise[4].

1    As to who is a representee see PARAS 733–739.

2    *Bloomenthal v Ford* [1897] AC 156 at 162, HL, per Lord Halsbury LC.

3    As to prospectuses, advertisements, etc see the cases cited in PARAS 713, 714.

4    Thus in company prospectus cases it has been considered of importance that the representee was a lawyer, whose knowledge of the world and experience must have taught him how little reliance was to be placed upon representations such as those in question (*Shrewsbury v Blount* (1841) 2 Man & G 475 at 504 per Tindal CJ); or a person well acquainted with dealings of shares in companies, with prospectuses, and with stock exchange transactions (*Bellairs v Tucker* (1884) 13 QBD 562 at 577, DC, per Denman J); or a man of business, who had himself turned his own business into a company, and taken shares in other companies, and was quite competent to form an opinion for himself (*Smith v Chadwick* (1884) 9 App Cas 187 at 197, HL, per Lord Blackburn); or a broker with experience of company promotions and undertakings (*Capel & Co v Sim's Ships Compositions Co Ltd* (1888) 58 LT 807 at 809); or an underwriter, as distinct from an investor, to which two classes of applicants for allotment totally different considerations apply (*Baty v Keswick* (1901) 85 LT 18). As to misrepresentation in offer documents generally see COMPANIES vol 15A (2016) PARA 1259 et seq.

As to an inference of inducement see PARA 764.

## (ii) Materiality

### 767. Meaning of 'materiality'.

A representation is material[1] when its tendency, or its natural and probable result, is to induce the representee[2] to act on the faith of it in the kind of way in which he is proved to have in fact acted[3].

1 'Materiality' is a distinct thing from inducement. Each is a question of fact, if there is any evidence at all, and each must be separately proved, although in certain cases inducement may be inferred, as a fact, from manifest materiality: see PARAS 764–765.
2 As to who is a representee see PARAS 733–739.
3 See *Smith v Chadwick* (1882) 20 ChD 27 at 44, CA, per Jessel MR; on appeal (1884) 9 App Cas 187 at 196, HL, per Lord Blackburn, who refers to a statement of such a nature as would be likely to induce a person to enter into a contract. As to the definition of a material representation see also *Downs v Chappell* [1996] 3 All ER 344 at 351 per Hobhouse LJ, CA. See also *Lonrho plc v Fayed (No 2)* [1991] 4 All ER 961 at 966, [1992] 1 WLR 1 at 5–6.

### 768. Belief of either party irrelevant.

Except in certain circumstances[1], for the purposes of determining the question of materiality no regard is had to the views entertained by either of the parties when the representation was made. If, in any ordinary case, a representation was not material, the mere fact that the representee[2] thought at the time that it was cannot make it so[3]. Conversely, if, in any such case, the representation was material, the mere fact that the representor[4] did not at the time regard it as such cannot make it otherwise[5].

1 See PARA 769.
2 As to who is a representee see PARAS 733–739.
3 See *Beachey v Brown* (1860) EB & E 796 at 803 per Crompton J, where it is said that non-disclosure of a fact which was material in the mind of the party seeking to set up the defence of non-disclosure was not enough. The observation would apply with even greater force in a case of misrepresentation.
4 As to who is a representor see PARAS 724–732.
5 See *Lindenau v Desborough* (1828) 8 B & C 586 at 592–593; *Dalglish v Jarvie* (1850) 2 Mac & G 231 at 243; *London Assurance v Mansel* (1879) 11 ChD 363 at 368. These cases were cases of non-disclosure, but the principles enumerated in them are equally applicable to cases of positive misrepresentation.

### 769. Materiality constituted by special circumstances.

'A tendency to induce' means a tendency to induce the particular representee[1] in the proved or admitted circumstances of the case. Where there is nothing special in those circumstances it is sufficient to prove that, in the ordinary course of events, the natural and probable effect of the representation was to influence the mind of a normal representee in the manner alleged[2]. However, there may be, to the knowledge of the representor[3], circumstances peculiar to the representee of such a character as to render the particular representation of importance to the particular representee to whom it was addressed, even though it would be utterly inoperative on the mind of a normal person under normal conditions. In all such cases the representation is material as between the parties.

The question frequently arises when the representation relates to the personality or identity of any individual who is alleged to be the owner, or late owner, of property offered to the representee for sale[4], or of the intended purchaser from the representee of any property[5], or of the representee's intended creditor in a monetary dealing[6], or when it relates to any person's independence of or connection with other persons or influences in the contemplated transaction[7]. In many such cases the representation has been held to be material, and the objection that it was immaterial to the contract (although, in one sense, this was true) has been overruled, because the objection presupposed that the contract had already been entered into, whereas the question was whether, but for the statement, the representee would ever have entered into the contract at all, or, in other words, whether the representation was material, not to the contract, but to the inducement[8]. In this type of case, unlike the ordinary type, it is obvious that the representor's knowledge or belief of the likely effect of the misrepresentation on the representee's mind is of the first importance, because it is precisely that knowledge or belief which makes a representation material as against him which would not be material as against anyone else[9].

1   As to who is a representee see PARAS 733–739.
2   For illustrations of the more obvious types of materiality see generally the cases cited in PARAS 788–796.
3   As to who is a representor see PARAS 724–732.
4   See eg *Fellowes v Lord Gwydyr* (1829) 1 Russ & M 83 at 89–90 per Lord Lyndhurst LC, who entertained no doubt that the representation would have been material if it had been shown that the representee would not have treated with anyone but Lord Gwydyr, but this was not sufficiently made out. The following are illustrations of the materiality of statements as to present or late ownership of goods offered for sale at auction: *Bexwell v Christie* (1776) 1 Cowp 395 (sale of goods and effects of a gentleman deceased at his house in the country); *Hill v Gray* (1816) 1 Stark 434 (sale of pictures as the property of a named collector); *Arkwright v Newbold* (1881) 17 ChD 301 at 314, CA, per James LJ (sale of picture under similar conditions); *Whurr v Devenish* (1904) 20 TLR 385 (sale of a horse as the property of a private gentleman, whereas at the actual moment of sale it had become the property of a jobmaster). As to auctions generally see AUCTION.
5   *Smith v Wheatcroft* (1878) 9 ChD 223 at 230, where Fry J recognised the principle that a misrepresentation of the identity of a purchaser may be a material one if the vendor would have been unwilling to enter into a contract in the same terms with anybody else, although he held that in that case the representee had failed to prove this essential fact; *Archer v Stone* (1898) 78 LT 34. See also *Lake v Simmons* [1927] AC 487 at 501, HL, per Lord Haldane. However, unless the contract is one in which some personal consideration forms a material ingredient, mere non-disclosure as to the person actually entitled to the benefit of a contract for the sale of real estate does not amount to misrepresentation, even though the contracting party knows that, if the disclosure were made, the other party would not enter into the contract: *Nash v Dix* (1898) 78 LT 445; *Dyster v Randall & Sons* [1926] Ch 932. As to the effect of mistakes as to the identity of a party to an intended contract see generally CONTRACT vol 22 (2012) PARA 207; MISTAKE vol 77 (2016) PARA 13.
6   *Smith v Kay* (1859) 7 HL Cas 750 at 758–759, 766–767; *Gordon v Street* [1899] 2 QB 641 at 647–649, CA.
7   *Fellowes v Lord Gwydyr* (1829) 1 Russ & M 83, where a person represented himself to be the agent of another, when in fact he was independent, being a purchaser from him; *Moens v Heyworth* (1842) 10 M & W 147, where goods were stated to have been invoiced to sellers as of first shipping quality by shippers of a distinct and independent position, whereas they were agents or partners; *Smith v Wheatcroft* (1878) 9 ChD 223. See also *Archer v Stone* (1898) 78 LT 34; *Gordon v Street* [1899] 2 QB 641, CA (both cases of statements by the representor of his independent individuality, when in reality he was identical with, or the instrument of, another person). It is doubtful whether a statement in a company prospectus that an expert's report on property purchased by the company was prepared for the directors, whereas in fact it was prepared on behalf of the vendors, is capable of being deemed a material misrepresentation, if there is no false statement in the report itself: see *Angus v Clifford* [1891] 2 Ch 449 at 456–458, CA, per Romer J, at 468 per Lindley LJ, and at 480 per Kay LJ, where differing views were expressed. As to misrepresentation in offer documents generally see COMPANIES vol 15A (2016) PARA 1259 et seq.
8   *Gordon v Street* [1899] 2 QB 641 at 645–646, CA, per AL Smith LJ.
9   *Archer v Stone* (1898) 78 LT 34; *Gordon v Street* [1899] 2 QB 641 at 648, CA, per AL Smith LJ, who laid great stress on the fact that the plaintiff himself was keenly alive to the importance, in his own interests, of suppressing his identity; *Whurr v Devenish* (1904) 20 TLR 385, where it was proved that the defendant was fully aware of the materiality of his representation that the horse was a private person's property (namely his own), and not that of a horse dealer, as tending to establish his good faith and the genuineness of the sale and to fetch better prices.

## 770. Burden of proving materiality on representee.

Materiality, if disputed, must be established by the representee[1] in addition to, and apart from, inducement[2]. This burden is usually discharged by comparison of the terms of the representation with the proved or admitted facts of the case. When once the circumstances are established, the question is, as a rule, the subject of argument only, but, in certain cases (for example where the representation is only an implied one from the external appearance of an object) it may be necessary to adduce some evidence of its tendency to deceive[3].

1　See generally the cases cited below; and PARAS 765, 767–769. As to who is a representee see PARAS 733–739.
2　*Mathias v Yetts* (1882) 46 LT 497 at 502, CA, per Jessel MR, and at 504 per Hannen LJ.
3　*London General Omnibus Co Ltd v Lavell* [1901] 1 Ch 135, CA; *Re Carvino Trade Mark* [1911] 2 Ch 572, CA. On the other hand, in *Gill v M'Dowell* [1903] 2 IR 463, and in *Patterson v Landsberg & Son* (1905) 7 F 675 at 681, Ct of Sess, per Lord Kyllachy, it was thought that the hermaphrodite animal in the one case, and the curio in the other, bore on its face the evidence of its capacity to induce and mislead.

## (iii) Inducement

## 771. What constitutes inducement.

The inducement which the representee[1] is required to establish is an inducement which was both the result and the object of the representation[2]. Neither element suffices without the other[3].

1　As to who is a representee see PARAS 733–739.
2　This proposition is frequently expressed in the formula of the Roman jurists that the misrepresentation must be one dans locum contractui: see eg *Attwood v Small* (1838) 6 Cl & Fin 232 at 444, HL, per Lord Brougham.
3　See PARAS 772–776.

## 772. Intention to induce without result.

There is nothing actionable in a proved intention to induce which fails of its effect altogether. A naked lie[1], or a lie in gross as it has otherwise been expressed[2], or an attempt to overreach, which misses its mark[3], comes to nothing[4]. Although a representee cannot normally succeed where he knows that the misrepresentation is false, since a man cannot be deceived where he knows the truth[5], it is not necessary as a matter of law to prove that the representee believed that the representation was true, and there may be circumstances in which a representee may know that the representation is false but nevertheless may be held to rely upon the misrepresentation as a matter of fact[6].

1　See *Pasley v Freeman* (1789) 3 Term Rep 51 at 56; *Langridge v Levy* (1837) 2 M & W 519 at 531.
2　See *Archer v Stone* (1898) 78 LT 34.
3　*Attwood v Small* (1838) 6 Cl & Fin 232 at 447–448, HL, per Lord Brougham.
4　*Coaks v Boswell* (1886) 11 App Cas 232 at 236, HL (if the vendor was not in fact misled, the contract could not be set aside). For instances of failure to prove inducement in fact, and consequent failure to obtain relief, see *Flinn v Headlam* (1829) 9 B & C 693; *Attwood v Small* (1836) 6 Cl & Fin 232; *Shrewsbury v Blount* (1841) 2 Man & G 475; *Vigers v Pike* (1842) 8 Cl & Fin 562, HL; *Hill v Balls* (1857) 2 H & N 299; *Re Northumberland and Durham District Banking Co, ex p Bigge* (1858) 28 LJ Ch 50; *Horsfall v Thomas* (1862) 1 H & C 90; *Way v Hearn* (1862) 13 CBNS 292 at 305, 307; *Mathias v Yetts* (1882) 46 LT 497 at 502, 504, CA; *Bellairs v Tucker* (1884) 13 QBD 562 at 578, 582, DC; *Salaman v Warner* (1891) 65 LT 132, CA; *Wasteneys v Wasteneys* [1900] AC 446 at 451, PC; *Baty v Keswick* (1901) 85 LT 18; *Stevens v Hoare* (1904) 20 TLR 407; *Sleigh v Glasgow and Transvaal Options Ltd* (1904) 6 F 420, Ct of Sess; *Seddon v North Eastern Salt Co Ltd* [1905] 1 Ch 326 at 335 per Joyce J; *Gamage Ltd v Charlesworth's Trustee* 1910 SC 257, Ct of Sess. See also *Kelly v Enderton* [1913] AC 191 at 194,

PC (alleged statement to vendor by agent of purchaser of an option on property that no other property transactions were proceeding in neighbourhood; statement, if made, fell far short of specific misrepresentation inducing contract); *H & JM Bennett (Potatoes) Ltd v Secretary of State for Scotland* 1990 SLT 189, HL.

5  See *Sprecher Grier Halberstam LLP v Walsh* [2008] EWCA Civ 1324, [2009] CP Rep 16 at [17].
6  See *Hayward v Zurich Insurance Co Plc* [2016] UKSC 48, [2017] AC 142, [2016] 4 All ER 628..

### 773. Necessity for existence of intention to induce.

It is not every false statement by which a person is in fact induced to alter his position for the worse which gives a right of action[1], but only such as the representor[2], either in fact or in contemplation of law, intended to operate as an inducement to the representee[3], or a class of which the representee is a member, to act on the representation in a particular manner[4].

It seems that such an intention may in certain circumstances be presumed on proof of the making of a statement which the representor must have foreseen would necessarily, or probably (in the ordinary course of events, or in the special circumstances of the case), produce the kind of effect on the representee's mind which it in fact produced[5].

Where such intent cannot be presumed, it must be established by direct evidence[6]. A claim does not arise in respect of a simple lie not intended to be acted upon in a case where the representor was under no duty to tell the truth[7], or where the representor was not only under no duty to give information correctly, but was under a positive duty to give it falsely[8].

1  Otherwise a person might sue another for damage suffered through relying on a conspicuous clock which was too slow (*Barley v Walford* (1846) 9 QB 197 at 208), or on the accuracy of a traveller's report as to conditions in a district abroad (*Gerhard v Bates* (1853) 2 E & B 476 at 485), or on the correctness of an address given inaccurately in a public directory (*Thiodon v Tindall* (1891) 65 LT 343 at 348, DC).
2  As to who is a representor see PARAS 724–732.
3  As to who is a representee see PARAS 733–739.
4  *Langridge v Levy* (1837) 2 M & W 519 at 531; *Tallerman v Dowsing Radiant Heat Co* [1900] 1 Ch 1 at 6 per Stirling J (on appeal [1900] 1 Ch 1 at 9, CA) (cited in PARA 779). See also eg *Peek v Gurney* (1873) LR 6 HL 377, where the object of the prospectus was merely to induce persons to apply for allotment of shares from the company, and a person who had not applied for allotment but had merely purchased shares after their allotment from the allottee had no cause of action. Cf *Andrews v Mockford* [1896] 1 QB 372, CA, where the publication of the prospectus was part of a scheme of fraud continued after allotment by other devices, and a purchaser of shares was held entitled to maintain a claim. As to misrepresentation in offer documents generally see COMPANIES vol 15A (2016) PARA 1259 et seq.
5  *Polhill v Walter* (1832) 3 B & Ad 114 at 123–124.
6  *Salaman v Warner* (1891) 65 LT 132, CA, where a statement of claim containing no averment of an intention to induce was struck out. On the other hand, there are cases where the statement of claim did contain sufficient allegations of such intention, and the demurrer was overruled: see *Barley v Walford* (1846) 9 QB 197; *Gerhard v Bates* (1853) 2 E & B 476. The following are cases where, on failure to show a purpose to induce, the representee was refused relief: *Way v Hearn* (1862) 13 CBNS 292 at 303, 305, 307; *New Brunswick and Canada Railway and Land Co v Conybeare* (1862) 9 HL Cas 711; *Thiodon v Tindall* (1891) 65 LT 343, DC; *Baty v Keswick* (1901) 85 LT 18; *Sleigh v Glasgow and Transvaal Options Ltd* (1904) 6 F 420, Ct of Sess; *Tackey v McBain* [1912] AC 186 at 191–192, PC. Cf *Andrews v Mockford* [1896] 1 QB 372, CA; *Gordon v Street* [1899] 2 QB 641, CA (fraudulent concealment by moneylender of his identity in order to induce borrower to contract with him). As to intent to induce see the cases cited in PARAS 733–739. As to the necessity that a representation should be intended to be acted upon in the manner in which it was in fact acted upon in order to found estoppel by representation see ESTOPPEL vol 47 (2014) PARA 372.
7  *Collins v Cave* (1859) 4 H & N 225 at 232 per Pollock CB.
8  See eg *Cave v Mills* (1862) 7 H & N 913 at 930 per Bramwell B (untruth told to a person seeking to buy poison to murder another).

## 774. Representation need not be the sole inducement.

It is sufficient to prove that the misrepresentation was an inducing cause, even if it may not have been the sole inducing cause[1]. When once it is established that it had an influence on the mind and conduct of the representee[2], the law places no burden on him, and confers no right on the representor[3], of instituting a conjectural inquiry as to what would have happened if certain things had been said, which in fact were not said, or had been said differently[4].

Thus it is no answer for the representor to suggest, or prove, that other considerations co-existed and co-operated with the misrepresentation in producing the result. If, as against the representor, the misrepresentation can be shown to have been an effective inducement, it need not have been the sole inducement[5].

1 See *JEB Fasteners Ltd v Marks Bloom & Co* [1983] 1 All ER 583, CA.
2 As to who is a representee see PARAS 733–739.
3 As to who is a representor see PARAS 724–732.
4 *Reynell v Sprye* (1852) 1 De GM & G 660; *Smith v Kay* (1859) 7 HL Cas 750 at 759 per Lord Chelmsford LC; *Re London and Leeds Bank, ex p Carling, Carling v London and Leeds Bank* (1887) 56 LJ Ch 321 at 323–324; *Gordon v Street* [1899] 2 QB 641 at 646, CA; *Drincqbier v Wood* [1899] 1 Ch 393 at 400; *Barton v Armstrong* [1976] AC 104, [1975] 2 All ER 465, PC; *JEB Fasteners Ltd v Marks Bloom & Co* [1983] 1 All ER 583, CA; *BFG Bank AG v Brown & Mumford Ltd* [1997] PNLR 202, [1996] EGCS 169, CA. See also *Bristol and West Building Society v Mothew* [1998] Ch 1, [1996] 4 All ER 698, CA (negligent advice; plaintiff did not need to show that he would not have acted as he did if he had been given the proper information).
5 *Attwood v Small* (1838) 6 Cl & Fin 232 at 448, HL; *Tatton v Wade* (1856) 18 CB 371 at 385, 387, Ex Ch; *Re Royal British Bank, Nicol's Case* (1859) 3 De G & J 387 at 422; *Higgins v Samels* (1862) 2 John & H 460 at 468; *Mathias v Yetts* (1882) 46 LT 497 at 502, CA; *Edgington v Fitzmaurice* (1885) 29 ChD 459 at 480–481, 483–485, CA; *Re London and Leeds Bank, ex p Carling, Carling v London and Leeds Bank* (1887) 56 LJ Ch 321; *Drincqbier v Wood* [1899] 1 Ch 393 at 404–405; *Assicurazioni Generali SpA v Arab Insurance Group (BSC)* [2002] EWCA Civ 1642 at [59], [2003] 1 All ER (Comm) 140 at [59], [2003] 1 WLR 577 at [59]; *Ross River Ltd v Cambridge City Football Club Ltd* [2007] EWHC 2115 (Ch), [2008] 1 All ER 1004, 117 ConLR 129; *Raiffeisen Zentralbank Osterreich AG v Royal Bank of Scotland plc* [2010] EWHC 1392 (Comm) at [173], [2011] 1 Lloyd's Rep 123 at [173], [2010] All ER (D) 111 (Jun); *Cassa di Risparmio della Repubblica di San Marino SpA v Barclays Bank Ltd* [2011] EWHC 484 (Comm) at [233], [467], [2011] NLJR 437, [2011] All ER (D) 189 (Mar). A court is at liberty to attach to one of two elements operating upon a person's mind the cause without which the loss would not have arisen: *Paul and Vincent Ltd v O'Reilly* (1913) 49 ILT 89.

## 775. Entirety of connected statements to be considered.

Where the inducing cause is alleged to be a document (such as a prospectus, advertisement or circular), or a batch of documents, containing a number of statements interconnected either by express reference and incorporation or by community of subject matter, it is a general rule that, for the purpose of determining the issue of inducement, the conjoint effect on the representee's[1] mind of the entirety of the statements or documents, in their mutual relation to and qualification of one another, is the question to be considered, rather than the effect of any particular statement or document apart from the others[2]. However, reliance may in certain circumstances be placed upon a representation in one of several associated statements or documents where that statement or document is not inseparably or necessarily bound up with the others[3].

1 As to who is a representee see PARAS 733–739.
2 *New Brunswick and Canada Railway and Land Co v Muggeridge* (1860) 1 Drew & Sm 363 at 379–380; *Arnison v Smith* (1889) 41 ChD 348 at 369, CA, per Lord Halsbury; *Aaron's Reefs v Twiss* [1896] AC 273 at 280, 291, HL; *Andrews v Mockford* [1896] 1 QB 372 at 382–383, CA; *Drincqbier v Wood* [1899] 1 Ch 393 at 404; *McConnel v Wright* [1903] 1 Ch 546 at 551, CA, per Collins MR; *R v Lord Kylsant* [1932] 1 KB 442, CCA; *R v Bishirgian* [1936] 1 All ER 586, CCA.

As to misrepresentation in offer documents generally see COMPANIES vol 15A (2016) PARA 1259 et seq.

3  See PARA 751.

## 776. Proof of inducement where representation ambiguous.

Where the representation is fairly capable of two or more constructions, in one of which it would be false and in the other or others true, it is for the representee[1] to allege and prove in which of its possible meanings he understood it, and, so understanding, was induced by it to alter his position[2].

1  As to who is a representee see PARAS 733–739.
2  See *Smith v Chadwick* (1882) 20 ChD 27 at 45, CA, per Jessel MR; and PARA 746.

### (iv) Alteration of Position

## 777. Necessity for showing alteration of position.

In order to sustain any claim or proceeding for misrepresentation it is necessary for the representee[1] to establish that he was induced by it, not merely to alter his mind, but to alter his position, that is to say, to effect a change in his material or temporal interests or situation[2].

This change may or may not be accompanied by ascertainable pecuniary loss or physical injury, which is damage[3]; and where it is necessary to prove damage, such resultant loss or injury must be shown in addition to the alteration of position itself, but not otherwise[4]. In any case, damage is a separate and distinct issue from alteration of position, and to establish the latter it is necessary and sufficient to prove that by reason of his belief in the truth of the representation the representee voluntarily altered his position[5].

1  As to who is a representee see PARAS 733–739.
2  A mere change of mind, without a change of position, is not enough; nor is a change of position which affects solely the representee's social, moral, political or spiritual condition. As to how the representee's position may be altered see PARA 778. As to the burden of proof see PARA 779.
3  As to damage see PARAS 790–792.
4  See PARAS 779–780, 789, 815.
5  There is a class of case in which it is not necessary to show that the representee altered his position at all, in the sense of doing anything on the faith of the representation, namely where he is shown to have suffered involuntary physical damage in consequence of it: see PARA 790.

## 778. How the representee's position may be altered.

There are various ways in which a representee[1] may act on the faith of a representation so as to alter his position. He may enter into a contract either with the representor[2] himself, or with a third person, or class of persons[3], or the alteration of position may take the form of a unilateral transaction of a binding nature, in the sense that it is not revocable except with the consent of the other party to it, such as a gift, licence or consent, a forbearance or a renunciation[4], or it may consist in an act, of whatever nature, the effect of which is to render the representee responsible in civil law to some third person[5], or even to render him amenable to criminal process, if such act would not have constituted any offence at all if the statement on the faith of which he committed it had been true[6]. Further, a person may physically alter his position by the act of using property, whether land or a chattel, in reliance on a representation (express, or implied from acts and conduct) that the place or chattel may be used without danger[7], and, generally, by the doing of or abstention from anything which has a bearing on his material interests, and which he is not legally compellable to do or to abstain from[8].

1  As to who is a representee see PARAS 733–739.

2  As to who is a representor see PARAS 724–732. A representee may alter his position by entering into a contract with the representor on material terms different to those he would have agreed to in the absence of the misrepresentation: *Huyton SA v Distribuidora Internacional de Productos Agricolas SA de CV* [2003] EWCA Civ 1104, [2004] 1 All ER (Comm) 402, [2003] 2 Lloyd's Rep 780.

3  See eg *Arnison v Smith* (1889) 41 ChD 348, CA, where the representees were induced to take debenture stock in a company by a misrepresentation by the directors of the company. As to the principle that a claim for deceit does not lie in respect of a representation as to the credit of a third person unless the representation was in writing see PARA 803.

4  As to gifts see *Haygarth v Wearing* (1871) LR 12 Eq 320 at 329; and GIFTS. As to compromises and consents see CIVIL PROCEDURE vol 12A (2015) PARA 1223 et seq. As to renunciations see *M'Carthy v Decaix* (1831) 2 Russ & M 614 at 620–623. Releases by deed and compromises come under the head of contracts proper: see eg *Hirschfeld v London, Brighton and South Coast Rly Co* (1876) 2 QBD 1; *Gilbert v Endean* (1878) 9 ChD 259, CA. See also CONTRACT vol 22 (2012) PARA 609.

5  *Adamson v Jarvis* (1827) 4 Bing 66.

6  *Burrows v Rhodes* [1899] 1 QB 816.

7  See PARA 790.

8  See generally the cases cited in PARAS 779, 790–792.

## 779.  Burden of proof.

The burden is on the representee[1] to allege and prove that the representor[2], actually or presumptively, intended him to act on the faith of the representation in the manner in which he did act, and it is not enough to prove damage to the representee unless it is also shown that it resulted from an alteration of position induced by that representation[3]. Whether there is any sufficient averment[4], or any evidence[5], of such matters are questions of law; but otherwise, and subject to the principle of law that a person is presumed to intend the natural consequences of his acts and statements, all matters connected with alteration of position are issues of fact[6].

1  As to who is a representee see PARAS 733–739.

2  As to who is a representor see PARAS 724–732.

3  See *Tallerman v Dowsing Radiant Heat Co* [1900] 1 Ch 1 at 5–6 per Stirling J (on appeal [1900] 1 Ch 1 at 9, CA) (although damage was caused to the plaintiffs by a misrepresentation alleged to constitute a passing off, the statements complained of were not intended to be acted on by the plaintiffs, and had not been acted upon by them); *Strover v Harrington* [1988] Ch 390, [1988] 1 All ER 769 (misrepresentation by vendor's agents; purchaser's solicitors subsequently informed that the statement was erroneous, but failed to inform purchaser; loss arose from their failure rather than the misrepresentation). As to inducement see PARAS 771–776. As to the principle that a party setting up estoppel by representation must have acted on the representation to his prejudice see ESTOPPEL vol 47 (2014) PARA 376.

4  *Behn v Kemble* (1859) 7 CBNS 260; *Salaman v Warner* (1891) 65 LT 132, CA.

5  See *Smith v Chadwick* (1884) 9 App Cas 187 at 195–196, HL.

6  As to questions of law and fact see PARAS 765–766.

# (9)  The Effect of Misrepresentation

## 780.  Remedies for fraudulent misrepresentation.

Where a representor[1] has, by way of fraudulent misrepresentation[2], induced a representee[3] to alter his position[4], other than by entering into a contract or other binding transaction[5] with the representor, the representee will be able to bring a claim for damages at common law[6] or for an account of profits in equity[7], but he will not be entitled to any other form of relief.

However, where the representee has been induced by fraudulent misrepresentation to enter into a contract or other binding transaction with the representor, he may either maintain a claim for damages at common law or under the Misrepresentation Act 1967[8], or rescind the contract or transaction, and, where he has been induced by the misrepresentation to incur loss in addition to entering into the contract, he may both rescind the contract and claim damages in respect of his further losses[9]. The representee may rescind the contract by instituting proceedings for rescission[10] or by simply communicating the decision to rescind to the representor[11], or may set up the fraudulent misrepresentation as a defence to any claim or proceeding instituted for the direct or indirect enforcement of the contract or transaction[12]. In circumstances where property is transferred under a contract, and the misrepresentation in question is fraudulent, the representee may rescind the contract by retaking possession of the property[13].

Where the representee has only altered his position by entering into a contract or other binding transaction, and has not been induced by the misrepresentation to incur any further loss, he may obtain relief either by way of rescission of the contract or damages, but not both[14]. However, these claims may be made alternatively in a single claim form[15], and a claim for relief by way of rescission of a contract will not, it seems, preclude an alternative or additional claim for the recovery of such further damage as may have been suffered by a representee who, as a result of a fraudulent misrepresentation, not only has entered into the contract but also has further altered his position and suffered damage by reason of that further alteration[16].

If the representee elects to sue for damages, the fact that he might first have avoided the contract or transaction, or taken proceedings to rescind it, or asserted his right to have it treated as void in any proceedings brought to enforce it, will not be a bar to his claim[17].

1  As to who is a representor see PARAS 724–732.
2  As to fraudulent misrepresentation see PARA 754 et seq.
3  As to who is a representee see PARAS 733–739.
4  As to materiality, inducement and alteration of position see PARA 764 et seq.
5  As to what is a binding transaction see PARA 778.
6  As to claims for damages see PARA 788 et seq.
7  As to account of profits see EQUITABLE JURISDICTION vol 47 (2014) PARA 105.
8  Because of the heavy onus of proof of fraud, pleaders may find it preferable to rely on the Misrepresentation Act 1967, which has the effect of reversing the onus of proof: see PARA 800.
9  *Archer v Brown* [1985] QB 401 at 415, [1984] 2 All ER 267 at 275.
10 As to claims for rescission see PARA 811 et seq. As to the representee's right to affirm or disaffirm the contract or transaction see PARA 783.
11 See PARA 811.
12 See PARA 784 et seq.
13 *Car and Universal Finance Co Ltd v Caldwell* [1965] 1 QB 525 at 554, [1964] 1 All ER 290 at 296, CA. This may be the case even where the representee is not aware of the representor's act in retaking the property: see *Car and Universal Finance Co Ltd v Caldwell*.
14 Ie the representee must elect between rescinding the contract and affirming it: see PARA 783.
15 See *Greenwood v Leather Shod Wheel Co* [1900] 1 Ch 421, CA; *Goldrei, Foucard & Son v Sinclair and Russian Chamber of Commerce in London* [1918] 1 KB 180, CA. A claimant may use a single claim form to start all claims which can conveniently be disposed of in the same proceedings: see CPR 7.3
16 See *Attwood v Small* (1838) 6 Cl & Fin 232 at 444, HL, per Lord Brougham; *Newbigging v Adam* (1886) 34 ChD 582 at 592, CA, per Bowen LJ; *Goldrei, Foucard & Son v Sinclair and Russian Chamber of Commerce in London* [1918] 1 KB 180 at 186, CA, per Pickford LJ (but cf at 190 per

Bankes LJ). A representee who had obtained rescission of a contract to take shares in a new company on grounds not involving fraud, but had not obtained restitution of money paid, might, it seems, in a subsequent claim for fraud recover from the directors or promoters, if the fraud were proved, the amount that had not been restored to him: see *Ship v Crosskill* (1870) LR 10 Eq 73 at 82–83, where the plaintiff's name was removed from the list of contributories for untrue statements in a prospectus, and it was held that in order to succeed in subsequent proceedings against directors or promoters to recover money paid on allotment it was necessary to prove fraud, but, as fraud was not established, the claim in the subsequent proceedings failed. See also *Stewart v Austin* (1866) LR 3 Eq 299; *Henderson v Lacon* (1867) LR 5 Eq 249. Cf *Redgrave v Hurd* (1881) 20 ChD 1 at 12, CA. As to misrepresentation in offer documents generally see COMPANIES vol 15A (2016) PARA 1259 et seq.

17 See *Arnison v Smith* (1889) 41 ChD 348 at 371, CA, per Cotton LJ.

### 781. Remedies for innocent misrepresentation.

Where a representee[1] entered into a contract or other binding transaction[2] with the representor[3] on the strength of an innocent misrepresentation[4], the representee is entitled to take proceedings for the purpose of having the contract rescinded[5] or for consequential relief[6] or to set up the misrepresentation as a defence in any proceedings by the representor to enforce the contract[7]. The representee may in some circumstances be entitled to damages, either because there is a special relationship between representor and representee which gives rise to a duty of care at common law[8] or because the representee can rely on the statutory right to damages[9].

1 As to who is a representee see PARAS 733–739.
2 As to what is a binding transaction see PARA 778.
3 As to who is a representor see PARAS 724–732.
4 As to innocent misrepresentations see PARAS 761–763.
5 As to claims for rescission see PARA 811 et seq.
6 See PARAS 811–812.
7 See PARA 784 et seq.
8 See *Hedley Byrne & Co Ltd v Heller & Partners Ltd* [1964] AC 465, [1963] 2 All ER 575, HL; PARAS 762–763, 797–799; and NEGLIGENCE vol 78 (2018) PARA 13.
9 See the Misrepresentation Act 1967 s 2(1); and PARA 800. Where the misrepresentation constitutes a misleading action under the Consumer Protection from Unfair Trading Regulations 2008, SI 2008/1277, reg 5 and Pt 4A (regs 27A-27L) the consumer may have special remedies against the trader: see CONSUMER PROTECTION vol 21 (2016)PARA 433 et seq.

### 782. Contracts induced by misrepresentation normally voidable, not void.

In general a contract induced by misrepresentation is valid until disaffirmed, not invalid ab initio, that is to say it is voidable, not void[1]. The consequences of this rule are of importance in relation both to the conditions of relief[2], and also to some of the affirmative defences which may be set up by the representor[3].

There is one exception, apparent rather than real, to the rule. When the misrepresentation relates to the essential nature of the contract which the representee[4] is induced by the misrepresentation to execute, for example to the type of transaction intended to be effected or the identity of the person with whom the representee is contracting, the effect of the misrepresentation may be wholly to negative the apparent consent of the representee to the contract and to render the contract void ab initio on the ground that when the representee executed it his mind did not accompany his outward act[5].

1 *Stevenson v Newnham* (1853) 13 CB 285 at 302–303, Ex Ch; *Feret v Hill* (1854) 15 CB 207 at 223–227; *Oakes v Turquand and Harding* (1867) LR 2 HL 325 at 346; *Ogilvie v Currie* (1868) 37 LJ Ch 541 at 546; *Reese River Silver Mining Co Ltd v Smith* (1869) LR 4 HL 64 at 69, 73–74; *Clough v London and North Western Rly Co* (1871) LR 7 Exch 26 at 34, Ex Ch; *Erlanger v New Sombrero Phosphate Co* (1878) 3 App Cas 1218 at 1227–1228, HL; *Re Scottish Petroleum Co*

(1883) 23 ChD 413 at 430–432, CA; *Aaron's Reefs v Twiss* [1896] AC 273 at 290–291, 294, HL; *Re Glubb, Bamfield v Rogers* [1900] 1 Ch 354 at 361–362, CA, per Lindley MR (gift); *United Shoe Machinery Co of Canada v Brunet* [1909] AC 330 at 339, PC; *Abram Steamship Co v Westville Shipping Co* [1923] AC 773 at 782–783, 787, HL, per Atkinson LJ.

2   See PARAS 813–816.

3   See PARA 824 et seq. As to who is a representor see PARAS 724–732.

4   As to who is a representee see PARAS 733–739.

5   In such cases the ground on which the contract is void is not the representation, but the mistake which is induced by the misrepresentation: see MISTAKE vol 77 (2016) PARA 13. See generally CONTRACT vol 22 (2012) PARA 207. See also FINANCIAL INSTRUMENTS AND TRANSACTIONS vol 49 (2015) PARAS 660, 671. Where a contract for the sale of goods is merely voidable on the ground of misrepresentation by the purchaser, the purchaser, until it is avoided, can transmit a good title to the goods to a third person taking them for value and without notice: see eg *Whitehorn Bros v Davison* [1911] 1 KB 463, CA; *Phillips v Brooks Ltd* [1919] 2 KB 243; and see SALE OF GOODS AND SUPPLY OF SERVICES vol 91 (2012) PARAS 151–153. As to the power to transmit a good title of a mercantile agent or a person who has agreed to buy goods where the agent or person is in possession of goods or documents of title to them with the apparent consent of the owner see AGENCY vol 1 (2017) PARAS 12, 134; SALE OF GOODS AND SUPPLY OF SERVICES vol 91 (2012) PARAS 155–156. However, where a contract has been induced by a misrepresentation as to the person with whom the representee is contracting such that it negatives his apparent consent and renders the contract wholly void, the representor cannot in general confer any title on a third person: see *Phillips v Brooks Ltd* [1919] 2 KB 243, HL; *Bell v Lever Bros Ltd* [1932] AC 161 at 217, HL, per Lord Atkin; and SALE OF GOODS AND SUPPLY OF SERVICES vol 91 (2012) PARAS 152–153. As to circumstances in which a representee may be estopped from denying the representor's authority to deal with goods see eg *Henderson & Co v Williams* [1895] 1 QB 521, CA. See also ESTOPPEL vol 47 (2014) PARA 361; AGENCY vol 1 (2008) PARAS 25–26.

## 783. Right of representee to affirm or disaffirm the contract.

A representee[1] who has been induced[2] by misrepresentation, whether fraudulent or innocent[3], to enter into a contract or other binding transaction with the representor[4], has, on discovery of the real facts, in the first instance, a right of election only. He may either affirm or disaffirm the contract or transaction, and, if he disaffirms it, give notice to the representor and demand from him a complete restoration of the status quo. In the event of his demand not being complied with he may, subject to certain conditions[5] and affirmative defences[6], institute proceedings for the purpose of having the contract or transaction declared void and rescinded by the court, in which event specific restitution and other relief consequential upon the declaration and rescission may be decreed[7]. The right of election, when exercised, is finally exhausted and a representee may not disaffirm a contract after he has once affirmed it, or treat a contract as subsisting after he has disaffirmed it[8]. The representee is not, however, bound to choose one course rather than the other; nor is he bound to make any choice at all within any particular period of time, although he delays doing so at his peril[9]. Further, should he choose to adhere to the contract, he is still entitled to all such remedies in damages as are available to a representee in such circumstances[10].

1   As to who is a representee see PARAS 733–739.

2   As to inducement see PARA 771 et seq.

3   As to fraudulent misrepresentation see PARA 754 et seq; and as to innocent misrepresentation see PARAS 761–763. If an innocent misrepresentation is subsequently incorporated as a term of the contract the representee may still rescind if the misrepresentation was made on or after 22 April 1967: see the Misrepresentation Act 1967 ss 1, 5; and PARA 703. Before that date the only claim available was one for breach of contract: *Pennsylvania Shipping Co v Compagnie Nationale de Navigation* [1936] 2 All ER 1167.

As to the right of the representee of fraudulent misrepresentation to retake possession of property see PARA 780.

4   As to who is a representor see PARAS 724–732.

5  See PARAS 829–833.
6  See PARAS 824–828.
7  As to claims for rescission see PARA 811 et seq. As to damages in lieu of rescission see PARA 832.
8  *Clough v London and North Western Rly Co* (1871) LR 7 Exch 26 at 34, 36, Ex Ch; *Re Thomas Edward Brinsmead & Sons, Tomlin's Case* [1898] 1 Ch 104; *Kwei Tek Chao (t/as Zung Fu Co) v British Traders and Shippers Ltd* [1954] 2 QB 459, [1954] 1 All ER 779.
9  See PARA 833.
10 Thus, having unsuccessfully sued the company in the names of the proper officers for rescission (see *Clarke v Dickson* (1858) EB & E 148), the representee, on afterwards suing the directors for the same misrepresentations (which were proved to be fraudulent), was held entitled to damages: see *Clarke v Dickson* (1859) 6 CBNS 453. As to the circumstances in which damages are available see PARAS 780–781.

## 784. Misrepresentation as a defence to proceedings.

Whenever a representee[1] is entitled to rescission of a contract[2], or other analogous relief, on the ground of misrepresentation, he is also in a position, if the representor[3] seeks to enforce the contract against him, to set up the misrepresentation as a defence to the claim[4], whether the proceedings instituted by the representor are brought to enforce the agreement directly, although not specifically, as in the case of a claim for money due under it[5], or to enforce it indirectly, as in proceedings to recover damages[6], or to enforce it specifically[7], and whether the representor's claim be asserted in the form of a claim or counterclaim[8], or in accordance with any authorised summary procedure[9] or otherwise. The representee need not in any such case counterclaim for rescission[10].

The conditions precedent to the validity of the defence are substantially the same as the conditions under which relief by way of rescission is granted[11]. With two exceptions[12], the evidence which will support the one will support the other, and what is a good answer to rescission constitutes an equally good answer to a defence setting up misrepresentation[13].

1  As to who is a representee see PARAS 733–739.
2  As to claims for rescission see PARA 811 et seq.
3  As to who is a representor see PARAS 724–732.
4  As to pleading generally see CIVIL PROCEDURE vol 11 (2015) PARA 340 et seq. See also LIMITATION PERIODS vol 68 (2016) PARA 943 et seq.
5  The following are examples of a plea of misrepresentation made in answer to claims for debt in covenant, or for liquidated sums alleged to be due, or to recover chattels the property in which was alleged to have passed under the contract, or otherwise for the purpose of directly, though not specifically, enforcing the contract: *M'Carthy v Decaix* (1831) 2 Russ & M 614 (agreement of compromise); *Stone v Compton* (1838) 5 Bing NC 142 (promissory note); *Mallalieu v Hodgson* (1851) 16 QB 689 (release, to which the reply of fraudulent misrepresentation was held good as against the defendant setting up the release, although the plaintiff failed because it was shown that both parties were defrauding creditors); *Evans v Edmonds* (1853) 13 CB 777 (money due under covenant in deed); *Bannerman v White* (1861) 10 CBNS 844 (price of goods); *Lee v Jones* (1864) 17 CBNS 482 (guarantee); *Dawes v Harness* (1875) LR 10 CP 166 (cheque); *Hirschfeld v London, Brighton and South Coast Rly Co* (1876) 2 QBD 1 (deed of release); *Eyre v Smith* (1877) 2 CPD 435 at 438, CA (liquidation by arrangement); *Aaron's Reefs v Twiss* [1896] AC 273, HL (call money on forfeited shares); *Gordon v Street* [1899] 2 QB 641, CA (promissory note); *Components' Tube Co v Naylor* [1900] 2 IR 1; *Re General Railway Syndicate, Whiteley's Case* [1900] 1 Ch 365, CA (calls on shares); *Shankland & Co v Robinson & Co* (1920) 57 Sc LR 400, HL (price of goods); *Far Eastern Shipping Co Public Ltd v Scales Trading Ltd* [2000] 1 All ER (Comm) 319, PC (guarantee). As to misrepresentation as an answer to a claim under a policy of insurance see INSURANCE vol 60 (2018) PARA 31 et seq.
6  *Wharton v Lewis* (1824) 1 C & P 529 (breach of promise of marriage); *Foote v Hayne* (1824) 1 C & P 545 (the same); *Canham v Barry* (1855) 15 CB 597 (breach of agreement to deliver possession).
7  As to claims for specific performance see generally SPECIFIC PERFORMANCE vol 95 (2017) PARA 501 et seq. The following are examples of refusal to grant specific performance on the

ground of the claimant's misrepresentation, set up by the defendant as a defence: *Cadman v Horner* (1810) 18 Ves 10; *Beaumont v Dukes* (1822) Jac 422; *Harris v Kemble* (1831) 5 Bli NS 730, HL; *Lord Brooke v Rounthwaite* (1846) 5 Hare 298; *Price v Macaulay* (1852) 2 De GM & G 339, CA in Ch (as to one of the two lots the subject of the sale); *Reynell v Sprye* (1852) 1 De GM & G 660 (as to the cross-action); *Higgins v Samels* (1862) 2 John & H 460; *Caballero v Henty* (1874) 9 Ch App 447; *Redgrave v Hurd* (1881) 20 ChD 1, CA; *Smith v Land and House Property Corpn* (1884) 28 ChD 7, CA; *Archer v Stone* (1898) 78 LT 34; *Jacobs v Revell* [1900] 2 Ch 858 (as to the defendant's counterclaim); *Lee v Rayson* [1917] 1 Ch 613 (similar case); *Holliday v Lockwood* [1917] 2 Ch 47 (similar case).

8   In the following cases the representee set up misrepresentation as a reply or answer to the representor's counterclaim or cross-bill: *M'Carthy v Decaix* (1831) 2 Russ & M 614; *Mallalieu v Hodgson* (1851) 16 QB 689; *Hirschfeld v London, Brighton and South Coast Rly Co* (1876) 2 QBD 1; *Eyre v Smith* (1877) 2 CPD 435, CA; *Reynell v Sprye* (1852) 1 De GM & G 660; *Jacobs v Revell* [1900] 2 Ch 858.

9   Eg the statutory proceedings for settling the list of contributories in the winding up of a company, which any person named in it as a contributory can resist on the ground of misrepresentation set forth in an affidavit: see COMPANY AND PARTNERSHIP INSOLVENCY vol 17 (2017) PARA 616 et seq.

10   A counterclaim for rescission was added in *Redgrave v Hurd* (1881) 20 ChD 1, CA; *Smith v Land and House Property Corpn* (1884) 28 ChD 7, CA; *Components' Tube Co v Naylor* [1900] 2 IR 1; *Shepherd v Croft* [1911] 1 Ch 521; *Hilo Manufacturing Co Ltd v Williamson* (1911) 28 TLR 164, CA. A cross-bill was filed for the like purpose in *Reynell v Sprye* (1852) 1 De GM & G 660.

11   As to conditions of the right to rescind see PARA 813 et seq.

12   See PARAS 785–786.

13   See *United Shoe Machinery Co of Canada v Brunet* [1909] AC 330 at 338, PC, where the constituent elements of a good defence are described, and appear to be substantially the same as the ingredients in a cause of action or proceedings for rescission. See also PARAS 813–816. As to the application of the principle (see PARA 783) that a representee cannot seek to avoid a contract which he has affirmed see *Wakefield and Barnsley Banking Co v Normanton Local Board* (1881) 44 LT 697, CA; *Hemmings v Sceptre Life Association Ltd* [1905] 1 Ch 365; *United Shoe Machinery Co of Canada v Brunet*. As to the necessity that specific restitution should be possible in order that misrepresentation may constitute a good defence see *Harris v Kemble* (1831) 5 Bli NS 730 at 751–752, HL; *Urquhart v Macpherson* (1878) 3 App Cas 831 at 838, PC (a case where a plea of fraud was raised in a reply); and cf PARA 829. As to the burden of proof see PARA 786.

### 785. Position where specific performance is sought.

Where the representor[1] is suing for specific performance of the contract, the jurisdiction being discretionary, less strong evidence will induce the court to give effect to the representee's[2] case than if he were claiming rescission[3], or were defending himself against a claim to enforce the contract otherwise than specifically[4]; for in the last two forms of proceeding the relief is such that the contract is avoided, or deemed a nullity, for all purposes; whereas, when specific performance is refused, it is merely a question of denying the party a particular remedy, leaving all others open to him, or of withholding relief except on equitable terms as to abatement of price, compensation or otherwise[5].

1   As to who is a representor see PARAS 724–732.

2   As to who is a representee see PARAS 733–739.

3   *Cadman v Horner* (1810) 18 Ves 10 at 12; *Re Banister, Broad v Munton* (1879) 12 ChD 131 at 142, CA. However, where the representee is in a position to apply for rescission, it is usually prudent to do so, and in some cases he comes to the court with a better equity if he adopts that course in preference to a waiting attitude: *Fenn v Craig* (1838) 3 Y & C Ex 216 at 222, where an insurance company applied to set aside a policy, instead of taking premiums until the death of the insured, and then disputing liability. On the other hand, where the representor company has forfeited the representee's shares, and there is, therefore, no contract to avoid, it is both prudent and proper to await the attack: *Aaron's Reefs Ltd v Twiss* [1896] AC 273 at 293, HL, per Lord Macnaghten. As to claims for rescission see PARA 811 et seq.

4   As to misrepresentation as a defence see PARAS 784, 787.

5　Thus specific performance was only granted with compensation in the following cases: *Scott v Hanson* (1829) 1 Russ & M 128 at 131 (as to part of the property); *King v Wilson* (1843) 6 Beav 124 at 128–129 (as to part of the property); *Hughes v Jones* (1861) 3 De GF & J 307. However, where it would be unjust to the representee (as in *Beaumont v Dukes* (1822) Jac 422 at 426) or it would be impracticable to make a decree subject to compensation (as in *Lord Brooke v Rounthwaite* (1846) 5 Hare 298 at 305, although there was an express condition of sale here providing for compensation), specific performance will be absolutely, and not conditionally, refused. Abatement or allowance may be forced on the representor as the condition of specific performance, but the representee who seeks specific performance has no right to this conditional remedy unless he derives it from some express term in the contract: see *Cordingley v Cheeseborough* (1862) 4 De GF & J 379 at 384–389 (misrepresentation by vendor as to measurement of property; purchaser rejected vendor's offer to vacate the contract; terms of contract applied; no deduction from purchase money); *Re Terry and White's Contract* (1886) 32 ChD 14 at 31, CA, per Lindley LJ (similar case; in this situation the vendor would sue in vain for specific performance without compensation; but that is quite a different thing from saying that the purchaser is entitled to insist upon specific performance without paying the price contracted for). See also *Molphy v Coyne* (1919) 53 ILT 177.

## 786.　Burden of proof of election to avoid contract.

In the case of proceedings to have the contract set aside it is not necessary for the representee[1] to allege or prove that he has exercised his right of election by avoiding the contract, the claim or counterclaim being itself sufficient[2], and the burden being on the representor[3] to prove affirmation and not on the representee to prove avoidance[4]. In the case of a defence, on the other hand, it appears that the burden is on the representee of proving not merely that the contract was induced by misrepresentation, but also that, having become voidable on that ground, it was in fact avoided by him within a reasonable time after discovery of the truth, and that he has restored, or is in a position to restore, any benefit obtained under it[5]. It seems that the fact that the representee has avoided the contract must be specifically pleaded in the defence[6].

1　As to who is a representee see PARAS 733–739.
2　*Hyde v Watts* (1843) 12 M & W 254 at 270; *Capel & Co v Sim's Ships Compositions Co* (1888) 58 LT 807 at 811.
3　As to who is a representor see PARAS 724–732.
4　As to affirmation as a defence see PARAS 827–828.
5　See *Dawes v Harness* (1875) LR 10 CP 166 at 167–168; *Urquhart v Macpherson* (1878) 3 App Cas 831 at 836–838, PC (where a plea of fraud was raised by a plaintiff in his reply); *United Shoe Machinery Co of Canada v Brunet* [1909] AC 330 at 338, PC; *First National Reinsurance Co v Greenfield* [1921] 2 KB 260 at 266, DC, per Lush J.
6　See *Meldon v Lawless* (1869) 18 WR 261; *Anderson v Costello* (1871) 19 WR 628 (both Irish cases); *Deposit and General Life Assurance Co v Ayscough* (1856) 6 E & B 761 at 762 per Crompton J. Cf *Dawes v Harness* (1875) LR 10 CP 166, where the defendant pleaded that the contract was induced by fraudulent misrepresentation, and the plaintiff was held entitled to rely on the defendant's failure in fact to disaffirm the contract, although he had not specifically raised the matter in his reply, since the defendant's plea of fraud was bad unless it imported an allegation that he had disaffirmed the contract, and the plaintiff's reply impliedly traversed this allegation.
　　Where proceedings to enforce calls on shares in a company and the shares have not been forfeited, a defendant alleging that the contract to take shares was induced by misrepresentation must not only plead and prove that he has disaffirmed the contract, but must normally also either plead and prove that he has taken proceedings for rectification of the company's register or join a counterclaim for rectification with his defence; it is not sufficient for him to plead merely that he is entitled to rectification, unless he has given an undertaking to begin rectification proceedings: see *Deposit and General Life Assurance Co v Ayscough*; *First National Reinsurance Co v Greenfield* [1921] 2 KB 260, DC, explaining *Bwlch-y-Plwm Lead Mining Co v Baynes* (1867) LR 2 Exch 324, and applying observations in *Aaron's Reefs Ltd v Twiss* [1896] AC 273, HL. See COMPANIES vol 15A (2016) PARA 1268.

## 787. Misrepresentation as a defence against representor's assignee.

In certain cases where proof that a contract was induced by misrepresentation would have afforded a good defence to the representee[1] in proceedings by the representor[2], it may not be a sufficient defence in proceedings by an assignee of the representor, for example in a case where the representee has been induced to execute a negotiable instrument and is sued upon it by a holder in due course[3]. However, where a debt is not secured by a negotiable instrument, it seems that a representee sued for the debt by an assignee of the representor is entitled to set up the defence that the contract under which the debt arose was induced by misrepresentation[4], even though he cannot set up against the assignee any claim for damages which he may have against the representor[5]. The rights of a third person to whom goods forming the subject of a voidable contract for sale, or land forming the subject of a voidable conveyance, have been transferred for value and without notice are mentioned elsewhere in this title[6].

1   As to who is a representee see PARAS 733–739.
2   As to misrepresentation as a defence see PARA 784. As to who is a representor see PARAS 724–732.
3   As to the general principle that a holder in due course holds free from defects in title see FINANCIAL INSTRUMENTS AND TRANSACTIONS vol 49 (2015) PARA 272. As to the burden of proof in a case of fraud see FINANCIAL INSTRUMENTS AND TRANSACTIONS vol 49 (2015) PARA 262.
4   See *Stoddart v Union Trust Ltd* [1912] 1 KB 181 at 189, CA, per Vaughan Williams LJ, and at 191 per Buckley LJ; and PARA 820. As to the general principle that an assignee of a chose or thing in action takes subject to equities see CHOSES IN ACTION vol 13 (2017) PARA 83.
5   *Stoddart v Union Trust Ltd* [1912] 1 KB 181, CA.
6   See PARAS 782, 820.

# 2. CLAIMS FOR DAMAGES

## (1) Damages for Deceit

### (i) Common Law Claim for Damages for Deceit

**788. Claim for damages for deceit.**

It may be preferable to frame a cause of action under the Misrepresentation Act 1967[1], rather than under the common law. However, where it is thought that a case is suitable for pleading under the common law, the following principles apply. On proof of the several matters subsequently mentioned[2], a claim[3] is maintainable at the suit of the representee[4] for damages in respect of fraudulent misrepresentation[5]. It is founded in tort[6], and the same principles of law and rules of evidence are applicable in whatever court the proceedings are instituted[7].

Since the claim is based on fraud, the period of limitation does not begin to run until the representee has discovered the fraud or could with reasonable diligence have discovered it[8].

1   See PARA 800.
2   See PARA 789. The particulars of the claim must be set out in the claim form and the claimant must specifically set out any allegation of fraud and/or details of any misrepresentation where he wishes to rely on them in support of his claim: see CPR PD 16–*Statements of Case* paras 1.1 et seq, 8.2(1), (3); and CIVIL PROCEDURE vol 11 (2015) PARA 347. See also *Newton Chemical Ltd v Arsenis* [1989] 1 WLR 1297, CA; *Garden Neptune Shipping v Occidental Worldwide Investment Corpn* [1990] 1 Lloyd's Rep 330, CA; *Movemain Ltd v Lewis* [1993] EGCS 130, CA. Where there is a charge of fraud, the claim in the Queen's Bench Division or the county court is tried with a jury unless the court is of opinion that the trial requires any prolonged examination of documents or accounts or any scientific or local investigation which cannot conveniently be made with a jury: see the Senior Courts Act 1981 s 69(1); the County Courts Act 1984 s 66(3); and JURIES vol 61A (2018) PARA 220. 'Fraud' here means the tort of deceit: see *Barclays Bank Ltd v Cole* [1967] 2 QB 738, [1966] 3 All ER 948, CA (decided under earlier legislation); and JURIES vol 61A (2018) PARA 220.
3   This includes a counterclaim: see *Redgrave v Hurd* (1881) 20 ChD 1, CA.
4   As to who is a representee see PARAS 733–739.
5   As to fraudulent misrepresentation see PARA 754 et seq.
6   Thus a claim for damages for fraudulent misrepresentation by which the plaintiff was induced to enter into a contract was not a claim upon or in relation to or in connection with the contract within the meaning of an arbitration clause in the contract, so as to enable the action to be stayed and referred to arbitration under the arbitration clause: see *Monro v Bognor UDC* [1915] 3 KB 167, CA. As to the general principles of tort see TORT vol 97 (2015) PARA 401 et seq.
7   The claim when brought at common law is sometimes called by its old name of 'action of deceit', and when brought in the Chancery Division it used to be described as an equitable claim for damages in the nature of, or analogous to, an action of deceit; but whatever distinctive terminology may be used, it has long been settled that the two forms of proceeding are precisely the same, and governed by the same principles: *Peek v Gurney* (1873) LR 6 HL 377 at 384, 390; *Arkwright v Newbold* (1881) 17 ChD 301 at 320, CA; *Smith v Chadwick* (1884) 9 App Cas 187 at 193, HL; *Schroeder v Mendl* (1877) 37 LT 452 at 454, CA; *Derry v Peek* (1889) 14 App Cas 337 at 360, HL. However, the necessity of proving fraud in proceedings for deceit has not narrowed the scope of the equitable remedy, which enables the court to award compensation for breach of a special duty in cases which, although classified in equity as fraud, do not necessarily import the element of dolus malus: *Nocton v Lord Ashburton* [1914] AC 932, HL; and see PARA 755. As to misrepresentation in offer documents and the principles governing proceedings for deceit as a result of fraudulent misrepresentations in offer documents see COMPANIES vol 15A (2016) PARA 1259 et seq.
8   See the Limitation Act 1980 s 32(1)(a); and LIMITATION PERIODS vol 68 (2016) PARAS 986, 1220 et seq. This extension of the limitation period applies even if the deliberate concealment of

facts relevant to a cause of action does not take place until after the accrual of the cause of action: *Sheldon v RHM Outhwaite (Underwriting Agencies) Ltd* [1996] AC 102, [1995] 2 All ER 558, HL.

## 789. Constituent elements of the claim for deceit.

In any proceedings for deceit the burden is on the representee[1] of alleging and (except in so far as any of them are either expressly or impliedly admitted before or at the trial) proving all of the following matters: (1) that the alleged representation consisted of something said, written or done which amounts in law to a representation[2]; (2) that the defendant was the representor[3]; (3) that the claimant was the representee; (4) that the representation was false[4]; (5) materiality and inducement[5]; (6) alteration of position[6]; (7) fraud[7]; and (8) damage[8]. Of these matters, the first six are common to all forms of proceeding for misrepresentation[9]. In proceedings for deceit, the concurrence of fraud and damage is essential if damages are to be recovered, and neither is sufficient without the other[10].

1 As to who is a representee see PARAS 733–739.
2 As to what amounts to a representation see PARA 702 et seq.
3 As to who is a representor see PARAS 724–732.
4 As to falsity see PARA 740 et seq.
5 As to materiality and inducement see PARAS 764–770.
6 As to alteration of position see PARAS 777–779.
7 As to fraudulent misrepresentation see PARA 754 et seq. As to the meaning of 'fraud' see PARAS 755–756.
8 As to damage see PARAS 790–792.
9 Ie not only claims for damages, but also proceedings for rescission (see PARA 811 et seq) and defences based upon misrepresentation (see PARAS 784–787).
10 This has been recognised from the earliest times: see *Baily v Merrell* (1615) 3 Bulst 94 at 95; *Pasley v Freeman* (1789) 3 Term Rep 51 at 56 per Buller J (fraud without damage, or damage without fraud, gives no cause of action; but when these two concur, an action lies); *Levy v Langridge* (1838) 4 M & W 337, Ex Ch; *Derry v Peek* (1889) 14 App Cas 337 at 343, HL, per Lord Halsbury LC. For illustrations of the principle that fraud must be alleged and proved see *Chandelor v Lopus* (1603) Cro Jac 4; *Horncastle v Moat* (1824) 1 C & P 166; *Childers v Wooler* (1860) 2 E & E 287, Ex Ch.

### (ii) Damage

## 790. What actionable damage includes.

In a claim for fraudulent misrepresentation[1] actionable damage includes actual and temporal injury, that is, some loss of money or money's worth, or some tangible detriment capable of being quantified and assessed[2]. It seems that actionable damage may now also extend to injured feelings, inconvenience and mental suffering[3].

It may include loss arising out of a contract entered into on the faith of the representation; loss of money paid to a third person or to the representor himself[4]; in certain circumstances, loss of profits, appointments or earnings[5]; or the equivalent in money of any destruction of, or injury to, property; or any expense, or detriment of any kind, which allows pecuniary computation[6].

The damage may consist in the personal and physical injury which results from doing some act on the faith of an express representation[7]. Also, where a representee[8] is induced by fraudulent misrepresentation to believe a certain state of things to exist, or a certain thing to have happened, and the misrepresentation is of such a nature that the mere making of it to a normal person, who believes it, is calculated to, and does, produce not merely mental distress but consequential physical and personal injury, then, even if he does nothing, but only suffers something by reason of his belief in its truth, his bodily suffering is damage of which the law takes notice in a claim founded on such misrepresentation[9].

1   As to fraudulent misrepresentation see PARA 754 et seq.

2   As to the principles on which damages are computed and quantified see PARA 804 et seq; and DAMAGES. The topic now under discussion concerns only the qualities and legal constituents of damage.

3   See eg *Archer v Brown* [1985] QB 401 (aggravated damages to compensate for injured feelings may be awarded in deceit on the same basis as in contract). It used to be the position that mental distress, unless accompanied by physical effects, or mere loss of social advantages to which no money value could be attached was not included: see *Chamberlain v Boyd* (1883) 11 QBD 407, CA (slander not actionable except on proof of actual damage, and therefore in point); *Mafo v Adams* [1970] 1 QB 548, [1969] 3 All ER 1404, CA (plaintiff was entitled to damages for loss of a regulated tenancy but not to exemplary damages for inconvenience caused by the defendant's deceit). See DAMAGES vol 29 (2014) PARA 429. As to the principles on which the court will act in cases where the damage suffered consists in the incurring of expenses resulting from criminal proceedings or the making of reparation for the consequences of a criminal act see *Askey v Golden Wine Co Ltd* [1948] 2 All ER 35. As to aggravated and exemplary damages see PARA 804; and DAMAGES vol 29 (2014) PARA 322 et seq.

4   Money paid to the representor himself is usually sued for as money had and received (see CONTRACT); but it may also be treated as damages, even though the amount is liquidated: *Kettlewell v Refuge Assurance Co Ltd* [1908] 1 KB 545 at 550, CA, per Alverstone CJ; on appeal sub nom *Refuge Assurance Co Ltd v Kettlewell* [1909] AC 243, HL. As to who is a representor see PARAS 724–732.

5   *Barley v Walford* (1846) 9 QB 197 (loss of profit on a design for silk handkerchiefs); *Denton v Great Northern Rly Co* (1856) 5 E & B 860 (missing an appointment); *Burrows v Rhodes* [1899] 1 QB 816 (loss of pay and earnings and capacity to earn); *4 Eng Ltd v Harper* [2008] EWHC 915 (Ch), [2009] Ch 91, [2008] 3 WLR 892 (loss of opportunity to purchase and profit from company). As to loss of profits see further PARA 808.

6   As to loss of property by reason of fraudulent misrepresentation see *Mullett v Mason* (1866) LR 1 CP 559 (loss of cow from cattle plague, and of other cows with which it was placed and which became infected with the same disease). As to expenses see *Barley v Walford* (1846) 9 QB 197 (in addition to his loss of profits, the plaintiff was put to trouble and expense in making inquiries and communicating with the persons falsely represented to be the registered owners of the design); *Milne v Marwood* (1855) 15 CB 778 (expense of fitting up a vessel); *Richardson v Silvester* (1873) LR 9 QB 34 (time and money spent in going to see the farm advertised); *Wilkinson v Downton* [1897] 2 QB 57 (expense of railway fares, inter alia); *Burrows v Rhodes* [1899] 1 QB 816 (fees paid for surgical operations); *Pritty v Child* (1902) 71 LJKB 512, DC (expense of sinking a well).

7   The following are examples of physical injury resulting from the use of a chattel, or of land, the qualities or condition of which had been misrepresented: *Levy v Langridge* (1838) 4 M & W 337, Ex Ch (gun); *Longmeid v Holliday* (1851) 6 Exch 761 (lamp; plaintiff failed on other grounds); *Burtsal v Bianchi* (1891) 65 LT 678 (illness caused by taking a house with defective drains; plaintiff failed on other grounds).

8   As to who is a representee see PARAS 733–739.

9   *Wilkinson v Downton* [1897] 2 QB 57; *Janvier v Sweeney* [1919] 2 KB 316, CA (both cases of tortious liability). As to the recovery, generally, of damages for illness caused by shock see NEGLIGENCE vol 78 (2018) PARA 11. See also DAMAGES vol 29 (2014) PARA 497.

### 791. Connection between the damage and the representation.

In every case where it is necessary to prove actionable damage[1] it is also necessary for the representee[2] to establish a causal connection, as distinct from a relation of mere sequence and succession, between the damage and the misrepresentation. The damage must be shown to have been a natural and direct result of the misrepresentation being acted on or, where the representee is induced by fraudulent misrepresentation to believe a certain state of things to exist[3], of the misrepresentation being believed[4]. Where this connection is not made out, then, even if he proves that he did in fact sustain the damage alleged by reason of his belief in the truth of the misrepresentation, the representee will not succeed in the claim[5]; but, where it is made out, he will succeed[6]. The representee is normally entitled to succeed if he is in a position to allege and prove that the representor[7] in fact intended the precise kind of damage which resulted[8]. Where a person suffers damage as a result of acting on a fraudulent misrepresentation made to another with the intention that it should, or the knowledge that it will, be so acted upon, damages are recoverable at his instance from the representor[9].

1  See PARA 790.

2  As to who is a representee see PARAS 733–739.

3  See PARA 790. As to fraudulent misrepresentation see PARA 754 et seq. As to inducement see PARAS 771–776.

4  See DAMAGES vol 29 (2014) PARA 430 et seq. There may be circumstances in which a representee may know that the representation is false but nevertheless may be held to rely upon the misrepresentation as a matter of fact: *Hayward v Zurich Insurance Co Plc* [2016] UKSC 48, [2017] AC 142, [2016] 4 All ER 628: see PARA 768.

5  *Collins v Cave* (1860) 6 H & N 131 at 134, Ex Ch; *Barry v Croskey* (1861) 2 John & H 1 (demurrer allowed); *Dashwood v Jermyn* (1879) 12 ChD 776; *Ajello v Worsley* [1898] 1 Ch 274 at 281–283; cf *Australian Steam Shipping Co Ltd v Devitt* (1917) 33 TLR 178.

6  *Polhill v Walter* (1832) 3 B & Ad 114 at 123–124; *Barley v Walford* (1846) 9 QB 197 at 206–209; *Mullett v Mason* (1866) LR 1 CP 559 at 563–564; *Wilkinson v Downton* [1897] 2 QB 57 at 59; *Janvier v Sweeney* [1919] 2 KB 316 at 324–325, CA, per Bankes LJ. A possible exception to this rule is where the damage is irrecoverable on grounds of public policy: see *Askey v Golden Wine Co Ltd* [1948] 2 All ER 35; *Shelley v Paddock* [1979] QB 120, [1978] 3 All ER 129; cf *Saunders v Edwards* [1987] 2 All ER 651, [1987] 1 WLR 1116, CA. See also DAMAGES vol 29 (2014) PARA 397.

7  As to who is a representor see PARAS 724–732.

8  See *Andrews v Mockford* [1896] 1 QB 372 at 378, CA, per Lord Esher MR, and at 384–385 per Rigby LJ.

9  *Levy v Langridge* (1838) 4 M & W 337, Ex Ch; *Longmeid v Holliday* (1851) 6 Exch 761 at 766; *Barry v Croskey* (1861) 2 John & H 1; *Gerhard v Bates* (1853) 2 E & B 476; *Clarke v Dickson* (1859) 6 CBNS 453; *National Exchange Co of Glasgow v Drew and Dick* (1855) 2 Macq 103, HL; *Peek v Gurney* (1873) LR 6 HL 377 at 410. As to the circumstances in which a person to whom a representation is passed on is a representee see PARA 734 et seq. As to the circumstances in which a person other than an original allottee of shares can maintain proceedings for deceit in respect of a misrepresentation in a company offer document see COMPANIES vol 15A (2016) PARAS 1270–1275.

## 792. Questions of fact and of law in relation to damage.

All questions of damage are questions of fact, the burden of establishing which lies upon the representee[1], subject to the following, which are questions of law, namely: (1) whether there is any evidence of the alleged damage having been sustained at all; (2) whether, if sustained, it is of the kind which the law recognises; (3) whether there is any evidence that the damage was in fact caused by the representee's belief in the truth of the misrepresentation; and (4) whether the proved damage was the natural and direct consequence of the misrepresentation[2].

1  *Baily v Merrell* (1615) 3 Bulst 94; *Pasley v Freeman* (1789) 3 Term Rep 51 at 53 per Grose J; *Smith v Chadwick* (1884) 9 App Cas 187 at 195–196, HL. As to who is a representee see PARAS 733–739.

2  *Vernon v Keys* (1810) 12 East 632 at 638 (affd (1812) 4 Taunt 488, Ex Ch); *Eastwood v Bain* (1858) 3 H & N 738; *Bear v Stevenson* (1874) 30 LT 177, PC; *Clydesdale Bank Ltd v Paton* [1896] AC 381 at 397–398, HL; *Tallerman v Dowsing Radiant Heat Co* [1900] 1 Ch 1 (on appeal [1900] 1 Ch 1 at 9, CA); *Stevens v Hoare* (1904) 20 TLR 407 at 409 per Joyce J.

## (iii) Parties

### 793. Who may sue and be sued.

The possible parties to a claim for damages for deceit are ordinarily the persons who were, or who are deemed to have been, the parties to the representation[1].

1 Deceit may arise in the context of domestic relations: *P v B (Paternity: Damages for Deceit)* [2001] 1 FLR 1041. As to who are representees and representors see PARAS 723–739. As to claims against companies and other corporations see COMPANIES vol 14 (2016) PARA 302 et seq; CORPORATIONS vol 24 (2010) PARA 477 et seq. As to the parties to a claim generally see CIVIL PROCEDURE vol 11 (2015) PARA 469 et seq. As to liability in tort generally see TORT vol 97 (2015) PARA 401 et seq.

### 794. Effect of death or disability or assignment of rights.

The survival of a cause of action in tort in the case of the death of the person entitled to sue or the person liable to be sued[1], the effect of bankruptcy[2] or winding up proceedings[3] upon the right to sue and liability to be sued, the liability in tort of minors[4] and persons who lack capacity[5], and the modes by which proceedings may be instituted and carried on by or against minors[6] and persons who lack capacity[7], are considered elsewhere in this work.

As regards assignments inter vivos, the bare right to sue for damages for misrepresentation is not transferable[8].

1 As to the survival of causes of action for the benefit of or against the estates of deceased persons, and the effect of the death of a party while a claim is proceeding, see CIVIL PROCEDURE vol 11 (2015) PARAS 489–490; WILLS AND INTESTACY vol 103 (2016) PARA 1277 et seq.
2 See BANKRUPTCY AND INDIVIDUAL INSOLVENCY vol 5 (2013) PARA 447 et seq. As to the principle that where a misrepresentation results in a pecuniary loss, and personal injury to the representee is only incidental, the right of action passes to the representee's trustee in bankruptcy see *Hodgson v Sidney* (1866) LR 1 Exch 313; and BANKRUPTCY AND INDIVIDUAL INSOLVENCY vol 5 (2013) PARA 448. As to the principle that the court will not restrain any action against a bankrupt to which his discharge would not be a defence see *Re Blake, ex p Coker* (1875) 10 Ch App 652; and BANKRUPTCY AND INDIVIDUAL INSOLVENCY vol 5 (2013) PARA 753.
3 See BANKRUPTCY AND INDIVIDUAL INSOLVENCY; COMPANY AND PARTNERSHIP INSOLVENCY.
4 See CHILDREN AND YOUNG PERSONS vol 9 (2017) PARAS 26–27.
5 See eg *Morriss v Marsden* [1952] 1 All ER 925; and MENTAL HEALTH AND CAPACITY vol 75 (2013) PARA 761.
6 See CHILDREN AND YOUNG PERSONS vol 10 (2017) PARA 1398 et seq.
7 See CPR 21.2; CPR PD 21–*Children and Protected Parties*; and MENTAL HEALTH AND CAPACITY vol 75 (2013) PARA 601.
8 *De Hoghton v Money* (1866) 2 Ch App 164 at 169, CA, per Turner LJ (the right to complain of fraud is not a marketable commodity). See also CHOSES IN ACTION vol 13 (2017) PARA 98. The rule applies equally to proceedings for rescission, where nothing is assigned but the bare right to sue: see PARA 819.

### 795. Capacity of member to sue company.

A person is not debarred from obtaining damages or other compensation from a company by reason only of his holding or having held shares in the company or any right to apply or subscribe for shares or to be included in the company's register in respect of shares[1].

1 Companies Act 2006 s 655. This provision has the effect of nullifying the rule in *Houldsworth v City of Glasgow Bank* (1880) 5 App Cas 317, HL, under which a subscriber for shares in a company could not claim damages for misrepresentation unless he severed his connection with the company: see *Soden v British and Commonwealth Holdings plc (in administration)* [1996] 3 All ER 951 at 959, [1996] 2 BCLC 207 at 215, CA, per Peter Gibson LJ; and COMPANIES vol 15A (2016) PARA 1276.

The rule did not affect the right of the shareholder to take any other kind of proceeding against the company in respect of the species of misrepresentation in question (*Western Bank of Scotland v Addie* (1867) LR 1 Sc & Div 145 at 163–164, HL) or to sue for damages in respect of any other species of misrepresentation (*Houldsworth v City of Glasgow Bank* at 329 per Lord Selborne).

As to the relief available where a partnership agreement or a purchase of a partnership share is induced by fraud or misrepresentation see PARTNERSHIP vol 79 (2014) PARAS 146–147.

## 796. Responsibility for the fraud of an agent.

A principal is responsible in tort for a representation made fraudulently by his agent, acting within the scope of his authority[1]. He is equally responsible where the representation was first made by the agent before the commencement of the agency but continued after its commencement, finally inducing a third person to enter into a contract which the agent made whilst acting within the scope of his authority[2]. Where an innocent misrepresentation[3] is made by an agent, the falsity of the facts of which are known to the principal, the principal will only be liable for deceit if he had expressly authorised the making of the misrepresentation or had deliberately employed the agent in order that the agent's ignorance might result in its being made[4]. A person becomes liable in tort for the fraudulent misrepresentation[5] of an alleged agent if, subsequent to the making of any such representation, he intervenes and adopts the benefit of it[6].

An agent is personally liable in tort for his own fraudulent misrepresentation[7].

1  *Lloyd v Grace, Smith & Co* [1912] AC 716, HL. See also *S Pearson & Son Ltd v Dublin Corpn* [1907] AC 351 at 357–358, HL, per the Earl of Halsbury; *Gordon v Selico Co Ltd* [1986] 1 EGLR 71, 18 HLR 219, CA; *Barclays Bank plc v Kalamohan* [2010] EWHC 1383 (Ch), [2010] All ER (D) 59 (Jun); and AGENCY vol 1 (2017) PARAS 136, 153 et seq. As regards the liability of a principal in tort for a criminal act by an agent see AGENCY vol 1 (2017) PARA 156. As to the liability of corporations for the torts of their agents or employees see CORPORATIONS vol 24 (2010) PARAS 477–478. See also COMPANIES vol 14 (2016) PARA 297. A friendly society has been held disentitled to retain money procured by the fraudulent misrepresentation of its agent: *Byrne v Rudd* [1920] 2 IR 12, Ir CA.
   A person may also be liable as a joint tortfeasor of the tort of deceit: *Dadourian Group International Inc v Simms* [2009] EWCA Civ 169 at [84], [2009] 1 Lloyd's Rep 601 at [84], [2009] All ER (D) 175 (Mar). It may also be open to a claimant to sue on a conspiracy to commit a tort: *Kuwait Oil Tanker Co SAK v Al Bader* [2000] 2 All ER (Comm) 271 at [127]–[129]; *London Allied Holdings Ltd v Lee* [2007] EWHC 2061 (Ch) at [252], [2007] All ER (D) 153 (Sep).
2  *Briess v Woolley* [1954] AC 333, [1954] 1 All ER 909, HL.
3  As to innocent misrepresentation see PARAS 761–763.
4  *Cornfoot v Fowke* (1840) 6 M & W 358; *Ludgater v Love* (1881) 44 LT 694, CA; *Gordon Hill Trust Ltd v Segall* [1941] 2 All ER 379, CA; *Armstrong v Strain* [1952] 1 KB 232, [1952] 1 All ER 139, CA; *Garnac Grain Co Inc v HMF Faure and Farclough Ltd* [1968] AC 1130n, [1967] 2 All ER 353, HL. See also AGENCY vol 1 (2008) PARAS 135, 152. As to the responsibility of an innocent member of a firm for the fraud of his partner see *Re Collie, ex p Adamson* (1878) 8 ChD 807 at 820, CA; and PARTNERSHIP vol 79 (2014) PARA 59 et seq.
   The statements in the text relate to liability for deceit. It may now be possible in appropriate cases to hold the principal liable for a careless statement by an agent or for so organising his business that although no one person can be said to be negligent, operations as a whole can be said to be negligent: see *WB Anderson & Sons Ltd v Rhodes (Liverpool) Ltd* [1967] 2 All ER 850. As to the liability of an agent for negligent misstatements made to a contractor to induce him to tender for the design and construction of a development see *J Jarvis and Sons Ltd v Castle Wharf Developments Ltd* [2001] EWCA Civ 19, [2001] Lloyd's Rep PN 328, [2001] All ER (D) 108 (Jan); and AGENCY vol 1 (2008) PARA 153. As to liability for careless misstatements see PARAS 762–763, 797–799; and NEGLIGENCE vol 78 (2018) PARA 13.
5  As to fraudulent misrepresentation see PARA 754 et seq.
6  *Wilson v Tumman* (1843) 6 Man & G 236 at 242; approved in *Keighley Maxted & Co v Durant* [1901] AC 240 at 246–247, HL, per Lord Macnaghten. As to the ratification by a principal of the acts of his agent see AGENCY vol 1 (2017) PARA 58 et seq.
7  *Eaglesfield v Marquis of Londonderry* (1878) 26 WR 540 at 541, HL; *Goldrei Foucard & Son v*

*Sinclair and Russian Chamber of Commerce in London* [1918] 1 KB 180, CA; and see AGENCY vol 1 (2008) PARAS 160, 164. See also *Convent Hospital Ltd v Eberlin and Partners* (1989) 23 ConLR 112, CA.

# (2) Damages for Negligent Words

### 797. Damages for negligent words at common law.

It was long believed to be a basic principle of English law that there was no liability for damages for financial loss caused by careless words in the absence of a contractual or fiduciary obligation to take care[1]. It is now clear that this view is wrong and that there may be a tortious claim for damages based upon a duty to take care, independent of contract or fiduciary obligations[2]. Such a claim may arise where there have been careless statements in the course of performing a contractual duty to take care[3] or in pre-contractual negotiations[4].

1   See *Le Lievre v Gould* [1893] 1 QB 491, CA; *Candler v Crane, Christmas & Co* [1951] 2 KB 164, [1951] 1 All ER 426, CA.
2   See *Hedley Byrne & Co Ltd v Heller & Partners Ltd* [1964] AC 465, [1963] 2 All ER 575, HL. For a discussion of this and later authorities see NEGLIGENCE vol 78 (2018) PARA 13. As to the Consumer Insurance (Disclosure and Representations) Act 2012 see PARA 762; and INSURANCE vol 60 (2018) PARA 29 et seq.
3   See PARA 798.
4   See PARA 799.

### 798. Careless statements made in the course of performing a contractual duty to take care.

The practice of a profession, art or calling which demands a special skill or ability carries with it a duty to exercise a reasonable amount of skill or ability. Before 1963[1] it was thought that where a person failed to use such reasonable skill or ability he was liable for breach of contractual duty[2] only and was not under a general duty in tort unless the failure was likely to cause physical injury to persons or property[3]. After 1963 it was at first assumed that this continued to be the case[4], but it is now clear that this is incorrect and that there may be a claim in tort for breach of duty of care in addition to a claim in contract[5]. The claims in contract and tort may coincide but different principles may apply to the assessment of damages, and in particular a different limitation period may be applicable for each cause of action[6].

1   Ie before the decision in *Hedley Byrne & Co Ltd v Heller & Partners Ltd* [1964] AC 465, [1963] 2 All ER 575, HL: see PARA 797.
2   See CONTRACT vol 22 (2012) PARA 210.
3   *Groom v Crocker* [1939] 1 KB 194, [1938] 2 All ER 394, CA; *Bean v Wade* (1885) 2 TLR 157, CA; cf *Nocton v Lord Ashburton* [1914] AC 932 at 952–956, HL, per Lord Haldane.
4   *Bagot v Stevens Scanlan & Co* [1966] 1 QB 197, [1964] 3 All ER 577, where a relationship creating a duty on the defendants to exercise reasonable skill and care arose out of the contractual relationship alone; *Clark v Kirby-Smith* [1964] Ch 506, [1964] 2 All ER 835, where the liability of a solicitor to his client for negligence was held to be a liability in contract and not in tort.
5   *Esso Petroleum Co Ltd v Mardon* [1976] QB 801, [1976] 2 All ER 5, CA, where a negligent representation was made by a person holding himself out as having special expertise in circumstances which gave rise to the duty to take reasonable care to see that the representation was correct; the duty of care existed during the pre-contractual negotiations and survived the making of the written contract, and the plaintiffs were held liable in the tort of negligence; *Batty v Metropolitan Property Realisations Ltd* [1978] QB 554, [1978] 2 All ER 445, CA, where the principle that a duty could be owed and a person could be liable both in contract and tort was held not to be confined to cases where a person owed a duty of care in relation to professional skills; *Midland Bank Trust Co Ltd v Hett, Stubbs & Kemp* [1979] Ch 384, [1978] 3 All ER 571, where

solicitors were held liable to their client in tort for breach of the duty of care, the decision in *Clark v Kirby-Smith* [1964] Ch 506, [1964] 2 All ER 835 being doubted and not followed. See also *JEB Fasteners Ltd v Marks Bloom & Co* [1983] 1 All ER 583, CA; *Tai Hing Cotton Mill Ltd v Liu Chong Hing Bank Ltd* [1986] AC 80 at 107, [1985] 2 All ER 947 at 957, PC (in this case, the Privy Council favoured the contractual analysis; but this decision may now be seen as argument against allowing a tortious duty of care more extensive than that provided for by the contract); *Central Trust Co v Rafuse* (1986) 31 DLR (4th) 481, Can SC; *Henderson v Merrett Syndicates* [1995] 2 AC 145, [1994] 3 All ER 506, HL; *White v Jones* [1995] 2 AC 207, [1995] 1 All ER 691, HL. See generally NEGLIGENCE; TORT vol 97 (2015) PARA 401 et seq.

6 See LIMITATION PERIODS vol 68 (2016) PARA 952 et seq. As to the measure of damages in tort and contract see generally DAMAGES vol 29 (2014) PARAS 408 et seq, 499 et seq.

## 799. Careless statements made in the course of pre-contractual negotiations.

Before 1963[1] careless statements made in the course of pre-contractual negotiations could only give rise to a claim to damages if the statements were either held to constitute a contractual term[2] or were not merely careless but fraudulent[3]. However, it is now clear that one contracting party may be under a duty of care in regard to statements made in pre-contractual negotiations, and breach of that duty may lead to liability in tort for negligence[4]. This is not to say that such a duty will always arise between negotiating parties; often it will not. However, the fact that the parties were in the course of negotiating a contract will not prevent a duty of care arising where the requirements of the law of tort are satisfied[5]. In the alternative, one contracting party may be liable to the other under the Misrepresentation Act 1967[6].

1 Ie before the decision in *Hedley Byrne & Co Ltd v Heller & Partners Ltd* [1964] AC 465, [1963] 2 All ER 575, HL: see PARA 797.
2 See PARA 798; and CONTRACT vol 22 (2012) PARA 354.
3 See PARA 788 et seq. As to fraudulent misrepresentation see PARA 754 et seq.
4 See *Esso Petroleum Co Ltd v Mardon* [1976] QB 801, [1976] 2 All ER 5, CA; PARA 798; and NEGLIGENCE vol 78 (2018) PARA 13; TORT vol 97 (2015) PARA 791 et seq. Thus it is possible that a solicitor acting for one side in the negotiation of the contract may owe a duty of care to the other party to the negotiations: *Gran Gelato Ltd v Richcliff (Group) Ltd* [1992] Ch 560, [1992] 1 All ER 865; cf *Hemmens v Wilson Browne* [1995] Ch 223, [1993] 4 All ER 826. All of these cases must now be read in the light of *White v Jones* [1995] 2 AC 207, [1995] 1 All ER 691, HL. See also *Dorsch v City of Weyburn* (1985) 23 DLR (4th) 379, Sask CA.
5 The duty of care may arise whether or not the pre-contractual negotiations result in the conclusion of a contract. Ordinarily, where a careless statement is made in negotiations which do not in fact lead to the completion of a contract, there would be no loss, but this is not necessarily so. For instance, a sub-contractor may make a carelessly low tender for work and a main contractor may rely on it in tendering successfully for the main contract; if the sub-contractor were to withdraw his tender before acceptance he would not be bound in contract but it may perhaps be argued that he is liable in tort. Such an argument has not been tested in the English courts but it has been rejected in New Zealand: see *Holman Construction Ltd v Delta Timber Co Ltd* [1972] NZLR 1081.
6 See PARAS 800, 810.

## 800. Statutory liability.

Under the Misrepresentation Act 1967[1], where a person has entered into a contract after a misrepresentation has been made to him by another party to it and as a result he has suffered loss, then, if the person making the misrepresentation would be liable to damages in respect of it had the misrepresentation been made fraudulently, that person is so liable notwithstanding that the misrepresentation was not made fraudulently, unless he proves that he had reasonable ground to believe and did believe up to the time the contract was made that the facts represented were true[2].

This statutory liability is similar to the common law liability for negligent misstatements[3], but it applies only where the misrepresentation induced the representee to enter into a contract with the representor, and not with a third party[4]. There are also important differences which make the statutory claim more attractive than the common law claim. Thus (1) the statutory provision applies to all contracts and there is no need to demonstrate a duty of care between the particular contracting parties[5]; and (2) the burden of proof is reversed, so that the representor[6] must prove his reasonable grounds for belief rather than the representee[7] having to prove that the representor failed to take reasonable care[8].

1 Ie the Misrepresentation Act 1967 s 2(1). Nothing in the Misrepresentation Act 1967 applies in relation to any misrepresentation or contract of sale which was made before the commencement of the 1967 Act (ie 22 April 1967): see ss 5, 6 (s 6(3) amended by the Sale of Goods Act 1979 ss 62, 63 and Sch 3).

2 Misrepresentation Act 1967 s 2(1). Section 2 does not entitle a person to be paid damages in respect of a misrepresentation if the person has a right to redress under the Consumer Protection from Unfair Trading Regulations 2008, SI 2008/1277, Pt 4A (regs 27A-27L) (see CONSUMER PROTECTION vol 21 (2016) PARA 433 et seq) in respect of the conduct constituting the misrepresentation: Misrepresentation Act 1967 s 2(4) (s 2(4), (5) added by SI 2014/870). The Misrepresentation Act 1967 s 2(4) does not prevent a debtor from bringing a claim under the Consumer Credit Act 1974 s 75(1) (see CONSUMER PROTECTION vol 21 (2016) PARA 232) against a creditor under a debtor-creditor-supplier agreement in a case where, but for the Misrepresentation Act 1967 s 2(4), the debtor would have a claim against the supplier in respect of a misrepresentation (and, where the Consumer Credit Act 1974 s 75 would otherwise apply, it accordingly applies as if the debtor had a claim against the supplier: Misrepresentation Act 1967 s 2(5)). As to the measure of damages under the Misrepresentation Act 1967 see PARA 810. Discovery of the misrepresentation between contract and completion does not preclude a claim for damages: see *Production Technology Consultants Ltd v Bartlett* [1988] 1 EGLR 182, CA. As to fraudulent misrepresentation see PARA 754 et seq.

3 See *Rust v Abbey Life Assurance Co Ltd* [1978] 2 Lloyd's Rep 386 at 391. As to negligent misstatements see PARAS 762–763, 797–799; and NEGLIGENCE vol 78 (2018) PARA 13.

4 See *Taberna Europe CDO II plc v Selskabet AF 1 September 2008* [2016] EWCA Civ 1262, [2017] QB 633, [2017] 3 All ER 1046.

5 See *Howard Marine and Dredging Co Ltd v A Ogden & Sons (Excavations) Ltd* [1978] QB 574, [1978] 2 All ER 1134, CA, where the owners of barges were held liable for damages under the Misrepresentation Act 1967 s 2(1) for misrepresentation made by their employee during pre-contractual negotiations as to the capacity of the company's barges which was a material matter on which the representees relied in concluding the contract; a claim in the alternative at common law for negligent misstatement failed.

6 As to who is a representor see PARAS 724–732.

7 As to who is a representee see PARAS 733–739.

8 See the Misrepresentation Act 1967 s 2(1). ). As to the measure of damages under the Misrepresentation Act 1967, which may be more advantageous than in the common law of negligence, see PARA 810.

# (3) Bars to Claims for Damages

## 801. Representee's knowledge of the truth.

A representee[1] who knows the truth is not deceived. Proof, therefore, of such knowledge is a complete answer to any proceeding founded on misrepresentation[2], and it is sufficient to show that the representee was aware of the real facts at any time before he altered his position on the faith of the false statement[3]. However, it must be established that the representee's knowledge was exact and complete; it is not enough to show partial and fragmentary information or mere suspicion[4]. Moreover, actual knowledge must be proved[5]. Imputed or constructive notice is not sufficient; thus, if the false statement was made to an agent of the representee, the representor is not allowed to protect himself by proving that the agent knew that the statement was untrue[6]. Nor is it of any use to establish merely that the representee had such means of knowledge and materials within his reach as would have enabled a person of ordinary business habits and normal intelligence to discover the whole truth, even though the representor himself may have supplied those means and materials, or even that the representee availed himself of them, if his investigation, whether perfunctory or diligent, did not in fact result in actual knowledge[7]. A person cannot be heard to complain that another has confided in a misrepresentation made, even if innocently, much less if fraudulently, for the purpose of inspiring that very confidence, or plead as an excuse that the person he has misled was at fault in not testing the statement by inquiry[8].

1   As to who is a representee see PARAS 733–739.
2   There are very few reported instances of the success of the plea in claims for damages, but see *Eaglesfield v Marquis of Londonderry* (1878) 26 WR 540 at 541, HL, per Lord Hatherley (damages proceedings); *Attwood v Small* (1838) 6 Cl & Fin 232 at 390, 448–450, HL; *Vigers v Pike* (1842) 8 Cl & Fin 562 at 648, HL; *Begbie v Phosphate Sewage Co* (1875) LR 10 QB 491 at 498–499 (on appeal (1876) 1 QBD 679, CA); *Re British Burmah Lead Co Ltd, ex p Vickers* (1887) 56 LT 815; *Wasteneys v Wasteneys* [1900] AC 446 at 449, PC; *Howarth v Pioneer Life Assurance Co Ltd* (1912) 107 LT 155, DC (actions for rescission). For cases where the plea has been successfully put forward by way of answer to a defence based on misrepresentation see *Dyer v Hargrave* (1805) 10 Ves 505; *Bawden v London, Edinburgh and Glasgow Assurance Co* [1892] 2 QB 534, CA (a case which has frequently been distinguished in subsequent cases: see eg *Newsholme Bros v Road Transport and General Insurance Co Ltd* [1929] 2 KB 356 at 367–375, CA, per Scrutton LJ). See INSURANCE vol 60 (2018) PARA 57 et seq. See also *Strover v Harrington* [1988] Ch 390, [1988] 1 All ER 769 (particulars of sale stated that a house had mains drainage; estate agent later informed the representee's solicitor that this was untrue; the solicitor did not pass this information to the representee; any loss flowed from the solicitor's failure rather than the misrepresentation, and the representee's claim was barred).
3   Where the representor corrects a misrepresentation before the representee enters into a contract, the latter will not be entitled to avoid the contract for misrepresentation: *Assicurazioni Generali SpA v Arab Insurance Group (BSC)* [2002] EWCA Civ 1642 at [63], [2003] 1 All ER (Comm) 140 at [63], [2003] 1 WLR 577 at [63]. As to the principle that a representation is deemed to continue until the representee acts upon it see PARA 753. As to alteration of position see PARA 777 et seq.
4   *Martin v Cotter* (1846) 3 Jo & Lat 496 at 507–508; *Wilson v Short* (1848) 6 Hare 366 at 376; *Hughes v Jones* (1861) 3 De GF & J 307 at 312; *Redgrave v Hurd* (1881) 20 ChD 1, CA; *Assicurazioni Generali SpA v Arab Insurance Group (BSC)* [2002] EWCA Civ 1642 at [64], [2003] 1 All ER (Comm) 140 at [64], [2003] 1 WLR 577 at [64]; *Clinicare Ltd v Orchard Homes and Developments Ltd* [2004] EWHC 1694 (QB) at [28], [2004] All ER (D) 244 (Jul).
5   As to where actual notice is constituted by registration see EQUITABLE JURISDICTION vol 47 (2014) PARA 131; REAL PROPERTY AND REGISTRATION vol 87 (2017) PARA 656.
6   See *Wells v Smith* [1914] 3 KB 722, where the representor made to the representee's agent a statement which the representor and the agent knew to be untrue, in order to induce the representee to act upon it. See also *Supersafe Supermarkets Ltd v Patel* (1970) 216 Estates Gazette 1135 (agent knowing true facts but unaware of misrepresentation; knowledge could not be imputed to principal). As to who is a representor see PARAS 724–732.
    In non-marine insurance cases, where an agent employed by the insurers to procure proposals fills in, or assists in filling in, the proposal form for the proposer, the knowledge of the agent is not normally to be imputed to the insurers: see INSURANCE vol 60 (2018) PARA 61.
7   *Dyer v Hargrave* (1805) 10 Ves 505 (as to two of the three misrepresentations which were the subject of the plea); *Dobell v Stevens* (1825) 3 B & C 623; *Pearson v Wheeler* (1825) Ry & M 303; *Bowring v Stevens* (1826) 2 C & P 337; *Harris v Kemble* (1831) 5 Bli NS 730 at 745, 750, HL; *King v Wilson* (1843) 6 Beav 124 at 129; *Reynell v Sprye* (1852) 1 De GM & G 660 at 687, 709–710; *Price v Macaulay* (1852) 2 De GM & G 339 at 346–347, CA in Ch; *Brandling v Plummer* (1854) 2 Drew 427 at 431–432; *Rawlins v Wickham* (1858) 3 De G & J 304 at 313–314; *Central Rly Co of Venezuela (Directors etc) v Kisch* (1867) LR 2 HL 99 at 118, 120–121, 123–124; *Caballero v Henty* (1874) 9 Ch App 447 at 450; *Redgrave v Hurd* (1881) 20 ChD 1 at 14, CA; *Mathias v Yetts* (1882) 46 LT 497 at 502, 504, CA; *Re London and Staffordshire Fire*

Insurance Co (1883) 24 ChD 149 at 154–156; *White v Haymen* (1883) Cab & El 101 at 103; *Arnison v Smith* (1889) 41 ChD 348 at 370–373, CA; *Moss & Co Ltd v Swansea Corpn* (1910) 74 JP 351; *Nocton v Lord Ashburton* [1914] AC 932 at 962, HL, per Lord Dunedin.

8  *Barley v Walford* (1846) 9 QB 197 at 209; *Wilson v Short* (1848) 6 Hare 366 at 377; *Reynell v Sprye* (1852) 1 De GM & G 660 at 710; *Price v Macaulay* (1852) 2 De GM & G 339 at 346–347, CA in Ch; *Central Rly Co of Venezuela (Directors etc) v Kisch* (1867) LR 2 HL 99 at 120–121; *Hunter v Walters* (1871) 7 Ch App 75 at 86; *Re Arnold, Arnold v Arnold* (1880) 14 ChD 270 at 281, CA (where the misrepresentation was assumed to be innocent); *Bloomenthal v Ford* [1897] AC 156 at 161–162, 168, HL (an estoppel case); *Betjemann v Betjemann* [1895] 2 Ch 474 at 479, 482, CA. Contributory negligence is not a defence to claims for fraud: *Alliance and Leicester Building Society v Edgestop Ltd* [1994] 2 All ER 38, [1993] 1 WLR 1462 (deceit); *Corporacion Nacional Del Cobre De Chile v Sogemin Metals Ltd* [1997] 2 All ER 917, [1997] 1 WLR 1396 (bribery).

The possibility has been recognised, however, in relation to non-fraudulent misrepresentation: see *Gran Gelato Ltd v Richcliff (Group) Ltd* [1992] Ch 560, [1992] 1 All ER 865.

## 802. Attempts to exclude liability for misrepresentation by contractual term.

Where the representor[1] and representee[2] have entered into a contract after the representation, the contract may contain a term purporting to exclude or restrict liability for misrepresentation. At common law such a clause will be ineffective if it seeks to exclude liability for fraudulent misrepresentation for a person cannot escape liability for his own fraudulent statements by inserting in a contract a clause that the other party is not to rely on them[3]. More generally the effect of such a term is governed by statute. The statutory provision applies to a contractual term which would exclude or restrict either any liability to which a party to a contract may be subject by reason of any misrepresentation made by him before the contract was made or any remedy available to another party to the contract by reason of such a misrepresentation[4]. If a term falls within the scope of this provision it is of no effect except in so far as it satisfies the requirement of reasonableness as stated in the Unfair Contract Terms Act 1977[5]; and it is for those claiming that the term satisfies that requirement to show that it does[6].

What is a representation and an exclusion for the purposes of this provision is to be approached in a broad and reasonable way; it will not suffice to make what would ordinarily be a representation accompanied by a statement that it is not to be treated as a representation[7]. On the other hand, it is permissible for a principal to state that an agent has no authority to make representations, and such a statement may ensure that what would otherwise be a representation within the agent's ostensible authority falls outside that authority and does not constitute a representation by the principal[8].

An 'entire agreement' clause[9], which is an agreement that the written contract expresses the entire agreement between the parties, does not preclude a claim in misrepresentation[10]. However, a clause which denies that a representation has been made, or that a representation, if made, has not been relied on, may be construed as in substance a clause which excludes or restricts liability for misrepresentation[11].

It should also be noted that a representation can itself become a collateral contract, the consideration for which is entry into the principal contract. Such a collateral contract can override express terms in the principal contract[12].

1  As to who is a representor see PARAS 724–732.
2  As to who is a representee see PARAS 733–739.
3  *S Pearson & Son Ltd v Dublin Corpn* [1907] AC 351 at 353–354, HL, per Lord Loreburn LC; and CONTRACT vol 22 (2012) PARA 388 et seq.

4   See the Misrepresentation Act 1967 s 3(1) (substituted by the Unfair Contract Terms Act 1977 s 8(1); renumbered by the Consumer Rights Act 2015 Sch 4 para 1). Set-off can be regarded as a remedy for the purposes of the Misrepresentation Act 1967 s 3: *Skipskredittforeningen v Emperor Navigation* [1997] 2 BCLC 398, [1998] 1 Lloyd's Rep 66. The Misrepresentation Act 1967 s 3 does not apply to a term in a consumer contract within the meaning of Consumer Rights Act 2015 Pt 2 (ss 61–76) , which contains separate provisions governing such cases (see CONSUMER PROTECTION vol 21 (2016) PARA 391–402): see s 3(2) (added by the Consumer Rights Act 2015 Sch 4 para 1).

5   Misrepresentation Act 1967 s 3(1). The effect of s 3 is to invalidate a clause in respect of claims based on misrepresentation; it has been held that, in so far as a claim applies to an alleged breach of contract, the Unfair Contract Terms Act 1977 scheme applies: *Skipskredittforeningen v Emperor Navigation* [1997] 2 BCLC 398, [1998] 1 Lloyd's Rep 66. See CONTRACT vol 22 (2012) PARA 419. In order to satisfy the requirement of reasonableness in the Misrepresentation Act 1967 s 3, the term must have been a fair and reasonable one to be included having regard to the circumstances which were, or ought reasonably to have been, known to or in the contemplation of the parties when the contract was made: see the Unfair Contract Terms Act 1977 s 11(1); and CONSUMER PROTECTION vol 21 (2016) PARAS 391, 392; CONTRACT vol 22 (2012) PARA 419.

     Neither the fact that the exclusion is contained in a well known standard form nor that the parties have been represented throughout by solicitors will of itself be sufficient evidence of reasonableness: *Walker v Boyle* [1982] 1 All ER 634 at 644–645, [1982] 1 WLR 495 at 507–508 per Dillon J (where a condition in the National Conditions of Sale did not satisfy the requirement of reasonableness). See also *South Western General Property Co Ltd v Marton* [1982] 2 EGLR 19; *Cooper v Tamms* [1988] 1 EGLR 257; *Swingler v Khosla* [1991] 1 EGLR 245; *Goff v Gauthier* (1991) 62 P & CR 388; *Inntrepreneur Estates (CPC) Ltd v Worth* [1996] 1 EGLR 84.

6   Misrepresentation Act 1967 s 3(1). See also the Consumer Rights Act 2015 Pt 2 (ss 61–76); and CONSUMER PROTECTION vol 21 (2016) PARA 391 et seq.

7   *Cremdean Properties Ltd v Nash* (1977) 244 Estates Gazette 547 at 551, CA, per Bridge LJ. See also *Walker v Boyle* [1982] 1 All ER 634 at 640, [1982] 1 WLR 495 at 501 per Dillon J.

8   *Overbrooke Estates Ltd v Glencombe Properties Ltd* [1974] 3 All ER 511, [1974] 1 WLR 1335; *Collins v Howell-Jones* [1981] 2 EGLR 108, CA. Cf *Museprime Properties Ltd v Adhill Properties Ltd* [1990] 2 EGLR 196, 61 P & CR 111. Such statements about the agent's authority are particularly common in sales by auction and house purchase transactions handled by estate agents. As to liability of agents for misrepresentation in such cases, and the effect of disclaimers, see *McCullagh v Lane Fox and Partners Ltd* [1996] 1 EGLR 35, (1995) 49 ConLR 124, CA; and AGENCY vol 1 (2017) PARA 136.

9   As to entire agreement clauses see CONTRACT vol 22 (2012) PARAS 221, 411.

10  *Inntrepreneur Pub Co v East Crown Ltd* [2000] 2 Lloyd's Rep 611 at [7]–[8], [2000] 3 EGLR 31 at [7]–[8]; *Deepak Fertilisers and Petrochemicals Corpn v Davy McKee (London) Ltd* [1999] 1 Lloyd's Rep 387, 62 ConLR 86, [1999] 1 All ER (Comm) 69, CA; *Ravennavi SpA v New Century Shipbuilding Co Ltd* [2006] EWHC 733 (Comm), [2006] 2 Lloyd's Rep 280, [2006] All ER (D) 23 (Apr); *BSkyB Ltd v HP Enterprise Services UK Ltd (formerly Electronic Data Systems Ltd)* [2010] EWHC 86 (TCC) at [382] et seq, 129 ConLR 147 at [382] et seq, [2010] IP & T 597 at [382] et seq; approved in *AXA Sun Life Services plc v Campbell Martin Ltd* [2011] EWCA Civ 133 at [92], [2012] 1 All ER (Comm) 268 at [92], [2011] 2 Lloyd's Rep 1 at [92]. As to entire agreement clauses generally see CONTRACT vol 22 (2012) PARA 221.

11  See *Cremdean Properties Ltd v Nash* (1977) 244 Estates Gazette 547, CA; *Raiffeisen Zentralbank Osterreich AG v Royal Bank of Scotland plc* [2010] EWHC 1392 (Comm) at [287], [2011] 1 Lloyd's Rep 123 at [287]; *JP Morgan Chase Bank v Springwell Navigation Corpn* [2010] EWCA Civ 1221 at [181], [2010] All ER (D) 08 (Nov); *Trident Turboprop (Dublin) Ltd v First Flight Couriers Ltd* [2008] EWHC 1686 (Comm) at [48], [2009] 1 All ER (Comm) 16 at [48], [2008] 2 Lloyd's Rep 581 at [48] (on appeal [2009] EWCA Civ 290, [2010] QB 86, [2009] 3 WLR 861); *First Tower Trustees Ltd v CDS (Superstores International) Ltd* [2018] EWCA Civ 1396, [2019] 1 WLR 637 (clause in lease excluding reliance on landlord's replies to pre-contract inquiries was a clause excluding liability for misrepresentation, but was unreasonable and so of no effect under Misrepresentation Act 1967 s 3(1)).

12  See *City and Westminster Properties (1934) Ltd v Mudd* [1959] Ch 129, [1958] 2 All ER 733.

## 803.   Statutory requirement as to representations concerning credit.

No claim may be brought by which to charge any person upon or by reason of a representation made concerning or relating to the character, conduct, credit, ability, trade or dealings of any other person, in order that such other person may obtain credit, money, or goods, unless the representation is made in writing, signed[1] by the party to be charged with it[2]. This applies only to claims for fraudulent misrepresentation[3], and not to a claim for damages for breach of duty founded on an innocent misrepresentation[4]; nor is it a defence to a claim at common law based on negligent representations[5].

Where the representations are partly oral and partly in writing, the claimant will succeed if he establishes that he was substantially induced by the written representations[6].

1   Personal signature of the principal is necessary: see eg AGENCY vol 1 (2017) PARAS 3, 19; FINANCIAL INSTRUMENTS AND TRANSACTIONS vol 49 (2015) PARA 679. The signature of a duly authorised officer or employee of a company is the signature of the company for this purpose: *UBAF Ltd v European American Banking Corpn* [1984] QB 713, [1984] 2 All ER 226, CA. See also COMPANIES vol 14 (2016) PARA 297.

2   Statute of Frauds Amendment Act 1828 s 6. The Statute of Frauds Amendment Act 1828 is commonly known as Lord Tenterden's Act. For decisions on this provision see *Lyde v Barnard* (1836) 1 M & W 101; *Haslock v Ferguson* (1837) 7 Ad & El 86; *Swann v Phillips* (1838) 8 Ad & El 457; *Devaux v Steinkeller* (1839) 6 Bing NC 84; *Turnley v MacGregor* (1843) 6 Man & G 46; *Craig v Watson* (1845) 8 Beav 427; *Tatton v Wade* (1856) 18 CB 371, Ex Ch; *Williams v Mason* (1873) 28 LT 232; *Swift v Jewsbury* (1874) LR 9 QB 301, Ex Ch; *Hosegood v Bull* (1876) 36 LT 617; *Pearson v Seligman* (1883) 48 LT 842, CA; *Bishop v Balkis Consolidated Co* (1890) 25 QBD 512, CA; *Hirst v West Riding Union Banking Co* [1901] 2 KB 560, CA; *Pearsons v Barclay & Co Ltd and Goddard* (1910) 103 LT 196, CA; *Banbury v Bank of Montreal* [1918] AC 626, HL. See also *UBAF Ltd v European American Banking Corpn* [1984] QB 713, [1984] 2 All ER 226, CA. See further FINANCIAL INSTRUMENTS AND TRANSACTIONS vol 49 (2015) PARA 677 et seq.

    On the true construction of the Statute of Frauds Amendment Act 1828 s 6, the representation must be made with the intent or purpose that the debtor should obtain 'money or goods upon credit': *Roder UK Ltd v Titan Marquees Ltd* [2011] EWCA Civ 1126, [2012] QB 752, [2012] 1 All ER 1305. See also *Contex Drouzhba Ltd v Wiseman* [2007] EWCA Civ 1201, [2008] 1 BCLC 631, [2008] BCC 301, CA (where a document executed by a director on behalf of a company contained a fraudulent representation, the director's signature on the document was sufficient evidence in writing for the purposes of the Statute of Frauds Amendment Act 1828 s 6 to enable an action in deceit to be brought against the director personally, since his signature was not only that of the company but also his personal signature).

    As to the application of the writing requirement to emails see *Lindsay v O'Loughnane* [2010] EWHC 529 (QB) at [95], [2010] All ER (D) 200 (Mar).

    The claimant must specifically set out any allegation of fraud and/or details of any misrepresentation where he wishes to rely on them in support of his claim: see CPR PD 16–*Statements of Case* para 8.2; and CIVIL PROCEDURE vol 11 (2015) PARA 347.

3   As to fraudulent misrepresentation see PARA 754 et seq.

4   *Banbury v Bank of Montreal* [1918] AC 626, HL. As to innocent misrepresentation see PARAS 762–763.

5   *WB Anderson & Sons Ltd v Rhodes (Liverpool) Ltd* [1967] 2 All ER 850 at 865 per Cairns J. It appears that the Statute of Frauds Amendment Act 1828 s 6 does apply to claims under the Misrepresentation Act 1967 s 2(1) (see PARA 800): *UBAF Ltd v European American Banking Corpn* [1984] QB 713 at 718–719, [1984] 2 All ER 226 at 229–230, CA, per Ackner LJ. As to negligent representation see PARAS 797–799.

6   *Tatton v Wade* (1856) 18 CB 371 at 385, 387–388, Ex Ch.

## (4) Measure of Damages

### 804. Claim for deceit.

The award in a claim for deceit, or its equitable equivalent[1], is of a gross sum in money, payable once and for all as compensation[2], to represent the present value of the entire net loss sustained by the representee[3] in the past, or likely to be sustained in the future[4], by reason of his being misled by the fraudulent misrepresentation[5].

The general rule as to the quantification of the damage is that the claimant should be restored to the position he would have been in if the representation had not been made. In applying this principle to consequential loss a broad approach should be taken, since it has been held that the defendant is bound to make reparation for all the actual damage flowing from the fraudulent inducement and cannot plead that the damage could not reasonably have been foreseen[6]. Although the loss need not have been foreseeable it must have been directly caused by the transaction[7].

1   See PARA 788.
2   See generally DAMAGES vol 29 (2014) PARAS 427–429. There used to be doubt as to whether exemplary damages might be recovered in deceit: see *Mafo v Adams* [1970] 1 QB 548, [1969] 3 All ER 1404, CA (differing views); *Cassell & Co Ltd v Broome* [1972] AC 1027 at 1076, [1972] 1 All ER 801 at 826, HL, per Lord Hailsham of St Marylebone LC, and at 1131 and 874 per Lord Diplock (against). However, there is now no obstacle if the general test for the award of exemplary damages is satisfied: *Kuddus v Chief Constable of Leicestershire Constabulary* [2001] UKHL 29, [2002] 2 AC 122; and such awards have in fact been made: *Parabola Investments Ltd v Browallia Cal Ltd* [2009] EWHC 901 (Comm), [2009] 2 All ER (Comm) 589 at [205]; *Axa Insurance UK plc v Financial Claims Solutions Ltd* [2018] EWCA Civ 1330, [2019] RTR 1. Aggravated damages may be recovered: *Archer v Brown* [1985] QB 401, [1984] 2 All ER 267. As to aggravated and exemplary damages see DAMAGES vol 29 (2014) PARA 322 et seq.
3   As to who is a representee see PARAS 733–739.
4   As to the meaning in law of damage, and the causal relation which it is necessary to establish between it and the misrepresentation, see PARAS 790–792.
5   As to fraudulent misrepresentation see PARA 754 et seq.
6   See *Doyle v Olby (Ironmongers) Ltd* [1969] 2 QB 158 at 167, [1969] 2 All ER 119 at 122, CA, per Lord Denning MR; and DAMAGES vol 29 (2014) PARAS 427–429. See also *Smith Kline & French Laboratories Ltd v Long* [1988] 3 All ER 887, [1989] 1 WLR 1, CA, where in order to place the representees in the position in which they would have been if the deceit had not been perpetrated, the value of the goods in question was ascertained by reference to the market value of the goods rather than the replacement cost.
      See further *Siametis v Trojan Horse (Burlington) Inc* (1979) 25 OR (2d) 120; *East v Maurer* [1991] 2 All ER 733, [1991] 1 WLR 461, CA; *Slough Estates plc v Welwyn Hatfield District Council* [1996] 2 EGLR 219, [1996] 2 PLR 50, *Clef Aquitaine SARL v Laporte Materials (Barrow) Ltd* [2001] QB 488, [2000] 3 All ER 493, CA.
7   *Smith New Court Securities Ltd v Citibank NA* [1997] AC 254 at 267, sub nom *Smith New Court Securities Ltd v Scrimgeour Vickers (Asset Management) Ltd* [1996] 4 All ER 769 at 779, HL, per Lord Browne-Wilkinson.

## 805. Assessment of damages.

Where the representee[1] has received no money or money's worth, and has simply parted with property or paid money which is irrecoverable in law[2] or in fact[3], or is under liability in that behalf which he is unable to dispute[4], the calculation of damages is simply a matter of addition, or (in the case of liability) an estimate of present values. However, where the representee's alteration of position assumes the form of a contract with the representor[5] or a third person, under which the representee has paid money and received in return property, rights or interests, for example a contract to take shares in, or debentures of, a company, the damages which the representee is entitled to recover from the representor are normally[6] the difference, if any, between the amount paid by the representee and the value of the property, rights or interests received by him[7]. If the real value of what the representee has received is nil[8], the representee is entitled to recover the full amount which he has paid; but the claim to this amount, although it may appear to be by way of a liquidated sum, is still in law a claim for damages[9].

1    As to who is a representee see PARAS 733–739.

2    See eg *Richardson v Silvester* (1873) LR 9 QB 34 (sums paid by the representee to third persons); *Wilkinson v Downton* [1897] 2 QB 57 (railway fares).

3    See eg *Mullett v Mason* (1866) LR 1 CP 559 (cows which perished); and the various misrepresentation of credit cases referred to in PARA 803 (goods delivered on credit, or money advanced, to insolvent persons).

4    Cf *Starkey v Bank of England* [1903] AC 114, HL (bank executed transfer of stock in reliance on forged power of attorney; bank liable to make restitution to stockholders; broker who had presented power of attorney liable to indemnify bank). In this case the broker had acted innocently and was liable on the ground of breach of warranty of authority (see AGENCY vol 1 (2017) PARA 162), but the bank's right of indemnity would have been the same if he had been guilty of fraudulent misrepresentation.

5    As to who is a representor see PARAS 724–732.

6    See *Clark v Urquhart* [1930] AC 28 at 67–68, HL, per Lord Atkin, reserving the right to consider in any future case whether the formula laid down in *McConnel v Wright* [1903] 1 Ch 546, CA was too rigidly expressed, on the ground that in all cases of transactions induced by fraudulent misrepresentation the measure of damages should be based on the actual damage flowing from the fraudulent inducement. See also *Hornal v Neuberger Products Ltd* [1957] 1 QB 247 at 259–260, [1956] 3 All ER 970 at 974, CA, per Lord Denning LJ. As to the measure of damages in tort see DAMAGES vol 29 (2014) PARA 408 et seq.

7    *McConnel v Wright* [1903] 1 Ch 546 at 554–555, CA, per Collins MR; and see COMPANIES vol 15A (2016) PARA 1275. See also *Heinemann v Cooper* [1987] 2 EGLR 154, 19 HLR 262, CA; *Downs v Chappell* [1996] 3 All ER 344, [1997] 1 WLR 426, CA. See, however, the criticism of the latter case in *Smith New Court Securities Ltd v Citibank NA* [1997] AC 254, sub nom *Smith New Court Securities Ltd v Scrimgeour Vickers (Asset Management) Ltd* [1996] 4 All ER 769, HL, where as the result of fraudulent misrepresentation the representee bought a large parcel of shares the true value of which was greatly reduced by a then undiscovered separate fraud practised on the company, and it was held that the representee could recover the whole of the difference between what it paid for the shares and the amount actually realised on the resale of the shares. Where the fraudulently obtained property consists of shares, their value should be calculated as of their date of purchase: *Great Future International Ltd v Sealand Housing Corpn* [2002] EWHC 2454 (Ch), [2002] All ER (D) 28 (Dec).

8    See *Twycross v Grant* (1877) 2 CPD 469, CA; *Jury v Stoker and Jackson* (1882) 9 LR Ir 385; *Thomson v Lord Clanmorris* [1900] 1 Ch 718, CA; *Goldrei, Foucard & Son v Sinclair and Russian Chamber of Commerce in London* [1918] 1 KB 180, CA; *McConnel v Wright* [1903] 1 Ch 546 at 554–555, CA, per Collins MR.

9    Thus a representee by putting his claim in the form of a demand for a liquidated sum, or labelling his cause of action money had and received, cannot alter its intrinsic nature or escape the disabilities attaching to it: see *Ship v Crosskill* (1870) LR 10 Eq 73; *Manners v Whitehead* (1898) 1 F 171, Ct of Sess. As to the principle that money paid to the representor may be sued for as money had and received or treated as damages see PARA 790.

## 806. Computation of benefits received by representee.

For the purpose of calculating damages, the value of the property, rights or interests received by the representee[1] under the contract means their real and actual value, to be determined by reference to the evidence adduced[2], and, in the case of marketable or saleable securities, without regard to market or current prices, which may be shown to have been manufactured by the same fraudulent means as gave the representee his cause of action[3]. The date at which the value is to be assessed is the date at which the property or rights were acquired, although subsequent events may be taken into account in determining the value at that date[4]. The representee is not bound to sell on discovery of the fraud, or at any subsequent time, but if he chooses to do so he must give credit for at least the sum received as purchase money[5], and if he delays selling after the date when he has had a reasonable time to consider his position, and if the price has gone down since that date, he may have to give credit for the higher price which he could have obtained at that date[6].

1  As to who is a representee see PARAS 733–739.
2  *Pearson v Wheeler* (1825) Ry & M 303 at 304.
3  *Twycross v Grant* (1877) 2 CPD 469 at 489–491, 503–505, 542–546, CA; *Jury v Stoker and Jackson* (1882) 9 LR Ir 385; *Arkwright v Newbold* (1881) 17 ChD 301 at 312–313, CA, per Fry J; *Peek v Derry* (1887) 37 ChD 541 at 591–594, CA (revsd without reference to this point sub nom *Derry v Peek* (1889) 14 App Cas 337, HL); *Glasier v Rolls* (1889) 42 ChD 436 at 455, CA, per Kekewich J; *McConnel v Wright* [1903] 1 Ch 546, CA; *Cackett v Keswick* [1902] 2 Ch 456 at 468, CA, per Farwell J; *Broome v Speak* [1903] 1 Ch 586 at 605–606, CA, per Buckley J, and at 623 per Collins MR (affd sub nom *Shepheard v Broome* [1904] AC 342, HL).
4  *Peek v Derry* (1887) 37 ChD 541 at 592–594, CA (revsd without reference to this point sub nom *Derry v Peek* (1889) 14 App Cas 337, HL); *Glasier v Rolls* (1889) 42 ChD 436 at 455, CA, per Kekewich J; *McConnel v Wright* [1903] 1 Ch 546, CA; *Broome v Speak* [1903] 1 Ch 586 at 609, CA, per Buckley J, and at 623 per Collins MR (affd sub nom *Shepheard v Broom* [1904] AC 342, HL).
5  *Peek v Derry* (1887) 37 ChD 541 at 593, CA; revsd without reference to this point sub nom *Derry v Peek* (1889) 14 App Cas 337, HL.
6  *Waddell v Blockey* (1879) 4 QBD 678, CA. If the representee is 'locked' into continuing to hold the property, any subsequent decrease in the property's value will be recoverable: see *Smith New Court Securities Ltd v Citibank NA sub nom Smith New Court Securities Ltd v Scrimgeour Vickers (Asset Management) Ltd* [1997] AC 254 at 266, 285, [1996] 4 All ER 769 at 778, 795, HL; *Standard Chartered Bank v Pakistan National Shipping Corp (SGS United Kingdom Ltd, Pt 20 defendant)* [2001] EWCA Civ 55, [2001] 1 All ER (Comm) 822; *Banks v Cox* [2002] EWHC 2166 (Ch), [2002] All ER (D) 376 (Oct); *4 Eng Ltd v Harper* [2008] EWHC 915 (Ch) at [55], [2009] Ch 91 at [55], [2008] 3 WLR 892 at [55]; *Parabola Investments Ltd v Browallia Cal Ltd* [2010] EWCA Civ 486 at [34] et seq, [2011] QB 477 at [34] et seq, [2011] 1 All ER (Comm) 210 at [34] et seq.

## 807. Duty to mitigate loss.

It is the duty of the representee[1] to take all reasonable steps to mitigate the loss sustained by him in consequence of the fraudulent misrepresentation[2], the question what is reasonable being one of fact, the burden of proof being on the representor[3].

1  As to who is a representee see PARAS 733–739.
2  As to fraudulent misrepresentation see PARA 754 et seq.
3  See DAMAGES vol 29 (2014) PARA 378 et seq. As to who is a representor see PARAS 724–732. The burden is on the representor to show both that the representee has failed to act reasonably and that the representee would have been in a more advantageous position if it had acted reasonably: *Standard Chartered Bank v Pakistan National Shipping Corpn* [2001] EWCA Civ 55, [2001] 1 All ER (Comm) 822.

## 808. Loss of profits.

It seems that a representee[1] may recover damages for loss of prospective profits if the loss is the natural and direct result of the representee acting upon the fraudulent misrepresentation[2], but he cannot recover for loss of prospective profits merely on the ground that he would have obtained them if the representation had been true[3].

1  As to who is a representee see PARAS 733–739.
2  See eg *Barley v Walford* (1846) 9 QB 197; and PARA 790. As to fraudulent misrepresentation see PARA 754 et seq.
3  See *Salvesen & Co v Rederi Aktiebolaget Nordstjernan* [1905] AC 302, HL; *Cassaboglou v Gibb* (1883) 11 QBD 797, CA; *Johnston v Braham and Campbell* [1917] 1 KB 586, CA (actions for breach of duty against agents); and AGENCY vol 1 (2008) PARA 86. Such a claim might lie if the representor had contracted that his statement was true, for then the representee would in principle be entitled to be put in the position he would have been in if the contract had been performed: see

DAMAGES vol 29 (2014) PARA 430.

See also *East v Maurer* [1991] 2 All ER 733, [1991] 1 WLR 461, CA (loss of profits could be recovered in an action for deceit as being actual damage directly flowing from the fraudulent representation; amount to be assessed on the basis of compensating for all the loss suffered rather than on the basis of putting the representee in as good a position as if the statement had been true; thus, where the representee bought a business as a result of the representor's fraud, the representee recovered damages which reflected not the profit which would have been made if the representations had been true but a reasonable return on the money which would otherwise have been invested in another business); *Clef Aquitaine SARL v Laporte Materials (Barrow) Ltd* [2001] QB 488, [2000] 3 All ER 493, CA (the successful claimant had not made a loss overall but less profit than if the fraudulent misstatement had not been made and the defendant's argument, that the rule of recovery was confined to cases of overall loss, was rejected; the claim was in accord with the 'overriding compensatory principle' of comparing the claimant's position before the fraudulent statement was made to him with his position as a result); and *Parabola Investments Ltd v Browallia Cal Ltd* [2010] EWCA Civ 486, [2011] QB 477, [2011] 1 All ER (Comm) 210 (a representee which had been induced to trade on an alternative trading system was entitled to the profits it would have accrued had it continued its previous trading practices).

As to who is a representor see PARAS 724–732.

### 809. Damages for negligent statements at common law.

It is clear that where damages are awarded for negligent misstatements[1] the cause of action is tortious and that accordingly damages should aim to restore the claimant to the position he was in before the statement, subject to the limitation that the loss suffered should be foreseeable[2].

1  See PARAS 762–763, 797–799.
2  As to the general principles governing the measure of damages see DAMAGES vol 29 (2014) PARAS 408 et seq, 499 et seq. Foreseeability being the test of remoteness of damage in negligence, the wider test employed in *Doyle v Olby (Ironmongers) Ltd* [1969] 2 QB 158, [1969] 2 All ER 119, CA, (see PARA 804) would not apply. As to the difference between the fraud and negligence measures see *Smith New Court Securities Ltd v Citibank NA* [1997] AC 254, sub nom *Smith New Court Securities Ltd v Scrimgeour Vickers (Asset Management) Ltd* [1996] 4 All ER 769, HL (see PARA 805); cf *South Australia Asset Management Corpn v York Montague Ltd* [1997] AC 191, [1996] 3 All ER 365, HL (where a valuer who negligently overvalued property was only liable for the foreseeable consequences of the information being wrong, and not for loss attributable to a general collapse of the property market), further explained in *Hughes-Holland v BPE Solicitors* [2017] UKSC 21, [2018] AC 599, [2017] 3 All ER 969.

See also *Naughton v O'Callaghan* [1990] 3 All ER 191. In this case, a racehorse was bought as a result of misrepresentations as to its pedigree and, although at the date of purchase this would have made no difference to its value, by the time the misrepresentation was discovered it was clear that the horse had little or no value as a racehorse. The purchaser recovered the difference between the purchase price and its present value rather than the difference between the purchase price and its actual value at the time of purchase, together with the costs of training and upkeep up to the date of discovery of the truth. See further *Jacovides v Constantinou* (1986) Times, 27 October; *Heinemann v Cooper* [1987] 2 EGLR 154, 19 HLR 262, CA; *Hussey v Eels* [1990] 2 QB 227, [1990] 1 All ER 449, CA; *First Interstate Bank of California v Cohen Arnold & Co* [1995] EGCS 188, (1995) Times, 11 December, CA.

As to the measure of damages in tort generally see DAMAGES vol 2014 (2014) PARA 408 et seq.

### 810. Damages under the Misrepresentation Act 1967.

Damages may be awarded under the Misrepresentation Act 1967[1], but the 1967 Act itself contains no guidance as to the principles upon which damages should be assessed. Some early cases suggested that damages might be recovered on contract principles, for example so as to recover foreseeable loss of profits[2]. But it is now clear that the better view is that this cause of action should be regarded as tortious[3]; and the same principles should be applied to claims under the statute as to claims for deceit[4].

1  Ie under the Misrepresentation Act 1967 s 2(1) (see PARA 800). Damages may also be awarded in

lieu of rescission under s 2(2) (see PARA 832). Damages awarded in lieu of rescission must be taken into account in assessing liability under s 2(1): see s 2(3); and PARA 832.

Damages under s 2(1) may be reduced for contributory negligence: see *Gran Gelato Ltd v Richcliff (Group) Ltd* [1992] Ch 560, [1992] 1 All ER 865. As to contributory negligence see NEGLIGENCE vol 78 (2018) PARA 75 et seq.

2  See *Jarvis v Swans Tours Ltd* [1973] QB 233 at 237, [1973] 1 All ER 71 at 73, CA, per Lord Denning MR; *Davis & Co (Wines) Ltd v Afa-Minerva (EMI) Ltd* [1974] 2 Lloyd's Rep 27; *Watts v Spence* [1976] Ch 165, [1975] 2 All ER 528.

3  *Andre & Cie SA v Ets Michel Blanc & Fils* [1979] 2 Lloyd's Rep 427, CA; *Chesneau v Interhome Ltd* (1983) Times, 9 June, CA. See also *Sharneyford Supplies Ltd v Edge* [1987] Ch 305, [1987] 1 All ER 588, CA.

4  See *Royscot Trust Ltd v Rogerson* [1991] 2 QB 297, [1991] 3 All ER 294, CA. In *Smith New Court Securities Ltd v Citibank NA* [1997] AC 254 at 283, sub nom *Smith New Court Securities Ltd v Scrimgeour Vickers (Asset Management) Ltd* [1996] 4 All ER 769 at 792, HL, Lord Steyn noted the 'trenchant academic criticism' of the *Royscot* decision, but declined to express a view whether it was correct. See also *Naughton v O'Callaghan* [1990] 3 All ER 191.

# 3. CLAIMS FOR RESCISSION

## (1) The Relief

**811. Nature and form of relief.**

The object of all proceedings based upon rescission of contracts induced by misrepresentation[1] is: (1) to obtain a judicial declaration and judgment that the contract in question has always been, and still is, voidable by reason of the misrepresentation[2]; (2) the annulment of the contract by the court, pursuant to its declaration, which annulment relates back to the date of the contract[3]; and (3) such consequential directions and relief as will restore the parties to the exact position in which they were before the contract was entered into, this being the inevitable operation of any avoidance ab initio[4]. The rescission is granted in total, or not at all[5], except where there are separate and severable covenants or stipulations[6], or where the instrument impeached may serve two purposes, or operate in two directions, in which case it may be rescinded in one of those purposes, whilst allowed to stand in the other[7].

1 As to rescission of contracts generally see CONTRACT vol 22 (2012) PARA 553 et seq. As to rescission on the grounds of mistake see MISTAKE vol 77 (2016) PARA 48 et seq. As to the rescission of contracts for the sale of land see BOUNDARIES vol 4 (2011) PARA 310; CONVEYANCING vol 23 (2016) PARA 445 et seq. As to the rescission of agreements for leases see LANDLORD AND TENANT vol 62 (2016) PARA 91. As to the avoidance of deeds see DEEDS AND OTHER INSTRUMENTS vol 32 (2012) PARA 267 et seq.

2 However, there may be alternative claims for rescission or for damages: see PARA 780.

3 *Reese River Silver Mining Co v Smith* (1869) LR 4 HL 64 at 73–74, 77–78, 81; *Abram Steamship Co Ltd v Westville Shipping Co Ltd* [1923] AC 773 at 781–782, HL, per Lord Atkinson. Rescission may be effected by the representee giving notice to the representor of his election to rescind and even, at least in a case of fraudulent misrepresentation, by an unequivocal overt act of election without successfully communicating with the representor: see *Car and Universal Finance Co Ltd v Caldwell* [1965] 1 QB 525, [1964] 1 All ER 290, CA. As to the rescission of a contract by retaking possession of property see PARA 780.

4 The transfer of legal property rights will still occur even if a contract has been tainted by misrepresentation. However, when a contract is rescinded, such rights will be revested in the representee: *Stevenson v Newnham* (1853) 13 CB 285 at 302–303. A representee with a right to rescind will have an equity to rescind: see PARA 820.

5 *Myddleton v Lord Kenyon* (1794) 2 Ves 391 at 408; *Beaumont v Dukes* (1822) Jac 422 at 426; *Clarke v Dickson* (1858) EB & E 148 at 155; *United Shoe Machinery Co of Canada v Brunet* [1909] AC 330 at 340, PC.

6 See *Henley v Stone* (1840) 3 Beav 355 (as to the power of a person partially interested to have a conveyance set aside, so far as it affected such partial interest, without disturbing the residue, or joining the parties having the other partial interests); *Bagot v Chapman* [1907] 2 Ch 222 (where the rule was correctly stated, although the application of it to the case has been commented on); *Howatson v Webb* [1908] 1 Ch 1 at 2–3, CA, per Cozens-Hardy MR, and at 2 per Farwell LJ.

7 *Haygarth v Wearing* (1871) LR 12 Eq 320; *Re Gomersall* (1875) 1 ChD 137, CA (affd sub nom *Jones v Gordon* (1877) 2 App Cas 616, HL). On a sale of property by auction a purchaser of more than one lot is not entitled to be granted rescission of the contract as to one lot on the ground of misrepresentation as to another lot, unless the inference can be drawn, from the situation, description or circumstances known and understood by vendor and purchaser at the time of sale, that the two transactions are interdependent, owing to matters known to both parties: see *Holliday v Lockwood* [1917] 2 Ch 47, where a claim for rescission failed. As to the exercise of the rule that rescission of part of a contract is not possible and its application where there is more than one contract see *De Molestina v Ponton* [2002] 1 All ER (Comm) 587, [2002] 1 Lloyd's Rep 271.

**812. Forms of proceedings; orders and directions.**

The ordinary form in which the aid of the court is invoked is a claim or counterclaim[1] for rescission, in which, on discharging the necessary burden of allegation and proof[2] and unless countervailed by any affirmative plea successfully raised by the representor[3], the representee[4] is entitled to relief of a nature to effect the objects already indicated[5], that is to say, an order rescinding or setting aside the contract, with or without a prefatory declaration[6], and, in certain special cases, an order for the delivery up of the instrument in which the contract is contained or recorded to be cancelled[7], or for rescission of the conveyance by which it was completed[8]; and such further orders for repayment of money with interest[9], reconveyance and retransfer[10], indemnity[11], injunction[12], accounts and inquiries[13], rectification of any entry in a statutory register which otherwise would or might import liability[14], and generally, and otherwise, all such directions as, in the circumstances of the particular case, may be required for the purposes of complete restitutio ad integrum. The representee, on his part, must also make all such corresponding repayments, retransfers and reconveyances as are necessary to restore the status quo on both sides[15].

Where the representee has simply paid money to the representor under the contract, and has received neither money nor money's worth in exchange, and so has nothing to restore, the proceeding assumes the form of a claim for money had and received[16], which succeeds or fails on precisely the same principles as if the claim were for rescission[17]; and, similarly, where the representee has parted with property or an instrument, without receiving any money or other benefit, the claim may be in conversion[18], or for the mere delivery up of the instrument to be cancelled[19], in which case, again, the same principles apply.

The court also has a statutory power to award damages in lieu of rescission where the misrepresentation was made otherwise than fraudulently[20].

1   See *Redgrave v Hurd* (1881) 20 ChD 1, CA (successful counterclaim for rescission). See also the cases cited in PARA 784.
2   As to the burden of allegation and proof see PARAS 813–815.
3   See PARA 824 et seq. As to who is a representor see PARAS 724–732.
4   As to who is a representee see PARAS 733–739.
5   See PARA 811. The numerous examples of claims (or counterclaims) for rescission in which the representee discharged his burden of proof and was not defeated by any affirmative plea, and in which therefore he obtained relief, may be roughly classified according to their subject matter as follows:
   (1)   sale, mortgage or lease of land (*Murray v Palmer* (1805) 2 Sch & Lef 474; *Kennedy v Green* (1834) 3 My & K 699; *Reynell v Sprye* (1852) 1 De GM & G 660; *Stanton v Tattersall* (1853) 1 Sm & G 529; *Torrance v Bolton* (1872) 8 Ch App 118; *Lindsay Petroleum Co v Hurd* (1874) LR 5 PC 221; *Lemprière v Lange* (1879) 12 ChD 675; *Re Arnold, Arnold v Arnold* (1880) 14 ChD 270, CA; *Nottingham Patent Brick and Tile Co v Butler* (1886) 16 QBD 778, CA; *Whittington v Seale-Hayne* (1900) 82 LT 49; *Baker v Moss* (1902) 66 JP 360; *Mahomed Kala Mea v Harperink* (1908) 25 TLR 180, PC; *Lee v Rayson* [1917] 1 Ch 613; *Bellotti v Chequers Developments Ltd* [1936] 1 All ER 89);
   (2)   sale or transfer of goods or securities (*Wilson v Short* (1848) 6 Hare 366; *Murray v Mann* (1848) 2 Exch 538; *Walsham v Stainton* (1863) 1 De GJ & Sm 678; *Maturin v Tredennick* (1864) 4 New Rep 15; *Donaldson v Gillot* (1866) LR 3 Eq 274; *Mathias v Yetts* (1882) 46 LT 497, CA; *Moorhouse v Woolfe* (1882) 46 LT 374; *Whurr v Devenish* (1904) 20 TLR 385);
   (3)   insurance (*Fenn v Craig* (1838) 3 Y & C Ex 216; *Traill v Baring* (1864) 4 De GJ & Sm 318; *Life and Health Assurance Association Ltd v Yule* (1904) 6 F 437, Ct of Sess);
   (4)   partnership, practice or business (*Stainbank v Fernley* (1839) 9 Sim 556; *Rawlins v Wickham* (1858) 3 De G & J 304; *Redgrave v Hurd* (1881) 20 ChD 1, CA; *Ferguson v Wilson* (1904) 6 F 779 at 783, Ct of Sess);
   (5)   compromises (*Davis v Chanter* (1855) 3 WR 321; *Brooke v Lord Mostyn* (1864) 2 De GJ & Sm 373 (revsd without affecting the law as laid down in the court below sub nom *Mostyn v Brooke* (1866) LR 4 HL 304); *Fane v Fane* (1875) LR 20 Eq 698; *Re Roberts, Roberts v Roberts* [1905] 1 Ch 704, CA);

(6)    contents of an instrument or document (*Lewellin v Cobbold* (1853) 1 Sm & G 376; *Lee v Angas* (1866) 7 Ch App 79n);

(7)    applications and subscriptions for shares in limited companies (see COMPANIES vol 14 (2016) PARA 446 et seq); and

(8)    miscellaneous (see eg *Cooper v Joel* (1859) 1 De GF & J 240 (guarantee); *A-G v Ray* (1874) 9 Ch App 397 (annuity); *Lemprière v Lange* (infancy); *Abram Steamship Co v Westville Shipping Co* [1923] AC 773, HL (assignment of benefit of contract)).

6   In all the cases cited in note 5 an order was made for rescission, and in most of them a declaration was prefixed to the decree or judgment.

7   As to the considerations which will move the court to order the physical surrender or destruction of an instrument see EQUITABLE JURISDICTION vol 47 (2014) PARA 84.

8   See PARA 816.

9   In all cases cited in note 5, where the representor had received any cash benefit under the contract he was ordered to refund it with interest at 4% or 5%, according to the circumstances, but it is thought that higher rates of interest would now be appropriate.

10  This is ordered where the representee was a vendor: see eg *Addis v Campbell* (1841) 4 Beav 401.

11  See *Stainbank v Fernley* (1839) 9 Sim 556; *Newbigging v Adam* (1886) 34 ChD 582, CA (on appeal sub nom *Adam v Newbigging* (1888) 13 App Cas 308, HL); *Whittington v Seale-Hayne* (1900) 82 LT 49.

An indemnity may be granted against expenses and liabilities incurred pursuant to obligations contained in the contract which is set aside; but, in a case where the misrepresentation was neither fraudulent nor negligent, it seems that an indemnity cannot be granted against liabilities which arose out of the contract but were not incurred in pursuance of contractual obligations, since to grant such an indemnity would be equivalent to the granting of damages, and damages cannot be recovered in respect of such a misrepresentation: see *Newbigging v Adam* at 589, 592, 594, 596; *Whittington v Seale-Hayne*, where on the setting aside of a lease of premises misrepresented to be sanitary, the plaintiff was granted an indemnity against the rent, rates, taxes and repairing expenses to which he had become liable thereunder, but not against loss of stock and profits owing to the insanitary condition of the premises. However, if the representation was fraudulent, it seems that the representee is entitled to such damages: see *Newbigging v Adam* at 589, 592; and PARAS 701, 780, 788 et seq or (now) if the representation was negligent, including under the Misrepresentation Act 1967: see PARAS 701, PARAS 797–800, PARAS 809–810.

12  *Walsham v Stainton* (1863) 1 De GJ & Sm 678 (injunction against transferring shares); *Henderson v Lacon* (1867) LR 5 Eq 249 (against calls); *Lemprière v Lange* (1879) 12 ChD 675 (against removal of furniture). See generally CIVIL PROCEDURE vol 12 (2015) PARA 1098 et seq. Where a representee shareholder has refused to pay calls on the ground of misrepresentation, the company will not be allowed to take advantage of the articles enabling it to forfeit the shares for such non-payment, and will be restrained by interim injunction from so doing until the trial of the claim, on the representee paying the amount of the calls into court: *Lamb v Sambas Rubber and Gutta Percha Co Ltd* [1908] 1 Ch 845; *Jones v Pacaya Rubber and Produce Co Ltd* [1911] 1 KB 455, CA, disapproving *Ripley v Paper Bottle Co* (1887) 57 LJ Ch 327.

13  *Haygarth v Wearing* (1871) LR 12 Eq 320; and see generally those of the cases cited in note 5 in which it was found necessary or desirable.

14  As to the rectification of the register of members of a limited company on the ground of misrepresentation see COMPANIES vol 15A (2016) PARA 1268.

15  See PARA 829.

16  As to claims for money had and received see CONTRACT.

17  See *Stone v City and County Bank* (1877) 3 CPD 282 at 294, 309–310, 312, CA; *Manners v Whitehead* (1898) 1 F 171, Ct of Sess. So, in *Kettlewell v Refuge Assurance Co Ltd* [1908] 1 KB 545, CA (on appeal sub nom *Refuge Assurance Co Ltd v Kettlewell* [1909] AC 243, HL), it was assumed, as the basis of the judgments, that in the case of an executed contract, if relief by way of rescission could not be granted, relief could not be granted in a claim for money had and received. As to the circumstances in which rescission of an executed contract may be granted see PARA 816. Representees have successfully asserted claims, in claims for money had and received, to recover deposits or other money paid on purchases of property or under a building contract (*Jones v Edney* (1812) 3 Camp 285; *Schneider v Heath* (1813) 3 Camp 506; *Flight v Booth* (1834) 1 Bing NC 370; *Dobell v Hutchinson* (1835) 3 Ad & El 355; *Hutchinson v Morley* (1839) 7 Scott 341; *Thornett v Haines* (1846) 15 M & W 367; *Moss & Co Ltd v Swansea Corpn Ltd* (1910) 74 JP 351); or money paid on applications for shares (*Stone v City and County Bank*); or premiums paid on insurance (*Duffell v Wilson* (1808) 1 Camp 401; *Blake v Albion Life Assurance Society* (1878) 4 CPD 94; *British Workman's and General Assurance Co Ltd v Cunliffe* (1902) 18 TLR 502, CA;

*Kettlewell v Refuge Assurance Co Ltd* [1908] 1 KB 545, CA; *Tofts v Pearl Life Assurance Co Ltd* [1915] 1 KB 189, CA; *Hughes v Liverpool Victoria Legal Friendly Society* [1916] 2 KB 482, CA; *Byrne v Rudd* [1920] 2 IR 12, Ir CA).

18 See *Jones v Keene* (1841) 2 Mood & R 348 (conversion of life policy). As to conversion generally see TORT vol 97 (2015) PARA 604 et seq.

19 *Moorehouse v Woolfe* (1882) 46 LT 374, where the defendant money-lender was ordered to deliver up the bill of sale to be cancelled, the plaintiff borrower having repaid all that was due.

20 See the Misrepresentation Act 1967 s 2(2); and PARA 832.

## (2) The Claim for Rescission

### (i) Conditions of the Right to Rescind

**813. Proof of fraud unnecessary.**

A contract or transaction induced by misrepresentation may be set aside, whether the representation was fraudulent or innocent[1] and notwithstanding that the misrepresentation has become a term of the contract or the contract has been performed[2]. This being so, fraud should not be charged when it cannot be proved, nor conduct be described as fraudulent when it cannot be maintained to have been dishonest[3]; and unnecessary and unproved allegations of fraud in any such proceedings are liable to attract costs[4], although it is no longer thought right to dismiss the claim entirely on that ground[5], unless it is framed in such a way that, after striking out of the claimant's pleading all allegations of fraud, no other cause of action or title to relief remains[6].

1 *Re Deposit and General Life Assurance Co, ex p Ayre's Case* (1858) 27 LJ Ch 579 at 583; *Ross v Estates Investment Co* (1868) 3 Ch App 682 at 685; *Redgrave v Hurd* (1881) 20 ChD 1 at 12–13, CA; *Derry v Peek* (1889) 14 App Cas 337 at 359, HL; *Re Metropolitan Coal Consumers' Association Ltd, Wainwright's Case* (1890) 63 LT 429 at 431, CA; *Stewart v Kennedy (No 2)* (1890) 15 App Cas 108 at 121–122, HL; *Ferguson v Wilson* (1904) 6 F 779 at 783, Ct of Sess; *Glasgow and South Western Rly Co v Boyd and Forrest* [1913] AC 404, HL; *Mair v Rio Grande Rubber Estates Ltd* [1913] AC 853 at 870, HL, per Lord Shaw of Dunfermline; *Glasgow and South Western Rly Co v Boyd and Forrest* as reported in 1915 SC 20, HL; *Faraday v Tamworth Union* (1916) 86 LJ Ch 436; *Armstrong v Jackson* [1917] 2 KB 822 at 825 per McCardie J; *Goldrei, Foucard & Son v Sinclair and Russian Chamber of Commerce in London* [1918] 1 KB 180 at 186, CA, per Pickford LJ, and at 192 per Sargant J; *Harrison v Knowles and Foster* [1918] 1 KB 608 at 610, CA, per Scrutton LJ; *Shankland & Co v Robinson & Co* (1920) 57 Sc LR 400, HL; *First National Reinsurance Co v Greenfield* [1921] 2 KB 260 at 272, DC, per McCardie J. See also *Museprime Properties Ltd v Adhill Properties Ltd* [1990] 2 EGLR 196, 61 P & CR 111. As to fraudulent misrepresentation see PARA 754 et seq; and as to innocent misrepresentation see PARAS 762–763.

2 See the Misrepresentation Act 1967 s 1; and PARAS 703, 816.

3 If the misrepresentation proves to be innocent, the court may award damages instead of rescission: see PARA 832. See also *Glasgow and South Western Rly Co v Boyd and Forrest* as reported in 1915 SC 20 at 25, HL, per Earl Loreburn.

4 *London Chartered Bank of Australia v Lemprière* (1873) LR 4 PC 572 at 597.

5 It was apparently the view of Lord Cottenham LC in *Wilde v Gibson* (1848) 1 HL Cas 605 at 620–621, 625 that, where fraud was alleged and not proved, the proceeding should be dismissed, although he afterwards either disclaimed, or modified, what he was reported to have said: *Archbold v Comrs of Charitable Bequests for Ireland* (1849) 2 HL Cas 440 at 459–460. See also *Espey v Lake* (1852) 10 Hare 260 at 264–265; *Parr v Jewell* (1855) 1 K & J 671 at 673–674; *Hickson v Lombard* (1866) LR 1 HL 324 at 331.

6 See *Anderson v Thornton* (1853) 8 Exch 425 at 428; *Thom v Bigland* (1853) 8 Exch 725 at 730–732; *Swinfen v Lord Chelmsford* (1860) 5 H & N 890 at 920–921; *Hickson v Lombard* (1866) LR 1 HL 324 at 336; *London Chartered Bank of Australia v Lemprière* (1873) LR 4 PC 572; *Connecticut Fire Insurance Co v Kavanagh* [1892] AC 473 at 479, PC; *Behn v Bloom* (1911) 132 LT Jo 87; *Nocton v Lord Ashburton* [1914] AC 932 at 965, HL, per Lord Dunedin, and at

967–968 per Lord Shaw of Dunfermline. As to pleading generally see CIVIL PROCEDURE vol 12 (2015) PARA 340 et seq.

### 814. Damage need not be proved.

If the representee[1] proves that he was misled by the misrepresentation into making the contract which he seeks to avoid, it is immaterial whether it has affected, or is likely to affect, his interests prejudicially or beneficially[2]. The representee is the sole judge; it is for him to elect whether, for reasons sufficient to himself, he will affirm, or rescind, the contract[3].

1   As to who is a representee see PARAS 733–739.
2   *Gillett v Peppercorne* (1840) 3 Beav 78 at 84 (a case of non-disclosure).
3   *Ayles v Cox* (1852) 16 Beav 23 at 24–25 per Romilly MR (purchaser was held not bound to take property sold as copyhold which turned out to be freehold; and it was said that it is unnecessary for a person who has contracted to purchase one thing to explain why he refuses to accept another). See also *Denny v Hancock* (1870) 6 Ch App 1 at 10 (a case where the representee was rejecting a claim for specific performance); *Hulton v Hulton* [1917] 1 KB 813, CA. As to affirmation of contracts see PARAS 827, 828.

### 815. Matters which must be proved.

With the exception of damage and, where the claim is for deceit, fraud[1], all the facts and matters which must be alleged and proved in a claim for damages for misrepresentation must be similarly alleged and proved in proceedings for rescission[2]. The representee[3] must further be prepared to show that the contract or transaction which he seeks to annul is an existing contract or transaction which, unless and until avoided, is valid and binding on the parties; for otherwise there is nothing in respect of which judicial intervention is required. The court can no more be asked to rescind than to enforce an alleged contract which has never in fact or in law come into being[4], or which was void ab initio[5], or which, having come into being, has been determined by the parties[6].

1   It is necessary to show both damage and fraud in a claim for damages for fraudulent misrepresentation (see PARAS 788–789), but it is not necessary for rescission: see PARAS 813–814. As to claims for damages for negligent words see PARA 797 et seq.
2   As to what must be proved in order to recover damages in a claim for deceit see PARA 789; and as to damages for negligent words see PARA 797 et seq.
3   As to who is a representee see PARAS 733–739.
4   See *Lagunas Nitrate Co v Lagunas Syndicate* [1899] 2 Ch 392 at 444, CA. Where, however, a person's name has been placed on the register of members of a company in pursuance of an alleged contract to take shares which never came into being, the court may rectify the register and remove the person's name from the list of contributors in any winding up of the company: see eg *Re Consort Deep Level Gold Mines Ltd, ex p Stark* [1897] 1 Ch 575, CA; *Re Etna Insurance Co, Slattery's Case* (1872) 7 IR Eq 245; *Re (Thomas Edward) Brinsmead & Sons, Tomlin's Case* [1898] 1 Ch 104. See also PARA 831. As to rectification of the register of members of a company see COMPANIES vol 15A (2016) PARA 1268. As to when negotiations become a concluded contract see CONTRACT vol 22 (2012) PARA 268.
5   Eg when the alleged contract was induced by a misrepresentation as to the person with whom the representee was contracting so that his apparent consent is negatived (see PARA 782); or where the contract is illegal or, although not illegal, is made void by statute (see CONTRACT vol 22 (2012) PARA 424 et seq).
6   Eg by forfeiture, pursuant to the articles of a company: see eg *Aaron's Reefs v Twiss* [1896] AC 273 at 293, HL. Where a forfeiture was a fraudulent device of the shareholders, in collusion with the company's secretary, the contract was held not to have been ended: *Re London and Provincial Starch Co, Gowers' Case* (1868) LR 6 Eq 77 at 81. As to the forfeiture of shares generally see COMPANIES vol 15A (2016) PARA 1400 et seq.

## 816. Rescission in regard to executed contracts.

It was formerly held that in certain circumstances the fact that the contract had been executed was a bar to its rescission[1]. However, since 22 April 1967[2], where a person has entered into a contract after a misrepresentation has been made to him, then, if otherwise he would be entitled to rescind the contract without alleging fraud, he is entitled to rescind, notwithstanding the misrepresentation has become a term of the contract or the contract has been performed[3].

1 See eg *Seddon v North Eastern Salt Co Ltd* [1905] 1 Ch 326. Cf *Bell v Lever Bros Ltd* [1932] AC 161, HL; *Mackenzie v Royal Bank of Canada* [1934] AC 468, PC; *Solle v Butcher* [1950] 1 KB 671 at 695–696, [1949] 2 All ER 1107 at 1121, CA, per Denning LJ, and at 703 and 1125 per Jenkins LJ.
2 Ie the commencement date of the Misrepresentation Act 1967 (ie 22 April 1967): see ss 5, 6 (s 6(3) amended by the Sale of Goods Act 1979 ss 62, 63 and Sch 3).
3 See the Misrepresentation Act 1967 s 1; and PARA 703.

### (ii) Parties

## 817. Who may sue and be sued.

The possible parties to proceedings for rescission or analogous relief are ordinarily the persons who were, or who are deemed to have been, the parties to the contract[1].

1 See *Northern Bank Finance Corpn Ltd v Charlton* [1979] IR 149 (rescission is prima facie a remedy which is only available against the other party to the contract). As to rescission where there is a chain of contracts see *Gross v Lewis Hillman Ltd* [1970] Ch 445 at 460 et seq, [1969] 3 All ER 1476 at 1482 et seq, CA; and see also PARA 735.
   As to who are deemed representees and representors see PARA 723 et seq. As to parties to claims generally see CIVIL PROCEDURE vol 11 (2015) PARA 469 et seq.

## 818. Effect of death or incapacity.

In case of the death or insolvency of the representee[1] or representor[2], the right to sue, or the liability to be sued, is transmissible to other persons in accordance with the same rules, and subject to the same conditions, as in the case of any other claim or proceeding founded on contract[3]. The liability of a minor who has obtained an advantage by misrepresentation of his age[4], and the mode by which proceedings may be instituted and carried on by or against minors[5] and persons who lack capacity[6], are considered elsewhere in this work.

1 As to who is a representee see PARAS 733–739.
2 As to who is a representor see PARAS 724–732.
3 As to the effect of death on rights under a contract see CONTRACT vol 22 (2012) PARA 639; WILLS AND INTESTACY vol 103 (2016) PARA 1277 et seq. As to the effect of the bankruptcy of the representor or the representee see eg *Re Blake, ex p Coker* (1875) 10 Ch App 652 (a stay was refused where the representor had filed a bankruptcy petition); *Motion v Moojen* (1872) LR 14 Eq 202 (undischarged bankrupt not capable of suing). See generally BANKRUPTCY AND INDIVIDUAL INSOLVENCY. As to the effect of the winding up of a company see COMPANY AND PARTNERSHIP INSOLVENCY.
4 See CHILDREN AND YOUNG PERSONS vol 9 (2017) PARA 23.
5 See CHILDREN AND YOUNG PERSONS vol 10 (2017) PARA 1398 et seq.
6 As to persons who lack capacity see MENTAL HEALTH AND CAPACITY vol 75 (2013) PARA 601 et seq.

## 819. Assignment of right to sue.

A bare equity to rescind a contract on the ground of misrepresentation is not assignable nor saleable[1]; but where property or an interest in property is assigned, there passes with it every such equity as is incidental to its effectual enjoyment, or necessary to secure it for the benefit of the assignee, including the equity of avoiding, or obtaining a court order to avoid, any conveyance or contract which stands in the way of such enjoyment, or destroys or prejudices such interest[2]. A claim for money had and received[3], or to any money or property which can be described as, in equity, the money or property of the representee[4], as distinct from a mere claim to damages, can also be assigned[5].

1    This is because an assignment of a bare right of litigation savours of champerty or maintenance: see *Wood v Downes* (1811) 18 Ves 120 at 125; *Prosser v Edmonds* (1835) 1 Y & C Ex 481 at 496–497, 500; *Dawson v Great Northern and City Rly Co* [1905] 1 KB 260 at 270–271, CA, per Stirling LJ; *Fitzroy v Cave* [1905] 2 KB 364 at 371, CA, per Cozens-Hardy LJ. See also CONTRACT vol 22 (2012) PARA 438.
2    *Prosser v Edmonds* (1835) 1 Y & C Ex 481 at 486–487, 499; *Wilson v Short* (1848) 6 Hare 366 at 384; *Cockell v Taylor* (1851) 15 Beav 103 at 116–117; *Stump v Gaby* (1852) 2 De GM & G 623 at 630–631; *Dickinson v Burrell* (1866) LR 1 Eq 337 at 342; *Dawson v Great Northern and City Rly Co* [1905] 1 KB 260 at 271, CA, per Stirling LJ.
3    See PARA 812; and CONTRACT.
4    As to who is a representee see PARAS 733–739.
5    It is on this principle that claims against delinquent directors and officers of a company are assignable and saleable: see COMPANIES; CHOSES IN ACTION.

## 820. Liability of assignee from representor.

Since choses or things in action are only assignable subject to equities, including the equity to rescind, any representee[1] who has become entitled to avoid a sale or transfer of a chose or thing in action as against the representor[2] is normally also entitled to avoid it against any other person who claims under or through the representor by assignment[3]. However, where a contract for the sale of goods is voidable on the ground of misrepresentation on the part of the purchaser and before it is avoided the representor sells the goods to a third person who buys them without notice of the representor's defect in title, the third person acquires a good title to the goods as against the representee[4]. Similarly, where a conveyance of an estate or interest in unregistered land is voidable on the ground of misrepresentation, the representee's equity to set aside the conveyance cannot be enforced against a purchaser for value without notice from the representor[5].

1    As to who is a representee see PARAS 733–739.
2    As to who is a representor see PARAS 724–732.
3    *Davis v Chanter* (1855) 3 WR 321; *Cockell v Taylor* (1851) 15 Beav 103 at 118; *Barnard v Hunter* (1856) 2 Jur NS 1213 at 1215. See also CHOSES IN ACTION vol 13 (2017) PARA 83. As regards negotiable instruments, which differ from other choses or things in action, see FINANCIAL INSTRUMENTS AND TRANSACTIONS vol 49 (2015) PARAS 262, 272 (burden of proof on holder in case of fraud; general principle that holder in due course takes free of defects in title).
4    Sale of Goods Act 1979 s 23. As to the intervention of a third party see PARA 830. The position is different where the contract is void and not merely voidable: see PARA 782.
5    See eg *Dunbar v Tredennick* (1813) 2 Ball & B 304 at 318; and EQUITABLE JURISDICTION vol 47 (2014) PARA 121. In the case of registered land the equity to rescind will be an interest in land and therefore whether a successor is bound depends on the general rules of priorities in registered land: see the Land Registration Act 2002 ss 28, 29, 116; and REAL PROPERTY AND REGISTRATION vol 87 (2017) PARAS 451 et seq, 458.

### (iii) Special Cases

## 821. Statutory procedure in company cases.

Where it is sought to rescind a contract to take shares in a limited company on the ground of misrepresentation[1], and for that purpose it is necessary or advisable to obtain a court order for rectification of the register of members[2] or, if the company is in liquidation, for variation of the list of contributories, a summary form of procedure is provided[3].

1  As to claims for rescission of contracts to take shares see COMPANIES vol 15A (2016) PARA 1260 et seq.
2  Otherwise the shareholder may lose the right to rescind: see PARA 831; and COMPANIES vol 15A (2016) PARA 1449.
3  See COMPANY AND PARTNERSHIP INSOLVENCY vol 17 (2017) PARA 622 et seq (statutory procedure for rectification of the register when the company is a going concern; variation of lists of contributories, and rectification of the register, when the company is being wound up).

## 822.  Procedure on sales by court order.

Where a purchaser of property, sold by judicial direction in any cause or matter, complains that he has been induced to purchase by misrepresentation, the proper mode of obtaining relief is by application to the judge in that cause or matter to be discharged from the purchase, and the application is governed by the same rules as those which regulate a claim for rescission[1].

1  *Martin v Cotter* (1846) 3 Jo & Lat 496 at 505; *Lachlan v Reynolds* (1853) Kay 52 at 55; *Brandling v Plummer* (1854) 2 Drew 427; *Whittemore v Whittemore* (1869) LR 8 Eq 603; *Re Banister, Broad v Munton* (1879) 12 ChD 131 at 141, CA; *Re Arnold, Arnold v Arnold* (1880) 14 ChD 270 at 273–274, 277, CA; *Mahomed Kala Mea v Harperink* (1908) 25 TLR 180, PC; *Re Longvale Brick and Lime Works Ltd* [1917] 1 IR 321 at 329–330, CA, per Sir Ignatius J O'Brien C. The purchaser was relieved in all the above cases, except in *Re Arnold, Arnold v Arnold*, and in most of them it was pointed out that the fact that the sale was under the court's direction, and that the misrepresentation was, in a sense, that of its officers, was a ground for granting relief not less, but more, readily than in an ordinary case.

## 823.  Statutory procedure in cases of sale of land.

Under the summary procedure authorised by statute for determining questions arising on the sale and purchase of land[1], a declaration may be obtained that the title shown is not such as the purchaser ought to be compelled to accept[2].

1  See the Law of Property Act 1925 s 49; and CONVEYANCING vol 23 (2016) PARA 470. This summary procedure does not apply to any question affecting the existence or validity of the contract: see s 49(1); and CONVEYANCING vol 23 (2016) PARA 470.
2  *Re Davis and Cavey* (1888) 40 ChD 601 at 609; and see CONVEYANCING vol 23 (2016) PARA 83. Further relief (eg return of a deposit) may raise a question which affects the validity of the contract, so that the purchaser may have to bring another claim to obtain relief: see *Re Davis and Cavey* at 609. As to implied covenants for title see the Law of Property (Miscellaneous Provisions) Act 1994 Pt I (ss 1–13); and CONVEYANCING vol 23 (2016) PARA 181.

# (3)  Bars to Rescission

## 824.  Defences to proceedings.

By way of answer to any proceedings for rescission or analogous relief, in whichever form[1] they may be instituted, the representor[2] may set up any of the affirmative pleas[3] which are special to proceedings of this nature, in addition to any other defence which may be available[4]. In the case of these pleas, the burden of allegation and, except so far as any averment may be expressly or impliedly admitted[5], of proof is on the representor[6].

1  As to forms of proceedings see PARA 812.
2  As to who is a representor see PARAS 724–732.
3  See PARA 825 et seq.
4  Ie either at common law, in equity or by statute. Certain statutory limitation periods, including

those for claims founded on tort and simple contract (see LIMITATION PERIODS vol 68 (2016) PARA 952 et seq), do not apply to claims for equitable relief except in so far as they may be applied by analogy with the application of earlier legislation: see the Limitation Act 1980 s 36(1); and LIMITATION PERIODS vol 68 (2016) PARA 954. As to the application of limitation periods to proceedings for rescission on the ground of fraud see LIMITATION PERIODS vol 68 (2016) PARA 986. See also EQUITABLE JURISDICTION vol 47 (2014) PARAS 262–263. As to the effect of fraud on periods of limitation see PARA 788. The Limitation Act 1980 does not affect any equitable jurisdiction to refuse relief on the ground of acquiescence or otherwise: see s 36(2); and LIMITATION PERIODS vol 68 (2016) PARAS 906, 919. As to the effect of delay on the right to rescission see PARA 833.

5   Ie admitted either at or before the trial (on pleading or disclosure). In the case of one of the affirmative pleas, namely liquidation of a company in a case where the contract sought to be rescinded is a contract by which the representee became a member of the company (see PARA 831), the admission of the fact usually appears from the very title of the proceedings. As to who is a representee see PARAS 733–739.

6   The very character of the defence ('affirmative') imports this. As to proof of delay on the part of the representee see *Aaron's Reefs v Twiss* [1896] AC 273 at 295, HL.

## 825.   Representee's knowledge of the truth.

The effect of the representee's[1] knowledge of the truth is common to proceedings for rescission and claims for damages, and has been dealt with elsewhere in this title[2].

1   As to who is a representee see PARAS 733–739.
2   See PARA 801.

## 826.   Contractual term limiting right to rescind.

A contract entered into after a misrepresentation may contain a term purporting to exclude or restrict[1] the right to rescind, or the right to any remedy that might be available. Such a term is subject to the statutory requirement of reasonableness[2].

1   This may include clauses which have the effect of excluding or restricting the right to remedy, even if such clauses are drafted as negating an element of the claim (eg a claim which denies that a representation has been made, or that a representation, if made, has not been relied on): see *JP Morgan Chase Bank v Springwell Navigation Corpn* [2010] EWCA Civ 1221 at [179] et seq, [2010] All ER (D) 08 (Nov). As to such clauses see PARA 802.
2   See the Misrepresentation Act 1967 s 3; and PARA 802. The Misrepresentation Act 1967 s 3 does not apply to a term in a consumer contract within the meaning of Consumer Rights Act 2015 Pt 2 (ss 61–76), which contains separate provisions governing such cases (see CONSUMER PROTECTION, PARAS 391–402: see s 3(2); and PARA 802.

## 827.   Affirmation of contract.

If, after discovery of the whole of the material facts giving him a right to avoid the contract[1], the representee[2] has, by word or act[3], definitely elected to adhere to it[4], the representor[5] has a complete defence to any proceedings for rescission[6]. The acts and conduct relied on as showing the representee's affirmation of the contract must be such as are more consistent, on a reasonable view of them, with that than with any other theory[7]. It is not sufficient to point to acts of a neutral character, or acts which are equally consistent with a possible ultimate intention to disaffirm[8], or with a mere suspension of judgment[9]. An affirmation which prevents rescission will not of itself be a bar to a claim for damages[10].

1   No less than this must be shown to support the plea. It is insufficient to prove partial information, giving rise to suspicion merely; there can be no effective affirmation or election which is not based on complete and exact knowledge: see *Jarrett v Kennedy* (1848) 6 CB 319 at 326; *Lachlan v*

*Reynolds* (1853) Kay 52 (in both cases, the plea failed on this ground). For illustrations of the kind and degree of knowledge required see *Ogilvie v Currie* (1868) 37 LJ Ch 541 at 544; *Sharpley v Louth and East Coast Rly Co* (1876) 2 ChD 663 at 685, CA (in both these cases, the plea succeeded).

2  As to who is a representee see PARAS 733–739.

3  In nearly all the cases cited in note 6, the affirmation was implied from acts and conduct rather than from word spoken or written; in no instance was an express agreement proved.

4  As to the right of election see PARAS 780, 783.

5  As to who is a representor see PARAS 724–732.

6  In the following cases, many of which related to company transactions, the representee's acts and conduct were held to signify affirmation, after he had full knowledge of the facts: *Campbell v Fleming* (1834) 1 Ad & El 40 (sale of shares); *Pulsford v Richards* (1853) 17 Beav 87 (purchase of further shares); *Re Royal British Bank, Mixer's Case* (1859) 4 De G & J 575 at 586–587 (receiving dividends); *Re Hop and Malt Exchange and Warehouse Co, ex p Briggs* (1866) LR 1 Eq 483 (instructing broker to sell shares at a premium, although no actual sale); *Re Cachar Co, Lawrence's Case, Re Russian (Vyksounsky) Iron Works Co, Kincaid's Case* (1867) 2 Ch App 412 (delay; payment of call without protest); *Re Russian (Vyksounsky) Iron Works Co, Whitehouse's Case* (1867) LR 3 Eq 790 at 793–794 (similar case); *Re Russian (Vyksounsky) Iron Works Co, Taite's Case* (1867) LR 3 Eq 795 at 798 (delay after giving notice of intention to take proceedings); *Scholey v Central Rly Co of Venezuela* (1868) LR 9 Eq 266n (receipt of a dividend, and payment of call without protest); *Ogilvie v Currie* (1868) 37 LJ Ch 541 (attempts to compromise after months of suspicion); *Re Bank of Hindustan, China and Japan, Campbell's Case, Hippisley's Case, Alison's Case* (1873) 9 Ch App 1 at 7, 15 (taking part in appointment of liquidators, and paying calls under balance orders without objection); *Sharpley v Louth and East Coast Rly Co* (1876) 2 ChD 663 at 677–684, CA (attending meetings, and pressing on the enterprise); *Cargill v Bower* (1878) 10 ChD 502 at 508–509 (action against company claiming cancellation of allotment of shares; support by plaintiff as contributory of petition for company's liquidation, with costs awarded to him in that character; dropping by him of claim for cancellation in action); *Re Wheal Unity Wood Mining Co, Chynoweth's Case* (1880) 15 ChD 13 at 17–18, CA (company seeking to put transferor's name on the register instead of transferee's, having demanded payment of calls from transferee and forfeited his shares for non-payment, held to have affirmed the contract with him); *Reid v London and Staffordshire Fire Insurance Co* (1883) 53 LJ Ch 351 (giving notice of discontinuance of former proceedings for rescission); *Re Dunlop-Truffault Cycle and Tube Manufacturing Co, ex p Shearman* (1896) 66 LJ Ch 25 (payment of allotment money and instalments after giving clear written notice of repudiation); *Re Metal Constituents Ltd, Lord Lurgan's Case* [1902] 1 Ch 707 at 710–711 per Buckley J (acts showing an intention to keep shares for the purpose of selling them at a premium); *Seddon v North Eastern Salt Co Ltd* [1905] 1 Ch 326 at 334 per Joyce J (continuing to carry on at a profit the business the purchase of which it was sought to set aside).

7  See *Watson v Burton* [1956] 3 All ER 929 at 937, [1957] 1 WLR 19 at 30 per Wynn-Parry J. For illustration of acts and conduct, or inaction, held not to amount to affirmation see *Re Metropolitan Coal Consumers' Association, ex p Edwards* (1891) 64 LT 561 (attending one meeting for a few minutes, and asking the secretary, on one occasion, the price of the shares); *Re Metropolitan Coal Consumer's Association, Karberg's Case* [1892] 3 Ch 1, CA (mere inaction and reasonably waiting for the result of a similar case); *Oelkers v Ellis* [1914] 2 KB 139 (no evidence of delay in taking proceedings after facts really ascertained); *Abram Steamship Co Ltd v Westville Shipping Co Ltd* [1923] AC 773, HL (consent to trivial alterations of plans after discovery of misrepresentations); *Laurence v Lexcourt Holdings Ltd* [1978] 2 All ER 810, [1978] 1 WLR 1128 (lessors misrepresented planning permission status of building; attempt by lessees to negotiate alternative arrangements with lessor did not amount to affirmation nor did lapse of a reasonable period for consideration after breakdown of these negotiations).

8  See eg *Wontner v Shairp* (1847) 4 CB 404 at 442–443, where the representee was present as a shareholder at a meeting of the company, but only for the purpose of proposing the very thing which it was the object of the proceedings to obtain.

9  See eg *Watson v Burton* [1956] 3 All ER 929, [1957] 1 WLR 19, where a purchaser of property completed payment of the deposit and asked for repairs to be done while seeking an accommodation with the vendor about a mistake discovered in the particulars. As to the effect of delay in taking proceedings for rescission see PARA 833.

10  *Production Technology Consultants Ltd v Bartlett* [1988] 1 EGLR 182, CA. See also PARAS 780, 783. As to a claim for damages see PARA 788 et seq.

## 828. Affirmation of contract induced by two distinct misrepresentations.

Affirmation of a contract induced by two distinct misrepresentations with knowledge of the true facts as regards the one, but not as regards the other, does not debar the representee[1] from relief[2]. Nor does the fact that the representee has claimed and recovered damages against one of two representors[3] who are parties to the contract preclude him from obtaining rescission against the other, even though the representors are partners[4]. However, where the contract was induced by a single representation, and the representee, with knowledge of its falsity in one particular, has affirmed the contract, he cannot escape from the consequences or defeat the representor's plea by proof that, since the affirmation, he has discovered another particular in which the same representation departed from the truth[5].

1   As to who is a representee see PARAS 733–739.
2   *Re London and Provincial Electric Lighting and Power Generating Co Ltd, ex p Hale* (1886) 55 LT 670.
3   As to who is a representor see PARAS 724–732.
4   *Rawlins v Wickham* (1858) 3 De G & J 304 at 315, 322.
5   *Campbell v Fleming* (1834) 1 Ad & El 40; *Re Russian (Vyksounsky) Ironworks Co, Whitehouse's Case* (1867) LR 3 Eq 790 at 794.

## 829. Impossibility or injustice of specific restitution.

The representee[1] may not be granted rescission where specific restitution is impossible, or on the intervention of a third party[2]. One of the conditions of rescission is actual restoration by the representee to the representor[3] of all property, if any, which he acquired under the contract, so far as it is capable of specific reconveyance or retransfer[4]. If the representor can show that the representee received under the contract anything which, whether a thing in possession or a thing in action, was on its acquisition capable of being specifically retransferred[5], and which the representee has either lost or destroyed, or so dealt with as to produce an entire alteration of its physical, commercial or legal character, quality and substance, as distinct from mere depreciation, decay or deterioration in the ordinary course of events[6], the plea is valid unless the representor, by his own conduct in standing by and tacitly permitting or encouraging the representee in his course of action, has precluded himself from taking the objection[7]. On the other hand, mere depreciation or deterioration of the subject matter of the contract, from no fault of the representee and without altering its character, is no bar to rescission[8]. Nor is commercial expansion of the subject matter of a contract of sale in the hands of the purchaser necessarily a bar to the granting of rescission to the vendor where the purchaser's misrepresentation was fraudulent[9].

There are cases which suggest that a broader approach may be taken if justice so requires in situations where, although specific restitution is no longer possible, effective restoration is possible by the payment of money[10].

1   As to who is a representee see PARAS 733–739.
2   See PARA 830.
3   As to who is a representor see PARAS 724–732.
4   See PARA 812. In a case where doubt existed as to the capacity of a party seeking rescission of an agreement to execute a reconveyance which was a necessary condition of the granting of rescission, an order was made providing that, if a reconveyance should be executed to the satisfaction of the court of first instance, rescission should take place, but that otherwise the proceedings should be dismissed: see *Lindsay Petroleum Co v Hurd* (1874) LR 5 PC 221 at 245 (allegation that the plaintiff company had ceased to exist). As to the availability of rescission where its effect would be to place the parties into a contractual relationship they had previously agreed to terminate see *Crystal Palace FC (2000) Ltd v Dowie* [2007] EWHC 1392 (QB) at [211]–[217], [2007] IRLR 682 at [211]–[217].

5  Where the representee has received nothing which he can restore, the plea has no application. It has no place, therefore, where the claim is one of money had and received, or conversion: see PARA 812. Nor does it apply where the representee has nothing to restore but money. In *Hulton v Hulton* [1917] 1 KB 813, CA, the court rescinded a deed of separation obtained by fraudulent misrepresentations of the husband as to his means, but refused to order the wife to repay the sums which she had for some years received under the deed, on the grounds that the money had been paid under a liability at common law which existed irrespective of the deed, and that the husband had received during the period very considerable advantages, eg freedom from molestation and proceedings by the wife for restitution of conjugal rights.

6  *Clough v London and North Western Rly Co* (1871) LR 7 Exch 26 at 34–35; *Compagnie Chemin de Fer Paris-Orléans v Leeston Shipping Co Ltd* (1919) 36 TLR 68 at 69 per Roche J (the principle of restitutio in integrum does not mean that a person is to be put back into the same position as before, but that he shall be put into as good a position as before). The following are illustrations of such alteration in the physical or mercantile properties of the subject matter as are sufficient to support this defence and to disentitle the representee to rescission: *Attwood v Small* (1838) 6 Cl & Fin 232 at 357, HL (working of collieries, iron mines and other property); *Vigers v Pike* (1842) 8 Cl & Fin 562 at 651, HL (mines worked out); *Clarke v Dickson* (1858) EB & E 148 at 153–155 (mines worked and legal character of securities altered from shares in a cost-book mine to shares in a joint stock company); *Western Bank of Scotland v Addie* (1867) LR 1 Sc & Div 145 at 165–166, HL (conversion of an unincorporated banking company into an incorporated joint stock company); *Sheffield Nickel Co v Unwin* (1877) 2 QBD 214, DC (position of both parties in relation to the patents and business in question materially changed); *Re Wheal Unity Wood Mining Co, Chynoweth's Case* (1880) 15 ChD 13 at 20, CA (having forfeited shares, the company had put it out of its power to restore the status quo); *Lagunas Nitrate Co v Lagunas Syndicate* [1899] 2 Ch 392, CA (where, after accrual of right to rescind, purchasers continued working a business at a profit, distributed dividends and called on the vendors to make outlays etc; the decision in this case might have been different if the vendors had been guilty of fraud: see at 433–434; and see comments in *Spence v Crawford* [1939] 3 All ER 271 at 280, HL, per Lord Thankerton, and at 288–289 per Lord Wright); *Glasgow and South Western Rly Co v Boyd and Forrest* as reported in 1915 SC 20, HL (completion of contract to construct railway after full knowledge of facts giving rise to right to rescind); *Steedman v Frigidaire Corpn* [1932] WN 248, PC (large part of refrigerating plant supplied let out to be operated by tenants of representee). Cf *Hulton v Hulton* [1917] 1 KB 813, CA, where the court rescinded a deed of separation obtained by fraudulent misrepresentations, although certain letters could not be restored by the representee by reason of their destruction under the terms of the deed, the court holding that the letters had been destroyed for the representor's benefit. If the representee has, before knowledge of the misrepresentation, assigned the benefit of the contract impeached to a third person, the right to rescind is lost; but if the representee in so assigning innocently passed on the misrepresentation to the assignee, who rescinds on discovery of the original misrepresentation, the right of the representee to rescind and his ability to make restitutio in integrum may be restored by the act of the assignee, even though the assignee has been obliged by the representee to bring proceedings to enforce his right to rescind the sub-contract and judgment had not been obtained in that action at the date when the representee began proceedings for rescission against the representor: *Abram Steamship Co Ltd v Westville Shipping Co Ltd* [1923] AC 773, HL.

7  See eg *Maturin v Tredennick* (1864) 4 New Rep 15.

8  *Western Bank of Scotland v Addie* (1867) LR 1 Sc & Div 145 at 165–166, HL; *Adam v Newbigging* (1888) 13 App Cas 308 at 323, 330–331, HL; *Oelkers v Ellis* [1914] 2 KB 139 at 152 per Horridge J; *Armstrong v Jackson* [1917] 2 KB 822.

9  *Spence v Crawford* [1939] 3 All ER 271, HL.

10  See *Atlantic Lines and Navigation Co Inc v Hallam Ltd, The Lucy* [1983] 1 Lloyds Rep 188; *Vadasz v Pioneer Concrete (SA) Pty Ltd* (1995) 130 ALR 570, Aust HC. See also *O'Sullivan v Management Agency and Music Ltd* [1985] QB 428, [1985] 3 All ER 351, CA; *Mahoney v Purnell* [1996] 3 All ER 61 (both cases of undue influence rather than misrepresentation). As to undue influence see CONTRACT vol 22 (2012) PARA 294 et seq.

See further *Smith New Court Securities Ltd v Citibank NA* [1997] AC 254 at 262, sub nom *Smith New Court Securities Ltd v Scrimgeour Vickers (Asset Management) Ltd* [1996] 4 All ER 769 at 774, HL, per Lord Browne-Wilkinson, doubting the assumption that the representees in a contract to buy shares in a public company could not rescind once they had sold the shares, since other shares could readily have been bought on the market.

**830. Intervention of a third party.**

The representee[1] may be precluded from exercising his right to rescind where an innocent third person has acquired an interest in the property which was the subject matter of the voidable contract[2]. In general the vital question will be whether the representee has communicated his decision to rescind to the representor[3] before the innocent third person has acquired an interest in the property.

In the case of the purchase of shares in a limited company, even where there is no question of the liquidation of the company[4], a representee ought to rescind speedily, if at all[5]; and this is particularly so when the misrepresentation alleged relates to matters disclosed in the constitution of the company[6].

1   As to who is a representee see PARAS 733–739.
2   *Clough v London and North Western Rly Co* (1871) LR 7 Exch 26 at 34–35; *Re Clarke, ex p Debtor v S Aston & Son Ltd* [1967] Ch 1121, [1966] 3 All ER 622, DC; *Society of Lloyd's v Leighs* [1997] CLC 1398, CA; *Crystal Palace FC (2000) Ltd v Dowie* [2007] EWHC 1392 (QB) at [210]–[217], [2007] IRLR 682 at [210]–[217]. See also PARAS 820, 833.
3   As to who is a representor see PARAS 724–732. As to the right of the representee of fraudulent misrepresentation to retake possession of property and whether that constitutes notice see PARA 780.
4   As to the effect of liquidation see PARA 831.
5   The reason is that, in the interim, persons may have become members of the company, as well as creditors, on the faith of the names they find on the register, which is a document to which the public have access: see COMPANIES vol 15A (2016) PARA 1263. The duty of the shareholder to move promptly was insisted on in *Directors of Central Rly Co of Venezuela v Kisch* (1867) LR 2 HL 99 at 125; *Scholey v Central Rly Co of Venezuela* (1868) LR 9 Eq 266n at 267n; *Ogilvie v Currie* (1868) 37 LJ Ch 541 at 546; *Re Hull and County Bank, Burgess's Case* (1880) 15 ChD 507 at 512; *Re Snyder Dynamite Projectile Co, Skelton's Case* (1893) 68 LT 210; *Aaron's Reefs v Twiss* [1896] AC 273 at 294, HL; *Re Christineville Rubber Estates Ltd* (1911) 28 TLR 38. See also *First National Reinsurance Co v Greenfield* [1921] 2 KB 260, DC. As to the position where the alleged contract to take shares never in fact came into existence see PARA 831.
     As to the effect of delay generally see PARA 833.
6   See *New Brunswick and Canada Railway and Land Co v Conybeare* (1862) 9 HL Cas 711 at 734; *Re Cachar Co, Lawrence's Case, Re Russian (Vyksounsky) Iron Works Co, Kincaid's Case* (1867) 2 Ch App 412; *Re Madrid Bank, Wilkinson's Case* (1867) 2 Ch App 536 at 540–541; *Re Barned's Banking Co, Peel's Case* (1867) 2 Ch App 674 at 684.

**831. Liquidation of company in cases of contracts to take shares.**

A defence for the representor[1] may arise where the contract sought to be rescinded is a contract by which the representee[2] became a member of a limited company. In this case, the winding up or insolvency of the company is a bar to any relief by way of rescission unless the representee has already begun proceedings for rescission or agreed with the company to be bound by such proceedings brought by some other person or has taken other appropriate steps to have his name removed from the register[3].

1   As to who is a representor see PARAS 724–732.
2   As to who is a representee see PARAS 733–739.
3   See COMPANY AND PARTNERSHIP INSOLVENCY vol 16 (2017) PARA 402. The principles which debar the granting of rescission in the case of a voidable contract to take shares do not prevent rectification of the register of members or the list of contributories where the alleged contract to take shares never came into existence: see COMPANIES vol 15A (2016) PARA 1268 et seq.

**832. Court's power to grant damages in lieu of rescission for non-fraudulent misrepresentation.**

Where a person has entered into a contract after a misrepresentation has been made to him otherwise than fraudulently[1], and he would be entitled, by reason of the misrepresentation, to rescind the contract[2], then if it is claimed, in any proceedings arising out of the contract, that the contract ought to be or has been rescinded, the court[3] may declare the contract subsisting and award damages in lieu of rescission if of the opinion that it would be equitable to do so[4].

1   As to innocent misrepresentation see PARAS 762–763. As to fraudulent misrepresentation see PARA 754 et seq.
2   As to claims for rescission see PARA 811 et seq.
3   An arbitrator has the same power as the court: Misrepresentation Act 1967 s 2(2).
4   Misrepresentation Act 1967 s 2(2). The court or arbitrator must have regard to the nature of the misrepresentation and the loss that would be caused by it if the contract were upheld, as well as to the loss that rescission would cause to the other party: see s 2(2). As to damages in respect of a misrepresentation if the person has a right to redress under the Consumer Protection from Unfair Trading Regulations 2008, SI 2008/1277, Pt 4A (regs 27A-27L) see Misrepresentation Act 1967 s 2(4), (5); and PARA 800.
        Damages may be awarded against a person under s 2(2), whether or not he is liable to damages under s 2(1) (see PARAS 800, 810); but where he is so liable any award under s 2(2) is to be taken into account in assessing his liability under s 2(1): s 2(3). Since damages may be awarded under this power even though the representor was in no way at fault, it seems possible that they should be assessed on a more cautious basis than where the right to damages depends on the proof of fraud or negligence: see *William Sindall plc v Cambridgeshire County Council* [1994] 3 All ER 932, [1994] 1 WLR 1016, CA (where the view was expressed that the correct measure of damages should be the cost of remedying the defect or the reduced market value attributable to the defect, although in this case there was held to be no misrepresentation); *Thomas Witter v TBP Industries Ltd* [1996] 2 All ER 573 at 591 per Jacob J (suggesting that damages under the Misrepresentation Act 1967 s 2(2) might be limited to loss in value and might exclude consequential loss, although in this case there was no consequential loss); *Floods of Queensferry Ltd v Shand Construction Ltd* [2000] BLR 81 (where it was considered inequitable to award damages where the claimant, if he knew the true position, would make a contract on the same terms with another) (on appeal in relation to liability for certain costs [2002] EWCA Civ 918, [2003] Lloyd's Rep IR 181). The party claiming damages must establish loss flowing from the misrepresentation: *Huyton SA v Distribuidora Internacional de Productos Agricolas SA de CV* [2003] EWCA Civ 1104 at [5], [2004] 1 All ER (Comm) 402 at [5]. 'Loss' includes financial loss, as well as detriment generally; the nature of the exercise required by the Misrepresentation Act 1967 s 2(2) is a balancing exercise in order to determine what would be equitable in the circumstances: *UCB Corporate Services Ltd v Thomason* [2005] EWCA Civ 225, [2005] 1 All ER (Comm) 601.
        After earlier conflicting first instance decisions as to whether the Misrepresentation Act 1967 s 2(2) applies where the right to rescind has become barred (see *Thomas Witter v TBP Industries Ltd* [1996] 2 All ER 573 at at 590-91; *Government of Zanzibar v British Aerospace (Lancaster House) Ltd* [2000] 1 WLR 2333 at 2343; *Floods of Queensferry Ltd v Shand Construction Ltd* [2000] BLR 81 at 91–93; *Pankhania v Hackney London Borough Council* [2002] EWHC 2441 (Ch), [2002] All ER (D) 22 (Aug) at [76]) the Court of Appeal has now held that the court has a discretion under s 2(2) only if rescission is available (or was available at the time the contract was rescinded), and therefore not where eg the contract has been affirmed, third party rights have intervened, an excessive time has elapsed or restitution has become impossible: *Salt v Stratstone Specialist Ltd* [2015] EWCA Civ 745, [2016] RTR 285 at [17].
        As to damages under the Misrepresentation Act 1967 see also PARA 810. As to who is a representor see PARAS 724–732.

## 833. Effect of delay.

Delay, or laches, falling short of the period prescribed by the statutory provisions relating to the limitation of claims[1] is not an absolute defence to a claim for rescission on the ground of misrepresentation[2]. The remedy of rescission is, however, an equitable one, and in cases where delay has occurred its validity as a defence will be assessed on equitable principles[3] and in relation to all the circumstances of the case[4]. Delay may therefore be taken as evidence of affirmation of the contract by the representee[5], or it may have resulted in change in the subject matter of the contract[6], or the intervention of a third party[7], or some other consequence which would prevent substantial justice being done between the parties by the granting of the remedy. In so far as this is the case, delay may be an important factor in the refusal to grant rescission. Moreover, the general presumption which the law makes in favour of the good faith and validity of transactions which have long stood unchallenged[8], and the general rule that equity aids the vigilant and not the indolent[9], further combine to support the proposition that claims for the rescission of contracts on the ground of non-fraudulent misrepresentation should be made promptly[10]. In cases of fraudulent misrepresentation there is no delay so long as the representee, without any fault of his own, remains in ignorance of the fraud[11].

1  As to the statutory provisions relating to the limitation of actions see PARA 824.
2  *Redgrave v Hurd* (1881) 20 ChD 1 at 13, CA.
3  *Leaf v International Galleries* [1950] 2 KB 86, [1950] 1 All ER 693, CA. A principal element in laches is acquiescence; in order to acquiesce, a person must be aware of facts constituting his title to relief: see EQUITABLE JURISDICTION vol 47 (2014) PARA 252 et seq.
4  *Lindsay Petroleum Co v Hurd* (1874) LR 5 PC 221 at 239, 246; *Leaf v International Galleries* [1950] 2 KB 86 at 92, [1950] 1 All ER 693 at 696, CA; *Salt v Stratstone Specialist Ltd* [2015] EWCA Civ 745, [2016] RTR 285 at [43].
5  *Clough v London and North Western Rly Co* (1871) LR 7 Exch 26 at 35, Ex Ch; *Lindsay Petroleum Co v Hurd* (1874) LR 5 PC 221 at 239–240; *Aaron's Reefs v Twiss* [1896] AC 273, HL; *Oelkers v Ellis* [1914] 2 KB 139 at 151–152 per Horridge J; *Kwei Tek Chao v British Trader and Shippers Ltd* [1954] 2 QB 459, [1954] 1 All ER 779. As to the importance of a change in the defendant's position see PARA 789; and EQUITABLE JURISDICTION vol 47 (2014) PARA 257. As to who is a representee see PARAS 733–739.
6  *Clough v London and North Western Rly Co* (1871) LR 7 Exch 26 at 35; *Lindsay Petroleum Co v Hurd* (1874) LR 5 PC 221 at 239–240; *Erlanger v New Sombrero Phosphate Co* (1878) 3 App Cas 1218 at 1277–1279, HL; *Armstrong v Jackson* [1917] 2 KB 822 at 828 per McCardie J.
7  *Clough v London and North Western Rly Co* (1871) LR 7 Exch 26 at 35. See also *Re Murray, Dickson v Murray* (1887) 57 LT 223.
8  *Vatcher v Paull* [1915] AC 372, PC. See also *Leaf v International Galleries* [1950] 2 KB 86 at 92, [1950] 1 All ER 693 at 696, CA, where Jenkins LJ that the principle of finality requires the purchaser either to verify or disprove the representation within a 'reasonable time'. See also *Leaf v International Galleries* at 91, 695 per Denning LJ.
9  See *Smith v Clay* (1767) 3 Bro CC 639n.
10  See *Lindsay Petroleum Co v Hurd* (1874) LR 5 PC 221 at 239–240; *Leaf v International Galleries* [1950] 2 KB 86, [1950] 1 All ER 693, CA; *Oscar Chess Ltd v Williams* [1957] 1 All ER 325 at 327, 330, [1957] 1 WLR 370 at 373–374, 377, CA, per Denning LJ. As to delay generally see EQUITABLE JURISDICTION vol 47 (2014) PARA 253 et seq.
11  *Rolfe v Gregory* (1865) 4 De GJ & Sm 576; *Molloy v Mutual Reserve Life Insurance Co* (1906) 94 LT 756, CA; *Oelkers v Ellis* [1914] 2 KB 139; *Armstrong v Jackson* [1917] 2 KB 822. As to the postponement of the limitation period in the case of fraud see PARA 788; and LIMITATION PERIODS vol 68 (2016) PARA 1220 et seq.

# INDEX

# Mines, Minerals and Quarries

COAL-MINING
SUBSIDENCE—*continued*
blighted property—
dwelling houses, purchase of 236
generally 235
claims—
agreements as to working of
minerals or leaving of minerals
unworked 246
double claims, avoidance of 245
expenses of claimant,
reimbursement of 247
statutory right to withdraw support,
in relation to 248
Coal Authority, duties of 62
Coal-Mining Subsidence Act 1991—
generally 201
reports on operation of 253
death or disablement, compensation
for 239
disputes—
arbitration of 250
generally 249
dwelling houses—
blighted houses, purchase of 236
home loss payments 228
temporary dispossession, relief
for 229
vacant houses, care of 230
ecclesiastical property affected by 226
emergency works, payments in respect
of 221
further damage—
effect of 224
stop notices. *See* stop notices *below*
historical background 200
inconvenience during works,
compensation for 231
information, offences with respect
to 254
land drainage—
Doncaster Drainage District 244
election by responsible persons 243
questions relating to, determination
of 242
remedial measures to be taken 241
listed buildings affected by 225
moveable property, compensation for
damage to 238
notices—
damage, as to 210
local authorities, to 252
owners and occupiers of property,
to 251

COAL-MINING
SUBSIDENCE—*continued*
payments in lieu of works—
depreciation payments—
discretionary payments 219
generally 217
obligatory payments 218
recipients of 220
discretionary payments—
depreciation payments 219
generally 216
generally 214
obligatory payments—
depreciation payments 218
generally 215
persons responsible for. *See*
responsible persons *below*
preventive measures—
existing buildings, structures or
works 240
land drainage. *See* land drainage
*above*
protected tenants' property affected
by 227
remedial action—
appropriate action, determination
of 211
duty to take 209
notice of damage 210
remedial works—
execution of 213
payments in lieu of. *See* payments in
lieu of works *above*
schedule of 212
responsible persons—
*meaning* 204
areas of responsibility 205
information to be provided by 207
more than one responsible person,
cases where 206
Secretary of State's powers as to 202
small firms, compensation for 237
stop notices—
further damage likely to occur,
where 222
review of 223
revocation of 223
subsidence adviser: meaning 208
subsidence damage: meaning 203
DEEP SEA MINING
arbitration awards 408
civil liability for breach of statutory
duty 412
disclosure of information 410

**References are to paragraph numbers; superior figures refer to notes**

**References are to paragraph numbers; superior figures refer to notes**

**References are to paragraph numbers; superior figures refer to notes**

OPENCAST WORKING OF
   COAL—*continued*
compulsory purchase, protection
   from 416
compulsory rights orders—
   agricultural holdings adjustments.
      *See* agricultural holding *above*
   allotment tenancy, termination
      of 460
   business tenancies 459
   challenge of 443
   chattels, right to remove 437
   compensation for. *See* compensation
      for compulsory rights orders
      *above*
   concurrent orders 497
   crop rights 436
   duration of 432
   effect of 433
   limitations on—
      general limitations 438
      particular limitations 439
      property not included in 440
   limited orders 498
   minerals other than coal, rights of
      working 434
   mining leases, restrictions on rents
      and royalties from 458
   mortgages, breach of terms and
      conditions of—
         after occupation 445
         during occupation 444
   nature of 431
   notification of 443
   procedure for making 442
   revocation of 432
   tenancies, breach of terms and
      conditions of—
         after occupation 445
         during occupation 444
   timber rights 435
   variation of 432
entry powers—
   generally 420
   incidents of power of entry 421
   notice of intended entry 422
ironstone district restoration—
   legislation 580
   modification of payments in lieu of
      restoration under ironstone
      leases 581
local inquiries 419
Opencast Coal Act 1958—
   appropriate national authority,
      powers of 417

OPENCAST WORKING OF
   COAL—*continued*
Opencast Coal Act 1958—*continued*
   Coal Authority, powers of 417
   compulsory purchase, protection
      from 416
   Crown land, application to 415
   emergency powers, replacement
      of 413
   inquiries under 419
   powers under 414
opencast planning permission—
   agricultural tenancies, provisions as
      to 428
   compulsory rights orders. *See*
      compulsory rights orders *above*
   drainage or water supply, rights as
      to 430
   farm business tenancies, provisions
      as to 429
   generally 423
   public rights of way, suspension
      of 424
   requirements in relation to 441
public rights of way—
   order suspending—
      circumstances for 424
      effect of 426
      procedure on application 425
      revocation of 427
subordinate legislation 418
QUARRY
   *meaning* 4
abandonment—
   duty to inform appropriate agency
      of 533
   fencing requirements 534
animals, care of 541
appointments, records of 525
beginning and ending of operations,
   notification requirements as
   to 532
breach of statutory duty 519
drinking water, provision of 540
free miners, leases for 620–700
generally 1
Gloucestershire, in. *See*
   GLOUCESTERSHIRE MINING
health and safety—
   documents—
      availability of 528
      service of 531
   exemptions, consents etc, powers as
      to 524

**References are to paragraph numbers; superior figures refer to notes**

# Misrepresentation